# NTA UGC NET/JRF/SET

# TEACHING AND RESEARCH APTITUDE

## General Paper 1
Compulsory


**AUTHORS**

Teaching & Research Aptitude *(Farah Sultan)*
Comprehension & Communication *(Mridula Sharma)*
Reasoning, Maths & Data Interpretation *(Varun Bali)*
Information and Communication Technology *(Neetu Gaikwad)*
People, Development and Environment & Higher Education System *(Dr. Rashmi Jain)*



arihant
SUCCESS AND NOTHING LESS

arihant
SUCCESS AND NOTHING LESS

## ARIHANT PUBLICATIONS (INDIA) LIMITED



卐 **Administrative & Production Offices**

**Regd. Office**

'Ramchhaya' 4577/15, Agarwal Road, Darya Ganj, New Delhi -110002
Tele: 011- 47630600, 43518550

卐 **Head Office**

Kalindi, TP Nagar, Meerut (UP) - 250002, Tel: 0121-7156203, 7156204

卐 **Sales & Support Offices**

Agra, Ahmedabad, Bengaluru, Bareilly, Chennai, Delhi, Guwahati, Hyderabad, Jaipur, Jhansi, Kolkata, Lucknow, Nagpur & Pune.

卐 **PRICE** ₹575.00

**PO No :** TXT-XX-XXXXXXX-X-XX

Published by Arihant Publications (India) Ltd.

For further information about the books published by Arihant, log on to www.arihantbooks.com or e-mail at info@arihantbooks.com

Follow us on

# About The Book

The National Eligibility Test (NET) also known as NTA-UGC-NET is a test to determine the eligibility of candidates opting for the post of Assistant Professor only or Junior Research Fellowship (JRF) and Assistant Professor both in Indian Universities and Colleges. On behalf of the University Grants Commission (UGC), the National Testing Agency (NTA) will conduct the NET Examination from December 2018.

This book 'NTA UGC NET/SET/JRF Teaching and Research Aptitude Paper 1' has been designed according to the latest syllabus and the latest pattern of the UGC NET General Paper-1. As per the syllabus applicable from June 2019, the book is divided into 10 Units (Teaching Aptitude, Research Aptitude, Comprehension, Communication, Mathematical Reasoning and Aptitude, Logical Reasoning, Data Interpretation, Information and Communication Technology, People and Environment and Higher Education System).

## Features of the book

- Easy to Understand Language Supported with Examples, Flowcharts, Figures, Diagrams, Latest Facts etc.
- Chapter/Unitwise 3000+ Multiple Choice Questions (MCQs) for Complete Practice.
- Chapter/Unitwise Previous Year Questions ( 2014-2019).
- 5 Practice Sets on Latest Examination Pattern with Online Practice.
- 2024-2019 Solved Papers with Detailed Explanations.

Huge efforts have been made from our side to keep this book error free, but inspite of that if any error is skipped in the book then that is purely incidental, apology for the same, please write to us about it so that it can be corrected in the further edition of the book.

In the end, we would like to wish Best of Luck to our readers!

Authors

# Contents

**Solved Paper, August 2024** 1-14
**Solved Paper, September 2024** 15-26
**Solved Paper, June 2023** 27-40
**Solved Paper, June 2023** 41-54
**Solved Paper, October 2022** (Shift II) 3-16
**Solved Paper, October 2022** (Shift I) 17-31
**Solved Paper, November 2021** (Shift I) 3-16
**Solved Paper, November 2020** 3-13
**Solved Paper, December 2019** (Shift I) 14-24
**Solved Paper, December 2019** (Shift II) 25-37
**Solved Paper, June 2019** 38-46

Unit 1 Teaching Aptitude 3-64
Unit 2 Research Aptitude 65-112
Unit 3 Comprehension 113-146
Unit 4 Communication 147-183
Unit 5 Mathematical Reasoning and Aptitude 184-245
Unit 6 Logical Reasoning 246-301
Unit 7 Data Interpretation 302-347
Unit 8 Information and Communication Technology 348-406
Unit 9 People, Development and Environment 407-457
Unit 10 Higher Education System 458-512

**Practice Sets (1-5)** 515-546

# Syllabus

## UNIT 1 Teaching Aptitude

- Teaching: Concept, Objectives, Levels of Teaching (Memory, Understanding and Reflective), Characteristics and Basic Requirements.
- Learner's Characteristics: Characteristics of Adolescent and Adult Learners (Academic, Social, Emotional and Cognitive), Individual Differences.
- Factors Affecting Teaching Related to: Teacher, Learner, Support Material, Instructional Facilities, Learning Environment and Institution.
- Methods of Teaching in Institutions of Higher Learning: Teacher Centred vs. Learner Centred Methods; Off-line vs. On-line Methods (Swayam, Swayamprabha, MOOCs etc.).
- Teaching Support System: Traditional, Modern and ICT based.
- Evaluation Systems: Elements and Types of Evaluation, Evaluation in Choice Based Credit System in Higher Education, Computer Based Testing, Innovations in Evaluation Systems.

## UNIT 2 Research Aptitude

- Research: Meaning, Types and Characteristics, Positivism and Post- Positivistic Approach to Research.
- Methods of Research: Experimental, Descriptive, Historical, Qualitative and Quantitative Methods.
- Steps of Research.
- Thesis and Article Writing: Format and Styles of Referencing.
- Application of ICT in Research.
- Research Ethics.

## UNIT 3 Comprehension

- A passage of text be given. Questions be asked from the passage to be answered.

## UNIT 4 Communication

- Communication: Meaning, Types and Characteristics of Communication.
- Effective Communication: Verbal and Non-Verbal, Inter-Cultural and Group Communications, Classroom Communication.
- Barriers to Effective Communication.
- Mass-Media and Society.

## UNIT 5 Mathematical Reasoning and Aptitude

- Types of Reasoning.
- Number Series, Letter Series, Codes and Relationships.
- Mathematical Aptitude (Fraction, Time and Distance, Ratio, Proportion and Percentage, Profit and Loss, Interest and Discounting, Averages etc.).

## UNIT 6 Logical Reasoning

- Understanding the Structure of Arguments: Argument Forms, Structure of Categorical Propositions, Mood and Figure, Formal and Informal Fallacies, Uses of Language, Connotations and Denotations of Terms, Classical Square of Opposition.
- Evaluating and Distinguishing Deductive and Inductive Reasoning.
- Analogies.
- Venn Diagram: Simple and Multiple Use for Establishing Validity of Arguments.
- Indian Logic: Means of Knowledge.
- Pramanas: Pratyaksha (Perception), Anumana (Inference), Upamana (Comparison), Shabda (Verbal Testimony), Arthapatti (Implication) and Anupalabddhi (Non-Apprehension).
- Structure and Kinds of Anumana (Inference), Vyapti (Invariable Relation), Hetvabhasas (Fallacies of Inference).

## UNIT 7 Data Interpretation

- Sources, Acquisition and Classification of Data.
- Quantitative and Qualitative Data.
- Graphical Representation (Bar-Chart, Histograms, Pie-chart, Table-Chart and Line-chart) and Mapping of Data.
- Data Interpretation.
- Data and Governance.

## UNIT 8 Information and Communication Technology (ICT)

- ICT: General Abbreviations and Terminology.
- Basics of Internet, Intranet, E-mail, Audio and Video-Conferencing.
- Digital Initiatives in Higher Education.
- ICT and Governance.

## Unit 9 People, Development and Environment

- Development and Environment: Millennium Development and Sustainable Development Goals.
- Human and Environment Interaction: Anthropogenic Activities and their Impacts on Environment.
- Environmental Issues: Local, Regional and Global; Air Pollution, Water Pollution, Soil Pollution, Noise Pollution, Waste (Solid, Liquid, Bio-Medical, Hazardous, Electronic), Climate Change and its Socio-Economic and Political Dimensions.
- Impacts of Pollutants on Human Health.
- Natural and Energy Resources: Solar, Wind, Soil, Hydro, Geothermal, Biomass, Nuclear and Forests.
- Natural Hazards and Disasters: Mitigation Strategies.
- Environmental Protection Act (1986), National Action Plan on Climate Change, International Agreements/Efforts -Montreal Protocol, Rio Summit, Convention on Biodiversity, Kyoto Protocol, Paris Agreement, International Solar Alliance.

## UNIT 10 Higher Education System

- Institutions of Higher Learning and Education in Ancient India.
- Evolution of Higher Learning and Research in Post Independence India.
- Oriental, Conventional and Non-Conventional Learning Programmes in India.
- Professional, Technical and Skill Based Education.
- Value Education and Environmental Education.
- Policies, Governance and Administration.

# NTA UGC NET/JRF/SET

*The University Grants Commission (UGC) of India is a statutory body set up by the Indian Union Government in 1956, and is charged with coordination, determination and maintenance of standards of higher education. It provides recognition to universities in India and disburses funds to recognised universities and colleges. From December 2018, the UGC-NET (Eligibility for Assistant Professor only or Junior Research Fellowship and Eligibility for both Assistant Professor) is to be conducted by NTA.*

## UGC NET-JRF

- The National Educational Testing Bureau of University Grants Commission (UGC) conducts National Eligibility Test (NET) to determine eligibility for lectureship and for award of Junior Research Fellowship (JRF) for Indian nationals in order to ensure minimum standards for the entrants in the teaching profession and research. The test is conducted in Humanities (including languages), Social Science, Forensic Science, Environmental Science, Computer Science and Applications and Electronic Science.
- UGC has allocated a number of fellowships to the universities for the candidates who qualify the test for JRF. The JRF is awarded to the meritorious candidates from among the candidates qualifying for eligibility for lectureship in the NET.

## ELIGIBILITY CRITERIA

- Candidates who have secured at least 55% marks (without rounding off) in Master s Degree OR equivalent examination from universities/institutions recognised by UGC in Humanities (including languages) and Social Science, Computer Science & Applications, Electronic Science etc. are eligible for this Test.
- The Other Backward Classes(OBC) belonging to non-creamy layer/Scheduled Caste(SC)/Scheduled Tribe(ST)/ persons with disability(PwD) category candidates who have secured at least 50% marks (without rounding off) in Master s degree or equivalent examination are eligible for this Test.
- Candidates who are pursuing their Master's degree or equivalent course or candidates who have appeared for their qualifying Masters degree (final year) examination and whose result is still awaited or candidates whose qualifying examinations have been delayed may also apply for this test.

  However, such candidates will be admitted provisionally and shall be considered eligible for award of Junior Research Fellowship/eligibility for Assistant Professor only after they have passed their Master's Degree OR equivalent examination with at least 55% marks (50% marks in case of OBC falling in Non-Creamy layer/SC/ST/PwD (persons with disability)) category candidates. Such candidates must complete their Masters degree or equivalent examination within two years from the date of NET result with required percentage of marks, failing which they shall be treated as disqualified.
- Candidates belonging to third gender in other words transgender would be eligible to draw the same relaxation in fee, age and qualifying criteria for NET (i.e. Junior Research Fellowship and Assistant Professor) as are available to SC/ST/PwD categories. The subject wise cut-offs for this category should be the lowest among those for SC/ST/PwD/OBC NCL categories in the corresponding subject.
- The Ph.D. degree holders whose Master s level examination had been completed by 19th September 1991 (irrespective of date of declaration of result) shall be eligible for a relaxation of 5% in aggregate marks (i.e. from 55% to 50%) for appearing in NET.
- Candidates are advised to appear in the subject of their post graduation only. The candidates, whose post graduation subject is not covered in the list of subjects, may appear in a related subject.

- Candidates having post-graduate diploma/certificate awarded by Indian University/ Institute or foreign degree/diploma/certificate awarded by the foreign University/institute should in their own interest, ascertain the equivalence of their diploma/degree/certificate with Master s degree of recognized Indian universities from Association of Indian Universities (AIU), New Delhi. (www.aiu.ac.in)

## SLET OR SET

While the UGC was drafting the concept of NET as a mandatory requirement for determining the eligibility for lectureship, it also gave an option to various state governments and union territories to conduct their independent tests. It was felt that an eligibility test at the national level might not completely be able to represent the subjects, which are regional.

There was a contention to permit candidates to take the test in their mother tongue. If it is NET at the national level, then SET is its counterpart at the state level. The SLET (State Level Eligibility Test for Lectureship Eligibility) has now been re-christened as SET (State Eligibility Test for Lectureship). The test is conducted both in English and in the vernacular languages. The only other difference being that unlike NET which makes you eligible to teach anywhere in the country, the SET entitles you to teach in any college or university in that particular state. The states or union territories that wish to conduct their own exam have to obtain UGC accreditation, which is granted for a stipulated period.

## PAPER PATTERN

### THE UGC-NET EXAMINATION CONSISTS OF TWO PAPERS

**Paper I** is of general nature and is used to assess the teaching research aptitude of the candidates. It is designed to test the reasoning ability, divergent thinking, general awareness and comprehension.

**Paper II** comprises Multiple Choice Questions (MCQs) based on the subject in which the candidate is taking the examination. There are 100 Objective Type Questions asked in this paper.

| Paper | Marks | Questions | Time |
|---|---|---|---|
| Paper-I | 100 | 50 questions<br>all are compulsory | 3 hrs (09.30 AM to 12.30 PM) |
| Paper-II | 200 | 100 questions<br>all are compulsory | |
| **Total** | **300** | | |

# UGC

# NET/JRF/SET

# Solved Paper, 2024

## (Exam Held on : 29 August 2024, Shift I)

## General Paper 1 (Teaching and Research Aptitude)

### *Instructions*

- This paper contains fifty Multiple Choice Questions, each question carries two marks.
- All questions are compulsory.
- Total time given for this paper is 1 hour.

**Directions** (Q. Nos. 1-5) *Read the following information carefully and answer the given questions.*

The following table presents the number of sports shoes produced by seven different companies *A-G* (in Lakh) along with the percentage (%) of sports shoes rejected and percentage (%) of sports shoes sold by these companies during the years 2022 and 2023. Based on the data in the table, answer the questions that follow.

**Company-wise details of sports shoes**

| Company | Year 2022 | | | Year 2023 | | |
|---|---|---|---|---|---|---|
| | Number (in lakh) | Rejected (%) | Sold (%) | Number (in lakh) | Rejected (%) | Sold (%) |
| *A* | 25 | 3 | 65 | 33 | 4 | 72 |
| *B* | 26 | 5 | 88 | 30 | 3 | 76 |
| *C* | 32 | 2 | 72 | 37 | 3 | 82 |
| *D* | 24 | 9 | 76 | 32 | 5 | 87 |
| *E* | 35 | 4 | 81 | 41 | 5 | 80 |
| *F* | 18 | 5 | 90 | 24 | 4 | 81 |
| *G* | 30 | 4 | 83 | 35 | 4 | 78 |

**1** What is the percentage rise in the production of sports shoes by Company *C* from the year 2022 to 2023?

(1) 15.375% (2) 20.625%
(3) 15.625% (4) 10.625%

***Ans.*** *(3)* Number of shoes produced in 2022 by Company $C = 32$ lakh

Number of shoes produced in 2023 by Company $C = 37$ lakh

$$\text{Percentage rise} = \frac{\text{New value} - \text{Old value}}{\text{Old value}} \times 100$$

$$= \frac{37-32}{32} \times 100$$

$$= 15.625$$

Thus, the percentage rise in the production of sports shoes by Company *C* is 15.625%.

**2** Total number of sports shoes sold by all companies in year 2023 is approximately ........ % of the total number of sports shoes produced by all the companies in that year.

(1) 84 (2) 79 (3) 72 (4) 75

***Ans. (2)*** Total shoes sold in 2023:

By Company $A$: $33 \times 0.72 = 23.76$ lakh

By Company $B$: $30 \times 0.76 = 22.8$ lakh

By Company $C$: $37 \times 0.82 = 30.34$ lakh

By Company $D$: $32 \times 0.87 = 27.84$ lakh

By Company $E$: $41 \times 0.80 = 32.8$ lakh

By Company $F$: $24 \times 0.81 = 19.44$ lakh

By Company $G$: $35 \times 0.78 = 27.3$ lakh

Total sold = 184.28 lakh

Total shoes produced in 2023:

$A$: 33 lakh  $B$: 30 lakh

$C$: 37 lakh  $D$: 32 lakh

$E$: 41 lakh  $F$: 24 lakh

$G$: 35 lakh

Total produced = 232 lakh

Percentage of shoes sold:

$$\left(\frac{\text{Total sold}}{\text{Total produced}}\right) \times 100 = \left(\frac{184.28}{232}\right) \times 100 = 79$$

So, approximately 79% of the total sports shoes produced in 2023 were sold.

**3** What is the percentage rise in the sale of sports shoes by Company $F$ from the year 2022 to 2023?

(1) 12%  (2) 25%  (3) 15%  (4) 20%

***Ans. (4)*** Sales in 2022: 18 lakh × 90% = 16.2 lakh

Sales in 2023: 24 lakh × 81% = 19.44 lakh

Difference: 19.44 lakh – 16.2 lakh = 3.24 lakh

$$\text{Percentage rise} = \left(\frac{3.24\text{ lakh}}{16.2\text{ lakh}}\right) \times 100 = 20$$

Therefore, the percentage rise in the sale of sports shoes by Company $F$ from 2022 to 2023 is 20%.

**4** What is the total number of rejected sports shoes from all the companies together in year 2022?

(1) 835000  (2) 835020

(3) 835040  (4) 835080

***Ans. (1)*** Rejected shoes in 2022:

By Company $A$ : 25 lakh × 3% = 75,000

By Company $B$ : 26 lakh × 5% = 130,000

By Company $C$ : 32 lakh × 2% = 64,000

By Company $D$ : 24 lakh × 9% = 216,000

By Company $E$ : 35 lakh × 4% = 140,000

By Company $F$ : 18 lakh × 5% = 90,000

By Company $G$ : 30 lakh × 4% = 120,000

Total rejected shoes:

75,000 + 130,000 + 64,000 + 216,000 + 140,000 + 90,000 + 120,000 = 835,000

Therefore, the total number of rejected sports shoes from all the companies together in year 2022 is 835,000.

**5** Percentage rise in the production of sports shoes from the year 2022 to 2023 is more than 25% for exactly ......... companies.

(1) 2  (2) 3  (3) 4  (4) 5

***Ans. (2)*** Percentage rise in production:

For Company $A$ : $\left(\frac{33-25}{25}\right) \times 100 = 32\%$

For Company $B$ : $\left(\frac{30-26}{26}\right) \times 100 = 15.38\%$

For Company $C$ : $\left(\frac{37-32}{32}\right) \times 100 = 15.63\%$

For Company $D$ : $\left(\frac{32-24}{24}\right) \times 100 = 33.33\%$

For Company $E$ : $\left(\frac{41-35}{35}\right) \times 100 = 17.14\%$

For Company $F$ : $\left(\frac{24-18}{18}\right) \times 100 = 33.33\%$

For Company $G$ : $\left(\frac{35-30}{30}\right) \times 100 = 16.67\%$

Companies with a percentage rise more than 25% are A, D and F.

Therefore, there are 3 companies with a percentage rise in production of more than 25% from 2022 to 2023.

**6** Which of the following are true about tropospheric or ground level ozone?

A. It is called as good ozone.
B. It is formed due to downward transfer of ozone from ozone layer.
C. It is formed due to the action of sunlight on oxides of nitrogen.
D. It is a greenhouse gas.

E. It is a key component of photochemical smog.

Choose the correct answer from the options given below.

(1) B, C, D and E

(2) A, B and C

(3) C, D and E

(4) A, D and E

***Ans. (1)*** Statements (B), (C), (D) and (E) are true about tropospheric or ground level ozone.
Ground level ozone, also known as tropospheric ozone, is a colourless, irritating gas that forms near the surface of the Earth. It is a secondary pollutant that's create when two primary pollutants, nitrogen oxides ($NO_x$) and volatile organic compounds (VOCs) react in sunlight and stagnant air.
Ground-level ozone is primarily formed at ground level due to chemical reactions, some ozone are transported downward from the stratosphere, contributing to the overall ozone concentration near the Earth's surface.

It is a greenhouse gas that contributes to global warming.

Ground-level ozone is a major component of photochemical smog, a type of air pollution that can cause respiratory problems and other health issues.

Statement (A) is incorrect because ground-level ozone is harmful to human health and the environment, while stratospheric ozone is beneficial as it protects us from harmful UV radiation.

**7** To teach a particular topic, a teacher first gives the students to watch the pre-recorded video of the lecture at home and then engages the students in discussions and problem solving activities in the class. This is an example of

(1) Lecture-demostration

(2) Flipped classroom

(3) Asynchronous learning

(4) Synchronous learning

***Ans. (2)*** To teach a particular topic, a teacher first gives the students a pre-recorded video of the lecture at home and then engages the students in discussions and problem-solving activities in the class. This approach is an example of a flipped classroom.

In a flipped classroom model, instructional content is delivered outside of class (e.g., through pre-recorded videos), and class time is used for engaging in interactive activities such as discussions and problem-solving.

**8** A teacher wants his students to watch pre-recorded videos and answer questions embedded in the videos. Which tool would be most suitable for this purpose?

(1) Edpuzzle

(2) Evernote

(3) Google Docs

(4) Strawpoll

***Ans. (1)*** The most suitable tool for embedding questions in pre-recorded videos is Edpuzzle. Edpuzzle allows teachers to integrate questions and interactive elements directly into videos, enabling students to engage with the content and assess their understanding as they watch.

**9** Match List I with List II.

| | **List I** (Scale of Measurement) | | **List II** (Example of Variable) |
|---|---|---|---|
| A. | Nominal | I. | Height of students |
| B. | Ordinal | II. | Time of day |
| C. | Interval | III. | Caste |
| D. | Ratio | IV. | Rank of Army personnel |

**Codes**

| | A | B | C | D | | A | B | C | D |
|---|---|---|---|---|---|---|---|---|---|
| (1) | I | II | III | IV | (2) | II | III | IV | I |
| (3) | III | IV | II | I | (4) | IV | I | II | III |

*Ans.* *(3)* The correct matching is A-III, B-IV, C-II and D-I.

**Nominal** involves categorical data with no intrinsic order. Caste is an example of a nominal scale.

**Ordinal** involves data with a meaningful order but not necessarily equal intervals. Rank of Army personnel is an example of an ordinal scale.

**Interval** involves numerical data with equal intervals but no true zero point. Time of day is an example of an interval scale.

**Ratio** involves numerical data with equal intervals and a true zero point. Height of students is an example of a ratio scale.

**10** Match List I with List II.

| | List I (Swayamprabha Channel No.) | | List II (Name) |
|---|---|---|---|
| A. | Channel : 04 | I. | Kautilya |
| B. | Channel : 05 | II. | Vidhik |
| C. | Channel : 06 | III. | Prabandhan |
| D. | Channel : 07 | IV. | Saaraswat |

**Codes**

| | A | B | C | D |
|---|---|---|---|---|
| (1) | III | II | IV | I |
| (2) | IV | III | II | I |
| (3) | I | II | III | IV |
| (4) | II | IV | I | III |

*Ans.* *(2)* The correct matching is A-IV, B-III, C-II and D-I.

**Channel : 04** SAARASWAT: CEC/UGC: Social Science , Education, Psychology, Home Science and related subjects.

**Channel : 05** PRABANDHAN: CEC/UGC: Social Science - 3, Management, Library Science, Information Science and related subjects.

**Channel : 06** VIDHIK: CEC/UGC: Social Science-4, Law, Legal Studies, Human Rights and related subjects.

**Channel : 07** KAUTILYA: CEC/UGC: Economics, Commerce and Finance.

**11** "Somdutta who is never seen eating during the day time is constantly gaining weight. Therefore, she must be eating during the night time". As per classical Indian philosophy which instrument of knowledge is used in the above statement?

(1) Perception (2) Analogy
(3) Verbal authority (4) Postulation

*Ans.* *(4)* The instrument of knowledge used in the given statement is Postulation. This involves making a hypothesis or assumption based on available information. The statement assumes that Somdutta is eating at night because she's gaining weight despite not eating during the day.

**12** Find the value of the expression

$$\frac{(0.12 \times 0.12 \times 0.12) + (0.012 \times 0.012 \times 0.012)}{(0.48 \times 0.48 \times 0.48) + (0.048 \times 0.048 \times 0.048)}$$

(1) $\frac{1}{16}$ (2) $\frac{1}{4}$
(3) 4 (4) $\frac{1}{64}$

*Ans.* *(4)*

$$\frac{(0.12 \times 0.12 \times 0.12) + (0.012 \times 0.012 \times 0.012)}{(0.48 \times 0.48 \times 0.48) + (0.048 \times 0.048 \times 0.048)}$$

$$= \frac{(0.12)^3 [(1 \times 1 \times 1) + (0.1 \times 0.1 \times 0.1)]}{(0.48)^3 [(1 \times 1 \times 1) + (0.1 \times 0.1 \times 0.1)]}$$

$$= \left(\frac{1}{4}\right)^3 = \frac{1}{64}$$

**13** Which of the following are routes for exposure to pollutants in humans ?

A. Inhalation
B. Consumption
C. Ingestion
D. Dermal
E. Digestion

Choose the correct answer from the options given below.

(1) A, B and C
(2) A, C and D
(3) B, D and E
(4) A, C and E

***Ans. (2)*** Among the given options, Inhalation, Ingestion and Dermal are the routes for the exposure to pollutants in humans.

**Inhalation :** Breathing in polluted air can expose individuals to various pollutants, including particulate matter, volatile organic compounds and gases.

**Ingestion :** This is synonymous with consumption and refers to the act of taking substances into the body through the mouth.

**Dermal :** Pollutants can also enter the body through the skin, especially if they are absorbed through cuts, scrapes or pores. Consumption and Digestion are not the routes for exposure to pollutants in humans because consumption of contaminated food or water can indirectly expose individuals to pollutants that have entered the food chain.
Digestion is the process of breaking down food and absorbing nutrients. While it is not a direct route of exposure to pollutants, it can be affected by pollutants that enter the body through other means.

**14** Which of the following are true about International Solar Alliance (ISA) ?

A. There are over 100 member countries in this alliance.
B. Its headquarter is in Geneva, Switzerland.
C. Most of its member countries lie between equator and Tropic of Cancer.
D. Primary objective of alliance is to efficiently use solar energy.
E. It is a collaborative initiative of India and France.

Choose the correct answer from the options given below.

(1) A, B and D

(2) A, D and E

(3) B, C and E

(4) C, D and E

***Ans. (2)*** Statements (A), (D) and (E) are correct about International Solar Alliance (ISA).

The International Solar Alliance (ISA) has 120 member countries.

Its main goal is to promote the efficient use of solar energy.

The ISA was founded by India and France. It is a collaborative initiative of India and France.

Statements (B) and (C) are incorrect because the ISA's headquarters is in Gurugram, India.

The ISA's members are primarily countries that lie between the Tropic of Cancer and the Tropic of Capricorn.

**15** Identify the threats to internal validity.

A. Selection threat
B. Maturation threat
C. Attrition threat
D. Testing threat

Choose the correct answer from the options given below.

(1) A, B and C

(2) B, C and D

(3) A, C and D

(4) A, B, C and D

***Ans. (4)*** All four options i.e., Selection, Maturation, Attrition and Testing are threats to internal validity.

Threats to internal validity are factors that can affect the ability to draw causal conclusions from an experiment.

Selection threat occurs when there are systematic differences between groups that could affect the outcome.

Maturation threat occurs when changes in participants over time affect the outcome, unrelated to the experimental treatment.

Attrition threat occurs when participants drop out of the study, which can affect the results.

Testing threat occurs when the act of testing itself affects the participants performance on subsequent tests.

**16** Which of the following were measures initiated by Lord Auckland?

A. Guaranteed the maintenance of oriental colleges
B. Publication of useful works for instruction in oriental languages
C. Selection of certain places for establishing central colleges for highest instruction

D. Closure of college libraries
E. Abolition of student scholarships

**Choose the correct answer from the options given below.**

(1) A, B and C (2) B, C and D
(3) C, D and E (4) A, D and E

***Ans. (1)*** Lord Auckland, during his tenure as the Governor-General of India, took several measures related to education. The specific measures initiated by Lord Auckland included :

Guaranteed the maintenance of oriental colleges was the part of his efforts to support and maintain the existing oriental colleges.

Publication of useful works for instruction in oriental languages by Auckland promoted the publication of works in oriental languages to support education.

Selection of certain places for establishing central colleges for highest instruction by Auckland and also initiated the establishment of central colleges for higher education.

Closure of college libraries and abolition of student scholarships were not initiated by Lord Auckland.

**17** **Identify the correct sequence of the following modes of communication.**

A. Written B. Face-to-face
C. Print D. Broadcasting
E. Datacasting

**Choose the correct answer from the options given below.**

(1) A, C, B, E, D (2) B, A, C, D, E
(3) C, D, E, A, B (4) D, E, A, B, C

***Ans. (2)*** The correct sequence from traditional to modern modes of communication is B, A, C, D, E.

Face-to-face is the most direct and personal form of communication.

Written involves recording messages in a more permanent form but still requires direct delivery.

Print involves the mass production of written material, such as newspapers and books.

Broadcasting involves transmitting information to a wide audience via radio or television.

Datacasting involves the delivery of data over broadcast networks, often used for digital content distribution.

**18** **A man invests ₹1550 in two parts, one part at the rate of 8% interest and another part at the rate of 6%. If the total interest earned in one year is ₹106, find the amount invested at each rate of interest, respectively.**

(1) ₹650 and ₹900 (2) ₹700 and ₹850
(3) ₹750 and ₹800 (4) ₹800 and ₹750

***Ans. (1)*** Let man invested ₹$x$ on Rate of interest 8%

And ₹$(1550 - x)$ on Rate of interest 6%

According to the Question,

We know, $SI = \frac{PRT}{100}$

Also, Given $SI_1 + SI_2 = 106$

$$\frac{x \times 1 \times 8}{100} + \frac{(1550 - x) \times 1 \times 6}{100} = 106$$

$$\frac{8x}{100} + \frac{9300 - 6x}{100} = 106$$

$$2x + 9300 = 10600$$

$$2x = 1300$$

$$\Rightarrow \quad x = 650$$

∴ First part = ₹650

and another part = ₹(1550 – 650) = 900

**19** **Which component of Baddeley's basic working memory model is involved in the task of rapid repetition of the word like 'See-Saw'?**

(1) Visuospatial sketchpad
(2) Bounded rationality
(3) Phonological loop
(4) Meta-cognition

***Ans. (3)*** The phonological loop is the component of Baddeley's basic working memory model responsible for processing verbal and auditory information, such as the rapid repetition of words like 'See-Saw'. It is involved in the short-term storage and rehearsal of verbal information.

**20** **The University Education Commission (1948-49) suggested a bachelor degree of**

(1) five years (2) four years
(3) three years (4) two years

***Ans.*** ***(3)*** The University Education Commission (1948-49), chaired by Dr. Sarvepalli Radhakrishnan, recommended a three-year bachelor's degree programme. This was a significant departure from the then-existing two-year degree programmes in India.

The commission's rationale for recommending a three-year degree was to provide students with more comprehensive and in-depth education, allowing for a more thorough exploration of their chosen subjects.

**21** **According to UGC Regulations 2018 on Plagiarism, which of the following percentages of similarity in a research article would result in debarring a university teacher from supervising a PhD. students for a period of two years?**

(1) 27% (2) 38% (3) 44% (4) 65%

***Ans.*** ***(3)*** The correct answer is 44%. As per the UGC Regulations 2018 on Plagiarism, if the similarity in a research article is found to be 40% to 60%, the consequences include debarring the faculty member from supervising new PhD. students for two years and not being allowed to publish for two years.

**22** **On the basis of the coverage area, identify the correct ascending order of the following four types of computer networks A-D.**

A. WAN B. LAN
C. MAN D. PAN

**Choose the correct answer from the options given below.**

(1) D, B, C, A
(2) B, C, A, D
(3) D, C, B, A
(4) A, B, D, C

***Ans.*** ***(1)*** The correct ascending order of the given computer networks based on their coverage area is D, B, C, A.

PAN (Personal Area Network) has the smallest coverage area, typically limited to a few meters. Examples include Bluetooth connections between devices.

LAN (Local Area Network) covers a smaller area, usually within a building or a campus. Examples include wired or wireless networks in offices or schools.

MAN (Metropolitan Area Network) covers a larger area, typically within a city or metropolitan region. Examples include networks connecting multiple LANs or institutions.

WAN (Wide Area Network) covers the largest area, spanning across countries or even continents. Examples include the internet.

**23** **An instructor uses portfolio assessments in an art class. What key components should be included in the students' portfolios?**

A. Collection of completed artworks
B. Reflective essays on their creative process
C. Standardised test scores
D. Peer feedback and critiques

**Choose the correct answer from the options given below.**

(1) B and C (2) A, B and D
(3) A and C (4) C and D

***Ans.*** ***(2)*** The correct answer is A, B and D.

A portfolio assessment in an art class focuses on showcasing the student's artistic progress and reflection. The key components of an art portfolio usually include

Collection of completed artworks demonstrates the student's creative output.

Reflective essays on their creative process allows students to articulate their thought process and growth.

Peer feedback and critiques helps to provide insights into the student's work from the perspective of their peers.

Standardised test scores are not part of an art portfolio, as the focus is on individual creativity and growth, rather than standardised assessment.

**24** "If one eats mushrooms after a long gap of time, one falls ill. I have been having some digestive issues since morning today, therefore there must have been mushroom in that mixed vegetable soup we had last night" which fallacy, if any, committed in the above argument?

(1) It is a valid argument

(2) Affirming the consequent

(3) Hasty Generalisation

(4) Begging the question

***Ans. (2)*** The fallacy in this argument is 'Affirming the consequent'. This fallacy occurs when the argument assumes that because the consequent (falling ill) is true, the antecedent (eating mushrooms) must also be true, which is not necessarily the case. In this argument, just because the person is ill, they assume it must be due to mushrooms, even though there could be other reasons for their illness.

**25** Which of the following propositions are contradictory ?

A. All squares are rectangles

B. No squares are rectangles

C. Some squares are rectangles

D. Some squares are not rectangles

Choose the correct answer from the options given below.

(1) C and D (2) A and D

(3) B and D (4) A and B

***Ans. (4)*** Propositions are contradictory if they cannot both be true or both be false at the same time. Let's analyse the propositions

All squares are rectangles is true because every square is indeed a rectangle.

No squares are rectangles is false because squares are a specific type of rectangle.

Propositions (A) and (B) are contradictory. If all squares are rectangles (A), then no squares can be non-rectangles (B) and *vice-versa*.

**26** According to David Holmes, the textual or behavioural qualities of communication are determined by the architecture of the particular .........

(1) Medium (2) Message

(3) Noise (4) Ideology

***Ans. (1)*** According to David Holmes, the architecture of the medium plays a crucial role in shaping the textual or behavioural qualities of communication. The medium through which communication occurs influences how messages are structured and perceived.

**27** Match List I with List II.

| | List I (Commission) | | List II (Recommendation) |
|---|---|---|---|
| A. | Hunter Commission | I. | University technological departments providing for research and teaching |
| B. | Sadler Commission | II. | Withdrawal of government support to colleges education |
| C. | Hartog Committee | III. | Development of mofussil colleges into future university centres |
| D. | Sargent plan | IV. | Enrichment of college libraries and concentration on Honours courses in select centres |

**Codes**

| | A | B | C | D | | A | B | C | D |
|---|---|---|---|---|---|---|---|---|---|
| (1) | I | II | III | IV | (2) | II | III | IV | I |
| (3) | III | IV | I | II | (4) | IV | I | II | III |

***Ans. (2)*** The correct matching is A-II, B-III, C-IV and D-I.

The **Hunter Commission** (1882) recommended that government funding should focus on primary and secondary education rather than collegiate education, suggesting a withdrawal of support at the college level.

The **Sadler Commission** (1917-1919) emphasised the development of rural or "mofussil" colleges and their potential to grow into university centers, focusing on expanding higher education in rural areas.

The **Hartog Committee** (1929) advocated for the improvement of college infrastructure, including libraries, and suggested concentrating Honours courses in select institutions to maintain quality in higher education.

The **Sargent Plan** (1944) proposed the creation of university-level departments focused on technological research and teaching to promote advancements in science and technology education.

**28** The Kothari Commission (1963-64) suggested spending ......... of national income on education.

(1) 3 percent (2) 6 percent
(3) 7 percent (4) 9 percent

***Ans. (2)*** The Kothari Commission (1963-64) recommended that 6 percent of the national income to be spent on education in order to improve the quality and accessibility of education in India.

**29** In a certain code language

'Bitter patience sweet fruit' is coded as: 'Bo Po So To'

'Art is sweet happiness' is coded as : 'Ao Io So Ho'

'Hoping is concealing bitter' is coded as: 'Hp Io Co Bo'

'Patience is art of hoping' is coded as : 'Po Io Ao Oo Hp'

How 'Patience is happiness' will be coded in this language ?

(1) Ho Io Po (2) Hp Ao Po
(3) Po Ao Hp (4) Po Io Ho

***Ans. (4)*** According to the question,

Bitter patience sweet fruit → Bo Po So To
Art is sweet happiness → Ao Io So Ho
Hoping is concealing bitter → Hp Io Co Bo
Patience is art of hoping → Po Io Ao Oo Hp

Hence, Patience is happiness → Po Io Ho

**30** The major difference between Television and Cinema is

(1) Eye movement
(2) Sound reverberation
(3) Bandwidth
(4) Liveness differential

***Ans. (4)*** The major difference between Television and Cinema is liveness differential. Cinema often involves a one-time, large-screen viewing experience that can be immersive and theatrical, while television is usually watched at home with ongoing access, and often involves live broadcasts or the possibility of time-shifted viewing.

**31** Arrange the datasets with the following means ($\overline{X}$) and standard deviations ($\sigma$) in decreasing order of their coefficients of variation.

A. $\sigma = 4.3, \overline{X} = 13.8$
B. $\sigma = 3.8, \overline{X} = 12.7$
C. $\sigma = 5.7, \overline{X} = 14.9$
D. $\sigma = 4.7, \overline{X} = 14.1$

Choose the correct answer from the options given below.

(1) A, B, C, D (2) B, C, D, A
(3) C, D, A, B (4) D, A, B, C

***Ans. (3)*** The coefficient of variation (CV) is a measure of relative dispersion. It is calculated as the ratio of the standard deviation ($\sigma$) to the mean ($\bar{x}$).

$$CV = \frac{\sigma}{\bar{x}}$$

We can calculate the CV for each dataset:

Dataset A: $CV = \frac{4.3}{13.8} = 0.3116$

Dataset B: $CV = \frac{3.8}{12.7} = 0.2992$

Dataset C: $CV = \frac{5.7}{14.9} = 0.3825$

Dataset D: $CV = \frac{4.7}{14.1} = 0.3333$

Arranging the datasets in decreasing order of their CVs, we get C, D, A, B.

**32** Match List I with List II.

| | List I (Concept) | | List II (Description) |
|---|---|---|---|
| A. | Closed text | I. | Verbal expressions |
| B. | Principle of safety | II. | Basic rhetorical structure |
| C. | Orality | III. | A text to elicit a single response |
| D. | Cluster | IV. | Avoidance of risk |

**Codes**

| | A | B | C | D |
|---|---|---|---|---|
| (1) | I | II | III | IV |
| (2) | II | III | IV | I |
| (3) | III | IV | I | II |
| (4) | IV | I | II | III |

***Ans.* (3)** The correct matching is A-III, B-IV, C-I and D-II.

**Closed text** is a text designed to elicit a single response or answer.

**Principle of safety** is the avoidance of risk or danger.

**Orality** is the use of spoken language, often characterised by features like repetition, parallelism and rhythm.

**Cluster** is a basic rhetorical structure that groups related ideas together.

**33** Which of the following is/are true?

A. If the selling price (SP) of an article is ₹ 40 and the gain is 15%, the cost price (CP) of the article is ₹ 32.

B. A man bought a toy for ₹ 150 and sold it at a profit of 8%. He sold the toy for ₹ 162.

C. A man buys a cycle for ₹ 500, but due to some problem, he sells it for ₹ 400. He thus incurs a loss of 22%.

D. Cost price of an article, if its SP is ₹ 210 and the loss is 30%, is ₹ 300.

Choose the correct answer from the options given below.

(1) A only (2) A and D only
(3) B and D only (4) B and C only

***Ans.* (3)** From Statement A

If the selling price (SP) of an article is 40 and the gain is 15%, the cost price (CP) of the article is 32.

$$\text{CP} = \left(\frac{100}{100 + P\%}\right) \times \text{SP}$$

$$\text{CP} = \frac{100}{115} \times 40 = 34.78$$

So, Statement A is incorrect.

From Statement B

A man bought a toy for ₹150 and sold it at a profit of 8%. He sold the toy for ₹162.

$$\text{SP} = \frac{100 + P\%}{100} \times \text{CP} = \frac{108}{100} \times 150 = 162$$

So, Statement B is correct.

From Statement C

A man buys a cycle for ₹500, but due to some problem, he sells it for ₹400. He thus incurs a loss of 22%.

$$\text{Loss} = 500 - 400 = 100$$

$$\text{Loss\%} = \frac{100}{500} \times 100 = 20\%$$

So, Statement C is incorrect.

From Statement D

Cost price of an article, if its SP is ₹210 and the loss is 30%, is ₹300.

$$\text{CP} = \frac{100}{100 - L\%} \times \text{SP} = \frac{100}{70} \times 210 = 300$$

So, Statement D is correct.

Hence, Statements B and D are correct.

**34** Which of the following methods of graphical representation of data would be useful in showing association between two variables?

(1) Ogive (2) Pie charts
(3) Histogram (4) Scatter plots

***Ans.* (4)** The method best suited for showing the association between two variables is scatter plots. Scatter plots display individual data points on a coordinate system, allowing you to observe and analyse the relationship or correlation between the two variables.

**35** If the statement "Some rectangles are squares" is given as true then which of the following statements can be inferred to be false?

A. All rectangles are squares.
B. Some rectangles are not squares.
C. Some squares are not rectangles.
D. No rectangles are squares.

Choose the correct answer from the options given below.

(1) B, C and D only (2) D only
(3) B and C only (4) A, B, C and D

***Ans.* (2)** "Some rectangles are squares" is true, the following can be inferred.

All rectangles are squares is false because only some rectangles are squares, not all.

Some rectangles are not squares can be true, as the statement "Some rectangles are squares" does not exclude the possibility that some rectangles are not squares.

Squares are not rectangles is false because squares are a specific type of rectangle.

No rectangles are squares is definitely false because "Some rectangles are squares" directly contradicts this statement.

So, the statement that can be inferred to be false is (D) No rectangles are squares.

**36** Consider the series given below. Find the number which can be inserted at the place of question mark (?).

5, 14, 39, 88, 209, ?, 667

(1) 378 (2) 297

(3) 299 (4) 375

*Ans. (1)* The pattern of the given series as follows

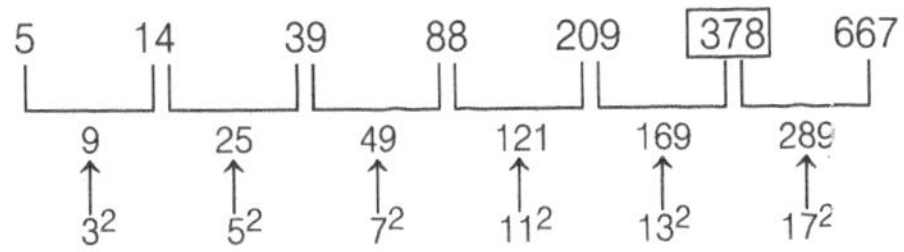


Hence, square of continuous prime numbers are adding.

**37** Match List I with List II.

| | List I (ICT Term) | | List II (Definition) |
|---|---|---|---|
| A. | VoIP | I. | A tool for real-time communication between two or more people sending text messages to their devices |
| B. | Instant Messaging (IM) | II. | A system of interlinked hypertext documents accessed via the Internet |
| C. | VPN | III. | A technology that allows you to talk with other people using the internet |
| D. | WWW | IV. | A network that protects data by encrypting network traffic |

**Codes**

| | A | B | C | D | | A | B | C | D |
|---|---|---|---|---|---|---|---|---|---|
| (1) | II | I | IV | III | (2) | IV | II | III | I |
| (3) | III | I | II | IV | (4) | III | I | IV | II |

*Ans. (4)* The correct matching is A-III, B-I, C-IV and D-II.

**VoIP** (Voice over Internet Protocol) is a technology that allows you to talk with other people using the Internet.

**Instant Messaging** (IM) is a tool for real-time communication between two or more people sending text messages to their devices.

**VPN** (Virtual Private Network) is a network that protects data by encrypting network traffic.

**WWW** (World Wide Web) is a system of interlinked hypertext documents accessed via the Internet.

**38** From the following identify the propositions that are logically equivalent.

A. Some books are novels
B. Some books are not non-novels
C. Some novels are not non-books
D. Some novels are books

Choose the correct answer from the options given below.

(1) C and D (2) A and D

(3) A and C (4) A, B, C and D

*Ans. (4)* All four propositions are logically equivalent. They all express the same idea, that there exists at least one book that is a novel.

**Some books are novels** This directly states that there exists at least one book that is a novel.

**Some books are not non-novels** This is a negation of the statement "All books are non-novels". If some books are not non-novels, then it implies that there must be at least one book that is a novel.

**Some novels are not non-books** This is a rephrasing of proposition (B). If some novels are not non-books, it means that there must be at least one book that is a novel.

**Some novels are books** This is a tautology, as it is always true that a novel is a book.

Therefore, all four propositions are equivalent and convey the same meaning.

**39** Identify the correct chronological order of the establishment of the following colleges.

A. Fort William College, Calcutta
B. Sanskrit College, Poona
C. Central Hindu College, Benares

D. Anglo-Vedic College, Lahore
E. Sanskrit College, Benares

Choose the correct answer from the options given below.

(1) A, B, C, E, D (2) C, D, B, E, A
(3) D, E, A, B, C (4) E, A, B, D, C

***Ans.*** ***(4)*** The correct chronological order of the establishment of the colleges are as follows

1. Sanskrit College, Benares (1791)
2. Fort William College, Calcutta (1800)
3. Sanskrit College, Poona (1821)
4. Anglo-Vedic College, Lahore (1886)
5. Central Hindu College, Benares (1898)

**40** The medium of Internet is described as

A. Restricted possibility
B. Unimpressive theology
C. Universalist
D. Redemptive
E. Electronic assembly

Choose the correct answer from the options given below.

(1) A, B and C
(2) B, C and D
(3) C, D and E
(4) A, B and E

***Ans.*** ***(3)*** The medium of the Internet is best described as C, D and E.

Universalist is described as universal because it connects people and resources globally, offering widespread accessibility and inclusivity.
Redemptive suggests that the Internet can bring improvement or recovery by providing access to education, social connections, and problem-solving resources, though it's a less common description.
Electronic assembly refers to the technological infrastructure of the Internet, emphasising its components and integration, but doesn't fully capture its global, inclusive nature.

**41** Leachate is a

(1) Green house gas
(2) Air pollutant
(3) Liquid extract from landfill site
(4) Ozone depleting substance

***Ans.*** ***(3)*** Leachate is a liquid that is formed when rainwater or other liquids percolate through waste in a landfill. It can contain a variety of pollutants, including heavy metals, organic compounds, and bacteria. These pollutants can contaminate groundwater and surface water, posing a risk to human health and the environment.

**42** Which of the following devices are computer output devices only?

A. Scanner B. Plotter
C. Light pen D. Projector
E. Speaker

Choose the correct answer from the options given below.

(1) A, B, D and E (2) D and E
(3) A, B and C (4) B, D and E

***Ans.*** ***(4)*** Among the given options, Plotter, Projector and Speaker are the output devices.

Output devices are hardware components that take data processed by the computer and present it to the user in a readable or perceivable form. They display, project, or produce output in various formats, such as text, images, audio or visuals. Common examples include monitors, printers, speakers, and projectors, etc.

Plotter is an output device used to create large, high-quality graphics or designs on paper, often for technical drawings or blueprints.

Projector displays visual output from the computer onto a large surface, like a screen or wall, for easier viewing by multiple people.

Speakers are output devices that convert digital audio signals from the computer into sound.

**43** **Which of the following is a software that displays unwanted or sometimes irritating pop-up advertisements which can appear on your computer or mobile phone?**

(1) Spyware
(2) Adware
(3) Worm
(4) Trojan Horse

***Ans. (2)*** Adware is a type of software that displays unwanted or intrusive advertisements on your computer or mobile device. These advertisements can appear as pop-ups, banners or other forms of online advertising. While adware itself is generally not malicious, it can be annoying and can slow down your device's performance.

**44** Microsoft Access is an example of an ......... .

(1) Operational resource toolkit system
(2) ERP system
(3) Database management system
(4) Knowledge management system

***Ans. (3)*** Microsoft Access is a popular Database Management System (DBMS). It is designed to help users create, manage and manipulate databases. It provides tools for organising, storing and retrieving data efficiently.

**45** **Which one of the following is considered as a prominent indoor air pollutant?**

(1) Mercury (2) Radon
(3) Helium (4) Argon

***Ans. (2)*** Radon is a naturally occurring radioactive gas that can seep into homes and buildings from the soil. It is considered a significant indoor air pollutant because it can increase the risk of lung cancer.

**Directions** (Q. Nos. 46-50) *Read the passage carefully and answer the questions that follows.*

Holidays are often a time of culinary indulgence even for people who are usually careful about diets for the rest of the year.

But there is more to holiday eating than avoiding excess calories. What we eat affects the health of the entire body, including the Immune system. Since the most of the body's immune system is concentrated in the gut and the trillions of healthy bacteria living there called the microbiome - what we eat has a direct impact on how the immune system functions. "A lot of people don't think about the effects of what they eat on immunity. But the science says it's crucial", says Heather Moday, MD, Founder of the Moday Centre for Functional and Intergrative Medicine in Norfolk, Virginia, and Philadelphia. And it's especially important at this time of year. Since the winter holidays occur around the time when illnesses like colds, flu and other respiratory illnesses peak.

While an occasional indulgence probably won't cause lasting damage, throwing caution to the wind till New year's Day is certainly unhealthy and might make you more susceptible to getting sick. "Even just a month of really just blowing it and not caring about nutrition can impact the microbiome", says Kristin Kirkpatrick, a registered dietitian at Cleveland Clinic's department of wellness and preventive medicine.

**46** **Which of the following statements is incorrect in the context of the given text?**

(1) There is a lot less harm done if four days out of the week you are eating pretty well
(2) To keep the immunity strong, one does not have to stop celebrating but needs to celebrate a little smarter
(3) What we eat has a direct impact on the immune system
(4) Occasional food indulgence will cause lasting damage

***Ans. (4)*** Statement (4) is incorrect as the passage explains that occasional indulgence likely won't cause lasting damage to the body. However, consistently neglecting nutrition over time, like throughout the holiday season, can negatively affect the immune system and microbiome.

**47** **Find out the correct statement that describes the primary focus of Heather Moday's statement in the text.**

(1) The benefits of a balanced diet
(2) The relationship between diet and immune system
(3) The important of regular exercise
(4) The effects of meditation on health

*Ans.* *(2)* Heather Moday emphasises that what we eat directly affects the immune system because a large portion of the body's immune system is located in the gut. The health of the microbiome, which is influenced by our diet, plays a crucial role in immune function.

**48** Which of the following are effects of diet on the body's immune system as discussed in the text?

(1) Increased cholestrol levels
(2) Direct impact on immune system functions
(3) Improved skin health
(4) Loss of appetite

*Ans.* *(2)* The passage explicitly states that "what we eat has a direct impact on how the immune system functions".

**49** Microbiomes are important as

(1) They create lots of sugar in the body
(2) They are healthy bacteria living in the body
(3) They may raise blood pressure and heart disease risk
(4) They increase the tendency for processed food

*Ans.* *(2)* The passage highlights that microbiomes are trillions of healthy bacteria in the gut that significantly impact the immune system. Their health is directly influenced by our diet, affecting how well our immune system functions.

**50** Important key message the above text conveys about holiday eating can be stated as follows

(1) It is important to completely avoid indulgence
(2) Occasional indulgence is unlikely to cause lasting damage
(3) Diet has no significant impact on the immune system
(4) Holidays are an ideal time to experiment with extreme diets

*Ans.* *(2)* The passage explains that occasional indulgence during the holidays probably won't lead to lasting harm, but regularly neglecting good nutrition can affect the microbiome and immune system. It's important to be mindful of diet to avoid increased susceptibility to illnesses.

# UGC
## NET/JRF/SET

# Solved Paper, 2024

### (Exam Held on : 02 September 2024, Shift I)

## General Paper 1 (Teaching and Research Aptitude)

***Instructions***

- This paper contains fifty Multiple Choice Questions, each question carries two marks.
- All questions are compulsory.
- Total time given for this paper is 1 hour.

**Directions** (Q. Nos. 1-5) *Read the following information carefully and answer the given questions.*

The following table shows the cumulative percentage distribution of the total number of visitors to Kullu and Manali together and cumulative number of visitors to Kullu on five different days, that is Monday to Friday. Based on the data in the table, answer the questions.

**Day-wise Distribution of visitors**

| Day | Cumulative percentage of visitors to Kullu and Manali | Cumulative number of visitors to Kullu |
|---|---|---|
| Monday | 15% | 360 |
| Till Tuesday | 40% | 1060 |
| Till Wednesday | 70% | 1540 |
| Till Thursday | 80% | 1700 |
| Till Friday | 100% | 1960 |

**Note** Total number of visitor to Kullu and Manali together in all five days is 4000.

**1** What is the ratio of the number of visitors to Manali on Wednesday to the number of visitors to Kullu on Thursday?

(1) 9 : 2 (2) 4 : 3 (3) 2 : 9 (4) 3 : 4

***Ans.*** *(1)* The total Percentage of visitors to Kullu and Manali together on Wednesday

$= 70 - 40 = 30\%$

The total number of visitors to Kullu and Manali together on Wednesday

$= 30\%$ of $4000 = 1200$

The number of visitors to Kullu on Wednesday is $= 1540 - 1060 = 480$

The number of visitors to Manali on Wednesday is $= 1200 - 480 = 720$

So, the number of visitors to Kullu on Thursday is $= 1700 - 1540 = 160$

Required ratio $= 720 : 160 = 9 : 2$

**2** The total number of visitors to Manali on Monday and Wednesday is ........% of the number of visitors to Kullu on Wednesday.

(1) 200 (2) 150

(3) 125 (4) 50

***Ans.*** ***(1)*** The total number of visitors to Kullu and Manali together by Monday = 15% of 4000

= 600

The number of visitors to Kullu by Monday is 360.

Therefore, the number of visitors to Manali on Monday is = 600 – 360 = 240

Total Percentage of visitors to Kullu and Manali together on Wednesday

= (70 – 40) = 30%

The total number of visitors to Kullu and Manali together by Wednesday

= 30% of 4000 = 1200

The number of visitors to Kullu on Wednesday is = 1540 – 1060 = 480

Therefore, the number of visitors to Manali on Wednesday = 1200 – 480 = 720

The total number of visitors to Manali on Monday and Wednesday is = 240 + 720 = 960

The number of visitors to Kullu on Wednesday is = 1540 – 1060 = 480

The total number of visitors to Manali on Monday and Wednesday as a percentage of the number of visitors to Kullu on Wednesday is

$$= \frac{960}{480} \times 100 = 200\%$$

**3** **What is the average number of visitors to Manali on all the days except Monday?**

(1) 560 (2) 520 (3) 490 (4) 450

***Ans.*** ***(4)*** Total number of visitors going to Kullu

= 1960

Total number of visitors going to Manali

= 4000 – 1960 = 2040

Number of visitors going to Kullu on Monday

= 360

Number of visitors going to Kullu and Manali going on Monday = 15% of 4000 = 600

Visitors going to Manali on Monday = Total visitors on Monday – Visitors going to Kullu on Monday = 600 – 360 = 240

Total visitors going to Manali except Monday

= 2040 – 240 = 1800

$$\text{Required average} = \frac{1800}{4} = 450$$

**4** **If 20% of the visitors to Kullu on Tuesday are foreigners and 40% of the visitors to Manali on Friday are foreigners, then what is the total number of visitors to Kullu on Tuesday who are not foreigners and to Manali on Friday who are foreigners?**

(1) 920 (2) 776 (3) 984 (4) 844

***Ans.*** ***(2)*** The cumulative number of visitors to Kullu by Monday is 360.

Therefore, the number of visitors to Kullu on Tuesday is = 1060 – 360 = 700

So, the number of foreigners on Tuesday

= 20% of 700 = 140

Number of non-foreigners = 700 – 140 = 560

Total number of visitors on Friday

= (100 – 80)% of 4000

= 20% of 4000

= 800

Visitors going to Kullu on Friday

= 1960 – 1700 = 260

Visitors going to Manali on Friday

= 800 – 260 = 540

Foreign visitors going to Manali on Friday

= 40% of 540 = 216

Required sum = 560 + 216 = 776

**5** **The average number of visitors to Kullu on Monday and Thursday is .........% less than the number of visitors to Manali on Wednesday.**

(1) 53.29 (2) 63.89 (3) 67.44 (4) 50.28

***Ans.*** ***(2)*** Number of visitors going to Kullu on Monday = 360

Number of visitors going to Kullu on Thursday = 1700 – 1540 = 160

Total number of visitors going to Kullu on Monday and Thursday = 360 + 160 = 520

$$\text{Average} = \frac{520}{2} = 260$$

Total number of visitors going on Wednesday

= (70 – 40)% of 4000

= 30% of 4000 = 1200

Number of visitors going to Kullu on Wednesday = 1540 – 1060 = 480

Number of visitors going to Manali on Wednesday = 1200 − 480 = 720

Difference = 720 − 260 = 460

$$\text{Required percentage} = \frac{460}{720} \times 100 = 63.89$$

**6** Which of the following are different types of ethnography?

A. Classical ethnography
B. Mainstream ethnography
C. Post-modern ethnography
D. Private ethnography
E. Expressive ethnography

Choose the correct answer from the options given below.

(1) A, B and C (2) B, C and D
(3) C, D and E (4) A, D and E

***Ans.*** ***(*)*** This Question has been dropped by NTA

Ethnography refers to a qualitative research method used to study cultures, societies, and human behaviours by observing and interacting with participants in their natural environments. The goal of ethnography is to provide a detailed, in-depth understanding of the practices, beliefs, and behaviours of people within a specific cultural group.

**Classical ethnography** This is a well-known type of ethnography, which focuses on the traditional, immersive study of cultures.

**Mainstream ethnography** This term is not commonly used in ethnographic literature and may not be a recognised type.

**Post-modern ethnography** This is a valid type of ethnography that emphasises the subjective nature of knowledge and challenges the traditional ways of studying cultures.

**Private ethnography** This is not a widely recognised type of ethnography.

**Expressive ethnography** This type of ethnography is recognised and focuses on representing cultural experiences through expressive forms, like performance or art.

**7** In a certain code language A is coded as Z, B is coded as Y, C is coded as X, and so on. How 'PERFECT' will be coded in that language?

(1) KVIUVXG (2) KVIVUXG
(3) KVIUVGX (4) KVUIVXG

***Ans. (1)*** In the given code language, each letter is replaced by its reverse counterpart in the alphabet (A $\rightarrow$ Z, B $\rightarrow$ Y, C $\rightarrow$ X, etc.). To decode "PERFECT"

P E R F E C T
↓ ↓ ↓ ↓ ↓ ↓ ↓
K V I U V X G

Thus, "PERFECT" is coded as KVIUVXG.

**8** What number would replace question mark (?) in the series given below?

1, 7, 16, 28, 43, 61, 82, ?

(1) 102 (2) 143 (3) 106 (4) 110

***Ans. (3)*** The pattern of the given series as follows,

1 7 16 28 43 61 82 106

+6 +9 +12 +15 +18 +21 +24

+3 +3 +3 +3 +3 +3

$\therefore$ ? = 106

**9** In ancient times, the oral communication system operated in an environment that was

(1) Literate (2) Urban
(3) Non-representative (4) Mediated

***Ans. (3)*** In ancient times, the oral communication system operated in a non-representative environment. This means that the information transmitted was often limited to a small group of people, and there was no way to record or preserve it for future reference. This was in contrast to later historical periods when writing and other forms of recording information became more widespread.

**10** SWAYAM is a programme initiated by

(1) Government of India
(2) National Council of Education Research and Training
(3) University Grants Commission
(4) Indira Gandhi National Open University

***Ans. (1)*** SWAYAM (Study Webs of Active-Learning for Young Aspiring Minds) is a flagship programmes initiated by the Government of India. It aims to provide quality education through online courses from top universities and institutions across the country. The programme is designed to achieve the three cardinal principles of the National Education Policy i.e. access, equity and quality.

**11** Sustainable Development Goal-7 is related to

(1) Gender equality

(2) Climate action

(3) Affordable and clean energy

(4) Quality education

***Ans.*** ***(3)*** Sustainable Development Goal-7 is related to affordable and clean energy.

Sustainable Development Goal-7 (SDG-7) specifically focuses on ensuring access to affordable, reliable, sustainable and modern energy for all. This includes both the expansion of renewable energy sources and the improvement of energy efficiency.

**12** **In the Buddhist system of education, higher education was placed at**

(1) the first level

(2) the second level

(3) the third level

(4) the fourth level

***Ans.*** ***(2)*** In the Buddhist system of education, higher education was placed at the second level. The first level focused on basic education, while the second level was for more advanced studies, including philosophy, religion and other subjects. Students who completed this level often became teachers or scholars.

**13** **Two persons $X$ and $Y$ invested ₹ 15,000 and ₹ 20,000 respectively, in a business. At the end of the year, they share the profit in the ratio of 3 : 1. If $X$ has invested his money for the whole year, for how many months $Y$ has invested his money?**

(1) 3 months (2) 6 months

(3) 5 months (4) 4 months

***Ans.*** ***(1)*** Let, $Y$ invested for $t$ months

The ratio of investments of $X$ and $Y$

$$= 15000 \times (12) : 20000\,(t) = 9 : t$$

Now we know that

ratio of share of investment = ratio of profit

$$\frac{9}{t} = \frac{3}{1}$$

$$t = 3$$

$Y$ invested for 3 months.

**14** **In the context of Computer Networks, which of the following best describes the transmission of a message using packet switching?**

1. Data packets may follow different routes and may arrive at different times in different order.
2. Data packets will always follow the same route and arrive at the same time in the same order.
3. Data packets will always follow the same route but could arrive at different times in different order.
4. Data packets may follow different routes but will always arrive at the same time in the same order.

***Ans.*** ***(1)*** In the context of Computer Networks, the transmission of a message using packet switching means data packets may follow different routes and may arrive at different times in different order. Packet switching divides data into packets that are sent independently through the network.

Because each packet can take a different path to the destination, they might arrive at different times and potentially in a different sequence than they were sent. This method is efficient and resilient, allowing for flexible routing and better utilisation of network resources.

**15** **If a conclusion incorporates a casual relationship between two or more variables it has measured**

(1) External validity

(2) Internal validity

(3) Replicability

(4) Conceptualisation

***Ans.*** ***(2)*** If a conclusion incorporates a casual relationship between two or more variables it has measured internal validity. Internal validity refers to the degree to which an experiment accurately measures the casual relationship between variables. It ensures that the observed effects are genuinely due to the variables being studied and not influenced by external factors. High internal validity means that the study effectively controls for confounding variables, making the causal link between variables more reliable.

**16** Which of the following are the characteristics of learner-centered approach?

A. It lays emphasis on skills.
B. It is centered on learner's needs.
C. It is centered on cooperative determination of subject matter.
D. Lays emphasis on variability of exposure.

Choose the most appropriate answer from the options given below

(1) C and D (2) A, B and C
(3) A, B, C and D (4) B and D

***Ans.*** ***(3)*** All the given options are the characteristics of learner-centered approach.

The learner-centered approach focuses on the needs, interests and learning styles of students, encouraging active participation and self-directed learning. It shifts the role of the teacher to a facilitator, guiding students as they take responsibility for their own learning.

In a learner-centered approach, the development of skills, especially critical thinking and problem-solving, is emphasised.

The approach focuses on the needs, interests and goals of the learner rather than just the curriculum or the teacher.

It is centered on cooperative determination of subject matter. The subject matter is often determined collaboratively, involving both the teacher and learners to make the learning experience more relevant.

The learner-centered approach values diverse learning experiences and exposure to different methods, materials and environments.

**17** Response of participants who are well aware of the fact that they are being studied is considered as

(1) Directed response
(2) Intentional response
(3) Desire effect
(4) Reactive effect

***Ans.*** ***(4)*** Response of participants who are well aware of the fact that they are being studied is considered as a reactive effect. This occurs when participants alter their behaviour or responses because they are aware that they are being observed or studied. This is common in research and can affect the validity of the study results.

**18** In an examination, average marks of six students is 50. However, during cross checking of the papers, it is found that the marks of one student has been misread as 48 instead of 84. Find the correct average marks of the students.

(1) 52 (2) 54 (3) 56 (4) 58

***Ans.*** ***(3)*** Total marks = Average marks × Number of students total marks = $50 \times 6 = 300$

Corrected total marks = Total marks − Incorrect marks + Correct marks

$$= 300 - 48 + 84 = 336$$

$$\text{Correct average} = \frac{336}{6} = 56$$

Therefore, the correct average marks of the students is 56.

**19** Which of the following are examples of organic pollutants in water?

A. Salts B. Pesticides
C. Dioxins D. Bases
E. Pigments

Choose the correct answer from the options given below.

(1) A, B and C (2) B, C and D
(3) C, D and E (4) B, C and E

***Ans.*** ***(4)*** Among the given options, Pesticides, Dioxins and Pigments are examples of organic pollutants in water.

Organic pollutants are toxic chemicals, often carbon-based, that persist in the environment, causing harm to ecosystems and human health.

**Pesticides** These are organic pollutants, as they are carbon-based compounds used to control pests.

**Dioxins** These are highly toxic organic pollutants resulting from industrial processes.

**Pigments** Some pigments can be organic compounds, especially those used in dyes. Salts and Bases are 'not the examples of organic pollutants in water.

**20** Montreal Protocol is related to protection of

(1) Biodiversity

(2) Glaciers

(3) Oceans

(4) Stratospheric ozone layer

*Ans.* ***(4)*** Montreal Protocol is related to protection of stratospheric ozone layer. The Montreal Protocol is an international treaty designed to protect the stratospheric ozone layer by phasing out the production and consumption of substances that deplete it, such as chlorofluorocarbons (CFCs).

**21** Individual who live in a particular community develop distinctively patterned system of

(1) Information distribution

(2) Media ownership

(3) Median marketing

(4) Information imperialism

*Ans.* ***(1)*** Individuals living in a particular community often develop distinctively patterned systems of information distribution, which refers to how information is shared, communicated and circulated within that specific community based on cultural, social and local norms.

**22** Any study of messages at the receivers stage is known as

(1) Communicator analysis

(2) Message analysis

(3) Noise analysis

(4) Audience analysis

*Ans.* ***(4)*** Any study of messages at the receivers stage is known as audience analysis.
It refers to the study of how messages are received, interpreted and understood by the audience. It focuses on the characteristics, needs and responses of the audience at the receiver's stage in the communication process.

**23** Which of the following are true regarding Fort William College?

A. Its medium of education was English.

B. Lord Wellesley taught here.

C. Ishwar Chandra Vidyasagar taught here.

D. It was here that Ishwar Chandra Vidyasagar studied along with Subhash Chandra Bose.

Choose the correct answer from the options given below.

(1) A, C and D

(2) B and D

(3) A, B, C and D

(4) A and C

*Ans.* ***(4)*** Statements A and C are true regarding Fort William College.

Fort William College was established to train British civil servants in Indian languages, but the medium of instruction initially included English.

Ishwar Chandra Vidyasagar, a noted educator and reformer, contributed to Fort William College by teaching and developing Bengali prose.

Statements B are D are false because

Lord Wellesley, the Governor-General of India, founded the college but did not teach there.

Ishwar Chandra Vidyasagar and Subhash Chandra Bose belonged to different generations, and they did not study together at Fort William College.

**24** Qualitative research makes use of

(1) Scaling

(2) Factoring

(3) Representative quotations

(4) SPSS

*Ans.* ***(3)*** Qualitative research makes use of representative quotations. It uses representative quotations from participants to illustrate themes, patterns and insights derived from the data. This method is key in understanding the experiences and perspectives of individuals in a detailed and nuanced way.

**25** If the statement "all lions are carnivorous animals" is given as true which of the following statements can be immediately inferred to be false?

A. No lions are carnivorous animals.

B. Some lions are carnivorous animals.

C. Some lions are not carnivorous animals.

D. Some carnivorous animals are lions.

Choose the correct answer from the options given below.

(1) C and D (2) A and C
(3) A and B (4) B and C

***Ans.*** ***(2)*** The correct answer is A and C.

The statement "all lions are carnivorous animals" is a universal affirmative statement. It asserts that every member of the set lions is also a member of the set carnivorous animals.

**No lions are carnivorous animals** This statement directly contradicts the given statement and is therefore false.

**Some lions are carnivorous animals** This statement is a weaker version of the given statement and can be inferred to be true.

**Some lions are not carnivorous animals** This statement contradicts the given statement and is therefore false.

**Some carnivorous animals are lions** This statement is a weaker version of the given statement and can be inferred to be true.

Therefore, the statements that can be immediately inferred to be false are A and C.

**26** According to National Education Policy 2020, which of the following universal human values will be considered as an integral part of holistic education?

A. Truth B. Sympathy
C. Righteous conduct D. Non-violence
E. Scientific temper

Choose the correct answer from the options given below.

(1) C and E
(2) B, D and E
(3) A, C, D and E
(4) A, B, C and D

***Ans.*** ***(3)*** According to the National Education Policy (NEP) 2020, the following universal human values are emphasised as an integral parts of holistic education.

**Truth** It emphasises the importance of honesty and integrity in all aspects of life. It encourages students to seek and uphold the truth in their academic and personal lives.

**Righteous conduct** It focuses on ethical behaviour and moral integrity, guiding students to act in ways that are fair, just and aligned with strong moral principles.

**Non-violence** It advocates for peaceful and respectful interactions, encouraging students to resolve conflicts through dialogue and non-violent means.

**Scientific temper** It promotes a mindset of inquiry, critical thinking and evidence-based reasoning. It encourages students to approach problems and questions with a scientific and rational perspective.

Sympathy is not an integral part of holistic education.

**27** Which of the following statements is true about Number system?

(1) The binary equivalent of the decimal number 57.625 is 111000.101
(2) $(145)_6 = (75)_{10}$
(3) $(1011)_2 + (1001)_2 = (20)_{10}$
(4) $(65)_{10} = (220)_5$

***Ans.*** ***(3)*** From option (1), 111000.101

$= 1\times 2^5 + 1\times 2^4 + 1\times 2^3 + 0\times 2^2 + 0\times 2^1 + 0\times 2^0 + 1\times 2^{-1} + 0\times 2^{-2} + 1\times 2^{-3}$

$= 32 + 16 + 8 + \frac{1}{2} + \frac{1}{8}$

$= 56 + 0.5 + 0.125$

$= 56.625$

$\therefore$ Option (1) is false.

From option (2), $(145)_6 = (75)_{10}$, it is not true.

From option (3), $(1011)_2 + (1001)_2$

$= [1\times 2^3 + 0\times 2^2 + 1\times 2^1 + 1\times 2^0] + [1\times 2^3 + 0\times 2^2 + 0\times 2^1 + 1\times 2^0]$

$= (8 + 2 + 1) + (8 + 0 + 0 + 1) = 11 + 9$

$= (20)_{10}$ it is true.

**28** As per classical Indian school of logic (Nyaya) which of the following fallacy is committed when the middle term is too wide?

(1) Anupasamhari
(2) Badhita
(3) Sadharana
(4) Asadharana

*Ans.* *(3)* As per classical Indian school of logic (Nyaya), Sadharana fallacy is committed when the middle term is too wide as leading to an invalid or weak syllogistic argument.

Anupasamhari fallacy occurs when the conclusion of a syllogism does not follow from the premises due to the premises being incomplete or insufficient. It involves the failure to properly link the premises to the conclusion.

Badhita fallacy arises when a syllogism is based on premises that are contradicted or disproven. It means that the argument is invalid because the premises are not true or have been shown to be false.

Asadharana fallacy occurs when the middle term is too specific or narrow, which may lead to an invalid argument. In this case, the specific middle term does not provide a sufficient link between the premises and the conclusion.

**29** A child of first class is trying to learn how to draw a circle on his own but is able to do with the help of his/her teacher. In the light of Vygotsky's theory, it highlights

(1) Assimilation

(2) Adoption

(3) Zone of Proximal Development

(4) Maturation

*Ans.* *(3)* A child of first class is trying to learn how to draw a circle on his own but is able to do with the help of his/her teacher. In the light of Vygotsky's theory, it highlights the Zone of Proximal Development.

In Vygotsky's theory, the Zone of Proximal Development (ZPD) refers to the range of tasks that a child can perform with the help of a more knowledgeable other (such as a teacher) but cannot yet accomplish independently. The child's ability to draw a circle with the teacher's assistance highlights their ZPD.

**30** Toxic substances that damange kidneys are called as

(1) Hematotoxic (2) Neurotoxic

(3) Cytotoxic (4) Nephrotoxic

*Ans.* *(4)* Toxic substances that damage the kidneys are referred to as nephrotoxic. Nephrotoxicity can lead to various kidney-related issues, including decreased kidney function and kidney failure. Such substances can impair the kidneys' ability to filter blood and maintain proper fluid and electrolyte balance.

**31** Which of the following statements are subalternate as per traditional square of opposition?

A. All plants are green organisms

B. No plants are green organisms

C. Some plants are not green organisms

D. Some plants are green organisms

Choose the correct answer from the options given below.

(1) A and D (2) B and D

(3) A and C (4) A and B

*Ans.* *(1)* The correct answer is (A) and (D).

In the traditional square of opposition, subalternation refers to the logical relationship where a universal statement (A or E) implies the truth of a corresponding particular statement (I or O), but not necessarily the other way around.

Specifically

**Universal Affirmative (A)** All S are P

**Particular Affirmative (I)** Some S are P

**Universal Negative (E)** No S are P

**Particular Negative (O)** Some S are not P

The statements relate as

A. All plants are green organisms (Universal Affirmative)

D. Some plants are green organisms (Particular Affirmative)

In this case, statement A (All plants are green organisms) implies that statement D (Some plants are green organisms) is true.

**32** Which of the following is a free and open-source content collaboration framework based on Javascript that enables existing CMSs and LMSs to create richer content?

(1) H5P (2) Plotagon

(3) Mindmeister (4) Labster

***Ans. (1)*** H5P is a free and open-source content collaboration framework based on Javascript that allows users to create, share and reuse interactive HTML5 content. It integrates with existing CMSs (Content Management Systems) and LMSs (Learning Management Systems) to enhance content creation capabilities.

**33** Project method of teaching was first propounded by

(1) Crow and Crow (2) John Dewey
(3) Robert Miller (4) Robert Mager

***Ans. (2)*** Project method of teaching was first propounded by John Dewey. Project method learning through engaging in projects and hands-on activities. This method is based on the idea that students learn best when they are actively involved in solving real-world problems and working on meaningful projects.

**34** An instrument used in structured observation that mentions the categories of behaviour to be observed is known as

(1) Category schedule
(2) Observation device
(3) Observation schedule
(4) Ontological tool

***Ans. (3)*** An instrument used in structured observation that mentions the categories of behaviour to be observed is known as observation schedule. An observation schedule is a structured tool used in observation studies that outlines the categories of behaviour to be observed and provides a systematic way to record and categorise the observed behaviours.

**35** Which one of the following is used as a reference to measure the Global Warming Potential (GWP) of a green house gas?

(1) Carbon dioxide ($CO_2$)
(2) Methane ($CH_4$)
(3) Chlorofluorocarbon (CFC)
(4) Hydrofluorocarbon (HFC)

***Ans. (1)*** Carbon dioxide ($CO_2$) is used as the reference gas to measure the Global Warming Potential (GWP) of other green house gases. The GWP of a gas is a measure of how much heat it traps in the atmosphere over a specific time period compared to $CO_2$.

**36** Which of the following statements are logically equivalent?

A. All cats are carnivorous animals.
B. All non-carnivorous animals are non-cats.
C. No cats are non-carnivorous animals.
D. Some carnivorous animals are cats.

Choose the correct answer from the options given below.

(1) A, B and C (2) B, C and D
(3) A, C and D (4) C and D

***Ans. (1)*** The logically equivalent statements are

All cats are carnivorous animals.

All non-carnivorous animals are non-cats.

No cats are non-carnivorous animals.

These statements express the same relationship between cats and carnivorous animals.

Statement D, "Some carnivorous animals are cats," is not equivalent but rather a weaker statement about the existence of cats among carnivorous animals.

**37** Consider the following snapshot of MS-Excel worksheet.

| | A | B | C | D |
|---|---|---|---|---|
| 17 | Day | Quantity | Sales Amount (₹) | |
| 18 | Monday | 1 | 234 | |
| 19 | Tuesday | 3 | 144 | |
| 20 | Wednesday | 6 | 367 | |
| 21 | Thursday | 5 | 674 | |
| 22 | Friday | 8 | 1099 | |
| 23 | Saturday | 3 | 233 | |

In cell D18, the value returned by the function.

=SUMIFS (C18 : C23, B18 : B23, ">3", C18 : C23, ">500") is ......... .

(1) 1466 (2) 2140 (3) 1773 (4) 26

***Ans. (3)*** The formula given is:

=SUMIFS (C18 : C23, B18 : B23, ">3", C18 : C23, ">500")

This formula sums the values in the range C18

Where two conditions are met:

The Quantity should be greater than 3.

The Sales Amount should be greater than 500.

Let's evaluate this step by step using the data in the table:

Let's check the rows that meet both conditions:

**Wednesday :** Quantity = 6 (greater than 3), but Sales Amount = 367 (not greater than 500).

**Thursday :** Quantity = 5 (greater than 3), and Sales Amount = 674 (greater than 500).

**Friday :** Quantity = 8 (greater than 3), and Sales Amount = 1099 (greater than 500).

Only **Thursday** and **Friday** meet both conditions.

Now, sum the Sales Amount for these days:

Thursday: 674

Friday: 1099

The total is 674 + 1099 = 1773

**38** Which of the following are main functions of mass communication?

A. Detachment of individual from society.
B. Indulge is message creation without worrying about moral consequences.
C. Survelliance of environment.
D. Transmission of social heritage.
E. Correlating the parts of society in response to environment.

Choose the correct answer from the options given below.

(1) A, B and C
(2) C, D and E
(3) A, B and D
(4) A, D and E

***Ans. (2)*** Statements C, D and E are the main functions of mass communication.
Mass communication is the process of transmitting information, ideas or messages to a large audience through various media channels, such as television, radio, newspapers and the internet.

**39** Which one of the following is a deemed to be university?

1. Periyar University, Salem
2. Nagaland University, Kohima
3. Guru Ghasidas Vishwavidyalaya, Bilaspur
4. Gandhigram Rural University, Madurai

***Ans. (4)*** Gandhigram Rural University is recognised as a deemed-to-be university, a category of higher education institution in India that has been granted the status of university by the University Grants Commission (UGC) but is not necessarily a full-fledged university.

**40** Which informal fallacy is committed in the following statement "Famous actor Jimmy Pecker has said in an interview that astrology is a real science, therefore scientists now must acknowledge that astrology is actually a science"?

(1) Appeal to inappropriate authority
(2) Red herring
(3) Strawman
(4) Appeal to ignorance

***Ans. (1)*** The fallacy is an appeal to inappropriate authority because the statement relies on Jimmy Pecker's status as a famous actor to validate a claim about astrology, rather than on credible scientific evidence. It mistakenly assumes that his opinion carries weight in a field where he lacks expertise.

**41** Which of the following is included among the core values promoted by NAAC (National Assessment and Accreditation Council) among the institutions of higher learning?

(1) Framing national education protocols
(2) Promoting religious education
(3) Total privatisation of education
(4) Fostering global competencies among students and teachers

***Ans. (4)*** The NAAC (National Assessment and Accreditation Council) promotes core values such as fostering global competencies among students and teachers, emphasising the importance of preparing learners for a globalised world. This contrasts with the other options, which are not aligned with NAAC's core values.

**42** A sum of money becomes ₹34800 in 2 years and ₹ 42000 in 5 years at simple interest per annum. Find the rate of interest and the sum of money respectively.

(1) 6%, ₹ 40000 (2) 7%, ₹ 30000
(3) 8%, ₹ 30000 (4) 5%, ₹ 35000

***Ans. (3)*** Amount after 2 years = ₹ 34800

Amount after 5 years = ₹ 42000

$\therefore$ SI of 3 years = 42000 − 34800 = 7200

$\therefore$ SI of 2 years $= \frac{7200}{3} \times 2 =$ ₹ 4800

$\therefore$ Principal = 34800 − 4800 = ₹ 30000

$$SI = \frac{PRT}{100}$$

$$\Rightarrow 4800 = \frac{30000 \times R \times 2}{100}$$

$$\Rightarrow R = \frac{4800 \times 100}{30000 \times 2} = 8\%$$

**43** Which of the following statements about Read Only Memory (ROM) are correct?

A. The contents of the memory remain intact even when the power to the ROM is turned off.
B. ROM is often used to store the start-up instructions when the computer is first switch on.
C. As the ROM becomes full, the processor has to continually access the hard disk.
D. ROM is a volatile memory.

Choose the correct answer from the options given below.

(1) A and B (2) B and C
(3) A and C (4) A, B, C and D

***Ans. (1)*** Statements A and B are correct about ROM.

**ROM** (Read Only Memory) is non-volatile memory that permanently stores data and instructions, which can only be read and not modified, used primarily during the computer's startup process.

ROM retains its contents even when the power is off. It is commonly used to store the start-up instructions, such as the BIOS, that are needed when the computer is first turned on.

Statements C and D are incorrect because ROM is not full like a hard disk; it is used for permanent storage of essential instructions, and accessing it does not involve continually using the hard disk.

ROM is non-volatile memory, meaning it does not lose its data when power is turned off.

**44** For preservation of their power the ruling elites seek from media channels.

(1) Societal intelligence
(2) Entrepreneurial partnership
(3) Digital technology diffusion
(4) Voices of dissent

***Ans. (1)*** Ruling elites often use media channels to gather societal intelligence, which helps them understand public opinion, trend and potential challenges to their power. This information allows them to strategise and maintain control more effectively.

**45** Which of the following statements is true about computers?

(1) The quality of the pictures taken by a digital camera depends on its resolution, which is measured in megabytes.
(2) USB stands for Universal Secure Bus.
(3) Microsoft Excel is an example of system software.
(4) The size of a computer monitor is measured diagonally across the screen.

***Ans. (4)*** Statement (4) is true about computers as the size of a computer monitor is measured diagonally across the screen from corner to corner. This measurement provides a standardised way to describe the screen size.

However, statements (1), (2) and (3) are false.

**Directions** (Q. Nos. 46-50) *Read the passage carefully and answer the questions that follows.*

The field ecologist has played a key role in shining the light on the species we love and admire. They have also underlined why conservation should not be just about caring for a few charismatic species-the cats, elephants, whales or Olive Ridleys. It's also about knowing the value of creatures many of us might consider annoying, even dangerous. For millennia, communities have attempted to protect animals and plants for practical and spiritual reasons. However, for around two centuries or so, an anthropocentric view of the world created an ecological discord of sorts. Utilitarian ideas began to dominate attitudes towards nature, which often meant that even conservation had a strictly commercial purpose. Modern environmental consciousness is perhaps about six decades old. In India, organisations such as the Bombay Natural History Society date back to the late 19th century and the endeavours of hunters-turned-conservationists played an important role in underlining the value of several species. But systematic efforts in mainstreaming ecology began much later and owed much to the works of pioneers like Salim Ali and M Krishnan.

**46** Identify the charismatic species based on the information given in the passage.

A. Deer
B. Whales
C. Elephants
D. Dogs

Choose the correct answer from the options given below.

(1) A and B (2) B and C
(3) C and D (4) A and D

***Ans.*** ***(2)*** According to the passage, charismatic species as animals like whales and elephants, which are often the focus of conservation efforts due to their appeal, while conservation should also extend beyond such species.

**47** Identify the correct statements.

A. Conservations is all about caring for the species we love and admire.
B. Communities have been living in ecological harmony for the last two centuries.
C. Field ecologists have contributed to our understanding about the value of different species in our lives.
D. Salim Ali is considered as pioneer in India in the field of mainstream ecology.

Choose the correct answer from the options given below.

(1) A and B (2) B and C
(3) C and D (4) A and D

***Ans.*** ***(3)*** Statements C and D are correct about the passage.

The passage states that field ecologists have helped us to understand the value of different species. The passage also mentions that Salim Ali was a pioneer in mainstreaming ecology in India.

**48** Modern environment consciousness is

(1) 20 years old (2) 40 years old
(3) 60 years old (4) 100 years old

***Ans.*** ***(3)*** According to the passage, modern environmental consciousness, which is about 60 years old, emerged as a response to the utilitarian view that had dominated for around 200 years.

**49** Utilitarian ideas started dominating attitudes towards nature about

(1) 2000 years ago (2) 60 years ago
(3) 100 years ago (4) 200 years ago

***Ans.*** ***(4)*** According to the passage, for around two centuries, utilitarian ideas began to dominate attitudes towards nature, leading to an anthropocentric view and ecological discord.

**50** Communities have been involved in the protection of plants and animals for the last

(1) Several thousand years
(2) 200 years only
(3) 60 years only
(4) Only recently

***Ans.*** ***(1)*** According to the passage, for millennia (several thousand years), communities have attempted to protect animals and plants for both practical and spiritual reasons.

# UGC

## NET/JRF/SET

# Solved Paper, 2023

(Exam Held on : 16 June 2023, Shift I)

## General Paper 1 (Teaching and Research Aptitude)

***Instructions***

- This paper contains fifty Multiple Choice Questions, each question carries two marks.
- All questions are compulsory.
- Total time given for this paper is 1 hour.

**Directions** (Q. Nos. 1-5) *Read the following extract and answer the questions that follows.*

Table-1 below shows the percentage (%) distribution of candidates who qualified in a competitive examination from six different state *A-F* during the two years 2021 and 2022, along with the ratio of males to females among them and Table-2 shows the total number of candidates who appeared and percentage (%) of candidates who qualified from all the six states *A-F* in same two years. Based on the data in the tables, answer the questions that follow :

**Table-1 : State-wise details of qualified candidates in 2021 and 2022**

| Year | 2021 | | 2022 | |
|---|---|---|---|---|
| State | Qualified(%) | Male : Female | Qualified(%) | Male : Female |
| *A* | 18% | 5 : 4 | 20% | 28 : 17 |
| *B* | 16% | 3 : 1 | 12% | 5 : 3 |
| *C* | 12% | 7 : 5 | 16% | 11 : 5 |
| *D* | 16% | 13 : 11 | 15% | 15 : 11 |
| *E* | 25% | 13 : 12 | 22% | 15 : 9 |
| *F* | 13% | 8 : 1 | 15% | 11 : 9 |

**Table-2 : Year-wise details of appeared and qualified (%) candidates**

| Year | Total Appeared from states *A-F* | Percentage (%) Qualified from States *A-F* |
|---|---|---|
| 2021 | 142000 | 45% |
| 2022 | 180000 | 52% |

**1** The number of female candidates who qualified from state *B* in 2021 is approximately ......... % of the male candidates who qualified from state A in 2022.

(1) 16 (2) 22

(3) 20 (4) 18

***Ans.*** ***(2)*** Total appeared candidates in 2021 from states *A-F* = 142000

Qualified percentage = 45%

Female qualified from state *B*

$$= \frac{1}{4} \times \frac{16}{100} \times \frac{45}{100} \times 142000$$

$$= 2556$$

Total appeared candidates in 2022 from states $A$-$F$ = 180000

Qualified percentage = 52%

Male qualified from state $B$

$$= \frac{28}{45} \times \frac{20}{100} \times \frac{52}{100} \times 180000$$

$$= 11648$$

$$\text{Required percentage} = \frac{2556}{11648} \times 100$$

$$= 21.94\% \approx 22\%$$

**2** **In 2022 for state $A$, if four female candidates who qualified are not eligible, then what is the average number of female candidates who qualified (and eligible) from all the six states together in the year 2022?**

(1) 5990 (2) 5900

(3) 5920 (4) 5940

***Ans. (1)*** Number of candidates qualified in 2022

$$= \frac{52}{100} \times 180000 = 93600$$

Number of female qualified in 2022 from state $A = \frac{17}{45} \times \frac{20}{100} \times 93600 - 4 = 7072 - 4 = 7068$

Number of female qualified in 2022 from state $B = \frac{3}{8} \times \frac{12}{100} \times 93600 = 4212$

Number of female qualified in 2022 from state $C = \frac{5}{16} \times \frac{16}{100} \times 93600 = 4680$

Number of female qualified in 2022 from state $D = \frac{11}{26} \times \frac{15}{100} \times 93600 = 5940$

Number of female qualified in 2022 from state $E = \frac{9}{24} \times \frac{22}{100} \times 93600 = 7722$

Number of female qualified in 2022 from state $F = \frac{9}{20} \times \frac{15}{100} \times 93600 = 6318$

Required average

$$= \frac{7068 + 4212 + 4680 + 5940 + 7722 + 6318}{6}$$

$$= \frac{35940}{6} = 5990$$

**3** **What is the ratio of the number of female candidates who qualified from states $A$ and $C$ together in 2021 to number of male candidates who qualified from the same two states in the year 2022?**

(1) 8307 : 21844 (2) 8407 : 21944

(3) 8307 : 21944 (4) 8307 : 20894

***Ans. (3)*** Number of female candidates who qualified from state $A$ in 2021 $= \frac{4}{9} \times \frac{18}{100} \times \frac{45}{100} \times 142000$

$$= 5112$$

Number of female candidates who qualified from state $C$ in 2021 $= \frac{5}{12} \times \frac{12}{100} \times \frac{45}{100} \times 142000$

$$= 3195$$

$A$ and $C$ together = 5112 + 3195 = 8307

Number of male candidates who qualified from state $A$ in 2022 $= \frac{28}{45} \times \frac{20}{100} \times \frac{52}{100} \times 18000$

$$= 11648$$

Number of male candidates who qualified from state $C$ in 2022 $= \frac{11}{16} \times \frac{16}{100} \times \frac{52}{100} \times 180000$

$$= 10296$$

Sum = 11648 + 10296 = 21944

Required ratio = 8307 : 21944

**4** **The number of male candidates who qualified from state $E$ in 2022 is approximately ......... % more than the number of male candidates who qualified from state $F$ in 2021.**

(1) 72 (2) 74

(3) 70 (4) 76

***Ans. (2)*** Number of male candidates who qualified in 2022 from state $E = \frac{15}{24} \times \frac{22}{100} \times \frac{52}{100} \times 180000$

$$= 12870$$

Number of male candidates who qualified in 2021 from state $F = \frac{8}{9} \times \frac{13}{100} \times \frac{45}{100} \times 142000$

$$= 7384$$

Difference = 12870 − 7384

$$= 5486$$

$$\text{Required percentage} = \frac{5486}{7384} \times 100$$

$$= 74.29\% \approx 74\%$$

**5** In the year 2021, the number of female candidates who qualified is more than 5000 in exactly ......... states.

(1) five (2) four

(3) three (4) two

***Ans.*** ***(4)*** The number of female candidates qualified in the year 2021.

$$\text{From state } A = \frac{4}{9} \times \frac{18}{100} \times \frac{45}{100} \times 142000$$

$$= 5112$$

$$\text{From state } B = \frac{1}{4} \times \frac{16}{100} \times \frac{45}{100} \times 142000$$

$$= 2556$$

$$\text{From state } C = \frac{5}{12} \times \frac{12}{100} \times \frac{45}{100} \times 142000$$

$$= 3195$$

$$\text{From state } D = \frac{11}{24} \times \frac{16}{100} \times \frac{45}{100} \times 142000$$

$$= 7668$$

$$\text{From state } E = \frac{12}{25} \times \frac{25}{100} \times \frac{45}{100} \times 142000$$

$$= 7668$$

$$\text{From state } F = \frac{1}{9} \times \frac{13}{100} \times \frac{45}{100} \times 142000$$

$$= 923$$

The number of female candidates who qualified is more than 5000 in exactly 2 states (*A* and *E*).

**6** In which method of collaborative learning the main purpose is to develop listening skills in the students?

(1) Circle of voices

(2) Problem solving

(3) Fishbowl strategy

(4) Jigsaw strategy

***Ans.*** ***(3)*** In the fishbowl strategy, students form two groups : one group engages in a discussion while the other group listens. The purpose of this strategy is to develop listening skills, as those outside the 'fishbowl' must listen carefully before contributing to the discussion.

**7** Which of the following individual differences may not affect learning?

A. Cultural background

B. Height

C. Blood Group

D. Age

E. Complexion

Choose the correct answer from the options given below.

(1) A, D and E only (2) B, C and E only

(3) B only (4) A, C and D only

***Ans.*** ***(2)*** Height, Blood Group and Complexion are individual differences that do not affect learning.

Whereas, Cultural background and Age can influence learning, as they are related to experiences, development, and context that impact how individuals engage in learning processes.

Individual differences refer to the distinct characteristics that make each person unique, including cognitive abilities, personality traits, learning styles, and social backgrounds. These differences influence how individuals perceive, process, and respond to information and learning experiences.

**8** Which of the following are the characteristics of mind mapping?

A. Built around a central topic

B. Use of long sentences and paragraphs to explain the content

C. The branches of a particular topic form a connected nodal structure

D. Use of images and symbols to represent ideas

Choose the correct answer from the options given below.

(1) A only (2) B and D only

(3) A, C and D only (4) B and C only

***Ans.*** ***(3)*** Statements (A), (C) and (D) are the characteristics of the mind mapping.

Mind mapping is a visual technique used to organise and represent information, where ideas branch out from a central concept in a structured, connected way. It typically uses keywords, images, and symbols to help generate, visualise, and organise ideas.

Characteristics of Mind mapping are as follows:

**Built around a central topic :** Mind mapping starts with a central idea or topic from which related ideas branch out.

**The branches of a particular topic form a connected nodal structure :** Ideas in a mind map are organised into a hierarchical or nodal structure, with connections between related topics.

**Use of images and symbols to represent ideas :** Mind maps often incorporate images and symbols to visually represent concepts.

Statement (B) is not a characteristic of mind mapping, as it focuses on concise points, keywords, and visuals rather than lengthy text.

**9** Match List-I with List-II.

| | List-I (Channel No.) | | List-II (Name) |
|---|---|---|---|
| A. | CH-04 | I. | Prabandhan |
| B. | CH-05 | II. | Kautilya |
| C. | CH-06 | III. | Saaraswat |
| D. | CH-07 | IV. | Vidhik |

**Codes**

| | A | B | C | D | | A | B | C | D |
|---|---|---|---|---|---|---|---|---|---|
| (1) | II | IV | I | III | (2) | IV | III | II | I |
| (3) | III | I | IV | II | (4) | I | II | IV | III |

***Ans.*** ***(3)*** The correct matching is A-III, B-I, C-IV and D-II.

Channel-04, on Swayam Prabha, it is called Saaraswat and covers topics such as social science, education, psychology, and home science.

Channel-05, Prabandhan is a Swayam Prabha channel that covers topics such as management, library science, information science, and related subjects.

Channel-06, on Swayam Prabha, it is called Vidhik and covers topics such as law, legal studies, human rights, and related subjects.

Channel-07, Kautilya is an economics and commerce channel on Swayam Prabha. It covers topics such as Kautilya's political views, his Saptanga Theory, and his ideas on war and diplomacy.

Swayam Prabha is a group of 40 DTH (Direct-to-Home) channels in India that broadcast high-quality educational content 24/7, covering a variety of subjects for school, college, and university students. It aims to provide access to learning resources across the country, particularly in areas with limited internet connectivity.

**10** Which of the following is a benefit of using rubrics for evaluation?

(1) Greater ease of grading

(2) Increased consistency in grading

(3) Increased subjectivity

(4) Greater test security

***Ans.*** ***(2)*** Increased consistency in grading is a benefit of using rubrics for evaluation. By providing clear criteria and scoring guidelines, rubrics help to ensure that all students are evaluated fairly and consistently.

A Rubric is a scoring guide that outlines specific criteria for evaluating student work. It provides clear guidelines for both students and teachers, ensuring consistent and fair assessment.

**11** According to the UGC Regulations, 2018 on plagiarism similarity of 42% refers to which of the following levels of plagiarism?

(1) 0 (2) 1

(3) 2 (4) 3

***Ans.*** ***(3)*** The UGC Regulations, 2018 on plagiarism define levels of plagiarism based on similarity percentages. A similarity of 42% is considered as Level 2 Plagiarism.

Provided Levels

Level 1: Similarities above 10% to 40%

Level 2: Similarities above 40% to 60%

Level 3: Similarities above 60%

Plagiarism is the act of using someone else's work or ideas as your own without giving credit to the original source. This includes copying and pasting text, paraphrasing without attribution or using someone else's ideas without citing them.

**12** The questions of whether a measure that is devised for a concept really does reflect the concept that it is supposed to be denoting, relates to

(1) Measurement validity
(2) Ecological validity
(3) Internal validity
(4) External validity

***Ans.*** *(1)* The questions of whether a measure truly represent the concept it intends to measure relates to Measurement validity.

Measurement validity refers to the extent to which a measurement instrument accurately measures the construct or concept, it is designed to assess. In other words, it ensures that the measure is valid and reliable for measuring the specific phenomenon of interest.

**13** Given below are two statements, one is labelled as Assertion (A) and the other is labelled as Reason (R).

**Assertion** (A) Surveys conducted over the internet have witnessed a huge growth since the late 1990.

**Reason** (R) Internet users always constitute an unbiased sample of the population.

In the light of the above statements, choose the correct answer from the options given below.

(1) Both A and R are true and R is the correct explanation of A.
(2) Both A and R are true, but R is not the correct explanation of A.
(3) A is true, but R is false.
(4) A is false, but R is true.

***Ans.*** *(3)* A is true, but R is false.

'Surveys conducted over the internet have witnessed a huge growth since the late 1990s. The rise of the internet has led to a significant increase in online surveys due to their convenience and cost-effectiveness.

Internet users always constitute an unbiased sample of the population. Internet users may not represent the entire population as they can be influenced by factors such as age, socio-economic status, and access to technology, leading to potential bias.

**14** Among the following types of sampling techniques, which one is also known as 'Judgemental' sampling?

(1) Quota sampling
(2) Convenience sampling
(3) Cluster sampling
(4) Purposive sampling

***Ans.*** *(4)* The type of sampling technique that is also known as 'Judgemental' sampling is Purposive sampling. This technique involves selecting samples based on the judgement of the researcher, who targets specific characteristics or criteria relevant to the research. It is often used when the researcher wants to focus on a particular group or specific attributes.

**15** Variations in time series data would be best represented by a

(1) Line chart (2) Pie chart
(3) Bar chart (4) Scatter plot

***Ans.*** *(1)* Variations in time series data would be best represented by a Line chart.

Line chart is particularly effective for displaying data points over a period of time, as it allows for easy visualisation of trends, patterns, and variations in the data across time intervals.

**16** The person who studies the symbiotic relationship between people and the media technologies which they create and use is identified as

(1) Media influencer
(2) Media sociologist
(3) Media anthropologist
(4) Media ecologist

***Ans.*** *(4)* The person who studies the symbiotic relationship between people and the media technologies which they create and use is identified as a Media ecologist.

A media ecologist studies the relationship between media technologies and society, considering how they influence and shape human culture and behaviour. They examine the ecological impact of media, including its effects on communication, social structures, and the environment.

**17** A political party broadcast is considered as a/an

(1) open text

(2) closed text

(3) lengthy text

(4) liberal text

***Ans.*** *(2)* A political party broadcast is considered a closed text because it is typically a one-way communication channel where the party presents its message to the audience without allowing for direct interaction or feedback. This differs from open text, which allows for two-way communication and exchange of ideas.

**18** The Buddhist concept of interpersonal communication emphasises

A. Flexible morality

B. Total isolation

C. Sensitive use of language

D. Truthfulness

E. Achievement of consensus

Choose the correct answer from the options given below.

(1) A, B and C only (2) B, C and D only

(3) C, D and E only (4) A, B and E only

***Ans.*** *(3)* The correct answer is (C), (D) and (E).

The Buddhist concept of interpersonal communication emphasises

**Sensitive use of language :** Buddhists believe in using language carefully and mindfully to avoid causing harm or misunderstanding.

**Truthfulness :** Honesty and integrity are highly valued in Buddhist communication.

**Achievement of consensus :** Buddhists strive for harmonious and mutually beneficial outcomes in their interactions, emphasising consensus and understanding.

**19** Given below are two statements.

**Statement** (I) The Hindu view of communication is based on the precept that reality is undivided.

**Statement** (II) According to the ancient Hindu view, language is a means to acquire knowledge.

In the light of the above statements, choose the correct answer from the options given below.

(1) Both Statement I and Statement II are correct.

(2) Both Statement I and Statement II are incorrect.

(3) Statement I is correct, but Statement II is incorrect.

(4) Statement I is incorrect, but Statement II is correct.

***Ans.*** *(1)* Both Statement I and Statement II are correct.

Statement I aligns with many Hindu philosophical concepts that view reality as non-dual (Advaita), suggesting a holistic understanding of existence where everything is interconnected.

Statement II is also correct, as ancient Hindu philosophy, particularly in texts like the Vedas and Upanishads, emphasises the importance of language (especially Sanskrit) as a medium through which knowledge and spiritual understanding are transmitted.

**20** Match List-I with List-II.

| | List-I (Scholars) | | List-II (Specialisation/ Concepts) |
|---|---|---|---|
| A. | Bharatha | I. | Grammar |
| B. | Bharthrahari | II. | Sadharanikaran |
| C. | Bhattanayaka | III. | Rasa theory |
| D. | Panini | IV. | Speech theory |

**Codes**

| | A | B | C | D | | A | B | C | D |
|---|---|---|---|---|---|---|---|---|---|
| (1) | I | II | III | IV | (2) | II | III | IV | I |
| (3) | III | IV | II | I | (4) | IV | I | III | II |

***Ans.*** *(3)* The correct matching is A-III, B-IV, C-II, D-I.

**Bharatha is associated with Rasa theory :** Bharatha, an ancient Indian sage, is credited with developing the Rasa theory in his work Natyashastra. This theory explains how various emotions (Rasas) in drama and art evoke specific responses from the audience.

**Bhartrhari is associated with Speech theory** : Bhartrhari, a philosopher and grammarian, introduced the Sphota theory, which deals with the concept of language and meaning. He focused on how the underlying unity of sound (speech) carries meaning, forming the basis of his speech theory.

**Bhattanayaka is associated with Sadharanikaran** : Bhattanayaka expanded on Bharatha's Rasa theory by introducing the concept of Sadharanikaran, which means "generalization." He suggested that art works by creating a universal emotional experience, transcending individual perspectives.

**Panini is associated with Grammar** : Panini was an ancient Sanskrit grammarian, known for his work Ashtadhyayi, a comprehensive and systematic analysis of Sanskrit grammar. His treatise laid the foundation for linguistic rules in ancient Indian language studies.

**21** A person $X$ can do a piece of work worth ₹3000 in 6 days. But he engages an assistant $Y$, and completes the work in 4 days. Find the share of the assistant $Y$ in completing the work.

(1) ₹800 (2) ₹1000 (3) ₹1500 (4) ₹1200

***Ans. (2)*** Person $X$ can do work in 6 days, $X$'s 1 day work $= \frac{1}{6}$ part of work

Both persons $X$ and $Y$ complete the work in 4 days

$Y$'s one day work $= \frac{1}{4} - \frac{1}{6} = \frac{1}{12}$

Ratio of their one day work $= \frac{1}{6} : \frac{1}{12} = 2:1$

$Y$'s share $= \frac{1}{3} \times 3000 =$ ₹1000

**22** A family consists of a husband and wife, their 3 daughters and 2 sons and their 2 wives. How many males and females respectively are there in this family?

(1) 5 and 4

(2) 3 and 6

(3) 4 and 5

(4) 6 and 3

***Ans. (2)*** Family diagram of the given information is as shown below.

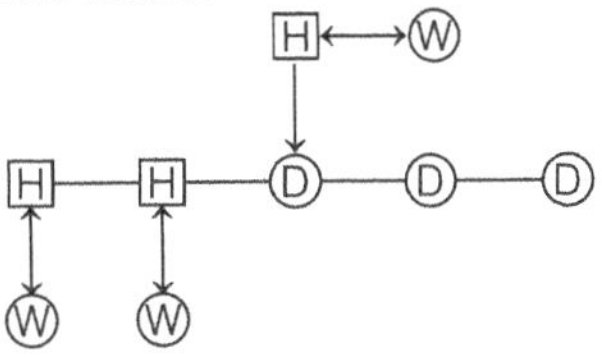


Hence, there are three males and six females in the family.

**Note** : This question has been dropped by UGC.

**23** What number would replace question marks (?) in the series given below?

1, 6, 14, 40, 108, 296, 808, ?

(1) 2208

(2) 1104

(3) 1212

(4) 1804

***Ans. (1)*** Given series and pattern followed is

$1 \xrightarrow{+5} 6 \xrightarrow{+8} 14 \xrightarrow{+26} 40 \xrightarrow{+68} 108 \xrightarrow{+188} 296 \xrightarrow{+512} \boxed{808} \xrightarrow{+1400} \boxed{?}$

We also see that difference also has some rule applied on it

26 = 2 (5 + 8)

68 = 2 (26 + 8)

188 = 2 (68 + 26)

512 = 2 (188 + 68)

So following this, next difference should be 2 (512 + 188) = 1400

Missing number = 808 + 1400 = $\boxed{2208}$

**24** The house of a man is facing towards South. From the front door of the house, the man starts walking and after walking for 20 meters straight, he turns to his left and walks for 50 meters. After this, the man turns to his right and walks for 80 meters and stops there. Find the distance from the point where the man stops to the front door of his house.

(1) $25\sqrt{5}$ m

(2) $50\sqrt{5}$ m

(3) 50 m

(4) 100 m

***Ans. (2)*** As per the information provided in question following diagram can be made

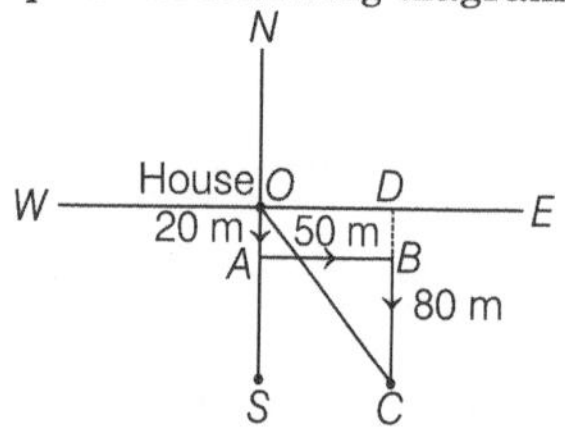


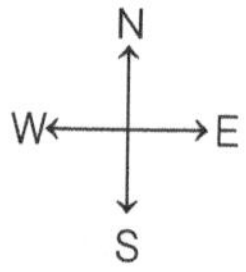


Given, $AB = OD = 50\text{ m}$

$$CD = BC + BD = 80 + 20 = 100\text{ m}$$

$$OC = ?$$

$$OC^2 = OF^2 + CD^2$$

$$OC^2 = (50)^2 + (100)^2$$

$$OC = \sqrt{12500} = 50\sqrt{5}\text{ m}$$

**25** In a certain coding language

(a) 'ON' is coded as 210.

(b) 'OFF' is coded as 540.

How 'SET' will be coded in that language?

(1) 1600 (2) 1850 (3) 1700 (4) 1900

***Ans. (4)*** For 'ON' $\rightarrow 210$

O = 15 (position in the alphabet); N = 14 (position in the alphabet)

Code $= 15 \times 14 = 210$

For 'OFF' $\rightarrow 540$

O = 15; F = 6

Code $= 15 \times 6 \times 6 = 540$

Now, let's apply this multiplication pattern to the word 'SET'

S = 19; E = 5; T = 20

Now, Code $= 19 \times 5 \times 20 = \boxed{1900}$

So, 'SET' will be coded as 1900.

**26** Which of the following statements are contrary to each other?

A. All movies are thrillers.

B. Some movies are not thrillers.

C. No movies are thrillers.

D. Some movies are thrillers.

Choose the correct answer from the options given below.

(1) A and C only (2) B and C only

(3) A and D only (4) C and D only

***Ans. (1)*** To determine which statements are contrary to each other, we need to analyse the relationships between them

**All movies are thrillers** This means every movie falls into the category of thrillers.

**Some movies are not thrillers** This suggests that there are at least some movies that do not belong to the thriller category.

**No movies are thrillers** This means that no movie falls into the category of thrillers at all.

**Some movies are thrillers** This indicates that at least some movies belong to the thriller category.

Pairs (A) and (C) are contrary because if all movies are thrillers, then it cannot be true that no movies are thrillers.

**27** If the statement "Some trucks are not polluting vehicles" is given as false then which of the following statements can be immediately inferred to be true?

A. All trucks are non-polluting vehicles.

B. All trucks are polluting vehicles.

C. Some trucks are polluting vehicles.

D. All polluting vehicles are trucks.

Choose the correct answer from the options given below.

(1) A and C only (2) C and D only

(3) B, C and D only (4) B and C only

***Ans. (4)*** Statements (B) and (C) are correct.

If the statement "Some trucks are not polluting vehicles" is false, it means that all trucks are polluting vehicles (B is true).

Since at least some of these trucks are polluting, some trucks are polluting vehicles (C is also true).

Statements (A) and (D) cannot be inferred from the given false statement.

**28** Which of the following statements is logically equivalent to the statement "All philosophers are realists"?

(1) No philosopher is non-realist.

(2) No realists are non-philosophers.

(3) No non-philosophers are non-realists.

(4) No non-realists are non-philosophers.

*Ans.* *(1)* The statement "All philosophers are realists" can be rephrased as "There are no philosophers who are non-realists", making it logically equivalent to the statement "No philosopher is non-realist".

**29** "I have listened to the Parliament speech of the President of the country XYZ once, from that I must conclude that he is a lousy speaker." Which fallacy is committed in the above statement?

(1) Begging the question

(2) Hasty generalisation

(3) Slippery slope

(4) Ad hominem

*Ans.* *(2)* The fallacy of hasty generalisation occurs when someone draws a broad conclusion based on limited or insufficient evidence. In this case, the speaker is concluding that the President is a lousy speaker based on only one speech, which is not enough to make a general judgement about his speaking abilities.

**30** Given below are two statements.

**Statement** (I) Nyaya syllogism is only inductive and material.

**Statement** (II) The Aristotelian syllogism is only deductive and formal.

In the light of the above statements, choose the correct answer from the options given below.

(1) Both Statement I and Statement II are correct.

(2) Both Statement I and Statement II are incorrect.

(3) Statement I is correct, but Statement II is incorrect.

(4) Statement I is incorrect, but Statement II is correct.

*Ans.* *(4)* Statement I is incorrect, but Statement II is correct.

Nyaya syllogism involves both inductive (reasoning from specific to general) and deductive (general to specific) reasoning, so it is not limited to inductive reasoning alone.

The Aristotelian syllogism is only deductive and formal, focusing on logical relationships between premises leading to a conclusion.

**31** Which of the following is a benefit that businesses receive from using the Internet?

(1) Easier use of satellite radio

(2) Faster connection with suppliers

(3) Improved methods of manufacturing

(4) The ability to call employees on the road

*Ans.* *(2)* The internet provides businesses with a faster and more efficient way to communicate and collaborate with suppliers, leading to improved supply chain management and reduced costs.

**32** Consider the equation $L + M = N$. Where $L = (100011)_2$ and $N = (101000)_2$

What is the value of $M$ as represented in decimal format?

(1) 40 (2) 35

(3) 10 (4) 5

*Ans.* *(4)* Given,

$$L + M = N$$

Where, $L = (100011)_2$

$$= 1\times 2^5 + 0\times 2^4 + 0\times 2^3 + 0\times 2^2 + 1\times 2^1 + 1\times 2^0$$

$$= 32 + 2 + 1 = 35$$

$$N = (101000)_2$$

$$= 1\times 2^5 + 0\times 2^4 + 1\times 2^3 + 0\times 2^2 + 0\times 2^1 + 0\times 2^0$$

$$= 32 + 8 = 40$$

$$M = N - L$$

$$M = 40 - 35 = 5$$

**33** A web page offers a link for users to request another web page. The requested web page contains HTML code and JavaScript code. In this context, identify the correct sequence of the following statements A-E.

A. The requested web page is displayed on the client computer.

B. The user clicks on the hyperlink and the web page is requested from the web server.

C. The requested web page content is transmitted to the client computer.

D. The client computer processes the JavaScript code using the web browser software.
E. The web server locates the requested web page.

Choose the correct answer from the options given below.

(1) B, E, C, A, D (2) B, E, D, C, A
(3) E, B, C, D, A (4) B, E, C, D, A

***Ans.*** ***(4)*** The correct sequence of the statements is B, E, C, D, A, when a user requests a web page.

1. The user clicks on the hyperlink and the web page is requested from the web server.
2. The web server locates the requested web page.
3. The requested web page content is transmitted to the client computer.
4. The client computer processes the JavaScript code using the web browser software.
5. The requested web page is displayed on the client computer.

**34** Given below are two statements.

**Statement** (I) Shareware is limited-functioning freeware and normally expires after a week or month.

**Statement** (II) Shareware code can be modified and redistributed.

In the light of the above statements, choose the correct answer from the options given below.

(1) Both Statement I and Statement II are correct.
(2) Both Statement I and Statement II are incorrect.
(3) Statement I is correct, but Statement II is incorrect.
(4) Statement I is incorrect, but Statement II is correct.

***Ans.*** ***(3)*** Statement I is correct, but Statement II is incorrect.

Shareware is typically a limited-functionality version of software that is distributed for free on a trial basis. After a certain period, often a week or month, the user may need to purchase a license to continue using the full version.

Shareware licenses typically restrict users from modifying or redistributing the software. This is to protect the developer's intellectual property and ensure that they receive revenue from the sale of the full version.

**35** Which of the following should always be regarded as security risks to computer systems?

A. Chat rooms B. Cookies
C. Pharming D. Virus
E. VoIP

Choose the correct answer from the options given below.

(1) A and D only
(2) C and D only
(3) B and D only
(4) A, D and E only

***Ans.*** ***(2)*** Pharming and Virus should always be regarded as security risks to computer systems.

Pharming is a serious security risk where users are redirected from legitimate websites to fraudulent ones, often without their knowledge, leading to data theft or malicious activities.

**36** When a water body gets enriched with nutrients, the process is called as

(1) Oligotrophication
(2) Eutrophication
(3) Mesotrophication
(4) Dystrophication

***Ans.*** ***(2)*** When a water body gets enriched with nutrients, the process is called as Eutrophication.

Eutrophication refers to the process where water bodies become enriched with nutrients, particularly nitrogen and phosphorus. This often leads to excessive growth of algae (algal blooms), which can deplete oxygen levels in the water and harm aquatic life.

**37** Which of the following statements are correct in respect of Greenhouse gases ?

A. They are generally of light green colour.
B. They absorbs thermal radiations emitted by Earth.
C. Water vapour is a greenhouse gas.
D. Greenhouse gases cause global warming.
E. Ammonia ($NH_3$) is a greenhouse gas.

Choose the correct answer from the options given below.

(1) A, B, C and D (2) A, C and E
(3) B, C and D (4) A, B, D and E

***Ans.*** ***(3)*** Statements (B), (C) and (D) are correct regarding Greenhouse gases.

Greenhouse gases trap heat by absorbing thermal radiation, contributing to the greenhouse effect.

Water vapour is a significant greenhouse gas and plays a crucial role in the Earth's climate system.

The accumulation of greenhouse gases in the atmosphere leads to an increase in global temperatures, commonly referred to as global warming.

Statements (A) and (E) are incorrect because Greenhouse gases are not characterised by their colour. They are colourless and odourless gases.

While ammonia can contribute to air pollution and affect ecosystems, it is not classified as a significant greenhouse gas compared to carbon dioxide, methane or nitrous oxide.

**38** Which of the following air pollutants help in the formation of photochemical smog?

(1) Carbon monoxide (2) Methane
(3) Oxides of sulphur (4) Oxides of nitrogen

***Ans.*** ***(1 & 4)*** Both carbon monoxide and oxides of nitrogen contribute to the formation of photochemical smog.

**Carbon Monoxide (CO)** This colourless, odourless gas is produced from incomplete combustion of fossil fuels. In the atmosphere, it can react with hydroxyl radicals (OH) to produce carbon dioxide and other secondary pollutants, exacerbating the effects of smog formation when combined with sunlight.

**Oxides of Nitrogen** ($NO_x$) Comprising primarily nitrogen monoxide (NO) and nitrogen dioxide ($NO_2$), these gases are emitted from vehicles and industrial processes. They play a crucial role in the formation of ground-level ozone, as they react with volatile organic compounds (VOCs) in the presence of sunlight, leading to the development of photochemical smog.

**39** Through enrichment process, concentration of which uranium isotope is increased in the natural uranium?

(1) U-234 (2) U-235
(3) U-238 (4) U-239

***Ans.*** ***(2)*** The enrichment process increases the concentration of the uranium-235 (U-235) isotope in natural uranium, which contains a higher proportion of uranium-238 (U-238). U-235 is the isotope that is fissile and used as fuel in nuclear reactors and for nuclear weapons.

**40** Three R's used for the mitigation of solid wastes are

A. Recover B. Reduce
C. Reuse D. Restrict
E. Recycle

Choose the correct answer from the options given below.

(1) A, B and C (2) B, C and D
(3) B, C and E (4) C, D and E

***Ans.*** ***(3)*** The three R's commonly used for the mitigation of solid waste are

**Reduce :** Minimise the amount of waste produced.

**Reuse :** Utilise items multiple-times before discarding them.

**Recycle :** Process materials to create new products.

Mitigation of solid waste involves strategies aimed at reducing waste generation, promoting the reuse of materials, and recycling items to minimise environmental impact.

Implementing the three R's (Reduce, Reuse, and Recycle) helps conserve resources and decrease landfill use.

**41** Which was the first education commission of independent India?

(1) Sargent Commission
(2) Kothari Commission
(3) Radhakrishnan Commission
(4) Mudaliar Commission

*Ans. (3)* The Radhakrishnan Commission, established in 1948, was the first education commission in independent India. It focused on the development of higher education and the need for a comprehensive educational framework in the country.

It was submitted its report in 1952. The commission was headed by Dr. Sarvepalli Radhakrishnan, who later became the second President of India.

Some objectives of this commission are

To examine the educational system in India and recommend improvements.

To address issues related to higher education and its relevance to society.

To promote the development of a national system of education that emphasises the importance of education for all.

**42** The National Education Policy document of 1986 revised in 1992 suggested

(1) use of multi-media for distance education.
(2) linking degrees with jobs.
(3) abolition of AICTE.
(4) focus on research, only for degrees.

*Ans. (1)* The National Education Policy of 1986, revised in 1992, aimed to improve access to education through distance learning by leveraging multi-media tools like television and radio. This approach was part of the effort to expand educational reach, especially in remote areas.

**43** The committee for the evolution of the New Education Policy recommended that no university in India should have more than ......... affiliated colleges.

(1) 50 (2) 60 (3) 75 (4) 100

*Ans. (4)* The committee for the evolution of the New Education Policy recommended that no university in India should have more than 100 affiliated colleges to ensure better management and quality of education.

**44** Which of the following universities have their locations in Bihar?

A, Vallabhi B. Vikramshila
C. Shridhanya Katak D. Odantapuri

Choose the correct answer from the options given below.

(1) A and D only (2) B and D only
(3) A and B only (4) B and C only

*Ans. (2)* Vikramshila and Odantapuri universities have their locations in Bihar.

Vikramashila situated in Bhagalpur district, Bihar, Vikramshila University was established by Dharmapala. This university was renowned for its studies in Buddhism and philosophy.

Odantapuri located in Nalanda district, Bihar, Odantapuri University was a major centre for the study of Buddhism. It was contemporary to Vikramshila University.

Vallabhi located in Bhavnagar district, Gujarat, Vallabhi University was a significant educational centre in ancient times. It played a crucial role in spreading Buddhism.

Shridhanya Katak information about this university is limited. Some believe it might have been located in Eastern India.

**45** Which of the following universities were established in the year 1857?

A. Calcutta University
B. Bombay University
C. Madras University
D. Allahabad University

Choose the correct answer from the options given below.

(1) A, B and D only
(2) A, B and C only
(3) B, C and D only
(4) A, C and D only

***Ans.*** ***(2)*** Calcutta University, Bombay University, and Madras University were all established in the year 1857. Allahabad University was founded later, in 1887.

Calcutta University established in 1857, it was the first modern university in India, inspired by the model of the University of London.

Bombay University also founded in 1857, it was established by the British to promote higher education in the Bombay Presidency.

Madras University founded in 1857, this institution was set-up to cater to the educational needs of southern India.

Allahabad University established later in 1887, it is one of the oldest modern universities in India, known for its academic excellence.

**Directions** (Q. Nos. 46-50) *Read the passage carefully and answer the questions that follows.*

Few of man's activities have zero environmental effect. For centuries, societies have suffered a wide variety to environmental damage, not least in terms of the air pollution that primitive, uncontrolled methods of combustion caused. People of Roman Britain, with fires in their huts, found the smoke a hazard to health and examination of human skulls shows a pitting that indicates a high frequency of sinusitis. The UK was the first country to widely experience massive industrial development based on coal. Between 1580 and 1680, imports of coal to London increased from 20000 tonnes year to 360000 tonnes and London became a city of 'great stinking fogs'. These were only really to disappear some years after the episode in December 1952 when cold temperatures and moist air resulted in the condensation of moisture on particles in the air from coal combustion. Over a radius of 20 miles, the resulting fog rendered the atmosphere opaque and its was found that in the week ending 13th December, 1952, there had been an excess of 2851 over the usual weekly number of deaths. In response the Clean Air Acts of 1956 and 1968 dealt mainly with smoke in cities. Two decades after the smog disaster the Control of Pollution Act (1947) was brought in and systematically began the long haul towards comprehensive improvements in air quality as part of overall environmental protection. Similar experiences were encountered across Europe and North America during the 20th century.

**46** London became a city of 'great stinking Jogs' as a result of

(1) household fires

(2) cold temperature

(3) coal combustion

(4) excusive moisture in the air

***Ans.*** ***(3)*** The passage states that London's 'great stinking fogs' were primarily caused by coal combustion, which contributed to significant air pollution in the city.

**47** Between 1580 and 1680 imports of coal to London increased

(1) marginally

(2) insignificantly

(3) negligibly

(4) substantially

***Ans.*** ***(4)*** Between 1580 and 1680, the imports of coal to London increased from 20000-360000 tonnes, which is a significant or substantial increase.

**48** The fog of London in the second week of December 1952

A. reduced the number of deaths.

B. increased the number of deaths.

C. rendered the atmosphere over a radius of 20 miles smoke free.

D. rendered the atmosphere over a radius of 20 miles opaque.

E. Did not make any difference to the air quality or to the number of deaths.

Choose the correct answer from the options given below.

(1) B, C and D only

(2) B and D only

(3) C, D and E only

(4) D and E only

***Ans.*** ***(2)*** Statements (B) and (D) are correct.

The fog increased the number of deaths (as mentioned in the passage, there were 2,851 excess deaths during that week). The fog rendered the atmosphere over a radius of 20 miles opaque.

Statements (C) and (E) are incorrect because the fog did not make the atmosphere smoke-free and it significantly impacted air quality and the number of deaths.

**49** The Control of Pollution Act

A. was brought in almost 20 years after the Clean Air Act of 1956
B. stopped all industrial activity
C. aimed at improving air quality
D. focused mainly on dealing with smoke in cities
E. focused on environmental protection

Choose the correct answer from the options given below.

(1) A and E only (2) B, C and D only
(3) A, C and E only (4) A, B, C and D only

***Ans.*** ***(3)*** According to the passage, statements (A), (C) and (E) are correct.

The Control of Pollution Act was brought in almost 20 years after the Clean Air Act of 1956. It aimed at improving air quality. It focused on environmental protection.

Statements (B) and (D) are incorrect because the passage does not state that the Act stopped all industrial activity or focused mainly on dealing with smoke in cities.

**50** The passage highlights mainly

(1) the association between vehicular pollution and development.
(2) air pollution and human health.
(3) the industrial development of UK.
(4) the similarities in development of UK, Europe and North America.

***Ans.*** ***(3)*** The passage highlights mainly the industrial development of UK.

According to the passage, London became a city of "great stinking fogs" due to the massive increase in coal imports and coal combustion, which polluted the air.

# UGC

# NET/JRF/SET

# Solved Paper, 2023

## (Exam Held on : 15 June, 2023, Shift I)

## General Paper 1 (Teaching and Research Aptitude)

***Instructions***

- This paper contains fifty Multiple Choice Questions, each question carries two marks.
- All questions are compulsory.
- Total time given for this paper is 1 hour.

**Directions** (Q.No 1-5) *Study the given table and answer the questions that follows.*

The following table shows the percentage (%) distribution of children in five different villages ($V_1$ to $V_5$) and percentage (%) distribution of children attending school from these five villages. Total number of children in all the five villages is 5800 and total number of children attending school from these five villages is 3600.

Based on the data in the table, answer the questions that follow.

**Village-wise percentage distribution of children**

| Villages | Percentage Distribution of | |
|---|---|---|
| | Number of children (5800) | Number of children attending school (3600) |
| $V_1$ | 16% | 15% |
| $V_2$ | 24% | 28% |
| $V_3$ | 11% | 14% |
| $V_4$ | 18% | 21% |
| $V_5$ | 31% | 22% |

**1** What is the total number of children who do not attend school from the villages $V_2$ and $V_3$ together?

(1) 528 (2) 508

(3) 518 (4) 628

***Ans.*** ***(3)*** Total number of children from the village

$$V_2 = \frac{24}{100} \times 5800 = 1392$$

Total number of children from the village

$$V_3 = \frac{11}{100} \times 5800 = 638$$

Total number of children from the village

$V_2$ who attend school $= \frac{28}{100} \times 3600 = 1008$

Total number of children from the village

$V_3$ who attend school $= \frac{14}{100} \times 3600$

$= 504$

Total number of children who do not attend school from the villages $V_2$ and $V_3$ together

$= 1392 + 638 - (1008 + 504)$

$= 518$

**2** The number of children attending school from village $V_1$ is approximately ......... % of the total number of children from that village.

(1) 58 (2) 60 (3) 53 (4) 54

***Ans. (1)*** Total number of children from the village

$$V_1 = \frac{16}{100} \times 5800 = 928$$

Total number of children from the village

$V_1$ who attend school $= \frac{15}{100} \times 3600 = 540$

Required percentage $= \frac{540}{928} \times 100 = 58.18 = 58\%$

**3** What is the average number of children who do not attend school from village $V_2$, $V_3$ and $V_5$ together?

(1) 512 (2) 508 (3) 540 (4) 532

***Ans. (2)*** Total number of children from the village $V_2$ who do not attend school

$$= \frac{24}{100} \times 5800 - \frac{28}{100} \times 3600$$

$$= 1392 - 1008$$

$$= 384$$

Total number of children from the village $V_3$ who do not attend school

$$= \frac{11}{100} \times 5800 - \frac{14}{100} \times 3600$$

$$= 638 - 504$$

$$= 134$$

Total number of children from the village $V_5$ who do not attend school

$$= \frac{31}{100} \times 5800 - \frac{22}{100} \times 3600$$

$$= 1798 - 792$$

$$= 1006$$

Required average $= \frac{384 + 134 + 1006}{3} = 508$

**4** The total number of children from the village $V_4$ and $V_5$ together is approximately ......% more than the total number of children who do not attend school from the same two villages.

(1) 118 (2) 124 (3) 122 (4) 120

***Ans. (4)*** The total number of children from the villages $V_4$ and $V_5$ = (18% + 31%) of 5800

$$= \frac{49}{100} \times 5800 = 2842$$

The total number of children who attend school from the villages $V_4$ and $V_5$

$$= (21\% + 22\%) \text{ of } 3600$$

$$= \frac{43}{100} \times 3600 = 1548$$

The total number of children who do not attend school from the villages $V_4$ and $V_5$

$$= 2842 - 1548 = 1294$$

Required percentage $= \frac{2842 - 1294}{1294} \times 100$

$$= \frac{1548}{1294} \times 100$$

$$= 119.62\% \approx 120\%$$

**5** What is the ratio of the total number of children from village $V_4$ to the number of children attending school from the same village?

(1) 22 : 21 (2) 29 : 28
(3) 29 : 21 (4) 31 : 23

***Ans. (3)*** The total number of children from village $V_4 = \frac{18}{100} \times 5800 = 1044$

The total number of children from village $V_4$ going to school $= \frac{21}{100} \times 3600 = 756$

Required ratio $= 1044 : 756 = 29 : 21$

**6** Which of the following are the examples of Scaffolding?

A. Providing hints and clues to solve a problem.
B. Allowing the students to figure out the problem on their own.
C. Providing the students with all the answers and solutions to a problem.
D. Asking leading questions to guide the students thinking.

Choose the correct answer from the options given below.

(1) B and C only (2) A and D only
(3) B and D only (4) A, B, C and D

**Ans.** ***(2)*** Statements (A) and (D) are the examples of Scaffolding.

Providing hints and clues to solve a problem is a form of scaffolding as it helps students approach a problem without giving them the direct answer.

Asking leading questions to guide the student's thinking also constitutes scaffolding, as it directs students toward their own understanding while still allowing them to explore and find solutions.

Statements (B) and (C) are not examples of Scaffolding because allowing the students to figure out the problem on their own does not provide support and is not scaffolding, as it removes guidance.

Providing the students with all the answers and solutions to a problem is the opposite of scaffolding, as it does not promote independent learning or critical thinking. Scaffolding is an educational technique that involves providing temporary support and guidance to help students achieve independence in learning and problem-solving.

**7** Which of the following are the humanistic approaches to learning?

A. It emphasises on self-motivation for better learning.
B. Its emphasis is on learning at the higher level.
C. It fosters curiosity.
D. It increases learner's reactivity.
E. It believes that learning becomes effective when it is need-based.

Choose the correct answer from the options given below.

(1) A and D only
(2) B, C and E only
(3) A, B, C, D and E
(4) B and D only

**Ans.** ***(3)*** All of the given statements reflect principles of humanistic approaches to learning, which emphasise personal growth, self-motivation, curiosity, and need-based learning.

Self-motivation is a key aspect of humanistic learning, promoting autonomy.

Learning at a higher level aligns with self-actualisation, a humanistic goal.

Fostering curiosity encourages intrinsic motivation, a core humanistic principle.

Learning is more effective when it addresses the learner's personal needs.

Need-based learning is central to the humanistic approach, focusing on the individual's unique learning requirements.

**8** Which of the following is an example of innovative approach to evaluation systems?

(1) Norm-referenced testing
(2) Peer evaluation
(3) Standardised testing
(4) Traditional grading

**Ans.** ***(2)*** Peer evaluation is an example of innovative approach to evaluation systems where students assess each other's work. It encourages collaboration, critical thinking, and active involvement in the learning process.

**9** In Swayam Prabha, Channel no-08 (Physical Sciences, Mathematics, Physics, Chemistry and related subjects) is named as

(1) Vageesh (2) Saaraswat
(3) Aryabhatta (4) Prabandhan

**Ans.** ***(3)*** In the Swayam Prabha platform, Channel no-08, which focuses on (Physical Sciences, Mathematics, Physics, Chemistry, and related subjects) is named as Aryabhatta, honouring the renowned ancient Indian mathematician and astronomer.

**10** Which of the following ICT tools are associated with Mind mapping?

A. Mindmeister B. X-mind
C. C-map D. Screen casto-matic
E. Adobephotoshop

Choose the correct answer from the options given below.

(1) B and D only (2) A, B and C only
(3) A, C and E only (4) D and E only

**Ans.** ***(2)*** Mindmeister, X-mind and C-map are ICT tools used for mind mapping, which help users visually organise information and ideas.

**11** Identify the disadvantages of closed ended questions in survey research.

A. It is difficult to make forced-choice answers exhaustive.
B. There is loss of spontaneity in respondent's answers.
C. They are time consuming for interviewers to administer.

Choose the correct answer from the options given below.

(1) A and B only (2) B and C only
(3) A and C only (4) A, B and C

***Ans.*** ***(1)*** Statement (A) and (B) are disadvantages of closed ended questions in survey research.
It is difficult to make forced-choice answers exhaustive : Closed-ended questions limit responses to pre-defined options, which may not cover all possible answers.
There is a loss of spontaneity in respondent's answer : Closed-ended questions restrict respondent's ability to provide detailed or nuanced answers.

**12** Given below are two statements.

**Statement** (I) Review of literature helps the researcher with the interpretation of his/her findings.
**Statement** (II) Review of literature is not of any help in learning different theoretical and methodological approaches to your research area.

In the light of the above statements, choose the correct answer from the options given below.

(1) Both Statement I and Statement II are correct.
(2) Both Statement I and Statement II are incorrect.
(3) Statement I is correct, but Statement II is incorrect.
(4) Statement I is incorrect, but Statement II is correct.

***Ans.*** ***(3)*** Statement I is correct, but Statement II is incorrect.
Statement I is correct as reviewing literature helps researchers to interpret their findings by providing context and comparison with previous studies.
Statement II is incorrect because a review of literature is crucial for learning about different theoretical and methodological approaches, which helps refine research questions and design.

**13** Given below are two statements.

**Statement** (I) Content analysis is an approach to the analysis of documents and texts that seeks to analyse them in qualitative terms.

**Statement** (II) Content analysis is a very transparent research method.

In the light of the above statements, choose the correct answer from the options given below.

(1) Both Statement I and Statement II are correct.
(2) Both Statement I and Statement II are incorrect.
(3) Statement I is correct, but Statement II is incorrect.
(4) Statement I is incorrect, but Statement II is correct.

***Ans.*** ***(4)*** Statement I is incorrect, but Statement II is correct.

Statement II is correct as content analysis is considered a transparent method, as the steps and procedures (such as coding categories) are usually well-documented and replicable.

Statement I is incorrect because content analysis can be both quantitative and qualitative. It involves systematically coding and interpreting the content of communication, which can be done using quantitative counts or qualitative thematic analysis.

**14** If you want to conclude that a given variable has a causal relation with a second variable, you have to be able to rule out other possible causal variables. The principle of causation involved here is the

(1) causal ambiguity rule
(2) temporal precedence rule
(3) covariance rule
(4) internal validity rule

***Ans.*** ***(4)*** The internal validity rule refers to the degree to which we can confidently conclude that a causal relationship exists between two variables, and that this relationship is not influenced by other confounding variables. Ensuring internal validity means ruling out other possible causal factors, which is essential in establishing causation.

**15** Which of the following diagrams would be useful in depicting the median value in the data?

(1) Bar chart (2) Box plot
(3) Pie chart (4) Scatter plot

***Ans.*** ***(2)*** Box plot would be useful in depicting the median value in the data.

A box plot (or box-and-whisker plot) is specifically designed to display the distribution of data based on five summary statistics: minimum, first quartile (Q1), median, third quartile (Q3) and maximum. It clearly indicates the median value and the variability of the data.

**16** The audiences of digital media are affected by

(1) limited geographical area
(2) fragmentation
(3) passive messages
(4) identity-crisis

***Ans.*** ***(2)*** The audiences of digital media are affected by fragmentation.

Fragmentation refers to the way digital media audiences are divided into smaller, diverse groups due to the vast array of content available, leading to varied preferences and interests. This affects how audiences engage with media, as they may only interact with specific niche content rather than a unified message.

**17** In films, close-ups are termed as

(1) Pro-active paradigms
(2) Static paradigms
(3) Visual paradigms
(4) Altered paradigms

***Ans.*** ***(3)*** In films, close-ups are termed as Visual paradigms.

A close-up in film is a shot that focuses on a specific detail or object, often a person's face. It is a visual paradigm because it is a specific way of framing a scene to convey a particular message or emotion to the viewer.

**18** Which of the following are the distinguishable features of Buddhist concept of communication?

A. Unidirectional
B. Process-oriented
C. Competitiveness
D. Creation of meaning
E. Behaviour-centred

Choose the correct answer from the options given below.

(1) A, B and C
(2) B, C and D
(3) C, D and E
(4) B, D and E

***Ans.*** ***(4)*** Among the given options, (B), (D) and (E) are the distinguishable features of concept of Buddhist communication.

Process-oriented : Buddhist communication emphasises the process of understanding and mindfulness rather than just the end result. Creation of meaning : It focuses on the shared creation of meaning through dialogue and interaction, reflecting the interconnectedness of all beings.

Behaviour-centred : This aspect relates to how communication is used to promote ethical behaviour and mindfulness in interactions.

**19** Given below are two statements.

**Statement** (I) The study of mass communication process is characterised by a macroscopic view of messages.

**Statement** (II) Semiology seeks a microscopic view of deconstructing messages.

In the light of the above statements, choose the correct answer from the options given below.

(1) Both Statement I and Statement II are correct.

(2) Both Statement I and Statement II are incorrect.

(3) Statement I is correct, but Statement II is incorrect.

(4) Statement I is incorrect, but Statement II is correct.

***Ans.*** *(1)* Both Statement I and Statement II are correct.

The study of mass communication processes focuses on the broader aspects of how messages are created, transmitted, and received within a society. It examines factors like media ownership, audience demographics, and the impact of media on public opinion. This macroscopic view looks at the big picture rather than focusing on individual messages.

Semiology, the study of signs and symbols, takes a microscopic approach to deconstructing messages. It examines the individual elements that make up a message, such as words, images, and sounds, and analyses how these elements convey meaning. Semiology seeks to understand the underlying structures and codes that shape communication.

**20** Given below are two statements.

**Statement** (I) The words-communication, community and communion are etymologically related.

**Statement** (II) As human society developed more and more simple systems of communication emerged.

In the light of the above statements, choose the correct answer from the options given below.

(1) Both Statement I and Statement II are correct.

(2) Both Statement I and Statement II are incorrect.

(3) Statement I is correct, but Statement II is incorrect.

(4) Statement I is incorrect, but Statement II is correct.

***Ans.*** *(3)* Statement I is correct, but Statement II is incorrect.

Statement I is correct as the words communication, community and communion share a common Latin root, communis, which means common. This indicates that these terms are etymologically related and share a common meaning or concept.

Statement II is incorrect because as human society developed, communication systems became more complex, not simpler. Early humans used simple forms of communication like gestures, grunts, and drumbeats. Over time, language developed, and written communication emerged, leading to increasingly complex systems of communication.

**21** In a certain coding language, 'KANPUR' is coded as 'JZMOTQ'. How 'MUMBAI' will be coded in that language?

(1) LTLAZH (2) NVNZBA

(3) NVNCBH (4) LTLZBH

***Ans.*** *(1)* The coding pattern seems to involve shifting each letter of the word back by 1 in the alphabet

| K | A | N | P | U | R |
|---|---|---|---|---|---|
| ↓−1 | ↓−1 | ↓−1 | ↓−1 | ↓−1 | ↓−1 |
| J | Z | M | O | T | Q |

Similarly,

| M | U | M | B | A | I |
|---|---|---|---|---|---|
| ↓−1 | ↓−1 | ↓−1 | ↓−1 | ↓−1 | ↓−1 |
| L | T | L | A | Z | H |

**22** When 18 is included in a list of natural numbers, the average of these numbers is increased by 2. When 8 is included in this new list of natural numbers, the average of these numbers in the new list remains the same. If there are $N$ natural numbers in the original list of numbers and their average is $X$, find the value of $N$ and $X$, respectively.

(1) 5, 6 (2) 6, 8

(3) 8, 6 (4) 6, 5

***Ans.*** ***(1)*** Given $X$ is the average of $N$ natural number

Sum of number = $NX$

Case 1 when 18 is added

$$NX + 18 = (X + 2)(N + 1)$$

$$NX + 18 = NX + X + 2N + 2$$

$$X + 2N = 16 \quad \ldots\text{(i)}$$

Case 2 when 8 is added

$$NX + 18 + 8 = (X + 2)(N + 2)$$

$$NX + 26 = NX + 2X + 2N + 4$$

$$X + N = 11 \quad \ldots(2)$$

Subtracting equation 2 from 1

$$N = 5$$

Putting in equation 2

$$X = 11 - 5 = 6$$

**23** **A girl walks 12 km South from her house, turns left and walks 26 km, again turns left and walks 37 km.**

**Again she turns right and walks 6 km to reach her office. In which direction is the office of the girl from her house?**

(1) South-East

(2) South

(3) North-East

(4) South-West

***Ans.*** ***(3)*** As per the information provided in the question, we can make following diagram. Where girl starts from $A$ and ends her journey at $E$. We see that $E$ is to North-East of $A$.

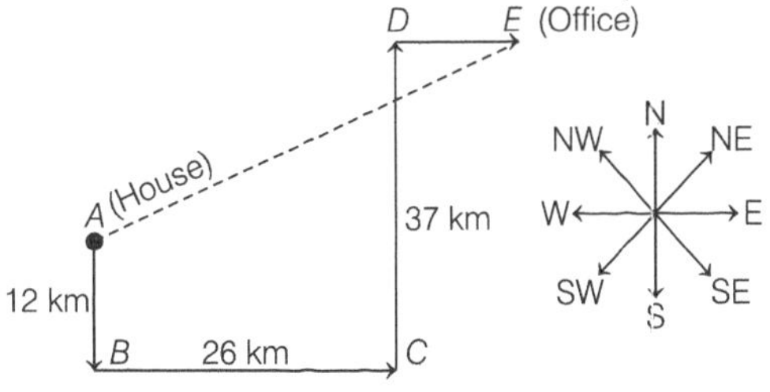


**24** **Find the number that can replace question mark (?) in the series given below.**

**20, 62, 189, 571, 1718, ?**

(1) 5160 (2) 2160

(3) 3160 (4) 4660

***Ans.*** ***(1)*** For the series

20, 62 189, 571, 1718, ?

Following is the rule followed to get the next term.

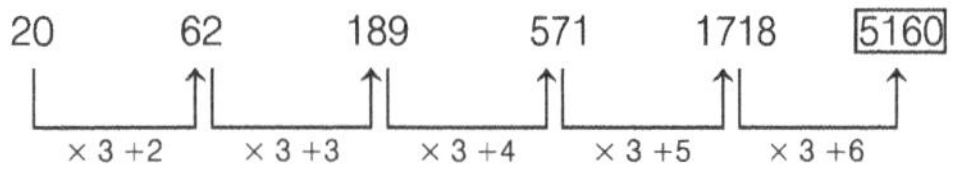


Thus, the missing term is 5160

**25** **The selling price of 30 articles is equal to the purchase price of 25 articles. Find the percentage of profit or loss.**

(1) 18% profit (2) $16\frac{2}{3}\%$ loss

(3) 18% loss (4) $16\frac{2}{3}\%$ profit

***Ans.*** ***(2)*** Given, SP of 30 articles = CP of 25 articles

$$\frac{CP}{SP} = \frac{30}{25} = \frac{6}{5}$$

Here, CP > SP

∴ There will be loss

$$\therefore \text{Loss percentage} = \frac{\text{CP} - \text{SP}}{\text{CP}} \times 100$$

$$= \frac{6-5}{6} \times 100 = \frac{100}{6}$$

$$= 16\frac{2}{3}\%$$

**26** **If the statement "All saints are materialists" is given as true which of the following statements could be inferred to be true?**

(1) No saints are materialists.

(2) Some saints are materialists.

(3) Some saints are not materialists.

(4) Some materialists are not saints.

***Ans.*** ***(2)*** If the statement "All saints are materialists" is true, it means that there is no saint who is not a materialist. This implies that at least some saints must be materialists.

**27** **Which of the following statements are logically equivalent?**

A. All saints are materialists.

B. No saints are non-materialists.

C. All non-materialists are non-saints.

D. No materialists are saints.

Choose the correct answer from the options given below.

(1) B, C and D only

(2) A and C only

(3) A and B only

(4) A, B and C only

***Ans.*** ***(4)*** Statements (A), (B) and (C) are logically equivalent

All saints are materialists. This statement means that there is no saint who is not a materialist.

No saints are non-materialists. This statement also means that there is no saint who is not a materialist. It's just a different way of expressing the same idea.

All non-materialists are non-saints. This statement means that if someone is not a materialist, then they must also be a non-saint. This is again equivalent to saying that there is no saint who is not a materialist.

**28** Which of the following statements are so related that they cannot both be false, though they can both be true?

A. Some saints are materialists.

B. All saints are materialists.

C. No saints are materialists.

D. Some saints are not materialists.

Choose the correct answer from the options given below.

(1) A and C only

(2) A and D only

(3) C and D only

(4) B and D only

***Ans.*** ***(2)*** The statements that are so related that they cannot both be false, though they can both be true, are (A) and (D) only.

Some saints are materialists. This means there is at least one saint who is a materialist.

Some saints are not materialists. This means that there is at least one saint who is not a materialist.

These can both be true; it is possible for some saints to be materialists while others are not. But these both statements cannot be false at the same time.

**29** "Of course XYZ political party is going to sweep the polls in the coming elections. Everybody is saying so".

Which informal fallacy is committed in the above statement?

(1) Appeal to emotion

(2) Begging the question

(3) Slippery slope

(4) Appeal to majority

***Ans.*** ***(4)*** The statement commits the Appeal to majority fallacy by suggesting that the XYZ political party will win simply because "everybody is saying so". This fallacy assumes that a claim is true or valid just because a large number of people believe it, rather than providing substantial evidence to support the claim.

**30** "All things are visible, because they are knowable". Which fallacy is committed in the above statement according to Classical Indian School of Logic (Nyaya)?

(1) Sadharana

(2) Anupasamhari

(3) Asadharana

(4) Viruddha

***Ans.*** ***(2)*** Anupasamhari is a fallacy in the Nyaya School of Classical Indian Logic, where a conclusion is drawn based on an over-generalisation or a faulty assumption that things with different properties can be treated as the same. In this case, the statement "All things are visible because they are knowable" commits this fallacy by falsely assuming that being knowable automatically makes something visible.

**31** Which of the following pairs of acronym and its expansion is incorrectly matched?

(1) GPS - Global Positioning System

(2) GSM - Global System for Management

(3) SIM - Subscriber Identity Module

(4) Wimax - Worldwide Interoperability for Microwave Access

***Ans.*** ***(2)*** Pair (2) is incorrectly matched because GSM actually stands for Global System for Mobile Communications, not "Global System for Management."

GSM (Global System for Mobile Communications) is a standard developed for mobile networks that allows users to make calls, send text messages and access data services. It is widely used across the world and supports international roaming, enabling seamless mobile communication between different countries.

**32** What does the following MS-EXCEL formula do?

= SUM (Sheet1 : Sheet4!D18)

(1) It adds data from all D18 cells in Sheet1, Sheet2, Sheet3 and Sheet4.

(2) It adds data from cell D18 of Sheet1 and cell D18 of Sheet4.

(3) It adds all data in the range A1 : D18 in Sheet1, Sheet2, Sheet3 and Sheet4.

(4) It adds data from cell A1 of Sheet1 and cell D18 of Sheet4.

***Ans.*** ***(1)*** The Excel formula = SUM (Sheet1 : Sheet4!D18) calculates the total of the values located in cell D18 across Sheet1, Sheet2, Sheet3 and Sheet4.

**33** Given below are two statements.

**Statement** (I)
$(11001000)_2 = (C8)_{16} = (200)_{10}$

**Statement** (II)
$(123)_{10} = (01111011)_2 = (7B)_{16}$

In the light of the above statements, choose the correct answer from the options given below.

(1) Both Statement I and Statement II are correct.

(2) Both Statement I and Statement II are incorrect.

(3) Statement I is correct, but Statement II is incorrect.

(4) Statement I is incorrect, but Statement II is correct.

***Ans.*** ***(1)*** Both Statement I and Statement II are correct.

For Statement (I)

$$(11001000)_2 = (C8)_{16} = (200)_{10}$$

Convert $(11001000)_2$ into decimal

$$1\times 2^7 + 1\times 2^6 + 0\times 2^5 + 0\times 2^4 + 1\times 2^3 + 0\times 2^2 + 0\times 2^1 + 0\times 2^0$$

$$= 128 + 64 + 8 = 200$$

Now, we have to convert $(200)_{10}$ to hexadecimal

$\frac{200}{16} = 12$ with reminder 8 and $12 = C$ in hexadecimal

The binary number 11001000 converted to hexadecimal is therefore equal to $(c8)_{16}$

For Statement II

$$(123)_{10} = (01111011)_2 = (7B)_{16}$$

Convert $(123)_{10}$ to binary

$(123)_{10} = (01111011)_2$ dividing by power of 2

Now $(123)_{10}$ in hexadecimal

$$\frac{123}{16} = 7 \text{ remainder } 11$$

The quotient is 7 and the remainder is 11. In hexadecimal, 11is represented by the letter B.

$(123)_{10} = 7B_{16}$

**34** Which of the following statements A-D apply to a laser printer?

A. It uses a rotating drum to transfer the image to the paper.

B. It uses powdered toner.

C. It uses nozzles to spray droplets on to the paper.

D. It uses a print head mechanism that moves side to side.

Choose the correct answer from the options given below.

(1) A and B only (2) C and D only
(3) A and C only (4) B and D only

***Ans.*** ***(1)*** Statements (A) and (B) can be applied to a laser printer.

This is a key component of a laser printer. The drum is charged with static electricity and then selectively discharged with a laser beam to create the image. The toner particles are attracted to the charged areas of the drum and then transferred to the paper. This is a key component of a laser printer.

Toner is a fine powder that is used to create the image on the paper. It is attracted to the charged areas of the drum and then transferred to the paper.

**35** One component of the internal memory of a computer is Random Access Memory (RAM). Which of the following statements are correct about characteristics of RAM?

A. RAM can be read from and written to.
B. RAM is volatile memory.
C. RAM is temporary storage.
D. Modern PCs typically have from 2TB upto 32 TB of RAM.

Choose the correct answer from the options given below.

(1) C and D only
(2) A, B and C only
(3) A and B only
(4) A, B, C and D

***Ans.*** ***(2)*** Statements (A), (B) and (C) are the characteristics of RAM.

RAM can be read from and written to. This is a fundamental characteristic of RAM. It allows the computer to both read data from and write data to the memory, enabling it to execute programs and store temporary data. RAM is volatile memory. This means that the contents of RAM are lost when the computer is turned off or restarted. Unlike non-volatile storage like hard drives or SSDs, RAM does not retain data when power is not supplied. RAM is temporary storage. RAM is primarily used for storing data that is currently being used by the computer. It is not intended for long-term storage of data.

RAM (Random Access Memory) is a type of computer memory that temporarily stores data and programs currently in use, allowing quick access and smooth operation. It is volatile memory, meaning it loses its contents when the computer is turned off.

**36** Given below are two statements.

**Statement** (I) Chlorine is one of the most commonly used and inexpensive chemical disinfectants for water.

**Statement** (II) Optimum fluoride levels in drinking water help prevent cavities in children.

In the light of the above statements, choose the correct answer from the options given below.

(1) Both Statement I and Statement II are correct.
(2) Both Statement I and Statement II are incorrect.
(3) Statement I is correct, but Statement II is incorrect.
(4) Statement I is incorrect, but Statement II is correct.

***Ans.*** ***(1)*** Both Statement I and Statement II are correct.

Chlorine is one of the most commonly used and inexpensive chemical disinfectants for water. It is effective in killing harmful bacteria and viruses that can cause waterborne diseases.

Fluoride is a naturally occurring mineral that is added to drinking water in many countries to help prevent cavities in children. Fluoride strengthens tooth enamel, making it more resistant to decay.

**37** What is the full form of NBOD?

(1) Neutral Biochemical Oxygen Damand
(2) Natural Biochemical Oxygen Demand
(3) Normalised Biochemical Oxygen Demand
(4) Nitrogenous Biochemical Oxygen Demand

***Ans.*** ***(4)*** NBOD stands for Nitrogenous Biochemical Oxygen Demand, which refers to the amount of oxygen required to break down nitrogenous compounds, such as ammonia, during the decomposition of organic matter in water.

**38** Soot particles

A. are also called black carbon
B. are mostly of coarse size range
C. are toxic
D. contribute in global warming
E. can penetrate in to deeper parts of lungs

Choose the correct answer from the options given below.

(1) A, B, C and D
(2) A, B, C and E
(3) A, C, D and E
(4) B, C, D and E

***Ans.*** ***(3)*** Among the given options, Soot particles are referred to as black carbon due to their dark colour.

Soot particles can be toxic, especially when they contain harmful substances like Polycyclic Aromatic Hydrocarbons (PAHs).

Soot particles absorb sunlight and heat, contributing to global warming.

As mentioned earlier, the fine size of soot particles allows them to penetrate deep into the lungs, potentially causing respiratory problems.

Soot particles also known as black carbon, are tiny carbon-based particles released from the incomplete combustion of fossil fuels, biomass, and other organic materials. They are harmful pollutants that contribute to air pollution, human health issues, and global warming by absorbing sunlight and heating the atmosphere.

**39** **Ozone layer which protects us from harmful ultraviolet radiations is situated in**

(1) Troposphere (2) Stratosphere
(3) Mesosphere (4) Ionosphere

***Ans.*** ***(2)*** Ozone layer which protects us from harmful ultraviolet radiations is situated in Stratosphere.

The ozone layer is situated in the Stratosphere, approximately 10 to 30 miles above the Earth's surface. It contains a high concentration of ozone ($O_3$) molecules, which absorb and block the majority of the Sun's harmful ultraviolet (UV) radiation. This protective layer is essential for maintaining life on Earth by reducing the risk of skin cancer and other UV-related health issues.

The Troposphere is the lowest layer of the Earth's atmosphere, extending from the surface up to about 7-10 miles.

The Mesosphere lies above the Stratosphere and extends from about 30 to 50 miles above the Earth. This layer is characterised by decreasing temperatures with altitude and is where meteoroids often burn up upon entering the atmosphere.

The Ionosphere is a region of the atmosphere that extends from about 30 to 600 miles above the Earth, characterised by ionized particles. It plays a crucial role in radio communication by reflecting radio waves back to Earth and is also involved in phenomena such as the auroras.

**40** **The latest amendment to Montreal protocol is**

(1) Kigali Amendment
(2) Nairobi Amendment
(3) Copenhagen Amendment
(4) Bangkok Amendment

***Ans.*** ***(1)*** The Kigali Amendment is the latest update to the Montreal Protocol, adopted in 2016, which targets the phase-down of hydrofluorocarbons (HFCs) due to their significant contribution to global warming. It aims to reduce HFC consumption in both developed and developing countries, promoting more environmentally friendly alternatives. This amendment represents a crucial step in global efforts to combat climate change and protect the ozone layer.

**41** **Raja Ram Mohan Roy was responsible for the establishment of**

(1) Agra College, Agra
(2) Hindu College, Kolkata
(3) Banaras Sanskrit College, Banaras
(4) Serampore College, Serampore

***Ans.*** ***(2)*** Raja Ram Mohan Roy played a significant role in the establishment of Hindu College in Kolkata in 1817, which was one of the first institutions in India to promote modern education and rational thinking.

**42** **What were the important observations of Education Commission (Pre-Independence) 1882-83?**

A. There is a need to replace the despatch of 1854.
B. It is necessary to refashion the general working of Indian universities.
C. There is also a need for local governments to extend the facilities of general education.
D. It is important to fund each college depending upon staff strength, maintenance expenses and locality requirements.

E. Special grants should be made available to improve the infrastructure of colleges.

Choose the correct answer from the options given below.

(1) A, B and C only

(2) B, C and D only

(3) C, D and E only

(4) A, D and E only

***Ans.*** ***(3)*** The important observations of the Education Commission (1882-83) during the pre-independence period among the statements are (C), (D) and (E).

There is a need for local governments to extend the facilities of general education.

It is important to fund each college depending upon staff strength, maintenance expenses, and locality requirements.

Special grants should be made available to improve the infrastructure of colleges.

These three points emphasises the development of educational infrastructure, funding mechanisms, and the role of local governments in expanding education.

**43** Match List-I with List-II.

| | List-I (Authorities/ Viceroys) | | List-II (Commission Chairmen) |
|---|---|---|---|
| A. | Lord Ripon | I. | Sarvepalli Radhakrishnan |
| B. | Lord Curzon | II. | Thomas Babington Macaulay |
| C. | William Bentinck | III. | WW Hunter |
| D. | Government of India | IV. | T. Raleigh |

**Codes**

| | A | B | C | D | | A | B | C | D |
|---|---|---|---|---|---|---|---|---|---|
| (1) | II | III | I | IV | (2) | I | II | IV | III |
| (3) | III | IV | II | I | (4) | IV | II | III | I |

***Ans.*** ***(3)*** The correct matching is A-III, B-IV, C-II, D-I.

Lord Ripon was the Viceroy of India during the time of the Indian Education Commission, which was headed by WW Hunter.

Lord Curzon was the Viceroy of India during the time of the Universities Commission, which was headed by T. Raleigh.

William Bentinck was the Governor-General of India during the time of the Indian Education Commission, which was headed by Thomas Babington Macaulay.

Government of India has appointed various commissions over time. One such commission, the Indian Education Commission, was headed by Sarvepalli Radhakrishnan.

**44** Given below are two statements.

**Statement** (I) Curriculum at Taxila was varied and included technical sciences.

**Statement** (II) Curriculum of Nalanda excluded technical sciences.

In the light of the above statements, choose the correct answer from the options given below.

(1) Both Statement I and Statement II are correct.

(2) Both Statement I and Statement II are incorrect.

(3) Statement I is correct, but Statement II is incorrect.

(4) Statement I is incorrect, but Statement II is correct.

***Ans.*** ***(1)*** Both Statement I and Statement II are correct.

The curriculum at Taxila was varied and included technical sciences, reflecting the educational breadth of that ancient institution. The curriculum of Nalanda, while it was broad, primarily focused on subjects like philosophy and the arts, and it is often noted that it did not emphasise technical sciences in the same way.

**45** Given below are two statements, one is labelled as Assertion (A) and the other is labelled as Reason (R).

**Assertion** (A) It is expected that a meaningful partnership will be formed between the States and the Union Government in managing education.

**Reason** (R) Education is concurrent subject as per the Constitutional Amendment of 1976.

In the light of the above statements, choose the correct answer from the options given below.

(1) Both A and R are true and R is the correct explanation of A.

(2) Both A and R are true, but R is not the correct explanation of A.

(3) A is true, but R is false.

(4) A is false, but R is true.

***Ans.*** *(1)* Both A and R are true and R is the correct explanation of A.

It is expected that a meaningful partnership will be formed between the States and the Union Government in managing education. This statement highlights the importance of collaboration between different levels of government to enhance educational governance and ensure that policies are effectively implemented across the country.

Education is a concurrent subject as per the Constitutional Amendment of 1976. This means that both the Central and State Governments have the authority to legislate on education. This constitutional framework supports the idea of a partnership, as it allows for shared responsibility and cooperation in managing educational policies and programmes.

**Directions** (Q. Nos. 46-50) *Read the following passage carefully and answer the questions that follows.*

Climate change will have broad impacts on human society. Changes projected to occur in the coming century or two won't have the apocalyptic, civilisation-destroying character of, say an all-out nuclear war or a direct hit from a large asteroid. But climate change will be disruptive in many ways to a civilisation whose planetary home is already under stress from the demands of billions of human beings.

The physical impacts of climate change won't be evenly distributed around the globe. Low-lying coastal regions', for example, will suffer more from sea-level rise; continental interiors will see more drought; and high latitudes will warm disproportionately. For that, reason alone, impacts will vary from country to country. But also alter the impact of a changing climate, social, political, and economic considerations. That's because wealthier countries are better able to adapt to and counter deleterious effects. Wealthy countries can build protective seawalls to ward off the rising oceans; they can engineer massive water projects to ensure continuing supplies of freshwater; they can outbid poorer countries if declines in domestic agriculture require increased food imports; their advanced healthcare systems can better cope with spreading tropical diseases; and their robust economies can speed recovery from extreme weather events. We are forced to the unfortunate conclusion that climate change will exacerbate the gap between rich and poor nations, as those with the fewest resources will be the most vulnerable. This conclusion should be especially troubling because anthropogenic climate change is almost 'entirely the result of fossil fuel consumption, deforestation, and other activities carried out by or for the benefit of the developed world.

**46** Impact of climate change on human society will be

(1) inconsequential

(2) as disastrous as the impact of a nuclear war

(3) disruptive

(4) mild

***Ans.*** *(3)* According to the passage, climate change would not have the catastrophic effects of a nuclear war, it will still be highly disruptive to human society, affecting various regions and countries differently. Wealthier nations may be better equipped to adapt, but poorer nations will be more vulnerable.

**47** In the context of climate change, which among the following statements are not correct?

A. Low-lying area will be threatened.

B. Agricultural production will be affected.

C. Developing countries will adapt better to it.

D. Health will be affected.

E. Developed countries will suffer less.

Choose the correct answer from the options given below.

(1) C and E only (2) A, B and C only
(3) A, C and E only (4) A, D and E only

***Ans.*** ***(1)*** According to the passage, the incorrect statements are (C) and (E).
The passage states that wealthier countries (not developing countries) will adapt better to climate change.
The passage suggests that developed countries will suffer less due to their ability to adapt more effectively, not equally as much as poorer nations.

**48** Climate change will impact the world

(1) uniformly
(2) the developing world less
(3) disparately
(4) the developed world more

***Ans.*** ***(3)*** The passage states that the physical impacts of climate change will not be evenly distributed and will vary significantly across different regions and countries.

**49** How will climate change affect the gap between the rich and poor countries?

(1) It will be increase the gap.
(2) It will reduce the gap.
(3) There will be no change in gap.
(4) It will bridge the gap.

***Ans.*** ***(1)*** The passage indicates that climate change will exacerbate the divide between rich and poor nations, as wealthier countries are better equipped to adapt to its effects.

**50** Given below are two statements.

**Statement** (I) The developed world can cope better with climate change.

**Statement** (II) The developed world is largely responsible for climate change.

In the light of the above statements, choose the correct answer from the options given below.

(1) Both Statement I and Statement II are correct.
(2) Both Statement I and Statement II are incorrect.
(3) Statement I is correct, but Statement II is incorrect.
(4) Statement I is incorrect, but Statement II is correct.

***Ans.*** ***(1)*** Both Statement I and Statement II are correct. The passage supports both statements: the developed world can cope better with climate change due to its resources and infrastructure, and it is largely responsible for climate change through activities such as fossil fuel consumption and deforestation.

NTA UGC

NET/JRF/SET

# Solved Paper 2022

# UGC
## NET/JRF/SET
# Solved Paper, 2022
(Exam Held on : 14 October, 2022, Shift II)

## General Paper 1 (Teaching and Research Aptitude)

*Instructions*
- This paper contains fifty Multiple Choice Questions, each question carries two marks.
- All questions are compulsory.
- Total time given for this paper is 1 hour.

**Directions** (Q.Nos 1-5) *Study the given table and answer the questions that follow.*
The following table shows the percentage (%) of colleges offering four IT courses on Python, Java, Multimedia and AI in four Indian states A-D, in a certain year. The table also presents the percentage-wise distribution of the number of colleges in the four states. The total number of colleges in the four states is 4000. Based on the data in the table, answer the questions.

**State-wise Percentage of Colleges offering IT Courses**

| State | % of Colleges offering | | | | % Distribution of Number of Colleges |
|---|---|---|---|---|---|
| | Python | Java | Multimedia | AI | |
| A | 86% | 74% | 59% | 56% | 35% |
| B | 80% | 92% | 82% | 84% | 15% |
| C | 74% | 88% | 84% | 86% | 20% |
| D | 68% | 64% | 68% | 70% | 30% |

**1** Number of colleges offering Java in State B is ……% of the number of colleges offering multimedia in State C.

(1) 78.15 (2) 80.23
(3) 82.25 (4) 84.52

***Ans. (2)*** Number of colleges offering Java in State B

$$= \frac{15}{100} \times 4000 \times \frac{92}{100} = 552$$

Number of colleges offering Multimedia in State C $= \frac{20}{100} \times 4000 \times \frac{86}{100} = 688$

$\therefore$ Required percentage $= \frac{552}{688} \times 100$

$= 80.23\%$

**2** If $M$ and $N$ represent the total number of colleges offering Python and Java respectively, in all the four states, then $M - N =$

(1) 64 (2) 96
(3) 48 (4) 32

***Ans. (4)*** Number of colleges offering Python

$$M = 4000\left(\frac{35}{100}\times\frac{86}{100}+\frac{15}{100}\times\frac{80}{100}+\frac{20}{100}\times\frac{74}{100}+\frac{30}{100}\times\frac{68}{100}\right)$$

$$= \frac{4000}{10000}(3010+1200+1480+2040)$$

$$= \frac{4000}{10000}\times 7730$$

$$= 3092$$

Number of colleges offering Java (N)

$$= 4000\left(\frac{35}{1000}\times\frac{74}{1000}+\frac{15}{1000}\times\frac{92}{1000}+\frac{20}{1000}\times\frac{88}{1000}+\frac{30}{1000}\times\frac{64}{1000}\right)$$

$$= \frac{4000}{10000}(2590+1380+1760+1920)$$

$$= \frac{4000}{10000}\times 7650 = 3060$$

Now, $M - N = 3092 - 3060 = 32$

**3** **The number of colleges offering the Python course is more than 460 in**

(1) All the four states

(2) Only three states

(3) Only two states

(4) Only one states

***Ans. (1)*** Number of colleges offering Python course in state

$$A = \frac{35}{100}\times\frac{86}{100}\times 4000 = 504$$

$$B = \frac{15}{100}\times\frac{80}{100}\times 4000 = 480$$

$$C = \frac{20}{100}\times\frac{74}{100}\times 4000 = 592$$

$$D = \frac{30}{100}\times\frac{68}{100}\times 4000 = 816$$

Hence, the number is more than 460 in all the four states.

**4** **The total number of colleges offering AI in all four states is**

(1) 2784 (2) 2816

(3) 2864 (4) 2952

***Ans. (2)*** Total number of colleges offering AI

$$= 4000\left(\frac{35}{1000}\times\frac{56}{1000}+\frac{15}{1000}\times\frac{84}{1000}+\frac{20}{1000}\times\frac{86}{1000}+\frac{30}{1000}\times\frac{70}{1000}\right)$$

$$= \frac{4000}{10000}(1960+1260+1720+2100)$$

$$= \frac{4}{10}\times 7040$$

$$= 2816$$

**5** **Ratio of the number of colleges offering Multimedia in State C to that of State D is**

(1) 2 : 3 (2) 11 : 13

(3) 14 : 17 (4) 13 : 16

***Ans. (3)*** Number of colleges offering Multimedia in State C

$$= \frac{20}{100}\times\frac{84}{100}\times 4000 = 672$$

Number of colleges offering Multimedia in State D

$$= \frac{30}{100}\times\frac{68}{100}\times 4000 = 816$$

$$\therefore \text{ Required ratio} = \frac{672}{816} = \frac{14}{17}$$

$$= 14:17$$

**6** **Which of the following statements is true regarding inductive argument ?**

(1) If all the premises are true, the conclusion must be true.

(2) It claims to support its conclusion only with some degree of probability.

(3) It claims to support its conclusion conclusively.

(4) Conclusion is completely contained already in the premises.

***Ans. (2)*** Statement (2) is true regarding about the inductive argument.

An inductive argument is an assertion that uses specific premises or observations to make a broader generalisation. Inductive arguments, by their nature, possess some degree of uncertainty. They are used to show the likelihood that a conclusion drawn from known premises is true. For example in the past, ducks have always come to our pond. Therefore, the ducks will come to our pond this summer.

**7** MIDI is associated with the storage of music files. MIDI is an acronym for

(1) Musical Interactive Digital Interface
(2) Musical Instructions Device Interpreter
(3) Mask Iterative Display Instance
(4) Musical Instrument Digital Interface

***Ans. (4)*** MIDI is an acronym for Musical Instrument Digital Interface. It is a protocol designed for recording and playing back music on digital synthesisers that is supported by many makes of personal computer sound cards. Originally intended to control one keyboard from another, it was quickly adopted for the personal computer.

**8** Match List I with List II.

| List I (Name of the Subject) | List II (Domain and Subject Matter) |
|---|---|
| A. Kavya | I. Agriculture, trade, commerce, animal husbandry |
| B. Anivikshiki | II. Etymology |
| C. Varta | III. Logic |
| D. Nirukta | IV. Imaginative and creative literature |

**Codes**

| | A | B | C | D |
|---|---|---|---|---|
| (1) | II | III | IV | I |
| (2) | IV | III | I | II |
| (3) | III | IV | II | I |
| (4) | II | IV | I | III |

***Ans. (2)*** The correct matching is A-IV, B-III, C-I and D-II.

**Kavya** is imaginative and creative literature. It was used by Indian court poets flourishing between 200 BCE and 1200 CE. This literary style, which includes both poetry and prose, is characterised by abundant usage of figures of speech such as metaphors, similes and hyperbole.

**Anvikshiki** generally denotes logic. It is a term in Sanskrit denoting roughly the science of inquiry and it should have been recognised in India as a distinct branch of learning as early as 650 BCE.

**Varta** denotes agriculture, trade, commerce and animal husbandry. Varta has been practiced in India probably since the Indus Valley Civilisation.

**Nirukta** is the study of etymology and is concerned with proper interpretation of the Sanskrit words, given their context in the ancient texts.

**9** Which among the following are the MOOCs Platforms?

A. Google Meet
B. Coursera
C. Zoom
D. Future Learn
E. Turnitin

**Codes**

(1) A, D and E (2) B, D and E
(3) B and D (4) C and D

***Ans. (3)*** Coursera and Future Learn are MOOCs platforms. Massive Open Online Courses (MOOCs) are free online courses available for anyone to enroll. Courera is a US-based MOOC founded in 2012 by Andrew Ng and Daphne Koller. Its headquarters is in California.

Future learn is a British digital learning education platform founded in 2012. It is MOOC expert track, micro credential and Degree Learning Platform.

**10** Given below are two statements.

**Statement I** Acute exposure to a chemical is a long- term continuous exposure by that chemical.

**Statement II** Chronic exposure to a chemical is a short-term exposure to that chemical.

In light of the above statements, choose the most appropriate answer from the options given below.

(1) Both the statements are correct.
(2) Both the statements are incorrect.
(3) Statement I is correct, but statement II is incorrect.
(4) Statement I is incorrect, but statement II is correct.

***Ans. (2)*** Both the statements are incorrect.

Acute exposure is a short contact with a chemical. It may last a few seconds or a few hours. Chronic exposure is continuous or repeated contact with a toxic substance over a long period of time (months or years). If a chemical is used every day on the job, the exposure would be chronic.

**11** **The price of a jewel, passing three hands rises on the whole by 65%. If the first and second sellers earned 20% and 25% profit respectively, find percentage profit earned by the third seller.**

(1) 10% (2) 15%
(3) 16% (4) 12%

***Ans. (1)*** Let the price of jewel = ₹ $x$

After first and second seller price of jewel

$$= x \times \frac{120}{100} \times \frac{125}{100} = 1.5x$$

$\therefore$ Cost price of third seller = $1.5x$

Selling price of third seller = $x \times \frac{165}{100} = 1.65x$

Percentage profit earned by third seller

$$= \frac{1.65x - 1.5x}{1.5x} \times 100$$

$$= \frac{0.15}{1.5} \times 100 = 10\%$$

**12** **Which of the following developmental areas of individual differences will be effected, if a child opts for frequent outbursts and throws tantrums ?**

(1) Social (2) Mental
(3) Emotional (4) Physical

***Ans. (3)*** If a child screams, cries and tantrums, then the emotional developmental area of individual differences is affected.

Emotional development develops in children during infancy. Emotions like anger, fear, jealousy, joy and love are found in this state. There is rapid development of emotions from infancy to childhood. The parts of happiness and sorrow are very effective in this period. Crying of a child (infant) after birth is considered to be the result of emotion. Emotional development begins to be rapid and distinct in childhood and becomes more intense during adolescence. The father of emotional development J V Watson is considered.

**13** **Find the next term in the series given below**

**124, 148, 196, 268, 364.**

(1) 484 (2) 584
(3) 464 (4) 268

***Ans. (1)*** The pattern of the series is

124 148 196 268 364 [484]

+24 +48 +72 +96 +120

+24 +24 +24 +24

$\therefore$ ? = 484

**14** **A 729 ml of a mixture contains milk and water in the ratio of 7 : 2. How much more water is to be added to get a new mixture containing milk and water in the ratio of 7 : 3?**

(1) 81 ml (2) 90 ml
(3) 85 ml (4) 75 ml

***Ans. (1)*** Quantity of milk in mixture $= \frac{7}{7+2} \times 729$

$$= \frac{7}{9} \times 729 = 567 \text{ ml.}$$

Quantity of water in mixture

$$= 729 - 567 = 162 \text{ ml.}$$

Let the amount of water to be added be $x$ ml, then,

$$\frac{567}{162 + x} = \frac{7}{3}$$

$\Rightarrow$ $1701 = 1134 + 7x$

$\Rightarrow$ $7x = 567$

$\therefore$ $x = 81$ ml

**15** Given below are two statements.

**Statement I** ROM is temporary memory that can be written to or read from and the contents of the memory can be changed.

**Statements II** RAM is permanent memory that can only be read from and contents of memory cannot be changed.

In light of the above statements, choose the most appropriate answer from the options given below.

(1) Both the statements are correct.
(2) Both the statements are incorrect.
(3) Statement I is correct, but statement II is incorrect.
(4) Statement I is incorrect, but statement II is correct.

***Ans. (2)*** Both the statements are correct.

Read Only Memory is a type of non-volatile memory used in computers and other electronic devices. Data stored in ROM cannot be electronically modified after the manufacture of the memory device. Random Access Memory (RAM) is a form of computer memory that can be read and changed in any order, typically used to store working data and machine code.

**16** Media messages consist of various layers of

(1) rationalisation
(2) complex resistance
(3) polymorphic meaning
(4) restrictive rituals

***Ans. (3)*** Media messages consist of various layers of polymorphic meaning. The language of word, pictures and music can be used to express many layered concepts and ideas about the world. Polymorphic mean that having more than one form or type as a result of discontinuous variation.

**17** Where is Chanakya said to have composed his Arthashastra ?

(1) Sarnatha (2) Takshashila
(3) Nalanda (4) Vikramashila

***Ans. (3)*** Chanakya composed Arthashastra in Takshashila. It is an Ancient Indian Sanskrit treatise on statecraft, political science, economic policy and military strategy. The text incorporates Hindu philosophy, includes ancient economic and cultural details on agriculture, mineralogy, mining and metals, animal husbandry, medicine, forests and wildlife.

**18** Which of the following are true regarding Classical Indian School of Logic?

A. It is deductive.
B. It is inductive.
C. It is formal.
D. It is material.
E. It always leads from universal to particular only.

Choose the correct answer from the options given below.

(1) A, B, C and D
(2) B and C
(3) A and D
(4) A, B, C, D and E

***Ans. (1)*** A, B, C and D are true regarding Classical Indian School of Logic. Classical Indian School of Logic is deductive, inductive, formal and material.

In deductive method, general rules and formulas are accepted as true and apply it to specific examples or situations. In this method, the help of concepts, basic elements and self-accomplishments is generally taken. Hence, Indian classical logics are deductive. An inductive argument is neither true nor false, but it is not completely false or true either. Proper inductive reasoning may be valid, valid or invalid. So it changes according to Indian classical logic. In addition, formative and materialistic regularly influence Indian classical logic.

**19** Which of the following are web search engines?

A. DuckDuckGo B. Google
C. Yahoo Search D. Bing
E. Pinterest

Choose the correct answer from the options given below.

(1) B, C and D (2) A, B, C and D

(3) B and E (4) A, C, D and E

***Ans. (2)*** DuckDuckGo, Google, Yahoo Search and Bing are web search engines.

Duck Duck Go search engine is an American company. It is especially used in America.

Yahoo Search is a search engine that works with BIG. Bing is a Microsoft ASP, MET based web search engine. It is available in 40 languages and offering its services.

Pinterest is a social media platform, in which photos and videos etc, are shared.

**20** A source of communicative inefficiency is

(1) desire for personal gratification

(2) implications of familiar relations

(3) peer pressure

(4) limited knowledge

***Ans. (4)*** Limited knowledge is a source of communicative inefficiency. Ineffective communication means that this message is lost at some point in the process and that the parties cannot understand the information conveyed in the same way. This can occur in the way the sender conveys the message or in the way the recipient interprets the message.

**21** One day a man left his home for a morning walk and went 12 km Southwards. He then turned right and walked 8 km. Again turned right and walked 12 km, turned left and walked 10 km. How many kilometres the man has to walk to reach straight to his home?

(1) 22 km (2) 18 km

(3) 20 km (4) 24 km

***Ans. (2)*** According to the question

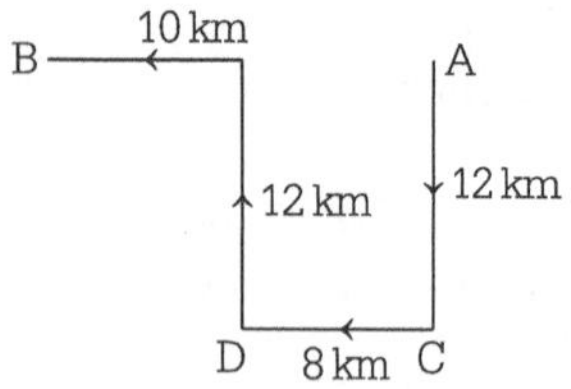


A = Starting point

B = End point

He has to walk straight distance from A to B

= 8+10 = 18 km

**22** Which of the following are elements of congenial classroom atmosphere?

A. Creating a conductive atmosphere

B. Engaging in individual efforts

C. Supportive team work

D. Negotiable movement inside the classroom

E. Immersive listening

Choose the correct answer from the options given below.

(1) A, B and E (2) A, C and E

(3) B, C and D (4) C, D and E

***Ans. (2)*** A, C and E are the elements of congenial classroom atmosphere.

A congenial classroom is a one where all students are welcome, all students are seen and given importance and all are known. The teachers make efforts to see their students more than as academic vessels. Creating a congenial classroom environment and management is one of the managerial skills which include promoting pupil participation, positive tone of teacher.

**23** Given below are two statements.

**Statement I** Positivism says that sciences need not be free from speculative and metaphysical approaches.

**Statement II** Positivism is suitable for natural sciences.

In light of the above statements, choose the most appropriate answer from the options given below.

(1) Both the statements are correct.

(2) Both the statements are incorrect.

(3) Statement I is correct, but statement II is incorrect.

(4) Statement I is incorrect, but statement II is correct.

***Ans. (2)*** Statement I is incorrect, but statement II is correct. Positivism is an empiricist philosophical theory that holds that all genuine knowledge is either true by definition or positive-meaning a posteriori facts derived by reason and logic from sensory experience.

Its goal is to formulate abstract and universal laws on the operative dynamics of the social universe.

**24** Virtual ethnography is located in a/an

(1) Natural environment
(2) Technical environment
(3) Political environment
(4) Economic environment

***Ans. (2)*** Virtual ethnography is located in a technical environment. It is a research approach for exploring the social interactions that take place in virtual (technical) environment.

These interactions often take place on the internet in sites such as newsgroups, chat rooms and web-based discussion forums. In the same way, virtual ethnographers study online communities and culture. They conduct their research on the Internet.

**25** Which aspect indicates to be the most relevant in decision-making process according to Kohlberg's theory of moral development?

(1) The age of the child
(2) Knowledge of Law
(3) Influence of friends and Siblings
(4) How the child arrives at conclusion

***Ans. (4)*** According to Kohlberg's theory of moral development, in the decision making process, it is known that how does the child draw conclusions. According to Kohlberg, there are eight stages of moral development. It is also called the principle of condition. This theory focuses on the thought process. This theory emphasises how one decides to respond to a moral dilemma rather than what one decides or actually does. According to Kohlberg, six stages of moral development can be easily identified. At each stage problems are identified.

**26** Community colleges are supposed to offer courses that are a mix of

(1) fine arts and life skills
(2) school and colleges education
(3) technical and traditional skills
(4) knowledge, technical and soft skills

***Ans. (4)*** Community colleges are expected to impart knowledge, technical and soft skills from a mix of courses offered. Knowledge, technology and soft skills are considered a symbol of totality. These are seen by connecting with practical knowledge. In the current environment, the nature of the courses should be such that the student gets familiar with the technical disciplines during the course of study, along with this soft skill are also developed in him.

Knowledge, technical and soft skills are considered to be the foundation. The Macaulay Commission, formed during the British rule, had also recommended this type of education, so that the all-round development of the students could take place.

**27** The major terms of reference for the National Knowledge Commission were

A. challenge developed countries in knowledge creation.
B. Westernise the Indian educational system.
C. promote creation of knowledge in science and technology laboratories.
D. promote knowledge applications in agriculture and industry.
E. build excellence in education system to meet the challenges of the 21st century.

Choose the correct answer from the options given below.

(1) A, B and C
(2) B, C and D
(3) C, D and E
(4) A, B and E

***Ans. (3)*** Statements C, D and E are correct with respect to National Knowledge Commission. This commission was constituted on 13th June, 2005 under the chairmanship of Sam Pitroda. The commission aimed to expand the Indian education system, it suggested the creation of approximately 1500 universities by the year 2015 by partly restructuring the existing universities.

The committee recommended the establishment of 50 new national universities and a nationalisation of higher education.

National Knowledge Commission focused on the need for excellence in the system, expansion of the higher education sector in the country.

**28** **The acronym 'SANKALP' introduced by the Ministry of Skill Development and Entrepreneurship, stands for**

(1) Skill Awareness and Knowledge Assessment of Livelihood Promotion
(2) Skill Addition and Knowledge Assessment of Livelihood Promotion
(3) Skill Acquisition and Knowledge Awareness of Livelihood Promotion
(4) Skill Attainment and Knowledge Assessment of Livelihood Promotion

***Ans. (3)*** The acronym 'SANKALP' stands for Skill Acquisition and Knowledge Awareness for Livelihood Promotion. SANKALP is a programme of the Ministry of Skill Development with loan assistance from the World Bank. It aims to improve short-term skill training qualitatively and quantitatively through strengthening institutions, bring in better market connectivity and inclusion of marginalised sections of the society.

SANKALP was launched on 19th January, 2018 and has tenure till March 2023. The outcomes in the project are measured through the results framework and Disbursement Linked Indicators (DLIs) agreed between MSDE and World Bank.

**29** **Which of the following is outside the Teacher Centric Method ?**

(1) Demonstration (2) Team teaching
(3) Inquiry approach (4) Lecture method

***Ans. (3)*** Inquiry approach does not come under teacher centered method. The use of inquiry approach generally stimulates the interest of the children and sufficient time is given for discussion before the knowledge words are introduced as part of the learning process. In addition, it provides equal opportunities to children for the application of concepts and principles, so inquiry approach comes under child-centred method of education, while demonstration, team teaching and lecture method are considered teacher-centred.

**30** **Mohit has sent an email to Bobby, Danny and Ashok as shown below.**

From : Mohit@gmail.com
To : Bobby@gmail.com
CC : Danny@gmail.com
Bcc : Ashok@gmail.com
Subject : Important Update
Dear Colleague
Please note that tomorrow's meeting has been cancelled.
Regard
Mohit

**Which of the following statements is correct?**

(1) Bobby and Danny are aware that Ashok received the email.
(2) Danny is aware that Ashok and Bobby received the email.
(3) Ashok is aware that Bobby and Danny received the email.
(4) All recipients are aware that the others received the email.

***Ans. (3)*** Statement (3) is correct because it is known from the e-mail sent that Ashok knows that Bobby and Danny have received the e-mail. Cc stands for carbon copy and Bcc stands for blind carbon copy. If you Cc someone in an e-mail, then people in both the To and Cc fields can see the other's e-mail, but Bcc is hidden by the blind carbon-copy, so it cannot see To and Cc . From the given question it is known that Ashok must have understood that both Bobby and Danny (To, Cc) must have read the e-mails.

**31** **One of the aims of qualitative data analysis is to**

(1) expand the Selected text of material
(2) analyse the researcher's credentials
(3) describe a phenomenon
(4) focus on binary dissection

***Ans. (3)*** The aim of qualitative data analysis is to describe a phenomenon. Qualitative Data Analysis (QDA) is the process of organising, analysing and interpreting qualitative data—non-numeric, conceptual information and user feedback—to capture themes and patterns, answer research questions and identify actions to take to improve your product or website.

**32** Which of the following are logically equivalent?

A. No P is S
B. Some S are non-P
C. Some non-P are not non-S
D. Some S are not P

Choose the correct answer from the options given below.

(1) B and C (2) C and D
(3) B, C and D (4) A, B, C and D

*Ans. (3)* B, C and D are logically equivalent.

**33** The period of Sendai Framework for Disaster Risk Reduction is

(1) 2015-2030
(2) 2020-2040
(3) 2015-2025
(4) 2020-2030

*Ans. (1)* The period of Sendai Framework for Disaster Risk Reduction is 2015-2030. The Sendai Framework was prepared in the year 2015. This framework was prepared by the member countries of UNO in Sendai (Japan). Under this, an innovation was signed on reducing the risk (due to natural disaster) at the global level. In parts of the world, natural disasters cause widespread loss of knowledge and material.

Underdeveloped and developing countries are most affected by such disasters. The main objective of the Sendai framework was to reduce such risks and to cooperate with each other on a global scale.

**34** Which of the following are advantages of content analysis?

It is a

A. transparent research method.
B. non-reactive method.
C. flexible method.
D. method that does not need a coding manual
E. method that is free of any kind of fame work.

Choose the correct answer from the options given below.

(1) A, B and C (2) B, C and D
(3) C, D and E (4) A, D and E

*Ans. (1)* The options A, B and C are advantages of content analysis. Content analysis is a research tool used to determine the presence of certain words, themes, or concepts within some given qualitative data (i.e. text). Using content analysis, researchers can quantify and analyse the presence, meanings and relationships of such certain words, themes, or concepts.

**35** Given below are two statements.

**Statement I** To address problem of climate change it is essential for the world to have 'Net Zero' carbon emissions by the year 2050.

**Statement II** There is zero carbon emission associated with the production of grey-hydrogen.

In the light of the above statements, choose the correct answer from the options given below.

(1) Both the statements are correct.
(2) Both the statements are incorrect.
(3) Statement I is correct, but statement II is incorrect.
(4) Statement I is incorrect, but statement II is correct.

*Ans. (3)* Among the given statements, statement I is true but statement II is false. To solve the problem of climate change, it is necessary for the world to achieve the goals of net zero carbon emissions by the year 2050. IPCC has given suggestions for this. According to a special report of the year 2018 by IPCC, the world should become a zero carbon emitter by 2050. Net zero refers to absorbing all the carbon released into the environment. Zero carbon emissions are not associated with the production of grey-hydrogen, but with the adoption of non-conventional energy in place of conventional energy sources and exploring its opportunities. India has set a target of net zero carbon emissions by the year 2070 at the Glasgow conference of COP 26.

**36** Which of the following can be categorised as non-verbal communication?

A. Pleasant voice
B. Postures
C. Gestures
D. Facial expressions
E. Vociferous greetings

Choose the correct answer from the options given below.

(1) A, B and C
(2) B, C and E
(3) C, D and E
(4) B, C and D

***Ans. (4)*** Postures, gestures and facial expressions can be categorised as non-verbal communication. Non-verbal communication is the transmission of messages or signals through a non-verbal platform such as eye contact, facial expressions, gestures, posture and body language. It includes the use of social cues, kinesics, distance and physical environments/appearance of voice and touch.

**37** The major ethical aspects of survey based research are

A. protection of participants from any kind of harm.
B. publicise the engagement of participants.
C. distinguish between different strata of people.
D. not to affect individual Privacy.
E. use individual Privacy for Private Profit.

Choose the correct answer from the options given below.

(1) A, B and C
(2) B, C and D
(3) A, C and E
(4) A and D

***Ans. (4)*** A and D are ethical aspects of survey based research. Survey methodology is 'the study of survey methods'. As a field of applied statistics concentrating on human-research surveys, survey methodology studies the sampling of individual units from a population and associated techniques of survey data collection, such as questionnaire construction and methods for improving the number and accuracy of responses to surveys. Survey methodology targets instruments or procedures that ask one or more questions that may or may not be answered.

**38** In an examination 42% students failed in Mathematics and 52% failed in Science. If 17% failed in both the subjects, find the percentage of those who passed in both the subjects.

(1) 23% (2) 25%
(3) 27% (4) 30%

***Ans. (1)*** According to question,

Percentage of students passed in both the subjects

$= 100 - (42 + 52 - 17)$
$= 100 - 94 + 17$
$= 117 - 94 = 23\%$

**39** "Considering the speech given by the School Principle today, I would conclude that he is not a good Public Speaker". Identify the informal fallacy committed in the above argument.

(1) Slippery Slope
(2) Ad Hominem
(3) Appeal to force
(4) Hasty Generalisation

***Ans. (4)*** If a listener, considering a speech given by the school principal today, tries to conclude that he is not a good speaker, then the listener identifies the idiosyncratic reasoning fallacy involving a quick generalisation device. Under this, speakers express their words or information in a rapid way. A skilled speaker clearly keeps his point on any factual subject, so that his words or information can reach the people easily. This is called 'implicit informal reasoning'.

**40** When inference is based not on causation but on uniformity of co-existence, what is it called as per Classical Indian School of Logic ?

(1) Kevalanvayi

(2) Samanyatodrsta

(3) Purvavat

(4) Sesavat

***Ans.*** ***(2)*** When inference is based not on causation but uniformity of co-existence, it is called Samanyatodrsta as per Classical Indian School of Logic. Samanyatodrsta inference is based on the relationship of co-existence rather than knowledge of a causal relationship. The presence of one can be assumed from the presence of the other based on the relationship of co-existence.

**41** Match List I with List II.

| **List I** (Types of Learning) | **List II** (Meaning ) |
|---|---|
| A. Factual Learning | I. This learning is used to organise information in logical structure. |
| B. Association Learning | II. This learning is used to develop personality and think coherently. |
| C. Conceptual Learning | III. This learning is used to organise sequence of activities to achieve a goal. |
| D. Procedural Learning | IV. This learning is used to connect with information more deeply and accurately. |

**Codes**

| | A | B | C | D |
|---|---|---|---|---|
| (1) | II | IV | I | III |
| (2) | II | I | III | IV |
| (3) | II | III | IV | I |
| (4) | III | I | IV | II |

***Ans.*** ***(1)*** The correct matching is A-II, B-IV, C-I and D-III.

**Factual learning** emphasises the acquisition and storage of information to be retrievable on demand.

**Conceptual learning** emphasises the kinds of things one is able to do with the information one has acquired.

**Associative learning** is the process through which organisms acquire information about relationships between events or entities in their environment.

**Procedural learning** the development of perceptual and motor skills through extensive practice is a crucial ability that facilitates efficient processing of and automatic responses to complex environmental stimuli.

**42** Given below are two statements.

**Statement I** Concentration of Volatile Organic Chemicals is generally 100-1000 times higher in surface water than underground water.

**Statement II** The most common method of treatment of Volatile Organic Chemicals is to aerate them to atmosphere.

In light of the above statements, choose the correct answer from the options given below.

(1) Both the statements are correct.

(2) Both the statements are incorrect.

(3) Statement I is correct, but statement II is incorrect.

(4) Statement I is incorrect, but statement II is correct.

***Ans.*** ***(4)*** Statement I is incorrect, true but statement II is correct. Total VOC concentrations in the wells range from below detection limits to more than 1000 micrograms per litre (µg/L). Volatile Organic Compounds (VOCs) are chemicals that both vaporise into air and dissolve in water.

VOCs are pervasive in daily life, because they're used in industry, agriculture, transportation and day-to-day activities around the home. When VOCs are spilled or disposed of on or below the land the VOC contaminants can migrate through soil and into the groundwater.

**43** Pyrolysis helps in addressing the problem of

(1) air pollution

(2) water pollution

(3) municipal solid wastes

(4) electronic wastes

***Ans. (3)*** Pyrolsis helps in addressing the problem of municipal waste. Pyrolysis is the heating of an organic material, such as biomass, in the absence of oxygen.

Biomass pyrolysis is usually conducted at or above 500° C, providing enough heat to deconstruct the strong bio-polymers mentioned above.

**44** Given below are two statements.

**Statement I** Most of the time, communication is loaded with power value.

**Statement II** Those who do not have the power of communication always seek to possess it.

In light of the above statements, choose the most appropriate answer from the options given below.

(1) Both the statements are correct.

(2) Both the statements are incorrect.

(3) Statement I is correct, but statement II is incorrect.

(4) Statement I is incorrect, but statement II is correct.

***Ans. (1)*** Both the statements I and II are correct.

Communication can shine a spotlight on problems, making them easier to see and offering a stage to popularise solutions. It can call people to the streets and it can bring people together.

Silence is communication and actions are messaging without words. Every organisation communicates every day.

**45** Match List I with List II.

| List I (Statements) | List II |
|---|---|
| A. The number of bits that make up a byte | I. 5 |
| B. Base-10 (denary) value of the binary number 001111 | II. 8 |
| C. Number of minutes to upload a 75 megabyte file at 2 Megabits per second upload speed | III. 10 |
| D. If there are $2^P$ bytes in a kilobyte then what is the value of P ? | IV. 15 |

**Codes**

| | A | B | C | D |
|---|---|---|---|---|
| (1) | I | II | III | IV |
| (2) | II | IV | I | III |
| (3) | III | IV | II | I |
| (4) | III | I | IV | III |

***Ans. (2)*** The correct matching is A-II, B-IV, C-I and D-III.

**For A,**

8 number of bits that make up a byte

1 byte = 8 bits

So, option II

**For B,**

$(001111)_2 = (?)_{10}$

$= 0\times 2^5 + 0\times 2^4 + 1\times 2^3 + 1\times 2^2 + 1\times 2^1 + 1\times 2^0$

$= 0+0+8+4+2+1 = 15$

$\therefore \quad (001111)_2 = (15)_{10}$

So, option (IV)

**For C,**

Duration = data transferred/speed

= 75 Megabyte/2 Mbps

$= \frac{75\times 8}{2}$ sec = 300 sec = $\frac{300}{60}$ min

Duration = 5 min

So, option I

**For D,** 1 Kilobyte = $2^P$ byte

$2^{10}$ byte = $2^P$ byte

$\therefore \quad p = 10$

So, option III

**Directions** (Q.No. 46-50) *Read the following passage and answer questions.*

Gandhi's speech in Banaras in February 1916 was, at one level, merely a statement of fact namely, that Indian nationalism was an elite phenomenon, a creation of lawyers and doctors and landlords. But, at another level, it was a statement of intent-the first public announcement of the returning expatriate's own desire to make Indian nationalism more properly representative of the Indian people. In the last month of that year, Gandhi was presented with an opportunity to put his precepts into practice. At a meeting held in Lucknow in December 1916, he was approached by a peasant from Champaran in Bihar. The peasant told him about harsh treatment of peasants by British Indigo planters.

Gandhi was to spend most of 1917 in Champaran. He was seeking to obtain for the peasants security of tenure as well as freedom to cultivate the crops of their choice. In 1918, Gandhi was involved in two campaigns in his home state of Gujarat.

First, he intervened in a labour dispute in Ahmedabad to better the conditions of textile mill workers. Then he joined peasants in Kheda for remission of taxes on peasants following the failure of their harvest. These initiatives marked Gandhi as a nationalist with sympathy for the poor. These were local struggles. During the World War I, the British had instituted press censorship and permitted detention without trial. The Rowlatt committee recommended the continuation of these tough measures. Gandhiji's call for a countrywide campaign brought life to standstill in North and West India.

**46** Which was the statement of fact in the Speech of Mahatma Gandhi at Banaras?

(1) Lawyers, doctors and landlords sided with the British.

(2) The Indian nationalism was elitist.

(3) Nationalism was of another level in India.

(4) The existing Indian nationalism was highly effective.

***Ans.*** ***(2)*** The fact in the speech of Mahatma Gandhi at Banaras was that the Indian nationalism was elitist. Indian nationalism is an instance of territorial nationalism, which is inclusive of all of the people of India, despite their diverse ethnic, linguistic and religious backgrounds. Indian nationalism can trace roots to pre-colonial India, but was fully developed during the Indian independence movement which campaigned for independence from British rule.

**47** Gandhiji could put his precept into practice during

(1) the Lucknow meeting

(2) the talks with landlords

(3) the Champaran campaign

(4) the interaction with nationalist leaders

***Ans.*** ***(3)*** Gandhiji put his percept into practice during the Champaran campaign. The Champaran Satyagraha of 1917 was the first Satyagraha movement led by Gandhi in India and is considered a historically important revolt in the Indian Independence Movement. It was a farmer's uprising that took place in Champaran district of Bihar, India, during the British colonial period.

**48** Gandhiji's speech expressed the intention of

(1) making Indian nationalism more representative.

(2) announcing the desire of expatriates to become politically active.

(3) criticising the activities of Indian nationalists.

(4) launching a new nationalist movement.

***Ans.*** ***(1)*** Gandhiji's speech expressed the intention of making Indian nationalism more representative. Assuming leadership of the Indian National Congress in 1921, Gandhi led nationwide campaigns for dealing with problems such as poverty, expanding women's rights, building religious and ethnic amity, ending untouchability and above all, achieving swaraj or self-rule.

**49** The main intent of the passage is to describe the

(1) British atrocities in India.

(2) different facets of Indian national movement.

(3) various campaigns against the British in India.

(4) emergence of Gandhiji as a representative national leader.

***Ans. (4)*** The main intent of the passage is to describe the emergence of Gandhiji as national leader. Mahatma Gandhi was a great learner. He brought changes in himself. He was a great leader because he created not only followers but also leaders.

The leaders coached by him served India and laid the foundation of the largest democracy in the world while the sibling was ruled by the military dictators.

**50** **Which issue propelled Gandhiji to the national stage for a wider movement?**

(1) Labour dispute of textile mill workers in Ahmedabad

(2) Agitation peasants in Kheda

(3) The revolt against British Indigo planters

(4) The Rowlatt Act

***Ans. (4)*** The Rowlatt Act propelled Gandhiji to the national stage of a wider movement. Rowlatt Acts legislation was passed by the Imperial Legislative Council the legislature of British India. The acts allowed certain political cases to be tried without juries and permitted internment of suspects without trial.

# UGC
# NET/JRF/SET
# Solved Paper, 2022
## (Exam Held on : 12 October, 2022, Shift I)

## General Paper 1 (Teaching and Research Aptitude)

*Instructions*
- This paper contains fifty Multiple Choice Questions, each question carries two marks.
- All questions are compulsory.
- Total time given for this paper is 1 hour.

**Directions** (Q.No 1-5) *Study the given table and answer the questions that follows.*

The following table presents the details about the percentage (%) distribution of teachers and the number of male teachers in six different cities (A-F). There is a total of 4500 teachers in all the six cities together.

**City-wise Distribution of Teachers**

| City ↓ | Percentage of (%) Teachers | Number of Male Teachers |
|---|---|---|
| A | 14% | 200 |
| B | 16% | 400 |
| C | 28% | 600 |
| D | 15% | 100 |
| E | 21% | 500 |
| F | 06% | 100 |

**1** What is the ratio of the number of male teachers in City-C to the number of female teachers in City-B?

(1) 11 : 15 (2) 15 : 11
(3) 15 : 8 (4) 8 : 15

***Ans. (3)*** Number of male teachers in City-C = 600 and number of female teachers in City-B

$$= \frac{16}{100} \times 4500 - 400$$

$$= 720 - 400 = 320$$

$$\therefore \text{ Required ratio} = \frac{600}{320} = 15 : 8$$

**2** The number of female teachers in City-D is approximately what percent of the total number of teachers in City-A?

(1) 75 (2) 81
(3) 95 (4) 91

***Ans. (4)*** Number of female teachers in City-D

$$= \frac{15}{100} \times 4500 - 100 = 675 - 100 = 575$$

Total number of teachers in City-A

$$= \frac{14}{100} \times 4500 = 630$$

$$\therefore \text{ Required percentage} = \frac{575}{630} \times 100$$

$$= 9126\% \approx 91\%$$

**3** What is the total number of male teachers in City-F, female teachers in City-C and female teachers in City-B together?

(1) 1080 (2) 1120
(3) 1180 (4) 1020

***Ans. (1)*** Number of male teachers in City-F = 100

Number of female teachers in City-C

$$= \frac{28}{100} \times 4500 - 600$$

$$= 1260 - 600 = 660$$

Number of female teachers in City-B

$$= \frac{16}{100} \times 4500 - 400$$

$$= 720 - 400 = 320$$

∴ Required sum = 660 + 100 + 320 = 1080

**4** In which city is the number of male teachers more than the number of female teachers?

(1) Only B (2) Only D
(3) Both B and E (4) Both E and F

***Ans. (3)*** Number of male teachers in City-B = 400

Number of female teachers in City-B = 320

Number of male teachers in City-D = 100

Number of female teachers in City-D = 575

Number of male teachers in City-E = 500

Number of female teachers in City-E

$$= \frac{21}{100} \times 4500 - 500$$

$$= 445$$

Numbers of male teachers in city-F = 100

Number of female teachers in city-F

$$= \frac{6}{100} \times 4500 - 100 = 170$$

Thus, Cities B and E, number of male teachers are more than number of female teachers.

**5** What is the difference between the total number of teachers in City-E and the number of female teachers in City-F?

(1) 625 (2) 775
(3) 675 (4) 725

***Ans. (2)*** Total number of teacher in City-E

$$= \frac{21}{100} \times 4500 = 945$$

and Number of female teachers in City-F

$$= \frac{6}{100} \times 4500 - 100 = 170$$

∴ Required difference = 945 – 170

= 775

**6** Match List I with List II.

| | List I | | List II |
|---|---|---|---|
| A. | National Education Policy | I. | 1993 |
| B. | National Policy on Education | II. | 2009 |
| C. | National Knowledge Commission | III. | 1986 |
| D. | Learning Without Burden Report of the National Advisory Committee | IV. | 2020 |

Choose the correct answer from the options given below.

| | A | B | C | D |
|---|---|---|---|---|
| (1) | IV | II | III | I |
| (2) | IV | III | I | II |
| (3) | IV | III | II | I |
| (4) | IV | I | II | III |

***Ans. (3)*** The correct matching is A-IV, B-III, C-II, D-I.

The **National Education Policy, 2020** has replaced the 34 year old National Education Policy, 1986. This new education policy has given priority to reorganise the present 10 + 2 school system into a new system of 5 + 3 + 3 + 4 curriculum and pedagogy for all children in the age group of 3 to 18 years. Along with this, special importance has been given to the all-round development of the children.

The **National Policy on Education** was announced in the year 1986, whose main objective was to establish rural universities, universal access to education, modernisation and commercialisation of education, emphasis on open universities and distance studies etc.

The **National Knowledge Commission** published its entire report in the year 2009 under the title 'Report in the name of the nation'. In this, special priority was given to the accessibility, creation, principles, services and applications of knowledge.

The **Learning Without Burden Report of the National Advisory Committee** was presented in the year 1993 by Professor Yashpal, a renowned educationist and former chairman of the University Grants Commission. In this report importance was given to education without burden.

**7** Given below are two statements, one is labelled as Assertion (A) and the other is labelled as Reason (R).

**Assertion** (A) There are certain psychological conditions under which inference takes place.

**Reason** (R) Absence of positive knowledge and will to infer its presence or absence are pre-requisites for inference to be drawn.

In the light of the above statements, choose the correct answer from the options given below.

(1) Both A and R are true and R is the correct explanation of A.
(2) Both A and R are true, but R is not the correct explanation of A.
(3) A is true, but R is false.
(4) A is false, but R is true.

***Ans. (1)*** Both Assertion (A) and Reason (R) are true and Reason (R) is the correct explanation of Assertion (A).

Inference is the process of drawing conclusions about general patterns of behaviour from specific observations. Inferences are pieces of missing information that an individual fills in through previous knowledge or through theories or prior belief.

For example, if someone walks into a room and notes that digital clocks are flashing, they can 'infer' that there must have been a recent power outage.

**8** The type of research in which the researcher gains familiarity with a phenomenon or to achieve new insights into it, is known as

(1) Diagnostic research study
(2) Exploratory research study
(3) Descriptive research study
(4) Hypothesis testing study

***Ans. (2)*** The type of research in which the researcher gains familiarity with a phenomenon or to achieve new insights into it, is known as exploratory research study.

Exploratory research is a research method that explores why something occurs when limited information is available. It can help researcher increase their understanding of a given topic, ascertain how or why a particular phenomenon is occurring and predict future occurrences. Exploratory research generally focuses on the 'why' questions. For example, a businessman might ask why customers aren't buying their product or how they can improve their sales process.

**9** Match List I with List II.

| List I | List II |
|---|---|
| A. Mist | I. Aerosols consisting of solid particles |
| B. Smoke | II. Aerosols produced by condensation of hot vapour of metals |
| C. Fume | III. Photochemical products of VOCs and NOx |
| D. Smog | IV. Aerosols consisting of liquid droplets |

Choose the correct answer from the options given below.

| | A | B | C | D |
|---|---|---|---|---|
| (1) | IV | I | II | III |
| (2) | III | II | IV | I |
| (3) | II | IV | III | I |
| (4) | IV | II | I | III |

***Ans. (1)*** The correct matching is A-IV, B-I, C-II, D-III.

**Mist** is a phenomenon caused by small droplets of water suspended in the cold air, usually by condensation. Mist is an example of aerosol where the dispersed phase is liquid.

**Smoke** is a suspension of airborne particulates and gases emitted when a material undergoes combustion or pyrolysis, together with the quantity of air that is mixed into the mass. Smoke is an example of solid aerosol in which dispersed phase is solid.

**Fumes** are the unpleasant and often unhealthy smoke and gases that are produced by fires or by things such as chemicals fuel or cooking.

**Smog** is composed mainly of tropospheric ozone ($O_3$), primary particulate matter such as pollen and dust, and secondary particulate matter such as sulphur oxides, volatile organic compounds, nitrogen oxides ($NO_x$) and ammonia gas.

***10*** **Match List I with List II.**

| List I | List II |
|---|---|
| A. Learning Management System | I. Blender |
| B. Web Conferencing System | II. Sakai |
| C. Animation Maker System | III. SPSS |
| D. Data Processing System | IV. Microsoft Teams |

**Choose the correct answer from the options given below.**

| | A | B | C | D |
|---|---|---|---|---|
| (1) | II | IV | I | III |
| (2) | IV | I | III | II |
| (3) | I | III | II | IV |
| (4) | III | II | IV | I |

***Ans. (2)*** The correct matching is A-II, B-IV, C-I, D-III.

**Blender** is a free and open-source 3D computer graphics software tool set used for creating animated films, visual effects, art, 3D-printed models.

**Sakai** is a free, community source, educational software platform designed to support teaching, research and collaboration.

**SPSS** statistics is a statistical software suite developed by IBM for data management, advanced analytics, multivariate analysis, business intelligence and criminal investigation.

**Microsoft Teams** is a proprietary business communication platform developed by Microsoft, as part of the Microsoft 365 family of products.

***11*** **Aman adds a video file to his social networking page. Which one of these describes a video that has been watched by a lot of people over a short period of time?**

(1) Digital (2) Tagged
(3) Viral (4) Open source

***Ans. (3)*** Aman adds a video file to his social networking page and it is watched by a lots of people, it will be a viral video.

A viral video is a video that has been watched by a lot of people over a short period of time. It has becomes popular through a viral process of Internet sharing, typically through video sharing websites such as YouTube, Instagram, Facebook, etc. as well as social media and email.

***12*** **Kavita's age is eight years more than thrice the sum of the ages of her two grandsons who are twins. Nine years later, Kavita's age will be one year more than two times the sum of the ages of her two grandsons. What was the age of Kavita when her grandsons were born?**

(1) 58 yr (2) 68 yr
(3) 65 yr (4) 28 yr

***Ans. (1)*** Let the age of each grandson be $x$ years and present age of Kavita be $y$ years

According to question,

$$x - 3y = 8 \quad \ldots\text{(i)}$$

After 9 years, $x + 9 - 2(y + 18) = 1$

$$x - 2y = 28 \quad \ldots\text{(ii)}$$

From equation (i) and (ii),

$$y = 20$$

$$\therefore \quad x = 3 \times 20 + 8 = 68$$

$\therefore$ Present age of both grandsons $= \frac{20}{2} = 10$ years

$\therefore$ Age of Kavita at the time of birth of her grandsons

$= 68 - 10 = 58$ years

**13** Match List I with List II.

| List I | List II |
|---|---|
| A. Fallacy that occurs due to appeal to non-rational methods of intimidation | I. Argumentum ad Hominem |
| B. Fallacy that occurs when an argument makes an appeal to the character of the person | II. Accident Fallacy |
| C. Fallacy that occurs when an argument is in the form of emotional 'appeal to the gallery' | III. Argumentum ad Populum |
| D. Fallacy that occurs when a general rule is applied to a case in which the rule is inapplicable | IV. Argumentum ad Baculum (force) |

Choose the correct answer from the options given below.

| | A | B | C | D |
|---|---|---|---|---|
| (1) | I | II | III | IV |
| (2) | III | II | I | IV |
| (3) | II | IV | I | III |
| (4) | IV | I | III | II |

***Ans. (4)*** The correct matching is A-IV, B-I, C-III, D-II.

**Argumentum ad Hominem** is fallacious argument that attacks not an opponent's beliefs, but his or her motives or character.

**The fallacy of accident** is an informal fallacy and a deductively valid, but unsound argument occurring in a statistical syllogism when an exception to a rule of thumb is ignored.

**In argumentation theory**, an Argumentum ad Populum is a fallacious argument, which is based on claiming a truth or affirming something is good because the majority thinks so.

**Argumentum ad Baculum** is the fallacy committed when one makes an appeal to force to bring about the acceptance of a conclusion.

**14** Match List I with List II.

| List I | List II |
|---|---|
| A. Phishing | I. The action of illegally installing malicious code which redirects a person to a fraudulent website with the purpose of obtaining that person's bank details. |
| B. Pharming | II. The action of sending text message to fraudulently obtain another person's bank details. |
| C. Spamming | III. The action of sending emails to fraudulently obtain another person's bank details. |
| D. Smishing | IV. Unsolicited bulk emails |

Choose the correct answer from the options given below.

| | A | B | C | D |
|---|---|---|---|---|
| (1) | I | III | IV | II |
| (2) | IV | I | III | II |
| (3) | III | I | IV | II |
| (4) | III | I | II | IV |

***Ans. (3)*** The correct matching is A-III, B-I, C-IV, D-II.

**Phishing** is where an attacker sends a fraudulent message designed to trick a person into revealing sensitive information or to deploy malicious software on the victim's infrastructure like ransomware.

**Pharming** is a cyberattack intended to redirect a website's traffic to another, fake site by installing a malicious program on the computer.

**Spamming** is the use of messaging systems to send multiple unsolicited messages to large numbers of recipients for the purpose of commercial advertising.

**Smishing** is the fraudulent practice of sending text messages purporting to be from reputable companies in order to induce individuals to reveal personal information, such as passwords or credit card numbers.

***15*** The reforms initiated under the Rashtriya Uchchatar Shiksha Abhiyan (RUSA) aim at

A. push for greater accountability and autonomy of state institution.
B. improving the quality of education and infrastructure.
C. formulation of stringent regulations to curb commercialisation of higher education.
D. increase in GER upto 50 percent.
E. efficient monitoring and continuous feedback mechanism.

Choose the correct answer from the options given below.

(1) A, B and C
(2) A and B
(3) A, B, C and D
(4) B, C, D and E

***Ans.*** ***(2)*** Statements A and B are correct with respect to RUSA. Following are the objectives of the reformative measures taken under Rashtriya Uchchatar Shiksha Abhiyan (RUSA):

Under this, more responsibility and autonomy of state institutions is emphasised and the quality of education and infrastructure is improved. Rashtriya Uchchatar Shiksha Abhiyan is a centrally sponsored scheme that was launched by the Government of India in the year 2013. It finances eligible higher education institutions of the states. The scheme has been allowed by the government to continue till 31st March, 2026 or till the next review (whichever is earlier). An amount of ₹ 12929.16 crore has been allocated in this proposal.

***16*** What comes next in the following sequence?

0.25, 2.25, 6.25, 12.25, ?

(1) 18.25
(2) 19.25
(3) 16.25
(4) 20.25

***Ans.*** ***(4)*** The pattern of the series is as follows

0.25 → (+2) → 2.25 → (+4) → 6.25 → (+6) → 12.25 → (+8) → **20.25**

***17*** Given below are two statements, one is labelled as Assertion (A) and the other is labelled as Reason (R).

**Assertion** (A) Universities play a key role in building a symbiotic relationship between the nation, state and society.

**Reason** (R) Universities are centres for creation and transmission of knowledge.

In the light of the above statements, choose the correct answer from the options given below.

(1) Both A and R are true and R is the correct explanation of A.
(2) Both A and R are true, but R is not the correct explanation of A.
(3) A is true, but R is false.
(4) A is false, but R is true.

***Ans.*** ***(2)*** Both Assertion (A) and Reason (R) are correct, but Reason (R) is not the correct explanation of Assertion (A).

Universities play a major role in building a symbiotic relationship between the nation, the state and the society, because it is in these universities that high value is imparted to the society through higher education, Like-equality, fraternity, rule of law, tolerance, technology etc; develop. Universities are the centers of creation and dissemination of knowledge, because the students studying here are given comprehensive and high quality education and degrees are distributed by taking examinations. The university does three special things for the students

- Personal development.
- To contribute for the betterment of the society.
- Getting good employment.

***18*** According to National Education Policy (2020), National Higher Education Regulatory Council will be the single point regulator for all disciplines except

(1) teacher education
(2) medical and legal education
(3) agricultural sciences
(4) management

*Ans. (2)* Except medical and legal education, NEP 2020 will be single point regulator for all the disciplines. This policy was started in place of Education Policy, 1986 under Right to Education Act, 2009. It changed existing 10 + 2 Model of Education to 5+ 3+ 3+ 4.

Benefits of NEP 2020 is that students will be given increased flexibility and choice of subjects to study, particularly in secondary school-including subjects in physical education, the arts and crafts, and vocational skills - so that they can design their own paths of study and life plans.

**19** Identify the correct order of the following major technological changes in computers based on fourth to first generation of computers.

A. Microprocessors
B. Vacuum Tubes
C. Integrated Circuits
D. Transistors

Choose the correct answer from the options given below.

(1) C, A, D, B (2) A, C, B, D
(3) A, C, D, B (4) D, B, A, C

*Ans. (3)* The correct order of technological change is A, C, D, B.

A microprocessor (1971-80) is a computer processor where the data processing logic and control is included on a single integrated circuit or a small number of integrated circuits.

An integrated circuit (1965-71) is a semiconductor wafer on which thousands or millions of tiny resistors, capacitors, diodes and transistors are fabricated.

A transistor (1959-65) can act as a switch or gate for electronic signals, opening and closing an electronic gate many times per second.

Used as on/off switches, vacuum tubes (1946-59) allowed the first computers to perform digital computations.

**20** Give below are two statements, one is labelled as Assertion (A) and the other is labelled as Reason (R).

**Assertion** (A) A proper name has only denotation, but no connotation.

**Reason** (R) Intension refers to set of adjectives. Extension refers to set of substantives.

In the light of the above statements, choose the correct answer from the options given below.

(1) Both A and R are true and R is the correct explanation of A
(2) Both A and R are true, but R is not the correct explanation of A
(3) A is true, but R is false
(4) A is false, but R is true

*Ans. (1)* Both Assertion (A) and Reason (R) are true and Reason (R) is the correct explanation of Assertion (A).

Intentions are mental states in which the agent commits themselves to a course of action. Intension and extension, in logic are correlative words that indicate the reference of a term or concept. Intension indicates the internal content of a term or concept that constitutes its formal definition and 'extension' indicates its range of applicability by naming the particular objects that it denotes.

**21** Match List I with List II.

| List I | List II |
|---|---|
| A. $H_0 : \mu = \mu_{H_0} = 100$ | I. Alternate hypothesis is that the population mean is not equal to 100 |
| B. $H_\alpha : \mu \neq \mu_{H_0}$ | II. Alternative hypothesis is that the population mean is greater than 100 |
| C. $H_\alpha : \mu > \mu_{H_0}$ | III. Null hypothesis is that the population mean is equal to the hypothesised mean 100 |
| D. $H_\alpha : \mu < \mu_{H_0}$ | IV. Alternative hypothesis is that the population mean is less than 100 |

Choose the correct answer from the options given below.

| | A | B | C | D |
|---|---|---|---|---|
| (1) | II | IV | III | I |
| (2) | IV | III | I | II |
| (3) | I | III | IV | II |
| (4) | III | I | II | IV |

***Ans.*** ***(4)*** The correct matching is A-III, B-I, C-II and D-IV.

Hypothesis tests are used to make decisions or judgements about the value of a parameter, such as the population mean.
Null hypothesis is denoted by $H_0$ and assumed to be true. Also, it contains the equal sign and has a specific value. Here specified value of population mean is 100.

$\therefore$ (A) $H_0 : \mu = \mu_{H_0} = 100$ (III)

Now, Alternate hypothesis is an alternate to the null hypothesis, denoted by $H_\alpha$ which might and might not be true. It contains the inequality sign such as $<, >$ and $\neq$.

(B) $H_\alpha : \mu \neq \mu_{H_0} \rightarrow$ (I)

(C) $H_\alpha : \mu > \mu_{H_0} \rightarrow$ (II)

(D) $H_\alpha : \mu < \mu_{H_0} \rightarrow$ (IV)

**22** The procedure of assigning numbers to various degrees of opinion, attitude and other concepts is called as

(1) regression
(2) scaling
(3) variance
(4) concordance

***Ans.*** ***(2)*** The procedures of assigning numbers to various degrees of opinion, attitude and other concepts is called as scaling. This is done in two ways i.e. making a judgement about some characteristic of an individual and this placing him directly on a scale that has been defined in terms of that characteristics and constructing questionnaires in such a way that the scores of individual's responses assign him a place on a scale. It may be stated that a scale is a continuum, consisting of the highest point (in terms of some characteristics e.g. preference, favourableness, etc.) and the lowest point along with several intermediate points between these two extremes points.

**23** Identify the correct sequence in decreasing order in terms of number of universities in the state.

A. Gujarat
B. Uttar Pradesh
C. Rajasthan
D. Karnataka
E. Madhya Pradesh

Choose the correct answer from the options given below.

(1) A, B, C, D, E
(2) B, C, D, A, E
(3) C, B, D, A, E
(4) C, B, A, D, E

***Ans.*** ***(*)*** Uttar Pradesh and Rajasthan has 83, Gujarat has 59, Madhya Pradesh has 39, Karnataka has 20 Universities.

As two states have same numbers of university, none of the given order is correct. NTA has DROP this answer.

**24** Identify the correct sequence for the technique of developing measurement tools.

A. Specification of concept dimensions
B. Selection of indicators
C. Concept development
D. Formation of index

Choose the correct answer from the options given below.

(1) A, B, C, D
(2) C, A, B, D
(3) B, C, A, D
(4) D, A, C, B

***Ans.*** ***(2)*** The correct sequence of measurement tools are C, A, B, D.
Concept development helps you evaluate your customers reactions to your product or service before your product launch.
Specify the dimensions of the concepts may either be accomplished by deduction i.e., by adopting a more or less intuitive approach or by empirical correlation of the individual dimensions with the total concept and/or the other concepts.

When selecting indicators, it is important to consider the long-term as well as the short-term objectives and how each will be measured.
An index is an accumulation of scores from a variety of individual items. To create one, you must select possible items, examine their empirical relationships, score the index and validate it.

**25** 1mm layer of pure ozone gas around Earth at normal temperature and pressure is equivalent to

(1) Dobson Unit (DU)
(2) 10 DU
(3) 100 DU
(4) 0.1 DU

***Ans.*** ***(3)*** 1 mm layer of pure ozone gas around the Earth at normal temperature and pressure is equivalent to 100 DU. One hundred Dobson Units of ozone would form a layer only 1 millimeter thick if it were compressed into a single layer, about the height of a dime. Compressed to sea-level pressure, the ozone in the atmosphere would form a layer about the height of two pennies stacked together.

**26** Organisational communication is ........ in nature.

(1) obtrusive
(2) contradictory
(3) non-behavioural
(4) applied

***Ans.*** ***(4)*** Organisational communication is applied in nature. Organisational communication is a field of study of all areas of communication and information flow that contribute to the functioning of a type of organisation.

Organisational communication continues to evolve, as a result of which the scope of organisations involved in this area of research has changed over time. Now traditionally for-profit companies, as well as non-governmental organisations and non-profit organisations, are a point of interest for scholars focused on the area of organisational communication.

**27** If 'All college professors are entertaining lecturers' is true in a square, of opposition which of the following can be inferred correctly from the given codes?

A. 'No college professors are entertaining lecturers' is false.
B. 'Some college professors are not entertaining lecturers' is true.
C. 'Some college professors are entertaining lecturers' is true.
D. 'Some college professors are entertaining lecturers' is false.

Choose the correct answer from the options given below.

(1) A and B (2) B and C
(3) C and D (4) A and C

***Ans.*** ***(4)*** 'All college professors are entertaining lectures' is true, in a square of opposition then statement A and C can be inferred correctly.

**28** What is the correct sequence of preparing vermi-compost?

A. Introduction of culture of worms into the pit.
B. Lining up with straw or dried grass and leaves.
C. Water the pit once or twice a week.
D. Construction of pit of half square meter area and one meter deep.
E. Putting into pit the organic wastes as and when generated.

Choose the correct answer from the options given below.

(1) D, E, B, A, C
(2) A, C, D, E, B
(3) E, A, B, C, D
(4) D, B, E, A, C

***Ans.*** ***(4)*** D, B, E, A, C is the correct sequence of preparing vermi-compost.

Vermi-compost is the product of the decomposition process using various species of worms, usually red wigglers, white worms and other earthworms, to create a mixture of decomposing vegetable or food waste, bedding materials and vermicast.

**29** Given below are two statements, one is labelled as Assertion (A) and the other is labelled as Reason (R).

**Assertion** (A) Bottom ash generated into the boilers of the thermal power plants are major cause of nearby river pollution.

**Reason** (R) The hot water generated from thermal power plants are discharged into the nearby rivers.

In the light of the above statements, choose the correct answer from the options given below.

(1) Both A and R are true and R is the correct explanation of A.
(2) Both A and R are true, but R is not the correct explanation of A.
(3) A is true, but R is false.
(4) A is false, but R is true.

***Ans. (2)*** Both Assertion (A) and Reason (R) are true, but Reason (R) is not the correct explanation of Assertion (A).

Bottom ash is part of the non-combustible residue of combustion in a power plant, boiler, furnace or incinerator. Bottom ash is used as a construction material in artificial reefs, roads, liners and daily covers for landfills, concrete masonry blocks and lightweight and partial replacement of aggregate.

Hot water generated from power plant is pumped from deep underground through a well under high pressure. When the water reaches the surface, the pressure is dropped, which causes the water to turn into steam. The steam spins a turbine, which is connected to a generator that produces electricity.

**30** Given below are two statements about Electronic Mail (e-mail).

**Statement I** You can create folders to store and organise your emails.

**Statement II** You can add attachments of any file size to an email.

In the light of the above statement , choose the correct answer from the options given below.

(1) Both statements I and II are true.
(2) Both statements I and II are false.
(3) Statement I is true, but statement II is false.
(4) Statement I is false, but statement II is true.

***Ans. (3)*** Statement I is true, but statement II is false.

An email attachment is a computer file sent along with an email message. One or more files can be attached to any email message and be sent along with it to the recipient. This is typically used as a simple method to share documents and images. Its services started in the year 1972.

The maximum size for any single email message including attachments is 25 MB.

**31** With reference to Likert-type scale, the correct set of options include.

A. Likert-type scale can be performed without a panel of judges.
B. Likert-type scales are not considered reliable.
C. Likert-type scale take more time to construct.
D. Each statement in Likert-type scale is given an empirical test for discriminating ability.
E. Likert-type scale can be used in respondent-centred studies.

Choose the correct answer from the options given below.

(1) A, B, C (2) B, C, D
(3) A, D, E (4) C, D, E

***Ans. (3)*** Statements A, D and E are correct with respect to Likert- type scale.

A Likert- scale is a psychometric scale commonly involved in research that employs questionnaires. It is the most widely used approach to scaling responses in survey research, such that the term is often used interchangeably with rating scale, although there are other types of rating scales. Likert type measurement can be done without consulting a group of judges. It can be used in respondent centered study.

**32** Under which initiative every student in the country will participate in a fun project/activity on 'The Languages of India', sometime in Grades 6-8?

(1) Make in India

(2) Digital India

(3) Padhe Bharat Badhe Bharat

(4) Ek Bharat Shrestha Bharat

***Ans.*** ***(4)*** Under 'Ek Bharat Shreshtha Bharat' initiative every student in the country will participate in a fun project/activity on 'The language of India' sometime in Grades 6-8. It is an initiative of the Ministry of Education. It was launched in 2015 to promote engagement amongst the people of different States/UTs so as to enhance mutual understanding and bonding between people of diverse cultures, thereby securing stronger unity and integrity of India.

**33** Given below are two statements.

**Statement I** It is not desirable to have all the interest areas around the outside of the classroom, leaving a large dead space in the middle.

**Statement II** It is not desirable to put bookshelves next to the reading area and games equipment by the game table.

In the light of the above statements, choose the most appropriate answer from the options given below.

(1) Both statements I and II are true.

(2) Both statements I and II are false.

(3) Statement I is true, but statement II is false.

(4) Statement I is false, but statement II is false.

***Ans.*** ***(3)*** Statement I is true, but statement II is false.

It is not desirable to have all the fields in the center of a class leaving a wide unused area around it. In the class, students should be taught a wide range of interesting subjects, so that the purpose of the class and the school is fulfilled. Therefore, this statement is correct.

It is not advisable to place bookshelves near the study area, sports equipment near the sports table. This statement is wrong, as it is intended to place the books near the study area and the game equipment near the game table. Through this process, according to the interest of the students in the class, they can take education and develop their personality.

**34** Given below are two statements.

**Statement I** The physical context of communication must be tangible.

**Statement II** The temporal context of message deals with the sequence of events.

In the light of the above statements, choose the correct answer from the options given below.

(1) Both statements I and II are true.

(2) Both statements I and II are false.

(3) Statement I is true, but statement II is false.

(4) Statement I is false, but statement II is true.

***Ans.*** ***(1)*** Both statements I and II are true.

The physical context is the environment where the communication takes place, such as a bedroom, hallway or bar. Within the environment, factors like the size of the space, the temperature and number of other people present will shape the communication that occurs. Temporal context in communication refers to the way that individuals rely on past behaviours to set the tone for communication.

**35** The population of a bacteria culture doubles every 2 minutes. How many minutes will it take for the population to grow from 1 to 1024?

(1) 10 (2) 14

(3) 18 (4) 20

***Ans.*** ***(4)*** The growth of population is in G.P.

1, 2, 4, 8 ........... 1024

$\because \quad 1024 = 2^{10}$

$\therefore$ Time taken $= 2 \times 10 = 20$ minutes

**36** Given below are two statements.

**Statement I** A fraction can be reduced to its lowest form by dividing the numerator and denominator with a common factor.

**Statement II** Two fractions can be compared by comparing their numerators if their denominators are equal.

In the light of the above statements, choose the correct answer from the options given below.

(1) Both statements I and II are true
(2) Both statements I and II are false
(3) Statement I is true, but statement II is false
(4) Statement I is false, but statement II is true

***Ans. (1)*** Statement I is true. Let the fraction be $\frac{26}{28}$ then it can be written as $= \frac{2\times 13}{2\times 14} = \frac{13}{14}$, where 2 is a common factor.

Statement II is also true. If denominators of two fractions are same then we can compare it by comparing the numerator.

Let $\frac{16}{51}$ and $\frac{7}{51}$ are true fractions with equal denominators '51'.

Hence, on comparing numerator, we get $\frac{16}{51} > \frac{7}{51}$.

**37** Identify the approaches to assessment that require performance in context.

A. Priming
B. Portfolios
C. Think-Pair-Share
D. Exhibitions
E. Token reinforcement

Choose the most appropriate answer from the options given below.

(1) B and D (2) A and C
(3) C and D (4) D and E

***Ans. (1)*** Portfolios and exhibitions are approaches to assessment that requires performance.

A portfolio is a collection of financial investments like stocks, bonds, commodities, cash and cash equivalents, including closed-end funds and Exchange Traded Funds (ETFs). An exhibition, in the most general sense, is an organised presentation and display of a selection of items.

**38** Types of communication distance on a continuum of ethnocentrism in sequence are

A. Indifference B. Avoidance
C. Disparagement D. Equality
E. Sensitivity

Choose the correct answer from the options given below.

(1) B, C, E, D, A
(2) D, E, A, B, C
(3) C, D, E, A, B
(4) A, B, C, E, D

***Ans. (2)*** Types of communication distance related to the continuity of ethnocentricity in the interpretation sequence is D, E, A, B, C.

Equality, sensitivity, indifference, avoidance, disparagement are the sequence of types of communication distance related to continuity of ethnocentrism.

Equality means equal access to all and opportunities without discrimination of caste, class, region, religion, gender etc. Sensitivity is the need to handle a topic or issue carefully, because it is likely to cause disagreement or make people angry or upset. Apathy, sadness or lacks of emotion are often caused by depression or alcohol or drug abuse. Avoidance means giving up people. Contempt means disobeying the order of the concerned person.

**39** Which of the following is not a fallacy of Ambiguity?

(1) Equivocation (2) Amphiboly
(3) Accent (4) Accident

***Ans. (4)*** Accident is not a fallacy of ambiguity. Fallacies of ambiguity involve some confusion over meaning, specifically over the members referred to by a term used in the argument. In a syllogism, there are of course, three terms that might be a source of confusion. A fallacy of ambiguity is committed whenever there is a word or phrase or whole passage that has more than one meaning and this lack of clarity of meaning leads to unwarranted conclusions.

be, in principle available often depends a great deal on the information that the local community gathers and the extent to which it can get its voice heard.

The shirking and absenteeism of village teachers for example are much more easily observed by the villagers themselves than by the government inspectors and the search for redress can be more effectively achieved with local activism. Besides, schools, hospitals and other facilities can be made more sensitive to the public needs if there is a local pressure in that direction, better than the directions from the above.

**46** What can bring the social opportunities within the reach of the people?

(1) The government directives

(2) Economic literature

(3) Actions of the public

(4) Success of social change

***Ans.*** ***(3)*** According to the passage, actions of the public can bring the social opportunities within the reach of the people. Public actions are a very public expression of a community's power in issue (voice) campaigns or electoral (vote) campaigns. Public actions can be an event held by an organisation or can be at either another organisation's or public body's event - such as a school board meeting.

**47** The effective quality of services depends upon making

(1) stricter rules for implementation

(2) local community involved

(3) redressal of grievances

(4) strong government vigilance

***Ans.*** ***(2)*** The effective quality of service depends upon making local community involved. Effective quality services boost sales. Customers that perceive a company's services as being high quality are more likely to do business with that company. Also, customers who buy from companies with high service quality are more likely to continue buying from those companies regularly. It saves marketing money.

**48** Positive functions of the government can be supported by

(1) public influence on policy-decisions

(2) focussing on education and social security

(3) centralised power structure

(4) top-down, one way general instructions

***Ans.*** ***(1)*** Public influence on policy decisions is the positive effect of the government. It enables good governance. It is the process of measuring how public institutions conduct public affairs and manage public resources and guarantee the realisation of human rights in a manner essentially free of abuse and corruption and with due regard for the rule of law.

**49** Adequate monitoring of public services is possible through

(1) expansion of essential services

(3) increasing social inclusivity

(2) improvement in quality of services

(4) effective public activism

***Ans.*** ***(4)*** Adequate monitoring of public services is possible through effective public activism. Effective activism simply means, well-being active for a cause, but the particular action you take and the cause for which you fight are up to you. Your voice really can make a difference in raising awareness of an issue and even changing laws and policies.

**50** What does the passage advocate to make services sensitive to public need?

(1) Pressure by beneficiaries

(2) Information gathering

(3) Government monitoring

(4) Checking absenteeism among public employees

***Ans.*** ***(1)*** Passage advocates pressure by beneficiaries to make services. Public need means an activity project that provides important tangible and intangible gains to society, that satisfies the expressed or observed needs of the public where accrued benefits significantly outweigh reasonably foreseeable detriments.

NTA
UGC
NET/JRF/SET

# SOLVED PAPER 2021

# UGC
## NET/JRF/SET

# Solved Paper, 2021

## (Exam Held on : 22 November, 2021, Shift I)

## General Paper 1 (Teaching and Research Aptitude)

***Instructions***

- This paper contains fifty Multiple Choice Questions, each question carries two marks.
- All questions are compulsory.
- Total time given for this paper is 1 hour.

**Directions** (Q. Nos. 1-5) *Read the following paragraph and answer the five questions which as follows*

The following table embodies the details about the enrollment of students in five different activities namely Swimming, Singing, Drawing, Dancing and Handicraft in the school during the session 2020-21. A total number of 3000 students including 1750 girls have been enrolled in various activities in the school. Based on the data in the table, answer the given questions.

**Activity-wise Enrollment of Students**

| **Activity** | **Percentage (%) of students enrolled** (Out of 3000) | **Percentage (%) of Girls enrolled** (Out of 1750) |
|---|---|---|
| Swimming | 16% | 14% |
| Singing | 21% | 28% |
| Drawing | 14% | 16% |
| Dancing | 24% | 20% |
| Handicraft | 25% | 22% |

**1** What is the ratio of the number of girls enrolled in Swimming to the number of boys enrolled in Swimming?

(A) 59 : 49 (B) 23 : 29

(C) 33 : 43 (D) 49 : 47

***Ans. (D)*** The number of girls enrolled in Swimming

$$= 1750 \times \frac{14}{100}$$

$$= 245$$

The number of boys enrolled in Swimming

$$= 3000 \times \frac{16}{100} - 245$$

$$= 480 - 245 = 235$$

$$\therefore \text{ Required ratio} = \frac{245}{235} = 49 : 47.$$

**2** What is the approximate percentage (%) of boys in the school?

(A) 42% (B) 28%

(C) 34% (D) 50%

***Ans. (A)*** Required ratio $= \frac{1250}{3000} \times 100$

$$= 41.66 \approx 42\%$$

**3** The number of girls enrolled in Dancing forms what per cent (%) of the total number of students in the school? (Round-off to two digit)?

(A) 9.32% (B) 10.67%
(C) 11.67% (D) 14.67%

***Ans. (C)*** The number of girls enrolled in Dancing.

$$= 1750 \times \frac{20}{100} = 350$$

$$\therefore \text{ Required per cent} = \frac{350}{3000} \times 100$$

$$= 11.666 = 11.67\%$$

**4** What is the total number of girls enrolled in Swimming and Drawing taken together?

(A) 505 (B) 515 (C) 525 (D) 535

***Ans. (C)*** Total number of girls enrolled in Swimming and Drawing together

$$= 1750 \times \frac{(14+16)}{100} = 1750 \times \frac{30}{100} = 525$$

**5** How many boys are enrolled in Singing and Handicraft taken together?

(A) 485 (B) 505
(C) 420 (D) 585

***Ans. (B)*** The number of boys enrolled in Singing

$$= 3000 \times \frac{21}{100} - 1750 \times \frac{28}{100}$$

$$= 630 - 490 = 140$$

The number of boys enrolled in Handicraft

$$= 3000 \times \frac{25}{100} - 1750 \times \frac{22}{100}$$

$$= 750 - 385 = 365$$

$\therefore$ The number of boys enrolled in Singing and Handicraft together

$$= 140 + 365 = 505$$

**6** Given below are two statements:

**Statement I** According to Nyaya philosophy an argument proceeds only on those issues that are completely unknown.

**Statement II** According to Nyaya philosophy an argument does not proceed on those issues that are well established.

In the light of the above statements. Choose the most appropriate answer from the options given below.

(A) Both Statement I and Statement II are correct
(B) Both Statement I and Statement II are incorrect
(C) Statement I is correct but Statement II is incorrect
(D) Statement I is incorrect but Statement II is correct

***Ans. (D)*** Nyaya is one of the six orthodox system of Indian philosophy. According to Nyaya philosophy, an argument does not proceed on those issues that are well established. An argument proceed only on known issue.

The major contribution of the Nyaya system is its working out in profound detail the means of knowledge known as inference. The Nyaya system is a philosophy of logic. It is also a system of epistemology. Nyaya is thus concerned with the means of right knowledge.

Thus, statement I is incorrect but statement II is correct.

Hence, option (D) is the correct answer.

**7** Match List I with List II:

| List I (Modalities of Teaching) | List II (Implementation) |
|---|---|
| A. Instruction | 1. One way Imposition of ideas from the teacher to the students |
| B. Training | 2. Associative presentation of ideas from teacher to students |
| C. Conditioning | 3. Disciplined drill conducted by teacher |
| D. Indoctrination | 4. Active Interchange of Ideas between teacher and students |

Choose the correct answer from the options given below:

| | A | B | C | D | | A | B | C | D |
|---|---|---|---|---|---|---|---|---|---|
| (A) | 2 | 1 | 4 | 3 | (B) | 1 | 2 | 3 | 4 |
| (C) | 4 | 3 | 2 | 1 | (D) | 3 | 4 | 1 | 2 |

***Ans. (C)*** The correct match of given lists are as follows

**Instruction** is the direction or order which is done between teachers and students. It is associated with the term 'curriculum' and generally refers to the teaching methods and learning activities that a teacher uses to deliver the curriculum in the classroom.

**Training** is a disciplined drill conducted by teacher. Teacher training refers to the policies, procedures, and provision designed to equip teachers with the knowledge, attitudes, behaviours, and skills they require to perform their tasks effectively in the classroom, school, and wider community.

**Conditioning** is associative presentation of ideas from teacher to students. Associative learning is a style of learning when two unrelated elements (objects, sights, sound, idea etc) become connected in our brain through process known as conditioning.

**Indoctrination** means causing someone to accept a set of beliefs uncritically through repeated instruction. Thus, it is a one way imposition of ideas from the teacher to the students.

**8** Identify the features of empirico-inductive paradigm of research

1. Research is concerned with the process rather than simply with outcomes or products
2. Based on logical positivist philosophy which assumes a single objective reality
3. Researchers are concerned with what are called 'participant perspectives'
4. Attempts to establish universal context free generalizations.

Choose the most appropriate answer from the options given below:

(A) 1 and 2 (B) 2 and 4 (C) 2 and 3 (D) 1 and 3

***Ans. (D)*** Among the given statements, 1 and 3 are correct. In an empirico-inductive paradigm, researcher collects empirical data (empirico) from specific cases to generalise (inductive) it's research finding. Research is concerned with the process rather than simply with outcomes or products and researchers are concerned with what are called participant perspective.

Empirical research makes use of quantitative and qualitative data gathering methods which may include surveys, experiments and methods of observation. This helps the researcher to gather empirical data, that is, data backed by evidence. It is not based on generalization.

**9** NEP-2020 proposes to establish which of the following new bodies?

I. SSSA  II. PARAKH
III. IITI  IV. NITI
V. NT

Choose the correct answer from the options given below:

(A) I, III, IV (B) I, II, III
(C) II, III, V (D) II, III, IV

***Ans. (C)*** NEP 2020 propose to establish PARAKH, IITI and NTA as new bodies. NEP 2020 (New Education Policy 2020) is an inclusive framework focusing on the elementary level of education to higher education in the country.

A new National Assessment Centre, PARAKH (Performance Assessment, Review, and Analysis of Knowledge for Holistic Development), will be set up as a standard-setting body for all recognized school boards under NEP 2020.

To ensure the preservation, growth, and vibrancy of all Indian languages, NEP recommends setting an Indian Institute of Translation and Interpretation (IITI), National Institute (or Institutes) for Pali, Persian and Prakrit, strengthening of Sanskrit and all language departments in HEIs, and use mother tongue/local language as a medium of instruction in more HEI (Higher Education Institution) programmes.

NEP 2020 proposed NTA (National Testing Agency) as the central exam conducting body for all the Higher Educational Institutes (HEIs).

**10** Given below are two statements :

**Statement I** Computer based testing promotes objectivity in assessment processes.

**Statement II** Choice-based credit system in Indian Higher Education is a new entry.

In the light of the above statements, choose the most appropriate answer from the options given below:

(A) Both Statement I and Statement Il are correct
(B) Both Statement I and Statement II are incorrect
(C) Statement I is correct but Statement II is incorrect
(D) Statement I is incorrect but Statement II is correct

***Ans. (A)*** Computer Based Test (CBT) simply refers to tests and assessments conducted through the use of the organised systems on computers. Computer based testing has many advantages, ranging from more efficient test creation, to faster test delivery and higher student engagement. It promotes objectivity in assessment processes. It is a new system of testing which is used extensively in Higher education.

Choice Based Credit System (CBCS) a new entry, is an initiative launched by UGC in 2016. CBCS is an educational model that offers students to opt for courses and subjects of their choice-core, elective courses, open or global electives and skill-based courses.
Hence, both statements I and II are correct.

**11** **With reference to Nyaya Philosophy, which of the following statements is true?**

(A) The linga or the middle term is not the Karana or operative cause of inference.
(B) The middle term may be a thing of the present but not of the past or the future.
(C) The middle term can function in an inference when past or future.
(D) The middle term can lead to the conclusion apart from the knowledge of vyapti or the universal relation between it and the major term.

***Ans.*** ***(A)*** With reference to Nyaya Philosophy, statement (A) is true.

Nyaya Philosophy states that nothing is acceptable unless it is in accordance with reason and experience. Nyaya is considered as a technique of logical thinking. In nyaya logic the term vyapti is a universal proposition or invariable relation between the middle term (linga/hetu) and the major term (sadya). According to the category of relation propositions are divided into categorical and the conditional.

**12** **Which of the following is an apex advisory and non statutory body?**

(A) NITI Aayog (B) NCTE
(C) AICTE (D) MCI

***Ans.*** ***(A)*** NITI Aayog is an apex advisory and non-statutory body.

In 2014, Prime Minister of India announced Planning Commission's abolition and created NITI Aayog through an executive resolution. NITI Aayog is neither a constitutional body nor a statutory body. A non-statutory body usually gets the power from an Executive order. For eg, NITI Aayog, National Development Council (NDC) etc.

The NITI Aayog serves as the apex public policy think tank of the Government of India, and the nodal agency tasked with catalysing economic development and fostering cooperative federalism through the involvement of State Governments of India in the economic policy-making process using a bottom-up approach.

**13** **Smita rode her scooty Northwards, then turned left and then again rode to her left 4 km. She found herself exactly 2 km West of her starting point. How far did she ride Northward initially?**

(A) 2 km (B) 5 km (C) 4 km (D) 6 km

***Ans.*** ***(B)*** According to the question,

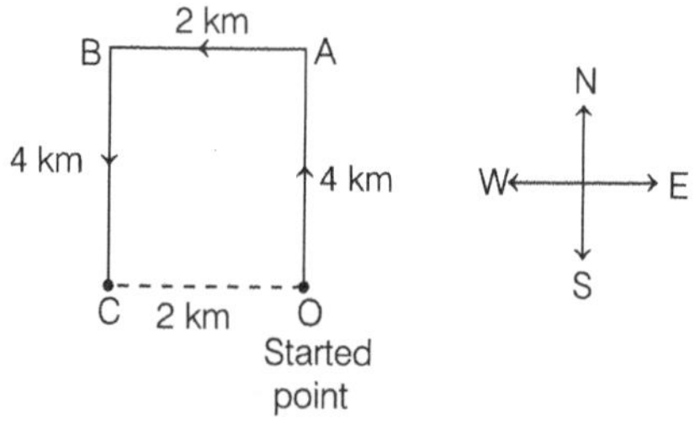


Hence, she ride Northward initially = 4 km.

**14** **The profit earned by selling a chair for ₹ 752 is 1.2 times the loss incurred when the same chair was sold for ₹ 400. What is the cost price of the chair?**

(A) ₹ 540 (B) ₹ 592
(C) ₹ 560 (D) ₹ 640

***Ans.*** ***(C)*** Let cost price of the chair be ₹ $x$.

According to the question,

$$752 - x = 1.2(x - 400)$$
$$\Rightarrow \quad 752 - x = 1.2x - 480$$
$$\Rightarrow \quad 1.2x + x = 752 + 480$$
$$\Rightarrow \quad 2.2x = 1232$$
$$\Rightarrow \quad x = \frac{1232}{2.2} = ₹\ 560$$

**15** **The global environmental issue of Ozone depletion is due to emission of**

I. Sulphur dioxide
II. Chlorinated hydrocarbons
III. Methane
IV. Carbone dioxide

**Choose the most appropriate answer from the options given below:**

(A) I and II (B) Only II
(C) III and IV (D) I, II and III

***Ans.*** ***(B)*** Among the given, option (B) is correct. The global environmental issue of Ozone depletion is due to emission of chlorinated hydrocarbons and carbon dioxide. Ozone layer depletion is the gradual thinning of the earth's ozone layer present in the upper atmosphere. It is caused by the release of chemical compounds containing gaseous chlorine or bromine from industry and other human activities. The thinning is most pronounced in the Polar regions, especially over Antarctica.

The main cause of ozone depletion and the ozone hole is manufactured chemicals, especially manufactured halocarbon refrigerants, solvents, propellants and foam-blowing agents CFCs, HCFCs, halons). Scientists noted that chlorine could destroy extensive amounts of ozone after it was liberated from CFCs by UV radiation.

**16** Given below are two statements: One is labelled as Assertion A and the other is labelled as Reason R.

**Assertion** (A) : A man pulls a loaded truck by his hair which becomes news.

**Reason** (R) : Unusual things make news called oddity and generate public interest.

In the light of the above statements, Choose the most appropriate answer from the options given below

(A) Both (A) and (R) are correct and (R) is the correct explanation of (A)
(B) Both (A) and (R) are correct but (R) is not the correct explanation of (A)
(C) (A) is correct but (R) is not correct
(D) (A) is not correct but (R) is correct

***Ans. (A)*** One man pulls a loaded truck by his hair which becomes news. As unusual things make news, called oddity and generate public interest. Oddity or queerness always helps to make facts interesting. The greater the degree of oddity in a story, the greater is its value as news.

Thus, both A and R are correct and R is correct explanation of A. Hence, oiption (A) is correct.

**17** Which of the following is designated as key behaviour of effectiveness of teaching as evident from researches?

(A) Using student ideas and contribution
(B) Structuring
(C) Teacher task-orientation
(D) Teacher affect

***Ans. (C)*** Teacher task – orientation is a key behaviour of effectiveness of teaching as evident from researchers. Task orientation is an important aspect of Effective Teaching because it relates to how much time the teacher actually spends on a designated instructional task. A task is a lesson that involves goals and activities that are designed to enhance student comprehension of identified concepts, skills or values.

Effective teaching and learning process depends on the attitude and behaviour of the teacher. Effective teacher behaviour is essential to bring out desirable student performance. Effective teacher spend more time in teaching academic subject rather than routing matters such as distributing handouts or taking attendance.

**18** Identify the correct order of following computer memory types ranked from slowest to fastest in terms of access time.

I. Cache II. CDROM
III. Hard Disk IV. RAM
V. Register

Choose the correct answer from the options given below:

(A) III, II, I, IV, V (B) V, I, IV, III, II
(C) II, III, IV, I, V (D) IV, I, V, II, III

***Ans. (C)*** Memory in a computer is required for storage and retrieval of the instructions and data. A system uses a variety of devices for storing these instructions and data that are required for its operation. The computer memory types ranked from slowest to fastest in terms of access time are CDROM, Hard Disc, RAM, Cache and Register.

Hence, option (C) is correct.

**19** Match List I and List II

| List I (Sampling Methods) | List II (Procedure involved) |
|---|---|
| A. Simple Random Sampling | 1. The first member is used as an informant to identify other. The process goes on like this |
| B. Stratified Random Sampling | 2. The units are chosen intact on the basis of their settings |
| C. Cluster Sampling | 3. The units are chosen from defined groups/ levels randomly |
| D. Snowball sampling | 4. The units are chosen by giving equal and independent chance to each mem |

Choose the correct answer from the options given below

| | A | B | C | D | | A | B | C | D |
|---|---|---|---|---|---|---|---|---|---|
| (A) | 1 | 2 | 3 | 4 | (B) | 4 | 3 | 2 | 1 |
| (C) | 3 | 4 | 1 | 2 | (D) | 2 | 1 | 4 | 3 |

***Ans. (B)*** The correct match of given lists is as follows

**Simple random sampling** In Simple Random the units are chosen by giving equal and independent chance to each member. It is a type of probability sampling in which the researcher randomly selects a subset of participants from a population.

**Stratified random sampling** In stratified random sampling the units are chosen from defined groups/levels randomly. It is a method of sampling that involves dividing a population into smaller groups called strata. The groups or strata are organized based on the shared characteristics or attributes of the members in the group.

**Cluster sampling** In cluster sampling, the units are chosen intact on the basis of their settings. It is a probability sampling technique where researchers divide the population into multiple groups (clusters) for research.

**Snowball sampling** In snowball sampling, the first member is used as an informant to identify other. The process goes on like this. It is where research participants recruit other participants for a test or study.

Hence, option (B) is correct.

**20** **Three men, four women and six children can complete a work in seven days. A woman does double the work a man does and a child does half the work a man does. How many women alone can complete this work in 7 days?**

(A) 7 (B) 8
(C) 9 (D) 12

***Ans. (A)*** Let 1 day's work of a man be $x$ units.

$\therefore$ 1 day's work of a woman = $2x$ units.

and 1 day's work of a child = $\frac{x}{2}$ units.

$$\therefore \text{Total work} = \left(3\times x + 4 + 2x + 6\times\frac{x}{2}\right)\times 7 \text{ units}$$
$$= (3x + 8x + 3x)\times 7 \text{ units}$$
$$= 14x\times 7 \text{ units}$$
$$= 98 \text{ units.}$$

$$\therefore \text{Required number of women} = \frac{98x}{7\times 2x} = 7$$

**21** **The next number P in the sequence of binary numbers 0, 10, 100, 110, P, ........, is**

(A) 111 (B) 1000 (C) 1010 (D) 1001

***Ans. (B)***

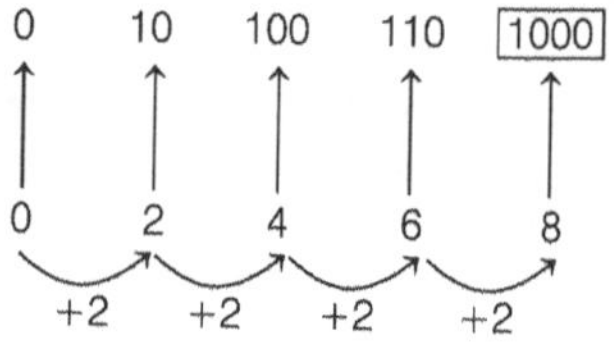


**22** **Why do we communicate?**

I. For social Interaction.
II. For happiness sake.
III. For messages to be understood.
IV. For sharing of experience.
V. For protection of traditions.

Choose the correct answer from the options given below:

(A) I, III, V (B) II, III, IV
(C) I, III, IV (D) I, II, V

***Ans. (C)*** We communicate for social interaction, for message to be understood and for our happiness sake. Communication is simply the act of transferring information from one place, person or group to another. It involves a sender, a message and a recipient.

**23** **'Whoever thrusts a knife into another person should be arrested. Surgeons thrust a knife into another person when operating. Therefore surgeons should be arrested'.**

**Which fallacy is committed in the following argument?**

(A) Hasty generalization
(B) Fallacy of accident
(C) Red Herring
(D) Appeal to unqualified authority

***Ans. (B)*** In the given argument Fallacy of accident has been committed. The fallacy of accident (also called destroying the exception or a dicto simpliciter ad dictum secundum quid) is an informal fallacy and deductively valid but unsound argument occurring in a statistical syllogism (an argument based on a generalization) when an exception to a rule of thumb is ignored. The fallacy of accident is committed by an argument that applies a general rule to a particular case in which some special circumstance ("accident") makes the rule inapplicable.

**24** Which of the following natural disasters are classified as topographies?

(A) Irritation (B) Avalanche
(C) Storm (D) Flood

***Ans.*** ***(B)*** Avalanche are classified as topographies. This disaster comes especially in the mountainous areas, in which the flow of snow occurs on the ground with the help of a gradient.

**25** Under Sustainable Development Goal 12-Sustainable Consumption and Production, one of the targets is to reduce per capita food waste at the retail and consumer levels by :

(A) $\frac{3}{4}$ (B) $\frac{1}{2}$
(C) $\frac{1}{3}$ (D) $\frac{1}{4}$

***Ans.*** ***(B)*** Sustainable Development Goal 12 ensures sustainable consumption and production patterns. It contains a wide range of targets, one of which is closely related to Think, Eat, Save. SDG Target 12.3 seeks to halve (1/2) per capita global food waste at retail and consumer levels, as well as to reduce food loss during production and supply. In order to measure food waste and losses, two indices have been proposed- a Food Waste Index (FWI) and a Food Loss Index (FLI).

**26** Which of the following values is related to self-transcendance?

(A) Security Value
(B) Value of Universalism
(C) Value of Freedom
(D) Value of Conformity

***Ans.*** ***(B)*** Value of Universalism is related to self-transcendence. Self-transcendence is a personality trait that involves the expansion of personal boundaries, including, potentially, experiencing spiritual ideas such as considering oneself an integral part of the universe. Benevolence and universalism fall under the motivational self- transcendence values.

**27** Given below are two statements

**Statement I** CPU executes software directly from secondary memory.

**Statement II** A software is termed as Open Source Software if it can be downloaded from the Internet.

In the light of the above statements, Choose the correct answer from the options given below :

(A) Both Statement I and Statement II are true
(B) Both Statement I and Statement II are false
(C) Statement I is true but Statement II is false
(D) Statement I is false but Statement II is true

***Ans.*** ***(B)*** CPU executes software directly from secondary memory. This statement is false. It is because secondary memory is not accessed directly by the Central Processing Unit (CPU). Instead, data accessed from a secondary memory is first loaded into Random Access Memory (RAM) and is then sent to the Processing Unit.

A Software is termed as Open Source Software if it can be downloaded from the internet. This statement is also false. Open-Source Software (OSS) is computer software that is released under a license in which the copyright holder grants users the rights to use, study, change, and distribute the software and its source code to anyone and for any purpose.
Thus, both statements I and II are false.

Hence, option (B) is the correct answer.

**28** If a 30 m ladder is placed against a 15 m wall such that it just reaches the top of the wall, the angle of elevation of the wall is

(A) 45° (B) 30° (C) 60° (D) 50°

***Ans.*** ***(B)*** Let $AB$ is a wall and $CA$ is a ladder.

Angle of elevation be $\theta$.

$\therefore \quad AB = 15\text{ m and } AC = 30\text{ m}$

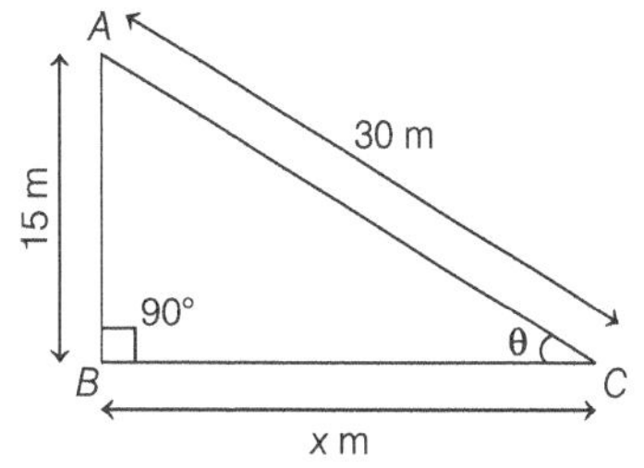


In $\Delta ABC$, $\sin\theta = \frac{AB}{AC}$ $\left(\because \sin\theta = \frac{P}{H}\right)$

$\Rightarrow \quad \sin\theta = \frac{15}{30}$

$\Rightarrow \quad \sin\theta = \frac{1}{2}$

$\theta = 30°$

**29** Given below are two statements

**Statement I** Action Research is used primarily to improve a given situation by a practitioner.

**Statement II** Applied research is directed at exploring applicability of principles already established.

In the light of the above statements, Choose the most appropriate answer from the options given below :

(A) Both Statement I and Statement II are correct

(B) Both Statement I and Statement II are incorrect

(C) Statement I is correct but Statement II is incorrect

(D) Statement I is incorrect but Statement II is correct

***Ans.*** ***(A)*** Action research is used primarily to improve a given situation by a practitioner. This statement is true. Action research is a form of investigation designed for use by teachers to attempt to solve problems and improve professional practices in their own classrooms. It involves systematic observations and data collection which can be then used by the practitioner-researcher in reflection, decision-making and the development of more effective classroom strategies.

Applied research is directed at exploring applicability of principles already established. This statement is true. Applied research refers to scientific study and research that seeks to solve practical problems. It is directed at exploring applicability of principles already established. This type of research can be used in a variety of ways. For e.g. it is used to find solutions to everyday problems, cure illness, and develop innovative technologies.
Thus, both statements I and II are correct. Hence, option (A) is the correct answer.

**30** When in a classroom communication, a teacher shows ability of creativity, correlation and analysis, it belongs to which category of skills?

(A) Thinking skills

(B) Expression skills

(C) Media utilization

(D) Human skills

***Ans.*** ***(A)*** When in a classroom communication, a teacher shows ability of creativity, creation and analysis, it belongs to thinking skills. Thinking skills enable us to process information, recall facts and apply knowledge to various situations. At a higher level, this can involve problem-solving and analysis, which are both useful in education.

**31** Who among the following was the first Chairman of UGC?

(A) Sh Humayun Kabir

(B) Sh C.D. Deshmukh

(C) Sh M. Moolgaokar

(D) Moolchand Sharma

***Ans.*** ***(B)*** Shri C.D. Deshmukh, CIE, ICS (14 January 1896 – 2 October 1982) was an Indian civil servant and the first Indian to be appointed as the Governor of the Reserve Bank of India in 1943 by the British Raj authorities. He worked as Chairman of UGC (1956–1961). He served as Vice-Chancellor of University of Delhi (1962–67). He was also the President of Indian Statistical Institute from 1945 to 1964. But the first Chairman of UGC was Dr. Shanti Swarup Bhatnagar (1953-1955). Presently (2022) K. Sanjay Murthy is the Chairman of UGC.

**32** Given below are two statements

**Statement I** A formal fallacy is one that may be identified through mere inspection of the form or structure of an argument.

**Statement II** Formal fallacies are found only in deductive arguments that have identifiable forms.

In the light of the above statements, Choose the correct answer from the options given below:

(A) Both Statement I and Statement II are true

(B) Both Statement I and Statement II are false

(C) Statement I is true but Statement II is false

(D) Statement I is false but Statement II is true

***Ans.*** ***(A)*** A formal fallacy is one that may be identified through mere inspection of the form or structure of an argument. Formal fallacies are deductively invalid arguments that typically commit an easily recognisable logical error.

A formal fallacy is a flaw in the structure of a deductive argument which renders the argument invalid, while an informal fallacy originates in an error in reasoning other than an improper logical form. Arguments containing informal fallacies may be formally valid, but still fallacious. Formal fallacies are found only in deductive arguments that have identifiable forms.
Thus, both Statements I and II are true. Hence, option (A) is the correct answer.

**33** Small hydro power potential in India is estimated approximately as

(A) ~ 60 MW (B) ~ 100 MW
(C) ~ 10 MW (D) ~ 20 MW

***Ans. (D)*** As per Ministry of New and Renewable Energy (MNRE), the estimated potential of small hydro power plant is 20 GW across the country. In India, hydro power plants of 25 MW or below capacity are classified as small hydro power plant.

India has large renewable energy potential from sources such as wind, solar, biomass, small hydro among others. As per estimates, India has a wind potential of more than 300 GW at a hub height of 100 metre, solar potential of 750 GW, assuming 3 per cent wasteland is made available, small hydro potential of 20 GW, and bio-energy potential of 25 GW.

**34** Match List I with List II

| List I (Digital Initiatives in Higher Education) | List II (Purpose) |
|---|---|
| A. SWAYAM | 1. Online store and access of academic awards namely degrees, mark-sheets etc. |
| B. SWAYAM PRABHA | 2. Store and access personal e-documents irrespective of physical location. |
| C. Digilocker | 3. MOOCs for high-quality education anywhere and anytime. |
| D. NAD | 4. Free DTH channel for high-quality education. |

**Codes**

| | A | B | C | D |
|---|---|---|---|---|
| (A) | 3 | 4 | 2 | 1 |
| (B) | 4 | 3 | 1 | 2 |
| (C) | 4 | 3 | 2 | 1 |
| (D) | 2 | 1 | 3 | 4 |

***Ans. (A)*** The correct match of given lists is as follows

**SWAYAM** stands for 'Study Webs of Active-Learning for Young Aspiring Minds'. It is an Indian Massive open online course (MOOC) platform for high –quality education anywhere and anytime. The SWAYAM initiative was launched by the then Ministry of Human Resource Development (M.H.R.D.), Government of India under Digital India to give a coordinated stage and free entry to web courses, covering all advanced education, High School and skill sector courses.

**SWAYAM Prabha** is an initiative of the Ministry of Human Resources Development to provide 32 High Quality Educational Channels through DTH (Direct to Home) across the length and breadth of the country on 24× 7 basis.

**DigiLocker** is an Indian digitization online service provided by Ministry of Electronics and Information Technology (MEIT), Government of India under its Digital India initiative. It provides an account in cloud to every Aadhaar holder to access authentic documents/ certificates , degree , mark-sheets.

**National Academic Depository** (NAD) is a 24× 7 online store house and access personal e-documents irrespective of physical location. Hence, option (A) is the correct answer.

**35** Match List I with List II

| List I (Types of communication) | List II (Function served) |
|---|---|
| A. Mass communication | 1. Corridor discussion |
| B. Intrapersonal communication | 2. Classroom teaching |
| C. Group communication | 3. For communication with oneself |
| D. Interpersonal communication | 4. For mechanical message transmission |

Choose the correct answer from the options given below

| | A | B | C | D |
|---|---|---|---|---|
| (A) | 4 | 3 | 2 | 1 |
| (B) | 1 | 2 | 3 | 4 |
| (C) | 2 | 3 | 4 | 1 |
| (D) | 3 | 2 | 1 | 4 |

***Ans. (A)*** The correct match of given lists is as follows

**Mass communication** is the process of imparting and exchanging information through mass media to large segments of the population. It is used for mechanical message transmission through multiple mediums, such as radio, television, social networking, billboards, newspapers, magazines, books, film, and the Internet.

**Intra-personal communication** is the process by which an individual communicates within themselves, acting as both sender and receiver of messages, and encompasses the use of unspoken words to consciously engage in self-talk and inner speech.

**Group communication** is used in classroom teaching-learning process. Group communication is the act of sending and receiving messages to multiple members of a group.

**Interpersonal communication** is an exchange of information between two or more people. It is used for corridor discussion. It is also an area of research that seeks to understand how humans use verbal and non-verbal cues to accomplish a number of personal and relational goals.
Hence, option (A) is the correct answer.

**36** Which of the following is an example of physical barrier to communication?

(A) Cultural disparity (B) Inattention
(C) Verbalism (D) Ill health

***Ans. (D)*** Ill health is an example of physical barrier to communication.

A physical barrier to communication can be defined as a physical factor that acts as a distraction to hinder the flow of communication. A physical barrier can be natural or human-made and is easy to spot. Noise, bad architecture, closed doors, ill health etc are all physical barriers to listening.

**37** The waste component of waste categorized as 'Trash' consists of

I. Paper, Cardboard cartons
II. Animal wastes
III. Industrial process wastes
IV. Vegetable wastes
V. Wood

Choose the correct answer from the options given below:

(A) I and V (B) I, III and V
(C) I, III, IV and V (D) I and V

***Ans. (A)*** Among the given, statements I and V are correct. The waste component of waste categorised as trash consists of paper, cardboard, cartons and wood, household wastes, electrical wastes and so on. Trash, garbage or rubbish is waste material that is discarded by humans, usually due to a perceived lack of utility.

**38** The NEP-2020 proposes to prepare which of the curriculum frameworks?

I. National Curriculum Framework for School Education
II. National Curriculum Framework for Adult Education
III. National Curriculum Framework for Teacher Education
IV. National Curriculum Framework for Technical Education
V. National Curriculum Framework for Vocational Education

Choose the correct answer from the options given below:

(A) I, III, V (B) I, II, III
(C) II, III, IV (D) III, IV, V

***Ans. (B)*** Among the given, statements I, II and III are correct .

National Education Policy- 2020 seeks to address the challenges including access, equity, quality, affordability and accountability faced by the current education system. It proposes to develop curriculum frameworks for School Education, Adult Education and Teacher Education.

NEP 2020 provides for reforms at all levels of education from school to higher education. It seeks to increase the focus on early childhood care, reform the current exam system, strengthen teacher training, and restructure the education regulatory framework. It also seeks to set up a National Education Commission, increase public investment in education, strengthen the use of technology and increase focus on adult education.

**39** Identify the indirect teaching strategies from the following list :

I. Gaining attention, informing the learner of the objective and presenting the stimulus material
II. Concept building through examples and non-examples
III. Explaining, exemplification and practice
IV. Problem based presentation with pair-share technique
V. Encouraging students to use references from their own experiences

Choose the correct answer from the options given below :

(A) II, IV and V (B) I, II and III
(C) II, III and IV (D) III, IV and V

***Ans.*** ***(A)*** Indirect teaching strategy is an approach to teaching and learning in which concepts, patterns and abstractions are taught in the context of strategies that emphasize concept learning, inquiry learning and problem-centered learning.

There are various ways to use indirect strategies: some have a higher degree of teacher-directed activities and others have students more actively involved in planning and designing instructional activities. For e.g. Concept attainment strategies, enquiry lessons, projects, reports, problems, discussion with students and their experiences, students self-evaluation, cooperative learning strategy and simulations.

Hence, option (A) is the correct answer.

**40** Given below are two statements

**Statement I** Mimamsakas and Vedantins agree with the Naiyayikas that the syllogism consists of five members or propositions.

**Statement II** Mimamsakas and Vedantins agree with the Naiyayikas that the syllogism is necessary only for pararthanumana or demonstrate inference not for svarthänumana or inference for oneself.

In the light of the above statements. Choose the most appropriate answer given below

(A) Both Statement I and Statement II are correct
(B) Both Statement I and Statement II are incorrect
(C) Statement I is correct but Statement II is incorrect
(D) Statement I is incorrect but Statement II is correct

***Ans.*** ***(D)*** Mimamsakas and Vedantins agree with Naiyayikas that the syllogism is necessary only for parathanuman or demonstrate inference and not for svarthanumana or inference for oneself. The Naiyayika maintains two modes or stages in perception. The first is called nirvikalpa (indeterminate), when one just perceives an object without being able to know its features and the second savikalpa (determinate), when one is able to clearly know an object.

The Naiyayikas believe that the bondage of the world is due to false knowledge, which can be removed by constantly thinking of its opposite (pratipakshabhavana), namely, the true knowledge.

Thus, statement I is incorrect but statement II is correct.

Hence, option (D) is the correct answer.

**41** Given below are two statements: One is labelled as Assertion A and the other is labelled as Reason R.

**Assertion** (A) Teaching support system whether traditional or modern is purportedly put in place for effecting economy and ensuring quality in teaching-learning transactions.

**Reason** (R) Learning outcomes in order to be congruent with stipulated instructional goals need scaffolds to begin with.

In the light of the above statements, Choose the most appropriate answer from the options given below :

(A) Both (A) and (R) are correct and (R) is the correct explanation of (A)
(B) Both (A) and (R) are correct but (R) is not the correct explanation of (A)
(C) (A) is correct but (R) is not correct
(D) (A) is not correct but (R) is correct

***Ans.*** ***(A)*** Teaching support system whether traditional or modern is purportedly put in place for effecting economy and ensuring quality in teaching-learning transactions. The given statement is true. The teaching support systems are used especially to make the teaching- learning effective and achieve the desired goals set by a teacher.

Learning outcomes in order to be congruent with stipulated instructional goals need scaffolds to begin with. This statement is true. According to the principle of congruence in instructional design (by Bloom's Taxonomy), in any situation learning goals, anticipated outcomes, instructional strategies, and assessment methods should be carefully matched when designing a learning strategy.

Thus, both A and R are correct and R is the correct explanation of A.

Hence, option (A) is the correct answer.

**42** Which of the following statements about wikis are True?

I. Wiki pages can be locked by moderators to prevent vandalism.

II. Every change that is made to a wiki page is logged and can be viewed in a history list.

III. A wiki is designed to allow people to collaborate easily.

Choose the correct answer from the options given below:

(A) I and II (B) II and III
(C) I and III (D) I, II and III

***Ans. (D)*** A protected page of wiki is a page where normal users are prevented from editing and/or moving at all. A user with moderator permission can edit or move a protected page.

Every change that is made to a wiki page is logged. A page history shows the order in which edits were made to any editable Wikipedia page, the difference between any two revisions, and a menu of special external tools. A page history is sometimes called revision history or edit history. A wiki is a collaborative tool that allows students to contribute and modify one or more pages of course related materials.

Hence, all statements are true.

**43** Given below are two statements: One is labelled as Assertion A and the other is labelled as Reason R.

**Assertion (A)** A research thesis has to follow a prescribed format and style of referencing.

**Reason (R)** This ensures the observance of research ethics.

In the light of the above statements, Choose the most appropriate answer from the options given below:

(A) Both (A) and (R) are correct and (R) is the correct explanation of (A)
(B) Both (A) and (R) are correct but (R) is NOT the correct explanation of (A)
(C) (A) is correct but (R) is not correct
(D) (A) is not correct but (R) is correct

***Ans. (C)*** A research thesis has to follow a prescribed format and style of referencing.

A good thesis should be clear and unambiguous and have a logical structure that should assist the reader's understanding the argument being presented and not obscure it.

A prescribed format and style of referencing does not ensure the observance of research ethics. Honesty, objective, carefulness , openness , transparency , accountability etc is the major point of research ethics.

Thus, statement A is correct but R is not correct. Hence, option (C) is the correct answer.

**44** In which method of research an independent variable is manipulated with an intent to observe concomitant changes in dependent variable?

(A) ExPost Facto method
(B) Case Study method
(C) Descriptive survey method
(D) Experimental method

***Ans. (D)*** The experimental method involves the manipulation of variables to establish cause and effect relationships. The key features are controlled methods and the random allocation of participants into controlled and experimental groups. In this method of research an independent variable is manipulated with an intent to observe concomitant changes in dependent variable.

The experimental method involves manipulating one variable to determine if changes in one variable cause changes in another variable. This method relies on controlled methods, random assignment and the manipulation of variables to test a hypothesis.

**45** A 108 m long train moving at a speed of 50 km/hr crosses a 112 m long train coming from the opposite direction in 6 sec. The speed of the second train is

(A) 48 km/h (B) 54 km/h
(C) 66 km/h (D) 82 km/h

***Ans. (D)*** Speed of first train = 50 km/h.

Let the speed of second train be $x$ km/h.

$\therefore$ Relative speed $= (50+x)$ km/h

$$= (50+x)\times\frac{5}{18} \text{ m/sec.}$$

According to the question,

$$6 = \frac{108+112}{(50+x)\times\frac{5}{18}} \quad \left[\because \text{Time} = \frac{\text{Distance}}{\text{Speed}}\right]$$

$$\Rightarrow \quad (50+x)\times\frac{5}{18}\times 6 = 220$$

$$\Rightarrow \quad 50 + x = \frac{220 \times 10}{5 \times 6}$$

$$\Rightarrow \quad 50 + x = 132$$

$$\Rightarrow \quad x = 132 - 50$$

$$= 82 \text{ km/h}$$

**Directions** (Q. Nos. 46-50) *Read the passage carefully and answer the question that follow*

As the world is becoming increasingly Interconnected, Global Citizenship Education (GCED), a response to contemporary global challenges, will be provided to empower learners to become aware of and understand global issues and to become active promoters of more peaceful, tolerant, inclusive, secure and sustainable societies.

As a part of holistic education, students at all HEIs will be provided with opportunities for internships with local industry, businesses, artists, crafts person etc. as well as research internship with faculty and researchers at their own or other HEIs/research institutions, so that students may actively engage with the practical side of their learning and, as a by-product, further improve their employability. India will be promoted as a global study destination providing premium education at affordable costs thereby helping to restore its role as a Vishwa Guru.

An international students office at each HEI hosting foreign students will be set up to coordinate all matters relating to welcoming and supporting students arriving from abroad. Research training collaboration and faculty/student exchanges with high quality foreign institution will be facilitated, and relevant mutually beneficial MOU with foreign countries will be signed. High Performing Indian Universities will be encouraged to set up campuses in other countries, and similarly, selected universities e.g. those from top 100 universities in the world will be facilitated and operate in India. A legislative framework facilitating such entry will be put in place and such universities will be given special dispensation regarding regulatory, governance and content norms on par with other autonomous institutions of India.

Furthermore, research collaboration and student exhanges between Indian institutions and global Institutions will be promoted through special efforts. Credits acquired in foreign universities will be permitted, where appropriate requirements of each HEI, to be counted for the award of a degree.

**46** Holistic education at HEIs is aimed at :

I. Research internship with researchers and faculty at different HEIs.

II. Recyling of traditional knowledge systems.

III. Providing opportunities for internships at local level.

IV. Keeping social sciences and natural sciences within distinct spheres of teaching and learning.

Choose the correct answer from the options given below :

(A) II and IV (B) I and III

(C) I and IV (D) III and IV

***Ans. (B)*** Among the given, statements I and III are correct. According to the passage , Holistic education at HEIs is aimed at research internship with research and faculty at different HEIs and providing opportunities for internships at local level.

As a part of holistic education , students at all HEIs will be provided with opportunity for internships with local industry , businesses , artists , craftsperson etc. as well as research internship with faculty and researchers at their own or other HEIs/research institution , so that student may actively engage with the practical side of their learning and as a by-product , further improve their employability.

**47** New National Education Policy is grounded in the assumptions that

I. There is increasing interconnectedness among nations at the global level.

II. Technical knowledge should replace traditional models of learning.

III. HEIs must focus on promotion of desirable ethical values.

IV. There is need for changes in legislative framework to facilitate free exchange of academic ideas and achievements.

Choose the correct answer from the options given below

(A) I, II and IV

(B) I and III

(C) I, III and IV

(D) III and IV

***Ans.* *(C)*** Among the given, statements I, III and IV are correct. According to given passage , New NEP is grounded in the assumption that there is increasing interconnectedness among nations at the global level and HEIs must focus on promotion of desirable ethical value . There is need for changes in legislative framework to facilitate free exchange of academic ideas and achievements. High performing Indian universities will be encouraged to set up campuses in other countries and similarly , selected universities ( Top 100) will be facilitated to operate in India.

**48** Which of the following statements most appropriately represent one of the chief concerns regarding higher education?

(A) It argues for only local production and of knowledge and its implementation.

(B) It emphasizes only upon implementation of foreign higher education models in India.

(C) It argues for mutual exchange of knowledge and learning among national and international institutions of higher education.

(D) It argues for practical learning alone for employability putting social issues aside.

***Ans.* *(C)*** According to the passage statement (C) is correct regarding higher education. It argues for mutual exchange of knowledge and learning among national and international institutions of higher education.

The modern higher education institution (HEI) is an organisation in transition.

The traditional roles of research and teaching are increasingly complemented by the ability to transfer knowledge and technology into other realms, where it will benefit industry, politics and wider society. Knowledge exchange (especially with the environment) is not an entirely new phenomenon and has always taken place at HEIs.

**49** Given below are two statements:

**Statement I** National Education Policy is framed with an objective of saving national HEIs from competition at the global level.

**Statement II** National Education Policy is framed with an objective of encouraging exchange of knowledge and expertise both at local and global level.

In the light of the above statements, Choose the most appropriate answer from the options given below:

(A) Both Statement I and Statement II are correct

(B) Both Statement I and Statement II are incorrect

(C) Statement I is correct but Statement II is incorrect

(D) Statement I is incorrect but Statement II is correct

***Ans.* *(D)*** According to passage, Statement I is incorrect but Statement II is correct. National Education Policy (NEP) is framed with an objective of encouraging exchange of knowledge and exchange both at local and global level. So, the statements regarding NEP of option (A) is false. NEP is not framed with an objective of saving national higher education institutions (HEIs) from competition at the global level.

**50** Given below are two statements

**Statement I** National Education Policy envisages learning as a process of inculcating values of tolerance, inclusion and sustainability.

**Statement II** National Education Policy lays stress on employability of learners in businesses and industries.

In the light of the above statements, Choose the most appropriate answer from the options given below :

(A) Both Statement I and Statement II are correct

(B) Both Statement I and Statement II are incorrect

(C) Statement I is correct but Statement II is incorrect

(D) Statement I is incorrect but Statement II is correct

***Ans.* *(A)*** According to the passage, NEP envisages learning as a process of inculcating values of tolerance, inclusion and suitability. NEP lays stress on employability of learners in business and industries. NEP will provide the much-needed tectonic shift in the pedagogical structure emphasising experiential and practical learning that will instill 21st-century skills in children.

Thus, both statements I and II are correct. Hence, option (A) is the correct answer.

# Solved Papers

## 2020 & 2019

# UGC
## NET/JRF/SET

# Solved Paper, 2020

(Exam Held on : 12 November, 2020)

## General Paper 1 (Teaching and Research Aptitude)

### *Instructions*

- This paper contains fifty Multiple Choice Questions, each question carries two marks.
- All questions are compulsory.
- Total time given for this paper is 1 hour.

**1** In the following statements, identify those which are related to characteristics and basic requirements of teaching at the understanding level.

1. Teaching stresses recitations of facts and information.
2. Teaching becomes an activity to promote seeing of relationship among facts and information.
3. The teacher expects that students will be able to translate and interpret the meanings in their own words.
4. The teacher insists on recall and recognition of facts presented.
5. The teacher gives a large number of examples to being home the main ideas.

Select the correct answer from the following options.

(A) 1, 2 and 3 only
(B) 3, 4 and 5 only
(C) 1, 4 and 5 only
(D) 2, 3 and 5 only

***Ans.*** *(D)* The teaching at the understanding level is of higher quality than the one at memory level. The characteristics and basic requirements of teaching related to the understanding level are :

- Teaching becomes an activity to promote seeing of relationships among facts and information.
- The teacher expects that students will be able to translate and interpret the meanings in their own words.
- The teacher gives a large number of examples to being home the main ideas.

Hence, option (D) is correct.

**2** There are two sets given below in which Set I offers types of learner's characteristics and Set II gives their description. Match the two sets :

| List-I (Learner's Characteristics) | List-II (Description) |
|---|---|
| A. Academic Characteristics | 1. Learner encodes and decodes relevant messages correctly. |
| B. Social Characteristics | 2. Learner selects different themes in his/her course when needed. |
| C. Emotional Characteristics | 3. Learner works as a team member of the peers. |
| D. Cognitive Characteristics | 4. Learner starts respecting the individual differences evident in likes and dislikes of members of his class. |

Choose the correct answer from the following options :

| | A | B | C | D | | A | B | C | D |
|---|---|---|---|---|---|---|---|---|---|
| (A) | 2 | 4 | 1 | 3 | (B) | 1 | 2 | 3 | 4 |
| (C) | 2 | 3 | 4 | 1 | (D) | 3 | 1 | 2 | 4 |

***Ans.*** *(C)* **Academic Characteristics** of learner include the education type, education level and knowledge. Learner selects different themes in his/her course when needed.

- **Social Characteristics** of learner often described as the process of establishing a sense of identity and establishing a role and purpose. Learner works as a team member of the peers.
- **Emotional Characteristics** Learner starts respecting the individual differences evident in likes and dislikes of members of his class.
- **Cognitive Characteristics** of learners can be described such as memory, mental pressure, solve problems, intellectual skills, remembers, organises and store information in the brain.

Learner encodes and decodes relevant messages correctly.

**3** Which of the following are the learner related factors in determining effectiveness of teaching?

1. Task relevant competencies of learner.
2. Content mastery of the teacher.
3. Choice of teaching methods.
4. Composition of the classroom.
5. Readiness level of student.

Choose the correct answer from the options given below.

(A) 2 and 3 only (B) 1 and 5 only
(C) 4 and 5 only (D) 2 and 5 only

***Ans.*** *(B)* The learner related factors in determining effectiveness of teaching are

- Task relevant competencies of learner.
- Readiness level of student.

Some other factors that determine good and effective teaching are

- An engaging personality.
- A passion for the subject matter.
- Demonstrated command of the subject matter.
- Willingness to acknowledge missteps.
- Being fair and transparent.

Hence, option (B) is correct.

**4** For organising effective teaching-learning systems in colleges, which of the following instructional strategies may be considered appropriate?

1. Replacing lecture work by computer-aided instruction.
2. Attuning teaching in terms of can do/will do analysis in respect of students' readiness levels.
3. Introduction of bio-metric based attendance in the class.
4. Diversifying teaching methods in terms of learners' needs.
5. Involving students, giving responsibility and recognising the accomplishments.

Choose the correct answer from the options given below.

(A) 2, 4 and 5 only (B) 1, 2 and 3 only
(C) 2, 3 and 4 only (D) 3, 4 and 5 only

***Ans.*** *(A)* For organising effective teaching-learning systems in colleges, there are some instructional strategies that may be considered appropriate :

- Attunning teaching in terms of can do/will do analysis in respect of students' readiness levels.
- Diversifying teaching methods in terms of learners' needs.
- Involving students, giving responsibility and recognising the accomplishments.

Hence, option (A) is correct.

**5** The research form which will be an appropriate fit for improving efficacy of formative assessment would be :

(A) Fundamental research
(B) Applied research
(C) Action research
(D) Ethnographic research

***Ans.*** *(C)* The research form that will be an appropriate fit for improving efficacy of formative assessment would be **'Action Research'**. It is a method of systematic enquiry that teachers undertake as researchers of their own practices.

- **Fundamental Research** is a type of scientific research with the aim of improving scientific theories for better understanding and prediction of natural or other phenomena.
- **Applied Research** is a methodology used to solve a specific, practical issue affecting an individual or a group.

- **Ethnographic Research** is a qualitative method where researchers observe and/or interact with a study's participants in their real life environment.

**6 In the two sets which follow, Set I gives certain terms used in research while Set II offers their description. Match the two sets.**

| List-I (Terms Used in Research) | List-II (Description) |
|---|---|
| A. A postulate | 1. It causes obtained results to vary in a particular direction. |
| B. A construct | 2. It is something which can change either quantitatively or qualitatively. |
| C. Variable | 3. It is the statement of the principle assumed, in the absence of direct evidence. |
| D. Systematic error | 4. Though not directly observable, is considered to exist. |

Select the correct answer from the following options :

| | A | B | C | D | | A | B | C | D |
|---|---|---|---|---|---|---|---|---|---|
| (A) | 1 | 2 | 3 | 4 | (B) | 3 | 4 | 2 | 1 |
| (C) | 2 | 1 | 3 | 4 | (D) | 4 | 3 | 1 | 2 |

*Ans.* *(B)* **A Postulate** It is the statement of the principle assumed, in the absence of direct evidence.

- **A Construct** Though not directly observable, is considered to exist.
- **Variable** It is something which can change either quantitatively or qualitatively.
- **Systematic Error** It causes obtained results to vary in a particular direction.

**7 A university teacher conducts research study where Lecture-cum Demonstration Method is used to assess the effect on students' level of participation in terms of the Socio-Economic Status (SES) of family and their habitat. Which variable in this study will be called an independent variable?**

(A) Lecture-cum Demonstration Method
(B) Students' level of participation
(C) SES of their family
(D) Habitat of the family

*Ans.* *(A)* If in a University, teacher conducts research study where Lecture-cum Demonstration Method is used to assess the effect on students' level of participation in terms of the Socio-Economic Status (SES) of faimly and their habitat then Lecture cum Demonstration Method will be called an Independent Variable.

This method is also known as Chalk and Talk Method. In this method, teacher is active and learner is passive. The essential qualities in learning science such as independent thinking, power of observation and reasoning can be developed in this method.

**8 When a researcher rejects the Null Hypothesis ($H_0$) in his/her study and accepts an Alternate Hypothesis ($H_1$), what type of error is likely to be?**

(A) Type I Error
(B) Type II Error
(C) Both Type I and Type II Error
(D) Neither Type I nor Type II Error

*Ans.* *(A)* When a researcher rejects the Null Hypothesis ($H_0$) in his/her study and accepts an Alternate Hypothesis ($H_1$), the type of error is likely to be Type I Error.

- **Type I Error** is a kind of error that occurs during the hypothesis testing when a Null Hypothesis is rejected, even though it is accurate and should not be rejected.
- **Type II Error** is the error caused by rejecting a Null Hypothesis when it is true.

**9 In which research design, the independent variable is 'selected' rather than 'manipulated'?**

(A) Experimental Research Design
(B) Historical Research Design
(C) Ex Post-Facto Research Design
(D) Descriptive Survey Research Design

*Ans.* *(C)* In Ex Post-Facto Research Design, the independent variable is 'selected' rather than 'manipulated'.

It is a method in which groups with qualities that already exist are compared on some dependent variables. An Ex-Post-Facto Research Design is considered quasi-experimental because the subjects are not randomly assigned, they are grouped based on a particular characteristic or trait.

**10** Inappropriate application of ICT in research is an example of :

(A) Technical lapse on the part of the researcher.
(B) Inadequate provision of ICT resources.
(C) Violation of research ethics.
(D) Absence of technical expertise of ICT resources.

***Ans.*** *(D)* Inappropriate application of ICT in research is an example of 'absence of technical expertise of ICT resources'. The Information Communication Technology (ICT) is an extensional term for Information Technology that stresses on the role of unified communications and the integration of tele-communications and computers, as well as necessary enterprise software, middleware, storage and audio-visual system, that enable users to access, store, transmit and manipulate information.

**11** Given below are two statements. One is labelled as Assertion (A) and other is labelled as Reason (R).

**Assertion** (A) While communicating with students, a teacher should go beyond what is prescribed.

**Reason** (R) Non-verbal cues definitely convey what is intended by the teacher.

In the light of the above statements, choose the correct option from those given below.

(A) Both A and R are true and R is the correct explanation of A.
(B) Both A and R are true, but R is not the correct explanation of A.
(C) A is true, but R is false.
(D) A is false, but R is true.

***Ans.*** *(B)* Teachers and students demonstrate respectful communication in the following ways :

- Use a tone that is honest and tactful. Choosing words that are appropriate to the situation and non-inflamentary.
- Non-verbal cues include all the communication between people that don't have a direct verbal translation.

Hence, Both (A) and (R) are true, but (R) is not the correct explanation of (A).

**12** Successful communication inside the classroom depends upon

1. detailed and long description of the topic.
2. describing the theme.
3. use of persuasive words and phrases.
4. clarity in explanations offered.
5. repetitive anecdotes.
6. unstructured delivery of message.

Choose the correct option from those given below :

(A) 1, 2 and 3 only (B) 2, 3 and 4 only
(C) 3, 4 and 5 only (D) 4, 5 and 6 only

***Ans.*** *(B)* Successful communication inside the classroom depends upon describing the theme, use of persuasive words and phrases and clarity in explanations offered.

Classroom communication exists in three categories, verbal, non-verbal and written.

Hence, option (B) is correct.

**13** If a teacher considers his or her students ill-informed, teacher's behaviour is described as :

(A) Single mindedness
(B) Having liberal view
(C) Pluralistic ignorance
(D) Conventional coding

***Ans.*** *(C)* If a teacher considers his or her students ill-informed, teacher's behaviour is described as pluralistic ignorance.

Pluralistic ignorance is a psychological state characterised by the belief that one's private thoughts are different from those of others.

It occurs when individual members of the group (a school, a team, workplace) believe that others in their group hold comparably more or less extreme attitudes, beliefs or behaviours.

**14** When the classroom communication is circular, the teacher-encoder will be a/an

(A) Active decoder (B) Passive observer
(C) Negative receiver (D) Restive coder

***Ans.*** *(A)* When the classroom communication is circular, the teacher-encoder will be a/an active decoder. A good understanding of the principle and process of communication will avail the classroom teacher to pass his/her pedagogical knowledge and skills across to the pupils in the classroom with ease.

**15** Communication begins usually with

(A) Confused ideas
(B) Semantic noise
(C) Apprehension
(D) Pictures in the mind

***Ans.*** *(D)* Communication begins usually with pictures in the mind. Communication is the process of creating, interpreting and negotiating meaning. Communication can be verbal, non-verbal or textual. It can be oral, visual or even physical. Although communication occurs in a variety of different ways, it is always a learned behaviour.

**16** MOTION is to RUN as EMOTION is to:

(A) FURIOUS (B) FEELING
(C) HEART (D) ENJOY

***Ans.*** *(B)* MOTION is to RUN as EMOTION is to FEELING.

**17** The missing letters in the given letter series are :

BCE, CDG, DEI, ......, FGM

(A) EFK (B) EGJ
(C) EFH (D) EGH

***Ans.*** *(A)* The given sequence of the series is

$$B \xrightarrow{+1} C \xrightarrow{+1} D \xrightarrow{+1} \boxed{E} \xrightarrow{+1} F$$
$$C \xrightarrow{+1} D \xrightarrow{+1} E \xrightarrow{+1} \boxed{F} \xrightarrow{+1} G$$
$$E \xrightarrow{+2} G \xrightarrow{+2} I \xrightarrow{+2} \boxed{K} \xrightarrow{+2} M$$

**18** If UGCNET = 35, then CSIRNET =

(A) 42 (B) 43
(C) 44 (D) 45

***Ans.*** *(C)* As, $\overset{21}{U}\,\overset{7}{G}\,\overset{3}{C}\,\overset{14}{N}\,\overset{5}{E}\,\overset{20}{T}$

$$\Rightarrow \frac{21+7+3+14+5+20}{2} = \frac{70}{2} = 35$$

In the similar way, $\overset{3}{C}\,\overset{19}{S}\,\overset{9}{I}\,\overset{18}{R}\,\overset{14}{N}\,\overset{5}{E}\,\overset{20}{T}$

$$\Rightarrow \frac{3+19+9+18+14+5+20}{2} = \frac{88}{2} = \boxed{44}$$

**19** A sum of money with compound interest becomes ₹ 400 in 2 years and ₹ 500 in 3 yr. Find the sum.

(A) ₹ 290 (B) ₹ 256
(C) ₹ 302 (D) ₹ 308

***Ans.*** *(B)* Net the principal be ₹ $P$ and rate of interest be $r$%.

$\therefore$ Compound interest in 2 yr $= P\left(1+\frac{r}{100}\right)^2$

$$400 = P\left(1+\frac{r}{100}\right)^2 \quad \ldots(i)$$

and compound interest in 3 yr

$$= P\left(1+\frac{r}{100}\right)^3$$

$$500 = P\left(1+\frac{r}{100}\right)^3 \quad \ldots(ii)$$

On dividing Eq. (ii) by Eq. (i),

$$\frac{500}{400} = \left(1+\frac{r}{100}\right)$$

$$\Rightarrow \frac{r}{100} = \frac{5}{4} - 1 = \frac{5-4}{4} = \frac{1}{4}$$

$$\Rightarrow r = \frac{1}{4} \times 100 = 25\%$$

Now, from Eq. (i),

$$400 = P\left(1+\frac{25}{100}\right)^2 = P\left(1+\frac{1}{4}\right)^2 = P\left(\frac{5}{4}\right)^2$$

$$\Rightarrow P = 400 \times \frac{4}{5} \times \frac{4}{5} = ₹\ 256$$

**20** Twenty times a positive integer is less than its square by 96. What is the integer?

(A) 24 (B) 20
(C) 30 (D) 14

***Ans.*** *(A)* Let the positive integer be $x$.

According to the question,

$$x \times 20 = x^2 - 96$$
$$\Rightarrow x^2 - 20x - 96 = 0$$
$$\Rightarrow x^2 - 24x + 4x - 96 = 0$$
$$\Rightarrow x(x-24) + 4(x-24) = 0$$
$$\Rightarrow (x+4)(x-24) = 0$$
$$\therefore x = 24 \text{ and } x = -4$$

Since, $x$ is a positive integer, neglect the negative value of $x$.

$$\therefore x = 24$$

**21** "Planets are big. Therefore, the atoms from which they are made are big". This inference commits which kind of fallacy?

(A) Fallacy of Division
(B) Fallacy of Ambiguity
(C) Fallacy of Equivocation
(D) Ad Populum

***Ans.*** *(A)* "Planets are big. Therefore, the atoms from which they are made are big." This inference commits Fallacy of Division. A fallacy of division is the error in logic that occurs when one reasons that something that is true for a whole must also be true of all or some of its parts. Two forms of the fallacy of division are :

- A person reasons that what is true of the whole must also be true of its parts.
- The person fails to justify that inference with the required degree of evidence.

**22** "Some teachers are not sincere" is an example of which category of proposition?

(A) Universal negative
(B) Universal affirmative
(C) Particular affirmative
(D) Particular negative

*Ans.* *(D)* "Some teachers are not sincere" is an example of particular negative category of proposition because all the teachers do not have the same quality or character, some particular may have different quality.

**23** Which of the following is correct about the sentence, "Some men are not married"?

(A) The subject is distributed.
(B) The predicate is distributed.
(C) Both subject and predicate are distributed.
(D) Neither subject nor predicate is distributed.

*Ans.* *(B)* In the sentence "Some men are not married", the predicate is distributed because here predicate is men and they are some married.

**24** Which one of the following is not a sense-organ according to Classical Indian School of Logic?

(A) Manas (B) Savikalpaka
(C) Caksuh (D) Srotra

*Ans.* *(B)* Savikalpaka is not a sense-organ according to Classical Indian School of Logic. Savikalpaka refers to one of the two types of Pratyaksa (Perception), according to Annambhatta and Kesava Misra (Tarkabhasa). Savikalpaka-Pratyaksa is that in which the cognition of an object is qualified by certain attributes like name, genus, quality, etc.

The given options - Manas, Cakush and Srotra are sense organs.

**25** "Have you stopped telling lies?"
This type of question commits which kind of fallacy?

(A) Fallacy of Complex Question
(B) Fallacy of Ambiguity
(C) Fallacy of Equivocation
(D) Fallacy of Accident

*Ans.* *(A)* 'Have you stopped telling lies'. This type of question commits Fallacy of Complex Question. Complex Question is a fallacy of induction that occurs when someone poses a question that pre-supposes an affirmative answer to an unasked question. A fallacy (also called sophism) is the use of invalid or otherwise faulty reasoning, or 'wrong moves' in the construction of an argument.

**Comprehension** (Q. Nos. 26-30) The following table gives the percentage of total students and also girl students enrolled in five Schools (A-E). The total number of students is 4500, while the total number of girl students is 2000. Based on the data of table, answer the questions that follow.

**Percentage of Total Number of Students and Girl Students in Five Schools**

| School Name | % of Total Students Enrolled | % of Girl Students Enrolled |
|---|---|---|
| A | 20% | 15% |
| B | 30% | 35% |
| C | 25% | 12% |
| D | 15% | 25% |
| E | 10% | 13% |

**26** The total number of girls enrolled in schools A and B together is

(A) 740 (B) 760
(C) 940 (D) 1000

**27** The total number of boys enrolled in schools C, D and E is

(A) 965 (B) 1250
(C) 1021 (D) 1325

**28** The number of girls enrolled in B, C and D constitutes what percentage (%) of total number of students in schools?

(A) 30% (B) 31%
(C) 32% (D) 33%

**29** The ratio of number of girls enrolled in school B to that of the number of boys enrolled in D is

(A) 1: 4 (B) 4 : 1
(C) 1: 3 (D) 3 : 1

**30** If 10% of the girls enrolled in C, change their school to E, then what will be the aggregate number of girls then in E?

(A) 214 (B) 234
(C) 274 (D) 284

**Solutions** (Q. Nos. 26-30) According to the information given in the comprehension,

Total number of students enrolled in School $A = 4500 \times \frac{20}{100} = 900$

Total number of students enrolled in school $B$
$= 4500 \times \frac{30}{100} = 1350$

Total number of students enrolled in school $C = 4500 \times \frac{25}{100} = 1125$

Total number of students enrolled in school $D = 4500 \times \frac{15}{100} = 675$

Total number of students enrolled in school $E = 4500 \times \frac{10}{100} = 450$

Now, total number of girls enrolled in school $A = 2000 \times \frac{15}{100} = 300$

Total number of girls enrolled in school $B = 2000 \times \frac{35}{100} = 700$

Total number of girls enrolled in school $C = 2000 \times \frac{12}{100} = 240$

Total number of girls enrolled in school $D = 2000 \times \frac{25}{100} = 500$

Total number of girls enrolled in school $E = 2000 \times \frac{13}{100} = 260$

and Total number of boys enrolled in school $A = 900 - 300 = 600$

Total number of boys enrolled in school $B = 1350 - 700 = 650$

Total number of boys enrolled in school $C = 1125 - 240 = 885$

Total number of boys enrolled in school $D = 675 - 500 = 175$

Total number of boys enrolled in school $E = 450 - 260 = 190$

***Ans.* 26.** *(D)* Required number of girls
$= 300 + 700 = 1000$

***Ans.* 27.** *(B)* Total number of boys enrolled in school $C, D$ and $E = 885 + 175 + 190 = 1250$

***Ans.* 28.** *(C)* Total number of girls enrolled in school $B, C$ and $D = 700 + 240 + 500 = 1440$

$\therefore$ Required percentage $= \frac{1440}{4500} \times 100 = 32\%$

***Ans.* 29.** *(B)* Ratio of number of girls enrolled in school $B$ to that of the number of boys enrolled in $D = \frac{700}{175} = \frac{4}{1} = 4:1$

***Ans.* 30.** *(D)* 10% of the girls enrolled in school $C = 240 \times \frac{10}{100} = 24$

$\therefore$ New number of girls enrolled in school
$E = 260 + 24 = 284$

**31** How many unique combinations of 0's and 1's can be made with 5-binary-digit code?

(A) 16 (B) 32 (C) 64 (D) 128

***Ans.*** *(B)* For unique combination of 1's and 1's can be made with $2^n$.

**From option** (A)

$16 = 2 \times 2 \times 2 \times 2 = 2^4$

Where, $n = 4$

So, it is wrong option

**From option** (B)

$32 = 2 \times 2 \times 2 \times 2 \times 2 = 2^5$

Where, $n = 5$

So, it is correct option

**From option** (C)

$64 = 2 \times 2 \times 2 \times 2 \times 2 \times 2 = 2^6$

Where, $n = 6$

So, it is wrong option

**From option** (D)

$128 = 2 \times 2 \times 2 \times 2 \times 2 \times 2 \times 2 = 2^7$

Where, $n = 7$

So, it is wrong option.

**32** The process through which an illegitimate website pretends to be a specific legitimate website is known as :

(A) Sniffing (B) Spoofing
(C) Back Doors (D) War Dialing

***Ans.*** *(B)* The process through which an illegitimate website pretends to be a specific legitimate website is known as Spoofing. Spoofing is the act of disguising a communication from an unknown source as being from a known, trusted source.

Spoofing can apply to emails, phone cells and websites, or can be more technical, such as a computer spoofing an IP Address, Address Resolution Protocol (ARP), or Domain Name System (DNS) Server.

**33** Which of the following keys of keyboard are called modifier keys?

1. Ctrl 2. Shift 3. End 4. Alt

**Codes**

(A) 1, 2 and 3 (B) 1, 2 and 4
(C) 1, 3 and 4 (D) 2, 3 and 4

***Ans.*** *(B)* A modifier key is a key that modifies the action of another key when the two are pressed together. Common modifier keys include Shift, Ctrl, Alt, Command, Option and Function.

**34** One aspect of E-governance deals with flow of information between the Government and Citizens. Which of the following are Government to Citizens (G2C) initiatives?

1. E-Help 2. E-Health
3. E-Tendering 4. E-Feedback

Choose the correct option from those given below.

(A) 1 and 2 only (B) 3 and 4 only
(C) 2 and 4 only (D) 2 and 3 only

***Ans.*** *(A)* One aspect of E-governance deals with flow of information between the government and citizens. In the given options, E-Help and E-Health are Government to Citizens (G2C) initiatives.

E-Help is support to ask anything. E-Health is relatively recent healthcare practice supported by electronic processes and communication.

**35** Which of the following portals include the list of 'Online Courses'?

1. ariia.gov.in
2. swayam.gov.in
3. mic.ac.in
4. nptel.ac.in

Choose the correct option from those given below.

(A) 1 and 3 only (B) 1 and 4 only
(C) 2 and 3 only (D) 2 and 4 only

***Ans.*** *(D)* swayam.gov.in and nptel.ac.in portals include the list of 'Online Courses'. SWAYAM is a programme initiated by Government of India and designed to achieve the three cardinal principles of Education Policy viz., Access, Equity and Quality.

SWAYAM seeks to bridge the digital divide for students who have hitherto remained untouched by the digital revolution and have not been able to join the mainstream of the knowledge economy.

National Programme on Technology Enhanced Learning (NPTEL) is a project of MHRD initiated by seven Indian Institutes of Technology (Bombay, Delhi, Kanpur, Kharagpur, Madras, Guwahati and Roorkee) alongwith the Indian Institute of Science, Bangalore in 2003, to provide quality education to anyone interested in learning from the IITs.

**36** Sustainable Development Goal- 'Life Below Water' aims at conserving and sustainably using

(A) Ground water resources
(B) Rivers, streams, ponds and lake resources
(C) Oceans, sea and marine resources
(D) Wetland resources

***Ans.*** *(C)* Sustainable Development Goal-'Life Below Water' aims at conserving and sustainably using oceans, sea and marine resources. Sustainable Development Goal 14 (Goal 14 or SDG 14) is about 'Life Below Water' and is one of the 17 Sustainable Development Goals established by the United Nations in 2015.

The official wording is "to conserve and sustainably use the oceans, sea and marine resources for sustainable development."

The Goal has ten targets to be achieved by 2030. Progress towards each target is being measured with one indicator each.

The first seven targets are "outcome targets": Reduce marine pollution; protect and restore ecosystems; reduce ocean acidification; sustainable fishing; conserve coastal and marine areas; end subsidies contributing to overfishing; increase the economic benefits from sustainable use of marine resources.

The last three targets are "means of achieving" targets which are as follows:

- To increase scientific knowledge, research and technology for ocean health.
- To support small scale fishers.
- To implement and enforce International Sea Law.

**37** From the following list, identify the Greenhouse Gases adopted in the Kyoto Protocol.

1. Carbon dioxide
2. Methane
3. Nitrous oxide
4. Hydroflurocarbons
5. Perflurocarbons
6. Sulphur hexafluoride

Select the most appropriate answer from the options given below :

(A) 1, 2, 4 and 5 only (B) 1, 4, 5 and 6 only
(C) 2, 4, 5 and 6 only (D) 1, 2, 3, 4, 5 and 6

***Ans.*** *(D)* Greenhouse Gases adopted in the Kyoto Protocol are Carbon Dioxide ($CO_2$), Methane ($CH_4$), Nitrous Oxide ($N_2O$), Hydrofluorocarbons (HFCs), Perfluorocarbons (PFCs) and Sulfur Hexafluoride ($SF_6$).

The Kyoto Protocol was adopted in Kyoto, Japan, on 11th December, 1997 and entered into force on 16th February, 2005. There are currently 192 parties (Canada withdrew from the protocol, effective from December 2012) to the Protocol.

The Kyoto Protocol implemented the objective of the UNFCCC to reduce the onset of global warming by reducing Greenhouse Gas concentration in the atmosphere "to a level that would prevent dangerous anthropogenic interference with the climate system".

**38** Climate pledges under Paris Agreement cover what fraction of greenhouse gas emissions reduction needed to limit the global warming below 2°C?

(A) 1/3 (B) 2/3 (C) 1/2 (D) 3/4

***Ans.*** *(A)* Climate pledges under Paris Agreement covers 1/3 fraction of Greenhouse Gas emissions reduction needed to limit the global warming below 2°C.

The Paris Agreement is an agreement within the United Nations Framework Convention on Climate Change (UNFCCC), dealing with Greenhouse Gas emissions mitigation, adaptation and finance, signed in 2016.

Its aim is to strengthen the global response to the threat of climate change by keeping a global temperature rise this century well below 2 degrees Celsius above pre-industrial levels and to pursue efforts to limit the temperature increase even further to 1.5 degrees Celsius.

**39** The impact of noise pollution on human health is governed by :

1. Intensity of noise
2. Duration of noise
3. Socio-economic status of an individual
4. Sensitivity of human ear
5. Frequency range of noise

Choose your answer from the options given below:

(A) 1, 2, 4 and 5 only
(B) 1, 2 and 3 only
(C) 1, 3, 4 and 5 only
(D) 1, 2, 3, 4 and 5

***Ans.*** *(A)* The impact of noise pollution on human health is governed by intensity of noise, duration of noise, sensitivity of human ear and frequency range of noise.

Noise pollution is an invisible danger.

It cannot be seen, but it is present nonetheless, both on land and under the sea. Noise pollution is considered to be any unwanted or disturbing sound that affects the health and well-being of humans and other organisms.

Noise pollution impacts millions of people on a daily basis.

The most common health problem it causes is Noise Induced Hearing Loss (NIHL). Exposure to loud noise can also cause high blood pressure, heart disease, sleep disturbances and stress. These health problems can affect all age groups, especially children.

**40** Polar Stratospheric Clouds are associated with which of the following environmental issues?

(A) Flash floods
(B) Acid rain
(C) Ozone layer depletion
(D) Photo-chemical smog

***Ans.*** *(C)* Polar Stratospheric Clouds are associated with Ozone layer depletion. Polar Stratospheric Clouds (PSCs) are clouds in the winter polar stratosphere at altitudes of 15,000-25,000 m (49,000-82,000 ft). One main type of PSC is madeup mostly of supercooled droplets of water and nitric acid and is implicated in the formation of Ozone holes.

Ozone layer depletion is the gradual thinning of the Earth's Ozone layer in the upper atmosphere.

**41** **The teaching in the universities of ancient India was controlled by the Board of Eminent Teachers. The affairs of which university were administered by the Board of Vikramsila University?**

(A) Jagaddala University
(B) Valabhi University
(C) Nalanda University
(D) Odantapuri University

***Ans.*** *(C)* The teaching in the universities of ancient India was controlled by the Board of Eminent Teachers. The affairs of Nalanda University were administered by the Board of Vikramsila University.

Nalanda University is situated in the Eastern state of Bihar. Nalanda University was once the most prominent seat of learning in India. The university is said to have flourished under the Reign of Gupta Dynasty back in 5th Century.

Vikramashila was one of the two most important centres of learning in India during the Pala Empire, alongwith Nalanda.

Its location is now the Site of Antichak village, Bhagalpur district in Bihar.

Vikramashila was established by the Pala Emperor Dharmapala in the late 8th or 9th Century in response to a supposed decline in the quality of scholarship at Nalanda.

**42** **For research in policy relevant areas, which of the following organisations is entrusted with the initiative 'Impress'?**

(A) IIAS (B) ICSSR
(C) ICPR (D) ICHR

***Ans.*** *(B)* For research in policy relevant areas, Indian Council of Social Science Research (ICSSR) organisation is entrusted with the initiative 'Impress'.

ICSSR was established in the year 1969. Impactful Policy Research in Social Science (IMPRESS) research in policy relevant areas so as to provide vital inputs in policy formulation.

The IMPRESS is an initiative of the Ministry of Human Resource Development, Government of India and is being implemented by the Indian Council of Social Science Research.

The scheme was sanctioned in August 2018 at a total cost of ₹ 414 crores for implementation upto 31st March, 2021.

**43** **Which of the following is a residential center for free and creative enquiry into the fundamental themes and problems of life and thought?**

(A) Dr Zakir Hussain Memorial College Trust
(B) Sri Lal Bahadur Shastri Rashtriya Sanskrit Vidyapeeth
(C) Indian Institute of Advanced Study
(D) National Assessment and Accreditation Council

***Ans.*** *(C)* The Indian Institute of Advanced Study (IIAS) is a residential center for free and creative enquiry into the fundamental themes and problems of life and thought.

IIAS is a research institute based in Shimla, India. It was setup by the Ministry of Education, Government of India in 1964 and it started functioning from 20th October, 1965.

The Institute is administered by a Society and a Governing Body.

**44** **Capturing the imagination and initiative of the student is of crucial importance in**

(A) Case Method of Teaching
(B) Concept Mapping
(C) Peer Instruction
(D) Quizzes

***Ans.*** *(A)* Capturing the imagination and initiative of the student is of crucial importance in Case Method of Teaching. It is an active form of instruction that focuses on a case and involves students' learning by doing. Cases are real or invented stories that include "an educational message" or recount events, problems, dilemmas, theoretical or conceptual issue that requires analysis and/or decision-making".

**45** **A vital role in human resource development of a country centered on skilled manpower, productivity and the quality of life of its people is focused on which of the following domains?**

(A) Professional education
(B) Formal education
(C) Lifelong education
(D) Technical education

***Ans.*** *(D)* A vital role in human resource development of a country centered on skilled manpower, productivity and the quality of life of its people is focused on technical education.

Technical education is entrusted with the responsibility of providing trained technical manpower for the technological upgradation of industrial production, services, productivity and innovation, contributing to the planned growth of the country's economy.

**Direction** (Q. Nos. 46 to 50) Read the passage given below carefully and answer the questions that follow :

The representative dimension of the new liberal political orders designed to protect individual rights, appeared as the best mechanism for actualising popular rule or sovereignty- indeed democracy. As a result, it is more beneficial to assess the meaning and value of 'rights' as historical and political practices, rather than conceptual forms (especially as counterparts to 'virtue'). In this respect, the discourse of rights reflected a new official mode of combining ethics and power for political conduct.

But the formally equal treatment of citizens belied a relatively arbitrary element, for the involvement of the citizenry in shaping the conduct of their representatives was left to elite influenced election procedures, qualifications and voluntary participation. Still, representation became the mythical means of transposing the authorising power of the people to the new authorities in government. Afterall, representatives had more time and money to perfect their virtue and skill in conducting their work and were not supposed to be corrupted by the power that attended their offices.

They were supposed to be better guardians and agents of public virtue than ordinary citizens as representation became institutionalised in the new states. The state wielded power over the people, diversifying rather than restricting the problems of demagoguery in ancient democracy that modern republics were supposed to correct.

**46** The aim of liberal democracy is to

(A) provide a mechanism to ignore popular voice
(B) safeguard individual rights
(C) understand the political order
(D) defocus representativeness

*Ans.* *(B)* The aim of liberal democracy is to safeguard individual rights. A liberal democracy is a representative democracy with protection for individual liberty and property by rule of law.

**47** What will be the more beneficial assessment of democracy?

(A) Considering rights as a political practice.
(B) Avoiding historical meanings of the concept.
(C) Emphasising on virtues.
(D) Examining the conceptual forms of democracy.

*Ans.* *(A)* Considering rights as a political practice will be the more beneficial assessment of democracy.

**48** What does the discourse of rights focus on?

(A) Election procedures
(B) Arbitrary freedom
(C) Reasonable political conduct
(D) New priests of power

*Ans.* *(C)* According to the given passsage, the Discourse of Rights focus on Reasonable Political Conduct. It reflected a new official mode of combining ethics and power for political conduct.

**49** What was expected of public representatives?

(A) Use power for personal gains.
(B) Behave like ordinary citizens.
(C) Become skilled in power politics.
(D) Safeguard representation of virtue.

*Ans.* *(D)* Safeguard representation of virtue was expected of public representatives. They were supposed to be better guardians and agents of public virtue than ordinary citizens as representation became institutionalised in the new states.

**50** According to the author of the passage, the modern republics should

(A) exercise power over people.
(B) institutionalise power and corruption.
(C) free themselves from the defects of ancient democracy.
(D) imitate the institutions of new states.

*Ans.* *(C)* According to the Author of the given passage, the modern republics should free themselves from the defects of ancient democracy.

# UGC
## NET/JRF/SET

# Solved Paper, December 2019

(Exam Date : 5/12/2019, Shift-I)

## General Paper 1 (Teaching Aptitude and Attitude)

***Instructions***

- This paper contains fifty Multiple-Choice Questions, each question carries two marks.
- All questions are compulsory.
- Total time given for this paper is 1 hour.

**1** The emphasis in memory level teaching is on which of the following?

(a) Organisation of thoughts and ideas
(b) Seeing of relationships among facts
(c) Systematic presentations to enable quick reproduction
(d) Critical thinking
(e) Mastery of correct sequencing of facts
(f) Segregating one feature from another

Choose the answer from the following options

(A) (a), (b) and (c) (B) (a), (c) and (e)
(C) (b), (c) and (d) (D) (d), (e) and (f)

***Ans.*** *(B)* Teaching is a purposeful activity. Through teaching the teacher brings a desirable change in the learners. Teachers teach students at three levels. He has to keep in mind about the developmental stage of the learners so that desired educational objectives can be achieved. Teaching is considered as the act of imparting instructions to the learners in the classroom situation.

These three levels are

- **Memory level** Thoughtless teaching
- **Understanding level** Thoughtful teaching
- **Reflective level** Upper thoughtful level

Memory level of teaching is the first and thoughtless level of teaching. At this level,

- the thinking ability does not play any role.
- students only cram the facts, information, formulas and laws that are taught to them.
- the teaching is nothing but learning the subject matter by rote.
- the role of the teacher is prominent and that of the student is secondary.
- the study material is organised and pre-planned.
- the teacher presents the study material in a sequential order.
- the memory level of teaching is usually used in lower classes.

Thus, option 2 is correct. Therefore, options (a), (c) and (e) are correct as the options (b), (d) and (f) are part of reflective level teaching.

**2** **A college teacher does research with a view to depict the reality situations relating to home conditions of students and hostels provided for. Which of the following research format will be helpful to do so?**

(A) Experimental research
(B) Descriptive research
(C) Participant observation based research
(D) Ethnographic research

*Ans. (C)* Participant observation is a qualitative research method in which the researcher not only observes the research participants, but also actively engages in the activities of the research participants. This requires the researcher to become integrated into the participants' environment while also taking objective notes about what is going on. Thus, option 3 is correct.

**3** **Classroom communication is**

(a) Like a computer-program
(b) Dictatorial
(c) Purposeful
(d) Pragmatic

Choose the correct option from those given below

(A) (a) and (c)
(B) (b) and
(c) (c) (b) and (d)
(D) (c) and (d)

*Ans. (D)* Classroom communication is always purposeful and pragmatic. It is because through classroom communication students-teachers interact with each other easily and exchange their ideas and thoughts in an effective way.

Thus, options (c) and (d) are correct because classroom communication could not be delivered like a computer program and in a dictatorial manner as given in the options (a) and (b).

**4** **"In this hospital, some nurses don't wear white dress, some doctors have private practice and medicines prescribed are of high cost. Therefore, treatment in this hospital is of poor quality." What fallacy does this argument make?**

(A) Fallacy of composition
(B) Slippery slope
(C) Fallacy of accident
(D) Fallacy of division

*Ans. (A)* The fallacy of composition occurs when someone assumes or argues "From the part to the whole, ignoring the fact that what is true of the part is not necessarily true of the whole."

In the argument given in the question, not wearing of the white dresses of the nurses and private practices a come of the doctors may lead to degradation of quality of the treatment to some extent but this reason can not be extended to the entire hospital.

Hence, this argument has fallacy of composition.

**5** **In which of the following steps of research, the scope for creativity and imagination is utmost?**

(A) Identifying the research problem and defining it
(B) Figuring out the related studies and the techniques used by other researchers
(C) Identifying variables and hypothesizing
(D) Data analysis and presentation of results

*Ans. (C)* A scientific research involves a systematic process that focuses on being objective and gathering a multitude of information for analysis so that the researcher can come to a conclusion.

This process is used in all research and evaluation projects, regardless of the research method. There are many steps in a research but the one which needs creativity and imagination is identifying variables and hypothesizing.

**6** **Which of the following is an example of maximum performance test?**

(A) Projective personality test
(B) Interest inventory
(C) Aptitude test
(D) Attitude scales

*Ans. (C)* Maximum Performance Tests are designed to test the limits of the persons' knowledge and abilities. It can either be Correct or Incorrect. Examples of this test are achievement and aptitude tests.

Aptitude test is designed to assess an individuals' skills or ability assessing how they perform in an area in which they have no prior training or knowledge. Schools used aptitude tests to determine if students are inclined to a certain area of study.

**7** Classroom interactions are influenced largely by

(A) Students commitment
(B) Teacher centric environment
(C) Organisational oversight
(D) Unsolicited interventions

***Ans.*** *(A)* Classroom interactions are largely influenced by students' commitment. Because it is the two-way process of communication between teacher and students.

If anyone of them fails to convey their thoughts the interaction may not be effective. Thus, the classroom interaction is very important for effective teaching.

**8** Identify the term '$X$' in the following series

3, 2, 11, 14, 27, 34, 51, $X$

(A) 62 (B) 69
(C) 60 (D) 71

***Ans.*** (A) Given series is,

| 3 | 2 | 11 | 14 | 27 | 34 | 51 | 62 |
|---|---|---|---|---|---|---|---|
| ↑ | ↑ | ↑ | ↑ | ↑ | ↑ | ↑ | ↑ |
| $1^2+2$ | $2^2-2$ | $3^2+2$ | $4^2-2$ | $5^2+2$ | $6^2-2$ | $7^2+2$ | $8^2-2$ |

$\therefore X = 62$

**9** The length of the side of a square (5.0 cm × 5.0 cm) is increased by 1%. By what percentage (%) the area of the square increases?

(A) 1% (B) 2%
(C) 2.5% (D) 4%

***Ans.*** *(B)* Area of square $= 5 \times 5 = 25 \text{ cm}^2$

$$\text{New edge of square} = 5 + \frac{1}{100} \times 5 = 5 + 0.05$$
$$= 5.05$$
$$\text{New area of square} = 5.05 \times 5.05 = 25.5025$$
$$\text{Required percent} = \frac{25.5025 - 25}{25} \times 100$$
$$= 0.5025 \times 4 = 2.01\% \approx 2\%$$

**10** The most characteristic feature of an adolescent learner which determines his/her social and moral development is the

(A) Tendency to be away from parents
(B) Concern for hero worshipping for emulating values and standards
(C) Mixing up with peers in the neighbourhood
(D) Identity crisis

***Ans.*** *(B)* Adolescence is a time when the young person is looking for his/her own identity and needs to experiment with different ways of looking. There is a constant preoccupation with appearance and body-image. Although this behaviour is more common among girls, boys are becoming more fashion-conscious and concerned about the way they look.

This is the time when teenagers looking for their idol hero and try to copy their style without giving any thought. Thus, option 2 is correct in this case.

**11** When a large number of students with different performance levels are there in the class, for uniform imparting of educative interactions, a teacher should opt for a communication which is:

(A) Top-down and linear
(B) Technology-enabled
(C) Individual-centric
(D) Self-projected

***Ans.*** *(B)* When a large number of students with different performance levels are there in the class. For uniform imparting of educative interactions, a teacher should opt for a communication which is technology enabled.

Integrating technology into the classroom is an effective way to connect with students of all learning styles. It gives students the opportunity to enhance the interaction with their classmates and instructors by encouraging collaboration. It helps students to stay engaged. Therefore, option (B) is correct.

**12** Which of the following statistical technique will be appropriate for data analysis when the observations are available in the form of frequencies?

(A) Parametric 't' test
(B) Non-parametric 'u' test
(C) Non-parametric 'chi-square' test
(D) Parametric correlated 't' test

***Ans.*** *(C)* The Chi-square statistic is a non-parametric (distribution free) tool designed to analyse group differences when the dependent variable is measured at a nominal level.

The Chi-square test is commonly used for testing relationships between categorical variables.

Like all non-parametric statistics, the Chi-square is robust with respect to the distribution of the data. It permits evaluation of both dichotomous independent variables and of multiple group studies. Each non-parametric test has its own specific assumptions as well. Some of the assumptions of the Chi-square include :

- The data in the cells should be frequencies rather than percentages.
- The levels or categories of the variables are mutually exclusive.
- Each subject may contribute data to one and only one cell in the $\times 2$.

**13** **In case, the population of research is heterogeneous in nature which of the following sampling techniques will ensure optimum representativeness of sample units?**

(A) Simple random sampling
(B) Stratified random sampling
(C) Cluster sampling
(D) Systematic sampling

***Ans.*** *(B)* Stratified random sampling, also called proportional random sampling or quota random sampling, is a method of sampling that involves the division of a population into smaller sub-groups known as 'strata'.

In stratified random sampling or stratification, the strata are formed based on members' shared attributes or characteristics such as income or educational attainment.

Stratified random sampling involves taking random samples from stratified groups in proportion to the population. Stratified random sampling breaks down the population into sub-groups and organises them by similar traits, characteristics and behaviour.

**14** **A person buys 3 items of ₹ 1500 each and 2 items of ₹ 1800 each from a shopping mall. On the total bill a discount of 10% is given. What is the average cost of the items?**

(A) 1650 (B) 1458 (C) 1658 (D) 1550

***Ans.*** *(B)* Total cost of purchased item

$= ₹(3 \times 1500 + 2 \times 1800)$

$= ₹(4500 + 3600) = ₹8100$

Cost after getting discount

$= ₹\left(8100 - \frac{10}{100} \times 8100\right)$

$= ₹(8100 - 810) = ₹\ 7290$

Average cost per item $= ₹\frac{7290}{5} = ₹1458$

**15** **Consider the following statements and choose the right option.**

**(a) Middle term should be distributed in atleast one premise**
**(b) Middle term should be present in the conclusion**
**(c) Both premises can be particular in a valid argument**
**(d) Both premises can be negative in a valid argument**

(A) (c) and (d) (B) Only (c)
(C) Only (a) (D) (b) and (c)

***Ans.*** *(C)* The middle term of a valid syllogism is distributed in at least one of the premises.

The fallacy of the undistributed middle occurs when this doesn't happen. For instance, the middle term (furry animals) in the following syllogism.

- All dogs are furry animals
- Some furry animals are cats
- Therefore, dogs are cats is not distributed and the argument is clearly fallacious.

**16** **A 50 years old man has a son whose age is 2/5 of his age. After how many years, the ratio of the age of the man to his son will be 5/3?**

(A) 10 yr (B) 15 yr (C) 20 yr (D) 25 yr

***Ans.*** *(D)* Age of man = 50 years

Age of son $= \frac{2}{5} \times 50 = 20$ years

Let after $x$ yr, the ratio of their age will be $\frac{5}{3}$,

then according to the question,

$$\frac{50 + x}{20 + x} = \frac{5}{3}$$

$$\Rightarrow \quad 150 + 3x = 100 + 5x$$

$$\Rightarrow \quad 2x = 50 \Rightarrow x = 25 \text{ yr}$$

**17** **Which of the following is true with reference to anupalabdhi as a means of knowledge?**

(A) I do not cognize the pot on the table, therefore it is absent there
(B) I directly perceive the absence of pot on the table
(C) I infer the absence of pot on the table since I do not find it to be there
(D) I know the absence of the pot on the table because I know its similarity with other absences

***Ans.*** *(A)* I do not at cognize the pot on the table, therefore it is absent there is true with reference to anupalabdhi as a means of knowledge.

**18** **The smallest integer greater than 1 which is simultaneously a square and a cube of certain integers is**

(A) 8 (B) 9 (C) 36 (D) 64

***Ans.*** *(D)* 64 is the square of 8, 64 is the cube of 4.

Hence, smallest integer greater than 1 which is simultaneously a square and cube of a number of 64.

**19** **"If it rains, then the drought will end. The drought has ended. Therefore, it rained." Which kind of fallacy does this commit?**

(A) Deductive fallacy (B) Inductive fallacy
(C) Abductive fallacy (D) Informal fallacy

***Ans.*** *(A)* If it rains, then the drought will end but if a drought has ended then it is not necessary that it is because of rain only; there can be many other reasons to it.

Therefore, it is a deductive fallacy.

**20** **Swapping of encoder-decoder roles in communication happens due to**

(A) Cognitive disruptions
(B) Semantic noise
(C) Feedback analysis
(D) Weak channelisation

***Ans.*** *(C)* In basic terms, humans communicate through a process of encoding and decoding. Encoding is the process of turning thoughts into communication.

The encoder uses a 'medium' to send the message like a phone call, email, text message, face-to-face meeting or other communication tool. Whereas, decoding is the process of turning communication into thoughts. Swapping of encoder-decoder roles in communication happens due to feedback analysis.

**21** **A research scholar while finally reporting the research results in the form of a thesis acknowledges the support of his/her supervisor in the preface. This will be treated as a**

(A) Sheer formality (B) Needed formality
(C) Superfluous act (D) Part of ethicality

***Ans.*** *(D)* Ethics are the moral principles that a person must follow, irrespective of the place or time. Behaving ethically involves doing the right thing at the right time. Research ethics focus on the moral principles that researchers must follow in their respective fields of research.

A research scholar while finally reporting the research results in the form of a thesis acknowledge the support of his/her supervisor in the preface it is treated as part of ethicality.

**22** **Which one of the following is the characteristic/ feature of an argument?**

(A) It is either valid or invalid
(B) It is neither valid nor invalid
(C) It is either true or false
(D) It is neither true nor false

***Ans.*** *(A)* An argument is valid if and only if it is necessary that if all the premises are true, then the conclusion is true, if all the premises are true, then the conclusion must be true; it is impossible that all the premises are true and the conclusion is false.

An argument is invalid if by assuming that all the premises are true and seeing whether it is still possible for the conclusion to be false.

If this is possible, then the argument is invalid. Therefore an argument can be either valid or invalid, there is no middle ground. You can't say that is somewhat valid or somewhat not valid.

**23** **Given below are two statements one is labelled as Assertion (A) and the other is labelled as Reason(R)**

**Assertion** (A) Classroom communication is pre-decided by social and institutional demands.

**Reasons** (R) Positive educative actions should guide learners to acquire knowledge of social significance.

**In the light of the above two statements, choose the correct option:**

(A) Both (A) and (R) are true and (R) is the correct explanation of (A)
(B) Both (A) and (R) are true, but (R) is not the correct explanation of (A)
(C) (A) is true, but (R) is false
(D) (A) is false, but (R) is true

**Ans.** *(A)* Classroom communication is a very effective tools which is used during teaching-learning process. Without it no information can be delivered to students by the teacher. It is pre-decided by social and institutional demands.
Thus, option (A) is correct.

**24** Which of the following teaching method(s) is/are contributive to direct learning?

(a) Team teaching and lecturing
(b) Simulation and role playing
(c) Lecture with or without use of audiovisuals
(d) Participation in workshop and assignments
(e) MOOCs and heuristics
(f) Interactive presentations

Choose your answer from the following options:

(A) (b), (d) and (e)
(B) (a), (b) and (c)
(C) (a), (b) and (c)
(D) (d), (e) and (f)

**Ans.** *(A)* Options (b), (d) and (e) are correct due to the following reasons :

- Role playing and simulations are forms of experiential learning. Both of these teaching methods function as learning tools for the students. It is a direct form of learning because students are actively involved in both self and peer assessment and obtain sustainable formative feedback.
- Simulated teaching is used prior to the classroom teaching practice with the objective of developing a specific skill of communication. It can be used for pre-service teachers to make them effective.
- Assignments and workshop provides a way to create an intensive educational experience in a short amount of time. Both contributes to direct learning as is a great way to teach hands-on-skills because it offers participants a chance to try out new methods.
- MOOC's provide interactive courses with user forums to support community interactions as well as provide immediate feedback to quick quizzes and assignments. While in neuristic method, students are put into the situation to learn by self-experience. It certainly develops self-confidence and self-reliance in the learners.

**25** Below are given two sets in which set I specifies the four behaviour modification techniques while set II indicates their exemplification. Match the two sets:

| Set I (Behaviour modification techniques) | Set II (Example) |
|---|---|
| A. Positive reinforcement | I. Withdrawal of a pleasant stimulus or application of an aversive stimulus to stop the behaviour |
| B. Negative reinforcement | II. Painful or aversive stimulus is presented to stop the occurrence of behaviour |
| C. Punishment | III. The behaviour increases in frequency after the removal of the stimulus |
| D. Extinction | IV. The behaviour increases in frequency after the presentation of a stimulus |

Choose your answer form following options.

(A) A-I, B-II, C-III, D-IV
(B) A-II, B-I, C-III, D-IV
(C) A-IV, B-III, C-II, D-I
(D) A-III, B-I, C-II, D-IV

**Ans.** *(C)* Behaviour modification is a means of changing behaviour through various techniques used to replace undesirable behaviours with desirable ones.

- Positive reinforcement uses a reward for positive behaviour to make sure the child continues with a desired behaviour. Through this reinforcement the behaviour increases in frequency after the presentation of a stimulus.
- Negative reinforcement means taking something unpleasant away to reinforce good behaviour. Through this reinforcement the behaviour increases in frequency after the removal of the stimulus.
- Punishment means when something is taken away in response to negative behaviour. Through this reinforcement painful or aversive stimulus is presented to stop the occurrence of behaviour.
- Extinction refers to the gradual weakening of a conditioned response that results in the behaviour decreasing or disappearing. Through this technique withdrawl of a pleasant stimulus or application of an aversive stimulus to stop the behaviour is achieved.

Hence, option (C) is the correct answer.

**Directions** (Q. Nos. 26-30) *Consider the following table that shows the amount of exports ( ₹ in crore) from three different Companies A, B and C over the years 2012-2018. Based on the data in the table, answer the given questions.*

**Year-wise amount of Exports from companies**

| Year | Amount of export (₹ in crore) | | |
|---|---|---|---|
| | A | B | C |
| 2012 | 40 | 90 | 70 |
| 2013 | 70 | 50 | 100 |
| 2014 | 50 | 70 | 130 |
| 2015 | 80 | 70 | 100 |
| 2016 | 110 | 90 | 70 |
| 2017 | 60 | 110 | 90 |
| 2018 | 130 | 150 | 110 |

**26** In how many of the given years, were the exports from Company A more than its average annual exports over the given years?

(A) 2 (B) 3
(C) 4 (D) 5

***Ans.*** *(B)* Average exports of Company

$$A = \frac{40+70+50+80+110+60+130}{7} = \frac{540}{7}$$

= ₹ 77.14 crore

In the year 2015, 2016 and 2018 the export is more than the average export.

Hence, option (B) is the correct answer.

**27** For which of the following pairs of years, the total exports from the three companies put together are equal?

(A) 2014 and 2017 (B) 2015 and 2017
(C) 2016 and 2017 (D) 2014 and 2015

***Ans.*** *(D)* In 2014, total exports = 50 + 70 + 130

= ₹ 250 crore

In 2015, total exports = 80 + 70 + 100

= ₹ 250 crore

Hence, in 2014 and 2015, the total exports from the three companies together are equal.

**28** In which year, the absolute difference between the exports from Companies A and B was the minimum?

(A) 2013 (B) 2014
(C) 2015 (D) 2016

***Ans.*** *(C)* In year 2015, the absolute difference between the exports from Companies A and B near minimum, which is 80 − 70 = ₹ 10 crore

**29** Average annual amount of exports during the given period for Company B is approximately what percent (%) of the average annual amount of exports for Company C?

(A) 89.64% (B) 91.21%
(C) 94.03% (D) 93.33%

***Ans.*** *(C)* Average annual exports of Company

$$B = \frac{90+50+70+70+90+110+150}{7}$$

$$= ₹\frac{630}{7} \text{ crore}$$

Average annual exports of Company

$$C = \frac{70+100+130+100+70+90+110}{7}$$

$$= ₹\frac{670}{7} \text{ crore}$$

$$\therefore \text{ Required percent} = \frac{\left(\frac{630}{7}\right)}{\left(\frac{670}{7}\right)} \times 100 = 94.03\%$$

**30** What was the difference between the average exports of three companies in 2017 and the average exports of three companies in 2012?

(A) ₹ 15.33 crore (B) ₹ 18.67 crore
(C) ₹ 25 crore (D) ₹ 20 crore

***Ans.*** *(D)* Average exports of companies in 2017

$$= \frac{60+110+90}{3} = \frac{260}{3} = ₹\ 86.66 \text{ crore}$$

Average exports of companies in 2012

$$= \frac{40+90+70}{3} = ₹\frac{200}{3} \text{ crore}$$

= ₹ 66.66 crore

Required difference = ₹ (86.66 − 66.66 crore)

= ₹ 20 crore

**31** Which among the following natural hazards has relatively slow onset?

(A) Volcanic eruptions (B) Droughts
(C) Wild fires (D) Land and slides

***Ans.*** *(B)* Drought is the natural calamity which is an event of prolonged shortages in the water supply, whether atmospheric, surface water or ground water.

It is relatively slow onset which can last for months or years or may be declared after as few as 15 days.

**32** Which one of the following represents the correct order of sequence for reading skills in the context ot research?

(A) Read, question, recall, review, survey
(B) Questions, survey, read, recall, review
(C) Recall, review, survey, question, read
(D) Survey, question, read, recall, review

*Ans. (D)* The correct sequence for reading skill in the context of research is survey, question, read, recall and review.

**33** Major sources of oxygen demanding waste in fresh water systems are

(a) Agricultural run-off
(b) Food processing
(c) Ore mining
(d) Sewage effluent
(e) Landfill sites

Choose the correct option from those given below

(A) (a), (d) and (e) (B) (b), (d) and (e)
(C) (a), (b) and (d) (D) (a), (b), (c) and (d)

*Ans. (C)* There are several classes of water pollutants. The first are disease-causing agents. A second category of water pollutants is oxygen-demanding wastes. These are the wastes that can be decomposed by oxygen-requiring bacteria. When large populations of decomposing bacteria are converting these wastes, it can deplete oxygen levels in the water. This causes other organisms in the water, such as fish, to die. Major sources of oxygen demanding wastes in the freshwater resources are agricultural run-off, food processing and sewage effluent and so on.

**34** Which of the following is a renewable natural resource?

(A) Biological diversity (B) Tin
(C) Natural gas (D) Salt

*Ans. (A)* A renewable resource is a resource which can be used repeatedly and replaced naturally. Biological diversity or biodiversity refers to all of the different kinds of life on Earth.

A collection of this biodiversity would include human beings, wildlife, sugar maples, oyster mushrooms, bacteria and the millions of other living organisms found on the Earth. It is also considered renewable natural resources and tin, natural gas and salt are the examples of non-renewable resources.

**35** Match List-I with List-II in the context of computer networking:

| List-I | List-II |
|---|---|
| A. VOIP | I. Makes use of light pulses to transmit data |
| B. Fibre-optic cable | II. Use of internet to make phone calls |
| C. URL | III. Most appropriate to connect computers in a small building |
| D. UTP cable | IV. Text used by web browsers to locate a web address on the Internet |

Choose the correct option:

(A) A-IV, B-I, C-II, D-III
(B) A-II, B-I, C-IV, D-III
(C) A-II, B-III, C-IV, D-I
(D) A-IV, B-III, C-II, D-I

*Ans. (B)* A computer network is a system in which multiple computers are connected to each other to share information and resources.

- **VOIP** or **Voice Over Internet Protocol**, also called IP telephony, is a method and group of technologies for the delivery of voice communications and multimedia sessions over Internet Protocol networks, such as the Internet. Through this we can use Internet to make phone calls.
- **A fibre-optic cable** is also known as optical-fibre cable, is an assembly similar to an electrical cable, but containing one or more optical fibres that are used to carry lights. So, it makes use of light pulses to transmit data.
- **URL** stands for Uniform Resource Locator and is used to specify addresses on the World Wide Web.
- **Unshielded Twisted Pair (UTP) cables** are widely used to connect computers in a small building.

**36** Which of the following communication technologies employ only asynchronous communication

(a) Video conferencing
(b) Email
(c) Forums
(d) Instant messaging

Choose the correct option

(A) (a) and (c) (B) (b) and (d)
(C) (b) and (c) (D) (a) and (d)

*Ans.* *(C)* In telecommunications, asynchronous communication is transmission of data, generally without the use of an external clock signal, where data can be transmitted intermittently rather than in a steady stream.

Any timing required to recover data from the communication symbols is encoded within the symbols. An asynchronous communication service or application does not require a constant bit rate. Examples are file transfer, email, forums and the World Wide Web.

**37** **In order to meet the demands of market economy and produce competent graduates, who can compete with their counterparts in international markets, the first and foremost change that needs to be introduced in the prevailing system of Indian higher education is related to:**

(A) Admission process
(B) Curriculum
(C) Educational technology
(D) Appointment of teachers

*Ans.* *(B)* In order to meet the new demands of market economy and produce competent graduates, who can compete with their counterparts in international markets, the first and foremost change that needs to be introduced in the prevailing system of Indian higher education is related to curriculum.

The curriculum is so designed to meet the professional demands of different companies and industries.

**38** **Which among the following is the flagship scheme of the Ministry of Skill Development and Entrepreneurship implemented by National Skills Development Corporation?**

(A) Robotics India
(B) Artificial Intelligence @ schools
(C) Make in India
(D) Pradhan Mantri Kaushal Vikas Yojana

*Ans.* *(D)* Pradhan Mantri Kaushal Vikas Yojana (PMKVY) is the flagship scheme of the Ministry of Skill Development and Entrepreneurship (MSDE) implemented by National Skill Development Corporation.

The objective of this Skill Certification Scheme is to enable a large number of Indian youths to take up industry-relevant skill training that will help them in securing a better livelihood.

**39** **Which of the following statement(s) is/are correct?**

**(a) For the sequence of integers represented in binary as 00111, 01001, 01011, P..... the next integer P would be represented as 01101.**

**(b) A byte is a binary number consisting of exactly 8 bits.**

Choose the correct option

(A) Only (a) (B) Only (b)
(C) Both (a) and (b) (D) Neither (a) nor (b)

*Ans.* (C) In binary number system,

00111 represents 7
01001 represents 9
01101 represents 11

So, the next term will be 13 because it is odd number series. In binary 13 respresents as 01101. A byte is a binary number which used for memory and it includes 8 bits.

So, statements (a) and (b) both are correct.

**40** **Biomass fuels have the potential to form a sustainable carbon-neutral energy source because they**

(A) Produce carbon dioxide on combustion as much as they consume when they grow.
(B) Produce less amount of carbon dioxide on combustion compared to the amount they use during their growth.
(C) Have carbon content same as fossil fuels.
(D) Do not produce hazardous emissions on combustion.

*Ans.* *(A)* Biomass fuels have the potential to form a sustainable carbon neutral energy source because they produce carbon dioxide in combustion as they consume when they grow.

**41** **Under Kyoto protocol, the parties in the second commitment period, have to reduce their greenhouse gas emissions with reference to 1990 levels by atleast**

(A) 10% (B) 12% (C) 15% (D) 18%

*Ans.* *(D)* Under Kyoto Protocol, the parties in the second commitment period have to reduce their Greenhouse gas emission with reference to 1990 levels by at least 18 percent.

The Kyoto Protocol is an international agreement linked to the United Nations Framework Convention on Climate Change (UNFCCC), which commits its parties by setting internationally binding emission reduction targets.

The first commitment period under the Kyoto Protocol was from 2008-2012 and the second commitment period is from January 2013 to December 2020.

**42** **In the age of four Vedas, students were admitted to the Vedic schools after performance of which ceremony, among the following?**

(A) Upanayana ceremony
(B) Utsarjana ceremony
(C) Satapatha brahmana
(D) Dhanurvidya ceremony

***Ans.*** *(A)* Upanayana is one of the traditional sanskaras or rites of passage that marked the acceptance of a student by a guru or teacher and an individual's entrance to a school in Hinduism.

The tradition is widely discussed in ancient Sanskrit texts of India and varies regionally. The sacred thread or janeu is received by the boy during this ceremony, that he continues wearing across his chest thereafter.
Generally, this ceremony should be done before the age of 12.

**43** **Select the option that includes file formats suitable for distributing sound files across the Internet.**

(A) wmv, mp4, wma, mp3
(B) avi, midi, wav, mp3
(C) avi, mov, wmv, mp3
(D) midi, wav, wma, mp3

***Ans.*** *(D)* **MIDI** stands for Musical Instrument Digital Interface. It is a technical standard that describes a communications protocol, digital interface and electrical connectors that connect a wide variety of electronic musical instruments, computers and related audio devices for playing, editing and recording music.

**WAV** stands for Waveform Audio File Format. It is an audio file format standard, developed by Microsoft and IBM, for storing an audio bitstream on PCs.

**WMA** stands for Windows Media Audio. It is a series of Audio codes and their corresponding audio coding formats developed by Microsoft.

**MP3** is a coding format for digital audio. All these include file formats suitable for distributing sound files across the internet.

**44** **Match the following study skills with their effective learning techniques :**

| | Study skills | | Learning techniques |
|---|---|---|---|
| A. | Elaborative interrogation | 1. | Mixing different kinds of problems together when studying |
| B. | Practice testing | 2. | Explaining what a section of text or an example problem means to you |
| C. | Self-Explanation | 3. | Testing yourself on the material you are trying to learn |
| D. | Interleaved practice | 4. | Answering why a fact is true |

Choose the correct option

| | A | B | C | D |
|---|---|---|---|---|
| (A) | 4 | 3 | 2 | 1 |
| (B) | 1 | 2 | 4 | 3 |
| (C) | 2 | 4 | 1 | 3 |
| (D) | 3 | 1 | 2 | 4 |

***Ans.*** *(A)* **Elaborative interrogation** is a strategy within this broad idea which involves asking 'how' and 'why' questions and finding those answers.

In **Practice testing students** are involved to test themselves on the basis of the materials provided them by a teacher.
By this material they test their learning and knowledge.

**Self explanation** is a learning strategy. Self explanation is the practice of thinking out loud. A person talks to him/herself as s/he works on a problem, in order to force a conscious awareness of the process his/her mind is going through.

**Interleaving** is a process where students mix or interleave, multiple subjects or topics while they study in order to improve their learning.

**45** **Which of the following is/are major issues arising out of the growing reliance on information technology?**

(a) Profitability (b) Security threats
(c) Privacy concerns

Choose the correct option:

(A) (a) and (b) (B) (a) and (c)
(C) (b) and (c) (D) (a), (b) and (c)

*Ans.* *(C)* The major issues arising out of the growing reliance on information technology are privacy concerns and security threats. These are the major challenges which give rise to cybercrimes.

Profitability is not a major issue as compared to security threats and privacy concerns. As profitability impacts a company to attract its investors for funding purposes.

**Directions** (Q. Nos. 46-50) *Read the following passage and answer the questions that follow.*

Anyone who has ever been in a classroom where the teacher's presentation was lifeless, static and without vocal variety can appreciate the commonsense value of the affective side of teaching. However, unlike the other behaviours, affect cannot be captured in transcripts of teaching or by classroom interaction instruments. Narrowly focussed research instruments otten miss a teacher's affective nature, which emerges from a more holistic view of the classroom. This affective nature is the foundation on which one can build a warm and nurturing relationship with his or her learness. What the instruments miss, the students see clearly. Students are good perceivers of the emotions and intentions underlying a teacher's actions and they often respond accordingly.

A teacher who is excited about the subject being taught and shows it by facial expressions, voice inflection, gesture and movement- thus communicating respect and caring for the learner- is more likely to hold the attention of students and motivate them to higher levels of achievement than one who does not exhibit these behaviours. Students take their cues from these affective signs and lower or heighten their engagement with the lesson accordingly. Enthusiasm is an important aspect of a teacher's affect. Enthusiasm is the teacher's vigour, power involvement excitement and interest during a classroom presentation and willingness to share this emotion with learners, who will want to respond in kind.

**46** The affective nature of teaching is reflected in

(A) Deeper understanding of the classroom environment
(B) Other behaviours of the teacher
(C) The recording of classroom interaction
(D) The limited reliance on research instruments

*Ans.* *(A)* The affective nature of teaching is reflected in deeper understanding of classroom environment.

**47** When does one feel the need for the value of affective aspects of teaching?

(A) When a teacher has a vocal variety
(B) When a teacher makes a dynamic presentation
(C) When a teacher's presentation is monotonous
(D) When a teacher's lecture is beyond expectation

*Ans.* *(C)* One feels the need for value of affective aspects of teaching when a teacher's presentation is monotonous.

**48** The passage focusses attention on

(A) Lifeless classroom presentation
(B) Affective factors of teaching
(C) Students as emotional learners
(D) Measuring teacher's affective nature

*Ans.* *(B)* The passage focuses attention on affective factors of teaching.

**49** The affective signs will provide students

(A) The basis for understanding contents
(B) Exhibitional behaviours
(C) Cues to hold attention
(D) A basis which triggers further enthusiasm

*Ans.* *(D)* The affective signs will provide students a basis which triggers further enthusiasm.

**50** Students respect a teacher who

(A) is emotional
(B) displays concern for students
(C) has a powerful voice
(D) has narcissitic attitude

*Ans.* *(B)* Students respect a teacher who displays concern for students. This is the very essential trait of an effective teacher.

# UGC
## NET/JRF/SET

# Solved Paper, December 2019

(Exam Date : 5/12/2019, Shift-II)

## General Paper 1 (Teaching Aptitude and Attitude)

### *Instructions*

- This paper contains fifty Multiple-Choice Questions, each question carries two marks.
- All questions are compulsory.
- Total time given for this paper is 1 hour.

**Directions** (Q. Nos. 1-5) *The following table presents the data on the number of vehicles of three different types (A, B and C) produced by a company during seven different years from 2012 to 2018. Based on the data in the table, answer the given questions.*

**Year-wise production of three types of vehicles**

| Year \ Vehicle | A-Type | B-Type | C-Type |
|---|---|---|---|
| 2012 | 5000 | 20000 | 15000 |
| 2013 | 15000 | 10000 | 22500 |
| 2014 | 10000 | 15000 | 30000 |
| 2015 | 17500 | 15000 | 23000 |
| 2016 | 25000 | 20000 | 15000 |
| 2017 | 13000 | 25000 | 20000 |
| 2018 | 30000 | 35000 | 25000 |

**1** In how many year was the production of A-type vehicles less than its average production over the given years?

(A) 2 (B) 4 (C) 3 (D) 1

***Ans.*** *(B)* Average production of A-type vehicles

$$= \frac{(5 + 15 + 10 + 17.5 + 25 + 13 + 30) \times 1000}{7}$$

$$= \frac{115500}{7} = 16500$$

$\therefore$ In 4 years, they are 2012, 2013, 2014, 2017, production of A-type vehicles less than its average production over the given years.

**2** In which of the following years was the total production of all the three types of vehicles 60000?

(A) 2013 (B) 2014
(C) 2015 (D) 2016

***Ans.*** *(D)* Total production of all three types in 2016.

$$= 25000 + 20000 + 15000 = 60000$$

**3** What was the average number of B-type vehicles produced by the company over the years?

(A) 20000 (B) 25000
(C) 15000 (D) 30000

***Ans.*** *(A)* Average number of B-type vehicles production

$$= \frac{(20 + 10 + 15 + 15 + 20 + 25 + 35) \times 1000}{7}$$

$$= \frac{140 \times 1000}{7} = 20000$$

**4** What was the average of all the three types vehicles produced by the company in the year 2012.

(A) 13333 (B) 13500
(C) 10500 (D) 11000

***Ans.*** *(A)* Required average

$$= \frac{5000 + 20000 + 15000}{3}$$

$$= \frac{40000}{3} \approx 13333$$

**5** The number of A-type vehicles produced in the year 2014 was what percent (%) of the number of C-type vehicles produced in the year 2016?

(A) ~ 33.33% (B) ~ 66.67%
(C) 50% (D) 15%

***Ans.*** *(B)* Required percentage

$$= \frac{10000}{15000} \times 100 \sim 66.67\%$$

**6** Which one of the following propositions is a contrary to "All poets are dreamers"?

(A) Some poets are dreamers
(B) Some poets are not dreamers
(C) No poets are dreamers
(D) No dreamers are poets

***Ans.*** *(C)* "No poets are dreamers" is a contrary to "All poets are dreamers".

**7** Which of the following was not a Millennium Development Goal (MDG)?

(A) Eradicate extreme poverty and hunger.
(B) Improve maternal health.
(C) Ensure healthy lives and promote well-being for all at all ages.
(D) Ensure environmental sustainability.

***Ans.*** *(C)* The United Nations Millennium Development Goals (MDG) are eight goals that all 191 UN member states have agreed to try to achieve by the year 2015.

The United Nations Millennium Declaration, signed in September 2000 commits world leaders to combat poverty, hunger, disease, illiteracy, environmental degradation and discrimination against women.

The Eight Millennium Development Goals are as follows :

- Eradicate extreme poverty and hunger;
- Achieve universal primary education;
- Promote gender equality and empower women;
- Reduce child mortality;
- Improve maternal health;
- Combat HIV/ AIDS, malaria and other diseases;
- Ensure environmental sustainability; and
- Develop a global partnership for development.

So ensure healthy lives and promote well-being for all at all ages is not a MDG. Hence, option (C) is right answer.

**8** Given below are two statements - one is labelled as Assertion (A) and the other is labelled as Reason (R).

**Assertion** (A) Skill development is a key feature in every individual's life.

**Reason** (R) An individual who wants to get employed, needs to possess good education only.

In the context of above two statements, choose the correct option.

(A) Both (A) and (R) are true and (R) is the correct explanation of (A)
(B) Both (A) and (R) are true, but (R) is not the correct explanation of (A)
(C) (A) is true, but (R) is false
(D) (A) is false, but (R) is true

***Ans.*** *(C)* Skill development refers to the identification of skill gaps and developing the existing skills to enable a person to achieve his/her goals. Skills play a very important role in every individual's life whether it is educational, professional or personal.

If a person wants to be successful she/he has to be accomplished in different spheres of life such as educational, personal, skill development techniques and so on.

Therefore, we can say that skill development is not only based on one sphere as mentioned in the reason statement. Hence, Assertion is true, but its Reason is false.

**9** **Arrange the steps of research in the sequence in which they are presented in the thesis.**

(A) Discussion, Review of Literature, Results, Conceptual, Framework, Problem
(B) Review of Literature, Problem, Conceptual Framework, Result, Discussion
(C) Problem, Review of Literature, Conceptual Framework, Results, Discussion
(D) Problem, Review of Literature, Conceptual Framework, Discussion, Results

***Ans.*** *(C)* Research is defined as careful consideration of study regarding a particular concern or a problem using scientific methods.

In other words, research is a process of systematic inquiry that entails collection of data; documentation of critical information and analysis and interpretation of that data/information, in accordance with suitable methodologies set by specific professional fields and academic disciplines.

The steps of research in which a thesis is presented are as follows :

(i) Selection of a Problem
(ii) Review of Literature
(iii) Conceptual Framework
(iv) Results
(v) Discussion

**10** **Given below are two statements - one is labelled as Assertion (A) and the other is labelled as Reason (R).**

**Assertion** (A) Government of India established higher educational statutory bodies to ensure quality of education.

**Reason** (R) There are some educational institutions in India which do not provide quality education.

In the context of above two statements, choose the correct option.

(A) Both (A) and (R) are true and (R) is the correct explanation of (A)
(B) Both (A) and (R) are true, but (R) is not the correct explanation of (A)
(C) (A) is true, but (R) is false
(D) (A) is false, but (R) is true

***Ans.*** *(A)* After independence in 1947, the Government of India has recognised and considered education as one of the most important and foremost aspects for building a modern, educated and highly civilised and progressive society based on high virtues.

In order to achieve this aim, the Indian Government has established a number of Higher Educational Statutory Bodies to ensure quality of education.

Some of the important among these are University Grants Commission (UGC), National Testing Agency (NTA), All India Council for Technical Education (AICTE), Council of Architecture (COA), Central Board for Secondary Education (CBSE),and so on.

Hence Assertion and Reason both are true.

**11** **By selling 70 pencils for ₹ 90- a person makes a loss of 25%. How many pencils should be sold for ₹ 234 to have a profit of 30%?**

(A) 95 (B) 100
(C) 105 (D) 110

***Ans.*** *(C)* Let the required number of pencils be $x$.

S.P as 70 Pencils = ₹ 90

S.P as 1 Pencil = ₹ $\frac{90}{70}$

C.P of 1 Pencil = ₹ $\frac{\frac{90}{70} \times 100}{75}$

New S.P as Pencil after 30% profit

$$= \frac{\frac{90}{70} \times 100}{75} \times \frac{130}{100}$$

According to the question,

$$\frac{\left(\frac{90}{70}\right) \times 130 \times x}{75} = 234 \Rightarrow \frac{9 \times 130 \times x}{7 \times 75} = 234$$

$$\Rightarrow \quad x = \frac{234 \times 7 \times 75}{9 \times 130} = 105$$

**12** **Which among the following is not the outcome of grounded theory research?**

(A) Concepts (B) Narrative
(C) Categories (D) Hypothesis

***Ans.*** *(B)* Grounded theory is a research method concerned with the generation of theory, which is 'grounded' in data that has been systematically collected and analysed.

It was developed in California, USA by Glaser and Strauss during their study 'Awareness of Dying'. It is used to uncover such things as social relationships and behaviours of groups, known as 'social processes'.

It is a general methodology for developing theory that is grounded in data which is systematically gathered and analysed. After conducting research one can create concepts, categories on the basis of generating hypothesis.

Thus, option 2 is correct.

**13** Which given of the following sets of letters when sequentially placed at the gaps in the latter series below shall complete it?

bb_ b_ ab _ cbba _ bcbb _

(A) a c b a c (B) a c b b b
(C) c b b b a (D) a b b b c

*Ans.* *(C)* Pattern of the given series is

b b c / b b a/b b c / b b a / b b c / b b a

**14** Which among the following is NOT a component of effective teaching?

(A) Questioning to check for the understanding of students
(B) Providing students with feedback
(C) Being flexible about how long it takes to learn
(D) Reactive mode of student's behaviour

*Ans.* *(D)* Effective teachers are valued by students, parents and society. They are highly regarded because being an effective teacher takes a special set of skills that engages students and inspires them to work harder. Such teachers need different components which make teaching very effective.

These components are :

- Planning
- Meet objectives of the curriculum/syllabus
- Show mastery of subject area
- Design pedagogically sound lessons
  - stated objectives
  - modeled activities
  - guided practice
  - checks for understanding
  - feedback/evaluation
- Review/closure
- Use methodology appropriate for class
- Provide balance of teacher/student talk
- Be flexible with students about how long they take to learn

Thus, option (D) is correct because reactive approaches tend not to be effective. By 'reactive' we many any approach that focuses on action after an incident. All difficult incidents require some degree of negotiation.

**15** Which one of the following is signified by Udaharana of Anumana (Inference) in India Logic?

(A) Statement of reason
(B) Proposition to be proved
(C) Conclusion proved
(D) Universal propositional along with an instance

*Ans.* *(D)* Universal proposition along with an instance is signified by Udaharana of Anumana (Inference) in India logic. Anumana is Indian philosophy, the second of the pramanas, or the five means of knowledge, inference occupies a central place in the Hindu school of logic (Nyaya).

**16** Identify the factors that do not contribute to the effectiveness of teaching from the options given below

(a) Socio - economic background of teacher
(b) Teacher's skill in pleasing the students
(c) Teacher's subject knowledge
(d) Teacher's personal contact with students

Choose the correct option

(A) (a), (c) and (d)
(B) (b), (c) and (d)
(C) (a), (b) and (c)
(D) (a), (b) and (d)

*Ans.* *(D)* The effective teaching is based on the knowledge, expertise and positive attitude of teachers and environment of teaching and learning.

Teachers' knowledge is the very important factor which affect the effectiveness of teaching learning of students.

Thus, option 4 is correct.

**17** Which of the following statements are true about a fuel cell?

(a) It is a device that uses electrochemical reactions to produce electric current.
(b) It consists of a positive electrode and a negative electrode separated by an electrolyte.
(c) Just like batteries it needs to be recharged with an electric current.

Choose the correct option from those given below

(A) (a) and (b) (B) (b) and (c)
(C) (a) and (c) (D) (a) (b) and (c)

***Ans.*** *(A)* A fuel cell is a device that converts chemical potential energy (energy stored in molecular bonds) into electrical energy. It consists of a positive electrode and a negative electrode separated by an electrode.

Hence, statements (a) and (b) are right.

**18** Which of the two statements from the following statements are correct?

(a) Sampling related error is subsumed under the category non-sampling error.
(b) Sampling error doesn't occur in multi-stage cluster sampling.
(c) Inaccurate sampling frame and non-response are examples of sampling-related error.
(d) There is an inverse relation between heterogeneity of population and sampling error.

Choose the correct option

(A) (a) and (c) (B) (a) and (d)
(C) (b) and (d) (D) (b) and (c)

***Ans.*** *(A)* Sampling is a process used in statistical analysis in which a predetermined number of observations are taken from a larger population.

The methodology used to sample from a larger population depends on the type of analysis being performed, but it may include simple random sampling or systematic sampling.

Survey results are typically subject to some error. Total errors can be classified into sampling errors and non-sampling errors. Sampling related error is subsumed under the category non- sampling error.

Inaccurate sampling frame and non-response are examples of sampling related errors.

Thus, both (a) and (c) statements are correct about sampling.

**19** In what ratio must a vendor mix two varieties of sugar work ₹ 60 per kg and ₹ 78 per kg so that by selling the mixture at ₹ 76.8 per kg, the vendor gains 20%?

(A) 7 : 4 (B) 7 : 2
(C) 5 : 3 (D) 5 : 2

***Ans.*** *(B)* Cost price of mixture $= \dfrac{76.8 \times 100}{120}$

$= ₹$ 64 per kg

According to the question,

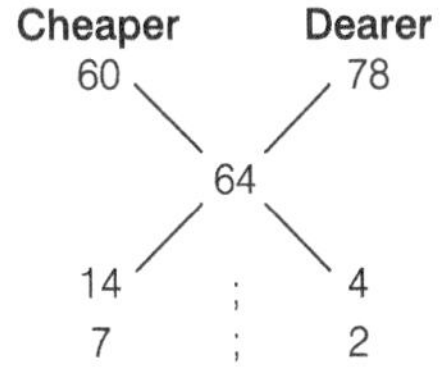


∴ Required ratio will be 7 : 2.

**20** Given below is a question followed by three statements. Identify the statements that are necessary to answer the question.

**Question** What is the percentage profit gained by a vendor when he sells an article?

**Statements**

(a) He gives a 10% discount on the marked price.
(b) He would have earned 25% profit if he did not give any discount.
(c) The cost price of the article is ₹ 8000

Choose the correct option from these given below

(A) (a) and (b) (B) (b) and (c)
(C) (a) and (c) (D) (a), (b) and (c)

***Ans.*** *(A)* Let the cost price of an article be $x$.

Marked price from statement (b) = $1.25x$

If he gives 10% discount from statements (a), selling price of the article

$$= 1.25x \times \frac{90}{100} = 1.125\,x.$$

∴ Required profit percent

$$= \frac{(1.25x - 1.125x)}{1.25x} \times 100 = 10\%$$

Therefore, statements (a) and (b) are required.

**21** Devdatta is fat and he does not eat during the day. Therefore, Devadatta is eating during the night.

The **above** example, in classical Indian School of Logic is a case of

(A) Comparison
(B) Implication
(C) Perception
(D) Verbal Testimony

*Ans.* *(B)* Devdatta is fat and he does not eat during the day. Therefore, Devdatta is eating during the night. In this argument the inference is clearly implied, therefore the above example is implication in the classical Indian School of Logic.

**22** Given below are two statements - one is labelled as Assertion (A) and the other is labelled as Reason (R).

**Assertion** (A) A blog is a form of social media.

**Reason** (R) A blog allows anyone to communicate to a public audience.

In the light of the above two statements, choose the correct option.

(A) Both (A) and (R) are true and (R) is the correct explanation of (A)
(B) Both (A) and (R) are true, but (R) is not the correct explanation of (A)
(C) (A) is true, but (R) is false
(D) (A) is false, but (R) is true

*Ans.* *(A)* A blog is a discussion and informational website published on the World Wide Web. It consists of discrete, often informal diary-style text entries or posts. Blog is a form of social media. It allows anyone to communicate to a public audience.

Hence, Assertion and Reason both are complimentary to each other so option (A) is right answer.

**23** Select the advantage of feedback in the process of communication, from the following

(A) It is beneficial in understanding of the subject matter
(B) It diagnosis the defects in receiver
(C) It clarifies the communication
(D) It explores the defects in receiver

*Ans.* *(C)* Communication is a process of creating and sharing ideas, information, views, facts, feelings, etc. among the people to reach a common understanding.

It is a continuous process which mainly involves three elements i.e. sender, message and receiver.

If a person understands what is being said, she/he gives immediate feedback which reflects his/her understanding.

So, the advantage of feedback in the process of communication is option (C).

**24** Choose two factors that do NOT affect the academic performance of students adversely

(a) Low self - efficacy belief
(b) Belief in God
(c) Indifferent attitude towards politics
(d) Teacher's low expectation from students

Choose the correct option

(A) (a) and (b) (B) (b) and (c)
(C) (c) and (d) (D) (b) and (d)

*Ans.* *(B)* Academic performance of students greatly depends on their self-efficacy, dedication, understanding, home- environment, parents' and teacher's attitudes and expectation from students and so on.

Thus, option 2 is correct.

**25** Match List - I with List II

| | List I (Digital Initative) | List II (Purpose) |
|---|---|---|
| A. | UMANG | (i) G2B Services |
| B. | BHIM | (ii) Learning platform |
| C. | eBiz | (iii) Unified Payment Interface |
| D. | SWAYAM | (iv) Single point of access to all government services |

Choose the correct option

| | A | B | C | D |
|---|---|---|---|---|
| (A) | (ii) | (i) | (iii) | (iv) |
| (B) | (iii) | (ii) | (iv) | (i) |
| (C) | (iv) | (iii) | (i) | (ii) |
| (D) | (i) | (iv) | (ii) | (iii) |

*Ans.* *(C)*

- **UMANG** stands for United Mobile Application for New-Age Government. It is envisaged to make a governance. It is a single point of access to all government services.
- **BHIM** (Bharat Interface for Money) is a mobile payment App developed by the National Payments Corporation of India (NPCI) based on the Unified Payments Interface (UPI).
- **eBiz** is being implemented by Infosys Technologies Limited under the guidance and aegis of Department of Industrial Policy and Promotion (DIPP), Ministry of Commerce and Industry, Government of India.

The focus of eBiz is to improve the business environment in the country by enabling fast and efficient access to Government-to-Business (G2B) services through an online portal.

- **SWAYAM** stands for Study Webs of Active Learning for Young Aspiring Minds. SWAYAM is the free online education which was developed by MHRD, Government of India and AICTE with the help of Microsoft. Thus, option (C) is correct.

**26** Which among the following is NOT related to qualitative research?

(A) Thematic analysis
(B) Case study
(C) Discourse analysis
(D) Survey method

*Ans.* *(D)*

- **Qualitative research** is a scientific method of observation to gather non-numerical data. This type of research refers to the meanings, concepts, definitions, characteristics, metaphors, symbols and description of things. This research seeks in-depth understanding of social phenomena within their natural setting. Thematic analysis, case study and discourse analysis are related to this type of research.
- **Thematic analysis** is one of the most common forms of analysis within qualitative research. It emphasised identifying, analysing and interpreting patterns of meaning within qualitative data.
- **A case-study** is a research strategy and an empirical inquiry that investigates a phenomenon within its real-life context.
- **Discourse analysis** is the study of social life, understood through analysis of language in its widest sense.

**27** Regarding E-governance, which of the following statements is/are correct?

(a) Decreasing transparency is an ICT enabled advantage of E-Governance.
(b) E-governance is related to the implementation of ICT in the government processes and functions.
(c) Common Service Centres (CSCs) help in providing and using E-Governance related services.

Choose the correct option

(A) (a), (b) and (c)
(B) (b) and (c)
(C) (a) and (c)
(D) (a) and (b)

*Ans.* *(B)* E-Governance can be defined as the application of Information Technology and Communication (ICT) for providing government services, exchange of information, transactions, integration of previously existing services and information portals. It makes the whole administrative process convenient, efficient, transparent, fully accountable and responsible.

Some effective examples of successful implementation of E-Governance to the governmental function include projects like; e-Mitra project (Rajasthan), e-Seva project (Andhra Pradesh), CET (Common Entrance Test).

Common Service Centres (CSCs) scheme is one of the mission mode projects under the Digital India Programme. These are the access points for delivery of essential public utility services, social welfare schemes, healthcare, financial, education and agriculture services, apart from host of B2C services to citizens in rural and remote areas of the country.

Hence, option (B) is right answer.

**28** In Social Sciences, a central issue is the question of whether the social world can be studied using the methods of natural sciences. This statement refers to the issue of

(A) Ontology
(B) Axiology
(C) Epistemology
(D) Etymology

*Ans.* *(C)* Epistemology is the branch of philosophy concerned with the theory of knowledge. Epistemology is the study of the nature of knowledge, justification and the rationality of belief.

Much debate in epistemology centers on four areas :

- The philosophical analysis of the nature of knowledge and how it relates to such concepts as truth, belief and justification,
- Various problems of skepticism,
- The sources and scope of knowledge and justified belief and
- The criteria for knowledge and justification.

Epistemology addresses such questions e.g. "What makes justified beliefs justified?", "What does it mean to say that we know something?" and fundamentally "How do we know that we know?"

In the same way, Epistemology also addresses that in social sciences, a central issue is the question of whether the social world can be studied using the methods of natural sciences.

- **Ontology** is the branch of metaphysics dealing with the nature of being.
- **Axiology** refers to the study of the nature of value and valuation, and of the kinds of things that are valuable.
- **Etymology** refers to the study of the origin of words and the way in which their meanings have changed throughout history.

**29** Given below are two statements, one is labelled as Assertion (A) and the other is labelled as Reason (R).

**Assertion** (A) Through on-line teaching a large number of students can be taught by very competent faculty.

**Reason** (R) On-line teaching helps students in developing critical thinking more than the off-line teaching can do.

In the light of the above two statements choose the correct option

(A) Both (A) and (R) are true and (R) is the correct explanation of (A)
(B) Both (A) and (R) are true, but (R) is not the correct explanation of (A)
(C) (A) is true, but (R) is false
(D) (A) is false, but (R) is true

*Ans.* *(C)* Due to new inventions in this modern time, a number of options are now available to save both money and time of people. It has now become possible for everyone to work as well as study simultaneously.

This credit goes to the many online courses and online teaching portals where a number of experts and courses are available just a click away.

But this type of teaching does not provide direct interaction of students and teachers. Also it does not develop any critical thinking in people as can be seen in the classroom teaching and learning.

Hence, Assertion is true but its Reason is not appropriate so option (C) is right answer.

**30** Select the alternative features from the following, which make open universities as non-traditional universities :

(a) Innovative method of teaching and learning.
(b) Innovative method of admission, curriculum and evaluation.
(c) Modern communication techniques.
(d) Teacher's friendly approaches.

Select the correct option:

(A) (b), (c) and (d) (B) (a), (b) and (c)
(C) (a), (c) and (d) (D) (a), (b) and (d)

*Ans.* *(B)* Open universities are non-traditional universities. These universities provide education through open-door academic policy.

These universities follow a system of education wherein admission is granted to the candidates on basis of minimum education and previous academic record, experience or references are not mandatory.

These universities do not follow traditional classroom teaching and learning and admission process but use innovative method of admission, curriculum and evaluation.

They mostly use Information and Communication Technology.

Thus, option (a), (b) and (c) are the alternative features from the following which make open universities as non- traditional universities.

**31** Match the following values with their distinguishing functions

| List I | List II |
|---|---|
| A. Sacrifice | (i) Working in a stipulated time |
| B. Sincerity | (ii) Confinement of individual mind on action |
| C. Self control | (iii) Showing love and affection |
| D. Altruism | (iv) Helping without selfish motives |

Choose the correct option from those given below :

| | A | B | C | D |
|---|---|---|---|---|
| (A) | (ii) | (i) | (iv) | (iii) |
| (B) | (iv) | (i) | (ii) | (iii) |
| (C) | (iii) | (iv) | (i) | (ii) |
| (D) | (i) | (iii) | (ii) | (iv) |

*Ans.* *(B)* The idea and practice of **sacrifice** play a profound role in different spheres of life whether it is religion, ethics and politics. Sacrifice is helping someone without selfish motives.

**Sincerity** is the virtue of one who communicates and acts in accordance with their feelings, beliefs, thoughts and desires. It is related to a person who shows sincerity in his/her work by completing it in a stipulated time.

**Self-control** is an aspect of inhibitory control. It is the ability to regulate one's emotions, thoughts and behaviour in the face of temptations and impulses. Self control is the confinement of individual mind on action.

**Altruism** is an ethical doctrine. It holds the moral value of an individual's actions depend solely on the impact on other individuals, regardless of the consequences on the individual itself. A person who has this shows love and affection with other individuals.

**32** Match the following soil orders with their descriptions

| List I | List II |
|---|---|
| A. Histosols | (i) Soil order that includes soils formed on volcanic ash. |
| B. Andisols | (ii) Soil order of cold regions including soils underlain by permafrost. |
| C. Gelisols | (iii) Soil order consisting of soils of dry climates. |
| D. Aridsols | (iv) Soil order consisting of soils with a thick upper layer of organic matter. |

Choose the correct option from those given below:

| | A | B | C | D |
|---|---|---|---|---|
| (A) | (iv) | (i) | (ii) | (iii) |
| (B) | (ii) | (iv) | (i) | (iii) |
| (C) | (i) | (ii) | (iii) | (iv) |
| (D) | (i) | (ii) | (iv) | (iii) |

*Ans.* *(A)* To identify, understand and manage soils, soil scientists have developed a soil classification or taxonomy system.

There are 12 soil orders:

- **Alfisols** Alfisols are moderately leached soils that have relatively high native fertility.
- **Andisols** Andisols are soils that have formed in volcanic ash or other volcanic ejecta.
- **Aridisols** Aridisols are calcium carbonate-containing soils of arid regions that exhibit at least some subsurface horizon development.
- **Entisols** Entisols are soils of recent origin.
- **Gelisols** Gelisols are soils of very cold climates that contain permafrost within 2 meters of the surface.
- **Histosols** Histosols are soils that are composed mainly of organic materials.
- **Inceptisols** Inceptisols are soils that exhibit minimal horizon development.
- **Mollisols** Mollisols are the soils of grassland ecosystems.
- **Oxisols** Oxisols are very highly weathered soils that are found primarily in the intertropical regions of the world.
- **Spodosols** Spodosols are acid soils characterised by a subsurface accumulation of humus that is complexed with AI and Fe.
- **Ultisols** Ultisols are strongly leached and acidic forest soils with relatively low fertility.
- **Vertisols** Vertisols are clay-rich soils that shrink and swell with changes in moisture content.

**33** As per the classical square of opposition, if 'A' proposition is given as true, then which one of the following is correct?

(A) "E" proposition is false, 'I' proposition is true and "O" proposition is false

(B) "E" proposition is true, "I" proposition is true and "O" proposition is true

(C) "E" proposition is false, "I" proposition is false and "O" proposition is true

(D) "E" proposition is true, "I" proposition is false and "O" proposition is false

*Ans.* *(A)* According to classical square of opposition, if 'A' proposition is given as true, then "E" proposition is false, "I" proposition is true and "O" proposition is false.

**34** Which of the following statements is/are correct?

(a) Software is loaded into secondary from RAM and is then execute by the CPU.

(b) A search engine is a software system that is designed to search for information on the www.

Choose the correct option :

(A) only (a) (B) only (b)
(C) Both (a) and (b) (D) Neither (a) nor (b)

*Ans. (B)* A web search engine or Internet search engine is a software system. It is designed to carry out web search or Internet search, which means to search the World Wide Web in a systematic way for particular information specified in a textual web search query.

Popular examples of search engines are Google, Yahoo! and MSN search. Search Engines utilize automated software applications (referred to as robots, bots or spiders) that travel along the web, following links from page to page, site to site.

**35** Match the following historic places with their distinguishing discipline of learning

| List I (Historic places) | List II (Discipline) |
|---|---|
| A. Takshila | (i) Astronomy |
| B. Ujjain | (ii) Buddhism |
| C. Sarnath | (iii) Art, Architecture and Painting |
| D. Ajanta | (iv) Medicine |

Choose the correct option from those given below :

| | A | B | C | D |
|---|---|---|---|---|
| (A) | (i) | (ii) | (iii) | (iv) |
| (B) | (ii) | (i) | (iv) | (iii) |
| (C) | (iii) | (iv) | (ii) | (i) |
| (D) | (iv) | (i) | (ii) | (iii) |

*Ans. (D)* **Takshila** The world's oldest university was established at Takshila (Bihar). It was flourished from 600 BC to 500 AD, in the kingdom of Gandhar.

A number of subjects were taught in this university some of these are vedas, languages, grammar, philosophy, medicine, surgery, archery, politics, warfare, astronomy, accounts, commerce and so on.

**Ujjain** Ujjain is an ancient city situated on the Eastern bank of the Kshipra River. It was the most prominent city on the Malwa plateau of central India.

It emerged as the political centre of central India around 600 BCE. It was prominent for astronomy for scholars.

**Sarnath** Sarnath is a place located North-East of Varanasi near the confluence of the Ganges and the Varuna rivers in Uttar Pradesh.

Sarnath is a famous place where Gautama Buddha first taught the Dharma and the Buddhist Sangha came into existence through the enlightenment of Kondanna.

**Ajanta** The Ajanta Caves are 30 (approximately) rock-cut Buddhist cave monuments which date from the 2nd century BCE to about 480 CE in Aurangabad district of Maharashtra. These caves are famous for art, architecture and paintings.

**36** Which of the following sequence represents the correct order of soil particles arranged in terms of particle size from the smallest to the largest?

(A) Gravel, Silt, Clay, Sand
(B) Silt, Clay, Gravel, Sand
(C) Clay, Silt, Sand, Gravel
(D) Silt, Clay, Sand, Gravel

*Ans. (C)* The upper layer of earth in which plants grow, a black or dark brown material typically consisting of a mixture of organic remains, clay, and rock particles is known as soil.

Soil is a mixture of organic matter, minerals, gases, liquids, and organisms that together support life. Soil texture consists of the particles that make up soil.

These are categorised into three groups by size i.e. clay, silt and sand. Sand particles are the largest and clay particles the smallest whereas silt is bigger than clay but smaller than sand.

**37** How many National Parks and Wildlife Sancturies were there in India till March 2011?

(A) 8 and 421 (B) 10 and 75
(C) 75 and 421 (D) 102 and 515

*Ans. (D)* Till March 2011, India had 102 National Parks and 515 Wildlife Sanctuaries. As per the National Wildlife Database, Wildlife Institute of India, there are 104 National Parks and 551 Wildlife Sanctuaries till May 2019.

**38** Consider the following statements with reference to the proposition "Some girls are not students".

(a) Subject term students is distributed.
(b) Predicate term girls is undistributed.
(c) Predicate term students is distributed.
(d) Subject term girls is undistributed.

Choose the correct option from those given below :

(A) (a) and (c) are correct
(B) (b) and (c) are correct
(C) (a) and (d) are correct
(D) (c) and (d) are correct

**Ans.** *(D)* "Some girls are not students". Here subject is "girls" and "students" is predicate.

Here predicate term "students" is distributed but subject term "Girls" is undistributed.

**39** Choose the person who has control over self, mode of communication and method of delivery in classroom from the following:

(A) Student (B) Teacher
(C) Audience (D) Visitor

**Ans.** *(B)* A teacher is a person who helps people to learn. A teacher often teaches in a classroom. During teaching- learning process, a teacher must have control over him/herself. He/She has the command over communication during teaching-learning process.

For effective teaching-learning, a teacher must use appropriate teaching aids, techniques and methods which should be age specific and based on the curriculum.

**40** Out of a total of 10 students, the average weight of 9 students is 60 kg. If the weight of the 10th student is 9 kg more than the average weight of all the 10 students, then the weight of the 10th student would be

(A) 61 kg (B) 69 kg (C) 70 kg (D) 71 kg

**Ans.** *(C)* Let the weight of the 10th student be $x$ kg.

According to the question,

$$\frac{60 \times 9 + x}{10} = (x - 9)$$

$$\Rightarrow \quad 540 + x = 10x - 90$$

$$\Rightarrow \quad 10x - x = 540 + 90$$

$$\Rightarrow \quad 9x = 630$$

$$\Rightarrow \quad x = \frac{630}{9} = 70 \text{ kg}$$

**41** Which of the following groups has the components of paralanguage communication?

(A) Voice, Emphasis and Impression
(B) Social Space, Voice and Impression
(C) Voice, Social Space and Expression
(D) Emphasis, Social Space and Voice

**Ans.** *(A)* Paralanguage refers to the non-verbal elements of communication used to modify meaning and convey emotion. Paralanguage may be expressed consciously or unconsciously and it includes the pitch, volume and in some cases, intonation of speech.

Sometimes the definition is restricted to vocally-produced sounds. The study of paralanguage is known as paralinguistics. The components of paralanguage communication are voice, emphasis and impression.

**42** Which among the following factors doesn't contribute to assessment bias?

(A) When language of the test and the tester is different from the languages of the students.
(B) Answers that support middle-class values.
(C) If assessment procedures are flexible and diverse to make disadvantaged students comfortable.
(D) Objective test for assessing abstract reasoning of the student.

**Ans.** *(C)* Assessment bias refers to qualities of an assessment instrument that unfairly penalize a group of students because of students' gender, race, ethnicity, socio-economic status, religion or other such group defining characteristics.

Assessment bias can be removed if teachers use fair test procedures which should be flexible and diverse to make disadvantaged students comfortable.

**43** Select the period in which India became a centre of higher learning?

(A) Gupta Period
(B) Buddha Period
(C) Mughal Period
(D) British Period

**Ans.** *(A)* The Gupta rulers encouraged higher learning by patronising centers of higher education at Nalanda, Takshila, Ujjain, Vikramshila and Vallabhi. Each university specialised in a particular field of study. Takshila specialised in the study of medicine, while Ujjain laid emphasis on astronomy.

Nalanda, being the biggest centre, handled all branches of knowledge. During the Gupta period India became a centre for higher studies by attracting scholars from all parts of India and from several foreign countries.

**44** Select the option that lists components for a cyberspace address (URL) in the correct order from beginning to end?

(A) Protocol, domain name of the host, path/file
(B) Path/file, protocol, domain name of the host
(C) Protocol, path/file, domain name of the host
(D) Domain name of the host, protocol, path/file

*Ans.* *(A)* Cyberspace is the global domain within the information environment consisting of the interdependent network of information technology infrastructures, including the Internet, telecommunications networks, computer systems, and embedded processors and controllers.

The components for a cyberspace address (URL) are protocol, domain name of the host, path/file.

**45** Match correctly the items of Column I with the items of Column II

| Column I | Column II |
|---|---|
| A. Ontology | (i) Ideographic |
| B. Epistemology | (ii) Realism |
| C. Methodolgy | (iii) Survey |
| D. Method | (iv) Positivism |

Choose the correct option :

| | A | B | C | D |
|---|---|---|---|---|
| (A) | (ii) | (iv) | (iii) | (i) |
| (B) | (ii) | (i) | (iii) | (iv) |
| (C) | (iv) | (ii) | (i) | (iii) |
| (D) | (ii) | (iv) | (i) | (iii) |

*Ans.* *(D)* **Ontology** is the philosophical study of being. It is related to realism. Broadly, ontology studies concepts that directly relate to being, in particular becoming, existence, reality, as well as the basic categories of being and their relations.

**Epistemology** is the study of the nature of knowledge, justification, and the rationality of belief. It is related to positivism.

**Methodology** is the systematic, theoretical analysis of the methods applied to a field of study. It comprises the theoretical analysis of the body of methods and principles associated with a branch of knowledge. Typically, it encompasses concepts such as paradigm, theoretical model, phases and quantitative or qualitative techniques.

It is associated with ideography.

**A method** means a pursuit of knowledge, investigation, mode of prosecuting such inquiry or system. In recent centuries it more often means a prescribed process for completing a task.

**Directions** (Q. Nos. 46-49) *Read the following passage and answer the questions that follow.*

Eventhough globalisation is one of the most discussed topics in the contemporary world. It is not altogether a well defined concept. A multitude of global interactions are put under the broad heading of globalisation.

Varying from the expansion of cultural and scientific influences across borders to the enlargement of economic and business relations throughout the world. A wholesale rejection of globalisation would not only go against global business.

It would also cut out movements of ideas, understanding and knowledge that can help all the people of the world, including the most disadvantaged members of the world population. A comprehensive rejection of globalisation can thus be powerfully counterproductive.

There is a strong need to separate out the different questions that appear merged together in the rhetoric of the antiglobalisation protests. The globalisation of knowledge deserves a particularly high profile recognition. Despite all the good things that can be rightly said about the importance of 'Local knowledge'.

Globalisation is often seen, both in journalistic discussions and in remarkably many academic writings, as a process of westernisation. Indeed, some who take an upbeat view of the phenomenon even sees it as a contribution of Western civilisation to the world.

**46** The attempt of the author in the passage is :

(A) Unconditioned advocacy of globalisation
(B) Unconditioned rejection of globalisation
(C) Unconditioned rejection of local knowledge systems
(D) Unbiased evaluation of globalisation

***Ans.*** *(D)* The attempt of the author in the given passage is unbiased evaluation of globalisation.

**47** **As per the passage, a wholesale rejection of globalisation would result in affecting**

(a) Global businesses
(b) Movement of Ideas
(c) Local knowledge systems

Choose the correct answer from the options given below

(A) (a) and (b) (B) (a) and (c)
(C) (c) and (b) (D) (a), (b) and (c)

***Ans.*** A wholesale rejection of globalisation would not only go against global business, it would also cut out movements of ideas, understanding and knowledge that can help all the people of the world, including the most disadvantaged members of the world population.

**48** **According to the passage, which one of the following is not a well defined concept?**

(A) Multiculturalism (B) Identity
(C) Globalisation (D) Local Knowledge

***Ans.*** *(C)* According to the passage, globalisation is one the most discussed topics in the contemporary world, but it is not altogether a well defined concept.

A multitude of global interactions are put under the broad heading of globalisation, varying from the expansion of cultural and scientific influences across borders to the enlargement of economic and business relations throughout the world.

**49** **According to the passage, which one of the following is counter productive?**

(A) Comprehensive support to globalisation
(B) Wholesale rejection of globalisation
(C) Comprehensive rejection of anti-globalisation protests
(D) Recognition of local knowledge systems

***Ans.*** *(B)* According to the given passage a comprehensive rejection of globalisation is the counterproductive.

**50** **According to the passage, what can be a comprehensive rejection of globalisation?**

(A) Powerfully counter productive
(B) Anti-globalisation
(C) Journalistic discussions
(D) Academic writings

***Ans.*** *(A)* A wholesale rejection of globalisation would not only go against global business, it would also cut out movements of idea, understanding and knowledge that can help all the people of the world.

With this fundamental thought, writer of this passage has a concept for comprehensive rejection of globalisation, which can thus be powerfully counter productive.

# UGC
## NET/JRF/SET

# Solved Paper, June 2019

### (Exam Date : 24/06/2019, Shift-II)

## General Paper 1 (Teaching Aptitude and Attitude)

***Instructions***

- This paper contains fifty Multiple-Choice Questions, each question carries two marks.
- All questions are compulsory.
- Total time given for this paper is 1 hour.

**1** Inclusive education implies

(A) Ensuring learning outcome of every child to be the same.

(B) Including the disabled in the main stream.

(C) Provides compulsory education for children below 14 years.

(D) Ensuring that no child is left behind in education.

***Ans.*** *(D)* Inclusive education implies that no child is left behind in education. It is about ensuring access to quality education for all students by effectively meeting their diverse needs in a way that is responsive, accepting, respectful and supportive.

Inclusive education is carried out in a common learning environment, that is, an educational setting where students from different backgrounds and with different abilities learn together in an inclusive environment. Here, students participate in the education programme through a common learning environment with support to diminish and remove barriers and obstacles that may lead to exclusion.

**2** The study of 'why does stressful living result in heart attack' can be classified as

(A) Descriptive research

(B) Explanatory research

(C) Correlational research

(D) Feasibility research

***Ans.*** *(B)* Explanatory research is conducted to explore the research questions which may or may not offer a final conclusion to the research conducted. It is conducted to handle new problem areas which have not been explored before. Exploratory research lays the foundation for more conclusive research and data collection.

So, in order to study why the heart attack occurs we must look forward towards explanatory research because the event has already been occurred.

**3** Listening is important for a teacher to

(A) Address the requirement of the learner

(B) Gain knowledge

(C) Keep the learner in good humour

(D) Evaluate the learner for the progress made

*Ans.* *(A)* Listening is the most important and key factor in teaching learning process because it is the most common medium through which we gain knowledge and even exchange ideas. Thus, in order to address the requirement of learner, the teacher must be an active listener.

He/she should listen attentively with an undivided attention.

**4** **During research, while recording observations if an observer rates an individual based on the rating given in another aspect of the interaction, this is termed as the**

(A) Evaluation effect
(B) Error of central tendency
(C) Halo effect
(D) Categorical effect

*Ans.* *(C)* Halo effect is a type of cognitive bias in which our overall impression of a person influences how we feel and think about his or her character. So, any kind of such research which record observation with respect to interaction is called Halo effect.

**5** **A hypothesis should be conceptually**

(A) Convoluted, complex and generic
(B) Complex, tough and general
(C) Simple, clear and specific
(D) Obscure, complicated and simple

*Ans.* *(C)* A Hypothesis is a precise, testable statement of what the researcher predict will be the outcome of the study. It is a tentative statement about relationship between two or more variables. A hypothesis is a statement that can be tested by Scientific research.

A hypothesis should be conceptually simple, clear and specific. All the concepts used in a hypothesis must be defined clearly.

**6** **Peer group interaction in a classroom helps in**

(A) Concept understanding
(B) Realisation of one's misunderstanding
(C) Rapport Building
(D) Questioning

*Ans.* *(A)* Having peer group interaction in class will make it more understandable for all to learn and group easily. It promotes active learning. This is because peer comprises of people of same age and belonging to same class.

So, if in a classroom we have a common interaction among the pupils, then we can broaden our knowledge and understanding about any of the given topic and subject matter to be studied.

**7** **The formulation of a research problem can be compared to**

(A) Laying the foundation of a building
(B) Building the walls of a home
(C) Polishing the doors of a building
(D) Constructing the ceiling of a house

*Ans.* *(A)* Research problem is said to be the foundation of the research thesis. It is important to make research problem concrete and explicit. There is no full proof method to be followed by the researcher in formulating significant questions about any research area in mind. But, there are certain working conditions which would help the researcher in formulating problem. Hence, the formulation of a research problem can be compared as 'laying the foundation of a building'.

Formulation of research problem is the first and most important step of research process.

**8** **Reflective practice implies use of one's**

(A) Cognition
(B) Metacognition
(C) Metacognition on cognition
(D) Reinforcement of learning

*Ans.* *(C)* Reflective practice is a method of assessing our own thoughts and actions for the purpose of personal learning and development. This practice implies the use of one's metacognition on cognition. Metacognition refers to one's awareness of and ability to regulate one's own thinking. It is often referred as 'thinking about thinking' or 'cognition of cognition'.

Learners often show an increase in self confidence when they build metacognitive skills. Metacognition allows person to take charge of their own learning.

**9** **When the learning outcomes of students are ensured with employment of less resources and effort on the part of a teacher and more initiative for self-learning is evident, which of the following expression will describe the teacher most appropriately?**

(A) Teacher is successful
(B) Teacher is effective
(C) Teacher is intelligent
(D) Teacher is practical

*Ans.* *(B)* A teacher is said to be effective when the learning outcomes of students are ensured with employment of less resources. A effective teacher also ensure that more initiative for self-learning is evident.

**10 Mailed questionnaire, observation, interview and collective questionnaire are instances of**

(A) Secondary sources (B) Personal sources
(C) Primary sources (D) Tertiary sources

*Ans.* *(C)* Primary resources in the research comprise of important and first hand data that includes mailed questionnaire, observation, interview and collective questionnaire. In primary sources we collect the data in raw format where things are just the collection and culmination of all the available data.

Primary source gives researcher direct access to the subject of his/her research topic.

**Directions** (Q. Nos. 11-20) *Read the following passage and answer the questions that follow.*

A business will usually go through a clear set of stages that will make up it organisational like cycle. These stages include introduction, early growth, continuous growth, maturity and decline. The first stage, the introduction stage, is the start-up phase where a business decides what its core strengths and capabilities are and starts selling its product or service. At this early stage, the founder or founders will be a part of every aspect of the daily process of the business. The main goal at this stage is to take off to a good start and make a place in the market.

The next stage, the early growth phase, aims at increased sales and more development. The focus at this stage remains on the original product or service but the effort is to increase the market share and venture into related products or services. The main goal is to move the founder to a more managerial role, so more time is spent on managing and building the business. At this stage, documents and policies need to be developed so any member of the organisation can see the business any time.

The third stage, the continuous growth stage, requires a systematic structure and more formal relationships among its participants. At this stage, the resource requirements of the business need careful handling. The focus is on the expansion of the business, keeping in mind its core strength and capability. A formal organisational structure and a clear delegation plan are important at this stage.

At the fourth stage of maturity, a business often slows down as the level of innovative energy may have become weak and the formal structures may have become obstacles. A lot of care is required to prevent decline.

**11 The slowing down of a business can happen if**

(A) there is a decline in the market share.
(B) the level of innovative energy weakens.
(C) the managerial roles are not clear.
(D) the level of investment declines.

*Ans.* *(B)* In the passage, it was mentioned in the fourth stage that any business will be slow down if the innovative level of energy is not upto the mark or weak. This will lead to the weakening and creating obstacle for the formal structure of the company. In such a case lot of care is taken so that one can prevent the decline in business.

**12 Venturing into related products and services does not mean that a business will**

(A) ignore the original product.
(B) move the founder to more managerial role.
(C) delegate more responsibilities.
(D) ignore the related products and services.

*Ans.* *(A)* In the stage of growth, the aim of any business is to expand the services and sales. For the expansion they tend to do ventures with other companies and their services but this doesn't mean that we get diverted from our original business and its services.

**13 The resource requirements of a business need careful handling at which stage?**

(A) Fourth (B) First
(C) Third (D) Second

*Ans.* *(C)* After the growth stage comes the third and the most crucial stage where we need to maintain continuous growth among the business. This stage requires more systematic structure and formal relationship among the participants. This requires careful handling of the resources. A formal organisational structure and a clear delegation plan are important in this stage.

**14 When will a business create its place in the market?**

(A) At maturity (B) At introduction
(C) At early growth (D) At late growth

***Ans.*** *(B)* Making place in the market need to be more strategic and said to be the introductory stage of any kind of business. The business must know about its strength and weakness and must be aware about the capabilities to make good place in the market. A good start will lead to good place in the market.

**15** The founder of a business does not move to a more managerial role at which stage?

(A) Early growth stage (B) Maturity stage
(C) Decline stage (D) Start up stage

***Ans.*** *(D)* Marginal roles comprise of looking for expansion, making partners, expanding product range etc. So at the introductory or start up level, founder is not concerned about these marginal roles rather they will be focusing more on their own business its strengths and capabilities and start selling its product or services.

**16** If the average of five numbers is – 20 and the sum of three of the numbers is 32, then what is the average of the other two numbers?

(A) – 66 (B) – 33
(C) – 34 (D) – 132

***Ans.*** *(A)* Average of 5 numbers = – 20

$$\text{Average} = \frac{\text{Total sum of numbers}}{\text{Total numbers}}$$

$\therefore$ Sum of 5 numbers $= -20 \times 5 = -100$

Sum of 3 numbers = 32

$\therefore$ Sum of 2 numbers $= -100 - 32$

$\therefore$ Average of 2 numbers $= -\frac{132}{2} = -66$

**17** Which of the following signifies non-verbal communication in an essential way?

(A) Instructions written on a question paper.
(B) Learner attending an online class.
(C) The dress code followed by an individual.
(D) Yoga instructor teaching yoga poses to the pupils.

***Ans.*** *(C)* In non-verbal communication, the sending or receiving of messages are done through the wordless messages. It means that communication is established other than oral or written. It is associated with the body language of the people. Non-verbal communication is the transfer of information through the use of body language includes eye contact, facial expression gestures and more. Among the given options 'the dress code followed by an individual' signifies non-verbal communication in an essential way.

**18** A trader mixes three varieties of refined oil costing ₹ 100, ₹ 40 and ₹ 60 per litre in the ratio 2 : 4 : 3 in terms of litre and sells the mixture at ₹ 66 per litre. What percentage of profit does he make?

(A) 12% (B) 10% (C) 9% (D) 8%

***Ans.*** *(B)* Cost Price (C.P) of 1 litre mixture

$$= \frac{2}{9} \times 100 + \frac{4}{9} \times 40 + \frac{3}{9} \times 60$$

$$= \frac{1}{9}(200 + 160 + 180) = \frac{1}{9} \times 540 = ₹\ 60$$

Selling Price (S.P) of 1 litre mixture = ₹ 66

$\therefore$ Profit = S.P – C.P = ₹ (66 – 60) = ₹ 6

$$\therefore \text{Profit\%} = \frac{\text{Profit}}{\text{C.P}} \times 100 = \frac{6}{60} \times 100 = 10\%.$$

**19** No Musicians are Japanese
All Barbers are Musicians
No Barbers are Japanese
*Identify the middle term in the above syllogism*

(A) Subject in the first premise and predicate in the second premise.
(B) Predicate in the first premise and subject in the second premise.
(C) Predicate in the both premises.
(D) Subject in both the premises.

***Ans.*** *(A)* According to question,

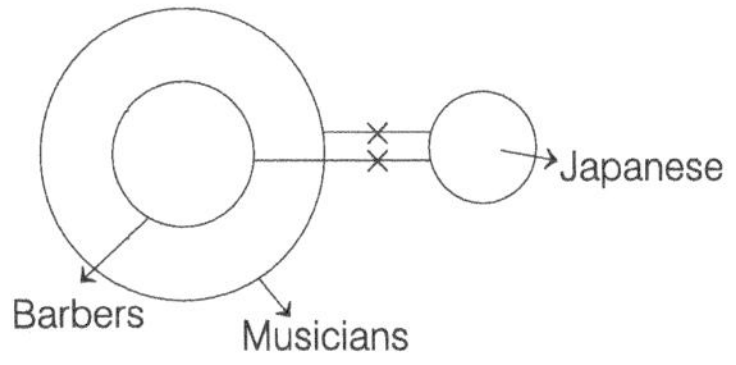


$\therefore$ Subject in the first premise and predicate in the second premise is the middle term.

**20** Inductive argument proceeds from

(A) Universal to Particular
(B) Particular to Universal
(C) Universal to Universal
(D) Particular to Particular

***Ans.*** *(B)* Inductive argument refers to the logical process, in which specific instances or particular situations are observed or analysed to establish general or universal principle.

Thus, inductive argument proceeds from particular to universal.

**21** **Assertion** (A) Communication presupposes a shared, symbolic environment, a social relationship even among non-participants.

**Reason** (R) It leads to social interaction, which in combination with other factors contributes to a sense of community.

*Choose the correct option given below*

(A) Both (A) and (R) are true and (R) is the correct explanation of (A).
(B) Both (A) and (R) are true but (R) is not the correct explanation of (A).
(C) (A) is true but (R) is false.
(D) (A) is false but (R) is true.

*Ans.* *(D)* Communication is an on-going process and it depends on the present environment in which one works. It is of many forms may be interpersonal, intrapersonal, group or mass communication. It is not presupposes shared and symbolic environment.

It is true to say that communication is a social interaction which in combination with other factors to contribute to the community.

Hence, Assertion (A) is false and Reason (R) is true.

**22** Consider the argument provided below. "Sound is permanent because it is a product like the jar".

*Identify the fallacy involved in the above argument on the basis of Indian logic from the options given below*

(A) Fallacy of contradictory reason
(B) Fallacy of wrong assertion
(C) Fallacy of irrelevant reason
(D) Fallacy of trivial reason

*Ans.* *(A)* Fallacy of contradictory reason works on the supposition that the proposition asserts and denies the same thing. This contradictory premises involve an argument that draws a conclusion from inconsistent or incompatible premises. The fallacy in the given argument is Fallacy of contradictory reason.

**23** Among the five friends, Vineet is taller than Monika, but not as tall as Ram. Jacob is taller than Dalip but shorter than Monika. Who is the tallest in their group?

(A) Ram (B) Monika (C) Vineet (D) Jacob

*Ans.* *(A)* According to the information given in the question the arrangement of persons with respect to height is

Ram > Vineet > Monika > Jacob > Dalip.

Hence, Ram is the tallest in the group.

**24** IF RED is coded as 6720, then how would GREEN be coded?

(A) 16717209 (B) 1677209
(C) 9207716 (D) 1677199

*Ans.* *(B)* As,

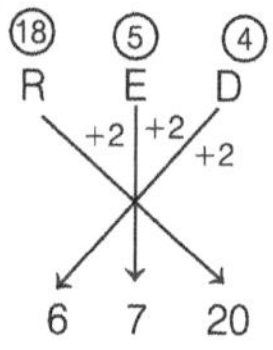


Position in English alphabet series

Similarly,

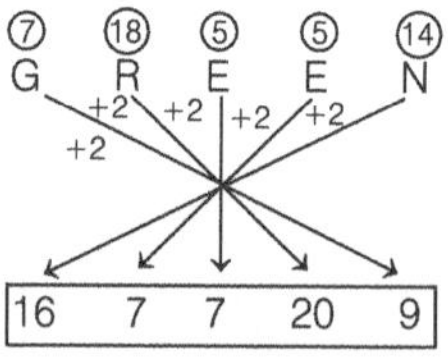


Position in English alphabet series

Hence, GREEN will be coded as 1677209.

**25** Which of the following is a characteristic of modern mass media?

(A) Capital intensive (B) Labour intensive
(C) Sustainable (D) Developmental

*Ans.* *(A)* Mass media means technology that is intented to reach a mass audience. It is the primary means of communication used to reach the vast majority of the general public. The most common platforms for mass media are newspapers, magazines, radio, television, internet etc.

Large audience, use of modern technology, capital intensive etc are some of the characteristics of modern mass media.

**26** If $0.75x = 0.02y$, then the value of $\left(\frac{y-x}{y+x}\right)$ is

(A) $\frac{73}{75}$ (B) $\frac{75}{77}$ (C) $\frac{73}{77}$ (D) $\frac{730}{75}$

*Ans.* *(C)* $0.75x = 0.02y$

$$\Rightarrow \frac{y}{x} = \frac{0.75}{0.02}$$

Applying componendo and dividendo,

$$\frac{y+x}{y-x} = \frac{0.75+0.02}{0.75-0.02}$$

$$\Rightarrow \frac{y+x}{y-x} = \frac{0.77}{0.73} \Rightarrow \frac{y-x}{y+x} = \frac{73}{77}$$

**27** A man travelled from the village to the railway station at the rate of 20 kmph and walked back at the rate of 5 kmph. If the whole journey took 5 hours, find the distance of the railway station from the village.

(A) 10 km (B) 15 km (C) 20 km (D) 40 km

*Ans.* *(C)* Let the required distance be $x$ km.

We know that, time $= \frac{\text{Distance}}{\text{Speed}}$

$\therefore \quad \frac{x}{20} + \frac{x}{5} = 5$

$\Rightarrow \quad x\left[\frac{1}{20} + \frac{1}{5}\right] = 5$

$\Rightarrow \quad x\left[\frac{1+4}{20}\right] = 5$

$\Rightarrow \quad \frac{5x}{20} = 5$

$\therefore \quad x = 20\,\text{km}$

**28** Consider the example given below.

Devadatta is growing fat.

He does not eat food during the day.

Therefore, he must be eating food during the night, other things being equal.

*Identify the logic involved in the example provided above by choosing the correct answer from options given below*

(A) Arthapatti (B) Anupalabdi

(C) Anumana (D) Sabda

*Ans.* *(A)* The logic involved in the given example is Arthapatti. Arthapatti is a Sanskrit term meaning 'presumption'. It refers to the way in which knowledge is derived from a set of circumstances. Arthapatti literally means that which is obtained through an established fact. It is considered as an important source of valid knowledge.

**29** Semantic barrier of communication is implied when the

(A) signal is lost before reaching the receiver.

(B) message transmitted by the source is unclear.

(C) receiver's attention is diverted.

(D) receiver does not understand the meaning of the message

*Ans.* *(D)* Semantic barrier refers to the misunderstanding between the sender and receiver arising due to the different meaning of words and other symbols used in the communication. Semantic barrier restricts effective communication. The semantic barrier can be caused in every type of communication. The semantic barriers usually arise when the information is not in the simple language and contains those words or symbols that have multiple meanings.

**30** Which of the following is a stage of intrapersonal communication?

(A) Phatic stage

(B) Intimate stage

(C) Personal stage

(D) Transcendental communication

*Ans.* *(D)* Intrapersonal communication takes place within the individual. Interpersonal communication is the method by which thoughts, feelings, meanings and ideas are exchanged face to face setting between two or more people. It is meant to reflect oneself to clarify something. This type of communication can be both descriptive or prescriptive. It is a form of transcendental communication. This is often understood in terms of individual so it is said to be transcendental in nature.

**Directions** (Q. Nos. 31-40) *Read the following passage and answer the questions that follow.*

Consider the following table that shows the production of fertilizers by a company (in 10000 tonnes) during the year 2011 to 2018.

**Answer the questions based on the table**

| Year | Production of Fertilizers |
|---|---|
| 2011 | 35 |
| 2012 | 50 |
| 2013 | 70 |
| 2014 | 55 |
| 2015 | 75 |
| 2016 | 60 |
| 2017 | 85 |
| 2018 | 90 |

**31** What was the approximate percentage increase in production of fertilizers in 2018 compared to that in 2011?

(A) 157% (B) 165%

(C) 177% (D) 182%

*Ans.* *(A)* Production of fertilizers in 2018 = 90 thousand tonnes Production of fertilizers in 2011 = 35 thousand tonnes.

∴ Required increase in percentage

$$= \frac{90-35}{35} \times 100$$

$$= 157.14\% \approx 157\%$$

**32** **In how many of the given years was the production of fertilizers more than the average production of the given years?**

(A) 2 (B) 3 (C) 4 (D) 5

*Ans.* *(C)* Average production of fertilizers

$$= \frac{35+50+70+55+75+60+85+90}{8}$$

$$= \frac{520}{8} = 65 \text{ thousand tonnes.}$$

∴ There are four years i.e., 2013, 2015, 2017 and 2018 in which the production of fertilizers is more than the average production of the given years.

**33** **In which year, the percentage increase in production as compared to the previous year was maximum?**

(A) 2012 (B) 2013 (C) 2015 (D) 2018

*Ans.* *(A)* Percentage increase in 2012

$$= \frac{50-35}{35} \times 100 = 42.85\%$$

Percentage increase in 2013

$$= \frac{70-50}{50} \times 100 = 40\%$$

Percentage increase in 2015

$$= \frac{75-55}{55} \times 100 = 36.36\%$$

Percentage increase in 2017

$$= \frac{85-60}{60} \times 100 = 4166\%$$

Percentage increase in 2018

$$= \frac{90-85}{85} \times 100 = 5.88\%$$

∴ Maximum increase in percentage is in the year 2012.

**34** **What was the percentage decline in the production of fertilizers from 2013 to 2014?**

(A) 20.4% (B) 21.4% (C) 22.6% (D) 24.2%

*Ans.* *(B)* Production in 2013 = 70 thousand tonnes

Production in 2014 = 55 thousand tonnes.

$$\therefore \text{Percentage decline} = \frac{70-55}{70} \times 100$$

$$= 2142\%$$

**35** **The average production of 2012 and 2013 was exactly equal to the average production of which of the following pairs of years?**

(A) 2011 and 2012 (B) 2011 and 2017
(C) 2012 and 2014 (D) 2015 and 2016

*Ans.* *(B)* Average production of 2012 and 2013

$$= \frac{50+70}{2} = 60 \text{ thousand tonnes.}$$

Average production in 2011 and 2017

$$= \frac{35+85}{2} = 60 \text{ thousand tonnes}$$

Hence, the average production of 2012 and 2013 was exactly equal to the average production in 2011 and 2017.

**36** **The mangroves exist in**

(A) Fresh water system (B) Temperate areas
(C) Semi-arid areas (D) Saline waters

*Ans.* *(D)* Mangrove is a shrub or small tree that grows in coastal saline or brackish water. There are about 80 different species of mangrove trees. Mangroves occur worldwide in the tropics and sub-tropics mainly between latitudes 25°N and 25°S. All of these trees grow in areas with low-oxygen soil, where slow moving water allows fine sediments to accumulate.

**37** **A/An .......... is a computer program that spreads by inserting copies of itself into other executable code or documents.**

(A) Operating system (B) Computer virus
(C) Firewall (D) Anti-virus

*Ans.* *(B)* Computer virus is a type of malicious software that, when executed, replicate itself by modifying other computer programs and inserting its own code. When this replication succeeds, the affected areas are then said to be 'infected' with computer virus.

**38** **The expansion of SANKALP is**

(A) Sanskrit Awareness and Knowledge Acquisition of Language Programme.
(B) Skills Acquisition and Karatae Awareness for Livelihood Promotion.
(C) Skills Acquisition and Knowledge Awareness for Livelihood Promotion.
(D) Sanskrit Awareness and Knowledge Acquisition for Livelihood Promotion.

*Ans.* *(C)* Skills Acquisition and Knowledge Awareness for Livelihood Promotion (SANKALP) project aims to implement the mandate of the National Skill Development Mission (NSDM), which was launched on 15th July by Ministry of Skill Development and Entrepreneurship.

The main objective of the project is to enhance institutional mechanisms for skills development and increase access to quality and market-relevant training for the work force.

It aims to provide access to skill training opportunities to the disadvantaged sections and also creating industry led and demand driven skill training capacity.

**39** **In which year the modern Indian University got established?**

(A) 1957 (B) 1857
(C) 1947 (D) 1964

*Ans.* *(B)* The Modern Indian Universities were established in the year 1857. These were the British style universities which were located at Calcutta (Kolkata), Bombay (Mumbai) and Madras (Chennai) in the year 1857. These learning centres were focussed on generating English speaking working class for the British administrative services.

**40** **Permafrost is defining characteristic of which biome?**

(A) Taiga (B) Tundra
(C) Grassland (D) Desert

*Ans.* *(B)* Permafrost is any ground that remains completely frozen – 32° F or colder – for atleast two years straight. These permanently frozen grounds are most common in regions with high mountains and in Earth's higher latitudes – near the North and South pole. Permafrost is found in Tundra biome.

**41** **Match the following**

| List I | List II |
|---|---|
| A First Generation | 1. Transistor |
| B Second Generation | 2. VLSI microprocessor |
| C Third Generation | 3. Vacuum tube |
| D Fourth Generation | 4. Integrated circuit |

**Codes**

| | A | B | C | D | | A | B | C | D |
|---|---|---|---|---|---|---|---|---|---|
| (A) | 3 | 4 | 1 | 2 | (B) | 3 | 1 | 4 | 3 |
| (C) | 3 | 1 | 2 | 4 | (D) | 1 | 3 | 4 | 2 |

*Ans.* *(B)* There are various generations of computer system operations which give birth to various technological advancements, like

| | |
|---|---|
| A First Generation | 3. Vacuum Tube |
| B Second Generation | 1. Transistor |
| C Third Generation | 4. Integrated Circuit |
| D Fourth Generation | 3. VLSI Micro Processor |

**42** **The report of which of the following Education Commissions carries the sub-title 'Education for National Development'?**

(A) Radhakrishnan Commission
(B) Mudaliar Commission
(C) Calcutta University Education Commission
(D) Kothari Commission

*Ans.* *(D)* Kothari Commission was set up under Dr. DS Kothari by Government of India to advise on the national pattern of education. The commission was set upto examine all aspects of the educational sector in India to evolve general pattern of education and to advise, frame policies for the development of education in India. The recommendations of this commission include

(i) Free and compulsory education upto 14 years.
(ii) Three Language Formula.
(iii) Training and Quality of teachers.
(iv) Development of education for agriculture and industry.

The sub-title of this commission is 'Education for National Development'.

**43** **Chemical oxygen demand in eutrophic water is**

(A) low (B) high
(C) medium (D) extremely low

*Ans.* *(B)* Chemical Oxygen Demand (COD) is a method of estimating the amount of oxygen needed to oxidise the organic matter present in water. Chemical Oxygen Demand in eutrophic water is high.

**44** **Which pollutant is the major source of marine pollution?**

(A) Agricultural run-off
(B) Oil spill
(C) Industrial waste water
(D) Sewage

*Ans.* *(D)* Sewage is the major source of marine pollution. It is reported that around 75% to 80% water pollution is caused by the domestic sewage. Domestic sewage contains toxicants, solid waste, plastic litters and bacterial contaminants which adversely affect marine life and cause water/marine pollution.

**45** **The target set by Indian Government for generating power from wind energy by the year 2022 is**

(A) 60 GW (B) 50 GW (C) 40 GW (D) 15 GW

*Ans.* *(A)* The target set by Indian Government for generating power from wind energy by the year 2022 is 60 GW. As of 30th June, 2018 the installed capacity of wind power in India was 34, 293 MW, mainly spread across Tamil Nadu, Maharashtra, Gujarat, Rajasthan, Karnataka, Andhra Pradesh and Madhya Pradesh. The Indian government's Ministry of New and Renewable Energy has also announced a new wind solar hybrid policy in 2018.

**46** **Which of the following is not a/an web browser?**

(A) Internet Explorer (B) Mozilla Firefox
(C) Google Chrome (D) Yahoo

*Ans.* *(D)* Web browser is the search engine through which we can get connected to the server and people around the globe. Yahoo is not that connecting server rather it is a webpage.

Yahoo is an internet portal that incorporates a search engine and a directory of world wide web sites. It is the largest web portal providing links to thousands of other web sites.

So, the major web browsing platforms are Internet Explorer, Mozilla Firefox and Google Chrome.

**47** **In which era given below, higher education in India got a set back?**

(A) British Era
(B) Buddhist Era
(C) Mughal Era
(D) Post-Independence Era

*Ans.* *(A)* Higher education in India got a set back in British Era. However, a marked difference occurred in the educational system with the arrival of British educational system.

In 19th century there were several commissions such as Wood's Dispatch, Hunter Commission and Sadler Commission that reform the education system and promote higher education in India.

**48** **One Tera Byte (TB) of memory is equal to**

(A) 1024 kB
(B) $1024\times 1024$ kB
(C) $1024\times 1024\times 1024$ kB
(D) $1024\times 1024\times 1024$ Bytes

*Ans.* *(C)* One Tere Byte (TB) is equal to $1024\times 1024\times 1024$ kB.

**49** **In Audio and Video compression, the term RGB means**

(A) Red, Grey, Blue
(B) Red, Green, Blue
(C) Red, Green, Black
(D) Red, Grey, Black

*Ans.* *(B)* In audio and video compression, the term RGB means 'Red, Green, Blue'. RGB is an additive colour, meaning that Red, Green and Blue all have a luminance value built in and a combination of different variations of Red, Green, Blue at different brightness will produce different colours.

**50** **Which of the following statements best explains the concept of sustainable development?**

(A) Use of natural resources minimally.
(B) Use of natural resources for our benefit.
(C) Use of natural resources judiciously so that they are available for future generations.
(D) Preserve our natural resources for our future generation.

*Ans.* *(C)* Sustainable development stands for preserving the resources and using it judiciously so that it can be made available for future generation. It is important to maintain sustainable development criteria because the resources are getting extincted.

It meets the need of the present without compromising the ability of future generations to meet their own needs.

# Teaching and Research Aptitude

## General Paper 1

*(Compulsory)*

# UNIT 01

# Teaching Aptitude

**CHAPTER ANALYSIS**

This unit is based on the updated syllabus of NTA UGC NET covering all the important topics of Teaching Aptitude. After thorough going the chapter you will be able to understand the Concept, Objectives and Levels of Teaching, Learner's Characteristics, Individual Differences, Factors Affecting Teaching, Methods of Teaching, Teaching Support System and Evaluation System.

Every year, 5 to 6 questions are asked from this unit in NTA UGC NET exam. Questions asked in exam are based on Levels of Teaching, Adult & Adolescent Learner, Online & Offline Methods of Teaching, Teaching Aids & Support System, SWAYAM, MOOCs, Evaluation, etc.

## CONCEPT OF TEACHING

Teaching is a methodology in which various activities are involved. The word 'teaching' is derived from the word 'to teach' which means 'to instruct'.

It means a process in which one individual gain knowledge or learn something from a more knowledgeable person. Teaching is skillful application of knowledge, experience and scientific principles with an objective to setup an environment to facilitate learning.

Teaching aptitude is a part of teaching in which a teacher tries to mould, shape and develop the behaviour of students according to the needs, cultures and thoughts of the society.

Teaching aptitude is made up of two words 'Teaching' and 'Aptitude' which refers to the quality of a teacher by virtue of which he teaches his students.

In other words, various teaching aids, teaching methodologies and teaching activities which are necessary for teaching are collelectively called teaching aptitude.

It is a part of teaching in which studies are above on the relationship of teacher and students in conducive and controlled environment.

**IN THIS UNIT**

- Teaching : Concept, Objectives, Levels of Teaching, Characteristics and Basic Requirements of Teaching
- Learner's Characteristics : Characteristics of Adolescent and Adult Learners, Individual Differences
- Factors Affecting Teaching Related to : Teacher, Learner, Support Material, Institutional Facilities, Learning Environment & Institution
- Methods of Teaching in Institutions of Higher Learning : Teacher Centred Vs. Learner Centred Methods; Offline Vs. Online Methods.
- Teaching Support System : Traditional, Modern and ICT Based
- Evaluation Systems : Elements and Types, Evaluation in CBCS in Higher Education, CBT, Innovations in Evaluation Systems.

## Definitions of Teaching

Some renowned scholars have define teaching which are given below:

**HC Morrison defines,** "Teaching is an intimate contact between a more mature personality and less mature one, which is designed to further the education of the latter."

According to **NL Gage,** "Teaching is a form of interpersonal influence aimed at changing the behaviour potential of another person."

**Albert Einstein defines**, "Teaching is a supreme art to awaken joy in creative expression and knowledge."

**Clerk** Teaching refers to activities that are designed and performed to produce in students behaviour.

According to **APJ Abdul Kalam**, "Teaching is a noble profession that shapes the character, calibre and future of an individual. If people remember me as a good teacher that will be a biggest honour for me."

**Edmund Amidon defines,** "Teaching as an interactive process primarily involving classroom talk which takes place between teacher and pupil and occurs during certain definable activity."

## Objectives of Teaching

Teaching is an interactive process between the students and the teaching sources. It is essential for the guidance, progress and development of students. The objective of teaching and learning must integrate at the end of the instruction. A good objective should be outcome based and measurable.

The objectives of the teaching are

- to bring desired changes in student's attitude.
- to shape behaviour and conduct of students.
- to develop children into a social and efficient member of society.
- to develop conceptual, intellectual and subject specific skills.
- to develop understanding.
- to improve the learning skills of students including methodological critical thinking, writing creatively, etc.

The overall objective of teaching is to build over all personality of the learners, the development of learner's capability thinkers and change in behaviour of students.

# LEVELS OF TEACHING

The activities of teaching and learning may be organised at various levels of abstraction; ranging from the use and application of simple mental powers to the most complex ones.

Through teaching the teacher brings a desirable changes in the learner. Both the concepts teaching and learning are interrelated to each other.

Development of all round personality of the learner is the final goal of teaching and learning.

During teaching, interaction takes place between an experienced person (teacher) and an in experienced person (student).

There are three identifiable levels of teaching and learning activities. These are

1. Memory Level of Teaching
   (Herbert's Teaching Model)
2. Understanding Level of Teaching
   (Morrisan Teaching Model)
3. Reflection Level of Teaching
   (Hunt's Teaching Model)

## 1. Memory Level of Teaching

The first level of teaching is memory level teaching. It is also called thoughtless teaching. **Herbert** is the main proponent of memory level ot teaching. At memory level teaching the focus is on memorisation. It is usually used in lower classes.

The instructional arrangement is such that the learner is helped in cramming the content presented to him. Here, the teaching learning process is mainly a Stimulus Response (S-R).

The famous educationist **Woodsworth** says "Memory is the direct use of what is learned". In this level emphasis is laid down on the presentation of the facts and informations and its cramming.

Teaching and learning at memory level are basically about committing factual material to our memory. It has three major aspects:

(a) Learning of the material
(b) Retention of the material
(c) Reproduction of the material as and when required

## Objectives

- Knowledge gained by the learner is basically factual that is acquired through memorisation and rote learning.
- It covers only the knowledge based objectives of Bloom's Taxonomy.
- The teaching is subject centered.
- Simple memorable things are taught to students.
- The subject material is well organised and simple in nature.
- The knowledge delivered is definite structured and observable.

## Structure

Herbert includes the following steps in Memory Level of Teaching

1. **Preparation** Questions are asked to test the previous knowledge.
2. **Statement of Aim** To acquaint the name of the topic.
3. **Presentation** Stimulating the mental activity, the pupils are provided with opportunities for self-learning.
4. **Association** Mutual relationship is established among facts, events and experts by comparison.
5. **Generalisation** Principles and laws are formulated for the future life situations.
6. **Application** New learnt knowledge is used in new situations.

## Psychological Basis

According to **Jean Piaget**, "Memory level is meant for starters. The learners are at pre-operational level of cognitive development in the school.

They cannot operate upon abstract concepts. As per their mental development, they can learn simple concepts without analysing their true meaning and nature."

Pavlov and Skinner advocated the conditioning theory that underlies the concept that correct response made by the individuals is strengthened by reinforcement to retain the learned subject matter longer and to facilitate ease in further learning.

The concept of Pavlov's classical conditioning considers the mechanical process as is applied at memory level teaching. Correct learning by the student is awarded and retained for future use.

## Teaching Method

Teaching method of this level is subject centered which aim is to make the students memorize the subject. The teaching methods include drill, review, revision and asking questions.

Drill refers to constant practice and repetitions to memorize a particular subject. Review relates to learners forming new associations with the subject. Next step is revising the concepts and asking questions is used to examine whether objectives are achieved or not.

Teacher's role is active as subject content, teaching technique and methods are decided by the teacher. Learner's role is passive.

**Teaching equipments** include teaching aids like audio-visual aids, models, charts, maps, pictures, TV, radio, etc.

## Evaluation System

The evaluation system mainly includes both essay and objective type questions. Oral tests are conducted to check the level of memorization.

The tests and tools need proper planning which could evaluate the students ability to comprehend, grasp, analyze, synthesize and discriminate. Fill up, matching, short answer, MCQ, recall type and recognition are some examples of evaluation system.

### Suggestions

- The teaching material should progress from simple to complex.
- The teaching material should be objective and useful.
- Teaching aids should be adequate, and parts of the content should be integrated and well sequenced.
- There should be scope for continuous reinforcement during the course of instruction.
- Systematic and organised way of presentation of subject matter should be there.

## 2. Understanding Level of Teaching

The main proponent of understanding level of teaching is **Morrison**. The teaching at the understanding level is of higher quality than the one at the memory level. It is more useful and thoughtful as it focus on the mastery of the subject.

Teaching is done to develop intellectual behaviour. Learners become more capable to think, present the facts in more logical manner, analyse them properly and also draw inferences. Motivation at the understanding level of teaching is extrinsic as well as intrinsic in nature.

Teaching-learning at the understanding level emphasizes seeing solitary facts in relation to general principles. It involves exploration, presentation, assimilation, organization and recitation through oral presentation or in the form of written paper. This type of teaching-learning can be carried out with the students in upper primary, middle and higher classes.

### Objectives

It is according to revised Bloom Taxonomy, understanding level of teaching aims at the following objectives

1. **Understanding Objectives** It is the understanding of instructional message by means of interpreting, exemplifying, classifying, comparing and inferring etc.
2. **Application objectives** includes the use of a proper procedure for executing and implementing the use of principle/rules in practical life situations.

### Structure

Morrison has divided the understanding level of teaching into five steps. These are

1. **Presentation** Content is presented, diagnosed and recapitulated till the students understand.
2. **Exploration** Testing previous knowledge, analysing the content.
3. **Assimilation** Generalisation, individual activities, working in laboratory and library, test of content.
4. **Organisation** Pupils are provided with the occasions for representation.
5. **Recitation** Pupil presents the content orally.

### Teaching Method

Teaching method of this level is subject centered as well as teacher centered. Teacher plans tha proceedings of the classroom in advance and works accordingly. Teacher adopts a permissive role and allows more freedom so that learners can interpret the information in their own way.

Teacher motivates the learners in their learning process. Teacher uses different type of methods in teaching such as lecture method, discussion method, inductive-deductive method, exemplification (explain by using examples), etc. Teacher's role is active as classroom activities and teaching methods are decided by the teachers. Learners are more active in comparison to learners at memory level of teaching.

### Evaluation System

Planned tests are prepared to evaluate the student's ability to comprehend, grasp, synthesize, descriminate, generalize and the insight to apply the generalised principles further. Besides asking questions for oral testing, written testing should be conducted. Comprehensive essays are also a tool for evaluation.

### Suggestions

- There should be effective classroom interaction
- Organised subject matter.
- Use of teaching aids.
- Proper classroom environment along with motivation by teachers.

## 3. Reflective Level of Teaching

Reflective level of teaching is also known as introspective level. **Hunt** is the main proponent of reflective level of teaching.

It is the highest and the most practical level of teaching. This level basically involves the use of scientific methods to understand the problems. The reflective level of teaching is highly thoughtful and useful. A learner can achieve this level only after memory level and understanding level.

Students at this level, develop curiosity, interest, inquiry and persistence which culminates in a scientifically determined conclusion or solution of a problem.

Teaching-learning at reflective level involves careful and critical examination of an idea or problem through the 'problem-solving approach'.

It is only possible at the high school level as older learners usually develop certain habits and abilities that were not strong in earlier years.

### Objective

- To develop insight into the learner to solve problems.
- To develop rational and critical thinking in the students.
- To develop the ability of independent thinking and decision making in the students.

### Structure

Hunt has divided the reflective level of teaching into further five steps. These are

- Creating a problematic situation.
- Formulation of the hypothesis
- Verify hypothesis
- Collection of data
- Testing of hypothesis

### Teaching Method

The teaching method of this level is student centered. There is lot of interaction between the teacher and learners.

Study material or classroom proceeding is neither organised nor pre-planned. The interaction is highly thoughtful and learners are allowed to bring up their own ideas to solve specific problem. Teacher played a democratic role in this level of teaching.

### Evaluation System

The Evaluation System at the reflective level of teaching should test the higher order cognitive abilities like reasoning, creativity, original thinking, problem-solving, critical thinking etc.

### Suggestions

- Proper atmosphere should be provided.
- Encourage independent learning and experessing the thoughts.
- Proper direction.
- Proper evaluation.

# OBJECTIVES OF TEACHING

An instructional objective should be specific, outcome based and measurable in nature. It describes an intended result of instruction rather than the process of instruction.

There are two ways of classifying instructional objectives i.e. first is given by Bloom while another classification is given by Gagne and Briggs.

Let us discuss both the classifications in detail.

## Bloom's Taxonomy

Bloom Taxonomy, a new vision of teaching was developed by the **Benjamin Bloom** in 1956. The Bloom's taxonomy is the set of three hierarchical models used to classify educational learning objectives into level of complexity and specificity.

The three lists cover the learning objectives in **cognitive**, **affective** and **psychomotor** domains.

### 1. The Cognitive Domain

The cognitive domain is a knowledge-based domain. It is broken into following six levels of objectives

(i) **Knowledge** It involves recognising or remembering facts, terms, basic concepts, or answers without necessarily understanding what they mean.

(ii) **Comprehension** It involves demonstrating understanding of facts and ideas by organising, comparing, translating, interpreting, giving descriptions and stating the main ideas.

(iii) **Application** It involves using acquired knowledge applying facts, techniques and rules.

(iv) **Analysis** It involves examining and breaking information into component parts, and determining how these parts relate to one another and finding evidences to support generalisations.

(v) **Synthesis** It involves building a structure or pattern from diverse elements.

(vi) **Evaluation** It involves presenting and defending opinions, by making judgements about information, the validity, or quality of work based on a set of criteria.

### 2. The Affective Domain

It is emotional based domain and moves through the lowest order processes to the highest. It is broken into following five levels

(i) **Receiving** It is about the student's memory and recognition as well.

(ii) **Responding** It involves participation of students in learning process.

(iii) **Valuing** It involves the value knowledge that are acquired by students.

(iv) **Organising** It involves the different values, information and ideas, that students accommodate on what has been learned.

(v) **Characterising** It involves to build abstract knowledge.

### 3. The Psychomotor Domain

It is an action-based domain that focus on change or development in behaviour or skill. Skills in the psychomotor domain describe the ability to physically manipulate a tool or instrument like a hand and hammer.

The psychomotor domain is broken into following five levels

(i) **Observing** It involves active mental attending of a physical event.

(ii) **Imitating** It involves attempted copying of a physical behaviour.

(iii) **Practicing** It involves trying a specific physical activities over and over.

(iv) **Adapting** It involves fine tuning, making minor adjustments in the physical activity in order to perfect it.

(v) **Naturalisation** It involves individual ability to adapt, modify or design the new techniques, methods or procedures according to the requirement of a situation.

Thus, learning takes place through three different channels i.e., cognitive, psychomotor and affective, it takes place as one process.

## Gagne and Briggs Model

This model is also called Gagne's Nine Conditions of Learning or Gagne's Taxonomy of Learning. According to this model, the educational learning objectives fall under following categories

(i) **Verbal Information** It refers to the ability to state knowledge that an individual acquires.

(ii) **Intellectual Skills** It refers to the ability to solve problem using rules. It includes concept learning, rule learning and problem solving.

(iii) **Cognitive Skills** It refers to the ability to solve problem by creating rules. It also includes methods and techniques for one's own learning, remembering and thinking skills.

(iv) **Motor Skills** It refers to motions that are carried out with the help of the brain, nervous system and muscles.

(v) **Attitudes** They are referred to an internal state of an individual.

## Nature and Characteristics of Teaching

Nature of teaching refers to those elements of teaching which are inherent with the concept of teaching. It means that there is no human influence on those elements of teaching. The nature of teaching can be understood through the following points

1. **Dynamic, Social and Humane** Teaching is not a fundamental concept because it is greatly influenced by social and human factors which are dynamic in themselves.
2. **Teaching is a Science** Teaching is a systematic activity. It is done with a definite aim and involves the use of scientific strategies and techniques. Different strategies are tested for their effectiveness and all observations along with scores of the students in tests are recorded. Therefore, teaching is a science.
3. **Teaching is an Art** Teaching involves the creativity of the teachers in explaining concepts to different type of learners. Teachers need to form strategies, adjust to various situations and understand the personality of each student. Therefore, teaching can also be considered as an art.
4. **Diverse Application** In application, teaching is of diverse nature. It may have various forms as formal, informal, directional, instructional, formational, training, conditioning, indoctrination, talking, showing, doing, remedial, etc.
5. **A System of Actions** Teaching is a system of actions varied in form and related with content and pupil behaviour under the prevailing physical and social conditions.
6. **A Professional Activity** Teaching is a professional activity involving teacher and student with a view to the development of students' personality.

   Professionalism helps teachers in being regular and making harmony with their students along with achievent of goals.
7. **An Interactive Process** Teaching is highly dominated by the communication skill. Teaching is an interactive process carried with purpose and objectives.
8. **Subjected to Analysis and Assessment** Teaching can be analysed and assessed based on the given task and also provide a feedback for further improvement.
9. **A Specialised Task** Teaching is a specialised task and may be taken as a set of skills for realisation of certain objectives.
10. **A Collection of Various Modes** Teaching is a collection of various modes of itself. It is a broader term. Terms like conditioning, training, instruction, indoctrination denote a kind of teaching.

    They are a part of teaching but not a synonym of teaching. These are various modes of teaching contributing towards teaching.
11. **A Continuous Process** : Teaching is not a static but an evolving, continuous and lifelong process. The concept of continuous learning has become important because it places priority on acquiring, adapting and learning from change.

## Basic Requirements of Teaching

Teaching is an interactional activity which requires a number of things to achieve certain aims.

Following are the basic requirements of teaching

### 1. Variables of Teaching

In teaching-learning process there are three types of variables i.e. **dependent variable**, **independent variable** and **intervening variable**.

These are

1. **Dependent Variable** (Student) The student is dependent variable whose all round development is shaped by the efforts of teacher and teaching process.

2. **Independent Variable** (Teacher) The teacher is an independent variable who plans, organises, leads and controls the process of teaching.
3. **Intervening Variable** (Curriculum) The curriculum, content, methods of teaching, tactics and strategies, management and institutional set–up are intervening variables which are essentially required for teaching.

### 2. Role of Infrastructure

A child spends his/her maximum time in school. Thus, school infrastructure becomes a basic requirement of teaching in a number of ways. These are

- School buildings, classrooms, playgrounds and libraries are the most important aspect of school infrastructure.
- Spacious and refurnished buildings and well-ventilated classrooms are most required things in schools.
- Well-equipped labs enable learners to perform lab activities more effectively.
- Facilities like extracurricular workshops, libraries, halls, games equipment, assembly area and proper sanitation facilities are some of the infrastructure essentials that every school should provide to its learners.

## PRINCIPLES OF TEACHING

The principles of teaching are closely related to maxims. Teaching methods are based on two types of principles such as general principles and psychological principles.

### 1. General Principles

(i) **Principle of Motivation** It creates curiosity among students to learn new things.

(ii) **Principle of Activity** (Learning by Doing) It includes both physical and mental activities. For example, students are asked to make charts and models. Froebel's Kindergarten (KG) system is based on this principle.

(iii) **Principle of Interest** It means by generation of genuine interest among the learner's community, the effectiveness of the teaching-learning process can be increased.

(iv) **Principle of Linking with Life** Life is for continuous experience and learning linked with life can be more enduring.

(v) **Principle of Definite Aim** This is important for optimum utilisation of teaching resource and making learning more focused.

(vi) **Principle of Recognising Individual Differences** Every student is unique in terms of intelligence, attitude, abilities, potentialities and socio-economic background. The teaching method should be devised in such a manner to make all students to avail equal opportunities of life.

(vii) **Principles of Selection** The horizon of knowledge is expanding every single day. The teacher should be able to pick contents that can be more relevant and updated to the learner's objectives.

(viii) **Principle of Planning** Every teacher has certain time bound objectives and hence teaching should be systematic to make maximum use of resources within the time limit.

(ix) **Principle of Division** To make learning easier, the subject matter should be divided into units and there should be link between the units.

(x) **Principle of Revision** To make learning enduring the acquired knowledge should be revised immediately and repeatedly.

(xi) **Principle of Creation and Recreation** This principle is must to make the classroom environment humorous and creative.

(xii) **Principle of Democratic Dealing** It entails students in planning and executing different activities. It helps in developing self-confidence and self-respect among the learners.

## 2. Psychological Principles

(i) **Principle of Motivation and Interest** A teacher needs to understand that every student is unique psychological entity. So a student can be motivated after identifying his/her motives and needs.

(ii) **Principle of Recreation** Recreation is necessary to tackle fatigue after attending lengthy classes. This breaks monotory and prepares students for learning again.

(iii) **Principle of Repetition and Exercise** This principle is applicable in case of small children.

(iv) **Principle of Expressing Creativity and** Self-Expression This is specifically applicable in subjects mathematics and in learning languages.

(v) **Principle of Reinforcement** Students should be suitable rewarded for their desired behaviour.

(vi) **Principle of Sympathy and Cooperation** This principle is required for the motivation of students.

(vii) **Principle of Imparting Training to Senses** The use of multi-media makes many senses get involved simultaneously, which is crucial for enduring learning.

(viii) **Principle of Remedial Teaching** This principle is necessary for the teacher to identify mistakes and suggest better answers to the problems.

# LEARNING

Learning is the process of assimilation of knowledge resulting from the interaction between the teacher and learner. Learning is a continuous process grounded in experience. Learning is the process of creating knowledge.

Learning is a natural process of growth or change in a person which is manifested as new modes or patterns of behaviour. The nature and processes involved in learning are studied in many fields, including educational psychology, neuropsychology, experimental psychology and pedagogy.

## Definitions of Learning

Learning may occur consciously or without conscious awareness. It is a relatively permanent change in behaviour and is the result of reinforced practice through the process of stimulus and response.

Some of the well known definitions of learning given by various thinkers are

According to **Skinner,** "Learning is a process of progressive behaviour through experience and training."

According to **Crow and Crow,** "Learning involves acquisition of knowledge, habits and attitudes."

According to **Gardner Murphy,** "Learning is the acquisition of new behaviour or the strengthening or weakening of old behaviour as the result of experience."

In the words of **Blair Jones and Simon,** "Any change of behaviour which is the result of experience and which causes people to face later situations differently may be called learning."

## Basic Conditions of Learning

**Contiguity** It is one of the basic conditions of learning. Contiguity is almost simultaneous occurrence of the stimuli and of the responses to them. It applies in teaching also.

**Practice** It is the repetition of response. Practice of S-R (Stimulus Response) is required in classical conditioning, operant conditioning, skill learning.

**Reinforcement** We can use reinforcement in different ways to produce different effects.

**Feedback** It means providing the knowledge that the responses are correct or that they require amendment.

**Generalisation and Discrimination** Both generalisations and discrimination are perhaps better defined as phenomena rather than as conditions of learning. We call them learning conditions because they are closely related to basic conditions of contiguity practice and reinforcement which are essential to all learning.

## Principles of Learning

To teach effectively, the teacher must understand the basic principles of learning as enumerated below

**Principle of Association** A teacher must know the state of learners' mind and capacity. As learning is continuous, teacher must start teaching at their level for better learning.

**Principle of Practice** Learning should always results in functional understanding of facts.

**Principle of Rewards** It means learning must be challenging and satisfying as well.

**Principle of Clarity** The practice must be continuously evaluated and redirected. Objectives must be clear to the teacher and learner.

**Principle of Multiple Exposure** To make someone learn may need set of practices. By using combination of teaching methods, the teaching will have cumulative effect on the learners. The percentages of learning and adoption will be higher with multiple experiences.

- **Principle of Varying Learning Ability** This is linked with the concept of individual differences also. Some may be slow learners, some could be fast learners. Learning depends upon communication and learning ability.
- **Principle of Theory and Practice** The 'why' and 'how' of an idea are explained by theory. So a teacher should balance theory and practice for better learning by the learners.
- **Principle of Effective Communication** Better learning can be achieved by integrating suitable audio-visual aids in teaching learning process.

# LEARNER

A learner is someone who is learning about a particular subject or how to do something. In other words, a learner is a person who is trying to gain knowledge or skill in something by studying, practising, or being taught.

## Classification of Learners

The learners can be classified in the following types

1. **Visual Learners** Visual learners learn best when information is presented using patterns, shapes and other visual aids in place of written or spoken words. One way teacher can differentiate their instruction for visual learners is by using graphic organisers to teach a lesson.
2. **Auditory Learners** To help auditory learners teachers can post audio recordings of lessons on the class website or incorporate group activities that require students to explain concepts. Various aspects of sound for example pitch, volume, tempo, rhythm resonance are important for auditory learners.
3. **Motor Learners** These learners learn through motor activity. Various aspects of action e.g. frequency, duration, intensity, pressure are important for them.
4. **Kinesthetic Learners** These learners learn best when they use tactile experiences and carry out physical activity to practice by applying new information. People who prefer this mode are connected to reality either through concrete personal experiences examples, practices or simulations.
5. **Logical Learners** These learners are the ones who are always making list, getting organised and trying to find the link between one piece of the puzzle and another. Logical learners are a natural fit for mathematics, science and other logic based subjects in schools.

## Characteristics of Adolescence and Adult Learner

Let's discuss in detail the characteristics of Adolescent and Adult Learners as per the Academic, Social, Emotional and Cognitive factors :

### 1. Adolescence Learner

Adolescence is a period of transition between childhood and adulthood that involves number of changes in body and mind.

Adolescence is a phase of life between 10 and 18 years according. The adults are mature, fully developed person and above the age of 18 years. An adult is regarded as independent, self-sufficient and responsible.

Now we will discuss the characteristics of adolescence and adult learners from the point of view of academic, social, emotional and cognitive.

### Characteristics of Adolescence Learners

(i) **Academic or Intellectual Development**

- Moving from concrete to abstract thinking.
- Prefers active over passive learning experiences.
- High achievement when challenged and engaged.
- An ability to be self-reflective.
- Demand relevance in learning and what is being taught.
- An intense curiosity and a wide range of intellectual pursuit, few of which are sustained over the long term.

(ii) **Social Development**

- As interpersonal skills are being developed, fluctuates between demand for independence and a desire for guidance and direction.
- Seeking approval of peers and others with attention-getting behaviours.
- Experimenting with ways of talking and acting as part of searching for a social position with peers.

(iii) **Emotional and Psychological Development**

- A desire to become independent and to search for adult identity and acceptance.
- Mood swings marked by peaks of intensity and by unpredictability.
- Self consciousness and being sensitive to personal criticism.
- Concern about physical growth and development.

(iv) **Moral Development**

- An understanding of the complexity of moral issues like question values, cultural expressions, etc.
- Being influenced by adult role models.
- Show compassion and are vocal for those who are downtrodden sections.
- Impatient nature regarding the pace of change.

## 2. Adult Learners

Adult Learner (mature student) is a person who is older and is involved in forms of learning.

Adults learner fall in a specific criteria of being experienced and don't always have a high school diploma. Many of adults learners go back to school to finish a degree, or earn a new one.

### Characteristics of Adult Learner

(i) **Academic Development**

The adult learners are more autonomous and self-directed. They are goal oriented and practical.

- Relevancy oriented and see reasons for learning something. They are not dependent on the others for direction.
- They appreciate an educational programme that is oragnised and has clearly defined elements.
- They evaluate learning in terms of results and its utility to their life situations.

(ii) **Social Development**

Adult person is well aware about the social environment in which he lives.

- He is bound by social customs traditions, rituals etc. He gives his own criticism and views on social customs.
- He carries out his social responsibilities efficiently and effectively and also capable of carrying out his teaching work.

(iii) **Emotional Development**

Adult learner is able to make emotionally correct decision. He understands ideas and facts through proper reasoning rather than taking decisions emotionally.

The learning process helps them in the development of their emotional instincts.

(iv) **Cognitive Development**

It focuses learning in the mental and psychological process of mind and not on behaviour.

- They are concerned with perception and the process of information. He is capable of taking right decision with regard to resolving factual, psychological and argumentative factors.
- The adult learners are efficient enough to analyse moral, social and religious values of teaching.

## Difference between Adolescent and Adult Learners

On the basis of learning, the difference between Adolescent and Adult Learners is discussed below:

| Elements | Adolescents | Adults |
|---|---|---|
| Learner | They are in search for personal identity. | Adults are more disciplined than adolescents. |
| Role of learner's expectation | They are in need of activities that meet their needs and learning expectations. | They have a clear understanding of their learning objectives. |
| Orientation to learning | They become disruptive when they lose interest in the lesson or feel bored. | They need to be involved in choosing what and how to learn. |
| Motivation for learning | They need help and support from the teacher and to be provided with constructive feedback. | They prefer to rely on themselves and work on their own pace. |
| Demand for learning | They can draw upon a variety of resources in the learning environment, including personal experience, the local community, and the Internet. | They come to the classroom with a wide range of knowledge, expectations, and experiences. |
| Climate | They need the teacher to build bridges between the syllabus and their world of interests and experiences. | They are able to do a wide range of activities. |
| Activities of learning | They can learn abstract issues and do challenging activities. | Adults learn at various rates and in different ways according to their intellectual ability, educational level, personality, and cognitive learning styles. |
| Evaluation | Their personal initiative and energy are moved into action through meaningful involvement with relevant and current content. | They come into the classroom with diverse experiences, opinions, thoughts, and beliefs which need be respected. |

# INDIVIDUAL DIFFERENCES

Individual differences stands for the variation or deviations among individuals in regard to a single characteristic or number of characteristics like height, weight, colour and complexion, strength etc., difference in intelligence, achievement, interest, attitude, aptitude, learning habits, motor abilities and skill. It is a known fact that two individuals are alike, not even the-twins. Each man has an intellectual capacity through which he gains experience and learning.

According to **Drever James,** "Variations or deviations from the average of the group, with respect to the mental or physical characters, occurring in the individual member of the group are individual differences."

According to **Skinner,** "Today we think of individual differences as including any measurable aspect of the total personality."

According to **CV Good,** "The variation or deviations among individual is regard to a single characteristics or a number of characteristics, those differences which in their totality distinguish one individual from another."

## Types of Individual Difference

1. **Physical Differences** Shortness or tallness of stature, darkness or fairness of complexion, fatness, thinness, or weakness are various physical individual differences.
2. **Differences in Intelligence** There are differences in intelligence level among different individuals. We can classify the individuals from super-normal to idiots on the basis of their intelligence level.
3. **Differences in Attitudes** Individuals differ in their attitudes towards different people, objects, institutions and authority.
4. **Differences in Motor Ability** There are differences in motor ability. These differences are visible at different ages. Some people can perform mechanical tasks easily, while others, even though they are at the same level, feel much difficulty in performing these tasks.
5. **Differences on Account of Gender**
   (i) Women have greater skill in memory while men have greater motor ability.
   (ii) Handwriting of women is superior while men excel in mathematics and logic.
   (iii) Women show greater skill in making sensory distinctions of taste, touch and smell etc., while men show greater reaction and conscious of size-weight illusion.
   (iv) Women are superior to men in languages, while men are superior in physics and chemistry.
6. **Racial Differences** There are different kinds of racial differences. Differences of environment is a normal factor in causing these differences. Karl Brigham has composed a list on the basis of differences in levels of intelligence among people who have migrated to United States from other countries. On the basis of these average differences between the races, the mental age of a particular individual cannot be calculated since this difference is based on environment.
8. **Differences due to Economic Status** Differences in children's interests, tendencies and character are caused by economic differences.
9. **Differences in Interests** Factors such as sex, family background level of development, differences of race and nationality etc., cause differences in interests.
10. **Personality Differences** There are differences in respect of personality. On the basis of differences in personality, individuals have been classified into many groups.

## Reasons of Individual Differences

1. **Heredity**
   One of the most significant and chief cause of individual differences is heredity. Some heretical traits bring a change from one individual to other. Au individual's height, size, shape, colour of hair, shape of face, nose, hands and legs, so to say the entire structure of the body is determined by his heretical qualities.
2. **Age**
   Age is another factor which is responsible in bringing individual differences. Learning ability and adjustment capacity naturally grow with age. When one grows in age, can aquire better control over our emotions and better social responsibilities.
3. **Sex**
   Due to sex variation, one individual differs from other. The physical development of the girl takes place a year or two earlier than the boys. The nature of girls is different from boys.
4. **Environment**
   Environment significantly influences individual differences. Changes in child's environment are reflected in the changes in his personality. Environment consists of physical, intellectual, social, moral, political, economic and cultural forces. All these forces cause individual differences.
5. **Education**
   Education is one major factor which brings individual differences. There is a wide gap in the behaviours of educated and uneducated persons.

## Educational Implications of Individual Differences

- The aims of education, curriculum method of teaching should be linked with individual differences considering the different abilities and traits of individual.
- The teacher should adopt types of methods of teaching considering individual differences related to interest, needs etc.
- Various methods such as playing methods, project method, story telling method are to be used considering/discovering how different students respond to task or problem.
- Some co-curricular activities like drama, music, literary activities should be assigned to children according to their interest.
- Curriculum should be modified to suit the need of all types of students.
- Teacher should impart educational guidance to the students while keeping in mind their individual differences.
- The teacher should assign the home task to the students while keeping in view individual differences.
- The students should be allowed to follow his own rate of learning in each of the subjects.

## Syllabus and Curriculum

Often Syllabus and Curriculum are interchangeable terms. They essentially refer to different things.

These can be described as follows

**Syllabus** In simple term syllabus is defined as the documents that consist of topics or portion covered in a particular subject. It is determined by the examination board and created by the professors. The professors are responsible for the quality of the course. It is made available to the students by the teachers, either in hard copy or electronic form to bring their attention towards the subject and take their study seriously.

A syllabus is considered as a guide to the incharge as well as to the students. It helps the students to know about the subject in detail, why it is a part of their course of study, what are the expectations from students, consequences of failure, etc. It contains general rules, policies, instructions, topics covered, assignments, projects, test dates, and so on.

**Curriculum** A Curriculum is basically a set of guidelines for different academic contents and chapters that are covered in a specific program offered by a particular school or college.

However, it covers the attitude, manner, knowledge, behaviour, performance, manner and the different skills that students will develop throughout the academic period.

Generally, a curriculum is well-planned and carefully designed by educational institutions or the government. Focusing on the overall learning experience provided by a course, it emphasizes essentially on the mental and physical development of the students.

### Differences Between Syllabus and Curriculum

The basic differences between Syllabus and Curriculum are :

| Syllabus | Curriculum |
|---|---|
| The syllabus is described as the summary of the topics covered or units to be taught in the particular subject. | Curriculum refers to the overall content, taught in an educational system or a course. |
| Syllabus varies from teacher to teacher. | Curriculum remains same for all the teachers. |
| It is descriptive in nature. | It is prescriptive in nature. |
| It is set for a particular subject. | It covers a particular course of study or a program. |
| It is prepared by teachers. | It is decided by the government or institution. |
| Duration of syllabus is for a year only. | Curriculum lasts till the completion of the course. |

# FACTORS AFFECTING TEACHING

There are number of factors that can affect teaching. These factors are as follows

1. **Teaching Skills** A teacher may know his subject well but for sharing, communicating and interactive various experience related to the learning of the subject, he needs specific teaching skills.

The proficiency and deficiency possessed by a teacher in this regard are quite responsible for turning the teacher learning process a big success or failure.

2. **Educational Qualification** A trained and more qualified teacher will help students to inculate the attitude of discussion questionnaire, investigation, inquiry and critical thinking in them. His or her lessons are rich in content and have relevance.
3. **Teacher's Attitude** The lack of coherence between the teachers' classroom attitudes and their expressed belief on active method of interaction may also affect teaching.

   To make teaching effective and productive following attitudes can be developed by a teacher
   - Physical, mental and emotional aspects should be given adequate weightage in developing teacher's attitude.
   - Teachers should be trained enough to be successful in catering student's varying needs and abilities in inclusive setting.
   - An effective professional development program should be designed to meet the specific needs of the school, community, including teachers.
   - Teacher should be flexible with the lesson plan.
4. **Learner's Attitude** Learner's attitude affect teaching–learning process in a number of ways. Negative or disturbing attitude of learner interrupts the learning process. Learner's participative attitude in the classroom generates a lively teaching environment. Attentive, curious and explorative attitude of learners create a productive teaching environment.
5. **Institutional or Administrative Set–up** Administrative set-up with variety and freedom of choice to the teachers generates a healthy teaching environment. Teachers are free to prepare their lesson plans and use a variety of teaching aids.

   Teacher, pupils, parents, staff member and schools should be kept in vertical supervision and horizontal accountability. The position and the responsibilities of teachers within the educational governance parameters should be clear.

   Administrative set–up of institution should be designed in such a manner so that balance of relationship among teachers, teacher–student, teacher–parents, school staff should be ensured.
6. **Teacher Training or Experience** Teacher training is a continuous process that promote teacher's teaching skills, master new knowledge, develop proficiency, which in turn improve student's learning. Teacher's training enables a teacher to understand cognitive domains of learners and plan his/her teaching accordingly. Teacher's training also enables a teacher to use technology in teaching–learning process.
7. **Economic Factors** Infrastructure, teacher's salaries and expenditure on student's facilities are a number of factors which affect teaching.

   Better salary structure with incentives generates a motivation among teachers for productive teaching. Expenditure on student's facilities such as scholarships, libraries, books and study materials motivate students to participate in teaching–learning process.
8. **Teaching–Learning Environment** Creating a good teaching–learning environment means taking into account both the psychological and the instructional perspectives. In an effective teaching–learning environment both the teachers and students play a significant role which are as follows
   - The learner must be active.
   - Learners should strive to comply with all behaviour expectations. Behavioural expectations are verbally outlined and posted as part of the classroom management plan.
   - Showing respect for self and others is one of the most important thing a student can do to contribute to a quality teaching–learning environment. A teacher can create a good teaching–

learning environment in the class by addressing psychological needs of the students.
- It is teacher's responsibility to provide clear behavioural and academic expectations right from the beginning.

9. **Physical Environment** The classroom is the basic structural unit of our educational system. Learners are constantly interacting with physical environment of their institutions during scheduled or unscheduled time consciously or unconsciously. The absence of minimum essential standard for a school drastically affects teacher's productivity output and classroom management.

   Ownership and engagement of space and equipment by both teacher and students in important for learning environment.
10. **Instructional Facilities** Instructional facilities also plays great role in effective teaching-learning process in institutions. These facilities include teaching aids, like traditional, modern and ICT based support systems i.e. T.V, radio, tape recorders, projectors, film strips, internet and so on. These Instructional facilities help to make teaching very effective.
11. **Classroom Management** Effective classroom management is a factor of successful teaching. Teacher has to give nurturing and engaging environment to the students. The climate of the classroom should be relaxed, pleasant without any time wastage, disruption or confusion.

# TEACHING AIDS OR SUPPORT MATERIAL

Support material is very essential which affects teaching-learning process. It is a valuable resource. It includes textbooks, institutional magazines, journals, periodicals etc. So, it is important to select such an effective support material which could be useful in transmitting knowledge among learners. Teaching aids are instrumental materials and devices that help the teacher in carrying out the teaching-learning process.

## Categories of Teaching Aids

Teaching aids can be categorised as following

### 1. Visual Aids

The traditional aids which involve the sense of vision are called visual aids. Types of visual aids are as follows

(i) **Blackboard** An efficient teacher always makes use of the blackboard. It focuses on technology and services to help students learn, not just one way but on their own way.

(ii) **Bulletin Board** It is a surface intended for the posting of public messages, for example to advertise items wanted or for sale, announce events, or provide information in the classroom.

(iii) **Real Objects** These are very important in the teaching of students on the basis of perception of objects, the students get apparent experience.

Objects like rocks, soils, minerals, etc can be shown in the class.

(iv) **Newspapers** A teacher can use a newspaper for finding parts of speech, teaching about life skills, or to keep student up to date by current news events.

(v) **Graphs** These are a wonderful teacher aids and can be used for any subject. Teachers can make their own graphs and use them for comparing population growth, numbers or ratios of objects, or even use them for charting student growth.

(vi) **Maps** A map is something to use when a teacher is describing where a city, state, country, or continent is located. Maps are great for social studies and science and give students a great understanding of spatial relations.

(vii) **Charts** A chart is a symbolised visualised teaching support system with pictures of relationships and charges which are used to tabulate a large mass of information or show a progression. Charts can help communicate different and dull subject matter in an interesting and effective way.

They are also helpful in summarising information and presenting abstract ideas in visual form.

(viii) **Magnetic Board** It can be a sheet of template and simply a type of chalk board, the surface of which is treated or coated with porcelain like substance. The base of the board is steel and pictures and objects can be pasted or mounted with small magnets and can easily be moved about. Here, objects can moved across the board easily to show the movement. Teacher and student both can get benefitted by using this.

(ix) **Three Dimensional Model** Real things may not be available all the time and in the desired form. Three Dimensional Model helps to overcome this problem. A model is a recognisable representation of real things in three dimensional view such as height, width and depth. This makes understanding better and easy. They are long lasting and inexpensive, so it is used in high class teaching institutes.

(x) **Power Point Presentation** It is a computer programme that allows the presenter to create and show slide to support his presentation. Here, one can combine text, graphics and content to create professional presentation. Through power point presentation, one can easily explain the context by showing a particular slide. It can used for teaching various concepts. It is used for educational purposes too. Many teachers take support of PPT and through this they can deliver their concepts well to students.

## 2. Audio Aids

The aids which involve the sense of hearing are called audio aids. These are the modern teaching aids.

Types of modern teaching support systems are as follows

(i) **Radio** Teachers have explored the use of radio in the classroom almost since radio technology entered into the mainstream of society. Radio offers teachers a mine of authentic sound documents to use in the classroom.

(ii) **Tape Recorder** Teachers use it to record some subject-matter that is presented according to the necessities. It is a very useful instrument for special education. It provides assistance to the student involved in mainstreamed content area classes.

(iii) **Gramophone** Teachers use it to correct the spoken languages and terms of the students.

(iv) **Digital Audio Player** A digital audio player is sometimes referred to as MP3 player and has the primary function of storing, organising and playing audio files. Some digital audio players are also referred to as portable media players as they have image viewing and video playing support. An ideal example is iPod (fourth generation audio instructional facilities). Through this, teachers can store their teachings and later students can listen this repeatedly to learn more effectively.

## 3. Audio-Visual Aids

The aids which involve the sense of hearing as well as the sense of vision are known as audio–visual aids. This is the most effective and useful than other teaching aids as it uses more than one sense simultaneously. These are ICT based teaching support systems.

Types of ICT based teaching support systems are as follows

(i) **Television** It is used to communicate information, idea, skills and attitudes. It enhance the quality of education and reduces the dependency on verbal teaching and teachers. It provides mass education opportunities.

(ii) **Computer** It is a good example of ICT based teaching support system. It can be defined as any electronic device that allows students to access the internet to research, create and complete the work.

It is greatly used for teaching purposes now a days. Well constructed programmes have the capacity to realistically present material which would not be available by other teaching methods.

(iii) **Films Strips and Films** Knowledge about various functions, discoveries and other information related to subject can be imparted with the help of film strips and films.

In the films and film strips each subject is given in systematic sequence and in detail and it gives clear knowledge of the subject.

(iv) **Multimedia** It is one of the techniques of improving the students to meet the academic needs and helps them developing language skill. Multimedia classroom provide the students chance for interacting with diverse texts that give them a solid background in tasks and content of mainstream college courses.

(v) **Pen Tab** It is a digital drawing tablet. It is a computer input device that enables the user to hand draw images animations and graphics with special pen like stylus similar to the way person drams images with pencil. It is also known as graphic tablet. It is useful in displaying the matter as one speaks the words are written on the monitor. Today, many teachers and professors are using this technique as it gives a feeling of online class.

## Edgar Dale's Cone of Experience

Edger Dale's Cone of Experience is a model that incorporates several theories to instructional design and learning process. During 1960s, Dale theorized that learners retain more information by what they 'do' as opposed to what is 'heard', 'read' or 'observed'. This research led to the development of the **Cone of Experience**. Now, this 'learning by doing, has become known as experimental learning or action learning.

Edgar Dale's Cone of Experience is a tool to help instructors make decisions about resources and activities.

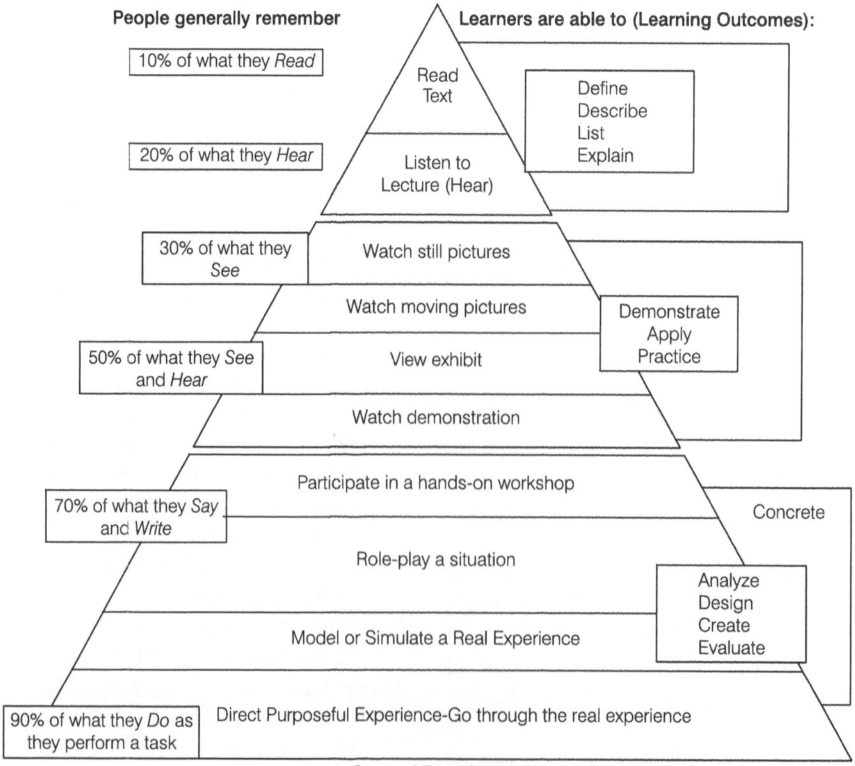


**Cone of Experience**

## Learning Environment

Learning Environment refers to the diverse physical locations, contexts and cultures in which student learn. It is the sum total of the surroundings in which individuals interact to enrich experiences and thus lead towards learning. It is only in the best environmental setting that the most effective learning takes place.

The requisitions, request and suggestions by the teacher can improvise the learning environment to a considerable extent. For instance, the teacher can suggest about lightening and ventilation arrangements which lead to restlessness and inattention in the classroom.

Hence, variations in the learning environment leads to different learning outcomes. A friendly atmosphere, conducive to learning has to be created in the classroom and freedom to acquire knowledge at once own pace could be the factors that enhance learning in the schools.

### Steps of Creating Positive Learning Environment

There is a need for positive learning environment that foster improved academic performance, with the ability to promote student's social and emotional well-being and progress inside and outside the classroom. Following are the steps required for positive learning environment :

***Step* 1. Make Learning Relevant**

Adjust teaching methods and strategies to meet the needs of the students on an individual basis as it will make students more engaged and attentive. On a whole, teacher must find ways to adapt the lesson or lecture to the interests of the students and to make learning more effective.

***Step* 2. Develop a code of Conduct**

The first step to establish a code of conduct is to ask students how they like being treated. Teacher should set the stage for appropriate classroom behaviours.

***Step* 3. Developing a Positive Action Curriculum**

Developing a positive action curriculum is one of the effective ways to teach and instill in students positive behaviours. Positive action curriculum should teach students:

- Positive actions lead to a good feeling and positive self-image.
- Positive actions such as problem-solving, decision-making and thinking skills develop the brain and make us smarter.
- Positive actions such as kindness and being respectful allow us to get along with others.
- Positive actions such as goal setting lead to personal growth and improvement.

***Step* 4. Develop Intrinsic Motivation**

Helping students learn that by changing a negative thought to a positive they can produce positive actions, and that positive actions will help them feel good about themselves is a powerful intrinsic motivator.

***Step* 5. Reinforce Positive Behaviours**

Certificates, stickers and other reward systems are great ways to recognize students and reinforce positive behaviours and achievement in the classroom.

***Step* 6. Always Respond With Positivity**

Regardless of situation or circumstances, there is always a way to respond to and interact with students in a positive way. Teaching students how to communicate and interact with each other in a positive manner is also a key to fostering a positive learning environment in the classroom.

## Institutional Facilities

Infrastructural resources are pre-requisites for providing proper environment to quality learning. The presence of institution does not always means that each and every minimum essential facility is available within the institution to make it running and the teaching-learning process effective.

Besides, the teachers and learners, the availability of adequate infrastructural facilities and teaching-learning materials constitute the core around which educational activities are organized.

In view of Grover and Singh, Physical Infrastructure includes adequate buildings with classrooms that allow instruction to take place without disruption and have enough space for the learners to participate in activities, clean and well-swept floors, well-ventilated spaces, drinking water and enough physical space for learners to engage in physical activities on campus grounds.

Hence, availability or non-availability of physical facilities affect the quality of education; provision of sufficient facilities in schools provides a challenging environment for students and effective teaching by teachers; lack of adequate facilities such as textbooks, ill-equiped classrooms, laboratories, workshops, library are responsible for poor performance in examination among the students.

## TEACHING FORMULA (MAXIMS)

Teacher is responsible for creating such an ambience which gives rise to maximum learning activities and various experiences may be achieved.

He use different methods, rules, principles etc in order to make his lesson effective and purposeful. The different maxims of teaching are discussed below

1. **From Known to Unknown** The maxims state that the new knowledge to be given to pupils must be logically linked with their previous knowledge. This maxim facilitates learning process and economises the efforts of the teacher.
2. **From Simple to Complex** This maxim states that difficulty should follow ease in teaching. Alternatively, the teacher should start with simple thing and proceed to difficult one in a logical, systematic and step wise manner.
3. **From Concrete to Abstract** Concrete things are solid things and they can be visualized but abstract things are only imaginative things. Through this process, the learners understand the materials more easily. Some power of imagination also develops in them.
4. **From Analysis to Synthesis** Analysis means breaking something into individual elements. Synthesis is just reverse of Analysis. It means joining the individual elements into one whole. In fact, these two are an integral part of cognitive domain of Bloom's taxonomy of Educational Objectives.
5. **From Particular to General** A teacher should always proceed from particular to general statements. General facts, principles and ideas are difficult to understand and hence the teacher should always first present particular things and lead to general things.
6. **From Whole to Part** This maxim is the offshoot Gestalt Theory of learning whose main emphasis was to perceive things or objects as whole and not in the form of parts. Whole is more understandable, motivating and effective than the parts.
7. **From Psychological to Logical** This maxim states that the sequence of teaching process should be psychological followed by logical. If the teaching process is not in logical order its organisation is not systematic then the entire teaching process will become haphazard.
8. **From Actual to Representative** Teaching is more effective when the teacher displays actual teaching aids instead of artificial ones before the pupils in the classroom. Researches have shown that the natural teaching material has more influence in the teaching process instead of artificial one.
9. **From Definite to Indefinite** A teacher should always start from definite because definiteness has its limited boundaries and jurisdiction than indefinite things. We learn easily indefinite things on the basis of definite things.
10. **From Induction to Deduction** The process of deriving general laws, rules or formulae from particular examples is called induction. It means drawing a conclusion from set of examples.

    Deduction is just opposite of induction. In it we derive a certain particular conclusion from general laws, rules or principles.

11. **From Empirical to Rational** It means that the empirical knowledge of a student should be made rational so that it becomes true and definite. (It may be recalled here that empirical knowledge is the one which a learner receives by observation.)

# METHODS OF TEACHING IN INSTITUTIONS OF HIGHER LEARNING

Methods of teaching refers to general principles, pedagogy and management strategies used for classroom instruction. Choice of teaching methods depends on educational philosophy, classroom demography, subject areas and organisation's mission.

Following are the methods of teaching

**Methods of Teaching**

- **Teacher-Centered Methods**
  - Lecture Method
  - Demonstration Method
  - Biographical Method
  - Historical or Banking Teaching Theory Method
  - Team Teaching or Collaborative Teaching Method
- **Learner's Centered Methods**
  - Laboratory Method
  - Project Method
  - Assignment Method
  - Discussion Method
  - Brainstorming Method
  - Seminar Method

## 1. Teacher-Centered Methods

These methods consider teachers as the main authority figure and students are viewed as empty vessels who passively receive knowledge from their teachers.

Teacher–centered methods are

### (i) Lecture Method

Lecture method is the oldest teaching method applied in educational institution. This method is one way channel of communication of information. Student's involvement in this teaching method is just to listen and sometimes pen down some notes if necessary during the lecture, combine the information and organise it.

Lecture method of teaching serves four basic purposes–to motivate, to clarify, to review and to expand. Before preparing a lecture, the teacher must be aware of audience, purpose of lecture, time and content of lecture.

#### Merits

- This method helps students to learn languages and students develop their learning skills.
- The teacher can control and direct the flow of information with greater precision.
- It stimulates the interest of students by providing advanced knowledge on the topic where up to date information is not available.
- Teacher delivers the same lecture to both students without recognising the individual differences.

#### Demerits

- Lecture are often forgotten by the students soon after, and attention level is not the same while student listening the lecture.
- It is highly authoritarian and undemocratic.
- The learner is a silent receiver of information.
- It does not provide scope to learners to ask questions, raise doubts or provide observations.

### (ii) Lecture Demonstration Method

In the demonstration method, the teacher or an assigned student or group show how a process is done while the students become observers. The demonstrator is knowledgeable in preparing the apparatus needed according to the steps to be followed. The rest of the class becomes focused on the activity and concentration on the subject is assured. Demonstration method is a visual approach to examining information, ideas and processes. Demonstration method of teaching is based on following principles

- Learning by doing maxim is followed
- Skills can be developed by imitation
- The perceptions help in imitation

This method is mainly applied in technical or training institutes. In teacher education programs it is used to develop skills in the student teacher. At school level, a teacher applies it in teaching science, biology, nature, study, arts and crafts. This method of teaching involves various senses to make learning permanent.

### Merits

- It allows students to see the teacher actively engaged as a learner and a model rather than merely telling then what they need to know.
- It focuses to achieve psychomotor and cognitive objectives.
- It develops interests in the learners and motivates them for their active participation.
- It is economical in terms of efforts, energy, resources and time.

### Demerits

- There is scarcity of audio-visual aids due to poor economic conditions of government schools and teachers are not so creative to produce handmade models for demonstration.
- It is highly controlled and dominating method of instruction.
- It does not provide opportunities to involve learners' participation.
- It requires precision, practice and accuracy to be really successful.

## (iii) Biographical Method

In Biographical Method of teaching, some biographies are used to analyse the author's personal life.

In this teaching method, teachers' role become significant and learners play their inductive role in learning process.

### Merits

- It is used to tackle pedagogical difficulties associated with the increasing marketisation of higher education and the depoliticised attitudes of the students.
- It is suitable at higher level of teaching where students are capable to reach at an inference on their own.

### Demerits

- Students can be damaged by engaging openly and publically with curricula that asks them to draw on their own biographies.
- Students sometimes get diverted into learning criminologic theories and end up being criminal later.

## (iv) Historical Method

Historical method of teaching is a technique of presenting information, in which a topic is considered in terms of its earliest phases and followed in a historical course through its subsequent evolution and development.

A leading international educator of the 20th century, named this form of teaching a banking teaching theory. In the banking concept of education, knowledge is a gift bestowed by those who consider themselves knowledgeable upon those who they consider to know nothing.

### Merits

- This method of teaching provides the student with deposits of knowledge like money in a bank.
- The teacher directs and controls students' behaviour, and provides a model to correct the responses.
- It evolves students speaking ability.

### Demerits

- It is a very confusing method for the weak students to follow.
- This method is more focussed on speaking and memorising skills, therefore it does not guarantee good writing ability of students.

## (v) Question Answer Teaching Method

Question answer teaching strategy is an old strategy also known as "Socratic Method of Teaching". It was developed by the famous philosopher Socrates.

According to Parke, "the question is the key to all educative activity above the habit-skill level. It strategy is focused on to achieve the cognitive objectives and bringing knowledge to the conscious level".

### Merits

- While asking questions, the teacher keeps in mind the abilities, needs and interest of the learner.
- It involves the learners' participation towards the subject matter and in teaching acts.

- It helps in achieving cognitive objectives and bringing knowledge at conscious level.
- Classroom verbal interaction is encouraged.
- It is a useful strategy at all the levels of education.

### Demerits

- It is difficult to prepare good questions, and arrange them logically.
- The whole content-matter cannot be taught by this strategy.
- The teacher wants the structured answers from the learners. There is no freedom for imaginative answers.

## (vi) TV or Video Presentation

It is an improved presentation of radio or audio presentation and it can virtually bring the whole world inside the classroom. Screening of video presentation is followed by discussion or task.

### Merits

- Specifically useful for adult learners.
- Easily accessible for learners in remote areas.
- Specifically useful for subjects, such as geography and astronomy.
- Many important personalities and experts are brought to the classroom through video presentations.

### Demerits

- Less possibility for two-way communication.
- There can be difficult in adjusting to complicate schedules to telecast period.

## (vii) Team Teaching Method

Team teaching involves a group of instructors working purposefully, regularly and cooperatively to help a group of students. In this method of teaching teachers set goals for course, design a syllabus, prepare individual lesson plans, teach students and evaluate the results.

The team teaching method allows for more interaction between teachers and students. Teachers evaluate students on their achievement of the learning goals, students evaluate teachers on their teaching proficiency. The team teacher's main contribution is that, the pupils can have maximum opportunities of facing maximum specialists.

Working in teams spreads responsibility, encourages creativity, deepens friendships, and builds community among teachers.

Hence, the pupils can gain the advantage of specific knowledge of the different teachers.

### Merits

- It provides stimulus to the ideas of the pupils and teachers.
- It develops the strong will and responsibility of participation among the pupils and teachers.
- It is very economical in terms of time and energy.

### Demerits

- In this method many teachers are required.
- It is not useful for all subjects.
- It requires much time for planning and scheduling.

### → Micro Teaching

Micro teaching is a teacher training technique. It was first time developed by **Dwight W Allen** and his colleagues at Stanford University. According to **Allen**, "Micro teaching is a scaled down teaching encounter in class size and class time."

The objective of Micro teaching is to build up skills and confidence, to experience a range of lecturing styles and to learn and practise giving constructive feedback. As a tool for teacher preparation, micro teaching trains teaching behaviours and skills in small group settings aided by video-recordings. In a protected environment of friends and colleagues, teachers can try out a short piece of what they usually do with their students and receive a well-intended collegial feedback. Micro teaching can be defined with the help of the following diagram.

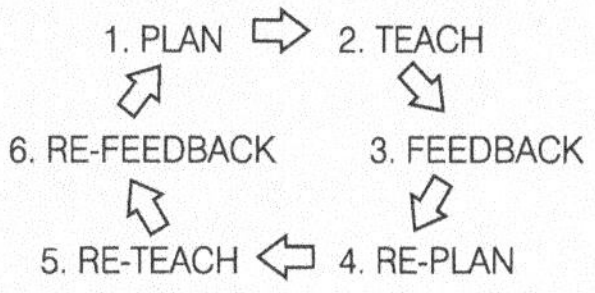

## 2. Learner's Centered Methods

In learner's centered methods of teaching, teachers and students play an equally active role in the learning process.

Following are the learner's centered methods of teaching

### (i) Laboratory Method

The laboratory method is a planned learning activity dealing with original or raw data in the solution of a problem. It is a procedure involving first hand experiences with materials or facts derived from investigations or experimentation. The primary aim of laboratory method of teaching is to give first hand experience to students.

#### Merits

- It is used to designate a teaching procedure in the physical sciences that use experimentation with apparatus.
- It builds scientific attitude and sense of achievement among learners.

#### Demerits

- It is not suitable for all the subjects because all knowledge cannot be verified through experiment.
- It is effective only in a small group.

### (ii) Project Method

Project method is one of the modern methods of teaching in which, the students point of view is given importance in designing the curricula and content of studies. This method is based on the philosophy of pragmatism and the principle of 'learning by doing'.

In this strategy pupils perform constructive activities in natural condition, realistic and experiential.

Project method of teaching encourages the spirit of scientific enquiry as it involves validation of hypothesis based on evidence gathered from field through investigation.

#### Merits

- It takes the student beyond the walls of the classroom and makes learning realistic and experimental.
- It encourages the spirit of scientific enquiry as it involves validation of hypothesis based on evidence gathered from field through investigation.
- It allows the students a great degree of freedom to choose from among the option given to them, hence it provides a psychological boost.

#### Demerits

- It is time consuming and can be extended endlessly.
- It requires meticulous planning and execution otherwise it can give unreliable results.
- There can be many uncontrolled social or natural factors which may affect the outcome of the project.
- In the absence of effective and alert supervision, a student may take the unreliable data.

### (iii) Assignment Method

Assignment method of teaching is an instructional technique comprises the guided information, self-learning, writing skills and report preparation among the learners.

Following precautions should be taken while executing assignment method of teaching.

- The assignment must be lesson concerned and related with the textbook and curriculum.
- The assignment must be explained with the availability of resources.
- The core of the subject or unit must be clarified.
- The tough and difficult portions of the assignment need to be explained well.

#### Merits

- It provides information analysis and research attitude to the learners.
- It develops the learning experiences from various sources.
- It inculcates the self-learning attitude among the students.

### Demerits

- There are always chances of plagiarism increasing chances of copy-paste.
- The slow learners need much more attention from the teacher, again it gives more burden for the teacher.
- The time limit given threatens the students which makes the substandard work.

## (iv) Discussion Method

Discussion method of teaching is a group activity involving the teacher and the student to define the problem and seek its solution. Discussion method is also described as a constructive process involving listening, thinking as well as the speaking ability of the student. Discussion method of teaching involves following steps

(a) **Orientation** provides the discussion topic and explains how students have to prepare for discussion.

(b) **Engagement** develops an environment of discussion in which an intensive session of questioning and answering is conducted.

(c) **Debrief** allows time to students to make their own notes.

### Merits

- It is a learner-centered method.
- It allows learners to take responsibility of their own learning thus, making them more mature and independent learners.
- It facilitates student reflection on what they learnt.
- It provides freedom of decision making and forming judgements.

### Demerits

- It is highly time consuming.
- It may lead to invalid and illogical interference.
- It encourages the dominance of a few members from the group of learners.

## (v) Brainstorming Method

It is a group creativity technique by which efforts are made to find a conclusion for a specific problem by gathering a list of ideas spontaneously contributed by its members.

The term was popularised by **Alex Faickney Osborn** in the 1953 book 'Applied Imagination'. According to him, people are able to think more freely and they suggest many spontaneous new ideas as possible. All the ideas are noted down and are not criticised and after brainstorming session the ideas are evaluated.

### Merits

- It popularises the group method of finding ideas.
- It applies to solve the goal of the group.
- It provides platform for everyone to speak and to create ideas.
- It is very economical.

### Demerits

- It may lead to constant arguing due to virtues.
- Team members who have displayed creativity are more likely to succeed.
- It can be over-applied easily.
- It is not a very systematic way of studying a subject.

## (vi) Seminar Method

It is a method in which a group of people come together for discussion and learn specific techniques and topics.

Usually there are several keynote speakers within each seminar, and these speakers are usually experts in their own fields or topics.

### Merits

- A wealth of knowledge usually, presented by many speakers at one time in one place.
- In this method individuals can meet to others with same interests/problems or concerns.
- A great way for those who do not like to read, or attend classes, to improve their knowledge of a specific subject.

### Demerits

- There are chances that the speakers share the incorrect knowledge.
- It is time consuming as well as costly.
- There are chances that attendees will expect too much from a seminar and may be disappointed.

## (vii) Heuristic Method

This method was proposed by **Armstrong**. The word Heuristic is derived from the Greek work 'Heuriskein' which means 'find'. The aim of this method is to make students learn curiously by discovery, instead of receiving information from teachers. Principles of activity, logical thinking, known to unknown purposeful experience, self-thinking, self-study etc. are used in Heuristic method.

In this method, the teacher gives a topic or problem to students and they have to find out the solution, using library, online resources, workshops, seminars etc.

### Merits

- It is student centered approach.
- The teacher encourages students to learn on their own.
- It focuses on developing scientific attitude in students for problem solving.
- It helps in all round development of students.

### Demerits

- It is not meant for students of primary level.
- Not all students possess the same set of skills. So below average students will not be comfortable with this method.
- It is important here for students to have access to library, laboratory and internet. Some institutes might not be able to provide these, so in such circumstances, it will be difficult to use this method.

## (viii) Kinesthetic Learning

This is also known as tactile learning or hands on learning. In such learning, there is more emphasis on physical activities, instead of lectures or demonstration. Students learn by experience, role playing, drama, sport etc.

### Merits

- It involves lesser use of technology.
- Such activities are good in engaging students so that they learn with greater interest and curiosity.
- It helps students in retaining what they have learnt.

### Demerits

- Not all subjects can be taught by using this method.
- Students might understand the working easily using this method but they will not have deep knowledge of concepts.
- To overcome this it should be used with lecturing but not as a substitute of lecturing.

## (ix) Computer Assisted Learning

Computer-assisted learning is concerned with the use of a computer to mediate the flow of information in learning process.

A computer has the ability to process information quickly, accurately and to adopt and respond to the learner's need difficulties and progress, which is much greater than that of a book or video tape.

### Merits

- It has more flexibility and better control in comparison to other methods.
- It can be effectively used for drilling and practicing simulation and modeling.

### Demerits

- It is impersonal and costly.

## (x) Case Study Method

The case study method is a participatory, discussion based way of learning where students gain skills in critical thinking, communication and group dynamics.

A case study is usually a description of an actual situation, commonly involving a decision, a challenge and opportunity, a problem, or an issue faced by a person or persons in a social setup such as an organisation. In learning with case studies, the students must deal with situations described in the case.

This method has application across disciplines, such as psychology, biology. Management, law, sociology, history etc.

The case study method becomes an efficient tool for the creation of a learner centered education rather than a teacher-centered education.

It is an important for bringing real world problems in to a classroom or workshop. This ensure active participation and may lead to innovative solution to the problems.

### Merits

- In enhances decision-making and problem solving skills.
- It provides opportunity to the participants to analysis critically, examine, evaluate and express reasoned opinions.
- It ensures active participation, which may lead to innovative solutions.

### Demerits

- It is impersonal and costly.

## (xi) Personalized System of Instruction (PSI)

It refers to a set of methods, strategies, experiences and techniques which are used to address the diverse needs, interests and aspirations of the students. It can be used for all subject matters except where the students are there to select the contents. It is a learner-centred method which consists of five basic elements that are :

(a) Mastery learning
(b) Self-pacing
(c) Stress on written material
(d) Proctors
(e) Lectures

### Merits

- Learning is self-paced.
- It is based on mastery learning.

### Demerits

- It cannot be used for primary level students.
- It is not suitable for psychomotor and affective domains.
- It is not valid for rapidly changing course contents.

## (xii) Flipped Classroom

A modern concept that has become popular since 2007, here the teacher records their lectures and share them with students. It is named as flipped classroom as it is the opposite of normal classroom. In a normal classroom set up, the teacher instructions the students and gives them assignments as homework.

But in flipped classroom, the teacher shares the link for video lectures with students and they watch these at their own pace at home. The students then work on assignments in the classroom.

### Merits

- Students can study video lectures and handout at their own pace.
- It helps in better discussion on assignments in the classroom.

### Demerits

- In this the teacher as well as the students should be aware of latest technology is which can be used for recording and sharing lectures.
- There could be problem if teachers and students do not have good internet connection.

# Another Model of Teaching Method

Map can be used to explore a multitude of topics and can incorporate visual learning, spatial thinking and quantative skills into lesson.

It has two types and they are as follows

## 1. Mind Mapping

Mind mapping as a method of teaching was developed by Tony Buzan. A mind map is a diagram for representing tasks, words, concepts or items linked to and arranged around a central concept or subject. It uses non-linear graphical layout the user to build an intuitive framework around a central concept.

It can turn a long list of monotonous information into a colourful, memorable and highly organised diagram that works in line with a learner's brain's natural way of doing things.

It is commonly used in presentations, critical thinking, brainstorming and decision-making.

Mobile learning as a form of e-learning is helpful for students to access information whenever and wherever they want.

### 2. Concept Mapping

Concept mapping is a great way to build upon previous knowledge by connecting now information back to it. It was started in 1984.

Concept mapping is a visual representations of information. Concept maps are visual display ideas, images, words, phrases and sentences that connect one another and present complex concept based on the knowledge of the mapper.

It works very well for classes or content that have visual elements or in times when it is important to see and understand relationship between different things.

## Offline and Online Methods of Teaching

### Offline Methods

Offline methods of teaching are considered traditional and are most commonly used methods of teaching in all institutions. These methods are prevalent in teaching-learning process.

These are both student-centric and teacher-centric methods. These include lecture method, demonstration method, team-teaching method, project method and all those methods of teaching which do not use any means of Information and Communication Technology.

#### Benefits of Offline Methods

- More personal face to face interaction with the teacher which makes the subject more interesting to learn.
- The teacher will be able to understand if they were able to get their point across correctly to each student by asking them to do activities related to the task.
- It is easier for students to get doubts and misconceptions clarified as and when the subject matter is being taught.
- The entire class-time in offline classes can be dedicated to teaching and learning.
- Offline classes are accessible to those who do not have a proper internet connection too.
- There is a chance for the teachers and students to bond with each other and form social relationships.
- There is more scope for classroom discussions and debates in offline classes.

The facial expressions and body language of the students will help the teacher understand if they are keeping the students interested in the class.

### Online Method

Online methods of teaching are modern methods of teaching which are based on technology and rarely used in institutions to impart education.

These are new methods which are based on ICT and online mode. For example, SWAYAM, Swayamprabha and MOOCs, etc.

#### Benefits of Online Methods

- **Time and Location Flexibility** A teacher can choose to teach at any time that suits him/her.
- **Better Organisation** Another major benefit of teaching online is that everything is well organised, avoiding any mismanagement.
- **Convenience** Online teaching doesn't require any travelling overhead.
- **Diverse Teaching Experiences** The online medium of teaching gives a teacher an opportunity and experience to connect with students from different disciplines, backgrounds and cultures.
- Online teaching can thus take the teaching experience from a regional level to national level and even further to an international level.
- **Student Engagement** Online teachers report that online teaching incorporates more engagement between student and the teacher.

## Online vs. Offline Method

The main difference between online and offline learning is location. With offline learning, participants are required to travel to the training location, typically a lecture hall, college or classroom.

With online learning, on the other hand, the training can be conducted from practically anywhere in the world.

Another difference is the flexibility offered. Online learning usually has a more flexible timescale. With offline learning, it is typically carried out between office hours and doesn't offer as much flexibility to the learner or the trainer.

Unlike offline learning method that requires us to shell out a lot of money, the online mode of learning is absolutely affordable and doesn't burn a hole in our pocket.

## E-Learning

E-learning is the acquisition of knowledge which takes place through electronic technologies and media. Typically, e-learning is conducted on the internet, where students can access their learning materials online at any place at any time.

Some examples of e-learning are :

### 1. SWAYAM

SWAYAM stands for Study Webs of Active-Learning for Young Aspiring Minds. It is a Massive Open Online Course (MOOC). This programme was launched by the Government of India in 2017 which is designed to achieve the three cardinal principles of Education Policy i.e. access, equity and quality to all especially to the most disadvantaged groups.

#### Aims

It aims to bridge the digital divide for students in e-education thus, promotes E-Learning. It is an instrument for self-actualisation which provides opportunities for a life-long learning.

Courses delivered through SWAYAM are available free of cost to the learners of school (from 9th class), under-graduate, post-graduate, engineering, law and other professional courses.

These programmes are offered by faculties of centrally funded institutions like IITs, IIMs and Central Universities. These courses can be accessed by anyone, anywhere at any time.

The courses hosted on SWAYAM are in four quadrants

(i) Video lecture.

(ii) Specially prepared reading material that can be downloaded or printed.

(iii) Self-assessment tests through tests and quizzes.

(iv) An online discussion forum for clearing the doubts.

#### Characteristics of SWAYAM

- SWAYAM is high quality learning experience using multimedia on anytime, anywhere basis.
- One-stop web location from interactive-content for all courses from school to university level.
- State of the art system that allows easy across, monitoring and certification.
- Peer group interaction and discussion forum to clarify doubts.
- Hybrid model that adds to be quality of class room teaching.

### 2. Swayamprabha

The Swayamprabha is a digital initiative of Government of India which was launched in 2017. It is a group of 32 DTH channels devoted to telecast high-quality educational programmes on 24 × 7 basis using the GSAT-15 satellite.

#### Aims

The programme is designed to provide new content everyday for atleast 4 hours which would be repeated 5 more times in a day, allowing the students to choose the time of their convenience.

These 32 channels are uplinked from BISAG, Gandhinagar. The study material/contents are provided by NPTEL, IITs, UGC, CEC, IGNOU, NCERT and NIOS the web portal is maintained by the INFLIBNET Centre. The 32 DTH Channels are set to cover

(i) **Higher Education** Curriculum-based course contents at post-graduate and undergraduate level.

All courses would be certified, ready in their detailed offering through SWAYAM.

(ii) **School Education** (9-12 Levels) Modules for teacher's training as well as teaching and learning aids for children.

(iii) **Curriculum-based Courses** that can meet the needs of life-long learners of Indian citizens in India and abroad.

(iv) **Assist students of (Class 11th and 12th)** to prepare for competitive exams.

### Characteristics of Swayamprabha

- This technology enables teachers to teach large number of students who are not physically present in the classes.
- The main advantage of this scheme is that it is being telecasted on DTH channels which are cheaper, easily accessible and it gives chance to rural people also to study from good teachers.
- It offers flexibility for people to learn at their own place.
- It also gives opportunities to the teachers to use their teaching abilities in a best way they can that increases their teaching capacity.
- The DTH e-classes provide curriculum-based course and contents for post-graduate and undergraduate level learners. Students hailing from disciplines such as arts, science, commerce, performing arts, social sciences and humanities, engineering, technology, law, medicine, agriculture, etc will get access to the required content through Swayamprabha channels.

## 3. MOOCs

MOOC stands for Massive Open Online Course. It is a web-based platform which provides unlimited number of students worldwide with a chance of distance education with the best institutes in the world. It was set up in 2008 and became more active in 2012 as a popular learning tool.

### Aims

It provides opportunities to its learners such as video lectures, downloading notes, contributing their own and sharing their point of view by communicating with peers, professors and Teaching Assistants (TAs).

There are various notable institutions, both non-profit and commercial, that offer these courses worldwide with the help of MOOC providers such as

- **NPTEL** (India) Indian Institute of Technology (IITs) and Indian Institute of Science (IISc) offer online courses through this platform which require no registration and are free of cost.
- **WiziQ** (India and USA) IIT Delhi, India offers this course through this platform which requires registration and fees to study courses offered by them.

  (i) **Open2Study** Based on Australia.

  (ii) **Coursera** Based out of USA.

  (iii) **edX** Based on USA.

  (iv) **udemy** Based on USA.

### Characteristics of MOOCs

- **Openness** is one of the core components of a MOOCs, along with self-organisation, connectedness, complexity, and chaos. Openness of information flow is a vital characteristic of a self-organising complex system and one that implies a system is willing to transform.
- **Barriers to Persistence** Both MOOC models have issues of high drop out rates. To mitigate this issue, researchers have examined the barriers to learning in this new environment.
- **Models** MOOCs began with a connectives model targeting an adult lifelong learning audience. The MOOC concept was then applied to postsecondary online education using the MOOC model, which was designed as a traditional teacher-directed course, yet automated, massive and online.

### E-Pathshala

E-Pathshala is a portal/app developed by the CIET, NCERT. It was initiated jointly by the Ministry of Human Resource Development and CIET, NCERT and launched in November 2015.

E-Pathshala hosts educational resources for teachers, students, parents, researchers and educators.

The platfrom offers a slew of educational resources, including NCERT textbooks for classes 1-12, audio-visual resources by NCERT, periodicals, supplements, teacher training modules and a variety of other print and non-print materials. These materials can be downloaded by the user for offline use with no limits on downloads. The app supports flip book format to provide a more realistic experience.

### Aims

It provides access to digital textbooks for all classes, graded learning materials and enables participation in exhibitions, contests, festivals, workshops, etc.

### Characteristics

- Access digital textbooks (e-textbooks) for all classes.
- Access graded learning materials (supplementary books).
- Know about events.
- Accessd-e-resources (audios, videos, interactive images, maps, question banks, etc.).
- Help children achieve expected learning outcomes.

### Bharat Padhe Online

'Bharat Padhe Online' is a campaign for crowdsourcing of ideas for improving the online education system in India.

It was launched by HRD Ministry in April 2020. The 'Bharat Padhe Online' is a one week programme.

It aims to invite all the best minds of the country to share their suggestions or solutions directly with the HRD Ministry in order to overcome the problems of online education alongwith promoting the available digital education platforms.

## TEACHING SUPPORT SYSTEM

Teaching Support System is basically a set of tools that helps to improve student achievement by building newer capacities in the teachers. It can be taken a kind of proces as well, it influences the way decisions are made and what information is passed on.

This helps us to know that how teachers acquire new skills and increase student achievement in areas they are under-performing. Though they are happening simultaneously, the movement has taken place from traditional to modern to ICT (Information and Communication Technology) based education.

### Traditional Teaching Support System

Traditional Teaching Method or System includes conventional methods of teaching that are used in the classroom for knowledge generation. It follows teacher-centred approach which aims at high test scores, grades, etc. This method was based on memorization of facts, objective information and correct knowledge. Here, the teacher relies on textbooks, lectures and written assignments.

Hence, the traditional teaching aids include Blackboards, Textbooks, Charts, Pictures, Models, Flashcards, Globes, Maps, Worksheets, etc. These aids involve a sense of vision and further enhance the observation skills of learners. This technique of teaching is a one-way flow of information i.e. from the teacher. This method is still being adhered in the schools as it has more interaction between the teacher and student.

### Modern Teaching Support System

Modern Teaching Method reflects educational progressivism as it is based on understanding, application, analysis, evaluation, innovation and critical thinking of facts. This method aims at learning, retention, accumulation of valuable knowledge and skills.

Hence, the modern teaching aids include Internet Surfing, Laptops, Computer Educational Games, Online Dictionaries, Power-point Slides and Games, Online e-books, Online Tests, Educational CDs and DVDs, Projectors, Interactive Whiteboards or Smart Boards, etc.

Digitization in teaching, learning assessment and feedback improves learning process and it also helps integrative and social responsibility and civic engagement. Collaborative learning and problem-solving or problem-based learning is a key aspect of Modern Teaching methods.

## ICT Based Teaching Support System

ICT is an electronic means of capturing, processing, storing and communicating information. ICT based teaching support facilitate and enhance learning through computer and communications technology.

ICT has proven to be a vital form of teaching in today's scenario, since it provides ease for the teacher and the student to store, retrieve and manipulate the information.

Teaching can thus take the shape of computer-assisted learning (distance learning), video-conferencing, projectors and even mobiles. This technology has the ability to not only engaging the students in subjective activities but also enhance their cognitive skills. ICT includes computers, internet, telephone, radio and other audio-visual equipments. Hence, the development of innovative practices and the generation of new competencies in ICT are fast becoming key issues for teacher and trainer training.

## Significance of Teaching Support System

- Students can learn better when they are motivated properly through different teaching aids.
- Teaching aids provide complete example for conceptual thinking.
- Proper use of teaching aids helps to retain concepts permanently.
- Teaching aids provide direct experience to the students.
- Teaching aids help to increase the vocabulary of the students.
- Teaching aids create the environment of interests for the students.
- Teaching aids make the classroom live and active.
- Teaching aids facilitate the proper understanding to the students which discourage the act of cramming.

# EVALUATION SYSTEM

Evaluation is the wider term and plays a very important role in teaching learning process. Evaluation means to determine the growth and changes, taking place in pupils as a result of teaching learning experiences.

Evaluation can be described as the systematic approach for collecting, providing and utilising information about an educational course or program to determine the nature, quality and efficiency of the teaching and learning in that course or program.

In its wider sense evaluation is the continuous inspection of all available information concerning the student, teacher, educational programme and the teaching–learning process to ascertain the degree of change in students and form valid judgement about the students.

According to **Gronlund** and **Linn** "Evaluation is a systematic process of collecting, analysing and interpreting information to determine the extent to which pupils are achieving instructional objectives."

According to **CE Beeby** "Evaluation is the systematic collection and interpretation of evidence leading as a part of process to a judgement of value with a view to action."

## Objectives of Evaluation

- To help in diagnosing weaknesses of students.
- To help in predicting future achievement.

- To test the development of skills and attitudes of students.
- To familiarise the teacher with nature of pupil learning development and progress.
- To serve as a means of improving school-community relation.

## Steps of Evaluation Process

1. **Purpose** For what the evaluation is being conducted.
2. **Audience** The audience will determine the type of information collected and reported.
3. **Resources** What resources will be needed to conduct the evaluation.
4. **Evidence** What type of data or information will be needed to answer the evaluation questions.
5. **Data-gathering Techniques** Multiple techniques are used to increase the validity of the results.
6. **Analysis** Different interpretations are used to analyse the outcome of evaluation.
7. **Reporting** An evaluation report is distributed to the identified audience.

## Characteristics of Evaluation

- Evaluation implies a systematic process omits the casual controlled observation of pupils.
- It is a continuous process. In an ideal situation the teaching learning process on the one hand and the evaluation procedure on the other hand, go together. It is certainly a wrong belief that the evaluation procedure follows the teaching learning process.
- It is the determination of the congruence between the performance and objectives.
- Evaluation emphasises the broad personality changes and major objectives of an educational programme. Therefore, it includes not only subjectmatter achievements but also attitudes, interests and ideals, ways of thinking, work habits and personal and social adaptability.
- Evaluation always assumes that educational objectives have previously been identified and defined.
- This is the reason why teachers are expected not to lose sight of educational objectives while planning and carrying out the teaching-learning process either in the classroom or outside it.
- Objectives and accordingly learning experiences should be so relevant that ultimately they should direct the pupils towards the accomplishment of educational goals.
- A comprehensive programme of evaluation involves the use of many procedures (for example, analytico-synthetic, heuristic, experimental, lecture, etc.); a great variety of tests (for example, essay type, objective type, etc.); and other necessary techniques (for example, socio-metric, controlled-observation techniques, etc.).

## Importance of Evaluation

1. **Ensuring Learning Takes Place** Assessment should provide information about the levels of understanding that students are reaching upto.

   Frequent feedback to learners is required so that learners monitor their learning and actively evaluate their strategies and their current levels of understanding.
2. **Ensuring Teacher Effectiveness** Teaching can be effective if teachers start by setting learning objectives, instead of about what the teacher will do.

   Teachers must assess their students based on these primary learning objectives rather than on arbitrary standards.
3. **For Creating a Quality Learning** A quality learning environment is ensured through evaluation.
   - (i) **Learner-Centred** It pays attention to the knowledge, skills, attitudes and beliefs that learners bring to the educational setting.
   - (ii) **Knowledge-Centred** It takes seriously the need to help students become knowledgeable by learning in ways that leadtounderstanding.

(iii) **Assessment-Centred** It provides opportunities for feedback and revision, and also about the fact that the assessment matches the students' learning goals.

(iv) **Community-Centred** This refers to several aspects of the community, including the classroom as community, the school as a community, and the degree to which students, teachers and administrators feel connected to the large community of homes, business, states, the nation and even the world.

## Elements of Evaluation

An effective evaluation system includes the following research-based essential elements. These are as follows

1. **Research-Based and Proven Performance Targets** To ensure that student performance continually improves through the work of excellent teachers and leaders, an evaluation system must use measurement of clearly articulated, research-based and proven performance targets.
2. **Include Evidence of Teaching and Student Learning from Multiple Sources** In most of the institutions it is seen that end-of-year tests are used commonly to measure students' learning which provide teachers with too little information too late and may not reflect the full breadth and depth of instruction. Researchers have found that combining a range of measures yield the greatest reliability and predictive power of a teachers gains with students.
3. **Use Information to Provide Constructive Feedback to Teachers** The aim of evaluation should be to improve teacher practice. For this, timely feedback is important which should be provided formally, informally or both.

   It is provided using multiple sources of evidence from a variety of different measures, including observations focused on professional practice and the extent of student learning, analysis of the improvement of student performance, analysis of artifacts including lesson plans, professional development plans, supplemental resources, participation-in coursework, improvement plans and so on.
4. **Standardised and Periodic Training for Evaluators** Evaluators who collect the measures of evidence and provide feedback must be highly trained to ensure that ratings are fair, accurate and reliable.

   Thus provide training to evaluators is important which should be based on conducting effective classroom observations and walk-through focused on the quality of instruction, assessing student data, interpreting survey information, effectively providing clear, constructive, timely and meaningful feedback and so on.
5. **Use of Evaluation Results** Ratings of educator's effectiveness guide the institution's decisions regarding determinations, recognition, development, interventions and policies that impact the extent of student learning.

   Highly effective educators use their evaluation results in such ways like, contributing through key leadership roles, assisting with the challenges of high need students, assuming other critical additional duties that contribute to a school system's overall success.

## Techniques of Evaluation

Evaluation technique is not the end of teaching-learning process, although it is a valid theory that change the thinking and understanding behaviour of the students.

Thus, a standard evaluation indicates the qualitative change in the behaviour of the students.

The evaluation techniques are divided into two i.e. **qualitative** and **quantitative** techniques.

### 1. Quantitative Techniques

The quantitative techniques can be categorised into three elements.

(i) **Written Examination** This technique or method is also known as paper-pencil test. It is one of the popular technique of evaluation in these days.

Further, it has four basic components i.e. very short, short, long and essay type question-answers.

(ii) **Oral Examination** This technique is supplementary to the written examination. Test of reading ability and pronunciation is the example of oral examination.

(iii) **Practical Examination** This technique is used for testing the experimental activities of the students as well as manipulative skills of students. It is done in subjects like science, agricultural craft, music and technology.

## 2. Qualitative Techniques

Qualitative techniques is focussed on understanding how students make meaning and experience their environment or world.

These techniques can be categorised into following

(i) **Interview** It comprises a number of open-ended, questions that result in responses that yield information.

It is common to engage in face-to-face verbal interviews with one individual or with a group of students.

It is because of the fact that students are usually more willing to talk than write.

(ii) **Observation** It does not require direct contact with the students, rather this type of data collection involves a teacher providing information-rich descriptions of behaviour, conversations, interactions of the students for outcomes of the students' behaviour.

(iii) **Checklist** It does not only give the observer a set of criteria to observe, but it allows the observer to show student progress over time and to correlate a number with a qualitative process.

(iv) **Rating Scale** It is used for applying the expression of opinion or judgement regarding some situation, object, or character.

(v) **Cumulative Records** It is used for knowing the details about students' behaviour. Cumulative records include anecdotal records, cumulative record cards and diaries of students.

**→ Assessment of Evaluation**

- Assessment is the process of objectively understanding the state or condition of a thing by observation and measurement. Thus, assessment of teaching means measurement of its effectiveness.
- Evaluation is the process of observing and measuring a thing for the purpose of judging it and of determining its value, either by comparison to similar things, or to a standard. Evaluation of teaching means passing judgement on the teaching as part of an administrative process.

# Types of Evaluation

Evaluation can be categorised as following

## 1. Formative Evaluation

Formative evaluation includes any form of classroom interaction that generates information on student learning, which is then used by faculty (teacher) and students to fine-tune their teaching and learning strategies, respectively, during the teaching-learning process.

**Michael Scriven** coined the term formative evaluation in 1967. But, in 1968, Benjamin Bloom popularised the term through his book "Learning for Mastery" and considers it as a tool for improving the teaching-learning process for students.

It can be rated on scales that produce a qualitative rather than a quantitative description of teaching and generally utilised a three-to-five point scale.

These scales are called quality scales by Barr (1980) and required rater judgment with regard to the presence or absence of traits or the degree to which they were present.

### Purpose of Formative Evaluation

- To provide feedback for teachers to modify subsequent learning activities and experiences.
- To identify and remediate group or individual deficiencies.
- To move focus away from achieving grades and onto learning processes, in order to increase self-efficacy and reduce the negative impact of extrinsic motivation.
- To improve students' metacognitive awareness of how they learn.
- To provide immediate feedback to both student and teacher regarding the success and failures.
- To provide information to the teacher for modifying instruction and use this instruction for improving learning and instruction.
- Frequent ongoing assessment allows both for fine-tuning of instruction and student focus on progress.
- It encourages teacher and peer dialogue around learning, and also encourages positive motivational beliefs and self-esteem.
- It provides opportunities to close the gap between current and desired performance.

## 2. Summative Evaluation

Summative evaluation refers to the assessment of participants where the focus is on the outcome of a program. This contrasts with formative assessment, which summarises the participants' development at a particular time.

It is also coined by **Michael Scriven** in 1967. Questionnaires, Surveys, Interviews, Observations, Testing, Projects (a culminating project that synthesises knowledge) are the most common methods of summative assessment which aim to summarise overall learning at the completion of the course or unit.

Summative assessment usually takes place after students have completed units of work or modules at the end of each term and/or year. The information it gives indicates progress and achievement usually in grade-related or numerical terms. It's the more formal summing-up of a student's progress.

Therefore, summative assessment gives pupils, parents and teachers valuable information about a pupil's overall performance at a specific point in their learning.

## 3. Diagnostic Evaluation

Diagnostic evaluation is concerned with finding out the reasons for student's persistent or recurring learning difficulties that cannot be resolved by standard corrective measures or formative evaluation.

The aim of diagnostic evaluation is to find out the causes of learning problems and plan to take remedial actions. Observational techniques or specially prepared diagnostic techniques can be used to diagnose the problem. It determines the level of competence of the students.

Diagnostic evaluation includes; pretest results, an evaluation of your child's reading strengths and reading needs, an instructional plan, a description of the tutoring that was conducted, post-test results, a summary of outcomes and recommendations for future instruction.

### Significance of Evaluation

- Evaluation aids in devising more effective instructional materials and procedures of instruction.
- Evaluation is important to the classroom teachers, supervisors and administrators in directing as well as guiding teaching and learning.
- Evaluation helps to measure the validity and reliability of instruction.
- Evaluation helps teachers to discover the needs of the learners.
- Evaluation, helps to provide objective evidences for effective cooperation between parents and teachers.
- Evaluation can be used to enforce external standards upon the individual class or school.
- Evaluation helps parents to understand learners growth, interests and potentials.

## Evaluation in Choice Based Credit System in Higher Education (CBCS)

The University Grants Commission (UGC) has initiated several measures to bring equity, efficiency and excellence in the Higher Education System of country. Majority of Indian higher education institutions have been following marks or percentage based evaluation system, which obstructs the flexibility for the students to study the subjects of their choice and their mobility to different institutions.

Thus, to remove this situation the University Grants Commission (UGC) introduced Choice Based Credit System (CBCS) in higher education from the year 2015.

With the help of CBCS students can choose interdisciplinary, intra-disciplinary and skill-based courses including core, elective/ minor or skill based courses of their choice. The courses can be evaluated following the uniform grading system, which is considered to be better than the conventional marks system.

CBCS gives emphasis on the Continuous and Comprehensive Evaluation, computation of the Cumulative Grade Point Average (CGPA) based on the performance of students in the examinations and semester system.

It gives 40% weightage to the internal assessment and remaining 60% to the final exam. Internal evaluation consists of one test for 20 marks, one assignment for 10 marks: 5 marks for the active participation in the class and 5 marks for overall conduct of the learners during class hours.

### Advantages of Choice Based Credit System

- It can be seen as a major shift from the teacher centre to learner centre education.
- Student may undertake as many credits as they can cope with (without repeating all courses in a given semester if they fail in one/more courses).
- It permits learners to choose soft courses of different interdisciplinary and intradisciplinary subjects with the core subjects.
- It also helps to the learners to pursue their courses at different times.
- It has broadened the base of education system.
- Stress and anxiety of learners can be reduced through it.
- Helpful in ensuring the uniformity in education system in terms of evaluation and assessment.
- Globally acclaimed education system can be maintained through it, as it has the provision of offering different courses at the same time.

### Disadvantages of Choice Based Credit System

- It is tough to measure or calculate the exact marks.
- One subject can be repeated three times, it makes the students irresponsible.
- Numbers of courses are imposed in the CBCS,which is an overburden for the student as well as teachers.
- Chance of subjectivity is maximum, as internal evaluation has 40 % weightage.
- Research work and innovation get hamper, as most of the time teachers have to be involved in setting papers and making arrangement for the examinations.

## Evaluation in Computer Based Testing (CBT)

Information and Communication Technology (ICT) has become an essential component in higher education in India for the last decade. Thus, evaluation system is shifting from traditional assessment to computer based testing which is considered more authentic and accurate. The trend to opt this system of evaluation is increasing in the Indian higher education system due to several cases of cheating or proxy testing in high-stakes competitive exams in the recent years.

As a result, an increasing number of higher education institutions in India are choosing to invest in Computer Based Testing (CBT) instead of paper-and-pencil format to reduce the default methods.

## Factors Responsible to use Computer Based Testing

1. **Growth in Number of Internet Users** According to recent studies the-number of internet users is increasing day by day in even smaller towns and cities in India.

   So, most of the students are aware of basics of computer. Thus, it creates possibilities to include Computer Based Testing system in education.

2. **CBT is User-Friendly** Computer-based tests are correctly perceived to be fairer, more convenient, reliable and user friendly.

   Though some tests like the Graduate Record Examinations (GRE) have been computer based since the 1990's, the focus has now shifted from mere standardisation and certification to building a complete delivery model that encompasses preparation, testing and assessment.

3. **Elimination of Human Error and Bias** CBT improves the quality and reliability of the test and eliminates the chance of human error or bias in grading answers. Besides, it allows large number of tests and student data to be securely stored and analysed so that the quality of future tests can be improved.

4. **Scheduling Flexibility and Accessibility** Greater flexibility for scheduling and growing numbers of test centers across India has improved accessibility. This accessibility in turn has opened new opportunities for population previously unaccounted for in competitive admissions and job selections.

5. **Cost Effectiveness** In earlier times, affordability was the major obstacle in switching to the computer based testing. But over the time, institutes and employers have realised that paper based exams take longer time for evaluation as compared to CBT.

   Apart from this, there are many cases of cheating, theft and fraud in paper based exams/testing which make the scores obtained in these exams far less reliable as compared to CBT. Computerisation of tests is cost effective for host organisations and provides them the best option to ensure fair scoring across a large number of candidates.

## Innovations in Evaluation Systems

The evaluation of teaching and learning is important. There is also need to improve our present evaluation system by innovating some new techniques and methods.

Some of these innovative methods are given below

1. **Questionnaires** can be used to explore more complex, and more relevant issues such as what students are learning, what aspects are most useful, what could be improved. Thus, questionnaires can be used in evaluation system depending on the purpose, but they may be useful at the beginning and end of an initiative.

2. **Student Interviews** are often a valuable means of evaluation. Interviews can be done with focus groups of students and can be arranged at appropriate times during the course.

3. Asking students to **keep a journal** of their experiences and their comments about the initiative can often be useful. Journals can be analysed to increase confidence and understanding and can be used to improve the teaching-learning process.

   Thus, journals can be included as part of student assessment.

4. **The Socratic Wheel** is a simple and powerful visual rating tool with multiple applications. It can be used to set learning goals on the basis of baseline conditions, monitor progress or evaluate final results using multiple criteria, or compare projects, activities and individual profiles using single criteria.

# Chapter Practice

## Teaching : Nature, Objectives, Characteristics and Levels

1 Teaching aptitude means
(A) an interest in the teaching work orientation implementing teaching principles and methods
(B) love for money
(C) it is a specific capacity or special ability
(D) Both (A) and (C)

2 Which of the following is/are not the characteristic(s) related to the concept of teaching?
(A) Teaching is an educational communication
(B) Teaching is an haphazard activity
(C) Teaching is a process in which the learners, teachers, curriculum and other variables are organised in a systematic way to attain pre-determined goals
(D) All of the above

3 "Teaching is a supreme art to awaken joy in creative expression and knowledge."
It is stated by
(A) H C Morrison
(B) B D Smith
(C) Albert Einstein
(D) N L Gage

4 Which of the following is/are related to the element(s) of nature of teaching?
(A) It is dynamic, social and humane
(B) It is both arts and science
(C) It is an interactive process carried with purpose and objectives
(D) All of the above

5 The good objective of teaching should be able to
(A) bring desired changes in student's attitude
(B) improve learning skills of students
(C) develop conceptual intellectual and subject specific skills
(D) All of the above

6 Arrange the following levels of cognitive domain in correct sequence.
1. Synthesis, Knowledge, Application, Evaluation, Analysis, Comprehension
2. Knowledge, Comprehension, Application, Analysis, Synthesis, Evaluation
3. Synthesis, Application, Evaluation, Comprehension, Analysis, Knowledge
4. Knowledge, Comprehension, Evaluation, Application, Synthesis, Analysis

**Codes**
(A) 1 and 2 (B) Only 2
(C) 1 and 3 (D) Only 4

7 Match the following.

| **List I** (Levels) | **List II** (Characteristics) |
|---|---|
| A. Receiving | 1. It involves participation of students in learning process. |
| B. Responding | 2. It involves the value knowledge that are acquired by students. |
| C. Valuing | 3. It involves to build abstract knowledge. |
| D. Characterising | 4. It is about student's memory and recognition as well. |

**Codes**

| | A | B | C | D |
|---|---|---|---|---|
| (A) | 4 | 1 | 2 | 3 |
| (B) | 2 | 1 | 3 | 4 |
| (C) | 3 | 2 | 1 | 4 |
| (D) | 1 | 3 | 4 | 2 |

8 Which of the following is/are the characteristic(s) of psycho-motor domain?
(A) It is a knowledge based domain
(B) It is an action based domain
(C) Skills in psycho-motor domain describe the ability to physically manipulate a tool or instrument like a hand and hammer
(D) Both (B) and (C)

9 According to Gagne and Briggs model the educational learning objectives fall under which of the following categories?
(A) Verbal information
(B) Naturalisation
(C) Cognitive skills
(D) Both (A) and (C)

10 Who is the exponent of memory level of teaching?
(A) Herbart (B) Briggs
(C) Bloom (D) Hunt

**11** Which of the following is/are incorrect about memory level of teaching?
(A) It is the first level of teaching
(B) The teaching learning process is mainly stimulus-response
(C) It focuses on the mastery of the subject
(D) The teacher forces the students to learn the syllabus content through the process of memorisation

**12** Which of the following is/are the merit(s) of understanding level of thinking?
(A) The students make use of their thinking abilities
(B) Knowledge acquired at this level forms the basis of reflective level of teaching
(C) The students at this level learn by understanding facts and information
(D) All of the above

**13** According to Hunt which of the following steps are included under the (Reflective syntax) model of teaching?
(A) Creating a problematic situation
(B) Formulation of hypothesis
(C) Mastery of the content
(D) Both (A) and (B)

**14** Which of the following is/are the characteristics of reflective level of teaching?
(A) It is also known as introspective level
(B) It basically involves the use of scientific method to the understanding of the problems
(C) The student's original thinking and creative abilities are developed
(D) All of the above

**15** Which of the following given below are the general principles of teaching?
(A) Principle of motivation and interest
(B) Principle of remedial teaching
(C) Principle of imparting training to senses
(D) Principle of democratic dealing

**16** Which of the following is/are the advantage(s) of teaching machine?
(A) Right answer is delayed
(B) It encourage students to take active part in the instruction process
(C) The teacher after knowing about the progress of student can give necessary supplementary reinforcement
(D) Both (B) and (C)

**17** A good teacher should possess which of these qualities to be an effective teacher?
(A) He/She should have superior learning skills
(B) He/She should always be ready to improve himself through self-analysis
(C) He/She should be well conversant with various teaching techniques
(D) All of the above

**18** Which of the following statement(s) is/are not true?
(A) Teaching is just an art
(B) Teachers can be trained only
(C) Teachers are born
(D) All of the above

**19** The main aim of classroom teaching is
(A) to give information
(B) to develop inquiring mind
(C) to develop personality of students
(D) to help students pass examinations

**20** Teaching in higher education implies
(A) presenting the information given in the textbook
(B) asking question in the class and conducting examinations
(C) helping students prepare for and pass the examination
(D) helping students to learn

**21** Teaching will be effective if the teacher
(A) is the master of the subject
(B) has much experience in teaching the subject
(C) starts from what students know already
(D) uses many instructional aids

**22** Which is the most desirable outcome of teaching in higher education?
(A) Increase in student achievement
(B) Increase in the level of independent thinking of students
(C) Higher percentage of result
(D) Increase in the number of students who opt for the subject

**23** The main objective of teaching at higher education level is
(A) to prepare students to pass examination
(B) to develop the capacity to take decisions
(C) to give new information
(D) to motivate students to ask questions during lecture

**24** Before explaining the need of the topic, it is important to
(A) maintain high discipline in the class
(B) get the attention of the learners
(C) raise few questions from the previous learning
(D) All of the above

**25** The most significant component of effective teaching is
(A) create a disciplined classroom environment
(B) teachers' commitment and integrity
(C) teacher's efforts to foster learning and understanding
(D) take attendance regularly

**26** The most important objective of teaching is to
(A) facilitate students when it comes to the construction of knowledge and understanding
(B) cover the prescribed syllabus
(C) create a relaxed teaching and learning environment
(D) take classes regularly

**27** Teaching helps in
(A) transmitting the social values and ideals to the young minds
(B) preparing children for competition
(C) preparing students for examination
(D) All of the above

**28** In the overall growth of a student, who plays an important role?
(A) Teacher
(B) Guardian
(C) School manager
(D) Principal

**29** "Education is the manifestation of perfection already in man" was stated by
(A) M K Gandhi
(B) R N Tagore
(C) Swami Vivekanand
(D) Sri Aurobindo

**30** Effective teaching is a function of
(A) teacher's satisfaction
(B) teacher's honesty and commitment
(C) teacher's making students learn and understand
(D) teacher's liking for professional excellence

**31** Effective teaching comprises of
(A) an active teacher, but the students may be passive
(B) active students, but the teacher may be passive
(C) both the teacher and the students are active
(D) All of the above

**32** In a lively classroom situation, there is likely to be
(A) occasional roars of laughter
(B) complete silence
(C) frequent teacher–student dialogue
(D) loud discussion among students

**33** Which one of the following statements is correct?
(A) Syllabus is an annexure to the curriculum
(B) Curriculum is the same in all educational institutions
(C) Curriculum includes both formal and informal education
(D) Curriculum does not include methods of evaluation

**34** According to Swami Vivekananda, teacher's success depends on
(A) his renunciation of personal gain and service to others
(B) his professional training and creativity
(C) his concentration on his work and duties with a spirit of obedience to God
(D) his mastery on the subject and capacity in controlling the students

**35** Which of the following teacher, will be liked most?
(A) A teacher of high idealistic attitude
(B) A loving teacher
(C) A teacher who is disciplined
(D) A teacher who often amuses his students

**36** Interaction inside the classroom should generate
(A) argument (B) information
(C) ideas (D) controversy

**37** A teacher can be successful if he/she
(A) helps students in becoming better citizens
(B) imparts subject knowledge to students
(C) prepares students to pass the examination
(D) presents the subject matter in a well organised manner

**38** Which of the following qualities is most essential for a teacher?
(A) He should be a learned person
(B) He should be a well dressed person
(C) He should have patience
(D) He should be an expert in his subject

**39** Suppose a student wants to share his problems with his teacher and he visits the teacher's house for the purpose, the teacher should
(A) contact the student's parents and solve his problem
(B) suggest him that he should never visit his house
(C) suggest him to meet the principal and solve the problem
(D) extend reasonable help to boost his morale

**40** Most often, the teacher-student communication is
(A) spurious (B) critical
(C) utilitarian (D) confrontational

**41** Attitudes, actions and appearances in the context of classroom communication are considered as
(A) verbal (B) non–verbal
(C) impersonal (D) irrational

**42** Which one of the following is considered a sign of motivated teaching?
(A) Students asking questions
(B) Maximum attendance of the students
(C) Pin drop silence in the classroom
(D) Students taking notes

**43** Teacher's role at higher education
(A) provide information to students
(B) promote self-learning in students
(C) encourage healthy competition among students
(D) help students to solve their problems

**44** At the primary school stage, most of the teachers should be women because they
(A) can teach children better than men
(B) know basic content better than men
(C) are available on lower salaries
(D) can deal with children with love and affection

**45** What is more desirable in a classroom?
(A) A teacher delivering a lecture on the basis of the text and his own research
(B) A teacher delivering a lecture on the basis of course content and standard books
(C) A teacher answering questions raised by students
(D) A teacher maintaining strict discipline and taking attendance regularly

**46** While presenting your ideas in a classroom it is better to
I. recognise that there can be other views
II. recognise that students are not a homogenous mass
III. take dissenting views also in consideration
(A) Both I and III (B) Only III
(C) II and III (D) I, II and III

**47** The most important challenge before a teacher is
(A) to maintain discipline in the class
(B) to make students do their homework
(C) to prepare question paper
(D) to make teaching–learning process enjoyable

**48** The psychological aspects of the classroom are best managed by
(A) the class teacher
(B) the subject teacher
(C) the principal
(D) the student themselves

**49** An effective teacher will ensure
(A) cooperation among his students
(B) laissez–faire role
(C) competition among students
(D) competition or cooperation as the situation demands

**50** A new teacher to start with will have to
(A) enforce discipline in class
(B) establish rapport with the students
(C) cut jokes with the students
(D) tell the students about his qualifications

**51** The basic requirement to teach efficiently is
(A) mastery over the topic
(B) mastery over different strategies of teaching
(C) mastery over technology
(D) All of the above

**52** If students do not understand what is taught in the classroom, the teacher should feel
(A) terribly bored
(B) to explain it in a different way
(C) that he is wasting time
(D) pity for the students

**53** A teacher will become an effective communicator if
(A) he uses instructional aids
(B) he helps students get meaning out of what he teaches
(C) he asks question in between teaching
(D) he helps students get correct answer to the questions on the topic

**54** An ideal situation in a classroom would be where
I. a teacher comes fully prepared to deliver his lecture
II. students come fully prepared and discuss the subject with each other in teacher's presence
III. teachers and students discuss the subject
IV. the teacher uses audio–visual aids while learning
(A) Both I and III (B) Both III and IV
(C) Only II (D) Only III

**55** Which one of the following is appropriate in respect of teacher student relationship?
(A) Very informal and intimate
(B) Limited to classroom only
(C) Cordial and respectful
(D) Indifferent

**56** Which of the following is not a prescribed level of teaching?
(A) Memory (B) Understanding
(C) Reflective (D) Differentiation

**57** The students who keep on asking questions in the class should be
(A) encouraged to find answer independently
(B) advised to meet the teacher after the class
(C) encourage to continue questioning
(D) advised not to disturb during the lecture

**58** The Verstehen School of Understanding was popularised by
(A) German Social Scientists
(B) American Philosophers
(C) British Academicians
(D) Italian Political Analysts

**59** Which of the following is the most important single factor in underlying the success of beginning as a teacher?
(A) Scholarship
(B) Communicative ability
(C) Personality and its ability to relate to the class and to the pupils
(D) Organisational ability

**60** A person can enjoy teaching as a profession when he
(A) has control over students
(B) commands respect from students
(C) is more qualified than his colleagues
(D) is very close to higher authorities

**61** Teachers who are passionate in classroom transactions
(A) involve their students in the teaching-learning process
(B) often lack deeper insight of the subject content
(C) use frivolous examples to hold the student's attention
(D) All of the above

**62** Success of the teaching profession depends upon
(A) policy to keep students happy
(B) maintaining of relationship with school administrators
(C) growth of both learners and teachers through the teaching–learning process
(D) finding avenues for personal growth

**63** Those teachers are popular among students who
(A) develop intimacy with them
(B) help them solve their problems
(C) award good grades
(D) take classes on extra tuition fee

**64** The primary responsibility for the teacher's adjustment lies with
(A) the children (B) the principal
(C) the teacher himself (D) the community

**65** Which one of the following is the most important quality of a good teacher?
(A) Punctuality and sincerity
(B) Content mastery
(C) Content mastery and reactive
(D) Content mastery and sociable

**66** A successful teacher is one who is
(A) compassionate and disciplinarian
(B) quite and reactive
(C) tolerant and dominating
(D) passive and active

**67** The primary duty of the teacher is to
(A) raise the intellectual standard of the students
(B) improve the physical standard of the students
(C) help all round development of the students
(D) imbibe value system in the students

**68** A teacher's most important challenge is
(A) to make students do their homework
(B) to make teaching–learning process enjoyable
(C) to maintain discipline in the classroom
(D) to prepare the question paper

**69** A teacher can establish rapport with his students by
(A) becoming a figure of authority
(B) impressing students with knowledge and skill
(C) playing the role of a guide
(D) becoming a friend to the students

**70** A teacher is said to be fluent in asking questions, if he can ask
(A) meaningful questions
(B) as many questions as possible
(C) maximum number of questions in a fixed time
(D) many meaningful questions in a fixed time

**71** On the first day of his class, if a teacher is asked by the students to introduce himself, he should
(A) ask them to meet after the class
(B) tell them about himself in brief
(C) ignore the demand and start teaching
(D) scold the student for this unwanted demand

**72** If the students do not understand what is taught in the class, the teacher should
(A) repeat the lesson once again
(B) teach the lesson again citing suitable examples
(C) check the previous knowledge of the students in the topic
(D) proceed to the next topic

**73** The best way to react to a wrong answer given by a student is
(A) to scold him for not having learnt the lesson
(B) to explain why the answer is wrong
(C) to ask another student to give the correct answer
(D) to ignore the wrong answer and pass on the next question

**74** When a student asks a question to which the teacher has no direct, correct answer he should
(A) give some vague answer and satisfy the student
(B) tell the student not to ask much irrelevant questions
(C) tell the student that he would give the correct answer later
(D) ask the student to find out the answer himself from the books in the library

**75** A teacher in the class should keep the pitch of his voice
(A) high enough
(B) low
(C) moderate
(D) sometime low and sometime high

**76** The best educational programme is the one which is framed keeping in mind the
(A) need of the child
(B) interest of the child
(C) ability of the child
(D) need of the society in addition to all these

**77** If majority of the students in your class are weak, then as a teacher you should
(A) slow the pace of your teaching
(B) increase the pace so that students speed up
(C) focus only on intelligent students
(D) keep your teaching slow and give extra guidance to bright pupils

**78** To stop the malpractice of cheating in the examinations, what step should be taken by the teacher?
(A) Punish the students as well as the parents
(B) Rusticate the student from the institution
(C) Explain the moral values attached to the event
(D) Severly punish the student

**79** If you get an opportunity to teach a differently abled student along with normal students, what type of treatment would you give?
(A) Take care of that student sympathetically in the class
(B) No extra attention as disability is the student's destiny
(C) No extra attention as majority of the students will suffer
(D) Arrange a seat in the front row and teach at a pace convenient to the student

## Teaching Aids and Teaching Support Systems

**80** Instructional aides are used by the teacher to
(A) glorify the class
(B) attract the students
(C) clarify the concepts
(D) ensure discipline

**81** Teaching aids can help teachers to make
(A) teaching interesting
(B) teaching less burdensome
(C) content easy and concrete
(D) lessons seem fancy

**82** An effective teaching aid is one which
(A) is colourful and good looking
(B) activates all faculties
(C) is visible to all students
(D) easy to prepare and use

**83** Which of the following statements is incorrect regarding Traditional Teaching Method?
(A) It follows teacher-centred approach.
(B) Based on memorization of facts, objective information and correct knowledge.
(C) Collaborative learning and problem-based learning is a key aspect of this method.
(D) It has more interaction between the teacher and student.

**84** Digitization in teaching, learning assessment and feedback improves ............
(A) learning process
(B) social responsibility
(C) civic engagement
(D) All of the above

**85** Which Teaching Method has the ability to engage the students in subjective activities and enhance their cognitive skills?
(A) Traditional teaching
(B) Modern teaching
(C) ICT-based teaching
(D) None of the above

**86** The use of teaching aids is justified if there is :
(A) attracting student's attention.
(B) effective engagement of students in learning.
(C) optimized learning outcomes.
(D) minimized indiscipline problems.

**87** For a teacher, which of the following methods would be correct for writing on the blackboard?
(A) Writing fast and as clearly as possible.
(B) Writing important points as clearly as possible.
(C) Writing the matter first and then writing the answer as stated by them.
(D) None of the above.

**88** You are planning to teach human anatomy. The most suitable teaching aid would be to
(A) put up a chart on human anatomy
(B) show the learners' model of the human body
(C) show them MS Power Point presentations and videos depicting location and functions of part of the human body
(D) read from the text and simultaneously explaining verbally

**89** A teacher uses audio-visual aids and physical activities in her teaching because they
(A) provide a diversion to learners
(B) utilise maximum number of senses to enhance learning
(C) provide relief to the teacher
(D) facilitate effective assessment

**90** A smart classroom is a teaching space which has
I. smart portion with a touch panel control system.
II. PC/Laptop connection and DVD/VCR player.
III. document camera and specialised software.
IV. projector and screen.
Select the correct answer from the codes given below
(A) I and II
(B) II and IV
(C) I, II and III
(D) I, II, III and IV

**91** **Assertion** (A) For an effective classroom communication at times it is desirable to use the projection technology.
**Reason** (R) Using the projection technology facilitates extensive coverage of course contents.
(A) Both A and R are true and R is the correct explanation of A
(B) Both A and R are true, but R is not the correct explanation of A
(C) A is true, but R is false
(D) A is false, but R is true

**92** Learning environment refers to :
(A) a way to describe the universal classroom.
(B) an ideal classroom.
(C) the physical, psychological and instructional atmosphere in a classroom.
(D) best environmental setting.

**93** How can teachers create a positive learning environment?
(A) Create bright, clean and organized spaces.
(B) Make learning relevant.
(C) Developing a positive action curriculum.
(D) All of the above.

**94** The essence of effective classroom environment is
(A) a variety of teaching aids
(B) lively student-teacher interaction
(C) strict discipline
(D) All of the above

**95** ............ are the pre-requisites for providing proper environment to quality learning.
(A) Infrastructural facilities or resources
(B) School activities
(C) Sports and games
(D) All of the above

## Learning and Learner's Characteristics

**96** Who said this that "Learning is a process of progressive behaviour through experience and training"?
(A) Crow and Crow
(B) Skinner
(C) Blair Jones and Simon
(D) Gardner Murphy

**97** "Learning helps in bring desirable change in behaviour" means
(A) learning is the process of bringing changes in behaviour
(B) it helps in introducing desired change in the behaviour of learner in all its domain
(C) it helps in proper growth and development
(D) Both (A) and (B)

**98** To teach effectively in classroom which of the following basic principles of learning are required?
(A) Principle of clarity
(B) Principle of effective communication
(C) Principle of varying learning abilities
(D) All of the above

**99** These learners learn best when they use textile experiences and carry out physical activity to practice by applying new information." They are which type of learners?
(A) Auditory learners
(B) Kinesthetic learners
(C) Visual learners
(D) Motor learners

**100** The academic characteristics of the adolescents are
(A) they show a wide range of intellectual development
(B) they tend to be curious
(C) they favour active or passive learning
(D) All of the above

**101** Which of the following is/are the cause(s) of individual differences among learners?
(A) Differences in Attitude
(B) Differences in Intelligence
(C) Differences in Age
(D) Differences in Achievement

**102** Moral values can be effectively inculcated among the students when the teacher
(A) frequently talks about values
(B) himself practices them
(C) tells stories of great persons
(D) talks of Gods and Goddesses

**103** When a normal student behaves in an erratic manner in the class, you would
(A) pull up the student then and there
(B) talk to the student after the class
(C) ask the student to leave the class
(D) ignore the student

**104** For an efficient and durable learning, learner should have
(A) ability to learn only
(B) requisite level of motivation only
(C) opportunities to learn only
(D) desired level of ability and motivation

**105** The students learn best by
(A) listening
(B) reading
(C) doing
(D) seeing

**106** Some students in a class exhibit great curiosity for learning. It may be because such children
(A) are gifted
(B) come from rich families
(C) show artificial behaviour
(D) create indiscipline in the class

**107** The most appropriate meaning of learning is
(A) acquisition of skills
(B) modification of behaviour
(C) personal adjustment
(D) inculcation of knowledge

**108** The learners always appreciate
(A) a well-researched and informative lecture
(B) a well-organised and presentable lecture
(C) a concise and stimulating lecture
(D) All of the above

**109** Learners can learn more effectively by
(A) listening
(B) taking detailed written notes
(C) actively participating
(D) All of the above

**110** Learners should not be encouraged to
(A) ask as many questions as possible both inside and outside the class
(B) actively interact with other learners in group work
(C) participate in as many co-curricular activities as possible
(D) memorise all the answers to questions which the teacher may ask

**111** Students can be classified into four types on the basis of their learning. Which one of the following seeks meaning and reasoning to the learning?
(A) Innovative learner
(B) Analytic learner
(C) Common sense learner
(D) Dynamic learner

**112** Which of the following learner characteristics is highly related to effectiveness of teaching?
(A) Peer groups of the learner
(B) Family size from which the learner comes
(C) Prior experience of the learner
(D) Educational status of the parents of the learner

**113** Verbal guidance is least effective in the learning of
(A) aptitudes (B) skills
(C) attitudes (D) relationship

**114** Which one is the highest order of learning?
(A) Chain learning
(B) Problem–solving learning
(C) Stimulus–response learning
(D) Conditioned–reflex learning

**115** Which of the following is not an aspect of learning?
(A) Elimination of errors
(B) Accumulation of knowledge
(C) Modification of behaviours
(D) Sensitisation of nerves

**116** The period of adolescence is known as the period of stresses and strains. What type of behaviour is unwanted from the learners at that period?
(A) Silence and hush-hush policy
(B) Attitude of independence
(C) Sympathetic understanding
(D) Individual thought process

**117** The ability to learn by an individual is
(A) acquired by the individual
(B) developed by the teacher
(C) absorbed from environment
(D) occurred from within

**118** Which of the following skills are needed for present day teacher to adjust effectively with the classroom teaching?
I. Knowledge of technology
II. Use of technology in teaching-learning
III. Knowledge of students' needs
IV. Content mastery
**Codes**
(A) I and III (B) II and III
(C) II, III and IV (D) II and IV

**119** Which is the least important factor in teaching?
(A) Punishing the students
(B) Maintaining discipline in the class
(C) Lecturing in impressive way
(D) Drawing sketches and diagrams on the blackboard

**120** Effective teaching depends on
(A) physical built of a teacher
(B) physical appearance of a teacher
(C) knowledge of a teacher
(D) behaviour of a teacher

**121** Teachers who are passionate in classroom transactions
(A) often lack deeper insight of the subject content
(B) use frivolous examples to hold the student's attention
(C) involve their students in the teaching-learning process
(D) All of the above

**122** A good teacher must be
(A) resourceful and autocratic
(B) resourceful and participative
(C) resourceful and authoritative
(D) resourceful and dominant

123 Attitude of the teacher that affects teaching pertains to
(A) affective domain
(B) cognitive domain
(C) connative domain
(D) psychomotor domain

124 "Spare the rod and spoil the child", gives the message that
(A) punishment in the class should be banned
(B) corporal punishment is not acceptable
(C) undesirable behaviour must be punished
(D) children should be beaten with rods

125 When some students are deliberately attempting to disturb the discipline of the class by making mischief, what will be your role as a teacher?
(A) Expelling those students
(B) Isolate those students
(C) Reform the group with your authority
(D) Giving them an opportunity for introspection and improve their behaviour

126 Classroom communication must be
(A) Teacher centric
(B) Student centric
(C) General centric
(D) Textbook centric

127 The teacher has been glorified by the phrase "Friend, philosopher and guide" because
(A) he has to play all vital roles in the context of society
(B) he transmits the high value of humanity to students
(C) he is the great reformer of the society
(D) he is a great patriot

128 Which among the following can make a class more effective?
(A) Clear and loud explanation of the subject matter
(B) Strict discipline in the class
(C) Making learning experiences learner centered
(D) Keeping students relaxed while teaching

129 While planning instructional procedures, what will be your goal?
(A) To enable students to score high grades
(B) To achieve all the developmental goals
(C) To ensure that students master the chapter/topic
(D) To make classroom procedure more interesting

130 Which maxim states that difficulty should follow ease in teaching?
(A) From centre to abstract
(B) From simple to complex
(C) From known to unknown
(D) None of the above

131 Which among the following maxim means to regulate the education of a pupil by observation?
(A) From definite to indefinite
(B) From induction to deduction
(C) From centre to abstract
(D) From empirical to rational

132 Which among the following is types of individual differences?
(A) Difference in attitudes
(B) Difference in achievement
(C) Physical difference
(D) All of the above

133 Difference in children's interests, tendencies & character are which differences?
(A) Personality differences
(B) Emotional differences
(C) Racial differences
(D) Economic differences

## Methods of Teaching in Institution of Higher Learning, Offline and Online Methods

134 Good teaching is best reflected by
(A) attendance of students
(B) number of distinctions
(C) meaningful questions asked by students
(D) pin drop silence in the class

135 To maintain interest among students in class, a teacher should
(A) make maximum uses of teaching aids
(B) discuss
(C) ask questions intermittently
(D) All of the above

136 In the classroom, the teacher sends the message either as words or images. The students are really
(A) encoders (B) decoders
(C) agitators (D) propagators

137 "A diagram speaks more than 1000 words." The statement means that the teacher should
(A) use diagrams in teaching
(B) speak more and more in the class
(C) use teaching aids in the class
(D) not speak too much in the class

**138** If you get an opportunity to teach a visually challenged student along with normal students, what type of treatment would you like to give him in the class?

(A) Not giving extra attention because majority may suffer
(B) Take care of him sympathetically in the classroom
(C) You will think that blindness is his destiny and hence you cannot do anything
(D) Arrange a seat in the front row and try to teach at a pace convenient to him

**139** Which of the following is not instructional material?

(A) Overhead Projector
(B) Audio cassette
(C) Printed material
(D) Transparency

**140** Books can be a powerful source of communication, provided

(A) the content is abstract
(B) the content is illustrative
(C) the medium is Hindi
(D) the content is presented through good print

**141** As regards the use of blackboard in the class, what arrangements should be made for the students with weak eyesight?

(A) They should be provided with spectacles
(B) They should be asked to read that is written on the blackboard
(C) They should be given front seats
(D) Special arrangement should be made for them

**142** If a seminar or conference is being conducted in your city concerning education, what will you do?

(A) I will take part in it without the permission of the principal
(B) I shall seek the permission of the principal
(C) I shall take leave from the school
(D) I shall take no interest in it

**143** Better classroom management means

(A) effective group work and interaction among the students
(B) proper planning and preparation in developing suitable teaching aids
(C) punctuality of the teachers and ability to complete course in time
(D) All of the above

**144** For maintaining an effective discipline in the class, the teacher should

(A) allow students to do what they like
(B) deal with the students strictly
(C) give the students some problem to solve
(D) deal with them politely and firmly

**145** Which of the following statements is correct?

(A) Syllabus is a part of curriculum
(B) Syllabus is an annexure to curriculum
(C) Curriculum is the same in all educational institutions affiliated to a particular university
(D) Syllabus is not the same in all educational institutions affiliated to a particular university

**146** Discussion in class will be more effective if the topic of discussion is

(A) not introduced
(B) stated before the start of the discussion
(C) written on the board without introducting it
(D) informed to the students in advance

**147** A teacher can achieve maximum involvement of the students in developing the lesson through the

(A) lecture method
(B) discussion method
(C) use of teaching aids
(D) demonstration method

**148** Questioning, in teaching, is most useful in

(A) ensuring active participation of learners in the class
(B) rote memorisation of facts by the learners
(C) disciplining the learners
(D) preparing learners for examination

**149** Arrange the following teaching process in order.

I. Relate the present knowledge with previous one
II. Evaluation
III. Re-teaching
IV. Formulating instructional objectives
V. Presentation of instructional materials

**Codes**

(A) I, II, III, IV, V
(B) II, I, III, IV, V
(C) V, IV, III, I, II
(D) IV, I, V, II, III

**150** Which of the following should a teacher adopt in a lecture?

(A) Precise and low tone
(B) Elongated tone
(C) Precise and high tone
(D) Moderate tone

151 The lecture method is an effective way to
(A) introduce new information/concepts
(B) introduce a new skill
(C) assess understanding of learners
(D) stimulate participation of learners

152 Lecture as a teaching method can be more effective if a teacher
(A) reads from his/her notes
(B) uses prepared pointers and organises discussions around the same
(C) teaches extempore
(D) enriches the content of lectures with appropriate examples from other disciplines

153 Which of the following is considered the oldest teaching method?
(A) Demonstration method
(B) Lecture method
(C) Micro-teaching method
(D) Seminar method

154 The lecture method is useful when a teacher is dealing with
(A) large group
(B) junior classes
(C) small group
(D) training the group

155 While delivering a lecture if there is some disturbance in the class, then a teacher should
(A) keep quiet for a while and then go on
(B) not bother about what is happening in the class
(C) punish those causing the disturbance
(D) All of the above

156 Which of the following statement is not correct?
(A) Lecture method can develop reasoning
(B) Lecture method can develop knowledge
(C) Lecture method is one way process
(D) During lecture method students are passive

157 Maximum participation of students during teaching is possible through
(A) lecture method
(B) demonstration method
(C) inductive method
(D) textbook method

158 Demonstration refers to a teaching method in which learners
(A) do the process on their own
(B) work in groups and complete the process
(C) read from the text and internalise the steps of the process
(D) are provided with an opportunity to observe for themselves the object or processes that they wish to learn

159 If the focus of learning is to increase skills, the most suitable methods of teaching would be
(A) learning by doing (B) demonstration
(C) discussion (D) All of these

160 Which one of the following is the best method of teaching?
(A) Lecture (B) Discussion
(C) Demonstration (D) Narration

161 Team teaching has the potential to develop
(A) competitive spirit
(B) cooperation
(C) the habit of supplementing the teaching of each other
(D) highlighting the gaps in each other's teaching

162 Which of the following methods of teaching encourages the use of maximum senses?
(A) Problem-solving method
(B) Laboratory method
(C) Self-study method
(D) Team teaching method

163 In order to promote direct learning which of the following methods would be best suited?
(A) Discussion session
(B) Project method
(C) Team teaching method
(D) Lecture with examples

164 Micro teaching is more effective
(A) during preparation for teaching practice
(B) during teaching practice
(C) after the teaching practice
(D) always

165 Which one of the following is a scaled down teaching situation?
(A) Macro teaching
(B) Team teaching
(C) Cooperative teaching
(D) Micro teaching

166 Maximum participation of students is possible in teaching through
(A) discussion method
(B) lecture method
(C) audio–visual aids
(D) textbook method

167 The best method of teaching is to
(A) impart information
(B) ask students to read books
(C) suggest good reference material
(D) initiate a discussion and participate in it

168 Discussion method can be used when
(A) the topic is very difficult
(B) the topic is easy
(C) the topic is difficult
(D) All of the above

169 Discussion in class will be more effective if the topic of discussion is
(A) not introduced
(B) stated before the start of the discussion
(C) written on the board without introducing it
(D) informed to the students in advance

170 Which method of teaching is known as "Socratic Method of Teaching"?
(A) Question and Answer Teaching Method
(B) TV or Video Presention
(C) Seminar Method
(D) Brain Storming Method

171 Which among the following method is used for drilling and practicing simulation and modelling?
(A) Kinesthetic Method
(B) Hemistric Method
(C) Compute assisted learning
(D) None of the above

172 Which of the following is/are considered as the offline method(s) of teaching?
I. Team-teaching method
II. Discussion method
III. Project method
IV. Demonstration method
**Codes**
(A) Only I (B) I, II and III
(C) II and IV (D) All of these

173 Which of the following is the example of online method of teaching?
I. SWAYAM II. Swayamprabha
III. MOOCs
**Codes**
(A) Only I (B) I and II
(C) II and III (D) All of these

174 SWAYAM online method of teaching was launched in which year?
(A) 2000 (B) 2003
(C) 2010 (D) 2017

175 Consider the following statements about SWAYAM.
I. SWAYAM is designed to achieve the three cardinal principles of education policy i.e. access, equity and quality to all.
II. It promotes E-learning.
III. It provides opportunities for a life-long learning.
Which of the following statements is/are correct?
(A) Only I (B) I and II
(C) II and III (D) All of these

176 Swayamprabha is an online learning platform which consists of how many T. V. channels?
(A) 12 (B) 20 (C) 32 (D) 44

177 MOOCs was set up in which year?
(A) 2000 (B) 2003
(C) 2008 (D) 2011

178 Choose the correct option.
(A) Computer aided education may replace teachers
(B) Online teaching is more effective than face to face teaching
(C) Teacher can be assisted by computer aided education
(D) Online and offline teaching can both replace each other

179 The teacher introduces a mathematical formulae and rules by showing a video. The teacher gives lot of meaningful examples to demonstrate the application. It is
(A) the deductive approach
(B) the inductive approach
(C) the laboratory method
(D) None of the above

## Evaluation System

180 Diagnostic evaluation ascertain
(A) students performance at the beginning of instructions
(B) learning progress and failures during instructions
(C) degree of achievements of instructions at the end
(D) causes and remedies of persistent learning problems during instructions

**181** Which of the following is not a characteristic of a good achievement test?
(A) Reliability
(B) Objectivity
(C) Ambiguity
(D) Validity

**182** By which of the following methods the true evaluation of the students is possible?
(A) Evaluation at the end of the course
(B) Evaluation twice in a year
(C) Continuous evaluation
(D) Formative evaluation

**183** In teaching, the most effective method of evaluation is
(A) continuous and comprehensive evaluation throughout the term
(B) conducting annual examination
(C) maintaining cumulative records of students
(D) semester system evaluation

**184** Evaluation of learning outcomes means
(A) gathering evidences related to students learning
(B) making judgements on the basis of gathered evidences related to students learning
(C) formal testing
(D) awarding numerical scores

**185** Which of the following indicates evaluation?
(A) Ram got 45 marks out of 200
(B) Mohan got 38 per cent marks in English
(C) Shyam got first division in final examination
(D) All of the above

**186** Which of the following is the most important characteristic of Open Book Examination System?
(A) Students become serious
(B) It improves attendance in the classroom
(C) It reduces examination anxiety amongst students
(D) It compels students to think

**187** Which one of the following types of evaluation assesses the learning progress to provide continuous feedback to both teachers and students during instruction?
(A) Placement evaluation
(B) Formative evaluation
(C) Diagnostic evaluation
(D) Summative

**188** While delivering lecture if there is some disturbance in the class, a teacher should
(A) keep quiet for a while and then continue
(B) punish those causing disturbance
(C) motivate to teach those causing disturbance
(D) not bother of what is happening the class

**189** Failure of teacher to communicate his ideals well to the students may result in
(A) classroom indiscipline
(B) loss of students interest in topic being taught
(C) increased number of absentees in the class
(D) All of the above

**190** Which of the following is not an advantage of Choice Based Credit System?
(A) It helps learners to pursue their courses at different times.
(B) It has broadened the base of education system.
(C) Stress and anxiety of learners can be reduced through it.
(D) Chance of subjectivity is maximum, as internal evaluation has 40% weightage.

**191** Which of the following is a true statement regarding Computer Based Testing?
(A) Online teaching techniques make the process of CBT.
(B) CBT focuses on a complete delivery model that encompasses preparation and testing.
(C) With CBT, the probability of error and bias increases.
(D) Although pricey, CBT is flexible and accessible.

**192** Sometimes test are taken without notice. What is their use?
(A) Surprise test help in correct evaluation of student's knowledge
(B) These tests can be taken when teacher has not prepared a lesson/topic
(C) They compel the students to study regularly
(D) All of the above

**193** Good evaluation of written material is not based on which of the following?
(A) Comprehension of subject
(B) Logical presentation
(C) Ability to write what is read
(D) Linguistic expression

# Previous Years' Questions

## UGC NET-December 2019

1 Classroom interactions are influenced largely by
(A) student's commitment
(B) teacher centric environment
(C) organisational oversight
(D) unsolicited interventions

2 The emphasis in memory level of teaching is on which of the following?
1. Organisation of thoughts and ideas
2. Seeing of relationship among facts
3. Systematic presentation to enable quick reproduction.
4. Critical thinking
5. Mastery of concept sequencing of facts
6. Segregating one feature from another

Choose the correct answer from the following options
(A) 1, 2 and 3
(B) 1, 3 and 5
(C) 2, 3 and 4
(D) 4, 5 and 6

3 Which of the following teaching method(s) is/are contributive to direct learning?
1. Team teaching and lecturing
2. Simulation and role playing
3. Lecture with or without use of audio-visuals
4. Participation in workshop and assignment
5. MOOCs and heuristics
6. Interactive presentation

Choose the correct answer from the following options
(A) 2, 4 and 5 (B) 1, 2 and 3
(C) 3, 4 and 6 (D) 4, 5 and 6

4 The most characteristic feature of an adolescent learner which determines his/her social and moral development is the
(A) tendency to be aware from parents
(B) concern for hero worshipping for emulating values and standards
(C) mixing up with peers in the neighbourhood
(D) identity crisis

5 Below are given two lists in which list I specifies the four behaviour modification techniques while list II indicates their exemplification. Match the two lists.

| **List I** (Behaviour Modification Techniques) | **List II** (Examples) |
|---|---|
| A. Positive reinforcement | 1. Withdrawal of present stimulus or application of an aversive stimulus to stop the behaviour. |
| B. Negative reinforcement | 2. Painful or aversive stimulus is presented to stop the occurrence of behaviour |
| C. Punishment | 3. The behaviour increases in frequency after the removal of a stimulus |
| D. Extinction | 4. The behaviour increases in frequency after the presentation of a stimulus |

Choose the correct options from the following

| | A | B | C | D |
|---|---|---|---|---|
| (A) | 1 | 2 | 3 | 4 |
| (B) | 2 | 1 | 3 | 4 |
| (C) | 4 | 3 | 2 | 1 |
| (D) | 3 | 1 | 2 | 4 |

6 Match the following study skills with their effective learning techniques.

| **List I** (Study Skills) | **List II** (Learning Techniques) |
|---|---|
| A. Elaborative Interrogation | 1. Mixing different kinds of problems together when studying |
| B. Practice Teaching | 2. Explaining what a section of text or an example problem means to you |
| C. Self-explanation | 3. Testing yourself on the material you are trying to learn |
| D. Interleaved practice | 4. Answering why a fact is true |

Choose the correct options from the following

| | A | B | C | D |
|---|---|---|---|---|
| (A) | 4 | 3 | 2 | 1 |
| (B) | 1 | 2 | 4 | 3 |
| (C) | 2 | 4 | 1 | 3 |
| (D) | 3 | 1 | 2 | 4 |

**7** In the age of four Vedas, students were admitted to the Vedic Schools after performance of which ceremony?
(A) Upanayana ceremony
(B) Ustarjana ceremony
(C) Satapatha ceremony
(D) Dhanurvidya ceremony

## UGC NET-June 2019

**8** Which of the learner characteristics will influence his/her perspective in a course of study?
1. Learner's commitment
2. Parents interest in the learner
3. Prior knowledge of the learner
4. Skill of the learner in the concerned area
5. Family size of the learner
6. Socio-economic background

Choose the correct answer from the options given below
(A) 1, 3 and 4 (B) 1, 2 and 3
(C) 3, 4 and 5 (D) 4, 5 and 6

**9** Which of the strategies in the list given below will be associated with direct teaching?
1. Providing examples and explanation
2. Promoting inquiry
3. Focussing on concepts
4. Giving review and recapitulation
5. Offering practice and feedback
6. Problem raising and problem-solving

Choose the correct answer from the options given below
(A) 1, 2 and 3 (B) 2, 3 and 4
(C) 1, 4 and 5 (D) 4, 5 and 6

**10** Which of the following is an online store house of all academic awards like certificates, diplomas, degrees, marksheets etc?
(A) SWAYAM
(B) National Digital Library
(C) National Academic Library
(D) National Academic Depositary

**11** Which of the following is a non-conventional learning programme in higher education?
(A) SWAYAM
(B) Face-to-face teaching-learning
(C) Tutorial class
(D) Seminar

**12** Who developed the theory of multiple intelligence?
(A) Alfred Binet (B) L Thurstone
(C) Charles Spearman (D) Howard Gardner

**13** Which among the following describes the emotional intelligence of learners?
1. Understand the emotion of other people and your own
2. Express oneself very strongly
3. Being rational in thinking
4. Adjusting one's emotion as per situation
5. Being creative and open to criticism
6. Accepting other people as they are

Choose the correct answer from the options given below
(A) 1, 4 and 6 (B) 4, 5 and 6
(C) 1, 2 and 3 (D) 2, 3 and 4

**14** Which of the following statements explain the concept of inclusive teaching?
(A) Teacher facilitates the learning of gifted students.
(B) Teacher facilitates the learning of weak students
(C) Teacher takes support of parents of the students to make them learn
(D) Teacher makes the students of different backgrounds to learn together in the same class

**15** To organise discussion method in teaching effectively which of the following conditions should be met?
1. Topic be easy
2. Topic be cleared in advance
3. Topic of common interest
4. Availability of more than one teacher
5. Language facility of participants

Select appropriate answer from the options given below
(A) 2, 3 and 5 (B) 1, 2 and 3
(C) 1, 2 and 5 (D) 3, 4 and 5

**16** From the list of the effective teaching behaviour, identify those which are called key behaviours.
1. Direct audible and oral delivery to all students.
2. Encouraging students to elaborate on an answer.
3. Warming and nurturing relationship with learners.
4. Varying modes of presentation.
5. Preventing misbehaviour with minimum of class disruption
6. Organising what is to come and summarising what has gone before.

Select your answer from the options given below

(A) 1, 4 and 5 (B) 1, 2 and 3
(C) 2, 3 and 4 (D) 4, 5 and 6

**17** In a classroom situation, a teacher organises group discussion to help arrive at a solution of a problem in terms of model of communication used, it will be called
(A) Transactional model
(B) Interaction model
(C) Horizontal model
(D) a Linear model

**18** When the learning outcomes of students are ensured with employment of less resources and effort on the part of a teacher and more initiative for self-learning is evident, which of the following expression will describe the teacher most appropriately?
(A) Teacher is successful
(B) Teacher is effective
(C) Teacher is intelligent
(D) Teacher is practical

**19** Peer group interaction in a classroom helps in
(A) concept understanding
(B) realisation of one's understanding
(C) rapport building
(D) questionnaire

**20** Listening is important for a teacher to
(A) address the requirement of the learner
(B) gain knowledge
(C) keep the learner in good humour
(D) evaluate the learner for the progress made

**21** Inclusive education implies
(A) ensuring learning outcomes of every child to be the same
(B) including the disabled in the mainstream
(C) provides compulsory education for children below 14 years
(D) ensuring that no child is left behind in education

**22** Reflective practice implies use of one is
(A) cognition
(B) meta-cognition
(C) meta-cognition on cognition
(D) reinforcement of learning

**23** In audio and video compression, the term RGB means
(A) Red, Grey, Blue
(B) Red, Green, Blue
(C) Red, Green, Black
(D) Red, Grey, Black

**24** Which of the following is an example of high order of cognitive learning outcome?
(A) Learning of facts and their sequences
(B) Learning roles and action sequences
(C) Learning of concepts and abstractions
(D) Learning of awareness and valuing

**25** Instructions which encourage live participation and interaction through online classes are called
(A) Synchronous instructions
(B) Asynchronous instructions
(C) Traditional instructions
(D) Theoretical instructions

**26** What are the elements of evaluation plan?
1. Purpose 2. Resource
3. Analysis 4. Authority

Select the correct answer from the options given below

(A) 1 and 3 (B) Only 2
(C) 2, 3 and 4 (D) 1, 2 and 3

**27** Which of the following is the key behaviour contributing to effective teaching?
(A) Summarising what was told by a student
(B) Encouraging students to elaborate on an answer
(C) Using direct and indirect questioning
(D) Explaining concepts in a logical step by step presentation

**28** Which type of evaluation focuses on the identification of deficiencies and difficulties of the learner?
(A) Summative evaluation
(B) Follow-up evaluation
(C) Diagnostic evaluation
(D) Criterion-referenced evaluation

**29** In which method of arriving at knowledge, the emphasis is on both proceeding from particular to general and from general to particular in a combined way?
(A) Inductive method (B) Deductive method
(C) Scientific method (D) Analogical method

**30** 'Gyanvani' launched by IGNOU to cover the educational needs of India refer to
(A) satellite based educational TV channel
(B) educational FM radio network
(D) global imitative of academic networks
(D) MOOCs

**31** 'Cone of Experience' related to teaching learning was suggested by
(A) John Dewey (B) Kilpatrick
(C) Froebel (D) Edgar Dale

**32** Which of the following is a social characteristic of a learner?
(A) Power of sensory perception
(B) Thinking ability
(C) Power of synthetic imagination
(D) Ability to relate oneself with others

**33** Which is the characteristic of formative evaluation?
(A) Evaluation occurs at the terminal point
(B) Evaluation is used before programme design
(C) Evaluation relates to indicating learning outcome of teaching
(D) Evaluation is conducted during teaching

**34** Which among the following is a non-cognitive characteristic of learner?
(A) Recalling
(B) Problem solving
(C) Identifying important sensory inputs
(D) Believing what is true

**35** The field of study which uses role playing, simulation and self-evaluation as strategies for adult learner is known as
(A) Pedagogy (B) Andragogy
(C) Anthropology (D) Psychology

**36** In a classroom, content produced for a specific user will lead to
(A) personality development
(B) content filtering
(C) personalisation
(D) general academic integration

## UGC NET-December 2018

**37** Below are given a number of key behaviours as well as helpful behaviours of effectiveness of teaching based on research evidence. Identify those which are key behaviours and indicate your answer by selecting from the codes.
1. Structuring through comments by the teacher in respect of what is to come.
2. Questioning through content and process level questions.
3. Lesson clarity implying the extent to which presentations are not involved.
4. Probing which implies statements to encourage students to elaborate.
5. Engagement rate devoted to learning when students are actually on task.
6. Rate at which students understand and correctly comprehend assignments and exercises.

**Codes**
(A) 2, 3 and 4 (B) 1, 4 and 5
(C) 1, 4 and 6 (D) 3, 5 and 6

**38** For organising an effective teaching-learning system which of the following combinations of statements would reflect the most appropriate concern? Select from the codes to indicate your answer.
1. Determining what will be the intended learning outcome.
2. Deciding as to what strategy and tactics will be used.
3. Formally approving the academic qualifications of teachers.
4. Determining the evaluation tool to be used.
5. Deciding the size of the classroom.
6. Assessing the prior academic experience of the learner.

**Codes**
(A) 3, 4, 5, 6 (B) 1, 2, 3, 4
(C) 1, 2, 4, 6 (D) 1, 3, 4, 5

**39** From the following list of learner characteristics identify those which will be helpful in ensuring effectiveness of teaching. Select your answer from the codes.
1. Extent to which learner obeys the school rules.
2. Learner's level of motivation.
3. Feelings of learners towards the social system.
4. Learner's interest in sports and games.
5. Prior experience of the learner.
6. Interpersonal relations of learners.

**Codes**
(A) 2, 5 and 6 (B) 1, 3 and 5
(C) 3, 4 and 5 (D) 1, 2 and 3

## UGC NET-July 2018

**40** Which of the following set of statements best describes the nature and objectives of teaching?
Indicate your answer by selecting from the codes
1. Teaching and learning are integrally related.
2. There is no difference between teaching and training.
3. Concern of all teaching is to ensure some kind of transformation in students.
4. All good teaching is formal in nature.
5. A teacher is a senior person.
6. Teaching is a social act whereas learning is a personal act.

**Codes**
(A) 1, 3 and 6 (B) 4, 5 and 6
(C) 1, 2 and 4 (D) 2, 3 and 5

**41** From the list of evaluation procedures given below identify those which will be called 'formative evaluation'. Indicate your answer by choosing from the codes.

1. A teacher awards grades to students after having transacted the course work.
2. During interaction with students in the classroom, the teacher provides corrective feedback.
3. The teacher gives marks to students on a unit test.
4. The teacher clarifies the doubts of students in the class itself.
5. The overall performance of a student is reported to parents at every three months interval.
6. The learner's motivation is raised by the teacher through a question–answer session.

**Codes**

(A) 1, 3 and 5 (B) 2, 4 and 6
(C) 1, 2 and 3 (D) 2, 3 and 4

**42** **Assertion** (A) All teaching should aim at ensuring/learning.

**Reason** (R) All learning results from teaching.

Choose the correct answer from the following codes.

(A) A is true, but R is false
(B) A is false, but R is true
(C) Both A and R are true and R is the correct explanation of A
(D) Both A and R are true, but R is not the correct explanation of A

**43** In the two lists given below list I indicates methods of teaching while list II provides the basic requirements for success/effectiveness.

Match the two lists and indicate your answer by choosing from the codes.

| List I (Method of Teaching) | List II (Basic Requirements For Success/Effectiveness) |
|---|---|
| A. Lecturing | 1. Small step presentation with feedback provided |
| B. Discussion in group | 2. Production of large number of ideas |
| C. Brainstorming | 3. Content delivery in a lucid language |
| D. Programmed Instructional Procedure | 4. Use of teaching aids |
| | 5. Theme based interaction among participants |

**Codes**

| | A | B | C | D | | A | B | C | D |
|---|---|---|---|---|---|---|---|---|---|
| (A) | 3 | 5 | 2 | 1 | (B) | 4 | 2 | 1 | 3 |
| (C) | 1 | 2 | 3 | 4 | (D) | 2 | 3 | 4 | 5 |

## UGC NET-November 2017

**44** On the basis of summative tests, a teacher is interpreting his/her students, performance in terms of their wellness lifestyle evident in behaviour. This will be called

(A) continuous and comprehensive evaluation
(B) norm–referenced testing
(C) criterion–referenced testing
(D) formative testing

**45** The spatial audio reproduction in a classroom can reduce the students

(A) respect for the teacher
(B) motivation for excellence
(C) interest in technology-orientation
(D) cognitive load in understanding

**46** **Assertion** (A) All teaching implies learning.

**Reason** (R) Learning to be useful must be derived from teaching.

Choose the correct answer from the following codes.

(A) Both A and R are true, but R is not the correct explanation of A
(B) A is true, but R is false
(C) A is false, but R is true
(D) Both A and R are true and R is the correct explanation of A

**47** Which of the following set of statements best represents the nature and objective of teaching and learning?

1. Teaching is like selling and learning is like buying.
2. Teaching is a social act while learning is a personal act.
3. Teaching implies learning whereas learning does not imply teaching.
4. Teaching is a kind of delivery of knowledge while learning is like receiving it.
5. Teaching is an interaction and is triadic in nature whereas learning is an active engagement in a subject domain.

**Codes**

(A) 2, 3 and 5 (B) 1, 2 and 3
(C) 1, 2 and 4 (D) 1, 4 and 5

**48** From the list given below identify the learner characteristics which would facilitate teaching-learning system to become effective. Choose the correct codes to indicate your answer.

1. Prior experience of learner
2. Learner's family lineage
3. Aptitude of the learner
4. Learner's stage of development
5. Learner's food habits and hobbies
6. Learner's religious affiliation

**Codes**

(A) 4, 5 and 6 (B) 1, 4 and 5
(C) 2, 3 and 6 (D) 1, 3 and 4

**49** Which one of the following is a key behaviour in effective teaching?

(A) Structuring
(B) Instructional variety
(C) Questioning
(D) Using student ideas and contribution

## UGC NET-January 2017

**50** **Assertion** (A) Formative evaluation tends to accelerate the pace of learning.
**Reason** (R) As against summative evaluation, formative evaluation is highly reliable.
Choose the correct answer from the following codes.

(A) Both A and R are true and R is the correct explanation of A
(B) Both A and R are true, but R is not the correct explanation of A
(C) A is true, but R is false
(D) A is false, but R is true

**51** Which of the following sets of statements represents acceptable propositions in respect of teaching–learning relationships? Choose the correct codes to indicate your answer.

1. When students fail in a test, it is the teacher who fails.
2. Every teaching must aim at ensuring learning.
3. There can be teaching without learning taking place.
4. There can be no learning without teaching.
5. A teacher teaches but learns also.
6. Real learning implies rote learning.

**Codes**

(A) 2, 3, 4 and 5 (B) 1, 2, 3 and 5
(C) 3, 4, 5 and 6 (D) 1, 2, 5 and 6

**52** In which teaching method learner's participation is made optimal and proactive?

(A) Discussion method
(B) Buzz session method
(C) Brainstorming session method
(D) Project method

**53** One of the most powerful affecting teaching effectiveness is related to the

(A) social system of the country
(B) economic status of the society
(C) prevailing political system
(D) educational system

## UGC NET-August 2016

**54** Which of the following learner characteristics are likely to influence the effectiveness of teaching aids and evaluation systems to ensure positive results?

(A) Learner's family background, age and habitation
(B) Learner's parentage, socio–economic background and performance in learning of the concerned subject
(C) Learner's stage of development, social background and personal interests
(D) Learner's maturity level, academic performance level and motivational dispositions

**55** A teacher in a classroom has immediate control over

(A) the self, selected methods of communication and the message
(B) the audience, the noise and the reception
(C) the feedback, the technology and the audience experience
(D) the communication channel, other communicators and external factors

**56** Internal and external factors that affect message reception by the students in the classroom are referred to as

(A) feedback
(B) fragmentation
(C) channelisation
(D) noise

**57** Which of the following factors affect teaching?
Choose the correct codes to indicate your answer.

1. Teacher's internal locus of control.
2. Learner–motivation.
3. Teacher's biographical data.

4. Teacher's self-efficacy.
5. Learner's interest in co-curricular activities.
6. Teacher's skill in managing and monitoring.
7. Teacher's knowledge of the subject including general knowledge.

**Codes**

(A) 1, 2, 4, 6 and 7
(B) 1, 2, 3, 4 and 5
(C) 3, 4, 5, 6 and 7
(D) 2, 3, 4, 5 and 6

**58** Which combination of methods of teaching is likely to optimise learning?

(A) Lecturing, discussions and seminar method
(B) Interactive discussions, planned lectures and Power Point based presentations
(C) Interactive lecture sessions followed by buzz sessions, brainstorming and projects
(D) Lecturing, demonstrations and Power Point based presentations

**59** **Assertion** (A) Teaching aids have to be considered as effective supplements to instruction.

**Reason** (R) They keep students in good humour.

Choose the correct answer from the codes given below

**Codes**

(A) Both A and R are true and R is the correct explanation of A
(B) Both A and R are true, but R is not the correct explanation of A
(C) A is true, but R is false
(D) A is false, but R is true

**60** Which of the following set of statements reflects the basic characteristics of teaching?

Select the correct alternatives from the codes.

1. Teaching is the same as training.
2. There is no difference between instruction and conditioning when we teach.
3. Teaching is related to learning.
4. Teaching is a 'task' word while learning is an 'achievement' word.
5. Teaching means giving information.
6. One may teach without learning taking place.

**Codes**

(A) 1, 2 and 3 (B) 3, 4 and 5
(C) 2, 3 and 5 (D) 1, 4 and 6

**61** The purpose of formative evaluation is to

(A) grade student's learning outcomes
(B) accelerate student's learning performance
(C) check student's performance graph
(D) provide feedback to teacher's effectiveness

**62** As a good classroom communicator, you are supposed to know your

(A) audience emotions
(B) silent cues
(C) artful pauses
(D) counter arguments

## UGC NET-July 2016

**63** A college level assistant professor has planned his/her lectures with an intent to develop cognitive dimensions of students centered on skills of analysis and synthesis. Below, given are two lists of items list I consisting of levels of cognitive interchange and list II comprising basic requirements for promoting them. Match the two lists and indicate your answer by choosing the correct alternative from the codes.

| List I (Levels of Cognitive Interchange) | List II (Basic Requirements for Promoting Cognitive Interchange) |
|---|---|
| A. Memory level | 1. Giving opportunity for discriminating examples and non–examples of a point |
| B. Understanding level | 2. Recording the important points made during the presentations |
| C. Reflective level | 3. Asking the students to discuss various items of information |
| | 4. Critically analysing the points to be made and discussed |

**Codes**

| | A | B | C | | A | B | C |
|---|---|---|---|---|---|---|---|
| (A) | 2 | 4 | 1 | (B) | 3 | 4 | 2 |
| (C) | 2 | 1 | 4 | (D) | 1 | 2 | 3 |

**64** The use of teaching aids is justified on the ground of

(A) attracting student's attention in the classroom
(B) minimising indiscipline problems in the classroom.
(C) optimising learning outcome of students
(D) effective engagement of students in learning tasks

**65** Select the alternative which consists of positive factors contributing to effectiveness of teaching.

List of factors

1. Teacher's knowledge of the subject.
2. Teacher's socio-economic background.
3. Communication skill of the teacher.

4. Teacher's ability to please the students.
5. Teacher's personal contact with students.
6. Teacher's competence in managing and monitoring the classroom transactions.

**Codes**

(A) 2, 3 and 4 (B) 3, 4 and 6
(C) 2, 4 and 5 (D) 1, 3 and 6

**66** Which set of learner characteristics may be considered helpful in designing effective teaching-learning systems? Select the correct alternative from the codes given below.

1. Prior experience of learners in respect of the subject.
2. Interpersonal relationships of learner's family friends.
3. Ability of the learners in respect of the subject.
4. Student's language background.
5. Interest of students in following the prescribed dress code.
6. Motivational–orientation of the students.

**Codes**

(A) 1, 2, 3 and 4 (B) 1, 3, 4 and 6
(C) 2, 3, 4 and 5 (D) 3, 4, 5 and 6

**67** Match the items of the first list with that of the second list in respect of evaluation system. Choose the correct codes

| List I | List II |
|---|---|
| A. Formative evaluation | 1. Evaluating cognitive and co-cognitive aspects with regularity |
| B. Summative evaluation | 2. Tests and their interpretations based on a group and certain yardsticks |
| C. Continuous and comprehensive | 3. Grading the final learning outcomes evaluation |
| D. Norm and criterion referenced | 4. Quizzes and discussions tests |

**Codes**

| | A | B | C | D | | A | B | C | D |
|---|---|---|---|---|---|---|---|---|---|
| (a) | 4 | 3 | 1 | 2 | (b) | 1 | 2 | 3 | 4 |
| (c) | 3 | 4 | 2 | 1 | (d) | 1 | 3 | 4 | 2 |

**68** **Assertion** (A) The purpose of higher education is to promote critical and creative thinking abilities among students.
**Reason** (R) These abilities ensure job placements.

Choose the correct answer from the following codes

(A) Both A and R are true and R is the correct explanationof A
(B) Both A and R are true, but R is not the correct explanation of A
(C) A is true, but R is false
(D) A is false, but R is true

**69** Identify the important element a teacher has to take cognisance of while addressing students in a classroom.

(A) Avoidance of proximity
(B) Voice modulation
(C) Repetitive pause
(D) Fixed posture

## UGC NET-December 2015

**70** What are the characteristics of continuous and comprehensive evaluation?

1. It increases the workload on students by taking multiple tests.
2. It replaces marks with grades.
3. It evaluates every aspect of the student.
4. It helps in reducing examination phobia.

Select the correct answer from the codes given below

(A) 1, 2, 3 and 4 (B) 2 and 4
(C) 1, 2 and 3 (D) 2, 3 and 4

**71** The main objectives of student evaluation of teachers are

1. to gather information about student weaknesses.
2. to make teachers take teaching seriously.
3. to help teachers adopt innovative methods of teaching.
4. to identify the areas of further improvement in teacher traits.

Identify the correct answer from the codes given below

(A) 1 and 2 (B) 2, 3 and 4
(C) 1, 2 and 3 (D) Only 1

**72** What are required for good teaching?

1. Diagnosis 2. Remedy
3. Direction 4. Feedback

Select the correct answer from the codes given below

(A) 1, 2, 3 and 4 (B) 1 and 2
(C) 2, 3 and 4 (D) 3 and 4

**73** Which one of the following statements is correct in the context of multiple choice type questions?
(A) They are more objective than true-false type questions
(B) They are less objective than essay type questions
(C) They are more subjective than short-answer type questions
(D) They are more subjective than true-false type questions

**74** Greater the handicap of the students coming to the educational institutions, greater the demand on the
(A) family (B) society (C) teacher (D) state

**75** Which of the following attributes denote great strengths of a teacher?
1. Full–time active involvement in the institutional management.
2. Setting examples.
3. Willingness to put assumptions to the test.
4. Acknowledging mistakes.

Select the correct answer from the codes given below
(A) 1, 2 and 4 (B) 2, 3 and 4
(C) 1, 3 and 4 (D) 1, 2, 3 and 4

**76** In a classroom, a communicator's trust level is determined by
(A) the use of hyperbole
(B) the change of voice level
(C) the use of abstract concepts
(D) eye contact

## UGC NET-June 2015

**77** Which of the following factors does not impact teaching?
(A) Classroom activities that encourage learning
(B) Socio–economic background of teachers and students
(C) Learning through experience
(D) Teacher's knowledge

**78** A good teacher is one who
(A) gives useful information
(B) explains concepts and principles
(C) gives printed notes to students
(D) inspires students to learn

**79** Technique used by a teacher to teach include
1. lecture
2. interactive lecture
3. group work
4. self-study

**Codes**
(A) 1, 2 and 3
(B) 1, 2, 3 and 4
(C) 2, 3 and 4
(D) 1, 2 and 4

**80** Which of the following statements about teaching aids are correct?
1. They help in retaining concepts for longer duration
2. They help students learn better
3. They make teaching learning process interesting
4. They enhance rote learning

**Codes**
(A) 1, 2, 3 and 4 (B) 1, 2 and 3
(C) 2, 3 and 4 (D) 1, 2 and 4

**81** Achievement tests are commonly used for the purpose of
(A) making selections for a specific job
(B) selecting candidates for a course
(C) identifying strengths and weaknesses of learners
(D) assessing the amount of learning after teaching

**82** Which of the following is the highest level of cognitive ability?
(A) Knowing
(B) Understanding
(C) Analysing
(D) Evaluating

# ANSWERS

## Chapter Practice

| | | | | | | | | | |
|---|---|---|---|---|---|---|---|---|---|
| 1 (D) | 2 (B) | 3 (C) | 4 (D) | 5 (D) | 6 (B) | 7 (A) | 8 (D) | 9 (D) | 10 (A) |
| 11 (C) | 12 (D) | 13 (D) | 14 (D) | 15 (D) | 16 (D) | 17 (D) | 18 (D) | 19 (B) | 20 (D) |
| 21 (C) | 22 (B) | 23 (B) | 24 (B) | 25 (C) | 26 (A) | 27 (A) | 28 (A) | 29 (C) | 30 (C) |
| 31 (C) | 32 (C) | 33 (C) | 34 (A) | 35 (B) | 36 (C) | 37 (D) | 38 (C) | 39 (D) | 40 (C) |
| 41 (B) | 42 (A) | 43 (B) | 44 (D) | 45 (A) | 46 (D) | 47 (D) | 48 (A) | 49 (D) | 50 (B) |
| 51 (D) | 52 (B) | 53 (B) | 54 (B) | 55 (C) | 56 (D) | 57 (A) | 58 (A) | 59 (C) | 60 (B) |
| 61 (A) | 62 (C) | 63 (B) | 64 (B) | 65 (C) | 66 (A) | 67 (C) | 68 (B) | 69 (B) | 70 (A) |
| 71 (B) | 72 (B) | 73 (B) | 74 (C) | 75 (A) | 76 (B) | 77 (A) | 78 (C) | 79 (D) | 80 (C) |
| 81 (A) | 82 (B) | 83 (C) | 84 (D) | 85 (C) | 86 (B) | 87 (B) | 88 (C) | 89 (B) | 90 (D) |
| 91 (B) | 92 (C) | 93 (D) | 94 (B) | 95 (A) | 96 (B) | 97 (D) | 98 (D) | 99 (B) | 100 (D) |
| 101 (C) | 102 (B) | 103 (B) | 104 (D) | 105 (C) | 106 (A) | 107 (B) | 108 (C) | 109 (C) | 110 (D) |
| 111 (B) | 112 (C) | 113 (B) | 114 (D) | 115 (D) | 116 (A) | 117 (D) | 118 (C) | 119 (A) | 120 (C) |
| 121 (C) | 122 (B) | 123 (A) | 124 (C) | 125 (D) | 126 (B) | 127 (B) | 128 (D) | 129 (B) | 130 (B) |
| 131 (D) | 132 (D) | 133 (A) | 134 (C) | 135 (D) | 136 (B) | 137 (C) | 138 (D) | 139 (D) | 140 (B) |
| 141 (C) | 142 (B) | 143 (D) | 144 (D) | 145 (A) | 146 (D) | 147 (B) | 148 (A) | 149 (D) | 150 (C) |
| 151 (A) | 152 (D) | 153 (B) | 154 (A) | 155 (B) | 156 (A) | 157 (C) | 158 (D) | 159 (B) | 160 (C) |
| 161 (C) | 162 (B) | 163 (B) | 164 (A) | 165 (D) | 166 (A) | 167 (D) | 168 (C) | 169 (D) | 170 (A) |
| 171 (C) | 172 (D) | 173 (D) | 174 (D) | 175 (D) | 176 (C) | 177 (C) | 178 (C) | 179 (B) | 180 (D) |
| 181 (C) | 182 (C) | 183 (A) | 184 (B) | 185 (D) | 186 (D) | 187 (B) | 188 (C) | 189 (D) | 190 (D) |
| 191 (B) | 192 (A) | 193 (A) | | | | | | | |

## Previous Years' Questions

| | | | | | | | | | |
|---|---|---|---|---|---|---|---|---|---|
| 1 (A) | 2 (B) | 3 (A) | 4 (B) | 5 (C) | 6 (A) | 7 (A) | 8 (A) | 9 (C) | 10 (D) |
| 11 (A) | 12 (D) | 13 (A) | 14 (D) | 15 (A) | 16 (A) | 17 (A) | 18 (B) | 19 (A) | 20 (A) |
| 21 (D) | 22 (B) | 23 (B) | 24 (C) | 25 (A) | 26 (D) | 27 (D) | 28 (C) | 29 (C) | 30 (B) |
| 31 (D) | 32 (D) | 33 (D) | 34 (D) | 35 (B) | 36 (C) | 37 (D) | 38 (C) | 39 (A) | 40 (A) |
| 41 (B) | 42 (A) | 43 (A) | 44 (C) | 45 (D) | 46 (D) | 47 (A) | 48 (D) | 49 (B) | 50 (C) |
| 51 (B) | 52 (A) | 53 (D) | 54 (D) | 55 (A) | 56 (D) | 57 (A) | 58 (C) | 59 (B) | 60 (B) |
| 61 (B) | 62 (C) | 63 (A) | 64 (D) | 65 (D) | 66 (B) | 67 (A) | 68 (C) | 69 (B) | 70 (D) |
| 71 (B) | 72 (A) | 73 (A) | 74 (C) | 75 (B) | 76 (D) | 77 (B) | 78 (D) | 79 (A) | 80 (B) |
| 81 (D) | 82 (D) | | | | | | | | |

UNIT 02

# Research Aptitude

## CHAPTER ANALYSIS

This unit is based on the updated syllabus of NTA UGC NET covering all the important topics related to Research Aptitude. After thorough going the chapter you will be able to understand the meaning , types and characteristics of Research, Positivism & Post positivism, Methods of Research, Steps of Research, Thesis & Article Writing, Research Ethics etc.

Every year 5 to 6 questions are asked from this unit in NTA UGC NET exam, which are based on types an characteristics of Research, Methods & Steps of Research and Research Ethics etc.

## CONCEPT OF RESEARCH

Research is composed of two words 're' and 'search' which means to 'search again' or to search for new facts or modify older ones in any branch of knowledge.

Research is a process of systematic inquiry that needs collection of data, documentation of critical information, analysis and interpretation of data. It is in accordance with suitable methodologies set by specific professional fields and academic disciplines.

Research aptitude is acquired or natural skill of an individual to do scientific and objective analysis of observations. Such aptitude contributes in the development of generalised principles. The curiosity in human mind gives birth to research aptitude. Research is a vast process which involves micro to macro observations of a problem.

### Definitions of Research

Research is defined as a careful consideration of study regarding a particular concern or a problem using scientific methods. It gives multiple solutions for a single problem and there are many possible ways to do research for a single problem.

**IN THIS UNIT**

- Research : Meaning, Types and Characteristics
- Positivism and Post-positivism Approach to Research
- Methods of Research : Qualitative, Historical, Quantitative, Experimental and Descriptive Methods
- Steps of Research
- Thesis and Article Writing : Format and Styles of Referencing
- Application of ICT in Research
- Research Ethics

Definitions given by some scholars are as follows

**Redman** and **Mory** define research as a "Systematic effort to gain new knowledge."

According to **Webster,** "Research is a studious inquiry or examination, critical and exhaustive investigation or experimentation, having its aim for discovery of new facts and their correct interpretation".

According to **J W Best,** "Research is considered to be the more formal, systematic, intensive process of carrying on the scientific methods of analysis.

It involves a more systematic structure of investigation, usually resulting in some sort of formal record of procedures and report of results or conclusions."

According to **John Creswell,** "Research is a process of steps used to collect and analyse information to increase our understanding of a topic or an issue."

According to **Morley,** "Research is a process of arriving at dependable solutions to problems through the planned and systematic collection, analysis and interpretation of data."

## Objectives of Research

Objectives are the goals, researcher set out to attain in their study. They inform the reader what the researcher wants to accomplish through the research work.

The objectives of research can be catagorised as:

- **Theoretical Objectives** It leads to the formulation of new theories and basic knowledge by exploring the association between different variables.
- **Factual Objectives** Studies at such objectives which aim at finding new facts.
- **Application Objectives** Such objectives suggest the use of already existing theories to new situations.
- **Variable Objectives** In fact they are of philosophical in nature in which the final result is obtained on the basis of philosophy.
- **Practical Objectives** These objectives are categorised as developmental research and in order to achieve them functional research is undertaken. Research objectives are the results sought by the researcher, to achieve at the end of the research study. Through, each research has its own specific purpose, research objectives that vary with its achievement

# TYPES OF RESEARCH

Research may be classified into different types for the sake of better understanding of the concept. Following are important types of research

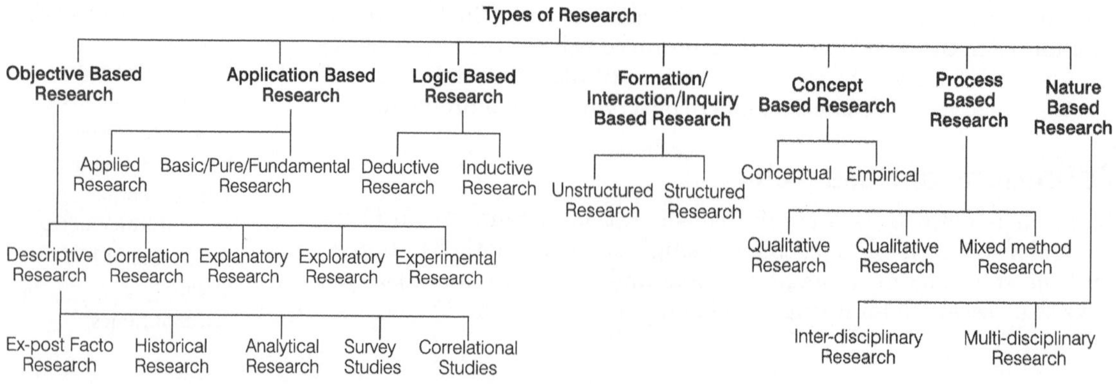

## Objective Based Research

Objective based research can be classified as descriptive, correlational, explanatory, exploratory and experimental research.

### 1. Descriptive Research

This research attempts to describe systematically a situational problem or a phenomenon and provides information about various subjects like living condition of a community.

It also includes surveys and fact-finding enquiries with adequate interpretation. The main characteristic of this method is that the researcher has no control over the variables, he can only report what has happened or what is happening. The purpose of descriptive research is collecting the information without disturbing the environment.

#### Types of Descriptive Research

(i) **Ex-post Facto Research** Ex-post facto research is systematic empirical inquiry based on a scientific and analytical investigation of dependent and independent variables. The ex-post facto research has a quasi-experimental nature because the subjects of research are not randomly assigned, they are grouped on particular characteristic or trait.

(ii) **Historical Research Wiersma** defines historical research as a process of critical inquiry into past events, in order to produce an accurate description and interpretation of such events.

It aims to discover the trends in past, in order to understand the present and to anticipate the future. It is advantageous because many socio, economic and political theories and issues can be understood in the light of past experiences.

(iii) **Analytical Research** The analytical research usually concerns itself with cause-effect relationships. In analytical research, the researchers use facts or informations which are already available and analyse these to make a critical evaluation of the material. In analytical research, the researchers hypothesis and specify their interpretations.

(iv) **Survey Studies** Survey research is another category of descriptive research. Surveys are forms of questioning that involves larger group of people.

They are conducted to create authentic description of existing situations, diagnose problems and make plans for changing the situation.

(v) **Correlational Studies** Correlational studies measure two or more relevant variables and assess a relationship between or among them.

### 2. Correlational Research

Correlational research measures the level of association or relationship between two or more variables.

In correlational research, variables must be quantifiable and usually represent at least ordinal scale of measures. A consistent relationship between variables is used to predict future events.

It aims to find out whether there is either :

(i) **Positive Correlation** In this correlation, both variables change in the same direction. For instance, as **height** increases, **weight** also increases.

(ii) **Negative Correlation** In this correlation, the variables change in opposite directions. For example, as **coffee consumption** increases, **tiredneess** decreases.

(iii) **Zero Correlation** In this correlation, there is no relationship between the varibales. For example, **coffee consumption** is not correlated with **height**.

### 3. Explanatory Research

Explanatory research is conducted for those problems which have not been researched before. The purpose of explanatory research is to explain why certain events occur and to build, elaborate, extend or test theory.

Explanatory research allows the researcher to test and verify specific theories and make amendments to those theories.

**Example** To analyse the effects of re-branding initiatives on the levels of customer loyalty.

## 4. Exploratory Research

Exploratory research is conducted for such problems which have not been clearly defined. It is flexible and can address research questions of all types (what, why, how). This research is often used to generate formal hypothesis.

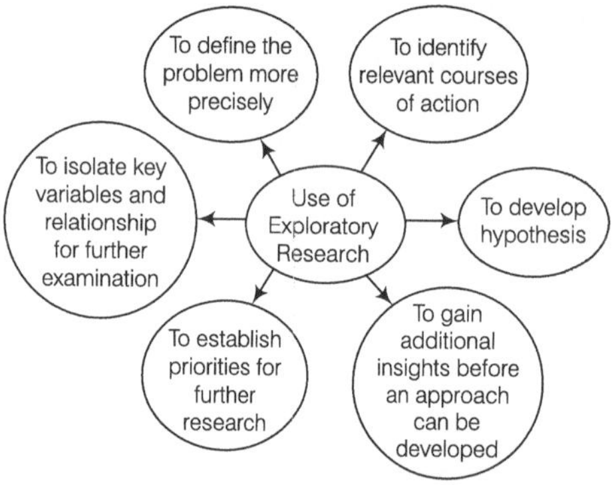


**Example** Alcoholism (drinking) is a serious issue in Indian society, but this behaviour is not clearly defined as it has some medical concern also. At the end of research the researcher explored numerous reasons of alcoholism and developed a hypothesis that alcohol is consumed by people for relaxation of body. It is exploratory research because there is still scope open for further research on this problem.

## 5. Experimental Research

Experimental research is a systematic and scientific approach to research, in which the researcher manipulates one or more variables. This research also controls and changes the other variables. The purpose of experimental research is to study the cause and effect relationship.

**Example** Education, a high degree of skill, sectors and experiences all are independent variables, which separately influence salary of an individual. If any of these variable is higher, the salary of an individual will be higher.

# Application Based Research

Application based research seeks to solve practical problems. This type of research plays an important role in solving everyday problems that often have an impact on life, work, health and overall well-being.

Following are the types of Application Based Research

## 1. Basic/Pure/Fundamental Research

Basic research involves the process of collecting and analysing data/information to develop or enhance theory. Basic research is conducted solely for the purpose of theory development and refinement.

Basic research advances fundamental knowledge about the human world. It focuses on refuting or supporting theories that explain how things operate, what makes things happen, why social relations have a certain way, and why society changes. It generates new ideas, principles and theories, which lays the foundations of modern progress and development in different fields.

**Example** A study, looking at how caffeine consumption impacts the brain.

## 2. Applied Research

Applied research is conducted to solve a specific practical problem of an individual or group or society.

It is used in medicine, business and education in order to find solutions that may cure diseases, solve scientific problems or develop technology. It uses the data directly from real world application.

The ultimate goal of an applied research is to improve the human condition.

**Example** Finding out the best way to approach and treat diseases like anxiety/depression/ asthma etc.

**Difference between Fundamental and Applied Research**

| Fundamental Research | Applied Research |
|---|---|
| It is the research which is generally conducted to develop some new theories. | It is the research which is generally conducted to solve the problem of the organisational setting. |
| It is inductive in nature. | It is deductive in nature. |
| It is also called as basic research or pure research. | It is also called as action research. |
| It is qualitative in nature. | It is quantitative in nature. |

## Logic Based Research

Logic based research is guided by the logical processes of induction and deduction.

Following are the types of Logic Based Research

### 1. Deductive Research

In deductive research the researcher studies what others have done, reads existing theories and then tests hypothesis that emerge from those theories. In deductive research the researcher moves from a more general level to a more specific level. The deductive method or approach involves these steps

(i) State the hypothesis based on the theory or research literature.
(ii) Collect data to test the hypothesis.
(iii) Make proper decision that hypothesis supported or not.

**Example** In a study conducted to analyse the impact of classroom environment on a child's mental health, a researcher deduced that lack of orderliness and basic supplies are associated with the behavioural issues that children show in classroom.

### 2. Inductive Research

In an inductive research a researcher collects the data that is relevant to his or her topic of interest.

The inductive approach also involves

(i) Observe the different events or phenomena in the world.
(ii) Try to identify the pattern between the different observations.
(iii) Make a general view about what is occurring.

**Example** A researcher collected data about depression and aggression among teenagers, after analysing the data the researcher established a pattern that a number of teenagers became depressed and aggressive after declaration of results of their board exams. The researcher developed a theory that overexpectation of parents from their child is the main reason of depression and aggression among them.

## Formation/Interaction/ Inquiry Based Research

Formation based research depends on the interaction of researcher with a set of people. The mode of interaction could be direct or indirect. Following are the types of Formation Based Research

### 1. Unstructured Research

In unstructured research the problem which has to be investigated is not pre-determined, rather they are spontaneous.

In this type of research, the researcher is free to explore nature of problem, issue or phenomenon without quantifying it.

**Example** Study of the diversity of food pattern in different parts of India.

### 2. Structured Research

A structured research (also known as systematic observation) is a data collecting method, in which researcher gather data without direct involvement with the participants. The data collection technique. It uses coding method for data collection.

The structured approach to inquiry is usually classified as quantitative research.

**Example** If Indian Standards Institution wants to gather data about a popularity of a certain food product. It will use structured research methodology to sort the data to find a quantitative outcome.

## Concept Based Research

On the basis of concept the research can be divided into two categories

### 1. Conceptual Research

This type of research is generally used by philosophers and thinkers to develop new concepts or to reinterpret the existing concepts.

### 2. Empirical Research

The empirical research relies on experiences or observation alone. It is a data based research coming up with conclusions that are capable of being verified by observation or experiment.

In this type of research the researcher must formulate a working hypothesis. He collects data to prove or disprove his/her hypothesis.

## Process Based Research

On the basis of process the research can be classified into three categories namely qualitative, quantitative and mixed research.

### 1. Qualitative Research

This is basically an approach and not just a method to conduct research. It is basically inductive or spiritual in nature and has a very different structure. In this type of research the main objective is to develop an understanding on human beings/ social science to know what people feel and think. Qualitative researchers are concerned with process rather than simply with outcomes or products.

- It seeks to obtain information and description of complex and dynamic processes using holistic, naturalistic and non-manipulative methods.
- No statistical tests are required.

### 2. Quantitative Research

This type of research is mostly associated with the positivist or post positivist paradigm. It involves collecting and converting data into numerical form. The quantitative research is based on logical positivist paradigm which utilises experimental method. This type of research is deductive in that it test theories which have already been proposed. It aims at analysing of data through the use of sophisticated statistical methods and software packages.

In quantitative research the experiments carefully plans the study including the test or other data collection instruments to be used. This type of research is based more directly on its original plans and its results are more readily analysed and interpreted.

### 3. Mixed Research

Mixed method research is a methodology for conducting research that involves collecting, analysing and intergrating quantitative (e.g., experiments surveys) and qualitative (e.g., focus groups, interviews) research.

## Nature Based Research

Research on the basis of nature is classified into two parts that are :

### 1. Inter-disciplinary Research

"Inter-disciplinary research is a mode of research by team or individuals that integrates information, data, techniques, tools, perspectives, concepts and theories from two or more disciplines or bodies of specialised knowledge to advance fundamental understanding or to solve problems whose solutions are beyond the scope of a single discipline or area of research practice."

### 2. Multi-disciplinary Research

Multi-disciplinary research is the blend of two or more subjects to expand on a topic in a manner that would not be possible through the discussion of only one subject.

Thus, in a multi-disciplinary research, various disciplines address scientific and social challenges independently rather than in collaboration and hence share goals.

## Characteristics of Research

The characteristics of a research are the qualities or features of the research, which give recognition to the outcome of the research.

Important characteristics of research are discussed below

1. **Objectivity** It means the research is being free from all bases. In other words it means, observation is unaffected by the observer's values, beliefs and preferences to the possible extent.
2. **Reliability** If the similar research is carried by time and again in a similar setting it must give similar result. So, the researcher must frame the research questions to make it reliable and provide similar outcomes. For example, if a respondent gives out a response to a particular item, he/she is expected to give the same response to that item even if he/she is asked repeatedly. If he/she is changing his/her response to the same item, the consistency will be lost.

3. **Validity** The meaning of validity in research is accuracy in research procedure and research instruments. There are multiple measuring tools available for research design but valid measuring tools are those which help a researcher in determining results according to the objective of research.

   Any measuring device can said to be valid if it measures what it is expected to measure and nothing else.

   (i) **Internal Validity** It is the most basic type of validity because it concerns the logic of the relationship between the independent variable and the dependent variable. This type of validity is an estimate of the degree to which inferences about causal relationship can be drawn based on the measure employed and research design.

   (ii) **External Validity** It means the external factors that can affect study must be controlled. It concerns whether results of the research can be generalised to another situation, different subjects settings and so on.

4. **Accuracy** It means truth or correctness of a statement or describing things exactly as they are and avoiding jumping to unwarranted conclusions either by exaggeration or fantasising.
5. **Credibility** It refers to the extent to which a research account is believable and appropriate, with particular reference to the level of agreement between participants and the researchers.
6. **Systematisation** It means attempting to find all the relevant data or collecting data in a systematic and organised way so that the conclusion drawn are reliable.
7. **Empirical** research is based on direct experience or observation by the researcher.
8. **Logical** research is based on valid procedures and principles.
9. **Cyclical** research starts with a specific problem, find solution for that problem and paves way to arise new problem.
10. **Generalisation** It is closely related to validity. It refers to the degree to which research findings can be applied to a larger population.

    Here, the sample considered is the representative of the whole population, so the findings should be applicable to the whole population.

    (i) **Analytical** research utilises proven analytical procedures in gathering data; whether historical, descriptive, experimental and case study.

    (ii) **Critical** research exhibits careful and precise judgements.

    (iii) **Methodological** research is conducted in a methodological manner without biasness, using systematic method and procedures.

    (iv) **Replicability** research design and procedures are repeated to enable the researcher to arrive at valid and conclusive results.

11. **Importance of cause and effect** Establishing cause and effect is a central goal of most researches. It demonstrates that a particular independent variable (the cause) has no effect on the dependent variable of interest (effect).

## RESEARCH APPROACHES

There are two important approaches famous among sociological researchers i.e. Positivism and **Post-Positivism**.

These approaches are discussed below

### Positivism

This approach was first formulated by the French thinker **Auguste Comte**. Thus, he is considered the 'Father of Positivism'.

He first described the epistemological perspective of positivism in 'The Course in Positive Philosophy' (1842) and 'System of Positive Polity' (1851). The positivism is based on scientific basis.

According to Comte, the whole universe is organised and operated by Unchangeable Natural Laws. Thus, it can be understood through scientific methods rather than theological or hypostatical manner.

Hence, positivism is to understand and acquiring knowledge about everything with the help of scientific methods which are based on analysis, synthesis, application and classification. It only discusses about those events which can be seen or felt directly and can be analysed.

**According to Comte steps of Positivism approach**

To select a topic to study

⇓

To collect the observable evidences related to the topic through evaluation

⇓

After analysis classify the collected evidences on the basis of general classification

⇓

To give conclusion

## Paradigm

A paradigm is a model of the functions and interpretations of a process a way of thinking about something and how to study it.

The emphasis on the concept of a paradigm in research philosophy in the recent decades is usually attributed to the work of **Thomas S. Kuhn** in the 1960's. He discussed paradigms in the context of "the progress of scientific discoveries in practice" and went on to define paradigms as "universally recognised scientific achievements that for a time provide model problems and solutions to a community of practitioners".

**Bryman** provides a useful definition of a paradigm. According to him, "it is a cluster of beliefs and dictates which for scientists in a particular discipline influence what should be studied, how research should be done and how results should be interpreted".

Hence, it is primarily a set of basic beliefs that defines the nature of the world and the place that individual holds in the world and it also guides individual's action.

The paradigms are grouped as positivist and interpretive paradigms. The pitfalls in the positivist approach led to the emergence of interpretivism, subjectivism, etc.

The new set of paradigms is referred by multiple names such as, interpretivism, phenomenology and subjectivism.

### Characteristics of Positivism

- Positivism is related to scientific point of view as well as scientific methodology.
- Positivism keeps itself away from religious and philosophical ideas.
- Positivism is a utility science and believes in the form that knowledge gained through positivism can be used as a means of social reconstruction.

### Limitations of Positivism

- Positivism relies on experience as a valid sources of knowledge.
- Positivism lacks empathy and consideration of the subjective, individual and hermeneutic aspects of social phenomenon.
- Its search for ideal and perfect scientific methodology and analysis are too unrealistic.
- Positivism sometimes is a rejection of metaphysics. It is a position that the goal of knowledge which is simply to describe the phenomena that we experiences.

# Post-Positivism

Post-positivism argues that by combining empirical comments with logical reasoning, a proper estimate can be made about an event. Post-positivism believes that there is no difference between the thinking and acts of scientists and our daily affairs.

The scientific logic and general logic are essentially the same process and there is no difference in between the two, only difference is in the fraction. According to Post-positivism, all observations are unstable and there is an error and all these principles are reusable. Post-positivism believes that the goal of science is to achieve the aim of truth with the help of correct methods either we achieve the aim or not.

Post-positivism gives emphasis on three developments such as

(i) Use of quantitative and qualitative strategies.

(ii) Desire of strategy based on question research.

(iii) Its pattern is based on quantitative v/s qualitative technique.

Hence, it promotes the triangulation of qualitative and quantitative methods that explores the diversity of researchable facts.

# METHODS OF RESEARCH

Research method may be understood as all those methods or techniques that are used for conducting a research.

In other words, all those methods which are used by the researcher during the course of studying his/her research problem are termed as research methods.

Since, the objective of research is to arrive at a solution for a given problem, the available data and unknown aspects of the problem have to be related to each other to make a solution possible.

However, keeping this in view, research methods can be put into the following categories

## 1. Historical Research Method

Historical study or method focuses on collection and objective evaluation of data related to past occurrences in order to test hypothesis concerning causes, effects or trends of these events that may help to explain present events and anticipate future events.

The purpose of historical method of research is to re-evaluate data in relation to selected hypothesis, theories and generalisations, and to understand how and why educational theories and practices developed.

### Steps of Historical Research

(i) Identify an idea, topic or research question.

(ii) Conduct a background literature review.

(iii) Refine the research ideas and questions.

(iv) Determine that historical method will be used.

(v) Identify and locate primary and secondary data sources.

(vi) Evaluate the authenticity and accuracy of source materials.

(vii) Analyze the data and develop a narrative exposition of the findings.

### Objectives of Historical Research

- The purpose of historical research is to discover unknown events.
- To study the cause and effect relationship between two events.
- To record and evaluate the accomplishments of individuals, institutions and other kinds of organisations.
- To provide understanding of the immediate phenomenon of concern.
- It tries to understand the significance of events that may be responsible for shaping a particular situation.

### Methods of Historical Research

(i) **Archival Data** The archival data or primary sources, are typically the resources that researchers rely most heavily on. It includes official documents and other items that would be found in archives, museums, etc.

(ii) **Secondary Sources** Secondary sources are the works of other historians.

(iii) **Running Records** Running records are the documentaries maintained by private or non-profit organisations.

(iv) **Recollections** Recollections include sources such as autobiographies, diaries or memoirs.

### Sources of Historical Research

There are two sources of historical research that are discussed below:

#### (i) Primary Sources

A primary source is a document that contains the original statement on the topic being investigated by the researcher.

These contain evidence that is closest to the event under investigation as recounted by observers and participants.

These include the following :

- Documents generated by the events themselves such as archival records (governmental, institutional, commercial, ecclesiastical, etc), internal letters and memoranda (memos), speeches, summaries or minutes of conferences and meetings, photographs of people, buildings and equipment, statistical information (such as tally sheets and surveys), lists of holdings (goods, equipment, etc) and reports and statements (mission statements, employee guidelines).
- Documents produced to record events such as chronicles, diaries, reports produces by journalists and interviews conducted by them, drawings and photographs, motion picture films, tape recordings and video recordings.
- Documents in supplementary forms produced much later in the form of oral sources, oral traditions and folklores, languages themselves, say fables, folktales, folklore etc are a good source; etc.

### (ii) Secondary Sources

A secondary source is the one derived or created from a primary source (that first reported the event being studied). It reports events based on use of primary and other secondary sources as basis of data collection. It contains information reported by a person who did not directly observe the event, object or condition (Key, 1997, p.1).

Thus, these report events by a person other than a direct observer or a participant in the events. A source becomes a primary or secondary source depending upon its proximity to the actual event under investigation (Powell, 1991, p.140). Examples of secondary sources are give below :

- Textbooks
- Encyclopedias
- Monographs
- Articles in magazines

## 2. Descriptive Research Method

It is a research method that describes the characteristics of the population or phenomenon that is being studied.

This methodology focuses more on the "what" of the research subject rather than the "why" of the research subject.

Thus, it does not make accurate predictions, and does not determine cause and effect.

It is a quantitative research method that attempts to collect quantifiable information to be used for statistical analysis of the population sample. It is a popular market research tool that allows to collect and describe the nature of the demographic segment.

In descriptive research, none of the variables are influenced in any way because it uses observational method to conduct the research. Hence, the nature of the variables or their behaviour is not in the hands of the researcher.

Descriptive research method is generally a cross-sectional study where different sections belonging to the same group are studied. The data collected and analyzed during this method can also be used by other research methods.

### Types of Descriptive Research

Descriptive research is classified into different type according to the kind of approach that is used in conducting descriptive research. The different types of descriptive research are highlighted below:

(i) **Descriptive-Survey Research** It uses surveys to gather data about varying subjects. This data aims to know the extent to which different conditions can be obtained among these subjects.

For example, a researcher wants to determine the qualification of employed professionals in India. He uses a survey as his research instrument, and each item on the survey related to qualifications is subjected to a Yes/No answer.

(ii) **Descriptive-Normative Survey** This is an extension of the descriptive-survey, with the addition being the normative element. In the descriptive-normative survey, the results of the study should be compared with the norm. For example, an organisation that wishes to test the skills of its employees by a team may have them a skills test.

The skill tests are the evaluation tool in this case and the result of this test is compared with the norm of each role.

(iii) **Descriptive-Status** This is a quantitative description technique that seeks to answer questions about real-life situations.
For example, a researcher researching the income of the employees in a company, and the relationship with their performance.

(iv) **Descriptive-Analysis Method** of research describes a subject by further analysing it, which in this case involves dividing it into two parts. For instance, a questionnaire is devised to analyse the job role of employees with similar salaries and work in same jobs.

(v) **Descriptive-Comparative** In descriptive-comparative research, the researcher considers two variables which are not manipulated, and establish a formal procedure to conclude that one is better than the other. For example, an examination body wants to determine the better method of conducting tests between paper-based and computer- based tests.

### Characteristics of Descriptive Research

- Descriptive research uses a quantitative research method by collecting quantifiable information to be used for statistical analysis of the population sample.
- It can also be carried out using the qualitative research method, to properly describe the research problem. This is because descriptive research is more explanatory than exploratory or experimental.
- In descriptive research, researchers cannot control the variables like do in experimental research.
- The results of descriptive research can be further analyzed and used in other research methods.

## 3. Experimental Method of Research

The experimental method is a systematic and scientific approach to research in which the researcher manipulates one or more variables, and controls and measures any change in other variables.

Experimenters manipulate certain stimuli, treatments or environmental conditions and observe how the condition or behaviour of the subject is affected or changed. An experiment involves the comparison of the effects of a particular treatment with that of a different treatment or no treatment.

It is the most systematic method as through this method cause-effect relationship of individuals behaviour can be established.The findings of experimental method are open to critical examination and verification.

One of the constraints of experimental method is that; human behaviour is changeable, identical behaviour of the same individual not occur under identical conditions at different times. This method is costly and time consuming.

## 4. Action Research

Action research is a process in which participants examine their own educational practice systematically and carefully using the techniques of research.

The term 'action research' was coined in 1940 by **Kurt Lewin**, a German American Social Psychologist.

Action research refers to a wide variety of evaluative, investigative and analytic research methods designed to diagnose problems or weakness. It helps the researcher to develop practical solutions to address them quickly and efficiently. It is conducted to address an immediate problem. It is a type of applied research.

### Objectives of Action Research

- To identify problem areas and improve the working conditions in school.
- To develop scientific attitude among teachers students, principals and administrators for studying, understanding and solving current academic problem.
- To bring potential in school functionaries.

### Features of Action Research

- It usually emerges out of situational needs and a solution to problem is also designed with respect to the situation.

- As problem emerges in practical real life situation, so action is to be taken in real world.
- The focus may be more on problems that need urgent attention.
- It is mostly on social situation such as in educational institutions.
- It is a small scale intervention.
- Quantitative and qualitative methods can be employed in conducting an action research.

Thus, the action research is focused on immediate application and not on the development of theory or general applications.

### Steps in Conducting Action Research

(i) Identification of a problem.

(ii) Defining, analysing and explaining a problem.

(iii) Listing and stating the probable causes.

(iv) Development of proposition/ formulation of hypothesis(es).

(v) Planning, development, implementation and evaluation of action research.

(vi) Drawing conclusions and taking decisions.

(vii) Sharing of results.

## 5. Quantitative Research Method

Quantitative research is a structured way of collecting and analysing data obtained from different sources.

This method involves the use of computational, statistical and mathematical tools to derive results.

The data collection tools for a qualitative research are surveys and experiments. Experiments can provide specific results regarding the cause and effect relationship of several independent or interdependent factors related to a particular problem.

As data is collected, analysed and presented in numbers, the results obtained from quantitative research are extremely reliable. Numbers do not lie, they present an honest picture of the conducted research without discrepancies and is also extremely accurate.

This research method offers no scope for personal comments or biasing of results. The results achieved are numerical and are thus, fair in most cases.

### Characteristics of Quantitative Research

- Quantitative research uses deductive or 'top-down' approach. The researcher formulates and uses hypothesis.
- It is based on logical-positive paradigm which utilises experimental methods and quantitative measures to test specific hypothetical generalisations with narrow- angle lens.
- Quantitative research uses scientific method like the researchers treat their subjects of study as having an existence independent of themselves and without any intrinsic meaning.
- Behaviour of the subjects under study is assumed to be regular and predictable.
- Most of the common research objectives in quantitative approach aim at description, explanation and prediction of social phenomenon.
- Quantitative research attempts to study behaviour under controlled conditions. The nature of observation is objective, is based on different observers.
- Closed ended structured questionnaires, tests, attitude scales, rating scales, etc. are used to collect quantitative data for precise measurement.
- The dominant sampling strategy in quantitative research is probability sampling, which depends on the selection of a representative sample from a larger population.
- Quantitative research is deductive in that it tests theories which have already been proposed. It aims at analysis of representative and validated quantitative data, through the use of sophisticated statistical methods.

## 6. Qualitative Research Method

During the late 18th century, philosophers such as Immanual Kant, William Dithey, Edmund Husserl and Maurice Merleu-Ponty believed that life consists of experiences and we live in a matrix of complex relationships with others.

The seminal work of these philosophers paved the way for the birth of naturalistic or qualitative research.

Qualitative research is a method of naturalistic inquiry, that seeks in-depth understanding of social phenomena within their natural setting. It focuses on the 'why' rather than the 'what' of social phenomena and relies on the direct experiences of human beings as meaning-making agents in their every day lives.

## Importance of Qualitative Research

- Establishment of causal relationships between independent and dependent variables,
- Law-like generalisability of phenomena,
- Replicability,
- Objective in the collection, analysis and interpretation of data, and reporting of results.

It is dominated by the largely unquestioned, natural science paradigm of hypothetico-deductive methodology. Quantitative research actually goes beyond just analysing numbers.

## Methods of Qualitative Research

(i) **In-depth Interview** This is the most common qualitative research method. It is a personal interview that is carried out with one respondent at a time.

The advantage of this research is that, it provides great opportunity to gather precise data about what people believe and what their motivation are.

The researchers can ask questions and follow-up questions during interviews which can help them to collect relevant informations.

(ii) **Focus Group** A focus group is also one of the commonly used qualitative research method. In focus group research method a limited number of respondents (6-12) based on topic of research is included.

The main aim of this research method is to find answers to the questions of–why, what and how.

(iii) **Ethnographic Research** Ethnographic research method focuses on the meaning of sociology through close field observation of sociocultural phenomena.

This research method studies people in their naturally occurring environment. In such research geographical constraints can be an issue while collecting data. This research method aims to understand the cultures, challenges, motivations and settings that occur.

(iv) **Text or Content Analysis** In this method, the researchers try to analyse the social life by decoding the words and images from a piece of the documents or other similar forms like film, music, documentary etc. The aim of content analysis is to identify important characteristics of the content, being researched and present in a simplified manner, so that it can be easily understood.

(v) **Phenomenology** Phenomenology describes the structures of experience as they present themselves to consciousness, without recourse to theory, deduction, or assumptions from other disciplines. Phenomenological method is particularly effective at bringing the experiences and perception of individuals from their own perspectives.

# Tools of Research

## 1. Paper

A research paper is a common form of academic writing which is based on analysis, interpretation, and research findings on a particular topic conducted by a researcher.

Research papers require writers to locate information about a topic, take a stand on that topic and provide evidence for that position in an organised report. The research paper may also refer to a scholarly article that contains the results of original research or an evaluation of research conducted by others.

Most scholarly articles must undergo a process of peer review before they can be accepted for publication in an academic journal.

## 2. Workshop

A workshop is an interactive session, often takes a full day or more, in which clients, researchers and other participants such as customers work intensively on an issue or question.

In a workshop, elements of qualitative research, brainstorming and problem solving are included. A workshop involves larger numbers of people than conventional group discussions and often involve more than one moderator or facilitator.

## 3. Seminar

Seminar is simply a group of people coming together for the discussion and learning of specific techniques and topics. It is a form of academic instruction, either at a university or offered by a commercial or professional organisation.

It brings together small groups for recurring meetings, focusing each time on some particular subject, in which everyone present is requested to actively participate. In a seminar, the instructor prepares the concepts and techniques to present and discuss through a combination of visual materials, interactive tools or equipment and demonstrations.

## 4. Conference

A conference is a formal meeting, where participants exchange their views on various topics. Conference can take place in different fields and it need not be academic in nature all the time.

Some of the examples of conference are-parent-teacher conference, sports conference, trade conference, journalist conference, doctors conference, conference of research scholar and so on.

A conference is a pre-arranged meeting which involves consultation and discussion on a number of topics by the delegates.

## 5. Symposium

Symposium is a formal gathering in an academic setting where participants are experts in their respective fields. These experts present or deliver their opinions or view points on a chosen topic of discussion. A symposium can be labelled as a small scale conference as the number of delegates is smaller.

# Steps or Process of Research

A research involves a systematic process that focuses on being objective and gathering a multitude of information for analysis, so that the researcher can come to a conclusion.

A research follows the following steps

Formulating Research Problem

⇓

Reviewing the Research Structure

⇓

Conducting the Literature Review

⇓

Developing the Hypothesis

⇓

Preparation of Research Design

⇓

Collection of Data

⇓

Analysis and Interpretation of Data

⇓

Concluding the Data and Formal Write-up of the Research Report

## Step 1 Formulating Research Problem

The first step in the formulation of research is to make a research problem concrete and explicit. There is no full proof method to be followed by the researcher in formulating significant questions about any research area in mind. But, there are certain working conditions which would help the researcher in formulating problem.

Generally, these stages are used to formulate a research problem.

***Stage* I Selection of a Research Area** Formulation of research problem begins with selection of a broad research topic from personal experience, literature, previous research and theories in which researcher is interested.

***Stage* II Dissect the Research Area into Sub-area** The subject area chosen by the researcher may be broad in that case researcher needs to dissect it into small areas or topics. For example, researcher chooses 'childhood nutrition' topic. It is a broad subject area and researcher need to dissect it more.

He can dissect it into childhood development series, malnutrition in children, child immunisation, childhood diseases, childhood mortality and childhood vaccines. There can be many other categories or you can select a category and sub-area among all of them.

***Stage* III Focus on the Selecting an Area of Interest** In this step, researcher may choose one or two areas of his interest. Rest sub-areas does can be avoided by the researcher if he did not have any interest in them.

***Stage* IV Generate Research Questions** Generate as many research questions as possible on the selected area or topic. Research questions should be formulated in such a way that they can be answered using scientific techniques and research procedures.

***Stage* V Decide about the Objectives** Objectives are the possible answers to the research question or the research problem that researcher have formulated. Objectives make you specific, as you conduct your study around the objectives that you have decided. The objectives need to be specific in nature but you can also generate general objectives.

***Stage* VI Formulating Final Statement of Research Problem** After establishing the significance, researchability and feasibility, then the researcher finally formulates a final statement of a research problem. A research problem could be in declarative or interrogative format.

## **Step 2** Reviewing the Research Structure

- Once the task of formulating the research problem is over, the researcher must review the research structure.
- This step provides foundational knowledge about the problem area.
- The review of structure, also educates the researcher about what studies have been conducted in the past, how these studies were conducted and the conclusions in the problem area.

## **Step 3** Conducting the Literature Review

Literature review is usually the longest stage in the research process. Actually, the literature review starts even before the formulation of research aims and objective, because you have to check if exactly the same research problem has been addressed before.

Nevertheless, the main part of the literature review is conducted after the formulation of research aims and objectives.

You have to use a wide range of secondary data sources such as books, newspapers, magazines, journals, online articles, etc.

The purpose of literature review is to

- The review of related literature enables the researcher to define the limits of his fields.
- It helps the researcher to delimit and define his problem.
- By reviewing the related literature, one can avoid unfruitful and useless problem areas. By reviewing the literature the researcher can avoid unintentional duplication of well established findings.
- It gives to the researcher an understanding of research methodology.
- The reason for reviewing the literature is to know about the recommendations of previous researchers listed in their studies for further research.

## Identify Variables and Formulate Hypothesis

The next step is to identify the variables of the study and formulate the hypothesis:

### Variables

It represents the measurable traits that can change over the course of an experiment or research. Variable is the central idea in research. A variable is defined as anything that varies or changes in value.

It can take two or more values because variable represents a quality that can exhibit differences in value, usually magnitude or strength. For instance–a person's attitude towards women empowerment is variable as it can range from highly favourable to highly unfavourable.

#### Selection of Variables

The researcher while selecting the variable should consider carefully as to which independent variable is to be selected and which variable are to be controlled so that changes can be made in independent variable. While selecting a controlled variable a researcher should see how he manipulates the independent variable.

A researcher while selecting variable should consider some behavioural things in mind./ The variables should not be too many. A researcher should also keep in mind the financial resources when selecting independent and dependent variables for his study. He should also be careful about time limit.

#### Types of Variables

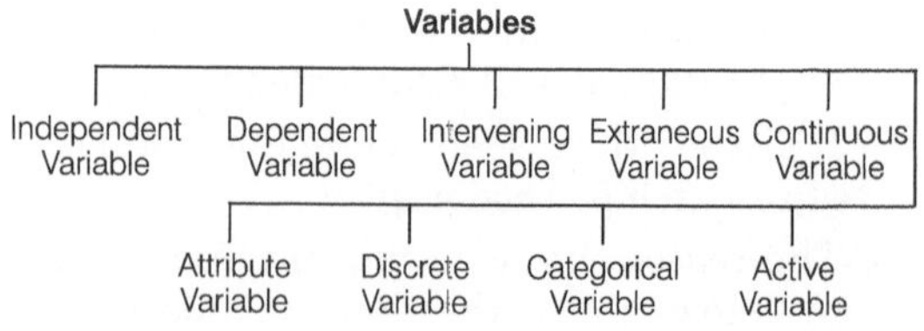


(i) **Independent Variable** It is the variable manipulated by the researcher in an experiment. It influences or affects another variable of the system.

(ii) **Dependent Variable** It is the variable that changes as a result of changes made on the independent variable. It does not influence or affect another variable of the system.

(iii) **Intervening Variable** It is a hypothetical variable used to explain casual links between other variables. These are variables through which one variable affects another variable.

(iv) **Extraneous Variable** These are variables which have an effect on the dependent variable, but are not part of the system. There can be many factors or variables that may affect the outcome. These variables are termed as extraneous variable.

(v) **Continuous Variable** These can be expressed continuously. They are numeric variables that have an infinite number of values between any two values. For example–the length of a part, date and time on which payment is received.

(vi) **Discrete or non-Continuous Variable** These are numeric values that have a countable number of values between any two values. For example, the number of customer complaints.

(vii) **Categorical Variable** It contains a finite number of categories or distinct groups. Categorical data might not have a logical order. For example, categorical predictors include gender, etc.

(viii) **Active Variable** An active variable is a variable that can be manipulated. Active variables are also called experimental variables.

(ix) **Attribute Variable** An attribute variable is a variable that cannot be manipulated. A researcher cannot use these variable as they are an inherent part of a person or object.

### Measuring Variables

Measurement of variables is central to research studies. There are four scales for measuring the variables such as detailed below:

- **Nominal Scale** A Nominal Scale enables the classification of individuals, objects or responses into sub-groups based on a common/shared property. A variable measured on a nominal scale may have one, two or more sub-categories depending upon the extent of variation.
- **Ordinal Scale** The lowest level of the ordered scale that is commonly used is the ordinal scale. The ordinal scale place events in order. It is used for variables which can be categorised as well as ranked. For example, when asked about the satisfaction of a service, respondent can vary in one of these responses : Very satisfied, satisfied, neutral, dissatisfied and very dissatisfied.
- **Interval Scale** It is used for variables involving quantity which can be categorised, ranked as well as can be expressed in increament. The scale has an arbitrary zero point with numbers placed at equally appearing intervals. It is used also in attitude measurement. Measuring temperature is an example of interval scale. The interval scale may either be numeric or semantic formats. The interval scales allow the calculation of averages like mean, median, mode and dispersion like range and standard deviation.
- **Ratio Scale** It is the highest level of measurement scales. Ratio scales allow the researcher to compare both differences in scores and relative magnitude of scores. Examples of ratio scale include weight, length and times. In the marketing research, most counts are ratio scale. It has absolute zero characteristics. This scale is used to calculate all the scientific variables. In the absence of a ratio scale, scientific variables cannot be measured.

## Step 4 Developing Hypothesis

The word hypothesis consists of two words hypo and thesis. Hypo means tentative or subject to the verification and thesis means statement about solutions of the problem. Thus, it can be defined as a tentative explanation of the research problem, a possible outcome of the research.

According to **Good and Hatt** "A hypothesis is a proposition which can be put to test in order to determine its validity."

While **Kerlinger** defines hypothesis as a conjectural while statement of the relation between two or more variables.

The hypothesis is a powerful research process to achieve dependable knowledge. It is the presumptive statement of a proposition or a reasonable guess based upon the available evidence which the researcher seeks to prove through his study. Hypothesis is formulated only as a suggested solution to the problems, with an objective that the ensuing study may lead either to rejection or retention.

### Features of Hypothesis

- It should be clearly and precisely stated.
- It should be testable.
- It should state the expected relationship between variables.
- It should be limited in scope.
- It should be consistent with most known facts.
- It should be stated in simple terms.

### Importance of Hypothesis

- It ensures the entire research methodologies are scientific and valid.
- It helps to assume the probability of research failure and progress.
- It helps to provide link to the underlying theory and specific research question.
- It helps in data analysis and measure the validity and reliability of the research.
- It provides a basis or evidence to prove the validity of the research.
- It helps to describe research study in concrete terms rather than theoretical terms.

### Types of Hypothesis

1. **Null Hypothesis** It means zero hypothesis. A researcher has nothing to do in developing it. The null hypothesis proposes that no statistical significance exists in a set of given observation.

2. **Directional and Non-Directional Hypothesis** Directional hypothesis states the direction of the differences or association. It tends to be more specific about the outcomes. On the other hand non-directional hypothesis states only the difference or association between variables and not the direction.
3. **Declarative Hypothesis** It is a hypothesis developed as a declarative statement. It generally states relationship between the variables concerned.

   When the researcher makes a positive statement about the outcome of the study, the hypothesis takes a declarative form.
4. **Complex Hypothesis** It shows the relationship between two or more dependent variables and two or more independent variables. Like eating more fruits and vegetables leads to weight loss, glowing skin and reduces the risk of many diseases.
5. **Statistical Hypothesis** A statistical hypothesis is sometimes called confirmatory data analysis. It is an assumption about a population parameter.
6. **Descriptive Hypothesis** It is a statement about the existence, size, form or distribution of a variable. It encourage researchers to think about the implications of a supported or rejected finding.
7. **Relational Hypothesis** A relational hypothesis is a statement about the relationship between two variables with respect to some case. Relational hypothesis may be correlational or explanatory (casual).
   (a) **Correlational Hypothesis** It is a statement indicating that variables occur together in some specified manner without implying that one causes the other.
   (b) **Explanatory Hypothesis** It is a statement that describes a relationship between two variables in which one variable leads to a specified effect on the other variable.
8. **Alternative Hypothesis** An alternative hypothesis is the opposite of null hypothesis where we can find some statistical importance or relationship between variables. Here, the researcher wants to show or prove some relationship between variables.

## Hypothesis Testing

The value of statistics is to be calculated and then it is compared with the tabulated value of the statistic. If the computed value lies within the range of tabulated value, then null hypothesis is not rejected.

The level of significance considered for tabulated value is generally 5% or 1%. Hypothesis testing or significance testing is a method for testing a claim or hypothesis about a parameter in a population, using data measured in a sample.

The main purpose of hypothesis testing is to help researcher in reaching a conclusion regarding population by examining a sample taken from a population.

The test only indicates whether the hypothesis is supported or not supported by the available data. Hypothesis testing is an act of statistics. These are four main steps in hypothesis testing

1. **State or Null and Alternate Hypothesis** It means after developing initial research hypothesis it is important to restate it as null ($H_0$) and alternate ($H_a$) hypothesis so that you can test it.

   The alternate hypothesis is usually initial hypothesis that predicts a relationship between variable. The null hypothesis is a prediction of no relationship between the variable the researcher interested in.
2. **Collect Data** For a statistical test to be valid it is important to perform sampling and collect data in a way that is designed to test hypothesis.
3. **Perform a Statistical Test** There are variety of statistical tests available, but they all are based on the comparison of **within-group variance** (how spread out the data is within a category) versus **between-group variance** (how different the categories are from one another).

4. **Decide Whether Null Hypothesis is Supported or Rejected** Based on the outcome of your statistical test the researcher has to decide whether null hypothesis is supported or rejected.

   In most cases, the cut off for rejecting the null hypothesis will be 0.05. It means when there is a less than 5% chance that you would see these results if the null hypothesis work true.

5. **Present Your Findings** The results of hypothesis testing will be presented in the results and discussion sections of the research paper. In the results section, a brief summary of data and summary of the results of the statistical test are presented. While in the discussion, person can discuss whether initial hypothesis was supported or refuted.

## Errors in Hypothesis Testing

There can be four different situations in testing hypothesis such as

- Null hypothesis is true but it has been rejected.
- The null hypothesis is true and it has not been rejected.
- The null hypothesis is false and it has been rejected.
- The null hypothesis is false and it has not been rejected.

The second and third are good conclusions but the first and fourth are errors. Type I error occur when true hypothesis get rejected. Type II error occurs when a false hypothesis does not get rejected.

## Generalisation and Interpretation

If in testing of the hypothesis, it has been supported by the data several times, then it can be used for generalisations and thus for formulating theories. This way research is used to solve real-life problem.

If the researcher has no hypothesis to start with, he might seek to explain his findings on the basis of some theory. It is known as interpretation. The process of interpretation may trigger off new questions which in turn may lead to further research.

# Step 5. Preparation of Research Design

According to **Russel Ackoff**, "Research design is the process of making decisions before a situation arises in which the decision is to be carried out." In this step, the researcher prepares the conceptual framework within which the research would be carried out.

Following are the significant aspects which must be kept in mind while preparing a research design

- Means of obtaining the information
- Tools of data collection
- Objectives of the research study
- Data analysis (qualitative and quantitative)
- Time available for each stage of the research
- Cost involved for the research

This step helps researcher to decide the course of action during various stages of the research, which saves time and resources of the researcher.

## Objectives of Research Design

Research design achieves the following aims of the researcher.

- It makes research efficient.
- It optimise the utilisation of researches.
- It makes reliability and flexibility.

To find solution of problem and questions in research

- To arrange research systematically
- To give clear direction with regard to research
- It helps to make research efficient.

## Types of Research Designs

There are different types of research design depending upon the nature of the problem and objectives of the study. Following are the types of research design

1. **Exploratory Research Design**

   Exploratory research intends merely to explore the research questions and does not intend to offer final and conclusive solutions to the existing problems. It is also known as 'formulative research design'.

This type of research is usually conducted to study a problem that has not been clearly defined yet. The objective in this type of research is development of theory or new ideas, by formulating a research problem for in-depth analysis or by establishing the working hypothesis. Such a research uses qualitative and unstructured methods of research.

2. **Conclusive Research Design** It is a research designed to assist the decision maker in deciding, evaluating and choosing the better course of action in a given situation. It is different from exploratory research as it is formal and structured.

   Data collected in this type of research is subject to quantitative analysis. Some types of conclusive research design are casual research design, longitudinal research design, cross-sectional research design, etc.

3. **Experimental Research Design** It is any research conducted with a scientific approach, where a set of variables are kept constant while the other sets of variables are being measured as the subject of experiment.

   Independent variables are manipulated in experiments and their effect on dependent variable is observed under controlled conditions to interpret the relationship. It can be categorised as pre-experimental design, quasi-experimental design and True–experimental design.

4. **Descriptive and Diagnostic Research Design** It is concerned with describing the characteristics of a particular individual or group. Meanwhile a diagnostic research determines the frequency with which a variable occurs or its relationship with another variable. In other words the study analysing whether a certain variable is associated with another comprises diagnostic research study.

   On the other hand a study that is concerned with specific predictions or with narration of facts and characteristics related to an individual, group or situation, are examples of descriptive research.

5. **Hypothesis–Testing Research Design** The researcher tests the hypothesis of the causal relationship between two or more variables.

   These studies require procedure that would only decrease biases and enhance reliability but also facilitate deriving inferences about the causality.

   Generally, experiments satisfy such requirements. Hence, when research design is discussed in such studies, it often refers to the design of experiments.

6. **Cross–Sectional Research Design** When data is collected on more than one case simultaneously i.e., at the same point of time, it is said to involve a cross- sectional design. This is used to collect a body of quantitative and quantifiable data with two or more variables. They are then scrutinised to identify connectivity patterns.

   Researcher who employ cross–sectional design are concerned with variation or differentiation. In this type of research design a sample is surveyed and is surveyed again on atleast one more occasion.

7. **Causal Comparative Research Design** This design seeks to find relationship between independent and dependent variables after an action or event has already occurred. It attempts to determine the causes or consequences of differences that exist between or among groups of individuals.

   It is less time consuming and economical. It gives chance to the researcher to analyse on the basis of his personal option and then come out with best possible solutions. The independent variable cannot be manipulated.

8. **Longitudinal Research Design** In this design, the time and cost involved is quite high. It is comparatively less used design in social research. It can be called as an extension of survey research as it includes the self-completion questionnaire or structured interview styled within the context of cross–sectional research design.

It is observational studies. It means that researcher record information about their subjects without manipulating the study environment. Here, the researcher is able to detect development or changes in the characteristics of target population at both the group and individual level.

## Step 6 Sampling

Sampling is the process by which a relatively small number of individuals or measures of individuals, objects or events is selected in order to find out something about population from which it was selected.

Usually four steps are involved in the process.

(i) **Defining the Population** A population refers to any collection of specified group of living beings or non–human entities such as educational institutions, geographical areas etc. some call it universe. If a population is not properly defined, a researcher does not know what units to consider when selecting the sample.

(ii) **Listing the Population** In order to select a sample from given population it is also necessary to have complete accurate and upto date list of all the units in the population.

(iii) **Selecting a Representative Sample** In this researcher after defining a population and listing all the units, selects a sample unit from the sampling frame.

(iv) **Obtaining an Adequate Sample** If the population under study is homogenous, a small sample is sufficient. On the other hand, a much larger sample is necessary if there is greater variability in the units of population.

### Types of Sampling

The method of selecting a sample is fundamental importance and depends upon the nature of data and investigation.

The techniques of selecting a sample can be classified as

(i) **Non-probability Sampling** It is a sampling procedure which is not the basis for estimating the probability that each item in the population has been included in the sample. In this type of sampling, items for the sample are selected at the discretion of the researcher. It is very cost and time-effective. It is also easy to use and can also be used when it is impossible to conduct probability sampling (e.g. when you have a very small population to work with). In non-probability sampling, while representing the population we cannot calculate confidence intervals and margins of error. This is the reason why probability sampling is considered first.

The types of non-probability sampling are enumerated as follows :

(a) **Judgement Sampling** The researcher uses his/her judgement to select population members who are likely to provide accurate information. This can be used for his historical or descriptive research.

(b) **Quota Sampling** Under quota sampling the interviewers are simply given quotas to be filled from the different strata. With some restrictions on how they are to be filled. This type of sampling is very convenient and is relatively less expensive.

(c) **Haphazard Sampling** It is a method where a researcher chooses item haphazardly, trying to stimulate randomness. However, the result may not be random at all and is often tainted by selection bias.

(ii) **Snowball Sampling** It is a technique used when desired sample characteristic is rare. It is also known as network, chain referral or reputation sampling method. It begin by collection of data on one or more contacts usually known to the person collecting data.

At the end of data collection process (e.g. questionnaire, survey or interview) the data collector asks the respondents to provide contact information for other potential respondents.

These potential respondents are contacted and provide more contacts. Snowball sampling helps in studying small informal social group and its impact upon formal organisational structure.

It is a non-probability sampling technique that is used by researcher to identify potential subjects in studies where subjects are hard to locate. The types of snowball sampling can be classified as linear, exponential and non–discriminative and exponential discriminative.

(iii) **Probability Sampling** Probability Sampling is also known as random sampling or chance sampling. Under this sampling design, every item of the universe has an equal chance of inclusion in the sample. With probability sample the researcher may be able to know the size of the sample needed to achieve any desired level to accuracy. He can specify the chance of each unit being selected. He can estimate the magnitude of error due to sampling. He can determine the level of confidence. There are different methods of selecting a probability sample these are discussed below

(a) **Simple or Restricted Random Sampling** In this type of sampling each unit of population is given an equal chance of being selected.

(b) **Stratified Random Sampling** Under stratified random sampling the population is divided into several sub-population that are more homogeneous than the total population (the different sub–population are called strate). Then, we select items from each stration to constitute a sample.

(iv) **Cluster Sampling** In cluster sampling the total population is divided into a number of relatively small sub–divisions which are themselves cluster of still smaller units and then some of these cluster randomly selected for inclusion in the over all sample.

(v) **Multi-Stage Sampling** It is used in large scale surveys for a more comprehensive investigation. The researcher may have to use two, three or four stage sampling.

## Step 7 Collection of Data

The next step in the research is collection of data. There are many alternatives available to collect relevant data. The researcher should select one of the methods of collecting data taking into consideration the nature of investigation, scope and objective of inquiry, financial cost, availability of time and desired accuracy. Data can be primary or secondary depending upon its source.

### (i) Primary Data

It is collected by the researcher specifically as per the requirement of study. The data collected by a researcher is through observation, interview method, questionnaires and schedules, are discussed below

(a) **Observation Method** It is the most commonly used method specially in studies related to behavioural sciences. Under this method the information is sought by way of investigator's own direct observation without asking from the respondents.

(b) **Interview Method** This method can be used through personal interviews or through telephone interviews. In personal interview the investigator follows structured approach and the questions are pre–conceived.

Here, the output/results also depend on the ability of the interviewer to a large extent. The interview approach must be friendly, courteous, conversational and unbiased.

(c) **Telephone Interview** This method of collecting information consists of contacting respondents on telephone itself. It is not widely used method. It is used when surveys has to be accomplished in a very limited time.

(d) **Mailed Questionnaires** This method of data collection is quite popular particularly in case of big inquires. The questionnaire is mailed to respondent who are expected to read and understand the questions. To write down the reply in the space meant for the purpose in the questionnaire itself. It is most commonly used method in business and economic surveys.

(e) **Schedules** In this method the enumerators are specially appointed and trained for collecting information. Schedules consist of relevant questions. The enumerators visit respondents with schedules, these schedules are filled up by the enumerators on the basis of replies given by the respondent.

(f) **Survey Method** This approach is most suitable for gathering descriptive information.

It is of two types i.e. structured and unstructured survey. Structured survey use formal lists of questions asked of all respondents in the same way. Whereas Unstructured survey allows the interviewer probe respondents and guide the interview according to their answers.

### (ii) Secondary Data

It means the data that is already available i.e. refers to the data which have already been collected and analysed by someone else. When the researcher utilises secondary data, then he has to look into various sources from where he can obtain them.

Secondary data may either be published data or unpublished data. Usually, published data is available in:

(a) Various publications of the central, state and local governments;
(b) Various publications of foreign governments or of international bodies;
(c) Technical and Trade Journals;
(d) Books, magazines and newspapers;
(e) Reports prepared by research scholars, economists, etc.
(f) Historical documents and other resources of published information.

## Step 8 Analysis and Interpretation of Data

In this step, the researcher analyses the data to identify common patterns within the responses and critically examines them to achieve aims and objectives.

### Process of Analysing Data

The next step after collecting the data is to analyse it. It needs a number of closely related operations such as establishment of categories to raw data through coding, tabulation and then drawing statistical inferences.

(i) **Editing** The purpose of cleaning data is called editing. The aim of editing is to identify and minimise errors, miscalculations, misclassification or any gap in information provided by the respondent. Editing improves the quality of data for coding.

(ii) **Coding** In this the first step is to ensure the nature of data i.e., whether it is quantitative or qualitative. The qualitative data may be descriptive the case history e.g. categorical or discrete, gender, attitude, strongly favourable favourable or unfavourable.

### Classification of Data

The classification of data is a process of arranging data in groups or classes on the basis of common characteristics.

It can be classified in these ways.

#### Classification According to Attributes

The data can be descriptive or numerical further the classification can be simple, manifold which are explained as

(i) **Simple Classification** In this classification the research consider only one attribute and divide the universe into two classes. One class consisting of items possessing the given attribute and the other class consisting of items which does not posses the given attribute.

(ii) **Manifold Classification** Here, the two or more attributes are considered simultaneously and divide the data into number of classes.

#### Classification According to Class Intervals

In this the classification is done with data relating to income, age, weight production, occupancy etc. Such quantitative data are known as the statistics of variables and are classified on the basis of class intervals.

**Tabulation** It is a part of technical procedure where the classified data are put in the form of tables. It is the process of summarising raw data and displaying the same in compact form for further analysis.

When data are large computers can be used for tabulation. It is an orderly arrangement of data in columns and rows. It is essential because of the following

- It conserves space and reduces explanatory and descriptive statement to minimum. It facilitates the process of comparison, the summation of items and detection of errors and omissions.

## Data Analysis

Analysis of the data is done with the help of different mathematical and statistical techniques like percentages, averages, correlation, regression etc. Analysis mainly depend whether the data is qualitative or quantitative.

### Analysis of Qualitative Data

Qualitative data can be observed and recorded. This type of data is not–numerical in nature. This type of data is collected through methods of observation, one–to–one interview.

There are no set ground rules for analysing qualitative data, it can be analysed on the basis of these approaches i.e., deductive and inductive. The deductive approach involves analysing qualitative data based on a structure that is pre-determined by the researcher.

The inductive approach on the contrary is not based on predetermined structure or set ground rules/framework. It is often used when a researcher has very little or no idea of the research phenomena.

Thus, qualitative data is usually based on interpretative philosophy.

### Analysis of Quantitative Data

Quantitative data is statistical and is structured in nature–meaning, it is more rigid and defined. This type of data is measured using numbers and values.

For quantitative data there are a variety of statistical analysis tools used to identify statistical relationships between variables. The data can be analysed manually or through computer.

(i) **Manual Data Analysis** This can be done if the number of respondents is reasonably small and if there are not many variables to analyse. This is useful for calculating frequencies and for simple cross tabulation.

(ii) **Data Analysis Using Computer** If a researcher wants to analyse data with the help of computer then he/she should be familiar with appropriate computer programme.

The most common software used is SPSS. In the process of analysis relationship or differences, supporting or conflicting with original or new hypothesis should be subjected to tests of significance.

## Step 9 Concluding the Data and Formal Write-up of the Research Report

This is the final step of research. On the basis of data interpretation some generalisation may arise. The generalisation made in this step should not be based on personal opinion rather, it should flow from the analysis based on data.

The validity of the research outcome depends on how accurately the findings of data have been incorporated in the conclusion.

**Format of Report**

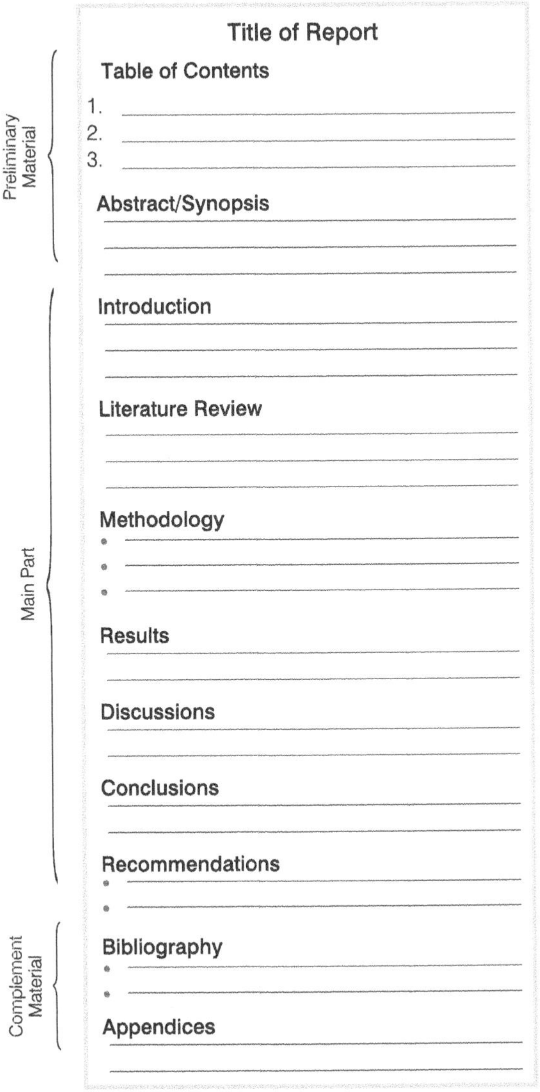


# THESIS WRITING

A thesis is a document written in support of obtaining an academic degree or qualification. It is usually longer than research paper and thus completed in a number of years.

A thesis, also called dissertation, is usually associated with postgraduate studies; i.e. research or master's degree, Ph. D or M. Phil level and is carried out under a supervision of a professor or the academician of the university.

Supervisor oversees and guides the progress of thesis writing. A thesis and a research paper, both require the demonstration of extent academic research and the evidence of capacity for critical analysis.

The completion of thesis, however, requires the input of original work and author's findings in the field of chosen topic. While chosing a topic for a thesis the author must take into consideration the expectation of originality in the field or the input of some relevant new information or ideas.

## Characteristics of Thesis Writing

The characteristics of thesis writing are given as

- The research management is a form of research in which the emphasis is not only on theoretical studies but is also based on behavioural studies.
- The research is done to carry out the basic facts, then accordingly find a solution to the related problem under study.
- In research the behavioural aspect is more reliable in comparison to theoretical aspect.
- A research should have the knowledge and skill to present its thesis effectively. The writing style can be developed through continuous practice.

## Content of Thesis Writing

1. **Introduction to Research** This includes research introduction and nature of research, its objective, area of research and related study material.
2. **Research Hypothesis** In this a brief description of hypothesis which are given related to research study.
3. **Research Methodology** In this, brief discussion of all research related methods are presented.
4. **Unit** In the research study, every part of the unit is presented with clarity. The entire research study is then divided into different units.

5. **Analysis of Data** It is the most crucial part of any research. It summarises the collected data. It also involves the interpretation of data gathered through the use of analytical and logical reasoning to determine patterns, relationships or trends.
6. **Result** In this the results of the research study are presented.
7. **Conclusion** A research should include well constructed conclusion of the entire research study and what the research is about.
8. **Research Comment** The comments are presented which includes about problem relating to classification, tabulation as well as possible defects and solution to research problem.
9. **Reference/Bibliography** The researcher gives in detail the reference material used by him and the books, newspaper and other sources used.
10. **Appendix** It contains the schedule of questionnaire description of difficult terms, charts, maps.

## Format and Styles of the Thesis Writing

The thesis is a lengthy experimental design, or theoretical report, with a problem method-results-discussion structure. This recurrent hypothetical deductive pattern of developing a thesis to solve a problem and then constructing a methodology and testing for results is common in research writing. Following format should be followed while writing a thesis.

### Front Matter

The front matter frames the thesis work. It includes the following elements

1. **Title Page** The title page should be informative, contain keywords and reveal the topic of the thesis. On this page title of the thesis, author's name, supervisor's name, place and date should be given.
2. **Abstract** The abstract should be given in about 100 to 150 words or roughly 5-10 sentences. In this section, the author of the thesis should briefly state the research problem, methodology, key results and conclusion.
3. **Table of Contents** In this section, a list of key subject headings and sub-headings of the thesis should be given with their page numbers. The author should ensure to include acknowledgements, appendixes and bibliography in the list.
4. **List of Figures** This section included the figure numbers, figure titles and page numbers.
5. **List of Tables** This section included the table numbers, table titles and page numbers of the tables.
6. **Nomenclature** (Optional) In this section, the author can give a list of terms, symbols, acronyms and their meanings.

### Body

The body of the thesis provides the introduction, narrative and analysis of the research work.

The body includes the following elements

1. **Introduction** In this section, the author should state the purpose of the investigation, the problem being investigated, the background of the problem, general approach of the thesis, and the criteria for the study's success.
2. **Theory** The author should develop the theoretical basis for research design or experimental work, including any governing equations. Detailed calculations go to an appendix.
3. **Materials Apparatus and Procedures** The author should give the list and describe key materials and apparatus. Then describe the procedure in full detail. For design studies, this section includes component design, fabrication, assembly and testing procedures. The author should use illustrations.
4. **Results** The author should present the results, usually with accompanying table and graphs. The author should characterise the patterns and quality of the results and estimate their accuracy and precision.

5. **Discussion** In this section, discuss the meaning of the results, stating clearly what their significance is, compare the results with theoretical expectations and account for anything unexpected.
6. **Conclusions** In this section, review the results in relation to the original problem statement. Assess the success of the study in light of the criteria of success mentioned in the introduction part.
7. **Recommendations** In this section, the author can recommend directions for future work.

### End Matter

The end matter is mainly referential material. It includes following elements

1. **Acknowledgement** In this section, the author should acknowledge assistance from advisors, sponsors, funding agencies, colleagues, technicians and so on.
2. **Appendixes** In this section, the author should provide detailed calculations, procedures, data in separate appendixes. Give each appendix a title, a letter (Appendix A, B, C) and an introductory paragraph.
3. **Bibliography** The author should give an alphabetical list of works referred during the study.

   It is suggested to follow bibliographical and footnote formats of the concerned department or of a prominent periodical published by a professional society in concerned field.

## ARTICLE WRITING

A research article is a detailed account of research activity written by the researcher. An article is not bound by the methodology adopted in writing a research paper.

A research covers the entire outcome of research while an article is a topic specific essay. The main aim of an article is to give detailed information on a particular topic.

### Format and Styles of Article Writing

Following format and styles should be followed while writing an article

### Front Matter

1. **Title Page** The title page should be informative, contain keywords and reveal the topic of the article. On this page, title of the article and author's name, should be given.
2. **Abstract** The abstract should be given in about 100 to 150 words or roughly 5-10 sentences. In this section, the author of the article should briefly state the research problem, methodology, key results and conclusion.

### Body

1. **Introduction** In this section, the researcher should state the reasons of the conducted study, its theoretical framework, the goal of the research, the problem statement and create hypothesis.
2. **Methodology** In this section, the researcher should include samples of the article, how he/she obtained/selected these, what materials (equipment, apparatus and measuring instruments) he used during the article writing and what procedures he/she used in this writing.
3. **Researcher** here uses different types of reading material (hibs) such as banks, magazines, internet site and other related material or sources used by the researcher.
4. **Results** The researcher should present the results, usually with accompanying text, table and graphs. The author should characterise the patterns and quality of the results and estimate their accuracy and precision.
5. **Discussion** The researcher should include the following points in the discussion of article writing such as
   (i) Non-technical interpretation of results.
   (ii) Linking results to original purposes and hypothesis.

(iii) Why the results turned out the way they did.
(iv) Identifying the study's limitations.
(v) Suggesting steps for further research.

### End Matter

It includes the following element

**Reference** The researcher must include the references he/she used during writing the article like internet sites, journals, magazines, books, thesis and other sources.

## APPLICATION OF ICT IN RESEARCH

Application of Information and Communication Technologies (ICTs) in research is referred to the use of advanced digital technologies to support research process. It plays a vital role in enabling users to explore new and innovative research opportunities. Without it, these discoveries and opportunities may not have otherwise been possible if only standard desktops or general purpose IT technology were used.

The researchers need to change with changing times and need to understand today's fast changing knowledge base and its peculiarities. ICT tools are mainly used by researchers for its ability to ease knowledge-gathering process and to enhance resource-development.

The use of ICT is based on the individual's logical assessment of how various applications increase his/her effectiveness and efficiency in work and provide ease in communication with peers. Generally, ICT tools help researcher in the following research related tasks

### Data Collection

Through the use of computers, internet and modern technology, data can be collected easily. The collection procedure is simple and less time consuming. This reduces the need for manual collection.

### Accessing Data

Data available online can be accessed with ease. Online portals provide relevant information about the surveys conducted. Government portals provide data such as census information that can be easily accessed.

Data.gov.in is an open portal from where data can be taken to support the researches. Similarly, e-books and manuscripts can also be easily accessed online.

### Storing Data

Data can be stored for present and future use in various ways such as in spreadsheets, cloud servers, google drive, etc. There are many software that enable the storing of data.

Microsoft Excel, Oracle, SQL are some of them. Data once stored can be used again and again in different researches. It can be protected through login credentials (password).

### Processing Data

ICT can be readily used to process the information. It can process huge data in very little time. Manual process is very time consuming. ICT provides various tools to process numerical data such as finding averages and standard deviation. Non-numerical data can also be easily processed by data analysing tools.

### Interpreting Data

ICT can also be used to interpret data in many ways such as through pie charts, bar graphs, histograms, etc. Visual presentations are easy to understand and interpret.

### Discussion of Research Findings

Researchers can publish their research papers by uploading it in various e-portals, e-journals and e-magazines.

This enables many readers across the world to go through the research papers, discuss about it and give valuable insights. Shodhganga is one such site of India.

## Role of Computer in Various Phases of Research Process

1. **Role of Computers in Literature Review** Computers help for searching the literature (for review of literature) and bibliographic references stored in the electronic databases of the World Wide Webs. It can thus be used for storing relevant published articles to be retrieved whenever needed.
2. **Role of Computers for Sample Size Calculation** Several softwares are available to calculate the sample size required for a proposed study. NCSS-PASS-GESS is such software. The standard deviation of the data from the pilot study is required for the sample size calculation.
3. **Role of Computers in Empirical Phase** Empirical phase consists of collecting and preparing the data for analysis. The data obtained from the subjects are stored in computers as word files or excel spreadsheets.

   This has the advantages of making necessary corrections or editing the whole layout of the tables if needed, which is impossible or time consuming in case of writing in papers.

   Thus, computers help in data entry, data editing, data management including follow up actions etc. Computers also allow for greater flexibility in recording the data while they are collected as well as at greater ease during the analysis of these data.
4. **Role of Computers in Data Analysis Phase** This phase consist of statistical analysis of the data and interpretation of results. Many softwares are now available to perform the 'mathematical part' of the research process i.e. the calculations using various statistical methods.
5. **Role of Computers in Research Dissemination Phase** This phase is the publication of the research study. The research article is typed in word format and converted to Portable Data Format (PDF) and stored and/or published in the World Wide Web.

### Main Tools of Computer Research

To analyse the data with the help of computer there are tools which help the researcher in carrying out his research

1. **Spreadsheet** A computer application that stimulates a paper worksheet. It displays multiple cells that together make a grid consisting of rows and columns. Each cell containing either alphanumeric text or numeric values. Microsoft–excel is a popular spreadsheet software. The other spreadsheet. packages are lotus1, 2, 3.

   It is used in many fields. It helps to create reports of questionnaire data in the form of graphical presentation. It is a powerful tool for data analysing and its also used for SPSS data entry.
2. **Word Processor Package** It is an ICT application used for the production, composition, editing formatting and possibly any sort of printable material. The word processing packages are Microsoft Word, Word Perfect.

   The purpose of word processor is to allow people to write. They make it lost easier to edit text. In this the document is stored easily on disk and can be retrived and used easily.
3. **Database Management Packages** (DBMS) It is an organised collection of information.

   A DBMS is software designed to manage the database. The various desktop databases are Microsoft Access, dBase, or dBase III + Fox Base, Visual Fox/Pro.

   They are very useful in creating and maintaining queries, the databases and generation of reports.
4. **Statistical Package for Social Sciences** (SPSS) It is used in Social Sciences. It is used by various kinds of researcher for complex statistical data analysis. SPSS is designed in such a way that it can handle a large set of variable data format.

The SPSS helps in research and data analysis programme in following ways
- Data transformation
- Regression Analysis
- ANOVA (Analysis of Variance)
- MANOVA (Multivariate Analysis of Variance)
- T-Tests

SPSS is used in many fields such as business, education, medicine and others. SPSS research tool can compare and explore the difference between responses to two or more questions. It is a powerful tool for data analysing.

SPSS is widely coveted due to its straight forward and English like command language.It is one of the most popular statistical package which can perform highly complex data manipulation and analysis with simple introduction.

5. **Web Browser** A browser or a web browser is a software application for accessing information on the world wide web. A web browser enables a user to display and interact with text images, videos, music, games and other information typically by accessing a web page found on a website.

   It is collectively provided in the world wide web. Some example of browsers are Microsoft Internet Explorer, Mozilla Firefox, Netscape Navigator, Opera Chrome (Google browser) etc.

# RESEARCH ETHICS

Research that involves human subjects or participants, raises unique and complex ethical, legal, social and political issues.

It refers to a diverse set of values, norms and institutional regulations that help constitute and regulate scientific activity.

Following are the objectives of Research Ethics
- To protect human participants.
- To ensure that research is conducted in a way that serves interests of individuals, groups and society as a whole.
- To examine specific research activities and projects for their ethical soundness, looking at issues such as the management of risk, protection of confidentiality and the process of informed consent.

Research involving vulnerable persons, which may include children, persons with developmental or cognitive disabilities, persons who are institutionalised, the homeless or those without legal status, raises ethical issues in research context.

Conduct of human research in developing countries, use of genetic material in research, protection of privacy in light of advances in technology and internet capabilities are serious concern for an ethical research.

## Components of Ethical Research

Following are the components of ethical research

1. **Voluntary Participation** In an ethical research all the participants in the research should be voluntary, which means their informed consent is required.

   The participants must be told about procedures and informed about potential risk. The consent should be documented in written form.

2. **No Harm to the Subjects** The research should be conducted in such a manner so that any harm to the participants could be minimised.

3. **Confidentiality of Participants** In an ethical research the participants must be guaranteed their autonomy, privacy, dignity and confidentiality.

## Main Approaches to Research Ethics

There are three major approaches to ethics such as

1. **Deontological Approach** It means one should identify and use a universal code in making ethical discussion. This is an absolute approach.

2. **Utilitarianism Approach** Decision regarding ethics in research should be based on an examination and comparison of cost and benefits that may arise from a study. If the expected benefits exceeded the expected risks, the study is presumed to be ethical.
3. **Ethical Scepticism Approach** It states that ethical standards are not universal but are relative to one's own particular culture and time. This is based on relativism.

## Suggestions for Research Ethics

Here are a few suggestions with regard to ethical research to the researcher

- **Avoid Bias** Objectivity in research means to avoid bias in the research process as it is considered unethical.
- **Using Inappropriate Research Methodology** The deliberate use of a highly biased sample, method or procedure is unethical.
- **Honesty** It means the researcher need to report honestly and that this applies to methods (What you did) your data, your results.
- **Carefulness** It means one should take care in carrying out research to avoid careless mistakes. Review your work carefully and critically to ensure that results are credible.
- **Openness** One should always be prepared to share his data and result along with any new tools developed.
- **Respect for Intellectual Property** One should never plagarise or copy, other people's work and try to pass it off as your own. You should seek permission before using other people's tools or methods.
- **Confidentiality** It means one should respect anything that has been provided in confidence.
- **Human Subjects Protection** It means if your research involves people, then your research method should not harm them.

## Errors in Research

Errors in research may occur due to various reasons. Every research is susceptible to errors. There are some common errors in research such as

- The error may arise due to some confusion in selecting the research methodology, data collection or data interpretation.
- Errors can also be due to biases and prejudices that the researcher introduced into the research analysis.
- Small errors can occur in research writers that go unnoticed during proofreading of the manuscript.
- Errors can also result due to research questions that does not prove to be well–defined and researchable.
- Population specification errors occur when the researcher does not understand who they should survey.

# Chapter Practice

## Research : Meaning, Objectives, Characteristics and Types

1 Research is
(A) searching again and again
(B) finding solution to any problem
(C) working in a scientific way to search for truth of any problem
(D) None of the above

2 Who said that "Research is a systematic effort to gain new knowledge"?
(A) Webster (B) Redman and Mory
(C) J W Best (D) None of these

3 Who said that "Research is a process of steps used to collect and analyse information to increase our understanding of a topic or an issue"?
(A) Morley (B) J W Best
(C) Creswell (D) Kerlinger

4 A good research aims at
(A) developing generalisations, theories and principles
(B) solving routine problems
(C) betterment of the society
(D) None of the above

5 Which of the following is/are the nature of research?
(A) It is objective and factual
(B) It is scientific in nature
(C) It is logical in nature
(D) All of the above

6 Which of the following is the objective of research?
(A) To gain familiarity with phenomena and achieve new insight into it
(B) To determine the frequency with which something occurs
(C) To describe, unexplained horizon of knowledge
(D) All of the above

7 In what ways the objectivity of the research can be enhanced?
(A) Through its impartiality
(B) Through its reliability
(C) Through its validity
(D) All of the above

8 Which is the main objective of research?
(A) To review the literature
(B) To summarise what is already known
(C) To get an academic degree
(D) To discover new facts or to make fresh interpretation of known facts

9 The quality of research can be judged by the
(A) relevance of research
(B) methodology adopted in conducting the research
(C) depth of research
(D) experience of researcher

10 A research is conducted to fulfil which of the following?
I. Generate new knowledge
II. Not to develop a theory
III. Obtain research degree
IV. Reinterpret existing knowledge
Select the correct answer from the following codes.
(A) I, III and II
(B) III, II and IV
(C) II, I and III
(D) I, III and IV

11 Which of the following statement(s) is/are true?
(A) In research, objectives can be worded in question form
(B) In research, objectives can be worded in statement form
(C) Objectives are to be stated in Chapter I of the thesis
(D) All of the above

12 Sine qua non (essential elements) of good research is
(A) a well-formulated hypothesis
(B) a good research supervisor
(C) adequate library
(D) a well-formulated problem

13 Research can be classified as
(A) basis, applied and action research
(B) quantitative and qualitative research
(C) philosophical, historical, survey and experimental research
(D) Both (b) and (c)

14 Which of the following is/are type(s) of field studies?
(A) Exploratory testing
(B) Hypothesis testing
(C) Both (A) and (B)
(D) None of the above

15 Which research is primarily concerned with finding out 'what is' or 'what was'?
(A) Explanatory research
(B) Correlational research
(C) Descriptive research
(D) None of the above

16 In which of the following researches 'manipulation' is always a part of?
(A) Historical research
(B) Fundamental research
(C) Descriptive research
(D) Experimental research

17 Which of the following is most appropriate about ex-post facto research?
(A) The research is carried out after the incident
(B) The research is carried out prior to the incident
(C) The research is carried out along with the happening of an incident
(D) The research is carried out keeping in mind the possibilities of an incident

18 Which type of research concerns itself with cause effect relationships?
(A) Ex-post Facto research
(B) Analytical research
(C) Correlational research
(D) Explanatory research

19 "To search measures to reduce the absentee rate among employees of a company" is the example of which type of research?
(A) Correlational research
(B) Analytical research
(C) Explanatory research
(D) Ex-post Facto research

20 Which research is conducted for those problems which have not been researched before?
(A) Explanatory research
(B) Exploratory research
(C) Historical research
(D) Analytical research

21 Which research is conducted for such problems which have not been clearly defined?
(A) Exploratory research
(B) Basic/fundamental research
(C) Experimental research
(D) None of the above

22 The process not needed in experimental researches is
(A) Observation
(B) Manipulation
(C) Controlling
(D) Content analysis

23 The experimental studies are based on
(A) the manipulation of the variables
(B) conceptual parameters
(C) replication of research
(D) survey of literature

24 Empirical research is based on
(A) direct experience of researcher
(B) direct observation of researcher
(C) writing skill of researcher
(D) Both (A) and (B)

25 Which of the following is the example of Basic/fundamental research?
(A) A study, assessing whether men or women are likely to suffer from depression
(B) A study, looking at how caffeine consumption impacts our brain
(C) A study, looking at how family environment influences the socialisation of a child
(D) All of the above

26 Fundamental research reflects the ability to
(A) synthesise new ideas
(B) expound new principles
(C) evaluate the existing material concerning research
(D) study the existing literature regarding various topics

27 The research that applies the laws at the time of field study to draw more and more clear ideas about the problem is
(A) Applied research
(B) Action research
(C) Experimental research
(D) None of the above

28 The principles of fundamental research are used in
(A) Action research
(B) Applied research
(C) Philosophical research
(D) Historical research

29 Research shows that the older a person is, the larger their vocabulary. This is an example of a
(A) Positive correlation
(B) Negative correlation
(C) Casual correlation
(D) Zero correlation

30 Which of the following is not a characteristic of research?
(A) Research is systematic
(B) Research is not a process
(C) Research is problem oriented
(D) Research is not passive

31 Which of the following is/are the characteristic(s) of an authentic research?
(A) Validity (B) Credibility
(C) Objectivity (D) All of these

## Positivism, Post-Positivism Approach to Research and Steps/Processes of Research

32 In the Positivism approach which method is mainly used?
(A) Theological (B) Hypostatical
(C) Scientific (D) All of these

33 The approach which is based on the assumption that social phenomena can be explained by observing cause and effect is
(A) Positivism (B) Interpretivism
(C) Qualitative (D) None of these

34 Which approach emphasise that researcher and reality are inseparable and reality is internal and socially constructed?
(A) Positivism (B) Interpretivism
(C) Qualitative (D) None of these

35 Positivism as a approach was first formulated by the French thinker ........ who is considered as the 'Father of Positivism'.
(A) Thomas Kuhn (B) Auguste Comte
(C) Catherine Dawson (D) None of these

36 Which of the following is emphasised by Post-Positivism approach in research?
(A) Desire of strategy based on question research.
(B) Use of quantitative and qualitative strategies.
(C) Pattern is based on quantitative *v/s* qualitative technique.
(D) All of the above

37 "To find out solutions for the betterment of tribal community in India" is an example of which research?
(A) Historical research
(B) Correlational research
(C) Explanatory research
(D) None of the above

38 "This research is a process of critical inquiry into past events." The statement indicates which type of research?
(A) Correlational research
(B) Explanatory research
(C) Historical research
(D) Ex-post facto research

39 The research that aims at immediate application is
(A) Action research
(B) Empirical research
(C) Conceptual research
(D) Fundamental research

40 Which of the following approaches is/are famous among sociological researchers?
(A) Analytical Approach
(B) Positivism Approach
(C) Post-Positivism Approach
(D) Both (A) and (C)

41 The key defining characteristic of experimental research is that
(A) The independent variable is manipulated
(B) Hypothesises are proved
(C) A positive correlation exists
(D) Samples are large

42 Action Research is
(A) an applied research
(B) a research carried out to solve immediate problems
(C) a longitudinal research
(D) simulative research

43 Which method of research uses deductive or top-down approach?
(A) Qualitative research
(B) Quantitative research
(C) Descriptive research
(D) Historical research

44 The first step of research is
(A) selecting a problem.
(B) searching a problem.
(C) finding a problem.
(D) identifying a problem.

45 When a research problem is related to heterogeneous population, the most suitable method is
(A) Cluster sampling
(B) Stratified sampling
(C) Convenient sampling
(D) Lottery method

46 When a possible solution to the problem has been written in desired direction, this type of hypothesis is called
(A) Directional hypothesis
(B) Non-directional hypothesis
(C) Declarative hypothesis
(D) None of the above

## Tools of Research, Process of Research, Variables, Hypothesis

47 The advantage of synopsis is
(A) it clearly shows the way of research
(B) it visualises the various difficulties related with different steps of research
(C) it helps in planning various steps of the research
(D) All of the above

48 The synopsis of research is called
(A) blue print
(B) mapping of problem
(C) base of a problem
(D) All of the above

49 The research papers writing methodology has slight variations in reference to
(A) the standards maintained by research journals
(B) the interests of the researchers
(C) the research traditions
(D) All of the above statements are correct with slight variations

50 A research paper can be presented in
(A) journals (B) symposium
(C) seminars (D) All of these

51 Who plays a pivotal role in a workshop?
(A) The participants
(B) The expert
(C) The director
(D) All of the above

52 Which of the following is/are step(s) of a research workshop?
(A) The presentation and explanation of the topic
(B) The practice of following an approach
(C) Follow-up and evaluation of a topic
(D) All of the above

53 Which of the following is/are characteristic(s) of research workshop?
(A) To attain the higher cognitive and psychomotor objectives of the research
(B) To comprehend the theoretical and practical aspects of the research
(C) To explore the possibilities of applied aspects of the research
(D) All of the above

54 A workshop is
(A) a conference for discussion on a topic
(B) a meeting for discussion on a topic
(C) a class at a college or a university in which a teacher and the students discuss a topic
(D) a brief intensive course for a small group emphasising the development of a skill or technique for solving a specific problem

55 Arrange the following steps of research in correct sequence.
I. Reviewing the research structure
II. Formulating research problem
III. Conducting the literature review
IV. Developing a hypothesis
V. Preparation of research design
VI. Collection of data

**Codes**
(A) I, II, III, IV, V and VI
(B) I, II, IV, III, V and VI
(C) II, I, III, IV, V and VI
(D) II, I, IV, III, V and VI

56 Attributes of objects, events or things which can be measured are called
(A) Qualitative measure
(B) Data
(C) Variables
(D) None of the above

57 Which variables are those that a researcher chooses to study in order to assess their possible effects on one or more other variables?
(A) Dependent variable
(B) Independent variable
(C) Extraneous variable
(D) None of the above

**58** Extraneous variables are essentially
(A) Independent variable
(B) Dependent variable
(C) Dependent or independent variable
(D) Neither independent nor dependent variable

**59** Which of the following is not an example of a continuous variable?
(A) Family size (B) Intelligence
(C) Height (D) Attitude

**60** Which of the following variables cannot be expressed in quantitative terms?
(A) Socio-economic status
(B) Marital status
(C) Numerical aptitude
(D) Professional attitude

**61** In research, something that does not vary is called a
(A) Variable
(B) Method
(C) Constant
(D) None of the above

**62** A manipulated variable is called
(A) Extraneous variables
(B) Intervening variables
(C) Subject variables
(D) Active variables

**63** The behaviour that is measured during an experiment is known as the
(A) Compounding variable
(B) Independent variable
(C) Dependent variable
(D) Control variable

**64** The objective(s) of a seminar is/are
(A) to develop critical and analytical capacities in a researcher
(B) to develop observational and experiential presenting capabilities in a researcher
(C) to develop synthetic and evaluation related abilities in a researcher
(D) All of the above

**65** When academicians are called to deliver lecture or presentation to an audience on certain topic or a set of topic of educational nature, it is called
(A) Training programme
(B) Seminar
(C) Workshop
(D) Symposium

**66** What is/are the advantage(s) of a conference?
(A) Mutual exchange of ideas
(B) Development of democratic values
(C) Guidance of new researchers
(D) All of the above

**67** The concepts in a hypothesis are stated as
(A) populations (B) variables
(C) ideas (D) theories

**68** Which of the following statements is true in the context of the testing of a hypothesis?
(A) Both, the alternative and the null hypothesis cannot be tested
(B) It is only the alternative hypothesis, that can be tested
(C) It is only the null hypothesis, that can be tested
(D) Both, the alternative and the null hypothesis can be tested

**69** Which of the following is/are define(s) declarative hypothesis?
(A) The declaration of the relationship among the variables
(B) The expression of the correlation among the variables
(C) Both of (A) and (B)
(D) None of the above

**70** A working hypothesis is
(A) a proven hypothesis for an argument
(B) not required to be tested
(C) a provisionally accepted hypothesis for further research
(D) a scientific theory

**71** Identify the incorrect statement.
(A) A hypothesis is made on the basis of limited evidence as a starting point for further investigations
(B) A hypothesis is a basis for reasoning without any assumption of its truth
(C) Hypothesis is a proposed explanation for a phenomenon
(D) Scientific hypothesis is a scientific theory

**72** A good hypothesis should be
(A) precise, specific and consistent with most known facts
(B) formulated in such a way that it can be tested by the data
(C) of limited scope and should not have global significance
(D) Both (A) and (B)

**73** A null hypothesis is
(A) when there is no difference between the variables.
(B) the same as research hypothesis.
(C) subjective in nature.
(D) when there is a difference between the variables.

**74** What is a cross-sectional design?
(A) A study of one particular section of society.
(B) One that is devised when the researcher is in a bad mood.
(C) The collection of a data from more than one case at a moment in time.
(D) Comparision of two or more variables.

**75** A systematic literature review is
(A) one which gives equal attention to the principal contributors.
(B) a responsible, professional process of time management for research.
(C) a replicable, scientific and transparent process.
(d) None of the above

**76** What is Research Design?
(A) A way of conducting research that is not grounded in theory
(B) The choice between using qualitative or quantitative methods
(C) The style in which you present your research findings e.g. a graph
(D) A framework for every stage of the collection and analysis of data

**77** This design seeks to find relationship between independent and dependent variables after an action or event has already occurred is
(A) Longitudinal research design
(B) Cross Sectional research design
(C) Causa-Comparative research design
(D) Experimental research design

## Sampling, Data Collection

**78** It is a non-probability sampling technique that is used by researcher to identify potential subjects in studies where subjects are hard to locate.
(A) Multistage
(B) Snowball
(C) Stratified
(D) Judgement sampling

**79** The primary data can be collected through
(A) Observation method
(B) Schedules
(C) Questionnaires, Interview method
(D) All of the above

**80** Match the following.

| List I (Variables) | List II (Characteristics) |
|---|---|
| A. Continuous | 1. It contains a finite number of categories or district group. |
| B. Categorical | 2. They have an effect on the dependent variable. |
| C. Discrete | 3. They are numeric variables that have an infinite number of values between any two values. |
| D. Extraneous | 4. These are numeric values that have a countable number of values between any two values. |

**Codes**

| | A | B | C | D |
|---|---|---|---|---|
| (A) | 2 | 4 | 3 | 1 |
| (B) | 3 | 1 | 4 | 2 |
| (C) | 1 | 2 | 3 | 4 |
| (D) | 4 | 3 | 2 | 1 |

**81** Tabulation is essential due to these reasons
(A) It conserves space and reduces explanatory and descriptive statements to minimum
(B) It provides the process of comparison the summation of item and detection of errors and omissions
(C) It provides the basis for various statistical computations
(D) All of the above

**82** Which of the following is/are incorrect about the analysis of qualitative data?
(A) It can be analysed on the basis of deductive and inductive approach
(B) Analysis is more rigid and defined
(C) It is measured using numbers and values
(D) It is useful for calculating frequencies and simple cross-tabulation

**83** Which one of the following is a non-probability sampling?
(A) Simple random
(B) Haphazard
(C) Systematic
(D) Stratified

**84** A data collection method in which the researcher does not interact with the subject(s) being studied is called
(A) an unobtrusive measure
(B) field research
(C) qualitative research
(D) None of the above

**85** Which of the following step(s) is/are involved in the process of sampling?
(A) Defining the population
(B) Listing the population
(C) Selecting representative sample and obtaining an adequate sampling
(D) All of the above

**86** In this type of scale variables can be systematically added, subtracted, multiplied and divided, in its absence scientific variables cannot be measured.
(A) Nominal Scale
(B) Interval Scale
(C) Ratio Scale
(D) Ordinal Scale

**87** Match the following.

| List I (Measuring Scale) | List II (Characteristics) |
|---|---|
| A. Nominal | 1. Places events in order. |
| B. Ordinal | 2. Used for variables involving quantity which can be categorised or ranked. |
| C. Interval | 3. It is the highest level of measurement scale. |
| D. Ratio | 4. Assigns number symbols to events in order to label them. |

**Codes**

| | A | B | C | D | | A | B | C | D |
|---|---|---|---|---|---|---|---|---|---|
| (A) | 4 | 1 | 2 | 3 | (B) | 1 | 2 | 3 | 4 |
| (C) | 2 | 3 | 4 | 1 | (D) | 1 | 4 | 3 | 2 |

**88** Which of the following sampling methods is not based on probability?
(A) Simple random sampling
(B) Stratified sampling
(C) Quota sampling
(D) Cluster sampling

**89** Cluster sampling is used when
(A) population is scattered and sample size is to be kept large
(B) population is heterogeneous
(C) long Survey is needed
(D) Both (A) and (C)

**90** An investigator wants to study the vocational aspirations of visually challenged children in a wide geographical area. He should select his sample by using
(A) Simple Random Sampling
(B) Stratified Sampling
(C) Purposive Sampling
(D) Convenient Sampling

**91** The type of sampling where each person in population has equal chance of being selected is
(A) Probability Sampling
(B) Non-Probability Sampling
(C) Judgement Sampling
(D) None of the above

**92** Which of the following should be included in a research proposal?
(A) Your academic status and experience
(B) The difficulties you encountered with previous reading on the topics
(C) Your choice of research methods and reason for choosing them.
(D) All of the above

**93** What is the purpose of the conclusion in a research report?
(A) It contains a useful review of literature.
(B) It explains how concept were defined and measured.
(C) It outlines the methological procedure.
(D) It summarises the key findings in relation to research question.

**94** A disadvantage of using secondary data sources is that
(A) The data may have been collected with reference to research questions that are not those of the researcher.
(B) The researcher may bring more detachment in viewing the data than original researchers could muster.
(C) Data have often been collected by teams of experienced researchers.
(D) Secondary data sets are often available and accessible.

## Thesis and Article Writing

**95** The quality of research thesis can be enhanced by
(A) by keeping aesthetic sense in its typography
(B) by giving good charts, flow diagrams and systematic graphs

(C) by keeping its excellent binding and title page
(D) All of the above

**96** Which of the following can be the most appropriate method of a thesis writing?
(A) Ethical and attractive
(B) Favourable in global interest
(C) Scientific
(D) Personal

**97** Which of the following is/are essential element(s) of report writing?
(A) Research methodology
(B) Reference
(C) Conclusion
(D) All of the above

**98** There is a provision of writing suggestions and recommendations at the last page of each thesis, because
(A) it enhances the reputation of the researcher
(B) it communicates the best qualities of the researcher
(C) it gives authenticity to the research work
(D) it is merely a tradition

**99** Bibliography given in a research report
(A) helps those interested in further research and studying the problem from another angle
(B) makes the report authentic
(C) Both (A) and (B)
(D) None of the above

**100** What is the advantage of writing a thesis in a scientific manner?
(A) It maintains global standardisation
(B) It generates global awakening
(C) It communicates globally
(D) None of the above

**101** The quality of research proposals will diminish when
(A) you will try to give extra importance to certain person
(B) you will become unbiased for all the persons who have directly or indirectly contributed in your work
(C) you will be giving thanks to persons in the light of your personal relations
(D) you will make a justice with all the persons

**102** An article
(A) is a topic specific essay
(B) covers entire outcome of research
(C) is also a dissertation
(D) None of the above

**103** The introduction section of an article contains
(A) reasons of the conducted study
(B) theoretical framework
(C) title
(D) Both (A) and (B)

**104** Which of the following is/are considered the basic component of computer?
(A) Keyboard (B) CPU
(C) Moniter (D) All of these

**105** A thesis statement is
(A) an observation (B) a fact
(C) an assertion (D) a discussion

**106** In a thesis, figures and tables are included in
(A) the appendix
(B) a separate chapter
(C) the concluding chapter
(D) the text itself

**107** There is a need for the qualities of labelling, page-numbering and refinement in the graphical figures in a researcher
(A) specific qualities
(B) artistic qualities
(C) appreciative qualities
(D) painter's qualities

**108** The main part of the research is
(A) title page
(B) trunk region
(C) posterior region
(D) All of the above

## Application of ICT in Research

**109** In which of the following way ICT tools helps researcher?
(A) Manage information
(B) Identify appropriate information source
(C) Use information of external communication knowledge across subject fields
(D) All of the above

110 Which of the following is the role of computers in various phases of research process?
(A) In reviewing literature
(B) Sample six and calculation
(C) Research dissemination phase
(D) All of the above

111 Which of the following is not the characteristic of spreadsheet
(A) A computer application that stimulates a paper worksheet
(B) It is used for production
(C) It is used in statistical data analysis
(D) It is designed to manage database.

112 Which of the following is correct about statistical package for social science?
(A) It is used in social sciences
(B) It is designed in such a way that it can handle large set of data variable format
(C) It is used for complex data analysis
(D) All of the above

113 A web browser is
(A) A software application for accessing information on the world wide web
(B) It enables web browser to display and interact with text images
(C) The web browser's examples are Microsoft, Mozilla, Firefox, Opera etc.
(D) All of the above

## Research Ethics

114 A good researcher lays his hands on
(A) a specific area and tries to understand it in great details
(B) a specific area and tries to understand it in minute details
(C) several areas and tries to understand them at basic level
(D) any area of his interest

115 Which of the following is/are ethical transgression?
(A) To follow ethical principles
(B) To define ethics
(C) To defy ethical principles
(D) All of the above

116 Research is not considered ethical if it
(A) tries to prove a particular point
(B) does not ensure privacy and anonymity of the respondent
(C) does not investigate the data scientifically
(D) is not of a very high standard

117 Each word of a research should be
(A) justifiable
(B) full of wisdom
(C) enjoyable
(D) entertaining

118 The 'ethics' in research is related to
(A) scientific method
(B) humanity
(C) reliability
(D) All of the above

119 In order to inculcate the ethical values in the researches, it is essential that it should be
(A) in accordance with the researcher's abilities
(B) providing opportunities to the researcher to work freely
(C) inculcate maturity in the researcher
(D) All of the above

120 In context of ethical issues a researcher should consider research as a
(A) Passive process
(B) Self-contained process
(C) Value-oriented process
(D) Discovery oriented process

121 Good 'research ethics' means
(A) not disclosing the holdings of shares/stocks in a company that sponsors your research
(B) assigning a particular research problem to one PhD/research student only
(C) discussing with your colleagues confidential data from a research paper that you are reviewing for an academic journal
(D) submitting the same research manuscript for publishing in more than one journal

122 Which one of the following belongs to the category of good 'research ethics'?
(A) Publishing the same paper in two research journals without telling the editors
(B) Conducting a review of the literature that acknowledges the contributions of other people in the relevant field or relevant prior work
(C) Trimming outliers from a data set without discussing your reasons in a research paper
(D) Including a colleague as an author on a research paper in return for a favour even though the colleague did not make a serious contribution to the paper

# Previous Years' Questions

## UGC NET-December 2019

1 Which among the following is not the outcome of grounded theory research?
(A) Concepts (B) Narrative
(C) Categories (D) Hypothesis

2 Which of the two statements from the following statements are correct?
(i) Sampling related error is subsumed under the category non-sampling error
(ii) Sampling error doesn't occur in multi-stage cluster sampling
(iii) Inaccurate sampling frame and non-response are examples of sampling related error
(iv) There is an inverse relation between heterogeneity of population and sampling error
Choose the correct option.
(A) (i) and (iii)
(B) (i) and (iv)
(C) (ii) and (iv)
(D) (ii) and (iii)

3 Which among the following is not related to qualitative research?
(A) Thematic analysis
(B) Case study
(C) Discourse analysis
(D) Survey method

4 A college teacher does research with a view to depict the reality situations relating to home conditions of students and hostels provided for which of the following research format will be helpful to do so?
(A) Experimental Research
(B) Descriptive Research
(C) Participant Observation Based Research
(D) Ethnographic Research

5 In which of the following steps of research, the scope for creativity and imagination is utmost?
(A) Identifying the research problem and defining it
(B) Figuring out the related studies and techniques used by other researchers
(C) Identifying variables and hypothesizing
(D) Data analysis and presentation of results

6 Which of the following statistical technique will be appropriate for data analysis when the observations are available in the form of frequencies?
(A) Parametric t-test
(B) Non-Parametric 'u' test
(C) Non-Parametric 'chi-square test'
(D) Parametric correlated 't' test

7 In case, the population of research is heterogeneous in nature, which of the following sampling techniques will ensure optimum representativeness of a sample units?
(A) Simple random sampling
(B) Stratified random sampling
(C) Cluster sampling
(D) Systematic sampling

8 A research scholar while finally reporting the research results in the form of a thesis acknowledges the support of his/her supervisor in the preface. This will be treated as a
(A) Sheer formality (B) Needed formality
(C) Superflous act (D) Part of ethicality

9 Which one of the following represents the correct order of sequence for reading skills in the context of research?
(A) Read, question, recall, review, survey
(B) Question, survey, read, recall, review
(C) Recall, review, survey, question, read
(D) Survey, question, read, recall, review

## UGC NET-June 2019

10 Which of the following action sets best represent an action research cycle?
(A) Reflect, act, plan and observe
(B) Plan, act, observe and reflect
(C) Observe, plan, reflect and act
(D) Act, plan, observe and reflect

11 A good review of research literature aims at
(A) subjective analysis of the content
(B) provides information about the authors and their affiliations
(C) generates research questions and validating those techniques
(D) conducts multiple task-based screening

**12** A researcher fails to reject the null hypothesis (Ho) in his/her research. What implications will it carry for his/her principal research hypothesis?
(A) Accepting the research hypothesis
(B) Rejecting the research hypothesis
(C) Not taking any decision on the research hypothesis
(D) Improving the research hypothesis

**13** Which one of the following is the main feature of qualitative research?
(A) Avoids positivist assumptions and data analysis
(B) Subscribes to pre-existing categories
(C) Collects data in numerical form
(D) Uses empirical method of data analysis

**14** Which of the following research formats focuses on hypothesis testing and generalisations?
(A) Experimental and ex-post facto research.
(B) Intervention based action research
(C) Phenomenological and narrative research
(D) Case study research

**15** A hypothesis is
(A) A certain and established finding
(B) A part of the research question
(C) A strategy of evaluating data
(D) A tentative statement providing explanation

**16** From the following list identity the qualitative research characteristics and select your answer from the codes given below
(i) Creating purpose statements and research questions
(ii) Stating the purpose and research questions in a broad way
(iii) Collecting the data based on words from a small number of individuals
(iv) Collecting numeric data and statistical analysis
(v) Using text analysis and interpreting larger meanings of the findings

**Codes**
(A) (ii), (iii) and (v)
(B) (i), (ii) and (iii)
(C) (i), (ii) and (iv)
(D) (i), (iii) and (v)

**17** Position papers are
(A) Compiling of academic articles
(B) Providing review articles
(C) Offering a synopsis of an extended research
(D) Highlighting of issues and depiction os status

**18** Case Studies are
(A) studies conducted in areas of genetics and microbiology
(B) in-depth examination of a subjects and its related conditions
(C) a report on the existing socio-political condition
(D) specialised research in the areas of health and sanitation

**19** Tertiary Source of data is
(A) Films hoardings and posters
(B) Government gazette , newspaper and magazines.
(C) Information derived from both primary and secondary sources.
(D) Data collected from policy papers.

**20** Through which research method, the manipulation of an independent variable and its effect on dependent variable is examined with reference to a hypothesis under controlled conditions?
(A) Ex-post Facto Research
(B) Descriptive Research
(C) Case Study Research
(D) Experimental Research

**21** Bibliography given in a research report
(A) helps those interested in further research
(B) shows the vast knowledge of the researcher
(C) makes the report authentic
(D) is an optional part of the report

**22** The research design is specifically related to which of the following features in research?
(i) Sample selection
(ii) Formulation of a plan
(iii) Deciding about the tool for data collection
(iv) Hypothesis making
(v) Choice of a field of inquiry

Select your answer from the options given below :
(A) (ii) (iii) and (iv) (B) (i), (ii) and (iii)
(C) (ii), (iv) and (v) (D) (iii), (iv) and (v)

**23** In which of the following research studies, interpretation and meaning get more attention than formation of generalisations?
(i) Historical Studies
(ii) Survey Studies
(iii) Philosophical Studies
(iv) Ethnographic Studies
(v) Hypothetico-deductive studies
(vi) Ex-post factor studies

Choose your answer from the options given below
(A) (i), (ii) and (iii) (B) (iv), (v) and (vi)
(C) (ii), (iv) and (v) (D) (i), (iii) and (iv)

**24** A hypothesis should be conceptually
(A) convoluted, complex and generic
(B) complex, tough and general
(C) simple, clear and specific
(D) obscure, complicated and simple

**25** Mailed questionnaire, observation, interview and collective questionnaire are instances of
(A) Secondary sources
(B) Personal sources
(C) Primary sources
(D) Tertiary sources

**26** The study of 'why does stressful living result in heart attack'? can be classified as
(A) Descriptive Research
(B) Explanatory Research
(C) Correlational Research
(D) Feasibility Research

**27** During research, while recording observation if an observer rates on individual based on the rating given in another aspect of the interaction, this is termed as the
(A) Evaluation Effect
(B) Error of Central Tendency
(C) Halo Effect
(D) Categorical Effect

**28** The formulation of a research problem can be compared to
(A) Laying the foundation of a building
(B) Building the walls of a home
(C) Polishing the doors of a building
(D) Construction the ceiling of a house

**29** A shift in attitude in respondents between two points during data collection is called
(A) Reactive effect (B) Maturation effect
(C) Regression effect (D) Conditioning effect

**30** From the list given below identify those which are called 'Non-probability sampling procedures
(i) Simple random sampling
(ii) Dimensional sampling
(iii) Snowball sampling
(iv) Cluster sampling
(v) Quota sampling
(vi) Stratified sampling
Choose the correct option.
(A) (i), (ii) and (iii) (B) (ii), (iv) and (v)
(C) (i), (iii) and (iv) (D) (ii), (iii) and (v)

**31** The major characteristic of correlation analysis is to see out
(A) differences among variables
(B) variations among variables
(C) association among variables
(D) regression among variables

**32** The conceptual framework in which a research is conducted is called a
(A) Synopsis of research
(B) Research design
(C) Research hypothesis
(D) Research paradigm

**33** Snowball sampling is the process of selecting a sample using
(A) Networks
(B) Groups
(C) Snowballs
(D) Computer Programmes

**34** A tentative proposition with unknown validity that specifies a relationship between two or more variables is called
(A) Research problem
(B) Research proposal
(C) Research design
(D) Research hypothesis

**35** In which of the following research paradigms the focus of concern is on interpreting reality in terms of participants perspective?
(A) Experimental Research
(B) Ex-post facto Research
(C) Ethnographic Research
(D) Survey Research

**36** Research design that needs to collect factual information on a continuing basis is classified
(A) Longitudinal Study Design
(B) Pre and Post Study Design
(C) Cross-Sectional Study Design
(D) Double Control Study Design

## UGC NET-December 2018

**37** Which of the following statements best reflect the meaning and characteristics of research? Select from the code to give your answer.

I. Research means challenging the status quo.
II. Research is an endeavour to collect facts and information.
III. Research is a synthesis of deductive and inductive processes.
IV. Research means proving one's assertions and beliefs.
V. Research is a careful review of reported studies.
VI. Research is a critical and passionate search for knowledge.

**Codes**

(A) I, V and VI (B) II, IV and V
(C) I, II and III (D) I, III and VI

**38** The paradigm of research which focuses on the development of professional expertise of the researcher practitioner is called

(A) Pure research (B) Applied research
(C) Qualitative research (D) Action research

**39** In the two lists given below, list I specifies the methods of research while list II describes the critical feature associated with a method of research. Match the two and select from the codes to indicate your answer.

| List I (Research Methods) | List II (Critical Features Associated) |
|---|---|
| A. Experimental method | I. Generalising to the population from a large sample. |
| B. Ex post facto method | II. Establishing the patterns of events which have happened, through primary and secondary sources. |
| C. Historical method | III. Studying shared behaviour patterns. |
| D. Ethnographic method | IV. Establishing cause and effect through control. |
| | V. Probing into the causal factors from the observed effects. |

**Codes**

| | A | B | C | D |
|---|---|---|---|---|
| (A) | IV | V | II | III |
| (B) | II | III | IV | V |
| (C) | II | I | IV | III |
| (D) | I | II | III | IV |

**40** In the two sets given below, list I provides the format of presentation and list II give the distinct features to go with them. Match the two lists and select from the codes to indicate your answer.

| List I (Format of Presentation) | List II (Distinctive Features) |
|---|---|
| A. Thesis/ dissertation | I. Based on free-wheeling of ideas |
| B. Research paper | II. Target oriented group based reflection |
| C. Workshop | III. Reflective deliberations based on specific themes |
| D. Seminar | IV. Presentation on a summary of research done |
| | V. Systematic prescribed format |

**Codes**

| | A | B | C | D |
|---|---|---|---|---|
| (A) | V | IV | II | III |
| (B) | I | II | III | V |
| (C) | II | III | IV | V |
| (D) | III | I | II | V |

## UGC NET-July 2018

**41** There are two lists given below list I specifies the types of research, while list II indicates their characteristics. Match the two and give your answer by selecting the appropriate codes.

| List I (Research Types) | List II (Characteristics) |
|---|---|
| A. Fundamental Research | I. Finding out the extent of perceived impact of an intervention. |
| B. Applied Research | II. Developing an effective explanation through use of interventions. |
| C. Action Research | III. Improving an existing situation through use of interventions. |
| D. Evaluative Research | IV. Exploring the possibility of a theory for use in various situations |
| | V. Enriching technological resources. |

**Codes**

| | A | B | C | D |
|---|---|---|---|---|
| (A) | I | II | III | IV |
| (B) | II | III | IV | V |
| (C) | II | IV | III | I |
| (D) | V | IV | III | II |

42 Which of the following sequences of research step is nearer to scientific method?
(A) Defining a problem, Identifying the causes of the problem, Defining a population, Drawing a sample, Collecting data and Analysing results.
(B) Identifying the casual factors, Defining the problem, Developing a hypothesis, Selecting a sample, Collecting data and arriving at generalisations and conclusions.
(C) Suggested solution of the problem, Deducing the consequences of the solution, Perceiving the problem situation, Location of the difficulty and testing the solutions.
(D) Perceiving the problem situation, Locating the actual problem and its definition, hypothesising, Deducing the consequences of the suggested solution and testing the hypothesis in action.

43 In which of the following activities, potential for nurturing creative and critical thinking is relatively greater?
(A) Participation in research conference
(B) Participation in a workshop
(C) Preparing research summary
(D) Presenting a seminar paper

44 The problem of 'research ethics' is concerned with which aspect of research activities?
(A) Defining the population of research
(B) Evidence based research reporting
(C) Following the prescribed format of a thesis
(D) Data analysis through qualitative or quantitative techniques

## UGC NET-November 2017

45 In finalising a thesis writing format which of the following would form part of supplementary pages?
(A) Table of contents
(B) Conclusions of the study
(C) Bibliography and appendices
(D) List of tables and figures

46 Which of the following is susceptible to the issue of research ethics?
(A) Faulty research design
(B) Choice of sampling techniques
(C) Reporting of research findings
(D) Inaccurate application of statistical techniques

47 A researcher attempts to evaluate the effect of method of feeding on anxiety-proneness of children. Which method of research would be appropriate for this?
(A) Experimental method
(B) Ex-post-facto method
(C) Survey method
(D) Case study method

48 In which of the following arrangements, a wider spectrum of ideas and issues may be made possible?
(A) Workshop mode
(B) Conference
(C) Symposium
(D) Research Article

49 Which of the following research types focuses on ameliorating the prevailing situations?
(A) Applied research
(B) Action research
(C) Experimental research
(D) Fundamental research

## UGC NET-June 2017

50 In which of the following research, the researcher attempt to trace an effect?
(A) Survey research
(B) Ex-post Facto research
(C) Historical research
(D) Summative research

51 In which of the following, reporting format is formally prescribed?
(A) Doctoral level thesis
(B) Conference of researchers
(C) Workships and seminars
(D) Symposia

## UGC NET-January 2017

52 Which of the sets of activities best indicate the cyclic nature of action research strategy?
(A) Act, Plan, Observe, Reflect
(B) Plan, Act, Observe, Reflect
(C) Reflect, Observe, Plan, Act
(D) Observe, Act, Reflect, Plan

53 Which sequence of research steps is logical in the list given below?
(A) Problem formulation, Analysis, Development of research design, Hypothesis making, Collection of data, Arriving at generalisations and conclusions

(B) Development of research design, Hypothesis making, Problem formulation, Data analysis, Arriving at conclusions and Data collection
(C) Problem formulation, Hypothesis making, Development of research design, Collection of data, Data analysis and Formulation of generalisations and conclusions
(D) Problem formulation, Deciding about the sample and data collection tools, Formulation of hypothesis, Collection and Interpretation of research evidence

**54** The Principal of a school conducts an interview session of teachers and students with a view to explore the possibility of their enhanced participation in school programmes. This endeavour may be related to which type of research?
(A) Evaluation research
(B) Fundamental research
(C) Action research
(D) Applied research

**55** Below are given two lists-research methods (List I) and data collection tools (List II). Match the two lists and indicate your answer by selecting the correct code.

| List I (Research Methods) | List II (Data Collection Tools) |
|---|---|
| A. Experimental method | I. Using primary and secondary sources |
| B. Ex post-facto method | II. Questionnaire |
| C. Descriptive survey method | III. Standardised tests |
| D. Historical method | IV. Typical characteristic tests |

**Codes**

| | A | B | C | D |
|---|---|---|---|---|
| (A) | II | I | III | IV |
| (B) | II | III | I | IV |
| (C) | III | IV | II | I |
| (D) | II | IV | III | I |

**56** The issue of 'research ethics' may be considered pertinent at which stage of research?
(A) At the stage of problem formulation and its definition
(B) At the stage of defining the population of research
(C) At the stage of data collection and interpretation
(D) At the stage of reporting the findings

## UGC NET-July 2016

**57** From the following list of statements identify the set which has negative implications for 'research ethics'.
I. A researcher critically looks at the findings of another research.
II. Related studies are cited without proper references.
III. Research findings make the base for policy making.
IV. Conduct of practitioner is screened in terms of reported research evidences.
V. A research study is replicated with a view to verify the evidences from other researches.
VI. Both policy making and policy implementing processes are regulated in terms of preliminary studies.

Which of the statements given above are correct?
(A) I, II and III (B) II, III and IV
(C) II, IV and VI (D) I, III and V

**58** The format of thesis writing is the same as in
(A) preparation of a research paper/article.
(B) writing of seminar presentation.
(C) a research dissertation.
(D) presenting a workshop/conference paper.

**59** A researcher intends to explore the effect of possible factors for the organisation of effective mid-day meal interventions. Which research method will be most appropriate for this study?
(A) Historical method
(B) Descriptive survey method
(C) Experimental method
(D) Ex-post facto method

**60** Which of the following is an initial mandatory requirement for pursuing research?
(A) Developing a research design
(B) Formulating a research question
(C) Deciding about the data analysis procedure
(D) Formulating a research hypothesis

**61** In a research on the effect of child-rearing practices on stress-proneness of children in completing school projects, the hypothesis formulated is that child rearing practices do influences stress proneness'.
At the data analysis stage a null hypothesis is advanced to find out the tenability of research hypothesis. On the basis of the

evidence available, the null hypothesis is rejected at 0.01 level of significance. What decision may be warranted in respect of the research hypothesis?

(A) The research hypothesis will also be rejected.
(B) The research hypothesis will be accepted.
(C) Both the research hypothesis and the null hypothesis will be rejected.
(D) No decision can be taken in respect of the research hypothesis.

**62** In qualitative research paradigm, which of the following features may be considered critical?

(A) Data collection with standardised research tools
(B) Sampling design with probability sample techniques
(C) Data collection with bottom-up empirical evidences
(D) Data gathering to take place with top-down systematic evidences

## UGC NET-December 2015

**63** Ethical norms in research do not involve guidelines for

(A) Data sharing policies
(B) Thesis format
(C) Copyright
(D) Patenting policy

**64** A researcher is interested in studying the prospects of a particular political party in an urban area. What tool should he prefer for the study?

(A) Schedule (B) Rating Scale
(C) Interview (D) Questionnaire

**65** Which of the following statements is not true in the context of participatory research?

(A) Its sole purpose is production of knowledge
(B) It recognises knowledge as power
(C) It emphasises on people as experts
(D) It is a collective process of enquiry

**66** Which of the following are the basic rules of APA style of referencing format?

I. Italicise titles of shorter works such as journal articles or essays.
II. Invert authors' name (last name first).
III. Italicise titles of longer works such as books and journals.
IV. Alphabetically index references list.

Select the correct answer using the codes given below.

(A) III and IV (B) I and III
(C) II, III and IV (D) I, II, III and IV

## UGC NET-June 2015

**67** The conclusions/findings of which type of research cannot be generalised to other situations?

(A) Historical research
(B) Descriptive research
(C) Experimental research
(D) Casual comparative research

**68** A good thesis writing should involve

I. reduction of punctuation and grammatical errors to a minimum.
II. careful checking of references.
III. consistency in the way the thesis is written.
IV. a clear and well written abstract.

Select the correct answer from the codes given below.

(A) II, III and IV (B) I, II and III
(C) I, II and IV (D) All of these

**69** Which of the following statements regarding the meaning of research are correct?

I. Research refers to a series of systematic activity or activities undertaken to find out the solution of a problem.
II. It is a systematic, logical and an unbiased process wherein verification of hypothesis, data analysis, interpretation and formation of principles can be done.
III. It is an intellectual enquiry or quest towards truth.
IV. It leads to enhancement of knowledge.

Select the correct answer from the codes given below.

(A) I, II and III (B) II, III and IV
(C) I, III and IV (D) All of these

**70** Which of the following steps are required to design a questionnaire?

I. Writing primary and secondary aims of the study.
II. Review of the current literature.
III. Prepare a draft of questionnaire.
IV. Revision of the draft.

Select the correct answer from the codes given below.

(A) I, II and III (B) I, III and IV
(C) II, III and IV (D) All of these

# ANSWERS

## Chapter Practice

| | | | | | | | | | |
|---|---|---|---|---|---|---|---|---|---|
| 1 (C) | 2 (B) | 3 (C) | 4 (A) | 5 (D) | 6 (D) | 7 (D) | 8 (D) | 9 (C) | 10 (D) |
| 11 (B) | 12 (A) | 13 (D) | 14 (D) | 15 (C) | 16 (D) | 17 (A) | 18 (B) | 19 (B) | 20 (A) |
| 21 (A) | 22 (D) | 23 (A) | 24 (A) | 25 (D) | 26 (B) | 27 (A) | 28 (B) | 29 (A) | 30 (B) |
| 31 (D) | 32 (C) | 33 (A) | 34 (B) | 35 (B) | 36 (D) | 37 (A) | 38 (C) | 39 (A) | 40 (D) |
| 41 (B) | 42 (B) | 43 (B) | 44 (C) | 45 (B) | 46 (A) | 47 (D) | 48 (D) | 49 (D) | 50 (D) |
| 51 (B) | 52 (D) | 53 (D) | 54 (D) | 55 (C) | 56 (C) | 57 (B) | 58 (A) | 59 (B) | 60 (B) |
| 61 (C) | 62 (D) | 63 (D) | 64 (D) | 65 (B) | 66 (D) | 67 (C) | 68 (B) | 69 (C) | 70 (C) |
| 71 (D) | 72 (D) | 73 (A) | 74 (C) | 75 (C) | 76 (D) | 77 (C) | 78 (B) | 79 (D) | 80 (B) |
| 81 (D) | 82 (A) | 83 (B) | 84 (A) | 85 (D) | 86 (C) | 87 (A) | 88 (C) | 89 (D) | 90 (B) |
| 91 (A) | 92 (C) | 93 (D) | 94 (A) | 95 (D) | 96 (B) | 97 (D) | 98 (D) | 99 (C) | 100 (C) |
| 101 (A) | 102 (A) | 103 (D) | 104 (D) | 105 (C) | 106 (D) | 107 (B) | 108 (D) | 109 (D) | 110 (D) |
| 111 (A) | 112 (D) | 113 (D) | 114 (B) | 115 (C) | 116 (D) | 117 (A) | 118 (D) | 119 (A) | 120 (C) |
| 121 (A) | 122 (B) | | | | | | | | |

## Previous Years' Questions

| | | | | | | | | | |
|---|---|---|---|---|---|---|---|---|---|
| 1 (B) | 2 (A) | 3 (D) | 4 (C) | 5 (C) | 6 (C) | 7 (B) | 8 (D) | 9 (D) | 10 (B) |
| 11 (C) | 12 (B) | 13 (A) | 14 (A) | 15 (D) | 16 (A) | 17 (D) | 18 (B) | 19 (C) | 20 (D) |
| 21 (A) | 22 (B) | 23 (D) | 24 (C) | 25 (C) | 26 (B) | 27 (C) | 28 (A) | 29 (C) | 30 (D) |
| 31 (C) | 32 (B) | 33 (A) | 34 (D) | 35 (C) | 36 (A) | 37 (C) | 38 (D) | 39 (A) | 40 (B) |
| 41 (D) | 42 (D) | 43 (A) | 44 (A) | 45 (C) | 46 (C) | 47 (B) | 48 (B) | 49 (B) | 50 (B) |
| 51 (A) | 52 (B) | 53 (C) | 54 (C) | 55 (B) | 56 (D) | 57 (C) | 58 (C) | 59 (D) | 60 (A) |
| 61 (B) | 62 (C) | 63 (C) | 64 (D) | 65 (D) | 66 (D) | 67 (B) | 68 (B) | 69 (C) | 70 (C) |

# UNIT 03

# Comprehension

## CHAPTER ANALYSIS

Reading Comprehension is the level of understanding of a text/passage. It includes a passage followed by a few questions. As per updated syllabus of NTA UGC NET 5 to 6 questions are asked from this unit. The natures of comprehension asked in the examination are Descriptive, Narrative, Explanatory, Persuasive and Argumentative and the word limit of Passage is 250 to 300 words.

The questions asked in the examination are based on Central idea of passage, Author's opinion, Explicit or Implicit information, Language Expressions and Statement.

**IN THIS UNIT**


- Nature of Passages Asked in Examination
- Nature of Questions Asked in Examination
- Solved Examples
- Previous Year Questions


## Nature of Passages Asked in Examination

Generally, following types of comprehension passages are asked in examination

1. **Descriptive** Such passages describe an event or journey, etc in a very systematic manner so that the reader can visualise the topic and enter into the writer's experience.
2. **Narrative** Such passages relate a series of events either real or imaginary or chronologically arranged information is provided to the readers with the help of a plot.
3. **Explanatory or Interpretative** Such passages are based on interpreting personalities, events, ideas or concepts. Focus is on interpretation rather than information.
4. **Persuasive** In such type of passages, a point of view is presented and the writer seeks to persuade a reader that the assertion or claim put forth by him is correct.
5. **Argumentative** Such passages contain arguments about both sides of an issue. It could be that both sides are presented in an equally balanced way or it could be that one side is presented more forcefully than the other.

## Nature of Questions Asked in Examination

We can classify the questions being asked in examination, are based on;

- **Main Theme or Central Idea** These type of questions are based on the passage as a whole; these questions test up to what extent the reader is able to understand the paragraph. Answers of such type of questions can be easily found from the text itself.
- **Author's Opinion or Attitude** Such questions are based on the author's viewpoint and the answers are not explicitly mentioned. They have to be derived from the key sentences used by the author to express his thoughts.
- **Explicit or Direct Information** These are direct questions based on the names, dates, figure, data, facts or opinions mentioned in the passage.
- **Implicit Information** Answers to these questions are not clearly stated but are to be inferred or deduced from the passage.
- **Language Expressions** These questions are based on specific words or phrases mentioned in the passage. Sometimes they are based on synonyms or antonyms which test an understanding of a word in the context of the passage.
- **Statements** In such type of questions two or three statements are provided and a candidate has to answer which of the statement or statements are true.

### → Right Approach to Answer Different Questions

- First read the passage once or twice to understand the main theme of the passage.
- Underline the main or key sentences of the passage.
- Underline the words related to vocabulary or English grammar, idioms, etc.
- Pay attention to the probable title of the given passage. Answer of such questions should be attempted only after reading and understanding the main theme or central idea of the passage.
- Read the questions thoroughly and try to understand what has been asked in the question and answer accordingly.

# Solved Examples

## Comprehension 1

**Directions** (Q. Nos. 1-5) Read the following passage carefully and answer the questions that follow.

What is immediately needed today is the establishment of a World Government or an International Federation of Mankind. It is the utmost necessity of the world today, and all those persons who wish to see all human beings happy and prosperous naturally feel it keenly. Of course, at times, we all feel that many of our problems of our political, social and cultural life would come to an end if there were one Government all over the world. Travellers, businessmen, seekers of knowledge and teachers of righteousness know very well that great impediments and obstructions are faced by them, when they pass from one country to another, exchange goods, get information and make an effort to spread their good gospel among their fellowmen. In the past religious sects divided one set of people against another, colour of the skin or construction of the body set one against the other. But today when philosophical light has exploded the darkness that was created by religious differences and when the scientific knowledge has falsified the theory of social superiority and when modern inventions have enabled human beings of all religious views and of all races and colours to come in frequent contact with one another, it is the governments of various countries that keep people of one country apart from those of another. They create artificial barriers, unnatural distinctions, unhealthy isolation, unnecessary fears and dangers in the minds of common men who by their nature want to live in friendship with their fellowmen. But all these evils would cease to exist if there were one government all over the world.

1. What is the urgent need of the world today?
   (A) The establishment of an international economic order
   (B) The establishment of a world government
   (C) The creation of a cultured international social order
   (D) The raising of an international spiritual army

***Ans*** *(B)* According to the passage the top priority need is to set up a world government. This will enable people to lead a happy and prosperous life.

2. What was the factor that set one man against another?
   (A) Material prosperity of certain people in the midst of grinding poverty
   (B) Superior physical strength of some persons
   (C) Colour of the skin or construction of the body
   (D) Psychological barriers

***Ans*** *(C)* It is the colour of the skin or construction of body that set one against the other. This was prevalent in the past as religious sects separated one type of people against another.

3. Which of the following problems has not been mentioned in the passage as likely to be solved with the establishment of a World Government?
   (A) Social problems (B) Political problems
   (C) Cultural problems (D) Economic problems

***Ans*** *(D)* The passage does not highlight the economic problems. But in the passage the author feels that most of the problems i.e., social, political and cultural would be resolved if a world government is established.

4. What do the government of various countries do to keep people of one country apart from those of another?
   (A) They create artificial barriers
   (B) They create unnatural distinctions
   (C) They foster unhealthy isolation
   (D) All of the above

***Ans*** *(D)* The government of different countries try to develop unnatural obstacles, distinctions and also create unwanted isolation.

The governments do this to keep people away from each other. According to the author all the above mentioned evils would come to an end if there is a presence of one world government.

5. What divide/divides people of one country against another?
   (A) Different religions
   (B) Different languages
   (C) Material advancement of few nations with imperialistic learnings
   (D) Government of various countries

***Ans*** *(D)* It is the governments of various countries that keep people of one country apart from those of another.

## Comprehension 2

**Directions** (Q. Nos. 1-5) Read the following passage carefully and answer the questions that follow.

The function of education is to prepare young people to understand the whole process of life. The end of education is not merely to pass some examinations and get a job and earn one's livelihood. If education is to make people understand life, then surely life is not merely a job or an occupation; life is something extraordinarily wide and profound, it is a great mystery, a vast realm in which we function as human beings. If we prepare ourselves only to earn a livelihood, we shall miss the whole point of life. To understand life is much more important than to get a degree or pass an examination for a job.

Life, with all its subtleties, is such a vast expanse. It has its extraordinary beauty, its sorrows and joys. It also has its hidden things of the mind such as envies, ambitions, passions, fears, fulfilment and anxieties. The birds, the flowers, the flourishing trees, the heavens, the stars, the rivers and the fishes therein all this is life. When we are young, we must seek and find out what life is all about. Thus, we cultivate intelligence with the help of education. Intelligence is the capacity to think freely, without fear, without a formula, so that we begin to discover for ourselves what is real and what is true.

Anyone who is gripped with fear will never be intelligent. Most of us have fear in one form or another. Where there is fear there is no intelligence. Thus, what education should do is to help us understand the need of freedom. Unless we are free we will not understand the whole process of living. When we are free we have no fear. We do not imitate but we discover.

**1** What is effect of fear on humans?

(A) We are not able to develop our intelligence
(B) We think freely
(C) We see the vast expanse of life
(D) We understand life's great mystery

***Ans*** (*A*) The impact of fear on people is that they are unable to develop their intelligence. Intelligence is the capacity to think freely.

**2** The aim of education is to make us realise the need of

(A) freedom (B) passing examinations
(C) jobs (D) understanding science

***Ans*** (*A*) The main purpose of education is to make one feel the importance of freedom in one's life. It is the freedom which allows an individual to speak and think or express without any feeling of fear.

**3** When we are young we should

(A) seek the meaning of life
(B) study and get a degree
(C) try for a good job
(D) study science

***Ans*** (*A*) At a young age we should seek the meaning of life. We should not strive for acquiring degree, or getting good jobs. The real education is to understand the whole process of life.

**4** Education helps us realise the

(A) way to develop our career
(B) need for good health
(C) meaning of fear
(D) necessity of freedom

***Ans*** (*D*) Education should help us to feel the need of freedom. When we are free we have no fear. One can realise the value of freedom.

**5** The passage is about

(A) education (B) freedom
(C) intelligence (D) livelihood

***Ans*** (*A*) The passage focuses on education.

## Comprehension 3

**Directions** (Q. Nos. 1-5) Read the following passage carefully and answer the questions that follow.

Traditional Indian values must both be viewed both from the angle of an individual and from that of a geographically delimited agglomeration of people or groups enjoying a common system of leadership which we call the 'State'. Indian State's special feature is the peaceful, coexistence of social groups of various historical provenances which mutually adhere in a geographical, economic and political sense, without ever assimilating to each other in social terms, in ways of thinking, or even in language.

Modern Indian law will determine certain rules, especially in relation to the regime of the family, upon the basis of how the loin-cloth is tied, or how the turban is worn, for this may identify the litigants as members of a regional group and therefore, as participants in its traditional law, though their ancestors left the region three or four centuries earlier. The use of the word 'State' above must not mislead us.

There was no such thing as a conflict between the individual and the State, atleast before foreign governments became established, just as there was no concept of state 'sovereignty' or of any church-and-state dichotomy.

Modern Indian 'secularism' has an admittedly peculiar feature : it requires the state to make a fair distribution of attention amongst all religions. These blessed aspects of India's famed tolerance (Indian kings so rarely persecuted religious groups that the exceptions prove the rule) at once struck the Portuguese and other European visitors to the West Coast of India in the sixteenth century and the impression made upon them in this and other ways gave rise, at one remove, to the basic Constitution of Thomas More's Utopia.

There is little about Modern India that strikes one at once as Utopian : but the insistence upon the inculcation of norms and the absence of bigotry and institutionalised exploitation of human or natural resources are two very different features which link the realities of India and her tradition with the essence of all Utopians.

**1** Which of the following is a special feature of the Indian State?

(A) Peaceful co-existence of people under a common system of leadership
(B) Peaceful co-existence of social-groups of different historical provenances attached to each other in a geographical, economic and political sense
(C) Social integration of all groups
(D) Cultural assimilation of all social groups

***Ans*** *(B)* In the passage, according to the author, the significant feature of the Indian state is peaceful co-existence of social groups of various historical provenances that mutually adhere in geographical, economic and political sense.

**2** The author uses the word 'State' to highlight

(A) antagonistic relationship between the state and the individual throughout the period of history
(B) absence of conflict between the state and the individuals upto a point in time
(C) the concept of state sovereignty
(D) dependence on religion

***Ans*** *(B)* The word 'state' in the passage signifies the absence of conflict between the state and the individual upto a point in time.

**3** Which one is the peculiar feature of modern Indian 'secularism'?

(A) No discrimination on religious considerations
(B) Total indifference to religion
(C) No space for social identity
(D) Disregard for social law

***Ans*** *(A)* The distinctive feature of modern Indian secularism is that there exists no discrimination on religious grounds.

**4** The basic construction of Thomas More's Utopia was inspired by

(A) Indian tradition of religious tolerance
(B) persecution of religious groups by Indian rulers
(C) social inequality in India
(D) European perception of Indian state

***Ans*** *(A)* The fundamental construction of Thomas More's Utopia was inspired by the Indian tradition of religious tolerance.

**5** What is the striking feature of modern India?

(A) Replica of Utopian State
(B) Uniform laws
(C) Adherence to traditional values
(D) Absence of Bigotry

***Ans*** *(D)* The salient feature of modern India is the non-existence of bigotry.

## Comprehension 4

**Directions** (Q. Nos. 1-5) Read the following passage carefully and answer the questions that follow.

Taylorism is a variation on the theme of efficiency; it is a late-19th-and-early-20th-century instance of the larger recurring theme in human life of increasing efficiency, decreasing waste, and using empirical methods to decide what matters, rather than uncritically accepting pre-existing ideas of what matters.

Taylor system is a theory of management that analyses and synthesises workflows, improving labour productivity. The core ideas of the theory were developed by Frederick Winslow Taylor in the 1880s and 1890s, and were first published in the monographs, shops management (1905) and The Principles of Scientific Management (1911).

Frederick Taylor believed that decisions based upon tradition and rules of thumb should be replaced by precise procedures developed after careful study of an individual at work. Its application is contingent on a high level of managerial control over employee work practices.

Thus, it is a chapter in the larger narrative that also includes, for example, the folk wisdom of thrift, time and motion study, Fordism, and lean manufacturing.

In management literature today, the greatest use of the concept of Scientific Management (or Taylorism) is as a contrast to a new, improved way of doing business.

It overlapped considerably with the efficiency movement, which was the broader cultural echo of scientific management's impact on business managers specifically. In political and sociological terms, Taylorism can be seen as the division of labour pushed to its logical extreme, with a consequent de-skilling of the worker and dehumanisation of the workplace.

**1** Scientific management is a theory of management
- (A) that promotes the rule of thumb
- (B) that promotes the democratic pattern in industrial organisation
- (C) that analyses and synthesises workflows, improving labour productivity
- (D) that promotes the unity of command within the organisation

***Ans*** (*C*) Scientific management is a theory of management that analyses and synthesises workflows, improving labour productivity.

**2** Frederick Taylor believed that
- (A) decisions based upon tradition and rules of thumb should be replaced by precise procedures developed after careful study of an individual at work.
- (B) decisions based upon precise procedures developed after careful study of an individual at work should be replaced by tradition and rules of thumb
- (C) strict discipline should be applied at the workplace
- (D) workers should be treated as a means of productivity like machine

***Ans*** (*A*) Frederick Taylor believed that decisions based upon tradition and rules of thumb should be replaced by precise procedures developed after careful study of an individual at work.

**3** Taylorism is based on
- (A) decreasing efficiency, increasing waste, and using empirical methods to decide what matters, rather than uncritically accepting pre-existing ideas of what matters
- (B) increasing efficiency, decreasing waste, and using empirical methods to decide what matters, rather than uncritically accepting pre-existing ideas of what matters
- (C) decreasing efficiency, increasing waste and using traditional methods for day-to-day decision.
- (D) decreasing efficiency, increasing waste, and applying completely democratic pattern within the organisation.

***Ans*** (*B*) Taylorism is based on increasing efficiency, decreasing waste and using emperical methods to decide what matters, rather than uncritically accepting pre-existing ideas of what matters.

**4** Scientific management
- (A) overlapped considerably with the efficiency movement, which was the broader cultural echo of scientific management's impact on business managers specifically
- (B) overlapped considerably with the effectiveness movement which was the broader cultural echo of scientific management's impact on business managers specifically
- (C) overlapped considerably with the democatic movement, which was the broader cultural echo of scientific management's impact on business managers specifically
- (D) overlapped considerably with the autocratic pattern, which was the broader cultural echo of scientific management's impact on business managers specifically

***Ans*** (*A*) Scientific management overlapped considerably with the efficiency movement which was the broader cultural echo of scientific management's impact on business managers specifically

**5** In political and sociological terms,
- (A) Taylorism can be seen as the division of labour pushed to its socialistic pattern, with a consequent de-skilling of the worker and dehumanisation of the workplace.
- (B) Taylorism can be seen as the division of labour pushed to its democratic pattern, with a consequent de-skilling of the worker and dehumanisation of the workplace.
- (C) Taylorism can be seen as the division of labour pushed to its democratic pattern, with a perfect skilling of the worker and humanisation of the workplace.

(D) Taylorism can be seen as the division of labour pushed to its logical extreme, with a consequent de-skilling of the worker and dehumanisation of the workplace.

***Ans*** *(D)* In political and sociological terms, Taylorism can be seen as the division of labour pushed to its logical extreme, with a consequent de-skilling of the worker and dehumanisation of the workplace.

## Comprehension 5

**Directions** (Q. Nos. 1-5) Read the following passage carefully and answer the questions that follow.

Human resource planning is strategy for acquisition, utilisation, improvement and preservation of the human resources of an enterprise. The objective is to provide right personnel for the right work and optimum utilisation of the existing human resources. It puts the objectives of the organisation on paper and plans into the number and kind of personnel needed to accomplish those objectives.

Thus, HRP involves determination of future manpower needs to help management in being upbeat. Manpower planning starts with examining the overall objectives of the organisation. In fact, manpower plan should be integrated into the overall objectives.

The number of employees required to perform various operations will be derived from the objectives of the organisation. Overall objectives of the organisation have to be understood in order to draw a good manpower plan. Manpower demand is the number of people required to handle the present jobs.

Forecasting the demand for manpower is the process of estimating the future quantity and quality of employees required. For instance, in a retail organisation, the manpower demand is forecasted based on the work to be performed in every retail store. Obviously the long-term corporate plans, budgets and annual plans would become basis for forecasting the demand for labour. Supply forecast is also known as manpower inventory.

The objective of preparing manpower inventory is to find out the number and quality of manpower available within the organisation to employ in various jobs identified in the organisation.

Development of supply of manpower data relating to present human resources in terms of components, number, designations and department wise should be developed. Here potential losses in the existing manpower should be considered.

The loss of manpower arises out of voluntary retirements, deaths, retirements, dismissals, layoffs, disablement due to ill health, accidents and other losses occurring due to poor attitude and low commitment to the organisation. Gap analysis is the process of identifying the difference in the estimated number of employees and actual number of employees available in the organisation. This enables to determine the quantity and quality of manpower needed. This gap reveals the number of personnel to be recruited to fill the gaps.

**1** Forecasting the demand for manpower

(A) is the process of estimating the future quantity and quality of employees required

(B) is the process of calculating current workforce engaged in different operations in the organisation

(C) is the process of estimating the critical situations, that may occur during the production process

(D) is the process of analysing the performance of the workers engaged in the organisation is past years

***Ans*** *(A)* Forecasting the demand for manpower is the process of estimating the future quantity and quality of employees required.

**2** According to this passage,

(A) the number of employees required to perform various operations will be determined by the government

(B) the number of employees required to perform various operations will be derived from the objectives of the organisation

(C) the number of employees required to perform various operations will be derived from the market forces

(D) the number of employees required to perform various operations will be determined by the Trade Unions

***Ans*** *(B)* According to the given passage the number of employees required to perform various operations will be derived from the objectives of organisation.

**3** Supply forecast is also known as

(A) manpower inventory

(B) manpower analysis

(C) manpower planning

(D) manpower forecasting

***Ans*** *(A)* Supply forecast is also known as manpower inventory.

**4** The objective of preparing manpower inventory is

(A) to find out the number and quality of manpower prescribed by government and other industrial regulating agencies
(B) to find out the number and quality of manpower required for future operations in the organisation
(C) to find out the number and quality of manpower available in the market
(D) to find out the number and quality of manpower available within the organisation to employee in various jobs identified in the organisation.

***Ans*** (*D*) The objective of preparing manpower inventory is to find out the number and quality of manpower available within the organisation to employ in various jobs identified in the organisation.

**5** Gap analysis is the process of

(A) identifying the total of the estimated number of employees and actual number of employees available in the organisation
(B) identifying the difference in the estimated number of employees and actual number of employees available in the labour market
(C) identifying the difference in the estimated number of employees and actual number of employees available in the organisation
(D) identifying the required number of employees and actual number of employees available in the organisation

***Ans*** (C) Gap analysis is the process of identifying the difference in the estimated number of employees and actual number of employees available in the organisation.

## Comprehension 6

**Directions** (Q. Nos. 1-5) Read the following passage carefully and answer the questions that follow.

'Desertification' is a term used to explain a process of decline in the biological productivity of an ecosystem, leading to total loss of productivity. While this phenomenon is often linked to the arid, semi-arid and sub-humid ecosystems, even in the humid tropics, the impact could be most dramatic. Impoverishment of human-impacted terrestrial ecosystems may exhibit itself in a variety of ways, such as accelerated erosion as in the mountain regions of the country, salinisation of land as in the semi-arid and arid 'green revolution' areas of the country, for example, in Haryana and Western Uttar Pradesh, and site quality decline– a common phenomenon due to general decline in tree cover and monotonous monoculture of rice/wheat across the Indian plains.

A major consequence of deforestation is that it relates to adverse alterations in the hydrology and related soil and nutrient losses. The consequences of deforestation invariably arise out of side degradation through erosive losses. Tropical Asia, Africa and South America have the highest levels of erosion.

The already high rates for the tropics are increasing at an alarming rate (For example, through the major river systems, such as the Ganga and the Brahmaputra in the Indian context), due to deforestation and ill-suited and management practices subsequent to forest clearing. In the mountain context, the declining moisture retention of the mountain context, the declining moisture retention of the mountain soils, drying up of the underground springs and smaller rivers in the Himalayan region could be attributed to drastic changes in the forest cover.

An indirect consequence is drastic alteration in the upland-lowland interaction, mediated through water. The current concern the tea planter of Assam has is about the damage to tea plantations due to frequent inundation along the flood-plains of Brahmaputra, and the damage to tea plantation and the consequent loss in tea productivity is due to rising level of the river bottom because of siltation and the changing course of the river system.

The ultimate consequences of site desertification are soil degradation, alteration in available water and its quality, and the consequent decline in food, fodder and fuel-wood yields essential for the economic well-being of rural communities.

**1** According to the passage, which of the following are the consequences of decline in forest cover?

1. Loss of topsoil
2. Loss of smaller rivers
3. Adverse effect on agricultural production
4. Declining of groundwater

Select the correct answer using the code given below

(A) 1, 2 and 3 (B) 2, 3 and 4
(C) 1 and 4 (D) 1, 2, 3 and 4

***Ans*** (*D*) According to the passage, loss of topsoil, Loss of smaller rivers, adverse effect on agricultural production and declining of groundwater are the consequences of decline in forest cover.

**2** Which of the following is/are the correct inference/inferences that can be made from the passage?

1. Deforestation can cause changes in the course of rivers.
2. Salinisation of land takes place due to human activities only.
3. Intense monoculture practice in plains is a major reason for desertification in Tropical Asia, Africa and South America.

Select the correct answer using the code given below.

(A) Only 1
(B) Both 1 and 2
(C) Both 2 and 3
(D) None of the above is a correct inference

***Ans*** (*A*) Deforestation can cause changes in the course of rivers is the correct inference that can be made from the given passage.

**3** With reference to 'desertification' as described in the passage, the following assumptions have been made:

1. Desertification is a phenomenon is tropical areas only.
2. Deforestation invariably leads to floods and desertification.

Which of the above assumptions is/are valid?

(A) Only 1 (B) Only 2
(C) Both 1 and 2 (D) Neither 1 nor 2

***Ans*** (*B*) Deforestation invariably leads to floods and desertification is a valid assumption.

**4** Which of the following depicts the passage after going through the paragraph?

(A) Decline in the biological loss of productivity
(B) Total loss of the productivity of soil.
(C) Combining (A) and (B)
(D) None of the above

***Ans*** (*C*) Decline in the biological loss of productivity and total loss of the productivity of soil that depicts the given passage after going through the paragraph.

**5** Which of the following sums up the site desertification of the soil?

(A) Soil degradation
(B) Alternation in available water
(C) Consequent decline in food and fodder
(D) All the above

***Ans*** (*D*) The ultimate consequences of site desertification are soil degradation, alteration in available water and its quality and the consequent decline in food and fodder.

# Chapter Practice

## Comprehension 1

**Directions** (Q. Nos. 1-5) Read the following passage carefully and answer the questions that follow.

The previous decade has reversed the presumptions about development and more than anything else, it has made it difficult to decide what is in store during the next decade. However, there are some things about which one can make claims with some confidence.

Firstly, education, health and productive employment are the decisive factors for development and impartiality. We believe that all these are the results of rapid economic development and to achieve these ends, development only can generate resources. In the present form, it will be best to view it as a better reason than as a result of development. In fact, in every case of successful development, the evaluation of previous reforms in education, technical skills, health, existence and productive tasks are included.

Secondly, technical ability is a vital resource and explains the high ratio of development in production and trade as compared to ratios of development in more traditional factors, such as natural resources or capital formation. There is no requisite capability in research. In fact, industrial momentum in a factory of farm is more important than the presence of a research organisation.

Thirdly, essentially required environment also cannot be ignored for a long time period, which is next only to the issue of disarmament in the list of international issues. At the national level, there has been a definite rise in ignorance towards the environment due to development.

In the context of India, at least two immediate factors increase the ratio mentioned above. The first one of these is the rise in population level. By giving momentum to expansion of population and the workforce, human resources development has achieved synergistic importance. An increase in population is also a factor but is not the most important one, which delineated environmental decay in rural and urban areas.

Second, as a large country, we cannot make an independent place for ourselves in the global system without developing appropriate ability for the development of one's self-respect. In order to achieve this objective, the achievement of technical skills is a decisive step.

So far, we have taken human resource development, technical and environmental issues as supporting factors of the main part of the plan. Along with the expansion of quality of basic infrastructure and targets of production (tonnes of steel and kilowatt hours of electricity), other targets of capacity (kilometers) and other targets (number of schools and students, number of electrified villages), known techniques, full use of natural resources and maximum possible use of available financial resources have been emphasised upon.

**1** According to this passage, what has been considered to be the most important by us out of the following?

(A) Basic facilities and increase in the number of achieved targets.

(B) Ideal use of available natural resources.

(C) Maximum use of available financial resources.

(D) All of the above

**2** According to the author of the passage, whose effect, out of the following is felt at the national level?

(A) Expansion of workforce of high quality

(B) Lack of care and activism for the protection of environmental resources

(C) Continuous decay of technical potentialities in urbanised countries

(D) Emphasis on a slower pace of disarmament as compared to disarmament in other nations

**3** According to the author of the passage, which of the following factors is of synergistic importance?

(A) Population growth

(B) Workforce

(C) Human resource development

(D) None of the above

**4** Which of the following areas has not been included among various 'targets' mentioned in the passage?
(A) Maximum use of financial resources
(B) Electricity production
(C) Population growth
(D) Number of schools and children

**5** Which of the following can be the most suitable title of the passage?
(A) Potential obstacles in economic development.
(B) Main factors of development.
(C) Targets in development process.
(D) Role of population growth in development.

## Comprehension 2

**Directions** (Q. Nos. 1-5) Read the following passage carefully and answer the questions that follow.

Though top leaders of the nationalist movement were the policy makers, the immediate day-to-day leadership was provided by the middle-class intellectuals. The rural origin of the industrial labour force together with rampant illiteracy and their simplistic docility attracted social workers, mainly drawn from the middle-class intellectuals. They had an obvious advantage. Not being employees, the leaders were free from fear of victimisation and immune towards the risks of leadership. Being generally well educated, they had a better perspective and sense of organisation. They could see the issue in broader context. They belonged to a higher social plane than the workers and with good education intellectual development comparable to the best among the employers they could meet the employers on their own plane and carry on negotiations on an equal footing.

According to Royal Commission on Labour in India, 'the effect of this surge was enhanced by the political turmoil which added to the prevailing feelings of unrest and assured to provide willing leaders of a trade union movement'. But outside leadership had led to the politicisation of the movement.

Politicisation of the labour movement in India contributed both to its strength and weakness. While economic hardship was present all along as a latent force, the major impetus for growth of unionism was primarily provided by major political currents, particularly the movement for national independence.

For the zeal and the organising ability, which the leaders of the nationalist movement brought to bear upon the Indian. Trade Union Movement, it would not have gained the dimensions and the position it had by 1909 within a decade of its formal start.

**1** Leadership to Trade Union was provided by middle-class intellectuals in India because
(A) they were the active participants in the nationalist movement.
(B) they were literates among the workers.
(C) they were able to negotiate with employers on equal terms.
(D) the workers did not want any one among them to be their leader.

**2** During the early years, Trade Union Movement gained greater dimensions because
(A) the workers accepted outside leaders
(B) it started along with the independence movement
(C) the leaders were well educated with broad perspectives
(D) the leaders were devoted to the welfare of workers

**3** The word 'surge' in the passage means
(A) decrease (B) support
(C) increase (D) slowness

**4** What could be the reason for workers not coming forward to take up the leadership in Trade Union Movement in the early years?
(A) Lack of time (B) Illiteracy
(C) Fear of victimisation (D) Risk in leadership

**5** According to the passage, which of the following leadership primarily led to the politicisation of the movement?
(A) Inside leadership (B) Outside leadership
(C) Both (A) and (B) (D) Illiterate leadership

## Comprehension 3

**Directions** (Q. Nos. 1-5) Read the following passage carefully and answer the questions that follow.

For years the managerial philosophers had called management's attention to its total responsibility. They indications of a moral oughtness we there, they stressed. As Stewards for stockholders, managers had a prime to the employees, the customers, and the community–along with their well-recognised responsibility to the owners.

By and large, these early pronouncements apparently fell on deaf ears. By the mid-thirties, however, heartening signs began to appear. In 1937, for example, Raymond Moley declared that while management remained legally and ethically a primary agent of the investors, its secondary responsibility to the public and labour had become relatively greater.

Four years later, Roger D Lapham asserted that in the narrow sense of the past, management had been considered solely responsible to its ownership–its stockholders–but there was a growing conviction that in the broader sense management's duty to its customers, to the public, and to its employees came first.

By 1951, this view was well established, and Frank Abraham's writing in the Harvard Business Review enunciated the new philosophy when he indicated that the job of management was to conduct the affairs of the enterprise in such a way as to maintain an equitable balance among the claims of the variously interested group. In the mid-sixties and early seventies, we have again recognised changes in philosophy that reflect management's gradual assumption of its moral and social obligation of good corporate citizenship.

We see it, for example, in management's assuming its social responsibility by cooperating with the federal government in withholding goods from countries if those goods would jeopardise our national security; in maintaining prices at a level consistent with a healthy economy, not raising them to a point considered critically inflationary; in training the unemployed; in cleaning up city ghettos; and in recognising and acting upon pollution problems. More examples could be cited, but the point of the broadened view taken by management of its total responsibility has been made.

**1** Raymond Moley advocated management's responsibility to
(A) owners of organisation only
(B) owners and employees only
(C) owners, public and labour
(D) owners, public, labour and customers

**2** Which of the following is not a part of corporate social responsibility?
(A) Controlling prices of prevent inflation
(B) Training of employees
(C) Acting upon pollution related problems
(D) Jeopardising the security of nation

**3** Corporate social responsibility comprises of
(A) Moral obligations of an organisation
(B) Social obligations of an organisation
(C) Moral and social obligations of an organisation
(D) None of the above

**4** Abraham is of the opinion that
(A) it is difficult to satisfy variously interested groups
(B) job management is to conduct affairs of enterprise
(C) there should be a balance among the interested groups
(D) None of the above

**5** In view of Lapham, management must take care of
(A) investors only
(B) stockholders and employees only
(C) stockholders, public and customers only
(D) stockholders, customers, public and employees

## Comprehension 4

**Directions** (Q. Nos. 1-5) Read the following passage carefully and answer the questions that follow.

Modern biotechnology, especially, the creation of Genetically Modified (GM) crops is often presented as a magical solution or universal panacea for the problems of poverty, inadequate nutrition and even environmental degradation across the world.

Conversely, there are people who present the picture of tech-generated monster and major human health hazards being created by science. Many of the technological changes currently being utilised in agriculture can have unforeseen consequences, and their safety and future viability are far from secure.

The reality, as always, is far more complex than either of these two extremes. Even today, the total food production in the world is adequate to feed the hungry of the world. The problems is rather one of unequal distribution, a large part of the population of developing countries engaged in agriculture, face many problems, such as lack of infrastructure, poor or unstable market access, volatile input and output prices, etc.

These issues cannot be addressed by biotechnology as their solution is a far cry. It is true that transgenic plants can offer a range of benefits (more effective pest resistance of seeds and crops through genetically controlled methods and leads to improved yield), which are above and beyond those that emerged from more traditional innovations.

A basic question, of course, is whether the new GM technology is safe, and whether this is absolutely crucial since the effect may only be known much later. The jury is still very much out on this matter and the controversy does not appear to resolve quickly. The trouble is that most governments in developing countries have relatively low food and beverage regulatory standards and public systems for monitoring and surveillance of such standards are either poor or non-existent. This leaves them open for entry and even dumping of a range of agricultural products of new technology, which may not pass the regulatory standards in more developed countries.

**1** Which of the following is true in context of the passage?

(A) Genetically modified crops have been universally recognised as a solution to poverty and environmental degradation.
(B) The only way to improve the deficit in food requirement and food production in world is by adapting genetically modified crops.
(C) Genetically modified crops produce more yield as compared to yield from traditional methods.
(D) Taking advantage of the absence of regulatory standards, scientists have been dumping new products in the market without appropriate approval.

**2** Choose the word/group of words which is most similar in meaning to open in the context of the passage?

(A) Vulnerable (B) Capable
(C) Threatened (D) Uncertain

**3** Choose the word/group of words which is most opposite in meaning to VOLATILE as used in the passage?

(A) Never-ending (B) Valuable
(C) Irreversible (D) Stable

**4** The author of the given passage seems to be definitely

(A) suggesting the use of traditional methods of agriculture as against biotechnological by developing countries owing to their poor regulatory standards.
(B) in favour of utilising biotechnology as a tool for the alleviation of poverty in the world.
(C) urging the policy markers to improve infrastructural facilities so that farmers can maximize the benefits of genetically modified crops.
(D) unconvinced of the long-term effects and rationale for immediate requirement of genetically modified products

**5** Why, according to the author, is genetic modification of crops not an answer to the problem of hunger in the world?

1. People being highly doubtful of the long-term effects of genetically modified crops of not buy the products grown by such methods.
2. The problem of hunger in the world is not due to inadequate production of food but due to unequal distribution of it.
3. Many developing countries have banned genetically modified products as developed countries have been using such countries as dumping groups for new genetically modified products.

(A) Only (1) (B) Only (2)
(C) Both (2) and (3) (D) Both (1) and (3)

## Comprehension 5

**Directions** (Q. Nos. 1-5) Read the following passage carefully and answer the questions that follow.

It should be remembered that the Nationalist Movement in India, like all nationalist movements was essentially a bourgeois movement. It represented the natural historical stage of development and to consider it or to criticise it, as a Working Class Movement is wrong.

Gandhi represented that movement and the Indian masses in relation to the movement to a supreme degree and he became the voice of Indian people to that extent. The main contribution of Gandhi to India and the Indian masses has been through the powerful movements that he launched through the National Congress.

Through nation-wide action, he sought to mould the millions and largely succeeded in doing so. He changed them from a demoralised, timid and hopeless mass, bullied and crushed by every dominant interest and incapable of resisting tyranny, and capable of united action and sacrifice for a larger cause.

Gandhi made people think of political and economic issues and every village and every bazaar hummed with argument and debate on the new ideas and hopes that filled the people.

That was an amazing psychological change. The time was ripe for it, of course, and circumstances and world conditions worked for this change. However, a great leader was necessary to take the advantage of those circumstances and conditions. Gandhi was that leader and he released many bonds that imprisoned and disabled our minds and none of us who experienced it can ever forget that great feeling of release and exhilaration that came over the Indian people.

Gandhi has palyed a revolutionary role of greatest importance in India because he knew how to make the most of the objective conditions and could reach the heart of the masses, whereas groups with a more advanced ideology functioned largely in air because they did not fit in with those conditions and could, therefore, not evoke any substantial response from the masses.

It is perfectly true the Gandhi, functioning in nationalist plane, did not think in terms of the conflict of classes, trying to compose their differences. However, the actions he indulged in and taught the people have inevitably raised mass consciousness tremendously the made social issues vital. Gandhi and the Congress must be judged by the policies they pursued and the action they indulged in. But behind this, personality counts and colours those policies and activities. In case of very exceptional people like Gandhi, the question of personality becomes especially important in order to understand and appraise him. To us, he represented the spirit and honour of India, the yearning of her sorrowing millions to be rid of their innumerable burdens and an insult to him by the British Government or others was as insult to India and her people.

**1** Which one of the following is true of the given passage?
(A) The passage is a critique of Gandhi's role in Indian movement for independence.
(B) The passage hails the role of Gandhi in India's freedom movement.
(C) The author is neutral on Gandhi's role in India's freedom movement.
(D) It is an account of Indian National Congress's support to the Working Class Movement.

**2** The change that the Gandhian movement brought among the Indian masses was
(A) physical (B) cultural
(C) technological (D) psychological

**3** To consider the Nationalist Movement or to criticise it as a Working Class Movement was wrong because it was a
(A) historical movement
(B) voice of the Indian people
(C) bourgeois movement
(D) movement represented by Gandhi

**4** Gandhi played a revolutionary role in India because be could
(A) preach morality
(B) reach the hearts of Indians
(C) see the conflict of classes
(D) lead the Indian National Congress

**5** Groups with advanced ideology functioned in air as they did not fit in with
(A) objective conditions of masses
(B) the Gandhian ideology
(C) the class consciousness of the people
(D) the difference among masses

## Comprehension 6

**Directions** (Q. Nos. 1-5) Read the following passage and answer the questions that follow.

It is no longer enough for us to talk about providing for universal access to education. Making available schooling facilities is an essential prerequisite, but it is insufficient to ensure that all children attend school and participate in the learning process. The school may be there, but children may not attend or they may drop out after a few months.

Through school and social mapping, we must address the entire gamut of social, economic, cultural and indeed linguistic and pedagogic issues, factors that prevent children from weaker sections and disadvantaged groups, as also girls, from regularly attending and complementing elementary education. The focus must be on the poorest and most vulnerable since these groups are the most disempowered and at the greatest risk of violation or denial of their right to education.

The right to education goes beyond free and compulsory education to include quality education for all. Quality is an integral part of the right to education.

If the education process lacks quality, children are being denied their right. The Right of Children to Free and Compulsory Education Act lays down that the curriculum should provide for learning through activities, exploration and discovery. This places an obligation on us to change our perception of children as passive receiver of knowledge and to move beyond the convention of using textbooks as the basis of examinations. The teaching-learning process must become stress-free and a massive programme for curricular reform should be initiated to provide for child-friendly learning system, that is more relevant and empowering. Teacher accountability systems and processes must ensure that children are learning and that their right to learn in a child-friendly environment is not violated. Testing and assessment systems must be reexamined and redesigned to ensure that these do not force children to struggle between school and tuition centres, and bypass childhood.

**1** Which one of the following does depict the school in the best possible manner?

(A) Through school and school mapping.
(B) The focus must be on the poorest sections of society.
(C) Both (A) and (B)
(D) None of the above

**2** According to the passage, which of the following is/are of paramount importance under the Right to Education?

1. Sending of children to school by all parents.
2. Provision of adequate physical infrastructure in schools.
3. Curricular reforms for developing child-friendly learning system.

Select the correct answer using the codes given below.

(A) Only 1 (B) 1 and 2
(C) Only 3 (D) None of these

**3** With reference to the above passage, the following assumptions have been made:

1. The Right to Education guarantees teacher's accountability for the learning process of children.
2. The Right to Education guarantees 100% enrolment of children in the schools.
3. The Right to Education intends to take full advantage of demographic dividend.

Which of the above assumption(s) is/are valid?

(A) Only 1 (B) 2 and 3 (C) Only 3 (D) 1, 2 and 3

**4** According to the passage, which one of the following critical in bringing quality in education?

(A) Ensuring regular attendance of children as well as teachers in school.
(B) Giving pecuniary benefits to teachers to motivate them.
(C) Understanding the socio-cultural background of children.
(D) Inculcating learning through activities and discovery.

**5** What is the essential message in this passage?

(A) The Right to Education now is a fundamental right
(B) The Right to Education enables the children of poor and weaker sections of the society to attend schools.
(C) The Right to Free and Compulsory Education should include quality education for all.
(D) The government as well as parents should ensure that all children attend schools.

## Comprehension 7

**Directions** (Q. Nos. 1-5) Read the following passage and answer the questions that follow.

Some religious leaders have taught that man is made up of a body and soul, but they have been silent about intellect. Their followers try to feed to the body to earth and save the soul from perdition after death-but they neglected the claims of the mind. Bread for the body and virtue for the soul, these are regarded as indispensable requisites of human welfare. Nothing is said about knowledge and education.

Thus, Jesus Christ spoke of feeding the hungry, healing the sick and converting the sinners, but he never taught the duty of teaching an ignorant and increasing scientific knowledge. He himself was not a well-educated man and intellectual pursuits were beyond his horizon.

Gautama Buddha also laid stress on morality, meditation and asceticism, but he did not attach great importance to history, science, art or literature. St. Ambrose deprecated scientific studies and wrote, 'To discuss the nature and position of the earth does not help us in our hope for life to come'. St. Basil said very frankly and foolishly, 'It is not a matter of interest to us whether the earth is a sphere, a cylinder or a disc'.

Thomas Carlyle also followed the Christian tradition and declared that he honoured only two kinds of men and no third, i.e., the manual labourer and the religious teacher. He forgot the scientist, the scholar and the artist. The cynics of Greece despised education at last.

**1** What have the religious teachers taught in the past?

(A) That man is made up of body only.
(B) That man is made up of soul only.
(C) That man is made up of bubbles.
(D) That man is made up of body and soul together.

**2** According to the passage, what is food for the soul?

(A) Bread (B) Virtue
(C) Vice (D) Education

**3** The following philosophers are mentioned in the paragraph.

1. Jesus 2. Gautama Buddha
3. St. Ambrose 4. Thomas Carlyle
5. St. Basil

Which of the following depicts the correct order as they appear in the paragraph?

(A) (1), (2), (3), (4) and (5)
(B) (1), (3), (4), (5) and (2)
(C) (1), (2), (3), (5) and (4)
(D) (2), (1), (3), (4) and (5)

**4** Intellectual pursuits have been neglected because

1. They are unnecessary and superfluous.
2. They make people dwarf.
3. They lead people to hell.

(A) Only (1) is correct
(B) Only (2) is correct
(C) Only (3) is correct
(D) Only (1) and (2) are correct

**5** The style of the passage is

(A) Narrative (B) Expository
(C) Critical (D) Analytical

## Comprehension 8

**Directions** (Q. Nos. 1-5) Read the following passage carefully and answer the questions given below it :

A great deal of the world's work is neither producing material things nor altering the things that Nature produces, but doing services of one sort or another.

Thoughtless people are apt to think a brickmaker more of a producer than a clergyman. When a village carpenter makes a gate to keep cattle out of a field of wheat, he has something solid in his hand which he can claim for his own until the farmer pays him for it. But when a village boy makes a noise to keep the birds off, he has nothings to show, though the noise is just as necessary as the gate. The postman does not make anything ..... The policeman does not make anything ..... The doctor makes pills sometimes; but that is not his real business, which is to tell you when you ought to take pills, and what pills to take, unless indeed he has the good sense to tell you not take them at all, and you have the good sense to believe him, when he is giving you good advice instead of bad. The lawyer does not make anything substantial ..... They are all in service.

**1** Thoughtless people think a brickmaker more of a producer than a clergyman because

(A) a clergyman is an idler
(B) a brickmaker produces something solid which he can keep with him till he gets its price
(C) a brickmaker, being physically stronger than a clergyman, can naturally produce more
(D) he cannot understand the philosophical lectures of the clergyman

**2** According to the author of the passage, a large number of persons :

(A) are producing material things
(B) are altering the things that Nature produces
(C) are doing nothing in particular
(D) offer services

**3** The writer thinks that :

(A) both the doctor and the patient are sensible when one makes pills and the other buys them
(B) the doctor is sensible and the patient is insensible
(C) the doctor is insensible and the patient is insensible
(D) both the doctor and the patient make sense when the doctor tells not to take the pills and the patient believes him

**4** The writer's description of the doctor's business :

(A) strengthens the main argument of the passage because the doctor's business is to make pills

(B) is irrelevant to the main argument of the passage
(C) weakens the main argument of the passage
(D) illustrates the difference between producing something and offering a service

**5** The word 'substantial' in the passage means
(A) of no importance
(B) of considerable importance
(C) of no value
(D) of low price

## Comprehension 9

**Directions** (Q. Nos. 1-5) Read the passage carefully, then answer the questions which are based on what is stated or implied in the passage.

Since the world has become industrialised, there has been an increase in the number of animal species that have either become extinct or have neared extinction. Bengal tiger, for instance, which once roamed the jungle in vast numbers, now number only 2300 and by the year 2025 their population is estimated to be down to zero. What is **alarming** about the case of Bengal tiger is that this extinction will have been caused almost entirely by poachers who according to some sources, are not interested in material gain but in personal gratification. This is an example of the callousness that is part of what is causing the problem of extinction. Animals like the Bengal tiger, as well as, those belonging to other endangered species, are a valuable part of the world's ecosystem. International laws protecting these animals must be enacted to ensure their survival, and the survival of our planet. Countries around the world have begun to deal with the problem in various ways.

Some countries, in order to circumvent the problem, have allocated large amount of land to animal reserves. They then charge admission fees to help defray the costs of maintaining the parks, and they often must also depend on world organisations for support. With the money get, they can invest in equipment and patrols to protect the animals. Another solution that is an attempt to **stem the tide** of animal extinction is an international boycott of products made from endangered species. This seems fairly effective, but it will not, by itself, prevent animals from being hunted and killed.

**1** What is the author's main concern in this passage ?
(A) Problems of industrialisation
(B) The Bengal tiger
(C) Endangered species
(D) Callousness of man

**2** According to the passage, poachers kill for :
(A) material gain
(B) personal satisfaction
(C) Both (A) and (B)
(D) None of the above

**3** Which of the following words is closest in meaning to the bold word 'alarming'?
(A) Serious (B) Dangerous
(C) Distressing (D) Frightening

**4** Certain species are becoming extinct because of :
(A) industrialisation
(B) poaching
(C) love of products made from them
(D) All of the above

**5** The Phrase 'Stem the tide' means :
(A) save (B) stop
(C) touch (D) spare

## Comprehension 10

**Directions** (Q. Nos. 1-5) Read the following passage carefully and answer the questions given below it:

Many people believe that science and religion are contrary to each other. But this notion is wrong. As a matter of fact, both are complementary to each other. The aim of both these institutions is to explain different aspects of life, universe and human existence. There is no doubt that the methods of science and religion are different. The method of science is observation, experimentation and experience. Science takes its recourse to progressive march towards perfection; the rules of religion are faith, intuition and spoken word of the enlightened; in general, while science is inclined towards reason and rationality, spiritualism is the essence of religion.

In earlier times when man appeared on earth, he was over-awed at the sight of violent and powerful aspects of nature. In certain cases, the usefulness of different natural objects of nature overwhelmed man.

Thus began the worship of forces of nature-fire, the sun, the rivers, the rocks, the trees, the snakes, etc. The holy scriptures were written by those who had developed harmony between external nature and their inner self. Their object was to ennoble, elevate and liberate the human spirit and mind. But the priestly class took upon itself the monopoly of scriptural knowledge and interpretation to its own advantage. Thus the entire human race was in chains. Truth was flouted and progressive, liberal and truthful ideas or ideas expressing doubt and skepticism were suppressed and their holders punished. It was in these trying circumstances, the science emerged as a saviour of mankind. But its path was not smooth and safe. The scientists and free thinkers were tortured. This was the fate of Copernicus, Galileo, Bruno and others. But, by and by science gained ground.

**1** Why does man worship the force of nature?
(A) The holy scriptures advocate the worship of forces of nature
(B) The worship elevates and liberates the human spirit and mind
(C) The worship makes man believe in faith and intuition
(D) Forces of nature reach us spiritualism

**2** Which of the following statements is true in the context of the passage?
(A) Science and religion are antagonistic to each other
(B) Science encourages worshipping of nature
(C) Religion is essential for external peace and harmony
(D) Regimental religion was replaced by scientific principles

**3** According to the passage, science and religion both :
(A) rely on the spoken word of the enlightened
(B) emerged out of the fear of man
(C) emerged from the desire of man to worship the forces of nature
(D) employ different methods of enquiry

**4** Why is it said in the passage that, 'science emerged as a saviour of mankind'?
(A) Many great thinkers contributed to the progress of science
(B) Science takes recourse to progressive march towards perfection
(C) Science is inclined towards reason and rationality
(D) Man was bound in chains by religious orthodoxy

**5** Which of the following statements is not true in the context of the passage?
(A) Man worships the forces of nature
(B) Methods of science and religion are different
(C) Regimental religion got degenerated into orthodoxy
(D) Galileo and Bruno were disciples of Copernicus

## Comprehension 11

**Directions** (Q. Nos. 1-5) Read the passage carefully and then choose the one best answer for each question given below :

The conservative is not an extreme individualist. He may be willing to concede numerous arguments of the unqualified individualists, for his own respect, for the dignity of the individual is not surpassed by that of any man. Yet, he cannot agree to the full implications of individualism, which is based so he thinks, on an incorrect appraisal of man, society, history, and government. In his own way, the individualist is as much a perfectionist as the Socialist, and with perfectionism the conservative can have no **truck**.

In particular, the conservative refuses to go all the way with economic individualism. His distrust of unfettered man, his recognition to groups, his sense of the complexity of the social process, his recognition of the real services that government can perform– all these sentiments make it impossible for him to subscribe to the dogmas and shibboleths of economic individualism : laissez-faire, the negative state, enlightened self-interest, the law of supply and demand, the profit motive. The conservative may occasionally have kind word for each of these notions, but he is careful to qualify his support by stating other, more important social truths. For example, he does not for a moment deny the prominence of the profit motive, but he insists that it be recognised for the selfish thing it is and be kept within reasonable, socially imposed limits.

**1** The conservative is
(A) a perfectionist
(B) an economist
(C) a socialist
(D) None of the above

**2** The conservative is against Economic Individualism for all the following reasons except:
(A) he does not trust free men
(B) he believes in the authority of the government
(C) he believes in groups
(D) he feels that social processes are important

**3** The author mentions all the following catchwords of economic individualism except:
(A) free trade
(B) the profit motive
(C) balance of trade
(D) the negative state

**4** Which of the following words can replace the bold word 'truck' ?
(A) Dealing
(B) Bargain
(C) Debate
(D) Transport

**5** Which of the following statements is true ?
(A) The socialist and the individualist tend to be broadly similar in their views
(B) The conservative believes that profit motive originates in selfishness
(C) The conservative is also an extreme individualist
(D) None of the above

# ANSWERS

**Comprehension 1**
1 (D) 2 (A) 3 (C) 4 (C) 5 (B)

**Comprehension 2**
1 (C) 2 (B) 3 (C) 4 (B) 5 (B)

**Comprehension 3**
1 (C) 2 (D) 3 (C) 4 (C) 5 (D)

**Comprehension 4**
1 (A) 2 (A) 3 (D) 4 (D) 5 (B)

**Comprehension 5**
1 (B) 2 (D) 3 (A) 4 (B) 5 (A)

**Comprehension 6**
1 (C) 2 (C) 3 (D) 4 (D) 5 (C)

**Comprehension 7**
1 (D) 2 (B) 3 (C) 4 (A) 5 (A)

**Comprehension 8**
1 (B) 2 (D) 3 (D) 4 (D) 5 (B)

**Comprehension 9**
1 (C) 2 (B) 3 (D) 4 (D) 5 (B)

**Comprehension 10**
1 (B) 2 (D) 3 (D) 4 (D) 5 (D)

**Comprehension 11**
1 (D) 2 (D) 3 (A) 4 (A) 5 (B)

# *Previous Years' Questions*

## UGC-NET June 2019

### Comprehension 1

**Directions** (Q. Nos. 1-5) *Read the following passage carefully and answer the questions that follow.*

All great thinkers live and move on a high plane of thought. It is only there, they can breathe freely. It is only in contact with spirits like themselves they can live harmoniously and attain that serenity which comes from ideal companionship. The studies of all great thinkers must range along the highest altitudes of human thought. I have always thought that the strongest argument in favour of the Baconian theory was, that no man, however, indubitable his genius, could have written the play and sonnets that have come down to us under Shakespeare's own name who had not the liberal education of Bacon.

The magnificent ideals that have ever haunted the human mind and given us our highest proofs of a future immortality by reason of the impossibility of their fulfillment here, are splintered into atoms by contact with life's realities. Hence, comes our sublime discontent. A habitual mediation on the vast problems that underline human life and are knit into human destinies-thoughts of immortality, of the littleness of mere man, of the greatness of man's soul, of the splendor of the universe that are invisible to the ordinary traffickers in the street, as the vastness of St. Peter's is to the spinder that weaves her web in a corner of the dome-these things do not fit men to understand the average human being, or tolerate with patience the sordid wretchedness of the unregenerated masses.

It is easy to understand, therefore, why such thinkers fly to the solitude of their own thoughts, or the silent companionship of the immortals and if they care to present their views in prose or verse to the world, that these views take a sombre and melancholy setting from 'the pale caste of thought' in which they were engendered.

**1** Great thinkers are content to live

(A) amidst crises of civilisations

(B) in lofty thoughts with exceptional calm

(C) at high altitudes in order to be away from society

(D) with complexities of and find solutions to them

***Ans*** (*B*) All great thinkers move and live on a high plane of thought. So, they are content to live in touring thoughts with tranquility or peace.

**2** Why do great thinkers love solitude?

(A) To be in pursuit of the ideal in the company of immortals

(B) To spend time in peace

(C) Because they are misanthropists

(D) Because the world is unhealthy for them

***Ans*** (*A*) According to the passage the great thinkers love loneliness because they want to be in search of the ideal in the company of immortals.

**3** Immortality is the crucial idea constantly being explored by

(A) Ordinary traffickers

(B) Great thinkers

(C) Gods who appear to the thinkers

(D) Scientists

***Ans*** (*B*) The great thinkers continuously search the crucial idea i.e. the eternal life.

**4** Baconian liberal education is

(A) a lofty and ideal fantasy

(B) instrumental in making human being rule over their destiny

(C) an engagement with the intricacies of the day-to-day life

(D) equivalent to ancient ideas of sublimity

***Ans*** (*C*) The passage describes the Baconian education as an arrangement with the complexities of the day-to-day life.

**5** According to the passage, our sublime discontent is due to

(A) realisation of our lack of contact with God

(B) acute sense of loneliness in a hostile world

(C) possibility of immortality through some channels to God and inability to get hold of it

(D) the contrast between the ideals in great literature and their opposite in the real life

***Ans*** (*D*) Our complete dissatisfaction is because of the difference between the principles in literature and their opposite in real life.

## Comprehension 2

**Directions** (Q. Nos. 1-5) Read the following passage carefully and answer the questions that follow.

There is a common thread running through the unravelling of India's statistical system. A modern economy with sound institutions is characterised by timely dissemination of credible data. A long-term policy needs an empirical basis and issues of veracity of data will influence investment decisions. In a country with a large population of youth, data on national development, especially in core sectors like agriculture, industry, health, education and employment, will be critical. Here comes the role of National Statistical Commission, a body created to establish standards.

Questioning the data veracity is a global phenomenon. The official narrative is always questioned by the people on the other side of the fence. Dissemination of economic data is essential to reach out to the public who lived their reality. Lack of data will adversely impact the quality of national policies. India must start strengthening institutions such as the Central Statistical Commission.

These institutions must be granted autonomy and insulated from external interferences. Enhanced operational autonomy will make their work credible. An indicator of operational autonomy is their ability to stick to a dissemination calendar regardless of what the data indicates.

1 What is important for a modern economy?

(A) A common thread
(B) Dissemination of credible data
(C) Unravelling of statistical system
(D) Selective distribution of data

***Ans*** (*B*) Dissemination is an integral part of survey research. In modern economy good institutions are distinguished if they publicise or disseminate the data with great transparency. It is then only the data is considered credible or reliable.

2 What is the work of National Statistical Commission?

(A) Establishing standards
(B) Questioning data veracity
(C) Questioning official narrative
(D) Supporting the public perception

***Ans*** (*A*) The National Statistical Commission, an advisory body on all statistical matters, was set up to enhance public trust in official statistics. Its main task is to lay down standards.

3 What does the passage ultimately suggest to National Statistical Commission?

(A) Restricting policy decisions
(B) Critically examining data veracity
(C) Stick to a calendar of data dissemination
(D) Support development in core sectors

***Ans*** (*C*) According to the passage, the National Statistical Commission needs to adhere to the fixed schedule as far as the data dissemination is concerned.

4 Investment decision are impacted by

(A) youth population
(B) national development
(C) issues of data veracity
(D) establishment of national institutes

***Ans*** (*C*) Data veracity is the degree to which data is accurate, precise and trusted. It helps to filter through what is important and what is not and it also generates a deeper understanding of data. Thus, the investment discussion are affected by the issues of data veracity.

5 How can the quality of national policies be improved?

(A) By living in reality
(B) By supporting external interferences
(C) By controlling autonomous institutions
(D) By enhanced operational freedom

***Ans*** (*D*) The quality of national policy can be made better by increasing the operational freedom. It means the national policy should be more functional in its working, then only the quality of national policy will strengthen.

## Comprehension 3

**Directions** (Q. Nos. 1-5) Read the following passage carefully and answer the questions that follow.

Perhaps what bothered the media in 1970s was the shift in liberty being suggested. For centuries, journalists had operated on the basis of negative liberty, or freedom from external restraints. Suddenly, however, the thrust was positive freedom, a freedom for pursuit of some predetermined goals. This new social responsibility seems grounded on a school of thought that sees negative liberty as insufficient and ineffective, somewhat like telling people they are free to walk without first making sure they are not crippled.

Who better than government is able to provide humanity with appropriate means?

Government, even a democratic government, is seen by social responsibility adherents as the only force strong enough to guarantee effective operation of freedom. This does not mollify observers who find social responsibility to be only slightly disguised version of authoritarianism. Media philosopher John Merrill has been one of the most outspoken critics of the theory.

To him, the proposition that pluralism of ideas should be governmentally mandated is ludicrous. Journalists, he says, must retain their freedom to make their own news and editorial judgements. Even well-intentioned attempts by outside groups seeking media improvement are self-serving, and inevitably lessen the autonomy of journalists, Merrill maintains. This leads us to the issue of media autonomy.

**1** What was the basis of the operation of journalists earlier?
(A) Freedom of limited choices
(B) Social responsibility
(C) Free from outside pressure
(D) Government control

***Ans*** (C) According to the passage, the journalists were free from outside pressure. They valued independence in their jobs. They had freedom from external restraints.

**2** According to John Merrill, seeking improvement in media, is
(A) appropriate (B) well-intentioned
(C) inevitable (D) self-serving

***Ans*** (*D*) According to media philosopher John Merrill looking for improvement in media is self-serving or working for self-interest.

**3** The passage critically analyses
(A) operation of journalists
(B) mandate for government
(C) social responsibility theory of media
(D) regimented autonomy of journalists

***Ans*** (*C*) The passage examines crucially social responsibility theory of media.

**4** Some scholars consider social responsibility aspect of media as
(A) negative freedom (B) pluralism
(C) democratisation of media
(D) authoritarianism

***Ans*** (*D*) According to the views of some scholars the social responsibility aspect of media is to be regarded as authoritarianism. Though in social responsibility theory the press is taken to be for the people and society.

**5** Positive freedom means
(A) grounded thought
(B) pursuing certain set goals
(C) freedom with conditions
(D) providing identified means

***Ans*** (*B*) In the passage positive freedom signifies that one should be free to pursue some predetermined goals.

## Comprehension 4

**Directions** (Q. Nos. 1-5) Read the following passage carefully and answer the questions that follow.

Michelangelo is famous for having successfully interpreted the human body. His great achievement is that of the painting of David whose hands reach out as a sign of human capability and potential. It is assumed that the time he lived was ripe for exchange of knowledge, development in science and matured enough to advance the horizon of investigation in all fields. Renaissance humanism stressed on a serious rethink on the nature of art that focussed on accurate details. In painting and sculpture, artists focussed on not so casual but verifiable and minute details. Michelangelo's paintings are no exception to it. In a study published in the journal of the Royal Society of Medicine, a group of surgeons are of the opinion that the great master was "afflicted by an illness involving his joints." They have used his portraits as evidence to argue their view. During his life, he complained of what he felt to be 'gout'. Later he complained of his sore and stiff hands which the doctors would find to be natural for someone who was engaged in handmade art. The doctors found corroboration of those claims in portraits of the artist that show a hanging left hand with both **degenerative** and **non-degenerative** changes.

They attribute the pain not just to arthritis, but to the stress of hammering and chiselling and note that though the master was seen hammering days before his death at an old age, he did not write or sign his own letters before his death. In recent times, there have been attempts to diagnose famous artists with diseases that were not known during their time. This practice has raised many questions, especially on the issue of ethics in research. It is also inferred from authentic analysis that Michelangelo persisted in his work until his last days. This theory would emphasise that his artistic subject defied his physical infirmities.

**1** What generalisation do people subscribe to?
(A) Establishing facts by DNA tests
(B) Inferring the essence of character from famous people's handwriting
(C) Carbon dating of the hair of celebrities to draw conclusion on their physical structure
(D) To retroactively diagnose famous artists and public figures of conditions that were not prevalent during their time

***Ans*** (*D*) People in recent times try to diagnose the popular artists and figures with diseases which were not common during their period. Hence, option 'D' is the correct answer.

**2** Renaissance painting in Europe was sceptical of
(A) the obsessive medieval method of accuracy
(B) the classical simplicity and lack of control
(C) the case and decorative excess of earlier art
(D) expressionist technique

***Ans*** (*C*) In Europe, the renaissance painting was inquisitive because artists focussed on not so causal but on minute details. The paintings depicted the decorative pieces of earlier art.

**3** The controversy that the passage above refers to is whether
(A) Michelangelo worked under duress
(B) Michelangelo could contain his physical infirmity by artistic excellence
(C) Michelangelo submitted to disease
(D) Michelangelo survived different diseases before pursing art

***Ans*** (*B*) According to the passage, Michelangelo continued his work until his last days but his artistic workmanship defied his physical weakness.

**4** Michelangelo lived during a time that lets us know that
(A) human aspirations are limitless and open to new vistas of knowledge
(B) cross cultural exchange in ideas is the only way for human progress
(C) it is progress of science and anatomy that contributes to civilisations exclusively
(D) human beings possess language which is the only key to knowledge

***Ans*** (*A*) The period during which Michelangelo lived tell us that desires of people were boundless and open to new perspectives of knowledge. The time was ripe for exchange of knowledge and development in all fields.

**5** What actually may be concluded from the above passage?
(A) Physical infirmities do dissuade people with capabilities from excelling
(B) Excellence in any form triumphs over extraneous factors including physical ailments
(C) Michelangelo's gout and other ailments lessened his efficiency
(D) The diseases Michelangelo faced were due to constant hammering

***Ans*** (*B*) The outstanding achievement in any form can be overcome despite physical illness. So, it may be concluded from the above passage that physical weakness cannot stop one's work. It means excellence in any form triumphs over outside factors, be it physical weakness.

## Comprehension 5

**Directions** (Q. Nos. 1-5) Read the following passage carefully and answer the questions that follow.

A business will usually go through a clear set of stages that will make up its organisational life cycle. These stages include introduction, early growth, continuous growth, maturity and decline. The first stage, the introduction stage, is the start-up phase where a business decides what its core strengths and capabilities are and starts selling its product or service. At this early stage, the founder or founders will be a part of every aspect of the daily process of the business. The main goal at this stage is to take off to a good start and make a place in the market.

The next stage, the early growth phase, aims at increased sales and more development. The focus at this stage remains on the original product or service but the effort is to increase the market share and venture into related products or services. The main goal is to move the founder to a more managerial role so more time is spent on managing and building the business. At this stage, documents and policies need to be developed so any member of the organisation can see the business any time.

The third stage, the continuous growth stage, requires a systematic structure and more formal relationships among its participants. At this stage, the resource requirements of the business need careful handling.

The focus is on the expansion of the business, keeping in mind its core strength and capability. A formal organisational structure and a clear delegation plan are important at this stage. At the fourth stage of maturity, a business often slows down as the level of innovative energy may have become weak and the formal structures may have become obstacles. A lot of care is required to prevent decline.

**1** The resource requirements of a business need careful handling at which stage?

(A) Fourth (B) First
(C) Third (D) Second

***Ans*** (*C*) According to the passage, the resource requirement of a business need careful handling at the third stage.

**2** Venturing into related products and services does not mean that a business will

(A) ignore the original product
(B) move the founder: to a more managerial role
(C) delegate more responsibilities
(D) ignore the related products and services

***Ans*** (*A*) At the early growth phase, a business aims to increase sales and development. The main focus is on the original product or service so a business cannot neglect original products.

**3** The founder of a business does not move to a more managerial role at which stage?

(A) Early growth stage (B) Maturity stage
(C) Decline stage (D) Start up stage

***Ans*** (*D*) At the start up stage the founder of the business does not move to a more managerial role. At this stage, a business decides what its main strength and capabilities are and they begin to sell its product or services.

**4** The slowing down of a business can happen if

(A) there is a decline in the market share
(B) the level of innovative energy weakens
(C) the managerial roles are not clear
(D) the level of investment declines

***Ans*** (*B*) The business can fall off if the level of innovative energy weakens. It is the stage of maturity. Thus, great care is needed to prevent business from decline.

**5** When will a business create its place in the market?

(A) At maturity (B) At introduction
(C) At early growth (D) At late growth

***Ans*** (*B*) According to passage at the introduction stage or first stage the business will build its place in the market. Here, the main aim is to take off a good start.

## Comprehension 6

**Directions** (Q. Nos. 1-5) Read the following passage carefully and answer the questions that follow.

An important difference between human beings and animals is the property of language. Animals have a rudimentary information process but this process does not have the sophistication and complexity of human language. If two dogs communicate, they pass on information but they can't discuss details the way humans can. While humans are blessed to possess the language faculty, most of the time they don't utilise it to its greatest potential.

Perhaps this is because human beings tend to react rather than respond. And a lot of the message of languages is lost in this reaction.

In the daily use of language, people forget the complex process involved in order to put even one word in place. The wonder of this process lies in the fact that it is involuntary in nature, the whole set of chain processes right from the command in the brain to the forming of words from the message required to the movement of the vocal chords and corresponding movements in the lungs and mouth takes place within seconds. Perhaps the whole suggestion of 'think before you speak', may lead to a silent world! In the world of daily interaction, language becomes a marker and a means of projecting identity.

The people around us identify us with a certain style of using language and unknowingly, each language user follows this style by habit. It is not a bad idea to record one's spoken communication from time to time, as this will assist in removing any unwanted elements that the speech may be expressing. Similarly, it is a good idea to step back once in a while and read one's written communication objectively.

**1** The world will become a silent place if people will think

(A) too much (B) before listening
(C) before responding (D) before speaking

***Ans*** (*D*) If people will think before speaking, the world will become a silent place.

**2** The process of language is a wonder because it is

(A) a reaction (B) a response
(C) smooth (D) involuntary

**Ans** (*D*) According to the passage, the process of language is a wonder because it is involuntary in nature.

**3** Which of the following forms is assumed by the language style of a person?

(A) A reaction (B) A habit
(C) A response (D) A thought

**Ans** (*B*) A habit is assumed by the language style of a person.

**4** When human beings react rather than respond

(A) they lose the message
(B) they lose control
(C) they become emotional
(D) they can't speak

**Ans** (*A*) Most of the times people try to react at once rather than respond. As a result most of the messages of languages is lost.

**5** Animals do not possess language because

(A) the power of speech is missing
(B) the life breath is missing
(C) the level of complexity is missing
(D) the information-sharing is missing

**Ans** (*C*) A rudimentary difference between animals and human beings is that animals do not possess the level of complexity of human language. Animals can pass on information but they cannot discuss details what people can do.

## Comprehension 7

**Directions** (Q. Nos. 1-5) Read the following passage carefully and answer the questions that follow.

Geography seeks to understand the physical and human organisation of the surface of the Earth. In the field of geography, inter-related themes are frequently seen. These are scale, pattern and process. Scale is defined as the level of structure or organisation at which a phenomenon is studied. Pattern is defined as the variation observed in a phenomenon studied at a particular scale.

The third theme, process, further connects the first two. Process is defined as the description of how the factors that affect a phenomenon act to produce a pattern at a particular scale. For instance, when a passenger on an aircraft looks out of the window, the view changes according to the scale.

At the global scale when the aircraft maintains its height, he can see the chunks of clouds in all their pattern, the sun or the moon, as per the time. When the aircraft loses a little height, passengers can see the land and water masses in their different colours and the shape of land masses. At the continental scale, the passengers can see the shapes of the land features and how they are distributed. The pattern emerges as the variation of land and water and the proportion of each. Looking carefully, passengers can note how each land mass aligns with the others and how each mountain bears the signs of the process through which it emerged.

The processes in a geography change in a regular and repetitive manner. One instance of this is the annual solar cycle of the sun and the earth. Most systems in nature display time cycles that are organised in a rhythm of their own as these time cycles and natural processes are always active, the environment of the earth is always in a state of dynamism. This environmental change is not only the result of natural process but also the result of human activity. Physical geography works towards understanding the interaction between man and nature and also the results of this interaction in order to manage global climate change better.

**1** The time cycles of the system of nature follow their own

(A) path (B) rhythm
(C) process (D) cycle

**Ans** (*B*) The system in nature shows that the time cycles are arranged in a rhythm of their own because these time cycles and natural proccess are always active.

**2** The view seen by a passenger looking out of the window of an aircraft; will be affected by the

(A) process (B) pattern
(C) scale (D) rhythm

**Ans** (*C*) According to the passage the view seen by a passenger seeing out of the window of an aircraft will be impacted by the scale.

**3** Physical geography studies the results of the interaction between man and nature in order to

(A) understand global climate change
(B) study the impact of man's activities on nature
(C) address the issue of global climate change
(D) reduce man-animal conflict

**Ans** (*C*) To manage the issue of global climate change physical geography studies the result of the interaction between man and nature.

**4** In geography, pattern studies the variation observed in a phenomenon at

(A) a particular scale (B) any scale
(C) every scale (D) most scale

***Ans*** (*A*) Pattern studies the differences seen in a phenomenon at a particular scale.

**5** The alignment of a landmass with other elements can be seen by a passenger on a flight on a

(A) global scale (B) continental scale
(C) local scale (D) time scale

***Ans*** (*B*) On a continental scale the alignment of a landmass with other elements can be seen by a passenger on a flight.

## UGC-NET December 2018

## Comprehension 8

**Directions** (Q. Nos. 1-5) Read the following passage carefully and answer the questions that follow.

One of the findings of the research into successful leadership is the fact that respect is always a two-way street. No matter how powerful you are, no matter what your experience, skills and accomplishments, you will not be respected by others if you consistently treat them disrespectfully. Friendliness i.e., treating others politely and showing interest in them-is a way of showing your respect for other people and in return they respect you. If as a manager you are respected, preventive maintenance strategy will be accepted as a sincere attempt to resolve problems rather than a mean-spirited attempt to cause problems.

As important as friendliness is, I want to make sure you are not mislead into believing that friendliness will replace or correct poor management. I have seen effective managers who did not use this friendliness element but could have been more effective if they did use it. I have seen very friendly managers who were ineffective because they were not doing effective management things. In other words, managers who intervene effectively in a friendly way are always more effective than managers who intervene effectively in a non-friendly way. Maintaining a friendly relationship is another part of maintaining work performance. It also helps you avoid having people try to hurt you because they do not like you. It might save your life.

**1** According to the passage, friendliness in management terms implies

(A) making management effective
(B) making management ineffective
(C) replacing poor management
(D) correcting ineffective management

***Ans*** (*A*) Friendliness is more important in making management effective because managers who intervene effectively in a friendly way are always more effective.
Therefore, friendliness in management terms implies making management effective.

**2** The central idea of the passage is

(A) friendliness improves the work-ethos
(B) friendliness avoids change of feeling hurt
(C) friendliness is necessary for management
(D) friendliness is a negative factor for management

***Ans*** (*A*) Friendliness, that means treating others politely and showing interest in workers, is a way of showing respect towards other people or workers. It leads to enhance the work-ethos. It is a reciprocal element such as give respect and take respect. Therefore, the central idea of the passage is friendliness improves the work-ethos.

**3** The passage highlights which of the following feature of a successful leadership?

(A) Reciprocity of the leader
(B) Least concern for relationship by the leader
(C) Independence of the leader
(D) Dependence of the leader

***Ans*** (*A*) Respect is always a reciprocal element. It is a two-way street. If someone shows respect to the other and in return they respect you and you easily resolve the problems rather than making a mean-spirited attempt to cause problems.
Therefore, reciprocity of the leader highlights his successful feature.

**4** What is reported in respect of successful leadership?

(A) Respect depends on the accomplishments of the leader
(B) Respect comes out of respect
(C) Respect depends on the skills of the leadership
(D) Respect depends on experience of the leadership

***Ans*** (*B*) One of the findings of the research into successful leadership is the fact that respect is always a two-way street. A successful leader will not be respected by others if he consistently treats them disrespectfully. Hence, option 'B' is correct.

**5** The preventive maintenance strategy used by a respected manager will mean to the subordinates.

(A) An attempt to become sincere.
(B) An attempt to become mean-spirited.
(C) An attempt to resolve problems.
(D) An attempt to cause problems.

***Ans*** (*C*) Maintaining a friendly relationship leads to good working performance and also leads to resolve the problems. It helps a manager to avoid those people who try to hurt him because they do not like him and might save his life. Thus, through showing a friendliness nature a manager can resolve the problem rather than a mean-spirited attempt to cause problems. Therefore, the preventive maintenance strategy used by a respected manager will mean to the subordinates as an attempt to resolve problems.

## UGC-NET July 2018

## Comprehension 9

**Directions** (Q. Nos. 1-5) *Read the following passage carefully and answer the questions that follow.*

If India has to develop her internal strengths, the nation has to focus on the technological **imperatives**, keeping in mind three dynamic dimensions : the people, the overall economy and the strategic interests. These technological imperatives also take into account a 'fourth' dimension, time, an offshoot of modern day dynamism in business, trade and technology that leads to continually shifting targets.

We believe that technological strengths are especially crucial in dealing with this fourth dimension underlying continuous change in the aspirations of the people, the economy in the global context and the strategic interests. The progress of technology lies at the heart of human history. Technological strengths are the key to creating more productive employment in an increasingly competitive market place and to continually upgrade human skills.

Without a pervasive use of technologies, we cannot achieve overall development of our people in the years to come. The direct linkages of technology to the nation's strategic strengths are becoming more and more clear, especially since 1990s. India's own strength in a number of core areas still puts it in a position of reasonable strength in geo-political context.

Any nation aspiring to become a developed one needs to have strengths in various strategic technologies and also the ability to continually upgrade them through its own creative strengths. For people-oriented actions as well, whether for the creation of large scale productive employment or for ensuring nutritional and health security for people or for better living conditions, technology is the only vital input.

The absence of greater technological impetus could lead to lower productivity and wastage of precious natural resources. Activities with low productivity or low value addition, in the final analysis hurt the poorest most. The technological imperatives to lift our people to a new life and to a life they are entitled to is important.

India, aspiring to become a major economic power in terms of trade and increase in GDP, cannot succeed on the strength of **turnkey** projects designed and built abroad or only through large-scale imports of plant and machinery, equipment and know how. Even while being alive to the short-term realities, medium and long-term strategies to develop core technological strengths within our industry are vital for envisioning a developed India.

**1** Envisioning a developed India requires

(A) focus on short-term projects
(B) development of core technological strengths
(C) aspiration to become a major economic player
(D) dependence upon projects designed abroad

***Ans*** (*B*) Envisioning a developed India requires the development of core technological strengths and capabilities within our industry. Alongwith short-term realities, we must focus on medium and long-term plans of action so that we do not depend totally on foreign machinery or projects.

**2** Absence of technology would lead to

1. less pollution.
2. wastage of precious natural resources.
3. low value addition.
4. hurting the poorest most.

Select the most appropriate answer from the following codes.

(A) 1, 2 and 4 (B) 2, 1 and 4
(C) 1, 2 and 3 (D) 2, 3 and 4

***Ans*** (*D*) Absence of technology means lower productivity and wastage of natural resources. Low productivity and low income eventually affects the poor most.

**3** According to the given passage, which of the following are indicative of the fourth dimension?

1. Aspirations of people.
2. Modern day dynamism.
3. Economy in the global context.
4. Strategic interests.

Select the most appropriate answer from the following codes.

(A) 1, 3 and 4
(B) 1, 2 and 4
(C) 1, 2 and 3
(D) 2, 3 and 4

***Ans*** (*A*) According to the given passage, continuous change in the aspirations of people, the economic growth in global perspective and strategic interests are indicative of the fourth dimension.

To develop India's internal strengths, the nation has to focus on the technological imperatives. The fourth dimension suggests an ever changing targets in business, trade and technology in modern days.

**4** More productive employment demands

(A) geo-political considerations
(B) large industries
(C) pervasive use of technology
(D) limiting competitive market place

***Ans*** (*C*) More productive employment demands extensive use of technology and upgrading of human skills according to the demands of technology.

Without extensive use of technology, overall development of any country is not possible. We must learn to change our strategies according to the need of time.

**5** The advantage of technological inputs would result in

(A) sidelining environmental issues
(B) lifting our people to a life of dignity
(C) unbridled technological growth
(D) importing plant and machinery

***Ans*** (*B*) There will be many advantages of extensive use of technology. The most important will be providing our people a life of dignity. More use of technology can lead to more productive employment to people, thereby generating more wealth for people of all strata specially the vulnerable ones.

Technology is the answer for ensuring nutritional and health security, better living conditions and overall dignified life for all.

## UGC-NET November 2017

## Comprehension 10

**Directions** (Q. Nos. 1-5) Read the following passage carefully and answer the questions that follow.

Climate change is considered to be one of the most serious threats to sustainable development, with adverse impacts on the environment, human health, food security, economic activity, natural resources and physical infrastructure. Global climate varies naturally. According to the Intergovernmental Panel on Climate Change (IPCC), the effects of climate change have already been observed, and scientific findings indicate that precautionary and prompt action is necessary. Vulnerability to climate change is not just a function of geography or dependence on natural resources; it also has social, economic and political dimensions which influence how climate change affects different groups. Poor people rarely have insurance to cover loss of property due to natural calamities i.e., drought, floods, super cyclones, etc.

The poor communities are already struggling to cope with the existing challenges of poverty and climate variability and climate change could push many beyond their ability to cope or even survive. It is vital that these communities are helped to adapt to the changing dynamics of nature. Adaptation is a process through which societies make themselves better able to cope with an uncertain future. Adapting to climate change **entails** taking the right measures to reduce the negative effects of climate (or exploit the positive ones) by making the appropriate adjustments and changes.

These range from technological options such as increased sea defences or flood-proof houses on **stilts** to behavioural change at the individual level, such as reducing water use in times of drought. Other strategies include early warning systems for extreme events, better water management, improved risk management, various insurance options and biodiversity conservation.

Because of the speed at which climate change is happening due to global temperature rise, it is urgent that the vulnerability of developing countries to climate change is reduced and their capacity to adapt is increased and national adaptation plans are implemented.

Adapting to climate change will entail adjustments and changes at every level from community to national and international. Communities must build their resilience, including adopting appropriate technologies while making the most of traditional knowledge and diversifying their livelihoods to cope with current and future climate stress. Local coping strategies and knowledge need to be used in synergy with government and local interventions. The need of adaptation interventions depends on national circumstances.

There is a large body of knowledge and experience within local communities on coping with climatic variability and extreme weather events. Local communities have always aimed to adapt to variations in their climate. To do so, they have made preparations based on their resources and their knowledge accumulated through experience of past weather patterns. This includes times when they have also been forced to react to and recover from extreme events, such as floods, drought and hurricanes.

Local coping strategies are an important element of planning for adaptation. Climate change is leading communities to experience climatic extremes more frequently, as well as new climate extremes. Traditional knowledge can help to provide efficient appropriate and time-tested ways of advising and enabling, adaptation to climate change in communities who are feeling the effects of climate changes due to global warming.

**1** To address the challenge of climate change, developing countries urgently require

(A) implementation of national adaptation policy at their level
(B) adoption of short-term plans
(C) adoption of technological solutions
(D) imposition of climate change tax

***Ans*** (*A*) To address the challenge of climate change, developing countries urgently require implementation of national adaptation policy at their level. It is very essential that these countries must increase their capacity to adjust and adopt to various changes at every level. It is imperative for the communities to adopt appropriate technology along with traditional knowledge and also be prepared to adopt diverse means of livelihood to cope with current and future climate stress.

**2** Given below are the factors of vulnerability of poor people to climate change.

1. Their dependence on natural resources.
2. Geographical attributes.
3. Lack of financial resources.
4. Lack of traditional knowledge.

Select the most appropriate answer from the following codes.

(A) 2, 3 and 4 (B) 1, 2, 3 and 4
(C) Only 3 (D) 1, 2 and 3

***Ans*** (*D*) The poor people or communities suffer the most due to climate change or climate variability. They do not have the financial resources to cope with any loss due to these variations or natural calamities. It is very important that these communities are helped to adapt to the changing patterns of nature.

**3** Adaptation as a process enables societies to cope with

1. an uncertain future.
2. adjustments and changes.
3. negative impact of climate change.
4. positive impact of climate change.

Select the most appropriate answer from the following codes.

(A) Both 1 and 3 (B) 2, 3 and 4
(C) Only 3 (D) 1, 2, 3 and 4

***Ans*** (*A*) The process of adaptation can help people to cope up with uncertainties and unfortunate circumstances related with any type of changes. If people are taught to change and adapt according to climate change, they will be able to survive and withstand the posses. So, learning adaptation is crucial for survival.

**4** The main focus of the passage is on

(A) co-ordination between regional and national efforts
(B) adaptation to climate change
(C) social dimensions of climate change
(D) combining traditional knowledge with appropriate technology

***Ans*** (*B*) The main focus of the passage is adaptation to climate change. The author talks about adaptation process through which a society or people can adopt effective measures to mitigate the negative effects occurring due to climate change. Adapt and adjust to changes are the keywords through which people can survive and combine their traditional knowledge with new innovative ways to face new climate extremes.

**5** The traditional knowledge should be used through

(A) improvement in national circumstances
(B) synergy between government and local interventions
(C) modern technology
(D) its dissemination

***Ans*** (*B*) The traditional knowledge of communities should be used through synergy between government and local interventions. The author is of the view that government agencies and local communities must co-operate with each other to find out means of coping with climatic changes and extreme weather. Local people keep evolving strategies to cope with natural calamities and their wisdom and knowledge can be useful for government agencies to plan and evolve new measures to fight problems related to climate changes.

## UGC-NET January 2017

## Comprehension 11

**Directions** (Q. Nos. 1-6) Read the following passage carefully and answer the questions that follow.

The last great war, which nearly shook the foundations of the modern world, had little impact on Indian literature beyond aggravating the popular **revulsion** against violence and adding to the growing disillusionment with the 'humane **pretensions'** of the Western World. This was eloquently voiced in Tagore's later poems and his last testament, 'Crisis in Civilisation'. The Indian intelligentsia was in a state of moral dilemma.

On the one hand, it could not help sympathising with England's dogged courage in the hour of peril, with the Russian fighting with their backs to the wall against the ruthless Nazi hordes, and with China groaning under the heel of Japanese militarism; on the other hand, their own country was practically under military occupation of their own soil and an Indian army under Subhas Bose was trying from the opposite camp to liberate their country.

No creative impulse could issue from such confusion of loyalties. One would imagine that the achievement of Indian Independence in 1947, which came in the wake of the Allies' victory and was followed by the collapse of colonialism in the neighbouring countries of South-East Asia, would have released an upsurge of creative energy.

No doubt it did, but unfortunately it was soon submerged in the great agony of partition, with its inhuman slaughter of the innocents and the uprooting of millions of people from their homeland, followed by the martyrdom of Mahatma Gandhi.

These tragedies, along with Pakistan's invasion of Kashmir and its later atrocities in Bangladesh, did indeed provoke a poignant writing, particularly in the languages of the regions most affected, Bengali, Hindi, Kashmiri, Punjabi, Sindhi and Urdu. But poignant or passionate writing does not by itself make great literature.

What reserves of enthusiasm and confidence survived these disasters have been mainly absorbed in the task of national reconstruction and economic development. Great literature has always emerged out of chains of **convulsions**. Indian literature is richer today in volume, range and variety than it ever was in the past.

**1** What was the impact of the last great war on Indian literature?

(A) It had no impact
(B) It aggravated popular revulsion against violence
(C) It shook the foundations of literature
(D) It offered eloquent support to the Western World

***Ans*** (*B*) The last great war of World War II had little effect on Indian literature as resentment of people against violence increased manifold. People were also disillusioned that Western countries were sympathetic towards humanity after bombing and killing of innocent people all around the world. People realised the hypocritic nature of Western political leaders.

**2** What did Tagore articulate in his last testament?

(A) Offered support to Subhas Bose
(B) Exposed the humane pretensions of the Western World
(C) Expressed loyalty to England
(D) Encouraged the liberation of countries

***Ans*** (*B*) Tagore, in his last testament 'Crisis in Civilisation' and in his later poem exposed the pretensions of the so called civilised England and other Western countries who were ruthless in their treatment to Indians while they themselves were experiencing the great wealth and luxury.

**3** What was the stance of Indian intelligentsia during the period of great war?

(A) Indifference to Russia's plight
(B) They favoured Japanese militarism
(C) They prompted creativity out of confused loyalties
(D) They expressed sympathy for England's dogged courage

***Ans*** (*D*) The Indian intelligentsia or the class of educated people were in a state of moral dilemma due to great World War. They had sympathy and admiration for the Britishers for their dauntless courage during the war but at the same time, this educated class was annoyed and frustrated with the Britishers over the way in which they were ruling over Indians and torturing people for their own self-interest.

**4** Identify the factor responsible for the submergence of creative energy in Indian literature.

(A) Military occupation of one's own soil
(B) Resistance to colonial occupation
(C) Great agony of partition
(D) Victory of Allies

***Ans*** (*C*) The creativity of Indians intelligentsia was lost in the wake of partition which had resulted in so much killing, displacement and agony of millions of Indians and finally assassination of Mahatma Gandhi. These factors were too disturbing for any creativity to flourish in any part of India.

**5** What was the aftermath that survived tragedies in Kashmir and Bangladesh?

(A) Suspicion of other countries
(B) Continuance of rivalry
(C) Menace of war
(D) National reconstruction

***Ans*** (*D*) The consequences or aftermaths after surviving tragedies in Kashmir and Bangladesh were national reconstruction and economical development. Main focus of everyone after these tragedies was rebuilding of our country and finding ways through planning for economic development and well being of people so that nation becomes self-sufficient and independent in real term.

**6** The passage has the message that

(A) disasters are inevitable
(B) great literature emerges out of chains of convulsions
(C) Indian literature does not have a marked landscape
(D) literature has no relation with war and independence

***Ans*** (*B*) It can be inferred from the passage that great literature blooms out of great political and violent social upheavals. This is true in case of Indian literature which has flourished after independence and partition of India. Indian literature today is enriched with great range, volume and variety of writing from different intellectuals and people from different parts of country.

## UGC-NET July 2016

## Comprehension 12

**Directions** (Q. Nos. 1-6) Read the following passage carefully and answer the questions that follow.

In terms of labour, for decades the relatively low cost and high quality of Japanese workers conferred considerable competitive advantages across numerous durable goods and consumer electronics industries (e.g. machinery, automobile, TV, radio). Then labour-based advantages shifted to South Korea, then to Malaysia, Mexico and other nations. Today, China appears to be capitalising best on the basis of labour. Japanese firms still remain competitive in markets for such durable goods, electronics and other products, but the labour force is no longer sufficient for competitive advantage over manufacturers in other industrialising nations.

Such shifting of labour-based advantage is clearly not limited to manufacturing industries. Today, a huge number of IT and service jobs are moving from Europe and North America to India, Singapore and like countries with relatively well-educated, low-cost workforces possessing technical skills.

However, as educational levels and technical skills continue to rise in other countries, India, Singapore and like nations enjoying labour-based competitive advantage today are likely to find such advantage cannot be sustained through emergence of new competitors.

In terms of capital, for centuries the days of gold coins and later even paper money restricted financial flows. Subsequently regional concentrations were formed where large banks, industries and markets coalesced. But today capital flows internationally at rapid speed. Global commerce no longer requires regional interactions among business players.

Regional capital concentrations in places such as New York, London and Tokyo still persist, of course, but the capital concentrated there is no longer sufficient for competitive advantage over other capitalists distributed worldwide. Only if an organisation is able to combine, integrate and apply its resources (e.g. land, labour capital, IT) in an effective manner i.e. not readily imitable by competitors can such an organisation enjoy competitive advantage sustainable overtime.

In a knowledge-based theory of the firm, this idea is extended to view organisational knowledge as a resource with atleast the same level of power and importance as the traditional economic inputs. An organisation with superior knowledge can achieve competitive advantage in markets that appreciate the application of such knowledge.

**1** Which country enjoyed competitive advantages in automobile industry for decades?

(A) South Korea (B) Japan
(C) Mexico (D) Malaysia

***Ans*** (*B*) Japan enjoyed competitive advantages in automobile industry for decades because of low cost and high quality of Japanese workers.

**2** Why labour-based competitive advantages of India and Singapore cannot be sustained in IT and service sectors?

(A) Due to diminishing levels of skill
(B) Due to capital-intensive technology making in roads
(C) Because of new competitors
(D) Because of shifting of labour-based advantage in manufacturing industries

***Ans*** (*C*) Labour-based competitive advantages of India and Singapore can't be sustained in IT and Service Sector because of new competitors. Now, a days a huge number of IT and Service Jobs are moving from Europe and North America to India and Singapore.

**3** How can an organisation enjoy competitive advantage sustainable overtime?

(A) Through regional capital flows
(B) Through regional interactions among business players
(C) By making large banks, industries and markets coalesced
(D) By effective use of various instrumentalities

***Ans*** (*C*) By making large banks, industries and market coalesced, an organisations enjoy competitive advantage sustainable overtime.

**4** What is required to ensure competitive advantages in specific markets?

1. Access to capital.
2. Common office buildings.
3. Superior knowledge.

Select the most appropriate answer from the following codes.

(A) Only 1 (B) Both 1 and 2
(C) Only 3 (D) All of these

***Ans*** (*C*) An organisation with superior knowledge is required to ensure competitive advantages in specific market.

**5** The passage also mentions about the trend of

(A) global financial flow
(B) absence of competition in manufacturing industry
(C) regionalisation of capitalists
(D) organisational incompatibility

***Ans*** (*C*) The given passage also mentions about the trend of regionalisation of capitalists.

## UGC-NET December 2015

# Comprehension 13

**Directions** (Q. Nos. 1-5) Read the following passage carefully and answer the questions that follow.

I did that thing recently where you have to sign a big card-which is a horror unto its especially as the keeper of the big card was leaning over me at the time. Suddenly I was on the spot, a rabbit in the headlights, torn between doing a fun message or some sort of in-joke or a drawing. Instead overwhelmed by the myriad options available to me, I decided to just write 'Good luck, best, Joel'. It was then that I realised, to my horror, that I had forgotten how to write. My entire existence is 'tap letters into computer'. My shopping lists are hidden in the notes function of my phone. If I need to remember something I send an e-mail to myself. A pen is something I chew when I am struggling to think. Paper is something I pile beneath my laptop to make it a more comfortable height for me to type on.

A poll of 1000 teens by the stationers, Bic found that one in 10 don't own a pen, a third have never written a letter, and half of 13 to 19 years-old have never been forced to sit down and write a thank you letter. More than 80% have never written a love letter, 56% don't have **letter paper** at home and a quarter have never known the unique torture of writing a birthday card. The most a teen ever has to use a pen is on an exam paper.

Bic, have you heard of mobile phones? Have you heard of e-mail, facebook and snap chatting? This is the future. Pens are dead. Paper is dead. Handwriting is a **relic**. "Handwriting is one of the most creative outlets we have and should be given the same importance as other art forms such as sketching, painting or photography."

1 According to the author, which one is not the most creative outlet of pursuit?

(A) Reading (B) Handwriting
(C) Photography (D) Sketching

*Ans* (*A*) As per the passage, handwriting is one of the most creative outlets we have and should be given the same importance as sketching, painting and photography.

So, 'Reading' is not the most creative outlet of pursuit.

2 When confronted with signing a big card, the author felt like 'a rabbit in the headlight'. What does this phrase mean?

(A) A state of pain
(B) A state of confusion
(C) A state of pleasure
(D) A state of anxiety

*Ans* (*B*) The author was torn between doing a fun message or some sort of in joke or a drawing, when he was confronted with signing a big card. So, the phrase 'a rabbit in the headlight' means that the author was in a state of confusion.

3 How many teens, as per the Bic survey do not own a pen?

(A) 100 (B) 800
(C) 560 (D) 500

*Ans* (*A*) As per the Bic Survey, 100 out of 1000 teens do not own a pen.

4 The entire existence of the author revolves round

1. computer.
2. mobile phone.
3. typewriter.

Select the correct answer using the codes given below.

(A) Both 2 and 3 (B) Only 2
(C) Both 1 and 2 (D) All of these

*Ans* (*C*) According to the passage, the entire existence of the author revolves round computer and mobile phone.

5 What is the main concern of the author?

(A) That the teens have forgotten the art of handwriting
(B) That the teens use social networks for communication
(C) That the teens use mobile phones
(D) That the teens use computer

*Ans* (*A*) The main concern of the author is that the teens have forgotten the art of handwriting. They are busy using their mobile phones and computers.

## UGC-NET June 2015

# Comprehension 14

**Directions** (Q. Nos. 1-6) Read the following passage carefully and answer the questions that follow.

Storytelling is not in our genes. Neither it is an evolutionary history. It is the essence of what makes us human. Human beings progress by telling stories. One event can result in a great variety of stories being told about it. Sometimes, those stories differ greatly. Which stories are picked up and repeated and which ones are dropped and forgotten often determines, how we progress. Our history, knowledge and understanding are all the collections of the few stories that survive.

This includes the stories that we tell each other about the future. And how the future will turn out depends partly, possibly largely, on which stories we collectively choose to believe. Some stories are designed to spread fear and concern. This is because some storytellers feel that there is a need to raise some tensions. Some stories are frightening, they are like totemic warnings. 'Fail to act now and we are all doomed. Then, there are stories that indicate that all will be fine so long as we leave everything upto a few especially able adults. Currently, this trend is being led by those who call themselves 'rational optimists'.

They tend to claim that it is human nature to compete and to succeed and also to profit at the expense of others. The rational optimists however, do not realise, how humanity has progressed overtime through amiable social networks and how large groups work in less selfishness and in the process accommodate rich and poor, high and low alike. This aspect in storytelling is considered by the 'Practical Possibles', who sit between those who say all is fine and cheerful and be individualistic in your approach to a successful future and those who **ordain** pessimism and fear that we are doomed.

What the future holds for us is, which stories we hold on to and how we act on them?

1 Our knowledge is a collection of

(A) all stories that we have heard during our life-time
(B) some stories that we remember
(C) a few stories that survive
(D) some important stories

***Ans*** (*C*) As per the passage, our history, knowledge and understanding is a collection of the few stories that survive.

**2** Storytelling is

(A) an art
(B) a science
(C) in our genes
(D) the essence of what makes us human

***Ans*** (*D*) Storytelling is not in our genes and neither it is an evolutionary history. It is the essence of what makes us human.

**3** How the future will turn out to be, depends upon the stories?

(A) We collectively choose to believe in
(B) Which are repeatedly narrated
(C) Designed to spread fear and tension
(D) Designed to make prophecy

***Ans*** (*A*) According to the given passage, how the future will turn out to be depends largely on which stories we collectively choose to believe in.

**4** Rational optimists

1. look for opportunities.
2. are sensible and cheerful.
3. are selfishly driven

Select the most appropriate answer from the following codes.

(A) Both 1, 2 and 3 (B) Only 1
(C) Both 1 and 2 (D) Both 2 and 3

***Ans*** (*A*) Rational optimists are selfishly driven. They look for opportunities and are sensible and cheerful.

**5** Humans become less selfish when

(A) they work in large groups
(B) they listen to frightening stories
(C) they listen to cheerful stories
(D) they work in solitude

***Ans*** (*A*) Humans become less selfish when they work in large groups and in the process accommodate rich and poor, high and low alike.

**6** 'Practical Possibles' are the ones who

1. follow midway path.
2. are doom-mongers.
3. are self-centred.

Select the most appropriate answer from the following codes.

(A) Both 2 and 3
(B) Only 1
(C) Only 2
(D) All of the above

***Ans*** (*B*) 'Practical Possibles' are the ones who follow the midway path. They are the ones who sit between those who say all is fine and cheerful and are individualistic in their approach and those who ordain pessimism and fear that we are doomed.

# UNIT 04

# Communication

## CHAPTER ANALYSIS

This unit is based on the updated syllabus of NTA UGC Net covering all the important topics related to communication. After going through the chapter thoroughly you will be able to understand the meaning, types and characteristics of communication, effective communication and types of effective communication (verbal, non-verbal, inter-cultural, group and classroom communication), models, barriers and mass-media & society.

Every year 4 to 5 questions are asked from this unit in NTA UGC Net exam. Questions asked in exam from this unit are based on types and characteristics of communication, classroom communication, effective communication and verbal & non-verbal communication etc.

## COMMUNICATION

The word 'communication' is derived from the Latin word 'communicare' and 'communis' which means 'to share'. The dictionary meaning of communication is to exchange information and feelings through words, expressions and writing. It means sharing of ideas and flowing of messages. Even, someone's gestures visible to eyes or sounds audible in ears can be called communication.

The communication process takes place when a sender sends message through a medium (such as sound, gesture, oral tone, speaking, writing, etc.) and the receiver responds to it by sending appropriate feedback.

Communication is the most integral part of human nature. Human beings need to communicate to deal with various situations of daily lives. They do so, by verbal communication such as speaking, writing and non-verbal communication such as facial expressions, body language, tone, etc. So, communication is a social process and comprises of countless ways in which persons keep in touch with each other.

### Definitions of Communication

According to **Keith Davis,** "Communication is the process of passing information and understanding from one person to another."

According to **Carl Howland,** "Communication is the process by which an individual transmits stimuli to modify the behaviour of the other individuals."

According to **Millet,** "The underlying aim of communication is the meeting of minds on common issue".

**IN THIS UNIT**


- Communication : Meaning, Types and Characteristics of Communication
- Effective Communication : Verbal and Non-verbal, Inter-cultural, Group and Classroom Communication
- Barriers to Effective Communication
- Mass Media and Society

According to **Oxford Dictionary,** "Communication is transferring or conveying of meaning."

According to **Berlo,** "Communication as **S-R Model** or **Sender-Receiver Model**, where 'sender' stands for 'stimulus' and 'receiver' stands for 'response'. This was later extended to S-M-C-R Model that stands for Sender-Message-Channel-Receiver.

It is the basic communication process. Thus, the above definitions make it clear that "the essence of communication is understanding the information, not transmitting the information."

## Characteristics of Communication

1. **Two Way Process** Communication is essentially a two way process. It does not merely means sending and receiving messages. It is not complete unless and until the message has been understood by the receiver in the same sense.

   For example, in a classroom, the teacher conveys information to a group of students.
2. **Knowledge of Language** To make the communication successful, the receiver should first of all understand the sender's message. For this, the sender must speak in a language that is known to the receiver. For example, if the receiver cannot understand English and the sender conveys his ideas in English then the communication will be a failure.
3. **Exchange of Ideas** Communication helps to exchange information or ideas between the sender and receiver. In order to complete the process of communication, there must be an exchange of ideas, orders, feelings, etc., among two or more than two persons.
4. **Continuous Process** Communication is an endless process, we cannot freeze it at any moment. So, it is a dynamic process of action. It also interacts towards a desired goal. For example, manager or any officer continuously assigns work to his subordinates. At the same time, he also tries to know the progress of the work as well as gives directions to achieve the desired goal.
5. **The Message should be Complete** The message must contain all facts needed for desired reaction. It must be clear, concise, correct and complete. It must be presented keeping the emotions and sentiments of the receiver.

## Elements of Communication

1. **The Sender** The communication process begins with the sender,who is also called the communicator or source. The sender has some kind of information – a command, request, question, or idea– that he or she wants to present to others.

   For that message to be received, the sender must first encode the message in a form that can be understood, such as by the use of a common language and then transmit it.
2. **The Receiver** The person to whom a message is directed is called the receiver or the interpreter. To comprehend the information from the sender, the receiver must first be able to receive the sender's information and then decode or interpret it.
3. **The Message** The message or content is the information that the sender wants to relay to the receiver. Additional sub-text can be conveyed through body language and tone of voice. Put all three elements together – sender, receiver, and message – and you have the communication process at its most basic.
4. **The Medium** It is also called the channel; the medium is the means by which a message is transmitted. Text messages, for example, are trnasmitted through the medium of cell phones.
5. **Feedback** The communication process reaches its final point when the message has been successfully transmitted, received and understood. The receiver, in turn, responds to the sender, indicating comprehension. Feedback may be direct, such as a written or verbal response, or it may take the form of an act or deed in response (indirect).

6. **Noise** This can be any sort of interference that affects the message being sent, received or understood. It can be as literal as static over a phone line or radio.
7. **Barriers** Barriers to the communication process can occur in the form of physical, psychological, mechanical and linguistics.
   (a) **Physical Barriers** The 'physical barriers' to the communication process includes environmental stress (A high temperature and humidity can contribute to distortions in the sending and receiving of messages), ignorance of the medium (The use of a medium with which the communicators are not familiar would turn the medium itself into a barrier), etc.
   (b) **Psychological Barriers** Each of us has a certain 'frame of reference' through which we look out at the world, at people, and events and situations. No two individuals possess exactly similar frames of reference, even if they are identical twins. So, this is another form of barrier in the communication process.
   (c) **Mechanical Barriers** Mechanical barriers are those raised by the channels employed for interpersonal, group or mass communication. This type of barrier includes any disturbance, which interferes with the fidelity of the physical transmission of the message.
   (d) **Linguistics and Cultural Barriers** Language is the expression of the thoughts and experiences of people in terms of their cultural environment. When the same language is made use of in a different culture, it takes an another colour, another meaning.

## Objectives of Communication

1. **Convey Information** The main objective of communication is to convey information to the receiver. The information that is conveyed can be rotated to news, policies, procedures, decisions, etc.
2. **Give Command** Communication is used to give commands to the receiver. The receiver of the command can be a junior, student or a member of the family.
3. **Make Decisions** Communication helps in making decisions. The relationship of communication and decision making is unseparable since decisioning must rely on information.
4. **Motivation** Communication is used for motivating people. Motivation is necessary to bring out the best in people and communication plays a big role in it.
5. **Coordination** Coordination is a basic management function. It involves linking the various functional departments of an organization without proper and timely coordination, achievement of organizational goals is not possible.

   Therefore, the objective of communication is to coordinate the functions of various departments for the attainment of organizational goals.

## Importance of Communication

The importance of communication has been divided into four parts. These are as under :

1. **In Personal Terms**
   - It provides subject-matter for knowledge.
   - It provides the way to achieve success.
   - It determines the personality of a person.
   - It helps in making a person social.
2. **In Social Terms**
   - It helps in bringing change in the society.
   - It makes the people in a society literate and employed.
   - It helps in dealing with contingencies.
3. **In Psychological Terms**
   - It provides a good environment for an individual to develop.
   - It increases the morale of a group.
   - It inspires people in an organization to work effectively.
   - It gives encouragement for establishing coordination.

4. **In Physical Terms**
   - It provides a platform for people to communicate with each other.
   - It provides tools for business control.

# TYPES OF COMMUNICATION

Communication involves a sender and a receiver of message to perform a function. The message is shared between two persons, where, either one reacts to the message or one does not react. It can be said that communication is social and cultural togetherness.

Therefore, types of communication are divided on the basis of following aspects:

## On the Basis of Relationship

On the basis of relationship, types of communication can be divided into the following

### 1. Interpersonal Communication

It is the process by which people exchange information, feelings and meanings with others. It is a face-to-face communication.

It is not just about what is actually said but how it is said. It is an ideal and effective communication, as one can get an immediate feedback. In this communication, ethics are important. It may be formal or informal and can take place anywhere by means of words, sounds, facial expressions, gestures and postures.

This type of communication depends on the mutual relationship between two partners in their status, communication, role and skills.

### 2. Intrapersonal Communication

It takes place within the individual. It is meant to reflect oneself to clarify one's thoughts. It is self-oriented to know what is true or false, good or bad, etc.

It might be descriptive or prescriptive. It is a learned idea of an individual. It is generally consistent with values, so that it is often emotional. Talking to oneself, relating to oneself, meditation, playing are all examples of intrapersonal communication.

### 3. Group Communication

Group communication is the exchange of information and ideas between individuals using interpersonal skills. In group communication, team members have to effectively participate to make the communication effective.

### 4. Mass or Mediated Communication

Communication with mass audience is called as mass communication. It is used as synonyms for convenience. The channel through which communication takes place is called mass media.

Any mechanical device that multiplies messages and takes it to a large number of people simultaneously is the example of mass communication. It is a special kind of communication in which the nature of the audience is considered.

Its feedback is different from that of interpersonal communication. Radio, TV, newspapers, films, magazines, etc. are the examples of mass communication.

## On the Basis of Purpose and Style

On the basis of purpose and style, communication can be divided in two forms. They are

### 1. Formal Communication

A formal communication is deliberately established by upper level of management for day-to-day transmission of official information.

Certain rules, protocols and regulations are followed in formal communication such as choice of words, correct use of language, proper pronunciation, etc. It follows a definite structure and hierarchy and mostly takes place in organisations. There are six networks of formal communication. They are :

(i) **Chain Network** In this communication, the information and message flow only up or down in hierarchical chain of command.

Chain Network

(ii) **Star Network** Under this communication, the information and message flow among the group members through a leader. In other words, the group members do not communicate with each other directly but rely on the leader.

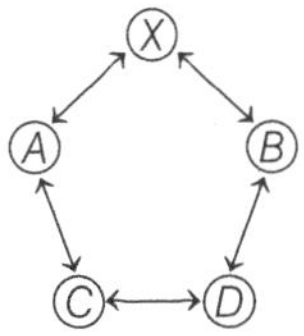


Star Network

(iii) **Circle Network** In this communication, the group members interact with the adjoining member only.

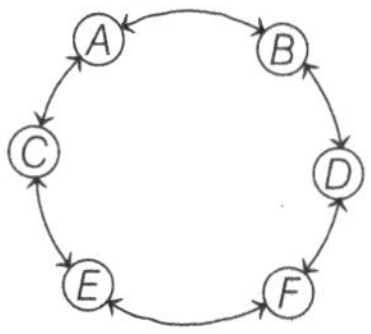


Circle Network

(iv) **All Channel Network** Under this communication, all members of a group actively communicate with each other freely. It is the most decentralised type of formal communication.

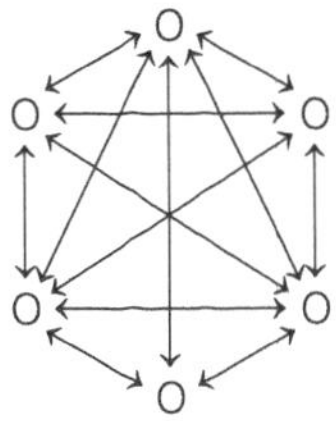

All Channel Network

(v) **Inverted-V Network**
Under this communication, a subordinate communicates with his immediate superior as well as second superior.

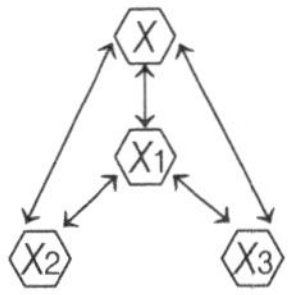


Inverted-V Network

(vi) **Y-Network** Under this communication, two subordinates through the hierarchical chain, communicate with the superior. In turn, the superior communicates with two superiors who are senior to him.

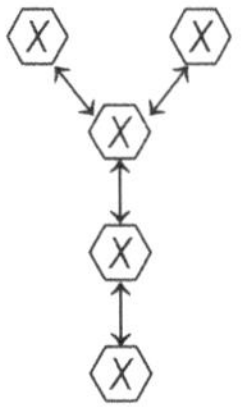


Y-Network

## Advantages

1. **Smooth Communication System** Formal communication moves through pre-determined channel and therefore, everyone is aware for where and how to send the message. So, it does not face any problem to flow.
2. **Increase in Efficiency**
Such communication increases overall efficiency of the management as organizational rules and procedures are required to be followed always.
3. **Permanent Record**
All formal communications like letters, reports and memos are kept permanently. So, it is helpful in future decision-making.
4. **Discipline** This communication creates the discipline in the mind of employees in any organization.
5. **Less Errors and Mistakes** It maintains all formalities of communication for which there is less chance of errors and mistakes.

## Disadvantages

1. **Authoritarian System** Formal communication states clear relationship between upper level management and lower level management. When there is a downward communication, there is an authoritarian tone to dominate lower level employees.
2. **Inflexibility** It is a rigid form of communication as make up or change cannot be considered easily when required.

3. **Costly** This sort of communication maintains all formalities of communication for which it involves more cost.
4. **Wastage of Time** Formal communication process passes through various stages or levels of an organization and therefore, requires more time to reach to its destination. This is ultimately the wastage of time.
5. **Delay in Decision-Making** Everyone has to maintain specific framework of communication in case of formal communication. Therefore, management requires more time which delays decision-making process.

## 2. Informal Communication

Informal communication is an unofficial communication taking place among employees of an organisation or between friends and family members. It do not follow any rules or regulations and mainly addresses the social needs of the people. It is inter-personal and face-to-face communication.

It takes place along with formal communication within an organisation such as unstructured conversation between an employee and his superior. Informal communication is also called grapevine communication as messages and information spread rapidly here.

**Keith Davis** has investigated the phenomena of **Grapevine**.

There are four types of Grapevine networks

(i) **Single Strand Network**
Under this communication, the information passes from one to one, that is one member communicates to another member who in turn communicates to another member and so on.

Single Strand Network

2. **Gossip Network**
Under this communication, the member communicates non-selectively, i.e. a member having information passes it on to everyone he meets.

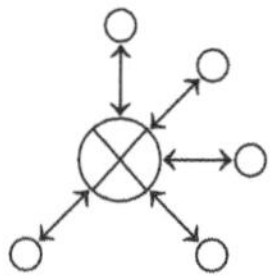

Gossip Network

3. **Probability Network**
Under this communication, information passes according to the law of probability, i.e. one member communicates randomly with others who in turn communicate to some others.

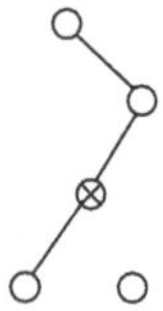

Probability Network

4. **Cluster Network**
Under this communication, the information passes selectively, i.e. one member communicates with only those members whom he trusts. In turn, they pass it on to some other selected members.
It is the most popular type of grapevine communication and widely prevalent in an organisation.

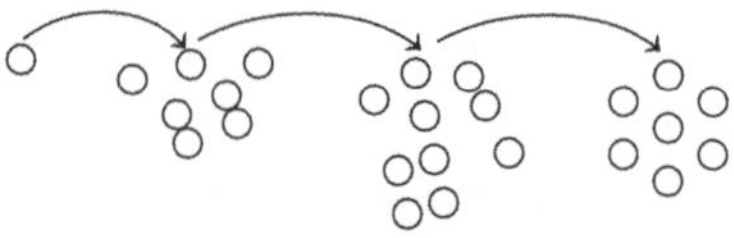

Cluster Network

## On the Basis of Direction

Communication flows through the networks in an organisation which may be of three types i.e. vertical, horizontal and diagonal.

### 1. Vertical Communication

This is basically a formal communication, where communication is most dominated. This follows the hierarchical chain of command. The vertical direction of communication can be upward (bottom-up) and downward (top-down).

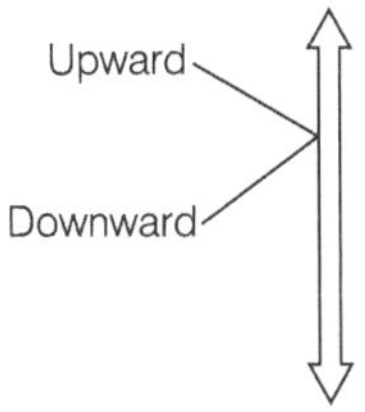


Vertical Communication

## 2. Horizontal or Lateral Communication

It is the communication where people can communicate with their colleagues and peers at same level in hierarchical chain of command. It is necessary for smooth coordination. It may combine both formal and informal communication. It is beneficial when organisations are very large. This leads to a successful interactive interpersonal communication.

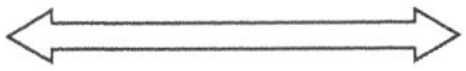

Horizontal Communication

## 3. Diagonal Communication

It is a free flow of communication, hence no barrier of hierarchy. It encourages the bonding between superior and subordinate as well as among the colleagues.

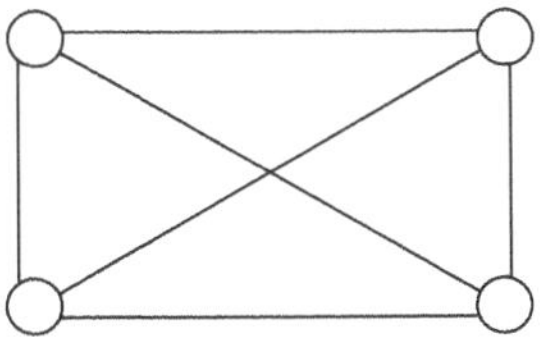

Diagonal Communication

# MODELS OF COMMUNICATION

Models of communication are conceptual models used to explain the human communication process. Models of communication simplify the process by providing a visual representation of the various aspects of a communication encounter. Basically, there are eight important models of communication. These are as follows

## 1. Transactional Model of Communication

Transactional Model of Communication is the exchange of messages between sender and receiver where each take turns to send or receive messages. Both sender and receiver are known as communicators.

In this model their role reverses each time in the communication process as both processes of sending and receiving occur at the same time.

The model is mostly used for interpersonal communication and is also called **Circular Model of Communication**. For example, transactional communication is not possible if the receiver is not listening to the sender.

The Transactional Model is the most general model of communication. Everyday talk and interactions are also a form of Transactional Model of Communication.

It is more efficient for communicators with similar environment and individual aspects. For instance, communication between people who know each other is more efficient as they share same social system.

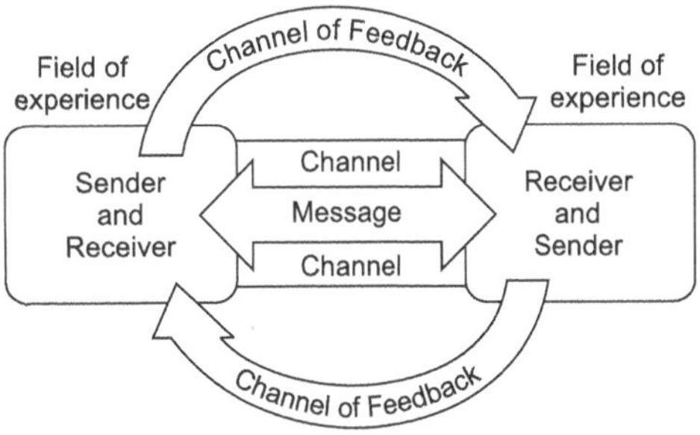


Transactional Model of Communication

## 2. Linear Model of Communication

Linear Model of Communication is considered as one way process where sender is the only one who sends message and receiver doesn't give feedback or response. The message signal is encoded and transmitted through channel in the presence of noise.

The sender is more prominent in Linear Model of Communication.

The Linear Model was founded by **Aristotle**, **Shannon** and **Weaver**, which was later adopted by **David Berlo** into his own model known as SMCR (Source, Message, Channel, Receiver) Model of Communication.

This model is also known as Transmission Model of Communication. Linear Model is applied in mass communication like TV, radio, etc. This model is not applicable in general human communication as general human communication has to have feedback and responses.

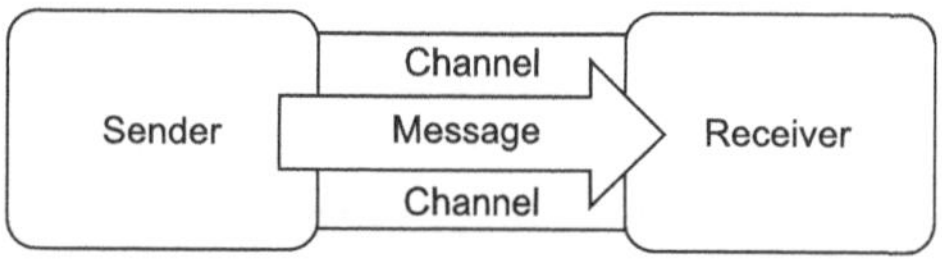


Linear Model of Communication

## 3. Interactional Model of Communication

The Interactional Model of Communication describes communication as a process in which participants alternate positions as sender and receiver and generate meaning by sending messages and receiving feedback within physical and psychological contexts.

Rather than illustrating communication as a linear, one-way process, the Interaction Model incorporates feedback, which makes communication a more interactive, two-way process. For example, a teacher may respond to a point which is raised during the class discussion by students or someone may point to the sofa when his/her roommate asks, where the remote control is?

**Wilbur Schramm** supported the Interactional Model of Communication. This model has two sender-receiver who exchange messages. Each participant alternates roles as sender and receiver in order to keep a communication encounter going. Although, this seems like a perceptible and deliberate process, we alternate between the roles of sender and receiver very quickly and often without conscious thought.

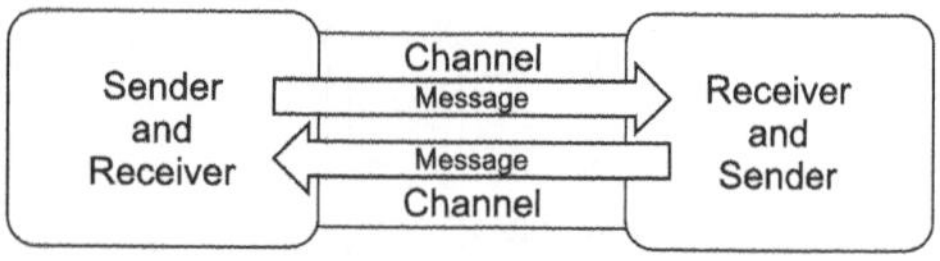


Interactional Model of Communication

## 4. Shannon-Weaver Model of Communication

The first major model for communication came in 1949 by **Claude Shannon** and **Warren Weaver Bell**, Laboratories. It laid the foundation for different communication models. It is a popular model and widely accepted. It provided visual mode of communication system in relation to electronic media popularly known as Mathematical Model of Communication.

The Shannon and Weaver Model represents the communication process in a linear form. It involves one- way communication from a sender transmitting message to a receiver.

The model contains basic elements as shown below.

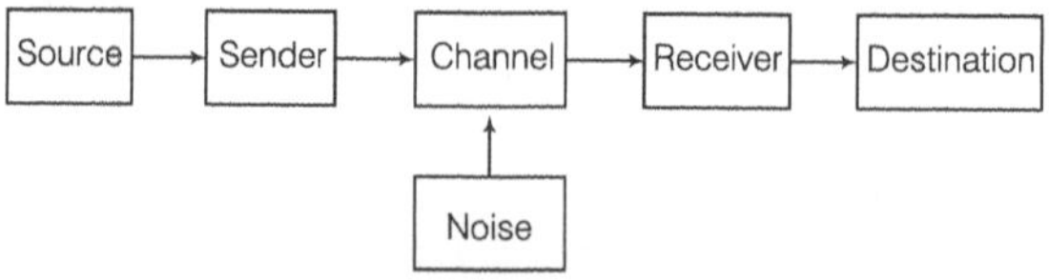


Shannon-Weaver's Model of Communication

Shannon and Weaver talked about the three levels of problems in the communication of information. The three levels are–technical (signal), semantic (interpretation of meaning) and influence (effectiveness).

It is best known for its ability to explain how messages can be mixed up and misinterpreted in the process between sending and receiving the message. The model explains the barriers to effective communication very well.

The model enables one to look at the critical steps in the communication of information from beginning to end. It can be applied more for interpersonal communication than group communication and mass communication.

Receiver plays the passive part in the communication process and sender plays the primary role. Feedback is taken as less important in comparison to messages sent by the sender.

## 5. Lasswell's Model of Communication

It was developed by communication theorist **Harold D Lasswell** in 1948. The model is also known as Action Model, Linear Model or One Way Model of Communication. It is regarded as one of the most influential communication models. This model is about the process of communication and its functions to society.

According to Lasswell, there are three functions for communication :

(a) Survillance of environment.

(b) Correlation of the components of society.

(c) Cultural transmission between generation.

The components of Lasswell's Model are :

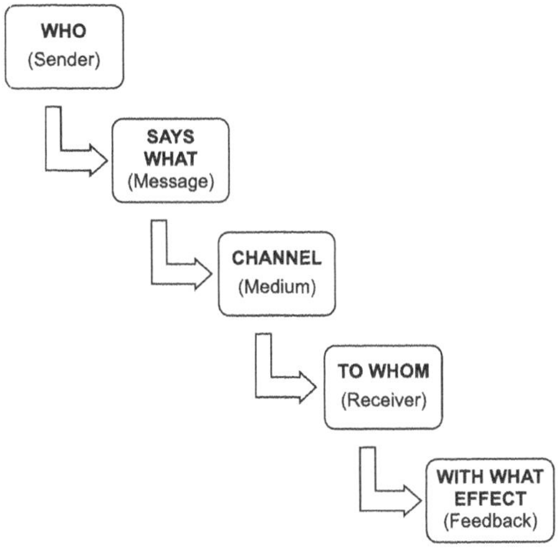


## 6. David Berlo's Model of Communication

In this model, he stressed on the relationship between the person sending the message and the receiver. According to this model, for the message to be properly encoded and decoded, the communication skills of both the source and the receiver should be good.

Berlo SMCR (Sender, Message, Channel Receiver) has four main components and each has its own sub-components.

Sender → Message → Channel → Receiver

It is a linear model of communication, where there is no two-way communication. There is no concept of feedback. There is no noise as well as no concept of barriers in communication.

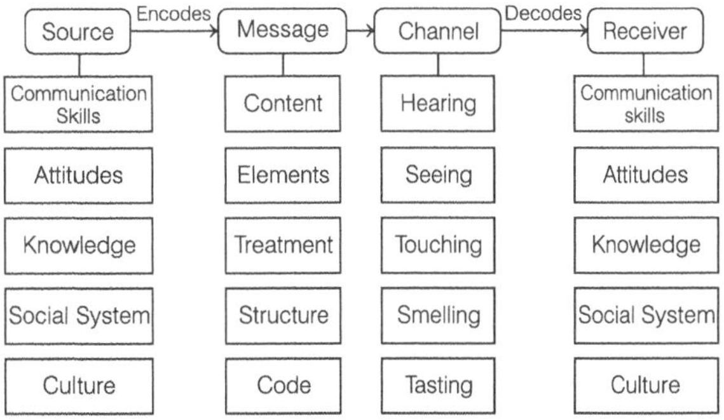


**Berlos's SMCR Model of Communication**

## 7. Aristotle Model of Communication

**Aristotle**, a great philosopher was the first to develop a communication model. This model is more focussed on public speaking than interpersonal communication. Aristotle Model of Communication is formed with three basic elements i.e. speaker, speech and audience.

In this model of communication, the sender sends the message to the receiver in an attempt to influence them to respond accordingly. The message has to be very impressive and convincing. So the sender must know and understand their audience well.

In this model, the sender is an active participant and receiver is passive. This concept is used in public speaking, seminars and lectures.

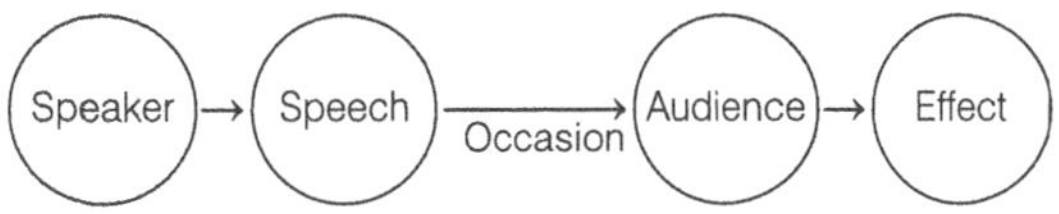


**Aristole's Model of Communication**

## 8. Helical Spiral Model

It was developed by **Frank Dance** in 1967. Helix is a three dimensional spring like curve in the shape of cyclinder or a cone.

The model is linear as well as circular combined and disagrees with the concept of linearly and circularity, individually.

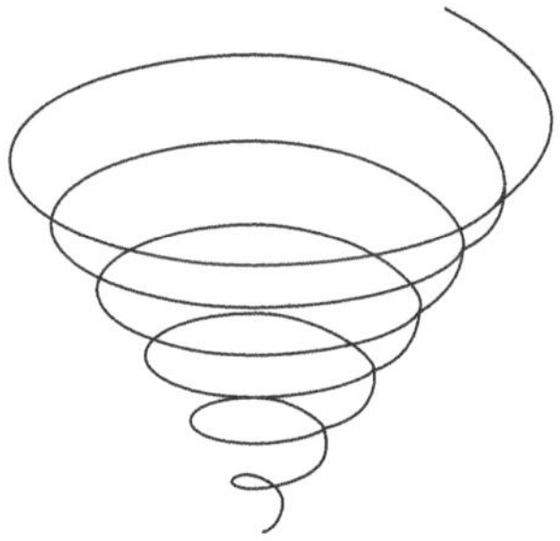

Helical Spiral Model of Communication

# Process of Communication

The process of communication consists of three steps that are discussed below :

- **Encoding** Encoding is the process of turning thoughts into communication. The encoder is the person who develops and sends the message. He/she must determine how the message will be received, the make adjustments so the message is received the way they want it to be received.
- **Medium** The encoder uses a 'medium' or channel to send the message– a phone call, email, text message, face-to-face meeting, or other communication tool. While the message is travelling through a channel, there is a scope of a noise that might interfere with the message.
- **Decoding** Decoding is the process of turning communication into thoughts. Once, the receiver receives the message he/she then decodes or interprets the message for themselves. After understanding the message, he/she sends a feedback starting a continuous chain of communication.

**Claude Shannon** and **Warren Weaver** developed the most widely used model of communication process. This model consists of eight components. They are

1. **Source** The source is the initiator of communication, who wants to transmit his ideas, thoughts, needs, intentions or other pieces of information to another person.
2. **Encoding** It is a process in which the ideas to be conveyed, are translated into a code or set of symbols or some other format of expression.
3. **Message** It is the actual physical product from the source-encoding. It represents the meaning which the source wants to convey.
4. **Channel** It is the medium through which the message transmits. It is the connecting link between the sender and the receiver.
5. **Decoding** It is the process which translates the message into a form that can be understood by the receiver.
6. **Receiver** It is the person to whom the message is directed (conveyed).
7. **Feedback** It is the response from the receiver which enables the sender (source) to determine whether the message is received and understood as originally intended.
8. **Noise** It includes those factors in each of the components of communication that reduces the accuracy of the message. Thus, it can occur at any stage of the communication process.

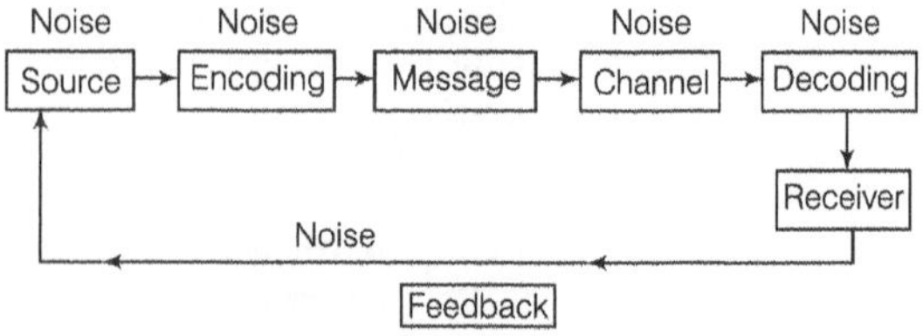


Process of Communication

# EFFECTIVE COMMUNICATION

Effective communication is defined as "The ability to convey information to another effectively and efficiently." It takes place when both the sender and receiver derive a common meaning from a message. There must be a mutual understanding and a common language between the sender and the receiver for the transmission of ideas or information. Listening is an important part of communication. Therefore, the receiver of information should be a good listener just as the sender should be a good communicator.

## Characteristics of Effective Communication

1. **Clarity of Purpose** The message to be delivered must be clear in the mind of sender. The person to whom it is targeted and the aim of the message should be clear.
2. **Completeness** The message delivered should be complete. It should be supported by facts and observations. It should be well planned and organised. No assumptions should be made by the receiver.
3. **Conciseness** The message should be concise. It should not include any un-necessary details. It should be short and complete.
4. **Feedback** Whether the message sent by the sender is understood in same terms by the receiver or not can be judged by the feedback received. The feedback should be timely and personal. It should be specific rather than general.
5. **Empathy** Empathy with the listeners is essential for effective verbal communication. The speaker should step into the shoes of the listener and be sensitive to their needs and emotions. This way he can understand things from their perspective and make communication more effective.
6. **Modify the Message According to the Audience** The information required by different people in the organisation differs according to their needs. What is relevant to the middle level management.

   Use of jargons (special words or expressions) should be minimised because it might lead to misunderstanding and misinterpretations. The message should be modified according to the needs and requirements of the targeted audience.

# TYPES OF EFFECTIVE COMMUNICATION

The types of effective communication are given below

1. Verbal Communication
2. Non-verbal Communication
3. Intercultural Communication
4. Group Communication
5. Classroom Communication

## 1. Verbal Communication

It refers to the form of communication in which message is transmitted, verbally i.e. by the use of sounds and words. Use of language in both spoken and written form is part of verbal communication.

In this type of communication, one has to remember the acronym KISS (Keep It Short and Simple). Verbal communication is further divided into two categories. These are **Oral** and **Written** communication.

### (i) Oral Communication

It includes face-to-face conversation, speech, telephonic conversation, video, TV, radio, internet, etc. Spoken words are also used in oral communication.

Oral communication is influenced by pitch, volume, speed and clarity of speaking. They all are termed as para language.

#### Factors Affecting Oral Communication

(a) **Pitch** It is a degree of highness or lowness of tone which depends on frequency of sound wave. It is an important device or element in teaching-learning process.

(b) **Volume** It depends on the number of people and proximity. It is measured in decibel.

(c) **Speed** While delivering the word, one should maintain the speed because a rhythmic voice makes sound more clear. Irregular speech may show a sign of uncertainty.

(d) **Clarity of Speaking** Proper pronunciation and smooth delivery of words make a message very effective.

### Advantages

- It brings quick feedback.
- It is voluntary and natural, easy for others to understand.
- It establishes a close relationship between speaker and listener.
- It also supports non-verbal communication.
- By reading facial expression and body language, one can guess whether one should trust, what is being said or not.

### Disadvantages

- The delivered words are temporary.
- What is heard is often forgotten.
- User is unable to think about what he is delivering.

### (ii) Written Communication

The communication which is performed through any written document is called written communication. Written language, signs, symbols are used to communicate in this communication.

Message can be trasmitted, via e-mail, letter, report, memo, etc. Therefore, written communication is the process of communication in which messages or information is exchanged or communicated within sender and receiver through written form.

Vocabulary, grammar, writing style, precision, clarity of the language, etc., influence messages, which are sent by the sender.

Written communication is the most common form of communication in business firms. Thus, it is considered as core, among the business skills.

### Advantages

- Message can be revised and edited many times before being sent, thus there is less chance of error.
- It provides record for every message sent and can be saved for later study.
- A written message enables receiver to fully understand it.
- Written message sends appropriate feedback.

### Disadvantages

- It does not bring instant feedback.
- It takes more time in composing a written message.
- Not everyone is good at writing.

**→ Mnemonic**

In general, a 'mnemonic' is a memory aid such as an abbreviation, rhyme or mental image that helps to remember something. Mnemonics can be used to remember phone numbers, names or the years of the reigns of the kings and queens, etc.

For example, to memorise the North American Great Lakes; the acronym 'HOMES' (Huron, Ontario, Michigan, Erie and Superior) which matches the letters of the five lakes is used. 'Knuckle' Mnemonic is used for the number of days in each month of Gregorian Calendar. Each Knuckle represents a 31 day month which is one of the examples of mnemonic.

## 2. Non-Verbal Communication

The non-verbal communications are those communications where the sending or receiving of messages is done through the wordless messages. It means that communication is established other than oral and written. It is all about the body language of the speaker and does not make use of words.

There are three distinct areas involved in this type of communication. They are:

(a) **Audio Sign** They play a very crucial role in non-verbal communication. Audio signs communicate the intended emotions in the form of sounds that are different for varying emotions.

For example, bell in a school, fire alarms, drumbeats, work shift alarms in factories and so on.

(b) **Body Language** It is that aspect of non-verbal communication which speaks without use of words. Each part of human body responds to different situation in a varied manner. It includes all actions i.e. physical or physiological postures, facial expressions, gestures and other body movements.

Our body movement includes our head, eyes, shoulders, lips, eyebrows, legs, arms and hands. All these can convey if we are uncomfortable, friendly, anxious or nervous.

(c) **Visual Sign** It is the act of using photographs, art, drawings, sketches, charts and graphs to convey information. For example, signed light (Red, Green and Blue).

### Advantages

- Information can be easily presented in non-verbal communication.
- This type of communication helps illiterate people to communicate with others by using gestures, facial expressions, eye contact, proximity, touching, etc.
- The message of non-verbal communication reach the receiver very fast. Thus, it reduces the time of both communicator and receiver.
- In this communication, people can repeat the verbal messages according to their need. For example, point in a direction while stating directions.

### Disadvantages

- Non-verbal communication is quite vague and imprecise.
- In this type of communication, long conversation and necessary explanations are not possible.
- As gestures and facial expressions are used in this communication, so it is difficult to understand quickly and requires a lot of repetitions to clarify the meaning of something.
- Non-verbal communication does not follow any rules, formality or structure like other communication.
- In non-verbal communication, there is a great possibility in distortion of information.

**→ Terms Related to Non-verbal Communication**

**Haptics** refers to touch behaviors that convey meaning during interactions. Touch operates at many levels, including functional-professional, social-polite, friendship-warmth, and love-intimacy.

**Vocalics** refers to the vocalized but not verbal aspects of non-verbal communication, including our speaking rate, pitch, volume, tone of voice and vocal quality. These qualities, also known as para language, reinforce the meaning of verbal communication, allow us to emphasize particular parts of a message, or can contradict verbal messages.

**Proxemics** refers to the use of space and distance within communication. Proxemics also studies territoriality, or how people take up defend personal space.

**Chronemics** refers the study of how time affects communication and includes how different time cycles affect our communication, including the differences between people who are past or future oriented and cultural perspectives on time as fixed and measured (monochronic) or fluid and adaptable (polychronic).

## 3. Intercultural Communication

This communication takes place between people of different cultures. Basically, 'inter' is a prefix that means 'between' and 'cultural' means 'from a culture'.

In this communication, we study about the communication across different cultures and social groups or how culture affects communication. Each culture has its own beliefs, values, rituals and morals which gets reflected in the people of that culture.

So, in inter-cultural communication, cultural values get shared when people of different cultures interact with each other. However, absence of a common language can be a barrier in this type of communication.

This type of communication plays a great role in understanding various disciplines of Social Sciences such as cultural studies, anthropology, linguistics, psychology and communication studies.

Intercultural communication is considered as the base for international businesses. This development of communication helps several cross-cultural service providers.

### Advantages

- It is important to establish and maintain positive intergroup relations.
- It can increase cultural knowledge and awareness, communication skills and tolerance.

### Disadvantages

- Sometimes, foreign students experience feelings of uncertainty and anxiety about how to integrate into their host society.
- It also creates incompatibility among students, intercultural conflicts and social alienation.

## 4. Group Communication

Group communication is the exchange of information and ideas between individuals using interpersonal skills.

In group communication, team members have to effectively participate for an effective communication.

It provides an opportunity for people to come together to discuss and exchange views of common interest. It includes collective decision-making, self-expression, increasing one's effect and elevating one's status. In group communication, there will be more resources, knowledge and ideas.

So, it's very effective. Group may be statistical (demographic arrangements), societal (common consciousness), social (actual association) and associational groups (formal structure).

Participation and sharing of information is central to the functioning of a group. A group can function on the basis of committees (small group for a specific purpose or conferences and large group).

### Advantages

- In group communication, people have chances to gain more information and knowledge.
- Through group communication, many goals can be achieved, like collective decision-making, self-expression, increasing one's effect, elevating one's status and relaxation and so on.
- By group communication, people eliminate all the biases that are generally introduced due to individual decision- making. It also reduces the unreliability of individual decisions.

### Disadvantages

- In group communication, group interaction is time consuming and often inefficient, especially in an emergency.
- In group communication, imbalances in status, skills and goals, may distort the process and the outcome sharply.

## 5. Classroom Communication

Classroom communication is the interaction between the teacher and the students in a classroom setting. It involves teacher who provides information, shares knowledge and experiences.

In such communication, there are students who grasp these informations. Effective classroom communication takes place when there is a two way flow of information.

For this, a teacher should be a good speaker so that he/she is able to communicate properly. Students should be active listeners, they should be open to ask their queries and raise doubts.

Classroom communication takes place effectively when teacher use teaching aids like charts, maps, slides, models, projectors, etc. Various methods of classroom communication can be adopted for effective interaction such as lecturing, discussion, debate, dialogues, demonstrations, etc.

### Principles of Classroom Communication

There are four principles of effective classroom communication, which are elaborated under the following heads:

#### (i) Principles for Teachers

(a) **Understand the Learners** A classroom teacher should have information about the learners' character such as previous knowledge and interests, as well as cognitive style. Thus, a teacher cannot treat all the students in the same manner because each individual is different.

(b) **Develop Effective Communication Skill** A teacher should have a great communication skill of both the aspects i.e. verbal and non-verbal. A teacher can record his/her own audio strength and analyse the same for identifying the strength and weakness in the spoken language. He remains open to feedback from his colleagues, peer groups, seniors as well as students too.

(c) **Knowledge of Pedagogy and Andragogy** A teacher should have knowledge of pedagogy and andragogy, therefore he enables to plan, organise, deliver and evaluate instructions. Thus, a teacher easily promotes the learning among the students.

(d) **Adopt Flexible Technique** A teacher should be flexible that helps him to modify the teaching techniques according to the needs of students.

(e) **Develop Proficiency in the Subject Matter** A teacher should be expert in his subject and should have potential to satisfy students by solving their queries while teaching.

### (ii) Principles for Message Design

(a) **Clear and Specified Objective** To be clear and specified, a message should be SMART. It means message should be Specific, Measurable, Achievable, Realistic and Time framed.

(b) **Proper Sequence** A message should be in proper sequence and organised as simple to complex, easy to difficult, concrete to abstract, known to unknown, observation to reasoning, etc.

(c) **Easy Language** The language of the message should be easy, simple and understandable to the learners. Technical jargon should be avoided.

(d) **Appropriate Symbols** Symbols used in messaging should be correct and standardised.

(e) **Relevant Exercise** The exercise given by the teacher should be of varying difficulty level and involve the learners meaningfully.

### (iii) Principles for Selection of Instructional Methods and Media

(a) **Relevant Methods and Media** The method should be appropriate and media operational processes should be relevant towards the objectives, content and context. Therefore, it is appropriate to the level of learners.

(b) **Variety of Methods and Media** A variety of methods and media are used by a teacher in order to provide individual differences among the learners and to discourage the monotony.

(c) **Better Quality of Media** A great quality of media is used in the classroom in terms of its colours, finishing, visibility and printing.

(d) **Integrate Media in Teaching-Learning** During the teaching-learning process, the media should not be isolated. Although it must be integrated, so that it boosts-up the understanding of the students or learners.

### (iv) Principles for Creating Conducive Learning Environment

(a) **Classes Should not be Overcrowded** The classes should not be overcrowded. If it is so, then it is difficult for a teacher to manage the class and not pay attention to each learner.

Therefore, the ratio between teacher-student should be specified.

(b) **Proper Seating Arrangement** For the successful learning, there should be a proper seating arrangement in the classroom. This helps a student to interact easily with the teacher.

(c) **Build Good Relationship with Student** A teacher should make good relationship with students. Therefore, he should know each and every student in the class by name and be friendly with them.

(d) **Encourage Cooperation and Healthy Competition** A teacher should encourage cooperation and healthy competition among the students by assigning group activities and pairing students with average or poor students.

(e) **Strengthening** A teacher should provide strengthening to the students for their desired communication behaviour through praise, rewards, social recognition, etc.

**→ Paraphrasing**

Paraphrasing is used to express something again using different words, so that it is easier to understand.

In a paraphrase, the ideas and meaning of the original source must be maintained and the main ideas need to come through but the wording has to be your own.

For example, telling the story of a movie you saw to your friend is paraphrasing. It is a solid means of truly and completely attempting to understand what the person is communicating with others i.e. what one is really trying to say.

Importance of paraphrasing in communication is as follows:

- It greatly enhances the impact of the conversation.
- It expresses the meaning of (the writer or speaker or something written or spoken) using different words, especially to achieve greater clarity.
- It helps to avoid impulsive or angry reactions.
- It prevents misunderstandings from occurring.

## Seven Cs of Effective Communication

The seven Cs of effective communication make sure that communication in the form of teaching-learning process is well constructed and clear. They are applicable to both written as well as oral communication.

These are as follows

1. **Completeness** The communication must be complete. It should convey all facts required by the learners. The sender of the message must take into consideration the receiver's mindset and convey the message accordingly.
2. **Conciseness** It means wordiness i.e. communicating what you want to convey in least possible words without forgoing the other Cs of communication. Conciseness is a necessity for effective communication.
3. **Consideration** It implies stepping into the shoes of others. Effective communication must take the audience into consideration i.e. the audience's viewpoints, background, mindset, education level, etc.
4. **Clarity** It implies emphasising on a specific message or goal at a time, rather than trying to achieve too much at once.
5. **Concreteness** It implies being particular and clear rather than fuzzy and general. It makes use of words that are clear and that build the reputation. It also strengthens the confidence.
6. **Courtesy** It implies the message should show the sender's expression as well as should respect the receiver. The sender of the message or teacher should be sincerely polite, judicious, reflective and enthusiastic.
7. **Correctness** It implies that there are no grammatical errors in the communication. It also checks for the precision and accurateness of facts and figures used in the message.

## Barriers of Effective Communication

Barriers of communication are those factors which produce obstacles in the way of reaching the message to the receiver. Following are the barriers of communication:

### 1. Language or Linguistic Barriers

Language means using words to deliver something to the receiver. It includes both verbal and non-verbal communication. Through the following points, we can understand easily, how language makes barriers to effective communication.

(i) **Insufficient Knowledge of a Language** If the language is constructed badly or faulty or there are mistakes in the message, then the receiver will find difficult to understand correctly.

(ii) **Incomplete Messages** There are certain assumptions underlying a communication. If the receiver is not clear about these assumptions, the purpose of the communication would be lost.

(iii) **Use of Jargons and Slangs** When communicating in same language, the terminology used in a message may act as a barrier if it is not fully understood by the receiver. For example, a message that includes a lot of specialist jargons (technical expressions) and abbreviations will not be understood by a receiver who is not familiar with the terminologies used.

(iv) **Translation Issues** If a message is written in one language and translated into another language, then, it is highly important that the translation should be free from errors or omissions. Therefore, the receiver can easily understand.

## 2. Semantic Barriers

The semantic barriers refers to the misunderstanding between the sender and receiver arising due to the different meanings of words, and other symbols used in the communication. The semantic barriers usually arise when the information is not in the simple language and contains those words or symbols that have multiple meanings.

## 3. Psychological or Emotional Barriers

Following are psychological or emotional barriers to the effective communication:

(i) **Forming Prior Judgements** Some people have the tendency to form a judgement before listening to the entire message.

(ii) **Pre-occupation of the Receiver** If the receiver is pre-occupied with other matters then he cannot properly listen to or attend to a message.

(iii) **Emotions as Hindrance** When emotions are strong, it is difficult to know the frame of mind of other person or group. Emotional attitudes of both, the communicators as well as the receivers inhibit free flow of transmission and understanding of messages.

(iv) **Attitude Related Issues** The attitude of a person to interpret the message in accordance with his self-concept, also affects communication. The communicator responds favourably to those messages that reinforce his self-concept. He also rejects those messages that are perceived to be a threat to his self-image.

## 4. Technical Barriers

Technical problems arising due to problems in hardware or software may hinder communication sent via emails, chats, text messages.

Sometimes, sender or receiver may have improper knowledge about technology and may not be able to use it successfully. Therefore, technical barriers may hinder the proper flow of information.

## 5. Cultural Barriers

Culture of a place impacts a person in a big way. It has implications on our behaviour, language, activities, rituals, traditions, norms, etc. This can create confusion and misunderstanding as every culture has different traditions.

Signs and symbols used positively in one culture may be understood differently in different cultures.

The rights and wrongs, morals and values also vary from culture to culture. In the absence of any effective communication, the cultural barriers can bring in conflict among different groups of people.

## 6. Sender-Oriented Barrier

The conditions or situations that create barriers in effective communication by the sender are sender-oriented barriers.

The sender's understanding, personal opinion, surroundings, environment, culture affect the information that is send by the sender. Therefore, the sender must have thorough knowledge about the information that he/she conveys. Any wrong interpretation can create communication barriers.

## 7. Receiver-Oriented Barrier

Receivers can also create communication barriers. These include lacking attention in understanding the message completely, receiver's personal opinion, attitude, values, beliefs, physical and emotional state of mind.

If the receiver is not able to properly interpret a message then it can create communication barriers.

## 8. Organisational Barriers

If an organisation does not believe in free flow of information to the lower levels or in any particular direction, then, there will be problems of understanding within the organisation. The rules and regulations may restrict or circumscribe the flow of information.

The hierarchical consciousness comes in the way of effective communication in the upward direction. If there are no adequate facilities for communication, there will be difficulties in ensuring effective communication.

Noise causes disturbance, distortion, confusion and interference in an organisation for transmission of messages.

## 9. Physical Barriers

Following are the physical barriers to effective communication

(i) **Medium Related**

Use of medium with which recipient is unfamiliar may lead to communication barrier.

(ii) **Environment Related**

Environmental stress such as high temperature, poor ventilation, etc., leads to barrier in the organisation or at any place.

- Subjective stress includes sleeplessness, ill-health, effects of drugs, mood swings, etc., also affect the communication.
- Surrounding area such as traffic noise, music, loudspeaker, etc., create some disturbance while communication takes place between two parties.

## 10. Mechanical Barriers

In the absence of communication facilities, there is difficulty in reaching of a message to the destination.

Channel noise, that includes any disturbance in physical transmission of a message, makes barrier to effective communication. For example, disturbances in radio transmission, blurredness on TV screens, inaudibility in telephone devices and so on.

## 11. Other Barriers

The various communication barriers at work places are as follows

- **Stereotyping** This means that the content of communication is determined by the expectations due to inadequate distinctions of objects or events. This interferes with effective communication.
- **Ideological Barriers** The members of the organisation do not share the same ideological perspectives and orientation. This affects the effective communication.
- **Filtering** It refers to the sender's purposeful and deliberate manipulation of information to be passed on to the receiver.

### → Communication Myths

Communication plays an important role in the success of the organisation because it can impact one's work and the level of satisfaction of other members of an organisation. However, while communication is a good means, there are quite a few myths that affect how we communicate and by revealing and understanding these myths one can become a better communicator.

Such myths are : meanings are in words, communication is a verbal process, telling is communicating, communication will solve all our problems, communication is a good thing, the more communication, the better response, communication can break down, communication is a natural ability and so on. Therefore, it can be said that myths have power but are imprecise.

## Suggestions to Overcome Barriers of Communication

In order to remove hindrances in the way of communication following suggestions need to be considered

1. **Clarify Ideas Before Communication** Any issue to be communicated to a subordinate should be completely studied and analysed by the superior.
2. **Use of Simple Language** Use of simple and clear words should be emphasised. Use of ambiguous words and jargons should be avoided.
3. **Have Clarity in Thoughts** It means one should be very clear about his objectives and what he wants to convey. One should arrange his thoughts in proper order and then convey.
4. **Motivation** Motivation also helps to remove some of the barriers, especially psychological and socio-cultural barriers.
5. **Proper Arrangement** Proper seating arrangements, visibility of the source and relatively comfortable environment facilitate communication.
6. **Appropriate Channel** Depending upon the type and objective of communication, selection of appropriate channel is crucial for success of communication.
7. **Conciseness** A communication should be concise and crisp. The sender should be clear headed and properly focussed in his vision.
8. **Open Mind** The people to communicate must have open minds. The information should not be withheld for personal interest or prejudice. The information should be interpreted without any bias.

# MASS MEDIA AND SOCIETY

The word 'media' comes from the plural of the Latin word 'medium' and it is used as a collective noun refer to TV, Radio, Newspapers, Magazines, Films, the International Network (Internet), etc. The media can be examined either in terms of broadcast media or print media.

Media and society are closely related to each other. With the advancement in technological area, our society has also observed the expansion in the thoughts and ideas of people.

Mass media has become an integral part of our society as we are just a clock away from any information that is available on the internet.

This could happen due to various media units of the country. Therefore, mass media is also known as the Fourth State or Pillar of a Democratic Nation. Media has become the most authentic source of information for people.

It helps in bringing considerable changes in the existing laws as per the prevailing social conditions, by playing the role of intermediary between the government and the mass. Many journalists and writers gave the following definitions about mass media such as:

- According to **Denis McQuail,** "Media is the mechanism of change of society."
- According to **Rashmi Bohra,** "Media is the mirror of society."
- According to **RK Majumdar,** "Media is the medium through which the society is educated."

## Objectives of Mass Media and Society

The main objective of mass media is to provide knowledge, educate and entertain people. The important objectives of mass media are given below

- To provide information about different aspects of human life. For example, education, government policies, programmes and so on.
- To convey cultural and educational programmes.
- To entertain people.
- To create public awareness.
- To establish international relations.
- To establish social contact and linkage.
- It also helps in facing disaster and calamity and so on.

## Functions of Mass Media

Mass media undertakes several functions in a societal set-up. Some of these are given below as

1. **Providing Information** The most important and foremost role of mass media is to provide information about different aspects of human life.

   For example, education, government policies, programmes, summits and so on. Its main function in a democratic country is to create awareness among the masses. Thus, mass media plays a great role in this respect.
2. **Providing Entertainment** Mass media plays an important role in providing entertainment on a larger extent. Operas, movies, stories (published), music, videos, photographs, internet, podcasts are used by the media to entertain and enthrall the audience. Mass media is a great source for the audiences, seeking the emotional release.
3. **Socialising People** Mass media connects people in the world. Through mass media, the world has become a 'Global Village'. Now, people can share their thoughts, opinions and views freely on social networking sites like Twitter, Whatsapp, Facebook, Telegram and so on.
4. **Work as a Responsible Source** Mass media works as a responsible source in the society. The media keeps watch on the government and others in power. Local news stations often have a segment in which they investigate problems for people.

   Entire, hour long news shows are devoted to exposes, which are stories designed to expose wrong doing.

   Government officials, who engage in bad behaviour know that, they will be on every news show and newspaper in the country, if they are caught.
5. **Providing Political Forum** The media also provides a forum to the political leaders belonging to different parties and ideologies. This function of the media becomes very active and important at the time of campaigns during elections. In this, candidates belonging to various parties often broadcast advertisements and debates on television. It is only through these mediums that voters learn about the candidates as well as the issues raised by them.
6. **Being the Common Carrier** Mass media plays a great role in exchanging news and information as well. Media acts in a dual manner. On one side, the people learn about the policies and ideologies of the government; while on the other side, media also helps in informing the government about what people really want.

## Social Media : New Form of Media

Today, internet has made everything almost possible. It became possible by social networking or social media. Social media is computer-based technology which facilitates the sharing of ideas, thoughts and information through the building of virtual networks and communities.

Examples of social media are Blogs, Facebook, Instagram, Twitter, Whatsapp, Wikipedia, YouTube, News Portal, etc., which successfully have created a unique place in the internet world. Different types of social media are given below as

### Facebook

It is an American online social media platform which was launched on 4th February, 2004, by Mark Zuckerberg. It is operated by Facebook Inc which is based in Menlo Park, California. Facebook can be accessed from devices with internet connectivity.

To become a facebook user, one has to create an account on facebook and after registering, user may join common-interest user groups organised by workplace, school hobbies and so on. It can also be used by companies for advertising their products.

### Instagram

It is a social networking service where people can create their accounts and can share their photos and videos. It was launched by **Kevin**

**Systrom** and **Mike Krieger** in 2010. It is owned by Facebook Inc. company.

### Twitter

It is an American online news and social networking service which can be used by any person by creating an account. Twitter was created in March 2006 by **Jack Dorsey**, **Noah Glass**, **Biz Stone** and **Evan Williams**.

On this social networking site, users can post and interact with messages known as 'tweets'. Before 2017, tweets were restricted to 140 characters, but from November 2017, this limit was doubled for all languages except Chinese, Japanese and Korean.

### YouTube

YouTube, LLC is a video-sharing website where anyone can upload, view rate and share, add to favourites, report, comment on videos and subscribe to other users.

It was created by **Chad Hurley**, **Steve Chen** and **Jawed Karim** in 2005. The headquarters of YouTube is in San Bruno, California, America. In 2006, Google bought this site.

### Whatsapp

Whatsapp was founded by Jan Koum and Brian Acton in 2009. It is a freeware and cross-platform messaging application which can be accessed by anyone who has a smartphone.

It is an alternative to SMS. It is owned by Facebook. The users of Whatsapp can send text messages, voice calls, video calls, images, documents and user location to each other.

### Blog

It is the short form of 'Weblog' which was coined by **Jorn Barger** on 17th December, 1997. The term 'Blog' was coined by **Peter Merholz** in 1999. Initially, some online journals were published which consisted of links of news, other information and about the details of bloggers.

These were known as 'Blogs' and the writers who used to write these blogs were known as 'Bloggers.' Gradually, blogs became popular but to write these blogs, bloggers needed to have knowledge about the computer programming languages like HTML language.

But after seeing possibilities, some websities provided free and easy equipments to write these blogs where bloggers did not need to know about the computer programming languages.

Blogs can be written about any aspect of life and in any language of the world. Blogs became more famous from the time when an American soldier wrote about his experience during the war when America attacked on Afghanistan.

## Effects of Mass Media

The effects of mass media can be seen through the following points:

### Positive Effects

- Mass media informs the public about government policies and programmes and how these programmes can be useful to them. This helps the people to voice their feelings and helps the government to make necessary changes in their policies or programmes.
- It can bring positive social changes.
- It entertains people.
- It acts as an agent of change in development.
- It helps the political and democratic processes of a country.
- It brings people of different countries closer to each other.
- It educates the public and promote trade and industry through advertisements.

### Negative Effects

- The traditional culture of country is adversely affected by mass media.
- Entertainment has become the main component of mass media. This affects the primary objectives of media i.e. to inform and educate people.
- Mass media promotes violence. Studies have proved that violence shown on television and cinema, have negative effects on children.
- It also promotes the desire in people to buy and own products that are advertised through the media but which may not be essential for them.

## Important Units or Institutions of Mass Media

The important mass media units of India are given below :

### All India Radio (Akashvani), 1927

Radio broadcasting was started in early 1920s. The first programme was broadcasted in 1923 by the Radio Club of Bombay. In 1927, broadcasting services were set up with two privately owned transmitters at Bombay (Mumbai) and Calcutta (Kolkata). The government took over the transmitters in 1930 and started operating them under the name of Indian Broadcasting Services.

It was changed to All India Radio (AIR) in 1936 and also popularised as Akashvani from 1957. There are 369 Radio Stations. Each of these radio stations function as the subordinate office of All India Radio.

### Press Trust of India (PTI), 1947

It is a non-profit sharing cooperative owned by the country's newspapers with a mandate to provide efficient and unbiased news to all its subscribers. It is the largest news agency of India. It was founded on 27th August, 1947 and it started functioning from 1st February, 1949. PTI offers its news services in the English and Hindi languages.

Bhasha is the Hindi language news service of the agency. All Major TV/Radio channels in India and several abroad, including BBC in London, receive PTI service.

### Hindustan Samachar, 1948

Hindustan Samachar is the first multi-lingual news agency in India, subscribed by more than 200 newspapers and almost all the news channels including Doordarshan. It was set up in 1948 by SS Apte offering its services in 10 languages such as Bengali, Oriya, Assamese, Telugu, Malyalam, Urdu, Punjabi, Gujarati, Hindi and Marathi.

In 1975, Hindustan Samachar was merged with Press Trust of India, United News of India and Samachar Bharati to form the media monopoly samachar.

### Central Board of Film, 1952

It was founded in 1952 with its headquarters at Mumbai. It is responsible for certifying the films produced in India as well as outside the country.

The board gives four categories of certificates i.e. 'U' for unrestricted public exhibition, 'A' for public exhibition restricted to adults only, 'UA' for unrestricted public exhibition with parental guidance for children below the age of 12 and 'S' for exhibition restricted audience such as doctors, etc.

### Children's Film Society, 1955

It was founded in 1955 and functions as an autonomous body under the administrative control of the Ministry of Information and Broadcasting. The society provides value based entertainment for children and also fulfils their psychological and educational needs through the medium of films.

### Press and Print Media, 1956

The office of the registrar of newspapers for India, more popularly known as RNI, came into being on 1st July, 1956 on the recommendation of the First Press Commission in 1953 and by amending the Press and Registration of Books Act, 1867.

The Press and Registration of Books Act contains the duties and functions of RNI. The Registrar of newspapers for India is required to submit an annual report to the Government about the Status of Newspapers before 31st December, every year.

### United News of India (UNI), 1959

It was founded in 1959 and has now grown into one of the largest news agencies in Asia.

UNI have correspondents in major cities such as Washington, London, Dubai, Colombo, Kathmandu, Islamabad, Dhaka, Singapore, Sydney and Vancouver, bringing to our subscribers stories of interest to Indian readers.

It has collaboration agreements with several foreign news agencies, including Reuters and DPA.

## Doordarshan, 1959

It was started in New Delhi on 15th September, 1959. The regular television services commenced in Delhi in 1965, Mumbai in 1972, Calcutta (Kolkata) in 1975 and in Chennai in 1975. The current form of Doordarshan was established on 15th September, 1976.

Doordarshan network consists of 64 Doordarshan Kendras/ Production Centres, 24 Regional News Units, 126 Doordarshan Maintenance Centres, 202 High Power Transmitters, 828 Low Power Transmitters, Very Low Power Transmitters, 18 Transposers, 30 Channels and DTH services. Doordarshan has started DD KISAN on 26th May, 2015 to provide information agricultural related schemes, programmes and also to educate the farmers.

## Film and Television Institute of India, 1960

The institute was set up in 1960 in Pune, as a premier institute for imparting training in the art and technique of film-making. Since 1974, it started giving training to Doordarshan employees in television production. The institution was renamed as Film and Television Institute of India in 1974.

## Indian Institute of Mass Communication (IIMC), 1965

It was inaugurated on 17th August, 1965 by the Ministry of Information and Broadcasting, **Smt. Indira Gandhi**. IIMC has provided many courses in the field of mass media. Its working is monitored by the government from time to time.

## Press Council of India (PCI), 1966

It was set up by Government of India in 1966 on the recommendations of the First Press Commission with the object of preserving the freedom of the press and of maintaining and improving the standards of press in India. The present council functions under the Press Council Act, 1978. It is a statutory, quasi judicial body which acts as a watchdog of the press.

## NAM News Network (NNN), 1976

It was founded in 1976. It is the transformation of the now-defunct NANAP or Non-Aligned New Agencies Pool.

It is also incumbent upon the NNN to assume the role of a creator to aware of the potential that exists for expanding trade and economic collaboration among NAM member countries through intelligence sharing and building of e-knowledge capacity.

### → Yellow Journalism

Yellow Journalism or Yellow Press is an American term for journalism. It is associated with newspapers that present little or no legitimate well-researched news while instead using eye-catching headlines for increase sales.

Nowadays, the term Yellow Journalism is used as a pejorative to decry any journalism that treats news in an unprofessional or unethical fashion.

In the United Kingdom, the term Yellow Journalism is equivalent to Tabloid Journalsm, meaning journalism is characteristic of tabloid newspapers, even if found elsewhere.

## Prasar Bharti, 1997

Prasar Bharti is a Public Service Broadcasting Centre in India with Akashvani (All India Radio) and Doordarshan as its two constituents. It came into existence on 23rd November, 1997 and mandated to organise and conduct public broadcasting services to inform, educate and entertain the public.

It also ensures a balanced development of broadcasting on radio and television. Therefore, it is also known as Broadcasting Corporation of India (BCI).

## Press Information Bureau (PIB)

The Press Information Bureau (PIB) is the nodal agency of the Government of India to disseminate information to the print and electronic media on government policies, programme initiatives and achievements.

It has 8 regional offices and 34 branch offices and information centres. The information material is released in English, Hindi, Urdu and other regional languages.

# Chapter Practice

## Meaning and Types of Communication

1 The English word 'Communication' is derived from the words
(A) communis and communicare
(B) communist and commune
(C) communism and communalism
(D) communion and commonsense

2 Each type of communication is affected by its
(A) Reception (B) Transmission
(C) Non-regulation (D) Context

3 Communication means
(A) transferring or conveying thoughts, views, emotions or information through specific signals and symbols.
(B) radio, TV, cinema, etc.
(C) telephone, telegram, fax, radio.
(D) None of the above

4 Communicating the message to each individual personally rather through a message hung on a board will be
(A) effective communication
(B) best communication
(C) bi-directional communication
(D) final communication

5 "Communication is the process of passing information and understanding from one person to another" is given by
(A) Carl Hovland (B) Keith Davis
(C) David Berlo (D) Harold D. Lasswell

6 Which of the following is the most fundamental component of the manager's job?
(A) Directing (B) Testing
(C) Communicating (D) Managing

7 Which one of the following is correct?
(A) Communication is not a mere transmission, it aims at understanding.
(B) Efficient communication minimises time and cost involved in the exchange process.
(C) Communication is a process involving a sender who sends a message, a channel through which a message is transmitted and a receiver.
(D) All of the above

8 The essence of communication is
(A) transmitting information
(B) sharing information
(C) imparting knowledge
(D) sharing and understanding information

9 Which type of communication is called as public relations?
(A) Across communication
(B) Interpersonal communication
(C) Internal communication
(D) External communication

10 Which of the following defines the nature of communication?
(A) Communication can be pervaded in every area of human existence.
(B) Communication has both the elements of Science and Art.
(C) It involves a systematic and continuous process of speaking, listening and understanding.
(D) All of the above

11 In interpersonal communication, ethics
(A) increase barriers to understanding.
(B) are not a consideration.
(C) stand in the way of honesty.
(D) are important.

12 Another name for interpersonal communication is
(A) mass communication.
(B) face-to-face public communication.
(C) dyadic communication.
(D) virtual reality.

13 Interpersonal communication occurs only when
(A) intimate conversation takes place.
(B) an individual converses with people they have no interest in knowing.
(C) an individual interacts with another person as a unique individual.
(D) three or more people are communicating with each other at the same time.

14 Intrapersonal communication helps one
(A) to know what others are thinking.
(B) learn about oneself.
(C) communicate with the general public.
(D) to become a talented public speaker.

15 Organisational communication can also be equated with
(A) intrapersonal communication
(B) interpersonal communication
(C) group communication
(D) mass communication

16 The type of communication that the teacher has in the classroom, is termed as
(A) interpersonal communication
(B) mass communication
(C) group communication
(D) face-to-face communication

17 Conversing with the spirits and ancestors is termed as
(A) transpersonal communication
(B) intrapersonal communication
(C) interpersonal communication
(D) face-to-face communication

18 The mode of communication that involves a single source transmitting information to a large number of receivers simultaneously, is called
(A) group communication
(B) mass communication
(C) intrapersonal communication
(D) interpersonal communication

19 In the field of communication, the word 'mass' is used to refer to
(A) common people
(B) large number of people
(C) Both 'A' and 'B'
(D) None of the above

20 Which of the following is/are the basic component(s) of mass communication?
(A) Mass audiences
(B) Mass messages
(C) Mass media
(D) All of the above

21 Users who use media for their own ends are identified as
(A) passive audience
(B) active audience
(C) positive audience
(D) negative audience

22 Formal communication can move
(A) upward (B) downward
(C) horizontal (D) All of these

23 Anything that interferes with a message in communication is known as
(A) Context (B) Noise
(C) Decoding (D) Feedback

24 Arrange the following ingredients of communication process in proper order.
I. Message II. Receiver
III. Encoder IV. Channel
V. Decoder
Select the correct answer from the codes given below.
(A) I, III, II, V, IV
(B) I, III, IV, II, V
(C) III, I, IV, V, II
(D) III, I, II, IV, V

25 The first theorist who developed communication as a significant aspect of organisational behaviour is
(A) Fayol (B) Simon
(C) Norbet Wiener (D) Barnard

26 **Assertion** (A) According to Herbert Simon, without communication there can be no organisation.
**Reason** (R) He views communication as a process whereby decisional premises are transmitted from one member of an organisation to another.
Select the correct answer from the codes given below.
(A) Both A and R are true and R is the correct explanation of A.
(B) Both A and R are true, but R is not the correct explanation of A.
(C) A is true, but R is false.
(D) A is false, but R is true.

27 Which of the following implies that the message should be sincerely polite, judicious, reflective and enthusiastic?
(A) Clarity (B) Courtesy
(C) Conciseness (D) Consideration

28 "Difficulties in communication arise when the sender and the receiver of the message use words or symbols in different senses." The statement signifies which type of communication barrier?
(A) Linguistic Barrier
(B) Semantic Barrier
(C) Emotional Barrier
(D) Organisational Barrier

29 Audience and feedback are the two main components of
(A) mass communication
(B) interpersonal communication
(C) intrapersonal communication
(D) None of the above

30 Arrange the following activities of interaction in logical order.
I. Analysis of the work done.
II. Planning and preparation.
III. Presentation of material.
IV. Modification and improvement.
Select the correct code from the options given below.
(A) I, II, III, IV (B) II, III, I, IV
(C) IV, I, II, III (D) I, III, IV, II

31 Which of the following methods of communication is the most effective?
(A) Presenting written material alongwith film projector.
(B) Presenting written material.
(C) Cannot be determined.
(D) Multimedia method.

32 Where accuracy of a communication is important then which communication type is desirable?
(A) One way communication
(B) Two way communication
(C) Both 'A' and 'B'
(D) None of the above

33 Which of the following is/are advantage(s) of having oral communication?
(A) Questions can be asked and answered.
(B) Feedback is immediate and direct.
(C) It is more persuasive and less expensive.
(D) All of the above

34 In order to understand verbal and non-verbal communication, which of the following things should we do?
(A) Accept cultural differences
(B) Studying your own culture
(C) Learn about other cultures
(D) All of the above

35 In which of the following communications the nature of audience is an important factor?
(A) Interpersonal Communication
(B) Business Communication
(C) Bottom-Top Communication
(D) Mediated Communication

36 Formal communication usually flows in
(A) six directions
(B) four directions
(C) three directions
(D) nine directions

37 Which of the following statements is true of diagonal communication?
(A) It combines both formal and informal communication.
(B) There is no barrier of hierarchy in diagonal communication.
(C) It is the most popular form of business communication.
(D) It creates barriers among superior and subordinate colleagues.

38 According to Keith Davis, how many types of grapevine chain occur?
(A) Two (B) Three
(C) Four (D) Five

39 Which of the following is the commonest grapevine chain in organisations?
(A) Single strand chain
(B) Gossip chain
(C) Probability chain
(D) Cluster chain

40 Which of the following is not true about the grapevine?
(A) It is faster at conveying information than an organisation's formal communication system.
(B) It is somewhere between 75 and 95 percent as accurate as the formal communication system.
(C) It is found in almost all organisations.
(D) Managers usually welcome its existence.

41 Under this communication network, the member communicates non-selectively is known as
(A) single strand network
(B) gossip network
(C) probability network
(D) cluster network

42 It is the process which translates the message into a form that can be understood by the receiver is called
(A) encoding
(B) receiver
(C) decoding
(D) feedback

## Communication Process, Models of Communication and Characteristics of Communication

**43** In the process of communication, which one of the following is in the chronological order?
(A) Communicator, Medium, Receiver, Effect, Message
(B) Medium, Communicator, Message, Receiver, Effect
(C) Communicator, Message, Medium, Receiver, Effect
(D) Message, Communicator, Medium, Receiver, Effect

**44** "The sender of information expresses his ideas into words, symbols or signs to convey the message." This is known as
(A) decoding
(B) encoding
(C) communication channel
(D) None of the above

**45** In circular communication, the encoder become a decoder when there is
(A) noise (B) audience
(C) criticality (D) feedback

**46** Which of the following can hamper the process of communication?
(A) Channel (B) Encoder
(C) Noise (D) Pollution

**47** The process of communication runs through
(A) a sender (B) a receiver
(C) a channel (D) All of these

**48** In the communication process, to encode means to
(A) block a pathway between the sender and receiver of a message.
(B) translate ideas into a code.
(C) speak to large group of people.
(D) interpret a code.

**49** Which of the following stages of communication process includes the conversion of symbols into a meaningful information?
(A) Encoding (B) Decoding
(C) Receiving (D) Channelising

**50** Which of the three components are part of human communication process?
(A) Message, Noise, Feedback
(B) Feedback, Message, Critquing
(C) Message, Recording, Feedback
(D) Noise, Feedback, Jargon

**51** Which of the following is/are the stage(s) of communication process?
(A) Encoding (B) Decoding
(C) Both 'A' and 'B' (D) None of these

**52** Following are the experimental learning activities adopted by a teacher. Arrange them in cyclic order.
I. Accommodation II. Converging
III. Assimilation IV. Diverging
Select the correct answer from the codes given below.
(A) I, II, III, IV (B) IV, III, II, I
(C) II, III, IV, I (D) III, I, II, IV

**53** Which of the following is also known as Circular Model of Communication?
(A) Transactional Model of Communication
(B) Linear Model of Communication
(C) Interactional Model of Communication
(D) None of the above

**54** The 'Linear Model' was founded by
(A) Aristotle (B) Shannon
(C) Weaver (D) All of these

**55** Who supported the Interactional Model of Communication?
(A) Aristotle
(B) David Berlo
(C) Weaver
(D) Wilbur Schramm

**56** Who among the following developed the most widely used model of communication process?
(A) Barnard
(B) Simon
(C) Norbert Wiener
(D) Shannon and Weaver

**57** Which was the first major model of communication that came into being in 1949?
(A) Shannon and Weaver Model of Communication
(B) Lasswell's Communication Model
(C) David Berlo Model of Communication
(D) Helical Spiral Model

**58** Which of the following is/are the characteristic(s) of David Berlo Model of Communication?
(A) It is a linear model
(B) There is no two-way communication
(C) There is no concept of feedback
(D) All of the above

**59** "In this type of model, focus is on public speaking than personal communication. This model is formed with three basic elements speakers, speech and audience." Name which model is this?
(A) Helical Spiral Model
(B) Shannon-Weaver Model
(C) Aristotle Communication Model
(D) Linear Model of Communication.

**60** "The Communication Theory reflects the fear or awe of mass media. In this, the receivers are passive and defenceless and takes whatever is shot at them." Name the theory.
(A) Psychological or Individual Difference Theory
(B) Personal Influence Theory
(C) Hypodermic or Bullet Theory
(D) Agenda Setting Theory

**61** Cultivation Theory was developed by whom in 1967?
(A) George Gerbner
(B) Paul & Lazarsfeld
(C) MC Combs and Donald Shaw
(D) Katz

**62** Which of the following is/are incorrect about Agenda Setting Theory?
(A) The theory is derived from the basic tenets of Marx and Engels.
(B) It envisages media to be under the control of working class.
(C) In this, the media sets agenda for masses which helps in bringing cognitive change in individuals.
(D) Both (A) and (B)

**63** Which of the following is/are the characteristic(s) of Uses and Gratification Theory?
(A) It is closely related to human psychology of needs, motives and influence.
(B) Audiences are active audience and uses media to fulfils their needs.
(C) It was developed by Katz in 1959.
(D) All of the above

**64** Name the theory that originated from Libertarian Theory.
(A) Social Responsibility Theory
(B) Communist Media Theory
(C) Free Press Theory
(D) Dependency Theory

**65** Which of the following is not the type of formal communication?
(A) Chain Network
(B) All Channel Network
(C) Circle Network
(D) Probability Network

**66** Under which type of Formal Communication, a subordinate communicates with his immediate superior as well as second superior?
(A) Circle Network
(B) Star Network
(C) Inverted V-Network
(D) Y-Network

**67** Which of the following statements explain the meaning of communication in administrative organisation?
I. Communication is the blood stream of administrative organisation.
II. The underlying aim of communication is the meeting of minds on common issues.
III. Communication is the heart of management.
IV. Communication is the shared understanding of a shared purpose.

Select the correct answer from the codes given below.
(A) I, II, III and IV
(B) I, II and IV
(C) II, III and IV
(D) II and IV

**68** To decode a message is to
(A) translate ideas into code
(B) interpret a message
(C) evaluate a message
(D) reject a message

**69** Which model of communication is not applicable in general human communication?
(A) Linear Model
(B) Interactional Model
(C) Transactional Model
(D) None of the above

**70** ......... implies the interchange of information and ideas among persons at the same level of authority.
(A) Horizontal Communication
(B) Downward Communication
(C) Upward Communication
(D) None of the above

**71** Which of the following is correct about Group Communication?

I. In this communication, people have chances to gain information and knowledge.
II. Through this communication, many goals can be achieved like collective decision-making, self-expression, etc.
III. In this communication, group interaction is time consuming.

Select the correct answer from the codes given below.

(A) I and II (B) II and III
(C) Only I (D) All of these

**72** Learning to communicate with others is the key to

(A) never being misunderstood.
(B) winning the approval of everyone around you.
(C) eliminating all of your listener's physiological noise.
(D) establishing rewarding relationships.

**73** Feedback is a listener's

(A) acceptance of a message.
(B) aversion to a message.
(C) verbal critique of your message.
(D) verbal or non-verbal response to a message.

**74** Which of the following is correct about paraphrasing?

(A) It greatly enhances the impact of the conversation.
(B) It helps to avoid impulsive or angry reactions.
(C) It prevents misunderstandings from occurring.
(D) All of the above

## Effective Communication

**75** Break-down in verbal communication is described as

(A) short circuit (B) contradiction
(C) unevenness (D) entropy

**76** Which of the following is/are the advantage(s) of having written communication?

(A) Message can be revised several times.
(B) It is a permanent record that can be saved.
(C) Receiver has more time to analyse the message.
(D) All of the above

**77** The term 'KISS' (Keep It Short and Simple) is almost used in which communication?

(A) Verbal (B) Non-verbal
(C) Intercultural (D) Group

**78** Kinesics, proxemics and para language are part of which communication?

(A) Non-verbal (B) Verbal
(C) Group (D) Intercultural

**79** Which of the following is/are correct in respect to non-verbal communication?

I. It helps illiterate people to communicate with others easily.
II. In this communication, people can repeat the verbal messages according to their need.
III. In this communication, there is a great possibility in distortion of information.

Select the correct answer from the codes given below.

(A) Only I (B) I and II
(C) II and III (D) All of these

**80** Classroom communication of a teacher rests on the principle of

(A) infotainment (B) edutainment
(C) entertainment (D) power equation

**81** Which of the following principles is a useful guide for establishing effective classroom communication?

(A) Principle of teachers
(B) Principle for selection of instructional methods and media
(C) Principle of creating conducive learning environment
(D) All of the above

**82** Classroom communication can be described as

(A) exploration
(B) institutionalisation
(C) unsignified narration
(D) discourse

**83** A smart classroom is a teaching space which has

I. smart portion with a touch panel control system.
II. PC/laptop connection and DVD/VCR player.
III. document camera and specialised software.
IV. projector and screen.

Select the correct answer from the codes given below.
(A) I and II
(B) II and IV
(C) I, II and III
(D) All of the above

**84** In the classroom, the teacher sends the message either as words or images. The students are really
(A) encoders (B) decoders
(C) agitators (D) propagators

## Barriers to Communication

**85** A jargon means
(A) a specialised language of a particular group of people.
(B) techniques of good writing.
(C) a special article written by an editor.
(D) None of the above

**86** Which of the following is not a barrier to effective communication associated with the media and channel?
(A) Noise
(B) Information overload
(C) Space proxemics
(D) Inappropriateness of media and/or channel

**87** Which of the following is described in the text as a contextual factor that can impact effectiveness of communication in an organisation?
(A) Organisational structure
(B) Organisation culture
(C) Technology
(D) All of the above

**88** What causes a lot of relevant information to be lost?
(A) Volume of information
(B) Timing of information
(C) Accuracy of information
(D) Flow of information

## Mass Media and Society

**89** Media is known as
(A) first estate (B) second estate
(C) third estate (D) fourth estate

**90** Who said that "Media is the mechanism of change of society"?
(A) Rashmi Bohra (B) Denis McQuail
(C) RK Majumdar (D) None of these

**91** Which of the following is the objective of mass media?
I. To provide information.
II. To convey cultural and educational programmes.
III. To entertain people.
IV. To establish social contact and linkage.
Select the correct answer from the codes given below.
(a) I and II (b) II, III, IV
(c) II and III (d) All of these

**92** Which of the following clearly defines the function of mass media?
(A) Providing information
(B) Work as a responsible source
(C) Providing a political forum
(D) All of the above

**93** Which of the following is/are type(s) of social media?
(A) Instagram (B) Blog
(C) YouTube (D) All of these

**94** Facebook was launched in which year?
(A) 1972 (B) 1980
(C) 1999 (D) 2004

**95** Instagram was launched in
(A) 2001 (B) 2005
(C) 2010 (D) 2013

**96** Which of the following is true about mass media?
(A) It can act as an agent of change in development.
(B) It has brought people of the world closer to each other.
(C) It can bring in positive social changes.
(D) All of the above

**97** Bengal Gazette, the first newspaper in India was started in 1780 by
(A) Dr. Annie Besant
(B) James Augustus Hicky
(C) Lord Cripson
(D) AGO Hume

**98** The largest circulated daily newspaper among the following is
(A) The Times of India
(B) The Indian Express
(C) The Hindu
(D) The Deccan Herald

**99** Communication *via* new media such as computers, teleshopping, internet and mobile telephony is termed as
(A) entertainment communication
(B) interactive communication
(C) development communication
(D) communitarian communication

**100** The term 'Yellow Journalism' refers to
(A) sensational news about terrorism and violence.
(B) sensational news prints on Yellow Paper.
(C) sensational news about arts and culture.
(D) Sensationalism and exaggeration to attract readers/viewers.

**101** Radio Broadcasting commenced in India in
(A) 1923 (B) 1927
(C) 1930 (D) 1936

**102** PIB stands for
(A) Personal Information Bureau
(B) Press Institute of Bombay
(C) Public Information Bureau
(D) Press Information Bureau

**103** The first Multi-Lingual News Agency of India was
(A) Samachar
(B) API
(C) Hindustan Samachar
(D) Samachar Bharati

**104** India's largest news agency is
(A) FBI (B) UTI
(C) UNI (D) PTI

**105** Prasar Bharti is also known as
(A) Broadcasting Centre of India
(B) Indian Broadcasting Authority
(C) Broadcasting Association of India
(D) Broadcasting Corporation of India

**106** The pioneer of the silent feature film in India was
(A) KA Abbas
(B) Satyajit Ray
(C) BR Chopra
(D) Dada Sahib Phalke

**107** Press censorship in India was imposed during the tenure of the Prime Minister
(A) Rajeev Gandhi (B) Narasimha Rao
(C) Indira Gandhi (D) Deve Gowda

**108** Children's Film Society of India was established in
(A) 1955 (B) 1956
(C) 1990 (D) 1959

**109** Who is the founder of Whatsapp?
(A) Brian Acton (B) Jan Koum
(C) Mark Zuckerberg (D) Both 'A' and 'B'

**110** The headquarters of YouTube lies in which country of the world?
(A) England (B) South Africa
(C) France (D) USA

**111** Twitter was created by
(A) Jack Dorsey
(B) Noah Glass
(C) Biz Stone and Evan Williams
(D) All of the above

**112** Prasar Bharti is related to
(A) Web Media
(B) Print Media
(C) Folk Media
(D) Broadcast Media

# *Previous Years' Questions*

## UGC NET-December 2019

**1** Classroom communication is

1. like a computer program
2. dictatorial
3. purposeful
4. pragmatic

Choose the correct option from those given below.

(A) 1 and 3 (B) 2 and 3
(C) 2 and 4 (D) 3 and 4

**2** Swapping of encoder-decoder roles in communication happens due to

(A) cognitive disruptions
(B) semantic noise
(C) feedback analysis
(D) weak channelisation

**3** Which of the following communication technologies employ only asynchronous communication?

1. Video-conferencing
2. E-mail
3. Forums
4. Instant messaging

Choose the correct option.

(A) 1 and 3 (B) 2 and 4
(C) 2 and 3 (D) 1 and 4

## UGC NET-June 2019

**4** Some of the barriers to effective communication are

1. Polysemy
2. Simple language
3. Use of cliches
4. Easy construction of sentence

Choose the correct answer from the codes given below.

(A) 1 and 2 (B) 2 and 3
(C) 3 and 4 (D) 1 and 3

**5** **Assertion** (A) The correlation function of mass media is vital for any society.

**Reason** (R) The interpretational aspect that include advertising and public relations shape and influence public opinion.

Choose the correct answer from the codes given below.

(A) Both A and R are true and R is the correct explanation of A
(B) Both A and R are true, but R is not the correct explanation of A
(C) A is true, but R is false
(D) A is false, but R is true

**6** The sequential order of elements in classroom communication is

(A) Knowledge, interest, evaluation, awareness
(B) Awareness, interest, evaluation, knowledge
(C) Evaluation, awareness, knowledge, interest
(D) Interest, knowledge, evaluation, awareness

**7** In a classroom, use of communication technology pre- supposes

(A) inattentive audience
(B) luxirious ambience
(C) extrapolation of contents
(D) new forms of expression and applications

**8** Connotative communication inside the classroom is

(A) direct (B) critical (C) implicit (D) explicit

**9** Communication through colours can result in

1. aesthetic codes 2. cultural code
3. semantic codes 4. binary codes

Choose the correct answer from the options given below.

(A) 1 and 3 (B) 2 and 3
(C) 2 and 4 (D) 1 and 2

**10** In the communication process, signs derive meanings through

(A) the subjectivity of various components.
(B) the objectivity of the decoder.
(C) the network of inter-relations.
(D) the neutrality of the channel.

**11** **Assertion** (A) Media entertainment does not enhance the cultural level of society.

**Reason** (R) Most media entertainment encourages escapism, not content quality.

Choose the correct answer from the options given below.

(A) Both A and R are true and R is the correct explanation of A
(B) Both A and R are true but R is not the correct explanation of A
(C) A is true but R is false
(D) A is false but R is true

**12** The dance of the honeybee conveying to other bees where nectar will be found, is an example of
(A) mass communication
(B) group communication
(C) interpersonal communication
(D) intrapersonal communication

**13** Choose the correct sequence of communication from the options given below.
(A) Information → exposure → persuasion → behavioural change
(B) Persuasion → information → behavioural change → exposure
(C) Exposure → information → persuasion → behavioural change
(D) Behavioural change → information → persuasion → exposure

**14** Which of the following is a function of mass media?
(A) To transmit culture
(B) To formulate national policies
(C) To help the judiciary take its decisions
(D) To stabilise the share market

**15** In a classroom situation, a teacher organises group discussion to help arrive at a solution of a problem.
In terms of Model of Communication uses, it will be called
(A) a Transactional Model
(B) an Interaction Model
(C) a Horizontal Model
(D) a Linear model

**16** Which of the following is a characteristic of modern mass media?
(A) Capital intensive
(B) Labour intensive
(C) Sustainable
(D) Developmental

**17** Which of the following signifies non-verbal communication in an essential way?
(A) Instructions written on a question paper.
(B) Learner attending an online class.
(C) The dress code followed by an individual.
(D) Yoga instructor teaching yoga poses to the pupils.

**18** Which of the following is a stage of intrapersonal communication?
(A) Phatic stage
(B) Intimate stage
(C) Personal stage
(D) Transcendental communication

**19** Semantic barrier of communication is implied when the
(A) signal is lost before reaching the receiver.
(B) message transmitted by the source is unclear.
(C) receiver's attention is diverted.
(D) receiver does not understand the meaning of the message.

**20** **Assertion** (A) Communication pre-supposes a shared, symbolic environment, a social relationship even among non-participants.
**Reason** (R) It leads to social interaction which in combination with other factors contributes to a sense of community.
Choose the correct answer from the options given below.
(A) Both A and R are true and R is the correct explanation of A
(B) Both A and R are true, but R is not the correct explanation of A
(C) A is true, but R is false
(D) A is false, but R is true

**21** Which of the following principles, a good communicator should follow?
1. He should stay organised.
2. He should avoid the use of visuals.
3. He should be authoritarian.
4. He must adjust to the medium.
5. He should prefer the method of story-telling.

Choose the correct answer from the options given below.
(A) 1, 2 and 3 (B) 2, 3 and 5
(C) 2, 4 and 5 (D) 1, 4 and 5

**22** Below are given two lists. List I describes the types of listeners in communication while list II indicates their characteristics.

| List I (Types of listeners involved in the communication) | List II (Characteristics) |
|---|---|
| A. Non-listener | 1. Is engaged in information other than the one need. |
| B. Marginal listener | 2. Receiving information without processing the significance in the context of communication. |
| C. Evaluative listener | 3. Looks into relevance of the information for understanding its implications. |
| D. Active listener | 4. Pays heed to the communi- cated information occasionally. |

Match the two sets and give your answer by choosing from the options.

| | A | B | C | D | | A | B | C | D |
|---|---|---|---|---|---|---|---|---|---|
| (A) | 4 | 3 | 2 | 1 | (B) | 3 | 4 | 1 | 2 |
| (C) | 2 | 1 | 3 | 4 | (D) | 1 | 4 | 2 | 3 |

**23** Which of the following elements a good classroom communication should adopt?

1. Concreteness
2. Courtsey
3. Filibustering
4. Fictionalisation
5. Coherence

Choose the correct answer from the options given below.

(A) 1, 2 and 4 (B) 2, 4 and 5
(C) 1, 2 and 5 (D) 1, 3 and 4

**24** Non-verbal communication is mostly

(A) mechanical (B) organic
(C) unstructured (D) structured

**25** Match list I with list II.

| List I (Media) | List II (Transmission/ Communication) |
|---|---|
| A. Audio | 1. Bandwidth |
| B. Advertising | 2. Linear communication |
| C. Internal | 3. Non-personal communication |
| D. Newspaper | 4. Frequency modulation |

Choose the correct answer from the options given below.

| | A | B | C | D | | A | B | C | D |
|---|---|---|---|---|---|---|---|---|---|
| (A) | 3 | 4 | 2 | 1 | (B) | 1 | 2 | 3 | 4 |
| (C) | 4 | 3 | 1 | 2 | (D) | 2 | 1 | 4 | 3 |

**26** "Mass media do not have pre-determined functions for everyone and people use them the way they like." This is suggestive of the fact that

(A) audiences are active.
(B) content is of little significance.
(C) contents lack plurality.
(D) audiences are homogeneous.

**27** A communication process can be considered complete when

(A) the sender transmits the message.
(B) the message enters the channel.
(C) the message leaves the channel.
(D) the receiver understands the message.

**28** A customer writes to a bank, "Kindly send me a statement of my transactions in my saving bank account 'A' during the last three months." In terms of communication, it will be called

(A) input (B) message
(C) output (D) feedback

**29** Identify the reasoning in the following argument, "Pre-active stage of classroom teaching is important just as pre-learning preparation stage of communication."

(A) Hypothetical
(B) Deductive
(C) Inductive
(D) Analogical

**30** In the context of communication, usual sequence is

(A) Language → Communication → Society → Civilisation
(B) Communication → Society → Language → Civilisation
(C) Communication → Language → Society → Civilisation
(D) Language → Society → Communication → Civilisation

## UGC NET-December 2018

**31** A teacher decides to form six groups of students and assigns a sub-theme to each group for discussion and reporting. Which kind of communication model will best describe his/her strategy in this regard?

(A) Transactional Model
(B) Linear Model
(C) Horizontal Model
(D) International Model

**32** Which of the following constitute the para language in communication?

1. Pitch of the voice
2. Internal noise
3. External noise
4. Use of pauses
5. Rate and volume of speech

Select the correct answer from from the codes given below.

(A) 2, 3 and 4 (B) 1, 4 and 5
(C) 1, 3 and 5 (D) 1, 2 and 3

**33** Which of the following would influence the effectiveness of communication in classroom instruction in a critical way?

(A) Subject knowledge of the teacher.
(B) Academic intelligence and personality characteristics of the teacher.
(C) Teaching aids used by the teacher while making presentations.
(D) Teaching style preferred by the teacher while transacting.

**34** While communicating in a classroom situation, which one of the following approaches will be considered the most appropriate?

(A) Empathetic and pragmatic
(B) Personal and emulative
(C) Technical and domineering
(D) Assertive and conformist

**35** Which of the following is a powerful determinant for effective assertive communication whether written or spoken?

(A) 'They' messages (B) 'I' messages
(C) 'We' messages (D) 'You' messages

## UGC NET-July 2018

**36** Identify the important element a teacher has to take cognizance of while addressing students in a classroom.

(A) Avoidance of proximity
(B) Voice modulation
(C) Repetitive pause
(D) Fixed posture

**37** **Assertion** (A) Classroom communication is a transactional process.

**Reason** (R) A teacher does not operate under the assumption that students responses are purposive.

Select the correct code for your answer.

(A) A is true, but R is false
(B) A is false, but R is true
(C) Both A and R are true and R is the correct explanation of A
(D) Both A and R are true, but R is not the correct explanation of A

**38** **Assertion** (A) To communicate well in the classroom is a natural ability.

**Reason** (R) Effective teaching in the classroom demands knowledge of the communication process.

Select the correct code for your answer.

(A) A is true, but R is false
(B) A is false, but R is true
(C) Both A and R are true and R is the correct explanation of A
(D) Both A and R are true, but R is not the correct explanation of A

**39** Which of the following set of statements are correct for describing the human communication process?

1. Non-verbal communication can stimulate ideas.
2. Communication is a learnt ability.
3. Communication is not a universal panacea.
4. Communication cannot break down.
5. More communication means more effective learning by students.

Select the correct answer from the codes given below.

(A) 2, 3 and 4 (B) 1, 4 and 5
(C) 1, 3 and 5 (D) 1, 2 and 3

## UGC NET-November 2017

**40** In a classroom, the probability of message reception can be enhanced by

(A) exposing the ignorance of students
(B) increasing the information load
(C) using high decibel audio tools
(D) establishing a viewpoint

**41** A good communicator begins his/her presentation with a

(A) non-sequitur (B) repetitive phrase
(C) ice breaker (D) complex question

**42** The classroom communication should essentially be

(A) empathetic (B) abstract
(C) non-descriptive (D) contrived

**43** Classroom communication must be

(A) teacher centric (B) student centric
(C) general centric (D) textbook centric

## UGC NET-January 2017

44 When verbal and non-verbal messages are contradictory, it is said that most people believe in
(A) indeterminate messages
(B) verbal messages
(C) non-verbal messages
(D) aggressive messages

45 Positive classroom communication leads to
(A) coercion
(B) submission
(C) confrontation
(D) persuasion

46 Classroom communication is the basis of
(A) social identity
(B) external (lack of sense or meaning)
(C) biased passivity
(D) group aggression

47 Effective communication pre-supposes
(A) non-alignment
(B) domination
(C) passivity
(D) understanding

48 Expressive communication is driven by
(A) passive aggression
(B) encoder's personality characteristics
(C) external clues
(D) encoder-decoder contract

## UGC NET-July 2016

49 Imagine you are working in an educational institution where people are of equal status. Which method of communication is best suited and normally employed in such a context?
(A) Horizontal communication
(B) Vertical communication
(C) Corporate communication
(D) Cross communication

50 As a teacher, select the best option to ensure your effective presence in the classroom.
(A) Use of peer command
(B) Making aggressive statements
(C) Adoption of well established posture
(D) Being authoritarian

51 What are the barriers to effective communication?
(A) Moralising, being judgemental and comments of consolation
(B) Dialogue, summary and self-review
(C) Use of simple words, cool reaction and defensive attitude
(D) Personal statements, eye contact and simple narration

52 The choice of communication partners is influenced by factors of
(A) proximity, utility, loneliness
(B) utility, secrecy, dissonance
(C) secrecy, dissonance, deception
(D) dissimilarity, dissonance, deviance

53 Every communicator has to experience
(A) manipulated emotions
(B) anticipatory excitement
(C) the issue of homophiles
(D) status dislocation

## UGC NET-December 2015

54 Every type of communication is affected by
(A) context
(B) reception
(C) transmission
(D) non-regulation

55 Aspects of the voice, other than the speech are known as
(A) delivery language
(B) physical language
(C) personal language
(D) paralanguage

56 In a classroom, a communicator's trust level is determined by
(A) eye contact
(B) the use of hyperbole
(C) the change of voice level
(D) the use of abstract concepts

## UGC NET-July 2015

57 The term 'Grapevine' is also known as
(A) downward communication
(B) upward communication
(C) informal communication
(D) horizontal communication

## UGC NET-June 2015

**58** In communication, the language is
(A) the verbal code
(B) intrapersonal
(C) the symbolic code
(D) the non-verbal code

**59** **Assertion** (A) Formal communication tends to be fast and flexible.

**Reason** (R) Formal communication is a systematic and orderly flow of information.

Select the correct code for your answer.
(A) Both A and R are true and R is the correct explanation of A
(B) Both A and R are true, but R is not the correct explanation of A
(C) A is true, but R is false
(D) A is false, but R is true

**60** Which of the following is not a principle of effective communication?
(A) Persuasive and convincing dialogue
(B) Participation of the audience
(C) One-way transfer of information
(D) Strategic use of grapevine

**61** Effectiveness of communication can be traced from which of the following?
1. Attitude surveys
2. Performance records
3. Students attendance
4. Selection of communication channel

Select the correct answer from the codes given below.
(A) 1, 2 and 4 (B) 1, 2 and 3
(C) 2, 3 and 4 (D) All of these

# ANSWERS

## Chapter Practice

| | | | | | | | | | |
|---|---|---|---|---|---|---|---|---|---|
| 1 (A) | 2 (D) | 3 (A) | 4 (A) | 5 (B) | 6 (C) | 7 (D) | 8 (D) | 9 (D) | 10 (D) |
| 11 (D) | 12 (C) | 13 (C) | 14 (B) | 15 (C) | 16 (D) | 17 (A) | 18 (B) | 19 (C) | 20 (D) |
| 21 (B) | 22 (D) | 23 (B) | 24 (C) | 25 (D) | 26 (A) | 27 (B) | 28 (B) | 29 (A) | 30 (B) |
| 31 (D) | 32 (B) | 33 (D) | 34 (D) | 35 (D) | 36 (A) | 37 (B) | 38 (C) | 39 (D) | 40 (D) |
| 41 (B) | 42 (C) | 43 (C) | 44 (B) | 45 (D) | 46 (C) | 47 (D) | 48 (B) | 49 (B) | 50 (A) |
| 51 (C) | 52 (B) | 53 (A) | 54 (D) | 55 (D) | 56 (D) | 57 (A) | 58 (D) | 59 (C) | 60 (C) |
| 61 (A) | 62 (D) | 63 (D) | 64 (C) | 65 (D) | 66 (C) | 67 (D) | 68 (B) | 69 (A) | 70 (A) |
| 71 (D) | 72 (D) | 73 (D) | 74 (D) | 75 (D) | 76 (D) | 77 (A) | 78 (A) | 79 (D) | 80 (B) |
| 81 (D) | 82 (D) | 83 (D) | 84 (B) | 85 (A) | 86 (B) | 87 (D) | 88 (A) | 89 (D) | 90 (B) |
| 91 (D) | 92 (D) | 93 (D) | 94 (D) | 95 (C) | 96 (D) | 97 (B) | 98 (A) | 99 (B) | 100 (D) |
| 101 (A) | 102 (D) | 103 (C) | 104 (D) | 105 (D) | 106 (D) | 107 (C) | 108 (A) | 109 (D) | 110 (D) |
| 111 (D) | 112 (D) | | | | | | | | |

## Previous Years' Questions

| | | | | | | | | | |
|---|---|---|---|---|---|---|---|---|---|
| 1 (D) | 2 (C) | 3 (C) | 4 (D) | 5 (A) | 6 (B) | 7 (D) | 8 (C) | 9 (D) | 10 (C) |
| 11 (A) | 12 (B) | 13 (C) | 14 (A) | 15 (B) | 16 (A) | 17 (C) | 18 (D) | 19 (D) | 20 (D) |
| 21 (D) | 22 (D) | 23 (C) | 24 (C) | 25 (C) | 26 (A) | 27 (D) | 28 (B) | 29 (D) | 30 (C) |
| 31 (A) | 32 (B) | 33 (D) | 34 (A) | 35 (B) | 36 (B) | 37 (A) | 38 (B) | 39 (C) | 40 (D) |
| 41 (C) | 42 (A) | 43 (B) | 44 (C) | 45 (D) | 46 (A) | 47 (D) | 48 (B) | 49 (A) | 50 (C) |
| 51 (A) | 52 (A) | 53 (B) | 54 (A) | 55 (D) | 56 (A) | 57 (C) | 58 (C) | 59 (D) | 60 (C) |
| 61 (B) | | | | | | | | | |

# UNIT 05

# Mathematical Reasoning and Aptitude

**CHAPTER ANALYSIS**

This unit is based on updated exam pattern of NTA UGC NET covering all the important topics of Mathematics; Reasoning & Aptitude. In Reasoning Section questions are asked from Series, Coding Decoding, Sitting Arrangement, Direction Sense Test, Blood Relation etc.

In Mathematical Aptitude Section questions are asked from Fraction, Ratio and Proportion, Percentage, Profit, Loss & Discount and Interest. Every year 4 to 5 questions are asked from this unit. With consistent practice, you can score full marks in these questions.

**IN THIS UNIT**

- Types of Reasoning
- Number Series, Letter Series
- Codes and Relationships
- Mathematical Aptitude (Fraction, Percentage, Ratio and Proportion, Average, Profit and Loss, Discounting, Interest, Time and Distance, etc.).

## REASONING

Reasoning is the process of thinking in a logical way in order to form the conclusion or judgement from an information. It basically tests one's ability to judge things in a complete situation. It analyses a student's ability to picturise data and rearrange it to reach to a solution. From a student's perspective, Reasoning as a subject does not require any formal learning of specific rules, but an exposure to find your own way to handle tricky questions.

There are three important methods of reasoning, deductive, inductive and abductive reasoning.

1. Deductive Reasoning
2. Inductive Reasoning
3. Abductive Reasoning

### 1. Deductive Reasoning

It is the process of reasoning from one or more statements (premises) to reach a logical certain conclusion.

***Example***

All humans are deathly. (first premise)

Rakesh is a human. (second premise)

Therefore, Rakesh is deathly. (conclusion)

## 2. Inductive Reasoning

It reaches conclusions through the citation of examples and is the most frequently used form of logical reasoning. It is also known as 'synthetical reasoning'.

***Example***

Rakesh is mortal. (first premise)

Ram is mortal. (second premise)

Mohan is mortal. (third premise)

Therefore, Human is mortal. (conclusion)

## 3. Abductive Reasoning

It is somewhat similar to inductive reasoning. It takes its clues from guessing, since conclusions drawn here are based on probabilities.

***Example***

The container is filled with red pebbles. (major premise)

Raman has a red pebble in his hand. (minor premise)

The red pebble in Raman's hand was taken out of the container. (conclusion)

By abductive reasoning, the possibility that Raman took the red pebble from the container is reasonable, though it is purely based on the speculation.

Anyone could have given the red pebble to Raman, or probably Raman could have bought a red pebble at a retail store.

## Types of Reasoning

Conventionally there are three important domains of reasoning.

### Logical Reasoning

It is the process of deriving a logical inference from a hypothesis through reasoning. It tests one's reading and understanding abilities.

It involves interpreting sentences, deriving conclusions from passages, extracting logics from statements, deriving courses of action from statements, arguments, assumptions, and conclusions from the given statements.

### Verbal Reasoning

It is the ability to logically understand the concepts and solve problems expressed in words. It includes questions based on analogy, classification, blood-relation etc.

### Non-verbal Reasoning

It is the ability to understand the concepts and solve problems expressed in numbers/letters/ figures in combination with words.

It involves identifying relationship, finding series of figures, image analysis, finding similarities and differences between shapes and pattern etc.

# SERIES

Series is a sequential order of letters, numbers or both arranged in such a way that each term in the series is obtained according to specific rules.

## Number Series

In questions based on Number Series, you are required to find the missing or wrong number in a sequence. The missing number may be at the beginning, middle or at the end of sequence.

### Types of Number Series

- **Even Series** The series in which all the numbers are even numbers followed in a sequence, is known as even series.
  e.g. 2, 4, 6, 8, 10, 12, 14, 16, 18, 20 etc.
- **Odd Series** The series in which all the numbers are odd numbers followed in a sequence, is known as odd series.
  e.g. 1, 3, 5, 7, 9, 11, 13, 15, 17, 19, 21 etc.
- **Prime Series** The series in which all the numbers are prime numbers followed in a sequence, is known as prime series.
  e.g. 2, 3, 5, 7, 11, 13, 17, 19, 23, 29, 31 etc.
- **Square Series** The series in which all the numbers are squares of natural numbers followed in a sequence is known as square series.

e.g. $\begin{bmatrix} 1^2, & 2^2, & 3^2, & 4^2, & 5^2, & 6^2, & 7^2, & 8^2 \ldots \\ \downarrow & \downarrow & \downarrow & \downarrow & \downarrow & \downarrow & \downarrow & \downarrow \\ 1, & 4, & 9, & 16, & 25, & 36, & 49, & 64 \ldots \end{bmatrix}$

- **Cube Series** The series in which all the numbers are the cube of natural numbers followed in a sequence, is known as cube series.

e.g. $\begin{bmatrix} 1^3, & 2^3, & 3^3, & 4^3, & 5^3, & 6^3, & 7^3 \cdots \\ \downarrow & \downarrow & \downarrow & \downarrow & \downarrow & \downarrow & \downarrow \\ 1, & 8, & 27, & 64, & 125, & 216, & 343 \cdots \end{bmatrix}$

- **Arithmetic Series** The series in which the difference between each successive terms is constant, is known as arithmetic series.

e.g. 84, 80, 76, 72, 68, 64, 60, 56, 52, 48, 44 (–4 each step)

- **Mixed Series** The series in which we get the next term, first by multiplying/dividing and then by adding/ subtracting, is known as mixed series.

e.g. 3, 7, 15, 31, 63, 127, 255 (×2+1 each step)

- **Geometric Series** (GP) The series in which the ratio between each successive term is constant, is known as geometric series.

e.g. 1, 3, 9, 27, 81, 243, 729 (×3 each step)

$$\text{ratio } (r) = \frac{3}{1} = \frac{9}{3}, \frac{27}{9}, \frac{81}{27}, \ldots\ldots = 3$$

$$(r) = 3$$

**Note** In this case we apply multiplication or division.

- **Arithmetico-Geometric Series** This series is formed by a peculiar combination of Arithmetic and Geometric series.

e.g. 1, 4, 8, 11, 22, 25, [?] (+3, ×2, +3, ×2, +3, ×2)

$\therefore$ $? = 25 \times 2 = 50$

- **Twin/Alternate Series** This type of series may consist of two series combined into a single series. The alternating terms of this series may form an independent series in itself.

e.g. 3, 4, 8, 10, 13, 16, [? ?] (4 → 10 → 16 → ?: +6, +6, +6; 3 → 8 → 13 → ?: +5, +5, +5)

$\therefore$ First '?' = 13 + 5 = 18

and Second '?' = 16 + 6 = 22

So, next two terms of the series should be 18 and 22 respectively.

## Examples

**Directions** (Example Nos. 1-7) *Find the next number in the series.*

**1** 1, 3, 6, 10, 15, _

(A) 21 (B) 23 (C) 20 (D) 19

***Sol.*** *(A)* The pattern of the series is,

1, 3, 6, 10, 15, [21] (+2, +3, +4, +5, +6)

**2** 87, 80, 74, 69, 65, _

(A) 61 (B) 62 (C) 65 (D) 66

***Sol.*** *(B)* The pattern of the series is,

87, 80, 74, 69, 65, [62] (–7, –6, –5, –4, –3)

**3** 40, 15, 30, 25, 20, 35, _

(A) 13 (B) 81 (C) 72 (D) 10

***Sol.*** *(D)* The pattern of the series is,

40, 15, 30, 25, 20, 35, [10] (40 → 30 → 20 → 10: –10, –10, –10; 15 → 25 → 35: +10, +10)

**4** 2, 15, 41, 80, ?

(A) 111 (B) 120

(C) 121 (D)132

***Sol.*** *(D)* The series has following pattern

2, 15, 41, 80, [132] (+13, +26, +39, +52)

Here, there is an increment of consecutive multiples of 13 in consecutive terms.

Hence, missing term is 132.

**5** 32, 87, 332, 1635, ?

(A) 9000 (B) 8775

(C) 9774 (D) 6549

***Sol.*** *(C)* The series pattern is

32, 87, 332, 1635, [9774] ((–3)×3, (–4)×4, (–5)×5, (–6)×6)

**6** Which is the number that comes next in the following sequence?

2, 6, 12, 20, 30, 42, 56, ?

(A) 60 (B) 64 (C) 72 (D) 70

***Sol.*** *(C)*

2 6 12 20 30 42 56 [72]

+4 +6 +8 +10 +12 +14 +16

+2 +2 +2 +2 +2 +2

**7** Determine the term 'X' in the following series

2, 9, 20, 35, 54, 77, 'X'

(A) 104 (B) 102 (C) 89 (D) 110

***Sol.*** *(A)* 2, 9 20, 35, 54, 77, X,

+7 +11 +15 +19 +23 +27

+4 +4 +4 +4 +4

∴ X = 77 + 27 = 104

## Letter Series

Letter series is a sequence of letters taken from English alphabet and such sequence follows a certain logical pattern.

In letter series, certain logical pattern means that every next element of the series is obtained according to a certain change. In this series candidates are required to find out the next letter in the series or the missing letter in the series or the letter which is wrong in the series.

To solve these kinds of problems, assign numbers 1 to 26 to the letters of the English alphabets as shown below.

⟵ ***Reverse order***

| 26 | 25 | 24 | 23 | 22 | 21 | 20 | 19 | 18 | 17 | 16 | 15 | 14 |
|---|---|---|---|---|---|---|---|---|---|---|---|---|
| A | B | C | D | E | F | G | H | I | J | K | L | M |
| 1 | 2 | 3 | 4 | 5 | 6 | 7 | 8 | 9 | 10 | 11 | 12 | 13 |

| 13 | 12 | 11 | 10 | 9 | 8 | 7 | 6 | 5 | 4 | 3 | 2 | 1 |
|---|---|---|---|---|---|---|---|---|---|---|---|---|
| N | O | P | Q | R | S | T | U | V | W | X | Y | Z |
| 14 | 15 | 16 | 17 | 18 | 19 | 20 | 21 | 22 | 23 | 24 | 25 | 26 |

***Forward order*** ⟶

Concept of 'EJOTY'

| Letter | E | J | O | T | Y |
|---|---|---|---|---|---|
| Number | 5 | 10 | 15 | 20 | 25 |

The candidates can determine the relative positions of various alphabets by just remembering the word 'EJOTY'.

Series of opposite English alphabets

| | | | | | | | | | | | | |
|---|---|---|---|---|---|---|---|---|---|---|---|---|
| A | B | C | D | E | F | G | H | I | J | K | L | M |
| Z | Y | X | W | V | U | T | S | R | Q | P | O | N |

### *Examples*

**Directions** (Example Nos. 8-12) *Find the next number in the series.*

**8** Find the next letter for the series YVSP_______.

(A) N (B) M

(C) O (D) L

***Sol.*** *(B)* Y V S P [M]

−3 −3 −3 −3

**9** Find the missing letter in the series.

A, B, D, G, ..., P

(A) K (B) L

(C) M (D) N

***Sol.*** *(A)* A B D G [K] P

+1 +2 +3 +4 +5

**10** Find the missing letters in the series.

AB, DE, GH, ... , MN

(A) HI (B) JK

(C) KL (D) None of these

***Sol.*** *(B)*

+1 +1 +1 +1 +1

AB DE GH [JK] MN

+2 +2 +2 +2

**11** DKY, FJW, HIU, JHS, ?

(A) LFQ (B) LGQ

(C) KGR (D) KFR

***Sol.*** *(B)*

D —+2→ F —+2→ H —+2→ J —+2→ [L]

K —−1→ J —−1→ I —−1→ H —−1→ [G]

Y —−2→ W —−2→ U —−2→ S —−2→ [Q]

**12** What are the missing letters in the following series?

pqr – –rsp rs – – spq –

(A) pqppq (B) spqpr (C) sqpqr (D) sqprq

***Sol.*** *(C)* Here, the block which is repeated, consists of four letters 'pqrs'. Rewriting the series, the series must be pqrs/qrsp/rspq/spqr so, that the missing letters are 'sqpqr'. Thus, (C) is the correct option.

# CLASSIFICATION

The questions based on classification are based on similarity or dissimilarity between certain items or objects.

Some objects are grouped together on the basis of some common characteristics. This test is also known as 'odd one out'. In this topic following types of questions are asked.

## Choosing Odd Word

In this type of questions certain words have some similarity between them except one, which is the odd one out. Examples of choosing odd word are given below.

### Examples

**1** Choose the odd word in the group.

(A) Peacock (B) Vulture
(C) Sparrow (D) Swan

***Sol.*** *(D)* Swan is the only water bird in the group.

**2** Choose the odd word in the group.

(A) Sun (B) Black hole
(C) Venus (D) Mars

***Sol.*** *(B)* All the terms except 'Black hole' are related to the solar system.

**3** Choose the odd word in the group.

(A) Artery (B) Ventricle
(C) Pharynx (D) Aorta

***Sol.*** *(C)* Except 'Pharynx', all other terms are related to 'heart'.

## Choosing Odd Pair of Words

In this type of questions some pair of words are given which have certain relationship between them, we have to choose the pair in which the words are differently related.

Examples of choosing odd pair of words are given below.

### Examples

**4** Choose the pair in which words are differently related.

(A) Joule : Energy (B) Ampere : Current
(C) Angle : Degree (D) Pascal : Pressure

***Sol.*** *(C)* In all the pairs except Angle : Degree, first is a unit to measure the second.

**5** Choose the pair in which words are differently related.

(A) Death : Disease (B) Milk : Butter
(C) Grape : Wine (D) Water : Oxygen

***Sol.*** *(A)* In all other pairs except Death:Disease, second is a product obtained from the first.

**6** Choose the pair in which words are differently related.

(A) Ice–Cube : Cold (B) Iron : Hard
(C) Marble : Smooth (D) Purse : Money

***Sol.*** *(D)* Except (D), in all other pairs, second denotes a property of the first.

## Choosing Odd Numeral/Odd Numeral Pair in the Group

In this type of questions, some numeral/ numeral pair are given. We have to choose the odd numeral/ numeral pair from given options. Example of choosing numeral/numeral pair is given below.

### Examples

**7** Choose the odd number.

(A) 22 (B) 121 (C) 34 (D) 110

***Sol.*** *(C)* Except 34, all the other numbers are divisible by 11. Hence, 34 is the odd one.

**8** Choose the number pair that is different from others.

(A) 3, 5 (B) 7, 2 (C) 6, 2 (D) 1, 7

***Sol.*** *(B)* In all other pairs except (7, 2) the sum of the given numbers is 8.

**9** Choose the number pair that is different from others.

(A) (29, 31) (B) (47, 49) (C) (5, 7) (D) (11, 13)

***Sol.*** *(B)* Except (47, 49), all other options have prime numbers.

**10** Choose the number pair that is different from others.

(A) (80, 9) (B) (64, 8) (C) (36, 6) (D) (49, 7)

***Sol.*** *(A)* Except (80, 9), in all other options the first number is the square of second.

## Choose the Odd Letter Group

In this type of questions, some groups of letters are given, all of which except one, share a common similarity. Example of choosing odd letter group is given below.

### *Examples*

**11** Choose the group of letters that is different from others.

(A) KLM (B) IJK (C) PQR (D) RST

***Sol.*** *(B)* No other group contains a vowel, so IJK is odd among all.

**12** Choose the group of letters that is different from others.

(A) DCEB (B) PNQST
(C) VKHUM (D) WPZLH

***Sol.*** *(A)* Except option (A), all other options have 5 letters whereas option (A) has four letters.

**13** Choose the group of letters that is different from others.

(A) HKI (B) UXV (C) CFD (D) MQN

***Sol.*** *(D)* Except MQN, all other follow similar pattern.

H K I (+3, −2) U X V (+3, −2)

C F D (+3, −2) M Q N (+4, −3)

# CODING AND DECODING

A 'Code' is a system of conveying a message through signals. It is a method of sending a message between sender and the receiver in such a way that only the sender and the receiver can know its meaning.

However, 'Coding' is done according to a certain pattern in the mind of the sender. Therefore, its meaning can be deciphered by a third person, only if he carefully studies this pattern. This process is called 'Decoding'.

## Letter Coding

In this type of coding, letters of the original word are rearranged or coded in a particular pattern. To obtain the answer, the code needs to be deciphered.

Examples of letter coding are given below.

### *Examples*

**1** If 'SILVER' is coded as 'ZXYBDQ ' and 'KAMAL' is coded as LNCNY, then what will be the code for 'VIKAS'?

(a) BXNLZ (b) ZXYCN
(c) BXLNZ (d) LNCBD

***Sol.*** *(c)* As,

S I L V E R → Z X Y B D Q and K A M A L → L N C N Y

Similarly, V I K A S → B X L N Z

**2** If in a certain code language MAN is coded as NBO. Which of the following will be the code for SKY ?

(A) TLZ (B) ZLT
(C) YKS (D) LTZ

***Sol.*** *(A)* As, M A N (+1 +1 +1) → N B O  Similarly, S K Y (+1 +1 +1) → T L Z

**3** If MOHAN is represented by the code KMFYL, then COUNT will be represented by

(A) AMSLR (B) MSLAR
(C) MASRL (D) SAMLR

***Sol.*** *(A)* As, M O H A N (−2 −2 −2 −2 −2) → K M F Y L

Similarly, C O U N T (−2 −2 −2 −2 −2) → A M S L R

**4** If in a certain code language 'MIGHT' is written as 'GHMTI', then how will 'EARTH' is written in that code ?

(A) RTEHA (B) RTEAM
(C) RTAEH (D) RETHA

***Sol.*** *(A)* As, MIGHT ⟶ GHMTI
12345 → 34152

Similarly, EARTH ⟶ RTEHA
12345 → 34152

**5** In a certain code 'GALIB' is represented by 'HBMJC'. 'TIGER' will be represented by

(A) UJHFS (B) UHJSF
(C) JHUSF (D) HUJSF

***Sol.*** *(A)* As,

| G | A | L | I | B |
|---|---|---|---|---|
| ↓ +1 | ↓ +1 | ↓ +1 | ↓ +1 | ↓ +1 |
| H | B | M | J | C |

Similarly,

| T | I | G | E | R |
|---|---|---|---|---|
| ↓ +1 | ↓ +1 | ↓ +1 | ↓ +1 | ↓ +1 |
| U | J | H | F | S |

## Letter and Numerical Coding

In these questions, either numerical values are assigned to a word or alphabetical code values are assigned to the numbers.

The candidate is required to analyse the code according to the directions. Examples of letter and numerical coding are given below.

### Examples

**6** In a given code, SISTER is coded as 535301. UNCLE as 84670 and BOY as 129. How is RUSTIC written in that code?

(A) 633185 (B) 185336
(C) 363815 (D) 581363

***Sol.*** *(B)* As,

S I S T E R → 5 3 5 3 0 1

U N C L E → 8 4 6 7 0 and B O Y → 1 2 9

Therefore, R U S T I C → 1 8 5 3 3 6

**7** In a certain code, REASON is written as 621754 and TRUTH as 86983. Find out the codes for TREASON.

(A) 7548261 (B) 8621754
(C) 7452861 (D) 2865614

***Sol.*** *(B)* As, R E A S O N → 6 2 1 7 5 4 and T R U T H → 8 6 9 8 3

Therefore, T R E A S O N → 8 6 2 1 7 5 4

## Coding using Position Number of Alphabet

We present the alphabets and assign number to them as follows

| A | B | C | D | E | F | G | H | I | J | K | L | M |
|---|---|---|---|---|---|---|---|---|---|---|---|---|
| 1 | 2 | 3 | 4 | 5 | 6 | 7 | 8 | 9 | 10 | 11 | 12 | 13 |
| N | O | P | Q | R | S | T | U | V | W | X | Y | Z |
| 14 | 15 | 16 | 17 | 18 | 19 | 20 | 21 | 22 | 23 | 24 | 25 | 26 |

Example of coding using position number of alphabet is given below.

### Examples

**8** If in a certain code language 'WORD' is coded as 2315184, then how will 'SIMPLE' be coded as ?

(A) 1991316125 (B) 9131912165
(C) 1319161259 (D) None of these

***Sol.*** *(A)* As, W O R D → 23 15 18 4 Similary, S I M P L E → 19 9 13 16 12 5

[English alphabetical series position]

**9** If HPU = 9, JNU = 9, then DU = ?

(A) 5 (B) 6 (C) 1 (D) 7

***Sol.*** *(A)* In the alphabet series

H = 8, P= 16, U = 21

8 + 16 + 21 = 45

45 ÷ 5 = 9

J = 10, N = 14, U = 21

10 + 14 + 21 = 45

45 ÷ 5 = 9

Similarly, D = 4, U = 21

4 + 21 = 25

25 ÷ 5 = 5

Hence, option (A) is correct.

## Symbol Coding

In symbol coding, various symbols are assigned to the letters of a word and based upon their correlation or similarity, the candidates are required to find the rules or pattern which is being followed.

Example of symbol coding is as follows;

### Example

**10** In a certain code language 'GONE' is written as '5%2#' and 'MEDAL' is written as '4 # 3 $ @', then how will 'GOLD' be written in that code language ?

(A) 5@%3 (B) 5%@3 (C) 5#@3 (D) 5%#3

***Sol.*** *(B)* As,

| G | O | N | E | and | M | E | D | A | L |
|---|---|---|---|---|---|---|---|---|---|
| ↓ | ↓ | ↓ | ↓ | | ↓ | ↓ | ↓ | ↓ | ↓ |
| 5 | % | 2 | # | | 4 | # | 3 | $ | @ |

Similarly,

| G | O | L | D |
|---|---|---|---|
| ↓ | ↓ | ↓ | ↓ |
| 5 | % | @ | 3 |

∴ GOLD ⇒ 5%@3

## Substitution Coding

In this type of coding, an object name is substituted with different object names, we should carefully trace the substitution and answer given question.

### Example

**11** If 'book' is coded as 'pencil', 'pencil' is coded as 'mirror', 'mirror' is coded as 'book'. Then, what is useful to write on a paper?

(A) book (B) pencil (C) mirror (D) pen

***Sol.*** *(C)* From the question, pencil is useful to write on a paper but pencil is coded as mirror, so the mirror is useful to write on a paper.

## Artificial Language Coding

In this type of questions, some messages are provided in the code language and some codes are assigned to each word of the message.

The candidates are required to decipher the code of each word by finding the common code for two words and this process is followed to decipher the code for each word thereafter and hence the entire message is decoded.

Examples of artificial language coding are given below.

### Examples

**12** In a certain code language 'he is great' is written as 'ka pa ra' and 'is ram hungry' is written as 'na sa ka'. Find the code for 'is'.

(A) na (B) sa (C) ka (D) ra

***Sol.*** *(C)* he (is) great → (ka) pa ra.

(is) ram hungry → na sa (ka)

Clearly, the code for 'is' is 'ka'.

**13** Given that in a code language, '645' means 'day is warm' ; '42' means 'warm spring' and '632' means 'spring is sunny'. Which digit represents 'sunny' ?

(A) 3 (B) 2

(C) 4 (D) 5

***Sol.*** *(A)* 645 → day is warm – I

42 → warm spring – II

632 → spring is sunny – III

From I and II, we can find that the common number is 4.

So, 4 stands for warm.

From I and III, common number is 6. So, 6 stands for 'is' and from II and III, we can find that the common number is 2, so 2 stands for spring. Now, from III we can see that 3 stands for 'sunny'.

## Conditional Coding

Under this pattern, letters/numbers are given and their codes are given right under them. Candidates are required to find out code for a particular letter group/word/number according to the given conditions.

### Examples

**14** In the question below, is given a group of numbers followed by four combinations of letters/symbols. You have to find out which of the combinations correctly represents the group of numbers based on the following coding system and the conditions that follow and mark your answer accordingly.

| **Digit** | 3 | 8 | 0 | 7 | 4 | 6 | 9 | 2 | 5 | 1 |
|---|---|---|---|---|---|---|---|---|---|---|
| **Code** | H | $ | R | A | M | % | L | K | E | @ |

Conditions

(i) If a number begins and ends with a non-zero odd digit, then the first and the last digits are to be coded as Y and #, respectively.

(ii) If a number begins and ends with an even digit (including zero), then the first and the last digits are to be coded as B and X, respectively.

What will be the code for 764981?

(A) A % M L $ @ (B) Y % M L $ @
(C) Y % M L $ # (D) A % M L $ #

***Sol.*** *(C)* When condition is not applied, the coding is done as follows

| 7 | 6 | 4 | 9 | 8 | 1 |
|---|---|---|---|---|---|
| ↓ | ↓ | ↓ | ↓ | ↓ | ↓ |
| Y | % | M | L | $ | # |

But here the number begins and ends with a non-zero odd digit and therefore condition (i) is applied here. As condition (i) is applied here, 7 and 1 will be coded as Y and #, respectively.

∴

| 7 | 6 | 4 | 9 | 8 | 1 |
|---|---|---|---|---|---|
| ↓ | ↓ | ↓ | ↓ | ↓ | ↓ |
| Y | % | M | L | $ | # |

∴ Code for 764981 ⇒ Y%ML$#

# BLOOD RELATIONSHIP

In such type of tests, the information about the blood relations of a group of persons is given in jumbled form. Candidate is asked to ascertain the relationship between any of two persons on the basis of the information provided.

## Developing a Family Relationship Tree

To develop a blood relation tree, some standard symbols may be used to tell about the relationship among the family members. Suppose A is male and B is a female. Generally, we use + sign for male and – sign for female.

| Condition | Sign |
|---|---|
| When A is male | (+) A |
| When B is female | (–) B |
| When A and B are married | (+) A ↔ (–) B |
| M is a child of N | N<br>↓<br>M |
| When P has two Children Q and R | P<br>↓ ↓<br>Q R |
| When T is the sibling of U | T ← U or T → U |

→ *Some of relations in the society have been given as below*

1. Grandfather's son : *Father or uncle*
2. Grandmother's son : *Father or uncle*
3. Grandfather's only son : *Father*
4. Grandmother's only son : *Father*
5. Mother's or father's mother : *Grandmother*
6. Mother's or father's father : *Grandfather*
7. Grandfather's only daughter-in-law : *Mother*
8. Grandmother's only daughter-in-law : *Mother*
9. Mother's or father's son : *Brother* or *oneself*
10. Mother's or father's daughter : *Sister* or *oneself*
11. Mother's or father's brother : *Uncle*
12. Mother's or father's sister : *Aunt*
13. Husband's or wife's sister : *Sister-in-law*
14. Husband's or wife's brother : *Brother-in-law*
15. Son's wife : *Daughter-in-law*
16. Daughter's husband : *Son-in-law*
17. Brother's son : *Nephew*
18. Brother's daughter : *Niece*
19. Uncle's or Aunt's son or daughter : *Cousin*
20. Sister's husband : *Brother-in-law*
21. Brother's wife : *Sister-in-law*
22. Children of same parents : *Siblings*
23. Common term for husband and wife : *Spouse.*

## Deciphering Relations based on Statement

In this type of questions, a person gives information to the another particular person either in a photograph or present in front of him.

Using this information, it is required to determine the relationship between the two people in the question. Examples of deciphering relation based on statement are given below.

### *Examples*

**1** Gopal said, pointing to Govind, "His father is my father's only son". How is Gopal related to Govind ?

(A) Grandfather (B) Grandson
(C) Son (D) Father

***Sol.*** *(D)* My father's only son → Myself

That means Gopal is talking about himself. Hence, Gopal is father of Govind.

**2** Pointing to a photograph, man said, "I have no brother or sister but that man's father is my father's son". Whose photograph was it ?

(A) His own (B) His son
(C) His father (D) His nephew

***Sol.*** *(B)* Since, the narrator has no brother or sister, his father's son means himself. So, the man who is talking is the father of the man in the photograph. Thus, the man in the photograph is his son.

## Relations Based on Fact

In this type of questions, the information is given in the form of a puzzle. It is required to analyse the information and answer the given questions. Examples of relations based on fact are given here.

### *Examples*

**3** If A is B's sister, C is B's mother, D is C's father and E is D's mother, then how is A related to D ?

(A) Granddaughter (B) Daughter
(C) Aunt (D) Father

***Sol.*** *(A)*

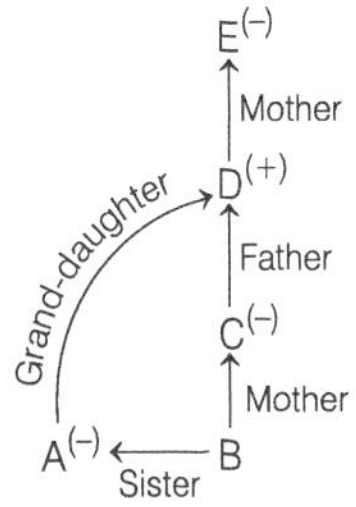


∴ A is the granddaughter of D.

**4** P is the father of R and S is the son of Q and T is the brother of P. If R is the sister of S, how is Q related to T ?

(A) Wife (B) Sister-in-law
(C) Brother-in-law (D) Daughter-in-law

***Sol.*** *(B)* Making relation diagram as per the given information.

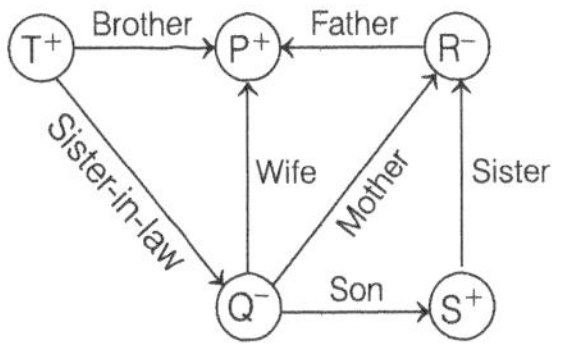


From above relation diagram we can say that Q is sister-in-law of T.

**5** A is father of B and C is sister of A, D is grandson of C. How is D related to B?

(A) Uncle (B) Nephew
(C) Cousin (D) Grandson

***Sol.*** *(B)*

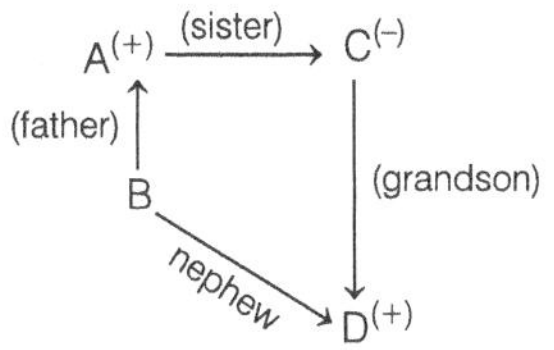


## Coded Relationship

In this type of questions certain symbols are used to represent the relationship. The candidate is required to decode the given information and answer the question based on it. Example of coded relationship is as follows.

### *Examples*

**Direction** (Example No. 6) *Read the following information and answer the question based on it.*

'A + B' means 'A is the daughter of B'.
'A × B' means 'A is the son of B'.
'A – B' means 'A is the wife of B'.

**6** If 'P × Q – S', which of the following is true ?

(A) S is the wife of Q (B) S is father of P
(C) P is daughter of Q (D) Q is father of P.

***Sol.*** *(B)* Let us draw a family diagram based on the given information.

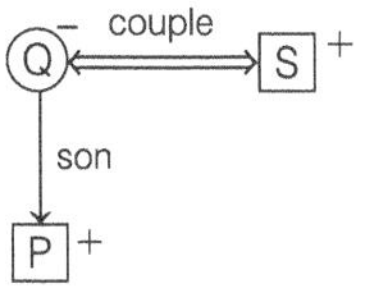


Clearly, S is the father of P.

**Directions** (Example Nos. 7 and 8) *Read the following information and answer the questions based on it.*

I. 'P × Q' means 'P is brother of Q'.
II. 'P – Q', means 'P is mother of Q'.
III. 'P + Q' means 'P is father of Q'.
IV. 'P ÷ Q' means 'P is sister of Q'.

**7** Which of the following means 'M is niece of N'?

(A) M × R – N (B) N ÷ J + M ÷ D
(C) N ÷ J + M (D) N × J – D ÷ M

*Sol.* *(B)* M is niece of N. So, M is female. Here option (A) is redundant. Also, gender of M cannot be determined using options (C) and (D).

Now, N ÷ J + M ÷ D

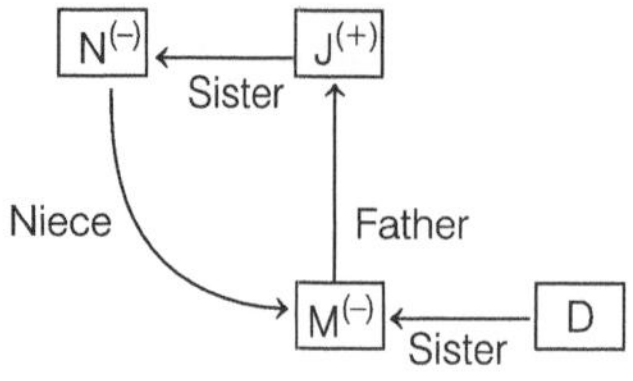


**8** Which of the following means B is the grandfather of F?

(A) B + J – F (B) B – J + F
(C) B × T – F (D) B ÷ T + F

*Sol.* *(A)* B is grandfather of F. So, B should be male. Hence, options (B) and (D) are redundant. By taking option (A).

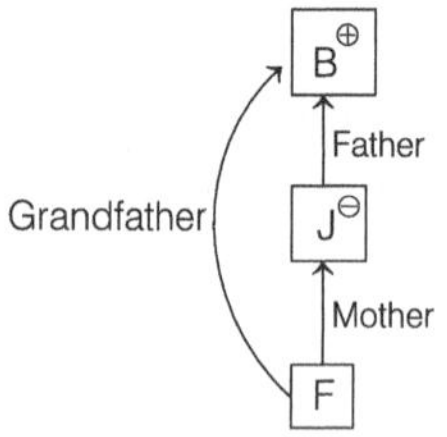


Hence, option (A) is true.

# DIRECTION SENSE TEST

There are four main directions–East, West, North, South as shown below

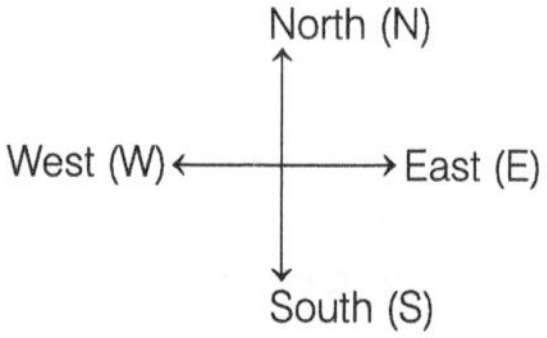


There are four cardinal directions– North-East (NE), North-West (NW), South-East (SE), and South-West (SW) as shown below

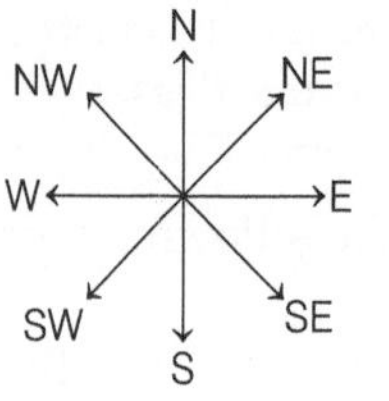


### → Some Important Points

- At the time of sunrise, the shadow of the object is always towards West.
- At the time of sunset, the shadow of the object is always towards East.
- At 12:00 Noon, the rays of the sun are vertically downward, hence there will be no shadow.
- Distances are also asked along with the directions in the questions related to the direction sense.
- The Pythagorus theorem is needed to find the distance. Therefore, according to Pythagorus theorem, in a right angle triangle;

$$(\text{Hypotenuse})^2 = (\text{perpendicular})^2 + (\text{Base})^2$$

## Examples

**1** After starting from a point, A walks 3 km towards East, then turning to his left he moves 3 km. After this, he again turns left and moves 3 km. In which direction is A from his starting point?

(A) North (B) East (C) West (D) South

*Sol.* *(A)* According to the question,

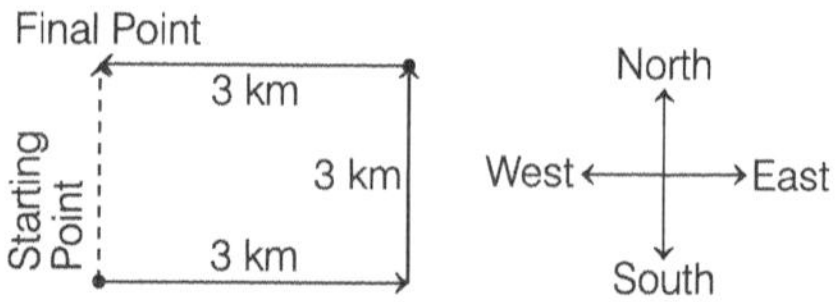


Thus, A is in North direction from his starting point.

**2** Ankit started walking towards North. After walking 30 m, he turned towards left and walked 40 m. He then turned left and walked 30 m. He again turned left and walked 50 m. How far is he from his original position?

(A) 10 m (B) 40 m
(C) 30 m (D) None of these

*Sol.* *(A)*

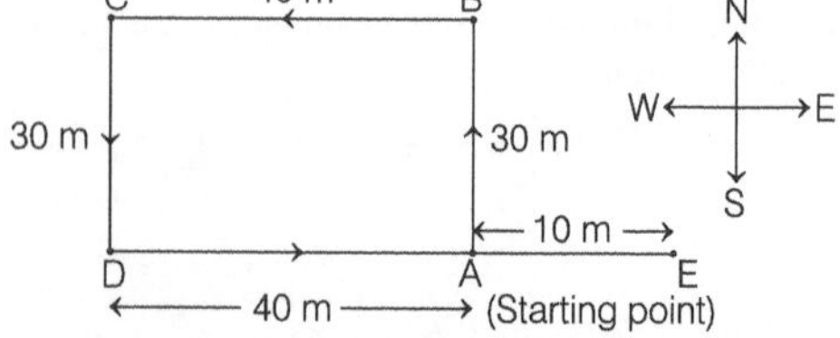


The final position of Ankit is E and starting point is A. Therefore, he is only 10 m away from his starting point. Hence, answer is the option (A).

**3** Lakshman went 15 km to the West from his house, then turned left and walked 20 km, he again turned towards East and walked 25 km and finally turned left and covered 20 km, how far is he now from his house?

(A) 15 km (B) 20 km (C) 25 km (D) 10 km

***Sol.*** *(D)*

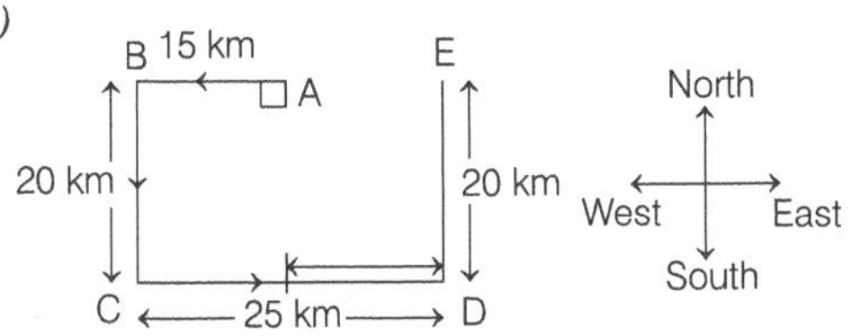


Points A and E show the starting and end positions respectively of Lakshman. From the diagram given above it is clear that E is 10 km away from A. Hence, option (D) is the correct answer.

**4** Ram walks 15 km to the West. Then, he turns South and walks 4 km. Again he turns to the East direction and walks 12 km. How far is he from his original position?

(A) 3 km (B) 4 km
(C) 5 km (D) 6 km

***Sol.*** *(C)*

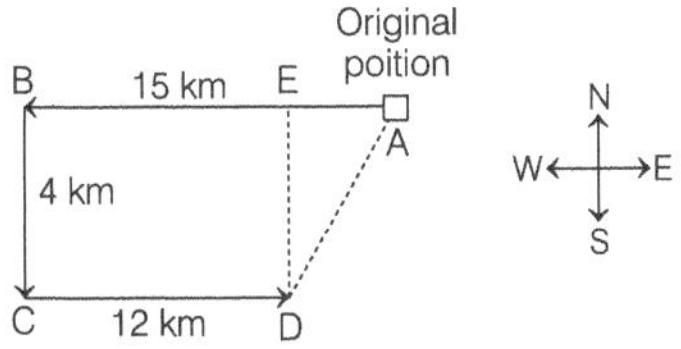


According to the above figure,

AB = 15 km, BC = 4 km

CD = 12 km, ED = BC = 4 km

EA = AB – BE, EA = 15 – 12 = 3 km

$\therefore \quad AD = \sqrt{AE^2 + DE^2}$

$= \sqrt{3^2 + 4^2} = \sqrt{9 + 16}$

$= \sqrt{25} = 5 \text{ km}$

**5** Mahesh walks 20 m North. Then, he turns right and walks 30 m. Now, he turns right and walks 35 m. Now turning left, he walks 15 m. Again, he turns left and moves 15 m. In which direction and how far is he from his original position?

(A) 15 m, East (B) 45 m, East
(C) 15 m, West (D) 45 m, West

***Sol.*** *(B)*

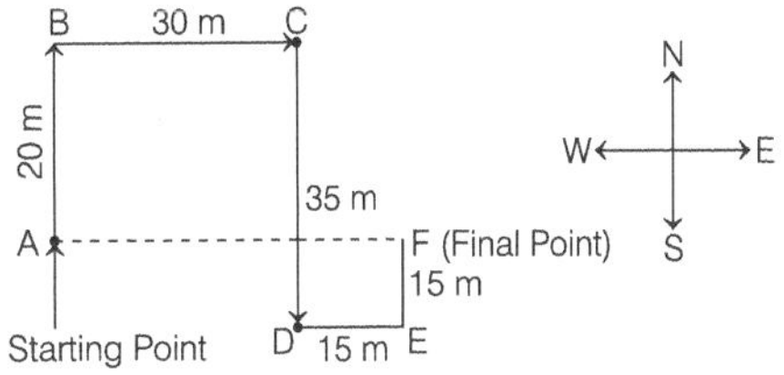


Mahesh's distance from his original position,

AF = BC + DE = 30 + 15 = 45 m

Also, 'F' lies to East of 'A'.

# ARRANGEMENT

The process of determining position, place or size of one or more than one person/thing on the basis of their relative comparison with other person/thing is called the Arrangement. There are two types of questions which are asked

1. Based on Order and Ranking
2. Based on Sitting Arrangement

## Based on Order and Ranking

In this type of questions, comparison of different objects based on some factors like ages, marks, size, height is given or the positon of person(s) from either of the two ends of a row is given.

In comparison type questions, the candidate is required to arrange the data in ascending or descending order and then answer the related question.

→ *While solving this type of question, keep the following points in mind*

1. Total number of persons in a row = (Rank of a person from left end/top + Rank of that person from right end/bottom) – 1
2. Rank of a person from right end/bottom = (Total number of person in row) – (Rank of that person from left end/top) + 1
3. Rank of a person from top/left end = (Total number of persons in row) – (Rank of that person from right end/bottom) + 1
4. In case of interchanging of positions
   (a) Total number of persons = [Initial position of 1st person+Interchanged position of 2nd person] –1
   (b) New position of 2nd person = [Difference in the two positions of 1st person] + [Initial position of 2nd person]

In position based questions, the candidate is required to find the total number of persons in the row or number of persons to the top/left or right/bottom of a particular person etc.

### Examples

**1** Ram is taller than Mohan and Sohan, while Sohan is taller than Shyam. Also, Mohan is taller than Sohan. Who amongst the following is the shortest?

(A) Shyam (B) Mohan
(C) Ram (D) Sohan

***Sol.*** *(A)* According to the question,

Ram > Mohan and Ram > Sohan
Sohan > Shyam
Mohan > Sohan

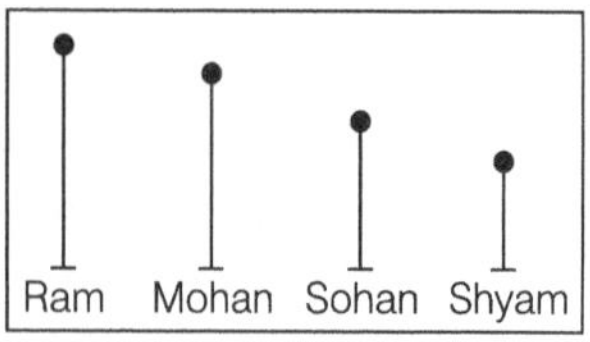


Arranging the above data, we get

Ram > Mohan > Sohan > Shyam

Clearly, Shyam is the shortest.

**2** In a row, position of Sandeep is 10th from left and 16th from right. How many people are there in the row?

(A) 30 (B) 26
(C) 25 (D) 16

***Sol.*** *(C)* Position of Sandeep from left (L) = 10

Position of Sandeep from right (R) = 16

∴ Total number of people in the row = (L + R) − 1
= 10 + 16 − 1
= 25

**3** In a queue of girls, Shama is 11th from the starting and 27th from the last. How many girls are there in the queue?

(A) 37 (B) 43
(C) 35 (D) 36

***Sol.*** *(A)* We know that,

Total number of girls in queue
= (Rank of girl from starting + Rank of girl from last) − 1
= 11 + 27 − 1 = 37

## Based on Sitting Arrangement

Questions of seating arrangement are based on a set of information containing certain conditions. Candidates are required to arrange the object either in a row or in a circle on the basis of such conditions.

Information given in the question is presented in distorted form to create confusion and to test candidate's ability to analyse the information step by step in order to answer the question correctly.

### Examples

**4** 6 persons are sitting in a row. They are A, B, C, D, E and F. C is not sitting beside D who is sitting on the extreme right. E is between A and C. A is not sitting beside F and D. B is between F and D. Who is at immediate right of A?

(A) B (B) C (C) D (D) E

***Sol.*** *(D)* According to the question, the arrangement is as follows.

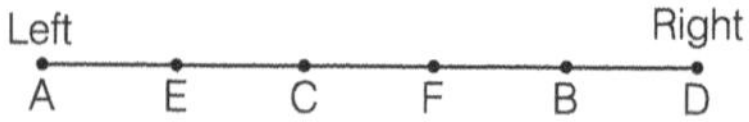


Clearly, E is sitting to the immediate right of A.

**5** A, B, C and D are playing cards. A and C and B and D are partners. D is to the right of C. The face of C is towards West. Find the direction that D is facing.

(A) West (B) East
(C) South (D) North

***Sol.*** *(C)* Arrangement according to the question is as follows

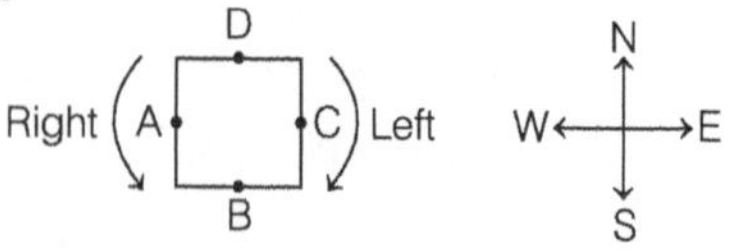


Clearly, D is facing South.

**6** Six persons are sitting in a circle facing the centre of the circle. Parikh is between Babita and Narendra. Asha is between Chitra and Pankaj. Chitra is to the immediate left of Babita. Who is to the immediate right of Babita?

(A) Parikh (B) Pankaj
(C) Narendra (D) Chitra

***Sol.*** *(A)* On the basis of information,

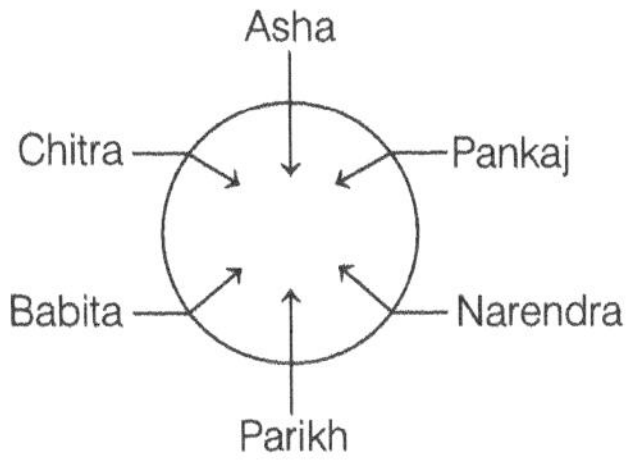


Clearly, Parikh is to the immediate right of Babita.

# MATHEMATICAL APTITUDE

Mathematical Aptitude simply means the ability of an individual to solve numerical and mathematical calculations. It also tests the quantitative skills along with logical and analytical skills.

In order to solve the question asked under this section, it is very important for the candidates to have knowledge of basic arithmetic.

## Basic Arithmetic

Questions based on Number system, fraction (Decimal), Average, Ratio & Proportion, Age, Percentage, Profit & loss, Discount, Interest, Unitary method, Time & Work, Speed, Distance & Time and Mensuration etc. come under Basic Arithmetic.

## Number System

A system, in which we study face and place values of the digits in a number, different types of number, divisibility tests by different number etc. is called number system.

- In a numeral, the face value of a digit is the value of the digit itself irrespective of its place in the numeral.

  For example, In the numeral 48532, the face value of 5 is 5.

- In a numeral (number), the place value of a digit changes according to the change of its place.

  For example, In the number 28354, the place value of 3 equals place value of hundredth digit i.e.

  $= (\text{Digit at hundredth place}) \times 10^2$

  $= 3 \times 10^2 = 300$

- Counting number are called natural numbers and these are denoted by N.

  For example, $N = \{1, 2, 3, ......\}$

- All natural numbers along with zero form a set of whole numbers and these are denoted by W.

  For example, $W = \{0, 1, 2, 3, ......\}$

- Whole numbers and negative numbers form is the set of integers and these are denoted by I.

  For example,
  $I = \{......, -4, -3, -2, -1, 0, 1, 2, 3, 4, ......\}$

- A counting number, which is divisible by 2, is called an even number.

  For example 2, 4, 6, 8, .........

- A counting number, which is not divisible by 2, is known as an odd number.

  For example 1, 3, 5, 7, 9, 11, .........

- A counting number is called prime number when it is exactly divisible by only 1 and itself.

  For example 2, 3, 5, 7, 11, 13, .........

### Examples

**1** Find the sum of face value and place value of 8 in 43836.

(A) 88 (B) 808 (C) 880 (D) 888

***Sol.*** *(B)* Place value of 8 = 800

Face value of 8 = 8

$\therefore$ Required sum = 800 + 8 = 808

**2** The number of all prime numbers less than 40 is

(A) 15 (B) 18
(C) 17 (D) 12

***Sol.*** *(D)* There are 12 prime numbers less than 40 which are 2, 3, 5, 7, 11, 13, 17, 19, 23, 29, 31, 37.

## Divisibility Tests

There are following rules to test the divisibility by different numbers

| | |
|---|---|
| ***Divisibility by 2*** | When the last digit of a number is either 0 or even, then the number is divisible by 2.<br>*For example* 12, 86, 472, 520, 1000 etc., are divisible by 2. |
| ***Divisibility by 3*** | When the sum of the digits of a number is divisible by 3, then the number is divisible by 3.<br>*For example*, (i) 1233 1+2+3+3=9, which is divisible by 3, so 1233 must be divisible by 3. |
| ***Divisibility by 4*** | When the number made by last two digits of a number is divisible by 4, then that particular number is divisible by 4. Apart from this, the number having two or more at the end, is also divisible by 4.<br>*For example* (i) 6428 is divisible by 4 as the number made by its last two digits, i.e. 28 is divisible by 4. |
| ***Divisibility by 5*** | Numbers having 0 or 5 at the end are divisible by 5.<br>*For example* 45, 4350, 135, 14850 etc., are divisible by 5 as they have 0 or 5 at the end. |
| ***Divisibility by 6*** | When a number is divisible by both 3 and 2, then that particular number is divisible by 6 also.<br>*For example* 18, 36, 720, 1440 etc., are divisible by 6 as they are divisible by both 3 and 2. |
| ***Divisibility by 7*** | A number is divisible by 7 when the difference between twice the digit at ones place and the number formed by other digits is either zero or a multiple of 7.<br>*For example* 658 is divisible by 7, because $65-2\times 8=65-16=49$.<br>As 49 is divisible by 7, so the number 658 is also divisible by 7. |
| ***Divisibility by 8*** | When the number made by last three digits of a number is divisible by 8, then the number is also divisible by 8. Apart from this, if the last three or more digits of a number are zero, then the number is divisible by 8.<br>*For example*<br>(i) 2256 As 256 (the last three digits of 2256) is divisible by 8, therefore 2256 is also divisible by 8. |
| ***Divisibility by 9*** | When the sum of all the digits of a number is divisible by 9, then the number is also divisible by 9.<br>*For example* , (i) 936819 9+3+6+8+1+9 = 36, which is divisible by 9.<br>Therefore, 936819 is also divisible by 9. |
| ***Divisibility by 10*** | When a number ends with zero, then it is divisible by 10.<br>*For example* 20, 40, 150, 123450, 478970 etc. are divisible by 10, as they all end with zero . |
| ***Divisibility by 11*** | When the sum of digits at odd and even places are equal or differ by a number divisible by 11, then the number is also divisible by 11.<br>*For example* (i) 2865423 Let us see<br>Sum of digits at odd places $(A)=2+6+4+3=15$<br>Sum of digits at even places $(B)=8+5+2=15$ $(\because A=B)$<br>Hence, 2865423 is divisible by 11. |
| ***Divisibility by 12*** | A number which is divisible by both 4 and 3, is also divisible by 12.<br>*For example* 2244 is divisible by both 3 and 4. Therefore, it is divisible by 12 also. |
| ***Divisibility by 14*** | A number which is divisible by both 7 and 2, is also divisible by 14.<br>*For example* 1232 is divisible by both 7 and 2. Therefore, it is divisible by 14 also. |
| ***Divisibility by 15*** | A number which is divisible by both 5 and 3, is also divisible by 15.<br>*For example* 1275 is divisible by both 5 and 3. Therefore, it is divisible by 15 also. |
| ***Divisibility by 16*** | A number is divisible by 16 when the number made by its last 4 digits is divisible by 16.<br>*For example* 126304 is divisible by 16 as the number made by its last 4 digits, i.e. 6304 is divisible by 16. |
| ***Divisibility by 18*** | A number is divisible by 18 when it is even and divisible by 9.<br>*For example* 936198 is divisible by 18 as it is even and divisible by 9. |
| ***Divisibility by 25*** | A number is divisible by 25 when its last 2 digits are either zero or divisible by 25.<br>*For example* 500, 1275, 13550 are divisible by 25 as last 2 digits of these numbers are either zero or divisible by 25. |

### Examples

**1** The seven-digit number 876p37q is divisible by 225. The value of p and q can be respectively

(A) 9,0 (B) 0, 0
(C) 0, 9 (D) 9, 5

***Sol.*** *(D)* Seven-digit number 876p37q is divisible by 225, if this number is divisible by 9 and 25. If this number is divisible by 9, then sum of its digits should be divisible by 9.

Now, sum of digits = 8 + 7 + 6 + p + 3 + 7 + q

31 p + q

p + q = 5 or p + q = 14

q = 5 because last two digits divisible by 25.

then p = 0 or 9.

**2** The five-digit number 375 $xy$ is divisible by 90. The value of $x$ and $y$ respectively

(A) 3, 0 (B) 0, 3
(C) 6, 5 (D) 5, 0

***Sol.*** *(A)* If 375 $xy$ is divisible by 90. Then, it will also divisible by 9 and 10 $y = 0$ (because 375 $xy$ is divisible by 10) this number also divisible by 9.

Then, sum of its digits is divisible by 9.

$= 3 + 7 + 5 + x + y = 15 + x + y$

$x + y = 3$

$x = 3$ $[\because y = 0]$

## Fraction

Fraction is a number that can be expressed in the form of $\frac{a}{b}$, where $a$ and $b$ are natural numbers. Here, $a$ is called the numerator and $b$ is called the denominator.

### Types of Fraction

(i) **Proper Fraction** When the numerator of a fraction is less than its denominator, then fraction is called proper fraction.

e.g. $\frac{1}{2}, \frac{15}{17}, \frac{21}{43}$ etc.

(ii) **Improper Fraction** When the numerator of a fraction is greater than its denominator, then fraction is called improper fraction.

e.g. $\frac{17}{13}, \frac{18}{14}, \frac{45}{19}$ etc.

(iii) **Simple Fraction** The fraction, which has denominator other than power of 10, is called simple fraction.

e.g. $\frac{2}{5}, \frac{5}{7}, \frac{11}{8}$ etc.

(iv) **Decimal Fraction** The fraction whose denominator is in the form of power of 10, is called the decimal fraction.

e.g. $\frac{7}{10} = 0.7, \frac{98}{1000} = 0.098$ etc.

are decimal fractions.

### Operations on Fraction

(i) **Addition and Subtraction** To add or subtract fractions, change the given fractions into equivalent fractions such that their denominators become same. For it, take the LCM of denominators.

Then, their sum $= \frac{\text{sum of numerators}}{\text{common denominator}}$

e.g. $$\frac{1}{4} + \frac{2}{3} = \frac{1}{4} \times \frac{3}{3} + \frac{2}{3} \times \frac{4}{4}$$
$$= \frac{3}{12} + \frac{8}{12} = \frac{3+8}{12} = \frac{11}{12}$$

(ii) **Multiplication** To multiply the fractions, multiply the numerators to get the resultant numerator and multiply denominators to get the denominator.

e.g. $$\frac{2}{3} \times \frac{4}{7} = \frac{2 \times 4}{3 \times 7} = \frac{8}{21}$$

(iii) **Division** To perform division on fractions, find the reciprocal of divisor fraction and multiply it with another one.

e.g. $$\frac{3}{4} \div \frac{1}{2} = \frac{3}{4} \times \frac{2}{1} = \frac{3}{2}$$

### Examples

**1** Find the sum of $1\frac{3}{5} + 1\frac{8}{9} + 2\frac{4}{5}$.

(A) $6\frac{19}{45}$ (B) $6\frac{16}{45}$ (C) $6\frac{17}{45}$ (D) $6\frac{13}{45}$

***Sol.*** *(D)* $1\frac{3}{5} + 1\frac{8}{9} + 2\frac{4}{5} = \frac{8}{5} + \frac{17}{9} + \frac{14}{5}$

$$= \frac{72 + 85 + 126}{45} = \frac{283}{45} = 6\frac{13}{45}$$

**2** $\frac{3}{4}$ of $\frac{5}{6}$ of $\frac{7}{10}$ of 1664 = ?

(A) 648 (B) 762 (C) 612 (D) 728

***Sol.*** *(D)* $? = \frac{3}{4} \times \frac{5}{6} \times \frac{7}{10} \times 1664 = 728$

**3** Simplify $7 - \left(2\frac{3}{4} + 2\frac{1}{2}\right)$.

(A) $2\frac{1}{4}$ (B) $1\frac{3}{4}$

(C) $2\frac{3}{4}$ (D) $1\frac{1}{4}$

***Sol.*** *(B)* $7 - \left(2\frac{3}{4} + 2\frac{1}{2}\right) = 7 - \left(\frac{11}{4} + \frac{5}{2}\right)$

$= 7 - \left(\frac{11}{4} + \frac{10}{4}\right) = 7 - \frac{21}{4}$

$= \frac{28}{4} - \frac{21}{4} = \frac{7}{4} = 1\frac{3}{4}$

## Comparison of Fractions

To compare fractions or to arrange them in ascending or descending order, write them in decimal form and compare.

**4** Write the fraction $\frac{5}{8}, \frac{7}{10}$ and $\frac{9}{13}$ in ascending order.

(A) $\frac{5}{8}, \frac{7}{10}, \frac{9}{13}$ (B) $\frac{5}{8}, \frac{9}{13}, \frac{7}{10}$

(C) $\frac{9}{13}, \frac{7}{10}, \frac{5}{8}$ (D) $\frac{9}{13}, \frac{5}{8}, \frac{7}{10}$

***Sol.*** *(B)* $\frac{5}{8} = 0.625$; $\frac{7}{10} = 0.7$; $\frac{9}{13} = 0.69$ $\left(\frac{5}{8} < \frac{9}{13} < \frac{7}{10}\right)$

Thus, ascending order of fractions is 0.625, 0.69, 0.7

**5** Arrange the fractions $\frac{5}{6}, \frac{3}{4}, \frac{4}{13}$ and $\frac{7}{9}$ in ascending order.

(A) $\frac{4}{13}, \frac{3}{4}, \frac{7}{9}, \frac{5}{6}$ (B) $\frac{3}{4}, \frac{7}{9}, \frac{4}{13}, \frac{5}{6}$

(C) $\frac{5}{6}, \frac{7}{9}, \frac{3}{4}, \frac{4}{13}$ (D) $\frac{5}{6}, \frac{4}{13}, \frac{7}{9}, \frac{3}{4}$

***Sol.*** *(A)* $\frac{5}{6} = 0.83$, $\frac{3}{4} = 0.75$, $\frac{4}{13} = 0.31$, $\frac{7}{9} = 0.78$

Thus, the ascending order of fractions is

0.31, 0.75, 0.78, 0.83

i.e. $\frac{4}{13} < \frac{3}{4} < \frac{7}{9} < \frac{5}{6}$

# Average

An average or arithmetic mean of given data is the sum of the given observations divided by number of observations.

$$\text{Average} = \frac{\text{Sum of observations}}{\text{Number of observations}}$$

### *Examples*

**1** Find out the average of 308, 125, 45, 120 and 102.

(A) 140 (B) 143 (C) 145 (D) 154

***Sol.*** *(A)* Required average $= \frac{\text{Sum of given observations}}{\text{Number of observations}}$

$= \frac{308 + 125 + 45 + 120 + 102}{5}$

$= \frac{700}{5} = 140$

**2** There are 30 boys and 60 girls in a class. If the average age of boys is 12 yr and average age of girls is 10 yr, find out the average of the whole class.

(A) 10.99 yr (B) 11 yr

(C) 10.66 yr (D) 10 yr

***Sol.*** *(C)* Average age of the whole class

$= \frac{30 \times 12 + 60 \times 10}{30 + 60}$

$= \frac{360 + 600}{90} = \frac{960}{90} = 10.66$ yr

**3** The number of observations in a group is 40. The average of the first 10 members is 4.5 and the average of the remaining 30 members is 3.5. The average of the whole group is

(A) 4 (B) 15/2 (C) 15/4 (D) 6

***Sol.*** *(C)* Average of whole group $= \frac{10 \times 4.5 + 30 \times 3.5}{10 + 30}$

$= \frac{45 + 105}{40} = \frac{150}{40} = \frac{15}{4}$

**4** A group of 210 students appeared in some test. The mean of 1/3rd of students is found to be 60. The mean of the remaining students is found to be 78. The mean of the whole group will be

(A) 72 (B) 80 (C) 76 (D) 74

***Sol.*** *(A)* Total number of students = 210

Now, 1/3 of total students = 70

∴ Total of 70 students = $70 \times 60 = 4200$

Remaining students = $210 - 70 = 140$

∴ Total of 140 students = $140 \times 78 = 10920$

∴ Mean of total students = $\frac{4200 + 10920}{210}$

$= \frac{15120}{210} = 72$

**5** The mean marks obtained by a class of 40 students is 65. The mean marks of half of the students is found to be 45. The mean marks of the remaining students is

(A) 85 (B) 60 (C) 70 (D) 65

***Sol.*** *(A)* Mean marks = $\frac{\text{Total marks}}{\text{Number of students}}$

$65 = \frac{\text{Total marks of 40 students}}{40}$

∴ Total marks of 40 students = 2600

Again, mean marks of 20 students

$= \frac{\text{Total marks of 20 students}}{20}$

$45 = \frac{\text{Total marks of 20 students}}{20}$

∴ Total marks of 20 students = 900

Thus, total marks of remaining 20 students

$= 2600 - 900 = 1700$

∴ Mean marks of remaining 20 students

$= \frac{1700}{20} = 85$ marks

**6** The mean of four numbers $a$, $b$, $c$ and $d$ is 100. If $c = 70$, then the mean of the remaining numbers is

(A) 30 (B) 85/2

(C) 170/3 (D) 110

***Sol.*** *(D)* Given, $c = 70$

According to the question,

$$\frac{a+b+c+d}{4} = 100$$

$\Rightarrow$ $a + b + c + d = 400$

$\Rightarrow$ $a + b + d + 70 = 400$ (putting the value of $c$)

$\Rightarrow$ $a + b + d = 400 - 70 = 330$

$\Rightarrow$ $a + b + d = 330$

$\Rightarrow$ $a + b + d = 3 \times 110$

∴ $\frac{a+b+d}{3} = 110$

Hence, mean of the remaining numbers are 110.

# Ages

In this type of questions, information is given about the present (current) age or the age of some years before or the age of some years after of some persons and candidates have to find the answer to the question based on this information.

If the present age of $A$ is $x$, then age $t$ years later/hence is equal to $x + t$ and age $t$ years ago is equal to $x - t$.

## Examples

**1** A father is twice as old as his son. 20 yr back, he was 12 times as old as his son. What is the present age of father?

(A) 44 yr (B) 23 yr

(C) 42 yr (D) 49 yr

***Sol.*** *(A)* Let the present age of son be $x$ yr.

∴ Present age of father is $2x$ yr.

According to the question,

$12(x - 20) = 2x - 20$

$\Rightarrow$ $12x - 240 = 2x - 20$

$\Rightarrow$ $10x = 220$

$\Rightarrow$ $x = \frac{220}{10} = 22$

∴ Present age of father = $2 \times 22$

= 44 yr

**2** The ratio of present ages of two children is 5 : 6. Two years hence, the ratio will be 7 : 8. What will be the ratio of their ages after 12 yr?

(A) 22 : 24 (B) 15 : 16

(C) 17 : 18 (D) 11 : 12

***Sol.*** *(C)* Let the present ages are 5 yr and 6 yr.

According to the question,

$$\frac{5x+2}{6x+2} = \frac{7}{8}$$

$\Rightarrow$ $40x + 16 = 42x + 14$

∴ $x = 1$

Hence, their ages after 12 yr will be 17 yr and 18 yr respectively.

∴ Required Ratio = $\frac{17}{18} = 17 : 18$

## Ratio and Proportion

1. **Ratio** A ratio is a comparison of two or more similar quantities. The ratio between $x$ and $y$ can be represented as $x:y$, where $x$ is called antecedent and $y$ is called consequent. i.e. $\frac{x}{y}$ or $x:y$

   **For example** 2 : 3 is a ratio in which 2 is antecedent and 3 is consequent.

   - A ratio $x:y$ is said to be in the simplest form if its antecedent '$x$' and consequent '$y$' have no common factor other than 1.

   **Example** The ratio 32 : 48 is not in the simplest form, because 16 is a common factor of its antecedent and consequent. The simplest form of this ratio is 2 : 3 (dividing the 1st term and 2nd term by 16)

2. **Proportion** An equality of two ratios is called the proportion.

   - If $\frac{a}{b}=\frac{c}{d}$ or $a:b=c:d$, then we can say that $a, b, c$ and $d$ are in proportion and can be written as $a:b::c:d$, where symbol '::' represents proportion.
   - If $x$ is divided into $a:b:c$, then

$$\text{first part} = \frac{ax}{a+b+c}$$

$$\text{second part} = \frac{bx}{a+b+c}$$

$$\text{and third part} = \frac{cx}{a+b+c}$$

### Examples

**1** The ratio of three positive numbers is 2 : 3 : 5 and the sum of squares is 608. Three numbers are

(A) 2, 3, 5 (B) 10, 15, 25
(C) 8, 12, 20 (D) 4, 6, 10

***Sol.*** *(C)* Let numbers are $2x$, $3x$ and $5x$.

According to the question,

$$(2x)^2 + (3x)^2 + (5x)^2 = 608$$

$$\Rightarrow 4x^2 + 9x^2 + 25x^2 = 608$$

$$\Rightarrow 38x^2 = 608$$

$$\Rightarrow x^2 = 608/38 = 16$$

$$\Rightarrow x = \sqrt{16} = 4$$

$\therefore$ Numbers are $2 \times 4$, $3 \times 4$ and $5 \times 4$, i.e. 8, 12 and 20 respectively.

**2** Salaries of Akash, Bablu and Chintu are in the ratio of 2 : 3 : 5. If their salaries were increased by 15%, 10% and 20% respectively, then what will be the new ratio of their salaries?

(A) 3 : 3 : 10 (B) 23 : 33 : 60
(C) 20 : 22 : 40 (D) None of these

***Sol.*** *(B)* Ratio of salaries of Akash, Bablu and Chintu $= 2:3:5$

Let the common ratio be $x$.

Then, salaries of Akash, Bablu and Chintu will be $2x$, $3x$ and $5x$ respectively.

Now, 15% increase in Akash's salary

$$= 15\% \text{ of } 2x = \frac{15 \times 2x}{100} = 0.3x$$

$\therefore$ New salary $= 2x + 0.3x = 2.3x$

Also, 10% increase in Bablu's salary

$$= 10\% \text{ of } 3x = \frac{10 \times 3x}{100} = 0.3x$$

$\therefore$ New salary $= 3x + 0.3x = 3.3x$

Again, 20% increase in Chintu's salary $= 20\%$ of $5x$

$$= \frac{20 \times 5x}{100} = 1x$$

$\therefore$ New salary $= 5x + x = 6x$

$\because$ New ratio $= 2.3x : 3.3x : 6x$

On multiplying with 10 and dividing by $x$, the ratio will be 23 : 33 : 60.

## Percentage

A per cent is a fraction whose denominator is 100 and the numerator of the fraction is called the rate per cent. 'Per cent' is denoted by '%' sign. Conventionally, these two terms per and cent are combined as a one which is called percent usually.

$$15\% = 15/100 = 0.15$$

### Conversion of Per cent into Fraction $x\% = \frac{x}{100}$

e.g. $25\% = \frac{25}{100} = \frac{1}{4}$

### Conversion of Fraction into Percentage

(fraction) $\frac{x}{y} \Rightarrow \frac{x}{y} \times 100\%$ (percentage)

e.g. $\frac{3}{8}$ is a fraction. $\frac{3}{8} \times 100 = 37.5\%$ is its percentage.

### Expressing One Quantity as a Per cent with Respect to Other

$$\frac{\text{1st quantity}}{\text{2nd quantity}} \times 100$$

2nd quantity (in respect of which percentage has to be obtained)

e.g. 60 kg is what per cent of 240 kg ?

Required percentage $= \frac{60}{240} \times 100 = \frac{100}{4} = 25\%$

**→ Some Important Formulae**

- When a number $x$ is increased or decreased by $y$%, then the new number will be $\frac{100 \pm y}{100} \times x$

  '+' sign in case of increase

  '–' sign in case of decrease
- If $x$ is $a$% more than $y$, then $y$ is $\left(\frac{a}{100+a} \times 100\right)\%$ less than $x$.
- If $x$ is $a$% less than $y$, then $y$ is $\left(\frac{a}{100-a} \times 100\right)\%$ more than $x$.
- When the value of an object is first changed (increased or decreased) by $a$% and then changed (increased or decreased) by $b$%, then

  $$\text{Net effect} = \left[\pm a \pm b + \frac{(\pm a)(\pm b)}{100}\right]\%$$

  Net effect is a increase or a decrease according to the + ve or – ve sign, respectively of the final result.
- If the price of the commodity increases or decreases by $a$%, then the decrease or increase in consumption, so as not to increase or decrease the expenditure is equal to $\left(\frac{a}{100 \pm a}\right) \times 100\%$.

### Examples

**1** The price of petrol increases by 25%. By what percentage must a customer reduce the consumption so that the earlier bill on the petrol does not alter?

(A) 20% (B) 25%
(C) 30% (D) 33.33%

***Sol.*** *(A)* Reduction percentage in consumption

$$= \left\{\frac{r}{(100+r)} \times 100\right\}\%$$

$$= \frac{25}{125} \times 100 = 20\%$$

**2** If the radius of a circle is increased by 50%, the perimeter of the circle will increase by

(A) 20% (B) 30%
(C) 40% (D) 50%

***Sol.*** *(D)* Let, radius of circle = 10 cm

Perimeter of circle $= 2\pi r = 2 \times \pi \times 10$
$= 20\pi$ cm

New radius (after 50% increment) $= 10 \times \left(\frac{150}{100}\right)$
$= 15$ cm

Perimeter of circle $= 2\pi r = 2 \times \pi \times 15$
$= 30\pi$ cm

Percentage change in perimeter $= \left(\frac{30\pi - 20\pi}{20\pi}\right) \times 100$
$= \frac{10\pi}{20\pi} \times 100 = 50\%$

**3** In an examination, 78% of the total students who appeared were successful. If the total number of failures was 176 and 34% got first class, then how many students got first class?

(A) 272 (B) 112
(C) 210 (D) 254

***Sol.*** *(A)* Let total students appeared in an exam = $x$

Then, 22% of $x = 176$

$\Rightarrow \frac{22}{100} \times x = 176$

$\Rightarrow x = \frac{176 \times 100}{22} = 8 \times 100$

$\Rightarrow x = 800$

Now, number of students who got first class

$= 34\%$ of $800 = \frac{34}{100} \times 800$

$= 34 \times 8 = 272$

## Profit and Loss & Discounting

Profit and Loss are the terms related to monetary transactions in trade and business. Whenever a purchased article is sold, then either profit is earned or loss is incurred.

### Some Important Terms Related to Profit and Loss

**Cost Price (CP)** This is the price at which an article is purchased or manufactured.

**Selling Price (SP)** This is the price at which an article is sold.

**Profit (*P*)** When SP of an article is more than its CP, then profit is earned.

**Loss (*L*)** When SP of an article is less than its CP, then loss is incurred.

**Overhead Charges** Those charges which are extra expenditures on purchased items apart from actual cost price, are known as overhead charges. Such charges include freight charges, rent, salary of employee etc. If these charges are given in the question, then these are considered with cost price.

### → Formulae Related to Profit and Loss

1. Profit = SP − CP
2. Loss = CP − SP
3. $\text{Profit \%} = \frac{\text{Profit}}{\text{CP}} \times 100\% = \frac{\text{SP} - \text{CP}}{\text{CP}} \times 100\%$
4. $\text{Loss \%} = \frac{\text{Loss}}{\text{CP}} \times 100\% = \frac{\text{CP} - \text{SP}}{\text{CP}} \times 100\%$
5. $\text{SP} = \left(\frac{100 + \text{P\%}}{100}\right) \times \text{CP}$ or $\text{CP} = \frac{\text{SP} \times 100}{(100 + \text{P\%})}$
6. $\text{SP} = \left(\frac{100 - \text{L\%}}{100}\right) \times \text{CP}$ or $\text{CP} = \frac{\text{SP} \times 100}{(100 - \text{L\%})}$

## Examples

**1** A girl buys a TV for ₹ 18500 and sells it for ₹ 15000. Calculate the loss per cent.

(A) 18% (B) 19%
(C) 18.91% (D) 17.85%

***Sol.*** (*C*) Here, SP = ₹ 15000 and CP = ₹ 18500

∴ Loss = CP − SP = 18500 − 15000 = ₹ 3500

$$\text{And loss\%} = \frac{\text{Loss}}{\text{CP}} \times 100\% = \frac{3500}{18500} \times 100\% = 18.91\%$$

**2** A cooler is bought for ₹ 5000 and sold at a profit of 25%. Find its selling price.

(A) ₹ 6250 (B) ₹ 5000
(C) ₹ 4250 (D) ₹ 6000

***Sol.*** (*A*) Here, *C*P = ₹ 5000 and Profit = 25%

From the formula,

$$\text{SP} = \frac{100 + \text{Profit\%}}{100} \times \text{CP} = \frac{100 + 25}{100} \times 5000 = 125 \times 50 = ₹\ 6250$$

⇒ SP = ₹ 6250

**3** By selling an article for ₹ 240, a person incurs a loss of 10%. At what price should he sell it so that he makes a profit of 10%?

(A) ₹ 300 (B) ₹ 293.33
(C) ₹ 285.50 (D) ₹ 310

***Sol.*** (*B*) Here, SP = ₹ 240, *L*% = 10%

$$\therefore \quad \text{CP} = \frac{\text{SP} \times 100}{(100 - L\%)} = \frac{240 \times 100}{90} = ₹\ \frac{800}{3}$$

Now, to get a profit of 10%,

$$\text{SP} = \frac{\text{CP} \times (100 + P\%)}{100} = \frac{800 \times 110}{3 \times 100} = ₹\ 293.33$$

**4** Rawan buys an old scooter for ₹ 4700 and spends ₹ 800 on it's repairing. What per cent profit will he get if he sells it for ₹ 5800?

(A) $5\frac{5}{11}\%$ (B) $6\frac{1}{11}\%$ (C) $5\frac{6}{11}\%$ (D) $6\frac{3}{11}\%$

***Sol.*** (*A*) CP = 4700 + 800 = ₹ 5500, SP = ₹ 5800

$$\therefore \text{ Profit per cent} = \frac{\text{SP} - \text{CP}}{\text{CP}} \times 100\% = \frac{5800 - 5500}{5500} \times 100\% = \frac{300}{5500} \times 100\% = \frac{300}{55}\% = \frac{60}{11}\% = 5\frac{5}{11}\%$$

**5** The cost price of 12 items is equal to the selling price of 8 items. Find the profit per cent.

(A) 40% (B) 48% (C) 50% (D) 60%

***Sol.*** (*C*) Here, *x* = 12, *y* = 8

$$\therefore \quad P\% = \frac{x - y}{y} \times 100\% = \frac{12 - 8}{8} \times 100\% = \frac{4}{8} \times 100\% = 50\%$$

### Marked Price (MP)

The price which is marked on an article, is known as marked price of the article.

### Discount (D)

While selling an article, when a shopkeeper sells the article less than the MP or gives some concession, then this concession is known as discount.

**Successive discount** If two successive discounts of $r_1$% and $r_2$% is given on an article, then

$$\text{Net discount} = r_1 + r_2 - \frac{r_1 r_2}{100}$$

### Examples

**6** The marked price of an article is ₹ 500. If it is sold for ₹ 400, find the rate of discount.

(A) 20% (B) 25%
(C) 30% (D) 10%

***Sol.*** (*A*) MP = ₹ 500, SP = ₹ 400

$\therefore$ D = MP − SP = 500 − 400 = ₹ 100

$$\therefore \text{Rate of discount} = \frac{D}{MP} \times 100\% = \frac{100}{500} \times 100\% = 20\%$$

**7** Find the equivalent discount of two consecutive discounts of 10% and 15%.

(A) 25% (B) 23.5%
(C) 22.5% (D) 20%

***Sol.*** (*B*) Here, $r_1 = 10\%$, $r_2 = 15\%$

Required equivalent discount

$$= \left(r_1 + r_2 - \frac{r_1 r_2}{100}\right)\%$$

$$= \left(10 + 15 - \frac{10 \times 15}{100}\right)\%$$

$$= (25 - 1.5)\%$$

$$= 23.5\%$$

**8** An item whose MP is ₹ 16000, is sold for ₹ 11400 after two successive discounts. If the first discount be 5%, find the second discount.

(A) 10% (B) 20%
(C) 15% (D) 25%

***Sol.*** (*D*) MP = ₹ 16000, SP = ₹ 11400, $d_1\% = 5\%$, $d_2\% = ?$

Using,

$$SP = MP \times \left(\frac{100 - d_1}{100}\right) \times \left(\frac{100 - d_2}{100}\right)$$

$$11400 = 16000 \times \left(\frac{100 - 5}{100}\right) \times \left(\frac{100 - d_2}{100}\right)$$

$$\Rightarrow \frac{114}{160} \times \frac{100}{95} = \left(\frac{100 - d_2}{100}\right)$$

$$\Rightarrow 100 - d_2 = 75$$

$$d_2 = 100 - 75 = 25\%$$

**9** Find the difference between two successive discounts of 36% and 4% on ₹1000 and a discount of 40% on the same amount.

(A) ₹ 144 (B) ₹ 14.40
(C) ₹ 1.44 (D) ₹ 14

***Sol.*** (*B*) Equivalent discount of 36% and 4%

$$= \left(r_1 + r_2 - \frac{r_1 r_2}{100}\right)\%$$

$$= \left(36 + 4 - \frac{36 \times 4}{100}\right)\%$$

$$= (40 - 1.44)\% = 38.56\%$$

Now, difference between the two types of discount

= 40% of 1000 − 38.56% of 1000

= 1.44% of 1000 = ₹ 14.40

## Interest

When a person borrows some money from an another person, he had to return some extra money for the usage of this money. This extra money given by the person is called the interest.

1. **Simple Interest** (SI) When interest is given on the borrowed sum or money, then it is called simple interest. It is denoted by SI.

$$SI = \frac{P \times r \times t}{100}$$

Where,

$P$ = Principal
= The amount of money that is borrowed,
$r$ = Rate per cent
= The rate at which SI is charged on the principal.
$t$ = Time
= The period for which principal is borrowed.

**Amount** Amount is the sum of principal and simple interest.

$$\therefore \quad A = P + SI$$

### Examples

**1** Find the SI on ₹ 1000 for 2 yr at the rate of 7%.

(A) ₹ 100 (B) ₹ 70 (C) ₹ 210 (D) ₹ 140

***Sol.*** (*D*) Here, $P$ = ₹ 1000, $r$ = 7%, $t$ = 2 yr

$$\therefore \quad SI = \frac{P \times r \times t}{100} = \frac{1000 \times 7 \times 2}{100} = ₹\ 140$$

**2** A sum amounts to ₹ 3120 at the rate of 4% in 5 yr. Find the sum.

(A) ₹ 3000 (B) ₹ 2500
(C) ₹ 2750 (D) ₹ 2600

***Sol.*** (*D*) Here, $A$ = ₹ 3120, $r = 4\%$, $t = 5$ yr

Using, $\text{SI} = \dfrac{P \times r \times t}{100}$

$$A - P = \frac{P \times r \times t}{100} \quad [\because A = P + \text{SI}]$$

$$\Rightarrow \quad 3120 - P = \frac{P \times 4 \times 5}{100}$$

$$\Rightarrow \quad 3120 - P = \frac{P}{5}$$

$$\Rightarrow \quad P + \frac{P}{5} = 3120$$

$$\Rightarrow \quad \frac{6P}{5} = 3120$$

$$\Rightarrow \quad P = 3120 \times \frac{5}{6} = ₹\ 2600$$

**3** What will be the simple interest on ₹ 1600 at $7\frac{1}{2}$% per annum for 3 yr 6 months?

(A) ₹ 420 (B) ₹ 360
(C) ₹ 400 (D) ₹ 340

***Sol.*** (*A*) $P$ = ₹ 1600, $r = 7\frac{1}{2}\% = \frac{15}{2}\%$,

$t$ = 3 yr 6 months $= 3\frac{1}{2}$ yr $= \frac{7}{2}$ yr

$$\therefore \quad \text{SI} = \frac{Prt}{100} = \frac{1600 \times 15 \times 7}{2 \times 2 \times 100} = ₹\ 420$$

**4** In what time, simple interest on the sum of ₹ 7500 will be ₹ 2160 at the rate of 8% per annum?

(A) 4 yr (B) 3.6 yr
(C) 5.5 yr (D) 6 yr

***Sol.*** (*B*) Here, $P$ = ₹ 7500, SI = ₹ 2160, $r = 8\%$, $t$ = ?

Using, $\text{SI} = \dfrac{Prt}{100}$

$$2160 = \frac{7500 \times 8 \times t}{100}$$

$$t = \frac{2160 \times 100}{7500 \times 8} = 3.6 \text{ yr}$$

**5** Rehana borrowed a sum of ₹ 10000 at the rate of 9% per annum. How much would she return at the end of two year?

(A) ₹ 12500 (B) ₹ 12800
(C) ₹ 11800 (D) ₹ 11500

***Sol.*** (*C*) $P$ = ₹ 10000, $r = 9\%$, $t = 2$ yr

$$\therefore \text{ Using, SI} = \frac{Prt}{100} = \frac{10000 \times 9 \times 2}{100} = ₹\ 1800$$

Thus, amount returned by Rehana = $P$ + SI
= 10000 + 1800
= ₹ 11800

2. **Compound Interest** (CI) Interest that is accrued on the initial principal and the accumulated interest of a prime debt is called compound interest. Compound interest is the addition of interest to the principal sum of a loan or deposit i.e. interest on interest. It is denoted by CI.

**Amount** The sum of principal and compound interest is known as amount. Amount is denoted by A.

Let principal = $P$, rate = $R$% per annum and time = $n$ yr

(i) If interest is compounded annually,

then $\text{Amount} = P\left(1 + \dfrac{R}{100}\right)^n$

Compound interest = Amount − Principal

$$\text{Compound interest} = P\left[\left(1 + \frac{R}{100}\right)^n - 1\right]$$

(ii) If interest is compounded half-yearly, then rate $= \dfrac{R}{2}$ and time $= 2n$

$$\text{Amount} = P\left(1 + \frac{R}{2 \times 100}\right)^{2n}$$

(iii) If interest is compounded quarterly, then rate $= \dfrac{R}{4}$ and time $= 4n$

$$\text{Amount} = P\left(1 + \frac{R}{4 \times 100}\right)^{4n}$$

(iv) If interest is compounded annually but time is in fraction

(Suppose time $= n\dfrac{a}{b}$ yr), then

$$\text{Amount} = P\left(1 + \frac{R}{100}\right)^n \times \left(1 + \frac{\left(\frac{a}{b}\right)R}{100}\right)$$

(v) If rates of interest are $R_1$%, $R_2$% and $R_3$% for 1st, 2nd and 3rd respectively, then

$$\text{Amount} = P\left(1 + \frac{R_1}{100}\right) \times \left(1 + \frac{R_2}{100}\right) \times \left(1 + \frac{R_3}{100}\right)$$

(vi) If difference between CI and SI is given for 2 yrs,

$$D = P\left(\frac{R}{100}\right)^2 = \frac{\text{SI} \times R}{200}$$

$D$ = Difference

## Examples

**6** Find the compound interest on ₹ 6000 at 5% per annum for 3 yr, compounded annually.

(A) ₹ 652.50 (B) ₹ 945.75
(C) ₹ 845.80 (D) ₹ 666.50

**Sol.** (B) Given that $P$ = ₹ 6000, $R$ = 5%, $n$ = 3 yr

$$\therefore \quad \text{Amount} = P\left(1 + \frac{R}{100}\right)^n = 6000\left(1 + \frac{5}{100}\right)^3$$

$$= 6000 \times \left(\frac{21}{20}\right)^3$$

$$= 6000 \times \frac{21 \times 21 \times 21}{20 \times 20 \times 20}$$

= ₹ 6945.75

Hence, CI = Amount − Principal

= 6945.75 − 6000 = ₹ 945.75

**7** Calculate the compound interest on ₹ 60000 in 2 yr at 5% per annum, if the interest being compounded half-yearly.

(A) ₹ 6228.77 (B) ₹ 6428.88
(C) ₹ 7358.75 (D) ₹ 5328.80

**Sol.** (A) Here, $P$ = ₹ 60000, $n$ = 2 yr and $R$ = 5%

$$\therefore \quad A = P\left(1 + \frac{R}{2 \times 100}\right)^{2n}$$

[∵ interest being compound half-yearly]

$$= 60000\left(1 + \frac{5}{200}\right)^{2 \times 2}$$

$$= 60000 \times \frac{41}{40} \times \frac{41}{40} \times \frac{41}{40} \times \frac{41}{40}$$

$$= \frac{2825761 \times 6}{256} = ₹\ 66228.77$$

Hence, CI = Amount ($A$) − Principal ($P$)

= 66228.77 − 60000 = ₹ 6228.77

**8** The compound interest accrued on an amount at the end of two years at the rate of 12% per annum is ₹ 2862. What is the amount?

(A) ₹ 12200 (B) ₹ 13500
(C) ₹ 11250 (D) ₹ 10550

**Sol.** (C) Let the principal be ₹ $P$, then

$$\because \quad \text{CI} = P\left[\left(1 + \frac{R}{100}\right)^n - 1\right]$$

$$\Rightarrow \quad 2862 = P\left[\left(1 + \frac{12}{100}\right)^2 - 1\right]$$

$$\Rightarrow \quad 2862 = P\left[\left(\frac{28}{25}\right)^2 - 1\right]$$

$$\Rightarrow \quad 2862 = P\left[\left(\frac{784 - 625}{625}\right)\right]$$

$$\Rightarrow \quad 2862 = P \times \frac{159}{625}$$

$$\therefore \quad P = \frac{2862 \times 625}{159} = ₹\ 11250$$

Hence, principal = ₹ 11250

**9** What is the difference between the simple and compound interest on ₹ 7300 at the rate of 6% per annum in 2 yr?

(A) ₹ 29.37 (B) ₹ 26.28
(C) ₹ 31.41 (D) ₹ 23.22

**Sol.** (B) Here, $P$ = ₹ 7300, $R$ = 6%

$$\therefore \quad \text{Difference} = \frac{P \times R^2}{(100)^2}$$

$$= \frac{7300 \times 6^2}{100 \times 100} = ₹\ 26.28$$

Hence, difference = ₹ 26.28

**10** What will be the compound interest on a sum of ₹ 50000 after 3 yr at the rate of 12% per annum?

(A) ₹ 80000 (B) ₹ 70000
(C) ₹ 70246.40 (D) ₹ 20246.40

**Sol.** (D) Given, $P$ = ₹ 50000, $R$ = 12% and time $n$ = 3 yr

$$\therefore \quad \text{Amount} = P\left(1 + \frac{R}{100}\right)^n = 50000\left(1 + \frac{12}{100}\right)^3$$

$$= 50000 \times \frac{28}{25} \times \frac{28}{25} \times \frac{28}{25}$$

= ₹ 70246.40

Hence, CI = $A - P$ = 70246.40 − 50000

= ₹ 20246.40

## Time and Work

- If a person can do a piece of work in $x$ days or hours, then that person's 1 day's work or 1 hour's work $= \frac{1}{x}$

- If a person's 1 day's (hour's) work $= \frac{1}{x}$, then the person will complete the work in $x$ days (hours).
- If a person is $x$ times efficient than second person, then work done by first person : Second person $= x:1$ and time taken to complete a work by first person : second person $= 1:x$.
- If ratio of number of men required to complete a work is $m:n$, then the ratio of time taken by them will be $n:m$.

### Examples

**1** Subhas can copy 50 pages in 10 h, Subhas and Prakash can copy 300 pages in 40 h. In how many hours can Prakas copy 30 pages?

(A) 12 h (B) 9 h (C) 13 h (D) 10 h

**Sol.** *(A)* Number of pages copied by Subhas in 10 h = 50

$\therefore$ Number of pages copied Subhas in 1 h $= \frac{50}{10} = 5$

and number of pages copied by Subhas in 40 h

$$= 40 \times 5 = 200$$

$\therefore$ Number of pages copied by Prakash in 1 h

$$= \frac{300}{40} - \frac{200}{40} = \frac{100}{40} = 2.5$$

$\therefore$ Time taken by Prakash to copy 30 pages

$$= \frac{30}{2.5} = 12\text{ h}$$

**2** $A$ and $B$ together can complete a work in 3 days. They started together but after 2 days, $B$ left the work. If the work is completed after 2 more days, $B$ alone could do the work in how many days?

(A) 5 (B) 6 (C) 7 (D) 10

**Sol.** *(B)* $(A+B)$'s 2 days work $= 2 \times \frac{1}{3} = \frac{2}{3}$

Remaining work $= 1 - \frac{2}{3} = \frac{1}{3}$

$A$ will complete $\frac{1}{3}$ work in 2 days, therefore $A$ will complete 1 work in 6 days.

$A$'s 1 day's work $= \frac{1}{6}$

$B$'s 1 day's work $= \frac{1}{3} - \frac{1}{6} = \frac{1}{3}$

Hence, $B$ will take 6 days to complete the work alone.

**3** If tap $A$ can fill a tank 2 times faster than tap $B$ and takes 20 min less than tap $B$ to fill the tank. If both the taps are opened simultaneously, then find the time taken to fill the tank by tap $A$.

(A) 20 min (B) 25 min
(C) 15 min (D) 16 min

**Sol.** *(A)* Let the time taken by tap $A$ to fill the tank be $x$ min then, time taken by tap $B$ to fill the tank be $2x$ min.

Then, according to the question,

$$2x - x = 20$$

$$\Rightarrow \quad x = 20$$

$\therefore$ Time taken by tap $A$ = 20 min

## Speed, Time and Distance

**Speed** The rate at which a body or an object travels to cover a certain distance is called speed of that body.

**Time** The duration in hours, minutes or seconds spent to cover a certain distance is called the time.

**Distance** The length of the path travelled by any object or a person between two places is known as distance.

$$\text{Speed} = \frac{\text{Distance}}{\text{Time}}$$

$$\text{Time} = \frac{\text{Distance}}{\text{Speed}}$$

$$\text{Distance} = \text{Speed} \times \text{Time}$$

### Conversion of Units

$$a\text{ km/h} = \frac{5a}{18}\text{ m/s (km/h to m/s)}$$

$$a\text{ m/s} = \frac{18a}{5}\text{ km/h (m/s to km/h)}$$

### Examples

**1** A train covers a distance of 200 km with a speed of 10 km/h. What is the time taken by the train to covers this distance ?

(A) 19 h (B) 21 h (C) 20 h (D) 15 h

**Sol.** *(C)* Speed = 10 km/h, Distance = 200 km

$$\text{Time} = \frac{\text{Distance}}{\text{Speed}} = \frac{200}{10}$$

$\therefore$ Required time = 20 h

**2** Raj and Prem walk in opposite direction at the rate of 3 km/h and 2 km/h, respectively. How far will they be from each other after 2 h?

(A) 8 km (B) 10 km

(C) 2 km (D) 6 km

***Sol.*** *(B)* Distance covered by Raj in 1 h = 3 km

Distance covered by Prem in 1 h = 2 km

Relative speed = (3 + 2) = 5 km

Distance covered by Raj and Prem in opposite direction in 2h = 5 × 2 = 10 km

**3** A person covers a distance of 12 km, while walking at a speed of 4 km/h. How much distance he would cover in same time, if he walks at a speed of 6 km/h?

(A) 10 km (B) 20 km

(C) 18 km (D) 16 km

***Sol.*** *(C)* Given, $D_1 = 12$ km, $S_1 = 4$ km/h, $D_2 = ?$

and $S_2 = 6$ km/h

Since, the time is kept constant. Therefore, according to the formula,

$$\frac{D_1}{S_1} = \frac{D_2}{S_2}$$

$$\Rightarrow \frac{12}{4} = \frac{D_2}{6}$$

$$\Rightarrow D_2 = 18 \text{ km}$$

Therefore, the person will cover 18 km.

**4** Three persons walk some distance $x$ along a street at the speed of 2 km, 3 km and 4 km per hour. Their average speed in km/h is

(A) $2\frac{1}{3}$ (B) $2\frac{3}{4}$

(C) $2\frac{10}{13}$ (D) $3\frac{1}{3}$

***Sol.*** *(C)* We know that, average speed of 3 persons is $\frac{3xyz}{xy + yz + zx}$

Hence, $x = 2$ km/h, $y = 3$ km/h and $z = 4$ km/h

$$\therefore \text{Average speed} = \frac{3 \times 2 \times 3 \times 4}{2 \times 3 + 3 \times 4 + 4 \times 2}$$

$$= \frac{3 \times 2 \times 3 \times 4}{6 + 12 + 8}$$

$$= \frac{72}{26} = \frac{36}{13}$$

$$= 2\frac{10}{13} \text{ km/h}$$

# MENSURATION

1. Area of a triangle

$= \frac{1}{2} \times \text{base} \times \text{height}$

$= \frac{1}{2} \times b \times w$

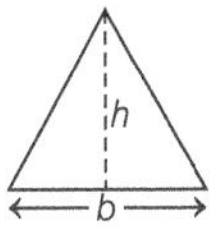


2. Area of an equilateral triangle

$= \frac{\sqrt{3}}{4} \times (\text{side})^2$

$= \frac{\sqrt{3}}{4} a^2$

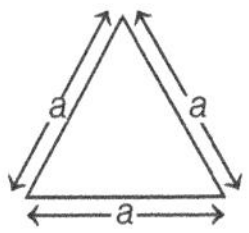


3. Area of a rectangle

$= \text{length } (l) \times \text{breadth } (b)$

4. Perimeter of a rectangle

$= 2 \times [\text{length } (l) + \text{breadth } (b)]$

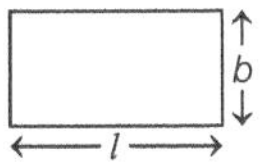


5. Area of a square = $[\text{side}]^2$

6. Perimeter of a square

$= 4 \times \text{side} = 4a$

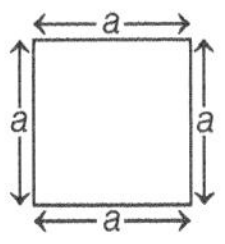


7. Area of a rhombus

$= \frac{1}{2} \times$ product of diagonals

$= \frac{1}{2} \times d_1 \times d_2$

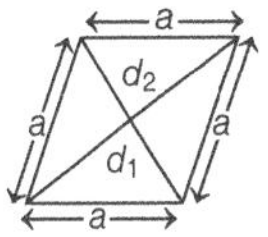


8. Perimeter of rhombus = $4 \times \text{side } (a)$

9. Area of a parallelogram

$= \text{Base } (B) \times \text{height } (h)$

10. Perimeter of a parallelogram

$= 2 \times [\text{Base } (B) + \text{Slant height } (A)]$

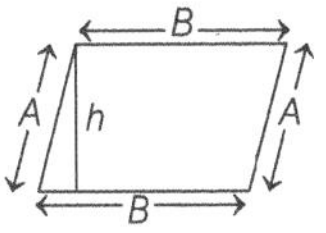


11. Area of a circle = $\pi \times (\text{radius})^2 = \pi r^2$

12. Perimeter (Circumference) of a circle = $2 \times \pi \times \text{radius}$

$= 2 \times \pi \times r$

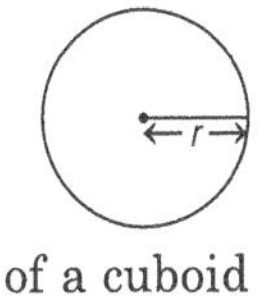


13. If length, breadth and height of a cuboid is $l$, $b$ and $h$ respectively. Then

(i) Volume of cuboid = $lbh$

(ii) Total surface area of cuboid = $2(lb + bh + hl)$

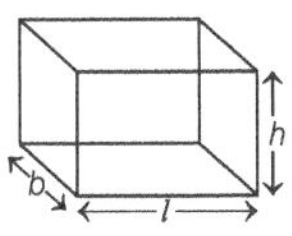

14. If a side of a cube is $x$, then
(i) Volume of cube = $x^3$
(ii) Total surface area of cube $= 6x^2$

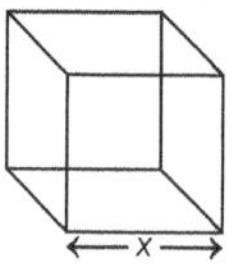


15. If radius of base and height of a circular cylinder are $r$ and $h$ respectively.
Then
(i) Volume of right circular cylinder = $\pi r^2 h$
(ii) Curved (lateral) surface area of cylinder = $2\pi rh$
(iii) Total surface area of cylinder $= 2\pi r(h + r)$

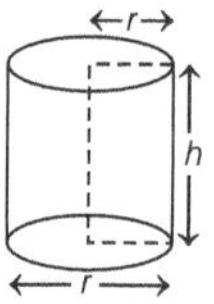


16. If radius of the base, height and slant height of a cone are $r$, $h$ and $l$ respectively.
(i) Volume of cone $= \frac{1}{3}\pi r^2 h$
(ii) Curved (lateral) surface area of cone = $\pi rl$
(iii) Total surface area of cone $= \pi r(l + r)$
(iv) Slant height $(l) = \sqrt{r^2 + h^2}$

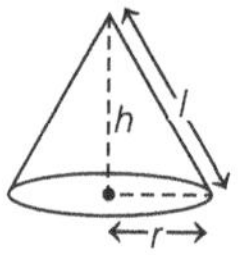


17. If radius of a sphere is $r$, then
(i) Volume of sphere $= \frac{4}{3}\pi r^3$
(ii) Curved (lateral) Surface Area of sphere = $4\pi r^2$

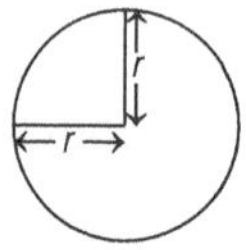


18. If radius of a hemisphere is $r$, then
(i) Volume of hemisphere $= \frac{2}{3}\pi r^3$
(ii) Curved (lateral) surface area of hemisphere = $2\pi r^2$
(iii) Total surface area of hemisphere = $3\pi r^2$

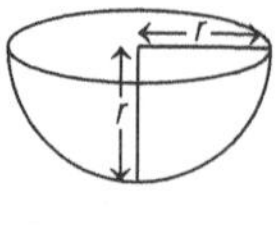


## Examples

**1** The area of an equilateral triangle is $\frac{\sqrt{243}}{4}$ sq cm. Find the length of its side.

(A) 3 cm (B) $3\sqrt{3}$ cm
(C) 9 cm (D) $\sqrt{3}$ cm

**Sol.** *(A)* According to the question,

$$\frac{\sqrt{3}}{4}a^2 = \frac{\sqrt{243}}{4}$$

$$\Rightarrow \quad a^2 = \frac{\sqrt{81 \times 3}}{\sqrt{3}} = \frac{9\sqrt{3}}{\sqrt{3}}$$

$$\therefore \quad a = \sqrt{9} = 3\text{ cm}$$

**2** A rectangle has 20 cm as its length and 200 sq cm as its area. If the area is increased to $1\frac{1}{5}$ times the original area by increasing its length only, then perimeter of the rectangle so formed (in cm) is

(A) 72 (B) 60 (C) 64 (D) 68

**Sol.** *(D)* $l_1 = 20$ cm, $A_1 = 200$ sq cm

$$\therefore \quad b_1 = \frac{200}{20} = 10\text{ cm}$$

Now, $A_2 = 200 \times \frac{6}{5} = 240$ sq cm;

$b_2 = 10$ cm

$$\therefore \quad l_2 = \frac{240}{10} = 24\text{ cm}$$

$A_1$ = Given area, $A_2$ = New area

$l_1$ = given length, $l_2$ = new length, $b_2$ = new width

$\therefore$ Perimeter of new rectangle $= 2(l_2 + b_2)$
$= 2(24 + 10)$
$= 2 \times 34 = 68$ cm

**3** A railing of 288 m is required for fencing a semi-circular park. Find the area of the park. (take $\pi = 22/7$)

(A) 4928 $m^2$ (B) 9865 $m^2$
(C) 8956 $m^2$ (D) 9856 $m^2$

**Sol.** *(A)* Let the radius of the park be $r$, then

$$\pi r + 2r = 288$$

$$\Rightarrow \quad (\pi + 2)r = 288$$

$$\Rightarrow \quad \left(\frac{22}{7} + 2\right)r = 288$$

$$\Rightarrow \quad r = \frac{288 \times 7}{36} = 56$$

$$\therefore \quad \text{Area of the park} = \frac{1}{2}\pi r^2 = \frac{1}{2} \times \frac{22}{7} \times 56 \times 56$$

$$= 4928\text{ m}^2$$

**4** If the areas of three adjacent faces of a cuboidal box are 120 sq cm, 72 sq cm and 60 sq cm respectively, then find the volume of the box.

(A) 820 $cm^3$ (B) 720 $cm^3$
(C) 750 $cm^3$ (D) 760 $cm^3$

*Sol.* (B) Given, $lb = 120$ sq cm, $bh = 72$ sq cm and $lh = 60$ sq cm

$$\therefore \quad lb \times bh \times lh = 120 \times 72 \times 60$$
$$\Rightarrow \quad (lbh)^2 = 120 \times 72 \times 60$$
$$\Rightarrow \quad lbh = \sqrt{120 \times 72 \times 60}$$
$$= \sqrt{12 \times 10 \times 12 \times 6 \times 10 \times 6}$$
$$= 12 \times 10 \times 6 = 720\,\text{cm}^3$$

**5** If the lateral surface area of a cylinder is 94.2 sq cm and its height is 5 cm, then find the radius of its base. ($\pi = 3.14$)

(A) 5 cm (B) 8 cm (C) 3 cm (D) 4 cm

*Sol.* (C) Given, lateral surface area = 94.2 sq cm

$$\Rightarrow \quad 2\pi rh = 94.2 \quad [r = r \text{ radius}]$$
$$\therefore \quad r = \frac{94.2}{2\pi h} = \frac{94.2}{2 \times 3.14 \times 5} \quad [h = \text{height}]$$
$$= 3\,\text{cm} \quad [\because h = 5\,\text{cm given}]$$

# CALENDAR

A calendar is the record of all the days of the year.

- The smallest unit of a calendar is a day.
- A week is group of 7 days.
- A month is 12th part of a year.
- A year is the time taken by Earth to complete one revolution around the Sun.
- A period of 100 years is called a *century*. There are two types of years.
  (a) **Ordinary year** An ordinary year is a year which has 365 days. Such years are not divisible by 4. e.g., 2001, 2002, 2003 etc. Ordinary years in the form of century are not exactly divisible by 400. e.g. 900, 1800, 2100, etc.
  (b) **Leap year** A leap year is a year which has 366 days. Such years are exactly divisible by 4. e.g. 2004, 2008, 2012 etc. Leap year in the form of a century are exactly divisible by 400. e.g. 2000, 2400, 2800 etc.
- **Odd days** In a given period, the number of days more than the complete weeks are called odd days. Or, we can say, when total number of days is divided by 7, then the remainder is called odd days.

1 ordinary year = 365 days = (52 weeks+1day)
1 leap year = 366 days = (52 weeks + 2 days)

### → Odd Days in Century Years

- 100 yr = 76 ordinary years + 24 leap years
  = (76 × 1 + 24 × 2) odd days
  = 124 odd days
  = (17 weeks + 5 days)
  = 5 odd days

∴ Number of odd days in 100 yr = 5
∴ Number of odd days in 200 yr
= (5 × 2) = 10 = (7 + 3) = 3 odd days

- Number of odd days in 300 yr
  = 5 × 3 = 15 days
  = 2 weeks +1 day
  = 1 odd day

Number of odd days in 400 yr
= (5 × 4) + 1 (for leap year)
= 20 + 1 = 21 days
= 3 weeks = 0 odd day

The first day of century cannot be Wednesday, Friday and Sunday.

The last day of century cannot be Tuesday, Thursday and Saturday.

## How to Find the Day on a Particular Date?

In order to find a particular day on the basis of given day and date the following steps are to be taken.

**Step I**

Find the total number of odd days between the reference date and the date for which the day is to be determined (exclude the reference day but count the given day for counting the total number of odd days)

**Step II**

(a) If the reference day was before that particular date– The day of the week on the particular date is equal to the total number of odd days ahead of the reference day.

*Or*

(b) If the reference day was ahead of that particular date– The day of the week on the particular date is equal to number of odd days before the reference day.

**Note** In order to find a day on a particular date, when reference day is not given, you have to find the number of odd days upto that date. Your required day will be determined according to the given table.

**Day of the Week Related to Odd Days**

| Number of days | Day |
|---|---|
| 0 | Sunday |
| 1 | Monday |
| 2 | Tuesday |
| 3 | Wednesday |
| 4 | Thursday |
| 5 | Friday |
| 6 | Saturday |

## Examples

**1** If March 27, 2011 was Sunday, what was the day on June 27, 2012?

(A) Monday
(B) Wednesday
(C) Sunday
(D) Saturday

***Sol.*** (*B*) Day on 27 March 2011 = Sunday

Number of odd days from 27 March 2011 to 27 June 2011 = 4 + 30 + 31 + 27 = 92

= 13 week + 1 odd day

Hence, day on 17 June 2011 = Sunday + 1

= Monday

Now, as 2012 is a leap year

∴ Day on 27 June 2012 = Monday + 2

= Wednesday

**2** I have a calendar of year 1997. When can I use it again?

(A) 2001 (B) 2003
(C) 2005 (D) 2007

***Sol.*** (*B*) The year 1997 has 365 days, i.e. 1 odd day, year 1998 has 365 days, i.e. 1 odd day. Likewise year 1999, 2001 and 2002 have 1 odd day each and year 2000 has 366 days, i.e. 2 odd days.

The sum of odd days, so calculated from years 1997 – 2002 = 1 + 1 + 1 + 2 + 1 + 1 = 7 days

= 0 odd days.

Hence, the year 2003 will have the same calendar as that of the year 1997.

# Chapter Practice

## Series

**Directions** (Q. Nos. 1-14) Find the missing term in the following series.

**1** 3, 8, 27, 112, ?, 3396
(A) 565 (B) 452 (C) 500 (D) 1530

**2** 2, 9, 28, 65, ?
(A) 121 (B) 195 (C) 126 (D) 103

**3** 17, 43, 81, 131, ?
(A) 375 (B) 468 (C) 300 (D) 193

**4** CE, GI, KM, OQ, ?
(A) TW (B) TV (C) SU (D) RT

**5** AZ, BY, CX, ?
(A) EW (B) EU (C) GH (D) DW

**6** AN, BO, CP, DQ, ?
(A) EG (B) ER (C) EH (D) EF

**7** SHG, RIF, QJE, PKD, ?
(A) NME (B) NLB (C) OLE (D) OLC

**8** AFI, JOR, MRU, ?
(A) GJN (B) HMP (C) PMO (D) RII

**9** Find the next term in the series.
A, D, G, J, ?
(A) K (B) L (C) M (D) N

**10** Find the next two terms of the given series.
Z, S, W, O, T, K, Q, G, ?, ?
(A) N, C (B) N, D (C) O,C (D) O, D

**11** abca_bcaab_ca_bbc_a
(A) ccaa (B) bbaa
(C) abac (D) abba

**12** _cb_ca_bacb_ca_bac_d
(A) badddb (B) bbbddd
(C) addddb (D) addbbb

**13** What comes in place of question mark (?) in the series given below?
P3C, R5F, T8I, V12L, ?
(A) Y17O (B) X16M
(C) X17O (D) X16O

**14** Replace the question mark (?) in the following series with suitable option.
C-3, E-5, G-7, I-9, ?, ?
(A) M-18, K-14 (B) K-11, M-13
(C) X-24, M-21 (D) O-15, X-24

## Classification

**Directions** (Q. Nos. 15-29) In each of the following questions, find the odd one.

**15** (A) Crimson (B) Scarlet
(C) Cardinal (D) Golden

**16** (A) Swim (B) Run
(C) Anticipate (D) Acrobat

**17** (A) Shorthand (B) Morse
(C) Semaphore (D) Record

**18** (A) Oil : Lamp (B) Water : Tap
(C) Oxygen : Life (D) Power : Machine

**19** (A) Circle : Arc (B) Line : Dot
(C) Hexagon : Angle (D) Square : Line

**20** (A) Captain-Team
(B) Boss-Gang
(C) Prime Minister-Cabinet
(D) Artist-Troupe

**21** (A) 1, 1 (B) 9, 729 (C) 7, 343 (D) 1, 100

**22** (A) 42, 4 (B) 36, 6 (C) 32, 2 (D) 15, 5

**23** (A) TPLI (B) YUQN (C) RNJF (D) SOKJ

**24** (A) dcba (B) zyxw (C) srpq (D) hgfe

**25** (A) 345 (B) 321 (C) 876 (D) 654

**26** (A) 345 (B) 821 (C) 236 (D) 182

**27** (A) 4-16 (B) 3-12 (C) 7-28 (D) 5-15

**28** (A) 22-12 (B) 32-22 (C) 62-22 (D) 52-42

**29** (A) 25, 50, 56 (B) 20, 40, 46
(C) 18, 36, 40 (D) 12, 24, 30

## Coding

**30** In a certain code, 'BELIEF' is written as AFKKDH'. How would 'SELDOM' be written in that code ?
(A) RDKCHL (B) RFKENM
(C) RFKFNO (D) TFKENP

**31** If PALE is coded as 2134, EARTH is coded as 41590, then how is PEARL coded as ?
(A) 29530 (B) 24153
(C) 25413 (D) 25430

**32** In a certain code language, 3a, 2b, 7c means 'truth is eternal', 7c, 9a, 8b, 3a' means 'enmity is not eternal' and 4d, 2b 8b means 'truth does not'. Which of the following means 'enmity' in that language?

(A) 3a (B) 7c
(C) 8b (D) 9a

**33** If 'MACHINE' is coded as 19-7-9-14-15-20-11, then how will you code 'DANGER' in the same code ?

(A) 11-7-20-16-11-24 (B) 13-7-20-9-11-25
(C) 10-7-20-13-11-24 (D) 13-7-10-11-25

**34** In a certain code, 'BASKET' is written as '5$3%#1' and 'TRIED' is written as '14★#2'. How is 'SKIRT' written in that code ?

(A) 3%★41 (B) 3★%41
(C) 3%#41 (D) 3#4%1

**35** In a certain code, the following numbers are coded by assigning signs

| 1 | 2 | 3 | 4 | 5 | 6 | 7 | 8 | 9 |
|---|---|---|---|---|---|---|---|---|
| < | + | = | □ | ↑ | → | > | ≠ | – |

Which number can be decoded from the given symbols ?

→ ≠ > = <

(A) 63181 (B) 68731
(C) 62781 (D) 63118

**36** In a certain code, the following alphabets are coded in a certain way by assigning numbers as follows.

| A | D | I | L | M | N | O | R | W |
|---|---|---|---|---|---|---|---|---|
| 1 | 2 | 3 | 4 | 5 | 6 | 7 | 8 | 9 |

Which word can be decoded from the following ?
1 6 3 5 1 4 9 7 8 4 2

(A) Animal world (B) Animal less world
(C) World of animals (D) Animals world

**37** Some letters are given below in the first line and numbers are given below them in the second line. Numbers are the codes for the alphabets and vice-versa. Choose the correct number code for the given set of alphabets.

| C | W | E | A | Z | X | J | Y | K | L |
|---|---|---|---|---|---|---|---|---|---|
| 3 | 9 | 5 | 7 | 4 | 8 | 1 | 0 | 2 | 6 |

Given set J W X C L Z

(A) 198364 (B) 198264
(C) 198354 (D) 197354

**38** Given below are capital letters in the first line and symbols in the second line, Symbols and letters are codes for each other. Choose the correct code for the given letters.

| A | C | E | G | H | I | O | N | P | R | T | S | B | D | M |
|---|---|---|---|---|---|---|---|---|---|---|---|---|---|---|
| + | – | ÷ | × | = | ( | ) | [ | ] | ≠ | $\Vert$ | # | $\vert$ | > | < |

BEAST

(A) $|+ + \neq|$ (B) $|+ \times \#|$
(C) $|\div + \#\|$ (D) $|+ + \neq =$

**39** If in a certain code 'DICKINSON' is written as 357950210 and 'DIPP' is written as 3566, then how can 'PICNIC' be written in the same code ?

(A) 650757 (B) 657057 (C) 657507 (D) 560757

**40** If CAT = 12 , then MAN = ?

(A) 14 (B) 24
(C) 16 (D) None of these

**41** In a certain code 'ter ner ger' denotes 'you can determine', 'fer ler ter kar' denotes 'can she help me' and 'mer der ger' denotes 'how are you'. Which word denotes 'determine' in that code ?

(A) ger (B) ter (C) fer (D) ner

**Directions** (Q. Nos. 42-44) Study the following information carefully to answer the given questions.

**Codes**

I. 'very large risk associated' is written as 'nu ta ro gi'.
II. 'risk is very low' is written as 'gi se nu mi'.
III. 'is that also associated is written as 'ta mi po fu'
IV. 'inherent risk also damaging is written as 'fu nu di yu'.

*(All the codes are two letters codes only)*

**42** Which of the following represents 'risk also large' ?

(A) nu fu po (B) nu gi ro
(C) ro po ta (D) nu fu ro

**43** What is the code for 'very' ?

(A) ta (B) fu (C) ro (D) gi

**44** What is the code for 'associated' ?

(A) mi (B) ta (C) ro (D) gi

**Directions** (Q. Nos. 45-46) In each question below, is given a group of letters followed by four combinations of digits/symbols numbered (a), (b), (c) and (d). You have to find out which of the four combinations correctly represents the group of letters based on the following coding system and the conditions that follow and mark the number of that combination as your answer. If none of the combinations correctly represents the group of letters, mark (e), i.e., 'None of these', as your answer.

| Letter | E | R | C | F | L | N | H | K | P | T | A | S | G |
|---|---|---|---|---|---|---|---|---|---|---|---|---|---|
| Code | % | 3 | 2 | 5 | @ | 7 | # | 6 | 1 | 8 | 4 | % | 9 |

(i) If the first letter is a vowel and the last letter is a consonant, both are to be coded as 0.

(ii) If the first letter is a consonant and the last letter is a vowel, both are to be coded as 0.

(iii) If the first letter as well as the last letter are vowels, both are to be coded as the code of the last letter.

**45** NFRSCA
(A) 753%20 (B) 053%24
(C) 0232%0 (D) 053%20

**46** ARFTHE
(A) %358#% (B) 4358#%
(C) 4358#4 (D) %385#%

## Blood-Relationship

**47** Q's mother is the sister of P and daughter of M. S is the daughter of P and sister of T. How is M related to T ?
(A) Grandmother
(B) Father
(C) Grandfather
(D) Grandfather/Grandmother

**48** Pointing to a man on the stage, Rita said, 'He is the brother of daughter of the wife of my husband. How is the man on the stage related to Rita ?
(A) Son (B) Husband
(C) Cousin (D) Nephew

**Directions** (Q. Nos. 49-51) Read the following information and answer the questions given below.
Anita is the niece of Prateek's mother. Anita's mother is Prateek's aunt. Rohan is Anita's mother's brother. Rohan's mother is Anita's grandmother.

**49** Rohan's mother is ....... to Anita's mother.
(A) aunt (B) mother
(C) no relation (D) sister

**50** Prateek's and Anita's mother are
(A) cousin sister (B) sister-in-law
(C) friends (D) sisters

**51** Rohan is Prateek's
(A) brother (B) brother-in-law
(C) uncle (D) cousin brother

**52** T, S and R are three brothers. T's son Q is married to K and they have one child Rahul blessed to them. M the son of S is married to H and this couple is blessed with a daughter Madhvi. R has a daughter N who is married to P. This couple has one daughter Karuna born to them. How is Madhvi related to S ?
(A) Daughter (B) Niece
(C) Granddaughter (D) None of these

**53** Markandey is Rajiv's mother's father. Markandey has three brothers. One of them has grandson Abhi. Rajan is son of Abhi. Rajan is related to Rajiv as
(A) brother (B) nephew
(C) cousin (D) uncle

**54** If 'A $ B' means that 'A is the father of B' 'A ✶ B' means that 'A is the mother of B' 'A @ B' means that 'A is the wife of B', then which of the following means that 'M is the grandmother of N' ?
(A) M ✶R $ T @ N (B) M ✶R @ T @ N
(C) M ✶T $ N @ R (D) M ✶T $ N @ R

**55** Read the following information carefully to choose best option for the question.
'L % M' means that 'M is brother of L'
'L × M' means that 'L is mother of M'
'L ÷ M' means that 'L is the sister of M'
'L = M' means that 'M is father of L'
Which of the following means, I is the nephew of Q' ?
I. Q % J = I II. Q ÷ M × B % I
III. C ÷ I = B % Q
(A) Only III (B) Only I
(C) Only II (D) None of these

**Directions** (Q. Nos. 56-58) Read the following information carefully to answer these questions.
A family consists of six members P, Q, R, X, Y and Z. Q is the son of R but R is not the mother of Q. P and R are a married couple. Y is the brother of R. X is the daughter of P. Z is the brother of P.

**56** Who is the brother-in-law of R ?
(A) P (B) Z (C) Y (D) X

**57** How many female members are there in the family ?
(A) One (B) Two (C) Three (D) Four

58 Which of these is a pair of brothers ?
(A) P and X (B) P and Z
(C) Q and X (D) R and Y

## Direction-Sense Test

59 Neha was going to her house from the school. She first moves 8 km southwards and then turning to her left moves 7 km. Then, turning to her left, she walked 8 km further. Again, she turned to her left and moved 6 km and reached her house. In which direction was her house from the school?
(A) North-West (B) East
(C) South (D) North

60 A postman was returning to the post office which was in front of him to the North. When the post office was 100 m away from him, he turned to the left and walked 50 m to deliver the last letter at CGO complex and moved another 50 m to meet his friend. Then he turned towards North and walked 100 m. How far is he from the post office?
(A) 150 m (B) 100 m
(C) 50 m (D) 75 m

61 Ravi walks 8 km North-East and then 6 km South-East. Find the total distance as well as shortest distance between starting and end points.
(A) 14 km, 12 km (B) 14 km, 10 km
(C) 10 km, 8 km (D) 8 km, 6 km

62 If South-West becomes North, then what will North-East be?
(A) North (B) South-East
(C) South (D) East

63 Five villages P, Q, R, S and T situated close to each other. P is to the West of Q, R is to the South of P, T is to the North of Q and S is to the East of T. Then, in which direction R is with respect to S?
(A) North-West (B) South-East
(C) South-West (D) Data inadequate

64 Shyam goes to 5 km in the North from his school. Now, turning to the left, he goes to 10 km and again turns to left and goes to 5 km. How far is he from his school and in which direction?
(A) 10 km, South from school
(B) 10 km, North from school
(C) 10 km, West from school
(D) 10 km, East from school

65 A boat moves from a jetty towards East. After sailing for 9 nautical miles, turns towards right and covers another 12 NM. If the boat wants to go back to the jetty, what is the shortest distance now from her present position?
(A) 21 NM (B) 20 NM (C) 18 NM (D) 15 NM

66 Raju wants to go to the planetarium. So, he walked 1.5 km towards East from the place and then turned to right and walked 2.5 km and then turned towards East walked 1 km and turned to South and walked 4 km and reached the place by walking 2.5 km towards West. At what distance is he from the starting point?
(A) 6.5 km (B) 9.5 km
(C) 10 km (D) 9 km

67 A person walks towards his house at 8:00 am and observes his shadow to his right. In which direction he is walking?
(A) North (B) South
(C) East (D) West

68 Starting from a point S, Mahesh walked 25 m towards South. He turned to his left and walked 50 m. Then, he again turned to his left and walked 25 m. He again turned to his left and walked 60 m and reached a point W. How far Mahesh is from point S and in which direction?
(A) 10 m, West (B) 25 m, North
(C) 10 m, East (D) 25 m, West

69 Rohit walked 25 m towards South. Then, he turned to his left and walked 20 m. He then turned to his left and walked 25 m. He again turned to his right and walked 15 m. At what distance is he from the starting point and in which direction?
(A) 35 m, East (B) 35 m, North
(C) 40 m, East (D) 60 m, East

## Arrangement

70 Five girls took part in a race. Sonam finished before Neha but after Pooja. Shivani finished before Anju but after Neha. Who won the race?
(A) Sonam (B) Pooja
(C) Neha (D) Shivani

71 In the name list of 48 students, Rohit's rank is 41th from bottom. Find his rank from top.
(A) 12th (B) 8th (C) 7th (D) 9th

**72** In a row of trees, one tree is 7th from either end of the row. How many trees are there in the row?
(A) 11 (B) 15 (C) 14 (D) 13

**Directions** (Q. Nos. 73 and 74) Read the following information carefully and then answer the questions that follow.

A group of seven singers, facing the audience, are standing in a line on a stage as follow.

I. D is to the right of C.
II. F is standing beside G.
III. B is to the left of F.
IV. E is to the left of A.
V. C and B have one person between them.
VI. A and D have one person between them.

**73** Who is on the extreme right?
(A) D (B) F (C) G (D) E

**74** If we start counting from left, on which position is C?
(A) 1st (B) 2nd (C) 3rd (D) 5th

**Directions** (Q. Nos. 75-78) Read the information carefully and answer the questions based on it.

Six persons are sitting in a circle. A is facing to B. B is to the right of E and left of C. C is to the left of D. F is to the right of A. Now, D exchanges his seat with F and E with B.

**75** Who will be sitting to the left of D?
(A) B (B) F (C) E (D) A

**76** Who will be sitting to the left of C?
(A) E (B) F (C) A (D) B

**77** Who will be sitting opposite to A?
(A) E (B) F (C) D (D) B

**78** Who will be sitting opposite to C?
(A) E (B) D (C) B (D) A

**Directions** (Q. Nos. 79-82) Study the following information carefully and answer the question given below.

P, Q, R, S, T, U, V and W are sitting around a circle facing at the centre. T is second to the left of P and third to the right of V. S is second to the right of W who is to the immediate right of T. Q is third to the right of U.

**79** In which of the following pairs is the third person sitting in between the first and the second persons?
(A) UST (B) VRU
(C) TQW (D) None of these

**80** Who is to the immediate left of T?
(A) Q (B) W
(C) R (D) Date inadequate

**81** Who is second to the right of P?
(A) S (B) V (C) U (D) Q

**82** What is R's position with respect to W?
(A) Third to the left (B) Fourth to the left
(C) Sixth to the right (D) Fifth to the left

**Directions** (Q. Nos. 83-87) Study the following information to answer the given questions.

(i) Eight persons E, F, G, H, I, J, K and L are seated around a square table-two on each side.
(ii) There are three lady members and they are not seated next to each other.
(iii) J is between L and F.
(iv) G is between I and F.
(v) H, a lady member, is second to the left of J.
(vi) F, a male member, is seated opposite to E, a lady member.
(vii) There is a lady member between F and I.

**83** Who among the following are the three lady members?
(A) E, H and J (B) E, G and J
(C) G, H and J (D) H, E and G

**84** Which of the following is true about J?
(A) J is a male member
(B) J is a female member
(C) Sex of J cannot be determined
(D) Position of J cannot be determined

**85** Who among the following is seated between E and H?
(A) I (B) J (C) F (D) K

**86** Who among the following is to the immediate left of F?
(A) G (B) J (C) I (D) K

**87** How many persons are seated between K and F?
(A) One (B) Two (C) Three
(D) Cannot be determined

## Number System

**88** Find the sum of the face values of 9 and 6 in 907364.
(A) 15 (B) 20 (C) 9 (D) 18

**89** The sum of place values of 2 in 2424 is
(A) 4 (B) 220
(C) 2002 (D) 2020

**90** The product of any number and the 1st whole number is
(A) 0 (B) 2 (C) 1 (D) −1

**91** Which of the following is a prime number?
(A) 35 (B) 53 (C) 88 (D) 90

**92** The sum of the natural numbers which are divisors of 100, is
(A) 116 (B) 117 (C) 21 (D) 217

**93** If $1x5x01$ is divisible by 11, then the value of $x$ is
(A) 6 (B) 4 (C) 8 (D) 9

**94** The number $(6x^2 + 6x)$ for natural number $x(x + 1)$ is always divisible by
(A) 6 and 12 (B) Only 12
(C) Only 6 (D) Only 3

**95** Find the number nearest to 2559, which is exactly divisible by 35?
(A) 2535 (B) 2555 (C) 2540 (D) 2560

**96** There were a total of 10 bicycles and tricycles. If the total number of wheels was 24, how many tricycles were there?
(A) 2 (B) 6 (C) 18 (D) 4

**97** The sum of five consecutive numbers is 190. What is the sum of the largest and the smallest numbers?
(A) 75 (B) 77 (C) 76 (D) 73

**98** If a number is multiplied by three-fourth of itself, then the value thus obtained is 10800. What is that number?
(A) 210 (B) 180 (C) 120 (D) 160

## Fraction

**99** Express 0.275 in vulgar form.
(A) 19/40 (B) 11/40 (C) 17/40 (D) 13/40

**100** $1 + \frac{1}{2} + \frac{1}{4} + \frac{1}{7} + \frac{1}{14} + \frac{1}{28} = ?$
(A) 2 (B) 5 (C) 4 (D) 6

**101** $8\frac{1}{3} \div 10\frac{5}{6} = ?$
(A) 5/6 (B) 2/3 (C) 10/13 (D) 11/13

**102** $1\frac{3}{5} + 1\frac{8}{9} + 2\frac{4}{5} = ?$
(A) $6\frac{19}{45}$ (B) $6\frac{16}{45}$ (C) $6\frac{17}{45}$ (D) $6\frac{13}{45}$

**103** What should be added to 7/42 to get 7/12?
(A) 1/6 (B) 5/6 (C) 5/12 (D) 7/12

**104** When the fractions $\frac{8}{9}, \frac{9}{12}, \frac{7}{8}, \frac{5}{6}$ and $\frac{17}{20}$ are arranged in ascending order, which comes fourth?
(A) 8/9 (B) 9/12 (C) 7/8 (D) 17/20

## Average, Age, Ratio & Proportion

**105** Find the average of the following set of scores.
253, 124, 255, 534, 836, 375, 101, 443, 760
(A) 427 (B) 413 (C) 141 (D) 409

**106** The average of some natural numbers is 15. If 30 is added to first number and 5 is subtracted from the last number and the average becomes 17.5, then the number of natural numbers is
(A) 20 (B) 15 (C) 30 (D) 10

**107** In a History examination, the average for the entire class was 80 marks. If 10% of the students scored 95 marks and 20% scored 90 marks. What was the average marks of the remaining students of the class?
(A) 65.5 (B) 85
(C) 75 (D) None of these

**108** Five years ago, the average age of $P$ and $Q$ was 15 yr. Now, average age of $P$, $Q$ and $R$ is 20 yr. What would be the age of $R$ after 10 yr?
(A) 35 yr (B) 40 yr (C) 30 yr (D) 50 yr

**109** Two numbers are in the ratio 2 : 5. If 16 is added to both the numbers, their ratio becomes 1 : 2. The number are
(A) 28, 70 (B) 32, 80 (C) 16, 40 (D) 20, 50

**110** Two numbers are such that the ratio between them is 3 : 5. If each is increased by 20, the ratio between the new numbers so formed is 7 : 9. Find the original numbers.
(A) 9, 15 (B) 24, 40 (C) 27, 45 (D) 15, 25

**111** Incomes of $X$ and $Y$ are in the ratio 4 : 3. Their expenditures are in the ratio 12 : 7. Both save ₹ 3200 at the end of the month, then the income of $X$ is
(A) ₹ 8000 (B) ₹ 4000 (C) ₹ 2000 (D) ₹ 6000

## Percentage, Profit, Loss & Discount

**112** From 2008 to 2009, the sales of a book decreased by 80%. If the sales in 2010 was the same as in 2008, by what per cent did it increases from 2009 to 2010?
(A) 80% (B) 100% (C) 120% (D) 400%

**113** The monthly income of a person is ₹ 5000. If his income is increased by 30%, then what is his monthly income now?
(A) ₹ 7000 (B) ₹ 5500
(C) ₹ 4500 (D) ₹ 6500

**114** A man spends 75% of his income. His income is increased by 20% and he increased his expenditure by 10%. His saving are increased by
(A) 10% (B) 25% (C) $37\frac{1}{2}\%$ (D) 50%

**115** The height of a triangle is increased by 10%. To retain the original area of the triangle, its corresponding base must be decreased by
(A) $9\frac{1}{11}\%$ (B) 10% (C) $9\frac{1}{8}\%$ (D) $9\frac{1}{7}\%$

**116** A person sells an article for ₹ 12750 at a loss of 15%. Find the cost price of that article.
(A) ₹ 18000 (B) ₹ 14000
(C) ₹ 15000 (D) ₹ 16000

**117** Amit buys an article for ₹ 500 and sells it for ₹ 750. Find the profit got by Amit.
(A) ₹ 100 (B) ₹ 150
(C) ₹ 200 (D) ₹ 250

**118** If cost of 15 eggs is ₹ 75, then find out the cost of 4 dozens eggs.
(A) ₹ 240 (B) ₹ 300
(C) ₹ 150 (D) ₹ 185

**119** Abhay sells a motor bike to Subhash at a profit of 15% and Subhash sells it to Dinesh at a loss of 5%. Calculate overall profit or loss per cent in this transaction.
(A) 9.25% (B) 10%
(C) 11.25% (D) 9%

**120** On a 20% discount sale, an article costs ₹ 596. What was the original price of the article?
(A) ₹ 720 (B) ₹ 735 (C) ₹ 745 (D) ₹ 775

**121** The difference between a discount of 30% on ₹ 2000 and two successive discounts of 25% and 5% on the same amount is
(A) ₹ 30 (B) ₹ 35 (C) ₹ 25 (D) ₹ 40

## Interest (Simple and Compound)

**122** Find the simple interest on a sum of ₹ 12000 at the rate of 18% for 5 yr.
(A) ₹ 10800 (B) ₹ 9600
(C) ₹ 12100 (D) ₹ 8800

**123** Find the sum which amount to ₹ 6944 in three years at the rate of 8% per annum.
(A) ₹ 5600 (B) ₹ 6000 (C) ₹ 5800 (D) ₹ 6250

**124** What will be the present worth of ₹ 169 due in 2 yr at 4% per annum compound interest?
(A) ₹ 156.25 (B) ₹ 160
(C) ₹ 150.50 (D) ₹ 154.75

**125** What is the difference between compound interest and simple interest for 2 yr on the sum of ₹ 1250 at 4% per annum?
(A) ₹ 3 (B) ₹ 4 (C) ₹ 2 (D) ₹ 8

**126** A sum of ₹ 2668 amounts to ₹ 4669 in 5 yr at the rate of simple interest. Find the rate per cent.
(A) 15.2% (B) 14.9% (C) 16% (D) 15%

## Time and Work, Speed, Distance and Time

**127** *A* and *B* working together can finish a piece of work in 12 days while *B* alone can finish it in 30 days. In how many days can *A* alone finish the work?
(A) 18 days (B) 20 days
(C) 24 days (D) 25 days

**128** *A* completes 1/3 part of a work in 5 days, while *B* completes 2/5 part of the same work in 10 days. In how many days will they complete doing the work together?
(A) $7\frac{3}{4}$ days (B) $9\frac{3}{8}$ days
(C) $8\frac{4}{5}$ days (D) 10 days

**129** *A* can do a piece of work in 8 days, *B* can do it in 10 days and *C* can do it in 20 days. In how many days can *A*, *B* and *C* together complete the work?
(A) $3\frac{7}{11}$ (B) $3\frac{5}{11}$ (C) $3\frac{2}{11}$ (D) $3\frac{9}{11}$

**130** A pipe can fill a cistern in 6 h. Due to a leak in its bottom, it is filled in 7 h. When the cistern is full, in how much time will it be emptied by the leak?
(A) 42 h (B) 40 h (C) 43 h (D) 45 h

**131** Two pipes *A* and *B* can independently fill a tank completely in 20 min and 30 min, respectively. If both the pipes are opened simultaneously, how much time will they take to fill the tank completely?
(A) 10 min (B) 12 min
(C) 15 min (D) 25 min

**132** John started from $A$ to $B$ and Vinod from $B$ to $A$. If the distance between $A$ and $B$ is 125 km and they meet at 75 km from $A$, what is the ratio of John's speed to that of Vinod's speed?
(A) 2 : 3 (B) 3 : 2 (C) 4 : 3 (D) 5 : 4

**133** If 27 March, 1995 was a Monday, then what day of the week was 1November, 1994?
(A) Sunday (B) Monday
(C) Tuesday (D) Wednesday

**134** What was the day on 2nd July, 1984?
(A) Wednesday (B) Tuesday
(C) Monday (D) Thursday

## Mensuration

**135** The base of a triangular wall is 7 times its height. If the cost of painting the wall at ₹ 350 per 100 sq m is ₹ 1225, then what is the base length?
(A) 50 m (B) 70 m (C) 75 m (D) 100 m

**136** Three sides of a triangular field are of lengths 15 m, 20 m and 25m long, respectively. Find the cost of sowing seeds in the field at the rate of ₹ 5 per sq m.
(A) ₹ 750 (B) ₹ 150 (C) ₹ 300 (D) ₹ 600

**137** If each of the dimensions of a rectangle is increased by 200%, the area is increased by
(A) 300% (B) 400% (C) 600% (D) 800%

**138** A rectangle has 30 cm as its length and 720 sq cm as its area. Its area is increased to $1\frac{1}{4}$ times its original area by increasing only its length. Its new perimeter is
(A) 123 cm (B) 125 cm (C) 119 cm (D) 121 cm

**139** The inner circumference of a circular race track 7 m wide is 440 m. Find the radius of the outer circle.
(A) 57 m (B) 68 m (C) 77 m (D) 69 m

**140** The wheel of an engine turns 350 times round its axle to cover a distance of 1.76 km. The diameter of the wheel is
(A) 150 cm (B) 155 cm (C) 165 cm (D) 160 cm

**141** From the four corners of a rectangular sheet of dimensions $25 \times 20$ cm, square of side 2 cm is cut off from four corners and a box is made. The volume of the box is
(A) 828 $cm^3$ (B) 672 $cm^3$
(C) 500 $cm^3$ (D) 1000 $cm^3$

**142** A pillar 14 cm in diameter is 5 m high. How much material was used to construct it?
(A) $(77 \times 10^2)\ cm^3$ (B) $(77 \times 10^4)\ cm^3$
(C) $(77 \times 10^5)\ cm^3$ (D) $(77 \times 10^3)\ cm^3$

**143** A rod of 2 cm diameter and 30 cm length is converted into a wire of 3 m length of uniform thickness. The diameter of the wire is
(A) 2/10 cm (B) $2/\sqrt{10}$ cm
(C) $1/\sqrt{10}$ (D) 1/10 cm

# *Previous Years' Questions*

## UGC NET-December 2019

**1** Which of the following numbers would occur next in the series
2, 6, 30, 60, 130, 210, ......?
(A) 330 (B) 350
(C) 370 (D) 376

**2** What is the missing term in the series given below?
2, 4, 6, 12, 10, 36, 14, ?, 18, 321,...
(A) 50 (B) 72 (C) 108 (D) 18

**3** Identify the term '$X$' in the following series
3, 2, 11, 14, 27, 34, 51, $X$
(A) 62 (B) 69 (C) 60 (D) 71

**4** The next term of the series is
1D3, 3H5, 5L7—,...
(A) 7 P 9 (B) 7 R 9
(C) 7 N 9 (D) 7 L 9

**5** The next term in the series
AT, EQ, IN, OK, ...... is
(A) UH (B) UP
(C) US (D) UU

**6** Choose the missing term out of the following
JAK, KBL, LCM, MDN, ....... .
(A) OEP (B) NEO
(C) MEN (D) PFQ

7 Choose the missing term out of the given alternatives
TEF, UGH, ...... , WKL
(A) CMN (B) UJI
(C) VIJ (D) IJT

8 In a certain code "CREDIT" is written as "EPGBKR". Using the same code "DEBIT" will be written as
(A) FDCGV (B) FGCDV
(C) FCDGV (D) FCDVG

9 In a certain code "ENGLAND" is written as "ULSNYLV". Using the same code "IRELAND" will be written as
(A) HQUNYLV (B) QHUNYLV
(C) QUHNYLV (D) HUQNYLV

10 If the word "TEACHER" is coded as "TCJACCV" and the word "SURGEON" is coded as "PMGETSU" is a certain code language, then which of the following will represent the word "CONCORD" in the language?
(A) FTQEPQF
(B) EQPEQTF
(C) FPQAPME
(D) EMPAQPF

11 In a certain coding language 'AEIOU' is written as 'TNHDZ'. Using the same coding language 'BFJPV' will be written as
(A) UOIEA (B) AEIOU
(C) WQKGC (D) DGKQW

12 If RED is coded as 6720, then how would GREEN be coded?
(A) 16717209 (B) 1677209
(C) 9207716 (D) 1677199

13 If DRIVER = 12, GOVERNMENT = 20, BELIEVED = 16, then BAT= ?
(A) 6 (B) 8
(C) 10 (D) 12

14 A shopkeeper sells a refrigerator for ₹ 22000.00 and make a profit of 10%. If he desires to make a profit of 18% what should be his selling price?
(A) ₹ 23600 (B) ₹ 39600
(C) ₹ 36000 (D) ₹ 24600

15 A circle has the same area as that of a square of diagonal of length 11 cm. What is the diameter of the circle?
(A) ~8.7cm (B) ~17.4 cm
(C) ~7.8 cm (D) ~15.6 cm

16 The two cities P and Q are 360 km apart from each other. A car goes from P to Q with a speed of 40 km/h and returns to P with a speed of 60 km/h. What is the average speed of the Car?
(A) 45 km/h (B) 48 km/h
(C) 50 km/h (D) 55 km/h

17 A student obtains overall 78% marks in his examination consisting of Physics, Chemistry, Mathematics, Computer Science and General English. Marks obtained in each subject and the maximum marks are indicated in the following table

| | Physics | Chemistry | Mathematics | Computer Science | General English |
|---|---|---|---|---|---|
| Subject | (200 max marks) | (100 max marks) | (200 max marks) | (200 max marks) | (100 max marks) |
| Marks Obtained | 155 | 80 | 165 | 140 | $x$ |

The marks ($x$) obtained by the student in General English would
(A) 60 (B) 74 (C) 84 (D) 90

18 A sum of money with compound interest becomes ₹ 2400 in one year and ₹ 3000 in two year. Find out the principal amount.
(A) ₹ 1900 (B) ₹ 1910
(C) ₹ 1915 (D) ₹ 1920

19 If $x : y = 7 : 9$ then, $3x - 5y : 4x + y$
(A) $\frac{-24}{37}$ (B) $\frac{-22}{37}$ (C) $\frac{15}{22}$ (D) $\frac{42}{37}$

20 If 3% of $(a + b)$ = 7% of $(ab)$ and 5% of $(a - b)$ = 4% of $(ab)$ then what percentage of $b$ is $a$?
(A) $\frac{47}{23}\%$ (B) $\frac{23}{47}\%$ (C) $\frac{4700}{23}\%$ (D) $\frac{2300}{47}\%$

21 A certain principal invested at compound interest payable yearly amounts to ₹ 10816.00 in 3 yr and ₹ 11248.64 in 4 yr. What is rate of interest ?
(A) 3% (B) 4% (C) 4.5% (D) 5.5%

22 What is the exact equivalent discount of three successive discounts of 10%, 15% and 20% by sale of an article?
(A) 32.8% (B) 35.0%
(C) 38.0% (D) 38.8%

23 The sum of a number and its inverse is – 4. The sum of their cubes is
(A) – 52 (B) 52 (C) 64 (D) – 64

## UGC NET-June 2019

**24** If REASON is coded as 5 and GOVERNMENT as 9, then what is the code for ACCIDENT?

(A) 6 (B) 7
(C) 8 (D) 9

**25** Pointing towards a man the woman said, "His wife's father is the husband of my mother's only daughter". How is the woman related to the man?

(A) Daughter (B) Sister–in–law
(C) Sister (D) Mother–in–law

**26** A, B, C, D, E and F are six members in a family in which there are two married couples., E, a teacher is married to a doctor who is the mother of C and F. B, the lawyer is married to A. A has one son and one grandson. One of the two married ladies is a house wife. There is also one student and one male engineer in the family. How is A related to C?

(A) Grandfather (B) Mother
(C) Sister (D) Grandmother

**27** Among the five friends, Vineet is taller than Monika, but not as tall as Ram. Jacob is taller than Dalip but shorter than Monika. Who is the tallest in their group?

(A) Ram (B) Monika
(C) Vineet (D) Jacob

**28** Six friends A, B, C, D, E and F are sitting i a closed circle facing the centre. E is to the left of D. C is between A and B, F is between E and A. Who is to the right of C?

(A) A (B) B (C) D (D) E

**29** ......... : Play :: Sing : Song

(A) Scene (B) Act
(C) Theater (D) Field

**30** If 60% of $(a - b)$ = 40% of $(a + b)$, then what per cent of $a$ is $b$?

(A) 20% (B) 25%
(C) 40% (D) 50%

**31** If the simple interest on a certain sum for 1 yr 3 months at 8½ % per annum exceeds the simple interest on the same amount for 8 months at 7½% per annum by ₹ 45, then the sum is

(A) ₹ 600 (B) ₹800
(C) ₹6000 (D) ₹8000

**32** 5% of the inhabitants of a village having died of malaria, a panic set in. During this, 20% of the remaining inhabitants left the village. The population is then reduced to 4750. Find the number of original inhabitants.

(A) 5000 (B) 5250
(C) 6250 (D) 7500

**33** If $x$ and $y$ are two positive numbers and $x$ is 25% greater than $y$, What is the value of ratio $y/x$?

(A) 0.75 (B) 0.80
(C) 1.2 (D) 1.25

**34** If the average of five numbers is – 20 and the sum of three of the n umbers is 32, then what is the average of the other two numbers?

(A) – 66 (B) – 33
(C) – 34 (D) – 132

**35** If $0.75x$ is equal to $0.02y$, then the value of $\frac{y-x}{y+x}$ is

(A) 73/75 (B) 75/77
(C) 73/77 (D) 730/75

**36** A man travelled from the village to the railway station at the rate of 20 km/h and walked back at the rate of 5 km/h. If the whole journey took 5 hs, find the distance of the railway station from the village.

(A) 10 km (B) 15 km
(C) 20 km (D) 40 km

**37** A trader mixes three varieties of refined oil costing ₹100, ₹40 and ₹60 per litre in the ratio 2:4:3 in terms of litre and sells the mixture at ₹66 per litre. What percentage of profit does he make?

(A) 12% (B) 10%
(C) 9% (D) 8%

**38** Which of the following fraction is the result of the sum of an integer and its reciprocal?

(A) 15/8 (B) 26/5
(C) 36/7 (D) 37/5

**39** Sanjay sold an article at a loss of 25%. If the selling price would have been increased by ₹175, there would have been a gain of 10%. What was the cost price of the article?

(A) ₹ 350 (B)₹ 400
(C) ₹ 500 (D) ₹ 750

**40** The average of 35 raw scores is 18. The average of first seventeen of them is 14 and that of last seventeen is 20. Find the eighteenth raw score.
(A) 42 (B) 46 (C) 52 (D) 56

**41** A train leaves Agra at 5 am and reaches Delhi at 9am. Another train leaves Delhi at 7am and reaches Agra at 10:30am. At what time do both trains cross each other?
(A) 6:36 am (B) 6:56 am
(C) 7 am (D) 7:56 am

**42** Average age of a class of 59 students is 18 yr. If the age of the teacher is included, then the average increases by 3 months. The age of teacher is
(A) 28 yr (B) 30 yr
(C) 33 yr (D) 35 yr

**43** Two cyclists start from the same place in opposite directions. One goes toward North at 9km/h and the other goes towards South and 10km/h. What time will they take to be 47.5 km apart?
(A) $2\frac{1}{2}$ h (B) $4\frac{1}{4}$ h
(C) $4\frac{1}{2}$ h (D) $2\frac{1}{4}$ h

**44** The price of item A increases by 50 Paisa every year while the price of item B increases by 25 Paisa every year. If in 2008, the price of item A was ₹3.20 and that of B was ₹5.30. In which year item A will cost 40 Paisa more than the item B?
(A) 2016 (B) 2017
(C) 2018 (D) 2019

**45** The number of marble slabs of size 20 cm × 30 cm required to pave the floor of a square room of side 300 cm × 300 cm.
(A) 150 (B) 25
(C) 100 (D) 225

**46** ₹9000 were divided among a certain number of persons. Had there been 20 more persons, each would have got ₹160 less. The original number of persons was
(A) 55 (B) 30
(C) 45 (D) 25

## UGC NET-December 2018

**47** The next term in the series
−1,5,15,29 ......... is
(A) 59 (B) 63
(C) 36 (D) 47

**48** In the sequence of numbers 2, 8, 26, 62, 122, 212, $x$,......... the term $x$ is
(A) 248 (B) 332 (C) 338 (D) 302

**49** Ther next term in the series
ABD, DGK, HMS, MTB, SBL, ......... is
(A) ZKW (B) KZU (C) ZKU (D) ZCA

**50** If VARANASI is coded as WCUESGZQ, then the code of KOLKATA will be
(A) ZELHOQO (B) LQOOFZH
(C) LOQOZEH (D) HLZEOOQ

**51** In a certain code, LIFE is written as KMHJEGDF. How is WORD written in that code?
(A) XVPNSQCE (B) XVPNSQEC
(C) VXNPQSCE (D) VXNPQSEC

**52** Two numbers are in the ratio 2 : 5. If 16 is added to both the numbers, their ratio becomes 1 : 2. The numbers are
(A) 28, 70 (B) 32, 80
(C) 16, 40 (D) 20, 50

## UGC NET-July 2018

**53** Introducing Rakesh to her husband a women said, "His brother's father is the only son of my grandfather". The woman is related to Rakesh as
(A) Sister (B) Daughter
(C) Aunt (D) Mother

**54** Rajesh, his sister, his son and his daughter are fond of golf and often play together. The following statements are true for all the four
I. The best player's twin and worst player are of the opposite sex.
II. The best player and the worst player are of the same age. Assuming that both twins are members of the group of four, who is the best player.
(A) Daughter of Rajesh (B) Son of Rajesh
(C) Rajesh (D) Sister of Rajesh

**55** Five persons Amit, Anil Ajay, Atul and Anand live in a five storey building on different floors. Amit lives above Ajay, but below Anand. Atul lives above, but below Amit. Anil lives below Anand, but above Atul. In which floor does Anil live?
(A) Third floor
(B) Second floor
(C) Either third floor or fourth floor
(D) Fourth floor

## UGC NET-November 2017

**56** In the series 1, 6, 15, 25, 45, ...... the next term will be
(A) 76 (B) 56 (C) 84 (D) 66

**57** The next term in the series ABD, DGK, HMS, MTB, ... is
(A) SBL (B) PSK (C) RUH (D) NSA

**58** In certain code, "COVALENT" is coded as BWPDUOFM. The code of "ELEPHANT" will be
(A) QMUBIADH (B) QFMFUOBI
(C) EPHNTEAS (D) MFUIQRTW

**59** Ajay is a friend of Rakesh. Pointing to an old man Ajay asked Rakesh wo is he? Rakesh said "His son is my son's uncle". The old man is related to Rakesh as
(A) Father–in–law (B) Father
(C) Uncle (D) Grandfather

**60** A postman walked 20 m straight from his office, turned right and walked 10 m. After turning left he walked 10m and after turning right walked 20m. He again turned right and walked 70m. How far he is from his office?
(A) 40 m (B) 60 m
(C) 20 m (D) 50 m

## UGC NET-January 2017

**61** The missing term in the series 1, 4, 27, 16, ?, 36, 343,...... is
(A) 30 (B) 49 (C) 125 (D) 81

**62** If A is coded as C, M as I, N as P, S as O, I as A, P as N, E as M, O as E and C as S, then the code of COMPANIES will be
(A) SPEINMOAC (B) NCPSEIOMA
(C) SMOPIEACN (D) SEINCPAMO

**63** The next term in the following series YEB, WFD, UHG, SKI,? will be
(A) TLO (B) QOL (C) QLO (D) GQP

**64** Ali buys a glass, a pencil box and a cup and pays ₹21 to the shopkeeper. Rakesh buys a cup, two pencil boxes and a glass and pays ₹28 to the shopkeeper. Preeti buys two glasses, a cup and two pencil boxes and pays ₹35 to the shopkeeper. The cost of 10 cups will be
(A) ₹40 (B) ₹60
(C) ₹80 (D) ₹70

## UGC NET-July 2016

**65** In the series 3, 11, 23, 39, 59, ......... the next term will be
(A) 63 (B) 73 (C) 83 (D) 93

**66** A person walks 10 m infront and 10 m to the right. Then, every time turning to his left, he walks 5, 15 and 15 m, respectively. How far is he now from his starting point?
(A) 20 m (B) 15 m
(C) 10 m (D) 5 m

**67** In certain code, SELECTION is coded as QCJCARGML. The code of AMERICANS will be
(A) YKCPGAYLQ
(B) BNFSJDBMR
(C) QLYAGPCKY
(D) YQKLCYPAG

**68** A is sister of B. F is daughter of G. C is mother of B. D is father of C. E is mother of D. A is related to D as
(A) granddaughter
(B) daughter
(C) daughter–in–law
(D) sister

**69** Two railway tickets from city A to B and three tickets from city A to C cost ₹177. Three tickets from city A to B and two tickets from city A to C cost ₹173. The fare for city B from city A will be
(A) ₹25 (B) ₹27
(C) ₹30 (D) ₹33

## UGC NET-December 2015

**70** The next term in the series B2E, D5H, F12K, H27N, ? is
(A) J58Q (B) J56I
(C) I62Q (D) Q62J

**71** P and Q are brothers. R and S are sisters. The son of P is brother of S. Q is related to R as
(A) father (B) son
(C) brother (D) uncle

**72** A party was held in which a grandmother, father, mother, four sons, their wives and one son and two daughters to each of the sons were present. The number of females present in the party is
(A) 24 (B) 12 (C) 14 (D) 18

**73** Anil after travelling 6 km towards East from his house realised that he has travelled in a wrong direction. He turned and travelled 12 km towards West, turned right and travelled 8 km to reach his office. The straight distance of the office from his house is

(A) 10 km (B) 20 km
(C) 14 km (D) 12 km

**74** At present a person is 4 times older than his son and is 3 yr older than his wife. After 3 yr the age of the son will be 15 yr. The age of the person's wife after 5 yr will be

(A) 42 yr (B) 48 yr
(C) 45 yr (D) 50 yr

**75** The next term in the series
2, 5, 9, 19. 37, ? is

(A) 73 (B) 75 (C) 78 (D) 80

**76** In a certain code MATHURA is coded as JXQEROX. The code of HOTELS will be

(A) LEQIBP (B) ELQBIP
(C) LEBIQP (D) ELIPQB

**77** A girl introduced a boy as the son of the daughter of the father of her uncle. The boy is related to the girl as

(A) brother (B) uncle
(C) nephew (D) son

**78** One day Prakash left home and walked 10 km towards South, turned right and walked 5 km, turned right and walked 10 km and turned left and walked 10 km. How many kilometer will he have to walk to reach his home straight?

(A) 10 (B) 20 (C) 15 (D) 30

## UGC NET-December 2014

**79** The next term in the series
2, 7, 28, 63, 126, ... is

(A) 215 (B) 245
(C) 276 (D) 296

**80** The next term in the series
BA, ED, IH, NM, ...... is

(A) TS (B) ST (C) TU (D) SU

**81** If STREAMERS is coded as UVTGALDQR, then KNOWLEDGE will be coded as

(A) MQPYLCDFD (B) MPQYLDCFD
(C) PMYQLDFCD (D) YMQPLDDFC

**82** The mean of the ages of father and his son is 27 yr. After 18 yr, father will be twice as old as his son. Their present ages are

(A) 42, 12 (B) 40, 14
(C) 30, 24 (D) 36, 18

**83** Two numbers are in the ratio 3:5. If 9 is subtracted from the numbers, the ratio becomes 12:23. The numbers are

(A) 30, 50 (B) 36, 60
(C) 33, 55 (D) 42, 70

## UGC NET-June 2014

**84** If the series 4, 5, 8, 13, 14, 17, 22, ......... is continued in the same pattern, which one of the following is not a term of this series?

(A) 31 (B) 32
(C) 33 (D) 35

**85** Complete the series BB, FE, II, ML, PP, ... by choosing one of the following option given

(A) TS (B) ST
(C) RS (D) SR

**86** A is the brother of B, B is the brother of C, C is the husband of D and E is the father of A. D is related to E as

(A) daughter (B) daughter-in-law
(C) sister-in-law (D) sister

**87** A man started walking from his house towards South. After walking 6 km, he turned to his left and walked 5 km. Then, he walked further 3 km after turning left. He, then turned to his left and continued his walk for 9 km. How far is he away from his house?

(A) 3 km (B) 4 km
(C) 5 km (D) 6 km

**88** In a post office, stamps of three different denominations of ₹7, ₹8 and ₹10 are available. The exact amount for which one cannot buy stamps is

(A) ₹19 (B) ₹20
(C) ₹23 (D) ₹29

**89** One writes all numbers from 50 to 99 without the digits 2 and 7. How many numbers have been written?

(A) 32 (B) 36
(C) 40 (D) 38

**90** Anil is twice as old as Sunita. 3 yr ago he was three times as old as Sunita. The present age of Anil is
(A) 6 yr (B) 8 yr
(C) 12 yr (D) 16 yr

**91** A person has to buy both apples and mangoes. The cost of one apple is ₹ 7 whereas that of a mango is ₹5. If the person has ₹38, the number of apples he can buy is
(A) 1 (B) 2 (C) 3 (D) 4

**92** The odd numbers from 1 to 45 which are exactly divisible by 3 are arranged in an ascending order. The number at 6th position is
(A) 18 (B) 24
(C) 33 (D) 36

**93** The sum of the ages of two persons A and B is 50. 5 yr ago, the ratio of their ages was 5/3. The present age of A and B are
(A) 30 and 20 (B) 35 and 15
(C) 38 and 12 (D) 40 and 10

# ANSWERS

## Chapter Practice

| | | | | | | | | | |
|---|---|---|---|---|---|---|---|---|---|
| 1 (A) | 2 (C) | 3 (D) | 4 (C) | 5 (D) | 6 (B) | 7 (D) | 8 (B) | 9 (C) | 10 (A) |
| 11 (C) | 12 (C) | 13 (C) | 14 (B) | 15 (C) | 16 (C) | 17 (D) | 18 (B) | 19 (C) | 20 (D) |
| 21 (D) | 22 (A) | 23 (C) | 24 (C) | 25 (A) | 26 (A) | 27 (D) | 28 (C) | 29 (C) | 30 (C) |
| 31 (B) | 32 (D) | 33 (C) | 34 (A) | 35 (B) | 36 (A) | 37 (A) | 38 (C) | 39 (B) | 40 (A) |
| 41 (D) | 42 (D) | 43 (D) | 44 (B) | 45 (A) | 46 (B) | 47 (D) | 48 (A) | 49 (B) | 50 (D) |
| 51 (C) | 52 (C) | 53 (B) | 54 (C) | 55 (C) | 56 (B) | 57 (B) | 58 (D) | 59 (B) | 60 (B) |
| 61 (B) | 62 (C) | 63 (C) | 64 (C) | 65 (D) | 66 (A) | 67 (B) | 68 (A) | 69 (A) | 70 (B) |
| 71 (B) | 72 (D) | 73 (C) | 74 (C) | 75 (D) | 76 (A) | 77 (A) | 78 (B) | 79 (D) | 80 (A) |
| 81 (C) | 82 (A) | 83 (D) | 84 (A) | 85 (D) | 86 (B) | 87 (C) | 88 (A) | 89 (D) | 90 (A) |
| 91 (B) | 92 (D) | 93 (C) | 94 (A) | 95 (B) | 96 (D) | 97 (C) | 98 (C) | 99 (B) | 100 (A) |
| 101 (C) | 102 (D) | 103 (C) | 104 (C) | 105 (D) | 106 (D) | 107 (C) | 108 (C) | 109 (B) | 110 (D) |
| 111 (A) | 112 (D) | 113 (D) | 114 (D) | 115 (A) | 116 (C) | 117 (D) | 118 (A) | 119 (A) | 120 (C) |
| 121 (C) | 122 (A) | 123 (A) | 124 (A) | 125 (C) | 126 (D) | 127 (B) | 128 (B) | 129 (A) | 130 (A) |
| 131 (B) | 132 (B) | 133 (C) | 134 (C) | 135 (B) | 136 (A) | 137 (D) | 138 (A) | 139 (C) | 140 (D) |
| 141 (B) | 142 (D) | 143 (B) | | | | | | | |

## Previous Years' Questions

| | | | | | | | | | |
|---|---|---|---|---|---|---|---|---|---|
| 1 (B) | 2 (C) | 3 (A) | 4 (A) | 5 (A) | 6 (B) | 7 (C) | 8 (C) | 9 (B) | 10 (C) |
| 11 (A) | 12 (B) | 13 (A) | 14 (A) | 15 (A) | 16 (B) | 17 (C) | 18 (D) | 19 (A) | 20 (D) |
| 21 (B) | 22 (D) | 23 (A) | 24 (B) | 25 (D) | 26 (D) | 27 (A) | 28 (A) | 29 (B) | 30 (A) |
| 31 (B) | 32 (C) | 33 (B) | 34 (A) | 35 (C) | 36 (C) | 37 (B) | 38 (B) | 39 (C) | 40 (C) |
| 41 (D) | 42 (C) | 43 (A) | 44 (C) | 45 (A) | 46 (D) | 47 (D) | 48 (C) | 49 (A) | 50 (B) |
| 51 (C) | 52 (B) | 53 (A) | 54 (A) | 55 (C) | 56 (D) | 57 (A) | 58 (B) | 59 (B) | 60 (D) |
| 61 (C) | 62 (D) | 63 (B) | 64 (D) | 65 (C) | 66 (D) | 67 (A) | 68 (A) | 69 (D) | 70 (A) |
| 71 (D) | 72 (C) | 73 (A) | 74 (D) | 75 (B) | 76 (B) | 77 (A) | 78 (C) | 79 (A) | 80 (A) |
| 81 (B) | 82 (A) | 83 (C) | 84 (C) | 85 (A) | 86 (B) | 87 (C) | 88 (A) | 89 (A) | 90 (C) |
| 91 (D) | 92 (C) | 93 (A) | | | | | | | |

# Hints & Solutions

## Chapter Practice

1 (*A*) 3 8 27 112 [565] 3396

(×2)+2 (×3)+3 (×4)+4 (×5)+5 (×6)+6

2 (*C*) 2 9 28 65 [126]

$(1)^3+1$ $(2)^3+1$ $(3)^3+1$ $(4)^3+1$ $(5)^3+1$

3 (*D*) 17 43 81 131 [193]

+26 +38 +50 +62

+12 +12 +12

4 (*C*) CE GI KM OQ [SU]

+4 +4 +4 +4 (first letters); +4 +4 +4 +4 (second letters)

5 (*D*) AZ BY CX [DW]

−1 −1 −1 (second letters); +1 +1 +1 (first letters)

6 (*B*) AN BO CP DQ [ER]

+1 +1 +1 +1 (second letters); +1 +1 +1 +1 (first letters)

7 (*D*) S $\xrightarrow{-1}$ R $\xrightarrow{-1}$ Q $\xrightarrow{-1}$ P $\xrightarrow{-1}$ [O]

H $\xrightarrow{+1}$ I $\xrightarrow{+1}$ J $\xrightarrow{+1}$ K $\xrightarrow{+1}$ [L]

G $\xrightarrow{-1}$ F $\xrightarrow{-1}$ E $\xrightarrow{-1}$ D $\xrightarrow{-1}$ [C]

8 (*B*) A F I J O R

+5 +3 +5 +3

M R U [H M P]

+5 +3 +5 +3

9 (*C*) Each next term of the series is next third letter of the alphabets (according to position)

A D G J [M]

+3 +3 +3 +3

10 (*A*) The given sequence is a combination of two series.

I. Z, W, T, Q, ? and II. S, O, K, G, ?

Now, Z $\xrightarrow{-3}$ W $\xrightarrow{-3}$ T $\xrightarrow{-3}$ Q $\xrightarrow{-3}$ [N]

S $\xrightarrow{-4}$ O $\xrightarrow{-4}$ K $\xrightarrow{-4}$ G $\xrightarrow{-4}$ [C]

11 (*C*) The pattern of the series is

abc / aabc / aabbc / aabbcc / a ⇒ abac

12 (*C*) The pattern of the series is

acbd / cadb / acbd / cadb / acbd ⇒ addddb

The sequence is made of repetition of two blocks 'acbd' and 'cadb' alternatively.

13 (*C*) The pattern of the series is as follows

P $\xrightarrow{+2}$ R $\xrightarrow{+2}$ T $\xrightarrow{+2}$ V $\xrightarrow{+2}$ [X]

3 $\xrightarrow{+2}$ 5 $\xrightarrow{+3}$ 8 $\xrightarrow{+4}$ 12 $\xrightarrow{+5}$ [17]

C $\xrightarrow{+3}$ F $\xrightarrow{+3}$ I $\xrightarrow{+3}$ L $\xrightarrow{+3}$ [O]

So, the next term be X17O.

14 (*B*) In this series, every letter is given in its alphabetical position and one letter is skipped in between each term.

C-3 E-5 G-7 I-9 [K-11 M-13]

+2 +2 +2 +2 +2

Hence, the missing terms are K-11 and M-13.

15 (*C*) Except 'Cardinal' all the terms are related to colours.

16 (*C*) Except 'Anticipate' all the terms are related to body movements or exercise.

17 (*D*) Except 'Record' all the terms are related to secret of sending messages.

18 (*B*) In all other pairs, except Water : Tap, second requires the first to continue its corresponding function.

19 (*C*) Hexagon is not made from an angle.

20 (*D*) Artist is just a part of a troupe. [where as in rest, the first denotes the head of the second]

21 (*D*) Except (*D*), in all other groups, the second number is the cube of the first number.

22 (*A*) Except option (*A*), in all other options, first number is the multiple of second number.

23 (*C*) Except RNJF, all others contain one vowel.

24 (*C*) Except option (*C*), in all the other options, the continuous letters in reverse order is given.

25 (*A*) All except '345' are in decreasing order of digits.

26 (*A*) All except '345' have sum of digits is equal to 11.

345 = 3 + 4 + 5 = 12;

821 = 8 + 2 + 1 = 11

236 = 2 + 3 + 6 = 11;

182 = 1 + 8 + 2 = 11

**27** (*D*) All options, except '5-15' have the second number four times the first number.

**28** (*C*) Except option (C) in each pair, the second number is ten less than the first number.

**29** (*C*) All except '18, 36, 40' have second number double the first number and third number 6 more than the second number.

**30** (*C*) As,

$B \xrightarrow{-1} A$
$E \xrightarrow{+1} F$
$L \xrightarrow{-1} K$
$I \xrightarrow{+2} K$
$E \xrightarrow{-1} D$
$F \xrightarrow{+2} H$

Similarly,

$S \xrightarrow{-1} R$
$E \xrightarrow{+1} F$
$L \xrightarrow{-1} K$
$D \xrightarrow{+2} F$
$O \xrightarrow{-1} N$
$M \xrightarrow{+2} O$

**31** (*B*) As,

| P | A | L | E |
|---|---|---|---|
| 2 | 1 | 3 | 4 |

and

| E | A | R | T | H |
|---|---|---|---|---|
| 4 | 1 | 5 | 9 | 0 |

Similarly,

| P | E | A | R | L |
|---|---|---|---|---|
| 2 | 4 | 1 | 5 | 3 |

**32** (*D*) According to the given information,

3a 2b 7c → truth is eternal ...(i)
7c 9a 8b 3a → enmity is not eternal ...(ii)
4d 2b 8b → truth does not ...(iii)

From Eqs. (i) and (ii), 7c/3a → is/eternal
From Eqs. (i) and (iii), 2b → truth
From Eqs. (ii) and (iii), 8b → not
Hence, 9a → enmity.

**33** (*C*) As,

$M \xrightarrow{+6} 19$
$A \xrightarrow{+6} 7$
$C \longrightarrow 9$

**34** (*A*) As,

| B | A | S | K | E | T |
|---|---|---|---|---|---|
| 5 | $ | 3 | % | # | 1 |

and

| T | R | I | E | D |
|---|---|---|---|---|
| 1 | 4 | ★ | # | 2 |

Similarly,

| S | K | I | R | T |
|---|---|---|---|---|
| 3 | % | ★ | 4 | 1 |

**35** (*B*) According to the given sign table,

| → | ≠ | > | = | < |
|---|---|---|---|---|
| 6 | 8 | 7 | 3 | 1 |

**36** (*A*) According to the given alphabet codes,

| 1 | 6 | 3 | 5 | 1 | 4 |
|---|---|---|---|---|---|
| A | N | I | M | A | L |

| 9 | 7 | 8 | 4 | 2 |
|---|---|---|---|---|
| W | O | R | L | D |

**37** (*A*) Here,

| J | W | X | C | L | Z |
|---|---|---|---|---|---|
| 1 | 9 | 8 | 3 | 6 | 4 |

**38** (*C*) Here,

| B | E | A | S | T |
|---|---|---|---|---|
| \| | ÷ | + | # | \|\| |

**39** (*B*) As,

| D | I | C | K | I | N | S | O | N |
|---|---|---|---|---|---|---|---|---|
| 3 | 5 | 7 | 9 | 5 | 0 | 2 | 1 | 0 |

and

| D | I | P | P |
|---|---|---|---|
| 3 | 5 | 6 | 6 |

Similarily,

| P | I | C | N | I | C |
|---|---|---|---|---|---|
| 6 | 5 | 7 | 0 | 5 | 7 |

**40** (*A*) As, $\overset{3}{C}\overset{1}{A}\overset{20}{T}$

$= (3 + 1 + 20) \div 2 = 24 \div 2 = 12$

Similarly, $\overset{13}{M}\overset{1}{A}\overset{14}{N}$

$= (13 + 1 + 14) \div 2 = 28 \div 2 = 14$

**41** (*D*) According to the given information,

ter ner ger → you can determine
fer ler ter kar → can she help me
mer der ger → how are you

It is clear from the above that the code for determine is 'ner'.

**Sol.** (Q.Nos. 42-46) According to the given information,

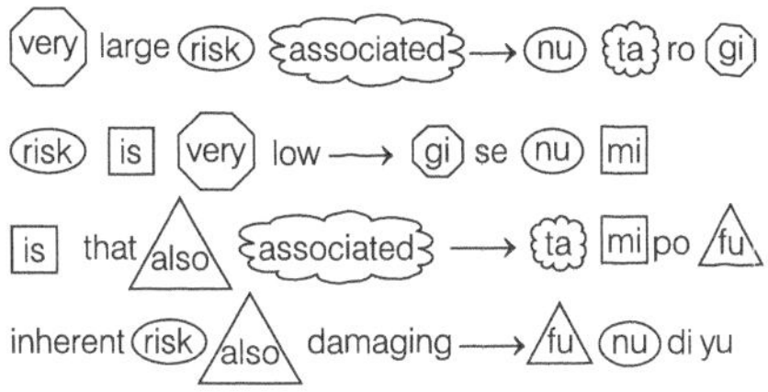


**42** (*D*) risk also large → nu fu ro

**43** (*D*) very → gi

**44** (*B*) associated → ta

**45** (*D*) From Statement II,

| N | F | R | S | C | A |
|---|---|---|---|---|---|
| ↓ | ↓ | ↓ | ↓ | ↓ | ↓ |
| 0 | 5 | 3 | % | 2 | 0 |

**46** (*A*) From Statement III,

If both the first and last letter are vowels, the both are coded as the last letter

| A | R | F | T | H | E |
|---|---|---|---|---|---|
| ↓ | ↓ | ↓ | ↓ | ↓ | ↓ |
| % | 3 | 5 | 8 | # | % |

**47** (*D*) We can summarise the information in a family tree

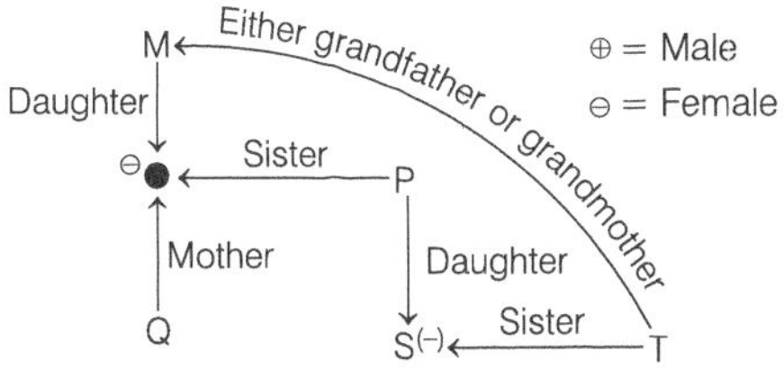


Hence, M is either the grandfather or the grandmother of T.

**48** (*A*) Brother of daughter means son. Wife of my husband means herself. So, the man is son of Rita.

**Sol.** (Q.Nos. 49-51) According to the given information, we can draw a relation diagram is as shown below

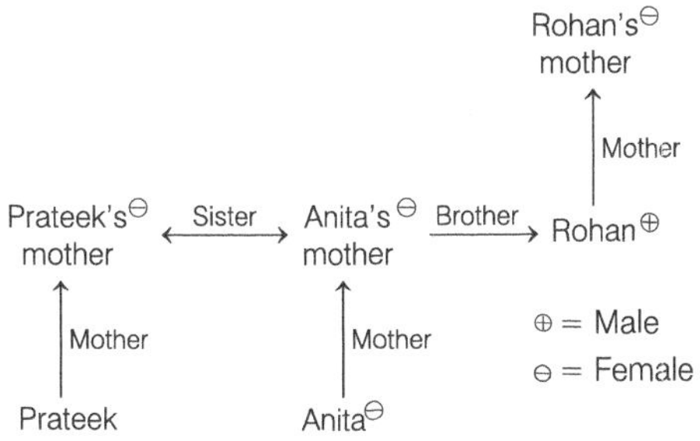


**49** (*B*) It is clear from the diagram that Rohan's mother is mother of Anita's mother.

**50** (*D*) Prateek's and Anita's mother are sisters.

**51** (*C*) Rohan is Prateek's uncle.

**52** (*C*) According to the question,

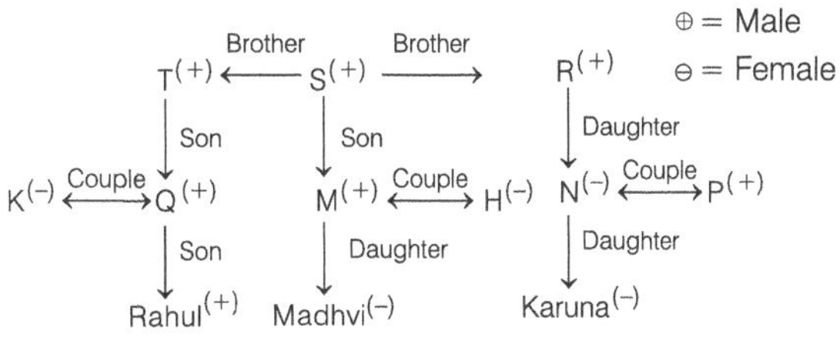


From the above generation tree, we see that Madhvi is the granddaughter of S.

**53** (*B*) According to the question,

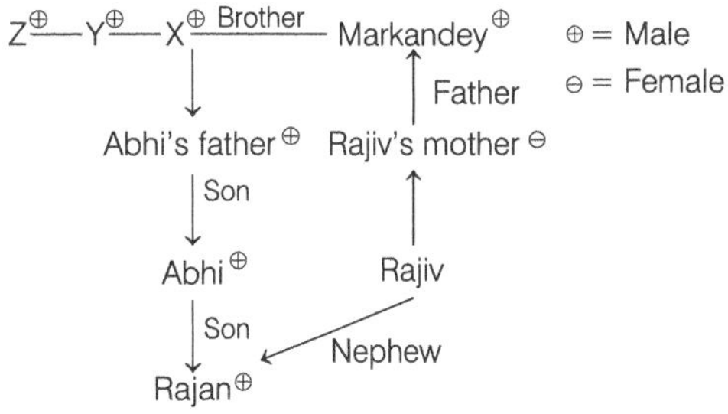


So, Rajan is nephew of Rajiv.

**54** (*C*) From option (C) M ✶T $ N @ R

M ✶T → M is the mother of T

T $ N → T is the father of N

N @ R → N is the wife of R.

From the given information, we can make a relation diagram.

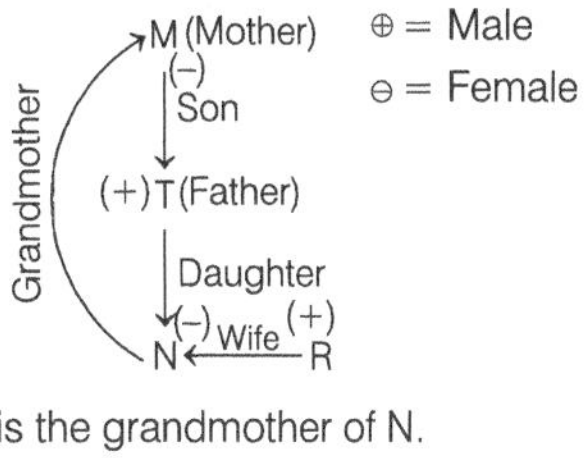


So, M is the grandmother of N.

**55** (*C*) I. Q % J = I

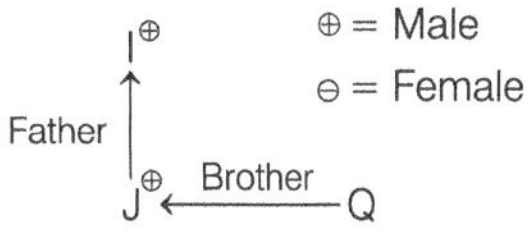


Here, I is the father of Q.

II. Q ÷ M × B % I

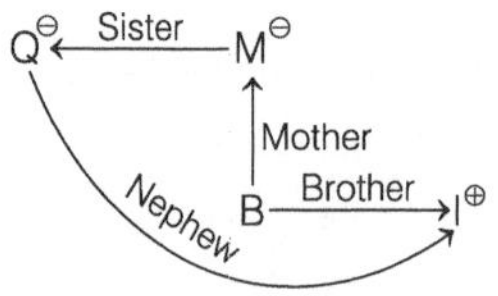


So, I is the nephew of Q.

III. C ÷ I = B % Q

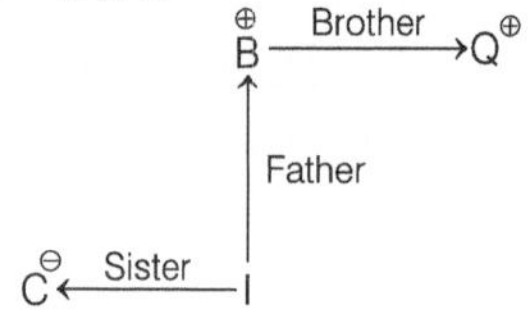


Here, the gender of I is not defined.

Hence, only Statement II means 'I is the nephew of Q'.

**Sol.** (Q.Nos. 56-58) From the information given data is arranged as

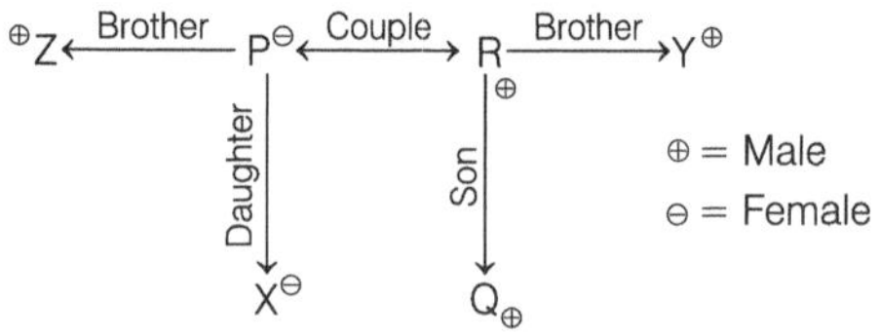


**56** (*B*) Z is brother-in-law of R.

**57** (*B*) X and P are females. i.e. there are two females.

**58** (*D*) R and Y are the pair of brothers.

**59** (*B*) The movement of Neha is shown in the figure below.

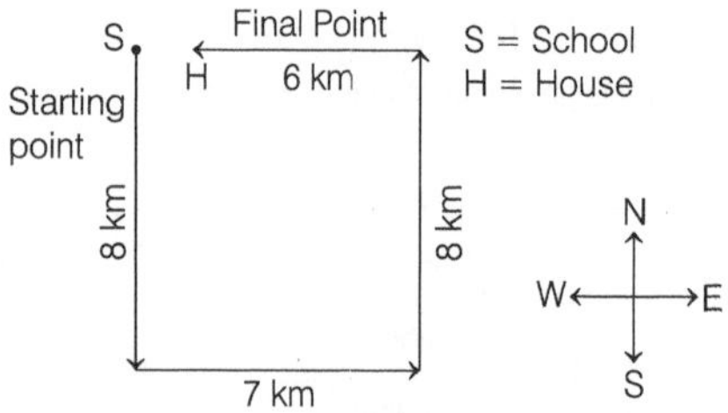


Clearly, Neha's house is to the East of her school.

**60** (*B*)

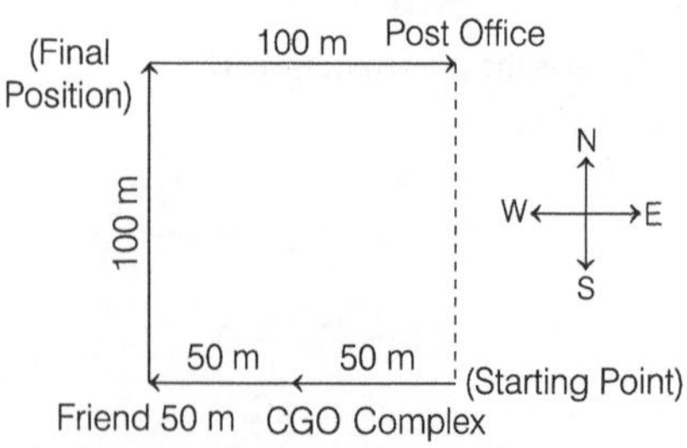


It is clear from the diagram that postman is 100 m away from the post office.

**61** (*B*) According to the question,

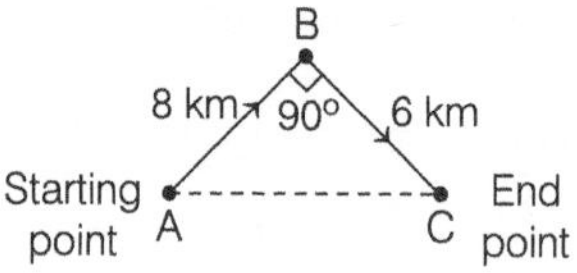


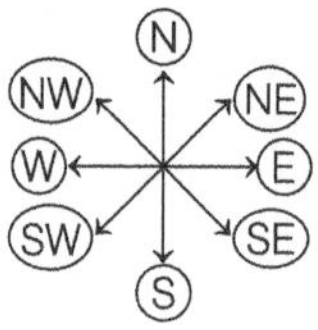

Here, total distance $= AB + BC$

$= 8 + 6 = 14$ km

and shortest distance

$$AC = \sqrt{AB^2 + BC^2}$$

$$= \sqrt{8^2 + 6^2} = \sqrt{64 + 36}$$

$$= \sqrt{100} = 10 \text{ km}$$

**62** (*C*) The diagrammatic representation of direction is as shown below

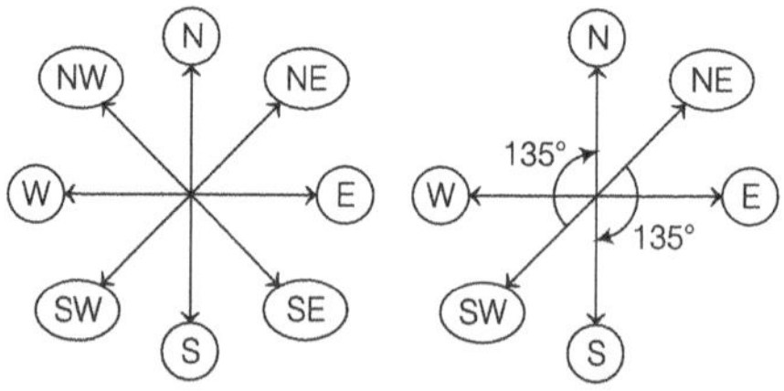


Clearly, directions are moving 135° clockwise. Hence, North-East will become South moving 135° clockwise.

**63** (*C*) According to the given information, locations of the five villages can be represented as shown below.

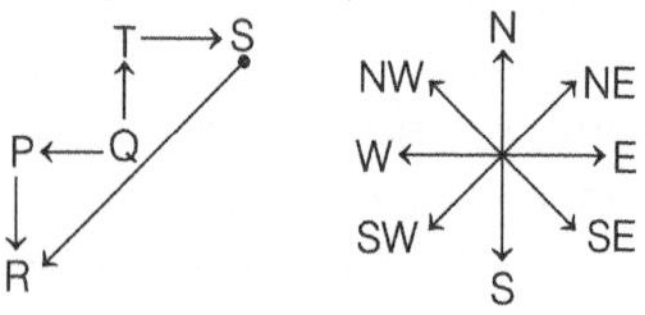

Clearly, R lies to the South-West of S.

**64** (*C*) The movements of Shyam are as follow

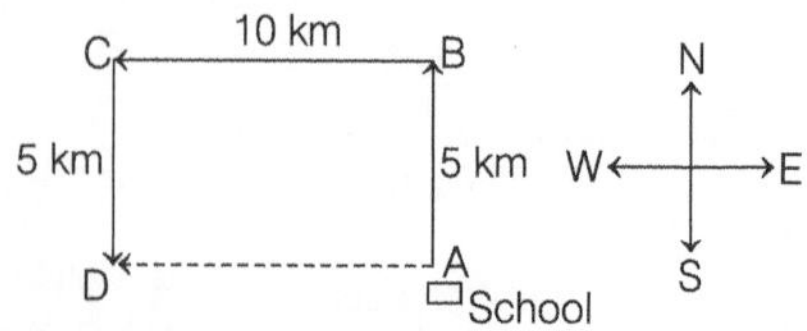


Let point A be the starting point, i.e. school of Shyam and point D be the final point.

From figure, AB = CD = 5 km

and AD = BC = 10 km

So, Shyam is 10 km far away from his school and in West direction from school.

**65** (*D*) According to the question,

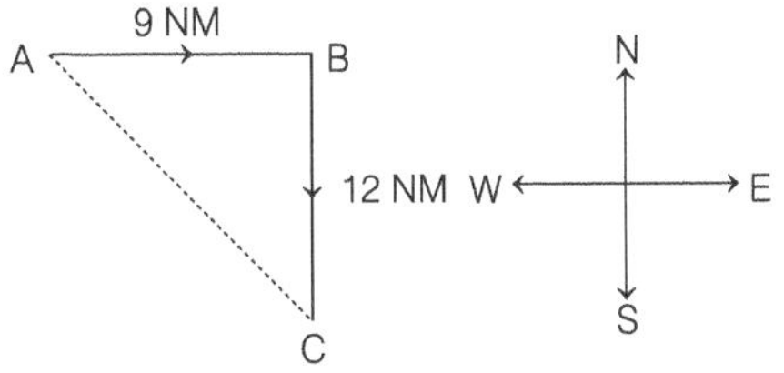


The shortest distance is AC.

$\therefore$ AC $\sqrt{(AB)^2 + (BC)^2}$

$= \sqrt{(9)^2 + (12)^2}$

$= \sqrt{81 + 144}$

$= \sqrt{225} = 15$ NM

**66** (*A*) The movements of Raju are as follows

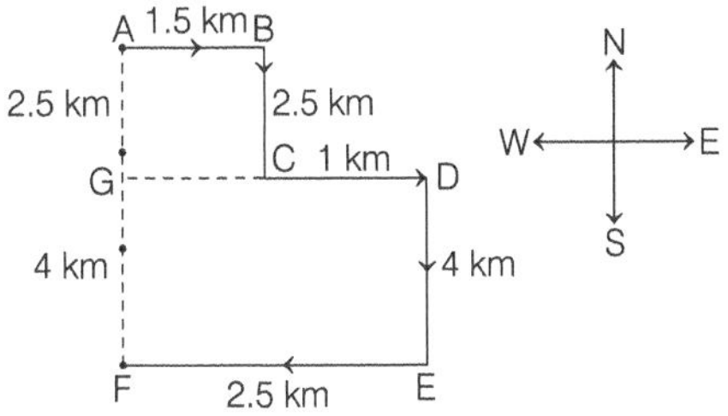


Let A be the starting point of Raju and F be the end point.

Now, GC = AB = 1.5 km,

GF = ED = 4 km

Now, distance of Raju from his starting point

= AG + GF = (2.5 + 4) = 6.5 km

**67** (*B*) At 8:00 am the Sun is in the East direction.

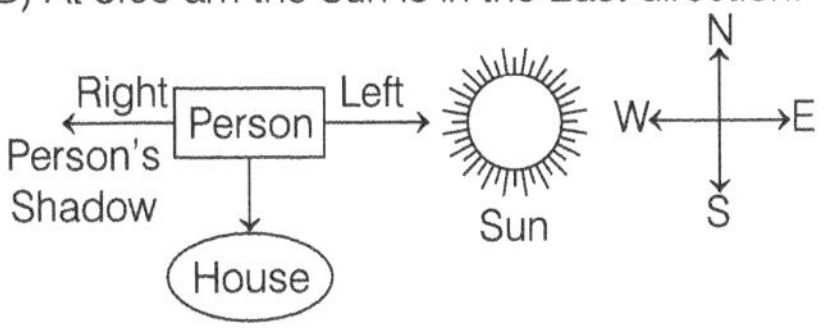


Clearly, the person is facing the South direction.

**68** (*A*) According to the question,

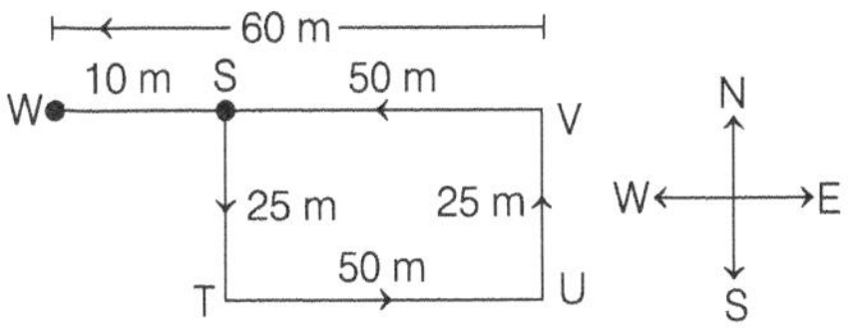


Mahesh is at a distance of 10 m away and in West direction from his starting point S.

**69** (*A*) The movements of Rohit are shown in figure given below

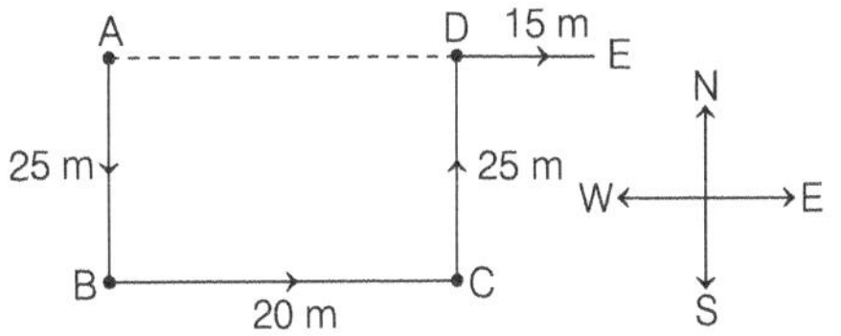


$\therefore$ Rohit's distance from starting point,

AE = AD + DE [$\because$ DE = 15m, BC = AD = 20m]

= 20 + 15 = 35 m

He is 35 m in East direction from the starting point.

**70** (*B*) According to the question,

Pooja > Sonam > Neha

and Neha > Shivani > Anju

Arranging the data in meaningful order, we get Pooja>Sonam>Neha>Shivani>Anju

Clearly, Pooja won the race.

**71** (*B*) Total number of students

= (Rank from top + Rank from bottom) − 1

48 = (T + 41) − 1 $\Rightarrow$ T = 8

$\therefore$ Rohit is 8th from top.

**72** (*D*) Here, position of tree from both the end is 7.

$\therefore$ Total number of trees = 7 + 7 − 1 = 13.

**Sol.** (Q.Nos. 73-74) On the basis of given information, the arrangement of the singers in a line is as follows.

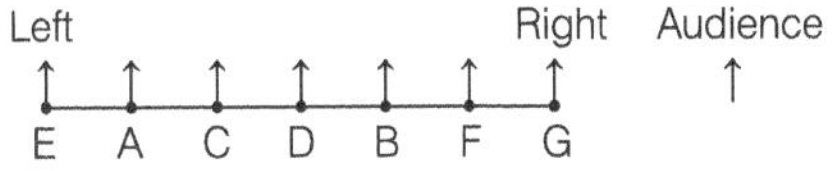


**73** (*C*) Clearly, singer G is on the extreme right.

**74** (*C*) C is third from the left.

**Sol.** (Q.Nos. 75-78) From the given information, sitting arrangement of all the persons is as follows

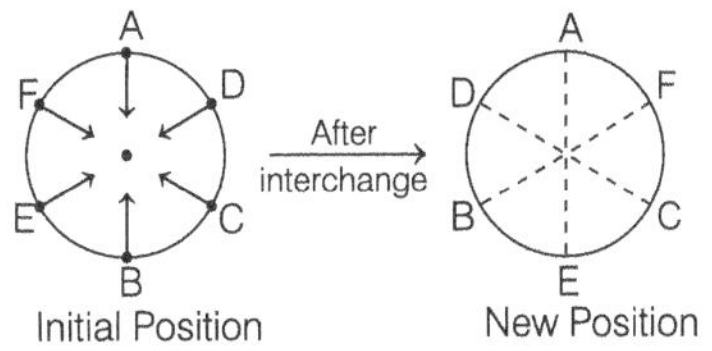


**75** (*D*) It is clear from the figure that A is to the left of D.

**76** (*A*) E is sitting to the left of C.

**77** (*A*) E is sitting opposite to A.

**78** (*B*) D is sitting opposite to C.

**Sol.** (Q.Nos. 79-82) On the basis of given information, the sitting arrangement is as follows

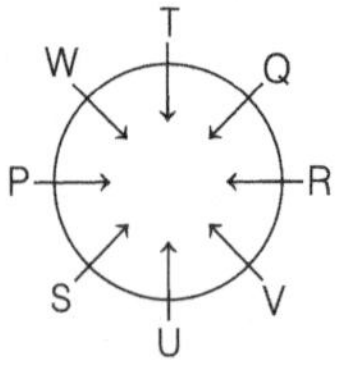


**79** (*D*) In none of pairs, the third person is sitting between the first and the second person.

**80** (*A*) Q is to the immediate left of T.

**81** (*C*) U is second to the right of P.

**82** (*A*) R is third to the left with respect to W.

**Sol.** (Q.Nos. 83-87) From the given information sitting arrangement of eight persons is as follows

**Note** (+ ) = Male, (–) = Female

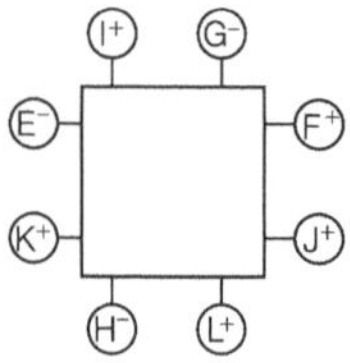


**83** (*D*) It is clear from the figure that the three lady members are H, E and G.

**84** (*A*) It is clear that, J is a male member.

**85** (*D*) K is sitting between E and H.

**86** (*B*) J is sitting to the immediate left of F.

**87** (*C*) There are three persons seated between K and F on either side.

**88** (*A*) The face value is the value of digit itself.

So, required sum = 9 + 6 = 15

**89** (*D*) Sum of place values of 2 in 2424

$= 2 \times 1000 + 2 \times 10 = 2000 + 20 = 2020$

**90** (*A*) 1st whole number = 0

Clearly, when any number is multiplied with 0 (the 1st whole number), then the result is 0.

**91** (*B*) 53 has only two factors i.e. itself and 1.

Hence, it is a prime number.

**92** (*D*) Here, divisors of 100 are 1, 2, 4, 5, 10, 20, 25, 50, 100.

∴ Required sum

$= 1 + 2 + 4 + 5 + 10 + 20 + 25 + 50 + 100 = 217$

**93** (*C*) When $1x\,5x\,01$ is divisible by 11, then sum of numbers at even place–sum of numbers at odd place = 0 or divisible by 11.

$\therefore \quad x + x + 1 - 6 = 11$

$x = 8$

**94** (*A*) $(6x^2 + 6x) = 6x(1 + x)$

If $x = 1$

$6(1)(1 + 1) = 6 \times 2$

then, it is clearly divisible by 6 and 12 as $x(x + 1)$ is even.

**95** (*B*)

$$35)2559(73$$
$$\underline{245}$$
$$109$$
$$\underline{105}$$
$$\underline{4}$$

The number nearest to 2559 as divisibles by 35 is $= 2559 - 4 = 2555$.

**96** (*D*) Let the required number of tricycles = $x$

Then, the number of bicycles = $10 - x$

According to the question,

$3x + 2(10 - x) = 24$

[∵ Tricycles = 3 wheels; Bicycle = 2 wheels]

$\Rightarrow \quad x + 20 = 24$

$\Rightarrow \quad x = 4$

Therefore, the required number of tricycles = $x = 4$

**97** (*C*) Let the five consecutive numbers be

$x - 2, x - 1, x, x + 1, x + 2$

Sum of numbers = 190

$\therefore x - 2 + x - 1 + x + x + 1 + x + 2 = 190$

$\Rightarrow \quad 5x = 190$

$\Rightarrow \quad x = 38$

Sum of largest and smallest numbers

$= x + 2 + x - 2$

$= 2x = 2 \times 38 = 76$

**98** (*C*) Let the number be $x$.

According to the question,

$$x \times \left(x \times \frac{3}{4}\right) = 10800$$

$$\Rightarrow \quad \frac{3x^2}{4} = 10800$$

$$\Rightarrow \quad x^2 = \frac{10800 \times 4}{3} = 14400$$

$$x = \sqrt{14400} = 120$$

**99** (*B*) $0.275 = \frac{275}{1000} = \frac{11}{40}$

**100** (*A*) $1 + \frac{1}{2} + \frac{1}{4} + \frac{1}{7} + \frac{1}{14} + \frac{1}{28}$

$$= \frac{28 + 14 + 7 + 4 + 2 + 1}{28} = \frac{56}{28} = 2$$

**101** (*C*) $? = \frac{25}{3} \div \frac{65}{6} = \frac{25}{3} \times \frac{6}{65} = \frac{10}{13}$

**102** (*D*) $1\frac{3}{5} + 1\frac{8}{9} + 2\frac{4}{5}$

$= (1 + 1 + 2) + \left(\frac{3}{5} + \frac{8}{9} + \frac{4}{5}\right)$

$= 4 + \frac{27 + 40 + 36}{45}$

$= 4 + \frac{103}{45} = 4 + 2\frac{13}{45} = 6\frac{13}{45}$

**103** (*C*) Let required number be $x$.

Then, according to the question,

$$x + \frac{7}{42} = \frac{7}{12} \Rightarrow x = \frac{7}{12} - \frac{7}{42}$$

$$= \frac{49 - 14}{84} = \frac{35}{84} = \frac{5}{12}$$

Thus, the required number is $\frac{5}{12}$.

**104** (*C*) $\frac{8}{9} = 0.89, \frac{9}{12} = 0.75, \frac{7}{8} = 0.875, \frac{5}{6} = 0.83$

$\frac{17}{20} = 0.85$

Therefore, ascending order of fractions is 0.75, 0.83, 0.85, 0.875, 0.89 i.e. $\frac{9}{12}, \frac{5}{6}, \frac{17}{20}, \frac{7}{8}, \frac{8}{9}$ and thus, the fourth fraction is $\frac{7}{8}$.

**105** (*D*) Required average $= \frac{\text{Sum of all scores}}{\text{Number of scores}}$

$$= \frac{\begin{bmatrix} 253 + 124 + 255 + 534 + 836 \\ + 375 + 101 + 443 + 760 \end{bmatrix}}{9}$$

$$= \frac{3681}{9} = 409$$

**106** (*D*) Let the total number of natural numbers be $x$.

Then, sum of natural numbers

$= 15 \times x$

Again, after adding 30 and subtracting 5 from it, we get sum

$= 15x + 25$

$\Rightarrow \quad 15x + 25 = 17.5 \times x$

$\Rightarrow \quad 17.5x - 15x = 25$

$\Rightarrow \quad x = 10$

**107** (*C*) Let there be 100 students.

Then, total marks of 10% students

$= 10 \times 95 = 950$

Total marks of 20% students

$= 20 \times 90 = 1800$

Rest marks = 8000 − (950 + 1800) = 5250

$\therefore$ Average marks $= \frac{5250}{70} = 75$

**108** (*C*) According to the question,

$$\left(\frac{P + Q}{2}\right) - 5 = 15$$

$\Rightarrow \quad \frac{P + Q}{2} = 20$

$\Rightarrow \quad P + Q = 40 \quad \ldots(i)$

and $\quad \frac{P + Q + R}{3} = 20$

$\Rightarrow \quad P + Q + R = 60 \quad \ldots(ii)$

On solving Eqs. (i) and (ii), we get $R = 20$ yr

$\therefore$ Age of $R$ after 10 yr from now

$= 20 + 10 = 30$ yr

**109** (*B*) Let, two numbers be $2x$ and $5x$.

According to the question,

$$\frac{2x + 16}{5x + 16} = \frac{1}{2}$$

$\Rightarrow \quad 4x + 32 = 5x + 16 \Rightarrow x = 16$

Hence, numbers are 32 and 80.

**110** (*D*) Let the two numbers be $3x$ and $5x$

Then, $\quad \frac{3x + 20}{5x + 20} = \frac{7}{9}$

$\Rightarrow \quad 27x + 180 = 35x + 140$

$\Rightarrow \quad 180 - 140 = 35x - 27x$

$\Rightarrow \quad 8x = 40 \Rightarrow x = \frac{40}{8} = 5$

Hence, the numbers are 15 and 25.

**111** (*A*) Let income of $X$ and $Y$ respectively $4a$ and $3a$ and their expenses are $12b$ and $7b$, respectively.

Then, according to the question,

$4a - 12b = 3200 \quad \ldots(i)$

and $\quad 3a - 7b = 3200 \quad \ldots(ii)$

On solving Eqs. (i) and (ii), we get

$a = 2000$ and $b = 400$

$\therefore$ Income of $X = 4a$

$= 4 \times 2000 =$ ₹ 8000

**112** (*D*) Let sale in 2008 = 100

Sales in 2009 = 20, Sale in 2010 = 100

$\therefore$ Required increase $= \frac{100 - 20}{20} \times 100$

$= \frac{80}{20} \times 100 = 400\%$

**113** (*D*) Monthly income of a person = ₹ 5000

Increment in income $= \frac{30}{100} \times 5000 = 1500$

$\therefore$ New income = 5000 + 1500 = ₹ 6500

**114** (*D*) Let the income of man initially be ₹ 100.

Expenditure = ₹ 75

$\therefore$ Savings = ₹ 25

Now, increase income = 120% of 100

$= \frac{120}{100} \times 100 = ₹120$

Increased expenditure = 110% of 75

$= \frac{110}{100} \times 75 = ₹\ 82.5$

New savings = ₹ 120 – 82.5 = ₹ 37.5

∴ Percentage increase in savings

$= \frac{37.5 - 25}{25} \times 100 = 50\%$

**115** (*A*) Let base (*b*) be 10 cm and height (*h*) be 10 cm.

∴ Area of triangle $= \frac{1}{2} \times b \times h$

$= \frac{1}{2} \times 10 \times 10 = 50\ cm^2$

If height is increased by 10%

then, new height = 11 cm and

$\frac{1}{2} \times b \times 11 = 50 \Rightarrow b = \frac{100}{11}$ cm

∴ Reduction in base $= \frac{\left(10 - \frac{100}{11}\right)}{10} \times 100\%$

$= \left(\frac{110 - 100}{11}\right) \times 10\%$

$= \frac{100}{11}\% = 9\frac{1}{11}\%$

**116** (*C*) Here, SP = ₹ 12750, *L*% = 15%

∴ $CP = \frac{SP \times 100}{(100 - L\%)} = \frac{12750 \times 100}{(100 - 15)}$

$= \frac{12750 \times 100}{85} = ₹\ 15000$

**117** (*D*) Here, CP = ₹ 500, SP = ₹ 750

Profit (*P*) = SP – CP = 750 – 500 = ₹ 250

**118** (*A*) ∵ Cost of 15 eggs = ₹ 75

∴ Cost of 1 egg $= ₹\frac{75}{15} = ₹\ 5$

∴ Cost of 4 dozens eggs = 4 × 12 × 5

= 5 × 48 = ₹240

**119** (*A*) Let CP of motor bike for Abhay = ₹ 100

When he sells to Subhash at 15% profit.

So, SP of motor bike for Abhay and CP of motor bike for Subhash $= 100 \times \frac{(100 + 15)}{100} = ₹\ 115$

When Dinesh purchases same and Subhash sells at 5% loss, then SP

$= 115 \times \frac{(100 - 5)}{100} = ₹\ 109.25$

So, overall profit = Actual SP – Actual CP

= 109.25 – 100 = 9.25%

**120** (*C*) Let the original price be ₹ *x*.

Since, after discount of 20% article costs ₹ 596.

∴ $596 = \frac{(100 - 20)}{100} \times x$

⇒ $x = \frac{596 \times 100}{80} = ₹\ 745$

**121** (*C*) ∵ Single equivalent discount per cent to 25% and 5%

$= \left(r_1 + r_2 - \frac{r_1 \times r_2}{100}\right)\% = \left(25 + 5 - \frac{25 \times 5}{100}\right)\%$

= (30 – 1.25)% = 28.75%

∴ Required difference $= \frac{(30 - 28.75) \times 2000}{100}$

$= \frac{1.25 \times 2000}{100} = ₹\ 25$

**122** (*A*) Here, *P* = ₹ 12000, *r* = 18%

*t* = 5 yr

∴ $SI = \frac{Prt}{100} = \frac{12000 \times 18 \times 5}{100} = ₹\ 10800$

**123** (*A*) Let the sum be *P*.

Here, *A* = ₹ 6944, *t* = 3 yr, *r* = 8%

Using, $SI = \frac{Prt}{100}$ [∵ *A* = *P* + SI]

⇒ $6944 - P = \frac{P \times 8 \times 3}{100}$

⇒ 694400 – 100*P* = 24*P*

⇒ $124P = 694400 \Rightarrow P = \frac{694400}{124} = ₹\ 5600$

**124** (*A*) Given, *R* = 4%, *n* = 2 yr and *A* = ₹ 169

∴ Amount $= P\left(1 + \frac{R}{100}\right)^n$

⇒ $169 = P\left(1 + \frac{4}{100}\right)^2 \Rightarrow 169 = P\left(\frac{26}{25}\right)^2$

⇒ $P = \frac{169 \times 25 \times 25}{26 \times 26} = ₹\ 156.25$

**125** (*C*) Given, *P* = ₹ 1250, *n* = 2 yr and *R* = 4%

∴ Difference $= \frac{PR^2}{(100)^2} = \frac{1250 \times (4)^2}{(100)^2}$

$= \frac{1250 \times 4 \times 4}{100 \times 100} = ₹\ 2$

**126** (*D*) Here, *P* = ₹ 2668, *T* = 5 yr, *A* = ₹ 4669

We know that,

Amount (*A*) = Principal (*P*) + Simple Interest (SI)

4669 = 2668 + SI

⇒ SI = 4669 – 2668 = ₹ 2001

Again, $SI = \frac{P \times R \times T}{100}$

$\therefore \quad 2001 = \dfrac{2668 \times R \times 5}{100}$

$\Rightarrow \quad R = \dfrac{2001 \times 100}{2668 \times 5} = \dfrac{2001 \times 5}{667} = 15\%$

$\therefore$ Rate of interest = 15% p.a.

**127** (*B*) $\because$ *A* and *B* do the work in 12 days.

$\therefore$ One day work of *A* and $B = \dfrac{1}{12}$

*B* alone do the work in 30 days.

$\therefore$ One day work of $B = \dfrac{1}{30}$

$\therefore$ One day work of $A = \dfrac{1}{12} - \dfrac{1}{30} = \dfrac{5-2}{60} = \dfrac{3}{60} = \dfrac{1}{20}$

Hence, *A* can do the work alone in 20 days.

**128** (*B*) $\because$ 5 days work of $A = \dfrac{1}{3}$

$\therefore$ 1 day work of $A = \dfrac{1}{3 \times 5} = \dfrac{1}{15}$

and 10 days work of $B = \dfrac{2}{5}$

$\therefore$ 1 day work of $B = \dfrac{2}{5 \times 10} = \dfrac{1}{25}$

$\therefore$ 1 day work of *A* and $B = \dfrac{1}{15} + \dfrac{1}{25} = \dfrac{5+3}{75} = \dfrac{8}{75}$

$\therefore$ Time taken by both together $= \dfrac{75}{8}$ days $= 9\dfrac{3}{8}$ days

**129** (*A*) *A*'s 1 day's work $= \dfrac{1}{8}$

*B*'s 1 day's work $= \dfrac{1}{10}$

*C*'s 1 day's work $= \dfrac{1}{20}$

$(A + B + C)$'s 1 day's work $= \dfrac{1}{8} + \dfrac{1}{10} + \dfrac{1}{20}$

$= \dfrac{5+4+2}{40} = \dfrac{11}{40}$

$\therefore (A + B + C)$ can finish the work in $\dfrac{40}{11}$ days or $3\dfrac{7}{11}$ days.

**130** (*A*) In 1 h, $\dfrac{1}{6}$ of the cistern can be filled.

In 1 h, only $\dfrac{1}{7}$ of the cistern can be filled due to leak in its bottom.

$\therefore$ In 1 h, $\dfrac{1}{6} - \dfrac{1}{7} = \dfrac{1}{42}$ of the cistern is empty.

Hence, the whole cistern will be emptied in 42 h.

**131** (*B*) Tank filled in 1 min by pipe $A = \dfrac{1}{20}$

Tank filled in 1 min by pipe $B = \dfrac{1}{30}$

Now, tank filled by both pipes in 1 min

$= \dfrac{1}{20} + \dfrac{1}{30} = \dfrac{3+2}{60} = \dfrac{5}{60} = \dfrac{1}{12}$

Hence, the time taken to fill the tank by both pipes is 12 min.

**132** (*B*) John's speed : Vinod's speed = 75 : (125 − 75)

= 75 : 50 = 3 : 2

**133** (*C*) Here, 27th March 1995 was Monday. Now, for calculating total number of odd days. First, we calculate total number of days till 1 November 1994.

$\therefore$ Number of days in March 1995 = 27

Number of days in February 1995 = 28

Number of days in January 1995 = 31

Number of days in December 1994 = 31

Number of days in November 1994 = 29

Total = 146 = 20 week + 6 odd days

Now, on November 1, 1994 = Monday − 6

= Tuesday

**134** (*C*) Number of odd days in 1600 yr = 0

Number of odd days in 300 yr = 1

$\therefore$ Number of odd days in 1900 yr = 1

Now, in 83 yr, there are 20 leap years and 63 ordinary years.

$\therefore$ Number of odd days in 83 yr = 40 + 63 = 103

= 14 weeks + 5 odd days.

$\therefore$ Number of odd days in 1983 yr = 5 + 1 = 6

Number of odd days from 1st January 1984 to 2nd July 1984 = 31 + 29 + 31 + 30 + 31 + 30 + 2

= 184 = 26 weeks + 2 odd days

$\therefore$ Total number of odd days = 6 + 2 = 8

= 1 week + 1 odd day

Day related to 1 odd day = Monday

Hence, the day on 2nd July 1984 was Monday.

**135** (*B*) Let the height of the triangle be $x$.

Then, base $BC = 7x$

Area of $\Delta ABC = \dfrac{1}{2} \times$ Base $\times$ Height

$= \dfrac{1}{2} \times 7x \times x = \dfrac{7}{2}x^2$

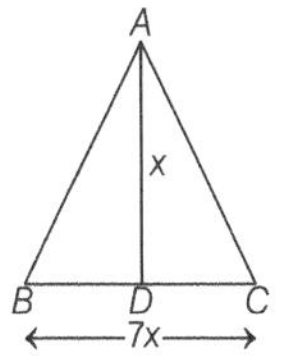


Area of painting in ₹ 350 = 100 sq m

$\therefore$ Area of painting in ₹ 1225 $= \dfrac{100}{350} \times 1225$

= 350 sq m

It means $\dfrac{7}{2}x^2 = 350 \Rightarrow x = 10$ m

$\therefore \quad$ Base $= 7x = 70$ m

**136** (*A*) Since, $AC^2 = (25)^2 = 625$

and $AB^2 + BC^2 = (15)^2 + (20)^2$

$= 225 + 400 = 625$

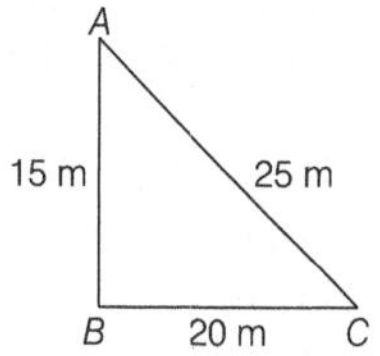


So, the triangle field is right angled at *B*.

$\therefore$ Area of the field $= \frac{1}{2} \times AB \times BC = \frac{1}{2} \times 15 \times 20$

$= 150 \text{ m}^2$

Since, the cost of sowing seed is ₹ 5 per sq. m.

$\therefore$ Cost of sowing seed for $150 \text{ m}^2 = 150 \times 5 =$ ₹ 750

**137** (*D*) Let the length and width of the rectangle be $x$ and $y$, respectively.

Then, area of rectangle $= xy$

Now, length of rectangle after increasing by

$200\% = x + \frac{200}{100}x = 3x$

Width of rectangle after increasing by 200%

$= y + \frac{200}{100}y = 3y$

$\therefore$ New area $= (3x)(3y) = 9xy$

$\therefore$ Percentage increase in area $= \frac{9xy - xy}{xy} \times 100$

$= \frac{8xy}{xy} \times 100 = 800\%$

**138** (*A*) Original breadth of rectangle $= \frac{720}{30} = 24$ cm

Now, area of rectangle $= \frac{5}{4} \times 720 = 900 \text{ cm}^2$

$\therefore$ New length of rectangle $= \frac{900}{24} = 37.5$ cm

$\therefore$ New perimeter of rectangle $= 2(l + b)$

$= 2(37.5 + 24)$

$= 2 \times 61.5 = 123$ cm

**139** (*C*) Here, $R$ = Radius of outer circle

and $r$ = Radius of inner circle

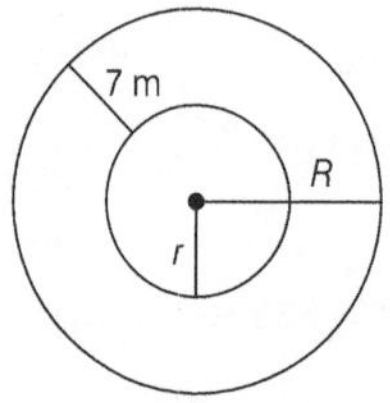


According to the question, $2\pi r = 440$

$\Rightarrow \quad r = \frac{440}{2\pi} = \frac{440}{2 \times \frac{22}{7}}$

$= \frac{440 \times 7}{44} = 70$ m

Clearly, $R - r = 7 \Rightarrow R - 70 = 7$

$\therefore \quad R = 70 + 7 = 77$ m

**140** (*D*) Distance covered in 1 round

$= \frac{\text{Total distance}}{\text{Total round}}$

$= \frac{1.76 \times 1000}{350} = \frac{176}{35}$ m

$\therefore \quad 2\pi r = \frac{176 \times 100}{35}$ cm

$\Rightarrow \quad 2r = \text{Diameter} = \frac{17600 \times 7}{22 \times 35}$

$= 160$ cm

**141** (*B*) Square of side 2 cm is cut from rectangular sheet as shown in the figure.

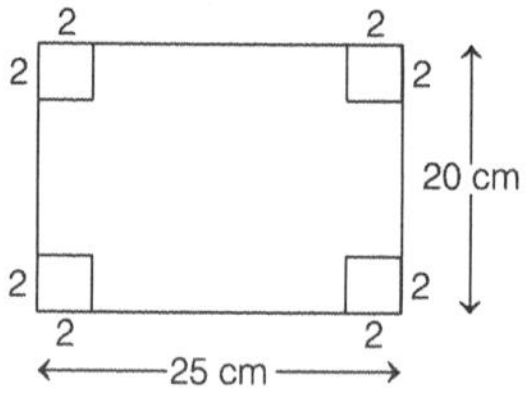


Then, length of the box $= 25 - (2 \times 2)$

$= 25 - 4 = 21$ cm

and breadth of the box $= 20 - (2 \times 2)$

$= 20 - 4 = 16$ cm

and height of the box will be 2 cm.

$\therefore$ Volume of the box = Length × Breadth × Height

$= 21 \times 16 \times 2 = 672 \text{ cm}^3$

**142** (*D*) Volume of the cylinder (pillar) $= \pi r^2 h$

$= \frac{22}{7} \times 7 \times 7 \times 500 = 77000 = (77 \times 10^3) \text{ cm}^3$

[$r$ = radius, $h$ = height of the pillar = 5 m = 500 cm]

**143** (*B*) Given, $r_1 = 1$ cm, $h_1 = 30$ cm

and $\quad h_2 = 300$ cm

$\therefore$ Volume of rod = Volume of wire

$\Rightarrow \quad \pi r_1^2 h_1 = \pi r_2^2 h_2$

$\Rightarrow \pi \times (1)^2 \times 30 = \pi \times r_2^2 \times 300$

$\Rightarrow \quad r_2^2 = \frac{30}{300}$

$\Rightarrow \quad r_2 = \frac{1}{\sqrt{10}}$ cm

$\therefore \quad \text{Diameter} = 2r_2 = 2 \times \frac{1}{\sqrt{10}} = \frac{2}{\sqrt{10}}$ cm

## Previous Years' Questions

**1** (*B*) 2, 6, 30, 60, 130, 210, ... .

$2 = 1^2 + 1 = 2$
$6 = 2^3 - 2$
$30 = 3^3 + 3$
$60 = 4^3 - 4$
$130 = 5^3 + 5$
$210 = 6^3 - 6$
$7^3 + 7 = 343 + 7 = 350$

**2** (*C*)

×3 ×3 ×3 ×3

2, 4, 6, 12, 10, 36, 14, **[108]** 18, 324

+4 +4 +4 +4

Therefore, $36 \times 3 = 108$

**3** (*A*) Given Series is,

3 2 11 14 27 34 51 **[62]**

$(1^2+2)$ $(2^2-2)$ $(3^2+2)$ $(4^2-2)$ $(5^2+2)$ $(6^2-2)$ $(7^2+2)$ $(8^2-2)$

$\therefore \quad X = 62$

**4** (*A*) 1 D 3, 3 H 5, 5 L 7, ...

+4 +4 +4

1 D 3 , 3 H 5 , 5 L 7 , **[7 P 9]**

+2 +2 +2 (inner) ; +2 +2 +2 (outer)

Therefore, the next term in the series is 7P9.

**5** (*A*)

−3 −3 −3 −3

A T E Q I N O K U H

+4 +4 +6 +6

Therefore, the next term in the series is UH.

**6** (*B*)

+1 +1 +1 +1

J A K , K B L , L C M , M D N , N E O

+1 +1 +1 +1 ; +1 +1 +1 +1

Hence, the missing term will be NEO.

**7** (*C*)

+2 +2 +2

T E F , U G H , V I J , W K L

+2 +2 +2 ; +1 +1 +1

Therefore, the missing term is VIJ.

**8** (*C*) As,

| C | R | E | D | I | T |
|---|---|---|---|---|---|
| +2 | −2 | +2 | −2 | +2 | −2 |
| E | P | G | B | K | R |

Similarly,

| D | E | B | I | T |
|---|---|---|---|---|
| +2 | −2 | +2 | −2 | +2 |
| **F** | **C** | **D** | **G** | **V** |

Therefore, the code for "DEBIT" will be "FCDGV".

**9** (*B*) As,

E N G L A N D → opposite alphabet +1 → U L S N Y L V

Similarly, I R E L A N D → opposite alphabet +1 → **Q H U N Y L V**

Hence, the code for "IRELAND" will be "QHUNYLV".

**10** (*C*) As,

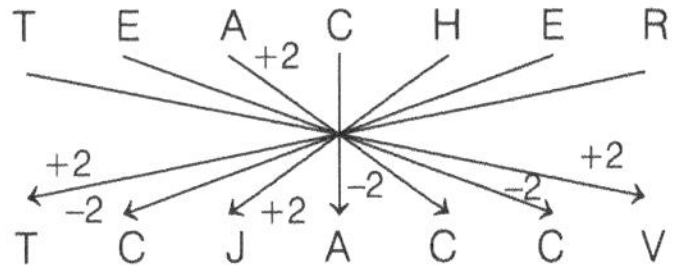


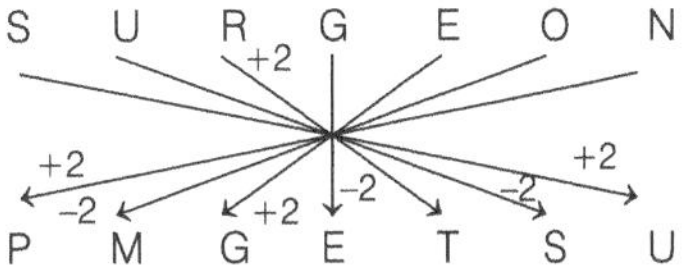


Similarly,

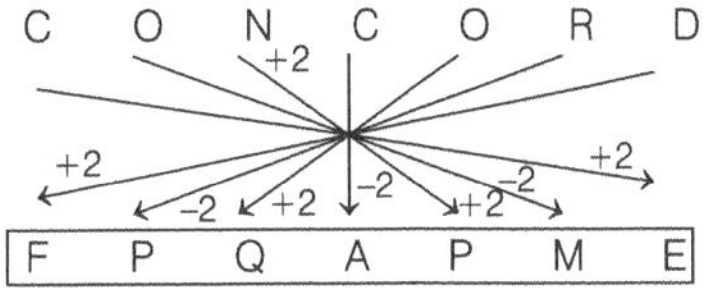


**11** (*A*) As,

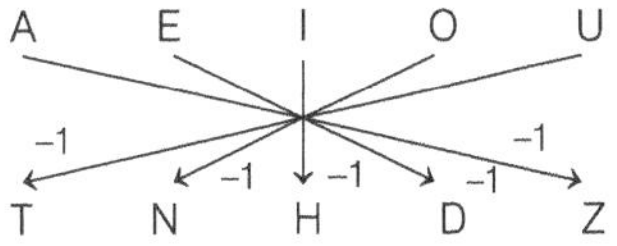


Similarly,

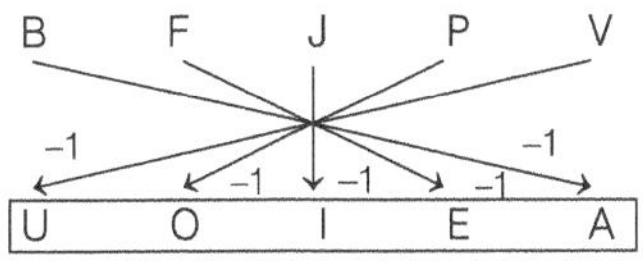

**12** (*B*) As,

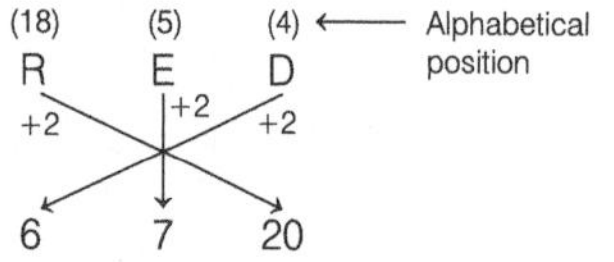


Similarly,

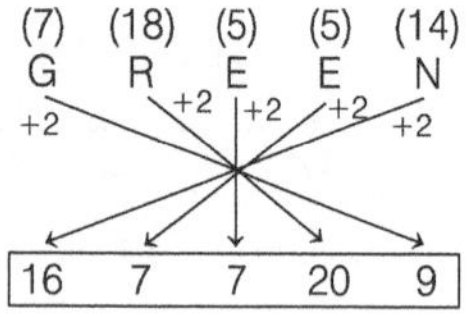


**13** (*A*) As, DRIVER = 12

The number of alphabets in DRIVER is 6

So the code = 6 × 2 = 12

Similarly, GOVERNMENT = 10 × 2 = 20

BELIEVED = 8 × 2 = 16

Similarly, BAT = 3 × 2 = 6

**14** (*A*) Let the price of refrigerator = $x$ then,

According to the quesiton,

$$SP = CP\left(1 + \frac{P}{100}\right)$$

SP = Selling Price

CP = Cost Price

P = Profit %

$$22000 = CP\left(1 + \frac{10}{100}\right)$$

CP = ₹ 20000

The selling price of refrigerator after 18% profit.

$$SP = 20000 \times \frac{118}{100} = ₹\, 23600$$

**15** (*A*) According to the question,

Area of circle = Area of Square

$$\pi r^2 = a^2$$

$$a = \sqrt{\pi r} \quad \ldots(i) \quad \begin{bmatrix} r = \text{raidus} \\ a = \text{side} \end{bmatrix}$$

$$d = \sqrt{2}a \quad [d = \text{diagonal}]$$

$$11 = \sqrt{2}a$$

$$\frac{11}{\sqrt{2}} = a \quad \ldots(ii)$$

Solving, Eqs. (1) and (2), we get

$$\frac{11}{\sqrt{21}} = \sqrt{\pi r}$$

$$\Rightarrow \quad r = \frac{\sqrt{7 \times 11}}{4}$$

$$d = \frac{2}{2}\sqrt{7 \times 11} \quad [\text{diameter } d = 2r]$$

$$d = \sqrt{7 \times 11}$$

$$d \approx 8.7 \text{ cm}$$

**16** (*B*) Distance of P to Q = 360 km

Speed of car from P to Q = 40 km/h

$$\text{then, time} = \frac{360}{40} = 9\text{ h} \quad \left[\because \text{time} = \frac{\text{distance}}{\text{speed}}\right]$$

Speed of Car from Q to P = 60 km/h

$$\text{then, time} = \frac{360}{60} = 6\text{ h}$$

$$\text{Average speed} = \frac{\text{total distance}}{\text{total time}}$$

$$= \frac{2 \times 360}{9\text{ h} + 6\text{ h}} = 48 \text{ km/h}$$

**Alternate Method** $x = 40$, $y = 60$

$$\text{Average speed} = \frac{2xy}{x + y}$$

$$= \frac{2 \times 40 \times 60}{40 + 60} = 48 \text{ km/h}$$

**17** (*C*) Total maximum number in all the subjects

= 200 + 100 + 200 + 200 + 100

= 800 marks

Total number student obtains in his examination

$$= 800 \times \frac{78}{100} = 624 \text{ marks}$$

Student gets marks in General Science

$$x = 624 - (155 + 80 + 165 + 140)$$

$$x = 624 - 540$$

$$\Rightarrow \quad x = 84 \text{ marks}$$

**18** (*D*) $\text{Amount} = \text{Principal}\left(1 + \frac{\text{Rate}}{100}\right)^{\text{Time}}$

$$2400 = P\left(1 + \frac{R}{100}\right)^1$$

$$2400 = P\left(1 + \frac{R}{100}\right) \quad \ldots(i)$$

$$3000 = P\left( + \frac{R}{100}\right)^2 \quad \ldots(ii)$$

On dividing Eq. (ii) by Eq. (i), we get

$$\frac{3000}{2400} = \frac{P\left(1 + \frac{R}{100}\right)^2}{P\left(1 + \frac{R}{100}\right)}$$

$$\frac{R}{100} = \frac{5}{4} - 1$$

$$\Rightarrow \quad R = 25\%$$

$$\text{Principal} = 2400 \times \frac{100}{125} = ₹\, 1920$$

**19** (*A*) $\frac{x}{y} = \frac{7}{9}$. Let $x = 7a$, then, $y = 9a$

$$= \frac{3(7a) - 5(9a)}{4(7a) + 9a} = \frac{21a - 45a}{28a + 9a}$$

$$= \frac{-24a}{37a} = \frac{-24}{37}$$

**20** (*D*) $\frac{3}{100} \times (a + b) = \frac{7}{100} \times (ab)$

$$3(a + b) = 7ab \quad \ldots(i)$$

$$\frac{5}{100} \times (a - b) = \frac{4}{100} \times (ab)$$

$$5 \times (a - b) = 4(ab) \quad \ldots(ii)$$

On dividing Eq. (i) by Eq (ii), we get

$$\frac{3(a + b)}{5(a - b)} = \frac{7ab}{4ab}$$

$$12a + 12b = 35a - 35b$$

$$47b = 23a$$

$$\frac{a}{b} = \frac{47}{23}$$

Percentage of $b$ respect to $a = \frac{23}{47} \times 100\% = \frac{2300}{47}\%$

**21** (*B*) Let principal = $P$

$$\text{Amount (A)} = \text{Principal (P)}\left(1 + \frac{\text{Rate}}{100}\right)^{\text{Time}}$$

for 3 yr $\quad 10816 = P\left(1 + \frac{R}{100}\right)^3 \quad \ldots(i)$

for 4 yr $\quad 11248.64 = P\left(1 + \frac{R}{100}\right)^4 \quad \ldots(ii)$

on dividin Eq (i) by Eq (ii), we get

$$\frac{10816}{11248.64} = \frac{P\left(1 + \frac{R}{100}\right)^3}{P\left(1 + \frac{R}{100}\right)^4}$$

$$1 + \frac{R}{100} = \frac{11248.64}{10816}$$

$$\frac{R}{100} = 1.04 - 1 \Rightarrow R = 4\%$$

**22** (*D*) $r_1 = 10\%$, $r_2 = 15\%$ and $r_3 = 20\%$

∴ Single equivalent discount for three successive discounts

$$= \left[1 - \left(1 - \frac{r_1}{100}\right)\left(1 - \frac{r_2}{100}\right)\left(1 - \frac{r_3}{100}\right)\right] \times 100\%$$

$$= \left[1 - \left(1 - \frac{10}{100}\right)\left(1 - \frac{15}{100}\right)\left(1 - \frac{20}{100}\right)\right] \times 100\%$$

$$= \left[1 - \frac{9}{10} \times \frac{4}{5} \times \frac{17}{20}\right] \times 100\%$$

$$= \frac{1000 - 612}{100} \times 100\%$$

$$= \frac{388}{1000} \times 100\% = 38.8\%$$

**23** (*A*) Let the number $= x$

Then, its inverse $= \frac{1}{x}$

According to the question, $x + \frac{1}{x} = -4$

Taking cube jkon both sides, we get

$$\left(x + \frac{1}{x}\right)^3 = (-4)^3$$

$$x^3 + \frac{1}{x^3} + 3x \times \frac{1}{x}\left(x + \frac{1}{x}\right) = -64$$

$$x^3 + \frac{1}{x^3} + 3(-4) = -64$$

$$x^3 + \frac{1}{x^3} = -64 + 12 = -52$$

**24** (*B*) As, REASON = 6 – 1 = 5

The number of alphabets of REASON is 6.

GOVERNMENT = 10 – 1 = 9

Similarly, ACCIDENT = 8 – 1 = 7

**25** (*D*)

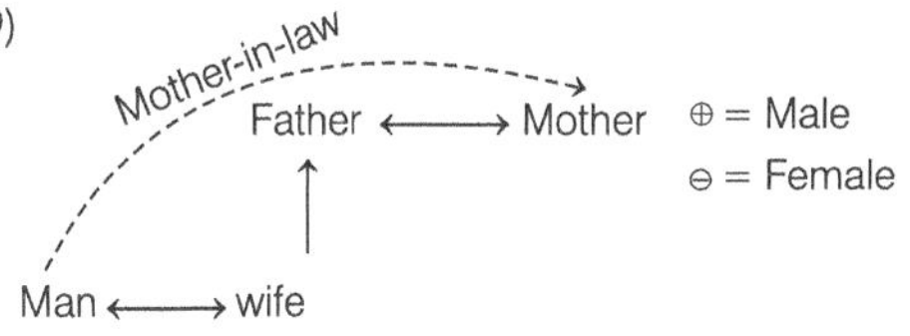


**26** (*D*)

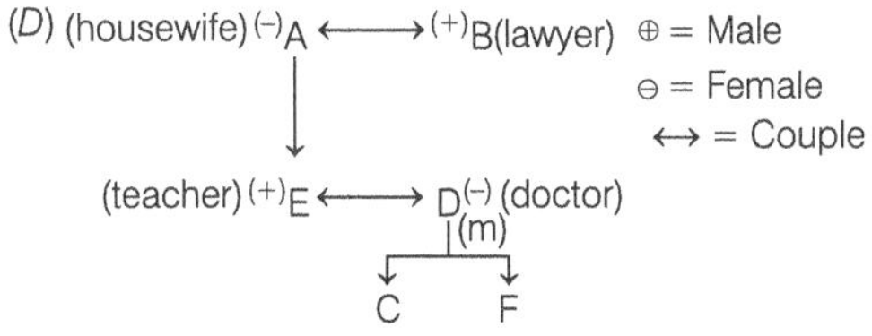


Either C or F can be a male or female.

From the above figure, it is clear that A is the grandmother of C.

**27** (*A*) Ram > Vineet > Monika ...(i)

Monika > Jacob > Dalip ...(ii)

From (1) and (2), we get

Ram > Vineet > Monika > Jacob > Dalip

Hence, Ram is the tallest in the group.

**28** (*A*)

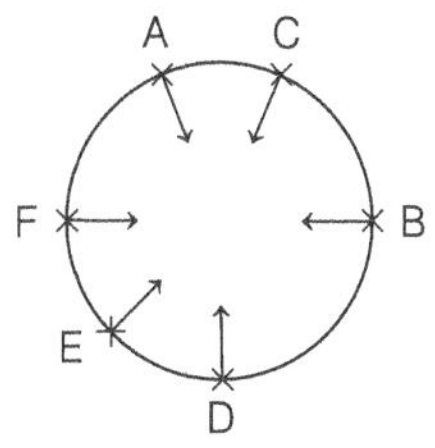


Hence, A is to the right of C.

**29** (*B*) As singing is the medium of expression of a song, similarly acting is the medium of expression for a play.

**30** (*A*) 60% of $(a-b)$ = 40% of $(a+b)$

$$\frac{60}{100}\times(a-b)=\frac{40}{100}\times(a+b)$$

$$3a-3b=2a+2b$$

$$\Rightarrow \quad a=5b$$

According to the question,

$$=\frac{b}{a}\times 100=\frac{b}{5b}\times 100=20\%$$

**31** (*B*) We know that,

$$\text{Simple interest}=\frac{\text{Principal}\times\text{Rate}\times\text{Time}}{100}$$

Let Principal = ₹$x$

According to the question,

$$\frac{x\times 1\frac{3}{12}\times 8\frac{1}{2}}{100}-\frac{x\times\frac{8}{12}\times 7\frac{1}{2}}{100}=45$$

$$\frac{x\times\frac{5}{4}\times\frac{17}{2}}{100}-\frac{x\times\frac{2}{3}\times\frac{15}{2}}{100}=45$$

$$\frac{85x}{8}-5x=4500$$

$$\frac{85x-40x}{8}=4500$$

$$45x=4500\times 8$$

$$x=₹\,800$$

**32** (*C*) Let the population of village = $x$

According to the question,

$$x\times\frac{95}{100}\times\frac{80}{100}=4750$$

$$x=4750\times\frac{100}{95}\times\frac{100}{80}$$

$$x=6250$$

**33** (*B*) According to the question,

$$x=y\times\frac{125}{100}\Rightarrow\frac{y}{x}=\frac{4}{5}=0.80$$

**34** (*A*) Average of five numbers = – 20

Sum of five numbers = – 20 × 5 = – 100

Sum of three numbers = 32

then, Sum of two numbers = – 100 – 32 = – 132

$$\text{Average of two numbers}=-\frac{132}{2}=-66$$

**35** (*C*) $0.75x=0.02y$

$$\frac{x}{y}=\frac{0.02}{0.75}\Rightarrow\frac{x}{y}=\frac{2}{75}$$

$$x=2a,\ y=75a$$

$$\text{Then, }\frac{y-x}{y+x}=\frac{75a-2a}{75a+2a}=\frac{73a}{77a}=\frac{73}{77}$$

**36** (*C*) Let the distance of railway station from village = $x$

$$\text{We know that } x=\frac{a\times b}{a+b}\times\text{total time}$$

$a$ = 20 km/h, $b$ = 5 km/h

$$x=\frac{20\times 5}{25}\times 5$$

$$x=20\text{ km}$$

**37** (*B*) CP = Cost price of mixture

SP = Selling price of mixture

The average price of mixture of the three varieties (CP)

$$=\frac{100\times 2+40\times 4+60\times 3}{2+4+3}$$

$$=\frac{200+160+180}{9}$$

$$\text{CP}=\frac{540}{9}=₹\,60 \quad \ldots\text{(i)}$$

$$\text{SP}=₹\,66 \quad \ldots\text{(ii)}$$

$$\text{The percentage of profit}=\frac{\text{SP}-\text{CP}}{\text{CP}}\times 100$$

$$=\frac{66-60}{60}\times 100$$

$$=\frac{6}{60}\times 100=10\%$$

**38** (*B*) Let the number = $x$

According to the question,

$$x+\frac{1}{x}=\frac{26}{5}$$

$$x+\frac{1}{x}=5+\frac{1}{5}$$

$$x=5$$

5 is an integer.

So, option (B) is correct.

**39** (*C*) Let the cost price of the article = ₹100$x$

$$\text{Selling price after 25\% Loss}=100x\times\frac{75}{100}=₹\,75x$$

$$\text{Selling price after 10\% Profit}=100x\times\frac{110}{100}=₹\,110x$$

According to the question,

$$100x-75x=₹\,175$$

$$x=₹\,5$$

Cost price of the article = 100 × 5 = ₹ 500

**40** (*C*) The average of 35 raw scores = 18

Total of 35 raw scores = 18 × 35 = 630

The average of first 17 raw scores = 14

Total of first 17 raw scores = 14 × 17 = 238

The average of last 17 raw scores = 20

Total of last 17 raw scores = 17 × 20 = 340

Required number = 630 – (238 + 340) = 52

**41** (*D*) Train A takes 4h to reach Delhi from Agra.

Train B takes 3.5h to reach Agra from Delhi.

Ratio of speeds of train A and train B = 3.5 : 4 = 7 : 8

Let speed of train $A = 7x$ km/h

then, speed of train $B = 8x$ km/h

Then, Distance between Agra and Delhi

$= 7x \times 4 = 28x$ km

Relative speed of trains in opposite direction $= 7x + 8x = 15x$ km/h

Train A leaves Agra at 5 am.

train A travels distance in 2h $= 7 \times 2 = 14x$

Remaining distance $= 28x - 14x = 14x$

Required time $= \dfrac{14x}{15x} = 56$ min

The time when both trains cross each other = 7:56 am.

**42** (*C*) Average age of a class of 59 students = 18 yr

Total age of a class = 18 × 59 = 1062

The age of the teacher is included, then the average of class = 18 yr 3 months then, total age of a class with teacher $= 18\frac{3}{12} \times 60 = \frac{73}{4} \times 60 = 1095$

The age of teacher = 1095 − 1062 = 33 yr

**43** (*A*) Speed of 1st cyclist = 9 km/h

Speed of 2nd cyclist = 10 km/h

In opposite direction

Relative speed of cyclists = 9 + 10 = 19 km/h

Required time $= \dfrac{47.5}{19} = 2\dfrac{1}{2}$ h.

**44** (*C*) The price of item A = ₹ 3.20

The price of item B = ₹ 5.30

The price of item A increases by = 50 Paisa

The price of item B increases by = 25 Paisa

The price of item A increases in per year more than that of item B = 50P − 25P = 25P

Required time $= \dfrac{5.30 - 3.20 + 0.40}{0.25} = \dfrac{2.50}{0.25} = 10$ yr

Item A will cost 40 Paisa more than item B

= 2008 + 10 = 2018

**45** (*A*) Required number of marble slabs

$= \dfrac{300 \times 300}{20 \times 30} = 150$

**46** (*D*) Let, the original number of person $= x$

According to question,

$$\frac{9000}{x} - 160 = \frac{9000}{x + 20}$$

$$\Rightarrow \frac{9000}{x} - \frac{900}{(x + 20)} = 160$$

$$\Rightarrow \frac{9000(x + 20) - 9000x}{x(x + 20)} = 160$$

$$\Rightarrow \frac{9000x + 180000 - 9000x}{x^2 + 20x} = 160$$

$$\Rightarrow x^2 + 20x - 1125 = 0$$

$$\Rightarrow x^2 + 45x - 25x - 1125 = 0$$

$$\Rightarrow x(x + 45) - 25(x + 45) = 0$$

$$\Rightarrow (x - 25)(x + 25) = 0$$

$\therefore$ $x = 25$

and $x = -45$

Negative value cannot be possible, therefore original number of person is 25.

**47** (*D*) The following pattern of given series

−1 5 15 29 [47]

+6 +10 +14 +18

+4 +4 +4

Hence, next term in the series is 47.

**48** (*C*) The series follows the pattern as

2 8 26 62 122 212 [x=338]

+6 +18 +36 +60 +90 +126

+12 +18 +24 +30 +36

+6 +6 +6 +6

**49** (*A*) The following pattern of series

A —+3→ D —+4→ H —+5→ M —+6→ S —+7→ [Z]

B —+5→ G —+6→ M —+7→ T —+8→ B —+9→ [K]

D —+7→ K —+8→ S —+9→ B —+10→ L —+11→ [W]

Hence, next term in series is 'ZKW'.

**50** (*B*) As, V A R A N A S I

+1 +2 +3 +4 +5 +6 +7 +8

W C U E S G Z Q

Similarly,

K O L K A T A

+1 +2 +3 +4 +5 +6 +7

[L Q O O F Z H]

**51** (*C*) As, K [L] M, H [I] J, E [F] G, D [E] F

−1 +1 −1 +1 −1 +1 −1 +1

L I F E ⟶ K M H J E G D F

Similarly, V [W] X, N [O] P, Q [R] S, C [D] E

−1 +1 −1 +1 −1 +1 −1 +1

W O R D ⟶ V X N P Q S C E

**52** (*B*) Let, two numbers be $2x$ and $5x$.

According to the question,

$$\frac{2x + 16}{5x + 16} = \frac{1}{2}$$

$\Rightarrow \quad 4x + 32 = 5x + 16$

$\Rightarrow \quad x = 16$

Hence, number are $2x$ and $5x$ = 32 and 80.

**53** (*A*) According to the question,

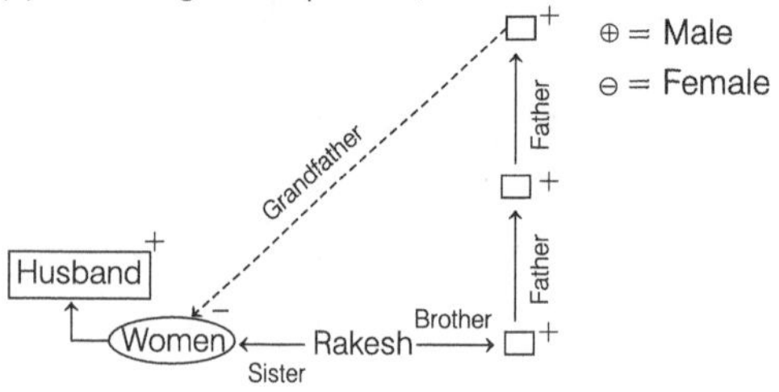


Hence, women is sister of Rakesh.

**54** (*A*) The diagram is like,

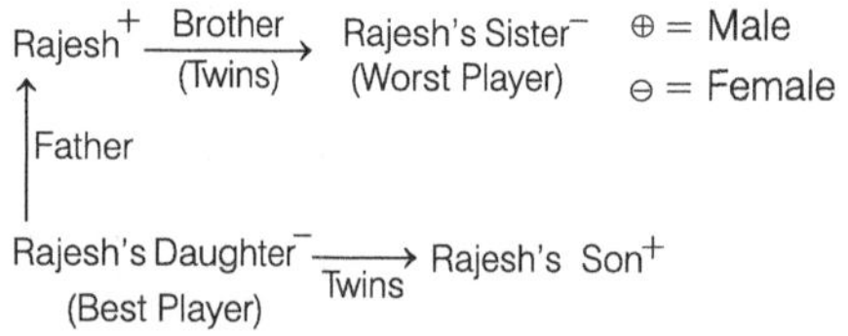


Clearly, best player is daughter of Rajesh.

**55** (*C*) Arrangement according to information given in the question as follows

5. Anand 4. Amit/Anil

3. Anil/Amit 2. Atul 1. Ajay

Therefore, Anil lives either on third floor or on fourth floor.

**56** (*D*) The pattern of the series is

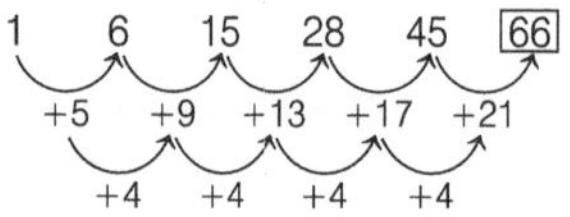


**57** (*A*) The pattern of the series is

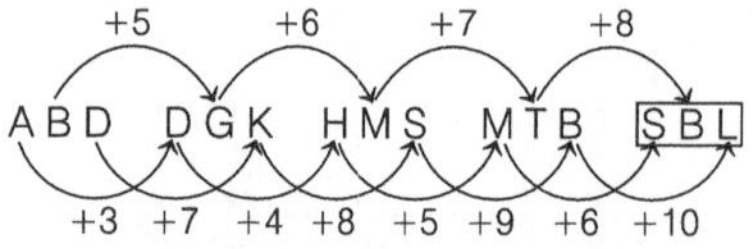


**58** (*B*) Here, the pattern of the coded word is

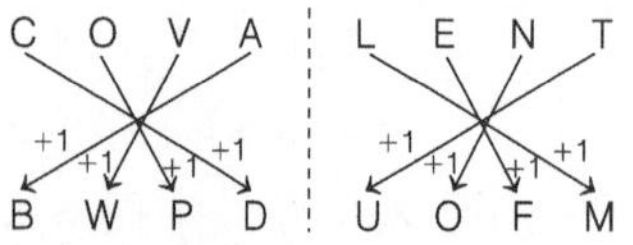


Similarly, the code of

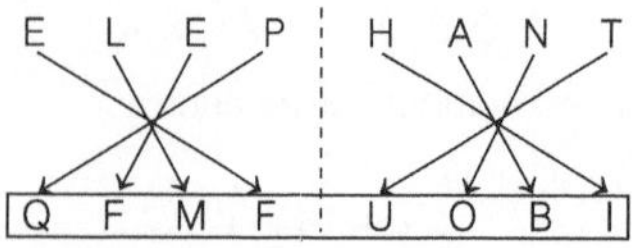


will be QFMFUOBI.

**59** (*B*)

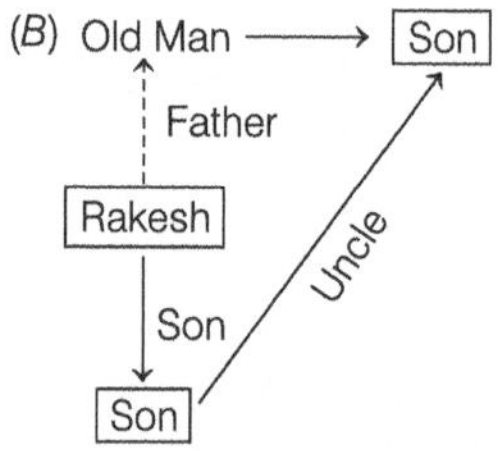


Hence, old man is the father of Rakesh.

**60** (*D*)

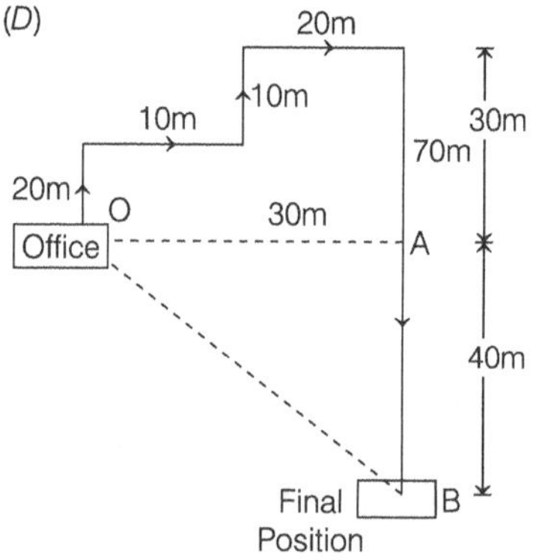


$OB = \sqrt{(30)^2 + (40)^2}$

$\Rightarrow \quad OB = \sqrt{900 + 1600}$

$\Rightarrow \quad OB = \sqrt{2500}$

$\Rightarrow \quad OB = 50\text{ m}$

**61** (*C*) Here, the pattern is

$1^3 = 1 \qquad 2^2 = 4$

$3^3 = 27 \qquad 4^2 = 16$

$5^3 = 125 \qquad 6^2 = 36$

$7^3 = 343$ and so on.

$\therefore \quad ? = 125$

**62** (*D*) According to the question,

A → C, M → I, N → P, S → O, I → A,

P → N, E → M, O → → E, C → S.

∴ C O M P A N I E S

↓ ↓ ↓ ↓ ↓ ↓ ↓ ↓ ↓

S E I N C P A M O

**63** (*B*)

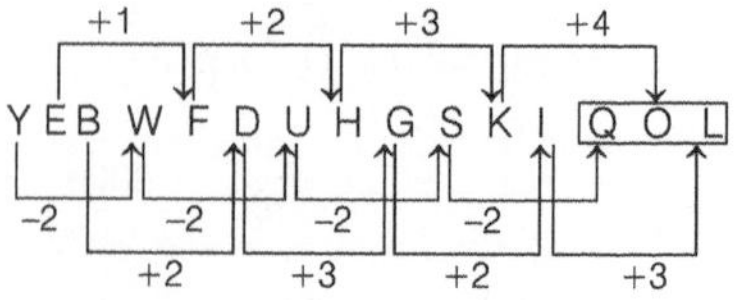


$\therefore \quad ? = QOL$

**64** (*D*) Let the cost of a glass, a pencil box and a cup be ₹ $x$, ₹ $y$ and ₹ $z$ respectively.

According to the question,

$$x + y + z = 21 \quad \ldots(i)$$
$$x + 2y + z = 28 \quad \ldots(ii)$$
$$2x + 2y + z = 35 \quad \ldots(iii)$$

Subtracting Eq. (i) from Eq. (ii), we get

$$y = 7$$

Subtracting Eq. (ii) from Eq. (iii), we get

$$x = 7$$

$\therefore$ $z = 7$

and $10z = 7 \times 10 =$ ₹70

**65** (*C*) The given series is as follows

3 → 11 → 23 → 39 → 59 → [83]

+8, +12, +16, +20, +24

+4, +4, +4, +4

So, next term = 83

**66** (*D*) According to given information,

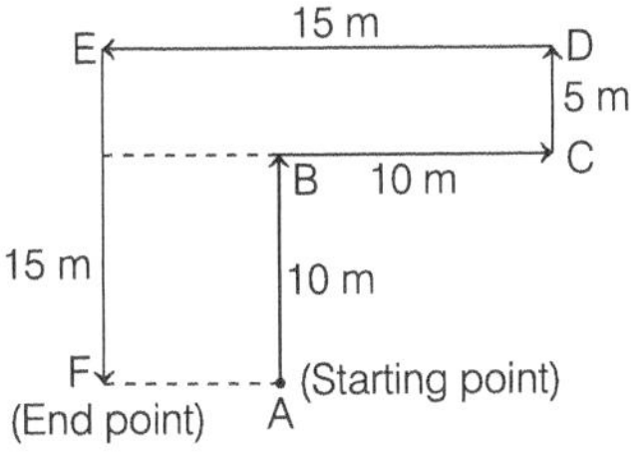


$\therefore$ Required distance, AF = DE − BC = 15 − 10 = 5 m

So, he is 5 m away from the starting point.

**67** (*A*) As,

S E L E C T I O N
−2 −2 −2 −2 −2 −2 −2 −2 −2
Q C J C A R G M L

Similarly,

A M E R I C A N S
−2 −2 −2 −2 −2 −2 −2 −2 −2
[Y K C P G A Y L Q]

**68** (*A*) According to the question,

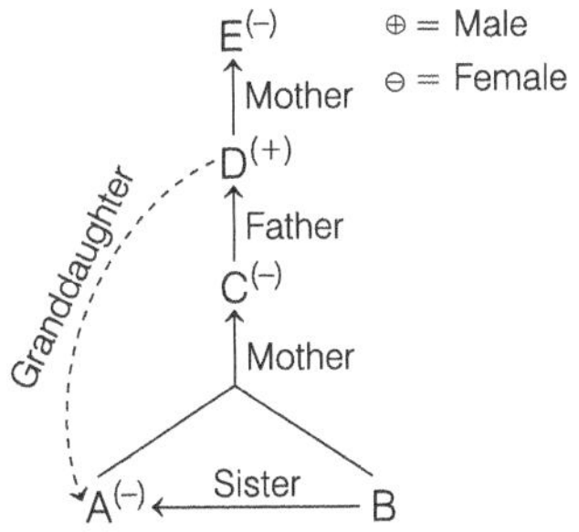


A is granddaughter of D.

**69** (*D*) Let the fare from A to B = ₹ $x$

and the fare from A to C = ₹ $y$

$$\therefore \quad 2x + 3y = 177 \quad \ldots(i)$$
$$3x + 2y = 173 \quad \ldots(ii)$$

And after solving Eqs. (i) and (ii), we get

$$x = 33$$

$\therefore$ Hence, the fare from city A to B is ₹ 33.

**70** (*A*) The sequence of the given series is as follows

B →(+2) D →(+2) F →(+2) H →(+2) [J]

2 →(×2+1) 5 →(×2+2) 12 →(×2+3) 27 →(×2+4) [58]

E →(+3) H →(+3) K →(+3) N →(+3) [Q]

Hence, the next term of the series is J58Q.

**71** (*D*) By making relation diagram, from the information given in the question, we have

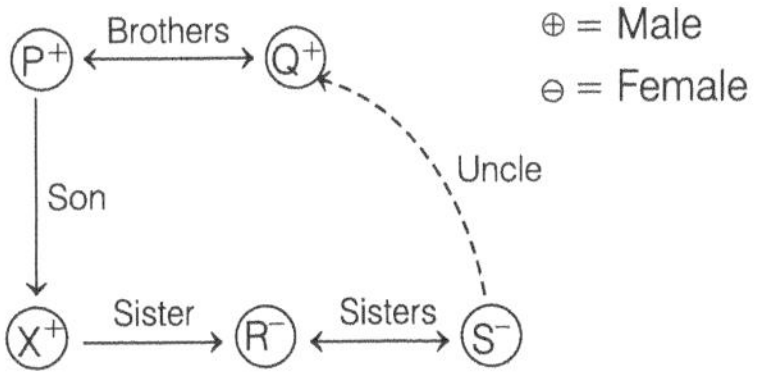


**72** (*C*) According to the question,

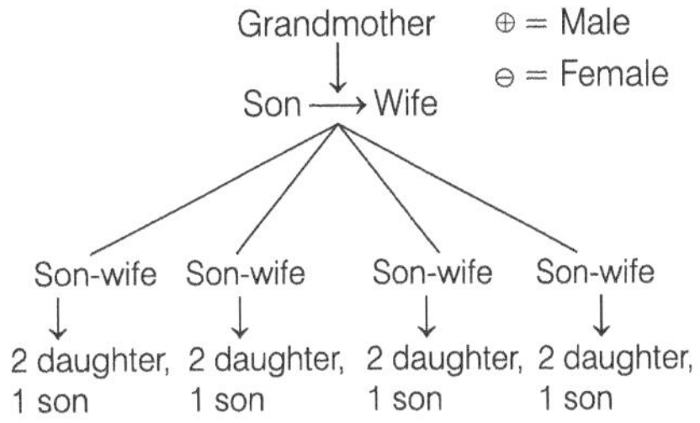


$\therefore$ Number of female members = 1 + 1 + 4 + 4 × 2

= 14

**73** (*A*) According to the question, the walking diagram of Anil is as given below

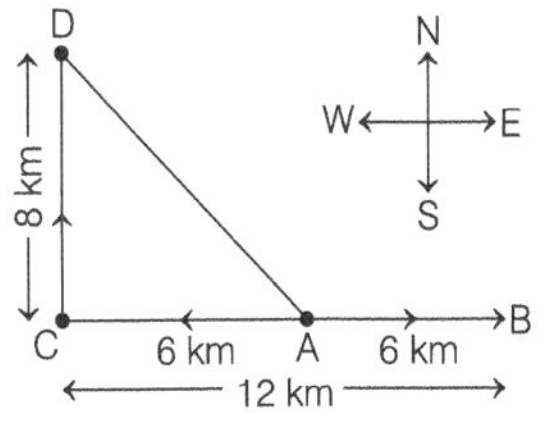


Let the point A shows Anil's house, where he travelled to 6 km upto point B and return back to the same direction upto 12 km, and point D is his office.

Here, AB = 6km, BC = 12 km, DC = 8 km

AC = BC − AB = 12 − 6 = 6 km, AD = ?

In ΔDCA,

$(AD)^2 = (DC)^2 + (CA)^2$ [by Pythagoras theorem]

$\Rightarrow \quad (AD)^2 = (8)^2 + (6)^2$

$\Rightarrow \quad (AD)^2 = 64 + 36 = 100$

$\therefore \quad AD = \sqrt{100} = 10$ km

Hence, straight distance of the office from Anil's house, $AD = 10$ km

**74** (*D*) Let the present age of son be $x$ yr.

Then, present age of father = $4x$ yr

and the present age of wife = $(4x - 3)$ yr

According to the question,

After 3 yr, the age of son will be 15 yr.

$x + 3 = 15$

$\therefore \quad x = 12$

Now, the age of wife after 5 yr will be

$= 4x - 3 + 5 = 4x + 2$

$= 4 \times 12 + 2 = 48 + 2 = 50$ yr

**75** (*B*) The pattern of given series is as follow

2 → 5 → 9 → 19 → 37 → [75]

×2+1 ×2–1 ×2+1 ×2–1 ×2+1

So, the next term is 75.

**76** (*B*) As, M A T H U R A

–3 –3 –3 –3 –3 –3 –3

J X Q E R O X

Similarly, H O T E L S

–3 –3 –3 –3 –3 –3

[E L Q B I P]

So, code for HOTELS will be ELQBIP.

**77** (*A*) The relation diagram is as follow

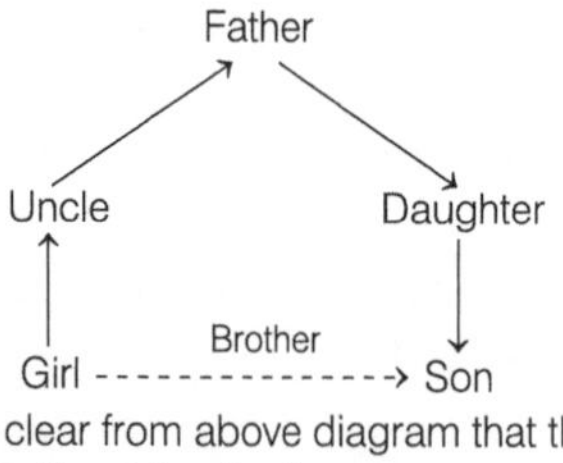


So, it is clear from above diagram that the boy is related to the girl as brother.

**78** (*C*) According to the question,

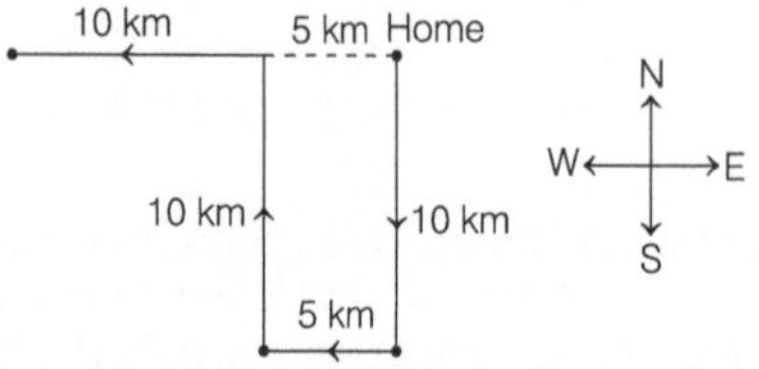


Hence, Prakash will have walk 10 + 5 = 15 km to reach his home.

**79** (*A*) $1^3 + 1 = 2, 2^3 - 1 = 7$

$3^3 + 1 = 28, 4^3 - 1 = 63$

$5^3 + 1 = 126, 6^3 - 1 =$ [215]

**80** (*A*) B A E D I H N M [T S]

–1 –1 –1 –1 –1

**81** (*B*) As, S T R E A M E R S

+2 +2 +2 +2 0 –1 –1 –1 –1

U V T G A L D Q R

Similarly, K N O W L E D G E

+2 +2 +2 +2 0 –1 –1 –1 –1

[M P Q Y L D C F D]

**82** (*A*) Mean of the present ages of father and son = 27 yr

∴ Total ages of father and son = 27 × 2 = 54 yr

After 18 yr, their total ages = 54 + 2 × 18 = 90 yr

At that time father will be twice as that of son. Let the age of son after 18 yr will be $x$, then the age of father after 18 yr will be $2x$.

$\therefore \quad 2x + x = 90$

$\Rightarrow \quad 3x = 90$

$\Rightarrow \quad x = 30$

Hence, the present age of son = 30 – 18 = 12yr

and the present age of father = 60 – 18 = 42 yr

**83** (*C*) Let the numbers be $x$ and $y$, then

$$\frac{x}{y} = \frac{3}{5}$$

$\Rightarrow \quad 5x - 3y = 0$ ...(i)

Now, $\quad \dfrac{x-9}{y-9} = \dfrac{12}{23}$

$\Rightarrow 23x - 23 \times 9 = 12y - 12 \times 9$

$\Rightarrow \quad 23x - 12y = 9(23 - 12) = 99$ ...(ii)

On multiplying Eq. (i) by 4 and then subtracting it from Eq. (ii), we get

$23x - 12y = 99$

$20x - 12y = 0$

$- \quad + \quad -$

$3x \quad = 99$

$\therefore x = 33$, then $y = 55$

Hence, numbers are 33 and 55.

**84** (*C*)

4 5 8 13 14 17 22 [23] [26] [31]

+1 +3 +5 +1 +3 +5 +1 +3 +5

[31] [32] [35] [40]

+1 +3 +5

All the terms except 33 is not a term of this series.

**85** (*A*)

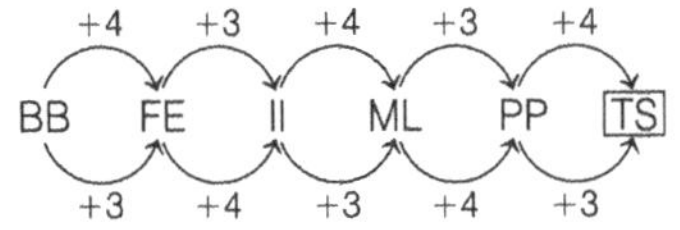


**86** (*B*)

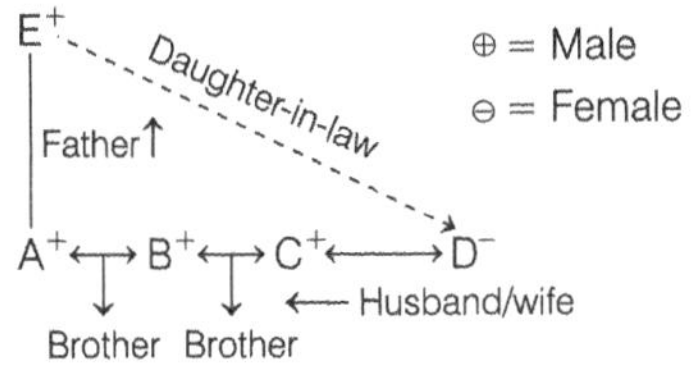


Since, E is the father of A and C is brother of A, then D, who is wife of C, is the daughter–in–law of E.

**87** (*C*) The diagram of walking of a man is below

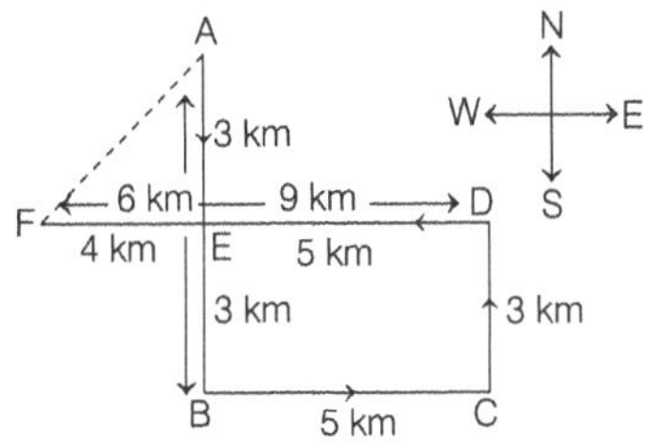


By diagram,

$AB = 6 \text{ km} \Rightarrow BC = ED = 5 \text{ km}$

$DC = BE = 3 \text{ km} \Rightarrow FD = 9 \text{ km}$

$FE = FD - ED = 9 - 5 = 4 \text{ km}$

$AE = AB - BE = 6 - 3 = 3 \text{ km}$

Now, in $\Delta AEF$,

$(AF)^2 = (FE)^2 + (AE)^2$ [by Pythagoras theorem]

$\Rightarrow (AF)^2 = (4)^2 + (3)^2$

$\Rightarrow (AF = 16 + 9 = 25$

$\Rightarrow AF = 5$

Hence, the man is 5 km away from his house.

**88** (*A*) Since, $20 = 2 \times 10$

$23 = 2 \times 8 + 7$

and $29 = 3 \times 7 + 8$

$19 = 1 \times 10 + 9$

But, there is no ticket costs ₹9.

Hence, the exact amount for which one cannot buy stamps is ₹19.

**89** (*A*) Total numbers between 50 and 99

$= 99 - 50 + 1 = 50$

Now, number made with digit 2 and 7 are 18

Which are 52, 57, 62, 67, 70, 71, 72, 73, 74, 75, 76, 77, 78, 79, 82, 87, 92, 97.

$\therefore$ Numbers have been written

$= 50 - 18 = 32$

**90** (*C*) Let the age of Sunita be $x$ yr.

$\therefore$ Age of Anil $= 2x$ yr

According to the question,

$2x - 3 = 3(x - 3)$

$2x - 3 = 3x - 9$

$-x = -6$

$\Rightarrow x = 6$

$\therefore$ Present age of Anil is

$2x = 2 \times 6 = 12$ yr

**91** (*D*) In this question, go through options is an easy way to solution,

So, let the number of apples = 4

$\therefore$ Number of apples × cost of one apple

+Number of mangoes × cost of one mango

$= 7 \times 4 + 5 \times 2 = 28 + 10 = 38$

**92** (*C*) The odd numbers from 1 to 45 which are exactly divisible by 3 are arranged in an ascending order is as follows

3, 9, 15, 21, 27, 33, 39, 45

Hence, the number at 6th position is 33.

**93** (*A*) Let the present age of A and B is $x$ yr and $y$ yr respectively.

Now, as per the question,

$x + y = 50$ ...(i)

and $\dfrac{x - 5}{y - 5} = \dfrac{5}{3}$

$\Rightarrow 3x - 15 = 5y - 25$

$\Rightarrow 3x - 5y = -10$ ...(ii)

Solving Eqs. (i) and (ii), we get

$x = 30$

$y = 20$

Hence, present age of $A = x = 30$ yr

and present age of $B = y = 20$ yr

# UNIT 06

# Logical Reasoning

CHAPTER ANALYSIS

This unit is based on updated exam pattern of NTA UGC Net covering all the important topics of Logical Reasoning. Every year 5 to 6 questions are asked from this unit. Some of these questions are based on theory and some questions are based on Statement form. In logical reasoning section questions are asked from structure & form of argument, categorical propositon, inference, mood & figure, fallacies, language, analogy, venn diagram, syllogism, statement & assumption, assertion & reason and Indian logic, etc.

## INTRODUCTION

The word 'logic' is derived from the Greek word 'logos' which means 'thoughts in language'. In other words, logic is the 'science of thought' expressed in language.

Logical reasoning is the process of deriving a logical inference from a hypothesis through reasoning. An important factor in logical reasoning is logical deduction. Deriving an inference from a set of arguments or statements is called **logical deduction**.

### Structure of Arguments

An argument is defined as a series of statements known as **premises** that are said to support a **conclusion**. In simple language, argument is a point of view on a particular matter supported by certain evidences.

The central parts of an argument include –

#### 1. Premise

A premise of an argument is something that is put forth as a truth, but is not proven. *e.g.*

- This is a beautiful car.
- The people of this town are angry.

If you are not satisfied with another person's argument, you can challenge the truth of their premises. The more complex the premise, the more opportunity there is to challenge it.

IN THIS UNIT

- Understanding the Structure of Arguments : Argument Forms, Structure of Categorical Propositions, Mood and Figure, Formal and Informal Fallacies
- Uses of Language, Connotations and Denotations of Term, Square of Oppositions
- Evaluating and Distinguishing Between Deductive and Inductive Reasoning
- Analogy
- Venn Diagram : Simple and Multiple Uses for Establishing validity of Argument.
- Indian Logic : Source of Knowledge
- Pramanas : Pratyaksha, Anumana, Upamana, Shabda, Arthapatti and Anupalabddhi
- Structure and Kinds of Anumana, Vyapti, Hetvabhasas

## 2. Conclusion

A conclusion is the statement that is reasoned or inferred from the argument's premises. *e.g.*

- We need to get out.
- You should buy this car.

A useful way of detecting a conclusion is that it will be a statement of necessity, saying what must or should happen. It will be framed to persuade the other person to do something or make some decision.

# Forms of Arguments

There are two forms of Arguments

- Deductive Argument
- Inductive Arguments

## Deductive Argument

Deductive argument means a form of logic in which specific inferences are drawn from multiple premises (general statements). It establishes the relationship between the proposition and conclusion.

When all the proposed statements are true, then the rules of deduction are applied and the result obtained is inevitably true.

## Inductive Argument

Inductive argument refers to the logical process, in which specific instances or situations are observed or analysed to establish general principles. In Inductive argument, there are certain possibilities that the conclusion drawn can be false, even if all the assumptions are true.

The argument vests on experience and observations that supports the apparent truth of the conclusion. Further the argument can be strong or weak, as it only describes the likelihood of the inference, to be true.

## Evaluating and Distinguishing between Deductive and Inductive Reasoning

- **Deductive Reasoning** The type of reasoning in which the conclusion is guaranteed to be true if the premises are true. The conclusions are based on premises and if one of the premises is not true then conclusion will also be not true.

  Premise All cats have long tail.

  Premise Tom is a cat.

  Conclusion Tom has long tail.

  Above is an example of deductive reasoning in which conclusion is deduced from premises.

- **Inductive Reasoning** The type of reasoning in which the conclusion is not fully guaranteed, there can be chance of error. On the basis of premises, the conclusion can be partially true or false or completely true or false.

  Premise : Most of the pulses contain proteins.

  Premise : Moong dal is a type of pulse.

  Conclusion : Moong dal contain proteins.

  The above conclusion can be completely true or partially true as it is mentioned in the premise the 'Most of the pulses', but is not mentioned 'all the pulses'.

  Therefore Moong dal may have proteins or may not have proteins but it is not totally guaranteed. So, this is an example of Induction reasoning.

# Categorical Propositions

In categorical proposition, there exists a relationship between the subject and the predicate without any condition. It means predicate is either affirmation or denial of the subject unconditionally. *e.g.*

I. All cups are plates.

II. No girl is boy.

The study of arguments using categorical statements (i.e. syllogisms) forms an important branch of deductive reasoning.

## Components of Proposition

A proposition, also known as a premise, is a grammatical sentence which comprises of a quantifier, subject, a predicate and a copula.

| e.g. All | aeroplanes | are | trains |
|---|---|---|---|
| ↓ | ↓ | ↓ | ↓ |
| Quantifier | Subject | Copula | Predicate |

- **Quantifier** The word 'All', 'No' and 'Some' are called quantifier as they specify a quantity.

'All' and 'No' are universal quantifiers and 'Some' is a particular quantifier.

- **Subject** (S) A subject is that part of a proposition about which something is said.
- **Predicate** (P) A predicate is that part of a proposition which is affirmed or denied about the subject.
- **Copula** (C) A copula is that part of a proposition which says about the relation between the subject and the predicate.

## Term

To find a logical deduction from two statements there should be three terms present. Those three terms are

1. **Major term** It is the predicate of the conclusion and is denoted by 'P' (for predicate).
2. **Minor term** It is the subject of the conclusion and is denoted by 'S' (for subject).
3. **Middle term** It is the term common to both the statements and is denoted by 'M' (for middle).

**Note** The middle term should not appear in the conclusion.

e.g. **Statements**

All ships are buses.

All cars are ships.

**Conclusion** All cars are buses.

Here, 'buses' is the predicate of the conclusion. Therefore, it is major term, P. 'Cars' is the subject of the conclusion. Therefore, it is the minor term, S. 'Ships' is the term common to both the statements. Therefore, it is the middle term, M.

## Major and Minor Statements

The 'major statement' is that in which the middle term is the subject and the 'minor statement' is that in which the middle term is the predicate.

e.g. **Statements**

All dogs are cats.

All cats are white.

Here, the middle term 'cats' is the subject of second statement. So, it is the major statement and the middle term, 'cats' is the predicate of first statement. So, it is the minor statement.

## Classification of Propositions

Propositions have been classified on the basis of quality and quantity of the propositions. Quality denotes whether the proposition is affirmative or negative in nature. Quantity denotes whether the proposition is universal or particular.

Types of proposition can be understood by the following diagram

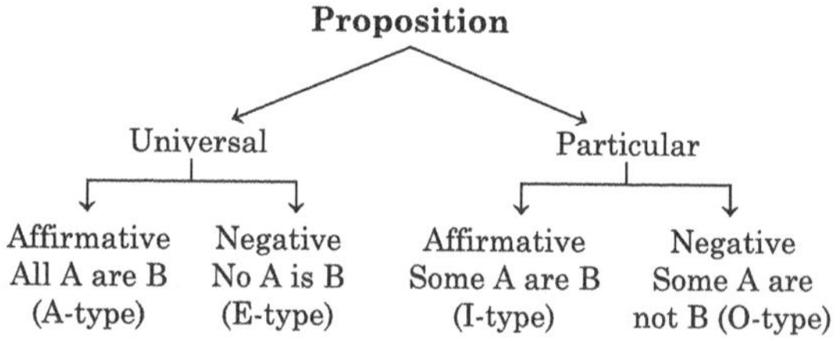


1. **Universal Affirmative Propositions (A)** This type of proposition denotes inclusion. Any universal affirmative propositions can be written as–All S is P.

   Its Venn Diagram Representation is

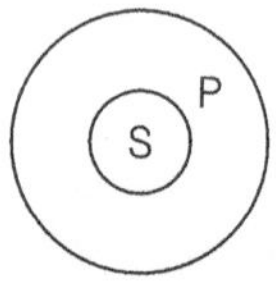


2. **Universal Negative Propositions (E)** This type of proposition denotes exclusion. Any universal negative proposition can be written as–No S is P.

   Its Venn Diagram Representation is

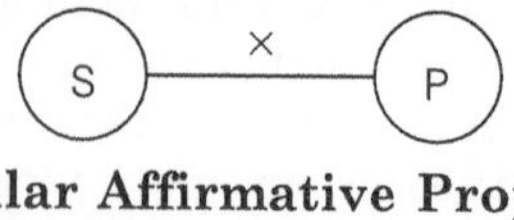


3. **Particular Affirmative Proposition (I)** This type of proposition denotes inclusion. Any particular affirmative proposition can be written as–Some S is P.

   Its Venn Diagram Representation is

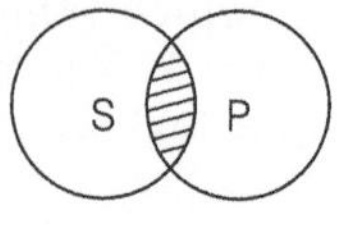

4. **Particular Negative Propositions (O)** This type of proposition denotes exclusion. Any particular negative proposition can be written as–Some S is not P.

Its Venn Diagram Representation is

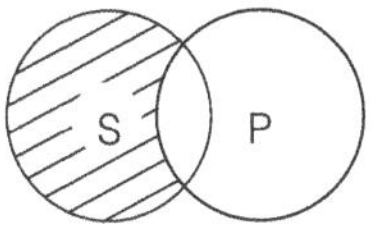


## Hidden Proposition

This type of proposition we have discussed so far are of standard nature. But there are propositions which do not appear in standard format but yet can be classified under any of the four types.

Let us now discuss the type of such propositions.

### 1. A-Type Propositions

(i) **All positive propositions** beginning with every, each, any are A-type propositions.

*e.g.*

(a) Every cot is mat.
All cots are mats.

(b) Each student of class V has passed.
All students of class V has passed.

(c) Anyone can do this job.
All (men) can do this job.

(ii) **A positive sentence** with a particular person as its subject is always an A-type proposition.

*e.g.*

(a) He can qualify the CAT written test.

(b) Mahatma Gandhi is known as the father of the nation.

### 2. E-Type Propositions

(i) **All negative sentences** beginning with no one, none, not a single, etc., are E-type proposition.

*e.g.*

(a) Not a single student could answer the question.

(b) None can cross the English channel.

(ii) **A negative sentence** with a very definite exception is also of E-type proposition.

e.g. No student except Ram has failed.

(iii) When an **interrogative sentence** is used to make an **assertion,** this could be deduced to an E-type proposition.

*e.g.* Is there any person who can scale Mount Everest?

None can climb Mount Everest.

### 3. I-Type Propositions

(i) **Positive propositions** beginning with words such as most, a few, mostly, generally, almost, frequently, often are to be deduced to the I-type.

*e.g.*

(a) Almost all the fruits have been sold.
Some fruits have been sold.

(b) Most of the students will qualify the exams.
Some of the students will qualify the exams.

(c) Girls are generally physically weak.
Some girls are physically weak.

(ii) **Negative propositions** beginning with words such as few, seldom, hardly, scarcely, rarely, little etc., are to be deduced to I-type.

*e.g.*

(a) Seldom players do not take rest.
Some players take rest.

(b) Few priests do not tell a lie.
Some priests tell a lie.

(c) Rarely IT professionals get a good job.
Some IT professionals get a good job.

(iii) **A positive sentence** with an exception which is **not definite,** is deduced to **I-type** proposition.

*e.g.*

(a) All students except three have passed.
Some students have passed.

(b) All innocents except a few are guilty.
Some innocents are guilty.

### 4. O-Type Propositions

(i) **All negative propositions** beginning with words such as 'all', 'every', 'any', 'each' etc. are to be reduced to O-type propositions.

*e.g.*

(a) All innocents are not guilty.
Some innocents are not guilty.

(b) All that glitters is not gold.
Some glittering objects are not gold.

(c) Everyone is not present.
Some are not present.

(ii) **Negative propositions** with words as most, a few, mostly, generally, almost, frequently are to be deduced to the O-type propositions.

*e.g.*

(a) Girls are usually not physically weak.
Some girls are not physically weak.

(b) Priests are not generally thieves.
Some priests are not thieves.

(c) Almost all the questions cannot be solved.
Some questions cannot be solved.

(iii) **Positive propositions** with starting words such as few, seldom, hardly, scarcely, rarely, little, etc. are to be deduced to the O-type.

*e.g.*

(a) Few girls are intelligent.
Some girls are not intelligent.

(b) Seldom are innocent guilty.
Some innocent are not guilty.

(iv) **A negative sentence** with an exception, which is not definite, is to be deduced to the O-type.

*e.g.*

(a) No students except Ram have passed.
Some students have not passed.

(b) No girls except a few are intelligent.
Some girls are not intelligent.

### Exclusive Propositions

Such Propositions start with 'only', 'done', 'none but', 'none else but' etc. and they can be reduced to either A ro E or I-type.

e.g. Only graduates are officers.
None graduate is officer (E-type)
All officers are graduates. (A-type)
Some graduates are officers. (I-type)

# INFERENCE

Inference is a logical conclusion derived from premises or statements known or assumed to be true.

## Types of Inferences

There are two types of inferences (conclusions), which are as given below

### 1. Immediate Inference

When an inference is drawn from a single statement, then it is known as 'immediate inference'. *e.g.*

**Statement** All books are pages.

**Conclusion** Some pages are books.

In the above example, conclusion is drawn from a single statement and does not require the reference of second statement. Hence, the inference is called an immediate inference.

#### Method to Draw Immediate Inference

There are various methods to draw immediate inferences like conversion, observation, contraposition, etc., but we are required to study only following two given methods

(i) **Implications** While drawing a conclusion through implication, subject remains the subject and predicate remains the predicate.

e.g. All boys are good.

Here, it is clear that if all boys are good, then some boys will definitely be good because some is a part of all.

e.g. No bags are roses.

Here, it is clear that if no bags are roses, then certainly some bags are not roses.

Immediate inference through implication can be presented as

| Types of Propositions | Types of Inferences |
|---|---|
| A | I |
| E | O |
| I | — |
| O | — |

(ii) **Conversions** In conversions, while drawing a conclusion, subject and predicate of a proposition are interchanged, but the quality of the proposition remains the same, i.e. the affirmative remains affirmative and the negative remains negative.

*e.g.*

I. **Statement** All lamps are mangoes.
**Conclusion** Some mangoes are lamps.

II. **Statement** No men are wise.
**Conclusion** No wise are men.

III. **Statement** Some rivers are ponds.
**Conclusion** Some ponds are rivers.

In above cases, subject and predicate change their positions but the quality remains same.

**Conversion Table**

| Types of Proposition | Gets converted into |
|---|---|
| A | I |
| E | E |
| I | I |
| O | Never gets converted |

## 2. Mediate Inference

In mediate inference, conclusion is drawn from two given statements.

e.g. **Statements** All dogs are cats
All cats are black.

**Conclusion** All dogs are black.

In the above example, conclusion is drawn from the two statements.

In other words, both the statements are required to draw the conclusion. Hence, the above conclusion is know as mediate inference.

### Method to Draw Mediate Inference

***Step* I** Properly align pair of propositions, i.e. the common term must be the predicate of the first proposition and the subject of the second.

*Let us consider the following pair of statements.*

I. Some bats are chairs
II. Some cats are bats
} Non-aligned pair

I. Some cats are bats
II. Some bats are chairs
} Aligned pair

**Priority order** The priority should be given while aligning. According to the following rule.

I E A →

i.e. importance for conversion should be given first to I-type statement, then to E-type statement and finally to A-type statement.

***Step* II** After having aligned statements, if required, inference can be drawn using the table as given below

| Types of I statement | | Types of II statement | | Types of inference |
|---|---|---|---|---|
| A | + | A | = | A |
| A | + | E | = | E |
| E | + | A | = | O* |
| E | + | I | = | O* |
| I | + | A | = | I |
| I | + | E | = | O |

The conclusion will follow the pattern in such a way that subject of the first statement is the subject of the inference and predicate of second statement is the predicate of the inference except the cases O* as shown in the table.

Where conclusion will follow the reverse pattern, i.e. subject of the first statement will be the predicate of inference and predicate of the second statement will be the subject of the inference.

The given table shows the combination of statements which produce definite and valid results. All other combinations will not produce definite inferences.

### Complementary Pair of Conclusions ('Either or' Situation)

In drawing mediate inference from given statements, students are required to be more attentive to select complementary pair of conclusions, where neither of the conclusions is definitely true but a combination of both makes a complementary pair.

Let us consider the example

**Statements** Some cars are scooters.
Some scooters are buses.

**Conclusions** I. Some cars are buses.
II. No cars are buses.

***Sol.*** Both the statements are properly aligned, therefore fulfil the first requirement but both the statements are of I-type and as per table for immediate inference, a combination I + I does not produce any valid mediate inference. Hence, no mediate inference can be drawn.

It is important to note here, that conclusion I, 'Some cars are buses' is not valid, because there is a possibility of 'No cars are buses', likewise conclusion II, 'No cars are buses' is invalid because there is a possibility of 'Some cars are buses'.

In other words, both the conclusions are invalid individually. However, we can say that either of conclusion I or II is true.

Hence, both the conclusions make a complementary pair of conclusions.

A complementary pair of conclusions must follow the following the conditions:

I. Both of them must have the same subject and the same predicate.

II. They are anyone of three types of pairs
(i) I-O type (ii) A-O type (iii) I-E type

**Note** Here, we have already discussed the A, E, I and O types of the statements.

## Venn Diagram Representation

**Statements** Some cars are scooters. Some scooters are buses.

Here, we can draw all possible cases as given below.

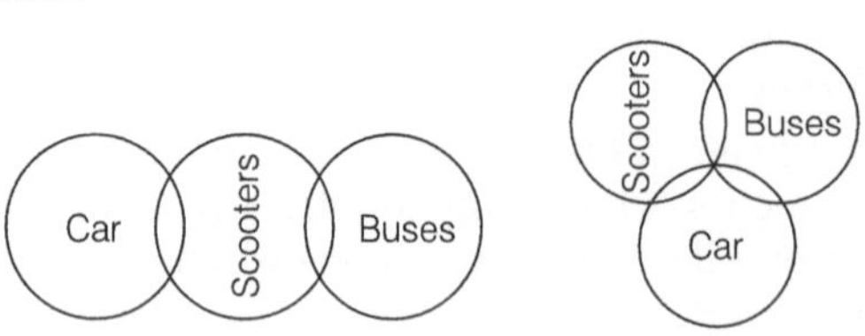


(a) (b)

Here, using both diagrammatical representations we can conclude either 'some cars are buses' or 'No cars are buses'. Hence, atleast one of the conclusions must be true.

**Possibility Cases in Syllogism and Solving them using Venn Diagrams** In syllogism, when there is no exact conclusion for the given statements, then possibility case arises.

If conclusion is **false** in one diagram and **true** in another diagram, then the conclusion is deduced as **partially true**.

In this case, partially true is considered as true.

**Statements** Some walls are roads.
All roads are floors.

**Conclusions**

I. All roads being walls is a possibility.

II. All walls being floors is a possibility.

***Sol.*** All possible diagrams are as follows

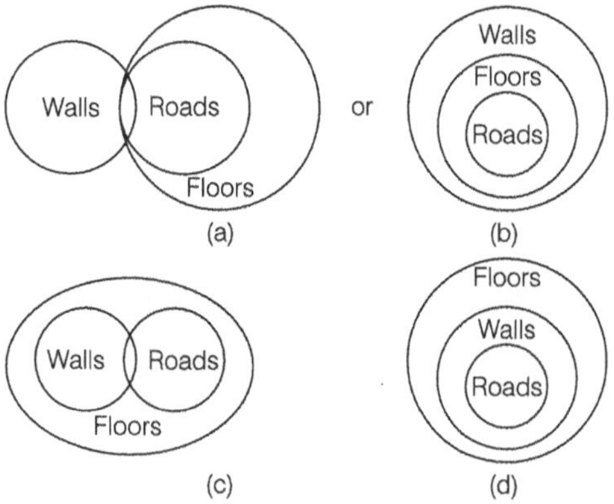


Here, the Conclusion I, i.e. 'All roads being walls is a possibility', is true in the diagrams (b) and (d).

And, the Conclusion II, i.e. 'All walls being floors is a possibility', is true in the diagrams (c) and (d).

Hence, both the conclusion follow.

## Examples

**1** Match the following.

| List-I | List-II |
|---|---|
| I. All S are P | 1. A proposition |
| II. No S are P | 2. E proposition |
| III. Some S are P | 3. I proposition |
| IV. Some S are not P | 4. O proposition |

**Codes**

| | I | II | III | IV | | I | II | III | IV |
|---|---|---|---|---|---|---|---|---|---|
| (A) | 1 | 2 | 3 | 4 | (B) | 2 | 4 | 3 | 1 |
| (C) | 4 | 3 | 2 | 1 | (D) | 3 | 2 | 4 | 1 |

***Sol.*** *(A)* 1 2 3 4

**2.** 'Some S is not P' is known as what type of proposition?

(A) Particular negative
(B) Particular affirmative
(C) Universal
(D) All of these

***Sol.*** *(A)* 'Some S is not P' is particular negative proposition.

**Directions** (Ex. 3-5) *Two statements are given in each of the following question, followed by two Conclusions I and II. You have to take the given two statements to be true even, if they seem to be at variance from commonly known facts. Read the conclusions and then decide which of the given conclusions logically follows from the two disregarding known facts.*

**Give Answer**

(A) If only Conclusion I follows
(B) If only Conclusion II follows
(C) If neither I nor II follows
(D) If both Conclusions I and II follow

**3. Statements**

All huts are mansions.
All mansions are temples.

**Conclusions**

I. Some temples are huts.
II. Some temples are mansions.

***Sol.*** *(D)* **Conclusion I** – A+ A= A

∴ All huts are mansions + All mansions are temples
= All huts are temples
$\xrightarrow{\text{conversion}}$ Some temples are huts.

So, Conclusion I follows.

**Conclusion II** All mansions are temples
$\xrightarrow{\text{conversion}}$ Some temples are mansions.

So, Conclusion II follows.

**Alternate Method** This shows the case of universal affirmative proposition.

So,

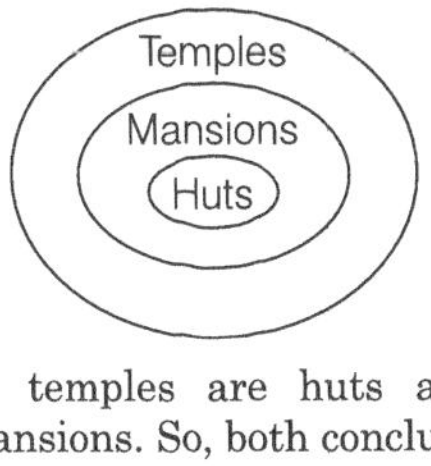


**Conclusions**
I. ✓
II. ✓

Clearly, some temples are huts as well as some temples are mansions. So, both conclusions follow.

**4. Statements**

Some camels are ships.
No ship is a boat.

**Conclusions**

I. Some ships are camels.
II. Some camels are not boats.

***Sol.*** *(D)* According to the question,

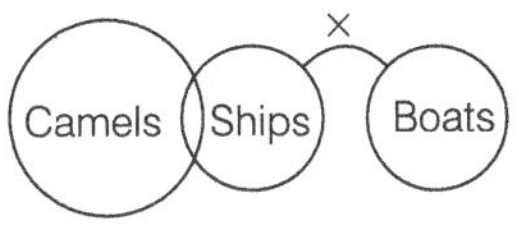


**Conclusions**
I. ✓
II. ✓

It is clear from diagram that both Conclusions I and II follow.

**5. Statements**

Some chalks are dusters.
All the dusters are boards.

**Conclusions**

I. Some chalks are boards.
II. No duster is a board.

***Sol.*** *(A)*

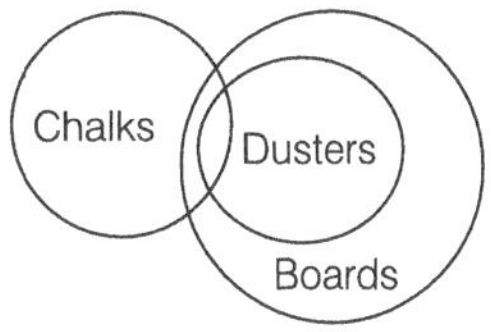


**Conclusions**
I. ✓
II. ✗

So, only Conclusion I follows.

**6.** In the following question, three statements numbered I, II and III and four conclusions are given. Select the correct answer from the options given.

**Statements**

I. Some newspapers are ACs.
II. Some ACs are trees.
III. All books are ACs.

**Conclusions**

1. Some books are newspapers.
2. All books are trees.
3. All trees are books.
4. Some books are not newspapers.

(A) Only 1 follows (B) 1 or 3 follows
(C) Either 1 or 4 follows (D) 2 and 3 follow

***Sol.*** *(C)* According to the question,

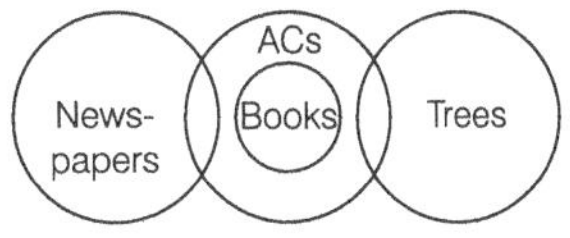


**Conclusions**
1. ✗
2. ✗
3. ✗
4. ✗
Either (1, 4)

Conclusion 1 does not follow. Conclusion 4 also does not follow.

But these two conclusions forms a complementary pair. Therefore, either 1 or 4 follows.

## Mood and Figures

A categorical proposition (syllogism) has two parts *i.e.* **Mood** and **Figures**. These are

1. **Mood** The mood of a categorical syllogism is a series of three letters corresponding to the type of proposition in major premise, the minor premise, and the conclusion are (A, E, I or O).

   **For Example,**
   No cat is dog.
   Some bears are dog.
   Some bears are cat.

   Now, the form of the premise and the conclusion.
   No S are P(E)
   Some S are P(I)
   Some S are not P(O)

   So, the mood of this proposition is "EIO".

   Here, cat is the major term, bears are the minor term and dog is the middle term.

2. **Figures** The figure of a categorical proposition (syllogism) is a number which corresponds to the placement of the two middle terms.

   Suppose, 'S' is the minor term, 'P' is the major term and 'M' is the middle term of the conclusion, then

   There are four possible figures

   **Figure I** When the middle term is on the left of P and on the right of S.

   **Figure II** When the middle term is on the right of both P and S.

   **Figure III** When the middle term is on the left of both P and S.

   **Figure IV** When the middle term is on the right of P and left of S.

| Figure I | Figure II | Figure III | Figure IV |
|---|---|---|---|
| (M) P | P (M) | (M) P | P (M) |
| S (M) | S (M) | (M) S | (M) S |
| S P | S P | S P | S P |

   Now, suppose there are arguments
   - All mammals are attractive.
   - All dogs are mammals.
   - Therefore, all dogs are attractive.

   Here, the major term is 'attractive', the minor term is 'dogs' and the middle term is 'mammals'.

   The mood of the above arguments is "AAA" since all three propositions are 'A' propositions (*i.e.* they are all of the form "All S are P".

   The figure of the above arguments is 'Figure I' since the middle term appears on the left and then on the right.

   **Figure I**

| | |
|---|---|
| Mammals (M) | Attractive (P) |
| Dogs (S) | Mammals (M) |

# FALLACIES

A fallacy is a defect in an argument which misleads the mind.

The defect may be intentional or unintentional. If the defect is intentional, we call it a sophism.

One's understanding of fallacies may be used for good, in order to avoid or expose error, or it may be used for evil in order to subtly deceive.

## Types of Fallacies

### 1. Formal Fallacies

A formal fallacy is one which involves an error in the form, arrangement or technical structure of an argument.

The question in view is not whether a conclusion is true or false, but whether the form of the argument is correct or incorrect, valid or invalid.

Here are some examples

#### Formally Valid Arguments

1. **True and Valid**
   All men are mortal.
   David is a man.
   Therefore, David is mortal.
2. **False but Valid**
   All men are green.
   David is a man.
   Therefore, David is green.

### Formally Invalid Arguments

3. **False and Invalid**
   Some men are green.
   David is a man.
   Therefore, David is green.
4. **True but Invalid**
   Some men are mortal.
   David is a man.
   Therefore, David is mortal.

### 2. Informal Fallacies

Informal fallacies refers to the unclear expression. It deals with the logic of the meaning of language. It basically focuses on the meaning of the arguments.

It involves things like misuse of language such as words or grammar, misrepresentation of facts or opinions, misconceptions due to underlying presuppositions or just plain illogical sequence of thoughts.

Informal fallacies develop when

1. The relationship between premises and conclusion does not hold up.
2. When premises are unsound.
3. Informal fallacies are more dependent on misuse of language and of evidence.

Informal fallacies cannot be reduced to symbolic formulas. They can be arranged into following categories.

### Informal Fallacy of Ambiguity

This fallacy involves imprecise use of language. Each language has its own "logic", the way the written symbols are arranged to convey certain meanings.

When a word or an expression is used in an imprecise manner, a door is opened for a misunderstanding which is called fallacy.

**For Example,**

- Logic teaches you how to argue.
- People argue entirely too much.

In the Statement 1, the word 'argue' is used to mean only the process of arranging propositions to flow logically from a premise to a conclusion. In the Statement 2, the word 'argue' is used to include such meanings as a heated discussion, a bitter disagreement, a dispute or a controversy.

### Amphibology or Semantic and Syntactic Ambiguity

This ambiguity occurs when a word, phrase or grammatical construction is used which can be understood more than one way.

**For Example,**

- Lots for sale [Semantic ambiguity : Allotments of land or numerous things]
- Laurie calls her mother when she is alone. [Syntactic ambiguity : who is alone, Laurie or her mother?]

A semantic ambiguity can be removed by defining the ambiguous word or by offering a synonym. It can be removed by reconstructing the sentence.

## LANGUAGE

Language is a system of conventional spoken, manual or written symbols by means of which human beings, as members of social group and participants in its culture, express themselves.

### Uses of Languages

The function of languages includes **informative**, **expressive** and **directive**.

These are

1. **Informative** The informative use of language involves giving and receiving of information. The general assumption is that the content is believable and valuable.
   **For example**, language is used to offer opinions, giving advice, make announcements, lectures etc.
2. **Expressive** Language expresses and evokes ideas, thoughts and feelings. Expressive function may or may not include any real information because the purpose of expressive use of language is to convey emotion.
3. **Directive** Language is used to establish and maintain social order. Directive use of language establishes norms of expected behaviour in certain situations. Laws rules, and policies are among the common

form of directive use of language that promote health and safety in society.

4. **To ask** Language is also used in asking questions. These questions can be written form as in books, papers, tests etc or in the oral form.
5. **To evaluate** Language can also be used to evaluate and express our judgements. There are three types of language used for evaluation—ethical, aesthetic, and technical. Ethical language is used for stating the right and wrong, rights and duties. Aesthetic language is used to talk about aspects like beauty and ugliness. Technical language is used for asserting the usefulness.
6. **Other uses** Language can be used in other ways such as to congratulate, apologize, affirm action, make a promise, etc.

### *Examples*

**5.** Which of the following statements denotes directive use of language?

(A) I am going to market today
(B) Eat your food
(C) This flower is beautiful
(D) None of the above

***Sol.*** *(B)* In 'Eat your food', a person is directing someone to do a certain task, that is eating food.

**6.** Which of the following denotes informative use of language?

(A) Hurrah! we won the match
(B) Don't break the law
(C) Sachin is a very good player
(D) Mobile phones are strictly prohibited

***Sol.*** *(C)* In option 'C', we are providing some information about Sachin that he is a good player.

## Connotations and Denotations

Connotations and denotations are properties of the terms in a proposition. They are also known as **intension** and **extension** of terms.

### Connotation

Connotation means to indicate an object or objects to which the name refers and also to suggest certain qualities residing in those objects.

**For Example** The term 'Man' refers to all human beings and it also implies the qualities of rationality and animality.

There are three views regarding the exact meaning of connotation.

1. **Objective View** According to this view, connotation means all the attributes contained in the term, both known and unknown. In logic, we are not concerned with anything unknown to our reason. It is concerned with relatively agreed and common attributes of a term.
2. **Subjective View** Here, only these attributes known to the subject or the speaker is taken into account. In other words, the subjective meaning of connotation may vary from person to person according to different views. If we accept this view there will be no agreement regarding the truth and the vary purpose of the logic will be defeated.
3. **Logical or Conventional View** According to this view, connotation means only the essential and fixed attributes of the object on account of which the term is applied to the object.

### Denotation

The function of indicating objects to which the term applies is called denotation. It suggests the extent of objects to which the term is applied.

## Square of Opposition

The square of opposition is a chart that was introduced within categorical logic to represent the logical relationship holding between certain propositions in virtue of their form.

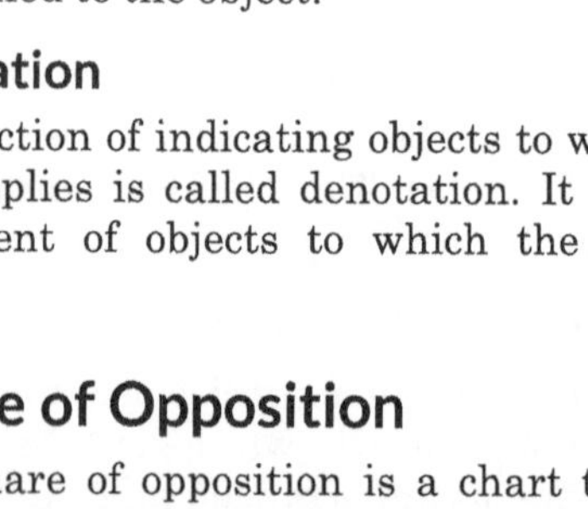


The four corners of this represent the four basic forms of propositions recognised in classical logic.

1. A proposition, or universal affirmatives take the form : All S are P.
2. E propositions, or universal negations take the form : No S are P.
3. I propositions, or particular affirmatives take the form : Some S are P.
4. O propositions, or particular negations take the form : Some S are not P.

### Contradictories

By contradictories, we mean two propositions, that cannot be both true and false together. 'A' and 'O' propositions are taken as contradictories and also 'E' and 'I' are also taken as contradictories. It has been also said that every statement has a contradictory opposite, because if a contradictory is true then it's opposite is false. Aristotle means a pair of affirmative and negative statements. These he refers as a contradictories.

There are many examples of contradictories like 'every woman is white' and 'not every woman is white' and 'no woman is white' and 'some man is white'.

## Contrary

By contrary statements, Aristotle means statement that both cannot be true at the same time. The universal affirmative and the universal, negative comes under this domain. Like "every woman is white" and "no woman is white".

They are not regarded as **contradictories** because both of them may be false. So, it has been said that the universal statements are contraries. It says that one proposition is true and another proposition is false, they can both be regarded as false. 'A' and 'E' are regarded as contraries.

## Sub-Contraries

It is regarded as the negations of universal statements. The medieval logicians call this as a 'particular' statements. The opposites of contraries are called sub-contraries. Two propositions can be regarded as both be true, but they cannot be regarded as both be false. I and O propositions are taken as sub-contraries. Aristotle says that sub-contraries can be regarded as both be true together. 'I' and 'O' propositions are not regarded as contrary or contradictory. Example of it is "some lunches are free" is false, then "some lunches are not, free" is true.

## Sub-Alternation

It means the two propositions that have the same subject and the same predicate terms. They agree on quality. It means the opposition between a universal and its particular.

'A' and 'I' and 'E' and 'O' are regarded as sub-alternation. It means the truth of the first helps us to implies the truth of the second.

It has been also said that the truth of a particular proposition does not imply the truth of the corresponding **universal proposition**. It has been said that, the truth of a proposition implies the truth of the I proposition. It has been said that, the truth of 'all cows have horns' does not imply the truth of 'some cows have horns'.

## Features of Square of Opposition

There are four ways, in which propositions may be 'opposed'-as contradictories, contraries, sub-contraries and as sub and superalterns. Relations exhibited by this square of opposition were believed to provide the logical basis for validating certain elementary forms of argument.

To explain these, we must first distinguish between immediate inferences and mediate inferences. When we draw a conclusion from one or more premises some inference must be involved. That inference is said to be mediate, when more than one premise is relied upon (as in a syllogism) because the conclusion is drawn from the first premise through the mediation of the second.

But, where a conclusion is drawn from only one premise there is no such mediation and the inference is said to be immediate.

A number of very useful immediate inferences may be readily drawn from the information embedded in the traditional square of opposition. Here are some examples

- If an A proposition is our premise, then (according to the square of opposition) one can validly infer that the corresponding O proposition (i.e., the O proposition with the same subject and predicate terms) is false.
- If an A proposition is our premise, then the corresponding I proposition is true.
- If an I proposition is our premise, its **corresponding** E proposition, which contradicts it, must be false.

Given the truth or the **falsehood**, of any of the four standard-form categorical propositions, it will be seen that the truth or falsehood of some or all of the others can be inferred immediately.

There are a considerable number of immediate inferences based on the traditional, **Square of Opposition**, we list them here

- **A** is given as true :
  **E** is false; **I** is true; **O** is false.
- **E** is given as true:
  **A** is false; **I** is false; **O** is true.
- **I** is given as true :
  **E** is false; **A** and **O** are undetermined.
- **O** is given as true :
  **A** is false; **E** and **I** are undetermined.
- **A** is given as false :
  **O** is true; **E** and **I** are undetermined.
- **E** isgiven as false :
  **I** is true; **A** and **O** are undetermined.
- **I** is given as false :
  **A** is false; **E** is true; **O** is true.
- **O** is given as false :
  **A** is true; **E** is false; **I** is true.

# ANALOGY

Analogy literally means 'similarity' i.e. having similar features. Questions on analogy, test the ability of a candidate to understand the relationship between two given objects and apply the same relationship to find the answer. Different types of analogies are given below.

## Word Analogy

In this type of analogy, word or pair of words are given which are related to each other in a particular manner. The candidate is required to identify the relationship between the words or pair of words.

Then, the candidate is required to pick the word or pair of words from the alternatives which bears exactly the same relationship to the given word or pair of words in the question.

### *Examples*

**1.** 'Melt' is related to 'Liquid' as 'Freeze' is related to

(A) Ice (B) Crystal
(C) Water (D) Cubes

**Sol.** *(A)* The term 'Melt' is associated with 'Liquid' because after melting of solid, we obtain liquid. Similarly, the state of 'Liquid' after freezing is 'Solid'.

**2.** 'Success' is related to 'Joy' in the same way as 'Failure' is related to

(A) Anger (B) Sorrow
(C) Happiness (D) Defeat

**Sol.** *(B)* 'Success' brings 'Joy'. Similarly, 'Failure' brings 'Sorrow'.

**3.** Find out the pairs in which the words bear the same relationship to each other as similar to the words of the given pair bear.

Horse : Mare

(A) Fox : Vixen
(B) Bullock : Doe
(C) Monk : Monkey
(D) Bee : Hen

**Sol.** *(A)* 'Mare' is the female 'Horse'. Similarly, 'Vixen' is the female 'Fox'.

**Directions** (Example Nos. 4 and 5) *In the following questions, out of the four given alternatives choose that alternative as your answer which is similar to the given words.*

**4.** Eyes : Tongue : Ear

(A) Finger (B) Thumb
(C) Knee (D) Nose

**Sol.** *(D)* All are human sense organs.

**5.** Pen : Pencil : Rubber

(A) Page (B) Cell (C) Pillow (D) T.V.

***Sol.*** *(A)* All are stationary items.

## Alphabet Analogy

In this type, two groups of letters, related to each other in a certain way, are given. The candidate is required to find out this relationship and choose either a letter-group that is related in the same way to the third group provided in the questions or a pair consisting of similarly related letter groups.

### Examples

**6.** LS is related to OH in the same way as '?' related to PC.

(A) PK (B) HP
(C) KX (D) XY

***Sol.*** *(C)* As,

L S ⟶ O H (opposite letter) Similarly, K X ⟶ P C (opposite letter)

**7.** What will come in the place of '?' in the following question?

BCD : EFG : : LMN : ?

(A) PQO (B) OPQ
(C) QPO (D) POQ

***Sol.*** *(B)* As, B C D → (+3, +3, +3) → E F G Similarly, L M N → (+3, +3, +3) → O P Q

∴ ? = OPQ

## Number Based Analogy

Such relationship is based on arithmetical operations like addition, subtraction, multiplication or division of numbers. One number of one of the pairs bears some arithmetical relationship with the second number.

Based on that relationship, the candidate is required to find the number of the another pair which bears the same relationship with the second number as in the first pair.

### Examples

**Directions** (Example Nos. 8 and 9) *Choose a number which bears the same relationship with the third/fourth number as the first two bear.*

**8.** 4 : 8 : : 16 : ?

(A) 28 (B) 18 (C) 20 (D) 32

***Sol.*** *(D)* As, 4 → ×2 → 8 Similarly, 16 → ×2 → 32

∴ ? = 32

**9.** 8 : 56 : : 9 : ?

(A) 10 (B) 63 (C) 7 (D) 9

***Sol.*** (B) As, $8 \times 7 = 56$ Similarly, $9 \times 7 = 63$

∴ ? = 63

## Alpha-Numeric Analogy

In this type of analogy, alphabets and numbers are given following a certain relationship. The relationship can be based on the position of alphabets, sum or product of position of alphabets in alphabetical series.

### Examples

**Directions** (Example Nos. 10 and 11) *Complete the second pair in which both the elements bears the same relationship as in the first pair.*

**10** NEWS : 14, 5, 23, 19 : : PAPER : ?

(A) 16, 5, 16, 1, 18
(B) 18, 5, 16, 1, 16
(C) 16, 1, 16, 5, 18
(D) 32, 2, 32, 10, 36

***Sol.*** *(C)* As,

N E W S → 14 5 23 19 ⟵ Alphabetical position

Similarly,

P A P E R → 16 1 16 5 18 ⟵ Alphabetical position

**11** FILM : 10 : : HOTEL : ?

(A) 12 (B) 16 (C) 18 (D) 30

*Sol. (A)* As,

F I L M
↓ ↓ ↓ ↓
6 + 9 + 12 + 13 = 40

$\frac{40}{4} = 10$ [∵ number of letters = 4]

Similarly,

H O T E L
↓ ↓ ↓ ↓ ↓
8 + 15 + 20 + 5 + 12 = 6

$\frac{60}{5} = 12$ [∵ number of letter = 12]

# VENN DIAGRAM

A venn diagram is a representation method for all possible relation that can exist between given group of elements in a single figure. There are two types of Venn diagram

## Relation Based Venn Diagram

In this type of questions, a candidate is required to find out the diagram which classify the given group correctly or illustrate the relation between them.

### Examples

**1** Which of the following diagram best depict the relationship between female and teacher?

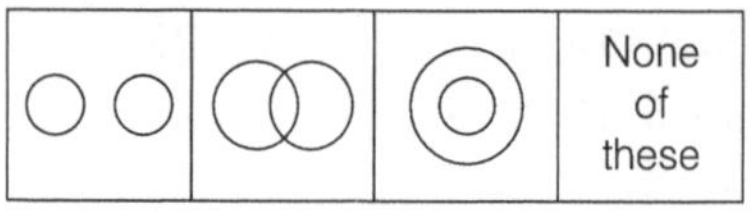


(A) (B) (C) (D)

*Sol. (B)* By profession some females can be teachers but there can also be some females who are not teachers. Also, there can be some male teacher.

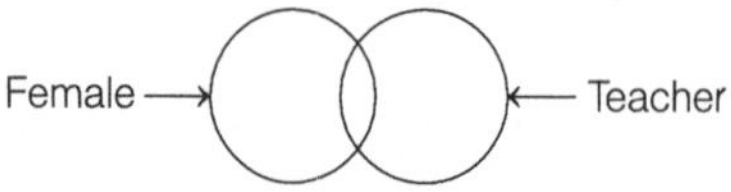


**2** Which of the following diagrams best depict the relationship between Doctors, Human beings and Cats?

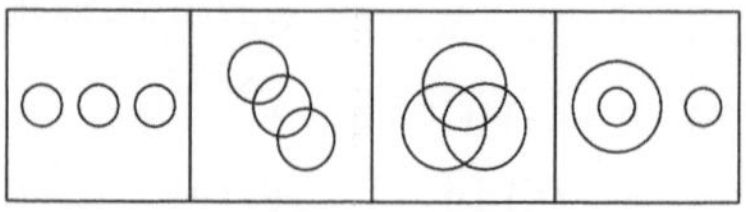

(A) (B) (C) (D)

*Sol. (D)* All Doctors can come under the group of Human beings but all Human beings do not come under the group of Doctors and Cats are entirely different from Doctors and Human beings.

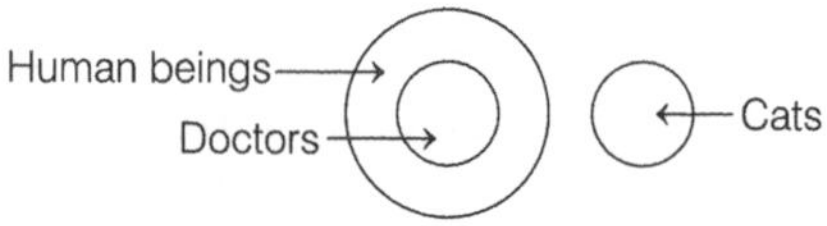


## Analysis Based Venn Diagram

In this type of questions, generally a venn diagram comprising of different geometrical figures is given. Each geometrical figure in the diagram represents a certain class.

The candidate is required to study and analyse the figure carefully and then answer the given questions based on it.

### Examples

**3** The given diagram represents those people who play Hockey, Cricket and Badminton. See the diagram and find out those people who play all the three games.

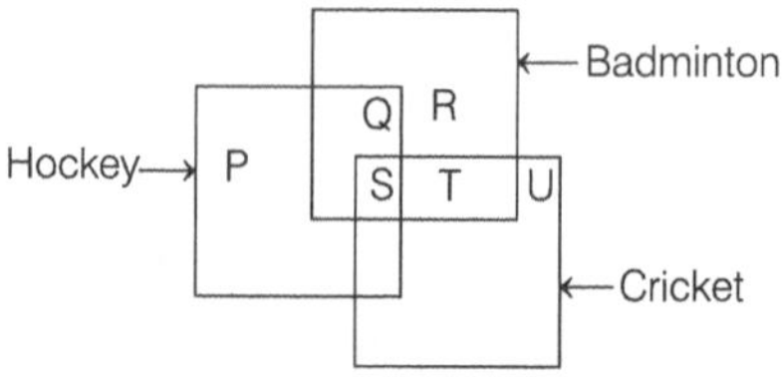


(A) T + U (B) Q + R
(C) P + Q + R (D) S

*Sol. (D)* S is that part which is common to all the three squares. It means that S represents those people who play all the three games.

**4.** Which one of the following diagrams best depicts the relationship among Seconds, Minutes and Hours?

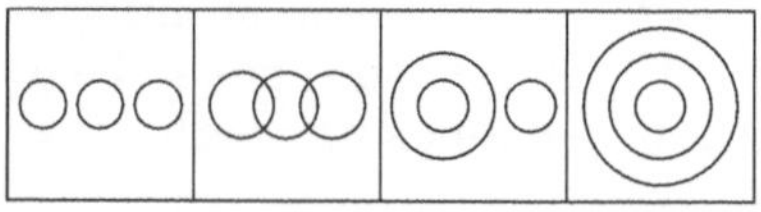

(A) (B) (C) (D)

*Sol. (D)* Seconds are the part of minute and minutes are the part of hour. This relation can be expressed by option (D).

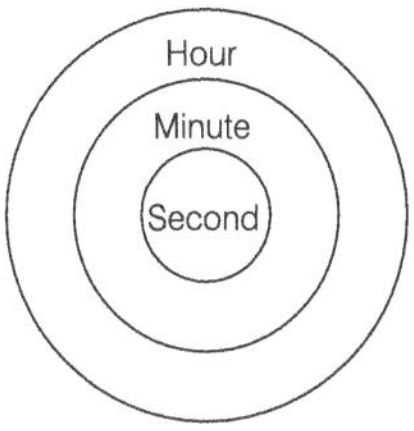


**5.** In the following figure, square represents lawyers, triangle represents cyclists, circle represents men and rectangle represents post-graduates. Which set of letters represents men who are not cyclists?

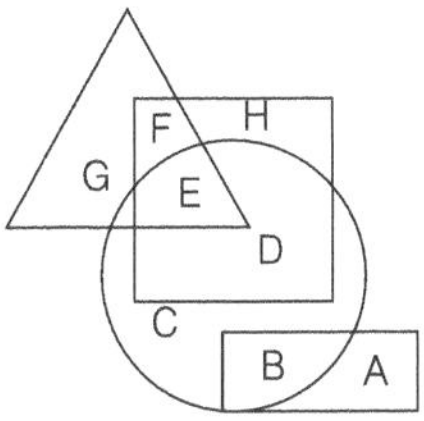


(A) B, C, D (B) E
(C) G, F (D) G, F, H, A

***Sol.*** *(A)* Set of letters B, C and D represent men who are not cyclists.

# SYLLOGISM

Syllogism is a Greek word which means inference or deduction. It is a deductive argument in which conclusion has to be drawn from the given statements. In this type of questions, a set of statements along with two or more conclusions is given. On the basis of these statements, candidates are required to check the correctness of conclusions whether the conclusion follows from the statement or not.

## Proposition

A proposition is a statement giving a relation between two terms. It is also known as premise.

### Classification of Proposition

This classification is based upon the quantity and quality of proposition.

Here, quantity denotes whether the proposition is universal or particular and quality denotes whether the proposition is affirmative or negative. There are four types of proposition which are as follows

| | Proposition | Quantity | Quality |
|---|---|---|---|
| A | All S are P | Universal | Affirmative |
| E | No S is P | Universal | Negative |
| I | Some S are P | Particular | Affirmative |
| O | Some S are not P | Particular | Negative |

### Venn Diagram Representation of Four Propositions

| Types of Propositions | Venn Diagram |
|---|---|
| A : All S are P | Always   |
| E : No S is P | Always   |
| I : Some S are P | Either   Some S are P [P are S ] |
| | or   Some S are P [All S are P] |
| | or   Some S are not P [All P are S] |
| O : Some S are not P | Either   Some S are not P [Some P are not S] |
| | or   Some S are not P [All P are S] |
| | or   Some S are not P [No S is P] |

### Examples

**Directions** (Example Nos. 1-3) *In each of the following questions two statements alongwith a set of conclusions is given. You have to take the statements to be true even if they seem to be at variance from the commonly known facts and decide which of the following conclusions logically follows from the given statements.*

**Give Answer**

(A) If only Conclusion I follows
(B) If only Conclusion II follows
(C) If neither Conclusion I nor II follows
(D) If both Conclusions I and II follow

***1.*** **Statements**

Some cars are scooters.
Some scooters are buses.

**Conclusions**

I. Some cars are buses.
II. No car is bus.

***Sol.*** *(C)* Here, we can draw all possible cases as given below

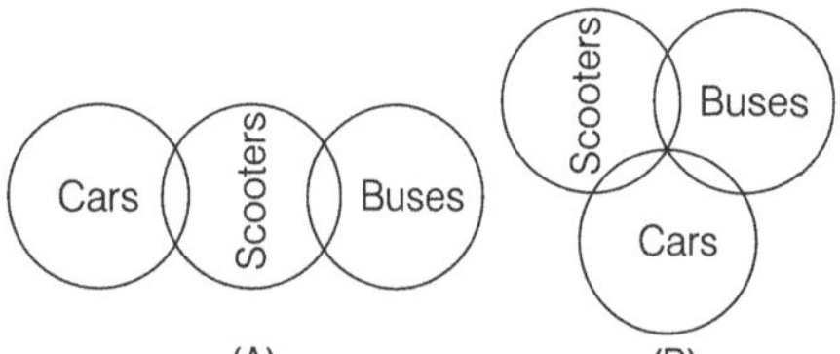


(A) (B)

**Conclusions** I. (✗) II. (✗)

Here, using both diagrammatical representations we can conclude either 'Some cars are buses' or 'No car is bus'. Hence, atleast one of the conclusions must be true.

***2.*** **Statements**

Some stars are planet.
All planets are galaxies.

**Conclusions**

I. Some stars are galaxies.
II. Some galaxies are planet.

***Sol.*** *(D)* According to the question, venn diagram is

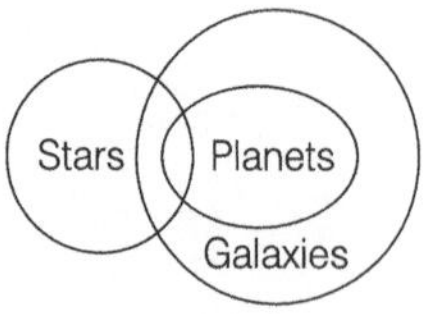


**Conclusions** I. (✓) II. (✓)

Hence, both the conclusions follow.

***3.*** **Statements**

All teachers are students.
No student is girl.

**Conclusions**

I. All girls are students.
II. Some girls are students.

***Sol.*** *(C)* According to the question, venn diagram is as follows

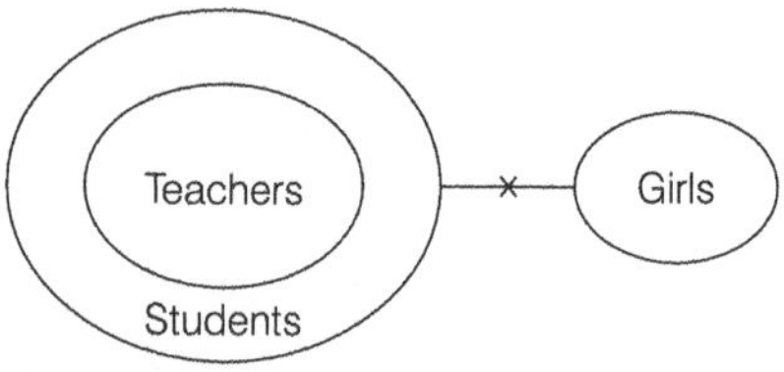


**Conclusions** I. (✗) II. (✗)

Hence, neither Conclusion I nor II follows.

***4.*** In the following question, three statements along with a set of four conclusions are given. Select the correct answer from the options given.

**Statements**

Some newspapers are ACs.
Some ACs are trees.
All books are ACs.

**Conclusions**

I. Some books are newspapers.
II. All books are trees.
III. All trees are books.
IV. No book is newspaper.

(A) Only I follows
(B) I or III follow
(C) Either I or IV follows
(D) II and III follow

***Sol*** *(C)* According to the question, venn diagram is as follows

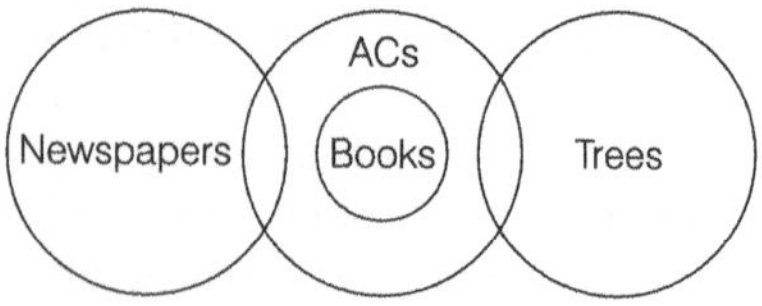


**Conclusions** I. (✗) II. (✗) III. (✗) IV. (✗)

Two Conclusions I and IV form a complementary pair. Therefore, either I or IV follows.

**5** Consider the following statements with reference to the proposition "Some girls are not students." **[UGC NET 2019]**

I. Subject term students is distributed
II. Predicate term girls is undistributed
III. Predicate term students is distributed
IV. Subject term girls is undistributed

Choose the correct option from those given below
(A) I and III are correct
(B) II and III are correct
(C) I and IV are correct
(D) III and IV are correct

***Sol.*** *(D)* "Some girls are not students". Here subject is "girls" and "students" is predicate.

Here predicate term students is distributed but subject term girls is undistributed.

# ASSERTION AND REASON

## Assertion (A)

It is a strong and forceful statement or claim made in regard with a thing, element for its use and effects.

## Reason (R)

It means a fact, event or statement that provides an explanation to the assertion. It is required to analyse whether the reason is an optimum and correct explanation of the assertion.

Sometimes, both assertion and reason are correctly stated facts but the reason does not correctly explain the assertion.

So, different possibilities can exist between these two statements and accordingly the correct answer is marked from the given alternatives.

### *Examples*

**Directions** (Example Nos. 1-3) *Choose the correct alternative from the following options for the Assertion (A) and Reason (R) given below*

**Give Answer**
(A) If both 'A' and 'R' are true and 'R' is the correct explanation of 'A'
(B) If both 'A' and 'R' are true but 'R' is not the correct explanation of 'A'
(C) If 'A' is true but 'R' is false
(D) If 'A' is false but 'R' is true

**1 Assertion** (A) Silver is not used to make wires.
**Reason** (R) Silver is a bad conductor.

***Sol.*** *(C)* Silver is not used to make wires. Hence, Assertion is true but Silver is not a bad conductor, it is a good conductor. Hence, Reason is false.

**2 Assertion** (A) In India, people elect their own representatives.
**Reason** (R) India is a democratic country.

***Sol.*** *(A)* India is a democratic country and people here elect their own representatives. Therefore, both the Assertion and Reason are correct. Since, India is a democratic country.

Hence, people elect their own representatives. Therefore, Reason (R) is the correct explanation of the Assertion.

**3 Assertion** (A) Aurangzeb failed in his deccan policy.
**Reason** (R) He could not follow the policy of appeasement.

***Sol.*** *(A)* 'R' explains 'A' as Aurangzeb failed in his deccan policy mainly due to political and religions intolerance.

**4.** Given below are two statements one is labeled as Assertion (A) and the other is labeled as Reason (R).
**Assertion** (A) Skill development is a key feature in every individual's life.
**Reason** (R) An individual who wants to get employed, needs to possess good education only.
In the context of above two statements, choose the correct option
(A) If Both 'A' and 'R' are true and 'R' is the correct explanation of 'A'
(B) If Both 'A' and 'R' are true but 'R' is not the correct explanation of 'A'
(C) If 'A' is true but 'R' is false
(D) If 'A' is false but 'R' is true

***Sol.*** *(C)* Skill development refers to the identification of skill gaps and developing the existing skills to enable a person to achieve his/her goals. Skills play a very important role in every individuals life whether it is educational, professional or personal.

If a person wants to be successful she/he has to be accomplished in different spheres of life such as educational, personal, skill development techniques and so on.

**5.** Given below are two statements one is labelled as Assertion (A) and the other is labelled as Reason (R)
**Assertion** (A) Classroom communication is pre decided by social and institutional demands.

**Reason** (R) Positive educative actions should guide learners to acquire knowledge of social significance.

In the light of the above two statements, choose the correct option

(A) If both 'A' and 'R' are true and 'R' is the correct explanation of 'A'

(B) If both 'A' and 'R' are true but 'R' is not the correct explanation of 'A'

(C) If 'A' is true but 'R' is false

(D) If 'A' is false but 'R' is true

***Sol.*** *(A)* Classroom communication is a very effective tools which is used during teaching learning process.

Without it no information can be delivered to students by the teacher. It is pre decided by social and institutional demands. Thus, option (A) is correct.

## STATEMENT AND ARGUMENTS

Argument is a fact that is being given by a person to support a statement in its favour or against it. These are of two types

### Strong Argument

It touches the practical and real aspect of the situation as described in the statement.

### Weak Argument

It is called weak, if it is not directly related to the given statement and it does not address all the points put forward in the given statement.

### *Examples*

**Directions** (Example Nos. 1-5) Each question below is followed by two arguments numbered I and II. You have to decide which of the arguments is a strong argument and which is a weak argument.

**Give Answer**

(A) If only Argument I is strong

(B) If only Argument II is strong

(C) If either I or II is strong

(D) If neither I nor II is strong

(E) Both Arguments I and II follow

***1*** **Statement** Should there be only a uniform rate of income tax irrespective of the level of income?

**Arguments**

I. Yes, this will substantially reduce the work of the officials of the income tax department.

II. No, this will reduce government tax collection to a large extent.

***Sol.*** *(B)* Argument I is weak because reduction of work load of IT officials is not too desirable a motive. Argument II is strong as reduced tax collection will have a bad impact on state activities.

***2*** **Statement** Should the sale of all the toys made in China be banned in India?

**Arguments**

I. Yes, these are very cheap and hence, will put the local toy manufacturers out of business.

II. No, Indian toys are of much better quality and their sale will not be affected.

***Sol.*** *(C)* Both are strong but both cannot be true at the same time. The sale will either be affected (as I says) or not be affected (as II says). Hence, either I or II is strong.

***3*** **Statement** Should all the annual examinations upto Std. V be abolished?

**Arguments**

I. Yes, the young students should not be burdened with such examinations which hampers their natural growth.

II. No, the students will not study seriously as they will get automatic promotion of the next class and this will affect them in future.

***Sol.*** *(E)* Clearly, neither the students can be burdened with studies at such a tender age, nor can they be left free to take studies casually, as this shall weaken their basic foundation. So, both the arguments follow.

***4*** **Statement** Should new big industries be started in Mumbai?

**Arguments**

I. Yes, it will create job opportunities.

II. No, it will further add to that pollution of the city.

***Sol.*** *(C)* Opening up of new industries is advantageous in opening more employment avenues and disadvantageous in that it adds to the pollution. So, either of the arguments holds strong.

**5 Statement** Should colleges be given the status of a university in India?

**Arguments**

I. Yes, colleges are in a better position to assess the student's performance and therefore the degrees will be more valid.

II. No, it is Utopian to think that there will not be nepotism and corruption in awarding degrees by colleges.

***Sol.*** *(D)* Clearly, at the college level, all the students are assessed according to their performance in the University Exams and not on the basis of any criteria of a intimate dealing with the students. So, Argument I is vague. Also, at this level the awarding of degrees in impartial and simply based on his performance. So, Argument II also does not hold.

# STATEMENT AND CONCLUSION

## Statement

A statement is a group of words arranged to form a meaningful sentence.

## Conclusion

A conclusion is a judgement or decision reached after consideration about the given statement. It is an opinion or decision that is formed after a period of thought or research on some facts or sentence stated by some one.

If an action is being undertaken and if such an action is always taken with a particular type of motive, then such motive must exist.

The use of word only makes the conclusion weak. Candidates are required to analyse the given statements understand their direct/ indirect implications and then decide which of the given conclusions follows logically.

### *Examples*

**Directions** (Example Nos. 1-3) *Each of these questions has a statement followed by two Conclusions I and II. Consider the statement and the following conclusions. Decide which of the conclusion follows from the statement.*

**Give Answer**

(A) If Conclusion I follows

(B) If Conclusion II follows

(C) If either Conclusion I or II follows

(D) If neither Conclusion I nor II follows

**1 Statement** Vegetable prices are soaring in the market.

**Conclusions**

I. Vegetables are becoming a rare commodity.

II. People cannot eat vegetables.

***Sol.*** *(D)* Both the conclusions are not related to the statement. Hence, neither I nor II follows.

**2 Statement** A friend in need is a friend indeed.

**Conclusions**

I. All are friends in good times.

II. Enemies in bad times are not friends.

***Sol.*** *(D)* A friend who offers help in time of need is a true friend. The use of term 'All' in Conclusion I makes it invalid. Conclusion II does not express the inherent meaning of the statement. Therefore, neither Conclusion I nor II follows.

**3 Statement** Quality has a price tag. India is allocating lots of funds to education.

**Conclusions**

I. Quality of education in India would improve soon.

II. Funding alone can enhance quality of education.

***Sol.*** *(A)* Only Conclusion I follows because funding along with other factors can improve quality of education but funding alone cannot guarantee the enhancement of quality of education.

**4** If the statement 'most of the students are obedient' is taken to be true which one of following pair of statements can be claimed to be true? **[UGC NET December 2012]**

I. All obedient persons are students

II. All students are obedient

III. Some students are obedient

IV. Some students are not disobedient

**Codes**

(A) I and II (B) II and III

(C) III and IV (D) II and IV

***Sol.*** (C) Statement III, 'Some students are obedient' and Statement IV 'some students are not obedient' can be claimed to be true.

**5** If the statement 'Some men are honest' is false, which among the following statements will be true? **[UGC NET June 2013]**

I. All men are honest.

II. No men is honest.
III. Some men are not honest.
IV. All men are dishonest.

**Codes**

(A) I, II and III (B) II, III and IV
(C) I, III and IV (D) II, I and IV

***Sol.*** (*B*) The Statements II, III and IV are the correct statements. Hence, option (B) is right.

# STATEMENT AND ASSUMPTIONS

## Statement

It is an information or a fact related to any general subject.

## Assumption

It is the hidden or unsaid part of the statement which a person assumes before stating some facts or statements. In this type of questions, a statement is followed by two or more assumptions. The candidate is required to assess the given statement and decide which of the given assumptions is implicit in the statement.

### *Examples*

**Directions** (Example Nos. 1-3) In each of the questions below is given a statement followed by assumption numbered I and II. Consider the statement and decide which of the given assumptions is implicit.

**Give Answer**

(A) If only Assumption I is implicit
(B) If only Assumption II is implicit
(C) If both I and II are implicit
(D) If neither I nor II is implicit

**1 Statement** It is faster to travel by air to Delhi from Patna.

**Assumptions**

I. Patna and Delhi are connected by air.
II. There are no other means of transport available to Delhi from Patna.

***Sol.*** (*A*) The given statement advises to travel by air between Delhi and Patna. Hence, no doubts, Assumption I is implicit. Assumption II is the contrary to the given statement. It is faster to travel by air' does not mean that other means of transport, slower than air transport, are available. Therefore, Assumption II is not implicit.

**2 Statement** Most of the classical dance themes are based on stories of Gods and Avatars.

**Assumptions**

I. Classical arts maintain their heritage by sticking to traditions.
II. New themes are not interesting.

***Sol.*** (*A*) Stories of Gods and Avatars carry the reflection of our tradition. Therefore, the statement implies that the classical arts endeavor to maintain their heritage by sticking to traditions.

Hence, Assumption I is clearly implicit. But, it is not given anywhere in the statement that new themes are not interesting. Therefore, Assumption II is not implicit.

**3 Statement** The anti-reservation movement was taken up by all the states.

**Assumptions**

I. If one state starts a movement, it is customary for the other states to follow it.
II. A major portion of the youths and employees all over the country were not in favour of reservation.

***Sol.*** (*B*) The anti-reservation movement could get acceptability by all the states only because major portion of the youths and employees were not in favour of reservation. Our statement is not based on the assumption that it becomes customary for the other states to follow a movement started by one state. Therefore, only Assumption II is implicit.

# STATEMENT AND COURSE OF ACTION

A course of action is a step taken to counter a given situation, problem or circumstance, so that either it may completely solve the problem or it may reduce the complexity of the problem and improve the situation.

A course of action is considered appropriate or acceptable only when it completely or partially solves the problem, otherwise it is not. In this type of questions, a situation is presented and some courses of actions are suggested in the context of that situation which is created by that problem. Course of action should be feasible and should relate with the practical aspect of life.

## Examples

**Directions** (Example Nos. 1-3) *In each of the questions below is given a statement followed by two courses of action numbered* I *and* II. *A course of action is a step or an administrative decision to be taken for improvement. On the basis of the information given in the statement you have to assume everything in the statement to be true and then decide which of the two given courses of action logically follow.*

**Give Answer**

(A) If only I follows
(B) If only II follows
(C) If either I or II follows
(D) If neither I nor II follows
(E) If both I and II follow

**1 Statement** A recent study shows that children below five die in the cities of the developing countries mainly from diarrhoea and parasitic intestinal worms.

**Courses of action**

I. Government of the developing countries should take adequate measures to improve the hygienic conditions in the cities.
II. Children below five years in the cities of the developing countries need to be kept under constant medication.

***Sol.*** (E) If Government concentrates to improve the hygienic condition in the cities, it may definitely reduce the impact of problem and this course of action appears to be feasible also.
Hence, this course of action follows. A constant medication is another practical feasible step, which would help minimise the cases of death due to diarrhoea and intestinal Worms. Therefore, course of action II also follows.

**2 Statement** The officer incharge of a company had a hunch that some money was missing from the safe.

**Courses of action**

I. He should get it recounted with the help of the staff and check it with the balance sheet.
II. He should inform the police.

***Sol.*** *(A)* Here, a hunch about the money being lost does not provide any ground for the incident having actually taken place and hence, action to inform the police will not lessen the problem but is more likely to aggravate the situation. A prudent step is to recount the money and tally with the books of account. Hence, course of action I is appropriate .

**3 Statement** Cell phone users have found that tariff plans are not as attractive as promoted by telecom companies and complained to regulatory authority about the same.

**Courses of action**

I. The regulatory authority should direct telecom companies to be transparent on the tariff structure of all plans.
II. The Government should restrict the number of telecom companies operating in the country.

***Sol.*** *(A)* Being 'not as attractive as promoted' is clear case of hiding things. Hence, transparency is the action to the problem and I follows. II goes against the spirit of free market and is not relevant to the problem either.

**4 Statement** The members belonging to two local clubs occasionally fight with each other on the main road and block traffic movement.

**Courses of Action**

I. The local police station should immediately deploy police personnel round the clock on the main road.
II. Those involved in fighting should be identified and put behind bars.
III. The local administration should disband the management of the two clubs with immediate effect.

(A) Both I and II follow
(B) Both II and III follow
(C) Both I and III follow
(D) All follow

***Sol.*** *(A)* A proper course of action would be serving notices to these clubs to behave themselves. Even police personnel may be deployed but only during the sensitive hours.

**5 Statement** Many students of the local school fell ill for the fourth time in a row in the last six months after consuming food prepared by the school canteen.

**Courses of Action**

I. The school management should immediately terminate the contract of the canteen and ask for compensation.

II. The school management should advise all the students not to eat food articles from the canteen.

III. The owner of the canteen should immediately be arrested for negligence.

(A) None follows
(B) Only II follows
(C) Only III follows
(D) Both I and II follow

*Sol.* (*A*) Courses of action I and III would be too harsh; II is absurd, efforts should be made to supervise the quality of the food prepared by the canteen.

# INDIAN LOGIC

Indian logic for knowledge (cognition) is divided into two parts **Prama** and **Aprama** i.e., true knowledge (or possess the property called Pramaya) and those that are not true (or do not possess the property of Pramanya).

## 1. Prama/Pramana

It means valid knowledge, which implies the manifestation of an object which is presented to us as it is. It has been said that if the knowledge has to pass the validity test, then it must correspond to reality.

### Types of Pramanas

Pramanas are the source of valid knowledge. According to Indian logic, there are six categories of Pramanas

(i) Pratyaksha (Perception)
(ii) Anumana (Inference)
(iii) Upamana (Comparison)
(iv) Shabda (Verbal Testimony)
(v) Arthapatti (Implication)
(vi) Anupalabdhi (Non-Apprehension)

### (i) Pratyaksha (Perception)

Perception is the direct and immediate cognition produced by the interaction between the object and sense-organs.

For perception, four elements are necessary. These are self, mind, sense organs and objects. The self is in contact with the mind (manas), the mind is in contact with the sense organs and lastly, the sense organs are in contact with the objects, as a result, we perceive objects.

There are two types of perceptions : Ordinary perception (laukika) and extraordinary perception (alaukika). Ordinary perception is further divided into two sorts; external (bahya) and internal (manas). External perceptions have five distractions because it is connected with five sense organs–auditory, visual, tactual, gustatory and olfactory.

In case of internal perception, the contacts occur between mind and the object. As a result, knowledge produces. Examples of internal perceptions are feelings, desiring, wishing etc.

Again, perceptions are divided in three sorts. These are indeterminate perception (Nirvikalpa), determinate perception (Sarvikalpa) and recognition (Prativijnana).

(a) **Indeterminate Perception** A perception is considered as indeterminate when we can't determine its features like colour, shape, size etc. which means it can't be explained through our vocabulary. This sort of knowledge arises when self has merely an awareness of the object without having any concrete knowledge of its name, form, qualities etc. It's existence is only proved through inferences, not by perception.

(b) **Determinate Perception** It arises when the knowledge of an object consists of character such as name, colour, shape etc. It gives knowledge of the object, as a result, we cognize 'It is a tree', 'He is a man' etc. In this case, an individual can identify and cognize the object as it is.

(c) **Recognition** The senses contact with the object and recalled that whether the same object had been encountered earlier or not. If it had encountered in the past and positively recapitulating the situation and the features of the object then it would be considered as recognition.

(d) **Extraordinary Perception** This is a perception that provides knowledge even without the senses-object contact. This sort of perception arises whenever the contacts between sense organs and objects occur in an unusual manner.

In this type of perception, an object is not directly presented to the sense organs, but it is retrieved in memory through the past cognition of it and is perceived through representation.

Suppose that a person has in the past experienced a piece of ice, its colour and its coldness. Owing to such invariable association of touch and colour, the person presents in his visual perceptions of ice and its coldness, this results him say, ice looks cold.

The following chart represents distinctions on perceptions

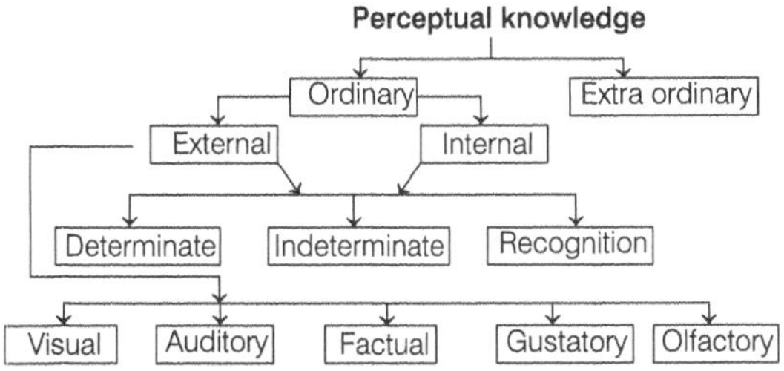


## (ii) Anumana (Inference)

Anumana (Inference) is such knowledge which follows from other knowledge. The word 'anu' stands for 'after' and 'mana' means 'cognition'. So, 'Anumana' means 'after cognition'.

**Constituents of Anumana (Inference)** An inference is constituted with atleast three statements or sentences and these three sentences are again constituted of three different terms.

These three sentences are named as 'major premise', 'minor premise' and conclusion respectively.

The major term is found in major premise. Similarly the minor term is found in minor premise and the term which is found in both major and minor premise is called a middle term. In the conclusion only major term and minor term is present. The middle term makes a link between minor term and major term. Major, minor and middle terms are used inter changeably as 'sadhya', 'paksa' and 'hetic'.

**For Example,**

- Major Premise : All things which have smoke have fire.
- Minor Premise : This hill has smoke.
- Conclusion : Therefore, this hill has fire.
  Major Term – Fire; Minor Term – Hill and Middle Term – Smoke

To explain the above example, it is stated that an individual saw the smoke on a hill from a distant place. By seeing the smoke he/she relates his/her previous knowledge that whenever there is a smoke there is fire.

Here, an inference, knowledge of an object is derived due to previous knowledge of some sign, mark or experience.

The previous knowledge is due to the universal relation between the major term and the middle term is being present in the minor term.

### Kinds of Anumana (Inference) Anumana

It is basically classified into following three kinds.

(a) **Purvavat** In Purvavat Anumana, we infer the unperceived effect from a perceived causes.

*e.g.* When from the presence of dark heavy clouds in the sky, we infer that there will be rainfall.

(b) **Sesavat** Here, we infer the unperceived cause from a perceived effect.

*e.g.* When we see a flood in a river, we infer that there was a heavy rain. This is called Sesavat inference.

(c) **Samanyatodrsta** This inference is based on certain observed points of general similarity.

*e.g.* When we see a animal with horns and infer that it has cloven hoofs, we have this kind of inference. There is a uniformity of co-existence between horns and cloven hoofs, though they are not casually related.

## (iii) **Upamana** (Comparison)

Upamana as a source of knowledge is derived from similarity between two things/objects. The word 'upamana' is derived from two words, 'upa' and 'mana'. The word 'upa' means similarity and 'mana' means 'cognition'.

*e.g.* If a person does not know that a 'squirrel' is ?, He is told that it is a small animal like rat, but it has a long fury tail and strips on its body. After some period of time, when he sees such an animal in the forest, he knows that it is a squirrel.

There are four steps involved in acquiring knowledge of an object in comparison (upamana).

(a) Having an authoritative statement that a word denotes objects of a certain description.
(b) One observes any such objects he has the knowledge of that it answers to the given description.
(c) There is a recollection of the descriptive statement received from the authority.
(d) There is a resulting knowledge that, this kind of objects are denoted by the word is same.

## (iv) **Shabda** (Verbal Testimony)

'Shabda' literally means verbal knowledge. It is the knowledge of objects derived from words or sentences. But all the verbal knowledge is not valid. Shabda is the instructive assertion of a reliable person, who is expert in certain matter and is willing to communicate his/her experience of it.

**For Example** If a lady ask a fisherman, who is fishing there that if she can cross the river. Since the fisherman is a local person over there and has no enmity with her replied that you can cross the river easily. Here, the word of the fisherman is to be accepted as a means of right knowledge called verbal testimony. There are two different kinds of Shabda Laukika and Shabda Alaukika.

## (v) **Arthapatti** (Implication)

Arthapatti refers to the way in which knowledge is derived from the set of circumstances.

It generally requires an observation of fact (s) and postulation based on such fact(s) we arrive at the information. It supposes a fact in order to support a well established fact.

*e.g.* Rahul, who is alive, but is not in his house, the vary knowledge of his being out of his house is based on perception. We ourselves look for him in the house, but we do not see him, so we conclude that since he is alive and is not inside the house, he must be somewhere outside his house.

## (vi) **Anupalabdhi** (Non-Apprehension)

Anupalabdhi recognises that things exist either in a positive or a negative relation to the observer and their surroundings. Positive relation means that they are perceived by the senses.

However in negative relation, or non-existence they cannot be perceived by the senses. So an alternative "mode of movement" is needed. The "mode of movement" of the mind is called Anupalabdhi.

Within the concept of Anupalabdhi there are four kinds of perceptions

(i) **Karana** Which is non-perception of casual condition.
(ii) **Vyapaka** Which is non-perception of pervader.
(iii) **Svabhava** Which is non-perception of the presence of itself.
(iv) **Viruddha** Which is non-perception of the opposed.

**Anumana** (Inference) In Indian logic, 'Anumana' means Inference. It is a knowledge that arises from other knowledge. In every anumana there are three terms

1. Major Term (Sadhya)
2. Minor Term (Paksa)
3. Middle Term (Hetu)

## 2. Aprama

It means invalid knowledge. It includes memory, doubt, error and hypothetical reasoning. Doubt is regarded as uncertainty in cognition. Hypothetical reasoning is regarded as no real knowledge.

So, Prama is always real whereas aprama gives us unreal knowledge. Prama is arrived by use of our reasoning, whereas Aprama is arrived by doubtful and defective knowledge and reasoning.

## Vyapti (Invariable Relation)

Vyapti refers to the state of pervasion. It is considered as the logical ground of inference which is one of the means of knowledge. No conclusion can be inferred without the knowledge of Vyapti. It guarantees the truth of conclusion.

**For Example**

If we observe smoke on the hill, we immediately perceive that there must be fire. But this inference is only made, if we already know that there is a relation between fire and smoke. This relation is called Vyapti.

So, here we infer the presence of fire on that hill on the basis of our past experience of that invariable association between smoke and fire.

This invariable association between smoke and the fire is called Vyapti.

### Basic Terms of Vyapti

In the example of smoke and fire, there is an unfailing relationship between them which is called Vyapti.

1. **Vyapya (Pervaded)** The consequence of the argument is called Vyapya, as in the above example 'smoke' is Vyapya as it is the consequence of fire.
2. **Vyapaka (Pervade)** The object of the action or consequence is called Vyapaka, as in the above example 'fire' is Vyapaka, as it causes smoke.

## Hetvabhasas (Fallacies of Inferences)

A fallacy in Inference is called Hetvabhasas. It means that a Hetic or a reason appears to be real or appropriate but in fact it is not.

Suppose there are two sentence below

(a) This is a horse, because it has horns.

(b) This is a bull, because it has horns.

This is an example of inconclusive reason and this fallacy in Indian logic is called Hetvabhasa. It means that the middle term appears to be a reason but is not a valid reason.

There are five kinds of Hetvabhasas

1. **Asiddha** It is referred to as a fallacy of the unproved middle. It has been said that when the middle term is not present in the minor term.
2. **Savyabhicara** It is regarded as the fallacy of the irregular middle.
3. **Satpratipaka** The middle term is contradicted by an other middle term in this fallacy.

   Here, the counter balanced reason by another reason is required.
4. **Badhita** It is regarded as the non-inferentially contradicted middle. The middle term is contradicted by some other pramana in this fallacy.
5. **Viruddha** It is referred as the contradictory middle. Here, the middle term is pervaded by the absence of major term.

# Chapter Practice

## Argument

1 'All S is P' is a form of which proposition?
(A) Universal Affirmative
(B) Universal Negative
(C) Particular Affirmative
(D) Particular Negative

2 'Every woman is white' and 'not every woman is white' comes under the domain of which square of opposition
(A) contradictory (B) contrary
(C) sub-contrary (D) sub-alternation

3 Match the following.

| List I | List II |
|---|---|
| I. A | 1. Universal Affirmative |
| II. E | 2. Universal Negative |
| III. I | 3. Particular Affirmative |
| IV. O | 4. Particular Negative |

**Codes**

| | I | II | III | IV | | I | II | III | IV |
|---|---|---|---|---|---|---|---|---|---|
| (A) | 1 | 2 | 3 | 4 | (B) | 4 | 3 | 2 | 1 |
| (C) | 1 | 4 | 3 | 2 | (D) | 2 | 4 | 3 | 1 |

4 Match the following.

| List I | List II |
|---|---|
| I. A proposition | 1. All non-P are non-S |
| II. E proposition | 2. No non-P are non-S |
| III. I proposition | 3. Some non-P are non-S |
| IV. O proposition | 4. Some non-P are not non-S |

**Codes**

| | I | II | III | IV | | I | II | III | IV |
|---|---|---|---|---|---|---|---|---|---|
| (A) | 1 | 2 | 3 | 4 | (B) | 4 | 3 | 2 | 1 |
| (C) | 1 | 4 | 3 | 2 | (D) | 4 | 2 | 3 | 1 |

5 Match the following.

| List I | List II |
|---|---|
| I. Subject term is distributed | 1. A proposition |
| II. Neither subject nor predicate is distributed | 2. O proposition |
| III. Subject and predicate is distributed | 3. E proposition |
| IV. Predicate term is distributed | 4. I proposition |

**Codes**

| | I | II | III | IV | | I | II | III | IV |
|---|---|---|---|---|---|---|---|---|---|
| (A) | 1 | 2 | 3 | 4 | (B) | 4 | 3 | 2 | 1 |
| (C) | 1 | 4 | 3 | 2 | (D) | 2 | 4 | 3 | 1 |

6 Match the following.

| List I | List II |
|---|---|
| I. Contrary | 1. Two statements cannot true at the same time |
| II. Contradictory | 2. A pair of affirmative and negative |
| III. Sub-contrary | 3. Opposite of contrary |
| IV. Sub-alternation | 4. The particular is the sub alternation of the universal |

**Codes**

| | I | II | III | IV | | I | II | III | IV |
|---|---|---|---|---|---|---|---|---|---|
| (A) | 1 | 2 | 3 | 4 | (B) | 4 | 3 | 2 | 1 |
| (C) | 4 | 2 | 3 | 1 | (D) | 1 | 4 | 3 | 2 |

7 Validity and Invalidity deals with
1. Arguments
2. Deductive arguments
3. Inductive arguments
4. Statements

(A) 1 and 3 (B) 2 and 3
(C) 1 and 2 (D) 1 and 4

8 Indicate which of the following pairs refer to E and O propositions?
(A) No men are good; some men are not good.
(B) All men are good, some men are good.
(C) All men are good, No men are good.
(D) Some men are good, some men are not good

9 Select the pair of contrary propositions
(A) I, O (B) A, E
(C) A, O (D) E, I

## Indian Logic

10 Match the following

| List-I | List-II |
|---|---|
| A. Perception | 1. Ordinary |
| B. Inference | 2. Vyapti |
| C. Comparison | 3. Analogy |
| D. Verbal Testimony | 4. Shabda |

**Codes**

| | A | B | C | D | | A | B | C | D |
|---|---|---|---|---|---|---|---|---|---|
| (A) | 1 | 2 | 3 | 4 | (B) | 4 | 3 | 2 | 1 |
| (C) | 1 | 4 | 3 | 2 | (D) | 3 | 4 | 2 | 1 |

**11** Vyapti means
1. Inference
2. Invariable concomittance
3. Existential fallacy
4. Referent fallacy

(A) 1 and 2 (B) 2 and 3
(C) 3 and 4 (D) 2 and 4

**12** Consider the following Inferences.
1. Tom is a rational animal.
2. All men are rational animals.
3. Tom is such a man.
4. Because Tom is a man.
5. Therefore, Tom is a rational animal.

The correct sequence of statements are
(A) 1 4 2 3 5 (B) 4 1 2 5 3
(C) 2 4 3 5 1 (D) 1 3 4 5 2

**13** Match the following.

| List I | List II |
|---|---|
| A. Major Term | 1. Hetu |
| B. Minor Term | 2. Sadhya |
| C. Middle Term | 3. Paksha |

**Codes**
(A) 2 3 1 (B) 1 2 3
(C) 3 2 1 (D) None of these

## Analogy

**14** 'Skirmish' is related to 'War' in the same way as 'Disease' is related to
(A) Infection (B) Epidemic
(C) Patient (D) Medicine

**15** 'Tree' is related to 'Root' in the same way as 'Smoke' is related to
(A) Cigarette (B) Fire
(C) Heat (D) Chimney

**16** Good : Bad : : Virtue : ?
(A) Blame (B) Sin (C) Despair (D) Vice

**17** Choose the proper alternative given in the codes to replace the question mark.
Bee-Honey, Cow-Milk, Teacher-?
(A) Intelligence (B) Marks
(C) Lessons (D) Wisdom

**18** Bird : Fly : : Snake : ?
(A) Timid (B) Clatter (C) Crawl (D) Hole

**19** Incandescent : Glowing
(A) Indefatigable : Untiring
(B) Boon : Oafish
(C) Tedious : Bore
(D) Flash : Flame

**20** Elevated : Exalted
(A) Promoted : Excellence
(B) Raise : Commensurate
(C) Disorderly : Unfaithful
(D) Dirty : Filthy

**21** GREAT : 25 : : NUMBER : ?
(A) 36 (B) 38
(C) 27 (D) 24

**22** 25 : 625 : : 35 : ?
(A) 1575 (B) 1205
(C) 875 (D) 635

**23** PST : 01 : : NPR : ?
(A) 3 (B) 4
(C) 1 (D) 7

**24** Dearth : Scarcity : : Substitute : ?
(A) Rumor (B) Assume
(C) Replace (D) Destroy

**Directions** (Q. Nos. 25-27) In the following questions, choose the missing word in place of sign (?) on the basis of the relationship between the words given on the left/right hand side of the signs.

**25** Water : Ocean : : Sand : ?
(A) Engine (B) River
(C) Desert (D) Waves

**26** Food : Stomach : : Fuel : ?
(A) Engine
(B) Automobile
(C) Rail
(D) Aeroplane

**27** STBP : 1920216 : : MNGO : ?
(A) 1314715 (B) 1413715
(C) 5173141 (D) 3114715

**Direction** (Q. No. 28) The numbers given in the bracket has same relations among them. Select the option in which the numbers have the same relationship as in the numbers given in the question.

**28** (81, 77, 69)
(A) (64, 61, 53) (B) (56, 52, 44)
(C) (92, 88, 79) (D) (75, 71, 60)

## Venn diagram

**29** Which diagram correctly represents the relationship between Politicians, Poets and Women?

(A) (B) (C) (D)

**30** Which of the following diagrams best represents the relationship among Uttar Pradesh, Kanpur, Jaipur?

(A) (B) (C) (D)

**31** Which one of the following diagrams represents the correct relationship among Teachers, Educated, Employed?

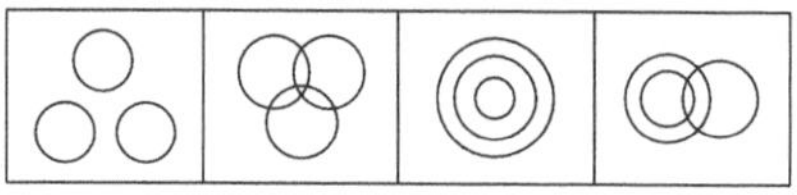

(A) (B) (C) (D)

**32** Which of the following diagrams represents the correct relationship between Herbivorous, Tigers and Animals?

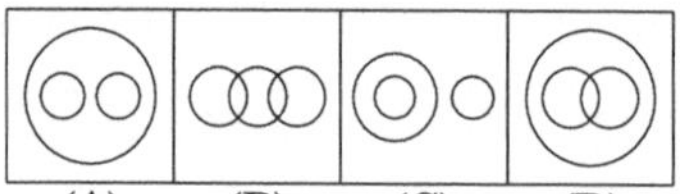

(A) (B) (C) (D)

**33** Which one of the following diagrams best represents the relationship between Snake, Lizard and Reptiles?

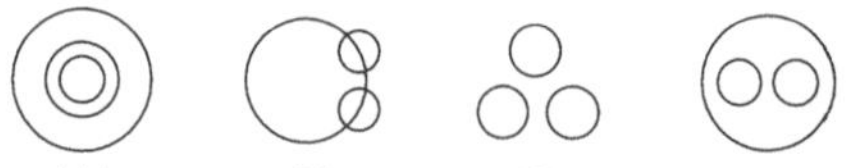

(A) (B) (C) (D)

**34** A result of survey of 1000 persons with respect to their knowledge of Hindi (H), English (E) and Sanskrit (S) is given below

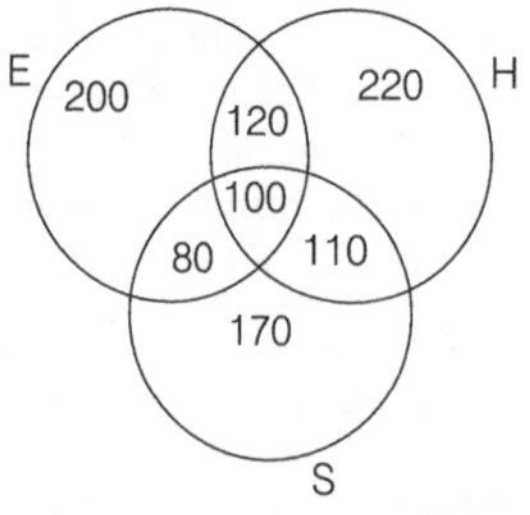


What is the ratio of those who know all the three languages to those who do not know Sanskrit?

(A) $\frac{5}{27}$ (B) $\frac{10}{17}$

(C) $\frac{1}{10}$ (D) $\frac{1}{9}$

**Directions** (Q. Nos. 35-39) Each of the following questions is based on the diagram given below. Study the diagram carefully and answer the questions.

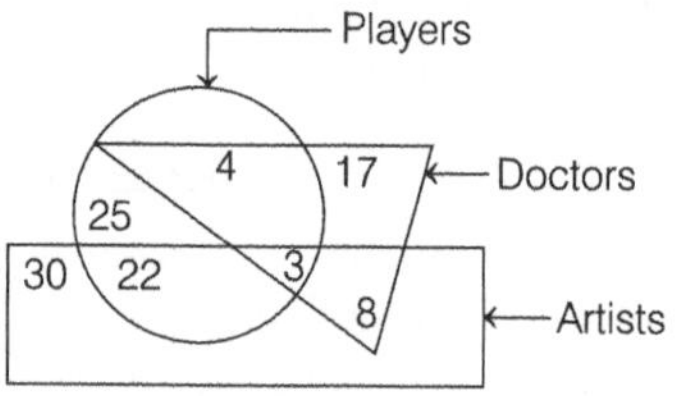


In the above diagram, rectangle represents 'artists', circle represents 'players' and triangle represents 'doctors'.

**35** How many players are neither artists nor doctors?

(A) 25 (B) 22

(C) 4 (D) 29

**36** How many artists are players?

(A) 22 (B) 3

(C) 25 (D) 8

**37** How many Artists are neither doctors nor players?

(A) 22 (B) 8

(C) 25 (D) 30

**38** How many doctors are neither players nor artists?

(A) 4 (B) 25

(C) 8 (D) 17

**39** How many doctors are players and artists both?

(A) 4 (B) 7

(C) 3 (D) None of these

## Syllogism

**Directions** (Q. Nos. 40 and 41) Two statements are given in each of the following questions, followed by two conclusions numbered I and II. You have to take the given two statements to be true even, if they seem to be at variance from commonly known facts. Read the conclusions and then decide which of the given conclusions logically follows from the two disregarding known facts.

**Give Answer**

(A) If only Conclusion I follows

(B) If only Conclusion II follows

(C) If neither I nor II follows

(D) If both Conclusions I and II follow

**40 Statements**

Some schools are laboratories.
All laboratories are theatres.

**Conclusions**

I. Some theatres are schools.
II. No school is a theatre.

**41 Statements**

Some birds are clouds.
Horse is a bird.

**Conclusions**

I. Some clouds are birds.
II. Horse is not a cloud.

**Directions** (Q. Nos. 42-46) Two/three/four statements are given in each of the following questions, followed by three/four conclusions numbered I, II, III and IV. You have to take the given statements to be true even, if they seem to be at variance from commonly known facts. Read all the conclusions and then decide which of the given conclusions logically follows from the given statements disregarding commonly known facts.

**42 Statements**

Some years are decades.
All centuries are decades.

**Conclusions**

I. Some centuries are years.
II. Some decades are years.
III. No century is a year.

(A) Conclusions I and II follow
(B) Conclusions I and III follow
(C) Either I or III and II follow
(D) Conclusion II follows

**43 Statements**

All clerks are superintendents.
All superintendents are managers.
All managers are supervisors.

**Conclusions**

I. All supervisors are clerks.
II. Some clerks are supervisors.
III. Some managers are clerks.
IV. All superintendents are clerks.

**44** Some statements are given followed by some conclusions. You have to consider the statements to be true even, if they seem to be at variance from commonly known facts. You have to decide which of the given conclusions, if any, follow from the given statements.

**Statements**

1. Some doctors are lawyers.
2. All teachers are lawyers.
3. Some engineers are lawyers.
4. All engineers are businessmen.

**Conclusions**

I. Some teachers are doctors.
II. Some businessmen are lawyers.
III. Some businessmen are teachers.
IV. Some lawyers are teachers.

(A) None follows
(B) Only I follows
(C) Only III follows
(D) II and IV follow

**45 Statements**

Some fans are coolers.
Some coolers are machines.
Some machines are computers.
All computers are televisions.

**Conclusions**

I. Some televisions are machines
II. Some machines are fans.
III. No machine is a fan.

(A) None follows
(B) Only I follows
(C) Only either II or III follows
(D) Only I and either II or III follow

**46 Statements**

All keys are staplers.
All staplers are blades.
Some blades are erasers.
Some erasers are sharpeners.

**Conclusions**

I. Some sharpeners are keys.
II. All keys are blades.
III. Some erasers are keys.

(A) I and II follow (B) Only I follows
(C) Only II follows (D) All follow

**Directions** (Q. Nos. 47-49) In these questions, four statements are given followed by four conclusions. One of which definitely does not logically follow (or is not a possibility of occurrence) from the given statements. That conclusions is your answer.

**47 Statements**

No toy is a doll.
All guns are toys.
All houses are dolls.
All dolls are baskets.

**Conclusions**

(A) All baskets are toys
(B) No gun is a house
(C) All guns being baskets is a possibility
(D) All houses are baskets

**48 Statement**

All references are mails.
All mentions are references.
All comments are mentions.
No mail is a declaration.

**Conclusions**

(A) No reference is a declaration
(B) All comments are mails
(C) No mention is a declaration
(D) All declaration being comments is a possibility

**49** Given below are two statements and four conclusions drawn from those statements. Select the code that expresses conclusion drawn validly from the statements (separately or jointly).

**Statements**

1. All dogs are mammals.
2. No cats are dogs.

**Conclusions**

I. No cats are mammals.
II. Some cats are mammals.
III. No dogs are cats.
IV. No dogs are non mammals.

(A) Only I
(B) I and II
(C) III and IV
(D) II and III

## Assertion and Reason

**50 Assertion** (A) There are more laws on the books today than ever before and more crimes being committed than ever before.

**Reason** (R) Because to reduce crime we must eliminate the laws.

Choose the correct answer from below

(A) 'A' is true, 'R' is doubtful and 'R' is not the correct explanation of 'A'
(B) 'A' is false, 'R' is true and 'R' is the correct explanation of 'A'
(C) 'A' is doubtful, R is doubtful and 'R' is not the correct explanation of 'A'
(D) 'A' is doubtful, R is true and R is not the correct explanation of 'A'

**Directions** (Q. Nos. 51-59) Each of these questions has an Assertion (A) and a Reason (R).

**Give answer**

(A) If both 'A' and 'R' are true and 'R' is the correct explanation of 'A'
(B) If both 'A' and 'R' are true but 'R' is not the correct explanation of 'A'
(C) If 'A' is true but 'R' is false
(D) If 'A' is false but 'R' is true

**51 Assertion** (A) A body weights less when immersed in water.

**Reason** (R) Newton's law explains the above phenomenon.

**52 Assertion** (A) The steam engine was invented by James Watt.

**Reason** (R) There was a problem of taking out water from flooded mines.

**53 Assertion** (A) We feel colder on mountains than on plains.

**Reason** (R) Temperature decreases with altitude.

**54 Assertion** (A) The colour of light with the shortest wavelength is violet.

**Reason** (R) One can notice this colour of light on one end of the rainbow which has seven colours of different wavelengths.

**55 Assertion** (A) Clothes are not washed properly in hard water.

**Reason** (R) Hard water contains many minerals

**56 Assertion** (A) Himalayas once laid under the sea.

**Reason** (R) Fossils of marine creatures are traced on the Himalayas.

**57 Assertion** (A) India is a secular country.

**Reason** (R) Indian people can practice any faith they like.

**58 Assertion** (A) Tamil Nadu gets most of the rainfall in winter.

**Reason** (R) Tamil Nadu gets rainfall from retreating monsoons.

**59 Assertion** (A) Eskimos reside in igloos.

**Reason** (R) No other material except snow is available.

## Statement and Arguments

**Directions** (Q. Nos. 60 and 61) Each question below is followed by two arguments numbered I and II. You have to decide which of the arguments is a strong argument and which is weak argument.

**Give answer**

(A) If only Argument I is strong
(B) If only Argument II is strong
(C) If either I or II is strong
(D) If neither I nor II is strong
(E) If both Arguments I and II are strong

**60 Statement** Should the organisations like the UNO be abolished?

**Arguments**

I. Yes, the cold war is going to an end, so there is no role of such organisations.
II. No, in the absence of these organisations, there will be a World War.

**61 Statement** Should small states be formed out of bigger states in India?

**Arguments**

I. Yes, there will be greater administrative convenience.
II. No, it will Jeopardise the national integration.

**Directions** (Q. Nos. 62-66) Each of these questions has a statement followed by three arguments I, II and III. Consider the statement and the arguments and decide which of the argument is strong and choose the correct option.

**62 Statement** Should there be a complete ban on setting up thermal power plants in India?

**Arguments**

I. Yes, this is the only way to control further addition to environmental pollution.
II. No, there is a huge shortage of electricity in most parts of the country and hence, generation of electricity needs to be augmented.
III. No, many developed countries continue to set up thermal power plants in their countries.

(A) None is strong
(B) Only I is strong
(C) Only II is strong
(D) Only III is strong

**63 Statement** Should the salary and perquisites of public sector undertaking employees be made equivalent to those in the private sector?

**Arguments**

I. Yes, this will help the public sector undertaking to attract and retain competent workforce.
II. No, public sector undertakings cannot afford to pay salaries to the level of private sector.
III. Yes, otherwise the public sector undertakings will not be able to compete with the private sector organisations.

(A) None is strong
(B) Only III is strong
(C) Only I is strong
(D) I and III are strong

**64 Statement** Should the Government ban export of all types of foodgrains for the next one year to tide over the unpredicted drought situation in the country?

**Arguments**

I. Yes, there is no other way to provide food to its citizens during the year.
II. No, the Government does not have its jurisdiction over private exporters for banning export.
III. Yes, the Government should not allow the exporters to export foodgrains and procure all the foodgrains held by such exporters and make it available for home consumption.

(A) I and II are strong
(B) II and III are strong
(C) I and III are strong
(D) None of the above

**65 Statement** Should smoking cigarettes and drinking alcohol by the actors be completely banned in the movies in India?

**Arguments**

I. Yes, this will significantly reduce the trend of smoking cigarettes and drinking alcohol among the youth in India.
II. No, there should be no such ban on the creative pursuits of the filmmaker.
III. No, the films portray the society and hence such scenes should be an integral part of the movie, if the storyline demands so.

(A) None is strong
(B) I and II are strong
(C) II and III are strong
(D) I and III are strong

**66 Statement** Should sale of vital human organs be made legal in India

**Arguments**

I. No, it goes against our culture.

II. No, this will lead to unhealthy practices.

III. Yes, this will bring an end to the illegal trading of human organs.

(A) None is strong
(B) I and II are strong
(C) Only III is strong
(D) II and III are strong

**67** If the statement 'most of the students are obedient' is taken to be true which one of the following pair of statements can be claimed to be true?

1. All obedient persons are students
2. All students are obedient
3. Some students are obedient
4. Some students are not disobedient

**Codes**

(A) 1 and 2 (B) 2 and 3
(C) 3 and 4 (D) 2 and 4

**68** If the statement 'Some men are honest' is false, which among the following statements will be true?

1. All men are honest.
2. No men are honest.
3. Some men are not honest.
4. All men are dishonest.

**Codes**

(A) 1, 2 and 3 (B) 2, 3 and 4
(C) 1, 3 and 4 (D) 2, 1 and 4

## Statement and Conclusions

**Directions** (Q. No. 69-73) Each of these questions (has/have statement/statements) followed by two or more Conclusions. Consider the statement/statements and the following conclusions. Decide which of the conclusion follows from the statement and choose the correct option.

**69 Statement** India's economy is depending mainly on forests.

**Conclusions**

I. Trees should be preserved to improve Indian economy.

II. India wants only maintenance of forests to improve economic conditions

(A) Only Conclusion I follows
(B) Only Conclusion II follows
(C) Both Conclusions I and II follow
(D) Neither Conclusion I nor II follows

**70 Statements**

1. Science has brought the gadgets of happiness, prosperity and wealth.
2. Science has not solved the problems of overpopulation.

**Conclusions**

I. Overpopulation is due to unscientific thinking.

II. Science has not helped world peace.

(A) Only Conclusion I follows
(B) Only Conclusion II follows
(C) Both Conclusion I and II follow
(D) Neither Conclusion I nor II follows

**71 Statement** This book can help because all good books help.

**Conclusions**

(A) This is not a good book
(B) This is a good book
(C) No good book help
(D) Some good books help

**72 Statements**

1. Best performance in Olympics fetches a gold medal.
2. Player 'X' got gold medal but later was found to be using a prohibited drug.

**Conclusions**

I. 'X' should be allowed to keep the gold medal.

II. Gold medal should be withdrawn and given to the next person.

(A) Only Conclusion II follows
(B) Neither Conclusion I nor II follows
(C) Both Conclusion I and II follow
(D) Only Conclusion I follows

**73 Statements**

1. There are monks among those who are felicitated for remarkable social service.
2. Jitananda and Vidyananda are among those felicitated.

**Conclusions**

I. Jitananda and Vidyananda did remarkable social service

II. All monks do social service

III. Jitananda and Vidyananda are not monks

IV. All monks are felicitated

(A) Only Conclusion I follows
(B) Only Conclusion II follows
(C) Both Conclusions I and II follow
(D) Neither Conclusion I nor III follows

## Statement and Assumptions

**Directions** (Q. Nos. 74-79) A statement is given in each of the following questions, followed by two assumptions numbered I and II. An assumption is something supposed or taken for granted. You have to consider the statement and the following assumptions and decide which of the assumptions is implicit in the statement.

**Given answer**

(A) If only I is implicit
(B) If only II is implicit
(C) If either I or II is implicit
(D) If neithe I nor II is implicit
(E) If both I and II is implicit

74 **Statement** The Government is making efforts to boost tourism in Jammu and Kashmir.

**Assumptions**

I. Tourism in Jammu and Kashmir dropped during last couple of years.
II. Special discount in the railway fare has been announced.

75 **Statement** "If you want to give any advertisement, give it in newspaper "X" - A tells B.

**Assumptions**

I. B wants to publicise his products.
II. Newspaper 'X' has a wide circulation.

76 **Statement** Buy pure milk of company 'X' an advertisement in a newspaper.

**Assumptions**

I. No other company supplies pure milk.
II. People read advertisements.

77 **Statement** It is dangerous to lean out of a moving train.

**Assumptions**

I. All those who lean out of a train take the risk of being hurt.
II. Generally, people do not like to get hurt.

78 **Statement** The driver of the huge truck pulled the emergency brakes to avoid hitting the auto rickshaw which suddenly came in front of the truck.

**Assumptions**

I. The auto rickshaw driver may be able to steer his vehicle away from the oncoming truck.
II. The truck driver may be able to stop the truck before it hits the auto rickshaw.

79 **Statement** The chairman of the company urged all the employees to refrain from making long personal calls during working hours in order to boost productivity.

**Assumptions**

I. Majority of the employees may respond positively to the chairman's appeal.
II. Most of the employees may continue to make long personal calls during working hours.

**Directions** (Q. Nos. 80-84) A statement is given in each of the following questions, followed by two assumptions numbered I and II. An assumption is something supposed or taken for granted. You have to consider the statement and the following assumptions and decide which of the assumptions is implicit in the statement.

**Give answer**

(A) If only I is implicit
(B) If only II is implicit
(C) If both I and II are Implicit
(D) If neither I nor II is implicit

80 **Statement** Double your money in five months. An advertisement.

**Assumptions**

I. The assurance is not genuine.
II. People want their money to grow.

81 **Statement** The medical department has asked people to use only boiled water in an attempt to prevent the spread of cholera in a town.

**Assumptions**

I. There is a doubt about the quality of water being supplied in the town.
II. There is some report of cholera in town.

82 **Statement** Food shortage is going to be a serious issue because of production shortage due to climate change and population increase all over the world.

**Assumptions**

I. Food prices are likely to increase.
II. Climate change is a serious issue.

83 **Statement** The local cultural club decided to organise a musical event to raise money for the construction of the club building.

**Assumptions**

I. The local residents may not allow the club to organise to musical event in the locality.

II. The money allocated by organising the musical event may be substantial enough for the club to start construction.

**84 Statement** The traffic police department has put up huge notice boards at all major junctions of the city warning drivers to refrain from using cell phones while driving or else their licences will be impounded.

**Assumptions**

I. The drivers of the vehicles may ignore the warning and continue using cell phones while driving.

II. The traffic police department may be able to nab most of the offenders and impound their licences.

## Statement and Courses of Action

**Directions** (Q. Nos. 85-87) In each of the questions below is given a statement followed by two courses of action. On the basis of the information given in the statement, you have to decide which of the given suggested courses of actions logically followed.

**Give answer**

(A) If only I follows
(B) If only II follows
(C) If either I or II follows
(D) If neither I nor II follows
(E) If both I and II follow

**85 Statement** Two local passenger trains collided while running in opposite directions on the same track as the signalling system failed for a short period.

**Courses of action**

I. The services of the motormen of the trains should immediately be terminated.

II. The Government should immediately constitute a task force to review the functioning of the signalling system.

**86 Statement** A major part of the local market in the city was gutted due to a short circuit causing extensive damage to goods and property.

**Courses of action**

I. The Government should issue strict guidelines for all establishments regarding installation and maintenance of electrical fittings.

II. The Government should relocate all the markets to the outskirts of the city

**87 Statement** Reports of steep and continued decline in the inflows into the Gobindsagar reservoir of the Bhakra Dam, coupled with a depleted stock of steam coal with the thermal power plants in the North, may lead to a serious power crisis in the region.

**Courses of action**

I. The supply of steam coal to the thermal power plants needs to be immediately stepped up by the Government.

II. The Government should set up hydraulic power plants on other rivers in the region.

**Directions** (Q. Nos. 88 and 89) In each question, a statement followed by three courses of action numbered I, II and III. Assume everything in the statement to be true. Decide which of the three given suggested courses of action logically follow for pursuing.

**88 Statement** Over 27000 bonded labourers identified and freed are still awaiting rehabilitation.

**Courses of action**

I. More cases of bonded labourers should be identified.

II. Till the proper rehabilitation facilities are available, the bonded labourers should not be freed.

III. The impediments in the way of speedy and proper rehabilitation of bonded labourers should be removed.

(A) None follows
(B) Only I follows
(C) Only II follows
(D) Only III follows

**89 Statement** In one of the accidents on a railway level crossing, fifty people died when a bus carrying them collided with a running train.

**Courses of action**

I. The train driver should immediately be suspended.

II. The driver of the bus should be tried in court for negligence on his part.

III. The railways authorities should be asked to man all its level crossings.

(A) None follows
(B) Only III follows
(C) Both I and II follow
(D) All follow

**Directions** (Q. Nos. 90 and 91) A statement is given followed by three courses of action. A course of action is taken improvement, follow-up etc. Read the statement carefully and pick the correct answer choice.

**90 Statement** The police has failed to protect the elderly citizens of the society. Only last week three old persons were killed at three different places.

**Courses of action**

I. The police should be asked to take special care of women and children.
II. The Government should bring a legislation against the killing of elderly people.
III. Criminals who are accused of killing elderly people should be prosecuted by the state.

(A) Only I follows (B) Only II follows
(C) Only III follows (D) None follows

**91 Statement** Many political activists have decided to stage demonstrations and block traffic movement in the city during peak hours to protest against the steep rise in prices of essential commodities.

**Courses of action**

I. The Government should immediately ban all forms of agitations in the country.
II. The police authority of the city should deploy additional forces all over the city to help traffic movement in the city.
III. The state administration should carry out preventive arrests of the known criminals staying in the city.

(A) Only I (B) Only II
(C) Only II (D) Both I and II

**Directions** (Q. Nos. 92-95) In each of the following questions a statement is given followed by two or three course of actions. You have to find out which courses of action follows and choose the correct option.

**92 Statement** India has been continuously experiencing military threats from its neighbouring countries.

**Courses of action**

I. India should engage into an all out war to stop the nagging threats.
II. India should get the neighbours into a serious dialogue to reduce the tension at its borders.

(A) Only I follows
(B) Only II follows
(C) Either I or II follows
(D) Neither I nor II follows

**93 Statement** Besides looks and appearances, it is also important to develop oneself from within.

**Courses of action**

I. One should not pay attention to fashion.
II. One should pay attention to fashion.
III. Books on self-development should be encouraged.

(A) Only I follows
(B) Only II follows
(C) Only III follows
(D) Neither I nor II follows

**94 Statement** The air and rail services have been severely disrupted due to thick fog in the northern part of the country.

**Courses of action**

I. The rail and air service should be temporarily suspended in the region.
II. People should be advised to make their travel plan keeping in mind the probable disruption resulting in delay or concellation of services.
III. The government should immediately install modern machines which will enable it to guide the rail and air services even if the thick fog develops.

(A) Only II follows
(B) Only III follows
(C) II and III follows
(D All follows

**95 Statement** Many complaints have been registered lately by commuters regarding unavailability of railway tickets during the peak travelling season.

**Courses of action**

I. The commuters should be advised to defer their travel plans till the peak season gets over.
II. Railways should try to accommodate as many commuters as possible by adding extra coaches to the trains.

(A) If only I follows
(B) If only II follows
(C) If either I or II follows
(D) If neither I nor II follows

# *Previous Years' Questions*

## UGC NET-December 2019

1 No Musicisans are Japanese
All Barbers are Musicians
No Barbers are Japanese
*Identify the Middle term in the above syllogism*
(A) Subject in the first premise and predicate in the second premise.
(B) Predicate in the first premise and subject in the second premise.
(C) Predicate in the both premises
(D) Subject in both the premises

2 Inductive argument proceeds from
(A) Universal to Particular
(B) Particular to Universal
(B) Universal to Universal
(C) Particular to Particular

3 **Assertion** (A) Communication presupposes a shared, symbolic environment, a social relationship even among non participants.
**Reason** (R) It leads to social interaction, which in combination with other factors contributes to a sense of community.
*Choose the correct option given below.*
(A) Both (A) and (R) are true and (R) is the correct explanation of (A)
(B) Both (A) and (R) are true but (R) is not the correct explanation of (A)
(C) (A) is true but (R) is false
(D) (A) is false but (R) is true

4 Consider the example given below.
Devadatta is growing fat.
He does not eat food during the day.
Therefore, he must be eating food during the night, other things being equal.
*Identify the logic involved in the example provided above by choosing the correct answer from options given below.*
(A) Arthapatti (B) Anupalabdi
(C) Anumana (D) Sabda

5 Consider the argument provided below.
"Sound is permanent because it is a product like the Jar".
*Identify the fallacy involved in the above argument on the basis of Indian logic from the options given below.*
(A) Fallacy of contradicatory reason
(B) Fallacy of wrong assertion
(C) Fallacy of irrelevant reason
(D) Fallacy of trival reason

6 The converse of 'All cats are mammals' is
(A) Some mammals are not cats
(B) No mammals are cats
(C) Some mammals are cats
(D) All mammals are cats

7 Mr X lives in a slum and is unemployed. Therefore, Mr X deserves to be minister.
Which kind of fallacy is committed in the argument?
(A) Fallacy of composition
(B) Ad misericordium
(C) Fallacy of Division
(D) Fallacy of Accident

8 In the statement "No dogs are reptiles", which terms are distributed?
(A) Only subject term
(B) Only predicate term
(C) Both subject and predicate terms
(D) Neither subject not predicate term

9 Which of the following is not a necessary step when you present an argument based on inference before the others according to the classical Indian school or Logic?
(A) Nigamana (B) Upamana
(C) Upanaya (D) Udaharana

10 Given below are two statements, one is labelled as Assertion (A) and the other is labelled as Reason (R)
**Assertion** (A) The spoken and written words are two media of many available for communication in the classroom.
**Reason** (R) Communication through any medium does not happen through attitudes of members.
In the light of the above two statements, choose the correct option from the option given below.
(A) Both (A) and (R) are true and (R) is the correct explanation of (A)
(B) Both (A) and (R) are true but (R) is not the correct explanation of (A)
(C) (A) is true, but (R) is false
(D) (A) is false, but (R) is true

11 'Some students are sincere' is an example of which preposition
(A) Universal Affirmative
(B) Universal Negation
(C) Particular Affirmative
(D) Particular Negation

12 Given below are two statements, one is laballed Assertion (A) and the other is lebelled as Reason (R)

**Assertion** (A) The clock speed of CPUs has not increased significantly in recent years

**Reason** (R) Software now being used is faster and therefore processors do not have to be faster.

In the light of the above two statements, choose the correct option from those given below.
(A) Both (A) and (R) are true and (R) is the correct explanation of (A)
(B) Both (A) and (R) are true but (R) is not the correct explanation of (A)
(C) (A) is true, but (R) is false
(D) (A) is false, but (R) is true

13 Given below are two stateemnts, one is labelled Assertion (A) and the other is labelled as Reason (R)

**Assertion** (A) pedagogy and social interaction are two major result-oriented activities of a teacher

**Reason** (R) Communication has a limited role in both these activities

In the light of the above two statements, choose the correct option from those given below.
(A) Both (A) and (R) are true and (R) is the correct explanation of (A)
(B) Both (A) and (R) are true but (R) is not the correct explanation of (A)
(C) (A) is true but (R) is false
(D) (A) is false but (R) is true

14 Given below are two statements: One is labelled as Assertion (A) and other is labelled as Reason (R)

**Assertion** (A) The internet is a collectio of interconnected computer networks, linked by transmission medium such as copper wires, fibreoptic cables, wireless connection etc.

**Reason** (R) World wide web is a collection of interconnected elements.

In the light of the above two statements, choose the correct answer.
(A) Both (A) and (R) are true and (R) is the correct explanation of (A)
(B) Both (A) and (R) are true but (R) is not the correct explanation of (A)
(C) (A) is true but (R) is false
(D) (A) is false but (R) is true

## UGC NET-June 2019

15 Identify the reasoning in the following argument:

'Writing on paper is similar to writing on the board'.
(A) Deductive (B) Hypothetical
(C) Analogical (D) Inductive

16 When subject and preducate of both the premises is same but they differ only in quantity, it is known as
(A) Subaltern (B) Contraries
(C) Subcontraries (D) Contradictories

17 All judges are fair minded is an example of ......... proposition.
(A) Universal affirmative
(B) Universal negative
(C) Particular affirmative
(D) Particular negative

18 "All tigers are animals" This is an example of which type of proposition?
(A) Particular Negative
(B) Particular Affirmative
(C) Universal Negative
(D) Universal Affirmative

19 Which of the following is converses of some S is P?
(A) Some S is not P (B) Some P is not S
(C) Some P is S (D) No P is S

20 Identify the minor term in the following syllogism: Some books are not edifying

All books are interesting

Therefore, some interesting things are not edifying.
(A) Subject of conclusion and predicate of second premise
(B) Predicate of the concliusion and predicate of the first premise
(C) Subject of the both premises
(D) Predicate of the both premises

**21** If proposition 'All republics are grateful' is taken to be true then which of the following propositions can be false?

(i) Republics are not grateful
(ii) some republics are not grateful
(iii) No republics are grateful
(iv) Some republics are grateful

Select the correct answer from the options given below:

(A) (i) only (B) (ii) only
(C) (i), (ii) and (iii) (D) (ii) and (iii)

**22** Given below are two premises with four conclusion drawn from them. Which of the following is valid conclusion drawn from the premises?

**Premises**

(i) All diaries are copies
(ii) No copy is book

**Conclusions**

(a) Some diaries are books
(b) Some books are copies
(c) No book is copy
(d) No diary is book

Choose the correct options

(A) (a) and (b) (B) (c) and (d)
(C) (b) and (c) (D) (a) and (d)

**23** According to traditional square of opposition if two proposition are so related that they cannot both be false, although they may both be true is called.

(A) Sub altern (B) sub contraries
(C) contradictory (D) Contrary

**24** Consider the following argument

**Statements** Some chairs are curtains
All curtains are bedsheets.

**Conclusion** Some charis are bedsheets.

What is the mood of the above proposition.

(A) IAI (B) IAA
(C) IIA (D) AII

**25** "All students cleared their examination" and "few students did not clear their examination". This is an instance of

(A) contradictories (B) Superaltern
(C) Subaltern (D) Contraries

**26** No farmer is teacher.
All professionals are farmers.
No professional is teacher.

Identify the middle term in the above syllogism

(A) Subject in the first premise and predicate in the second premise
(B) Predicate in the first premise and subject in the second premise
(C) Preedicate in both premises
(D) Subject in the both the premise

**27** The reasoning which would be helpful in finding new knowledge of facts about the world is

(A) Speculative (B) Inductive
(C) Deductive (D) Analogical

**28** Given below are two premises with four conclusions drawn from them. Which of the following conclusions could be validly drawn from the premises?

**Premises**

(i) All fans are tubes
(ii) Bulbs are not tubes

**Conclusions**

(A) Fans are not bulbs (B) All tubes are fans
(C) Fans are bulbs (D) No tubes is bulb

**29** Consider the example given below:

Devadatta is growing fat.

He does not eat food during the day.

Therefore, he must be eating food during the night other things being equal.

Identify the logic involved in the example provide above the choosing the correct answer from the options given below.

(A) Arthapatti (B) Anupalabdi
(C) Anumana (D) Sabda

**30** The proposition 'No Red is black' is equivalent to which of the following propositions?

(i) No black is red
(ii) All red are black
(iii) Some red are not black
(iv) Red is not black

Select the correct answer from the options given below

(A) (i), (ii), and (iv) (B) (iii) only
(C) (i) and (iv) (D) (iv) only

**31** Consider the argument provided below:

"Sound is impermanent because it is invisible"

Identify the fallacy involved in the above argument on the basis of Indian logic.

(A) Fallacy of irrelevant reason
(B) Fallacy of wrong assertion
(C) Fallacy of trivial reason
(D) Fallacy of contradictory reason

**32** Consider the argument provided below:

"Sound is permanent because it is a product like the jar"

Identify the fallacy involved in the above argument on the basis of Indian logic from the options given below:

(A) Fallacy of contradictory reason
(B) Fallacy of wrong assertion
(C) Fallacy of irrelevant reason
(D) Fallacy of trivial reason

**33** Identify the reasoning in the following argument:

Pre active stage of classroom teaching is important just as pre-learning preparation stage of communication

(A) Hypothetical (B) Deductive
(C) Inductive (D) Analogical

**34** Consider the example provide below:

"This gavaya is like my cow"

This is an example of which means of knowledge (Prammana):

(A) Comparison (B) Implication
(C) Perception (D) Inference

**35** When the subject and predicate of both the premises are the same but they differ in quality only, it is known as

(A) Contradictories (B) Contraries
(C) Subaltern (D) Super Altern

**36** If the proposition 'all pens are not pencils' is taken to be true then which of the following propositions can be false?

(A) All pens are pencils
(B) Some pencils are pens
(C) No pen is pencil
(D) Some pens are pencils

**37** Inference (anumana) in Indian logic is rooted in

(A) Variable relation between minor term and major term
(B) Invariable relation between middle term and minor term
(C) Variable concomitance between middle term and major term
(D) Invariable concomitance between middle term and meta term

**38** The proposition 'all leaves are green' is equivalent to which of the following propositions?

(1) No leaves are green
(2) No leaves are non green
(3) No leaves are in other colour than green
(4) No green is leaf

Select the correct answer from the options given below:

(A) 2, 3 and 4 (B) 1 and 2
(C) 2 only (D) 2 and 3

**39** In which of the following arguments 'the relation that exist between premises and conclusion is that of logical necessity'?

(A) Inductive (B) Deductive
(C) Demonstrative (D) Analogical

**40** Given below are two premises with four conclusions drawn from them. Which of the following conclusions could be validly drawn from the premises?

**Premises**

(a) Some bags are tables
(b) All bags are chairs

**Conclusions**

(i) Some tables are chairs
(ii) No chair is table
(iii) Some chairs are bags
(iv) Some bags are not tables

Select the correct answer from the options given below:

(A) i and iii (B) ii, iii, and iv
(C) i and iv (D) ii only

**41** Given below are two statements, one is labeled as Assertion (A) and the other is labeled as Reason (R)

**Assertion** (A) Through on line teaching a large number of students can be taught by very competent faculty.

**Reason** (R) Online teaching helps students in developing critical thinking more than the off line teaching can do

In the light of the above two statements choose the correct option

(A) Both (A) and (R) are true and (R) is the correct explanation of (A)
(B) Both (A) and (R) are true but (R) is not the correct explanation of (A)
(C) (A) is true but (R) is false
(D) (A) is false but (R) is true

**42** Given below are two statements - one is labeled as Assertion (A) and the other is labeled as Reason (R)

**Assertion** (A) Government of India established higher education statutory bodies to ensure quality of education.

**Reason** (R) There are some educational institutions in India which do not provide quality education.

In the context of above two statements, choose the correct

(A) Both (A) and (R) are true and (R) is the correct explanation of (A)
(B) Both (A) and (R) are true, but (R) is not the correct explanation of (A)
(C) (A) is true but (R) is false
(D) (A) is false but (R) is true

**43** Consider the following statements with reference to categorical proposition

(a) "Some birds are mammals" is a particular affirmative proposition and it distributes subject term alone.
(b) "Some birds are mammals" is a particular affirmative proposition and it distributes predicate terms alone.
(c) "Some birds are mammals" is a particular affirmative proposition and it distributes both subject and predicate terms
(d) "Some birds are mammals" is a particular affirmative proposition and it distributes neither subject term nor predicate terms.

Choose the correct option from below

(A) Only a and d are correct
(B) Only c and d are correct
(C) Only b is correct
(D) Only d is correct

**44** Which one of the following is not a part of immediate deductive inference

(A) Conversion (B) Obversion
(C) Syllogism (D) Contra position

**45** Given below are two statements one is labelled as Assertion (A) and the other is labelled as Reason (R)

**Assertion** (A) The governor has the power to ask for any information from the Chief Minister regarding the administration of the state.

**Reason** (R) The governor is the real Head of the state Administration

In the context of the above two statements choose the correct options

(A) Both (A) and (R) are true and (R) is the correct explanation of (A)
(B) Both (A) and (R) are true but (R) is not the correct explanation of (A)
(C) (A) is true but (R) is false
(D) (A) is false but (R) is true

**46** Given below are two statements, one is labelled as Assertion (A) and the other is labelled as Reason (R)

**Assertion** (A) Defining the objectives of the logic of discussion is not necessarily the first step in classroom communication.

**Reason** (R) Clear definition of objectives make students understand the topic well.

In the light of the above two statements, choose the correct option from the choice given below.

(A) Both (A) and (R) are true and (R) is the correct explanation of (A)
(B) Both (A) and (R) are true but (R) is not the correct explanation of (A)
(C) (A) is true, but (R) is false
(D) (A) is false, but (R) is true

**47** Given below are two statement, one is labelled as Assertion (A) and other as Reason (R)

**Assertion** (A) Sniffing may be used to steal data or information over a network.

**Reason** (R) Sniffing is or process of monitoring and capturing all data packets passing through given network.

In the light of the above stated two statement, choose the correct option from the choices given below.

(A) Both (A) and (R) are true and (R) is the correct explanation of (A)
(B) Both (A) and (R) are true but (R) is not the correct explanation of (A)
(C) (A) is true, but (R) is false
(D) (A) is false, but (R) is true

**48** Given below are two statements, One labelled as Assertion (A) and the other is labelled as Reason (R)

**Assertion** (A) The impact of natural disasters does not depend on socio economic factors.

**Reason** (R) Natural disasters do not discrimination between people of a society and other communities.

In the light of the above statements, choose the correct answer.

(A) Both (A) and (R) are true and (R) is the correct explanation of (A)
(B) Both (A) and (R) are true but (R) is not the correct explanation of (A)
(C) (A) is true but (R) is false
(D) (A) is false but (R) is true

**49** **Assertion** (A) The correlation function of mass media is vital for any society.

**Reason** (R) The interpretation aspects that include advertising and public relations shape and influence public opinion.

Choose the correct answer from the codes given below

(A) Both (A) and (R) are true and (R) is the correct explanation of (A)
(B) Both (A) and (R) are true but (R) is not the correct explanation of (A)
(C) (A) is true but (R) is false
(D) (A) is false but (R) is true

**50** Which one of the following propositions is a contrary to All poets are dreamers?

(A) some poets are dreamers
(B) Some poets are not dreamers
(C) No poets are dreamers
(D) No dreamers are poets

**51** Which one of the following is signified by Udaharana of Anumana (Inference) in India Logic?

(A) Statement of reason
(B) proposition to be proved
(C) conclusion proved
(D) Universal propositional along with an instance

**52** Given below are two statements - one is labeled as Assertion (A) and the other is labeled as Reason (R).

**Assertion** (A) A blog is a form of social media

**Reason** (R) A blog allows anyone to communicate to a public audience.

In the light of the above two statements, choose the correct option.

(A) Both (A) and (R) are true and (R) is the correct explanation of (A)
(B) Both (A) and (R) are true but (R) is not the correct explanation of (A)
(C) (A) is true but (R) is false
(D) (A) is false but (R) is true

## UGC NET-December 2018

**53** Which one among the following is a presupposition in inductive reasoning?

(A) Harmony in nature
(B) Uniformity of nature
(C) law of identity
(D) Unchangeability in nature

**54** Which one of the following statements is not correct in the context of Venn diagram method?

(A) It requires two overlapping circles for the two premises of a standard form categorical syllogism.
(B) It can be used to represent classes as well as propositions
(C) It is a method of testing the validity of arguments.
(D) It represents both the premises of a syllogism in one diagram.

**55** Superiority of intellect depends upon its power of concentration one theme in the same way as a concave mirror collects all the rays that strike upon it into one point.

What type of reasoning is entailed in the above statement?

(A) Analogical (B) Deductive
(C) Mathematical (D) Psychological

**56** Given below are two premises with four conclusions drawn them (taken singly or together) which conclusions are validly drawn? Select the correct answer from the code given below.

**Premises**

I. All politicians are honest person.
II. All honest persons are fair.

**Conclusions**

1. Some honest persons are politicians.
2. No honest person is politician.
3. Some fair persons are politicians.
4. All fair persons are politicians

(A) 2 and 4 (B) 1 and 3
(C) 1, 2 and 4 (D) 2 and 3

**57** **Assertion** (A) The initial messages to students in the classroom by a teacher need not be critical to establish interactions later.

**Reason** (R) More control over the communication process means more control over what the students are learning.

**Codes**
(A) A is true, but R is false.
(B) A is false, but R is true.
(C) Both A and R are true and R is the correct explanation of A.
(D) Both A and R are true, but R is not the correct explanation of A.

**58** **Assertion** (A) Classroom communication is a transactional process.

**Reason** (R) A teacher does not operate under the assumption that students' responses are purposive.

Select the correct codes for your answer.
(A) A is true, but R is false.
(B) A is false, but R is true.
(C) Both A and R are true and R is the correct explanation of A.
(D) Both A and R are true, but R is not the correct explanation of A.

**59** **Assertion** (A) To communicate well in the classroom is a natural ability.

**Reason** (R) Effective teaching in the classroom demands knowledge of the communication process.

Select the correct codes for your answer.
(A) A is true, but R is false.
(B) A is false, but R is true.
(C) Both A and R are true and R is the correct explanation of A.
(D) Both A and R are true, but R is not the correct explanation of A.

**60** **Assertion** (A) Indoor air pollution is a serious health hazard.

**Reason** (R) The dispersal of air pollutants is rather limited in indoor environment.

Choose the correct answer from the codes given below.
(A) A is true and R is false.
(B) Both A and R are false.
(C) Both A and R are true and R is the correct explanation of A.
(D) Both A and R are true, but R is not the correct explanation of A.

## UGC NET-July 2018

**61** Given below is a statement followed by three assumptions made from it. Which assumptions are implicit in the context of the given statement ?

Select the correct answer from the code given below.

**Statement** 'Smoking is injurious to health'–A warning printed on the cigarette packets.

**Assumptions**
1. People read printed matter on a cigarette packet.
2. People make careful note of a warning.
3. Non-smoking primates health.

(A) 2 and 3 (B) Only 1
(C) Only 2 (D) 1 and 2

**62** Given below are two premises (A and B). Four conclusions are drawn from them. Select the code that states validly drawn conclusion(s) (taking the premises individually or jointly).

**Premises**
a. Most of the dancers are physically fit.
b. Most of the singers are dancers.

**Conclusions**
1. Most of the singers are physically fit.
2. Most of the dancers are singers.
3. Most of the physically fit persons are dancers.
4. Most of the physically fit persons are singers.

**Codes**
(A) 3 and 4 (B) 4 and 1
(C) 1 and 2 (D) 2 and 3

**63** If the proposition 'domestic animals are hardly ferocious' is taken to be false, which of the following proposition/propositions can be claimed to be certainly true? Select the correct code.

**Propositions**
1. All domestic animals are ferocious.
2. Most of the domestic animals are ferocious.
3. No domestic animal is ferocious.
4. Some domestic animals are non-ferocious.

**Codes**
(A) 3 and 4 (B) Only 2
(C) Both 1 and 2 (D) Only 1

**64** **Assertion** (A) All teaching should aim at ensuring/learning.

**Reason** (R) All learning results from teaching.

Choose the correct answer from the following

**Codes**

(A) 'A' is true, but 'R' is false

(B) 'A' is false, but 'R' is true

(C) Both 'A' and 'R' are true and 'R' is the correct explanation of 'A'

(D) Both A and R are true, but R is not the correct explanation of 'A'

## UGC NET-November 2017

**65** Given below are two premises (1 and 2). From those two premises four conclusions (I), (II), (III) and (IV) are drawn. Select the code that states the conclusion/ conclusions drawn validly (taking the premises singularly or jointly)

**Premises**

1. All bats are mammals.
2. No birds are bats.

**Conclusions**

I. No birds are mammals.
II. Some birds are not mammals.
III. No bats are birds.
IV. All mammals are bats.

(A) I and II only (B) III Only

(C) III and IV only (D) I only

**66** Given below are four statements. Among them two are related in such a way that they can both be true but they cannot both be false. Select the code that indicates those two statements:

**Statements**

1. Honest people never suffer.
2. Almost all honest people do suffer.
3. Honest people hardly suffer.
4. Each and every honest person suffers.

**Codes**

(A) 1 and 3 (B) 1 and 4

(C) 2 and 3 (D) 1 and 2

**67** **Assertion** (A) In urban areas, smog episodes occur frequently in winters.

**Reason** (R) In winters, a lot of biomass is burnt by people for heating purposes or to keep themselves warm.

Choose the correct answer from the codes given below.

(A) Both 'A' and 'R' are true but 'R' is not the correct explanation of 'A'

(B) 'A' is true, but 'R' is false

(C) Both 'A' and 'R' is false.

(D) Both 'A' and 'R' are true and 'R' is the correct explanation of 'A'

**68** **Assertion** (A) All teaching implies learning

**Reason** (R) Learning to be useful must be derived from teaching.

Choose the correct answer from the following.

(A) Both 'A' and 'R' are true but 'R' is not the correct explanation of 'A'

(B) 'A' is true, but 'R' is false

(C) 'A' is false, but 'R' is true

(D) Both 'A' and 'R' are true and 'R' is the correct explanation of 'A'

## UGC NET-January 2017

**69** If the statement None but the brave wins the race is false, which of the following statements can be claimed to be true?

(A) Al brave persons win the race

(B) Some persons who win the race are not brave

(C) Some persons who win the race are brave

(D) No person who wins the race is brave

**70** Among the following propositions two are related in such a way that they cannot both be true but can both be false. Select the code that those two propositions.

**Statements**

1. Every student is attentive
2. Some students are attentive
3. Students are never attentive.
4. Some students are not attentive.

**Codes**

(A) 1 and 2 (B) 1 and 3

(C) 2 and 3 (D) 3 and 4

**71** **Assertion** (A) Sustainable development is critical to well being of human society.

**Reason** (R) Environmentally sound policies do not harm the environment or deplete the natural resources.

Choose the correct code

(A) Both (A) and (R) are correct and (R) is the correct explanation of (A)

(B) Both (A) and (R) are correct but (R) is not the correct explanation of (A)

(C) (A) is true and (R) is false

(D) (A) is false and (R) is true

## UGC NET-June 2016

**72** If the proposition 'All men are mortal' is false which of the following propositions can be claimed certainly to be true

**Proposition**

(A) Some men are mortal
(B) Some men are not mortal
(C) No man is mortal
(D) No mortal person is man

**73** If the proposition 'All farmers are poor' is false, then which of the following propositions can be claimed certainly to be true?

**Propositions**

(A) Some farmers are poor
(B) Some farmers are not poor
(C) No farmer is poor
(D) No poor person is a farmer

**74** Consider the following statement and select the correct code stating the nature of the argument involved in it.

To assume that the earth is the only populated world in the infinite space is as absurd as to assert that in an entire field of millet only one grain will grow.

(A) Astronomical (B) Anthropological
(C) Deductive (D) Analogical

**75** Given below are two premises and four conclusions are drawn from them (taking singly or together).

Select the code that states the conclusions validly drawn.

**Premises**

(I) All religious persons are emotional.
(II) Ram is a religious person.

**Conclusions**

(A) Ram is emotional
(B) All emotional people are religious
(C) Ram is not a non religious person
(D) Some religious people are not emotional

**Codes**

(A) (A), (B), (C) and (D) (B) (A) only
(C) (A) and (C) only (D) (B) and (C) only

**76** Among the following propositions two are related in such a way that one is the denial of the other.

Which are those propositions? Select the correct code.

**Propositions**

(A) All women are equal to men
(B) Some women are equal to men
(C) Some women are not equal to men
(D) No women are equal to men.

**Codes**

(A) (A) and (B) (B) (A) and (D)
(C) (C) and (D) (D) (A) and (C)

**77** Select the option which is not correct about Venn diagram.

(A) Venn diagram represents propositions as well as classes.
(B) It can provide clear method of notation
(C) It can be either valid or invalid
(D) It can provide the direct method of testing the validity.

**78** Select the code which is not correct in the context of deductive argument with two premises.

(A) An argument with one true premise, one false premise and a false conclusion may be valid.
(B) An argument with two true premises and a false conclusion may be valid.
(C) An argument with one true premise, one false premise and a true conclusion may be valid.
(D) An argument with two false premises and a false conclusion may be valid.

**79** **Assertion** (A) Conserving our soil resources is critical to human survival.

**Reason** (R) Soil is home to many microorganisms and it contains minerals.

Choose the correct code from the following options.

(A) Both (A) and (R) are true and (R) is the correct explanation of (A)
(B) Both (A) and (R) are true but (R) is not the correct explanation of (A)
(C) (A) is true but (R) is false
(D) (A) is false but (R) is true

**80** **Assertion** (A) The purpose of higher education is to promote critical and creative thinking abilities among students.

**Reason** (R) These abilities ensure job placements

Choose the correct answer from the following code.

(A) Both (A) and (R) are true and (R) is the correct explanation of (A)
(B) Both (A) and (R) are true but (R) is not the correct explanation of (A)
(C) (A) is true but (R) is false
(D) (A) is false but (R) is true

## UGC NET-December 2015

**81** Among the following following statements two are contradictory to each other. Select the correct code that represents them.

**Statements**

1. All poets are philosophers.
2. Some poets are philosophers
3. Some poets are not philosophers
4. No philosopher is a poet

**Codes**

(A) 1 and 2
(B) 1 and 4
(C) 1 and 3
(D) 2 and 3

## UGC NET-June 2015

**82** Consider the statement which is followed by two Arguments I and II

**Statement** India should have a very strong and powerful Lokpal.

**Arguments**

I. Yes, it will go a long in eliminating corruption in bureaucracy.

II. No, it will discourage honest officers from Making quick decisions.

**Codes**

(A) Only Argument I is strong
(B) Only Argument II is strong
(C) Both the arguments are strong
(D) Neither of the arguments is strong

**83** Consider the following Assertion (A) and Reason (R) and select the correct code given below

**Assertion** (A) No man is perfect.

**Reason** (R) Some men are not perfect.

**Codes**

(A) A is false but R is true
(B) Both A and R are true, but R does not provide sufficient reason for A
(C) Both A and R are true and R provides sufficient reason for A
(D) A is true but R is false

**84** **Assertion** (A) Formal communication tends to be fast and flexible.

**Reason** (R) Formal communication is a systematic and orderly flow of information.

**Codes**

(A) A is false but R is true
(B) Both A and R are true, but R does not provide sufficient reason for A
(C) Both A and R are true and R provides sufficient reason for A
(D) A is true but R is false

# ANSWERS

## Chapter Practice

| | | | | | | | | | |
|---|---|---|---|---|---|---|---|---|---|
| 1 (A) | 2 (A) | 3 (A) | 4 (A) | 5 (C) | 6 (A) | 7 (C) | 8 (A) | 9 (B) | 10 (A) |
| 11 (C) | 12 (D) | 13 (A) | 14 (B) | 15 (B) | 16 (B) | 17 (C) | 18 (C) | 19 (A) | 20 (D) |
| 21 (A) | 22 (D) | 23 (A) | 24 (C) | 25 (C) | 26 (A) | 27 (A) | 28 (B) | 29 (D) | 30 (A) |
| 31 (A) | 32 (C) | 33 (D) | 34 (D) | 35 (C) | 36 (A) | 37 (A) | 38 (C) | 39 (C) | 40 (D) |
| 41 (B) | 42 (C) | 43 (A) | 44 (D) | 45 (C) | 46 (A) | 47 (A) | 48 (A) | 49 (A) | 50 (A) |
| 51 (C) | 52 (A) | 53 (A) | 54 (B) | 55 (B) | 56 (A) | 57 (A) | 58 (A) | 59 (C) | 60 (E) |
| 61 (E) | 62 (C) | 63 (C) | 64 (D) | 65 (D) | 66 (A) | 67 (C) | 68 (B) | 69 (A) | 70 (D) |
| 71 (B) | 72 (A) | 73 (A) | 74 (A) | 75 (B) | 76 (B) | 77 (A) | 78 (B) | 79 (A) | 80 (B) |
| 81 (B) | 82 (A) | 83 (B) | 84 (D) | 85 (B) | 86 (A) | 87 (A) | 88 (D) | 89 (B) | 90 (A) |
| 91 (B) | 92 (B) | 93 (C) | 94 (D) | 95 (B) | | | | | |

## Previous Years' Questions

| | | | | | | | | | |
|---|---|---|---|---|---|---|---|---|---|
| 1 (A) | 2 (B) | 3 (D) | 4 (A) | 5 (A) | 6 (C) | 7 (A) | 8 (A) | 9 (D) | 10 (C) |
| 11 (A) | 12 (C) | 13 (B) | 14 (B) | 15 (A) | 16 (C) | 17 (B) | 18 (C) | 19 (B) | 20 (A) |
| 21 (A) | 22 (B) | 23 (B) | 24 (A) | 25 (C) | 26 (A) | 27 (A) | 28 (D) | 29 (A) | 30 (B) |
| 31 (A) | 32 (D) | 33 (D) | 34 (B) | 35 (A) | 36 (C) | 37 (A) | 38 (D) | 39 (C) | 40 (A) |
| 41 (D) | 42 (A) | 43 (C) | 44 (C) | 45 (C) | 46 (C) | 47 (B) | 48 (D) | 49 (A) | 50 (C) |
| 51 (D) | 52 (A) | 53 (B) | 54 (A) | 55 (A) | 56 (B) | 57 (B) | 58 (A) | 59 (B) | 60 (C) |
| 61 (C) | 62 (D) | 63 (C) | 64 (A) | 65 (B) | 66 (B) | 67 (D) | 68 (B) | 69 (A) | 70 (A) |
| 71 (D) | 72 (A) | 73 (A) | 74 (D) | 75 (C) | 76 (D) | 77 (C) | 78 (B) | 79 (B) | 80 (B) |
| 81 (A) | 82 (B) | 83 (B) | 84 (A) | | | | | | |

# *Hints & Solutions*

## Chapter Practice

**1** (*A*) Universal Affirmative

**2** (*A*) Contradictory

**3** (*A*) A → Universal Affirmative
E → Universal Negative
I → Particular Affirmative
O → Particular Negative

**4** (*A*) A proposition → All non-P are non-S
E proposition → No non-P are non-S
I proposition → Some non-P are non-S
O proposition → Some non-P are not non-S

**5** (*C*) A. Subject term is distributed → A proposition
B. Neither subject nor predicate distributed → I proposition
C. Subject and Predicate distributed → E proposition
D. Predicate term is distributed → O proposition

**6** (*A*) A. Contrary → Two statements can't be true at some time
B. Contradictory → A pair of Affirmative and Negative
C. Sub-contrary → Opposite of Contrary
D. Sub-alternation → The particular is the sub alternation of the universal

**7** (*C*) 1 and 2 i.e. Arguments and deductive arguments.

**8** (*A*) "No men are good" and "some men are not good" refers to E and O proposition

**9** (*B*) A, E are contrary propositions.

**10** (*A*) Perception : Ordinary; Inference : Vyapti comparison : Analogy; Verbal Testimony : Shabda

**11** (*A*) Vyapti means both inference and Invariable Concomittance.

**12** (*A*) The correct sequence is 14235

**13** (*A*) Major Term : Sadhya ; Minor Term : Papsha
Middle Term : Hetu

**14** (*B*) 'Skirmish', if uncontrolled gives rise to 'War'. In the same way, 'Disease', if uncontrolled gives rise to 'Epidemic'

**15** (*B*) 'Tree' originates from 'Root'. Likewise 'Smoke' originates from 'Fire'.

**16** (*B*) As 'Good' and 'Bad' are opposite, in the same way 'Virtue is' opposite to 'Sin'.

**17** (*C*) As, 'Bee' gives 'Honey', 'Cow' gives 'Milk', in the same way 'Teacher' gives 'Lessons' to the 'Students'.

**18** (*C*) As 'Birds' can 'Fly', in the same way 'Snake' can 'Crawl'.

**19** (*A*) 'Incandescent' and 'Glowing' are synonyms to each other. Likewise 'Indefatigable' and 'Untiring' are synonyms to each other.

**20** (*D*) 'Elevated' means 'Exalted'. Similarly, 'Dirty' is synonym to 'Filthy'

**21** (*A*) In word GREAT, the number of alphabets = 5

∴ GREAT $= (5)^2 = 25$

In the same way, in word NUMBER, the number of alphabets = 6

∴ NUMBER $= (6)^2 = 36$

**22** (*D*) As, New Number

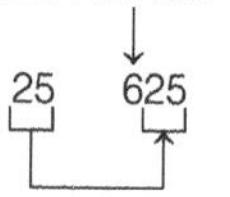


Similarly, New Number

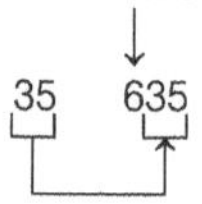


**23** (*A*) As,

Positional value: P → 16, S → 19, T → 20

16 + 19 + 20 = 55

Digit's sum = 5 + 5 = 10

Again, digits's sum = 1 + 0 = 1

Similarly,

Positional value: N → 14, P → 16, R → 18

14 + 16 + 18 = 48

Digit's sum = 4 + 8 = 12

Again, digit's sum = 1 + 2 = 3

**24** (*C*) Dearth' is the synonym of 'Scarcity' and similarly 'Substitute' is the synonym of 'Replace'.

**25** (*C*) 'Water' is contained in 'Ocean'. Likewise 'Sand' is contained in 'Desert'.

**26** (*A*) 'Food' is consumed in the 'Stomach' and 'Fuel' is consumed in 'Engine'.

**27** (*A*) As.

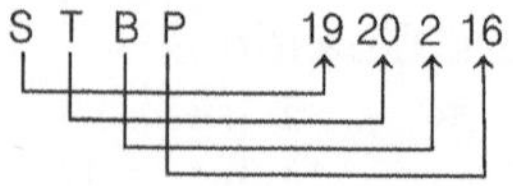


Similarly,

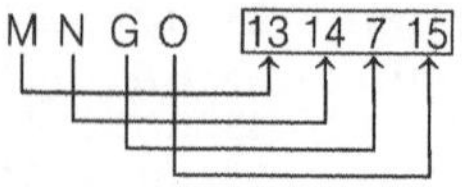


∴ ? = 1314715

**28** (*B*) Here, 81 → 77 → 69 (−4, −8)

Similarly, 56 → 52 → 44 (−4, −8)

**29** (*A*) Some women are poets. Some women are politicians. Some women politicians are poets. This can be expressed as given in option (A)

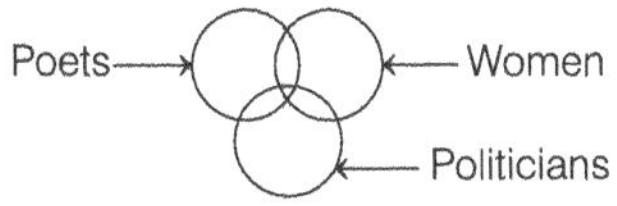


**30** (*C*) Kanpur is a city in the state of Uttar Pradesh while Jaipur is entirely different as it is a city in Rajasthan. This can be expressed as given in option (C)

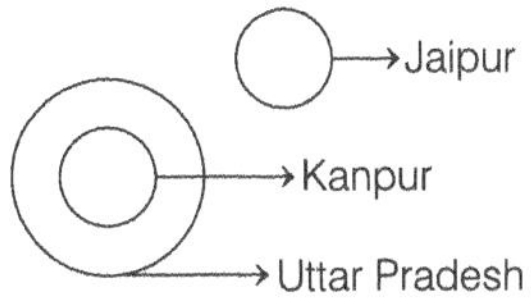


**31** (*D*) All the teachers are educated but some are employed. This can be expressed as given in option (D)

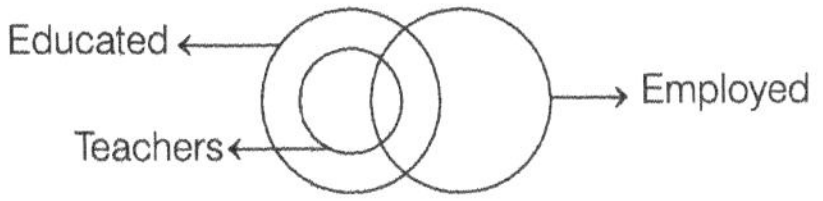


**32** (*A*) Tigers are animals but not herbivorous. This can be expressed as given in option (A)

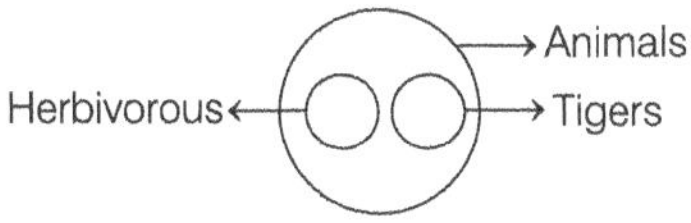


**33** (*D*) Snake and lizard are entirely different but both belong to the class of reptiles. This can be expressed as given in option (D)

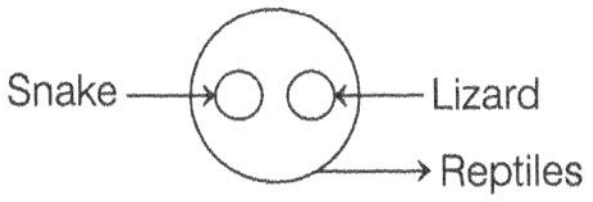


**34** (*A*) The persons knowing all the three languages are represented by the region which is common to all the three circles. Hence, number of such persons = 100. The persons who do not know Sanskrit are represented by the region outside Circle S. So, number of such persons = (200 + 120 + 220) = 540.

$\therefore$ Required ratio $= \frac{100}{540} = \frac{5}{27}$

**35** (*A*) There are 25 players who are neither artist nor doctors because this is the only region of the circle which is not common to either rectangle or triangle.

**36** (*C*) Required number = 22 + 3 = 25

**37** (*D*) There are 30 artists who are neither doctors nor players because this is the only region of the rectangle which is not common to either circle or triangle.

**38** (*D*) There are 17 Doctors who are neither players nor artists because this is the only region of the triangle which is not common with either circle or rectangle.

**39** (*C*) The region 3 is common to triangle, circle and rectangle and hence, represents doctors who are players as well as artists.

**40** (*A*) According to the question,

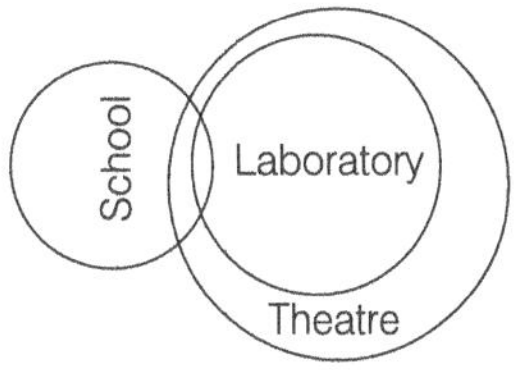


It is clear from diagram only Conclusion I follows.

**41** (*A*) According tot he question

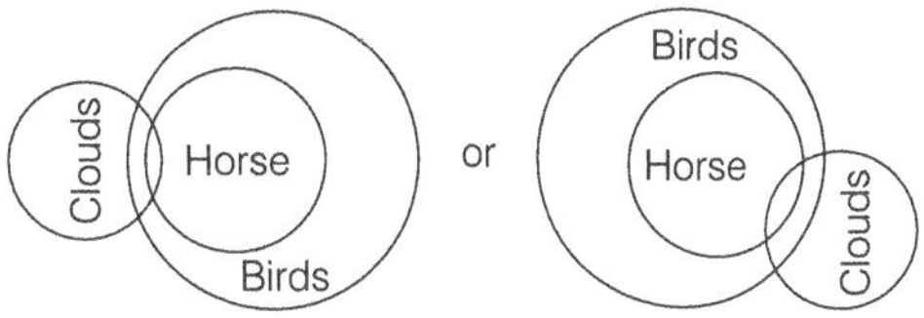


It is clear from diagram only Conclusion I follows.

**42** (*D*)

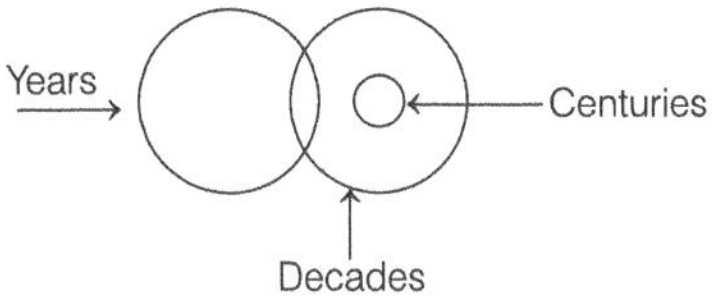


**Conclusions**

I. (✗) II. (✓) III. (✗)

∴ Only Conclusions II follows.

**43** (*C*) According to the statements, venn diagram is as,

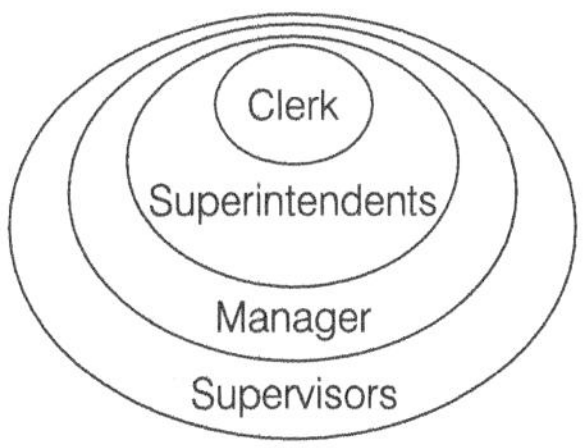


**Conclusions**

I. (✗) II. (✗) III. (✓) IV. (✗)

Clearly, only Conclusion III follows.

**44** (*D*) According to the question.

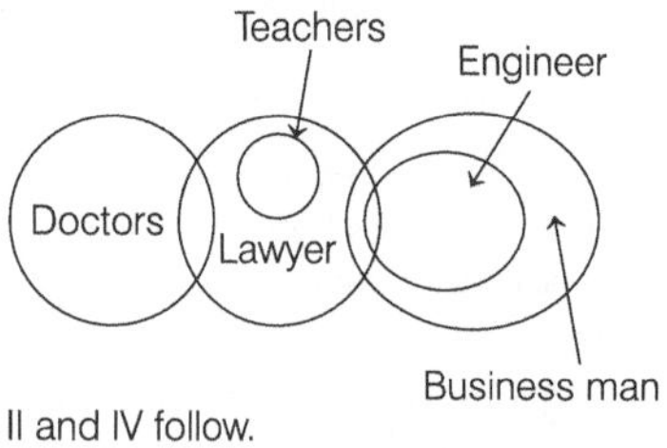


So, II and IV follow.

**45** (*B*)

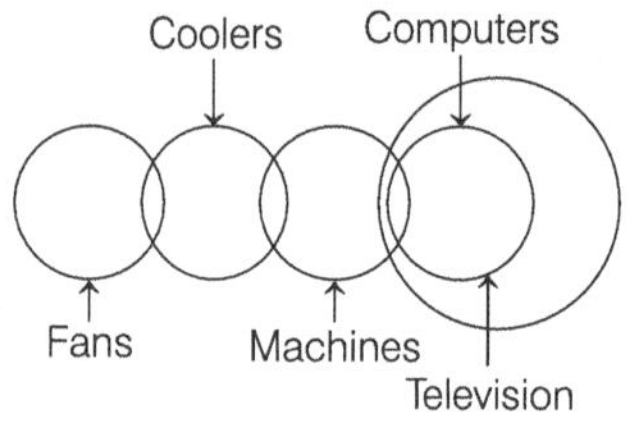


**Conclusions**

(I) Some televisions are machines. (✓)
(II) Some machines are fans. (✗)
(III) No machine is fan. (✗)

**46** (*C*)

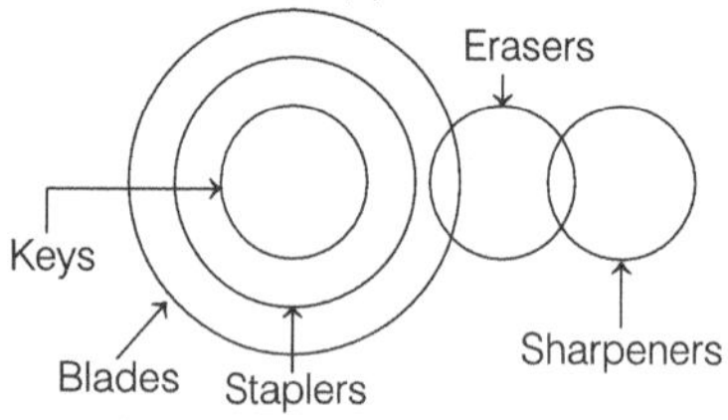


**Conclusions**

(I) Some sharpeners are keys.(✗)
(II) All keys are blades. (✓)
(III) Some erasers are keys. (✗)

**47** (*A*) According to the statements venn diagram is as,

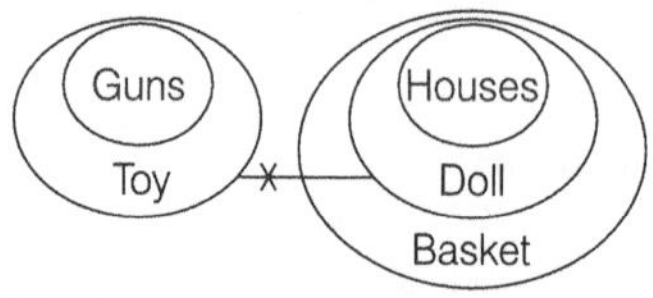


**Conclusions**

(A) False (B) True (C) True (D) True

Hence, conclusion (A) does not follow from the given statements.

**48** (*D*) According to the statements venn diagram is as,

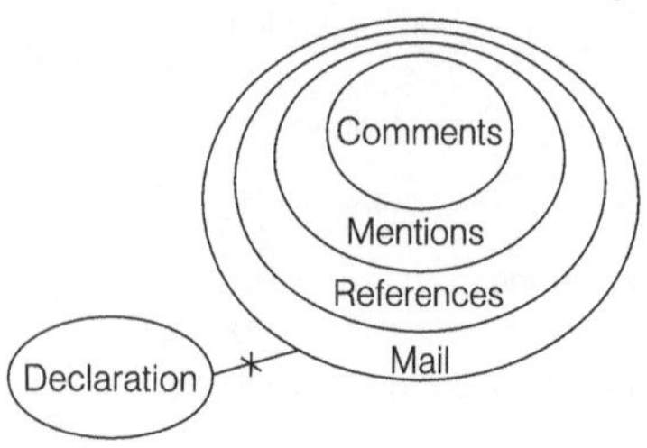


Conclusions

(A) True (B) True
(C) True (D) False

Hence, conclusion (D) does not follow from the given statements.

**49** (*C*) According to the question

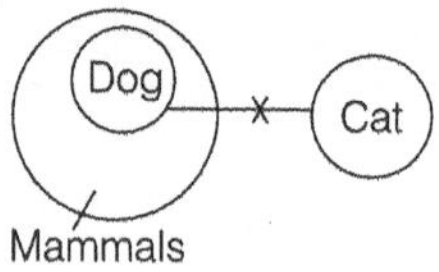


From above figure, we can say that the Conclusions III and IV are valid.

**50** (*A*) Here, Assertion (A) is true because today more and more laws are being introduce but still more and more crime is being committed.
Reason (R) is doubtful because eliminating law to reduce crime is not a solution and hence explanation is not correct.

**51** (*C*) 'A' is true and 'R' is false. A body weights less when immersed in water but this law was given by Archimedes, not by Newton.

**52** (*A*) Both 'A' and 'R' are true and 'R' is the correct explanation of A. The problem of pumping out water from the flooded mines required the need of a self-working engine which led James Watt to invent the engine.

**53** (*A*) Both 'A' and 'R' are true and 'R' is the correct explanation of 'A'. Above the sea level, temperature decreases with a increase in altitude which makes mountain peaks colder than plains.

**54** (*B*) Both 'A' and 'R' are true but 'R' is not the correct explanation of 'A'.

**55** (*B*) Both A and R are true but R is not the correct explanation of A. Clothes are not washed properly in hard water because hard water does not form lather with soap. However, it is true that hard water contains many minerals.
Both 'A' and 'R' are true and 'R' is the correct explanation of 'A'.

**56** (*A*) Himalayas are the young fold mountains which at one time are believed to lie inside the Tethys sea. This is evident from the recovery of fossils of marine creatures on its peak.

**57** (*A*) Both 'A' and 'R' are true and 'R' is the correct explanation of 'A'. Since, India is a secular country, people of India can practice any faith they like.

**58** (*A*) Both 'A' and 'R' are true and 'R' is the correct explanation of 'A' as, rainfall in Tamil Nadu is caused by the retreating which occurs in winter.

**59** (*C*) 'A' is true, but 'R' is false. Eskimos live in snow houses called igloos as such houses are warm inside

60 (*E*) Argument II is strong as the presence of UNO ensures friendly relations among various countries. Argument I is also strong because now-a-days the presence of UNO is felt undesirable.

61 (*A*) Only Argument I is strong as there will be greater administrative convenience by forming small states out of bigger states in India. Argument II is absurd.

62 (*C*) Argument I is weak because of the use of word only : Argument II is strong as the country's power need cannot be ignored. Argument III is weak because it is a argument based on example.

63 (*C*) Competent work force is desirable. Hence, Argument I is strong. Argument II does not appear to be true for all PSUs. And even it is true, an argument that takes recourse in helplessness seems to fall short on merit. Argument III is strong as competition is desirable.

64 (*D*) Argument I is weak as it is not true. Argument II is also weak on the same grounds. Argument III is strong as it elaborates on how banning exports would help tackle the drought situation.

65 (*D*) Argument I is strong because such a reduction in trend will be a desirable consequence. Argument II is weak as it doesn't explain as to what effect the ban will have on the creative pursuits. III is strong as a ban will take away from the power of the portrayal.

66 (*A*) Argument I is weak because talking of culture is irrelevant in this case. Infact, Argument I is not even true. Argument II is weak because it is simplistic. We are not told what these unhealthy practices will be. Argument III is weak because it is superfluous.

67 (*C*) Statement 3, 'Some students are obedient' and Statement 4 'some students are not obedient' can be claimed to be true.

68 (*B*) The statements 2, 3 and 4 are the correct statements. Hence, option (B) is right

69 (*A*) I follows because trees are a part of forest and India's economy depends mainly on forest. II is not correlated with the statement. So, it does not follow. Hence, Statement I follows.

70 (*D*) Neither Conclusion I nor II follows. Over population is a result of several factors. Therefore, only unscientific thinking cannot be held responsible for overpopulation.

71 (*B*) This is a good book, can be concluded.

72 (*A*) If a player is found guilty of doping, his medal is confiscated. Therefore, only Conclusion II follows.

73 (*A*) From both the statements, it is clear that Conclusion I is true i.e. Jitananda and Vidyananda did remarkable social series.

74 (*A*) The Government is making efforts to boost tourism in Jammu and Kashmir on the assumption that tourism in Jammu and Kashmir dropped during last couple of years,
Therefore, Assumption I is implicit in the statement.

75 (*B*) The word 'if in the statement implies that B may or may not be willing to publicise his products. Statement further suggests that advertisement should be given in newspaper 'X'. This means that 'X' will help advertise better. In other words, newspaper 'X' has a wide circulation. So, only Assumption II is Implicit

76 (*B*) I is definitely not mentioned in the advertisement. II is Implicit, otherwise company 'X' would not have given the advertisement.

77 (*A*) Instruction in the statement is based on the assumption that those who lean .out of a train are in the risk of being hurt. It is not inferred from the statement that people do not like to get hurt. Hence, only I is implicit.

78 (*B*) The driver does not have control on what the auto driver will do. Hence, I is invalid. But II is a valid assumption because if one takes an action he assumes its outcome.

79 (*A*) When we urge someone to do something, we assume a positive response. Hence, Assumption I is implicit while for the same reason Assumption II becomes invalid.

80 (*B*) Only Assumption II is implicit. People have desire to grow their money and they will respond the advertisement positively.

81 (*B*) It is clear that, on the basis of some report the medical department has asked people to use only boiled water in an attempt to prevent the spread of cholera in the town. So, only Assumption II is correct.

82 (*A*) It is clear that food prices are likely to increases because of food shortage. So, Assumption I is correct.

83 (*B*) Assumption I is implicit, such a decision would not be taken. Assumption II is implicit in the purpose of fund raising that has been mentioned in the statement.

84 (*D*) Assumption I is invalid because when a warning is given it is assumed that it will be heeded to. Further, Assumption II is not believed to be the motive behind a warning. Hence, II is also invalid.

85 (*B*) Motormen should not be made the scapegoat for the failure of the Signalling system. Hence, course of action I does not follow, course of action II follows.

86 (*A*) I follows as a measure of caution. But, II wont solve the problem and poor electrical fittings would wreak havoc where ever the market be.

87 (*A*) Statement points out the crisis faced by the power plants and one of the crisis is depletion of stock of steam coal with the thermal power plants in the North. Therefore, it is the right course of action to

supply the steam coal to the thermal power plants. Secondly, since the water inflows into the Gobindsagar has declined, setting up of another hydraulic power plant will be futile.

**88** (*D*) The problem discussed here clearly hints at the need for quick rehabilitation of bonded labourers. So, only III follows.

**89** (*B*) Only III logically follows because such accidents should not be repeated. The railways authourities should be asked to man all its level crossings.

**90** (*D*) I is invalid as the given statement talks about elderly people and not women and children. II and III are proper courses of action, yet they do not follow because such provisions are already there. Infact killing elderly people is a punishable offence under section 300 and 302 of IPC while murderers as a rule are prosecuted by the state. Therefore, II and III are not new suggestions. Infact, they are already in practice. Hence, I, II and III all are Invalid.

**91** (*B*) I is not feasible in a democracy. III does not follow because the problem is not concerned with 'criminals'. II is the only course of action the authorities can resort to.

**92** (*B*) Clearly, war is the last resort. First, peaceful talks and negotiations should be indulged in, to settle the issues of dispute. So, only course II follows.

**93** (*C*) The statement stresses the need for all round personality development of an individual. So, only III follows.

**94** (*D*) Keeping in mind the safety and convenience of passangers, both I and II follow. III clearly suggests a remedy to the problem and hence it also follows.

**95** (*B*) Only action II follows. During peak travelling season number of commuters increases rapidly so instead of saying them to defer their travel plans. Railway should try to accommodate as many commuters as possible by adding extra coaches to the trains.

## Previous Years' Questions

**1** (*A*) According to question,

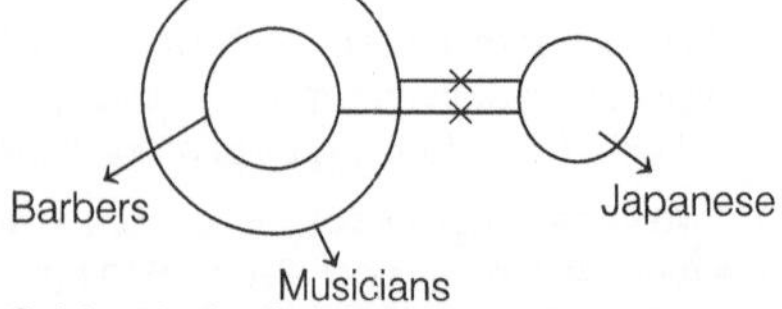


∴ Subject in the first premise and predicate in the second premise is the middle term.

**2** (*B*) Inductive argument refers to the logical process, in which specific instances or particular situations are observed or analysed to establish general or universal principle.

Thus, inductive argument proceeds from particular to universal.

**3** (*D*) Communication is an on-going process and it depends on the present environment in which one works. It is of many forms may be interpersonal, intrapersonal, group or mass communication. It is not presupposes shared and symbolic environment.
It is true to say that communication is a social interaction which in combination with other factors to contribute to the community.
Hence, Assertion (A) is false and Reason (R) is true.

**4** (*A*) The logic involved in the given example is Arthapatti. Arthapatti is a sanskrit term meaning 'presumption'. It refers to the way in which knowledge is derived from a set of circumstances.

**5** (*A*) Fallacy of contradictory reason works on the supposition that the proposition asserts and denies the same thing. This contradictory premises involve an argument that draws a conclusion from inconsistent or incompatible premises. The fallacy in the given argument is Fallacy of contradictory reason.

**6** (C) According to the question,

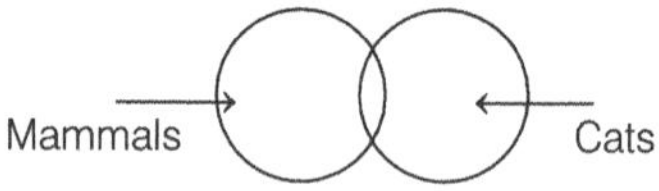


Hence, the converse is 'some mammals are cats'.

**7** (*B*) The fallacy of the argument is Ad misericordium Hence Option (B) is the correct choice

**8** (C) According to the question,

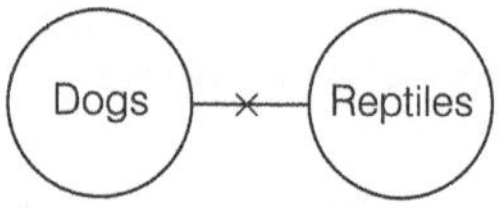


Hence, both subject and predicate term are distributed.

**9** (*B*) From the question, upamana is not a necessary step when an argument is presented based on interference before the others, according to the classical Indian school of logic.

**10** (C) There are many at modes of communication in the classroom and among them spoken and written words are two easy media available.
Whereas, the reason given is false and also does not explains the assertion.

**11** (C) From the question "some students are sincere" is an example of particular Affirmative.

**12** (C) From the given two statements, the assertion is true as the clock speed of CPUs has been the same in recent years. Whereas, the reason is not true and is also not relevant to the assertion statements Hence, option (C) is correct choice

**13** (*C*) From the above two statements, Pedagogy and social interference are the two important result oriented activities of a teacher; Also communication plays a major role in performing both these activities Hence, option (C) is the correct choice.

**14** (*B*) From the given two statements, both Assertion and Reason are true. Whereas, Reason (R) does not explain the assertion statement (A) correctly.

**15** (*A*) 'Writing on paper is similar to writing on board' is a type of deductive reasoning.

**16** (*C*) When subject and predicate of both the premises is same but differ only in quantity is known as sub-contraries.

**17** (*A*) 'All judges are fair minded' is an example of Universal Affirmative.

**18** (*D*) According to the question,

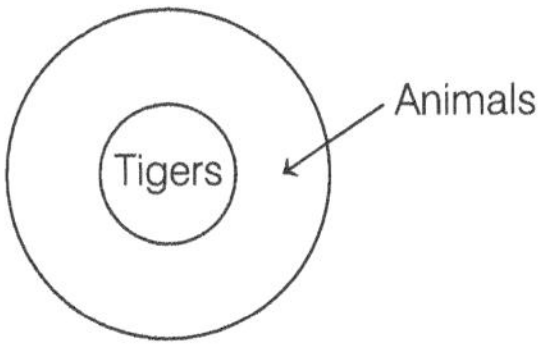


∴ This is an example of universal Affirmative.

**19** (*C*) According to the question,

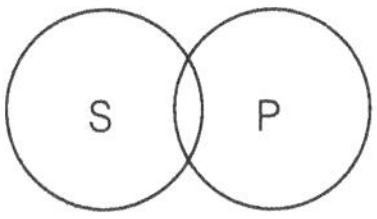


The converse which will be true is some P is S.

**20** (*A*) From the questions.

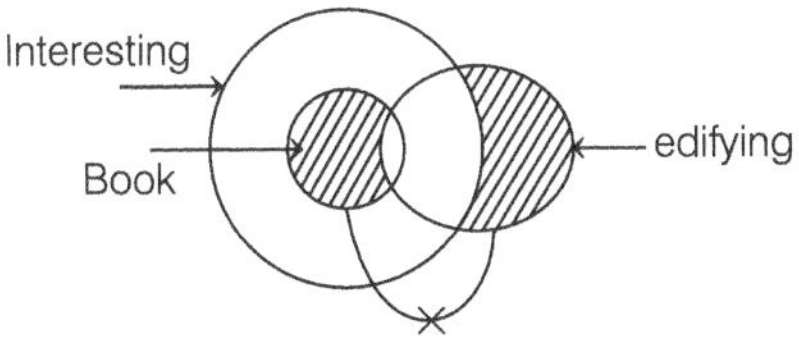


Hence, for some interesting things are not edifying subject of conclusion and predicate of second premise are minor terms.

**21** (*C*) From the given question,

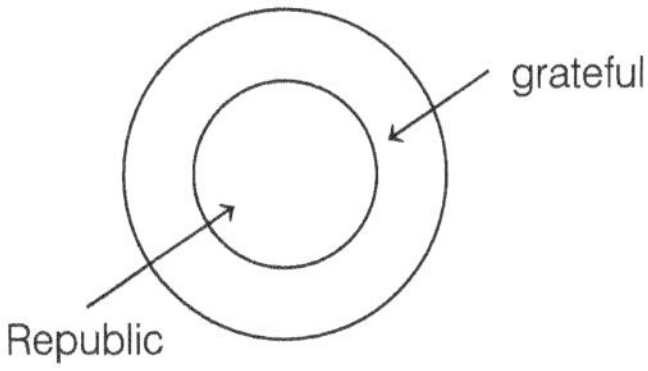


**Proposition**

(i)

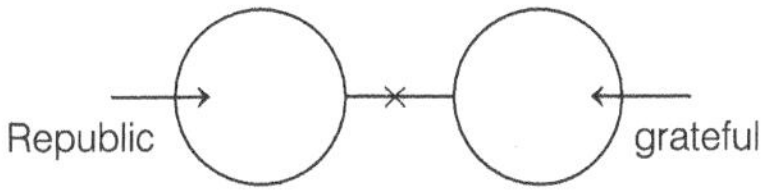


(ii)

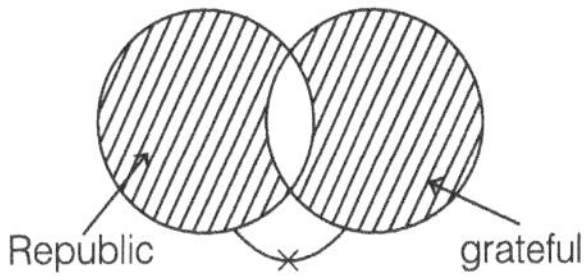


(iii)

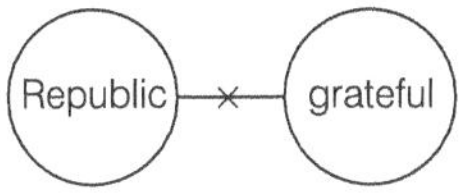


(iv)

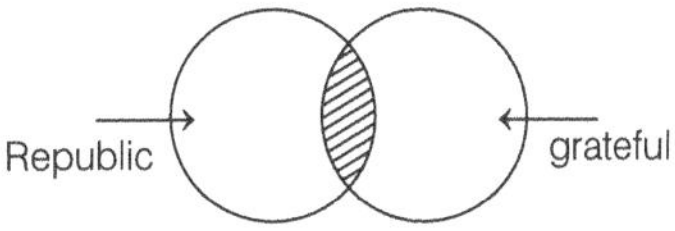


Hence, (C) is the correct option

**22** (*B*) According to the question,

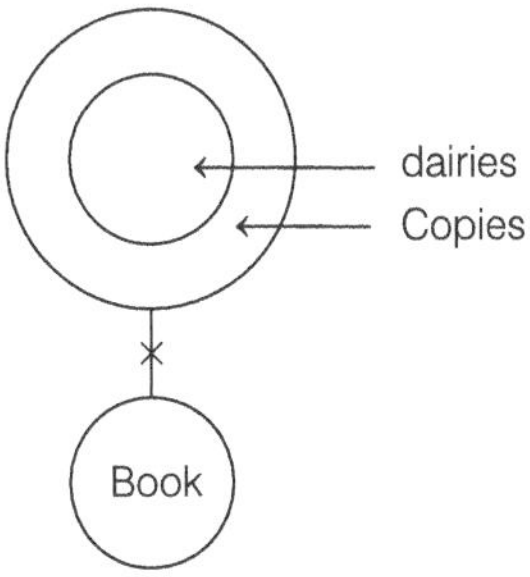


**Conclusions**

(A) × (B) × (C) ✓ (D) ✓

Hence, conclusion (C) and (D) are true

**23** (*B*) According to the given statement in the question, option (B) is correct.

**24** (*A*) According to the question,

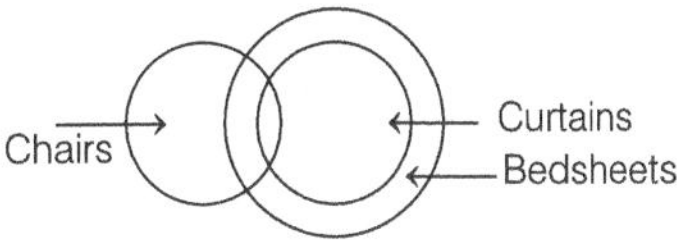


**Conclusion**

Hence, the mood of the above proposition is IAI.

**25** (*A*) According to the question,

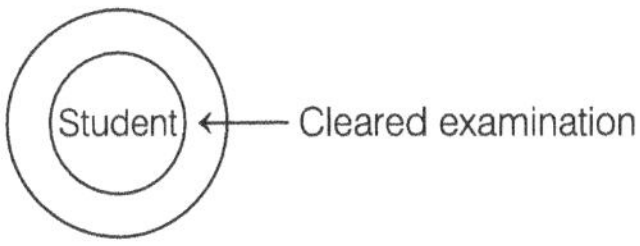


Hence, the statements are contradictories.

**26** (*A*) According to the question,

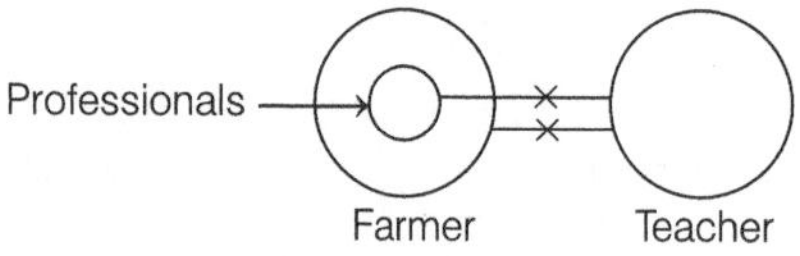


Hence, the middle term in subject in the first premise and predicate is the second premise.

**27** (*B*) Inductive reasoning help in finding new knowledge of facts about the world.

**28** (*B*) From the question,

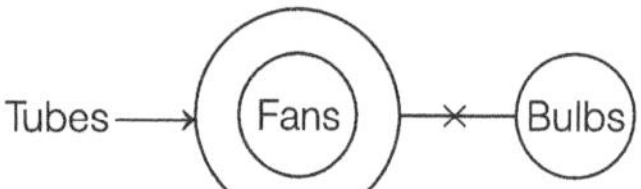


**Conclusions**

(A) ✓ (B) × (C) × (D) ×

Hence, (A) is the correct choice

**29** (*A*) Arthapatti

**30** (*C*) From the question,

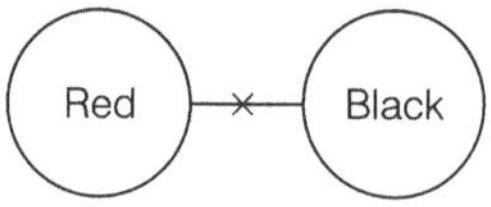


**Proposition**

(i)

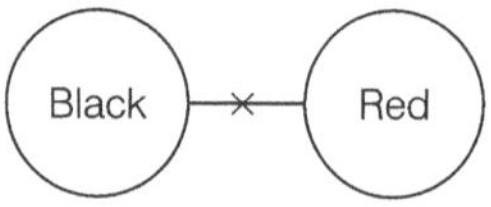


(ii)

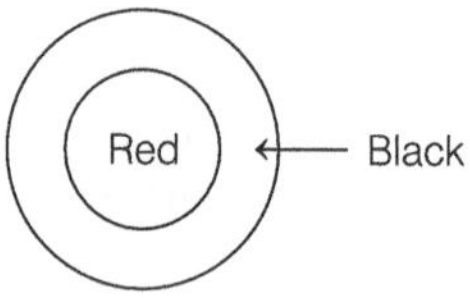


(iii)

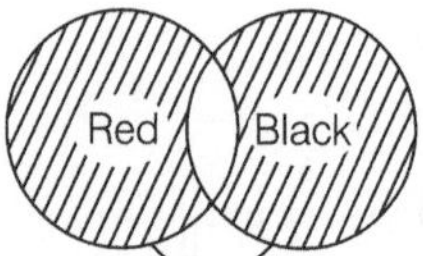


(iv)

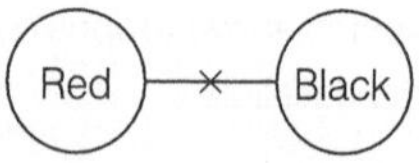


Hence (C) is the correct choice.

**31** (*A*) 'Sound is impermanent because it is invisible' on the basis of Indian logic, this is a fallacy of irrelevant reason.

**32** (*D*) 'Sound is permanent because it is a product like the jar'.
According to Indian logic, this a fallacy of trivial reason.

**33** (*D*) Since, in the given statement there is a correlation between pre-action stage of classroom teaching and pre-learning preparation stage of communication. Hence, this is an Analogical argument.

**34** (*B*) 'This gavaya is like my cow'. This is 'implication' type of knowledge.

**35** (*A*) When the subject and predicate of both the premises are the same but they differ in quality only, it is known as contradictories.

**36** (*A*) According to the question,

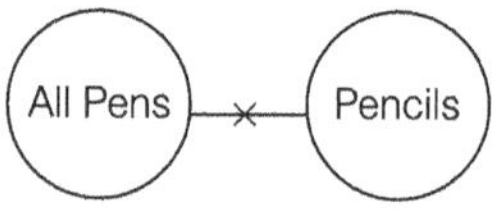


Hence, option (A) is correct choice

**37** (*A*) 'Anumana' is a Variable relation between minor term and major term.

**38** (*D*) From the question,

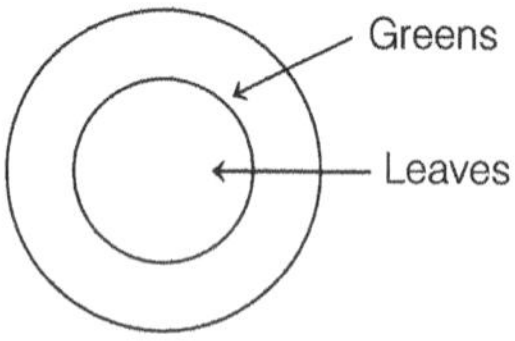


**Propositions**

1.

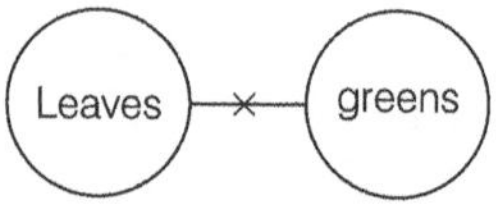


2.

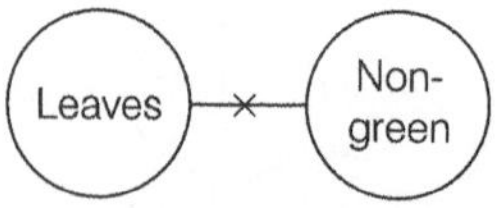


3.

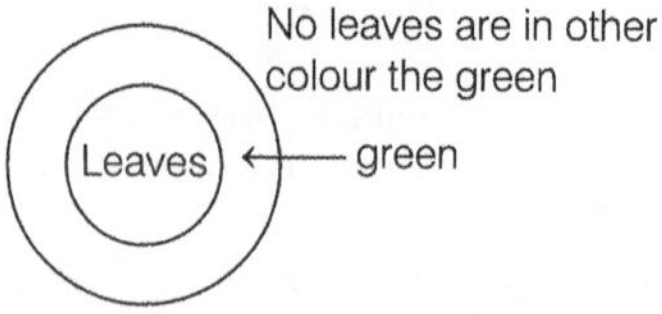


4.

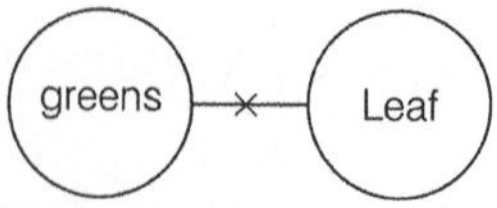


**39** (*C*) In demonstrative arguments, 'the relation that exist between premises and conclusion is that of logical necessity'.

**40** (*A*)

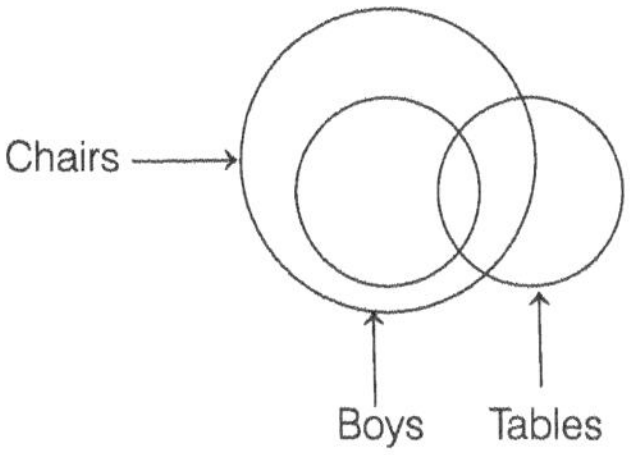


**Conclusions**

(i) ✓ (ii) × (iii) ✓ (iv) ×

Hence, only (i) and (iii) follows.

**41** (*C*) Due to new inventions in this modern time, a number of options are now available to save both money and time of people. It has now become possible for everyone to work as well as study simultaneously.

This credit goes to the many online courses and online teaching portals where a number of experts and courses are available just a click away. But this type of teaching does not provide direct interaction of students and teachers and also does not develop any critical thinking in people as can be seen in the classroom teaching and learning.

**42** (*A*) After independence in 1947, the Government of India has recognized and considered education as one of the most important and foremost aspects for building a modern, educated and highly civilised and progressive society based on high virtues. In order to achieve this aim, the Indian Government has established a number of Higher Educational Regulatory Bodies to ensure quality of education. Some of the important among these are University Grants.

Commission (UGC), National Testing Agency (NTA), All India council for Technical Education (AICTE), Council of Architecture (COA), Central Board of Secondary Education (CBSE), and so on.

**43** (*D*) According to the question,

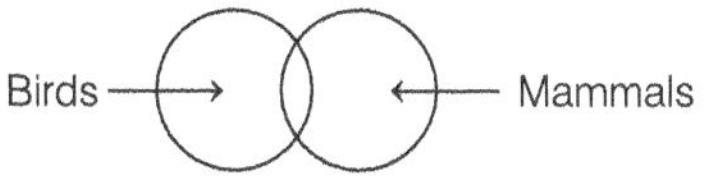


∴ "Some birds are mammals" is a particular affirmative proposition and it distributes neither subject term nor predicate term.

**44** (*C*) Syllogism is not a part of immediate deductive inference, whereas, conversion, obversion and contraposition are part of immediate deductive inference.

**45** (*C*) The first statement that is the assertion is correct, as the Governor has the power to ask for any information from the Chief Minister regarding the administration of the state

Whereas, the reason is not true

The Chief Minister and not the governor is the head of the state Administration

∴ Option (C) is correct option.

**46** (*D*) The first step in any classroom communication is always defining the objectives of the logic of discussion. So, the assertion becomes invalid.

But the reason, which state that clear definition of objectives make students understand the topic well is always true.

**47** (*A*) As sniffing is a process of monitoring and capturing all data packets passing through given network. It can be used to steal data as information over a network.

∴ Both (A) and (R) are true and (R) is the correct explanation of (A)

**48** (*D*) If precaution are taken ahead of any natural disasters, the impact of it can be minimised. Hence, the impact of natural disaster depend on the socio-economic factors, which is responsible for proper infrastructural developments as well as planning preventive measures.

When any natural disaster strikes any area it do not choose between communities but the whole community is affected.

Hence, Only (R) is true.

Assertion (A) is true.

**49** (*A*) The above two statement are true and also correlates each other.

**50** (*C*) No poets are dreames is a contrary to "all poets are dreamers".

**51** (*D*) Universal proposition along with an instance is signified by Udharaha of Anumana (Inference) in India logic.

**52** (*A*) A blog is a discussion and informational website published on the World Wide Web. It consists of discrete, often informal diary-style text entries or posts. Blog is a form of social media. It allows anyone to communicate to a public audience.

**53** (*B*) Uniformity of nature is a presupposition in inductive reasoning.

**54** (*A*) Venn diagram is graphical method of representing categorial proposition and testing the validity of categorical syllogisms.

**55** (*A*) The analogical reasoning is the process of reasoning from particular to particular. It derives a conclusion from one's experience in one or more similar situations. It also can be defined as any type of thinking that relies upon analogy, which indicates the comparison between two objects, or systems of objects, that highlights respects in which they are thought to be similar.

**56** (*B*) Ven-diagram drawn from the premises,

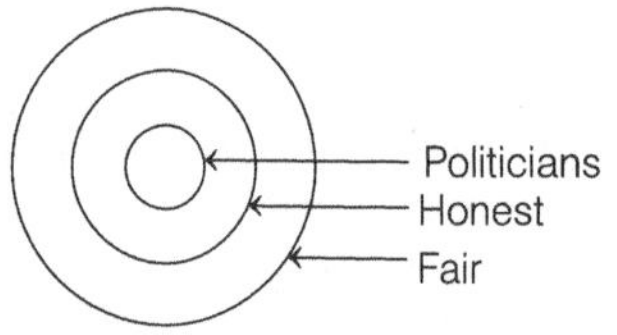


**Conclusions**

(A) ✓ (B) ✗ (C) ✓ (D) ✗

Hence, conclusions, 1 and 3 follow.

**57** (*B*) Assertion (A) is false, but Reason (R) is true because control over the communication will more control over what the student are learning.

**58** (*A*) A is true, but R is false.

**59** (*B*) Communicate well in the classroom is not a natural ability. It is learning process. So, Assertion (A) false, but statement given in Reason (R) is correct.

**60** (*C*) R is the correct explanation of A as Indoor air pollution must be in limit as it is a serious health hazard.

**61** (*C*) 'Smoking is injurious to health'. This warning printed on cigarette packets does not conclude that 'Non-smoking promotes health', so this is not an assumption for this pointed warning.

'People make careful not of a warning'. This is the implicit assumption for this warning.

**62** (*D*) According to the information, venn diagram is as follows

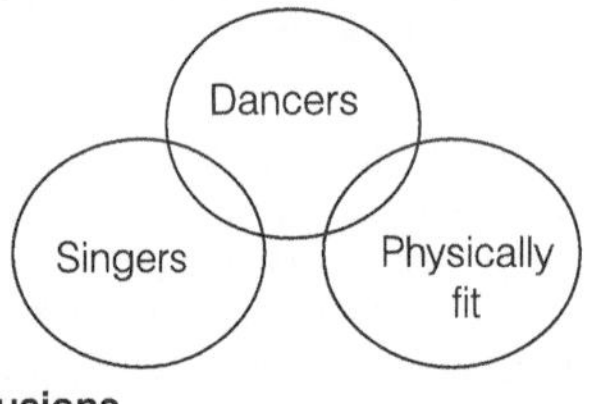


**Conclusions**

1. ✗ 2. ✓ 3. ✓ 4. ✗

So, conclusion 2 and 3 are true.

**63** (*C*) Given statement 'domestic animals are hardly ferocious' is taken to be false, then from this its clear that all domestic animals are ferocious and also can say most of the domestic animals are ferocious.

**64** (*A*) Learning is actually a specific term. Different people use different words to define learning within educational psychology, but in general, we're talking about a step-by-step process in which an individual experiences permanent, lasting changes in knowledge, behaviours, or ways of processing the world. Therefore, all the learning results from teaching is not correct.

However, in the learning and teaching environment which provide effective support and stimulating reflection on the role of teaching in the learning process all contribute to quality teaching.

**65** (*B*)

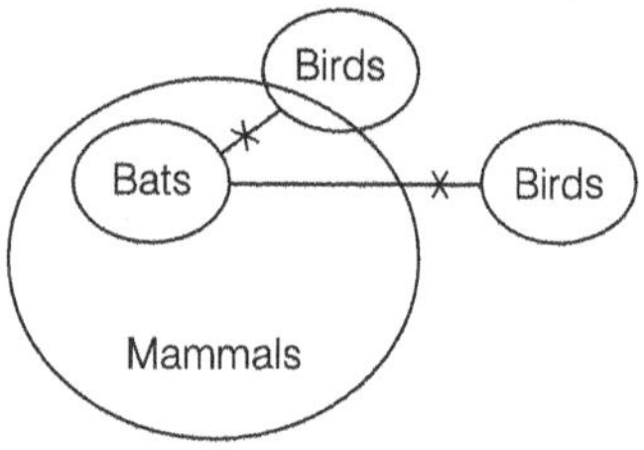


**Conclusions**

(I) No birds are mammals. (Doubtful)

(II) Some birds are not mammals. (✗)

(III) No bats are birds. (✓)

(IV) All mammals are bats. (Doubtful)

So, only Conclusion (III) is true

**66** (*A*) Among the given statements, both Statement '2' and Statement '3' can be true. Also, in the given pair both the statements are contradictory hence both cannot be false. Statement '1' and '3' both can both be true at a time but cannot ever be false at a time.

**67** (*A*) Smog episodes during winter (December - February) are mainly caused by limited dilution of air pollution, under unfavourable meterological conditions: little wind (from continental directions) and a temperature inversion.

Little wind results in very little horizontal dispersion (spread) of the pollution, while temperature inversions hinder vertical dispersion.

**68** (*D*) Blares says "no teaching without learning". Both are interrelated to each other. Therefore, all teaching implies learning because learning to be useful must be derived from teaching.

**69** (*B*) If the statement 'None but the brave wins the race' is false, then the statement

Some persons who win the race are not brave is true.

**70** (*A*) Statement 1 : Every student is attentive.

Statement 2 : Some students are attentive.

The above two statements are related in such a way that they cannot both be true but can both be false.

**71** (*B*) Sustainable development is development that meets the needs of the present, without compromising the ability of future generations to meet their own needs. Environmentally friendly or environment friendly are and sustainability are marketing terms referring to goods and services, laws, guidelines and policies that claim reduced, minimal or no harm upon ecosystems or the environment.

**72** (*A*) Since, the given proposition 'All men are mortal' is false. Hence, the true statement will be 'some men are mortal'.

**73** (*A*) Since, the given proposition 'All farmers are poor' is false. Hence, the true statement will be 'Some farmers are poor' is definitely true.

**74** (*D*) The semblance is between earth's features and grain. We need to focus on the word, as absurd as to assert that makes them analogical.

**75** (*C*)

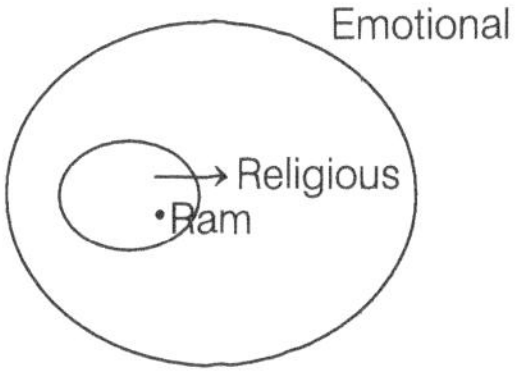


**76** (*D*) First proposition: All women are equal to men' is given among the answer choice. WE can start with that.

All women are equal to men also mean that some women are equal to men. It is based on the rules of syllogism, which means that what applies to all also applies to part of it. Now, the denial of it is some women are not equal to men. That is the third proposition.

**77** (*C*) Venn diagram uses overlapping circles or other shapes to illustrate the logical relationships between two or more sets of items. Often, they serve to graphically organize things, highlighting how the items are similar and different.

**78** (*B*) Deductive argument is based on the claim that the truth of its premises guarantees the truth of its conclusion. The terms valid and invalid are used to characterize deductive arguments. A deductive argument succeeds when, if we accept the evidence as true (the premises), we must accept the conclusion.

An argument is valid if and only if it is necessary that if all of the premises are true, then the conclusion is true; if all the premises are true, then the conclusion must be true; it is impossible that all the premises are true and the conclusion is false.

**79** (*B*) 'Assertion' is true as conservation of soil resources is critical to human survival. The 'Reason', that soil is home to many microorganisms and it contains minerals is also true but it doesn't explain the 'Assertion' correctly.

**80** (*B*) 'Assertion' is true as purpose of higher education is to promote critical and creative thinking abilities among students. The 'Reason' that, these abilities ensure job placements doesn't properly explain the Assertion.

**81** (*B*) Statement in option (1) says All poets are philosophers and statement in option (4) says No philosopher is a poet

So, both the statements contradicts each other.

**82** (*A*) Lokpal will definitely help in eliminating corruption therefore Argument I is strong.

**83** (*B*) Both A and R are true, but R does not provide sufficient reason for A. Given Assertion is true as each person has lack something in itself. Also, the given reason is true, being imperfect cause of lacking some assets a man is not perfect.

**84** (*D*) The formal channel of communication is very effective way of storing and presserving the available information and knowledge in a very handy manner.

Formal communication includes written, printed and audio-video media, it is a systematic and orderly flow of information. It does not tend to be fast, rather it is more organised and formal.

UNIT 07

# Data Interpretation

CHAPTER ANALYSIS

This unit is based on updated exam pattern of NTA UGC NET covering all the important topics of Data Interpretation. After thoroughgoing the chapter you will be able to know about the Data and its classification, Graphical Representation of Data, Data Interpretation, Table Chart, Pie Chart, Bar Graph, Line Chart, Histogram etc. Every year 5 questions asked from this unit.

Earlier, questions were mostly based on bar graph and pie chart; but now the pattern has changed, from last few years the question are based on data given in tabular form.

IN THIS UNIT

- Sources, Acquisition and Classification of Data
- Quantitative and Qualitative Data
- Graphical Representation (Table Chart, Bar Chart, Histogram, Line Chart and Pie Chart)
- Data Mapping
- Data Interpretation
- Data and Governance

## DATA

Data are information in raw or unorganised form (such as alphabets, numbers or symbols) that refer to conditions, ideas or objects. Infact they are individual pieces of factual information recorded and used for the purpose of analysis. It is usually collected for research purposes and it is closely related with sampling as well.

For example, marks of student in a class, temperature of various places in country, etc.

### Sources of Data

Normally we gather data from two sources namely **primary** and **secondary**.

#### 1. Primary Data Sources

Primary data is the data that you gather considering your analysis needs. The source of primary data is a population place from which you gather information in the form of questionnaire focusing on targeted size and kind of sample.

#### 2. Secondary Data Sources

Secondary data is the data acquired from optional sources like magazines, books, documents, journals, reports, the web and more.

## Data Acquisition

Data acquisition is the process of gathering and measuring information on targeted or desired variables, which enables one to evaluate outcomes and answer relevant questions.

It is a component of research in all fields of study including physical and social sciences, humanities and business.

The goal for all data collection is to capture quality evidence that allows analysis which lead to the formulation of convincing and credible answers to the questions that have been posed.

A formal data acquisition process is necessary as it ensures that the data gathered are both defined and accurate and that subsequent decisions based on arguments present in the findings are valid.

## Classification of Data

Data can be classified in following two types:

### 1. Qualitative Data

This type of data is basically descriptive in nature and a bit difficult to analyse. This type of data can be classified into categories, on the basis of physical attributes and properties of the object. It is concerned with the data that is observable in terms of smell, appearance, taste, feel, texture, gender etc.

The methods of collecting qualitative data are

- Focus Group
- Observation
- Interview

### 2. Quantitative Data

This type of data basically deals with quantity or numbers. It refers to the data which computes the values and can express it in numerical terms.

It can be used in computation and statistical test. It is concerned with measurements like height, weight, volume, length, size etc. The methods of collecting quantitative data are

- Surveys
- Experiments
- Observations and Interview

# GRAPHICAL REPRESENTATION

Data can be sorted and assigned in many ways, some of which are as follows.

- Table chart
- Histogram
- Bar chart
- Line chart
- Pie chart or circle graph

## Table Chart

Table Chart is the most systematic way of representing quantitative data in a tabular form to understand the given information and to demonstrate the problem in a certain field of study. In a table, data is arranged systematically in columns and rows. Generally, the information is arranged in a table in alphabetical order, chronological order, monthwise, yearwise, etc.

### Parts of Data Table

A table generally has the following five integral parts

1. **Table Title** The title of the table gives a general idea of the type and often the purpose of information presented.
2. **Stub** This section of the table contains row headings that tell us about the specific kind of information given in that row.
3. **Column Headings** The column headings tell us about the specific kind of information given in that column.
4. **Body** This section of the table consists of numerical figures or data.
5. **Footnotes** This section of the table consists an additional piece of information of the table.

Table title

| | | Percentage breakup of people of different age groups (years) in 2019 | | |
|---|---|---|---|---|
| | | Upto 20 | 20-30 | 30-40 |
| Cities | Delhi | 12 | 15 | 25 |
| | Mumbai | 8 | 17 | 17 |
| | Bengaluru | 9 | 21 | 20 |
| | Pune | 8 | 19 | 23 |

Stub | Column headings | Body

Total number of people surveyed is 15000000

Footnotes

## Histogram

A histogram is a graphical representation of a frequency distribution with class intervals as the base and frequency as the height of the graph. Unlike a bar graph that depicts decrete data, histograms depict continuous data, so they have bars without any space between them and the rectangular bars need not be of equal width. e.g. The following graph show 70 men of different age group.

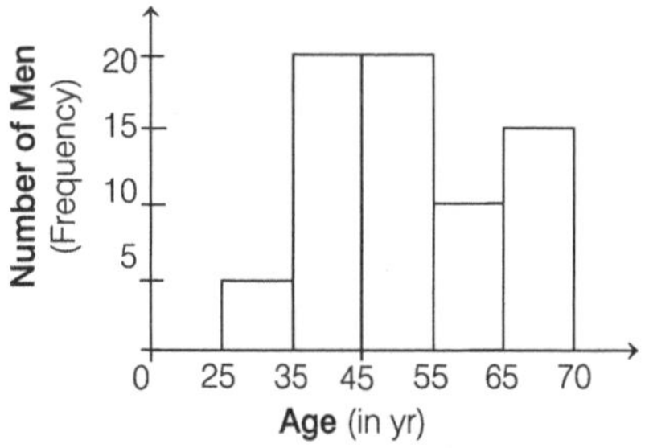


## Bar Chart

Bar chart is a chart or graph that presents categorial data with rectangular bars with heights or lengths proportional to the values that they represent.

The bars can be plotted vertically or horizontally. A bar graph shows comparisons among discrete categories. One axis of chart shows the specific categories being compared and the other axis represents a measured value.

Following are the main bar charts

1. **Simple Bar Chart** A simple bar chart relates to only one variable.
2. **Multiple Bar Chart** In this type, two or more bars are constructed adjoining each other which represent either different components of a total or to show multiple variables.

### Parts of a Bar Chart

Let's look at the components of a bar chart individually.

- **Graph Title** The graph title gives an overview of the information being presented in the graph. The title is given at the top of the graph.
- **Axis and Their Labels** Each graph has two axis. The axis labels tell us what information is presented on each axis. One axis represents data groups while the order represents the amounts or frequencies of the data groups.
- **Grouped Data Axis** The grouped data axis is always at the base of the bars. This axis displays the type of data being graphed.

**Price and Quantity Demanded of Various Items Per Week**

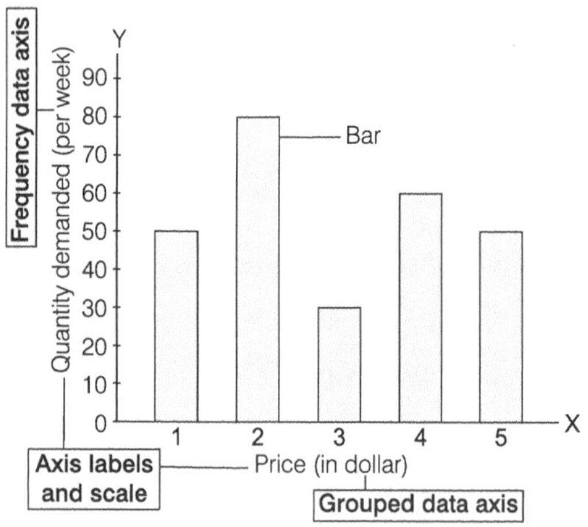


- **Frequency Data Axis** The frequency axis has a scale that is a measure of the frequencies or amounts of the different data groups.
- **Axes Scale** Scale is the range of the values being presented along the frequency axis.
- **Bars** The bars are rectangular blocks that can have their base at either vertical axis or horizontal axis. Each bar represents the data for one of the data groups.

## Line Chart

A line chart indicates the variation of a quantity with respect to the two parameters plotted on $X$ and $Y$-axis, respectively. It shows the quantitative information or a relationship between two changing quantities (variables) with a line or curve that connects a series of successive data points.

### Parts of a Line Chart

- **Title** The title of the line chart tells us what the graph is about.

- **Labels** The horizontal label across the bottom and the vertical label along the side tell us what kinds of facts are listed.
- **Scales** The horizontal scale across the bottom and the vertical scale along the side tell us how much or how many kinds of facts are there.
- **Lines** The lines connecting the points give estimates of the values between the points. e.g. various parts of a line graph can be shown with the help of a line graph.

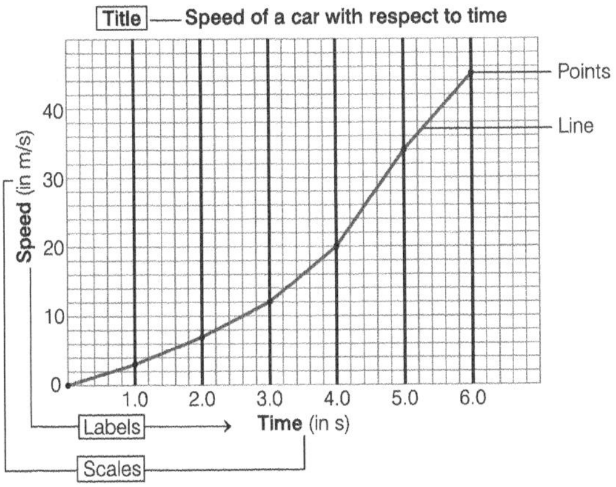


## Pie-Chart

It is a circular chart divided into sectors, in which its arc length, central angle and area are proportional to the quantities that it represents. Here, the total quantity is distributed over a total angle of 360° or 100%.

e.g. Among 18000 patients, the following pie-chart shows percentage breakup of patients suffering from different diseases.

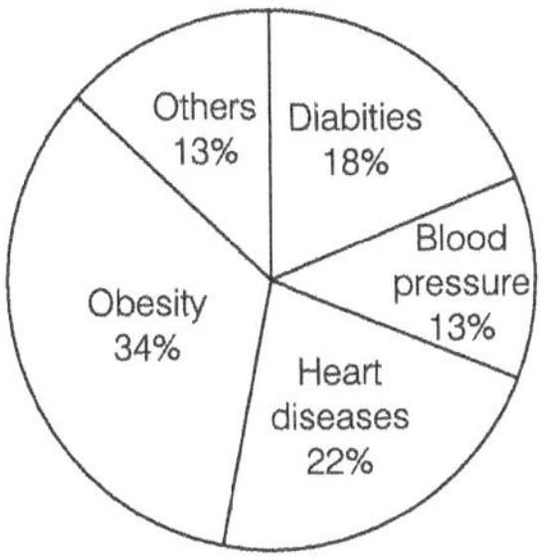


(i) If the data given in pie-chart is specialised in degree, then Value of any sector

$$= \frac{\text{Angle of that sector}}{360°} \times \text{Total value}$$

(ii) If the data given in pie-chart is specialised in percentage, then

Value of any sector

$$= \frac{\text{Percentage of that sector}}{100} \times \text{Total value}$$

# DATA INTERPRETATION

It is a process of analysing and calculating the given or present data to obtain a desired result or reaching a conclusion.

Some scales can be taken to compare the data. They are as follows,

**Nominal Scale** It is also known as nominal data. This is a type of data that is used to label variables without providing any quantitative value. It is the simplest form of a scale of measure.

**Ordinal Scale** It consists two categories that are exclusive and exhaustive but with a logical order. Quality ratings and agreement ratings are examples of ordinal scales.

There are following two types of data analysis

## 1. Qualitative Data Analysis

It is concerned with transforming raw data by searching, evaluating, recognising, coding, mapping, exploring and describing patterns, trends and categories in the raw data, in order to interpret them.

## 2. Quantitative Data Analysis

It is a set of process by which numerical data is analysed. It involves the use of statistical modeling, such as mean, median, frequency distribution, class interval and standard deviation.

The following is a description of some terms for statistical units.

**Class Interval** It refers to the numerical width of any class in a particular distribution.

Mathematically, it is defined as the difference between the upper class limit and the lower class limit.

For example, class interval for the data 1, 2, 2, 3, 3, 4, 5, 5 is 1 to 5 or 1-5, where 1 is lower class limit and 5 is upper class limit.

$\therefore$ Class interval = Upper class limit − Lower class limit

**Class Mark** The middle of a class interval is called a class mark. It is also defined as the average of the upper and lower class limits.

$$\therefore \text{ Class mark} = \frac{\text{Lower class limit} + \text{Upper class limit}}{2}$$

**Frequency** A frequency is the number of times a data value occurs. It is often represented by the letter $f$.

For example, If ten students score 80 in statistics, then the score of 80 has a frequency of 10.

**Mean** The mean or average of a data set is found by adding all the numbers in the data set and then dividing by the number of values in the set.

- If data set is unclassified, then

$$\text{Mean } (\bar{x}) = \frac{\text{Sum of observations}}{\text{Noumber of observations}} = \frac{\Sigma x}{n}$$

- If frequency is given, then

$$\text{Mean } (\bar{x}) = \frac{\Sigma fx}{\Sigma f}$$

Where $x \rightarrow$ observation (term), $n \rightarrow$ number of observations and $f \rightarrow$ frequency.

**Median** If the total number of observations $(n)$ is an odd number, then

$$\text{Median} = \left(\frac{n+1}{2}\right) \text{ term}$$

- If the total number of observations $(n)$ is an even number, then

$$\text{Median} = \frac{\left(\frac{n}{2}\right)^{\text{th}} \text{term} + \left(\frac{n}{2}+1\right)^{\text{th}} \text{term}}{2}$$

**Standard deviation** It is a measure spread of numbers and represented by symbol σ(sigma).

$$\therefore \quad \sigma = \sqrt{\frac{x - \bar{x}}{n}}, \text{ where } \bar{x} \text{ is a mean.}$$

## Principles used in Data Interpretation

The principles used in data interpretation are as below

### 1. Percentage

Percentage is a very useful tool for comparison in the analysis of data.

In percentage, $x\%$ of $y$ = $y\%$ of $x$

e.g. 30% of 50 = 50% of 30

$$\because \quad 30\% \text{ of } 50 = \frac{30 \times 50}{100} = 15$$

$$\text{and} \quad 50\% \text{ of } 30 = \frac{50 \times 30}{100} = 15$$

When a quantity is increased or decreased by same amount, then

(i) Percentage increase in the quantity

$$= \frac{\text{Total increment}}{\text{Initial value}} \times 100\%$$

e.g. If a number 40 is increased by 20, then

$$\text{percentage increase} = \frac{20}{40} \times 100 = 50\%$$

(ii) Percentage decrease in the quantity

$$= \frac{\text{Total decreased}}{\text{Initial value}} \times 100\%$$

e.g. If a number 60 is decreased by 20, then

$$\text{percentage decrease} = \frac{20}{60} \times 100 = 33\frac{1}{3}\%$$

#### Interpretation of Data Involving the Percentage

- To find by how much per cent $x$ is more or less than $y$ (or over $y$) or compared to $y$.

Required percentage

$$= \frac{\text{Value of } x - \text{Value of } y}{\text{Value of } y} \times 100 \text{ (when } x > y)$$

$$= \frac{\text{Value of } y - \text{Value of } x}{\text{Value of } y} \times 100 \text{ (when } x < y)$$

The denominator part contains the value with which the comparison is made.

This concept is also used for percentage change.

When, new number $(x) >$ original number $(y)$.

There is a percentage increase.

When, new number $(x) <$ original number $(y)$.

There is a percentage decrease.

## 2. Average

Average is the middle value that summarizes or represents the general significance of a set of values.

It is defined as

$$\text{Average} = \frac{\text{Sum of all items in the group}}{\text{Number of items in the group}}$$

Average is also called the 'Arithmetic mean' or mean value of all the values.

If $x_1, x_2, x_3, \ldots, x_n$ be $n$ numbers, then their average $= \frac{x_1 + x_2 + x_3 + \ldots + x_n}{n}$

## 3. Ratio

Ratio is compared by division of the measure of two quantities of the same kind.

In other words, ratio is a comparison of two numbers by division. If the two quantities are $x$ and $y$, then ratio of $x$ and $y$ is represented as $\frac{x}{y}$ or $x : y$.

- If a number $x$ is divided into two parts in the ratio of $a:b$, then first part $= \frac{a}{a+b} \times x$ and second part $= \frac{b}{a+b} \times x$.
- If a number $x$ is divided into three parts in the ratio of $a : b: c$, then first part $= \frac{a}{a+b+c} \times x$, second part $= \frac{b}{a+b+c} \times x$ and third part $= \frac{c}{a+b+c} \times x$.

## 4. Profit/Loss and Discount

The concepts of Profit/Loss and Discount play a very important role in trade and business. Whenever a purchased item is sold, then either profit is earned or loss is incurred.

- **Profit** If a person sells an article at price greater than the cost price, then he gets profit.

$$\text{Profit} = \text{SP} - \text{CP}$$

$$\text{Profit per cent} = \frac{\text{SP} - \text{CP}}{\text{CP}} \times 100\%$$

$$\text{SP} = \text{CP}\left(\frac{100 + \text{profit\%}}{100}\right)$$

and

$$\text{CP} = \text{SP}\left(\frac{100}{100 + \text{profit\%}}\right)$$

- **Loss** If a person sells an article at price less than the cost price, then he gets loss.

$$\text{Loss} = \text{CP} - \text{SP}$$

$$\text{Loss per cent} = \frac{\text{CP} - \text{SP}}{\text{CP}} \times 100\%$$

$$\text{SP} = \text{CP}\left(\frac{100 - \text{loss \%}}{100}\right)$$

and

$$\text{CP} = \text{SP}\left(\frac{100}{100 - \text{loss \%}}\right)$$

### Discount

If a person sells an article at price less than its marked price, then he actually gives a discount.

If marked price of an article is ₹$x$ and discount given by shopkeeper is $a$ %, then

$$\text{SP} = x\left(1 - \frac{a}{100}\right)$$

or

$$x = \text{SP}\left(\frac{100}{100 - a}\right)$$

- If marked price of an article is ₹$x$ and successive discounts given by shopkeeper are $a$%, $b$% and $c$ % respectively, then

$$\text{SP} = x\left(1 - \frac{a}{100}\right)\left(1 - \frac{b}{100}\right)\left(1 - \frac{c}{100}\right)$$

and

$$x = \text{SP}\left(\frac{100}{100 - a}\right)\left(\frac{100}{100 - b}\right)\left(\frac{100}{100 - c}\right)$$

Solved examples from various topics of DI are given below

## 1. Data Table

**Directions** (Example Nos. 1-4) Read the table and answer the questions. The following table gives demand and supply of sugar in million tonnes, for the period 2007 to 2012. Surplus is defined as excess of supply over demand.

**[UGC NET 2012]**

| Year | Demand | Supply |
|---|---|---|
| 2007 | 43.3 | 46.4 |
| 2008 | 47.2 | 47.8 |
| 2009 | 49.5 | 50.7 |
| 2010 | 53.4 | 54.2 |
| 2011 | 54.5 | 57.3 |
| 2012 | 62.7 | 63.4 |

**1** In how many years, the supply (in million tonnes) of sugar was more than the average supply for 2007 to 2012?

(A) 5 (B) 2 (C) 3 (D) 4

***Sol.*** *(C)* Average supply of sugar from the year 2007 to 2012

$$= \frac{[46.4 + 47.8 + 50.7 + 54.2 + 57.3 + 63.4]}{6}$$

$$= \frac{319.8}{6} = 53.3 \text{ million tonnes}$$

∴ In three years *viz.* 2010, 2011 and 2012, supply of sugar was more than the average supply.

**2** The average surplus (in million tonnes) of sugar for the period 2008 to 2012 is

(A) 1.44 (B) 1.84 (C) 1.53 (D) 1.22

***Sol.*** *(D)* Surplus of sugar in

$$2008 = 47.8 - 47.2 = 0.6$$
$$2009 = 50.7 - 49.5 = 1.2$$
$$2010 = 54.2 - 53.4 = 0.8$$
$$2011 = 57.3 - 54.5 = 2.8$$
$$2012 = 63.4 - 62.7 = 0.7$$

∴ Required average surplus

$$= \frac{0.6 + 1.2 + 0.8 + 2.8 + 0.7}{5}$$

$$= \frac{6.1}{5} = 1.22 \text{ million tonnes}$$

**3** The surplus of sugar was lowest for the year

(A) 2012 (B) 2008
(C) 2009 (D) 2010

***Sol.*** *(B)* It is clear from above solutions that surplus of sugar was lowest for the year 2008.

**4** The percentage increase in demand of sugar was the lowest as compared to its previous year in

(A) 2011 (B) 2008
(C) 2009 (D) 2010

***Sol.*** *(A)* Percentage increase in demand of sugar as compared to its previous year in

$$2008 = \frac{47.2 - 43.3}{43.3} \times 100\% = 9\%$$

$$2009 = \frac{49.5 - 47.2}{47.2} \times 100\%$$

$$= 4.8\% \approx 5\%$$

$$2010 = \frac{53.4 - 49.5}{49.5} \times 100\%$$

$$= 7.88\% \approx 8\%$$

$$2011 = \frac{54.5 - 53.4}{53.4} \times 100\%$$

$$= 2.05\% \approx 2\%$$

Thus, percentage increase was lowest in the year 2011.

**Directions** (Example Nos. 5-7) The following table shows the number of people in different age groups who responded to a survey about their favourite style of music. Use this information to answer the questions that follow.

**[UGC NET 2016]**

| Style of Music \ Age | Number of People | | |
|---|---|---|---|
| | Years 15-20 | Years 21-30 | Years 31+ |
| Classical | 6 | 4 | 17 |
| Pop | 7 | 5 | 5 |
| Rock | 6 | 12 | 14 |
| Jazz | 1 | 4 | 11 |
| Blues | 2 | 3 | 15 |
| Hip-hop | 9 | 3 | 4 |
| Ambient | 2 | 2 | 2 |

**5** Approximately what percentage of the total people were aged 21-30?

(A) 31% (B) 23%
(C) 25% (D) 14%

***Sol.*** *(C)* Total sample of (15 - 20)

$$= 6 + 7 + 6 + 1 + 2 + 9 + 2 = 33$$

Total sample of (21-30)

$= 4+5+12+4+3+3+2=33$

Total sample of 31 +

$= 17+5+14+11+15+4+2=68$

∴ Required percentage

$= \frac{33}{134} \times 100\%$

$= 24.62\% \approx 25\%$

**6** Approximately what percentage of the total people indicates that Hip-hop is their favourite style of music?

(A) 6% (B) 8%

(C) 14% (D) 12%

***Sol.*** *(D)* Required percentage $= \frac{9+3+4}{134} \times 100\%$

$= \frac{16}{134} \times 100\% \approx 12\%$

**7** What percentage of respondents aged 31+ indicated a favourite style other than classical music?

(A) 64% (B) 60%

(C) 75% (D) 50%

***Sol.*** *(C)* Required percentage $= \frac{68-17}{68} \times 100\%$

$= \frac{51}{68} \times 100\% = 75\%$

**Directions** (Example Nos. 8-13) Given below in the table is the decadal data of Population and Electrical Power Production of a country.

**[UGC NET 2015]**

| Year | Population (million) | Electrical Power Production (GW)* |
|---|---|---|
| 1951 | 20 | 10 |
| 1961 | 21 | 20 |
| 1971 | 24 | 25 |
| 1981 | 27 | 40 |
| 1991 | 30 | 50 |
| 2001 | 32 | 80 |
| 2011 | 35 | 100 |
| | | *1 GW = 1000 million watt |

Based on the given table, answer the questions below.

**8** In which decade, the average power availability per person was maximum?

(A) 1971-1981 (B) 1981-1991

(C) 1991-2001 (D) 2001-2011

***Sol.*** *(D)* Average power availability per person in the year 2001-2011

$= \frac{1}{2}\left[\frac{80 \times 1000}{32} + \frac{100 \times 1000}{35}\right]$

$\approx \frac{1}{2}(2500 + 2857) = \frac{5357}{2} = 2678.5 \text{ W}$

Similarly, in year

1991-2001 = 2083.5 W

1981-1991 = 1574 W

1971-1981 = 1261.5 W

It is clear from the above detail that average power availability per person was maximum in the year 2001-2011.

**9** By what percentage the power production increased from 1951 to 2011?

(A) 900% (B) 100%

(C) 300% (D) 600%

***Sol.*** *(A)* Power production increased from 1951-2011

$= \frac{(100-10)}{10} \times 100\%$

$= 900\%$

**10** Average decadal growth rate (%) of the population is

(A) ~5% (B) ~12.21%

(C) ~9.82% (D) ~6.73%

***Sol.*** *(C)* Percentage increase in between 1951 to 1961

$= \frac{21-20}{20} \times 100\%$

$= \frac{100}{20}\% = 5\%$

Percentage increase in between 1961-1971

$= \frac{24-21}{21} \times 100\%$

$= \frac{3}{21} \times 100\% = 14.29\%$

Percentage increase in between 1971-1981

$= \frac{27-24}{24} \times 100\%$

$= \frac{3}{24} \times 100\% = 12.50\%$

Percentage increase in between 1981-1991

$= \frac{30-27}{27} \times 100\%$

$= \frac{3}{27} \times 100\% = 11.11\%$

Percentage increase in between 1991-2001

$= \frac{32 - 30}{30} \times 100\%$

$= \frac{2}{30} \times 100\% = 6.67\%$

Percentage increase in between 2001-2011

$= \frac{35 - 32}{32} \times 100\%$

$= \frac{3}{32} \times 100\% = 9.38\%$

Average of percentage growth rate

$= \frac{1}{6} (5.00 + 14.29 + 12.50 + 11.11 + 6.67 + 9.38)$

$= \frac{1}{6} \times 58.95$

$= 9.825\% \approx 9.82\%$

Average decadal growth rate ≈ 9.82%

**11** In the year 1951, what was the power availability per person?

(A) 500 W (B) 100 W
(C) 200 W (D) 400 W

***Sol.*** *(A)* Power availability per person in the year 1951

$= \frac{10 \times 1000}{20} = \frac{1000}{2} = 500 \text{ W}$

**12** Which decade registered from the maximum growth rate (%) of population?

(A) 2001-2011 (B) 1961-1971
(C) 1971-1981 (D) 1991-2001

***Sol.*** *(B)* The maximum growth rate of population was in the year (1961-1971).

**13** Based on the average decadal growth rate, what will be the population in the year 2021?

(A) 36.62 million
(B) 40.34 million
(C) 38.49 million
(D) 37.28 million

***Sol.*** *(C)* We know that, average decadal growth rate = 9.82%

∴ Population in year 2021

$= \left(35 + 35 \times \frac{9.82}{100}\right)$ million

$= 38.437 \approx 38.49$ million

## Histogram

**1** Adjoining figure is the histogram of marks obtained in an examination of total marks 1000 and minimum pass marks is 300. The number of students who got more than or equal to 80% of marks are

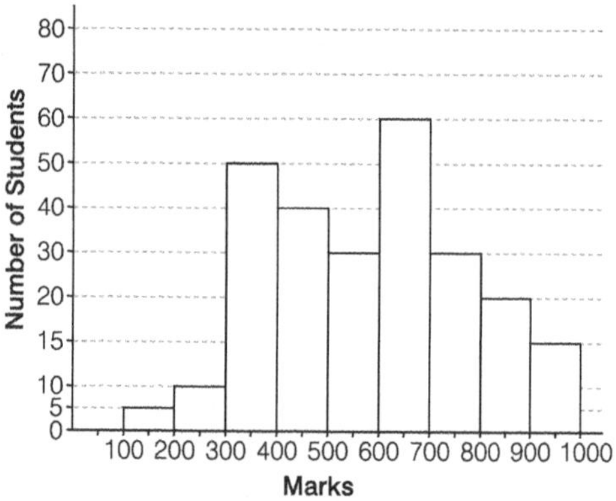


(A) 20 (B) 70 (C) 35 (D) 275

***Sol.*** *(C)* Number of students who got more than or equal to 80% (i.e. more than or equal to 800 marks) is $= 20 + 15 = 35$

**2** Adjoining histogram of weekly wages of 4300 workers. Ratio of the number of workers receiving less than or equal to ₹ 500 wages to the number of workers receiving more than or equal to ₹ 600 is

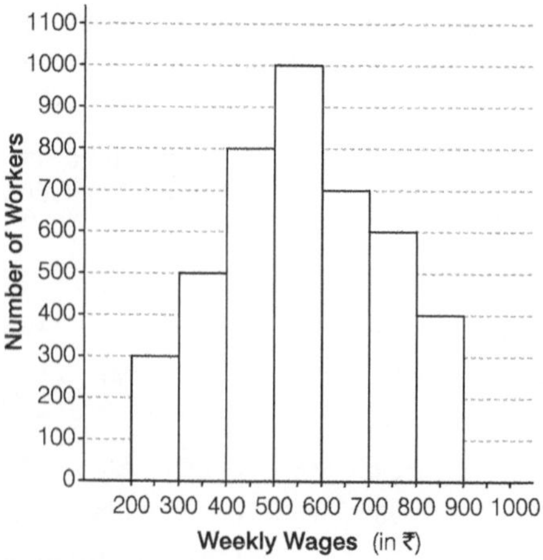


(A) 17 : 16 (B) 16 : 17
(C) 9 : 11 (D) 17 : 19

***Sol.*** *(B)* The number of workers receiving less than or equal to ₹ 500

= 300 + 500 + 800 = 1600

Total number of workers receiving more than or equal to ₹ 600

= 700 + 600 + 400 = 1700

∴ Required ratio = 1600 : 1700 = 16 : 17

**Directions** (Example Nos. 3-7) Study the following histogram and answer the questions.

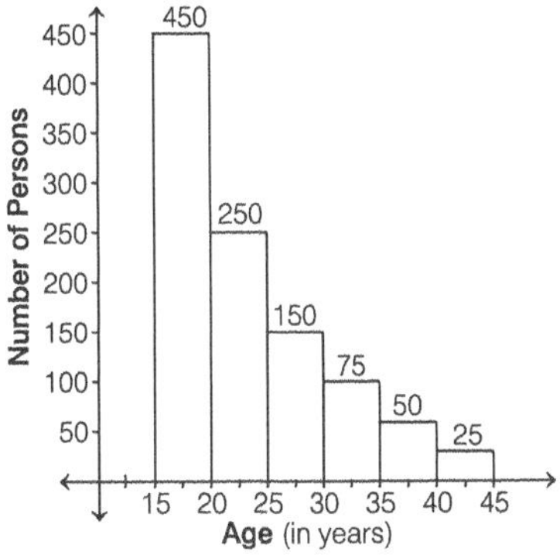


**3** The total number of persons in the age group of 15 yr to 45 yr is

(A) 450 (B) 800
(C) 1000 (D) 500

***Sol.*** *(C)* Total number of persons

= 450 + 250 + 150 + 75 + 50 + 25

= 1000

**4** The number of persons in the age group (20-30) yr is

(A) 475 (B) 400
(C) 300 (D) 700

***Sol.*** *(B)* Number of persons = 250 + 150 = 400

**5** The ratio of the number of persons between the age group of (20-25) and (30-35) yr is

(A) 1 : 3 (B) 2 : 1 (C) 10 : 3 (D) 6 : 1

***Sol.*** *(C)* Required ratio = 250 : 75 = 10 : 3

**6** The ratio of maximum population in an age group to the total number of persons under study is

(A) 4 : 5 (B) 9 : 10
(C) 9 : 20 (D) 2 : 5

***Sol.*** *(C)* Maximum population = 450

Total population = 1000

Required ratio = $\frac{450}{1000} = \frac{9}{20}$ or 9 : 20

**7** The percentage of population under study which is in the age group of (40-45) yr is

(A) 2.5 (B) 3.5 (C) 1.5 (D) 5

***Sol.*** *(A)* Required percentage = $\frac{25}{1000} \times 100 = 2.5\%$

**Directions** (Example Nos. 8-12) In the graph, classification show as per age, patients admitted in hospital in a day. Study the graph carefully and answer the question.

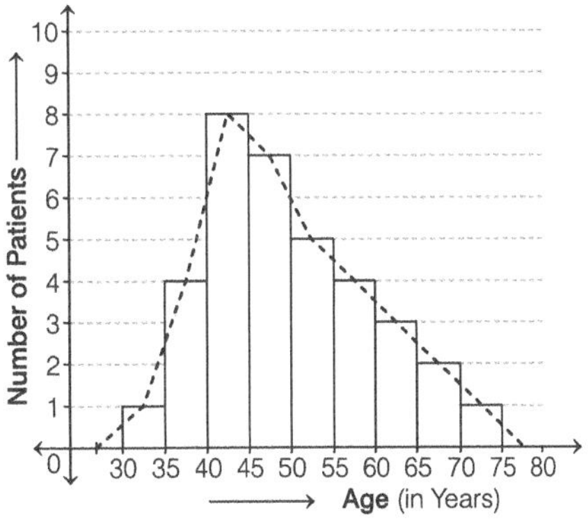


**8** Find total number of patients between 55 yr to 60 yr, admitted in hospital in a day.

(A) 6 (B) 4 (C) 28 (D) 8

***Sol.*** *(B)* From graph, it is clear that the number of patients between 55 to 60 yr = 4

**9** Find total number of patients who is more than 55 yr of age admitted in hospital.

(A) 4 (B) 7 (C) 10 (D) 9

***Sol.*** *(C)* From graph, it is clear that the number of patients who are more than 55 yr, admitted in hospital

= 4 + 3 + 2 + 1 = 10

**10** Find total number of patients who is more than 40 yr but less than 55 yr of age, admitted in hospital.

(A) 20 (B) 30
(C) 15 (D) 12

***Sol.*** *(A)* From graph, it is clear that the number of patients who are more than 40 yr but less than 55 yr = 8 + 7 + 5 = 20.

**11** Percentage of patients of age less than 45 yr, who got admitted to the hospital on that day is approximately equal to

(A) 14% (B) 20% (C) 37% (D) 62%

***Sol.*** *(C)* From graph, it is clear that the total number of patients = 1+ 4 + 8 + 7 + 5 + 4 + 3 + 2 + 1 = 35

Number of patients who are less than 45 yr of age

$= 1 + 4 + 8 = 13$

∴ Required percentage

$= \frac{13}{35} \times 100\% = \frac{13}{7} \times 20\%$

$= \frac{260}{7}\% = 37.14\% \approx 37\%$

**12** About 11% of the patients who got admitted to the hospital on that particular day were of age

(A) either between 35 yr and 40 yr or between 55 yr and 60 yr
(B) between 60 yr and 65 yr
(C) between 35 yr and 40 yr
(D) between 35 yr and 40 yr and between 55 yr and 60 yr

***Sol.*** *(D)* From graph, it is clear that the total number of patients between 35 yr and 40 yr and between 55 yr and 60 yr = 4 and total number of patients = 35

∴ Required percentage $= \frac{4}{35} \times 100\% = \frac{4}{7} \times 20\%$

$= \frac{80}{7}\% = 11.42\% \approx 11\%$

## Bar Graph

**Directions** (Example Nos. 1-3) A watch company produces four different products. The sale of these products in lakh during 2005 and 2010 are shown in the following bar diagram. Study the graph and answer the questions.

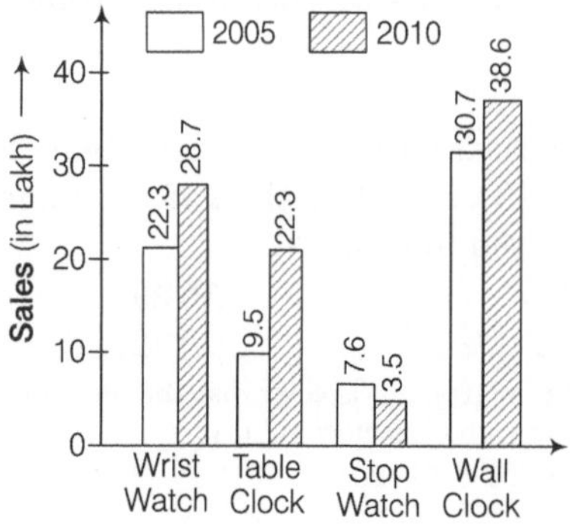


**1** The sales in percentage of wrist watch in 2010 more than the sales of table clock in 2010 was nearly by

(A) 26.7% (B) 27.7%
(C) 28.7% (D) 21.7%

***Sol.*** *(C)* The sales in percentage

$= \frac{28.7 - 22.3}{22.3} \times 100\% = 28.69\% \text{ or } 28.7\%$

**2** The ratio of sales of stop watch in 2010 to the sale of table clock in 2005 is

(A) 6 : 19 (B) 7 : 6 (C) 19 : 6 (D) 7 : 19

***Sol.*** *(D)* Ratio of sale of stopwatch in 2010 to the sale of table clock in 2005

$= \frac{3.5}{9.5} = 7 : 19$

**3** The sales of table clock in 2005 was less than the sales of wall clock in 2005 is nearly by

(A) 70.05% (B) 69.05%
(C) 68.05% (D) 62.05%

***Sol.*** *(B)* Required percentage $= \frac{30.7 - 9.5}{30.7} \times 100\,\%$

$= 69.05\%$

**Directions** (Example Nos. 4-9) Study the following chart and answer the questions given below the chart.

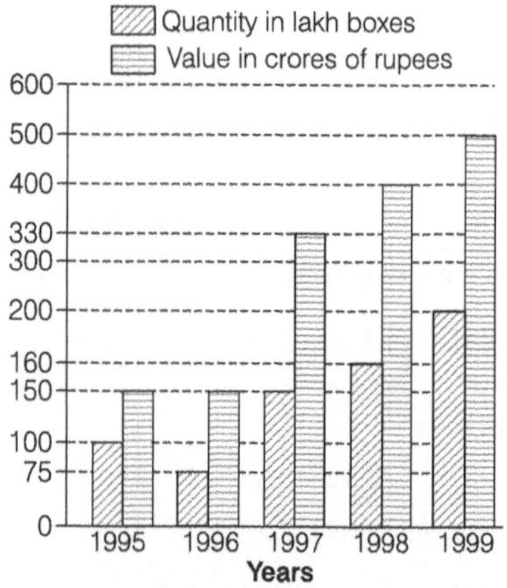


**4** If in the year 1998, the boxes were exported at the same rate per box as that in 1997, what would be the value (in crores of ₹) of export in 1998?

(A) 330 (B) 400 (C) 352 (D) 375

**Sol.** *(C)* Per box export rate in 1997 = $\frac{330 \times 10000000}{150 \times 100000}$ = 220

Now, boxes exported in the year 1998 = 160 lakh

∴ Export value in 1998 = 160 × 2.2 = 352 crore

**5** What is the difference between boxes (in lakhs) exported in the years 1996 and 1997?

(A) 50 (B) 25
(C) 100 (D) None of these

**Sol.** *(D)* Number of boxes exported in year 1997 = 150 and number of boxes exported in year 1996 = 75

∴ Required difference = 150 − 75 = 75 lakh

**6** In which year was the value per box the minimum?

(A) 1996 (B) 1998
(C) 1999 (D) 1995

**Sol.** *(D)* Per box value in 1995 = $\frac{15000}{100}$ = ₹ 150

Per box value in 1996 = $\frac{15000}{75}$ = ₹ 200

Per box value in 1997 = $\frac{33000}{150}$ = ₹ 220

Per box value in 1998 = $\frac{40000}{160}$ = ₹ 250

Per box value in 1999 = $\frac{50000}{200}$ = ₹ 250

So, it is clear from above that the value of per box was minimum in the year 1995.

**7** What is the difference between the boxes exported in the years 1997 and 1998?

(A) 100000 (B) 1000000
(C) 10 (D) 1000

**Sol.** *(C)* Boxes exported in the year 1998 = 160 lakh

Boxes exported in the year 1997 = 150 lakh

∴ Required difference = (160 − 150) = 10 lakh

**8** What was the approximate percentage increase in export value from the year 1995 to 1999?

(A) 375 (B) 200
(C) 233.3 (D) None of these

**Sol.** *(C)* Export value in 1995 = ₹ 150 crore

Export value in 1999 = ₹ 500 crore

∴ Required percentage increase

$$= \frac{500 - 150}{150} \times 100\%$$

$$= \frac{350}{150} \times 100\% = 233.33\%$$

**9** What was the percentage drop in export quantity from the years 1995 to 1996?

(A) 75 (B) 25
(C) 50 (D) None of these

**Sol.** *(B)* Quantity of export in 1995 = 100 lakh box

Quantity of export in 1996 = 75 lakh box

∴ Required percentage drop in export quantity

$$= \frac{75 - 100}{100} \times 100\% = \frac{-25}{100} \times 100\% = -25\%$$

Here, negative sign shows the percentage drop in export quantity.

## Line Chart

This information can be represented by the line graph which is shown below

**1** The adjoining diagram is frequency polygon for the scores of students in a test. What is the total number of students appeared in the test?

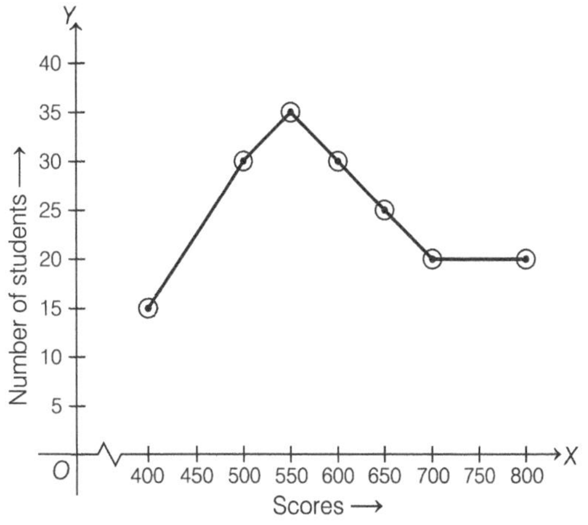


(A) 250 (B) 175 (C) 180 (D) 200

**Sol.** *(B)* From the figure,

Total number of students

= 15 + (30 × 2) + 35 + 25 + (20 × 2)

= 15 + 60 + 35 + 25 + 40

= 175 students

**Directions** (Example Nos. 2-5) A motorist and a scooterist made a journey of 120 km at the same time and from the same place. The graph shows the progress of the journey made by each person. Study the graph and answer the question.

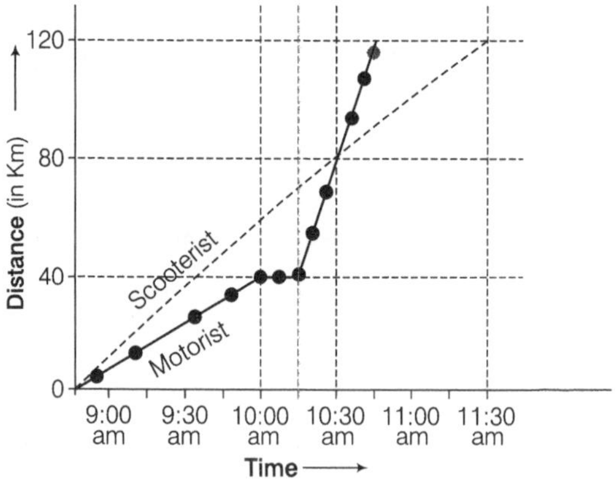


**2** At what time, did the motorist meet the scooterist?

(A) 10 : 30 am (B) 10 : 45 am
(C) 10 : 15 am (D) 10 : 20 am

***Sol.*** *(A)* Motorist and scooterist meet at 10 : 30 am. Since, both lines are intersecting at 10 : 30 am.

**3** What was the speed of the scooterist (in km/h) during the journey?

(A) 45 (B) 48 (C) 42 (D) 46

***Sol.*** *(B)* Total time taken $= 2\frac{1}{2}$ h

$\therefore$ Speed of scooterist $= \frac{120}{5/2} = 48$ km/h

$\left(\because \text{Speed} = \frac{\text{Distance}}{\text{Time}}\right)$

**4** The scooterist completes the journey in

(A) 3 h (B) 2 h
(C) $2\frac{1}{2}$ h (D) $3\frac{1}{2}$ h

***Sol.*** *(C)* From the diagram, scooterist completes the journey in $2\frac{1}{2}$ h.

**5** How far, from the start (in km), did the motorist meet the scooterist?

(A) 75 (B) 70 (C) 90 (D) 80

***Sol.*** *(D)* From the graph, motorist and scooterist meet at a distance of 80 km.

## Pie Chart

**Directions** (Example Nos. 1 and 2) Study the following pie chart carefully to answer the questions that follows.

Percentagewise distribution of teachers who teach six different subjects

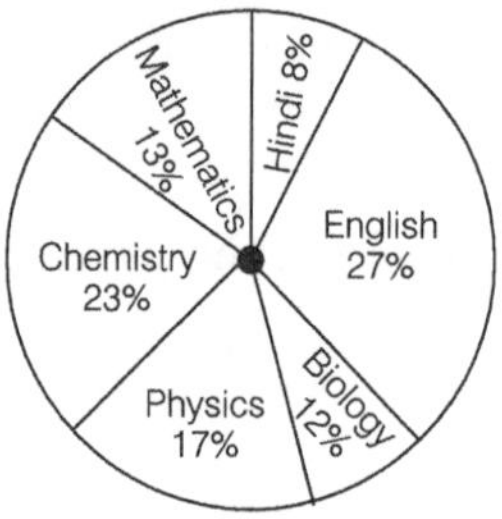


**Total number of teachers = 1800**

**1** If two-ninth of the teachers who teach Physics, are female, then number of male Physics teachers is approximately what per cent of the total number of teachers who teach Chemistry?

(A) 57% (B) 42% (C) 63% (D) 69%

***Sol.*** *(A)* Number of teachers in Physics

$= 1800 \times \frac{17}{100} = 306$

Female teachers in Physics $= 306 \times \frac{2}{9} = 68$

Male teachers in Physics $= 306 - 68 = 238$

Number of teachers in Chemistry

$= 1800 \times \frac{23}{100} = 414$

$\therefore$ Required percentage $= \frac{238}{414} \times 100\% \approx 57\%$

**2** What is the total number of teachers teaching Chemistry, English and Biology?

(A) 1226 (B) 1116 (C) 1176 (D) 998

***Sol.*** *(B)* Total number of teachers teaching Chemistry, English and Biology $= 1800 \times \frac{(23+27+12)}{100} = 1116$

**Directions** (Example Nos. 3-7) The following pie chart shows the expenditure incurred on the construction of a house in a city. Study the chart and answer the following questions.

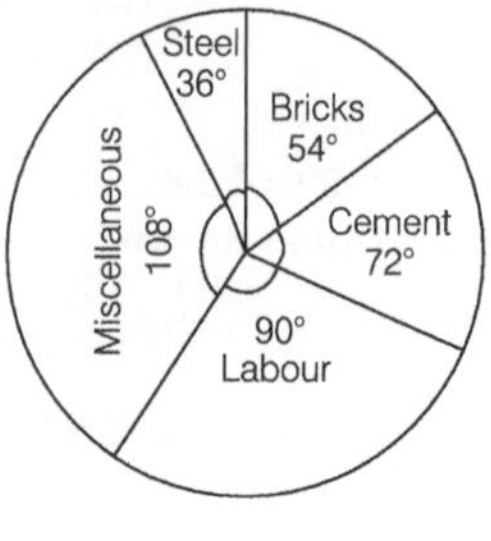

**3** The mean of the expenditure is on

(A) brick (B) cement (C) steel (D) labour

***Sol.*** *(B)* Mean expenditure = $\frac{360^\circ}{5} = 72^\circ$ i.e., cement

**4** The ratio expenditure on Steel, Cement and Bricks is

(A) 2 : 4 : 3 (B) 4 : 2 : 3
(C) 3 : 2 : 4 (D) 4 : 3 : 2

***Sol.*** *(A)* Required ratio = 36 : 72 : 54 = 2 : 4 : 3

**5** The highest expenditure percentage is

(A) 40% (B) 30% (C) 45% (D) 60%

***Sol.*** *(B)* Highest expenditure in percentage = $\frac{100}{360} \times 108^\circ$

$= 30\%$

**6** What part of expenditure on labour is in respect of total expenditure?

(A) $\frac{3}{10}$ part (B) $\frac{5}{8}$ part
(C) $\frac{1}{4}$ part (D) $\frac{7}{18}$ part

***Sol.*** *(C)* Part of labour expenditure to total expenditure

$= \frac{90}{360} = \frac{1}{4}$ part

**7** Of the total expenditure the percentage of expenditure on steel and bricks together is

(A) 90% (B) 20%
(C) 25% (D) 30%

***Sol.*** *(C)* Total per cent expenditure on steel and bricks

$= \frac{100}{360} \times (36 + 54)$

$= \frac{100}{360} \times 90 = 25\%$

# DATA MAPPING

Data mapping is defined as the relationship between two data systems. Data mapping connects two different types of data models together. It is a process of finding out as how an application or database connects to another application or database.

**For example,** Suppose there are two different databases, out of which one contains the list of names of persons in an organisation and other contains the list of their phone numbers.

Now, if we wish to connect both of the lists together, we will take the help of data mapping applications or softwares.

## Data Mapping Task

All the tasks under data mapping fall into two categories. These are

1. **Data Migration** This process focuses on mainly moving information from one data model to another data model. It creates a way between source data model and the destination data model.

   This way is facilitated by data mapping software which makes the migration process easy and efficient.

   For example, Suppose, if we want to move all the data that contains contact number, text messages and photos from one mobile to another, we use a software or a feature like bluetooth to get the job done. This is how data migration works.

2. **Data Integration** This process mainly focuses on new information. It creates a way between a new data model and an old data model and makes them connected to each other.

   By connecting both of the data models it becomes easier to access data from both of the sources.

# DATA AND GOVERNANCE

Data governance is a four way framework comprising availability, applicability, integrity and security. It is a set of processes, used by the stakeholders who use technology, to ensure that the important and critical data is managed and protected.

It involves a streamlined coordination for individuals, methods and innovation (technology) in such an order that it results in realising the value of data for any organisation. It has to be implemented as a disciplined work flow within the organisation, without that disciplines data would never be treated as a valuable commodity.

## Importance of Data and Governance

Data governance is required to ensure that an organisation's information assets are formly, properly, proactively and efficiently managed throughout the enterprise to secure its trust and accountability data governance comprises the collecting of data, revising and standardising it and making it good for use.

It makes the data consistent. It ensures that critical data is available at the right time to the right person, in a standardised and reliable form. Adopting and implementing data governance can result in improved productivity and efficiency of an organisation.

## Tools of Data and Governance

It is becoming very important to monitor business data for hacking and controlling it to meet regulatory standards.

A quality data governance program should include a governing body that defines procedures and creates an executable plan.

Data governance tools helps you to handle your data and ensure it to meet regulations. Some of the data governance tools available in the market are as follows

- TAG INSPECTOR
- ACAVEO
- AGILITY
- A.K.A
- ASIGRA
- CLEARSWIFT

## Data Sufficiency

Data sufficiency covers many different topics of quantitative aptitude. In data sufficiency, a question is followed by two or three statements.

You need to determine whether any of the statements individually or together are required to find the answer.

You are not required to do the complete solution, you just have to check whether with the help of given data you can find the required answer or not.

### Examples

**Directions** (Example Nos. 1-2) In each of the questions below consists of a question and two or three statements given below it. Read the question carefully and determine which of the given statements is/are necessary to answer the question.

**1** What is the two-digit number?

I. The digit in ten's place is 4 more than the digit in the unit's place.

II. The difference between the original number and the number obtained by interchanging the digits is 36.

(A) Only I
(B) Only II
(C) Both the statements
(D) None of the above

***Sol.*** *(D)* Let one's and ten's digit of the 2-digit number be $x$ and $y$ respectively.

From Statement I, $y = x + 4$

$\Rightarrow \quad y - x = 4$

From Statement II,

$(10y + x) - (10x + y) = 36$

$\Rightarrow \quad y - x = \frac{36}{9} = 4$

Now, if we see each of the statements separately, we find same equation.

Hence, we can't find the answer even by using both the statements together.

**2** What is the present age of Rahul?

I. The present age of Rahul is half of his father's age.

II. After five years, the ratio of ages of Rahul and his father is 4 : 7.

III. Rahul is younger to his brother by five years.

(A) I and II
(B) II and III
(C) All of these
(D) Cannot be determined

***Sol.*** *(A)* From the Statement I;

Let the father's age be $2x$ yr, then Rahul's age will be $x$ yr.

From the Statement II;

$$\frac{x + 5}{2x + 5} = \frac{4}{7}$$

$\Rightarrow \quad 7x + 35 = 8x + 20$

$\Rightarrow \quad 8x - 7x = 35 - 20$

$\Rightarrow \quad x = 15$

From Statement III : We cannot create any relation.

Therefore, with the helps of only I and II, present age of Rahul is 15 yr.

# Chapter Practice

## Classification of Data

1 Which type of data represents the temperature of different cities in a particular day?
(A) Quantitative data (B) Qualitative data
(C) Analytical data (D) None of these

2 Which of the following is a primary data source?
(A) Photograph collection
(B) News paper
(C) Articles
(D) None of the above

3 Taste, feel, texture etc. are kinds of which type of data?
(A) Quantitative data
(B) Qualitative data
(C) Both (A) and (B)
(D) None of the above

4 .......... software converts the data into electronic data interchange file format.
(A) Data planning
(B) Data collecting
(C) Data Mining
(D) Data Mapping

5 A data governance programme is usually adopted to maintain the ....... the data of an organisation.
(A) availability (B) Integrity
(C) security (D) All of these

## Table Chart

**Directions** (Q. Nos. 6-10) Classification of 100 students based on the marks obtained by them in Physics and Chemistry in an Examination.

| Subject / Marks out of 50 | 40 and above | 30 and above | 20 and above | 10 and above | 0 and above |
|---|---|---|---|---|---|
| Physics | 9 | 23 | 80 | 92 | 100 |
| Chemistry | 4 | 21 | 66 | 81 | 100 |
| **Average** (Aggregate) | 7 | 27 | 73 | 87 | 100 |

6 What is the difference between the number of students passed with 30 as cut-off marks in Chemistry and those passed with 30 as cut-off marks in aggregate?
(A) 3 (B) 4 (C) 5 (D) 6

7 If atleast 60% marks in Physics are required for pursuing higher studies in Physics, how many students will be eligible to pursue higher studies in Physics?
(A) 27 (B) 32 (C) 34 (D) 41

8 The percentage of number of students getting at least 60% marks in Chemistry over those getting at least 40% marks in aggregate, is approximately
(A) 21% (B) 27% (C) 29% (D) 31%

9 The number of students scoring less than 40% marks in aggregate is
(A) 13 (B) 19
(C) 20 (D) 27

10 If it is known that at least 23 students were eligible for a Symposium on Chemistry, then the minimum qualifying marks in Chemistry for eligibility to Symposium would lie in the range
(A) 40-45 (B) 30-40
(C) 20-30 (D) Below 20

**Directions** (Q. Nos. 11-15) The following table gives the sales of batteries manufactured by a company over the years.

**Number of Different Types of Batteries Sold by a Company Over the Years** (Numbers in thousand)

| Years / Types of Batteries | 4 AH | 7 AH | 32 AH | 35 AH | 55 AH | Total |
|---|---|---|---|---|---|---|
| 1992 | 75 | 144 | 114 | 102 | 108 | 543 |
| 1993 | 90 | 126 | 102 | 84 | 126 | 528 |
| 1994 | 96 | 114 | 75 | 105 | 135 | 525 |
| 1995 | 105 | 90 | 150 | 90 | 75 | 510 |
| 1996 | 90 | 75 | 135 | 75 | 90 | 465 |
| 1997 | 105 | 60 | 165 | 45 | 120 | 495 |
| 1998 | 115 | 85 | 160 | 100 | 145 | 605 |

**11** What was the approximate percentage increase in the sales of 55 AH batteries in 1998 compared to that in 1992?
(A) 28% (B) 31% (C) 33% (D) 34%

**12** The total sales of all the seven years is the maximum for which battery?
(A) 4 AH (B) 7 AH
(C) 32 AH (D) 35 AH

**13** What is the difference in the number of 35 AH batteries sold in 1993 and 1997?
(A) 24000 (B) 28000
(C) 35000 (D) 39000

**14** The percentage of 4 AH batteries sold to the total number of batteries sold was maximum in the year?
(A) 1994 (B) 1995 (C) 1996 (D) 1997

**15** In case of which battery there was a continuous decrease in sales from 1992 to 1997?
(A) 4 AH (B) 7 AH
(C) 32 AH (D) 35 AH

**Directions** (Q. Nos. 16-20) Study the following table carefully and answer the questions given below.

**Details of Sales and Profit of Six Booksellers in Two Years**

| Booksellers | Number of outlets | | Average sales (in ₹ lakh) per outlet | | Total profit (in ₹ lakh) of all the outlets | |
|---|---|---|---|---|---|---|
| | 2010 | 2011 | 2010 | 2011 | 2010 | 2011 |
| P | 2 | 3 | 50 | 55 | 40 | 60 |
| Q | 4 | 6 | 170 | 180 | 125 | 200 |
| R | 1 | 3 | 60 | 70 | 40 | 50 |
| S | 5 | 6 | 90 | 120 | 120 | 180 |
| T | 3 | 4 | 180 | 175 | 150 | 160 |
| U | 5 | 5 | 40 | 30 | 15 | 15 |

**16** Profitability is the ratio of profit to sales. For which bookseller was the profitability per outlet the highest in 2010?
(A) *P* (B) *Q* (C) *R* (D) *S*

**17** Which bookseller experienced the highest percentage increase in profits per outlet in 2011 over that in 2010?
(A) *T* (B) *Q* (C) *P* (D) *S*

**18** Profit is equal to total sales (sales of all outlets) minus total investment. What was the total investment of *U* in 2010?
(A) ₹ 190 lakh (B) ₹ 165 lakh
(C) ₹ 185 lakh (D) ₹ 150 lakh

**19** For which bookseller had the total sales been the highest in 2010?
(A) *P* (B) *Q*
(C) *T* (D) *R*

**20** What was the ratio of percentage increase in sales to the percentage increase in profits for *S* in all the outlets in 2011 over 2010?
(A) 8 : 9 (B) 11 : 13
(C) 17 : 19 (D) 6 : 5

**Directions** (Q. Nos. 21-25) Study the following table carefully and answer the questions given below.

**Number of Males and Females staying in various Societies**

| Societies | Males | Females |
|---|---|---|
| A | 250 | 350 |
| B | 400 | 150 |
| C | 300 | 275 |
| D | 280 | 300 |
| E | 180 | 250 |
| F | 325 | 300 |

**Percentage of Children**
(Males and Females in the Societies)

| Societies | Children | Male Children | Female Children |
|---|---|---|---|
| A | 25% | 40% | 60% |
| B | 40% | 75% | 25% |
| C | 16% | 25% | 75% |
| D | 25% | 80% | 20% |
| E | 40% | 50% | 50% |
| F | 24% | 46% | 54% |

**21** What is the respective ratio of the number of adult females to the total number of female children staying in all the societies together?
(A) 243 : 82 (B) 112 : 71
(C) 82 : 243 (D) 71 : 112

**22** What is the total number of female children staying in all the societies together?
(A) 314 (B) 433
(C) 410 (D) 343

**23** What is the respective ratio of the total number of adult males in societies *A* and *B* together to the total number of adult males in societies *E* and *F* together?
(A) 75 : 79 (B) 14 : 17
(C) 79 : 75 (D) 17 : 14

**24** What is the total number of members staying in all the societies together?
(A) 3520 (B) 3360
(C) 4289 (D) 3000

**25** What is the difference between the number of male children in society *B* and number of male children in society *F*?
(A) 84 (B) 14
(C) 96 (D) 26

## Histogram and Bar Chart

**Directions** (Q. Nos. 26-30) The histogram, given below, shows the number of families of a locality having various daily incomes, as obtained by a survey. Observe the graph and answer the questions based on it.

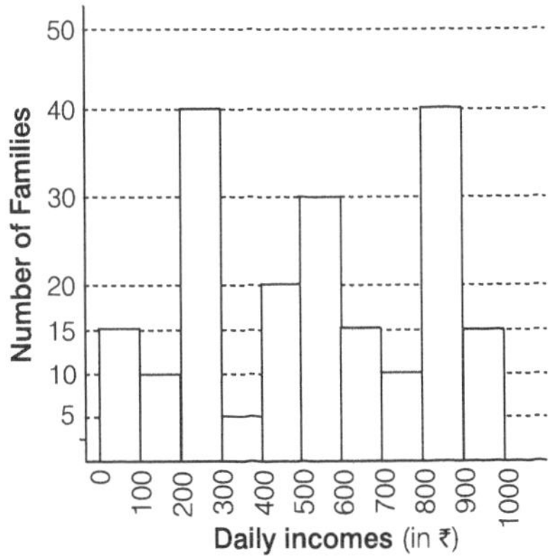


**26** In all, how many families were surveyed?
(A) 235 (B) 220
(C) 200 (D) 195

**27** The number of families, whose daily incomes are ₹ 800 or above, is
(A) 50 (B) 55
(C) 5 (D) 80

**28** The number of families, whose daily incomes are below ₹ 200, is
(A) 25 (B) 20 (C) 15 (D) 10

**29** The number of families, whose daily incomes are between ₹ 500 and ₹ 800 is
(A) 35 (B) 40 (C) 45 (D) 55

**30** What per cent of families have their daily incomes less than ₹ 500?
(A) 90 (B) 45 (C) 30 (D) 20

**Directions** (Q. Nos. 31-34) Study the following bar graph and answer the questions. The bar graph gives the annual rates of inflation in percentages for 1975 and 1987.

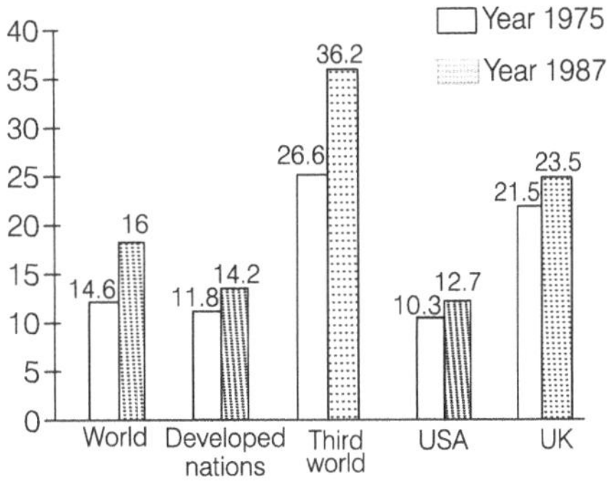


**31** From 1975 to 1987, inflation rate increased in the third world countries approximately by
(A) 10% (B) 20% (C) 30% (D) 36%

**32** The change in rate of inflation was least in which of the following?
(A) Developed nations (B) UK
(C) World (D) Third world

**33** Comparing the figures for USA *vis-a-vis* the developed nations, it can be concluded that
(A) USA had better control on inflation
(B) Developed nations had better control on inflation
(C) The inflation rate continues to be the same for USA and developed nations
(D) No conclusion can be drawn

**34** In the year 1987, the inflation rate in the third world countries *vis-a-vis* the world jumped approximately by
(A) 135% (B) 126%
(C) 122% (D) 200%

**Directions** (Q. Nos. 35-38) Study the bar graph and answer the questions.

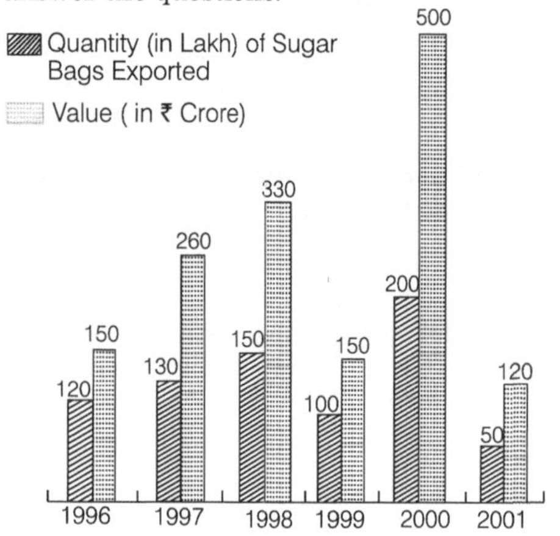


**35** Percentage fall in value from 2000 to 2001 is

(A) 75% (B) 25%
(C) 50% (D) 40%

**36** Value per bag was minimum in the year

(A) 1999 (B) 2001
(C) 1997 (D) 1996

**37** The difference between the bags exported in 1999 and 2000 was

(A) 15000000 (B) 5000000
(C) 10000000 (D) 20000000

**38** The approximate percentage increase in quantity from 1997 to 1998 was

(A) 15.38% (B) 15.9%
(C) 20.38% (D) 14.38%

**Directions** (Q. Nos. 39 and 40) Study the graph given below and answer the following questions.

**Demand and Production of Colour TVs of Five Companies for March, 2015**

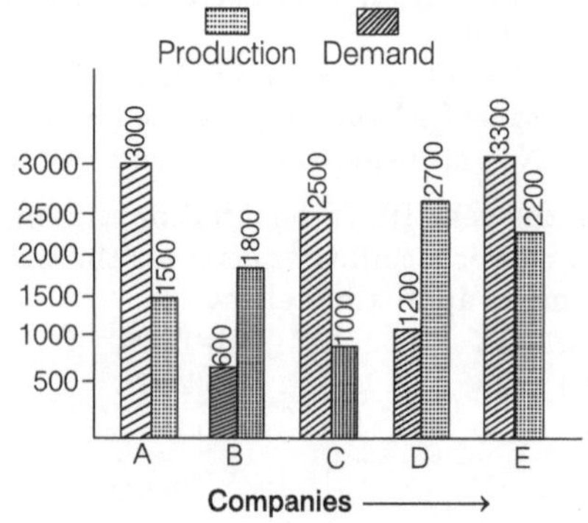


**39** What is the ratio of the number of companies having more demand than production to that of the companies having more production than demand?

(A) 3 : 2 (B) 2 : 3
(C) 4 : 1 (D) 1 : 4

**40** What is the difference between average demand and average production of TVs of all companies combined together?

(A) 380 (B) 280
(C) 480 (D) None of these

**Directions** (Q. Nos. 41-45) Sales of books (in thousands numbers) from six Branches–B1, B2, B3, B4, B5 and B6 of a publishing company in 2009 and 2010. Study the graph and answer the questions.

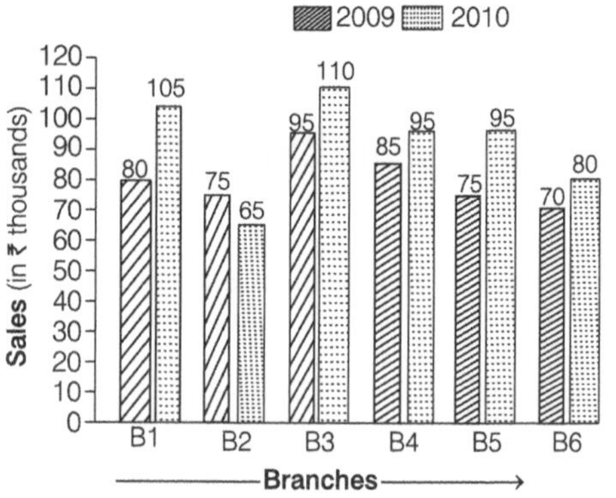


**41** The ratio of the total sales of Branch B2 for both years of the total sales of Branch B4 for both years is

(A) 7 : 9 (B) 2 : 3
(C) 4 : 5 (D) 3 : 5

**42** Total sales of branch B6 for both the years is $x$% of the total sales of Branches B3 for both the years. The value of $x$ is

(A) 68.54% (B) 73.17%
(C) 71.11% (D) 75.55%

**43** $x$% of the average sales of Branches B1, B2 and B3 in 2010 in the average sales of Branches B1, B3 and B6 in 2009. The value of $x$ is

(A) 77.5% (B) 87.5%
(C) 82.5% (D) 75%

**44** The average sales of all the branches for the year 2009 is (in thousands)

(A) 73 (B) 83
(C) 80 (D) 88

**45** Total sales (in thousands) of Branches B1, B3 and B5 together for both the years is

(A) 250 (B) 310
(C) 435 (D) 560

**Directions** (Q. Nos. 46-50) Study the following graph carefully to answer these questions. Number of students in College A and College B over the years.

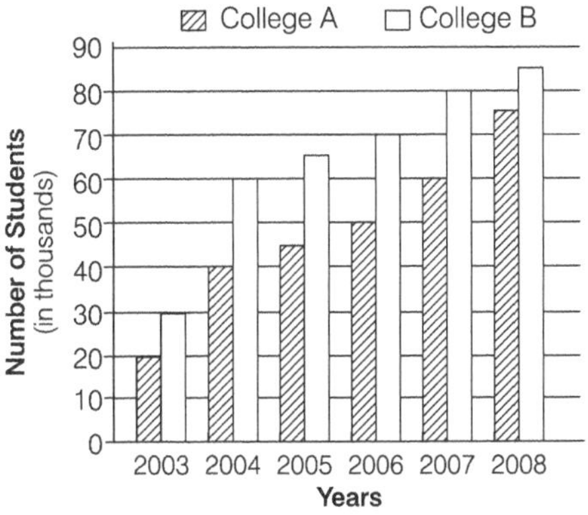


**46** What is the average number of students in College A for all the years together ?

(A) 45000 (B) 50000
(C) 52000 (D) 48000

**47** What is the approximate percentage rise in the number of students of College B from 2005 to 2006?

(A) 8 (B) 12
(C) 4 (D) 15

**48** What is the ratio between the total number of students of College A in year 2004, 2006 and 2007 together and the total number of students of College B in years 2003, 2004 and 2008 respectively?

(A) 35 : 32
(B) 33 : 37
(C) 34 : 31
(D) 32 : 35

**49** Number of students of College B in year 2005 is what per cent of total students of College B in all the years together? (rounded off to two digits after decimal)

(A) 20.61 (B) 23.79
(C) 21.79 (D) 17.29

**50** For which college(s) and in which year was the per cent rise in number of students from the previous year the highest?

(A) College A in year 2004 and College B in year 2005
(B) Only College B in year 2004
(C) College A in year 2004 and College B in year 2004
(D) College A in year 2007 and College B in year 2004

**Directions** (Q. Nos. 51-55) Study the given Histogram and answer the questions.

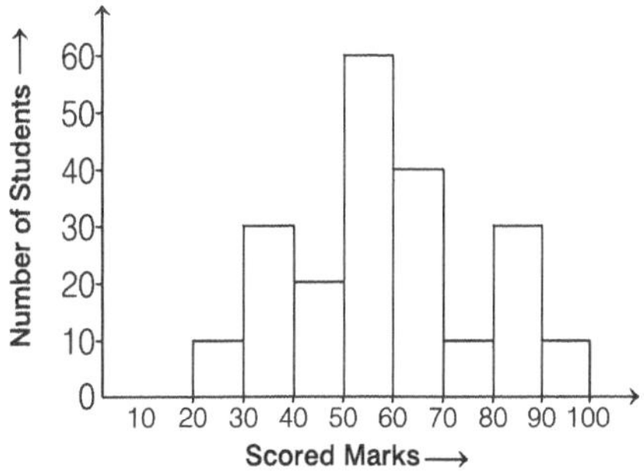


**51** What are the total number of students who are surveyed?

(A) 220 (B) 190
(C) 200 (D) 210

**52** What are the number of students who scored marks between 90-100?

(A) 40 (B) 30
(C) 10 (D) 20

**53** Find the percentage of the students who scored below 50 marks.

(A) $47\frac{13}{21}\%$ (B) $28\frac{4}{7}\%$
(C) $23\frac{13}{21}\%$ (D) $27\frac{5}{7}\%$

**54** Which of the following scores are scored by maximum number of students?

(A) 60-70 (B) 80-90
(C) 50-60 (D) 30-40

**55** Students scoring marks between 30-40 is how much percentage more than the scoring between 20-30?

(A) 200% (B) 300%
(C) 250% (D) 100%

## Line Graph (Chart)

**Directions** (Q. Nos. 56 and 57) Study the following graph carefully to answer the questions that follow.

Cost of three different fruits (in rupees per kg) in five different cities

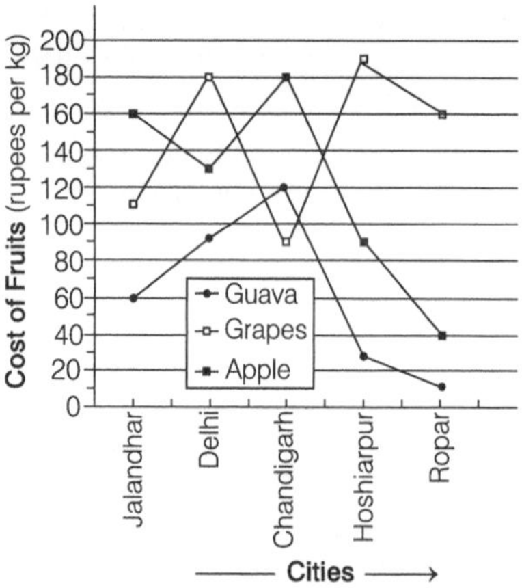


**56** In which city is the difference between the cost of 1 kg of apple and the cost of 1 kg of guava the second lowest?
(A) Jalandhar (B) Delhi
(C) Chandigarh (D) Ropar

**57** The cost of 1 kg of guava in Jalandhar is approximately what per cent of the cost of 2 kg of grapes in Chandigarh?
(A) 66 (B) 24 (C) 28 (D) 34

**Directions** (Q. Nos. 58 and 59) Study the following line chart carefully and answer the question given below. The following line chart represents the number of employee recruited in different years in a company.

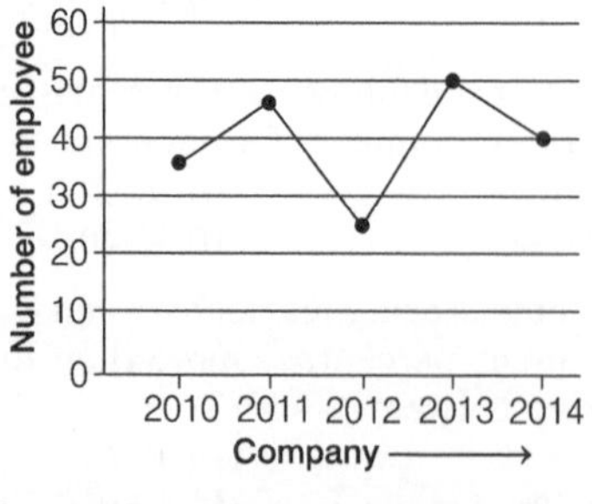


**58** If the total number of employees before the year 2010 was 640, then the total number of employee after 2014 was
(A) 840 (B) 835 (C) 560 (D) 720

**59** What was the ratio of number of employees recruited in year 2011 to that in year 2013?
(A) 8 : 5 (B) 9 : 5 (C) 9 : 10 (D) 2 : 3

**Directions** (Q. Nos. 60-64) Study the following graph carefully and answer the questions that follow.

**Number of Girls** (in thousand)
**Enrolled in Three Different Schools**

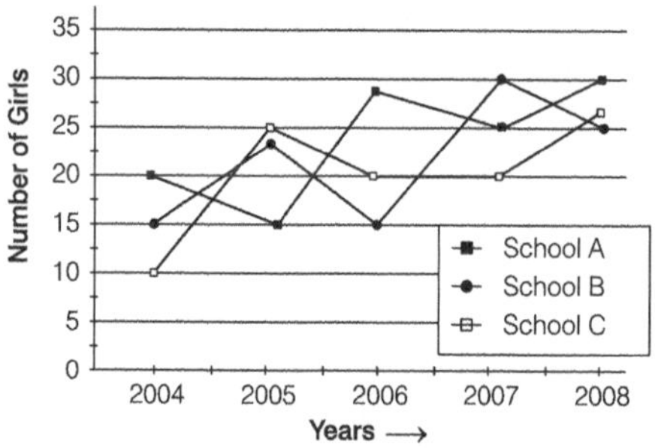


**60** What was the respective ratio between the number of girls enrolled in the school C in the year 2007 and total number of girls enrolled in school A and school B together in the same year?
(A) 11 : 3 (B) 3 : 11
(C) 4 : 11 (D) 4 : 7

**61** In which school was the difference between the number of girls enrolled in the year 2008 and 2004 minimum?
(A) Only School A
(B) Only School B
(C) Only School C
(D) Both School A and School B

**62** What was the approximate average number of girls enrolled in the year 2006 in all the three schools together?
(A) 20800 (B) 23000
(C) 20000 (D) 22500

**63** Total number of girls enrolled in the three school in the year 2004 was what percentage of the number of girls enrolled in School C in the year 2007?
(A) 220 (B) 210
(C) 45 (D) 225

**64** In which year was the total number of girls enrolled in all the three schools together second highest?
(A) 2008 (B) 2005
(C) 2006 (D) 2007

**Directions** (Q. Nos. 65-67) The following line graph gives the ratio of the amounts of imports by a company to the amount of exports from that company over the period from 1995 to 2001.

**Ratio of Value of Imports to Exports by a Company Over the Years**

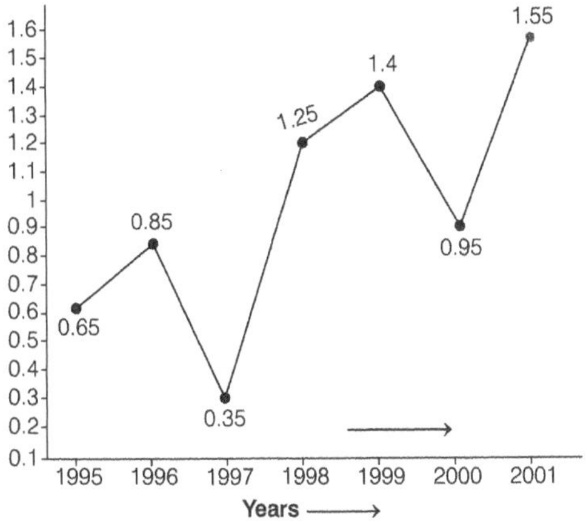


**65** If the imports in 1998 was ₹ 250 crore and the total exports in the years 1998 and 1999 together was ₹ 500 crore, then the imports in 1999 was

(A) ₹ 250 crore (B) ₹ 300 crore
(C) ₹ 357 crore (D) ₹ 420 crore

**66** The imports were minimum proportionate to the exports of the company in the year

(A) 1995 (B) 1996
(C) 1997 (D) 2000

**67** What was the percentage increase in imports from 1997 to 1998?

(A) 72
(B) 56
(C) 28
(D) Data inadequate

## Pie Chart or Circle Graph

**Directions** (Q. Nos. 68-72) Read the information carefully and answer the questions.

Total cost of production of a firm is ₹ 250 lakh. Following pie chart shows the percentage of costs of production in different purposes. Letter A,B,C,D represents the following

A = Cost of raw materials
B = Cost of packing materials
C = Cost of labour
D = Maintenance cost

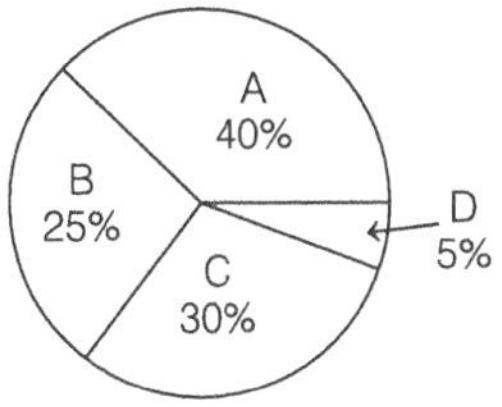


**68** If the production increases to five times of the present cost, then the percentage increase of the cost is

(A) 50% (B) 500%
(C) 300% (D) 400%

**69** If the total maintenance cost increases from ₹ 12.5 lakh to ₹ 50 lakh, then the percentage increase of the maintenance cost is

(A) 400% (B) 25%
(C) 75% (D) 300%

**70** Cost of packing materials and raw materials together amounts to

(A) ₹ 137.5 lakh
(B) ₹ 162.5 lakh
(C) ₹ 87.5 lakh
(D) ₹ 175 lakh

**71** If the cost of production doubles in a period of three years, then the corresponding maintenance cost will be

(A) ₹ 25 lakh (B) ₹ 125 lakh
(C) ₹ 12.5 lakh (D) ₹ 75 lakh

**72** If the packing cost increases by 2%, then the new packing cost will

(A) ₹ 5 lakh (B) ₹ 62.5 lakh
(C) ₹ 1.25 lakh (D) ₹ 63.75 lakh

**Directions** (Q. Nos. 73 and 74) The pie chart given shows the data on number of foreign collaboration approved with various countries. Some of these foreign collaborations are technical while others include foreign investment too. Study the pie-chart and answer the questions below it.

Total = 1200

2013

**73** By how much did the number of foreign collaboration approved with USA increase from 2013 to 2014?
(A) 216
(B) 99
(C) 315
(D) None of the above

**74** What is the ratio of the number of foreign collaborations approved with UK in 2013 to those in 2014?
(A) 13 : 15
(B) 7 : 17
(C) 14 : 15
(D) None of the above

**Directions** (Q. Nos. 75-77) In the following questions, the expenses of a country for a particular year is given in pie chart. Read the pie chart and answer the questions.

**75** The per cent of less money spent on non-plan than that on defence is
(A) 15% (B) 12% (C) 5% (D) 10%

**76** The per cent of excess money spent on others than that on sports, is
(A) 26% (B) 25%
(C) 27% (D) 28%

**77** The per cent of the total spending on health, is
(A) 25% (B) 30%
(C) 20% (D) 15%

**Directions** (Q. Nos. 78 and 79) The adjoining pie chart represents the proposed outlay of the fifth-five year plan of ₹ 40000 (in crores). Examine the chart and answer the questions.

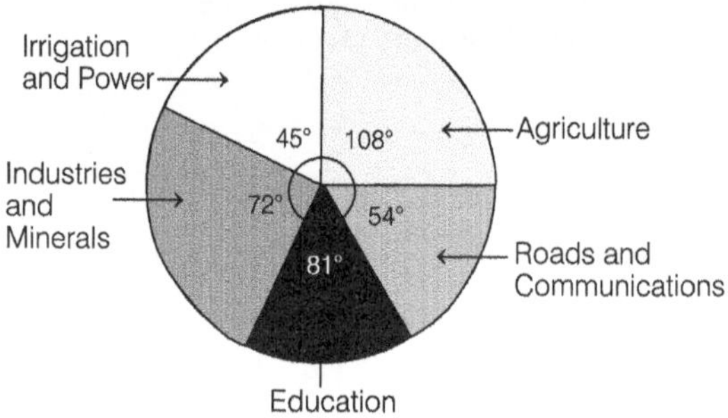


**78** The amount proposed on agriculture is more than that on industries and minerals by
(A) 7.5% (B) 10% (C) 12% (D) 12.5%

**79** The amount (in ₹ crores) proposed on irrigation and power is less than that on industries an minerals by
(A) 3000 (B) 3500
(C) 2000 (D) 2500

**Directions** (Q. Nos. 80-83) The following pie chart represents the transport used by children. Study the graph and answer the questions that follow.

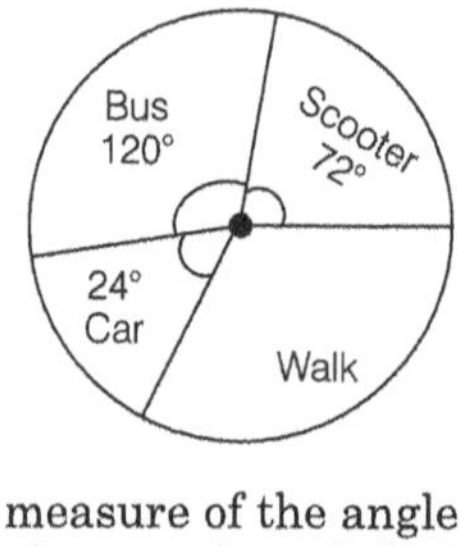


**80** What is measure of the angle at the centre representing people walking?
(A) 144° (B) 48° (C) 36° (D) 72°

**81** What is the percentage of children using scooter?
(A) 20% (B) $33\frac{1}{3}\%$ (C) 15% (D) 40%

**82** If 10 students come by car, how many come by bus?
(A) 60 (B) 50 (C) 30 (D) 100

**83** If 180 students come walking to school, what is the strength of the school?
(A) 540 (B) 450
(C) 360 (D) 600

## Data Sufficiency

**Directions** (Q. Nos. 84-86) In the following questions, each question is accompanied by two Statements I and II. You have to determine which statement(s) is/are sufficient to answer the question.

(A) Only Statement I is sufficient
(B) Only Statement II is sufficient
(C) Both the Statements are sufficient
(D) None of the statement is sufficient

**84** What is the number?

I. 20% of the number is $\frac{1}{5}$ of that number.
II. 5/6 of the number is 15 less than that number.

**85** How much is the profit percentage?

I. The toy is bought for ₹ 25.
II. The toy is sold for ₹ 30.

**86** What is the ratio of investment of $A, B$ and $C$?

I. Total investment is ₹ 10000 in which $A$'s contribution is ₹ 4000.
II. Ratio of investment of $A$ to $B$ is 3 : 4 and that of $B$ to $C$ is 3 : 2.

**Directions** (Q. Nos. 87 and 88) In the following questions, each question is accompanied by three Statements I, II and III. You have to determine which statement(s) is/are sufficient to answer the question.

(A) Only I and II
(B) Only II and III
(C) Only I and III
(D) All I, II and III

**87** What is the speed of Train A?

I. Train A crosses Train B, which is 200 m in length, in the opposite direction in 20 s.
II. Speed of Train B is 60 km/h.
III. Length of Train A is twice the length of Train B.

**88** What is the average age of 50 students standing in a class?

I. Ratio of boys and girls is 3 : 2 in the class.
II. Average age of boys and girls is 15.2 yr and 13.4 yr respectively.
III. Number of boys is more than number of girls in the class.

# *Previous Years' Questions*

## UGC NET-December 2019

**Directions** (Q. Nos. 1-5) The following table presents the data on the number of vehicles of three different types (A, B and C) produced by a company during seven different years from 2012 *to* 2018. *Based on the data in the table, answer the given questions.*

**Year-wise production of three types of vehicles**

| Vehicle/Year | A-Type | B-Type | C-Type |
|---|---|---|---|
| 2012 | 5000 | 20000 | 15000 |
| 2013 | 15000 | 10000 | 22500 |
| 2014 | 10000 | 15000 | 30000 |
| 2015 | 17500 | 15000 | 23000 |
| 2016 | 25000 | 20000 | 15000 |
| 2017 | 13000 | 25000 | 20000 |
| 2018 | 30000 | 35000 | 25000 |

**1** In how many year was the production of A-type vehicles less than its average production over the given years?

(A) 2 (B) 4 (C) 3 (D) 1

**2** In which of the following years was the total production of all the three types of vehicles 60000?

(A) 2013 (B) 2014
(C) 2015 (D) 2016

**3** What was the average number of B-type vehicles produced by the company over the years?

(A) 20000 (B) 25000
(C) 15000 (D) 30000

**4** The number of A-type vehicles produced in the year 2014 was what per cent (%) of the number of C-type vehicles produced in the year 2016?

(A) ~ 33.33% (B) ~ 66.67%
(C) 50% (D) 15%

**5** What was the average of all three types vehicles produced by the company in the year 2012?
(A) 13333 (B) 13500 (C) 10500 (D) 11000

**Directions** (Q. Nos. 6-10) The following table shows, the percentage (%) profit earned by Company A, income of Company B and expenditure of Company B during the years, 2013-18 as well as formula to compute percentage (%) profit. Based on the data in the table, answer the given questions.

**Year-wise Financial Details (in ₹ lakhs)**

| Year | Per Cent Profit of A | Income of B (in ₹ lakhs) | Expenditure of B (in ₹ lakhs) |
|---|---|---|---|
| 2013 | 40% | 48.6 | 36 |
| 2014 | 25% | 35 | 25 |
| 2015 | 60% | 62.4 | 48 |
| 2016 | 40% | 77 | 44 |
| 2017 | 10% | 80 | 50 |
| 2018 | 20% | 72 | 45 |

Where, Profit per cent

$$= \frac{\text{Income} - \text{Expenditure}}{\text{Expenditure}} \times 100$$

**6** In the expenditure of Company A in year 2017 was ₹ 45 lakhs, then the net profit (in ₹ lakhs) of Company A is what per cent of net profit (in ₹ lakhs) of Company B in the same year?
(A) 15% (B) 25%
(C) 40% (D) 75%

**7** If the income of Company A in the year 2018 was ₹ 90 lakhs, then the net profit (in ₹ lakhs) of Company B in 2018 is what per cent more than net profit (in ₹ lakhs) of Company A?
(A) 30% (B) 60% (C) 75% (D) 80%

**8** The per cent profit of Company B was maximum in the year
(A) 2014 (B) 2015
(C) 2016 (D) 2017

**9** In the income of the Company A in the year 2014 happened to be ₹ 32.5 lakhs, then what was the sum of the net profit (in ₹ lakhs) of Company A and Company B in 2014?
(A) ₹ 12.8 lakhs (B) ₹ 13.2 lakhs
(C) ₹ 15 lakhs (D) ₹ 16.5 lakhs

**10** What is the difference between per cent (%) profit of Company A and Company B in the year 2013?
(A) 5% (B) 7%
(C) 12% (D) 15%

**Directions** (Q. Nos. 11-15) Consider the following table that shows the amount of exports (₹ in crore) from three different Companies A, B and C over the years 2012-2018. Based on the data in the table, answer the given questions.

**Year-wise Amount of Export from Companies**

| Year | Amount of export (₹ in crore) | | |
|---|---|---|---|
| | A | B | C |
| 2012 | 40 | 90 | 70 |
| 2013 | 70 | 50 | 100 |
| 2014 | 50 | 70 | 130 |
| 2015 | 80 | 70 | 100 |
| 2016 | 110 | 90 | 70 |
| 2017 | 60 | 110 | 90 |
| 2018 | 130 | 150 | 110 |

**11** In how many of the given years, were the export from Company A more than its average annual export over the given years?
(A) 2 (B) 3
(C) 4 (D) 5

**12** For which of the following pairs of years, the total exports from the three companies put together are equal?
(A) 2014 and 2017
(B) 2015 and 2017
(C) 2016 and 2017
(D) 2014 and 2015

**13** In which year, the absolute difference between the exports from Companies A and B was the minimum?
(A) 2013 (B) 2014
(C) 2015 (D) 2016

**14** Average annual amount of export during the given period for Company B is approximately what per cent (%) of the average annual amount of export for Company C?
(A) 89.64% (B) 91.21%
(C) 94.03% (D) 93.33%

**15** What was the difference between the average export of three companies in 2017 and the average export of three companies in 2012?
(A) ₹ 15.33 crore (B) ₹ 18.67 crore
(C) ₹ 25 crore (D) ₹ 20 crore

## UGC NET-June 2019

**Directions** (Q. Nos. 16-20) Consider the following table that shows expenditure of a company (in lakh rupees) per annum over the given years. Answer the questions based on data contained in the table.

**Item of expenditure**

| Year | Salary | Transport | Bonus | Interest on Loans | Taxes |
|---|---|---|---|---|---|
| 2008 | 150 | 90 | 2.00 | 20.0 | 80 |
| 2009 | 180 | 100 | 2.50 | 30.5 | 95 |
| 2010 | 200 | 110 | 2.75 | 35.5 | 105 |
| 2011 | 240 | 115 | 3.00 | 40.0 | 85 |
| 2012 | 250 | 125 | 3.25 | 42.5 | 100 |

**16** Total expenditure of all the items in 2008 was approximately what, percentage of the total expenditure in 2012?
(A) 66% (B) 69% (C) 72% (D) 75%

**17** The total amount of bonus paid by the company during the given period is approximately what per cent of the total amount of salary paid during this period?
(A) 0.9% (B) 1.3% (C) 1.6% (D) 2.0%

**18** The approximate ratio between the total expenditure on taxes for all the years and the total expenditure on transport for all the years is
(A) 31 : 40 (B) 25 : 36
(C) 27 : 30 (D) 31 : 36

**19** The approximate ratio between the total expenditure of the company in the year 2008 and the total expenditure of the company in the year 2009 is
(A) 57 : 75 (B) 52 : 68
(C) 57 : 68 (D) 68 : 57

**20** What is the average amount of interest per year which the company had to pay (in rupees) during this period?
(A) 30.5 lakh (B) 32.7 lakh
(C) 33.7 lakh (D) 35.5 lakh

**Directions** (Q. Nos. 21-25) *Consider the following table that shows the production of fertilizers by a company (in 10000 tonnes during the year 2011 to 2018).*

**Answer the questions based on the data contained in the table**

| Year | 2011 | 2012 | 2013 | 2014 | 2015 | 2016 | 2017 | 2018 |
|---|---|---|---|---|---|---|---|---|
| Production of Fertilizers | 35 | 50 | 70 | 55 | 75 | 60 | 85 | 90 |

**21** What was the approximate percentage increase in production of fertilizers in 2018 compared to that in 2011?
(A) 157% (B) 165%
(C) 177% (D) 182%

**22** What was the percentage decline in the production of fertilizers from 2013 to 2014?
(A) 20.4% (B) 21.4%
(C) 22.6% (D) 24.2%

**23** In which year, the percentage increase in production as compared to the previous year was maximum?
(A) 2012 (B) 2013
(C) 2015 (D) 2018

**24** The average production of 2012 and 2013 was exactly equal to the average production of which of the following pairs of years?
(A) 2011 and 2012 (B) 2011 and 2017
(C) 2012 and 2014 (D) 2015 and 2016

**25** In how many of the given years was the production of fertilizers more than the average production of the given years?
(A) 2 (B) 3 (C) 4 (D) 5

**Directions** (Q. Nos. 26-30) Consider the following table that shows the total number of tickets sold of five movies, P, Q, R, S and T across 2 cinema houses A and B on a particular day. In accordance with the table, answer the questions that follow :

**Sale of Movie Tickets Cinema House-wise**

| Movies | Cinema | |
|---|---|---|
| | A | B |
| P | 200 | 300 |
| Q | 350 | 400 |
| R | 250 | 350 |
| S | 300 | 350 |
| T | 400 | 250 |

**26** What is the average number of tickets sold at Cinema B for Movies T and S together?
(A) 360 (B) 320 (C) 300 (D) 340

**27** What is the difference between the total number of tickets sold of all movies together at Cinema A and number of tickets sold of all movies together at Cinema B?
(A) 180 (B) 170 (C) 150 (D) 160

**28** What is the total number of tickets sold of Movie Q and R together at both the Cinemas A and B together?
(A) 1050 (B) 1200 (C) 1250 (D) 1350

**29** What is the ratio of the number of tickets sold of Movie P at Cinema B to the number of tickets sold of Movie Q at Cinema B?
(A) 2 : 3 (B) 3 : 4 (C) 1 : 2 (D) 3 : 5

**30** The number of tickets sold of Movie T at Cinema A in what per cent of the number of tickets of Movie P sold at Cinema A?
(A) 220% (B) 200%
(C) 210% (D) 190%

**Directions** (Q. Nos. 31-35) Consider the following table that shows the distribution of students in two Sections A and B in a school according to the marks obtained by them. There is a total of 45 students in each of the Sections A and B. Answer the questions based on the data contained in the table.

Marks obtained by students

| Marks | Number of students | |
|---|---|---|
| | Section-A | Section-B |
| 0-9 | 2 | 4 |
| 10-19 | 5 | 5 |
| 20-29 | 10 | 9 |
| 30-39 | 4 | 4 |
| 40-49 | 8 | 7 |
| 50-59 | 4 | 5 |
| 60-69 | 7 | 5 |
| 70-79 | 5 | 6 |

**31** How many students in Section A have obtained 30 or more marks but less than 50?
(A) 12 (B) 14
(C) 10 (D) 13

**32** If the passing marks is 40, approximately what is the percentage of successful students in Section B?
(A) 48% (B) 51% (C) 50% (D) 47%

**33** How many students in Section A and Section B have obtained 50 or more than 50 marks?
(A) 23 (B) 43 (C) 32 (D) 34

**34** If the passing marks is 30, what is the number of failures in both the sections together?
(A) 43 (B) 35 (C) 16 (D) 26

**35** How many students in Section A and Section B together have obtained marks less than 10?
(A) 10 (B) 11 (C) 12 (D) 6

## UGC NET-December 2018

**Directions** (Q.Nos. 36-40) The table below embodies data on the production, exports and percapita consumption of rice in Country P for the five years from 2012 to 2016. Answer the questions 36-40 based on the data contained in the table.

**Year-wise Production, Exports and Per Capita Consumption of Rice**

| Year | Production (in million kg) | Exports (in million kg) | Per Capita Consumption (in million kg) |
|---|---|---|---|
| 2012 | 186.5 | 114 | 36.25 |
| 2013 | 202 | 114 | 35.2 |
| 2014 | 238 | 130 | 38.7 |
| 2015 | 221 | 116 | 40.5 |
| 2016 | 215 | 88 | 42 |

Where, Per Capita Consumption = (Consumption in million kg) ÷ (population in million) and consumption (in million kg) = Production – Exports

**36** In which year, the population of country was the highest?
(A) 2015 (B) 2016 (C) 2013 (D) 2014

**37** The ratio of exports to consumption in the given period was the highest in the year
(A) 2014 (B) 2015 (C) 2012 (D) 2013

**38** What is the population of the country in the year 2014 (in million)?
(A) 2.79 (B) 2.85 (C) 2.64 (D) 2.72

**39** The percentage increase in the consumption of rice over the previous year was the highest in which year?
(A) 2015 (B) 2016
(C) 2013 (D) 2014

**40** What is the average consumption of rice (in million kg) over the years 2012-2016?
(A) 108 (B) 100.1
(C) 104 (D) 102.1

## UGC NET-July 2018

**Directions** (Q. Nos. 41-45) In accordance with the tables I and II, answer the questions that follow. Consider the following two tables (I and II) in which table I shows the percentage of students who joined and successfully completed the Ph.D programme from the Universities A to G and table II shows the number of foreign Ph.D students enrolled in the University C. These percentages have been rounded to the nearest whole number. There are the total of 855 Ph.D students in the University C and A total of 5700 students successfully completed the Ph.D programme from all the seven universities together.

**I. Students University-wise**

| Name of University | Percentage of Students who Joined Ph.D | Percentage of Students who Successfully Completed Ph.D (Out of 5700) |
|---|---|---|
| A | 22 | 18 |
| B | 15 | 17 |
| C | 10 | 13 |
| D | 17 | 16 |
| E | 08 | 09 |
| F | 12 | 15 |
| G | 16 | 12 |

**II. Foreign Ph.D Students in University C**

| Foreign Students | Number of Ph.D Students in University C |
|---|---|
| American | 65 |
| Australian | 46 |
| African | 25 |
| European | 35 |

**41** In case, there are 21 African students in University E, then approximately, what is their per cent in that university?
(A) 5% (B) 2% (C) 3% (D) 4%

**42** What is the ratio of students who successfully completed the Ph.D programme to the students who joined in the University G ?
(A) 1 : 2 (B) 9 : 17 (C) 3 : 4 (D) 6 : 11

**43** What percentage of students in University C is that of foreign students ?
(A) 20% (B) 15% (C) 25% (D) 30%

**44** The number of students who completed the Ph.D programme from Universities A and D together exceeds the number of students who joined the Universities C and E together, by
(A) 369 (B) 399 (C) 409 (D) 419

**45** Which university has the highest percentage of students who successfully completed the Ph.D programme out of the students who joined that university?
(A) E (B) F (C) B (D) C

## UGC NET-November 2017

**Directions** (Q. Nos. 46-50) Answer the questions based on the data given below.

**Table : Number of Registered Vehicles in India and India's Population**

| Year | Total vehicles (lakhs) | Two wheelers (lakhs) | Cars, jeeps, taxis (lakhs) | Buses (lakhs) | Goods vehicles (lakhs) | Other (lakhs) | Population (India) (Millions) |
|---|---|---|---|---|---|---|---|
| 1961 | 6.65 | 0.88 | 3.1 | 0.57 | 1.68 | 0.42 | 439.23 |
| 1971 | 18.65 | 5.76 | 6.82 | 0.94 | 3.43 | 1.70 | 548.15 |
| 1981 | 53.91 | 26.18 | 11.60 | 1.62 | 5.54 | 8.97 | 683.32 |
| 1991 | 213.74 | 142.00 | 29.54 | 3.31 | 13.56 | 25.33 | 846.42 |
| 2001 | 549.91 | 385.56 | 70.58 | 6.34 | 29.48 | 57.95 | 1028.73 |
| 2011 | 1417.58 | 1018.65 | 191.23 | 16.04 | 70.64 | 121.02 | 1210.19 |

**46** What was the per capita ownership of two wheelers in India in the year 2011?
(A) ~ 0.0084% (B) ~ 8.84%
(C) ~0.068% (D) ~0.084%

**47** What was the average decadal growth in the number of cars during 1961-2011?
(A) ~68% (B) ~ 217%
(C) ~ 157% (D) ~ 131%

**48** In the year 2001, out of the total number of vehicles, the number of passenger vehicles (4 wheelers) accounted for
(A) ~24% (B) ~31% (C) ~43% (D) ~14%

**49** The maximum decadal growth in population of India is registered in the period
(A) 1991-2001 (B) 2001-2011
(C) 1981-1991 (D) 1961-1971

**50** In which year the decadal growth (%) in number of cars surpassed that of the two wheelers?
(A) 2001 (B) 1981 (C) 2011 (D) 1991

## UGC NET-January 2017

**Directions** (Q. Nos. 51-53) The table below embodies data on the sales revenue (₹ in lakh) generated by a publishing house during the years 2012-15 while selling books, magazines and journals as three categories of items. Answer the questions based on the data contained in the table.

| | **Sales Revenue** (₹ in lakh) | | | |
|---|---|---|---|---|
| Years/Items | 2012 | 2013 | 2014 | 2015 |
| Journals | 46 | 47 | 45 | 44 |
| Magazines | 31 | 39 | 46 | 51 |
| Books | 73 | 77 | 78 | 78 |
| Total | 150 | 163 | 169 | 173 |

**51** In 2015, approximately what per cent of total revenue came from books?
(A) 45% (B) 55% (C) 35% (D) 25%

**52** The number of years in which there was an increase in revenue from atleast two categories of items, is
(A) 0 (B) 1 (C) 2 (D) 3

**53** If the year 2016 shows the same growth in terms of total sales revenue as the year 2015 over the year 2014, then the revenue in the year 2016 must be approximately
(A) ₹ 194 lakh (B) ₹ 187 lakh
(C) ₹ 172 lakh (D) ₹ 177 lakh

**Directions** (Q. Nos. 54-56) A university professor maintains data on MCA students tabulated by performance and gender of the students. The data is kept on a compute hard disk, but accidently some of it is lost because of a computer virus. Only the following could be recovered.

**Number of MCA Students**

| Performance | Average | Good | Excellent | Total |
|---|---|---|---|---|
| **Gender** | | | | |
| Male | | | 10 | |
| Female | | | | 32 |
| Total | | 30 | | |

Panic buttons were pressed but to no avail. An expert committee was formed, which decided that the following facts were self-evident.
(A) Half the students were either excellent or good.
(B) 40% of the students were females.
(C) One-third of the male students were average.

Answer the questions based on data table above.

**54** How many female students are excellent?
(A) 0 (B) 8 (C) 16 (D) 32

**55** What proportion of female students are good?
(A) 0 (B) 0.25
(C) 0.50 (D) 0.75

**56** Approximately, what proportion of good students are male?
(A) 0 (B) 0.73
(C) 0.43 (D) 0.27

**Directions** (Q. Nos. 57-60) The table below embodies data on the production, exports and percapita consumption of rice in country P for the five years from 2012 to 2016. Answer the questions, based on the data contained in the table.

**Year-wise Production, Export and Per Capita Consumption of Rice**

| Year | Production (in million kg) | Exports (in million kg) | Per Capita Consumption (in kg) |
|---|---|---|---|
| 2012 | 186.5 | 114 | 36.25 |
| 2013 | 202 | 114 | 35.2 |
| 2014 | 238 | 130 | 38.7 |
| 2015 | 221 | 116 | 40.5 |
| 2016 | 215 | 88 | 42 |

Where, Per Capita Consumption
= (Consumption in million kg) ÷ (population in million)
and consumption (in million kg)
= Production − Exports

**57** In which year, the population of country was the highest?
(A) 2015 (B) 2016
(C) 2013 (D) 2014

**58** The ratio of exports to consumption in the given period was the highest in the year
(A) 2014 (B) 2015
(C) 2012 (D) 2013

**59** What is the population of the country in the year 2014 (in million)?
(A) 2.79 (B) 2.85
(C) 2.64 (D) 2.72

**60** The percentage increase in the consumption of rice over the previous year was the highest in which year?
(A) 2015 (B) 2016
(C) 2013 (D) 2014

## UGC NET-June 2016

**Directions** (Q. Nos. 61-63) The following table shows the percentage profit (%) earned by two Companies A and B during the years 2011-15. Answer the questions based on the data contained in the table.

**Profit Earned by Two Companies**

| Year | Percentage Profit Per Cent | |
|---|---|---|
| | A | B |
| 2011 | 20 | 30 |
| 2012 | 35 | 40 |
| 2013 | 45 | 35 |
| 2014 | 40 | 50 |
| 2015 | 25 | 35 |

where,

$$\text{Per cent profit} = \frac{\text{Income} - \text{Expenditure}}{\text{Expenditure}} \times 100\%$$

**61** If the total expenditure of two companies was ₹9 lakh in the year 2012 and the expenditure of A and B were in the ratio 2 : 1, then what was the income of the Company A in that year?
(A) ₹ 9.2 lakh (B) ₹ 8.1 lakh
(C) ₹ 7.2 lakh (D) ₹ 6.0 lakh

**62** What is the average percentage profit earned by the Company B?
(A) 35% (B) 42% (C) 38% (D) 40%

**63** In which year, the percentage profit earned by the Company B is less than that of Company A?
(A) 2012 (B) 2013 (C) 2014 (D) 2015

## UGC NET-June 2015

**Directions** (Q Nos. 64-69) Questions are based on the tabulated data given below.

**A company has 20 employees with their age** (in yr) **and salary** (in thousand rupees per month) **mentioned against each of them**

| S. No. | Age (in years) | Salary (in thousand rupees per month) |
|---|---|---|
| 1. | 44 | 35 |
| 2. | 32 | 20 |
| 3. | 54 | 45 |
| 4. | 42 | 35 |
| 5. | 31 | 20 |
| 6. | 53 | 60 |
| 7. | 42 | 50 |
| 8. | 51 | 55 |
| 9. | 34 | 25 |
| 10. | 41 | 30 |
| 11. | 33 | 30 |
| 12. | 31 | 35 |
| 13. | 30 | 35 |
| 14. | 37 | 40 |
| 15. | 44 | 45 |
| 16. | 36 | 35 |
| 17. | 34 | 35 |
| 18. | 49 | 50 |
| 19. | 43 | 45 |
| 20. | 45 | 50 |

**64** Classify the data of age of each employee in class interval of 5 yr. Which class interval of 5 yr has the maximum average salary?
(A) 35-40 yr (B) 41-45 yr
(C) 46-50 yr (D) 51-55 yr

**65** What is the frequency (%) in the class interval of (30-35) yr?
(A) 20% (B) 25% (C) 30% (D) 35%

**66** What is the average age of the employees?
(A) 40.3 yr (B) 38.6 yr
(C) 47.2 yr (D) 45.3 yr

**67** What is the fraction (%) of employees getting salary ≥ 40000 per month?
(A) 45% (B) 50% (C) 35% (D) 32%

**68** What is the average salary (in thousand per month) in the age group (40-50) yr?
(A) 35 (B) 42.5
(C) 40.5 (D) 36.5

**69** What is the fraction of employees getting salary less than the average salary of all the employees?
(A) 45% (B) 50% (C) 55% (D) 47%

## UGC NET-2014

**Directions** (Q. Nos. 70-74) Read the following table carefully to answer the questions that follow.

**Net Area under Irrigation by Source in a Country**
(in thousand hectares)

| Year | Government canals | Private canals | Tanks | Tube wells and other wells | Other sources | Total |
|---|---|---|---|---|---|---|
| 1997-98 | 17117 | 211 | 2593 | 32090 | 3102 | 55173 |
| 1998-99 | 17093 | 212 | 2792 | 33988 | 3326 | 57411 |
| 1999-2000 | 16842 | 194 | 2535 | 34623 | 2915 | 57109 |
| 2000-01 | 15748 | 203 | 2449 | 33796 | 2880 | 55076 |
| 2001-02 | 15031 | 209 | 2179 | 34906 | 4347 | 56672 |
| 2002-03 | 13863 | 206 | 1802 | 34250 | 3657 | 53778 |
| 2003-04 | 14444 | 206 | 1908 | 35779 | 4281 | 56618 |
| 2004-05 | 14696 | 206 | 1727 | 34785 | 7453 | 58867 |
| 2005-06 | 15268 | 207 | 2034 | 35372 | 7314 | 60196 |

**70** Find out the source of irrigation that has registered the maximum improvement in terms of percentage on net irrigated area during 2002-03 and 2003-04.
(A) Government canals
(B) Tanks
(C) Tubewells and other wells
(D) Other sources

**71** In which of the following years, net irrigation by tanks increased at the highest rate?
(A) 1998-99
(B) 2000-01
(C) 2003-04
(D) 2005-06

**72** Identify the sources of irrigation that has recorded the maximum incidence of negative growth in terms of net irrigated area during the years given in the table.
(A) Government canals
(B) Private canals
(C) Tubewells and other wells
(D) Other sources

**73** In which of the following years, share of the tubewells and other wells in the total net irrigated area was the highest?
(A) 1998-99
(B) 2000-01
(C) 2002-03
(D) 2004-05

**74** Which of the following sources of irrigation has registered the largest percentage of decline in net area under irrigation during 1997-98 and 2005-06?
(A) Government canals
(B) Private canals
(C) Tanks
(D) Other sources

## UGC NET-December 2014

**Directions** (Q. Nos. 75-80) For a country $CO_2$ emissions (million metric tonne) from various sectors are given in the following table. Answer the questions based on the data given.

**$CO_2$ Emissions (million metric tonne)**

| Sector/ Year | Power | Industry | Commercial | Agriculture | Domestic |
|---|---|---|---|---|---|
| 2005 | 500 | 200 | 150 | 80 | 100 |
| 2006 | 600 | 300 | 200 | 90 | 110 |
| 2007 | 650 | 320 | 250 | 100 | 120 |
| 2008 | 700 | 400 | 300 | 150 | 150 |
| 2009 | 800 | 450 | 320 | 200 | 180 |

**75** What is the percentage growth of $CO_2$ emissions from power sector during 2005 to 2009?
(A) 60% (B) 50%
(C) 40% (D) 80%

**76** Which sector has recorded maximum growth in $CO_2$ emissions during 2005 to 2009?
(A) Power (B) Industry
(C) Commercial (D) Agriculture

**77** By what percentage, the total emissions of $CO_2$ have increased from 2005 to 2009?
(A) ~ 89.32% (B) ~ 57.62%
(C) ~ 40.32% (D) ~ 113.12%

**78** What is the average annual growth rate of $CO_2$ emissions in power sector?
(A) ~ 12.57% (B) ~ 16.87%
(C) ~ 30.81% (D) ~ 50.25%

**79** What is the percentage contribution of power sector to total $CO_2$ emissions in the year 2008?
(A) ~ 30.82% (B) ~ 41.18%
(C) ~ 51.38% (D) ~ 60.25%

**80** In which year, the contribution of industry to total $CO_2$ emissions was minimum?
(A) 2005 (B) 2006
(C) 2007 (D) 2009

# ANSWERS

## Chapter Practice

| | | | | | | | | | |
|---|---|---|---|---|---|---|---|---|---|
| 1 (A) | 2 (A) | 3 (B) | 4 (D) | 5 (D) | 6 (D) | 7 (B) | 8 (C) | 9 (D) | 10 (C) |
| 11 (D) | 12 (C) | 13 (D) | 14 (D) | 15 (B) | 16 (C) | 17 (D) | 18 (C) | 19 (B) | 20 (D) |
| 21 (A) | 22 (C) | 23 (D) | 24 (C) | 25 (C) | 26 (C) | 27 (B) | 28 (A) | 29 (D) | 30 (B) |
| 31 (D) | 32 (C) | 33 (B) | 34 (B) | 35 (A) | 36 (D) | 37 (C) | 38 (A) | 39 (A) | 40 (B) |
| 41 (A) | 42 (B) | 43 (B) | 44 (C) | 45 (D) | 46 (B) | 47 (A) | 48 (D) | 49 (C) | 50 (C) |
| 51 (D) | 52 (C) | 53 (B) | 54 (C) | 55 (A) | 56 (B) | 57 (D) | 58 (B) | 59 (C) | 60 (C) |
| 61 (D) | 62 (A) | 63 (D) | 64 (D) | 65 (D) | 66 (C) | 67 (D) | 68 (D) | 69 (D) | 70 (B) |
| 71 (A) | 72 (D) | 73 (B) | 74 (C) | 75 (C) | 76 (B) | 77 (D) | 78 (B) | 79 (A) | 80 (A) |
| 81 (A) | 82 (B) | 83 (B) | 84 (B) | 85 (C) | 86 (B) | 87 (D) | 88 (A) | | |

## Previous Year Questions

| | | | | | | | | | |
|---|---|---|---|---|---|---|---|---|---|
| 1 (B) | 2 (D) | 3 (A) | 4 (B) | 5 (A) | 6 (A) | 7 (D) | 8 (C) | 9 (D) | 10 (A) |
| 11 (B) | 12 (D) | 13 (C) | 14 (C) | 15 (D) | 16 (A) | 17 (B) | 18 (D) | 19 (C) | 20 (C) |
| 21 (A) | 22 (B) | 23 (A) | 24 (B) | 25 (C) | 26 (C) | 27 (C) | 28 (D) | 29 (B) | 30 (B) |
| 31 (A) | 32 (B) | 33 (C) | 34 (B) | 35 (D) | 36 (B) | 37 (C) | 38 (A) | 39 (D) | 40 (B) |
| 41 (C) | 42 (A) | 43 (A) | 44 (B) | 45 (D) | 46 (D) | 47 (D) | 48 (D) | 49 (D) | 50 (C) |
| 51 (A) | 52 (C) | 53 (D) | 54 (A) | 55 (B) | 56 (B) | 57 (B) | 58 (C) | 59 (A) | 60 (D) |
| 61 (B) | 62 (C) | 63 (B) | 64 (D) | 65 (D) | 66 (A) | 67 (A) | 68 (B) | 69 (C) | 70 (D) |
| 71 (D) | 72 (A) | 73 (C) | 74 (C) | 75 (A) | 76 (D) | 77 (A) | 78 (A) | 79 (B) | 80 (A) |

# Hints & Solutions

## Chapter Practice

**1** (*A*) Quantitative data

**2** (*A*) Photograph collection

**3** (*B*) Qualitative data

**4** (*D*) Data Mapping

**5** (*D*) All of these

**6** (*D*) Required difference = (Number of students scoring 30 and above marks in aggregate) – (Number of students scoring 30 and above marks in Chemistry)

$= 27 - 21 = 6$

**7** (*B*) We have, 60% of 50 $= \frac{60}{100} \times 50 = 30$

$\therefore$ Required number = Number of students scoring 30 and above marks in Physics $= 23 + 9 = 32$

**8** (*C*) Number of students getting atleast 60% marks in Chemistry = Number of students getting 30 and above marks in Chemistry = 21

Number of students getting atleast 40% marks in aggregate = Number of students getting 20 and above marks in aggregate = 73

$\therefore$ Required percentage $= \left[\frac{21}{73} \times 100\right]\%$

$= 28.76\% \approx 29\%$

**9** (*D*) We have, 40% of 50 $= \left(\frac{40}{100} \times 50\right) = 20$

$\therefore$ Required number = Number of students scoring less than 20 marks in aggregate

= 100 – Number of students scoring 20 and above marks in aggregate $= 100 - 73 = 27$

**10** (*C*) Since, 66 students get 20 and above marks in Chemistry and out of these 21 students get 30 and above marks, therefore to select top 45 students in Chemistry, the qualifying marks should lie in the range 20-30.

**11** (*D*) Required percentage $= \left[\frac{(145 - 108)}{108} \times 100\right]\%$

$= 34.26\% \approx 34\%$

**12** (*C*) The total sales (in thousands) of all the seven years for various batteries are

For 4AH $= 75 + 90 + 96 + 105 + 90 + 105 + 115 = 676$

For 7AH $= 144 + 126 + 114 + 90 + 75 + 60 + 85 = 694$

For 32AH $= 114 + 102 + 75 + 150 + 135 + 165 + 160 = 901$

For 35AH $= 102 + 84 + 105 + 90 + 75 + 45 + 100 = 601$

Clearly, sales are maximum in case of 32 AH batteries.

**13** (*D*) Required difference $= [(84 - 45) \times 1000] = 39000$

**14** (*D*) The percentage of sales of 4 AH batteries to the total sales in different years are

For 1994 $= \left(\frac{96}{525} \times 100\right)\% = 18.29\%$

For 1995 $= \left(\frac{105}{510} \times 100\right)\% = 20.59\%$

For 1996 $= \left(\frac{90}{465} \times 100\right)\% = 19.35\%$

For 1997 $= \left(\frac{105}{495} \times 100\right)\% = 21.21\%$

Hence, required percentage is maximum in 1997.

**15** (*B*) From the table, it is clear that the sales of 7 AH batteries have been decreasing continuously from 1992 to 1997.

**16** (*C*) In the year 2010, profitability per outlet for the

bookseller $P = \frac{1}{2}\left(\frac{40 \text{ lakh}}{50\text{lakh}}\right) = 0.40$ lakh

bookseller $Q = \frac{1}{4}\left(\frac{125\text{lakh}}{170\text{lakh}}\right) = 0.18$ lakh

bookseller $R = \frac{1}{1}\left(\frac{40\text{lakh}}{60\text{lakh}}\right) = 0.66$ lakh

bookseller $S = \frac{1}{5}\left(\frac{120\text{lakh}}{90\text{lakh}}\right) = 0.27$ lakh

bookseller $T = \frac{1}{3}\left(\frac{150\text{lakh}}{180\text{lakh}}\right) = 0.28$ lakh

bookseller $U = \frac{1}{5}\left(\frac{15\text{lakh}}{40\text{lakh}}\right) = 0.075$ lakh

Thus, for the bookseller *R*, the profitability per outlet is maximum.

**17** (*D*) Percentage increase in profit per outlet in 2011 over that in 2010 for the

bookseller $P = \left(\frac{\frac{60}{3} - \frac{40}{2}}{\frac{40}{2}} \times 100\right)\%$

$= \left(\frac{20 - 20}{20} \times 100\right)\% = 0\%$

bookseller $Q = \left(\frac{\frac{200}{6} - \frac{125}{4}}{\frac{125}{4}} \times 100\right)\%$

$= \left(\frac{400-375}{12} \times \frac{4}{125} \times 100\right)\% = 6.67\%$

bookseller $R = \left(\frac{\frac{50}{3} - \frac{40}{1}}{\frac{40}{1}} \times 100\right)\% = -\text{ve}$

bookseller $S = \left(\frac{\frac{180}{6} - \frac{120}{5}}{\frac{120}{5}} \times 100\right)\%$

$= \left(\frac{30-24}{24} \times 100\right)\% = 25\%$

bookseller $T = \left(\frac{\frac{160}{4} - \frac{150}{3}}{\frac{150}{3}} \times 100\right)\% = -\text{ve}$

bookseller $U = 0\%$

Hence, required bookseller is $S$.

**18** (*C*) Profit = Total sales – Total investment

⇒ Total investment = Total sales – Profit

∴ In the year 2010, total investment of $U$

= 5 × 40 lakh –15 lakh = ₹185 lakh

**19** (*B*) In the year 2010, total sales of

bookseller $P$ = 50 × 2 lakh = ₹100 lakh

bookseller $Q$ = 170 × 4 lakh = ₹680 lakh

bookseller $R$ = 60 × 1 lakh = ₹60 lakh

bookseller $S$ = 90 × 5 lakh = ₹450 lakh

bookseller $T$ = 180 × 3 lakh = ₹540 lakh

bookseller $U$ = 40 × 5 lakh = ₹200 lakh

Hence, total sales is highest for bookseller $Q$.

**20** (*D*) Percentage increase in sales

$= \left(\frac{120 \times 6 - 90 \times 5}{90 \times 5} \times 100\right)\%$

$= \left(\frac{720-450}{450} \times 100\right)\% = 60\%$

Percentage increase in profit

$= \left(\frac{180-120}{120} \times 100\right)\% = 50\%$

Hence, required ratio $= \frac{60\%}{50\%} = 6:5$

**Sol.** (Q. Nos. 21-25)

Number of children in society $A \rightarrow 600 \times \frac{25}{100} = 150$

Number of female children $= 150 \times \frac{60}{100} = 90$

Number of male children = 150 – 90 = 60

In society $B \rightarrow 550 \times \frac{40}{100} = 220$

Number of female children $= 220 \times \frac{25}{100} = 55$

Number of male children = 220 – 55 = 165

In society $C \rightarrow 575 \times \frac{16}{100} = 92$

Number of female children $= 92 \times \frac{75}{100} = 69$

Number of male children = 92 – 69 = 23

In society $D \rightarrow 580 \times \frac{25}{100} = 145$

Number of female children $= 145 \times \frac{20}{100} = 29$

Number of male children = 145 – 29 = 116

In society $E \rightarrow 430 \times \frac{40}{100} = 172$

Number of female children $= 172 \times \frac{50}{100} = 86$

Number of male children = 172 – 86 = 86

In society $F \rightarrow 625 \times \frac{24}{100} = 150$

Number of female children $= 150 \times \frac{54}{100} = 81$

Number of male children = 150 – 81 = 69

**21** (*A*) Number of female children

= 90 + 55 + 69 + 29 + 86 + 81 = 410

Number of adult females

= (350 + 150 + 275 + 300 + 250 + 300) – 410

= 1625 – 410 = 1215

∴ Required ratio = 1215 : 410 = 243 : 82

**22** (*C*) Number of all female children = 410

**23** (*D*) Number of adult males in societies $A$ and $B$

= (250 – 60) + (400 – 165)

= 190 + 235 = 425

Number of adult males in societies $E$ and $F$

= (180 – 86) + (325 – 69)

= 94 + 256 = 350

∴ Required ratio = 425 : 350 = 17 : 14

**24** (*C*) Number of all members

= (250 + 350) + (400 + 150) + (300 + 275)
+ (280 + 300) + (180 + 250) + (325 + 300) + 150
+ 220 + 92 + 145 + 172 + 150 = 4289

**25** (*C*) Required difference = 165 – 69 = 96

**26** (*C*) Total number of families surveyed

= 15 + 10 + 40 + 5 + 20 + 30 + 15 + 10 + 40 + 15

= 200 families

**27** (*B*) Number of families having daily income ₹ 800 and above = 40 + 15 = 55 families

**28** (*A*) Number of families having daily income below ₹ 200 = 15 + 10 = 25 families

**29** (*D*) Number of families having daily income between ₹ 500 and ₹ 800 = 30 + 15 + 10 = 55 families

**30** (*B*) Total families below 500 = 15 + 10 + 40 + 5 + 20 = 90

$\therefore$ Percentage $= \frac{90}{200} \times 100 = 45\%$

**31** (*D*) Required increase $= \frac{36.2 - 26.6}{26.6} \times 100\% \approx 36\%$

**32** (*C*) Least change in the world = 16 − 14.6 = 1.4 only

**33** (*B*) Percentage increase in inflation of developed nations $= \frac{14.2 - 11.8}{11.8} \times 100 = 20.34\%$

USA $= \frac{12.7 - 10.3}{10.3} \times 100 = 23.30\%$

Clearly, developed nations had better control on inflation.

**34** (*B*) Required percentage $= \frac{36.2 - 16}{16} \times 100\% \approx 126\%$

**35** (*A*) Required percentage fall $= \frac{500 - 120}{500} \times 100\%$

$= \frac{380}{500} \times 100\%$

$= 76\% \approx 75\%$

**36** (*D*) Here, value per bag

in 1996 $= \frac{150 \text{ Cr}}{120 \text{ lakhs}} =$ ₹ 125/bag

in 1997 $= \frac{260 \text{ Cr}}{130 \text{ lakhs}} =$ ₹ 200/bag

in 1999 $= \frac{150 \text{ Cr}}{100 \text{ lakhs}} =$ ₹ 150/bag

in 2001 $= \frac{120 \text{ Cr}}{50 \text{ lakhs}} =$ ₹ 240/bag

So, value per bag was minimum in 1996.

**37** (*C*) Required difference = (200 − 100) lakhs = ₹ 10000000

**38** (*A*) Approximate percentage increase in quantity from 1997 to 1998 $= \frac{150 - 130}{130} \times 100\%$

$= \frac{20}{130} \times 100\% = 15.38\%$

**39** (*A*) Number of companies having more demand than production = 3

Companies having more production than demand = 2

$\therefore$ Required ratio = 3 :2

**40** (*B*) Required difference

= Average demand − Average production

Average production

$= \frac{1500 + 1800 + 1000 + 2700 + 2200}{5}$

$= \frac{9200}{5} = 1840$

Average demand

$= \frac{3000 + 600 + 2500 + 1200 + 3300}{5}$

$= \frac{10600}{5} = 2120$

$\therefore$ Required difference = 2120 − 1840 = 280

**41** (*A*) Total sales of Branch B2 in both years

= 75 + 65 = 140 thousands

Total sales of Branch B4 in both years

= 85 + 95 = 180 thousands

$\therefore$ Required ratio $= \frac{140}{180} = \frac{7}{9} = 7 : 9$

**42** (*B*) Total sales of Branch B6 in both years

= 70 + 80 = 150 thousands

Total sales of Branch B3 in both years

= 95 + 110 = 205 thousands

Now, according to the question,

$x\%$ of 205 = 150

$\Rightarrow \quad 205 \times \frac{x}{100} = 150$

$\Rightarrow \quad x = \frac{100 \times 150}{205}$

$\Rightarrow \quad x = \frac{3000}{41}$

$\Rightarrow \quad x = 73.17\%$

**43** (*B*) Average sales of Branches B1, B2 and B3 in the year 2010 $= \frac{105 + 65 + 110}{3} = \frac{280}{3}$ thousands

and average sales of Branches B1, B3 and B6 in the year 2009 $= \frac{80 + 95 + 70}{3} = \frac{245}{3}$ thousands

Now, according to the question,

$x\%$ of $\frac{280}{3} = \frac{245}{3}$

$\Rightarrow \quad \frac{280}{3} \times \frac{x}{100} = \frac{245}{3}$

$\Rightarrow \quad x = \frac{100 \times 245}{280} = \frac{2450}{28}$

$\Rightarrow \quad x = \frac{1225}{14} = 87.5$

$\Rightarrow \quad x = 87.5\%$

**44** (*C*) Average sales of all the branches in year 2009

$$= \frac{80+75+95+85+75+70}{6} \text{ thousands}$$

$$= \frac{480}{6} = 80 \text{ thousands}$$

**45** (*D*) Sales of Branch B1 in both years

$= 80 + 105 = 185$ thousands

Sales of Branch B3 in both years

$= 95 + 110 = 205$ thousands

Sales of Branch B5 in both years

$= 75 + 95 = 170$ thousands

Now, total sales of all three branches in both years

$= 185 + 205 + 170$

$= 560$ thousands

**46** (*B*) Average number of students in College A

$$= \left(\frac{20+40+45+50+70+75}{6}\right) \text{thousands}$$

$= 50000$

**47** (*A*) Percentage increase $= \left(\frac{70-65}{65} \times 100\right)$

$= 7.69 \approx 8\%$

**48** (*D*) Required ratio $= (40 + 50 + 70) : (30 + 60 + 85)$

$= 160 : 175 = 32 : 35$

**49** (*C*) Total number of students in College B over all the years $= (30+60+65+70+80+85)$ thousands

$= 390$ thousands

Number of students in College B in 2008

$= 85$ thousands

$\therefore$ Required percentage $= \frac{85}{390} \times 100 = 21.79\%$

**50** (*C*) It is obvious from the diagram, the rise in the year 2004 was 100% for both the Colleges A and B.

**51** (*D*) Total number of students surveyed

$= 10 + 30 + 20 + 60 + 40 + 10 + 30 + 10 = 210$

**52** (*C*) According to the given Histogram, the number of students who scored between 90-100 are 10.

**53** (*B*) Number of students who scored below 50 marks

$= 10 + 30 + 20 = 60$

$\therefore$ Required percentage $= \frac{60}{210} \times 100\%$

$= \frac{200}{7} = 28\frac{4}{7}\%$

**54** (*C*) According to the given Histogram, maximum number of students scored 50-60 marks.

**55** (*A*) Number of students who scored between 30-40 marks = 30

Number of students who scored between 20-30 marks = 10

$\therefore$ Required percentage $= \frac{30-10}{10} \times 100$

$= \frac{20}{10} \times 100\% = 200\%$

**56** (*B*) Cost of 1 kg apple in Jalandhar = ₹ 160

Cost of 1 kg guava in Jalandhar = ₹ 60

Difference = 160 – 60 = ₹ 100

Similarly, in Delhi → ₹ (130 – 90) = ₹ 40

In Chandigarh → ₹ (180 – 120) = ₹ 60

In Ropar → ₹ (40 – 10) = ₹ 30

Hence, the second lowest difference between price of 1 kg apple and 1 kg guava is in Delhi.

**57** (*D*) Cost of 1 kg of guava in Jalandhar = ₹ 60

Cost of 2 kg of grapes in Chandigarh = ₹ 90 × 2

= ₹ 180

$\therefore$ Required percentage $= \frac{60}{180} \times 100 = \frac{1}{3} \times 100$

$= 33.33\% \approx 34\%$

**58** (*B*) Total number of employees before the year 2010

$= 640$

According to the line chart,

Total number of employees after 2014

$= 640 + 35 + 45 + 25 + 50 + 40$

$= 835$

**59** (*C*) $\frac{\text{Number of employees recruited in 2011}}{\text{Number of employees recruited in 2013}} = \frac{45}{50} = \frac{9}{10}$

$\therefore$ Ratio $= 9 : 10$

**60** (*C*) Required ratio $= 20 : (25 + 30)$

$= 20 : 55 = 4 : 11$

**61** (*D*) For School A = (30 – 20) thousands

= 10 thousands

For School B = (27.5 – 15) thousands

= 10 thousands

For School C = (27.5 – 10) thousands

= 17·5 thousands

$\therefore$ For both the Schools A and B the difference was minimum.

**62** (*A*) Required average $= \left(\frac{27.5+20+15}{3}\right) = 20833$

$\approx 20800$

**63** (*D*) Total number of girls admitted in 2004

$= (20 + 15 + 10) = 45$ thousands

Required percentage $= \frac{45}{20} \times 100 = 225\%$

**64** (*D*) Total number of girls

Year 2005 = $(25 + 22.5 + 15)$ thousands

= 62.5 thousands

Year 2006 = $(27.5 + 20 + 15)$ thousands

= 62.5 thousands

Year 2007 = $(30 + 25 + 20)$ thousands

= 75 thousands

Year 2008 = $(30 + 27.5 + 25)$ thousands

= 82.5 thousands

**65** (*D*) The ratio of imports to exports for the years 1998 and 1999 are 1.25 and 1.40 respectively.

Let the exports in the year 1998 = ₹ $x$ crore

Then, the exports in the year 1999 = ₹ $(500 - x)$ crore

$\Rightarrow \quad x = \frac{250}{1.25} = 200$ [using ratio for 1998]

Thus, the exports in the year 1999 = ₹ (500 − 200)

= ₹ 300 crore

Let the imports in the year 1999 = ₹ $y$ crore

Then, $\quad 1.40 = y/300$

$\Rightarrow \quad y = (300 \times 1.40) = 420$

∴ Imports in the year 1999 = ₹ 420 crore

**66** (*C*) The imports are minimum proportionate to the exports implies that the ratio of the value of imports to exports has the minimum value.

Therefore, the required year is 1997.

**67** (*D*) The graph gives only the ratio of imports to exports for different years. To find the percentage increase in imports from 1997 to 1998, we require more details such as the value of imports or exports during these years.

**68** (*D*) According to the question,

New cost = $5 \times 250$ = ₹ 1250 lakh

∴ Percentage increase $= \frac{1250 - 250}{250} \times 100\% = 400\%$

**69** (*D*) Old maintenance cost = ₹ 12.5 lakh

New maintenance cost = ₹ 50 lakh

∴ Percentage increase $= \frac{50 - 12.5}{12.5} \times 100\% = 300\%$

**70** (*B*) Cost of packing materials + Raw materials

= 25% of 250 + 40% of 250

= 62.5 + 100

= ₹ 162.5 lakh

**71** (*A*) Since, cost of production doubles, so maintenance cost will also be double.

So, new maintenance cost = $12.5 \times 2$ = ₹ 25 lakh

**72** (*D*) Old packing cost = 25% of 250

$= \frac{25}{100} \times 250 = 62.5$ lakh

∴ New packing cost = 62.5 + 2% of 62.5

= 63.75 lakh

**73** (*B*) Foreign collaboration approved with USA during the year 2013 $= \frac{1200}{360} \times 64.8 = 216$

Foreign collaboration approved with USA in 2014

$= \frac{1500}{360} \times 75.6 = 315$

∴ Difference = 315 − 216 = 99

**74** (*C*) Here, foreign collaboration approved with UK in 2013

$= \frac{1200}{360} \times 50.4 = \frac{60480}{360} = 168$

Foreign collaboration approved with UK in 2014

$= \frac{1500}{360} \times 43.2 = 180$

∴ Required ratio = 168 : 180 = 14 : 15

**75** (*C*) Money spent on non-plan

$= \frac{36°}{360°} \times 100\% = 10\%$

Money spent on defence = 15%

Difference = 15% − 10% = 5%

**76** (*B*) Money spent on sports $= \frac{18°}{360°} \times 100\% = 5\%$

Money spent on others = 30%

Difference = 30% − 5% = 25%

**77** (*D*) Money spent on health $= \frac{54°}{360°} \times 100 = 15\%$

**78** (*B*) Required percentage $= \frac{108° - 72°}{360°} \times 100\%$

$= \frac{36°}{360°} \times 100\%$

$= \frac{1}{10} \times 100 = 10\%$

**79** (*A*) Required amount $= \frac{72° - 45°}{360°} \times 40000$

$= \frac{27°}{360°} \times 40000$ = ₹ 3000 crores

**80** (*A*) We know that, the sum of total angles at centre in any circle = 360°

Therefore, bus + car + scooter + walk = 360°

$\Rightarrow \quad 120° + 24° + 72° + x = 360°$

$\Rightarrow \quad 216° + x = 360°$

$\Rightarrow \quad x = 360° - 216°$

$\Rightarrow \quad x = 144°$

Hence, the measure of the angle at the centre representing people walking = 144°

**81** (*A*) Percentage of children using scooter

$$= \frac{72°}{360°} \times 100\% = \frac{1}{5} \times 100\% = 20\%$$

**82** (*B*) Centre angle, come by car = 24°
and centre angle, come by bus = 120°

Now, angle of 24° = 10 students

$\therefore$ Angle of 1° $= \frac{10}{24}$ students

$\therefore$ Angle of 120° $= \frac{10}{24} \times 120 = 50$ students

So, 50 students come by bus.

**83** (*B*) Centre angle of walking people = 144°

Now, angle of 144° = 180 students

$\therefore$ Angle of 360° $= \frac{180}{144} \times 360 = 450$ students

**84** (*B*) Let the number be $x$.

From Statement I, 20% of $x = \frac{1}{5}$ of $x$

$\Rightarrow \quad x \times \frac{20}{100} = x \times \frac{1}{5}$

$\therefore$ From Statement I, we cannot find the answer.

From Statement II, $x \times \frac{5}{6} = x - 15$

$\Rightarrow \quad x - \frac{5}{6}x = 15 \Rightarrow \frac{x}{6} = 15$

$\therefore \quad x = 90$

Therefore, only Statement II is sufficient to answer the question.

**85** (*C*) From Statement I, cost price of toy = ₹ 25

From Statement II, selling price of toy = ₹ 30

From both the statements,

$$\text{Profit }\% = \frac{SP - CP}{CP} \times 100\%$$

$$= \frac{30 - 25}{25} \times 100\% = 20\%$$

Therefore, both the statements are required to answer the question.

**86** (*B*) We can't find the ratio of *A*, *B* and *C* from Statement I.

From Statement II, $A : B = 3 : 4 \Rightarrow \frac{A}{B} = \frac{3 \times 3}{4 \times 3} = \frac{9}{12}$

and $B : C = 3 : 2 \Rightarrow \frac{B}{C} = \frac{3 \times 4}{2 \times 4} = \frac{12}{8}$

$\therefore A : B : C = 9 : 12 : 8$

Therefore, Statement II is required.

**87** (*D*) From Statement I, length of Train B = 200 m

Crossing time = 20 s

From Statement II, speed of Train B = 60 km/h

$$= 60 \times \frac{5}{18} = \frac{50}{3} \text{ m/s}$$

From Statement III, length of Train A

= 2 × length of Train B.

= 2 × 200 = 400 m

From Statements I, II and III

$$\text{Crossing time} = \frac{\text{Length of Train A} + \text{Length of Train B}}{\text{Speed of Train A} + \text{Speed of Train B}}$$

$$\Rightarrow \quad 20 = \frac{200 + 400}{\text{Speed of Train A} + \frac{50}{3}}$$

$$\Rightarrow \quad 600 = 20 \times \text{speed of Train A} + \frac{1000}{3}$$

$$\Rightarrow 20 \times \text{speed of Train A} = 600 - \frac{1000}{3}$$

$$\therefore \text{Speed of train A} = \frac{1800 - 1000}{3 \times 20} = \frac{40}{3} \text{ m/s}$$

Therefore, all the statements are required to answer the question.

**88** (*A*) From Statement I,

$3x + 2x = 50 \Rightarrow 5x = 50$

$\Rightarrow \quad x = \frac{50}{5} = 10$

$\therefore$ Number of boys = 3 × 10 = 30

Number of girls = 2 × 10 = 20

From Statement II, average age of boys and girls is 15.2 yr and 13.4 yr respectively.

From Statements I and II,

$$\text{Average age of boys and girls} = \frac{30 \times 15.2 + 20 \times 13.4}{30 + 20}$$

$$= \frac{456 + 268}{50}$$

$$= \frac{724}{50} = 14.48 \text{ yr}$$

Quantitative information is not obtained from Statement III.

Therefore, only Statements I and II are necessary to answer the question.

## Previous Years' Questions

**1** (*B*) Average production of A type vehicles

$$= \frac{(5+15+10+17.5+25+13+30)\times 1000}{7}$$

$$= \frac{115500}{7} = 16500$$

∴ In 4 yr, 2012, 2013, 2014 and 2017, production of A-type vehicle is less than its average production.

**2** (*D*) Total production of all three types in 2016

$$= 25000 + 20000 + 15000 = 60000$$

**3** (*A*) Average number of B-type vehicles production

$$= \frac{(20+10+15+15+20+25+35)\times 1000}{7}$$

$$= \frac{140 \times 1000}{7} = 20000$$

**4** (*B*) Required percentage $= \frac{10000}{15000} \times 100 = \sim 66.67\%$

**5** (*A*) Required average $= \frac{5000 + 20000 + 15000}{3}$

$$= \frac{40000}{3} = 13333.33 \approx 13333$$

**6** (*A*) Expenditure of Company A in 2017= ₹ 45 lakhs

Let income of Company A in 2017 = ₹ $x$ lakhs

Then, Profit per cent $= \frac{\text{Income} - \text{Expenditure}}{\text{Expenditure}} \times 100$

$$10 = \frac{x - 45}{45} \times 100$$

$$\Rightarrow \quad \frac{450}{100} = x - 45$$

$$\therefore \quad x = ₹\,\frac{99}{2} \text{ lakhs}$$

Net profit of Company A in 2017 = Income – Expenditure

$$= \frac{99}{2} - 45 = \frac{9}{2} \text{ lakhs}$$

Net profit of Company B in 2017 = Income – Expenditure

$$= 80 - 50 = ₹\,30 \text{ lakhs}$$

∴ Required percentage $= \frac{\frac{9}{2}}{30} \times 100 = 15\%$

**7** (*D*) Income of Company A in the year 2018 = ₹ 90 lakhs

Let expenditure of Company A in the year 2018 = ₹ $x$

Then, Profit percent $= \frac{\text{Income} - \text{Expenditure}}{\text{Expenditure}} \times 100$

$$20 = \frac{90 - x}{x} \times 100$$

$$x = 450 - 5x \Rightarrow x = \frac{450}{6}$$

$$x = ₹\,75 \text{ lakhs}$$

Net profit of Company A in the year 2018

$$= 90 - 75 = ₹\,15 \text{ lakhs}$$

Net profit of Company B in the year 2018

$$= 72 - 45 = 27 \text{ lakhs}$$

∴ Required percentage $= \frac{27 - 15}{15} \times 100$

$$= 80\%$$

**8** (*C*) The percentage profit of Company B

**In 2014**

$$\left[\text{Profit} = \frac{\text{Income} - \text{Expenditure}}{\text{Expenditure}} \times 100\right]$$

Profit per cent $= \frac{35 - 25}{25} \times 100 = 40\%$

**In 2015**

Profit per cent $= \frac{62.4 - 48}{48} \times 100 = 30\%$

**In 2016**

Profit per cent $= \frac{77 - 44}{44} \times 100 = 75\%$

**In 2017**

Profit per cent $= \frac{80 - 50}{50} \times 100 = 60\%$

The percentage of profit of Company B was maximum in the year 2016.

**9** (*D*) The income of Company A in the year 2014 = ₹ 32.5 lakhs

Let the expenditure of Company A in the year 2014 = ₹ $x$ lakhs then,

Profit per cent $= \frac{\text{Income} - \text{Expenditure}}{\text{Expenditure}} \times 100$

$$25 = \frac{32.5 - x}{x} \times 100$$

$$\Rightarrow \quad x = 130 - 4x \Rightarrow x = \frac{130}{5}$$

$$x = ₹\,26 \text{ lakhs}$$

Net profit of Company A in the year 2014

$$= \text{Income} - \text{Expenditure}$$

$$= 37.5 - 26 = ₹\,6.5 \text{ lakhs}$$

Net profit of Company B in the year 2014

$$= 35 - 25 = 10 \text{ lakhs}$$

Net profit of Company A and Company B in 2014

$$= 10 + 6.5 = ₹\,16.5 \text{ lakhs}$$

**10** (*A*) The percentage profit of Company B in the year 2013

Profit per cent $= \frac{\text{Income} - \text{Expenditure}}{\text{Expenditure}} \times 100$

$= \frac{48.6 - 36}{36} \times 100 = 35\%$

The percentage profit of Company A in the year 2013

$= 40\%$ (given)

$\therefore$ Required difference $= 40\% - 35\% = 5\%$

**11** (*B*) Average exports of Company A

$= \frac{40 + 70 + 50 + 80 + 110 + 60 + 130}{7}$

$= \frac{540}{7} =$ ₹ 77.14 crore

In the year 2015, 2016 and 2018 the export is more than the average export.

**12** (*D*) In 2014, total exports

$= 50 + 70 + 130 =$ ₹ 250 crore

In 2015, total exports $= 80 + 70 + 100$

= ₹ 250 crore

Hence, in 2014 and 2015, the total exports from the three companies together are equal.

**13** (*C*) In year 2015, the absolute difference between the exports from Companies A and B near minimum, which is $80 - 70 =$ ₹ 10 crore

**14** (*C*) Average annual exports of Company B

$= \frac{90 + 50 + 70 + 70 + 90 + 110 + 150}{7}$

= ₹ $\frac{630}{7}$ crore

Average annual exports of Company C

$= \frac{70 + 100 + 130 + 100 + 70 + 90 + 110}{7}$

= ₹ $\frac{670}{7}$ crore

$\therefore$ Required per cent $= \frac{\left(\frac{630}{7}\right)}{\left(\frac{670}{7}\right)} \times 100 = 94.03\%$

**15** (*D*) Average exports of companies in 2017

$= \frac{60 + 110 + 90}{3} = \frac{260}{3} =$ ₹ 86.66 crore

Average exports of companies in 2012

$= \frac{40 + 90 + 70}{3} =$ ₹ $\frac{200}{3}$ crore

= ₹ 66.66 crore

$\therefore$ Required difference = ₹ (86.66 − 66.66) crore

= ₹ 20 crore

**16** (*A*) Total expenditure of all items in 2008 (in lakh rupees)

$= (150 + 90 + 2 + 20 + 80)$

= ₹ 342 lakh

Total expenditure of all the items in 2012

$= (250 + 125 + 3.25 + 42.5 + 100)$

= ₹ 520.75 lakh

$\therefore$ Required percentage $= \frac{342}{520.75} \times 100 \approx 66\%$

**17** (*B*) Total amount of bonus paid by the company during the given period

$= (2 + 2.5 + 2.75 + 3 + 3.25)$

= ₹ 13.5 lakh

Total amount of salary paid by the company during given period $= (150 + 180 + 200 + 240 + 250)$

= ₹ 1020 lakh

$\therefore$ Required percentage $= \frac{13.5}{1020} \times 100 \approx 1.3\%$

**18** (*D*) Total expenditure on taxes for all the years

$= 80 + 95 + 105 + 85 + 100$

= ₹ 465 lakh

Total expenditure on transport for all the years

$= 90 + 100 + 110 + 115 + 125$

= ₹ 540 lakh

$\therefore$ Required ratio $= 465 : 540 = 31 : 36$

**19** (*C*) Total expenditure of company in the year 2008

= ₹ 342 lakh

Total expenditure of company in the year 2009

$= 180 + 100 + 2.5 + 30.5 + 95$

= ₹ 408 lakh

$\therefore$ Required ratio $= 342 : 408 = 57 : 68$

**20** (*C*) The average amount of interest on loans in all the years

$= \frac{20 + 30.5 + 35.5 + 40 + 42.5}{5}$

$= \frac{168.5}{5} =$ ₹ 33.7

**21** (*A*) The production of fertilizers in 2011 = 35

The production of fertilizers in 2018 = 90

$\therefore$ Required percentage $= \frac{90 - 35}{35} \times 100$

$= \frac{55}{35} \times 100 \approx 157\%$

**22** (*B*) The production of fertilizers in 2013 = 70

The production of fertilizers in 2014 = 55

$\therefore$ Required percentage $= \dfrac{70-55}{70} \times 100$

$= \dfrac{15}{70} \times 100 = 21.4\%$

**23** (*A*) Required percentage

in 2012 $= \dfrac{50-35}{35} \times 100\% = 42.85\%$

in 2013 $= \dfrac{70-50}{50} \times 100\% = 40\%$

in 2015 $= \dfrac{75-55}{55} \times 100\% = 36.36\%$

in 2017 $= \dfrac{85-60}{60} \times 100\% = 41.67\%$

in 2018 $= \dfrac{90-85}{85} \times 100\% = 5.88\%$

The percentage increase in production as compared to the previous year was maximum in 2012.

**24** (*B*) Average production of 2012 and 2013

$= \dfrac{50+70}{2} = \dfrac{120}{2} = 60$

Average production of 2011 and 2017 $= \dfrac{35+85}{2}$

$= \dfrac{120}{2} = 60$

Then, Average production of 2012 and 2013 was exactly equal to the average production of 2011 and 2017.

**25** (*C*) The average production of fertilizers of the given years

$= \dfrac{35+50+70+55+75+60+85+90}{8}$

$= \dfrac{520}{8} = 65$

The production of fertilizers more than the average production in 2013, 2015, 2017 and 2018.

**26** (*C*) The average number of tickets sold at Cinema B for the Movies T and S together

$= \dfrac{350+250}{2} = \dfrac{600}{2} = 300$

**27** (*C*) Total number of tickets sold of all the movies together at Cinema A

$= 200 + 350 + 250 + 300 + 400 = 1500$

Total number of tickets sold of all the movies together at Cinema B $= 300 + 400 + 350 + 350 + 250 = 1650$

$\therefore$ Required difference $= 1650 - 1500 = 150$

**28** (*D*) Total number of tickets sold of Movie Q at both the Cinemas A and B $= 350 + 400 = 750$

Total number of tickets sold by Movie R at both the Cinemas A and B $= 250 + 350 = 600$

$\therefore$ Required sum $= 750 + 600 = 1350$

**29** (*B*) Number of tickets sold of Movie P at Cinema B $= 300$

Number of tickets sold of Movie Q at Cinema B $= 400$

$\therefore$ Required ratio $= 300 : 400 = 3 : 4$

**30** (*B*) Number of tickets sold of Movie T at Cinema A $= 400$

Number of tickets sold of Movie P at Cinema A $= 200$

$\therefore$ Required percentage $= \dfrac{400}{200} \times 100 = 200\%$

**31** (*A*) The number of students in Section A have obtained 30 or more marks but less than 50

$= 4 + 8 = 12$

**32** (*B*) Total students in Section B

$= 4+5+9+4+7+5+5+6 = 45$

Number of students in Section B have obtained 40 or more marks $= 7 + 5 + 5 + 6 = 23$

$\therefore$ Required percentage $= \dfrac{23}{45} \times 100 \approx 51\%$

**33** (*C*) Number of students in Section A have obtained 50 or more marks $= 4 + 7 + 5 = 16$

Number of students in Section B have obtained 50 or more marks $= 5 + 5 + 6 = 16$

$\therefore$ Required sum $= 16 + 16 = 32$

**34** (*B*) Number of students in Section A have obtained marks less than $30 = 2 + 5 + 10 = 17$

Number of students in Section B have obtained marks less than $30 = 4 + 5 + 9 = 18$

$\therefore$ Required number $= 17 + 18 = 35$

**35** (*D*) Number of students in Section A have obtained marks less than $10 = 2$

Number of students in Section B have obtained marks less than $10 = 4$

$\therefore$ Required sum $= 2 + 4 = 6$

**36** (*B*) In year 2016,

Total consumption (in million kg) $= 215 - 88 = 127$

$\therefore$ Population (in million) $= \dfrac{127}{42} = 3.02$

In year 2015,

Total consumption (in million kg) = Production – Export

$= 221 - 116 = 105$

$\therefore$ Population (in million) $= \dfrac{\text{Consumption in million kg}}{\text{Per capita consumption}}$

$= \dfrac{105}{40.5} = 2.59$

In year 2014,

Total consumption (in million kg) $= 238 - 130 = 108$

$\therefore$ Population in million $= \dfrac{108}{38.7} = 2.79$

In year 2013,

Total consumption (in million kg) = 202 − 114 = 88

$\therefore$ Population in million $= \frac{88}{35.2} = 2.5$

Hence, the population of country is highest in year 2016.

**37** (*C*) In year 2015, Export = 116

Consumption = 221 − 116 = 105

$\therefore \quad \text{Ratio} = \frac{116}{105} \approx 1.10$

In year 2014, Export = 130

Consumption = 238 − 130 = 108

$\therefore \quad \text{Ratio} = \frac{130}{108} \approx 1.20$

In year 2013, Export = 114

Consumption = 202 − 114 = 88

$\therefore \quad \text{Ratio} = \frac{114}{88} \approx 1.29$

In year 2012,

Export = 114

Consumption = 186.5 − 114 = 72.5

$\therefore \quad \text{Ratio} = \frac{114}{72.5} \approx 1.57$

Hence, the ratio of export to consumption is highest in year 2012.

**38** (*A*) Total consumption in year 2014 (in million)

= 238 − 130 = 108

$\therefore$ Population in year 2014 (in million)

$$= \frac{\text{Consumption}}{\text{Per capita consumption}}$$

$$= \frac{108}{38.7} = 2.79$$

**39** (*D*) Percentage increase in consumption in year 2014

$$= \left(\frac{38.7 - 35.2}{35.2}\right) \times 100 = 9.9$$

Percentage increase in consumption in year 2015

$$= \left(\frac{40.5 - 38.7}{38.7}\right) \times 100 = 4.65$$

Percentage increase in consumption 2016

$$= \left(\frac{42 - 40.5}{40.5}\right) \times 100 = 3.7$$

Hence, highest percentage increase in year 2014.

**40** (*B*) Required average

$$= \frac{(186.5 - 114) + (202 - 114) + (238 - 130) + (221 - 116) + (215 - 88)}{5}$$

$$= \frac{72.5 + 88 + 108 + 105 + 127}{5}$$

$$= \frac{500.5}{5} = 100.1$$

**41** (*C*) According to the given information,

Total number of Ph.D students completed the programme successfully from all the seven universities = 5700

Total number of Ph.D students in the University C = 855 i.e. 10% of total.

$\therefore$ Total number of Ph.D students in the University E

$$= \frac{855}{10} \times 8 = 684$$

African students in the University E = 21 (given)

$\therefore$ Required percentage $= \frac{21}{684} \times 100 \approx 3\%$

**42** (*A*) Total number of students who successfully completed Ph.D programme in the University G

$$= \frac{5700 \times 12}{100} = 684$$

Total number of students in the University G, who joined Ph.D $= \frac{855}{10} \times 16 = 1368$

$\therefore$ Required ratio $= \frac{684}{1368} = \frac{1}{2}$

**43** (*A*) Total number of Foreign Ph.D students in University C = 65 + 46 + 25 + 35 = 171

Total number of Ph.D students in the University C = 855

$\therefore$ Required percentage $= \frac{171}{855} \times 100 = 20\%$

**44** (*B*) Total number of students who completed the Ph.D programme from Universities A and D together

$$= (18 + 16) \times \frac{5700}{100} = 1938$$

Total number of students who joined the Universities C and E together = 855 + 684 = 1539

$\therefore$ Required difference = 1938 − 1539 = 399

**45** (*D*) Required percentage of University E

$$= \frac{513}{684} \times 100 = 75\%$$

Required percentage of the University F

$$= \frac{855}{1368} \times 100 = 62.5\%$$

Required percentage of the University B

$$= \frac{969}{1881} \times 100 = 51.5\%$$

Required percentage of the University C

$$= \frac{741}{855} \times 100 = 86.6\%$$

Therefore, required percentage of University C is the highest.

**46** (*D*) Number of registered two wheelers in 2011

= 1018.65 lakh

Population of India in 2011 = 1210.19 millions

Per capita ownership of two wheelers in India in 2011

$$= \frac{1018.65 \times 10^5}{1210.19 \times 10^6} \approx 0.084\%$$

**47** (*D*) Growth in number of cars during year 1961-1971

$$= \frac{6.82 - 3.1}{3.1} = 1.2$$

Similarly, Growth during year 1971-1981

$$= \frac{11.60 - 6.82}{6.82} = 0.70$$

Growth during year 1981-1991$= \frac{29.54 - 11.60}{11.60} = 1.54$

Growth during year 1991-2001 $= \frac{70.58 - 29.54}{29.54} = 1.38$

Growth during year 2001-2011 $= \frac{191.23 - 70.58}{70.58} = 1.70$

Now, average decadal growth during 1961-2011

$$= \frac{(1.2 + 0.70 + 1.54 + 1.38 + 1.70)}{5} \times 100\%$$

$$= 130.4\% \approx 131\%$$

**48** (*D*) Number of registered Cars, Jeeps, Taxis in 2001

= 70.58 (lakhs)

Number of registered Buses in 2001 = 6.34 (lakhs)

Total number of registered vehicles = 549.91 (lakhs)

$\therefore$ Required percentage $= \frac{70.58 + 6.34}{549.91} \times 100\%$

$$= \frac{76.92}{549.91} \times 100\% \approx 14\%$$

**49** (*D*) Decadal growth in population of India during 1961-1971 $= \frac{548.15 - 439.23}{439.23} \times 100\% = 24.79\%$

Similarly, for year 1981-1991

$$= \frac{846.42 - 683.32}{683.32} \times 100\% = 23.86\%$$

For year 1991-2001

$$= \frac{1028.73 - 846.42}{846.42} \times 100\% = 21.53\%$$

For year 2001-2011

$$= \frac{1210.19 - 1028.73}{1028.73} \times 100\% = 17.63\%$$

$\therefore$ Decadal growth in population of India is maximum during 1961-1971.

**50** (*C*) Decadal growth in number of cars during 1971-1981

$$= \frac{11.60 - 6.82}{6.82} \times 100\% = 70.08\%$$

and that of two wheelers

$$= \frac{26.18 - 5.76}{5.76} \times 100\% = 354.5\%$$

Decadal growth in number of cars during 1981-1991

$$= \frac{29.54 - 11.60}{11.60} \times 100\% = 154.65\%$$

and that of two wheelers

$$= \frac{142.00 - 26.18}{26.18} \times 100\% = 442.4\%$$

Now, decadal growth in number of cars during 2001-2011

$$= \frac{191.23 - 70.58}{70.58} \times 100\% = 170.94\%$$

and that of two wheelers

$$= \frac{1018.65 - 385.56}{385.56} \times 100\% = 164.20\%$$

So, in the year 2011 decadal growth in the number of cars surpassed that of two wheelers.

**51** (*A*) In 2015, total revenue = 173 lakh

$\therefore$ Required percentage $= \frac{78}{173} \times 100\% = 45\%$

**52** (*C*) In 2012-2013 and 2013-2014, there was an increase in revenue from atleast two categories of items.

**53** (*D*) Increase in sales from 2014 to 2015 = 173 − 169

= ₹ 4 lakh

$\therefore$ Revenue in 2016 = 173 + 4 = ₹ 177 lakh

**Sol.** (Q. Nos. 54-56)

**Number of MCA Students**

| → Performance<br>Gender ↓ | Average | Good | Excellent | Total |
|---|---|---|---|---|
| Male | 16 | 22 | 10 | 48 |
| Female | 24 | 8 | 0 | 32 |
| Total | 40 | 30 | 10 | 80 |

**54** (*A*) From the above table, it is clear that 0 (no) female student is excellent.

**55** (*B*) Required proportion = 8 / 32 = 0.25

**56** (*B*) Required proportion = 22/30 = 0.73

**57** (*B*) In year 2016, total consumption (in million kg)

$= 215 - 88 = 127$

$\therefore$ Population in million $= \dfrac{127}{42} = 3.02$

In year 2015, total consumption (in million kg)

$= 221 - 116 = 105$

$\therefore$ Population in million $= \dfrac{105}{40.5} = 2.59$

In year 2014, total consumption (in million kg)

$= 238 - 130 = 108$

$\therefore$ Population in million $= \dfrac{108}{38.7} = 2.79$

In year 2013, total consumption (in million kg)

$= 202 - 114 = 88$

$\therefore$ Population in million $= \dfrac{88}{35.2} = 2.5$

Hence, the population of country is highest in year 2016.

**58** (*C*) In year 2015,

Export = 116

Consumption = 221 – 116 = 105

$\therefore$ Ratio $= \dfrac{116}{105} \approx 1.10$

In year 2014, Export = 130

Consumption = 238 – 130 = 108

$\therefore$ Ratio $= \dfrac{130}{108} \approx 1.20$

In year 2013, Export = 114

Consumption = 202 – 114 = 88

$\therefore$ Ratio $= \dfrac{114}{88} \approx 1.29$

In year 2012, Export = 114

Consumption = 186.5 – 114 = 72.5

$\therefore$ Ratio $= \dfrac{114}{72.5} \approx 1.57$

Hence, the ratio of export to consumption is highest in year 2012.

**59** (*A*) Total consumption in year 2014 (in million)

$= 238 - 130 = 108$

$\therefore$ Population in year 2014 (in million)

$= \dfrac{\text{Consumption}}{\text{Per capita consumption}} = \dfrac{108}{38.7} = 2.79$

**60** (*D*) Percentage increase in consumption in year 2013

$= \left(\dfrac{88 - 72.5}{72.5}\right) \times 100 = 21.38\%$

In year 2014 $= \left(\dfrac{108 - 88}{88}\right) \times 100 = 22.73\%$

In year 2015 $= \left(\dfrac{105 - 108}{108}\right) \times 100 = -2.78\%$

In year 2016 $= \left(\dfrac{127 - 105}{105}\right) \times 100 = 20.95\%$

Clearly, percentage increase in consumption of rice is maximum in 2014.

**61** (*B*) Expenditure of A $= \dfrac{2}{3} \times 9 =$ ₹ 6 lakh

$\because$ Profit of A in 2012 = 35%

So, income of A = 6 + 35% of 6

= 6 + 2.1 = ₹ 8.1 lakh

**62** (*C*) Required average $= \dfrac{30 + 40 + 35 + 50 + 35}{5}$

$= \dfrac{190}{5} = 38\%$

**63** (*B*) In the year 2013, the profit percentage of A is 45 and that of B is 35. So, it is in 2013.

**64** (*D*) According to the given information,

| Age Interval | Number of Employees | Average Salary |
|---|---|---|
| 30-35 | 7 | $\dfrac{200}{7} = 28.57$ |
| 36-40 | 2 | $\dfrac{75}{2} = 37.5$ |
| 41-45 | 7 | $\dfrac{290}{7} = 41.42$ |
| 46-50 | 1 | $\dfrac{50}{1} = 50$ |
| 51-55 | 3 | $\dfrac{160}{3} = 53.33$ |

The maximum average salary shows in the age group of (51-55) yr.

**65** (*D*) Per cent frequency in the class interval of (30-35) yr

$= \dfrac{7}{20} \times 100\% = 35\%$

**66** (*A*) Average age of the employees

$$= \frac{(44+32+54+42+31+53+42+51+34+41+33+31+30+37+44+36+34+49+43+45)}{20}$$

$$= \frac{806}{20} = 40.3 \text{ yr}$$

**67** (*A*) Total number of employees who are getting salary $\geq$ 40000 /month $= \frac{9}{20} \times 100\% = 45\%$

**68** (*B*) Average salary in (40-50) yr $= \frac{340}{8}$

$$= 42.5 \text{ thousand}$$

**69** (*C*) Average salary of all the employees

$$= \frac{(35+20+45+35+20+60+50+55+25+30+30+35+35+40+45+35+35+50+45+50)}{20}$$

$$= \frac{775}{20} = 38.75 \text{ thousand}$$

Per cent number of employees, who are getting salary less than the average salary of all the employees

$$= \frac{11}{20} \times 100\,\% = 55\%$$

**70** (*D*) Every source of irrigation that has registered improvement during the year 2002-03 to 2003-04, is as under

Improvement in Government canals

$$= \frac{(14444 - 13863) \times 100\%}{13863} = 4.19\%$$

Improvement in private canals

$$= \frac{206 - 206}{206} \times 100\% = 0$$

Improvement in tanks

$$= \frac{1908 - 1802}{1802} \times 100\% = 5.88\%$$

Improvement in tubewells and other wells

$$= \frac{35779 - 34250}{34250} \times 100\% = 4.46\%$$

Improvement in other sources

$$= \frac{4281 - 3657}{3657} \times 100\%$$

$$= 17.06\%$$

It is clear from above detail that the maximum improvement is done in other sources during the year 2002-03 to 2003-04.

**71** (*D*) Net irrigation by tanks in the year 1998-99

$$= \frac{2792 - 2593}{2593} \times 100\% = 7.67\%$$

Net irrigation by tanks in the year 2000-01

$$= \frac{2449 - 2535}{2535} \times 100\% = -3.39\%$$

Net irrigation by tanks in the year 2003-04

$$= \frac{1908 - 1802}{1802} \times 100\% = 5.88\%$$

Net irrigation by tanks in the year 2005-06

$$= \frac{2034 - 1727}{1727} \times 100\% = 17.77\%$$

It is clear from above detail that net irrigation by tanks increased at the highest rate in the year 2005-06.

**72** (*A*) It is clear from the given table that Government canals have recorded the maximum incidence of negative growth in terms of net irrigated area during the given years.

**73** (*C*) Share of tubewells and other wells in the total net irrigated area

In the year 1998-99

$$= \frac{33988}{57411} \times 100\% = 59.2\%$$

In the year 2000-01

$$= \frac{33796}{55076} \times 100\% = 61.36\%$$

In the year 2002-03

$$= \frac{34250}{53778} \times 100\% = 63.68\%$$

In the year 2004-05 $= \frac{34785}{58867} \times 100\% = 59.09\%$

It is clear from above that share of the tubewells and other wells in the total net irrigated area was the highest in the year 2002-03.

**74** (*C*) Detail of the largest percentage of decline in net area under irrigation during 1997-98 and 2005-06 is as below

Government canals $= \frac{15268 - 17117}{17117} \times 100\%$

$$= -10.8\%$$

Private canals $= \frac{207 - 211}{211} \times 100\% = -1.89\%$

Tanks $= \frac{2034 - 2593}{2593} \times 100\% = -21.55\%$

Other sources $= \frac{7314 - 3102}{3102} \times 100\% = 135.78\%$

Hence, from above detail we can say that the largest percentage of decline in net area irrigation is in the tanks.

**75** (*A*) Percentage growth of $CO_2$ emission

$$= \frac{CO_2 \text{ emission in 2009} - CO_2 \text{ emission in 2005}}{CO_2 \text{ emission in 2005}} \times 100$$

$$= \frac{800 - 500}{500} \times 100\%$$

$$= \frac{300}{500} \times 100\% = 60\%$$

**76** (*D*) Power sector $= \frac{800 - 500}{500} \times 100\%$

$$= \frac{300}{500} \times 100\% = 60\%$$

Industry sector $= \frac{450 - 200}{200} \times 100$

$$= \frac{250}{200} \times 100\% = 125\%$$

Commercial sector $= \frac{320 - 150}{150} \times 100$

$$= \frac{170}{150} \times 100\% = 113.33\%$$

Agriculture sector $= \frac{200 - 80}{80} \times 100$

$$= \frac{120}{80} \times 100 = 150\%$$

Therefore, required sector is Agriculture sector.

**77** (*A*) Total $CO_2$ emission in 2005

$$= 500 + 200 + 150 + 80 + 100 = 1030$$

Total $CO_2$ emission in 2009

$$= 800 + 450 + 320 + 200 + 180 = 1950$$

Percentage growth $= \frac{1950 - 1030}{1030} \times 100\%$

$$= \frac{920}{1030} \times 100\% = 89.32\%$$

**78** (*A*) Average annual growth

in the year 2005-06,

$$\frac{600 - 500}{500} \times 100\% = 20\%$$

in the year 2006-07,

$$\frac{650 - 600}{600} \times 100\% = 8.33\%$$

in the year 2007-08,

$$\frac{700 - 650}{650} \times 100\% = 7.69\%$$

in the year 2008-09,

$$\frac{800 - 700}{700} \times 100\% = 14.28\%$$

∴ Average annual growth rate

$$= \frac{20 + 8.33 + 7.69 + 14.28}{4}$$

$$= \frac{50.3}{4} = 12.57\%$$

**79** (*B*) Percentage contribution of power sector to total $CO_2$ emission in the year 2008

$$= \frac{CO_2 \text{ emission by power sector in 2008}}{\text{Total emission in 2008}} \times 100\%$$

$$= \frac{700}{700 + 400 + 300 + 150 + 150} \times 100\%$$

$$= \frac{700}{1700} \times 100\%$$

$$\approx 41.18\%$$

**80** (*A*) In 2005, the contribution of industry to total sectoral $CO_2$ emission was minimum, and it was 19.42%.

# UNIT 08

# *Information and Communication Technology*

## CHAPTER ANALYSIS

In this digital era, Information and Communication Technology (ICT) plays an important role in almost all spheres of our life. This unit is based on the updated syllabus of NTA UGC Net covering all the important topics of Information and Communication Technology (ICT).

After a thorough study of this chapter, you will be able to understand ICT and its general abbrevations, terminologies, basics of internet, intranet, e-mail, audio and video-conferencing, digital initiatives in higher education, ICT and governance and so on. From these topics, around 4-5 questions are asked in the exam. Most of the questions asked in exam are based on ICT, computer, binary number system, digital initiatives, etc.

ICT is a common term which refers to the technologies used for collecting, storing, editing and communicating information in various formats. It includes all communication devices or applications like, radio, TV, cellular phones, computers, networks, satellite system and so on. ICT plays a vital role in the current and future development of society and nation.

ICT can be defined as all the digital devices, tools, content and resources which are used to achieve the goals of teaching-learning process as well as management of the education system.

ICTs can be divided into two components as

(i) **Information Technology** (IT) refers to the hardware and software of information collection, storage, processing and presentation.

(ii) **Information and Communication Infrastructure** (ICI) refers to physical tele-communications systems and networks and the services that utilize ICT tools.

### IN THIS UNIT

- ICT : General Abbreviations and Terminologies
- Basics of Internet, Intranet, E-mail, Audio and Video-Conferencing
- Digital Initiatives in Higher Education
- ICT and Governance

## Components of ICT

There are 6 most common components that make up an ICT system:

- **Data** It includes raw facts/figures/ statistics.
- **Hardware** It contains physical components in a computer or peripherals such as input/ output devices, storage, processor, etc.
- **Software** It is a set of computer programs which provides the step by step instructions to get the job done.
- **Information** It is the result from processing data.
- **Procedures** These are actions conducted in a series of a certain order to ensure the system will run smoothly.
- **People** Individuals are needed to supply the data to the ICT system.

## Scope of ICT

### In Education

- Teaching models have changed with the introduction of ICT, as now learners participate actively on online computer based platforms instead of being passive listeners.
- ICT makes learning interactive, self directed and independent. It facilitates learner-centered learning with the use of computer and internet.
- E-learning platforms have emerged as one of the best measures that can help the students continue their studies during emergency situations like the COVID-19 outbreak.
- Considering the impact of ICT, various digital initiatives are launched by Ministry of HRD for school students and even those seeking UG and PG level education. E.g. DIKSHA, e-Pathshala, Swayam, Swayam Prabha, etc.

### In Healthcare

- Through ICT, the data can be transferred to the patient or to the doctor for consultation. The patient can have medical record in hand that can be used anywhere, anytime.
- In light of COVID-19, where people are forced to stay healthy indoors, mobile health (m Health) apps have come to our rescue. At present, there are approx 200,000 m-Health apps available in the apps stores which help people to know their health status and also helps interaction between patients and doctors.

### In Governance

- e-Governance is about leading the transformation of government to provide efficient, convenient and transparent services to citizens and businesses through the use of ICT.
- Government launched MyGov.in app, an innovative citizen engagement platform for direct participation of citizens in governance. It provides avenue for channelizing their ideas, comments and creative suggestions to central ministries and associated organisations.
- Other apps which have been launched by the government are cVIGIL, UMANG, mAadhaar, mPassport Seva, etc.

## Advantages of ICT

- **Communication** ICT offers a more efficient, time and money saving way of communication through apps like Whatsapp, Zoom, Skype, GoTo Meeting, etc.
- **Creation of Jobs** The best advantage of ICT has been creation of new and interesting jobs in IT sectors. Advancement of technology has created great employment opportunities in fields such as web designing, database administration, etc.
- **Cost Effectiveness** ICT has made everything cost effective. Nowadays, business meetings take place over video-conferencing apps such as Zoom. ICT saves money as it provides almost every facility including shopping.
- **Bridging the Cultural Gap** Greater access to the ICT has helped to bridge the cultural gap by helping people from different cultures to communicate with each another and allowing the exchange of views and ideas.
- **Greater Availability** ICT has made it possible for people to avail almost every facility at any time $24 \times 7$.

- **Education** ICT has allowed educational facilities to reach everyone while making learning easier and more effective.

## Disadvantages of ICT

- **Lack of Job Security** Experts believe that ICT has made job security a big issue. As technology keeps on changing nearly every day, individuals need to be constantly studying the changes in their profession, if they want to feel secure in their jobs.
- **Overriding Cultures** While ICT may have made the world a global village, it has also contributed to one culture to predominate over others. As a result, many a time, the traditional values of another comparatively weaker culture are lost.
- **Privacy** Though information technology may have made communication quicker, easier and more convenient, it has also brought along privacy issues. From cell phone signal interceptions to e-mail hacking, people are now worried about their once private information becoming public knowledge.
- **Reliance on Technology** With ICT, people relying on technology for everything. Consequently, they become prone to sedentary lifestyle which can lead to various problems.
- **Reliability of Information** Anyone with access to a computer and an internet connection internet can start a blog or post something up on a website, so just because something's on the web doesn't mean it's reliable. Hence, ICT is not a reliable medium of data.
- **Reduced Personal Interaction** ICT makes working or communicating from remote areas possible. This reduces all forms of personal interactions among friends, families and even colleagues.

# COMPUTER

- The term 'Computer' is derived from the Latin word 'Computare' which means 'to calculate'.
- A computer is an electronic machine that accepts data (input) from the user, processes the data by performing calculations and operations on it and then, generates the desired results (output) to the user. It processes both qualitative and quantitative data quickly and accurately.

### → Important Facts

- Charles Babbage also known as 'Father of Computer', who invented the Analytical Engine (first general purpose computer) and difference engine.
- 'Abacus' is a first mechanical calculating device and used for addition and subtraction.
- 'Pascaline' was a first mechanical adding machine developed by Blaise Pascal.
- 'ENIAC' was a first electronic digital computer.
- 'EDVAC' was a binary computer developed by John Von Neumann.

## Generations of Computer

A generation refers to the state of improvement in the development of system.
There are five generations of computer:

| Generations | Switching Devices | Speed | Operating Systems | Languages | Applications |
|---|---|---|---|---|---|
| First (1940-56) | Vaccum Tubes Thermionic Valve Machine | milliseconds | Batch operating system | Machine language | Used for scientific purpose e.g. ENIAC, UNIVAC, MARK-1, etc. |
| Second (1956-63) | Transistors (made of semi-conductor) | microseconds | Batch processing OS, Multitasking OS | Assembly languages | Used for commercial production, e.g. IBM 7094, CDC 1604, etc. |
| Third (1964-71) | Integrated Circuits (ICs) (made of silicon) | nanoseconds | Time sharing and multi-programming OS | High level language | Database management system e.g. IBM 360 series. Honeywell 6000 series, etc. |

| Generations | Switching Devices | Speed | Operating Systems | Languages | Applications |
|---|---|---|---|---|---|
| Fourth (1971-1980) | Very Large Scale Integrated (VLSI) circuits/ microprocessor | picoseconds | Time sharing, GUI interface, distributed systems | All high level languages | Personal Computers, e.g. IBM 4341, DEC 10, Intel 4004 micro processor, etc. |
| Fifth (19801 and onwards) | Ultra Large Scale Integrated (ULSI) chips | — | Parallel processing and AI systems | Natural language | Artificial intelligence e.g. Robotics, Laptop, etc. |

## Classification of Computer

The computer systems can be classified on the following basis:

### Based on Size

**Micro Computers** They are the least powerful, yet the most widely used and fastest growing types of computers also called 'Portable computers'. These are Laptops, Personal computers, Tablet computers, Handheld computers, Personal Digital Assistant (PDA), etc.

**Mini Computers** They are smaller in size, faster, cost lower than mainframe computers. Initially, it was designed for control, implementation, human interaction and communication but now are used for engineering and CAD (Computer Aided Design) calculations, etc. and even as midsize servers.
e.g. DEC PDP and vax series, HP-2100 series, etc.

**Mainframe Computers** They have large internal memory and processors that process billions of simple calculations and real time transactions. The mainframe computers are critical to commercial databases, transaction servers and applications that require high resiliency security and agility.

e.g. IBM Z series, UNIVAC 1110, etc.

**Super Computers** They are the fastest and most expensive machines which have high processing speed and speed is measured in FLOPS. e.g. CRAY 1, PARAM, etc.

### Based on Data Handling

**Analog Computer** An analog computer (spelt analogue in British English) is a form of computer that uses continuous physical phenomena such as electrical, mechanical, or hydraulic quantities to model the problem being solved.

**Digital Computer** A computer that performs calculations and logical operations with quantities represented as digits, usually in the binary number system.

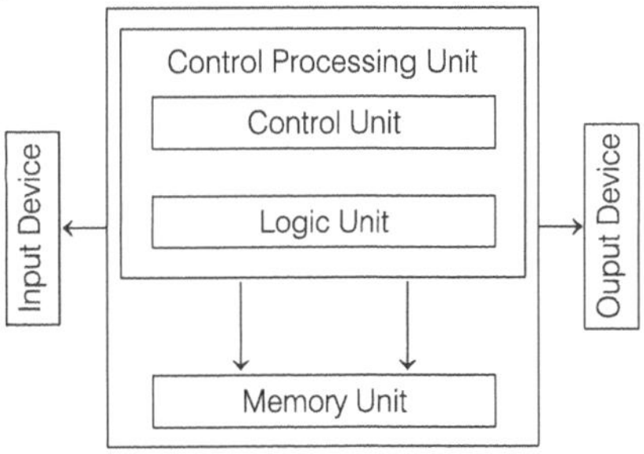


**Hybrid Computers** They are the combination of analog and digital computers. Machines used in hospitals like ECG and DIALYSIS are the commonly used hybrid computer.

### Based on Purpose

**General Purpose Computers** They are used to solve variety of problems by changing the program or instructions, e.g. to make small database, calculations, accounting, etc.

**Special Purpose Computers** They are used to solve a single and dedicated type of problem, e.g. Automatic aircraft landing, Multimedia computer, etc.

**Note** A personal computer uses a number of chips mounted on a circuit board called Motherboard.

## Components of Computer

A computer consists of following main components :

1. Input Unit
2. Output Unit

3. Central Processing Unit
4. Memory Unit

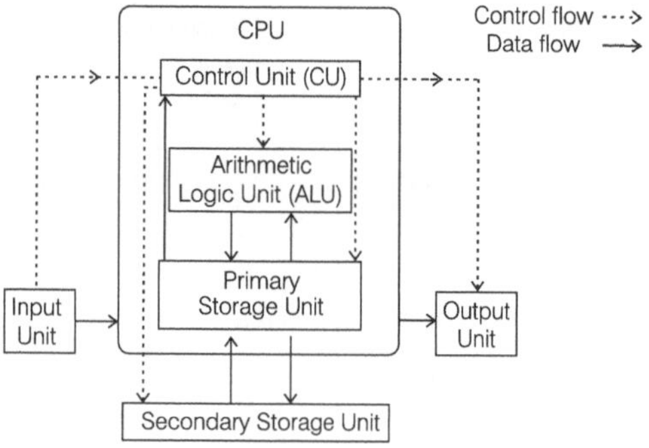


**Computer Architecture**

## 1. Input Unit

The computer accepts coded information through input unit by the user. It is a device that is used to give required information to the computer.

Some of the commonly used input devices are :

i. Keyboard
ii. Pointing devices: Mouse, Track ball, Joystick, Light pen.
iii. Barcode Reader
iv. Optical Mark Reader (OMR)
v. Optical Character Recognition (OCR)
vi. Magnetic Ink Character Recognition (MICR)
vii. Smart Card Reader
viii. Biometric Sensor
ix. Scanner
x. Microphone (Mic)
xi. Webcam, etc.

**Note** Ctrl, Shift and Alt keys are called modifier keys.

## 2. Output Unit

This unit sends the processed results to the user. It is mainly used to display the desired result to the user as per input instructions.

Some of the commonly used output devices are:

i. Monitor : CRT, LCD, LED, 3-D, TFT
ii. Printers provide hard copy. They are
   (a) **Impact Printers** Dot matrix printer, daisy wheel printer, line printer, drum printer.
   (b) **Non-Impact Printers** Inkjet printer, thermal printer, laser printer, electromagnetic printer, electrostatic printer.
iii. Plotter
iv. Speaker
v. Headphones
vi. Projector, etc.

## 3. Central Processing Unit (CPU)

It consists a set of registers, arithmetic logic unit and control unit, which together interpret and execute instructions in assembly language.

The primary functions of the CPU are as follows:

- The CPU transfers instructions and input data from main memory to registers, i.e. internal memory.
- The CPU executes the instructions in the stored sequence.
- When necessary, CPU transfers output data from registers to main memory.

Central Processing Unit is often called the 'Brain of Computer'. The CPU is fabricated as a single Integrated Circuit (IC) and is also known as 'microprocessor'.

**→ USB**

USB (Universal Serial Bus) is a plug and play interface that allows a computer to communicate with peripheral and other devices.

CPU consists of following main sub-systems:

### (i) Arithmetic Logic Unit (ALU)

ALU is responsible for performing calculations and contains decision-making mechanism.

Most ALUs can perform the following operations :

- Logical operations (AND, NOT, OR, XOR).
- Arithmetic operations (addition, subtraction, multiplication and division).
- Bit-shifting operations (shifting or rotating a word by a specified number of bit to the left or right with or without sign extension).
- Comparison operations (=, <, < =, >, > =).

### (ii) Control Unit (CU)

CU or clock coordinates with the input and output devices of a computer. It directs the computer to carry out stored program instructions by communicating with the ALU and the registers.

## 4. Memory Unit

Memory is a part of the computer, which holds data and instructions. This unit is responsible to store programs or data on a temporary or permanent basis.
In general, the memory is classified into two categories as follows:

### (i) Primary or Main Memory

The memory unit that communicates directly with the CPU is called the main memory or the internal memory.

Primary memory can be further classified in two categories which are as follows:

(a) **Random Access Memory** (RAM) It is also known as read/write memory or volatile memory that allows CPU to read as well as write data and instructions into it. It is used for the temporary storage that means it loses its content when the power supply button is switched off.

There are two categories of RAM as follows:

I. Dynamic RAM (DRAM)

II. Static RAM (SRAM)

(b) **Read Only Memory** (ROM) It is also known as non-volatile memory or permanent storage. It does not lose its content when the power is switched off. It holds the computer startup routine.

When a computer is booting, BIOS (Basic Input/Output System) is loaded to the memory by ROM.

There are three categories of ROM as follows:

I. Programmable Read Only Memory (PROM)

II. Erasable Programmable Read Only Memory (EPROM)

III. Electrically Erasable Programmable Read Only Memory (EEPROM)

**→ Cache Memory**

It is a storage buffer that stores the data which is used more often, temporarily and makes them available to CPU at a fast rate. It compensates the gap in speeds of processor and main memory.

**→ Virtual Memory**

It is an illusion of extremely large main memory that allows the execution of processes that are not completely in main memory.

### (ii) Secondary or Auxiliary Memory

This memory stores much larger amount of data and information for extended periods of time. Data in secondary memory cannot be processed directly by the CPU, first it must be copied into primary storage, i.e. RAM. This memory is also known as non-volatile memory.

Secondary memory devices are as follows:

(a) **Hard Disk Drive** (HDD) It is a non-volatile, random access digital data storage device. HDD is a data storage device used for storing and retrieving digital information using rotating disks (platters) coated with magnetic material. Hard disk is divided into tracks which are further subdivided into sectors.

(b) **Floppy Disk** (Diskette) It is used to store small amount of data and is slower to access than hard disks. They are composed of a thin and flexible disk of a magnetic storage medium of square shape.

(c) **Magnetic Tapes** These tapes are made of a thin, magnetizable coating on a long, narrow strip of plastic film to store data permanently. Data can be read as well as recorded. These tapes can store data in a sequential manner.

(d) **Compact Disc** (CD) It is the most popular and the least expensive type of optical disc which is used as a data storage device.

CDs are categorised into three main types as follows:

I. CD-ROM (Compact Disc-Read Only Memory)

II. CD-R (Compact Disc- Recordable)

III. CD-RW (Compact Disc- ReWritable)

(e) **Digital Video Disc** (DVD) It is also known as Super Density Disc (SDD) or Digital Versatile Disc. DVDs offer higher storage capacity than compact discs while having the same dimensions.

Depending upon the disc type, DVD can store several Gigabytes of data (4.7 GB-17.08 GB).

DVDs come in three varieties as follows :

I. DVD-ROM (Digital Video Disc-Read Only Memory)

II. DVD-R (DVD-Recordable)

III. DVD-RW (DVD-ReWritable)

(f) **Blu-ray Disc** (BD) It is an optical disc storage medium designed to recapture the data normally in DVD format. Blu-ray disc contains 25 GB (23.31 GB) per layer space. Blu-ray can hold almost 5 times more data than a single layer DVD.

(g) **Pen/Thumb Drive** Pen drive is also known as flash drive. A flash drive is a data storage device that consists of flash memory (key memory) with a portable USB (Universal Serial Bus) interface.

**Note** A new laptop has been produced using the solid state hard drive technology. This technology weighs less, is smaller and uses less power.

**Basic Units of Memory Measurements**

| | |
|---|---|
| 1 Bit | Binary Digit (0 or 1) |
| 4 Bits | 1 Nibble |
| 8 Bits | 1 Byte |
| 1024 Byte | 1 KB (Kilo Byte) |
| 1024 KB | 1 MB (Mega Byte) |
| 1024 MB | 1 GB (Giga Byte) |
| 1024 GB | 1 TB (Tera Byte) |
| 1024 TB | 1 PB (Peta Byte) |
| 1024 PB | 1 EB (Exa Byte) |
| 1024 EB | 1 ZB (Zetta Byte) |
| 1024 ZB | 1 YB (Yotta Byte) |
| 1024 YB | 1 BB (Bronto Byte) |
| 1024 BB | 1 Geop Byte |

**→ Motherboard**

The main circuit board contained in any computer is called a Motherboard. It is also known as the Main Board, Logic Board, System Board or Planar Board. All other electronic devices and circuits of computer system are attached to this board like CPU, ROM, RAM, expansion slots, PCI slots and USB ports.

# DATA REPRESENTATION

It refers to those methods which are used internally to represent information stored in a computer.

## Number System

It defines a set of values that is used to represent quantity. Digital computers internally use the binary number system to represent the data and perform arithmetic calculations.

The number systems generally used by a computer are as follows :

1. **Binary Number System** This system is very efficient for computers, but not for humans. It contains only two unique digits 0s and 1s. It is also known as Base 2 System. The binary numbers 0 and 1 are called a bit. The computer always calculates input in binary form.

   e.g. $(10101)_2$

2. **Decimal Number System** It consists of 10 digits from 0 to 9. These digits can be used to represent any numeric value. It is also known as base 10 system or positional number system.

   e.g. $(1275)_{10}$, $(10406)_{10}$

   There are minimum 8 bits required to store any 3 digits decimal number.

3. **Octal Number System** It consists of 8 digits from 0 to 7. It is also known as base 8 system. Each position of the octal number represents a successive power of eight.

4. **Hexadecimal Number System** It provides us with a shorthand method of working with binary numbers. It is represented by four binary digits.

   These are 0 to 9 and A to F, where A denotes 10, B denotes 11 ....... F denotes 15. It is also known as Base 16 System or simply Hex.

   So, each position of the hexadecimal number represents a successive power of 16.

**Decimal, Binary, Octal and Hexadecimal Equivalents**

| Decimal | Binary | Octal | Hexadecimal |
|---|---|---|---|
| 0 | 0000 | 0 | 0 |
| 1 | 0001 | 1 | 1 |
| 2 | 0010 | 2 | 2 |
| 3 | 0011 | 3 | 3 |
| 4 | 0100 | 4 | 4 |
| 5 | 0101 | 5 | 5 |
| 6 | 0110 | 6 | 6 |
| 7 | 0111 | 7 | 7 |
| 8 | 1000 | | 8 |
| 9 | 1001 | | 9 |
| 10 | 1010 | | A |
| 11 | 1011 | | B |
| 12 | 1100 | | C |
| 13 | 1101 | | D |
| 14 | 1110 | | E |
| 15 | 1111 | | F |

## Conversion Between the Number Systems

Different types of conversion between the number systems are discussed below:

### 1. Decimal to Binary

To convert decimal to binary, following steps are involved :

***Step* 1** Divide the given number by 2.

***Step* 2** Note the quotient and remainder. Remainder should be 0 or 1.

***Step* 3** If quotient ≠ 0, then again divide the quotient by 2 and back to step 2.

If quotient = 0, then stop the process.

***Step* 4** First remainder is called as 'Least Significant Bit' (LSB) and last remainder is called as 'Most Significant Bit' (MSB).

***Step* 5** Arrange all remainders from MSB to LSB.

**Example** $(43)_{10} \rightarrow (?)_2$

| | | Remainder |
|---|---|---|
| 2 | 43 | 1 → LSB |
| 2 | 21 | 1 |
| 2 | 10 | 0 |
| 2 | 5 | 1 |
| 2 | 2 | 0 |
| 2 | 1 | 1 → MSB |
| | 0 | |

Then, $(43)_{10} \rightarrow (101011)_2$

### 2. Binary to Decimal

To convert binary to decimal, following steps are involved :

***Step* 1** Multiply all the binary digits by powers of 2.

***Step* 2** The power for integral part will be positive and for fractional part will be negative.

***Step* 3** Add all the multiplying digits.

**Example** $(1101.10)_2 \rightarrow (?)_{10}$

$$(1101.10)_2 = 1\times 2^3 + 1\times 2^2 + 0\times 2^1 + 1\times 2^0 + 1\times 2^{-1} + 0\times 2^{-2}$$
$$= 8 + 4 + 0 + 1 + 0.5 + 0$$
$$= 13.5$$

Then, $(1101.10)_2 \rightarrow (13.5)_{10}$

## Computer Codes

In computer, any characters like alphabet, digit or special character are represented by collection of 1s and 0s in a unique coded pattern.

The binary coding schemes that are most commonly used as follows :

## BCD

It is a number system where four bits are used to represent each decimal digits. BCD (Binary Coded Decimal) is a method of using binary digits to represent the decimal digits (0-9).

## ASCII

These are standard character codes used to store data so that it may be used by other software programs. Basically, ASCII (American Standard Code for Information Interchange) codes are of two types which are as follows :

1. **ASCII-7** It is a 7-bits standard ASCII code. It allows $2^7 = 128$ (from 0 to 127) unique symbols.
2. **ASCII-8** It is an extended version of ASCII-7. It is an 8-bits code, allows $2^8 = 256$ (0 to 255) unique symbols or characters.

## EBCDIC

In EBCDIC (Extended Binary Coded Decimal Interchange Code), characters are represented by 8-bits. These codes store information which is readable by other computers. It allows $2^8 = 256$ (0-255) combinations of bits.

# SOFTWARE

It is a collection of computer programs and related data that provide the instructions for telling a computer what to do and how to do. Software is an interface between user and computer.

Software can be divided into various categories as :

## 1. System Software

It helps the computer to manage internal resources. It consists of several programs, which are directly responsible for controlling, integrating and managing the individual hardware components of a computer system. Some common examples of system software are:

### (i) Operating System

An Operating System (OS) is a software, or a series of programs, which perform various types of functions in order to manage and organise files.

It is the first program run on a computer, when the computer boots up. Functions of an operating system are :

- Process management
- Memory management
- File management
- Input/output management

An operating system can be classified as follows :

- **Single-user** Allows only one user at a time.
  e.g. MS-DOS, Windows XP.
- **Multi-user** Allows two or more users to run programs at the same time.
  e.g. Unix, Linux, Windows 2000/7.
- **Multi-tasking** Allows more than one program to be run concurrently.
  e.g. Linux, Unix, Windows 95.
- **Multi-processing** Supports running a program on more than one CPU.
  e.g. Unix, Windows NT/2000.
- **Real-time** Used for real-time based applications like satellite launch, weather-forecasting, etc.
  e.g. Linux, HP-RT.

### (ii) Device Drivers

A software,which is written with the objective of making a device functional when it is connected to the computer is called device driver. Every device, whether it is a printer, monitor, mouse or keyboard has a driver program associated with it for its proper functioning.

## 2. System Utilities

They are used to support, enhance, expand and secure existing programs and data in the computer system.

System utility mainly consists of the following functions:

(i) **Disk Compression** It increases the amount of information that can be stored on any secondary storage device by compressing all information stored on a hard disk.

(ii) **Disk Fragmenter** It can be used to rearrange files and unused space in storage device.

(iii) **Back up Utilities** They can make a copy of all information stored on a disk and restore either the entire disk or selected files.

(iv) **Disk Cleaners** They are used to find files that have not been used for a long time. This utility also serves to increase the speed of a slow computer.

(v) **Anti-virus** It is the utility which is used to scan computer for viruses and prevent the computer system files from being corrupt, e.g. Norton, Quick Heal, etc.

## 3. Application Software

It is a computer software designed to help the user to perform singular or multiple tasks. Application softwares are also called the end-user programs.

There are two types of application software:

### (i) General Purpose Software

These are used for any general purpose or function.These softwares allow users to do simple (general) computer tasks.

e.g. Word processing software, Electronic spreadsheets, DBMS, Desktop publishing, Multimedia software, etc.

### (ii) Specific Purpose Software

These are created to execute one specific task. e.g. Inventory management, Payroll, Hotel management, Reservation, Report card generator, Billing system, HR management system, etc.

## 4. Open Source Software

It refers to something that can be modified and shared as its design is publicly accessible. Thus, open source software is a software whose source code is available for modification or enhancement by anyone. It contains certain criteria that must be met as follows:

- Software must be available free or at a low cost.
- Source code must be included.
- Anyone must be allowed to modify the source code.
- Modified versions can be redistributed.

Some examples of Open Source Software are : Linux, Open Office, Apache, HTTP Server, Mozilla Firefox, Google Chrome, Python, etc.

# PROGRAMMING LANGUAGE

It is a set of keywords, symbols and a system of rules for constructing statements by which humans can communicate the instructions to be executed by a computer. It is mainly categorised as :

## 1. Low Level Language

These are designed to operate and handle the entire instruction set of a computer system and directly interact with hardware.

It is divided into two parts :

(i) **Machine Language** It is sometimes, referred to as machine code or object code. It is a collection of binary digits or bits that computer reads and interprets.

(ii) **Assembly Language** It is used to interface with computer hardware. It uses instructed commands as substitutions for numbers allowing human to read the code more easily than binary.

## 2. Medium Level Language

It serves as the bridge between raw hardware and programming layer of a computer system.

## 3. High Level Language

A high level language is a programming language designed to simplify computer language. It is a language that is several steps removed from the actual code of the computer processor.

E.g. Basic, C, FORTRAN, Java, Pascal, etc.

**Some High Level Languages and their Application Areas**

| Languages | Years | Developers | Application Areas |
|---|---|---|---|
| FORTRAN (Formula Translation) | 1957 | IBM | Calculation |
| ALGOL(Algorithmic Language) | 1958 | A Committee of European | Scientific Purpose |
| COBOL(Common Business Oriented Language) | 1989 | A Committee | Business Management |
| BASIC(Beginner's All-purpose Symbolic Instruction Code) | 1964 | John G.Kemeny and Thomas E.Kurtz | Programming for Educational Purpose |
| Pascal | 1970 | Niklaus Wirth | Education |
| C | 1972 | Dennis Ritchie | System Programming |
| C++ | 1985 | Bjarne Stroustrup | System Object Programming |
| Java | 1995 | James Gosling | Internet Oriented Programming |

## Language Translator

It helps in converting programming languages to machine language.The translated program is called object code.

There are three different kinds of language translators

1. **Assembler** It is used to convert the assembly language into machine language (i.e. in the form of 0 or 1).This language consists of mnemonic codes, which are difficult to learn and is machine dependent.
2. **Compiler** It is used to convert the source code (written in high level language) into machine language. Compiler reads whole source code in a single run and traps the errors and informs to the programmer.
3. **Interpreter** This program converts a high level language program into machine language by converting it line-by-line and inform to the user as an error occurs.

# MICROSOFT WINDOWS (MS-WINDOWS)

Microsoft Windows stands for 'Microsoft Wide Interactive Network Development for Office Work Solution.' Microsoft windows is a series of graphical interface operating system developed, marketed and sold by Microsoft.

## Desktop

When we turn ON the computer then the first screen, which will be display on the computer is known as 'desktop'. The background image of desktop is called 'wallpaper'. A small arrow or blinking symbol, moving on the desktop, is called 'cursor'. Desktop contains start menu, task bar, icons, gadgets, etc.

## Files

These are the collection of data stored on auxiliary storage media. In windows, files are the basic unit to store data. The name given to a file or document by the user is called 'file name'. Each file has a specific file name and has a 'file extension' that identifies the file type.

Some common filename extensions are as follows :

| | |
|---|---|
| .rtf | WordPad document |
| .txt | Notepad text file |
| .eml | E-mail file |
| .exe | Executable file |
| .htm | HTML file (Web page) |
| .html, .pptx | MS-PowerPoint Presentation |
| .png | Portable Network Graphic |
| .gif | Graphics Interchange Format |
| .bmp | Bitmap |

## Folders

User organises files by storing them in folders. Folders can also store other folders, i.e. sub-folders. You can create any number of sub-folders and each can hold any number of files and additional sub-folders.

# MICROSOFT OFFICE (MS-OFFICE)

Microsoft Office was developed by Microsoft Inc in 1988. It is a collection of softwares, based on specific purpose and mainly used in office work.

## Microsoft Word (MS-Word)

MS-Word is a word processing application. Word processing software is mainly used in the creation of text based documents. It provides tools for composing, editing, formatting and printing of documents smaller than 45 KB.

E.g. WordStar, Easy Word, Notepad for windows.

When a user starts or opens MS Word, by default the name of the blank document is Document1 .docx where .doc or .docx is the extension.

### Features of Microsoft Word

MS-Word is the most popular word processing application due to its user-friendly features as described below :

- **Text Editing** It provides tremendous flexibility in terms of editing, adding and deleting text, modification of text content, i.e. cut, copy and paste.
- **Format Text** It offers to modify the text in any of the available hundreds of text designs, format text in various styles such as bold, italic, underline, etc.
- **Indentation** It denotes the distance of text boundaries and page margins. It offers three types of indentation– positive, hanging and negative.
- **Page Orientation** It facilitates selection of typed text printed or visible in horizontal view or vertical view on a specified size of the page. Word offers two types of page orientation : Portrait–vertically oriented and Landscape– horizontally oriented.
- **Bullets and Numbering** A list of bullets and numbering features used for tables, lists, pages and tables of content. Bullets are arranged in unordered lists and numbering are arranged in ordered lists.
- **Mail-Merge** Word provides a mail-merge of addresses of a large number of recipients with a common text document.
- **Graphics** It provides the facility of incorporating drawings in the documents which enhances their usefulness.
- **Horizontal and Vertical Scroll Bars** They enable one to move up and down or left and right across the window.

  The horizontal scroll bar is located above the status bar to back and forth the document. The vertical scroll bar is located along the right side of the screen to move up and down the document.

## Microsoft Excel (MS-Excel)

An electronic spreadsheet is used for analysing, sharing and managing information for accounting purpose performing mathematical calculations, budgeting, billing, etc.

A spreadsheet or worksheet is a matrix of rows and columns similar to an accounting ledger. Default extension of MS-Excel is .xlsx.

## Microsoft PowerPoint (MS-PowerPoint)

The application software that can create professional looking visual aids is called presentation graphics software.

The presentation software is used for creation of the slides and to display the information in the form of presentation of slides.

## Microsoft Access (MS-Access)

Database is a collection of logically related and similar data. Microsoft access is an application which allows the creating of databases. By default, .accdb is the extension of a MS Access.

# DATABASE

It is a collection of logically related information in an organised way so that it can be easily accessed, managed and updated. Database is inter-related records that performs adding, updating and deleting data.

## Components of a Database

A database consists of several different components. Database components are described below

### 1. Tables

These are the building blocks or relation of any relational database model where all the actual data is defined and entered.

Tables consist of cells at the intersection of records (rows) and fields (columns), which are described below :

(i) **Field** It is an area (within the record) reserved for a specific piece of data. e.g. customer number, customer name, street address, city, state, phone number, current address, etc. Field of a table is also known as 'column'.

(ii) **Record** It is the collection of data items of all the fields pertaining to one entity, i.e. a person, company, transition, etc. Record of a table is also known as 'row' or a 'tuple'.

### 2. Queries

These are basically questions based on the data available in a database. A query consists of specifications indicating which fields, records, and summaries a user wants to fetch from a database.

### 3. Forms

Like tables, forms can be used to view and edit your data. However, forms are typically used to view the data in an underlying table one record at a time.

### 4. Reports

When you want to print the records fetched from your database you need to design a report.

## Data Hierarchy

It refers to the systematic organisation of data, often in a hierarchical form.

Database
↑
Files
↑
Records
↑
Fields
↑
Bytes (Character)
↑
Bits

# COMPUTER NETWORK

A computer network is a collection of two or more computers which are connected together to share information and resources. User can share its its files as well as devices in computer network.

## Types of Computer Network

Types of computer network are as follows:

**Local Area Network** (LAN) A network that connects a group of computers in a small geographical area such as home, office, building, etc.

**Metropolitan Area Network** (MAN) It is a data network designed for a town or a city. e.g. a cable TV network.

**Wide Area Network** (WAN) It spans large locality and connects countries together. e.g. Internet.

**Wireless Local Area Network** (WLAN) It uses radio waves as its carrier. Areas may range from a single room to an entire office.

**Personal Area Network** (PAN) It is used for communication among computer and different information technological devices close to one person.

**Virtual Private Network** (VPN) The links between nodes are carried by virtual circuits in some larger network (e.g. Internet) instead of by physical wires.

## Network Topology

Topology can be referred as the geometric arrangement of a computer system. Each computer system in a topology is known as node. It includes :

1. **Bus Topology** In this topology, there is a single cable line to which all nodes are connected. If the cable is broken, the entire segment fails.

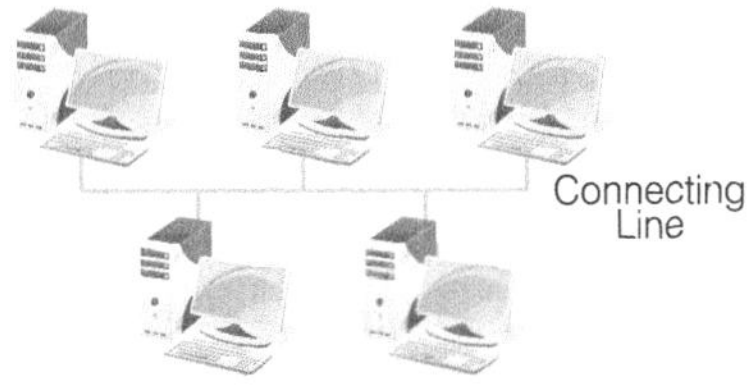


Bus Topology

2. **Ring or Circular Topology** In this topology, each node is connected in a circular way, to exactly two other nodes. Data travels from node to node, with each node handling every bit of data.

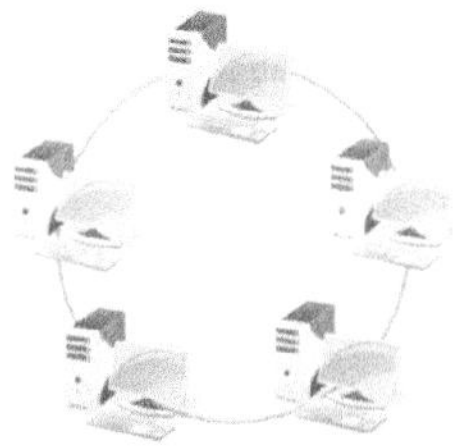

Ring Topology

3. **Star Topology** In this topology, the peripheral nodes are connected to a central node which is called hub.

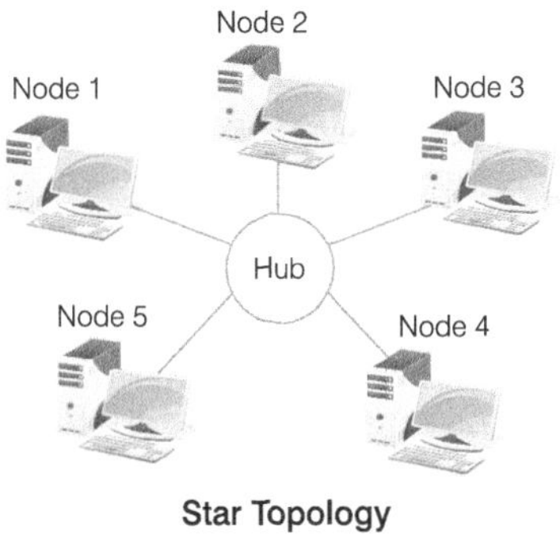


Star Topology

4. **Mesh Topology** In this topology, every node has a dedicated point to point link to every other node. It is also known as completely inter-connected topology.

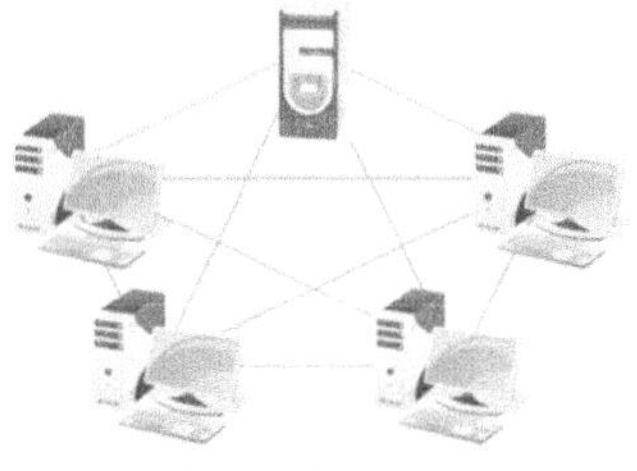

Mesh Topology

5. **Tree Topology** A tree network is a hybrid network topology in which star networks are interconnected via bus networks. This network is hierarchal in nature.

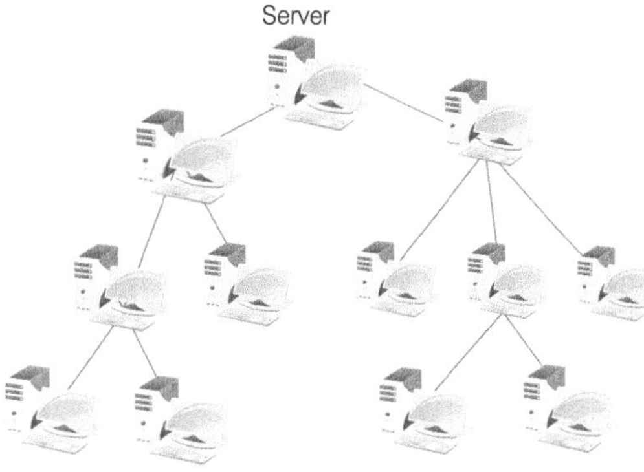


Tree Topology

## Communication

The term 'communication' means 'sending or receiving information'. When we communicate, we share information or data.

A communication system can be defined as the collection of hardware and software that facilitates intersystem exchange of information between different devices.

### Communication Media

Communication media of a network refer to the transmission media or the connecting media used in the network. It can be :

1. **Guided Media or Wired Technologies** It is bound by the cabling system that guides the data signal along specific path. It includes ethernet cable, coaxial cable and fibre optic cable.

2. **Unguided Media or Wireless Technologies** It is the transfer of information over a distance without the use of enhanced electrical conductors or wires. It includes radiowave, microwave, satellite, infrared wave and bluetooth.

# INTERNET

Internet stands for Interconnected Network, which began in 1950s by **Vint Cerf**, the Father of Internet. The Internet is a world wide network of networked computers that connects millions of people all over the world.

## History of Internet

In 1969, the University of California at Los Angeles and the University of Utah were connected as the beginning of the ARPANET (Advanced Research Projects Agency Network) using 50 kbits circuits.

It was the world's first operational packet switching network. The goal of this project was to connect computers at different universities and U.S. defence.

In mid 80s, another federal agency, the National Science Foundation created a new high capacity network called NSFNET, which was more capable than ARPANET. The only drawback of NSFNET was that it allowed only the academic research on its network and not any kind of private business on it.

So, private organisations and people started working to build their own networks, which were later interconnected with ARPANET and NSFNET to form the Internet.

### → Intranet and Extranet

**Intranet** is a private network that is contained within an enterprise. It may consist of many interlinked local area networks and also use leased lines in the wide area network. Typically, an intranet includes connections through one or more gateway computers to the outside Internet. The main purpose of an intranet is to share company information and computing resources among employees.

**Extranet** is a private network that is used for Internet protocol and the public tele-communication to share part of a business information.

## Types of Internet Connections

Some of the Internet connections available for Internet access are :

1. **Dial-up Connection** It is a method of connecting to the Internet using an existing telephone.

   The modem connects the computer through the standard phone lines, which serve as the data transfer medium.

2. **Broadband Connection** The term commonly refers to high speed Internet access that is always on and faster than the traditional dial-up access.

   It uses a telephone line to connect to the Internet. Broadband includes several high speed transmission technologies such as :

   (i) DSL (Digital Subscriber Line)
   (ii) Cable Modem
   (iii) Fibre Optic
   (iv) BPL (Broadband over Power Line),etc.

3. **Wireless Connection** Wireless broadband connects a home or business to the Internet using a radio link between the customer's location and the service provider's facility.

   Some ways to connect wirelessly are :

   (i) Wi-Fi (Wireless Fidelity)
   (ii) WiMAX (Worldwide Interoperability for Microwave Access
   (iii) Mobile Wireless Broadband Service
   (iv) Satellite, etc.

## Interconnecting Protocols

A protocol is a set of rules that govern data communications. Generally, some of protocols used to communicate via an Internet are as follows

1. **Transmission Control Protocol/Internet Protocol** (TCP/IP) The Internet protocol suits are the set of communication protocols used for the Internet. The details of TCP/IP are as follows :

   - **Transmission Control Protocol** (TCP) It provides reliable transport service, i.e. it ensures that message sent from sender to receiver is properly routed.

- **Internet Protocol** (IP) It allows different computers to communicate by creating a network of networks. IP handles the dispatch of packets over the network.

**Note** TCP/IP is necessary if one is to connect to the LAN.

2. **Simple Mail Transfer Protocol** (SMTP) It is the standard protocol for E-mail services on a TCP/IP network. It provides the ability to send and receive mail messages.
3. **Post Office Protocol 3** (POP3) It is the most recent version of a standard protocol for receiving E-mail. It is a client/server protocol in which E-mail is received and held for you by your Internet server.
4. **Internet Message Access Protocol** (IMAP) It is a standard protocol for accessing E-mail on a remote server from a local client. IMAP is an application layer Internet protocol.
5. **File Transfer Protocol** (FTP) It can transfer files between any computers that have an Internet connection and also works between computers using totally different operating systems.
6. **HyperText Transfer Protocol** (HTTP) It defines how messages are formatted and transmitted and what actions should be taken by the web servers and browsers in response to various commands. HTTP is called a 'stateless protocol'.
7. **Telnet Protocol** Telnet is a program that runs on the computer and connects PC to a server on the network. Telnet session will get started by entering valid username and password.
8. **Usenet Protocol** The usenet service allows a group of Internet users to exchange their views/ideas and information on some common topic that is of interest to all the members belonging to that same group.
9. **Point-to-Point Protocol** (PPP) It is a dial account which puts your computer directly on the Internet.
10. **Wireless Application Protocol** (WAP) A WAP browser is a commonly used web browser for small mobile devices such as cell phones.
11. **Voice over Internet Protocol** (VoIP) It allows delivery of voice communication over IP networks. e.g. IP calls.

## Terms Related to Internet

Some terms related to internet are as follows:

### World Wide Web (WWW)

WWW was introduced on 13th March, 1989, by Tim Berners Lee. The World Wide Web is a system of Internet servers that supports hypertext and multimedia to access several Internet protocols on a single interface.

The World Wide Web is a way of exchanging information between computers on the Internet, try to tie them together into a vast collection of interactive multimedia resources (Graphics, Audio, Video, Animation and Text).

### Web Page

The backbone of the World Wide Web is made of files, called 'pages' or 'web pages', containing information and links to resources- both text and multimedia - throughout the Internet. It is created using HTML.

There are basically two main types of web pages as static and dynamic. The main or first page of a website is known as home page.

### Website

A group of web pages that follow the same theme and are connected together with hyperlinks is called **website**.

e.g. http://www.carwale.com is a website while http://www.carwale.com/new/ is a web page.

### Web Browser

Web browsers are programs used to explore the Internet. We can install more than one web browsers on a single computer. The user can navigate through files, folders and websites with the help of a browser.

There are two types of web browser as follows :

(i) **Text Web Browser** A web browser that displays only text-based information is known as text web browser. e.g. Lynx.

(ii) **Graphical Web Browser** A web browser that supports both text and graphic information is known as graphical web browser.

e.g. Internet Explorer, Firefox, Netscape, Safari, Google Chrome and Opera.

**Note** The first graphical web browser was NCSA Mosaic and Netscape.

## Web Server

It is a computer program that requested HTML pages or files. A web client is the requesting program associated with the user.

The web browser is a client that requests HTML files from web servers. The server computer will deliver those web pages to the computers that requested them.

Every web server that is connected to the Internet is given a unique address, i.e. IP address made up of a series of four numbers between 0 to 255 separated by periods(.). e.g. Apache HTTP Server, Internet Information Services, Lighttpd, etc.

## Web Address and URL

A web address identifies the location of a specific web page on the Internet, such as http://www.learnyoga.com. On the web, web addresses are called URLs. URL stands for Uniform Resource Locator. Tim Berners Lee created the first URL in 1991 to allow the publishing of hyperlinks on the world wide web.

e.g."http://www. google.com/services/index.htm"

| | | |
|---|---|---|
| http | — | Protocol identifier |
| www | — | World Wide Web |
| google.com | — | Domain name |
| /services/ | — | Directory |
| index.htm | — | Web page |

## Domain Name

Domain is a group of network resources assigned to a group of users. A domain name is a way to identify and locate computers connected to the Internet. It always has two or more parts, separated by period/dot (·).

e.g. google.com, yahoo.com, etc.

## Domain Abbreviation

Domains are organised by the type of organisations and by country. A three-letter abbreviation indicating the organisation and usually two-letter abbreviation indicating the country name.

Most common domain abbreviations for organisations are as follows :

| Names | Entities |
|---|---|
| .info | Informational organisation |
| .com | Commercial business |
| .gov | Government agencies |
| .edu | Educational institutions |
| .org | Non-profit organisation |

Some domain abbreviations for country are as follows :

| Names | Entities |
|---|---|
| .in | India |
| .au | Australia |
| .fr | France |

**Note** MAC, Hardware and Physical Addresses are same.

## Blogs

A blog is a website or web page in which an individual records opinions, links to other site on regular basis. A typical blog combines text, images, and links to other blogs, web pages and other media related to its topic.

## Newsgroups

An area on a computer network especially the Internet, devoted to the discussion of a specified topic is known as Newsgroup.

## Search Engine

It is a website that provides the required data on specific topics. Search engines turn the web into a powerful tool for finding information on any topic. Here are some of the most popular search engines:

| | |
|---|---|
| Google | http://www.google.com |
| AltaVista | http:/www.altavista.com |
| Yahoo | http://www.yahoo.com |
| Hotbot | http://www.hotbot.com |
| Lycos | http://www.lycos.com |
| Excite | http://www.excite.com |
| WebCrawler | http://www.webcrawler.com |

## Services of Internet

Some of the important services provided by the Internet are as follows :

### Chatting

It is the online textual or multimedia conversation that takes place over the Internet. Chat with people using the Internet is somewhat similar to using the telephone for the same purpose. e.g. Skype, Whatsapp, Messenger, Google Talk, etc.

### E-mail

E-mail (Electronic-mail) is an electronic version of sending and receiving letter. Electronic mail lets you send and receive messages in electronic form.

The E-mail is transmitted between computer systems, which exchange messages or pass them onto other sites according to certain Internet protocols or rules for exchanging E-mail.

#### E-mail Addressing

To use E-mail, a user must have an E-mail address. The E-mail address contains all information required to send or receive a message from anywhere in the world. Storage area for E-mail messages is called mail box.

E-mail address consists of two parts separated by @ symbol – the first part is user name and the second part is host name (domain name). However, spaces are not allowed within the E-mail address.
e.g. arihantbooks@gmail.com

Here, arihantbooks is a username and gmail.com is a domain name.

#### Mailbox : Inbox and Outbox

A mailbox is the storage location of electronic mail messages that is found on a remote server. Software e-mail commonly divide the mailbox into separate folders, notably the inbox, outbox, sent items and deleted items.

- **Inbox** A place where e-mail messages are received. The inbox is the default location for all incoming mails unless rules have been setup to forward messages to another program or folder.
- **Outbox** A term used to describe the location or folder where e-mail is stored before being sent. It gives the opportunity to the user to review, edit and delete messages before they are sent.
- **Drafts** The drafts folder contains items that have not yet been sent. An e-mail is saved to the drafts folder when a user composes an e-mail and then click the Save and Close button.
- **Sent Items** This folder contains all items that have been sent but not deleted. It saves all the messages that were successfully sent.
- **Delete Items** When an e-mail is deleted, it is automatically sent to the trash. Items in your trash will remain there for approximately 30 days before it is automatically emptied and permanently deleted.

#### Creating and Sending a New E-mail

After login, if a user wants to create an e-mail, click on COMPOSE button and the following window will display on the screen.

New Message Window

There are various options which are accessible within an e-mail like Text formatting, Cc (Carbon copy), Bcc (Blind carbon copy), etc.

Some of these are as follows:

- **Cc** (Carbon copy) This allows an E-mail to be send to a large number of people by writing their respective addresses separated by commas.

- **Bcc** (Blind carbon copy) This is Cc, except that the recipient does not see the list of people in the Bcc field.
- **Signature** This is one of the basic elements of an E-mail message. By this, you are often able to set a signature, meaning a few lines of text which will be added to the end of the document.
- **Attachment** The files which are stored in computer can be sent through e-mail, with the help of attach files option in New Message window, user can send .doc, .pdf and .jpg files.

## Other Services of Internet

Some other services of Internet are as follows:

### Social Networking

It is a website that allows people with similar interests to come together and share information, photos and videos. This type of collaboration and sharing is known as social media. The most popular sites are currently Facebook, Twitter, Instagram, MySpace, etc.

### E-commerce

E-commerce (Electronic-commerce) includes sharing business information, maintaining business relationships and conducting business transactions by means of tele-communication networks or process of trading goods over Internet.

### Video-Conferencing

This term usually refers to communication between three or more users who are in atleast two locations, rather than one-to-one communication. Each user or group of users who are participating in a video conference typically must have a computer, a camera, a microphone, a video screen and a sound system. It can be classified audio-visual two way.

### Audio-Conferencing

It is the practice of connecting multiple parties on a single audio conference call, with multiple lines connected through a conferencing bridge. Audio conferencing participants can either be dialed directly by the meeting host or dial in manually to be conferencing bridge to join the call.

### E-banking

E-banking (Electronic-banking) is also known as Internet banking or Online banking. E-banking means any user with a personal computer and a browser can get connected to his bank's website to perform any of the virtual banking functions. All the services that the bank has permitted on the Internet are displayed in menu.

### E-shopping

E-shopping (Electronic-shopping) or Online shopping is the process of buying goods and services from merchants who sell on the Internet.

Books, clothing, household appliances, toys, hardware, software and health insurance are just some of the hundreds of products, consumers can buy from an online store. Some E-shopping sites are Naaptol, Flipkart, Yebbi, Homeshop 18, etc.

### E-reservation

E-reservation (Electronic-reservation) means making a reservation for a service *via* Internet.

You need not personally go to an office or a counter to book/reserve railways, airways tickets, hotel rooms, tourist packages, etc.

Examples of E-reservation sites are as follows:

(i) www.irctc.com
(ii) www.makemytrip.com
(iii) www.yatra.com
(iv) www.bookingsite.com

### E-learning

E-learning (Electronic-learning) refers to the electronic mode of delivering learning, training educational programs to users.

It is the mode of acquiring knowledge by means of the Internet and computer based training programs.

### M-commerce

M-commerce (Mobile-commerce) provides the application for buying and selling goods or services through wireless Internet enabled handheld devices. It involves new technologies, services and business models.

# COMPUTER SECURITY

It is also known as Cyber Security or IT Security. Computer security is a branch of information technology known as 'information security', which is intended to protect computers.

## Components of Computer Security

Basic components of computer security system are:

- **Confidentiality** It ensures that data is not accessed by any unauthorised person.
- **Integrity** It ensures that information is not altered by any unauthorised person.
- **Authentication** It ensures that users are the persons they claim to be.
- **Availability** It ensures that systems work promptly and service is not denied to authorised users.
- **Privacy** It ensures that an individual has the right to use the information and allows another to use that information.
- **Cryptography** It is the science of writing information in a 'hidden' or 'secret' form and is an ancient art. It protects the data in transmit and also the data stored on the disk. Some terms commonly used in cryptography are:
  - **Plain Text** It is the original message that is an input.
  - **Cipher** It is a bit-by-bit or character-by-character transformation without regard to the meaning of the message.
  - **Cipher Text** It is the coded message or the encrypted data.
  - **Encryption** It is encoding or scrambling data for transmission across a network. It secures the transmission.
  - **Decryption** It is the reverse of encryption, i.e. converting cipher text to plain text.

## Malware : Threats to Computer Security

Malware stands for Malicious Software. It is a broad term that refers to a variety of malicious programs that are used to damage computer system, gather sensitive information, or gain access to private computer systems.

It includes:

1. **Virus** VIRUS stands for Vital Information Resources Under Siege. Viruses copy itself and attach (rebooting) itself to other programs which further spread the infection.
2. **Worms** A computer worm is a standalone malware computer program that replicates itself in order to spread to other computers. Worms are hard to detect because they are invisible files.
3. **Trojan** A Trojan, or Trojan Horse, is a non-self replicating type of malware which appears to perform a desirable function but instead facilitates unauthorised access to the user's computer system. Trojans do not attempt to inject themselves into other files like a computer virus.
4. **Spyware** It is a program which is installed on a computer system to spy on the system owner's activity and collects all the information which is misused afterwards.

## Some Other Threats to Computer Security

There are some other threats to computer security, such as:

1. **Spoofing** It is the technique to access the unauthorised data without concerning to the authorised user.
2. **Hacking** It is an act of intruding into someone else's computer or network.
   A hacker is someone, who does hacking process.
3. **Cracking** It is an act of breaking into computers. Cracking tools include password crackers, trojans, virus, war-dialers, etc.

4. **Phishing** It is characterised by attempting to fraudulently acquire sensitive information such as passwords, credit cards details, etc.
5. **Spam** It is the abuse of messaging systems to send unsolicited bulk message in the form of E-mails. It is also called junk E-mails.

## Solutions to Computer Security Threats

Some safeguards to protect a computer system from accidental access aren :

1. **Antivirus Software** It is an application software that is designed to prevent, search for, detect and remove viruses and other malicious softwares. e.g. Avast, McAfee, Quick heal, Avg, etc.
2. **Digital Signature** It is an electronic form of a signature that can be used to authenticate the identity of the sender of a message.
3. **Firewall** Its primary objective is to control the incoming and outgoing network traffic by analysing the data packets and determining whether it should be allowed through or not, based on a predetermined rules.
4. **Password** It is a secret word or a string of characters used for user authentication to prove identity or access approval to gain access to resources, which should be kept secret from those who are not allowed to get access.

# DIGITAL INITIATIVES IN HIGHER EDUCATION

Higher education is changing very fast due to the Internet revolution and digital technology. Digitisation of higher education is now a global phenomenon, with large number of students going for it.

This shift from traditional forms of education points to the rapid globalisation and easy access to knowledge across the world. Digitisation gives increasing number of choices about what, how and where to go about for education.

In this regard, the Government of India has taken various steps to use this enormous opportunity to improve the standard of higher education.

## Innovative Methods for Enhancing the Teaching and Learning Process

Universities create knowledge associated with creativity and innovation, thus contributing to society. Today, universities in India have to provide quality education to a large number of students. The students attending universities doubled in the 1990s, and the demand continues to rise.

India's rich demographic dividend may soon be a disaster if the need of at least 800 new institutions of higher education is not met by 2020. This will raise the age participation rate in university education from 12.4% to 30%. In order to cope with this influx of students, four major digital initiatives in higher education are taken at present in India.

These initiatives are as follows :

### 1. SWAYAM

SWAYAM meaning 'self' is a Hindi acronym that stands for 'Study Web of Active learning for Young Aspiring Minds' is an Indian massive open online course platform. It is an initiative launched by the MHRD under Digital India on 9th July, 2017 to give free entry to all courses including all advanced education, high school and skill sector. The online portal swayam.gov.in presents the list of all courses and related information that can be accessed online. The salient features of Swayam are as follows:

- **Approve the Course on Offer** The list of courses which are being offered for the coming semester is available on www.swayam.gov.in. All VCs (Vice Chancellors) and Heads of Institutions need to take approval of the Competent Authority (Academic Council/ Senate) for these courses so that students can opt for them and seek transfer of credits.

- **Publicise the Courses** The Swayam courses shall be published by printing posters, WhatsApp messages, Facebook posts and Twitter accounts of the universities. The objective is to reach as many people as possible so that students can get benefit of these courses.
- **Prepare New Courses** If there are talented teachers in the universities who are willing to place their course on Swayam, they should be encouraged. Such proposals may be sent to the National Coordinator for approval and for providing funding to prepare the courses.
- **Retrain Teachers** All teachers may be asked to use the Swayam courses during their own teaching process so that we can have a blended learning process. The flipped classroom model, where the Swayam videos are seen at home and there is a discussion in the class would help in improving the quality of learning.
- **Monitoring Cell** Every university should have a Digital Learning Monitoring Cell which reviews the current use of these digital resources and suggests way to improve their utilisation further in the university and the affiliated institutions.

## 2. Swayam Prabha

Swayam Prabha is an initiative of the MHRD to provide 32 High Quality Educational Channels through DTH across the length and breadth of the country 24 × 7. It has curriculum based course content covering diverse disciplines. Its primary aim is to make quality learning resources accessible to remote areas where internet availability is still a challenge.

The Vice Chancellors of universities are instructed to do the following:

- **Buy DD Dish for Accessing Swayamprabha Channels** Every VC may instruct buying of the DD Free Dish from the market (₹1400 one-time cost only) and configure these channels in their office first and later install in as many class-rooms as possible.
- **Mandate Other Affiliated Colleges** The same message may be given to all the affiliated institutions for setting up these channels and operationalising them immediately.
- **Orient the Teachers** VCs may hold orientation sessions for all the teachers so that they see and use these channels while teaching their courses.

## 3. National Digital Library (NDL)

The third initiative is to give access to an online library where students can get resource materials. All institutions and the affiliated colleges may immediately join the National Digital Library at https://ndl.iitkgp.ac.in/.

This will help students to access more than 80 lakh digital resources at no cost. The library provides universal access so that all the students log-in and join the NDL. While doing the class work/assignments, they may be asked to use these resources.

All books in the libraries may be digitised and shared with the NDL at IIT Kharagpur so that it would add to the digital resources and there is greater sharing of the digital resources by all institutions.

## 4. National Academic Depository (NAD)

It is an initiative of the UGC that provides an online store house of all academic awards i.e certificates, diplomas, degrees, mark sheets etc.

NAD ensures easy access, retrievals and safe storage of all the documents. All the institutions are required to upload their documents on NAD.

# Other Digital Initiatives

Apart from the above mentioned, four major initiatives taken to digitize higher education, there are several minor initiatives, which are as follows :

(i) **Digital Campus** All campus processes like admissions, academic calendar, attendance, assessments, result declaration, administration, pay roll, financial and such other processes shall be computerised.

(ii) **Smart Campus** Every campus shall plan for efficient and economical use of water, electricity and waste. Use of solar power and water recycling systems may be planned for, as they would bring sustainability and saving in the long run.

(iii) **Clean Campus** Every campus shall participate in the Swachh Bharat Abhiyaan and achieve clean campus that has clean toilets, systems for solid/liquid waste management.

There will be swachhata rankings of all institutions and the best institutions would be rewarded.

(iv) **National Digital Payment Mission** Every institution should move towards a complete digital payment system in their campus covering all transactions by the institution.

The digital payment modes like BHIM App should be introduced to all students and commercial establishments on the campus, including the canteens.

(v) **Unnat Bharat Abhiyaan** Every institution to adopt atleast 5 villages and help in translating their knowledge for the use of the rural poor.

(vi) **Innovation Drives** Students may be encouraged to think out-of-the box and arrive at solutions that are innovative. For this, competitions may be organised for all students covering various areas. Every institution should try to participate in the hackathons that are being organised by various agencies, apart from government.

(vii) **Innovations in Improving the Administration of Institutions** Some progress has already been made in this regard during the last few years, such as conducting online admission tests in IITs, IIITs, IIMs and some other universities. Besides conveying knowledge to the student, education has to impart values, rational thinking, knowledge and self-sufficiency.

This can be done in a better way by giving more autonomy to educational institutions so that they can work within a broad framework.

Similarly, execution of the innovative practices will add to the skills, knowledge and personality development of both the faculties and the students. Academic flexibility is also important so that students can take enrollment according to their needs.

For this, all the educational institutions are required to make a comprehensive plan for future. The procedure for planning is summerised below. Every institution should plan for the future.

They should constitute a group within the campus for preparing the following :

(a) **A 15-year vision** to determine where the institution would like to be.

(b) **A 7-year strategic plan** to work out medium term plans to reach there.

(c) **A 3-year action plan** for immediate improvement of the quality of learning.

(viii) **Major Efforts Involving the Community for Improving Livelihoods** Strategic planning for comprehensive community and societal involvement is much more than adopting new technology.

At university level, we have to urgently think about the issues, problems and community solutions for the adoption of best practices.

Forecasting the emergence and impact of new technologies along with quickly adapting to the rapid changes is also required. These efforts can be grouped as follows :

(a) **Assessment of Courses on Specific Livelihood Benchmarks**

The courses should be assessed on key areas such as research and information collection, communication, collaboration, critical thinking and problem solving, as well as creativity and innovation.

(b) **Integration with National Priorities** Higher education needs to evolve to ensure that it meets the requirements of the future workforce.

It should provide the skills needed to drive this continuous change through integration with national priorities such as Digital India and Smart cities mission.

(ix) **Promoting Research** Research as- individual interest and for innovation and values can be undertaken properly and effectively through online sources.

The principles for promoting research and freedom will primarily focus on students as learners, respect and adjust for diversity, provide context-specific information and support, facilitate meaningful internationalisation, dialogue and engagement, adaptable, flexible and responsive approach to experimentation and evidence in a globalised world.

(x) **Research Accessibility and Accountability** To ensure accessibility to research and for accountability to capture core ideas from the published research, flexibility is required to accommodate the variety of different learning and teaching contexts within which teachers and learners work for example offshore, onshore, online in large and small groups.

Thus, digitization of education can help in research.

# ICT AND GOVERNANCE

With the rising awareness among the citizens and their better experiences with the private sector, the demand for better services from government departments have increased.

The application of Information and Communication Technology (ICT) has played a prominent role in strengthening such as demand. Consequently, the government moved at slow pace with scarce public resources.

## e-Government and e-Governance

The two terms 'e-Government' and 'e-Governance' are independent concepts. e-Government is understood as the use of Information and Communication Technology (ICT) to promote more efficient and cost effective government, facilitate more convenient government services and allow greater public access to information, and make government more accountable to citizens.

### Scope of e-Governance

Governance is all about flow of information between the government and citizens, the government and businesses and the government and government.

e-Governance covers all these relationships as follows :

- Government to Citizen (G2C)
- Citizen to Government (C2G)
- Government to Government (G2G)
- Government to Business (G2B)

### Government to Citizen

Government to citizen relationship is the most basic aspect of e-Governance. The G2C relation includes the services provided by the Government to the Citizens.

In modern times, government deals with many aspects of the life of a citizen which include the public utility services i.e. tele-communication, transportation, post, medical facilities, electricity, education, etc. The relation of a citizen with the government starts with the birth and ends with the death of the citizen.

Therefore, e-Governance in G2C relationship will involve facilitation of the services flowing from Government towards Citizens with the use of Information and Communication Technology.

Some examples of G2C are as follows:

(i) **e-Citizenship** It will include the implementation of ICT for facilitation of government services relating to citizenship of an individual. It may involve online transactions relating to issue and renewal of documents like ration cards, passports, election cards, identity cards, etc.

It is required for the government to create a virtual identity for every citizen so as to enable them to access the Government services online. For the same, Government would need to create a citizen database which is a huge task.

(ii) **e-Registration** It will cover the online registration of various contacts. Many of these contacts and transactions require registration for giving it legality and enforceability. Such registration may also be made ICT enabled. e-registration will help to reduce a significant amount of paperwork.

(iii) **e-Transportation** It includes ICT enabled services of Government, relating to transport by road, rail, water or air.

(iv) **e-Health** It includes ICT enabled health services of the government. Under this, interconnection of all hospitals may take place. Patient database and local pharmacy database may also be created.

(v) **e-Help** It refers to the facilitation of disaster and crisis management using ICT. It includes the use of technologies like Internet and SMS for the purpose of reducing the response time of the government agencies to the disasters.

Online information relating to disasters, warnings and calls for help can assist the government and the NGOs to coordinate their work and speed up the rescue work.

## Citizen to Government

Citizen to Government relationship will include the communication of citizens with the Government arising in the democratic process like voting, campaigning, feedback, etc.

Some examples are as follows:

(i) **e-Democracy** The true concept of democracy includes the participation of citizens in the democratic and governing process. Today due to the increased population, the active participation of the citizens in governing process is not possible. The ICT can help to enable the true democratic process including voting, public opinion, feedback and Government accountability.

(ii) **e-Feedback** It includes the use of ICT for the purpose of giving feedback to the Government. Use of ICT can enable online feedback to the Government, online debates as to the Government services.

## Government to Government

G2G relationship includes the relationship between Central and State Government and also the relationship between two or more Government departments.

Some examples of G2G are as follows:

(i) **e-Administration** It would include the implementation of ICT in the functioning of the government, internally and externally. Implementation of ICT can reduce the communication time between the government departments and governments. It can substantially reduce paper work if properly used. E-administration will also bring speed and transparency to the administration of government departments.

(ii) **e-Police** The concept of e-Police is little different from cyber police. Cyber police require technology experts to curb the electronic/cyber crimes. e-Police refers to the use of ICT for the purpose of facilitating the work of the Police department in investigation and administration. The concept of e-Police includes databases of police officers, their performances, criminal databases – wanted as well as in custody, the trends in crimes and much more. ICT can help reduce the response time of the Police department and also reduce cost by reducing paperwork.

(iii) **e-Court** The concept of e-Court includes the use of ICT in the judicial process. Technology may help distant hearing, online summons and warrants and online publication of judgement and decrees.

## Government to Business

G2B means to help the business class interact with the government in a smooth manner. Its purpose is to establish transparency in the business environment and when interacting with the government.

Some examples of G2B are as follows :

(i) **e-Taxation** Corporate sector pays many taxes, duties and dues to the Government. Payment of these taxes and duties will be made easier by e-Taxation.

Online taxing and online payment of taxes can help reduce cost and time required for physical submission of taxes. ICT can also help cross check the frauds and deficiencies in payment, further bringing accuracy and revenue to the government.

(ii) **e-Licensing** Companies have to acquire various licenses from the government, similarly the companies have to acquire various registrations. With ICT, the licensing and registration take less time and cost.

(iii) **e-Tendering** It will include the facilities of online tendering and procurement. It also helps in online submission of tenders and online allotment of work. It will reduce time and cost involved in the physical tendering system.

# Objectives of e-Governance

- **To Build an Informed Society** An informed society is an empowered society. Only informed people can make a responsible government. Access to every piece of information of the government and of public importance is one of the basic objectives of e-Governance.
- **To Increase Government and Citizen Interaction** e-Governance aims to build a feedback framework, to get feedback from the people and to make the government aware of people's problems and to find solutions with their active involvement.
- **To Encourage Citizen Participation** e-Governance aims to restore democracy to its true meaning by improving citizen participation in the governing process, by improving the feedback, access to information and overall participation of the citizens in the decision-making.
- **To Bring Transparency in the Governing Process** e-Governance carries an objective of making the governing process transparent by making all the government data and information accessible to people. It makes people aware of the decisions, and policies of the government.
- **To Make the Government Accountable** Government is responsible and answerable for every decision taken by it. e-Governance aims to help the government to be more accountable than now by bringing transparency and making the citizens more informed.
- **To Reduce the Cost of Governance** e-Governance also aims to reduce the cost of governance by cutting down expenditure on physical delivery of information and services particularly by cutting down on stationary, which amounts to the most of the government expenditure.
- **To Reduce the Reaction Time of the Government** Normally, due to red-tapism and other reasons, the government takes long to reply to people's queries and problems. e-Governance aims to reduce the reaction time of the government to the people's queries and problems.

## Advantages of e-Governance

Following are the important advantages of e-Governance :

- **Speed** Technology ensures fast communication. Internet, phones and cell phones have reduced the time taken in normal communication.
- **Cost Reduction** Paper-based communication needs lots of stationary, printers, computers, etc. which calls for continuous heavy expenditure. Internet and phones make communication cheaper saving valuable money for the government.
- **Transparency** Use of ICT makes governing process transparent. This is possible when every piece of information of the government is uploaded on the Internet and is available for the public to peruse.

  Current governing process leaves many ways to conceal the information from the people. ICT helps the information available online, eliminating all possibilities of concealing information.

## e-Government Initiatives in India : An Overview

From the early 90s, information technologies were supplemented by ICT technologies to extend its use for sector-wide applications with policy emphasis on reaching out to rural areas and taking in greater inputs from NGOs and private sector.

There has been an increasing involvement of international donor agencies under the framework of e-Governance to catalyse the development of e-Governance laws and technologies in developing countries.

Some initiatives taken for e-Governance in India :

1. **Bhoomi Project** (Karnataka) It is used for online delivery of land records. It is a key sustainable e-Governance project for the computerised delivery of 20 million rural land records to 6.7 million farmers of Karnataka.
2. **KHAJANE** (Karnataka) It is end to end automation of Government Treasury System. It has been implemented mainly to eliminate systemic deficiencies in manual treasury system.
3. **E-Courts** It is launched by Department of Justice, Ministry of Law and Justice. Its aim is improve the provision of judicial services to citizens.
4. **E-District** It is launched by Department of Information Technology. Its aim is to deliver citizen centric services at the district level such as issue of birth/death certificate, income and caste certificates etc.
5. **E-Office** It is launched by Department of Administrative Reforms and Public Grievances. It aim is significantly improve the operational efficiency of the government by transistioning to a less paper office.
6. **MCA 21** It is launched by the Ministry of Corporate Affairs. The project aims to provide electronic services to the companies registered under the Companies Act.

### Limitations

In spite of the massive opportunities and advantages, there are many constraints and challenges in ICT implementation process. Creation of infrastructure and the diffusion of technologies in moving towards e-Governance have been rather slow. This may primarily be attributed to the following reasons :

- **Lack of IT Literacy and Awareness Regarding Benefits of e-Governance** Lack of IT literacy is also major drawback. The administrative structure is not geared for maintaining, and retrieving the governance information electronically.
- The general tendency is to obtain the data from the files as and when required rather

than using Document Management System (DMS) and workflow technologies. DMS and workflow technologies are usually used in those departments where there is a lack of workforce.

- **Underutilization of Existing ICT Infrastructure** To a larger extent, the computers in many departments are used for the purpose of word processing only, resulting in the underutilization of the computers in terms of their use in data mining for supporting management decisions.
- **Attitude of Government Departments** Traditionally, the government servants have derived their sustenance from the fact that they are important repositories of government data.

  Thus, any effort to implement DMS and workflow technologies or bringing out the change in the system is met with resistance from the government servants.
- **Lack of Coordination between Government Departments and Solution Developers** At present, the users in government departments do not contribute enough to design the solution architecture. Consequently, the solution developed and implemented does not address the requirements of an e-Governance project and hence does not get implemented.
- **Resistance to re-engineering of Departmental Processes** Successful implementation of e-Governance projects requires lots of restructuring in administrative processes, redefining of administrative procedures and formats which find the resistance in almost all the departments at all the levels.

  Additionally, there is lack of expertise of departmental MIS (Management Information System) executives in exploiting data mining techniques, and collection and updation of real time content onto website etc. In such a scenario, it is difficult for any e-Governance solution to achieve its intended results.
- **Lack of National Level Infrastructure for Sustaining e-Governance** Infrastructure to support e-Governance initiatives does not exist within government departments. Whatever efforts have been made by various government organisations may be defined as islands of computerization.

# Computer Terminology

## A

**Abacus** A simple device for calculating, consisting of a frame with rows of wires or grooves along which beads are slide.

**Active Cell** It refers to the currently selected cell in a spreadsheet.

**Active Window** It is the currently focused window in the current window manager or explorer.

**Analog Computer** A computer that operates on data in the form of continuous variable physical quantities.

**Android** It is a LINUX based operating system designed primarily for touchscreen mobile devices such as smartphones and tablets computers.

**Antivirus Software** It consists of computer programs that attempt to identify threats and eliminate computer viruses and other malicious softwares (malwares).

**Application Software** It is a subclass of computer software that employs the capabilities of a computer directly to a task that the user wishes to perform.

**Arithmetic Logic Unit (ALU)** ALUs are capable of calculating the results of a wide variety of basic arithmetical and logical computations.

**Artificial Intelligence** AI is basically the stimulation of human intelligence in machines that are programmed to think and act like humans. Fifth generation computing devices, based on artificial intelligence, are still in development, though some applications, such as voice recognition, are being used today.

**American Standard Code for Information Interchange (ASCII)** It is a character set and a character encoding standard for electronic communication. It is based on the Roman alphabet as used in Modern English and other Western European languages.

**Assembler** A program that translates mnemonic statement into executable instructions.

**Assembly Language** A low-level symbolic code converted by an assembler.

**Auxiliary Memory** It is a non-volatile memory which is not directly accessible by CPU.

## B

**Backspace** This key is used on the keyboard to delete the text. Backspace will delete the text to the left of cursor.

**Backup** A default copy of a file or other item of data made in case the original is lost and damaged.

**Basic Input/Output System (BIOS)** It is also known as ROM BIOS. It provides an abstraction layer for the hardware.

**Batch Processing** The processing of previously collected jobs in a single batch.

**Binary** A numbering scheme in which there are only two possible values for each digit 0 and 1.

**Binary Coded Decimal (BCD)** A coding system in which a 4 digit binary number represents each decimal digit from 0 to 9.

**Bit** It is the most basic information unit used in computing and information theory.

**Blog** It is a discussion or informational site published on the world wide web (www).

**Bluetooth** A protocol that permits a wireless exchange of information between computers, cell phones and other electronic devices within a radius about 30 feet.

**Booting** It is a bootstrapping process which starts the operating system when a computer is switched ON.

**Browser** A special software that enables users to read/view web pages and jump from one web page to another.

**Bug** A software bug is an error, flaw, failure, or fault in a computer program or system that produces an incorrect or unexpected result.

**Byte** It is commonly used as a unit of storage measurement in computers, regardless the type of data being stored.

## C

**Cache Memory** It is a very high speed memory that is placed between the CPU and main memory. It holds frequently requested data and instructions so that they are immediately available to the CPU when needed.

**Compact Disc-Recordable (CD-R)** A blank compact disc which can be recorded at once only.

**Compact Disc-ReWritable (CD-RW)** A blank compact disc that can be erased and recorded many times.

**Central Processing Unit (CPU)** It performs the actual processing of data.

**Channel** A medium for transferring information, also called a line or circuit.

**Chat** Typing text into a message box on a screen to engage in dialog with one or more people *via* the Internet or other network.

**Chip** A tiny wafer of silicon containing small electric circuits that can store millions of bits of information.

**Co-axial Cable** A kind of copper cable used by cable TV companies between the community antenna and user homes and businesses.

**Communication** The transmission of data from one computer to another or from one device to another is called communication.

**Compact Disc (CD)** It is a digital optical disc data storage format made up of plastic and is coated with reflective metal.

**Compiler** It is a computer program that translates a series of instructions written in one computer language (called the source language) into another computer language (also called the object or target language).

**Computer Network** It is a system for communication among two or more computers.

**Computer Worm** It is a self-replicating computer program, similar to a computer virus.

**Control Unit** It is the part of a CPU that directs its operation.

**Cursor** A movable indicator on a computer screen identifying the point that will be affected by input from the user.

## D

**Data** It is a collection of facts and figures which are not in directly usable form.

**Database** A collection of data files integrated and organised into a single comprehensive file system which is arranged to minimise duplication of data.

**Data Processing** Converting data into information is called data processing.

**Data Redundancy** It is a condition created within a database or data storage technology in which same piece of data is held in two separate places.

**DBMS** It is a collection of programs that enable you to store, modify and extract information from a database.

**Debugging** It is a methodical process of finding and reducing the number of bugs, or defects in a computer program.

**Demodulation** The process is used at the receivers end to recover the original signal coming from the sender end in modulating form.

**Desktop** The area of a display screen where images, windows, icons and other graphical items appear.

**Device Driver** (often called a driver) It is a computer program that enables another program, typically, an operating system to interact with a hardware device.

**Digital Computer** A computer that operates with numbers expressed directly as digits.

**Disk Operating System (DOS)** An operating system which contains the disk oriented commands and uses disk devices for permanent storage.

**Display Unit** A device with a screen that displays characters or graphics representing data in a computer memory.

**Domain Name** A unique name that identifies a particular website and represents the name of the server where the web pages reside.

**Dots Per Inch (DPI)** It is defined as the measure of the resolution of a printer, scanner or monitor. It refers to the number of dots in one inch line.

**Drag-and-Drop** In graphical user interface, drag and drop is the action of clicking on a virtual object and dragging it to a different location or onto another virtual object.

**Digital Video Disc (DVD)** It is an optical disc storage media format that can be used for data storage including movies with high quality video and sound.

**Dynamic Random Access Memory (DRAM)** It is a type of random access memory which stores each bit of data in a separate capacitor.

## E

**E-Commerce (Electronic Commerce)** It is a type of industry where buying and selling of products or services is conducted over electronic systems such as the Internet and other computer network.

**Editing** The process of changing information by inserting, deleting, replacing, rearranging and reformation.

**E-mail (Electronic mail)** It is a method of composing, sending, storing and receiving messages over electronic communication systems.

**End User** Any individual who uses the information generated by a computer based system.

**Ethernet** It is a modern technique which is used to connect local computers in Local Area Network (LAN).

**Excel** It allows you to create spreadsheets much like paper ledgers that can perform automatic calculations.

## F

**Fiber Optics** It is a cable made up of glass or fiber through which data can be transferred from one place to another.

**File** A collection of information stored electronically and treated as a unit by a computer. Every file must have its own distinctive name.

**File Extension** It is a suffix to the name of a computer file applied to indicate the encoding of its contents or usage.

**File Server** A computer on a network that stores the programs and data files shared by the users of the network.

**Firewall** A security system usually consisting of hardware and software that prevents unauthorised persons from accessing certain parts of a program database or network.

**Font** It is a fixed typeface of a particular size and style.

**File Transfer Protocol** (FTP)This protocol is used to transfer files from one place to another on Internet.

## G

**Gigabyte** It is a unit of information or computer storage equal to approximately one billion bytes.

**GigaHertz (GHz)** A measurement used to identify the speed of the Central Processing Unit (CPU). 1 gigahertz is equal to 1 billion cycles per second.

**Graphical User Interface (GUI)** It is a method of interacting with a computer through a metaphor of direct manipulating of graphical images.

**Graphic Tablet** It is an input device which is used to create images, etc.

## H

**Hacker** A computer criminal who penetrates and tempers with computer programs or systems.

**Hard Copy** Printed version of soft copy of information or data. It is the permanent output provided by computer.

**Hard Disk** It is a non-volatile data storage device that stores data on a magnetic surface layered onto disk platters.

**Hardware** The mechanical, magnetic, electronic and electrical components that comprises a computer system such as CPU, monitor, keyboard and mouse, etc.

**Hexadecimal Number System** It is a number system that has base 16.

**HLL (High-Level Language)** It is a programming language designed to simplify computer programming. It is an abstract from of low-level computer processor operations such as memory accesses.

**Home Page** It refers to the web page that identifies a website and contains the hyperlink to other web page in the website.

**Hyperlink** An image or a portion of text on a web page that is linked to another web page.

**Hybrid Computer** These computers are made by taking the best features of the analog computer and digital computer.

**HyperText Markup Language (HTML)** This language is used to write web page and for designing.

**HyperText Transfer Protocol (HTTP)** It is an important protocol used on the world wide web for moving hypertext files across the Internet.

## I

**Icon** A symbol (such as picture or a folder) that represents a certain function on your computer.

**Impact Printers** These printers transfer the image onto paper through a printing mechanism that strikes the paper called ribbon.

**Information** It is the summarisation of data according to a certain pre-defined purpose.

**Input Device** These devices are used to put data and instructions in a computer.

**Instant Messaging (IM)** A chat program that offers real time communication over the Internet.

**I/O Port** This circuit is used to connect input and output devices to computer.

**Instruction** A command or an order given to a computer to perform a task.

**Integrated Circuits** Multiple electronic components combined on a silicon chip.

**Interface** A device or program that helps a user to communicate with a computer.

**Interpreter** A program that converts and executes the source code into machine code line by line.

**Internet** It is the worldwide, publicly accessible system of interconnected computer networks that transmit data by packet switching using the standard Internet protocol.

**Internet Surfing** To search something on Internet is called Internet surfing.

**Internet Protocol (IP) Address** These addresses are assigned to each and every computer on a TCP/IP network. It ensures that data on a network goes where it is supported to e.g. 192.168.2.250.

## J

**JAVA** It is a programming language. This language is used to create mobile applications, softwares, etc.

**Joint Photographic Experts Group (JPEG)** It is a commonly used method of lossy compression for digital photography.

**Joystick** It is a computer peripheral or general control device consisting of a handheld stick that pivots about one end and transmits its angle in two or three dimensions to a computer.

## K

**Keyboard** This is the standard input device attached to all computers. The layout of keyboard is just like the traditional typewriter of the type QWERTY.

**Kilobyte** It is a unit of information or computer storage equal to 1024 bytes. It is commonly abbreviated KB.

## L

**Language Processor** These softwares are used to convert other high or low level language programs in machine language. e.g. compiler, assembler, etc.

**Laptop** It is a small, lightweight and portable battery-powered computers that can fit onto your lap.

**Light Pen** A light sensitive style for forming graphics by touching coordinates on a display screen, thereby seeming to draw directly on the screen.

**LINUX** It is an open source operating system, meaning that the source code of the operating system is freely available to the public.

**Local Area Network (LAN)** In a LAN, the connected computers are geographically close together. They are either in the same building or within a smaller area.

**Low-level Language (LLL)** A programming language that deals with a computer's hardware components and constraints. It operates and handles the entire hardware and instructions set architecture of a computer directly.

## M

**Machine Language** The language of computer also called binary language. Instructions in this language are written as a sequence of 0's and 1's.

**Main Memory** A volatile and speedy memory that is divided into two parts RAM and ROM.

**Malware** It is a software that disrupts normal computer functions or sends a users personal data without the user's authorisation.

**Megabyte (MB)** 1 Megabyte is equal to 1048576 bytes, usually rounded off to 1 million bytes.

**Memory** Temporary storage for information, including applications and documents.

**Menu Bar** The horizontal strip across the top of an application's window. Each word on the strip has a context sensitive drop down menu containing features and actions that are available for the application in use.

**Microcomputer** A microprocessor-based computer, consisting of an MPU, internal semiconductor memory, input and output sections and a system bus, all on one, or several monolithic IC chips inserted into one or several PC boards.

**Microprocessor** A complete Central Processing Unit (CPU) contained on a single silicon chip.

**Modem (Modulator-Demodulator)** It refers to specific equipment that provides a means of communication between two computer systems over conventional telephone lines.

**Monitor** The visual readout device of a computer system. A monitor can be in several forms; a cathode ray tube (CRT), a liquid crystal display (LCD), or a flat-panel, full-color display.

**Motherboard** Main circuit board of a micro computer that contains the CPU, BIOS, memory, mass storage interfaces, serial and parallel ports, expansion slots and all the controllers required to control standard peripheral devices.

**Mouse** A manually operated input device for moving or entering positional information and other data or commands by accessing (pointing to) images on a monitor.

**Multimedia** Software programs that combine text and graphics with sound, video and animation. A multimedia PC contains the hardware to support these capabilities.

**Multitasking** It can simultaneously work with several programs or interrelated tasks that share memories, codes, buffers and files.

**Multireading** It is a facility available in an operating system that allows multiple functions from the same application packages.

**Multiuser** The term describing the capability of a computer system to be operated at more than one terminal at the same time.

**Multiplexer** It is a device that combines multiple input signals into an aggregate signal for transmission.

## N

**Network** A group of two or more computers linked together in a way that they can share data and resources.

**Node** The endpoint of a network branch or the junction of two or more branches.

**Non-Impact Printer** In this printer, chemical and inkjet technique is used. By these printers, high quality images are printed.

**Non-Volatile Memory** A memory where stored data remains undisturbed by the removal of electrical power.

## O

**Octal Number** A number system in which 8 digits are used. These digits are 0, 1, 2, 3, 4, 5, 6 and 7 and thus it is also called base 8 number system.

**Offline** It refers to the state in which a computer is temporarily or permanently unable to communicate with another computer.

**Online** It refers to the state of being connected to the networked computer system or the Internet.

**Operating System** A set of instructions that tell a computer on how to operate when it is turned on.

**Output** Data that come out of a computer device. e.g. information displayed on the monitor, sound from the speakers and information printed to paper.

## P

**Peripheral** A term designating the various kinds of machines and devices that work in conjunction with a computer but are not necessarily part of the computer structure.

**Personal Computer (PC)** A single-user computer containing a Central Processing Unit (CPU) and one or more memory circuits.

**Piracy** The illegal copying of software or other creative works.

**Pixels** The smallest element (a dot) on a display screen.

**Portrait** A term that designates the position of conventional printing across the width of a page.

**Post Office Protocol (POP)** A protocol that specifies how a personal computer can connect to a mail server on the Internet and download E-mail.

**Printer** A mechanical device for printing a computer's output on paper.

**Program** A set of instructions to perform a specific task.

**Programming Language** A vocabulary and set of grammatical rules for instructing a computer to perform specific tasks.

**Protocols** A set of rules that defines exactly how information is to be exchanged between two systems over Internet.

## Q

**QWERTY** It is one of the standard computer keyboards, with the characters Q, W, E, R, T and Y on the top row of letters.

## R

**Random Access Memory (RAM)** A volatile, semiconductor storage structure that accesses temporary data with a random or direct accessing method.

**Read Only Memory (ROM)** A semiconductor memory whose data cannot be erased, or overwritten; it can only be accessed (read) for used by the CPU.

**Register** A temporary storage unit for quick, direct accessibility of a small amount of data for processing.

**Router** A network device that enables the network to reroute messages, it receives that are intended for other networks.

**Routing** The process of choosing the best path throughout the LAN.

## S

**Scanner** An electronic device that uses light-sensing equipment to scan paper images such as text, photos and illustrations and translates the images into signals.

**Search Engine** Software that makes it possible to look for and retrieve information on the Internet, particularly the Web. Some popular search engines are AltaVista, Google, HotBot, Yahoo!, Web Crawler and Lycos.

**Secondary Memory** It is a permanent and non-volatile memory that remains undisturbed by the removal of electrical signals.

**Server** A computer that shares its resources and information with other computers on a network. This is a mainframe computer that serves the other computers attached to it.

**Software** The set of computer programs, procedures and associated documentation related to the effective operation. Software includes: system software and application software.

**Source Code** (Source Program) A set of computer instructions in hard-copy or stored form. When written in a language other than machine language, the source code requires translation by an assembler (or macroassembler), interpreter, or compiler into object code.

**Spam** Irrelevant or unsolicited messages sent over Internet, typically to large number of users, for the purpose of advertising, phishing, spreading malwares, etc.

**Spreadsheet** Software that allows one to calculate numbers in a format that is similar to pages in a conventional ledger.

**Static RAM** It is a type of RAM, that contains its contents only whenever current supply is ON.

**Super Computer** The largest mainframe computer featuring exceptionally high speed operation while manipulating huge amounts of information.

**Synchronisation** This method ensures that the receiving end can recognise characters in order, in which the transmitting end sends them in a serial data transmission.

**System Software** A general term for software that supervises, sequences and coordinates programs. System software may include programs, such as: operating systems, language translators.

## T

**TCP/IP (Transmission Control Protocol/ Internet Protocol)** This is a large grouping of programs and standards that govern how information moves around the Internet.

**Template** A pre-established format for a document, stored in a computer.

**Terabyte** (TB) It's about a trillion bytes. Actually it's 2 to the 40th power or 10095111627776 bytes.

**Time Sharing** It refers to the allocation of computer resources in a time dependent fashion to run several programs simultaneously.

**Topology** The structure of the network including physical connection such as wiring schemes and logical interactions between network devices.

**Trackball** Input device that controls the position of the cursor on the screen; the unit is mounted near the keyboard and movement is controlled by moving a ball.

## U

**Uniform Resource Locator (URL)** The specific Internet address for a resource such as an individual or organisation.

**UNIX** This is an operating system developed by AT & T. It's a big push that it allows one server to serve many different end users at one time.

**Upload** The processes of transferring information from a computer to a website (or other remote location on a network).

**Utility** A software program designed to perform a computer system's routine housekeeping functions, like copying, deleting files and/or providing techniques to simplify the execution of a program.

## V

**Video Display Terminal** A device for displaying input signals as characters on a screen, typically a monitor.

**Video Teleconferencing** A remote 'face-to-face chat', when two or more people using a webcam and an Internet telephone connection chat online.

**Virus** A piece of computer code designed as a prank or malicious act to spread from one computer to another by attaching itself to other programs.

**Volatile Memory** A memory whose contents are irretrievably lost when power is OFF.

## W

**Wide Area Network (WAN)** A network of a large number of computers that cover a large area like a city, state or even a whole country.

**Webcam** A video camera/computer setup that takes live images and sends them to a Web browser.

**Web Browser** An application or a program which is used to view and interact with web pages and to navigate between them.

**Website** A collection of web pages or hyperlinked webpage, which owned by an individual, a company or an organisation.

**Window** A portion of a computer display used in a graphical interface that enables users to select commands by pointing to illustrations or symbols with a mouse.

**Word Processing** A program that enables to compose a document within computer system with edit, store, format and print the specific document or insert, delete, copy and include text/graphics from other files.

**World Wide Web** ('WWW' or 'The Web') A network of servers on the Internet that use hypertext-linked databases and files.

**Workstation** The work area and/or equipment used for computer operations, including Computer Aided Design (CAD).

# Computer General Abbreviations

## A

| | |
|---|---|
| **AI** | Artificial Intelligence |
| **ALGOL** | Algorithmic Language |
| **ALU** | Arithmetic Logic Unit |
| **ASCII** | American Standard Code for Information Interchange |

## B

| | |
|---|---|
| **BASIC** | Beginner's All purpose Symbolic Instruction Code |
| **BCD** | Binary Coded Decimal |
| **BD** | Blu-ray Disc |
| **BIOS** | Basic Input/Output System |
| **Bit** | Binary Digit |
| **BPL** | Broadband over Power Line |
| **BPS** | Bits Per Second |

## C

| | |
|---|---|
| **CAD** | Computer Aided Design |
| **CD** | Compact Disc |
| **C-DAC** | Centre for Development of Advanced Computing |
| **CD-R** | Compact Disc-Recordable |
| **CD-ROM** | Compact Disc-Read Only Memory |
| **CD-RW** | Compact Disc-ReWritable |
| **CD-R/W** | Compact Disc-Read/Write |
| **CLI** | Command Line Interface |
| **COBOL** | Common Business Oriented Language |
| **CPS** | Characters Per Second |
| **CPU** | Central Processing Unit |
| **CRT** | Cathode Ray Tube |
| **CU** | Control Unit |

## D

| | |
|---|---|
| **DB** | Database |
| **DBA** | Database Administrator |
| **DBMS** | Database Management System |
| **DMS** | Document Management System |
| **DNS** | Domain Name System |
| **DOS** | Disk Operating System |
| **DPI** | Dots Per Inch |
| **DRAM** | Dynamic Random Access Memory |
| **DSL** | Digital Subscriber Line/Domain Specific Language |
| **DVD** | Digital Video Disc/Digital Versatile Disc |
| **DVD-R** | Digital Video Disc-Recordable |
| **DVD-ROM** | Digital Video Disc-Read Only Memory |
| **DVD-RW** | Digital Video Disc-ReWritable |

## E

| | |
|---|---|
| **EDVAC** | Electronic Discrete Variable Automatic Computer |
| **EBCDIC** | Extended Binary Coded Decimal Interchange Code |
| **EDP** | Electronic Data Processing |
| **EDSAC** | Electronic Delay Storage Automatic Calculator |
| **EPROM** | Erasable Programmable Read Only Memory |
| **EEPROM** | Electrically Erasable Programmable Read Only Memory |
| **E-Mail** | Electronic Mail |
| **ENIAC** | Electronic Numerical Integrator And Computer |
| **EXE** | Executable |

## F

| | |
|---|---|
| **FORTRAN** | Formula Translation |
| **FTP** | File Transfer Protocol |

## G

| | |
|---|---|
| **Gb** | Gigabit |
| **GB** | Gigabyte |
| **GUI** | Graphical User Interface |
| **GHZ** | GigaHertz |

## H

| | |
|---|---|
| **HDD** | Hard Disk Drive |
| **HLL** | High Level Language |
| **HTML** | HyperText Markup Language |
| **HTTP** | HyperText Transfer Protocol |

## I

| | |
|---|---|
| **ICT** | Information and Communication Technology |
| **ICR** | Intelligent Character Recognition |
| **IM** | Instant Messaging |
| **IMAP** | Internet Message Access Protocol |
| **I/O** | Input/Output |
| **IP** | Internet Protocol |
| **ISDN** | Integrated Services Digital Network |
| **ISO** | International Organisation for Standardisation |
| **ISP** | Internet Service Provider |
| **IT** | Information Technology |

## J

| | |
|---|---|
| **JPEG** | Joint Photographic Experts Group |

## K

| | |
|---|---|
| **Kb** | Kilobit |
| **KB** | Kilobyte |
| **Kbps** | Kilobits Per Second |
| **KHz** | KiloHertz |

## L

| | |
|---|---|
| **LAN** | Local Area Network |
| **LASER** | Light Amplification by Stimulated Emission of Radiation |
| **LCD** | Liquid Crystal Display |
| **LED** | Light Emitting Diode |
| **LISP** | List Processing |
| **LLL** | Low-Level Language |
| **LPM** | Lines Per Minute |
| **LSB** | Least Significant Bit |
| **LSI** | Large Scale Integration |

## M

| | |
|---|---|
| **MAC** | Media Access Control |
| **MAN** | Metropolitan Area Network |
| **M-Banking** | Mobile Banking |
| **Mb** | Megabit |
| **MB** | Megabyte |
| **MHz** | MegaHertz |
| **MICR** | Magnetic Ink Character Recognition |
| **MIDI** | Musical Instrument Digital Interface |
| **MIPS** | Million Instructions Per Second |
| **MODEM** | MOdulator-DEModulator |
| **MSB** | Most Significant Bit |
| **MS-DOS** | Microsoft-Disk Operating System |
| **MU** | Memory Unit |

## N

| | |
|---|---|
| **NAD** | National Academic Depositary |
| **NDL** | National Digital Library |
| **NIC** | Network Interface Card |
| **NOS** | Network Operating System |
| **NT** | New Technology (Windows) |

## O

| | |
|---|---|
| **OCR** | Optical Character Recognition |
| **OMR** | Optical Mark Reader |
| **OOP** | Object Oriented Programming |
| **OS** | Operating System |
| **OOS** | Open Source Software |

## P

| | |
|---|---|
| **P2P** | Peer-to-Peer |
| **PAN** | Personal Area Network |
| **PC** | Personal Computer |
| **PDA** | Personal Digital Assistant |
| **PDF** | Portable Document Format |
| **PPI** | Pixels Per Inch |
| **PPM** | Pages Per Minute |
| **PPP** | Point-to-Point Protocol |
| **PROM** | Programmable Read Only Memory |
| **PSTN** | Public Switched Telephone Network |

## Q

| | |
|---|---|
| **QoS** | Quality of Service |

## R

| | |
|---|---|
| RAM | Random Access Memory |
| RDBMS | Relational Database Management System |
| RGB | Red, Green and Blue |
| ROM | Read Only Memory |

## S

| | |
|---|---|
| SMTP | Simple Mail Transfer Protocol |
| SRAM | Static Random Access Memory |

## T

| | |
|---|---|
| TB | Terabyte |
| TCP | Transmission Control Protocol |
| TFT | Thin Film Transistor |

## U

| | |
|---|---|
| UNIVAC | Universal Automatic Computer |
| UI | User Interface |
| UPS | Uninterruptible Power Supply |
| URI | Uniform Resource Identifier |
| URL | Uniform Resource Locator |
| USB | Universal Serial Bus |

## V

| | |
|---|---|
| VDU | Visual Display Unit |
| VGA | Video Graphics Array |
| VLSI | Very Large Scale Integration |
| VoIP | Voice over Internet Protocol |
| VPN | Virtual Private Network |

## W

| | |
|---|---|
| WAN | Wide Area Network |
| WAP | Wireless Application Protocol |
| Wi-Fi | Wireless Fidelity |
| WiMAX | Worldwide Interoperability for Microwave Access |
| WWAN | Wireless Wide Area Network |
| WWW | World Wide Web |

## Y

| | |
|---|---|
| Yb | Yottabyte |

## Z

| | |
|---|---|
| Zb | Zettabyte |

# Chapter Practice

## ICT : Meaning, Advantages, Disadvantages and Uses

1 Which of the following statements regarding the term IT is/are False?

M. IT refers to the use of hardware and software for storage, retrieval, processing and distributing.

N. IT is an acronym that stands for Internet Technology.

Select the correct answer using the codes given below.

(A) Only M
(B) Only N
(C) Both M and N
(D) Neither M nor N

2 The statement "the study, design, development, implementation support or management of computer-based information systems, particularly software applications and computer hardware" refers to

(A) Information Technology (IT)
(B) Information and Collaborative Technology (ICT)
(C) Information and Data Technology (IDT)
(D) Artificial Intelligence (AI)

3 Read the following two statements.

I. Information and Communication Technology (ICT) is considered a subset of Information Technology (IT).

II. The 'right to use' a piece of software is termed as copyright.

Which of the given statement(s) is/are correct?

(A) Both I and II (B) Neither I nor II
(C) Only II (D) Only I

4 Information and Communication Technology includes

(A) online learning
(B) web based learning
(C) learning through the use of EDUSAT
(D) All of the above

5 Which of the following statements regarding the term ICT is / are TRUE?

P. ICT is an acronym that stands for Indian Classical Technology.

Q. Converging technologies that exemplify ICT include the merging of audio- visual, telephone and computer networks through a common cabling system.

Select the correct answer using the codes given below.

(A) P and Q (B) Neither P nor Q
(C) Only P (D) Only Q

## Computer : An Introduction

6 The word computer has been derived from which of the following word?

(A) Greek (B) English
(C) Hindi (D) Latin

7 It is an electronic device that can store, retrieve and process both qualitative and quantitative data quickly and accurately.

(A) Computer (B) Convergence
(C) Modem (D) None of these

8 Who is known as father of computer?

(A) Leonardo (B) Dennis Gason
(C) Charles Babbage (D) Percy L Spencer

9 Analytical engine developed by

(A) Blaise Pascal
(B) Charles Babbage
(C) Dennis Ritchie
(D) Alan Turing

10 Read the following two statements.

I. Abacus was the first calculating device.

II. Abacus is used for addition and subtraction operation.

Which of the given statement(s) is /are correct?

(A) Only I (B) Only II
(C) Both I and II (D) None of these

11 Who was the inventor of mechanical calculator for adding numbers?

(A) Charles Babbage (B) Peano
(C) Newton (D) Pascal

12 ENIAC was

(A) an electronic calculator
(B) a memory device
(C) first electronic digital computer
(D) an engine

13 Match the following.

| Invention | Inventor |
|---|---|
| A. Pascaline | I. John von Neumann |
| B. Difference Engine | II. Blaise Pascal |
| C. EDVAC | III. Charles Babbage |

Select the correct match using the codes given below.

| | A | B | C | | A | B | C |
|---|---|---|---|---|---|---|---|
| (A) | I | II | III | (B) | II | III | I |
| (C) | III | II | I | (D) | I | III | II |

14 First generation computer systems used
(A) transistors (B) vaccum tubes
(C) magnetic cores (D) silicon chips

15 Computer size was very large in
(A) first generation (B) second generation
(C) third generation (D) fourth generation

16 Which of the following statements regarding the term generation is/are TRUE?
P. Third generation's computers have real time operating system.
Q. First generation's computers have time-sharing operating system.
Select the correct answer using the codes given below.
(A) Only P (B) Only Q
(C) Neither P nor Q (D) Both P and Q

17 Transistors are associated with which of the following?
(A) First generation (B) Fifth generation
(C) Second generation (D) None of these

18 Speed of third generation computer is
(A) milli second ($10^{-3}$)
(B) micro second ($10^{-6}$)
(C) nano second ($10^{-9}$)
(D) pico second ($10^{-12}$)

19 Artificial intelligence is an example of
(A) first generation computer
(B) second generation computer
(C) third generation computer
(D) fifth generation computer

20 ...... is not a microcomputer, which is least powerful, yet the most widely used and fastest growing type of computers.
(A) Desktop computer
(B) Laptop
(C) Tablet PC
(D) Mainframe computer

21 A computer also known as server computer is
(A) super computer
(B) mainframe computer
(C) mini computer
(D) micro computer

22 Which of the following is the fastest and most expensive computer?
(A) Super computer (B) Micro computer
(C) Mini computer (D) None of these

23 Seismograph is an example of
(A) analog computer (B) digital computer
(C) hybrid computer (D) All of these

24 Which of the following computers are not categorised based on size?
(A) Micro computer
(B) Mini computer
(C) Super computer
(D) Digital computer

25 A hybrid computer is the one having the combined properties of
(A) super and micro computers
(B) mini and micro computers
(C) analog and digital computers
(D) super and mini computers

26 General purpose computers are used for
(A) creating a small database
(B) performing calculation
(C) accounting
(D) All of the above

27 Which type of computer is used in automatic aircraft landing?
(A) General computer
(B) Super computer
(C) Special purpose
(D) Micro computer

28 A personal computer uses a number of chips mounted on a circuit board called
(A) microprocessor
(B) system board
(C) daughter board
(D) mother board

29 Which of the following is the correct order of the four major functions of a computer?
(A) Process, Output, Input, Storage
(B) Input, Output, Process, Storage
(C) Process, Storage, Input, Output
(D) Input, Process, Output, Storage

**30** Computers gather data, which means that they allow users to ....... data.
(A) present (B) input
(C) output (D) store

**31** Which of the following is not an input device?
(A) Monitor (B) Microphone
(C) Keyboard (D) Joystick

**32** A barcode reader is an example of
(A) processing device (B) storage device
(C) input device (D) output device

**33** The retrival of information from the computer is defined as
(A) collection of data
(B) data retrieval operations
(C) output
(D) data output collection

**34** Match the following.

| List I | List II |
|---|---|
| A. Dot Matrix Printer | I. Input Device |
| B. Joystick | II. Storage |
| C. Compact Disc | III. Output Device |

Select the correct match using the codes given below.

| | A | B | C | | A | B | C |
|---|---|---|---|---|---|---|---|
| (A) | I | II | III | (B) | II | III | I |
| (C) | II | I | III | (D) | III | I | II |

**35** Which of the following is not an output device?
(A) Printer (B) Speaker
(C) Monitor (D) Keyboard

**36** The .... also called the brain of the computer, is responsible for processing data.
(A) motherboard
(B) memory
(C) RAM
(D) Central Processing Unit (CPU)

**37** What is the full form of USB as used in computer related activities?
(A) Universal Security Block
(B) Universal Serial Bus
(C) United Serial Bus
(D) Ultra Security Block

**38** ALU stands for
(A) American Logic Unit
(B) Alternate Local Unit
(C) Alternating Logic Unit
(D) Arithmetic Logic Unit

**39** The ...... is responsible for performing calculations and contains decision making mechanisms.
(A) CPU (B) MU
(C) ALU (D) CU

**40** Control unit of a digital computer is often called the
(A) clock
(B) nerve centre
(C) Both (A) and (B)
(D) IC

**41** What is the temporary storage memory chips that form the computers primary work space? The contents are lost if power is disrupted?
(A) Outputs (B) Windows
(C) ROM (D) RAM

**42** ...... is a type of memory circuitry that holds the computer's start up routine.
(A) RIM (Read Initial Memory)
(B) RAM (Random Access Memory)
(C) ROM (Read Only Memory)
(D) Cache Memory

**43** When a computer is booting, BIOS is loaded to the memory by
(A) RAM (B) ROM
(C) CD-ROM (D) TCP

**44** With regard to computer memory, which of the following statements is TRUE?
P. Read Only Memory (ROM) is 'volatile' memory.
Q. Random Access Memory (RAM) is 'volatile' memory.
R. Secondary Memory is 'volatile' memory.
Select the correct answer using the codes given below.
(A) P and Q (B) P and R
(C) Only P (D) Only Q

**45** Which of the following is the high speed memory which compensates the gap in speeds of processor and main memory?
(A) Cache memory (B) PROM
(C) EPROM (D) SRAM

**46** Virtual memory is
(A) an extremely large main memory
(B) an extremely large secondary memory
(C) an illusion of extremely large main memory
(D) a type of memory used in super computers

**47** A hard disk is divided into tracks which is further subdivided into
(A) clusters (B) sectors
(C) vectors (D) heads

**48** Read the following three statements.
I. The tracks are divided into pie-shaped sections known as sectors.
II. Blu-ray discs contain 20 GB per layer space.
III. USB stands for Universal Serial Bus.
Which of the given statements are correct?
(A) I and II (B) II and III
(C) I and III (D) I, II and III

**49** A compact disc is a data storage of the type, which is used to store digital data and relatively cheap storage.
(A) Magnetic (B) Optical
(C) Electrical (D) Electro mechanical

**50** The process of copying files to CD-ROM is known as
(A) burning (B) zipping
(C) digitising (D) ripping

**51** DVD technology uses an optical media to store the digital data. DVD is an acronym for
(A) Digital Vector Disc
(B) Digital Volume Disc
(C) Digital Versatile Disc
(D) Digital Visualisation Disc

**52** A new laptop has been produced that weighs less, is smaller and uses less power than previous laptop models.
Which of the following technologies has been used to accomplish this?
(A) Blu-ray Drive
(B) Solid State Hard Drive
(C) Universal Serial Bus Mouse
(D) Faster Random Access Memory

**53** Which of the following correctly lists computer memory types from highest to lowest speed?
(A) Secondary Storage; Main Memory (RAM); Cache Memory; CPU Registers
(B) CPU Registers; Cache Memory; Secondary Storage; Main Memory (RAM)
(C) CPU Registers; Cache Memory; Main Memory (RAM); Secondary Storage
(D) Cache Memory; CPU Registers; Main Memory (RAM); Secondary Storage

## Data Representation

**54** In a computer, a byte generally consists of
(A) 10 bits (B) 4 bits
(C) 8 bits (D) 16 bits

**55** A gigabyte is equal to
(A) 1024 megabytes
(B) 1024 kilobytes
(C) 1024 terabytes
(D) 1024 bytes

**56** Which of the following represents billion characters?
(A) Megabytes (B) Kilobytes
(C) Gigabytes (D) Terabytes

**57** Put the following units of storage into the correct order, starting with the smallest unit first and going down to the largest unit.
1. Kilobyte 2. Byte
3. Megabyte 4. Terabyte
5. Gigabyte 6. Bit
Choose the correct chronological order using the codes.
(A) 6, 2, 1, 3, 5, 4 (B) 6, 2, 1, 4, 3, 5
(C) 6, 2, 1, 3, 4, 5 (D) 6, 2, 1, 4, 5, 3

**58** 1 GB is equal to
(A) 2^30 bits (B) 2^30 bytes
(C) 2^20 bits (D) 2^20 bytes

**59** Digital computers internally use the ......... to represent data and perform arithematic calculations.
(A) octal number system
(B) binary number system
(C) decimal number system
(D) hexa decimal number system

**60** Decimal number system is the group of ...... numbers.
(A) 0 or 1 (B) 0 to 9
(C) 0 to 7 (D) 0 to 9 and A to F

**61** Minimum number of bits required to store any 3 digits decimal number is equal to
(A) 3 (B) 5
(C) 8 (D) 10

**62** A hexadecimal number is represented by
(A) three digits
(B) four binary digits
(C) four digits
(D) All of the above

**63** It provides us with a shorthand method of working with binary numbers. What does It here?
(A) Hexa decimal number system
(B) Decimal number system
(C) Binary number system
(D) None of the above

**64** Which one of the following represents the binary equivalent of the decimal number 25?
(A) 10101 (B) 01101
(C) 11001 (D) 11011

**65** If the binary equivalent of the decimal number 48 is 110000, then the binary equivalent of the decimal number 51 is given by
(A) 110011 (B) 110010
(C) 110001 (D) 110100

**66** Which one of the following is correct?
(A) $(17)_{10} = (17)_{16}$
(B) $(17)_{10} = (17)_8$
(C) $(17)_{10} = (10111)_2$
(D) $(17)_{10} = (10001)_2$

**67** Which one of the following is correct?
(A) $(1101.10)_2 \rightarrow (12.5)_2$
(B) $(1011.10)_2 \rightarrow (13.5)_{10}$
(C) $(1101.10)_2 \rightarrow (13.5)_{10}$
(D) $(1001.10)_2 \rightarrow (11.5)_{10}$

**68** MSB refers as
(A) Most Significant Bit
(B) Many Significant Bit
(C) Multiple Significant Bit
(D) More Significant Bit

**69** Match the following.

| List I | List II |
|---|---|
| A. $(43)_{10}$ | I. $(99)_{10}$ |
| B. $(1100011)_2$ | II. $(110101)_2$ |
| C. $(1000000)_2$ | III. $(101011)_2$ |
| D. $(53)_{10}$ | IV. $(64)_2$ |

Select the correct match using the codes given below.

| | A | B | C | D |
|---|---|---|---|---|
| (A) | III | I | IV | II |
| (B) | I | II | III | IV |
| (C) | I | IV | III | II |
| (D) | III | I | II | IV |

**70** An ASCII is a character-encoding scheme that is employed by personal computers in order to represent various characters, number and control keys that the computer user selects on the keyboard. ASCII is an acronym for
(A) American Standard Code for Information Interchange
(B) American Standard Code for Intelligent Information
(C) American Standard Code for Information Integrity
(D) American Standard Code for Isolated Information

**71** ............ is a method of using binary digits to represent the decimal digits.
(A) ASCII
(B) BCD
(C) EBCDIC
(D) Hexadecimal system

**72** Most commonly used the codes for representing bits are
(A) ASCII (B) BCD
(C) EBCDIC (D) All of these

## Software

**73** Which is a set of computer programs that interface between user and computer?
(A) An instruction (B) Software
(C) Memory (D) A processor

**74** Software refers to ......... procedures and related data that provide the instructions for telling a computer what to do and how to do it.
(A) the physical components that a compute is made of
(B) firmware
(C) programs
(D) people ware

**75** The two broad categories of software are
(A) word processing and spreadsheet
(B) transaction and application
(C) widows and Mac OS
(D) system and application

**76** Which of the following statements regarding the term system software is/are true?
M. It helps the computer to manage internal resources

N. It is responsible for controlling, integrating and managing the hardware components of a computer system.

Select the correct answer using the codes given below.
(A) Only M
(B) Only N
(C) Both M and N
(D) Neither M nor N

**77** It runs on computer hardware which performs various type of functions in order to manage and organise file
(A) operating system
(B) application software
(C) programs
(D) peripherals

**78** It is the first program, runs on a computer, when the computer boots up
(A) System software
(B) Operating system
(C) System operations
(D) Processing system

**79** Which one of the following is not the function of operating system?
(A) Resource management
(B) File management
(C) Networking
(D) Processor management

**80** Which of the following operating systems is also known as single user operating system?
(A) Windows (B) Linux
(C) Unix (D) MS-DOS

**81** Windows XP is the name of a/an
(A) application software
(B) hardware
(C) system software
(D) None of the above

**82** The primary purpose of the Windows operating system is
(A) to make the most efficient use of the computer hardware
(B) to allow people to use the computer
(C) to keep system programmer's employed
(D) to make computers easier to use

**83** The simultaneous processing of two or more programs by multiple processors, is
(A) Multi-programming
(B) Multi-tasking
(C) Time-sharing
(D) Multi-processing

**84** Utility programs include
(A) virus scanning software
(B) backup software
(C) disk defragmenter
(D) All of the above

**85** …… is a Windows utility program that locates and eliminates unnecessary fragment and rearranges files and unused to disk space to optimise operations.
(A) Backup (B) Disk cleanup
(C) Disk defragmenter (D) Restore

**86** Disk cleaner helps to free …… which also serves to increase the speed of a slow computer.
(A) data (B) recycle bin
(C) spaces (D) information

**87** Read the following two statements.
I. Application software performs specific task for computer users.
II. Application softwares are also called the end-user programs.

Which of the given statement(s) is/are incorrect?
(A) Only I (B) Only II
(C) Both I and II (D) Neither I nor II

**88** Word processing, spreadsheet and photo-editing are examples of
(A) application software
(B) system software
(C) operating system software
(D) platform software

**89** Which of the following is not open source software?
(A) Internet Explorer
(B) Linux
(C) Open Office
(D) Apache HTTP server

**90** Which of the following is an open source software?
(A) Acrobat Reader (B) MS Word
(C) Windows (D) Mozilla Firefox

## Programming Language

**91** Languages which can easily interact with the hardware are called
(A) high level languages
(B) low level languages
(C) middle level languages
(D) All of the above

**92** Match the following.

| List I | List II |
|---|---|
| A. C++ | I. Vint Cerf |
| B. Java | II. Bjarne Stroustrup |
| C. Internet | III. Tim Berners Lee |
| D. WorldWide Web | IV. James Gosling |

Select the correct match using the codes given below.

| | A | B | C | D |
|---|---|---|---|---|
| (A) | I | II | IV | III |
| (B) | III | II | I | IV |
| (C) | IV | II | I | III |
| (D) | II | IV | I | III |

**93** Computer language used for calculation is
(A) LOGO (B) FORTRAN
(C) BASIC (D) C++

**94** A computer program used for business application is
(A) LOGO (B) COBOL
(C) BASIC (D) FORTRAN

**95** C language developed by Dennis Ritchie in
(A) 1970 (B) 1971
(C) 1972 (D) 1973

**96** The language used for development of various games is
(A) C (B) C++
(C) Java (D) SQL

**97** Which of the following is not a programming language?
(A) Pascal (B) Microsoft Office
(C) Java (D) C++

**98** Computer language used on Internet is
(A) PASCAL (B) Java
(C) BASIC (D) LOGO

**99** The function of an assembler is
(A) to convert basic language into machine language
(B) to convert high level language into machine language
(C) to convert assembly language into machine language
(D) to convert assembly language into low level language

**100** The ...... program is used to convert mnemonic code to machine code.
(A) debug (B) C++
(C) FORTRAN (D) assembler

**101** A compiler is a software, which converts
(A) characters to bits
(B) high level language to machine language
(C) machine language to high level language
(D) words to bits

**102** A computer program that translates a program statement by statement into machine language is called a/an
(A) compiler (B) simulator
(C) translator (D) interpreter

## Microsoft Windows

**103** Background of screen is known as
(A) application (B) window
(C) desktop (D) frame

**104** The background image of desktop is called
(A) desktop (B) discover
(C) wallback (D) wallpaper

**105** A...... is a collection of information saved as a unit.
(A) folder (B) file
(C) path (D) file extension

**106** The name given to a document by the user is called
(A) filename (B) program
(C) data (D) record

**107** Which of the following contained at the end of the file name and help to determine the type of file?
(A) File property (B) File nomenclature
(C) File name (D) File extension

**108** Which one of the following is a file?
(A) Floppy disk
(B) Magnetic drum
(C) Magnetic tape
(D) None of the above

**109** What are .bas, .eml, .htm examples of in computing?
(A) Extensions (B) Protocols
(C) Database (D) Domains

**110** Which of the following statements is a false conceiving file name?
(A) Every file in the same folder must have a unique name
(B) The file name comes before the dot (.)
(C) The extension is another name for the type
(D) The file extension comes before the dot (.) followed by the file name

111 Which one of the following is not an/a image/graphic file format?
(A) PNG (B) GIF
(C) BMP (D) GUI

112 You organise files by storing them in
(A) archieves (B) lists
(C) indexes (D) folders

113 ...... may be included in other folder while making hierarchical structure folder.
(A) Mini folder
(B) Tiered folder
(C) Sub-folder
(D) Object

114 Microsoft Office was developed by........ in...... .
(A) Microsoft Inc, 1970s
(B) Microsoft Inc, 1980s
(C) Sun Microsoft, 1980s
(D) Sun Microsoft, 1970s

115 Which of the following is a collection of softwares, based on specific purpose and mainly used in office work
(A) MS-Word
(B) MS-Excel
(C) MS-PowerPoint
(D) All of the above

116 Read the following three statements.
I. MS-Word provides tool for composing, editing, formating and printing of documents.
II. Mail merge denotes the distance text boundaries and page margins.
III. Word offers Portrait-horizontally oriented.
Which of the given statement(s) is/are correct?
(A) Only I (B) Only II
(C) I and II (D) II and III

117 You can start Microsoft Word by using
(A) New (B) Start
(C) Program (D) All of these

118 When you start MS-Word, the opening document has the name as
(A) DOC-1 (B) Document 1
(C) Document (D) Workbook

119 The file extension of MS-Word document in Office 2007 is
(A) .pdf (B) .doc
(C) .docx (D) .txt

120 With regard to word processing software, the process of combining static information in a publication together with variable information in a data source to create one merged publication is called
(A) electronic mail (B) data sourcing
(C) mail merge (D) spam mail

121 Which of the following enables us to send the same letter to different persons in MS-Word?
(A) Mail merge (B) Mail join
(C) Mail copy (D) Mail insert

122 It is a software tool that lets one enter, calculate, manipulate set of numbers.
(A) Speedsheet (B) Spreadsheet
(C) Slidesheet (D) All of these

123 It is a grid of cells made up of horizontal and vertical columns.
(A) Worksheet (B) Sheet
(C) Excel sheet (D) Page

124 The extension of saved file in MS-Excel is
(A) .xis (B) .xas (C) .xlsx (D) .xll

125 Which software is used to create presentation?
(A) Microsoft Word
(B) Microsoft Excel
(C) Microsoft PowerPoint
(D) Microsoft Access

## Database

126 A collection of inter-related records is called a
(A) utility file (B) database
(C) spreadsheet (D) datasheet

127 ......... are the building blocks or relation of any relational database mode.
(A) Tables (B) Fields
(C) Queries (D) Forms

128 ......... are distinct items that don't have much meaning to you in a given context.
(A) Fields (B) Data
(C) Queries (D) Properties

129 A collection of related files is called a
(A) character (B) field
(C) database (D) record

130 Rows of a relation are called
(A) relation (B) tuples
(C) data structure (D) entity

131 What is a stored question about information in a database?
(A) Query (B) Sort
(C) Report (D) Record

132 Which of the following objects is/are contained in database?
(A) Table (B) Query
(C) Form (D) All of these

133 Which of the following places the common data elements in order from smallest to largest?
(A) Character, File, Record, Field, Database
(B) Character, Record, Field, File, Database
(C) Character, Field, Record, File, Database
(D) Bit, Byte, Character, Record, Field, File, Database

134 The data storage hierarchy consists of
(A) bits, bytes, fields, records, files and database
(B) bits, bytes, records, files and database
(C) bits, bytes, fields, files, records and database
(D) bytes, bits, fields, records, files and database

## Computer Network

135 A combination of hardware and software that allows communication and electronic transfer of information between computers is a
(A) network (B) backup system
(C) server (D) peripheral

136 A computer connected to another computer for sharing information form
(A) node (B) router
(C) server (D) network

137 What type of resource is most likely to be a shared common resource in a computer network?
(A) Printers
(B) Speakers
(C) Floppy disk drives
(D) Keyboards

138 What do we call a network whose elements may be separated by some distance? It usually involves two or more network and dedicated high speed telephone lines.
(A) LAN (B) WAN
(C) URL (D) Server

139 A(n) ...... area is a small group of computers and peripherals linked together in a small geographic area.
(A) MAN (B) PAN
(C) CAN (D) LAN

140 Which of following types of network is a data network designed for a town or a city?
(A) LAN (B) MAN
(C) PAN (D) WAN

141 There is a network that can connect networks ranging from small location or area to a bigger range including public packet network and large corporate networks. That network's enterprise allows users to share access to applications, services and other centrally located resources. Its ability for a huge geographical access has transformed networking. Which among the following is that network?
(A) SAN (B) CAN
(C) LAN (D) WAN

142 Which of the following refers to a small, single-site network?
(A) PAN (B) DSL
(C) RAM (D) USB

143 Choose the correct answer of the network according to their decreasing size of extension/coverage.
(A) WAN, LAN, MAN, PAN
(B) WAN, MAN, LAN, PAN
(C) MAN, LAN, PAN, WAN
(D) MAN, PAN, WAN, LAN

144 Geometric arrangement of devices on the network is called
(A) topology (B) protocols
(C) media (D) LAN

145 Consider the following statement about topology.
I. In bus topology, there is a single line to connect the nodes.
II. In ring topology, each node is connected in a circular way.
III. Mesh topology is also known as completely inter connected topology.
Which of these statements are correct?
(A) I, II and III (B) I and III
(C) II and III (D) I and II

146 ...... of a network refer to the transmission media or the connecting media used in the network.
(A) Communication media
(B) Topology
(C) Protocol
(D) None of the above

147 Which of the following is bound by the cabling system that guide the data signal along specific path?
(A) Guided Media
(B) Wired Technology
(C) Both (A) and (B)
(D) Unguided Media

148 A device that connects to a network without the use of cables is said to be
(A) distributed (B) cabled
(C) centralised (D) wireless

## Internet and E-mailing

149 The vast network of computers that connects millions of people all over the world is called
(A) LAN (B) Web
(C) hypertext (D) Internet

150 Which is not the feature of Internet?
(A) E-mail (B) News groups
(C) Chat (D) Designing

151 The Internet allows to
(A) send electronic mail.
(B) view web pages.
(C) connect to servers all around the world
(D) All of the above

152 Internet was developed in the
(A) 1950s (B) 1960s (C) 1970s (D) 1980s

153 A/An ........., is a private network that is contained within an enterprise.
(A) Intranet (B) Internet
(C) Extranet (D) Logical net

154 Consider the following statements about Internet facility.
I. It serves as the largest online information system.
II. It provides the most dependable and latest mode for sending e-mail.
III. Recurring expenditure on communicating e-mail is very high.
IV. It is often misused and has triggered cyber-crimes.

Which of these statement are correct?
(A) I, II and IV (B) I and IV
(C) II, III and IV (D) II and III

155 Protocol consists of ........., which suits are the set of communication protocols used for the Internet.
(A) TCD/IT (B) TCP/IP
(C) TCP/IT (D) TCT/IP

156 TCP/IP is necessary if one is to connect to the
(A) phone lines (B) LAN
(C) Internet (D) a server

157 ...... is a protocol used by e-mail clients to download e-mails to your computer.
(A) TCP (B) FTP
(C) SMTP (D) POP

158 POP3 and IMAP are e-mail accounts in which
(A) one automatically gets one's mail everyday
(B) one has to be connected to the server to read or write one's mail
(C) one only has to be connected to the server to send and receive email
(D) one does not need any telephone lines

159 The acronym FTP stands for
(A) File Transfer Protocol
(B) Fast Transfer Protocol
(C) File Tracking Protocol
(D) File Transfer Procedure

160 Which of the following is the communication protocol that sets the standard used by every computer that accesses web-based information?
(A) XML (B) DML
(C) HTTP (D) HTML

161 'WWW' stands for
(A) Work With Web (B) Word Wide Web
(C) World Wide Web (D) Worth While Web

162 The Internet service that provides a multimedia interface to available resources is called
(A) FTP (B) World Wide Web
(C) Domain name (D) Web Browser

163 ...... is collection of web pages and ...... is the very first page that we seen on opening of website.
(A) Home page, web page
(B) Website, home page
(C) Web page, home page
(D) Web page, website

**164** The first web browser is
(A) Internet explorer (B) Netscape
(C) World Wide Web (D) Firebox

**165** Internet explorer is a type of
(A) operating system (B) compiler
(C) browser (D) IP address

**166** Identify the IP address from the following.
(A) 300·215·317·3 (B) 302·215@417·5
(C) 202·50·20·148 (D) 202-50-20-148

**167** What is the name for a web page address?
(A) Directory (B) Protocol
(C) URL (D) Domain

**168** URL identifies the location of a specific web page on the Internet, here URL stands for
(A) Uniform Read Locator
(B) Uniform Resource Locator
(C) Unicode Research Location
(D) United Research Location

**169** Which of the following domains is used for profit business?
(A) .net (B) .edu
(C) .com (D) .org

**170** Which one of the following is not the same as the other three?
(A) MAC address (B) Hardware address
(C) Physical address (D) IP address

**171** Which is an instant messenger that is used for chatting?
(A) AltaVista (B) MAC
(C) Microsoft (D) Google Talk

**172** Which of the following is an instant messaging application?
1. WhatsApp 2. Google Talk
3. Skype
Select the corrrect answer using the codes given below.
(A) Only 1 (B) 1and 2
(C) 2 and 3 (D) 1, 2 and 3

**173** Given the following email fields, which of the mail addresses will 'swami' be able to see when he receives the message?
To : ram@test.com
Cc : raj@test.com; ravi@test.com
Bcc : swami@test.com; rama@test.com
(A) ram@test.com; rama@test.com
(B) ram@test.com; rama@test.com; raj@test.com; ravi@test.com
(C) ram@test.com
(D) ram@test.com; raj@test.com; ravi@test.com

**174** Sending an E-mail is similar to
(A) writing a letter (B) drawing a picture
(C) talking on the phone (D) sending a package

**175** Which of the following is the appropriate format of URL of e-mail?
(A) www_mail.com (B) www@mail.com
(C) WWW@mail.com (D) www.mail.com

**176** Video conferencing can be classified as one of the following types of communication.
(A) Visual one way
(B) Audio-visual one way
(C) Audio-visual two way
(D) Visual two way

**177** ...... is the encompassing term that involves the use of electronic platforms-intranet, extranet and the Internet to conduct a company's business.
(A) e-Commerce (B) e-Marketing
(C) e-Procurement (D) e-Business

**178** Which of the following is characteristic of Web 2.0 applications?
(A) Multiple users schedule their time to use Web 2.0 applications one by one
(B) Web 2.0 applications are focussed on the ability for people to collaborate and share information online
(C) Web 2.0 applications provide users with content rather than facilitating users to create it
(D) Web 2.0 applications use only static pages

**179** Riya tells her friends, Priya (priya@gmail.com), Sahil (sahil@gmail.com) and Muskan (muskan@yahoo.com), date of her anniversary party through an E-mail as shown below:
To : muskan@gmail.com
Cc : priya@gmail.com
Bcc : sahil@gmail.com
Subject : My Anniversary Party is on 05/02/2019.
Hello Friends,
I want to invite you on my Anniversary party. You can call me when you will come.
Riya
Which of the following cannot be derived from this E-mail?
(A) Sahil does not knows that both Muskan and Priya receives the mail.
(B) Muskan knows that Priya receives the mail.
(C) Priya knows that Sahil receives the mail
(D) Sahil knows that the anniversary party will be held on 05/02/2019.

**180** Sandeep tells his business partner, Saleem (saleem@gmail.com), Durgesh (durgesh@gmail.com) and Arif (arif@yahoo.com), date of seminar through an email as shown below:

To : saleem@gmail.com
Cc : durgesh@gmail.com
Bcc: arif@yahoo.com
Subject : Seminar held on 28/01/2019
Good Morning,
I would like to tell about the seminar for our new project E-Books which held on 28/01/2019. Please come on time and ensure me your presence.
Thanking you.
M.D.
Sandeep

Which of the following can not be derived from this E-mail?
(A) Saleem knows that both Durgesh and Arif receives mail.
(B) Durgesh knows that Arif receives the mail.
(C) Durgesh knows that seminar will be held on 28/01/2019.
(D) Arif knows that Durgesh receives mail.

**181** Yash tells his friends, Vaibhav (vaibhav@gmail.com), Aryan (aryan@gmail.com) and Kirti (kirti@gmail.com), date of his brother's birthday party through an E-mail as shown below.

To : vaibhav@gmail.com
Cc : aryan@gmail.com
Bcc : kirti@gmail.com
Subject : Brother's Birthday Party Invitation
Hello Friend,
How are you? I hope you are alright. I want to invite you on my brother Akshay's Birthday party is on 30/01/2019.
You have to come.
Bye
Yash

Which of the following can be derived from this E-mail?
(A) Vaibhav knows that Aryan receive mail
(B) Aryan knows that Sahil receive mail
(C) Kirti knows that both Aryan and Vaibhav receive mail
(D) Vaibhav knows that Kirti receive mail

**182** ......... is the practice of connecting multiple called parties on a single audio conference call with multiple lines connected through a conferencing bridge.
(A) Video conferencing
(B) Audio conferencing
(C) Audio call
(D) None of the above

## Computer Security

**183** If you are allowing a person on the network based on the credentials to maintain the security of your network, then this act refers to the process of
(A) authentication (B) automation
(C) firewall (D) encryption

**184** Encoding or scrambling data for transmission across a network is known as
(A) protection (B) detection
(C) encryption (D) decryption

**185** If your computer rebooting itself then it is likely that
(A) it has a virus.
(B) it does not have enough memory.
(C) there is not printer.
(D) there has been a power surge.

**186** Match the following.

| List I | List II |
|---|---|
| A. Virus | I. They are hard to detect |
| B. Worms | II. It is copied itself |
| C. Trojan | III. Non-self replicating type of malware |

Select the correct match using the codes given below.

| | A | B | C | | A | B | C |
|---|---|---|---|---|---|---|---|
| (A) | II | I | III | (B) | I | II | III |
| (C) | II | III | I | (D) | I | III | II |

**187** A program designed to destroy data on your computer which can travel to infect other computers, is called a
(A) disease (B) torpedo
(C) hurricane (D) virus

**188** Which of the following refers to dangerous programs that can be 'caught' of opening e-mail attachments and downloading software from the Internet?
(A) Utility (B) Virus
(C) Honey Pot (D) Spam

**189** Viruses, trojan horses and worms are
(A) able to harm computer system
(B) unable to detect if present on computer
(C) user-friendly applications
(D) harmless applications resident on computer

**190** It is a self-replicating program that infects computer and spreads by inserting copies of itself into other executable code or documents.
(A) Keylogger (B) Worm
(C) Virus (D) Cracker

**191** A computer virus normally attaches itself to another computer program is known as a
(A) host program (B) target program
(C) backdoor program (D) trojan horse

**192** It is the technique to access the unauthorized data without concerning to the authorized user.
(A) Spoofing (B) Forging
(C) IP spoofing (D) All of these

**193** It is an act of intruding into someone else's computer or network.
(A) Hacking (B) Cracking
(C) Adware (D) Spyware

**194** A person who uses his or her expertise to gain access to other people computers to get information illegally or do damage is a
(A) spammer
(B) hacker
(C) instant messenger
(D) All of the above

**195** ...... are often delivered to PC through an e-mail attachment and are often designed to do harm.
(A) Viruses (B) Spams
(C) Portals (D) E-mail messages

**196** An unsolicited e-mail, message sent to many recipients at once is a
(A) worm (B) virus
(C) threat (D) spam

**197** An antivirus is a(n)
(A) program code (B) computer
(C) company name (D) application software

**198** A digital signature is
(A) scanned signature
(B) signature in binary form
(C) electronic form of signature
(D) handwritten signature

**199** ......... primary objective is to control the incoming and outgoing network traffic by analysing the data packets.
(A) Firewall (B) Password
(C) Antivirus (D) Phishing

**200** It is a secret word or a string of characters used for user authentication to prove identity or access approval.
(A) Mailer (B) Password
(C) Macro (D) Firewall

**201** A term used to describe the location or folder where E-mail is stored before being sent.
(A) Inbox (B) Draft
(C) Outbox (D) Sent Items

## Digital Initiatives in Higher Education

**202** NMEICT stands for
(A) National Mission on E-learning through ICT
(B) National Mission on Education through ICT
(C) National Mission on E-governance through ICT
(D) National Mission on E-governance through ICT

**203** The online portal ......... presents the list of all courses and related information that can be accessed online.
(A) swayam.gov.in (B) ndl.itkgp.ac.in
(C) course.gov.in (D) None of these

**204** It is a DTH channel service in which new academic content will be aired by the universities and they will be regularly updated.
(A) Swayam (B) NDL
(C) Swayamprabha (D) NAD

**205** On institution future plan, which of the following is correct matching?

| List I | List II |
|---|---|
| A. 15 year vision | I. For immediate improvement of the quality of learning. |
| B. 7 year vision | II. To work out medium term plants to reach there. |
| C. 3 year vision | III. To determine where the institution would like to be. |

**Codes**

| | A | B | C |
|---|---|---|---|
| (A) | I | II | III |
| (B) | II | III | I |
| (C) | I | III | II |
| (D) | III | II | I |

**206** .......is an initiative of the UGC that provides an online store house of all academic awards i.e. certificates, diplomas etc.
(A) National Academic Depository
(B) National Digital Library
(C) Swayam
(D) Swayamprabha

**207** Higher education needs to evolve to ensure that it meets the requirements of the ....... .
(A) Forcasting (B) Future workforce
(C) Future needs (D) All of these

## ICT and Governance

**208** Government to citizen relationship is the most basic aspect of ......... .
(A) e-Government (B) e-Governance
(C) e-Citizenship (D) e-Relationship

**209** Which of the following statements regarding the term e-Governance is/are True?
M. e-Citizenship will include the implementation of ICT for facilitation of government services relating to citizenship.
N. e-Help refers to the facilitation of disaster and crisis management using ICT.
Select the correct answer using the codes given below:
(A) Both M and N
(B) Only M
(C) Only N
(D) Neither M nor N

**210** Which of the following require technology experts to curb the electronic cyber crimes?
(A) Police
(B) Expert police
(C) Cyber police
(D) None of the above

**211** ......... can help to enable the true democratic process including voting, public opinion, feedback and Government accountability.
(A) IT (B) ICT
(C) NDL (D) NAD

**212** Which of the following aims to reduce the reaction time of the government to the people's queries and problems?
(A) e-Registration (B) e-Help
(C) e-Governance (D) e-Health

**213** Which of the following is/are advantage(s) of e-Governance which make(s) e-Governance more informative?
(A) Speed
(B) Cost reduction
(C) Transparency
(D) All of the above

**214** DMS and workflow technologies are usually used in those departments where there is a lack of workforce. What does DMS stand for?
(A) Data Management Service
(B) Document Management Service
(C) Document Management System
(D) Data Management System

# Previous Years' Questions

## UGC NET Dec 2019

**1** Which of the following communication technologies employ only asynchronous communication

1. Video conferencing
2. Email
3. Forums
4. Instant messaging

Choose the correct option

(A) (1) and (3) (B) (2) and (4)
(C) (2) and (3) (D) (1) and (4)

**2** Select the option that includes file formats suitable for distributing sound files across the Internet

(A) wwv, mp4, wma, mp3
(B) avi, midi, wav, mp3
(C) avi, mov, wmv, mp3
(D) midi, wav, wma, mp3

**3** Which of the following statement(s) is/are correct

1. For the sequence of integers represented in binary as 00111, 010011, P ...... The next integer P would be represented as 01101
2. A byte is a binary number consisting of exactly 8 bits.

Choose the correct option

(A) Only (1) (B) Only (2)
(C) Both (1) and (2) (D) Neither (1) nor (2)

**4** Match List-I with List-II in the context of computer networking

| List I | List II |
|---|---|
| A. VOIP | I. Makes use of light pulses to transmit data |
| B. Fibre-optic cable | II. use of internet to make phone calls |
| C. URL | III. Most appropriate to connect computers in a small building |
| D. UTP cable | IV. Text used by web browsers to locate a web address on the Internet |

**Codes**

| | A | B | C | D |
|---|---|---|---|---|
| (A) | IV | I | II | III |
| (B) | II | I | IV | III |
| (C) | II | III | IV | I |
| (D) | IV | III | II | I |

**5** Match List I with List II

| List I (Digital Initative) | List II (Purpose) |
|---|---|
| A. UMANG | (i) G2B services |
| B. BHIM | (ii) Learning Platform |
| C. eBiz | (iii) Unified Payment Interface |
| D. SWAYAM | (iv) Single point of access to all government services |

Choose the correct options

| | A | B | C | D |
|---|---|---|---|---|
| (A) | (ii) | (i) | (iii) | (iv) |
| (B) | (iii) | (ii) | (iv) | (i) |
| (C) | (iv) | (iii) | (i) | (ii) |
| (D) | (i) | (iv) | (ii) | (iii) |

**6** Regarding E-governance, which of the following statements is/are correct

1. Decreasing transparency is an ICT enabled advantage of E - Governance
2. E-Governance is related to the implementation of ICT in the government process and function
3. Common service Centrs (CSCs) helop in providing and Using E - Governance related services

Choose the correct option

(A) (1), (2) and (3) (B) (1) and (3)
(B) (1) and (3) (D) (1) and (2)

**7** Which of the following statements i/are correct?

1. Software is loaded into secondary from RAM and is then execute by the CPU
2. A search engine is a software system that is designed to search for information on the www.

Choose the correct option:

(A) Only (1) (B) Only (2)
(C) Both (1) and (2) (D) Neither (1) nor (2)

**8** Select the option that lists components for cyberspace address (URL) in the correct order from beginning to end?

(A) Protocol, domain name of the host, path/file
(B) Path/file, protocol, domain name of the host
(C) Protocol, path/file, domain name of the host
(D) Domain name of the host, protocol, path/file

## UGC NET June 2019

**9** Identify the encompassing term that involves the use of electronic platform to conduct a company's business

1. E - Business  2. E - Commerce
3. E - Marketing  4. E- Governance

**Codes**

(A) 1 (B) 2 (C) 3 (D) 4

**10** Which of the following is generally associated with the domain name of an educational institution?

1. .org  2. .edu
3. .com  4. .inst

**Codes**

(A) 1 (B) 2 (C) 3 (D) 4

**11** Which of the following devices enables a computer to transmit data over telephon lines?

1. CPU  2. HUB
3. Switch  4. Modem

**Options**

(A) 1 (B) 2 (C) 3 (D) 4

**12** What is SWAYAM?

(A) Non - Governmental organisation
(B) Digital programme to achieve the principles of education
(C) on line platform
(D) Name of a web site

**13** Which of the following is not considered as a form of se ondary storage?

1. RAM  2. Floppy Disk
3. Optical Disk  4. Flash Drive

**Option**

(A) 1 (B) 2
(C) 3 (D) 4

## UGC NET 2019 June

**14** Wile sending an e-mail, to differentiate among To: CC; and BCC; field, which one of th following statements is True?

1. Recipients in the To: field cna see the email addresses that are in the BCC; and Cc: field
2. Recipients in the Cc : field can see the email addresses that are in the To : and BCC : fields
3. Recipients in the Bcc : field can see the email addresses that are in the To : and CCc : fields
4. Only the recipients in the Cc : field can see the other email addresses in the Bcc : field

(A) 1 (B) 2 (C) 3 (D) 4

**15** A group's access to digital technology and another group's lack of access to it, will cause a disparity known as

1. Internet inequality
2. Web inequality
3. Technological imbalance
4. Digital divide

**Options**

(A) 1 (B) 2 (C) 3 (D) 4

**16** Which one of the following is an educational FM radio network

1. Gyan Darshan  2. Gyan Vani
3. Gyan Dhara  4. GIAN

**Options**

(A) 1 (B) 2 (C) 3 (D) 4

**17** Software that you can download for free, but have to pay to continue its use after a trial period is called

1. Public domain software
2. Freeware
3. open source software
4. shareware

**Options**

(A) 1 (B) 2
(C) 3 (D) 4

**18** Which one of the following computer components is fastest in terms of speed of access?

1. USB Drive  2. Solid State Drive
3. Ram  4. Hard Disk Drive

**Option**

(A) 1 (B) 2
(C) 3 (D) 4

**19** A terabyte is equal to

(A) 1024 megabytes (B) 1024 kilobytes
(C) 1024 Gigabytes (D) $1024 \times 1024$ kilobytes

**20** The binary equivalent of $(-23)_{10}$ is (2's complement system for negative numbers is used)

(A) 01001 (B) 10111
(C) 01010 (D) 01000

**21** The full form of PDF is

(A) Portable Data format
(B) Portable Document Form
(C) Portable Document Format
(D) Portable Data form

22 Which of the given statements are true?
(i) Modem is a networking device
(ii) Modem is a voltage stabilizer
(iii) Modem converts analogue signal to digital signal and vice versa.

**Options**
(A) (ii) and (iii) (B) (i) and (iii)
(C) (i) and (ii) (D) (i), (ii) and (iii)

## UGC Net December 2018 Paper 1

23 If the binary equivalent of the decimal number 53 is 110101, then the binary equivalent of the decimal number 50 is given by
(A) 110011 (B) 110010
(C) 110001 (D) 110100

24 Which one of the following is not part of suite of products of Microsoft Office?
(A) Microsoft Excel
(B) Microsoft PowerPoint
(C) Microsoft Publisher
(D) Microsoft Window

25 The internet began with the development of
(A) USENET (B) Internet
(C) ARPANET (D) Intranet

26 RFID is an acronym for
(A) Roaming Frequency Identification
(B) Radio Frequency Identification
(C) Runtime Frequency Identification
(D) Remote Frequency Identification

27 Bluetooth is an example of
(A) PAN (B) LAN
(C) MAN (D) WAN

## UGC NET July 2018

28 Which of the following statements, regarding the term ICT is/are True
P : ICT is an acronym that stands for Indian Classical Technology.
Q : Converging technologies that examplify ICT include the merging of audio - visual, telephone and computer networks through a common cabling system.
(A) P Only (B) Q Only
(C) P and Q (D) Neither P nor Q

29 A new laptop has been produced that weighs less, is smaller and uses less power than previous laptop models.
Which of the following technologies has been used to accomplish this
(A) Universal Serial Bus Mouse
(B) Faster Random Access Memory
(C) Blue Ray Drive
(D) Solid State Hard drive

30 Given the following email fields, which of the email addresses will swami be able to see when he receives the massage

| | |
|---|---|
| To.... | ram@test. com |
| Cc... | raj@test. com; ravi@test. com |
| Bcc... | Swami@test.com;rama@test.com |

(A) ram@test.com
(B) ram@test.com; raj@test.com; ravi@test.com
(C) ram@test.com; rama@test.com
(D) ram@test.com; rama@test.com; raj@test.com; ravi@test.com

31 Put the following units of storage into the correct order, starting with the smallest unit first and going down to the largest unit.
(a) Kilobyte (b) byte
(c) megabyte (d) Terabyte
(e) Gigabyte (f) Bit

**Codes**
(A) (f), (b), (a), (c), (d), (e)
(B) (f), (b), (a), (d), (e), (c)
(C) (f), (b), (a), (c), (e), (d)
(D) (f), (b), (a), (d), (c), (e)

32 With regard to computer memory, which of the following statement (s) / is / are TRUE?
P : Read only memory (ROM) is volatile memory
Q : Random Access Memory (RAM) is volatile memory
R : Secondary memory is volatile memory
(A) P only (B) Q only
(C) P and Q only (D) P and R only

33 What is the name for a webpage address?
(A) Domain (B) Directory
(C) Protocol (D) URL

34 The data storage hierarchy consists of
(A) Bytes, bits, fields, records, files and databases
(B) Bits, bytes, fields, records, files and databases
(C) Bits, bytes, records, fields, files and databases
(D) Bits, bytes, fields, files, records and databases

**35** Which of the following domains is used for profit businesses?

(A) .org (B) .net
(C) .edu (D) .com

**36** What is the full form of USB as used in computer related activities

(A) Ultra security Block
(B) Universal Security Block
(C) Universal Serial Bus
(D) United Serial Bus

**37** Which of the following repressents billion characters?

(A) Terabytes (B) Megabytes
(C) Kilobytes (D) Gigabytes

**38** Whic]h of the following statement(s) is/are TRUe

S1 : the decimal number 11 is larger than the hezxadecimal number
S2 : In the binary number 110.101, the fractional part has the decimal value as 0.625

(A) S1 only (B) S2 only
(C) Both S1 and S2 (D) Neither S1 nor S2

**39** Read the following two statements.

I. Information and communication Technology (ICT) is considered as a subset of Information Technology (IT)
II. The right to use a piece of software is termed as copyright.

Which of the above mentioned statement(s) is/are CORRECT?

(A) Both I and II (B) Neither I nor II
(C) II only (D) I only

**40** Which of the following correctly lists the types of the computer memory from highest to lowest speed?

(i) Secondary storage
(ii) Main memory (RAM)
(iii) Cache memory
(iv) CPU registers

**Codes**

(A) (i), (ii), (iii), (iv) (B) (iv), (iii), (i), (ii)
(C) (iv), (iii), (ii), (i) (D) (iii), (iv), (ii), (i)

**41** Which of the following is a characteristic of Web 2.0 applications?

(A) Multiple users schedule their time to use Web 2.0 applications one by one
(B) Web 2.0 applications are focused on the ability for people to collaborate and share information online
(C) Web 2.0 applications provide users with content rather than facilitating users to create it
(D) Web 2.0 applications use only static pages

**42** With regard to a word processing software, the process of combining static information in a data source to create one merged publication is called

(A) Electronic mail (B) Data sourcing
(C) Mail merge (D) Spam mail

**43** DVD technology uses an optical media to store the digital data. DVD is an acronym for

(A) Digital Vectors Disc
(B) Digital Volume Disc
(C) Digital Versatile Disc
(D) Digital Visualization Disc

**44** ......... is a type of memory circuity that holds the computer's start up routine

(A) RIM (Read Initial Memory)
(B) RAM (Random Access Memory)
(C) ROM (Read only memory)
(D) Cache Memory

**45** An ASCII is a character encoding scheme that is employed by personal computers in order to represent various characrters, numbers and control keys that the computer user selects on the keyboard. ASCII is an acronym for

(A) American standard Code for information Interchange.
(B) American Standard Code for Intelligent Information
(C) American Standard Code for Information Integrity
(D) American Standard Code for Isolated Information

**46** The process of copying files to a CD - ROM is known as

(A) Burning (B) Zipping
(C) Digitising (D) Ripping

**47** An unsolicited e-mail message sent to many recipients at onece is a

(A) Worm (B) Virus
(C) Threat (D) Spam

**48** The statement the study, design, development, implementation support or management of computer based information stems, particularly software applications and computer Hardware refers to

(A) Information Technology (IT)
(B) Information and collaborative Technology (ICT)
(C) Information and Data Technology (IDT)
(D) Artificial Intelligence (AI)

**49** Which of the following is an instant messaging application
(i) Whats App
(ii) Google Talk
(iii) Viber
Select the correct answer from the codes given below
(A) (i) and (ii) only (B) (ii) and (iii) only
(C) (i) only (D) (i), (ii) and (iii)

**50** In a computer, a byte generally consists of
(A) 4 bits (B) 8 bits
(C) 16 bits (D) 10 bits

**51** Which of the following is not an input device
(A) Microphone (B) Keyboard
(C) Joystick (D) Monitor

**52** Which of the following is an open source software
(A) MS word (B) Windows
(C) Mozilla Firefox (D) Acrobat Reader

**53** Which of the following enables us to send the same letter to different people in MS Word?
(A) Mail Join (B) Mail copy
(C) Mail insert (D) Mail merge

**54** NMEICT stands for
(A) National Mission on Education through ICT
(B) National Mission on e-governance through ICT
(C) National Mission on E-commerce through ICT
(D) National Mission on E-learning through ICT

**55** Which of the following represents one billion characters?
(A) Kilobyte (B) Megabyte
(C) Gigabyte (D) Terabyte

**56** Which of the following is not open source software?
(A) Internet explorer
(B) Fedora Linux
(C) Open office
(D) Apache HTTP server

**57** Which one of the following represents the binary equivalent of the decimal number 25
(A) 10101 (B) 01101
(C) 11001 (D) 11011

**58** Encoding or scrambling data for transmission across a network is known as
(A) Protection (B) Detection
(C) Encryption (D) Decryption

**59** Which of the following is not an output device?
(A) Printer (B) Speaker
(C) Monitor (D) Keyboard

**60** Symbols A - F are used in which one of the following
(A) Binary number system
(B) Decimal number system
(C) Hexaadecimal number system
(D) Octal number system

**61** Which one of the following is not a search engine?
(A) Google (B) Chrome
(C) Yahoo (D) Bing

**62** CSS stands for
(A) Cascading Style sheets
(B) Collecting Style Sheets
(C) Comparative Style Sheets
(D) Comprehensive Style Sheets

**63** MOOC stands for
(A) Media Online Open Course
(B) Massachusetts Open Online Course
(C) Massive open online Course
(D) Myrind open online course

**64** Binary equivalent of decimal number 35 is
(A) 100011 (B) 110001
(C) 110101 (D) 101011

**65** The terms gif, jpmg, bmp, png are used as extensions for files which store
(A) audio data (B) image data
(C) video data (D) text data

**66** The acronuym FTP stands for
(A) File Transfer Protocol
(B) Fast Transfer Protocol
(C) File Tracking Protocol
(D) File transfer Procedure

**67** Which one of the following is not a/an image/graphic file format
(A) PNG (B) GIF
(C) BMP (D) GUI

**68** The first web browser is
(A) Internet Explorer (B) Netscape
(C) World Wide Web (D) Firefox

**69** When a computer is booting, BIOS is loaded to the memory by
(A) RAM (B) ROM
(C) CD - ROM (D) TCP

**70** Which one of the following is not the same as the other three
(A) MAC address (B) Hardware address
(C) Physical address (D) IP address

**71** Identify the IP address from the following
(A) 300 . 215 . 317 . 3 (B) 302 . 215@417 . 5
(C) 202 . 50.20 . 148 (D) 202 - 50 - 20 - 148

# ANSWERS

## Chapter Practice

| | | | | | | | | | |
|---|---|---|---|---|---|---|---|---|---|
| 1 (B) | 2 (A) | 3 (A) | 4 (D) | 5 (D) | 6 (D) | 7 (A) | 8 (C) | 9 (B) | 10 (C) |
| 11 (D) | 12 (C) | 13 (B) | 14 (B) | 15 (A) | 16 (C) | 17 (C) | 18 (C) | 19 (D) | 20 (D) |
| 21 (C) | 22 (A) | 23 (A) | 24 (D) | 25 (C) | 26 (D) | 27 (C) | 28 (D) | 29 (D) | 30 (B) |
| 31 (A) | 32 (C) | 33 (C) | 34 (D) | 35 (D) | 36 (D) | 37 (B) | 38 (D) | 39 (C) | 40 (B) |
| 41 (D) | 42 (C) | 43 (B) | 44 (D) | 45 (A) | 46 (C) | 47 (B) | 48 (C) | 49 (B) | 50 (A) |
| 51 (C) | 52 (B) | 53 (C) | 54 (C) | 55 (A) | 56 (C) | 57 (A) | 58 (B) | 59 (B) | 60 (B) |
| 61 (C) | 62 (B) | 63 (A) | 64 (C) | 65 (A) | 66 (D) | 67 (C) | 68 (A) | 69 (A) | 70 (A) |
| 71 (C) | 72 (D) | 73 (B) | 74 (C) | 75 (D) | 76 (C) | 77 (A) | 78 (B) | 79 (C) | 80 (D) |
| 81 (C) | 82 (D) | 83 (D) | 84 (D) | 85 (C) | 86 (C) | 87 (D) | 88 (A) | 89 (A) | 90 (D) |
| 91 (B) | 92 (D) | 93 (B) | 94 (B) | 95 (C) | 96 (C) | 97 (B) | 98 (B) | 99 (C) | 100 (D) |
| 101 (B) | 102 (D) | 103 (C) | 104 (D) | 105 (B) | 106 (A) | 107 (D) | 108 (D) | 109 (A) | 110 (D) |
| 111 (D) | 112 (D) | 113 (C) | 114 (B) | 115 (D) | 116 (A) | 117 (B) | 118 (B) | 119 (B) | 120 (C) |
| 121 (A) | 122 (B) | 123 (A) | 124 (C) | 125 (C) | 126 (B) | 127 (A) | 128 (A) | 129 (D) | 130 (B) |
| 131 (A) | 132 (D) | 133 (C) | 134 (A) | 135 (A) | 136 (A) | 137 (A) | 138 (B) | 139 (D) | 140 (B) |
| 141 (D) | 142 (A) | 143 (B) | 144 (A) | 145 (A) | 146 (A) | 147 (C) | 148 (D) | 149 (D) | 150 (D) |
| 151 (D) | 152 (B) | 153 (A) | 154 (A) | 155 (B) | 156 (C) | 157 (C) | 158 (B) | 159 (A) | 160 (C) |
| 161 (C) | 162 (B) | 163 (B) | 164 (B) | 165 (C) | 166 (C) | 167 (C) | 168 (B) | 169 (C) | 170 (D) |
| 171 (D) | 172 (D) | 173 (D) | 174 (A) | 175 (B) | 176 (C) | 177 (A) | 178 (B) | 179 (C) | 180 (B) |
| 181 (C) | 182 (B) | 183 (A) | 184 (C) | 185 (A) | 186 (A) | 187 (D) | 188 (B) | 189 (A) | 190 (B) |
| 191 (D) | 192 (A) | 193 (A) | 194 (B) | 195 (A) | 196 (D) | 197 (D) | 198 (C) | 199 (A) | 200 (B) |
| 201 (C) | 202 (B) | 203 (A) | 204 (C) | 205 (D) | 206 (A) | 207 (B) | 208 (B) | 209 (A) | 210 (C) |
| 211 (B) | 212 (C) | 213 (D) | 214 (D) | | | | | | |

## Previous Years' Questions

| | | | | | | | | | |
|---|---|---|---|---|---|---|---|---|---|
| 1 (C) | 2 (D) | 3 (C) | 4 (B) | 5 (C) | 6 (B) | 7 (B) | 8 (A) | 9 (B) | 10 (B) |
| 11 (D) | 12 (B) | 13 (A) | 14 (C) | 15 (D) | 16 (B) | 17 (D) | 18 (C) | 19 (C) | 20 (A) |
| 21 (C) | 22 (B) | 23 (B) | 24 (D) | 25 (C) | 26 (D) | 27 (A) | 28 (B) | 29 (D) | 30 (B) |
| 31 (C) | 32 (B) | 33 (D) | 34 (B) | 35 (D) | 36 (C) | 37 (D) | 38 (B) | 39 (B) | 40 (C) |
| 41 (B) | 42 (C) | 43 (C) | 44 (C) | 45 (A) | 46 (A) | 47 (D) | 48 (A) | 49 (D) | 50 (B) |
| 51 (D) | 52 (C) | 53 (D) | 54 (A) | 55 (C) | 56 (A) | 57 (C) | 58 (D) | 59 (C) | 60 (D) |
| 61 (C) | 62 (B) | 63 (A) | 64 (C) | 65 (A) | 66 (B) | 67 (A) | 68 (D) | 69 (C) | 70 (D) |
| 71 (C) | | | | | | | | | |

# UNIT 09

# *People, Development and Environment*

CHAPTER ANALYSIS

This unit is based on the updated syllabus of NTA UGC Net covering all the important topics related to People, Development & Environment. After going through the chapter you will be able to understand the Millennium and Sustainable Development Goals, human and environment interaction, environmental issues, climate change, natural & energy resources, national agreements or efforts, natural hazards etc.

Every year 4 to 5 questions are asked from this unit in NTA UGC Net exam, which are based on environment, pollution, MDG & SDG, resources, national /international action plan etc.

## DEVELOPMENT AND ENVIRONMENT

The term 'development' refers to the theory of social change that aims at the improvement in the country's economic and social conditions. It refers to the improvements in the ways of managing a region's natural and human resources. It is, then, a process that transforms the society such that it satisfies human wants and aspirations.

This understanding of development completely ignored the overexploitation of natural resources, climate change and pressure on the ecosystems. The adverse effect of such ignorance displayed the fact that the prevalent understanding of development has misinterpreted the concept of real development.

As a result, a new approach towards development was introduced. This new approach worked for securing not only the social and economic development, but was also focussed on sustainability of the environment. This approach was called Sustainable Human Development.

In order to meet the social, economic and environmental aspects of Sustainable Human Development, various goals were set up by the United Nations.


IN THIS UNIT

- Development and Environment : MDG and SDG
- Human and Environment Interaction : Anthropogenic Activities and their Impacts on Environment
- Environmental Issues : Air Pollution, Water Pollution, Soil Pollution, Noise Pollution, Waste : Climate Change and Its Socio-Economic and Political Dimensions
- Impacts of Pollutants on Human Health
- Natural and Energy Resources
- Natural Hazards and Disasters and their Mitigations
- National Agreements/Efforts : International Environmental Protection Act (1986), National Action Plan on Climate Change, Montreal Protocol, Rio Summit, Convention on Biodiversity, Kyoto Protocol, Paris Agreement, International Solar Alliance.

## Millennium Development Goals (MDGs)

The United Nations Millennium Development Goals are eight goals that all 191 UN member states have agreed to try to achieve by 2015.

The United Nations Millennium Declaration signed in September 2000, commit world Leader to combat poverty, hunger, disease, illiteracy environmental degradation and discrimination against women.

These were the time bound targets with a deadline of 2015. These goals have become known as the Millennium Development Goals (MDGs).

The eight millennium development goals are

1. to eradicate extreme poverty and hunger
2. to achieve universal primary education
3. to promote gender equality and empower women
4. to reduce child mortality
5. to improve maternal health
6. to combat HIV/AIDS, malaria and other diseases
7. to ensure environmental sustainability and
8. to develop a global partnership for development

### Millenium Development Goals Report

The MDGs Report in 2015 studied the work done so far found the following–

- As per the first goal, there has been a decline in number of people living in extreme poverty and hunger by more than half.
- Improvement in the primary school enrollment rate in developing regions.
- Improvement in the enrollment rate of female students.
- Fall in under five mortality rate by more than half and maternal mortality by 45 percent.
- Decline in the proportion of undernourished people in developing regions.
- Greater facility for treatment of HIV / AIDS, malaria and other diseases.
- Increase in the access to sources of water.

But, later it was found that progress towards the goals was uneven thus, in 2016, MDGs was replaced by the Sustainable Development Goals (SDGs) and the targets have to be achieved by 2030.

**→ Human Development Index (HDI)**

HDI is a part of Human Development Report that is published by UNDP.

Human Development Index emphasizes that people and their capabilities should be the ultimate criteria for assessing the development of a country, not economic growth alone. HDI measures average achievement of a country in three basic dimensions of human development:

- A long and healthy life.
- Access to knowledge.
- A decent standard of living.

India was ranked 129th, out of 189 countries on the 2019 Human Development Index (HDI) improving from the 130th position in 2018. The focus of the 2019 Report is on 'Inequality in Human Development'.

## Sustainable Development Goals (SDGs)

The sustainable development has been derived from Brundtland's Our Common Future, 1987 report of the World Commission on Environment and Development. "Sustainable development is the development that meets the needs of the present without compromising the ability of future generations to meet their own needs".

United Nations Development Programme helps in implementing the SDGs in 170 countries. These goals focus on eradicating poverty, protecting environment, ensuring peace and prosperity around the world. These goals came into effect from 2016 and is targeted to achieve by 2030.

### Objectives of Sustainable Development

- Environmental friendly patterns of activity.
- Energy efficiency.
- Conservation of natural and man-made resources.
- Provision of buildings and areas with lasting quality and character. This relates to design

quality to high standards of comfort and amenity, safety and convenience.

- Development of production opportunities.

The sustainable development goals are a set of 169 targets aiming at 17 goals.

## Characteristics of Sustainable Development

- It attempts to minimise greenhouse gases, and reduce global warming.
- It emphasises on green architecture and eco-friendly building practices.
- Use of natural, biodegradable building materials.
- Use of renewable resources of water.
- Emphasis of renewable energy sources such as solar and wind.
- Protection of natural habitat.
- Non-polluting construction practices and industries.
- Planned development of any resource used.

### Sustainable Development Goals and Targets

| | Goals | Targets |
|---|---|---|
| 1. | No Poverty | End poverty in all its form everywhere. It aims to eradicate extreme poverty by 2030. |
| 2. | Zero Hunger | End hunger achieve food security and improve nutrition. |
| 3. | Good Health and Well-being | Ensure healthy living and promote well-being for all at all ages. |
| 4. | Quality Education | Ensure inclusive and equitable quality education and promote life long learning opportunities for all. |
| 5. | Gender Equality | Achieve gender equality and empower all women and girls. |
| 6. | Clean Water and Sanitation | Ensure availability and sustainable management of water and sanitation for all. |
| 7. | Affordable and Clean Energy | Ensure access to affordable, reliable sustainable energy for all. |
| 8. | Decent Work and Economic Growth | Promote sustained, inclusive and sustainable economic growth, full and productive employment and decent work. |
| 9. | Industry, Innovation and Infrastructure | Build resilient infrastructure, promote inclusive and sustainable industrialisation and foster innovation. |
| 10. | Reduced Inequalities | Reduced inequalities within and among countries. |
| 11. | Sustainable Cities and Communities | Make cities and human settlements inclusive safe, resilient and sustainable. |
| 12. | Responsible Consumption and Production | Ensure sustainable consumption and production patterns. |
| 13. | Climate Action | Take urgent action to combat climate change and its impact. |
| 14. | Life Below Water | Conserve and sustainable use of the oceans, seas and marine resources. |
| 15. | Life on Land | Protect, restore and promote sustainable use of terrestrial ecosystem. |
| 16. | Peace, Justice and Strong Institutions | Promote peaceful and inclusive societies for sustainable development. |
| 17. | Partnerships for the Goals | Strengthening the means of implementation and revitalise the global partnerships for sustainable development. |

## UNDP Strategic Plan (2018-2021)

The Strategic Plan developed by United Nations help countries to achieve their sustainable development goals. UNDP (United Nations Development Plan) provide guidelines and support to developing nations in settting up their targets for sustainable development.

### Key Areas of UNDP Strategic Plan

- Eradicating poverty.
- Addressing climate change.
- Improving adolescent and maternal health.
- Achieving gender equality and empowerment of women and girls.
- Ensuring greater availability and use of disaggregated data for sustainable development.

### Features of UNDP Strategic Plan

- Strong committment to cradicate poverty.
- Become a trusted partner to evolve development in member countries.
- Be innovative and enterprising.
- Take and manage risks.
- Utilize resources judiciously.
- Become a thought leader.

# HUMAN AND ENVIRONMENT INTERACTION

Human and environment interaction can be defined as the interaction between the human social system and the ecosystem. Human have changed the physical, ecological and biological components of the Earth's planetary systems to an astonishing degree. Those environmental changes impact human population in return and continue to shift, often in unanticipated ways.

## Anthropogenic Activities and their Impacts on Environment

Anthropogenic activities are those that are derived from human activities, as opposed to those occurring in natural environments without human influences. The term is often used in the context of environmental externalities in the form of chemical or biological wastes that are produced as by-products of otherwise purposeful human activities. For instance, it is widely believed that the production of carbon dioxide is the primary factor deriving anthropogenic climate change.

Let us discuss the effects or impacts of anthropogenic activities on environment:

## Impacts on Environment

1. **Impact on Agriculture** The anthropogenic activities in the environment cause topographic changes that have strong repercussions like deforestation, soil erosion, depletion of nutrients, etc.

   Agricultural activities contribute to soil contamination by introducing pollutants or toxic substances such as cadmium by application of mineral phosphate fertilizers.

2. **Impact on Marine Fisheries** Anthropogenic impact on the water ecosystem can be defined as a cumulative manifestation of all kinds of human activity which cause hidden disturbances in the natural structure and functions of water biotic communities, diminishing fisheries and other negative effects of ecological, economic or socio - economic nature.

   Large inputs of waste of domestic and industrial nature including oil pollution has burdened the marine environment, which further reduced biodiversity.

3. **Arctic Melting** The changes in the Earth's climate from human influences are occurring particularly intensely in the Arctic region, evidenced by widespread melting of glaciers, thinning sea ice and permafrost temperatures.

   With some of the most rapid and severe climate change on Earth, "the Arctic regions melting contributed to sea levels rising globally by an average of about three inches in the past twenty years.

4. **Mining Activities** Mining refers to the extraction of minerals and metals from the Earth. It can cause environmental and health problems due to leaching of toxic substances into the ground and surface water. It can also lead to ecosystem degradation. Overburden dumps are man-made habitat causing multi-farious environmental problems ranging from erosion and enhancing sediment load in receiving water bodies, dust pollution, etc.

5. **Impact of Construction Activities** Construction activities impact on the environment throughout the life cycle of development. These impacts occur from initial work on site through the construction period, operational period and to the final demolition.

# ENVIRONMENT

Everything that surrounds or affects an organism during its life time, is collectively known as its environment. Environment is derived from the French word *'Environ'* which means 'our surroundings'.

Environment makes up our surroundings and affects our quality to live on the earth. The air we breathe, the water that covers most of the earth surface, the plants and animals around us and so on come in our environment.

## Components of Environment

There are two types of components of environment.

1. **Abiotic Components** These components include all the physical and chemical component in the environment which affect ecosystems. Abiotic component play an important part in the lives of all organisms. Some examples of abiotic components include soil, wind, water, sunlight and temperature etc.
2. **Biotic Components** These components are described as any living components that affects another organism or shapes the ecosystem. Biotic components include plants, animals, fungi and bacteria etc.

## Structure of Environment

Our environment can be divided into following four segments

### 1. Lithosphere

It is the solid crust or the hard top layer of the earth. It is made up of rocks and minerals and covered by a thin layer of soil. It constitutes about 29% part of the Earth, which is mainly composed of plants and animals or living organisms.

### 2. Hydrosphere

The domain of water is referred to as hydrosphere. It comprises various sources of water and water bodies like rivers, lakes, seas, oceans, ponds, streams, etc. It is essential for all living organisms. Only less than 1% of water resources are available for human exploitation.

### 3. Atmosphere

Atmosphere consists of a number of gases, dust and water vapour. The changes in the atmosphere produce changes in the weather and climate. It consists of different layers like :

(i) **Troposphere** It is the lowest layer of atmosphere. Almost all weather developments occur in the troposphere. Air in the troposphere thins as altitude increases and the temperature also decreases. This layer is also known as a connective layer.

(ii) **Stratosphere** It is the second layer of the atmosphere and extends from the tropopause to about 50 km. Temperature increases due to the absorption of the ultraviolet radiations of the Sun by ozone present in this layer.

(iii) **Mesosphere** This layer extends upto 50 and 80 km above the surface of the earth. It has the coldest temperature in the atmosphere dipping as low as −100°C. The phenomenon of shooting stars also occur in this layer.

(iv) **Thermosphere** In this layer temperature rises very rapidly with increasing height. It extends between 80 – 400 km. This layer helps in radio transmission.

Thermosphere is divided into two parts

(a) **Ionosphere** It is extended between 80-400 km and consist of electrically charged particles known as ions. Because of the electric charge, radio waves transmitted from the Earth are reflected back to the Earth by this layer and due to this, radio broadcasting has become possible.

(b) **Exosphere** This is the uppermost layer of the atmosphere. This layer has very thin air. The light gases such as helium and hydrogen float into the space from here. Many weather satellites orbit Earth in the atmosphere.

### 4. Biosphere

Plant and animal kingdom together make biosphere or the living world. It is a narrow zone of the earth where land, water and air interact with each other to support life.

## ENVIRONMENTAL ISSUES

Environmental issues are the concerns for the environment which arises due to environmental imbalance. Human activities create imbalance in nature, thereby disrupting the natural food chain, altering atmospheric gases and disturbing the hydrological cycle. Environmental issues affects people at local, national and global level.

The issues can be divided into three levels such as local, regional and global. These are discussed as follows:

1. **Local Issues** These relate to issues like water shortage in certain areas, soil erosion of local forests, different pollution level in the same city, landslides etc. These need to be solved or tackled at the local level. Thus, these issues are specific to local area.
2. **Regional Issues** These relate to the issues such as desertification and droughts, flood and soil erosion and deforestation. Regional issues also include rise in sea level, beach erosion, saltwater entry or intrusion resulting in increased salinity, flood and flood damages, threats to coastal wetlands and threats to agriculture. The regional issues can have greater extent than a local area but they are not spread globally.
3. **Global Issues** The global issues includes climate change and global warming, melting of ice caps, acidification, ozone depletion, degradation of ecosystem. These issues have global implications.

## POLLUTION

It is an undesirable change in the physical, chemical or biological characteristics of air, water and soil, that may create potential health hazard.

## Types of Pollution

Generally, pollution is divided into various types as under

1. Air Pollution
2. Water Pollution
3. Noise Pollution
4. Soil Pollution
5. Waste Pollution
6. Radioactive Pollution

## 1. Air Pollution

Air pollution refers to the release of pollutants into the air that are detrimental to human health and the planet as a whole.

### Sources of Air Pollution

Sources of air pollution can be based on two pollutants

1. Primary Air Pollutants
2. Secondary Air Pollutants

#### 1. Primary Air Pollutants

Primary pollutants can be emitted from many sources including automobiles, thermal power plants, natural gas power plants, biomass burning, forest fires, volcanoes, etc. They enter directly from the source.

Types of primary pollutants include:

(i) **Sulphur Dioxide** ($SO_2$) is a gas formed when Sulphur is exposed to oxygen at high temperatures during fossil fuel combustion, oil refining or metal smelting. $SO_2$ is toxic at high concentrations, but its principal air pollution effects are associated with the formation of acid rain and aerosols.

(ii) **Nitrogen Oxides** (No and $NO_2$) Highly reactive gases are formed when Oxygen and Nitrogen react at high temperatures during combustion or lightning strikes. In the atmosphere, it reacts with Volatile Organic Compounds (VOCs) and Carbon Monoxide to produce ground level Ozone through a complicated chain reaction mechanism.

(iii) **Carbon Monoxide** (CO) is an odourless, colourless gas formed by incomplete combustion of carbon in fuel. The main source is motor vehicle exhaust, along with industrial processes and biomass burning. Low exposures can aggravate cardiac ailments, while high exposures cause central nervous system impairment or death.

(iv) **Volatile Organic Compounds** (VOCs) VOCs including hydrocarbons (CxHy) but also other organic chemicals are emitted from a wide range of sources, including fossil fuel combustion, industrial activities and natural emissions. Large VOCs oxidize in the atmosphere to produce non-volatile chemicals that condense to form aerosols. Short lived VOCs interact with NO to produce high ground level Ozone in polluted environments.

(v) **Particulate Matter** is the term for a mixture of solid particles (dust, pollen, soot smoke) and liquid droplets found in the air.

(vi) **Lead** The major sources of lead emissions to the air are ore and metals processing. The highest air concentrations of lead are usually found near lead smelters. Other stationary sources are waste indicators, utilities, paints and lead acid battery manufacturers.

(vii) **Ammonia** It is a colourless, pungent, hazardous caustic gas composed of nitrogen and hydrogen. Livestock farming, animal waste and fertilizer application are the biggest sources of atmospheric ammonia emissions within the agricultural sector. Gaseous ammonia is a dangerous air pollutant which can cause death.

## 2. Secondary Air Pollutants

A secondary air pollutant is not directly emitted as such, but forms when other pollutions (primary pollutants) react in the atmosphere.

Secondary air pollutants include pollutants as

(i) **Smog** It is the combination of fog and smoke. There are two major kinds of smog which have been seen. They are

(a) **Photochemical Smog or Los Angeles Smog** It is the result of the interaction of Sunlight with certain chemicals in the atmosphere. It is formed due to chemical reaction involving nitrogen oxide, ozone, hydrocarbons and peroxyacetyl nitrate (PAN) in the presence of Sunlight. It consists of brown hazy fumes which causes irritation in eyes and lungs damage, etc.

(b) **Sulphurous Smog or London Smog** It is a mixture of sulphur dioxide in the air. It is more prevalent during the morning hours of winter season. London smog causes throat irritation and difficulty in breathing.

(ii) **Ground Level Ozone** It is a highly reactive secondary pollutant. This formation occurs when primary pollutants, like hydrocarbons and nitrogen oxides react with Sunlight. Ground level ozone causes aggravated symptoms to people with asthma, bronchitis, emphysema, when they are exposed to it.

(iii) **Fly Ash** It is very fine powder and tends to travel far in the air. It is composed of aluminium silicate, silicon dioxide ($SiO_2$), calcium oxide (CaO), toxic heavy metals like lead, arsenic, cobalt and copper.

If fly ash is not captured and disposed off properly, it can pollute air and water considerably. It settles on leaves and crops in fields in areas near to thermal power plants and lowers the plant yield.

(iv) **Acid Rain** Acid rain is a precipitation with pH level of less than 5.65. The term acid rain was coined by a Scottish Chemist **Angus Smith**, in 1852. Acid rain occurs usually due to injection of sulphur compounds or nitrogen oxides into the atmosphere, the chemicals combine with water to form sulphuric acid and nitric acid.

It is mainly caused by combustion of fossil fuels which results in emissions of sulphur dioxide ($SO_2$) and nitrogen oxides ($NO_x$).

**Impacts of Acid Rain**

- Acid rain shows an adverse impact on the forests, freshwaters, solid and aquatic life. It also kills the soil organisms.
- Acid rain is capable of damaging the buildings and historic monuments which are made up of rocks such as limestone and marble. This is because rocks contain a large amount of calcium carbonate, which reacts with the sulphuric acid to create gypsum and gypsum flakes off easily.
- Acid rain has adverse effect on vegetation. It results in poor germination of seeds, suppression of growth, leaf drop and reduction in production.

## Measures to Control Air Pollution

- Greater use of activated carbon to clean the air of any possible toxins.
- Change in fuel technique such as use of low surface fuel.
- Use of electric utility, use of natural gas as a fuel.
- Use of biofiltration.

## Effects of Air Pollution

- **Damage to Human Health** It means due to air pollution several heart and respiratory problems develop.
- Air pollution has major effect on plants and animals.
- Air pollution also damages crops.
- Air pollution can effect global climate change.
- Ground level ozone gas is poisonous gas that is created by chemical reactions involving air pollutants.
- Volcanoes, dust storms and forest fires are effect of air pollution.

## Government Initiatives of Air Pollution

(i) **Air Prevention and Control of Pollution Act, 1981** It was enacted by the Parliament in 1981 with an objective to prevent, control and reduce air pollution. The decisions were taken at UN conference on human environment held in Stockholm in June, 1972.

India takes appropriate steps for preservation of the natural resources of the Earth which, among other things, include the preservation of the quality of air and control of air pollution.

(ii) **National Ambient Air Quality Standards** The National Ambient Air Quality Standards (NAAQS) was notified in 1982 and duly revised in 1994. They are based on health criteria and land uses. The NAAQS have been revisited and revised in November, 2009 for 12 pollutants which include

| | |
|---|---|
| (a) Lead | (b) Nickel |
| (c) Benzene | (d) Ammonia |
| (e) Ozone | (f) Benzopyren |
| (g) Sulphur dioxide | (h) Nitrogen dioxide |
| (i) $PM_{10}$ | (j) PM 2.5 |
| (k) Arsenic | (l) Carbon monoxide |

(iii) **National Air Quality Monitoring Programme** Central Pollution Control Board (CPCB) is executing a nationwide programme of ambient air quality monitoring known as National Air Quality Monitoring Programme (NAQMP). It is undertaken in India to determine status and trends of ambient air quality.

The objectives of NAQMP are as follows

- To determine statistics and trends of ambient air quality.
- To ascertain whether the prescribed ambient air quality standards are violated.
- To identify non–attainment cities.
- To obtain the knowledge necessary for developing, preventing and corrective measures.

(iv) **Air Quality Index** India launched its first air quality index in April, 2015. It aims to monitor the air quality in major cities across the country on the real time basis.

It is colour based index and shows the quality of air by different colours.

| Remark | AQI | Colour Code |
|---|---|---|
| Good | 0-50 | Dark green |
| Satisfactory | 51-100 | Light green |
| Moderate | 101-200 | Yellow |
| Poor | 201-300 | Orange |
| Very poor | 301-400 | Red |
| Severe | 401-500 | Dark red (Maroon) |

The objective of air quality index are as follows

- To inform public regarding overall status of air quality through a summation parameter that is easy to understand.
- To inform citizens about associated health impacts of air pollution exposure.
- To rank cities/town for prioritising action based on measure of air quality index.
- To measure the emergences of pollution and to make remedial actions immediately.

(v) **Bharat Stage Emission Standards** (BSES) These are emission standards instituted by the Government of India to regulate the output of air pollutants from internal combustion engines and spark-ignition engines equipment. The standards are based on European regulation.

In 2016, BSES announced that the country would adopt BS-VI norms by 2020. The Petroleum Ministry of India has decided on 15th November, 2017, to bring forward the date of BS-VI grade auto fuels in NCT of Delhi with effect from 1st April, 2018 instead of 1st April, 2020.

(vi) **National Electric Mobility Mission Plan** (NEMMP) Government of India launched the NEMMP-2020 in 2013. It aims to achieve national fuel security by promoting hybrid and electric vehicles in the country. Government has launched the scheme namely Faster Adoption and Manufacturing of Hybrid and Electric Vehicles (FAME India) under NEMMP-2020.

**→ SAFAR (System of Air Quality and Weather Forecasting)**

The Ministry of Earth Sciences the Government of India has introduced a major national initiative 'System of Air Quality and Weather Forecasting and Research known as' 'SAFAR' for greater metropolitan cities of India.

**SAFAR** is the first mobile application service in India to provide a current and advanced forecast for air quality. The application was developed by scientist at Indian Institute of Tropical Meteorology (IITM), Pune.

It enables citizens to check their city's air quality in real time. The app provides current data and a forecast for air quality in the user's current location through a colour coded system.

## 2. Water Pollution

It takes place when bodies of water like rivers, lakes or groundwater are contaminated with either chemicals or natural forms of pollution that harm wildlife and plants.

### Sources of Water Pollution

Sources of water pollution can be classified as point and non-point sources of water.

(i) **Point Source** It occurs when harmful substances are emitted directly into a body of water such as by a pipe, drain, channel, tunnel, etc.

Point source pollution is usually monitored and regulated. An example of a point source of water pollution is a pipe from an industrial facility discharging effluent directly into a river.

(ii) **Non-Point Source** It occurs when pollutants indirectly enter a water body such as due to rainfall, snow melt, water run off, etc.

Non-point sources are much more difficult to monitor and control, and today they account for the majority of contaminants in streams and lakes. An example of a non-point source of water pollution is when fertilizer from a farm field is carried into a stream by rain (i.e. run-off).

Other sources of pollution of water could be :

- Oil, gasoline and additives also contribute to water pollution, caused by oil spills as well as by drips of oil and fuel, and drips from industrial machinery.

- Chemical and industrial processes.
- Sewage, untreated sewage, poorly treated sewage, or overflow from under-capacity sewage treatment facilities can send disease bearing water into rivers and oceans.

**→ Biological Oxygen Demand (BOD)**

Biological Oxygen Demand (BOD) represents the amount of oxygen consumed by bacteria and other microorganisms while they compose organic matter under aerobic at a specified temperature. The BOD value is most commonly expressed in milligrams of oxygen consumed per litre of sample during five days of incubation at 20°C. BOD reduction is used as a gauge of the effectiveness of wastewater treatment plants.

BOD is an important water quality parameter because it provides an index to assess the effect. It is used extensively for wastewater treatment as decomposition of organic waste by microorganism is commonly used for treatment.

## Measures to Control Water Pollution

- Reducing soil erosion or improving water treatment, attempt to stop contaminants from entering natural water systems through run-off or seepage.
- Clean Water Act or other such acts should be regulated.
- Reducing the amount of sediment in water.
- Utility companies have improved the controls in their treatment plants and fixed broken pipes, etc.
- Reducing the amount of sewage and chemical detergents released into water supplies.

## Effects of Water Pollution

The effects of water pollution depends upon the type of pollutants and its concentration and location of water bodies.

- Water pollution drastically affects aquatic life. It affects their metabolism, alters behaviour, causes illness and death.
- The effect of water pollution can have huge impact on food chain.
- Human are affected by pollution and can contract diseases such as hepatitis through faecal matter in water sources. Poor water treatment and contaminated water can cause an outbreak of infectious disease like cholera.
- The ecosystem can be critically affected, modified and destructed because of water pollution.

## Government Steps to Control the Water Pollution

The following steps are taken by the Government of India to reduce water pollution

- Formulation of environmental regulations.
- Promotion of cleaner production processes.
- Comprehensive amendments to various waste management rules including municipal solid waste, plastic waste, hazardous waste, bio-medical waste and electronic waste.
- Notification of construction and demolitions.
- Ban on burning of leaves, biomass, municipal solid waste.
- Revision of existing environmental standards and formulation of new standards.
- Issuance of directions under Section 5 of Environment (Protection) Act, 1986 and under Section 18(1) (b) of Water (Prevention and Control of Pollution) Act, 1974 and Air (Prevention and Control of Pollution) Act, 1981.
- Implementation of National River Conservation Plan for abatement of pollution in identified stretches of various rivers.
- Preparation of action plan for sewage management and restoration of water quality by state governments.

### **The Water** (Prevention and Control of Pollution) **Act, 1974**

The Act was enacted in 1974 to provide for the prevention and control of water pollution and for the maintaining or restoring of wholesomeness of water in the country. The Act was amended in 1988.

Under the Act, government has power to restrict any unit and to take samples of effluents and get them analysed in central or state laboratories.

Government also setup boards at centres and state level for prevention and control of water pollution and to promote cleanliness of the states.

**→ Hydrogen Sulphide**

Hydrogen sulphide ($H_2S$) indicates the level of pollution of water. If there is no $H_2S$ produced the water is considered to be clear. If $H_2S$ level is produced and

- **Small in quantity** The water colour is changed to light black which indicates low level of pollution.
- **Medium in quantity** The water colour is changed to black which indicates moderate water pollution.
- **High in quantity** The water colour is changed to dark black which means the water is more polluted.

## 3. Noise Pollution

Noise pollution is defined as unwanted sounds that disrupt normal sound in the environment. Noise coming from factories, vehicles, playing of loudspeaker during festivals or other occasions can contribute to outdoor noise pollution. On the other hand, loudly played music system or radio and other electronic gadgets can contribute to indoor noise pollution.

It can lead to loss of memory, deafness or in some cases psychiatric disorders. Sensitivity to different sound frequencies is measured using the A - weighted decibels Scale (dBA).

The acceptable amount of sound level is about 60 to 65 dBs, which equals to that of a normal conversation. Sound levels higher than 85 dBs are harmful depending on the duration of exposure and if one has hearing protection or not.

### Sources of Noise Pollution

On an average, the sources of noise pollution are divided into the following two categories

(i) **Natural Sources** It includes clouds thunder, hurricanes, tornados etc.

(ii) **Anthropogenic Sources** It can be further divided into three categories

(a) **Industrial Unit** It includes sound from industrial machines.

(b) **Means of Transportation** It includes sound from different means of transportation like bus, truck, motorcycle, etc.

(c) **Means of Entertainment** It includes sound generated in religious festivals, parties, etc.

### Effects of Noise Pollution

Some of the hazardous effects of noise pollution are as follows:

(i) **Physical Effects** It includes respiratory agitation, high blood pressure, headaches, and in case of extremely loud, constant noise can even lead to heart attacks.

(ii) **Pshychological Effects** Noise can cause attacks of stress, fatigue, depression, anxiety among the individuals.

(iii) **Sleep and Behavioural Disorders** Noise above 45 dB stops an individual from falling asleep. Loud noise can have latent effects on our behaviour causing aggressive behaviour and irritability.

(iv) **Memory and Concentration** Noise may affect people's ability to focus, which can lead to low performance over time. It lowers down the concentration level among the individuals.

### Measures to Control Noise Pollution

- Apply insulation which can reduce the noise.
- Volume reduction can reduce the speed of sound.
- Formation of green belt in areas of intense noise pollution through **Green Muffler** techniques.

**→ Green Muffler**

It is a technique of reducing noise pollution by planting 4-6 rows of trees around polluted areas or noisy places like roadsides, industrial areas, near highways.

It is carried out so that dense trees reduce noise pollution as they filter out the noise and obstruct it reaching the people. It is also known as green belt vegetation. It is a device for decreasing the amount of noise emitted by the exhaust of an internal combustion engine.

Under this scheme Ashoka and Neem plants are planted near residential localities to reduce noise pollution.

## 4. Soil Pollution

It can be defined as the changes in physical, chemical and biological conditions of the soil by human intervention or misuse of land. This reduces the quality and productivity of the soil. Improper solid waste disposal also leads to soil pollution.

Dumping garbage, waste and other toxins also make the land contaminated or polluted.

### Sources of Soil Pollution

(i) **Industrial Wastes** It includes chemicals such as mercury, lead, copper, zinc, cadmium, cyanides etc.

(ii) **Agricultural Wastes** Agricultural practices such as use of non-organic products in crops and livestock production lead to soil pollution. These substances include artificial chemical pesticides, herbicides and fertilizers.

(iii) **Nuclear Wastes** Radioactive elements from mining and nuclear power plants find their way into water and then into the soil.

(iv) **Mining and Smelting Sources** Mining activities cause soil pollution on a large scale. Hazardous materials that leak from mining activities including harmful dust particles are deposited on the surrounding soils.

### Effects of Soil Pollution

- Plants growing in polluted soil may accumulate high concentrations of soil pollutants through a process known as bio-accumulation.
- Crop yield is greatly affected by this form of pollution due to decrease in availability of nutrients.
- The short term effects of human exposure to polluted soil includes headaches, nausea, irritation of the skin, fatigue and weakness.
- Soil ecosystem is disturbed due to deforestation.
- Pollution often increases the salinity of soil, making it inhospitable for the growth of plant life.

### Control of Soil Pollution

Some of the measures to control soil pollution are as follows

- Waste can be recycled or incinerated to lessen pollutants.
- Dump mining waste, which comes from mining into pits.
- Rules and regulations regarding wastes should be addressed and enforced strictly.

**→ Acidification**

It is the process of turning something into acid by natural or man-made processes. The term acidification is used in mainly two important matter that is soil and water.

**Soil Acidification**

It occurs naturally very slowly as soil is weathered, but this process is accelerated by productive agriculture. Soil acidification occurs because the concentration of hydrogen ions in the soil increases. Ammonium based fertilisers are major contributors to soil acidification, especially if the nitrogen reaches the soil rather than taken up by plants.

**Ocean Acidification**

It occurs when carbon dioxide gas ($CO_2$) is absorbed by the ocean and reacts with sea water to produce acid. It is occurred mainly as a result of human activities such as burning fossil fuels.

As $CO_2$ is absorbed, it reacts with the water to form carbonic acid. This leads to the release of hydrogen ions-charged particles that are derived from the hydrogen in the water. The greater the hydrogen ion concentration, the more acidic the substance is.

## 5. Waste Pollution

Waste is defined as any substance which constitutes a scrap material, or an effluent or other unwanted surplus substance arising from application of any process.

According to its properties, waste is classified as inert, toxic and inflammable. If these wastes remain untreated, it leads to air, water, soil and solid waste pollution. Hence, waste may be in the form of solid, liquid and gas.

## (i) Solid Waste

Solid wastes are categorized as municipal wastes, industrial wastes and hazardous wastes. It is a term for man-made waste (basically, consisting of plastic litter) discarded in the environment and often found in sea or along the coastline, either floating on the surface or submerged.

Municipal waste arises from domestic activities of human beings. Industrial waste arises from industrial activities and hazardous wastes are the substances which causes hazards to plants, animals and humans. Few of the common hazardous wastes are radioactive substances, chemicals, biological wastes, flammable wastes and explosives.

### Solid Waste Management

Different methods are used for management of solid wastes and choice of proper methods depend upon the land area availability and disposal cost.

Let us discuss the methods to manage solid waste :

(a) **Disposal** It is done mostly through a sanitary landfill or through incineration.
- **Sanitary Landfills** It is a process of dumping waste in a scientifically designed area spreading waste in thin layers, in smallest volume and covering with soil on a daily basis. Methane is produced due to anaerobic decomposition of organic matters in solid waste.
- **Incineration** It is the process of burning municipal solid waste in a properly designed furnace under suitable temperture and operating conditions. It reduces the municipal solid waste by about 90% and 75% by weight.

(b) **Composting** Bacterial decomposition of organic components of the municipal waste result in the formation of humus or compost and the process is known as composting. It helps in disposal of solid waste and production of valuable manure for crops. It is also termed as Biodegradation.

(c) **Pyrolysis** It is defined as thermal degradation of waste in the absence of air. External source of heat is employed in this process. By this process, the chemical constituents and chemical energy of some organic wastes are recovered. The organic constituents split up into gaseous liquid and gaseous frictions like carbon dioxide, carbon monoxide, tar, methane, etc.

(d) **Recycling** It means reusing some components of the waste that may have some economic value. Recycling conserves resources, reduce the energy used during manufacture and also reduce pollution.

(e) **Source Reduction** It is one of the fundamental ways to reduce waste. This can be done by using less material when making a product, reusing products, designing products packaging to reduce their quantity.

(f) **Land Treatment** It is a process by which solid waste, such as sludge from wastes is applied onto or incorporated into the soil surface.

### Impacts of Solid Waste

There are potential risks to environment and living organisms due to improper handling of solid wastes. Some of the impacts are:

- It degrades water and soil quality.
- It leads to chemical poisoning through chemical inhalation.
- Choking of drains by solid wastes results in water logging which facilitates breeding of mosquitoes and results in the spread of diseases like malaria and plague.
- Waste products when burnt like plastic and rubber pollute the atmosphere with noxious fumes.

## (ii) Liquid Waste

It can be defined as such liquids as wastewater, fats, oils or grease (FOG), used oil, liquids, solids, gases, or sludge and hazardous household liquids. These liquids are hazardous or potentially harmful to human health and the environment.

### Sources of Liquid Waste

(a) **Household Wastewater** Wastewater from households contains many pollutants which are hazardous for human as well as environment.

(b) **Industrial wastewater** Water is used in industries for cooling and cleaning purpose. This water contains huge amount of chemicals which discharge into water bodies and make them dirty.

(c) Inorganic and organic wastewater.

(d) Oil and water mixtures.

### Effects of Liquid Waste Pollution

The wastewater and other liquid waste badly affect water bodies, land and our environment. This ultimately affects human health.

### Management of Liquid Waste

These are the following main ways to deal with liquid waste:

(a) **Primary or Physical Treatment** It is the process of mechanically removing the solid materials present in the water through metal screening. This treatment removes sixty percent of the floating solid materials.

(b) **Secondary or Biological Treatment** It is a biological oxidation of organic matter. It is achieved by filter method or by a sludge process. In this process, complex compounds are broken down into water, carbon dioxide, methane and ammonia.

(c) **Tertiary or Chemical Treatment** This method is an advanced form of chemical and physical process.

The most common methods in this treatment is precipitation of suspended particles, filtration with carbon to resolve, dissolve organic compounds by passage through a membrane to remove dissolve organic and inorganic materials.

## (iii) Bio-medical Waste

It means any waste, which is generated during the diagnosis, treatment or immunization of human beings or animals in research activities pertaining thereto or in the production or testing of biologicals.

### Sources of Biomedical Waste

- Discarded blood, sharps, unwanted microbiological cultures and stocks, identifiable body parts, other human or animal tissue, used bandages and dressings, discarded gloves, other medical supplies that may have been in contact with blood and body fluids and laboratory waste etc.
- Waste sharps include potentially contaminated used (and unused discarded) needles, scalpels, lancets and other devices capable of penetrating skin.

### Biomedical Waste Management

- Segregation is the most essential step in bio-medical waste management. It refers to the primary division of different categories of waste generated.
- Storage and accumulation of bio-medical waste is basically done in the areas and steps between the point of waste generation and location of waste treatment and disposal.
- Designing eco-friendly bio-degradable bio–medical plastic is the need of the hour.
- Periodic monitoring of the safe management of healthcare waste systems is recommended.

## (iv) Hazardous Waste

Hazardous waste is waste that has potential threats to human health and the environment.

"Any solid waste, other than radioactive wastes, which by reasons of physical or chemical or reactive or toxic, explosive, corrosive or other characteristics causing danger or likely to cause danger to health or environment whether alone or when coming in contact with other waste of environment."

### Sources of Hazardous Wastes

- Batteries
- Pesticides
- Equipment containing mercury
- Lamps containing mercury
- Paints and solvents
- Automotive wastes (used motor oil, antifreeze)
- Pesticides (insecticides, herbicides, fungicides)
- Mercury-containing wastes (thermometers, switches, fluorescent lighting, etc.)

- Electronics (computers, televisions, cell phones)
- Aerosols/Propane cylinders
- Caustics/Cleaning agents
- Refrigerant-containing appliances
- Some special batteries (e.g. lithium, nickel cadmium, or button cell batteries)
- Ammunition

## (v) e-Waste (Electronic Waste)

Electronic waste (e-waste) is a discarded electrical or electronic devices. In other words, used electronics which are destined for reuse, resale, salvage, recycling or disposal are considered as e-waste.

### Sources of e-Waste

- Waste generated from the products used for data processing such as computers, computer devices like monitor, speakers, keyboards, printers etc.
- Electronic devices used for entertainment like TV, DVDs and CD players.
- Equipment or devices used for communication like phones, landline phones, fax etc.
- Household equipments like vacuum cleaner, washing machines, air conditioners etc.
- Audio-visual components such as VCRs stereo equipment etc.

### Effects of e -Waste

The processes of dismantling and disposing of electronic waste in developing countries led to a number of environmental impacts

- Liquid and atmospheric release end up in bodies of water, groundwater, soil and air and therefore causes harmful infection.
- Levels of carcinogens in ponds, rice paddies etc., exceeded.
- Heavy metal found in road dust causes skin cancer, respiratory diseases, etc.
- Prenatal exposure to e-waste causes several adverse birth outcomes such as still birth, low birth rate etc.

### e-Waste Control

The first effort made to control e-waste was in 1992 under Basel Convention. Under this, there is a provision of recycling of 60% e-waste in developed countries.

**e-Waste Management Rule 2016** e-waste management until 2011 was dealt under the Hazardous Waste Management Rules. In 2011 the e-waste (Management and Handling) rules 2011 was enacted under the Environmental Protection Act 1986. In 2016, the e-waste management rule was enacted which replaced the 2011 rules and was eventually amended in 2018.

It covers producers, consumers, collection centres dismantlers and recyclers, manufactures, dealers, refurbishers and Producer Responsibility Organisation (PROs).

This rule is applicable on several equipments, components, Compact Fluroscent Lamp (CFL) and other mercury containing lamp.

**→ e-Waste Microfactory**

In April 2018, an Indian origin scientist has developed world's first microfactory that can transform the components of electronic waste items into valuable materials for reuse.

## 6. Radioactive Pollution

Radioactive pollution is the deposition of or presence of radioactive substances on the surfaces or within solids, liquids or gases where their presence is unintended or undesirable.

Radioactive contamination or pollution presents a hazard because of the radioactive decay of the contaminants, which emit harmful ionising radiation such as alpha particles or beta particles, gama rays or neutrons.

### Sources of Radioactive Pollution

Radioactive contamination can be due to

- release of radioactive gases, liquids or particles.
- an inevitable result of certain processes, such as the release of radioactive xenon in nuclear fuel reprocessing.
- nuclear fallout.

## Effects of Radioactive Pollution

- Radioactive pollution affects the person, who receives high doses of radiation. It could increase the chances of cancer and also affects the human skin.
- It causes an acute radiation syndrome.
- Following an atmospheric nuclear weapon discharge or a nuclear reactor containment breach, the air, soil, people, plants and animals in the vicinity will become contaminated by nuclear fuel and fission products.
- A spilled vial of radioactive material like uranyl nitrate may contaminate the ground.
- Cases of widespread radioactive contamination include the Bikini Atoll, the Rocky Flats plant in Colorado, the Fukushima Daiichi Nuclear Disaster, the Chernobyl Disaster and the area around the Mayak Facility in Russia.

## Control and Monitoring of Radioactive Pollution

- Make a concrete surface for free radioactive contamination and dispose it.
- Before access to radioactive areas, a variety of techniques to be applied such as barriers, changes of clothing and footwears.
- Use of contamination control products such as fixatives strippable coatings, and decontamination gels.
- Emphasise on containment.

# POLLUTANTS

A pollutant is a substance or energy introduced into the environment that has undesired effects or adversely affects the usefulness of resources. It is a chemical or biological substance, which harms water layer or land quality.

Pollutants can be classified as follows

## 1. On the Basis of Existence in Nature

(i) **Quantitative Pollutants** These are those substances normally occurring in the environment, but are termed as pollutants when their concentration (quality) increases in the environment. For example, $CO_2$ is present in the environment in greater quality than normal and is thus termed as quantitative pollutants.

(ii) **Qualitative Pollutants** These are those substances which are not normally present in the environment and are added by human beings and are polluted by nature, e.g. insecticides, pesticides.

## 2. On the Basis of Form

(i) **Primary Pollutants** The pollutants which are directly emitted from the source and remain in that form are termed as primary pollutants. For example, Smoke, ash, dust, nitric acid and sulphur dioxide.

(ii) **Secondary Pollutants** These are those substances which are formed by chemical reaction between the primary pollutants and constituents of the environment (i.e. which are already present in the environment) For example, Smog, ozone, and nitrogen oxide.

## 3. On the Basis of Disposal are

(i) **Biodegradable Pollutants** These are the pollutants that get degraded by natural means. Heat or thermal pollution and domestic sewage are considered in this category as these can be quickly decomposed by natural processes or engineered system such as municipal treatment plants.

(ii) **Non-Biodegradable Pollutants** These are the substance that either do not degrade or degrade very slowly in the natural environment.

For example, DDT, aluminium cans. These non-biodegradable pollutants accumulate and are biologically magnified as they move in the biological cycle and along food chains in ecosystem.

## Impacts of Pollutants on Human Health

The health effects or impacts caused by air pollutants may range from subtle bio-chemical and psychological changes to difficulty in breathing, coughing and aggravation of existing respiratory and cardiac conditions.

The human health effects of poor air quality are far reaching, and principally affect the body's respiratory system and cardiovascular system. Individual reactions towards air pollutants depend on the type of pollutant a person is exposed to, the degree of exposure, the individual's health status and genetics.

**Major Pollutants and their Impact on Human Life**

| Pollutants | Impact on Human |
|---|---|
| Oxides of Carbon | $CO_2$ has a major role in greenhouse effect, produces weak carbonic acid adding to acid rains.<br>Carbon monoxide affects human health by binding to haemoglobin, which may result in asphyxia. |
| Oxides of Sulphur | It damages human and other animal lungs and is important precursor to acid rain.<br>Its adverse impacts include corrosion of paint, metals and injury or death of animals and plants. |
| Oxides of Nitrogen | It damages the tissue.<br>It causes irritation to eyes, viral infections like influenza. |
| Hydrocarbons | It can have carcinogenic effect on humans.<br>Some of hydrocarbons are more reactive with sunlight and produce photochemical smog. |
| Liquid Droplets | It contributes to acid rains and corrosion.<br>It damages various life forms. |
| Suspended Particulate Matter (SPM) | It affects the respiratory system.<br>It causes greatest lung damage.<br>It interferences with absorption of $CO_2$ and release of $O_2$. |
| Photochemical Oxidants | It produces irritation to eyes, nose and throat.<br>It damages the respiratory system. |

# CLIMATE CHANGE

It is a long term shift in weather conditions identified by climatic factors such as rise in temperature, irregular rainfall, change in seasonal pattern, etc., over longer durations. Natural events and human activities are believed to be contributing to climate change.

## Causes of Climate Change

The causes for climate change are many. They can be grouped into **natural causes** and **man-made causes**.

### 1. Natural Causes of Climate Change

The natural causes of climate change are as follows

(i) **Ocean Currents** Ocean currents are the major component of the climatic system which is driven by horizontal wind forces causing the displacement of water against the sea surface. Due to temperature variation of the water, the climate of the region is largely influenced.

(ii) **Continental Drift** The continents of the world are constantly drifting. This drift in past had an impact on climate due to change in physical features of the landmass, their position and position of water bodies.

(iii) **Milankovitch Cycles** (Variation in Earth's Orbit) Earth's eccentricity, changes in axial tilt and precession of equinoxes taken together constitute Milankovitch cycles. This has large impact on climate change and are notable for their correlation with glacial and interglacial periods.

(iv) **Volcanic Activity** Eruption of volcanoes causes outburst of gases and dust particles. These partially block the incoming rays of the Sun which lead to cooling of the weather.

### 2. Man-made Causes of Climate Change

The anthropogenic or man-made causes of climate change are as follows

(i) **Deforestation** Forests act as carbon sink and play an important role in fight against global warming. When forest is disturbed or cleared, carbon stored is released as carbon dioxide causing global warming.

(ii) **Burning of Fossil Fuel** Burning of carbon-based fossil fuels causes release of carbon dioxide in the atmosphere. This has led to increase in concentration of Carbon Dioxide ($CO_2$) in the atmosphere.

(iii) **Modern Agricultural Practices** Agricultural practices adopted in recent years contribute to a large extent towards global warming. Flooded field used for rice cultivation is a major contributor of methane gas, a potent greenhouse gas.

(iv) **Industrialisation and Urbanisation** The excessive exploitation of resources for industrial activities has large impact on climate change. Cutting down forests to create industrial complexes and settlements had led to changes in the amount of sunlight reflected from the ground back into space.

**→ Greenhouse Gases (GHGs)**

The primary GHGs are carbon dioxide ($CO_2$), chlorofluorocarbon (CFCs), methane ($CH_4$), nitrous oxide ($N_2O$) and ozone ($O_3$).

Some other gases such as nitric oxide (NO) and carbon monoxide (CO) easily react with GHGs and affect their concentration in the atmosphere.

Greenhouse gases come out from burning of fossil fuels for energy, cutting down and burying forest to create pastures and plantations, carbon accumulates in our atmosphere. Certain waste management and agricultural practices aggravated the problem by releasing other potent global warming gases.

## Social Dimension of Climate Change

The social dimensions of climate change is an interplay between climate as a phenomenon, its related policy and society – including the role of people as victims and as agents of climate change.

The impacts of climate change increasingly affect the daily lives of people everywhere in terms of employment and livelihoods, health, housing, water, food security and nutrition. The inclusion of social dimension in climate change policy ensures that human rights are respected and gender equality is followed. Social dimension is essential to understand the consumption habits and patterns of the people so that climate policy can be integrated.

There is a need for successful adaptation to the effects of climate change which is possible with the right policy tools in place, strong political will, participation, effectively targeted funding, access to information and productive dialogue between communities and policymakers.

There is also a need for energy planning which includes the analysis of environment protection, energy security for the poor and social inclusion. Therefore, the transition to dispersed, localised renewable energy provides opportunities which broaden the momentum of social and political change.

## Political Dimensions of Climate Change

It includes national or global political action, planning and missions to combat climate change, as it results in huge loss of income and resources. Therefore, government needs to take up action plans and measures.

Some of the key developments as per political dimensions are discussed below–

- The **World Meteorigical Organization** and **United Nations Environment Programme**, established the Inter-governmental Panel on Climate Change in 1988 to investigate and report on international responses to climate change.
- The **IPCC** reports about the scientific, technical and socio-economic knowledge on climate change. It is an inter-governmental panel and accesses the impact of climate change all over the world.
- **The Kyoto Protocol** in Japan made an international treaty to reduce greenhouse gas emmissions that causes global warming. It was adopted on 11 December, 1997, but came into effect from 16 February, 2005.

- Yearly conferences are done by UNFCCC (United Nations Framework Convention on Climate Change) to access progress in dealing with climate change.
- Initiatives taken by Indian government to combat climate change includes formation of **National Action Plan on Climate Change (NAPCC)** in 2008. This consist of eight other missions to adapt to climate change.

## Various Measures to Control Climate Change

1. **Carbon Offset** A carbon offset is a reduction in emissions of carbon dioxide or greenhouse gases made in order to compensate for or to offset an emission made elsewhere. One ton of carbon offset represents the reduction of one ton of carbon dioxide or its equivalent in other greenhouse gases.

   Carbon offset usually supports project that reduces the emission of greenhouse gases in the short or long term. A common project type is production of renewable energy through windfarms, biomass energy or hydroelectric dams.
2. **Carbon Tax** It is a pollution tax on energy sources which emits carbon dioxide. The objective of carbon tax is to reduce the harmful and unfavourable levels of carbon dioxide emissions.

   Thereby deaccelerating climate change and its negative effect on environment and human health. Generally, carbon tax is determined by carbon tax rate and the quantity of carbon emission of a company in its manufacturing process. It is represented as the amount paid for every ton of greenhouse gas released in the atmosphere.
3. **Carbon Trading** It is another form of carbon pricing under cap and trade systems. It is a process of buying and selling permits and redits to emit $CO_2$.

   The Government set a cap on carbon emission for the whole country, then limits the amount of carbon dioxide that companies are allowed to release.
4. **Carbon Sequestration** (removal) It is the process of removing carbon from the atmosphere and storing it in a carbon sink i.e. a reservoir, ocean water or aquifer. It is one method of reducing the amount of carbon dioxide in the atmosphere with the goal of reducing global climate change.

# NATURAL RESOURCES

Natural resources are something which comes from nature without any actions of humankind. This includes all valued characteristics present on Earth including Sunlight, atmosphere, water, land (includes all minerals) along with all vegetation, crops and animal life that is collected by the humans for a better life.

## Classification of Natural Resources

Natural resources are classified into 2 categories:

1. **Renewable Natural Resources** Renewable resources are those which can be generated again after they are used. For example, water, wood and Sunlight are some of the examples of renewable resources.
2. **Non-Renewable Natural Resources** A non-renewable resource is that which exhausts after frequent usage and sometimes, it takes a long time to get generated like natural gas.

Some of the commonly used natural resources are:

### 1. Forest Resources

Forest is a natural ecosystem that has multi species and multi-aged trees. Forests have diverse functions.

They provide timber, forest products like lac, honey, wax, herbs, bamboo, roots, tuber, etc. They are useful in regulation of soil, water and air. Forests are vital for the preservation of biodiversity and play a significant role in maintaining ecological balance.

They provide fresh oxygen and also act as carbon sinks.

## Exploitation of Forest Resources

Deforestation is only responsible for the exploitation of indigenous forests and woodlands. It has resulted in the reduction of indigenous forests to four fifths of their pre agricultural area.

Following are main causes of deforestation:

(i) **Population Explosion** It possess a great threat to the environment. Vast areas of forest land are cleared to claim land for human settlement.

(ii) **Forest Fires** It is caused by both natural and human activities. Human clearing forest for habitation, agriculture, firewood, construction of roads etc. Therefore, they fire the forest.

Heat wave during summers cause forest fires naturally.

(iii) **Grazing Animals** Trampling of the forest soil in the course of overgrazing by livestock. It has affected the porosity of soil leading to soil erosion and desertification of the previously fertile forest area.

(iv) **Expansion of Agriculture** Farmers clear forests to get more land for planting crops. Many small farmers clear a few acres to fedd their families by cutting down trees and burning them in a process known as slash and burn agriculture.

(v) **Timber Harvesting** Timber resource is an important asset of a country. Many industries flourish due to high demand of commercial wood. Therefore, it leads to 14% of deforestation.

## India State of Forest Report, 2019

The Ministry for Environment Forests and Climate change relased the India State of Forest Report (ISFR), 2019. The 2019 Report for the first time assessed the qualitative nature of the forest cover including listing its biodiversity and the type of plants and trees found.

Some key highlights of the report are:

- The total forest and tree cover of the country is 80.73 million hectare. It is 24.56% of the total geographical area of the country.
- The forest and tree cover has incresed by more than 130 million hectares in the last 4 years.
- Area-wise, Madhya Pradesh has the largest forest cover in the country.
- In terms of forest cover as percentage of total geographical area, the top five states are Mizoram (85.41%), Arunachal Pradesh (79.63%), Meghalaya (76.33%), Manipur (75.46%) and Nagaland (75.31%).
- The top 3 states showing increase in forest cover are Karnataka (1,025 sq. km) followed by Andhra Pradesh (990 sq km) and Kerala (823 sq km).
- Top three states showing mangrove cover increase are Gujarat (37 sq km) followed by Maharashtra (16 sq km) and Odisha (8 sq km).
- There are 62,466 wetlands covering 3.8% of the area with the Recorded Forest Area (RFA)/ Green Wash (GW) of the country.

### → Social Forestry

It is the management and protection of forests. It aims to plant more trees to improve the environment. Afforestation is done on barren and unused lands also. Trees are planted along railway lines, roadside, river banks, etc. The term was first used in India in 1976 by the National Commission on Agriculture.

## Indian Forest Act, 2006

India Forest Act was passed on 18 December, 2006. It deals with rights of forest dwelling communities over forest land and resources. Schedule tribes and other traditional forest dwellers who have been residing in forests for generations get the right to use certain parts of the forest. These communities also help in conservation of the forests.

**Forest Conservation Movement**

| Name/Year | Description |
|---|---|
| Chipko Movement (1973) | It was launched in Reni village of Chamoli district of Uttarakhand where people embraced the trees to prevent them for being cut down.<br>It was led by Sunderlal Bahuguna, Gaura Devi, Chandi Prasad Bhatt etc. |
| Silent Valley Movement (1973) | It was started in Palakkad district of Kerala to save the Silent Valley Reserve Forest from being flooded by a hydroelectric project.<br>It was led by Sugatha Kumari and Kerala Sasthra Sahithya Parishad (KSSP). |
| Bishnoi Movement (1730) | This movement was started in village Khejarli in Rajasthan. When Maharaja of Jodhpur ordered to gather wood for new palace.<br>It was first led by Amrita Devi who hug the tree. After killing 363 Bishnoi villagers, Maharaja stopped cutting the trees. |
| Appiko Movement (1973) | It was started by Appu and Mamtha in Gubbi Gadde village of Uttarakhand.<br>It was second time started by Pandurang Hegde. |
| Narmada Movement (1985) | It was started by Medha Patkar and Baba Amte against the forest cutting for building a large dam. |
| Navadanya Movement (1987) | It was founded by Vandana Shiva which promotes biodiversity conservation, organic farming, the rights of farmers and the process of seed saving. |

## 2. Soil Resources

Soil resources form a fundamental part of the environment. They provide the physical base to support the productivity and cycling of biological resources, provide the source of nutrients and water for agricultural and forestry systems and fulfil a complex buffering role against environmental variability (ranging from dampening diurnal and seasonal change in temperature and water supply to the storage and binding of a range of chemical and biological agents).

They are also highly biodiverse. Soils themselves vary greatly – a soil with favourable mix of physical, chemical and biological characteristics will have a much higher potential for productivity in gross terms than one less favoured.

**Major Soils of India and their Properties**

| Soil | Formation | Characteristics | Distribution | Crops |
|---|---|---|---|---|
| Alluvial Soil | Silt brought by rivers. | Very fertile, fine grained both in new alluvium (Khadar) and old alluvium. | Punjab Haryana, U.P., M.P., Bihar, West Bengal | Rice, wheat, sugarcane, cotton, oilseeds and jute. |
| Black Soil (Regur) | Weathering of volcanic rocks. | Water retentive cracks develop when dry. | Maharashtra, Madhya Pradesh, Gujarat, Andhra Pradesh, Tamil Nadu | Cotton, sugarcane, oilseeds, tobacco. |
| Red and Yellow Soil | Decomposition of granite, gneiss and metamorphic rocks. | Not water retentive. When fertilizer added, soil becomes productive. | Tamil Nadu, Kerala, Karnataka | Bajra, maize, pulses, potatoes, fruits. |
| Laterite Soil | Leaching of laterite rocks. | Agriculturally less important. Bricks are made for house construction. | Peculiar to India. Andhra Pradesh, Tamil Nadu, West Bengal, Odisha, Rajasthan and Maharashtra | Cashew, coffee rubber. |
| Saline Soil (reh, kallar, usar, thu, rakar, chopan) | Accumulation of soluble salts. | Unproductive soil. In Punjab and Haryana gypsum is added to improve the soil. | Bihar, U.P., Haryana, Punjab, Rajasthan and Maharashtra | Berseem, Dhaincha, leguminous crops. |
| Forest Soil | Decomposition of organic matter. | Heterogeneous, character changes with parent rocks, and climate, require good quantity of fertilizers to work with. | Himalayan region, Western and Eastern Ghats | Temperate fruits, spices, tea, coffee. |

### Soil Erosion and Degradation

The destruction of the top soil cover is described as soil erosion, while decrease in its fertility is soil degradation. Wind and water are powerful agents of soil erosion because of their ability to remove soil and transport it. Wind erosion is significant in arid and semi-arid regions.

In regions with heavy rainfall and steep slopes, erosion by running water is more significant. Soil erosion can be divided into three types

(i) **Run-off Erosion** It is due to rills and gullies. The worst affected areas are those of Chambal, Betwa and Ken rivers.

(ii) **Sheet Erosion** It is the main problem in Rajasthan, where sandy soil is removed by run-off process.

(iii) **Splash Erosion** It is the problem of broad leaf dense forest in the region of Madhya Pradesh, North–East India and Chota Nagpur.

### Cause of Soil Erosion

Deforestation is one of the major causes of soil erosion. Plants keep soils bound in locks of roots and thus, prevent erosion. Soil in irrigated zones of India is becoming saline because of over-irrigation. Chemical fertilizers in the absence of organic manures are also harmful to the soil fertility. Unless the soil gets enough humus, chemicals harden it and reduce its fertility in the long-run.

### Soil Conservation

- Afforestation is the process of planting trees in a barren land devoid of any trees to create a forest cover. It is an important method to conserve the soil.
- Checking overgrazing and shifting cultivation is also helpful in order to reduce soil erosion and soil conservation.
- Through contour bunding and terracing soil erosion can be minimised. In this method, the hill slopes are divided into numerous small slopes, which reduce surface run-off and soil erosion.
- Developing shelter belts of trees and agro-forestry in arid and semi-arid areas may be helpful to protect cultivable lands from encroachment by sand dunes.

# ENERGY RESOURCES

Energy resources are the estimated maximum capacity for energy production given all available resources on Earth. In simple words, they are natural fuels that are used to produce heat, power, motion and electricity.

Energy resources can also be classified into two types: renewable and non-renewable.

## Renewable Energy Resources

Renewable energy resources are resources which are naturally replenished on a human timescale, such as sunlight, wind, rain, tides, waves, and geothermal heat. Such resources never run out and thus their supply is not limited.

### 1. Solar Energy

Sun is a big source of energy. The energy that we get from the Sun is called solar energy. All the natural phenomena like the flowing of wind, water cycle etc., are possible due to solar energy. Now-a-days, solar energy is being used to cook food with the help of solar cookers, heat water, light streets, pump water for irrigating fields etc.

#### Advantages

- It is readily available, inexhaustible, uninterrupted and continuous source of energy.
- Solar devices can be installed in remote areas such as small village in interior regions. Such as deserts, mountains.
- It is possible to produce solar energy in large quantities across many regions in the world especially tropical regions.
- It is clean. It creates electricity without contributing to global warming and pollution.

### Disadvantages

- It can be produced in tropical and sub-tropical areas only.
- Technology is still expensive and involves high installation cost.
- Difficult to store and run heavy machines.
- Silicon used in the production of SPV (Solar Photo Voltaic) cells is a pollutant.
- Solar panel are not being massed produced due to lack of material and technology.

## 2. Hydro-Energy

Water plays an important role in our life. Humans need water for many purposes, such as drinking, cooking etc.

Water flowing into the river or water stored in a dam is a source of hydro-energy. The simple method to use hydro-energy is to convert it into electrical energy.

### Advantages

- It is renewable as this method uses water to produce electricity.
- It is a clean and green alternative source of energy. It will not produce any greenhouse gases or toxins that will pollute the environment.
- It requires low maintenance and operating cost.

### Disadvantages

- It causes environmental damage.
- Construction cost is very expensive.
- It creates problem of shortage of water supply.

## 3. Wind Energy

Wind is converted into electricity through wind mills. These wind mills are generally established only at places where most of the days experience strong winds.

The energy from these wind mills is used for grinding grain, pumping water and to produce electricity. In India, many windmills have been setup in different states such as Maharashtra, Tamil Nadu, Karnataka, Rajasthan, Kerala, West Bengal, Odisha and Gujarat.

### Advantages

- It is inexhaustible source of energy.
- No pollution and emission of GHGs.
- Possibility of large scale production.
- They can generate power immediately after installation.
- Land around wind turbines can be used for other purposes such as farming.
- Wind turbines have low maintenance cost.

### Disadvantages

- Wind turbines generate noise pollution.
- Due to large scale construction of wind turbines on remote location, it could be a threat to wildlife.
- Lack of coordination among stakeholders.
- Wind turbines are suited to the coastal regions which receive wind throughout the year to generate power. So, places that do not have any coastal areas may not be benefitted by this power.

## 4. Biogas

It is another type of fuel which is a mixture of gases such as methane, carbon dioxide, hydrogen etc., which is obtained by decomposition of animal and plant wastes with the help of microorganisms in the presence of water. It is used as fuel in gas stove especially in rural areas.

### Advantages

- It is renewable and clean source of energy like solar and wind power.
- It is simple and low cost technology. It needs little investment of work and time, small bio-digesters can be used at home utilising, kitchen waste and animal manure.

### Disadvantages

- After refinement and compression, biogas still contains impurities.
- Biogas generation is also affected by weather. The optimal temperature bacteria need to digest waste is around 37°C. In cold climates, digesters require heat energy to maintain constant biogas supply.
- The systems used in the production of biogas are not efficient.

## 5. Biomass

It is waste material from plants or animals that is not used for food or feed. It can be waste from farming like wheat stalks or horticulture like yard waste, food processing like corn cobs, animal farming like manure rich in nitrogen and phosphorus or human waste from sewage plants.

It is used in various industrial processes, like energy production or as raw materials for manufacturing chemicals. It can either be used directly *via* combustion to produce heat or indirectly after converting it to various forms of biofuel.

### Advantages

- It is always and widely available as a renewable source of energy.
- It reduces the use of fossil fuels.
- It is less expensive than fossil fuels.
- Biomass production adds a revenue source for its manufacturers.

### Disadvantages

- Biomass energy is not as efficient as fossil fuels.
- Biomass plants require a lot of space.
- It can lead to deforestation since wood is one of the most used source of biomass energy.
- While biomass is carbon neutral, the use of animal and human waste esclates the amount of methane gas, which is also damaging the environment.

## 6. Biofuel

It is a fuel that is produced directly from plants or indirectly from agricultural, commercial, domestic and/or industrial wastes.

Renewable biofuels generally involves contemporary carbon fixation, such as those that occur in plants or microalgae through the process of photosynthesis.

Other renewable biofuels are made through the use or conversion of biomass that referring to recently living organisms, most often referring to plants or plant derived materials.

### Advantages

- It posses less risk to human health.
- It provides economic benefits.
- It is more readily available and sustainable.

### Disadvantages

- Biofuels have a lower energy output than traditional fuels and therefore require greater quantities to be consumed in order to produce the same energy level.
- To refine biofuels to more efficient energy outputs and to build the necessary manufacturing plants a high initial investment is required.
- Massive quantity of water is required for proper irrigation of biofuel crops as well as to manufacture fuel.

## 7. Tidal Energy

It is a form of hydropower that converts the energy from tides to electricity. Tides are caused by the combined effects of gravitational forces exerted by the Moon, the Sun and the rotation of the Earth.

Tidal energy presents an evolving technology with tremendous potential. However, it can only be installed along coastlines. Coastlines often experience two high tides and two low tides on a daily basis.

The difference in water levels must be at least 5 meters high to produce electricity. Tidal electricity can be created from tidal barrages, tidal fences and tidal turbines erected near sea.

### Advantages

- Tidal energy arise from being renewable it is also an environment friendly energy.
- It is predictable. It means these currents are highly predictable, developing with well known cycles which makes it easier to construct tidal energy system.
- It is effective at low speeds.

### Disadvantages

- Tidal energy is considered as a limited source of energy as it can provide electricity only during tides.
- It is expensive to setup.

- Bad weather and storms such as hurricanes that occur along coastline can damage tidal power plants.

## 8. Geothermal Energy

It is the heat of the Earth emerging from the shallow ground to hot water and hot rocks found a few miles below the Earth's surface and from molten rocks. Geothermal heat pumps can tap this resource.

It consists of a heat pump, an air delivery system and a heat exchanges system of pipes. All these equipments are buried in the shallow ground near the building and finally electricity is generated through these wells.

### Advantages

- Geothermal energy compared to other renewable source such as wind, solar or biomass is that it is not constant source of energy. It means it is not dependent on wind or Sun and available all the time.
- It is relatively easier to predict the output of geothermal plant. It does not have the same energy fluctuations as wind or solar.
- There is no shortage of geothermal energy unlike traditional energy source such as coal and fossil fuel.
- Using geothermal energy does not create pollution and help in creating clean environment.

### Disadvantages

- It is only suitable for regions where temperature below the Earth are quite low. And it can produce steam over a long period of time.
- Geothermal sites may contain some poisonous gases which can escape through the holes drilled by the construction. Thus, it may release harmful gases.
- This energy is not widely used therefore the unavailability of equipment, staff, infrastructure poses hindrances to the installation of geothermal plants.

# Non-Renewable Energy Resources

These are those natural resources that are available in limited quantity. These resources cannot be renewed or replenished in short duration. Therefore, they are also known as exhaustible resources. For example, Coal, natural gas, petroleum etc.

## 1. Fossil Fuel

They are found deep inside the Earth and are made by natural processes over many centuries. Their quantity is limited and they take thousands of years to get renewed.

Following are fossil fuels which are discussed below

(i) **Coal** It is also known **as black diamond.** Coal is used as a fuel to generate electricity in factories and steam engines.

(ii) **Natural Gas** It is used as a fuel called Compressed Natural Gas (CNG). Some wells dug into the Earth to produce only natural gas.

Natural gases are good alternative to petrol and diesel and is used as CNG. It burns easily and produces a lot of heat. It is good source of hydrogen.

(iii) **Petroleum** It is also known as mineral oil or crude oil. This liquid mineral is refined to make fuels such as petrol, diesel, cooking gas and kerosene.

Plastic, cosmetics and lubricants are also products of petroleum. It is found deep inside the Earth or under the sea floor. It is taken out by drilling wells deep into the Earth or under the seabed.

## 2. Nuclear Energy

The fuel used for nuclear energy is generally uranium, which is in a limited supply. Production of electricity from nuclear energy does not release carbon dioxide. Thus, use of nuclear energy is safe for the environment.

Although, there is a great deal of radiation danger associated with nuclear energy. It is capable of causing genetic disorders. Thus, if someone is once exposed to these radiations, it can affect the generations to come adversely.

### Advantages

- It is more cost effective.
- It does not use as much fuel in the process.
- It produces less waste and does not produce carbon dioxide or smoke.
- Power station has very long life time.
- Nuclear power stations are usually very compact when compared to the thermal station. Although the initial cost of building a nuclear plant is high. The maintenance and running costs are relatively low.
- It produces no pollution gases.

### Disadvantages

- There is a great deal of radiation danger associated with nuclear energy. It is capable of causing genetic disorder.
- Storage of nuclear wastes can lead to disastrous effects if not disposed or stored in a proper manner.
- Radioactive minerals are unevenly distributed around the world and are found in limited quantities.
- Starting a nuclear plant requires huge capital investment and advanced technology.
- It cannot react quickly to changes in electricity.

## Exploitation of Natural and Energy Resources

The exploitation of natural and energy resources started to emerge in the 19th century. During 20th century, energy consumption rapidly increased.

Today, about 80% of the world's energy consumption is sustained by the extraction of fossil fuels, which consists of oil, coal and gas.

Another non-renewable resource that is exploited by humans are subsoil minerals such as precious metals that are mainly used in the production of industrial commodities.

### Problems Arising from the Exploitation of Natural and Energy Resources

Some of the problems arising from the exploitation of natural and energy resources are

#### 1. Depletion of Fossil Fuels

The use of fossil fuels leads to its depletion due to

- industrial revolution increased energy demands.
- consumption of fossil fuels increased.
- rate of fossil fuels consumption is larger than rate of formation.
- depletion of fossil fuels reserve leads to problem for future generation.

#### 2. Deforestation

It leads to damage of the quality of land. It also means clearing of forests on a massive scale, resulting in damage to habitat, biodiversity loss and aridity.

Daily trees are cut down for

- selling fuel or timber.
- land used for settlements, cultivation etc.
- construction of dams for irrigation facilities.

#### 3. Greenhouse Gas Increases

Due to industrial revolution carbon dioxide emission rapidly increased that also leads to global warming. The greenhouse gas increases due to

- combustion of fossil fuels.
- combustion of wood.
- emissions from automobiles.
- emissions from industries.

#### 4. Water Pollution

It is considered as an essence of life, but rapid industrialisation and increasing urbanisation, results in the water pollution. Many pollutants are discharged into water bodies which affect the aquatic plants, organisms and the entire biological communities.

#### 5. Soil Erosion

It occurs naturally, but due to deforestation, construction of roads, urbanisation etc., it occurs with the rate of 40%. It happens so thus, resulting in land degradation, sedimentations of aquatic ecosystems and so on.

Although, the exploitation of natural and energy resources are a key factor in economic growth and development but, they are not without serious negative environmental and socio- economical impacts.

# NATURAL HAZARDS AND DISASTERS AND THEIR MITIGATIONS

Natural hazards are naturally occurring physical phenomena caused either by rapid or slow onset of events which can be geo-physical (earthquakes, landslides, tsunamis and volcanic activity), hydrological (avalanches and floods), and climatological (extreme temperatures, drought and wildfires).

In other words, natural hazards are the result of naturally occurring processes that act as a threat to humans and the environment.

Different types of natural hazards and their mitigation are given here:

## 1. Earthquake

It is a sudden release of energy accumulated in deformed rocks of Earth crust causing the ground to tremble or shake.

It can occur suddenly any time of the year without any warning causing severe loss of life and property. Earthquakes are caused due to disequilibrium in any part of the crust of the Earth such as, volcanic eruptions, faulting and folding, hydrostatic pressure of man-made water body etc.

### Mitigation of Earthquakes

- Follow certain building codes and guidelines for safe construction of buildings against earthquakes.
- Architectural and engineering inputs need to be put together to improve building design and construction practices.
- Educating the public about causes and characteristics of an earthquake.
- Preparedness measures helps to a certain extent in mitigating the natural disaster.

### → Earthquake Areas in India

**Least Damage Risk (Zone I)**

This zone includes the places of some parts of Punjab and Haryana, plain areas of Uttar Pradesh, portions of plains of North Bihar and West Bengal, delta areas of Godavari, coastal plain areas of Maharashtra and Kerala, desert areas of Rajasthan and most areas of Gujarat except Kutch region.

**Low Damage Risk (Zone II)**

This zone includes Southern Punjab and Haryana, Southern parts of plains of Uttar Pradesh, Eastern Rajasthan, coastal districts of Odisha, Tamil Nadu etc.

**Moderate Damage Risk (Zone III)**

This zone includes the areas of Southern and South - Eastern Rajasthan, most of Madhya Pradesh, Maharashtra and Karnataka, Southern Bihar, Northern and North-Western Odisha.

**High Damage Risk (Zone IV)**

This zone includes Jammu and Kashmir, Himachal Pradesh, Northern Punjab and Haryana, Delhi, Western Uttar Pradesh, terai and bhabar regions and Himalayan regions of Uttarakhand and Bihar and Sikkim areas.

**Very High Damage Risk (Zone V)**

It includes parts of Jammu and Kashmir, some parts of Himachal Pradesh, Uttarakhand, extreme North Bihar, entire North Eastern India and Kutch region of Gujarat.

## 2. Tsunamis

Tsunami is a phenomenon where a series of waves in a water body is caused by the displacement of a large volume of water. It occurs generally in an ocean or large lake. Sometimes the waves reach the heights in many meters. Earthquakes, volcanic eruptions and other underwater explosions below the water have the potential to generate a tsunami.

Tsunamis occur more frequently in the Pacific ocean particularly along 'Pacific Ring of Fire'. This zone is found at the Northern edge of the Pacific plate and most active fields of the Earth.

Several times a year a strong earthquake of atleast 7 on Richter Scale results in tsunamis. East Asian and Western North and South American coasts experience this hazard the most.

Tsunamis destroy everything in their way and cause huge damages to all kinds of structures and causes deaths in large numbers.

### Mitigations of Tsunamis

- Find out if your house is in danger and know the height of your street above sea level.
- Be familiar with warning signs.
- Make evacuation plans with more than one route and pick an elevated inland location.

## 3. Volcano

It is a landform at the end of a conduct or pipe which rises from below the crust and vents to the surface. Volcano is usually in the form of a peak which may be cone-shaped or dome-shaped.

The margin of the Pacific ocean is the area where the largest number of active volcanoes are situated. India is not prone to this hazard. The only active volcano in India is the Barren Island in Andman Nicobar Islands. It damages human settlements and the ash and dust injected into the atmosphere can be hazardous to health. It may damage aircrafts when accumulated around the engines.

The liquid magma erupting from volcano may bury human settlements and all kinds of structures. Large areas of cultivable land may be covered by this debris and rendered uncultivable.

### Mitigation of Volcanoes

- The best way to protect oneself against harm is to move away at first warning or sign of eruption in a volcano.
- Generally, there are signs of eruption much before the actual eruption in most volcanoes and monitoring agencies issue warnings for likely eruptions. One must follow these warnings to stay away from active volcanoes.

## 4. Cyclones

It refers to any spinning storm that rotates around a low pressure centre. Cyclone erupts with a terrifying energy. The strong winds whirls at a tremendous velocity of 120–200 km/per hr. It is accompanied by thunder lighting and rain. They occur mainly in the tropical and temperate regions of the world. The damages caused by cyclone are very severe.

The cyclonic storm damages installations, dwellings, communication system, trees, etc. Heavy rainfall from a cyclone usually spread over a large area cause large scale soil erosion and weakening of embankments. Cyclones may also cause prolonged heavy rains. This may lead to floods causing heavy losses. Water becomes contaminated and people may suffer from various water borne diseases.

Coastal regions of Andhra Pradesh, Odisha and West Bengal are among the areas that experience maximum damage due to cyclone. Tropical cyclones are known by different names in different parts of the world, such as, typhoons (South China Sea), depressions or strom (Bay of Bengal), and willy-willy (Australia).

Another variant of tropical storms is a tornado that is typically an American storm.

### Mitigation of Cyclones

- Efforts can be made to reduce the fury of waves by creating some structures along the coast.
- Planting mangroves along the coast.
- An early warning system about the movement and development of cyclones must be installed.
- Preparedness against cyclones also requires suitable measures in construction of houses and relocation of people.
- Belts of trees can help in reducing wind velocities by acting as wind breakers.

## 5. Flood

A flood is a general and temporary condition where two or more acres of normally dry land or two or more properties are inundated by water or mudflow.

Flooding occurs most commonly from heavy rainfall when natural water sources do not have the capacity to carry excess water. However, floods are not always caused by heavy rainfall.

They can result from other phenomena, particularly in coastal areas where inundation can be caused by a storm surge associated with a tropical cyclone.

### Mitigation of Floods

- Aforestation can check the frequency and intensity of floods.
- Floods can be prevented by making embankments and dykes.
- Monitoring of the flow of water in the rivers during the rainy season and timely warning to people and evacuation of those areas can help in reducing the damages caused by floods.
- Preparedness for such disasters and good communication networks can help reduce damages due to floods significantly.

## 6. Drought

It is an event that results from lower than normal expected rainfall over a season or period. The low rainfall is insufficient to meet the needs of human beings, plants, animals and agriculture.

Shortfall in rainwater results in drying of rivers, lakes, reservoirs and drying of wells due to excessive withdrawal and poor recharge of groundwater and loss of crop yield due to shortage of water are some of the main indicators of drought.

### Mitigation of Drought

- A regular monitoring of rainfall and checking the water availability in reservoirs, lakes and rivers.
- Use of efficient methods of irrigation and sowing low water consuming crops are some important measures to overcome drought.
- Rain water harvesting increases the water availability.

## 7. Cloudbursts

A cloudburst is an extreme amount of precipitation in a short period of time, sometimes accompanied by hail and thunder, which is capable of creating flood conditions.

The term cloudburst started from the notion that clouds were akin to water balloons and could burst resulting in rapid precipitation. Uttarakhand is one of the example for seeing cloudbursts, causing very heavy rainfall, flooding, landslides leading to death of thousands of people.

### Mitigation of Cloudbursts

- To build the canals and combined these canals with sewer system to level out the excess rainfall.
- To cope with the effects of climate change and chiefly aims at fixing acceptable limits of flooding on the streets.
- To erect an early warning system.

## 8. Landslides

These are a hazard in the mountainous regions. A landslide is a rapid down slope movement of rocks and soil along with vegetation growing there. It occur in large numbers in mountain areas especially in the rainy season. The soil and rocks become saturated with water in rainy season and become heavier and loose.

Landslides may be triggered by earthquakes also. They may destroy not only forests and settlements in their path, they might cover large tracts of cultivated land with debris.

### Mitigation of Landslides

- Techniques of slope stabilisation can help in checking the occurrence of landslides.
- Landslide prone zones along highways etc., can be identified and structures like retaining walls can be constructed to prevent movement of rocks.
- Maintaining a good tree cover on mountains can also help in checking the frequency of landslides.

## 9. Avalanches

An avalanche is a down-slope movement of snow and rocks similar to fall of debris in a landslide. However, avalanches are a hazard confined to high altitude areas where large amounts of snow accumulate on the mountain slopes.

Though, many such movements of ice result from accumulation of large amounts of snow on steep slopes and movement thereof under gravity. Some are triggered by factors like earthquakes. Large masses of snow thus move at very high velocity and bury settlements and vegetation in their path.

### Mitigation of Avalanches

- Monitoring the amount of snow accumulation on steep slopes and development of any cracks therein can be checked and precautions can be taken to contain the likely damage.
- Planning and creation of any infrastructure or settlements in such areas should take into account the extent of this hazard.
- Trapping the avalanche by control measures.
- Disposing the avalanche potential snow packs by artificial triggering.
- Predicting the occurrence of avalanches by through stability analysis and issuing warring (forth coming) about impending avalanete. Guiding the residents about emergency evacuation shelters.

## 10. Forest Fires

They are a very common hazard in forested areas during summer season. Since, there is a large amount of combustible material in the forest, the forest fires spread to large areas very rapidly.

Some of the forest fires may be caused due to natural reasons such as friction between trees and lightening, but many of them are a result of human activities.

Forest fires often become difficult to control.

### Mitigation of Forest Fires

- To keep a vigil in forest areas against fire.
- To maintain fire lines in forest is very important.
- Scientific methods should be employed to control fire in forest areas whenever such an event occurs so that the damage is contained and confined to the smallest possible area.

**→ National Green Tribunal (NGT)**

The National Green Tribunal has been established on 18th October, 2010 under the National Green Tribunal Act, 2010, for effective and expeditious disposal of cases relating to environmental protection and conservation of forests and other natural resources.

It is a specialised body equipped with the necessary expertise to handle environmental disputes involving multi-disciplinary issues. The Tribunal shall not be bound by the procedure laid down under the Code of Civil Procedure, 1908, but shall be guided by principles of natural justice. The principal bench of NGT is setup in New Delhi. Regional benches are in Pune (West Zone), Chennai (South Zone), Kolkata (East Zone) and Bhopal (Central Zone).

## Disaster Management

Mitigation is a complex process and challenging task. There are three key stages of activities in disaster management.

(i) **Before a Disaster** It means to reduce the potential for human material or environmental losses caused by hazards. And to ensure that these losses are minimised when disaster strikes.

(ii) **During a Disaster** To ensure that the needs and provisions of victims are met to remove and minimise suffering.

(iii) **After a Disaster** To achieve rapid and durable recovery. It means returning to normal life. The recovery includes debris clean up financial assistance to individuals and governments. Rebuilding of roads and bridges and providing main facilities. Sustained mass care for displaced human and animal populations.

### Disaster Management Act, 2005

The Disaster Management Act, 2005 has been enacted as the central Act deal with management of disasters. This act envisaged a three tier Disaster management structure in India at the National, state and district levels. It ensures measures by various wings of the Government for the prevention and mitigation of disasters. Every Ministry/Department of Central and State Governments to make provisions for funds to carry out activities set out in its disaster management plan.

## National Disaster Management Policy, 2009

The national policy on disaster management was approved by the Government in November, 2009. IT lays down policy on every aspect of disaster management in the country.

The main objectives of the policy are as follows

- Promoting a culture of prevention, preparedness and resilience at all levels through knowledge, innovation and education.
- Encouraging mitigation measures based on technology, traditional wisdom and environment sustianability.
- Ensuring efficient mechanism for identification, assessment and monitoring of disaster risks.
- Developing contemporary forecasting and early warning system.
- Ensuring efficient response and early relief measures.
- Undertaking reconstruction.

## National Disaster Management Plan 2016

National Disaster Management Plan (NDMP) 2016, the first ever national plan prepared in the country for disaster management.

With this Plan, India has signed our National Plan with Sendai Framework for Disaster Risk Reduction 2015-2030 to which India is a signatory. Its salient features are

- National Disaster Management Plan aims to make India disaster resilient and significantly reduce the loss of lives and assets.
- National Disaster Management Plan is based on four priority themes of the Sendai Framework understanding disaster risk, improving disaster risk, governance investing in disaster risk reduction and disaster preparedness, early warning.
- NDMP covers all phases of disaster management, i.e. prevention, mitigation response and recovery.
- It also identifies major activities, such as early warning, information dissemination, medical care, fuel, transportation, search and rescue, evacuation etc., to serve as a checklist for agencies responding to a disaster.

### Environment Related Important International Agreements/Conference

| | |
|---|---|
| UN Conference on the Human Environment | Stockholm (1972) |
| Convention on Migratory Species | Bonn (1979) |
| Convention for the Protection of the Ozone Layer | Vienna (1985) |
| Protocol on Substances that Deplete the Ozone Layer | Montreal (1987) |
| Convention on the Transboundary Movement of Hazardous Wastes | Basel (1989) |
| Earth Summit (UN Conference on Environment and Development) | Rio de-Janeiro (1992) |
| Convention on Prior Informed Consent | Rotterdam (1998) |
| UN Conference on Sustainable Development | Rio de-Janeiro (2012) |
| Nagoya Protocol on Genetic Resources | Nagoya (2010) |
| Convention on Biological Diversity (CBD-CoP-11) | Hyderabad (2012) |
| UN Climate Change Conference (CoP-20) | Lima (2014) |
| Paris Climate Conference (CoP-21) | Paris (2015) |
| Bonn Climate Conference (CoP-23) | Bonn (2017) |
| Katowice Climate Conference (CoP-24) | Poland (2018) |

# Environmental Conservation

Environmental conservation is the protection, preservation, management, or restoration of natural environments and the ecological communities that inhabit them. It is an umbrella term that defines anything we do to protect our planet and conserve its natural resources so that every living thing can have an improved quality of life.

It includes the management of human use of natural resources for current public benefit and sustainable social and economic utilization. In simple words, it is meant to protect nature by protecting vital resources, and it is also a way of living that works against the irresponsible practices of businesses and large corporations.

## Importance of Environmental Conservation

Due to the pressures of overconsumption, population growth and technology, the environment is being degraded, sometimes permanently. Then, conservation becomes important mainly for the following reasons:

- To repair some of the damage done by humans and maintain the environment for future generations.
- To maintain species diversity for our benefit and that of wildlife.
- To provide opportunities for education and the enjoyment of the environment.

# National and International Efforts to Conserve Environment

The importance of environmental conservation has been recognized by the governments who have begun placing restraints on activities that cause environmental degradation. They have come up with various acts, agreements and action plans to do so. Some of them are:

## 1. Environment Protection Act, 1986

After the Bhopal Gas Tragedy, the Government of India enacted the Environment Protection Act of 1986 under Article 253 of the Constitution.

The Environment Protection Act, 1986 came into effect on 19th November, 1986. In this Act, main emphasis is given to "**Environment**", defined to include water, air and land and the interrelationships with human.

The Act provides a framework for Central Government.

The main provisions of Environment Protection act are enumerated as

- The Act explicitly prohibits discharge of environmental pollutants in excess of prescribed regulatory standards.
- The Act provides provisions for penalities. For each failure or violation the punishment included a prison term up to 5 years or fine up to ₹ 1 lakh.
- The Act imposed an additional fine of up to ₹ 5000 for each day of continuing violation.
- If a failure or violation occurs for more than one year, the offender may be punished with imprisonment which may be extended up to 7 years.
- The Central Government shall have the power to take all such measures as it deems necessary or useful for protecting and improving the quality of the environment and preventing/ controlling and decreasing environmental pollution.

The Ramsar Convention of Wetlands is an international treaty for the conservation of wetlands i.e fresh or saline water marshy areas. The Convention was signed in 1971 and named after the city when it was held for the first time i.e. Ramsar in Iran. India has 37 wetland sites. Some of them are Asthamudi (Kerala), Bhoj (Madhya Pradesh), Renuka (Himachal Pradesh), Hoker (Jammu & Kashmir), etc.

## 2. National Action Plan on Climate Change (NAPCC)

- Government of India launched eight missions in 2008 as part of the National Action Plan on Climate Change (NAPCC) in specific areas, i.e. solar energy, enhanced energy efficiency, sustainable habitat, water, sustaining the Himalayan ecosystem, Green India, sustainable agriculture and strategic knowledge for climate change, which include assessment of the impact of climate change.
- The NAPCC focus on promoting understanding of climate change, adaptation and mitigation, energy efficiency and natural resource conservation.

  The 8 missions are

  (i) **National Mission for Sustainable Agriculture, 2008** The plan aims to support sustainable agricultural practices by use of manures, crop insurance, etc.

  (ii) **National Mission for Enhanced Energy Efficiency, 2009** It aims to promote energy efficiency by providing energy- saving certificates to companies, financing public- private partnerships to reduce energy consumption and reducing taxes on energy-efficient appliances like LED bulbs.

(iii) **National Solar Mission, 2010** The NAPCC aims to promote the development and use of solar energy for power generation and other uses. Other objectives include the establishment of a solar research centre, increased international collaboration on technology development, strengthening of domestic manufacturing capacity and increased Government funding and international support.

(iv) **National Mission on Strategic Knowledge for Climate Change, 2010** To gain a better understanding of climate changes and its impact through proper research. It also encourages private sector initiatives to develop mitigation technologies.

(v) **National Mission on Sustainable Habitat, 2010** Aim is to promote public transport, better waste management, recycling and sustainable energy generation.

(vi) **National Water Mission, 2011** With water scarcity worsening as a result of climate change, this plan sets a goal of a 20% improvement in water use efficiency.

(vii) **National Mission for Sustaining the Himalayan Ecosystem, 2014** The plan aims to conserve biodiversity, forest cover and Himalayan region, where glaciers that are a major source of India's water supply are projected to recede as a result of global warming.

(viii) **National Mission for a Green India, 2014** Goals include the afforestation of 6 million hectares of degraded forest land, expanding forest cover from 23% to 33% and enhance annual $CO_2$ sequestration.

## 3. Montreal Protocol, 1989

The Montreal Protocol is an international treaty signed by 197 countries to protect ozone layer by reducing production of substances responsible for ozone depletion. Signed in 1987, this universally ratified protocol came into force in 1989.

The Montreal Protocol (MP) aims at phasing out ozone depleting substances such as chlorofluorocarbons (CFCs) and hydro–chlorofluorocarbons (HCFCs) that were mostly used in air conditioning, refrigerating and foam industry by 2030.

## 4. Rio Summit, 1992

In June 1992, the United Nations Conference on Environment and Development (UNCED), also known as the Rio Earth Summit, was held in Rio de Janeiro in Brazil. The issues addressed included:

- **Patterns of Production** Particularly the production of toxic components, such as lead in gasoline, or poisonous wastes are being scrutinised by the UN and Governments alike.
- Alternative sources of energy are being sought to replace the use of fossil fuels which are linked to global climate change.

Another conference was held in June 2012, in Rio namely, the United Nations Conference on Sustainable Development. It is also commonly called Rio + 20 or Rio Earth Summit 2012.

## 5. Convention on Biodiversity, 1992

The Convention on Biological Diversity (CBD) enacted in 1992, is an international treaty that covers biodiversity at all levels: ecosystems, species and genetic resources. It also covers biotechnology through the Cartagena Protocol on Bio-safety.

It has three main objectives

1. The conservation of biological diversity.
2. The sustainable use of the components of biological diversity.
3. The fair and equitable sharing of the benefits arising out of the utilisation of genetic resources.

## 6. Kyoto Protocol, 1997

It is an international agreement which is linked to the United Nations Framework Convention on Climate Change. The Kyoto Protocol was adopted in Kyoto, Japan, in December, 1997 which came into force in February, 2005.

In this, 37 industrialised countries and the European community committed to reduce GHG emissions by atleast 18 per cent below 1990 levels in the eight-year period from 2013 to 2020.

## 7. Paris Agreement (CoP 21), 2015

The 21st Conference of Parties under the UNFCCC agreed on adoption of the Paris Agreement on post-2020 actions on climate change. This universal agreement is to succeed the Kyoto Protocol.

This agreement provides a framework for all countries to take steps to curb climate change including mitigation, adaptation, loss and damage, finance, technology development and transfer and capacity building.

## 8. International Solar Alliance, 2015

The International Solar Alliance (ISA) is an initiative launched by Prime Minister Narendra Modi at the India-Africa Summit on 30th November, 2015. It is an alliance of 121 countries, most of them being sunshine countries, which lie either completely or partly between the Tropic of Cancer and the Tropic of Capricorn.

The primary objective of the alliance is to work for efficient exploitation and utilisation of solar energy to reduce dependence on fossil fuels.

**Marrakech Climate Change Conference, 2016** The 2016 United Nations Climate Change Conference was an international meeting of political leaders and activists to discuss environmental issues. It was held in Marrakech, Morocco on 7-18 November, 2016. The purpose of the conference was to discuss and implement plans about combating climate change. The focal issue was that of water scarcity, water cleanliness and water related sustianability, a major problem in the developing world.

## 9. Bonn, Germany (CoP 23), 2017

23rd annual CoP under the UN Framework Convention on Climate Change (UNFCCC) was held in November, 2017, at Bonn (Germany). It was presided over by Fiji's PM Vorege 'Frank' Bainimarama who called for a sense of Urgency in implementing the 2015 Paris accord on combating climate change, because Fiji is already suffering from the impacts of global warming.

Key outcomes of CoP 23 were as follows

- It was decided that the negotiators will keep working for one year and finalise the rule book by December, 2018.
- It was agreed that the financial issues regarding the climate change must be addressed and the rich countries must take the responsibility of it.
- It was also decided that the Adaptation Fund under Kyoto Protocol can also become the part of the Paris Agreement to deal with the financial crunch.

## 10. Katowice, Polland (CoP 24), 2018

From 2nd December 2018, the 24th meeting of Conference of Parties (CoP 24) to the United Nations Framework Convention on Climate Change (UNFCCC) also known as **Katowice Climate Change Conference** was held at Katowice, Poland with an aim to finalise guidelines for implementation of the Paris Agreement adopted in 2016.

Vision of the CoP 24 meeting were as follows

- Adoption of a decision ensuring full implementation of the Paris Agreement.
- Meeting the target of global warming to below 1.5° Celsius.

## 11. Madrid Conference (CoP-25), 2019

The 2019 United Nations Climate Change Conference also known as CoP 25 was held in Madrid, Spain from 2-13 December, 2019. Under the Presidency of Chilean Government. The summit could not reach a final agreement of important issues.

However, its important features are:

- The summit passed the declaration calling on countries to improve their current pledges to reduce greenhouse emissions.
- It also endorsed to help poor countries that are suffering the effects of climate change.
- It also called on the 'urgent need' to cut planet-heating greenhouse gases in line with the goals of the 2015 Paris Climate Change Accord.

# Chapter Practice

## Development and Environment, Human and Environment Interaction

1 India was ranked ...... out of 189 countries on the 2019 Human Development Index.
(A) 130th (B) 129th
(C) 150th (D) 140th

2 Which of the following statements is correct regarding Human Development Index?
(A) It emphasizes that people and their capabilities should be the ultimate criteria for assessing the development of a country.
(B) It measures average achievement of a country through a decent standard of living.
(C) It measures how much capital each country loses through lack of education and health.
(D) Only (A) and (B)

3 Millennium Development Goals were adopted in which year?
(A) 1985 (B) 1995 (C) 2000 (D) 2005

4 Consider the following statement about Millennium Development Goals.
I. In 2000 the world leaders adopted MDGs in New York.
II. These were the time bound targets with a deadline of 2020.
III. Later MDGs were replaced by the Sustainable Development Goals.
Which of the above statements is/are not correct?
(A) Only I (B) I and III
(C) Only II (D) All of these

5 Which of the following are the goals of Millennium Development Goals?
(A) To eradicate extreme poverty and hunger
(B) To provide employment
(C) To improve maternal health
(D) Both (A) and (C)

6 In which year Millennium Development Goals were replaced by the Sustainable Development Goals?
(A) 2001 (B) 2005
(C) 2010 (D) 2016

7 "The development that meets the needs of the present without compromising the ability of future generations to meet their own needs" refers to
(A) Millennium Development Goals
(B) Sustainable Development Goals
(C) Environment Development
(D) None of the above

8 The objectives of sustainable development include
(A) Environmental friendly patterns of activity
(B) Energy efficiency
(C) Conservation of natural and man-made resources
(D) All of the above

9 Consider the following statements.
I. The sustainable development has been derived from Brundt Land's Our Common Future, 1987 report of the World Commission on Environment and Development.
II. It aims to develop production opportunities.
III. It came to coverage with the post 2015 Millennium Development Goals.
Which of the above statements is/are correct?
(A) Only I (B) I and II
(C) II and III (D) All of these

10 How many goals are there in Sustainable Development Goals?
(A) 10 (B) 12
(C) 17 (D) 21

11 **Assertion** (A) Sustainable development is critical to well-being of human society.
**Reason** (R) Environmentally, sound policies do not harm the environment or deplete the natural resources.
Choose the correct code.
**Codes**
(A) Both (A) and (R) are correct and (R) is the correct explanation of (A)
(B) Both (A) and (R) are correct, but (R) is not the correct explanation of (A)
(C) (A) is true and (R) is false
(D) (A) is false and (R) is true

12 Consider the following statements.

I. Environment and development are interrelated which cannot be separated from each other.

II. Development is a continuous and constant process.

III. Development has a edge over the environment.

Which of the above statements is/are not correct?

**Codes**

(A) Only I (B) I and II
(C) Only III (D) All of these

13 **Assertion** (A) Human environment interaction is always dependent on the degree of human activity.

**Reason** (R) Human activities have harmed ecosystems which have resulted in the loss of biodiversity.

Choose the correct option.

(A) Both (A) and (R) are true and (R) is the correct explanation of (A).
(B) (A) is false but (R) is true.
(C) Both (A) and (R) all true but (R) is not the correct explanation of (A).
(D) (A) is true but (R) is false.

14 Which of the following is not an anthropogenic activity?

(A) Mining (B) Industrialisation
(C) Weathering (D) Deforestation

15 Which of the following statements is incorrect regarding the impact on agriculture due to anthropogenic activities?

(A) Anthropogenic activities cause topographing changes that lead to soil. erosion, depletion of nutrients, etc.
(B) It leads to soil contamination through toxic substances.
(C) It impacts the socio-economic nature of soil.
(D) All of the above

16 Elements of environment are

(A) Nitrogen, carbon dioxide and oxygen
(B) Nitrogen, oxygen and ozone
(C) Carbon dioxide, oxygen and ozone
(D) Lithosphere, atmosphere, hydrosphere and biosphere

17 Consider the following statements about lithosphere.

I. It is a solid crust or the hard top layer of the Earth.

II. It constitutes about 39% part of the Earth.

III. It is the domain that provides us forests, lands for agriculture and human settlements.

Which of the above statements is/are correct?

(A) Only I (B) I and II
(C) II and III (D) All of the above

18 A hydrosphere is

(A) the domain of water
(B) comprises all forms of water bodies
(C) it covers 70% of Earth's surface
(D) All of the above

19 In which of the following layers of the atmosphere, ozone ($O_3$) gas is present?

(A) Stratosphere (B) Exosphere
(C) Troposphere (D) None of these

20 Which of the following is/are not the characteristic(s) of stratosphere?

(A) It is the lowest layer of the atmosphere
(B) It is free from cloud and associated weather phenomena
(C) It provides ideal flying condition for large jet planes
(D) In this layer temperature increases due to the absorption of the ultraviolet radiation of the Sun

21 Beginning from the surface of Earth, what is the sequence of different layers of atmosphere?

(A) Stratosphere, Troposphere, Ionosphere, Exosphere
(B) Troposphere, Stratosphere, Ionosphere, Exosphere
(C) Troposphere, Stratosphere, Ionosphere
(D) None of the above

22 Biosphere is

(A) the solid shell of inorganic materials on the surface of the Earth
(B) it is the narrow zone of the Earth where land water and air interact with each other to support life
(C) the sphere which occupies the maximum volume of all the spheres
(D) All of the above

## Environmental Issues

23 Which of the following is the major concern of Environmental issues?

(A) Air pollution (B) Water pollution
(C) Soil pollution (D) All of these

**24** Which of the following consists of the primary air pollutants?

(A) (B) CFC

(C) $CO_2$ (D) All of these

**25** Which of the following is/are the characteristic(s) of Sulphurous Smog or London Smog?

(A) It is a mixture of sulphur dioxide in the air.

(B) Its name is given as it affected London for a very long time.

(C) It is more prevalent during the morning hours of winter season.

(D) All of the above

**26** Fly ash is composed of

(A) aluminium silicate (B) silicon dioxide

(C) calcium oxide (D) All of these

**27** Which of the factors is/are the adverse impact of acid rain

(A) It shows adverse impact on forests, fresh water solid and acquatic life

(B) It has adverse impact on the nutrients such as magnesium

(C) Acid rain can damage the buildings and historic monuments which are made up of rocks such as limestone and marbles

(D) All of the above

**28** Acid rain is caused by which two gases?

(A) carbon dioxide are nitrogen

(B) carbon monoxide and carbon dioxide

(C) ozone and carbon dioxide

(D) nitrous oxide and sulphur dioxide

**29** The effect of air pollution can be seen on

(A) plants and animals

(B) global climate change

(C) surface water can be polluted

(D) Both (A) and (B)

**30** The objective of National Air Quality Monitoring Programme is

(A) To determine statistics and trends of ambient air quality

(B) To ascertain whether the prescribed ambient air quality standards are violated

(C) To identify non-attainment cities

(D) All of the above

**31** The National Ambient Air Quality Standards was revised in November, 2009 for pollutants like

(A) lead (B) ozone

(C) benzene (D) All of these

**32** India's first Air Quality Index was launched in which year?

(A) 2000 (B) 2005

(C) 2010 (D) 2015

**33** Which of the following is/are the objective of Air Quality Index?

(A) To inform public regarding overall status of air quality through a summation parameter that is easy to understand

(B) To inform citizen about associated health impacts of air pollution exposure

(C) To rank cities/towns for prioritising action based on measure of air quality index

(D) All of the above

**34** Which of the following is the first mobile application service in India to provide a current and advanced forecast for air quality?

(A) Air Quality Index (B) SAFAR

(C) NEMMP (D) NAAQS

**35** Which of the following are the important sources of water pollution?

(A) Agricultural wastes

(B) Industrial wastes

(C) Domestic wastes

(D) All of the above

**36** Some sources are much more difficult to monitor and control. These are

(A) point sources

(B) non-point sources

(C) other sources

(D) None of the above

**37** Due to which type of water pollution oxygen level decreases in water and new species take over?

(A) Surface water pollution

(B) Thermal water pollution

(C) Marine pollution

(D) Groundwater pollution

**38** Which of the following is the important measure to control water pollution?

(A) Reducing soil erosion or improving water treatment, attempt to stop contaminants from entering natural water systems through run-off or seawage

(B) Clean water act or other such acts should be regulated

(C) Reducing the amount of sediment in water

(D) All of the above

**39** Which of the following is/are the important government steps to control water pollution?

(A) Issuance of directions under Section 5 of Environment (Protection) Act, 1986 and under Section 18 (1) (B) of Water (Prevention and Control of Pollution) Act, 1974 and Air (Prevention and Control of Pollution) Act, 1981

(B) Implementation of National River Conservation Plan for abatement of pollution in identified stretches of various rivers

(C) Preparation of action plan for sewage management and restoration of water quality in aquatic resources by state governments

(D) All of the above

**40** Measuring BOD (Biological Oxygen Demand) is primarily used for

(a) estimating the types of microbes

(b) determining the level of oxygen

(c) waste water treatment as decomposition of organic waste by microorganism

(d) None of the above

**41** In which year noise pollution included in the Air Act (PCP)?

(A) 1981 (B) 1988

(C) 1995 (D) 2000

**42** The effect of noise pollution can be

(A) temporary or permanent deafness

(B) abortion

(C) it weakens the edifice of buildings

(D) All of the above

**43** Noise above ...... stops an individual from falling asleep.

(A) 40 dB

(B) 45 dB

(C) 50 dB

(D) None of the above

**44** Smog is a combination of

(A) fog (B) dust

(C) vapour (D) All of these

**45** Consider the following statements regarding 'Green Muffler'.

I. A technology for reducing pollution.

II. A method of afforestation.

III. Plantation along roadsides to reduce noise pollution.

IV. A process of reduce vibration.

Which of the above statements is/are correct?

(A) Only I (B) Only II

(C) Only III (D) All of these

**46** The source of soil pollution is

(A) nuclear wastes

(B) agricultural wastes

(C) industrial wastes

(D) All of the above

**47** Which of the following is the important measure to control soil pollution?

(A) Much of our waste can be recycled or incinerated to lessen pollutants

(B) Pre-determined holes are used to dump mining waste, which comes from mining

(C) Rules and regulations regarding wastes should be addressed and enforced

(D) All of the above

**48** What is ocean acidification?

(A) It occurs naturally very slowly

(B) It occurs mainly as a result of human activities

(C) It occurs when $_2$ is absorbed by the ocean and reacts with sea water to produce acid

(D) Both (B) and (C)

**49** The term Municipal Solid Waste (MSW) is generally used to describe

(A) wastes from industrial processes, concentration and demolition debris.

(B) wastes from private homes, commercial establishments and institutions.

(C) mining wastes

(D) agricultural wastes

**50** Which of the following processes is used through burning municipal solid waste in a properly designed furnace under suitable temperature and operating conditions?

(A) Sanitary landfills

(B) Incineration

(C) Composting

(D) Pyrolysis

**51** ...... term is defined as thermal degradation of waste in the absence of air.

(A) Composting (B) Incineration

(C) Pyrolysis (D) Sanitary landfills

**52** The radioactive pollution can be resulted in

(A) Acute radiation syndrome

(B) Cancer

(C) Both (A) and (B)

(D) None of the above

53 Liquid waste disposal consists of
(A) dewatering (B) sedimentation
(C) composting (D) All of these

54 ……… is the process of mechanically removing the solid materials present in the water through metal screening.
(A) Primary treatment
(B) Biological treatment
(C) Chemical treatment
(D) None of the above

55 ………. means any waste which is generated during the diagnosis, treatment or immunization of human beings or animals in research activities.
(A) Hazardous waste (B) Bio-medical waste
(C) E-waste (D) None of the above

56 The sources of e-waste are
(A) electronic devices used for entertainments such as DVDs and CD players
(B) waste generated from products used for data processing such as computers
(C) equipment devices used for communication like phones fax etc.
(D) All of the above

57 When was the first effort made to control E-waste under Basel Convention?
(a) 1990 (b) 1992 (c) 1993 (d) 1994

58 In which year world's first micro factory was developed which can transform the components of electronic waste items into valuable materials for reuse?
(A) 2000 (B) 2005
(C) 2011 (D) 2018

59 Match the following.

| List I (Pollutants) | List II (Impact on Human) |
|---|---|
| A. Oxides of nitrogen | 1. It damages various life forms |
| B. Liquid droplets | 2. It can have carcinogenic effect |
| C. Photochemical oxidants | 3. It damages tissues |
| D. Hydrocarbons | 4. It damages the respiration |

**Codes**

| | A | B | C | D | | A | B | C | D |
|---|---|---|---|---|---|---|---|---|---|
| (A) | 1 | 2 | 3 | 4 | (B) | 4 | 3 | 2 | 1 |
| (C) | 3 | 1 | 4 | 2 | (D) | 4 | 1 | 3 | 2 |

60 Pollutants that can be classified on the basis of nature are
(A) primary pollutant and secondary pollutant
(B) qualitative pollutant and quantitative pollutant
(C) biodegradable pollutant and non-bio degradable pollutant
(D) Both (A) and (C)

61 Smoke, ash, dust and nitric acid are which type of pollutants?
(A) Secondary pollutants
(B) Primary pollutants
(C) Biodegradable pollutants
(D) Qualitative pollutants

62 Pollutant released majorly by atmospheric reaction is
(A) Hydrocarbons
(B) Carbon compound
(C) Nitrogen compound
(D) Sulphur compound

63 Which pollutant damages human and animal lungs and is important precursor to acid rain?
(A) Hydrocarbons
(B) Oxides of nitrogen
(C) Oxides of sulphur
(D) Liquid droplets

64 Which type of pollutant irritates eyes, nose and throat?
(A) Photochemical oxidants
(B) Hydrocarbons
(C) Oxides of nitrogen
(D) Suspended particulate matter

## Climate Change

65 Climate represents ……
(A) long term average weather and its statistical variation for a given region.
(B) weather averaged over a year.
(C) measure of variation in the amount of precipitation.
(D) None of the above

66 Which of the following are the natural causes of climate change?
(A) Internal variability
(B) Ocean currents
(C) Volcanic activity
(D) All of the above

**67** How does climate change affect human health ?
(A) By increasing illnesses such as heat stress, cardiovascular disease and kidney disease.
(B) By increasing respiratory illnesses such as asthma.
(C) By increasing bacterial infections.
(D) All of the above

**68** The Greenhouse gas present in very high quantity is
(A) ethane (B) carbon dioxide
(C) propane (D) methane

**69** Burning of fossil fuels
(A) increases oxygen level
(B) increases greenhouse gases
(C) decreases greenhouse gases
(D) increases ethane level

**70** **Assertion** (A) Climate change mitigation and adaptation policies and measures should be prepared in transparent manner.
**Reason** (R) It will provide full access to information to all stakeholders.
**Codes**
(A) Both (A) and (R) are true and (R) is the correct explanation of (A).
(B) Both (A) and (R) all true but (R) is not the correct explanation of (A).
(C) (A) is true but (R) is false.
(D) (A) is false but (R) is true.

**71** Inter-governmental Panel on Climate Change was established to ......
(A) report and investigate on scientific evidence on and possible international response to climate change.
(B) establish developed country emissions.
(C) stabilize GHG concentrations in the atmosphere at a level.
(D) None of the above

**72** ...... is the process of removing carbon from the atmosphere and storing it in a carbon sink.
(A) Carbon trading
(B) Carbon sequestration
(C) Carbon tax
(D) Carbon offset

## Natural and Energy Resources

**73** Which of the following is/are the main causes of deforestation?
(A) Population explosion (B) Forest fires
(C) Timber harvesting (D) All of these

**74** What is social forestry?
(A) It refers to the management and protection of forests and afforestation on barren lands
(B) The objective of social forestry is to raise plantation by common man
(C) The practice also aims to protect agriculture from adverse climatic conditions by improving the environment
(D) All of the above

**75** Forest Act 2006 has also been called:
(A) The Tribal Rights Act
(B) The Tribal Bill
(C) The Tribal Land Act
(D) All of the above

**76** In which year the term Social Forestry was used in India by the National Commission on Agriculture, Government of India?
(A) 1977 (B) 1976
(C) 1976 (D) 1967

**77** According to the India state of Forest Report, 2019 the total forest and tree cover of the country is:
(A) 802, 088 sq km (B) 712, 249 sq km
(C) 807, 276 sq km (D) 708, 273 sq km

**78** The maximum loss of forest lands in India is caused by
(A) river valley projects
(B) industries
(C) means of transportation
(D) agriculture

**79** Deforestation during the recent decade has led to
(A) soil erosion (B) landslide
(C) loss of biodiversity (D) All of these

**80** Deforestation leads to an increase in atmospheric carbon dioxide because
(A) decaying trees release carbon dioxide
(B) living trees remove carbon dioxide from the atmosphere *via* photosynthesis
(C) burning wood releases carbon dioxide into the atmosphere
(D) All of the above

**81** Which of the following statement(s) is/are correct about Silent valley movement?
(A) It was started in the year 1987
(B) It was led by Sujatha Kumari
(C) To save valley Reserve Forest from being flooded by hydroelectric project
(D) All of the above

82 Match the following.

| List I (Soil types) | List II (Characteristics) |
|---|---|
| A. Black soil | 1. Agriculturally less important |
| B. Laterite soil | 2. Very fertile |
| C. Alluvial soil | 3. Heterogenous character changes with parent rock and climate |
| D. Forest soil | 4. Not water retentive when fertiliser added, soil becomes productive |

**Codes**

| | A | B | C | D | | A | B | C | D |
|---|---|---|---|---|---|---|---|---|---|
| (A) | 4 | 1 | 2 | 3 | (B) | 1 | 2 | 3 | 4 |
| (C) | 1 | 4 | 2 | 3 | (D) | 4 | 3 | 2 | 1 |

83 Soil erosion can be divided into
(A) run - off erosion (B) sheet erosion
(C) splash erosion (D) All of the above

84 Which of the following is measured by the porometer?
(A) Soil fertility (B) Soil salinity
(C) Soil acidity (D) All of these

85 The soil's fertility can be increased by growing more of
(A) food grains (B) leguminous plants
(C) fibre crops (D) None of these

86 Which of the following is true about laterite soils?
(A) They are formed as a result of leaching
(B) They are rich in minerals such as aluminium and iron
(C) They are found in hot and wet tropical areas
(D) All of the above

87 Which of the following is not a renewable natural resource?
(A) Clean air (B) Fresh water
(C) Fertile soil (D) Salt

88 Which of the following types of energy resources can last indefinitely or for a very long time due to judicious use?
(A) Non-renewable (B) Renewable
(C) Domestic (D) None of these

89 The ultimate source of energy is
(A) plants (B) animals
(C) bacteria (D) sun

90 The disadvantage of solar energy are
(A) it is difficult to store and run heavy machines
(B) it can be produced in tropical and sub tropical areas only
(C) its technology is still expensive and involves high installation
(D) All of the above

91 Which of the following statement is/are incorrect about tidal energy?
(A) It is a form of hydropower that converts the energy from tides to electricity
(B) It consist of a heat pump air delivery system and a heat exchange system of pipes
(C) It is an environment friendly energy
(D) It is effective at low speeds

92 The fuel used in the conventional nuclear reactor is
(A) cadmium (B) radium
(C) uranium (D) thorium

93 Thermal power generation in India is carried out by burning
(A) natural gas (B) coal
(C) oil (D) All of these

94 Which one of the following is not a renewable energy source?
(A) Solar (B) Coal
(C) Wave (D) Wind

95 The nuclear fuel used in the fast breeder reactor is
(A) cadmium (B) radium
(C) uranium (D) thorium

96 Hydroelectric power is
(A) produced with the help of dams
(B) renewable energy source
(C) not contributing to global warming
(D) All of the above

97 The second most important source after fossil fuels contributing to India's energy needs is
(A) solar energy
(B) nuclear energy
(C) hydro-power
(D) wind energy

98 Which of the following is a conventional source of energy?
(A) Coal (B) Wind energy
(C) Solar energy (D) Natural gas

**99** Biomass gasification is considered to be one of the sustainable solutions to power crises in India. In this context, which of the following statemnts is/are correct?

1. Coconut shells, groundnut shells and rice husk can be used in biomass gasification.
2. The combustible gases generated from biomass gasification consist of hydrogen and carbon dioxide only.
3. The combustible gages generated from biomass generation can be used for direct heat genertion but not in internal combustion engines.

Select the correct answer using the codes given below.

(A) Only 1 (B) Only 2 and 3
(C) Only 1 and 3 (D) 1, 2 and 3

## Natural Hazards and Disasters and their Mitigation

**100** Occurrence of Natural Hazards is affected by

(i) Land use changes
(ii) Drainage and construction
(iii) Ozone depletion
(iv) Climate change

Choose the correct answer from the codes given below.

(A) (i), (ii) and (iii)
(B) (i), (ii) and (iv)
(C) (i), (iii) and (iv)
(D) (ii), (iii) and (iv)

**101** Match the following.

| List I (Zones) | List II (Areas) |
|---|---|
| A. Least damage risk zone | 1. The areas of Southern and South |
| B. Moderate damage risk zone | 2. Jammu and Kashmir, Himachal Pradesh |
| C. High damage risk zone | 3. Kutch region of Gujarat |
| D. Very high dmage risk zone | 4. Portions of plains of North Bihar and West Bengal |

**Codes**

| | A | B | C | D |
|---|---|---|---|---|
| (A) | 4 | 1 | 2 | 3 |
| (B) | 1 | 2 | 3 | 4 |
| (C) | 3 | 2 | 1 | 4 |
| (D) | 4 | 3 | 1 | 2 |

**102** What is the main cause for the occurrence of tsunamis?

(A) Because of ocean floor movement, induced by an earthquake and producing gigantic waves
(B) As a result of hurricane
(C) Volcanic eruption in the sea
(D) None of the above

**103** The main effect of volcanic eruptions is

(A) flying of ash contents
(B) mud slides
(C) low temperatures on earth's surface
(D) All of the above

**104** Which of the following is a method to prevent flood?

(A) Levees
(B) Winding streams
(C) Efficient sewage systems
(D) All of the above

**105** Which of the following is an effective protection against cyclones and tsunamis?

(A) Shrimp farms (B) Building walls
(C) Mangrove forests (D) None of the above

**106** Which of the following is/are the main objectives of National Disaster Management policy 2009?

(A) Promoting a culture of prevention, preparedness and resilience at all levels through knowledge, innovation and education
(B) Promoting a productive and proactive partnership with media for disaster management
(C) Ensuring efficient response and relief with a caring approach towards the need of poor section of society
(D) All of the above

**107** Match List I and List II and select the correct answer from the codes given below.

| List I | List II |
|---|---|
| A. Flood | 1. Lack of rainfall of sufficient duration |
| B. Drought | 2. Tremors produced by the passage of vibratory waves through the rocks of the Earth |
| C. Earthquake | 3. A vent through which molted substances come out |
| D. Volcano | 4. Excess rain and uneven distribution of water |

**Codes**

| | A | B | C | D | | A | B | C | D |
|---|---|---|---|---|---|---|---|---|---|
| (A) | 4 | 1 | 2 | 3 | (B) | 2 | 3 | 4 | 1 |
| (C) | 3 | 4 | 2 | 1 | (D) | 4 | 3 | 1 | 2 |

**108** Which of the following is wrong statement?
I. Floods can be caused by natural, ecological or anthropogenic factors.
II. Anthropogenic activities such as deforestation and shifting cultivation can also contribute to floods.
Which of the following statements is/are correct?
(A) Only I (B) Only II
(C) Both I and II (D) None of these

**109** 'Lahar' is a natural disaster involving
(A) eruption of large amount of material
(B) strong winds
(C) strong water waves
(D) strong winds and water waves

**110** The cyclone 'Hudhud' hit the coast of which state?
(A) Andhra Pradesh (B) Karnataka
(C) Kerala (D) Gujarat

**111** Which of the following types of natural hazards have the highest potential to cause damage to humans?
(A) Earthquakes
(B) Forest fires
(C) Volcanic eruptions
(D) Droughts & floods

**112** Important measure to mitigate landslide is/are
(A) Techniques of slope stablilisation can help in checking the occurrence of landslides.
(B) Landslide prone zones along highways etc., can be identified and structures like retaining walls can be constructed to prevent movement of rocks
(C) Maintaining a good tree cover on mountains can also help in checking the frequency of landslides
(D) All of the above

**113** Which of the following is the objective of National Solar Mission of NAPCC?
(A) To create solar energy competition with fossil fuel based energy options
(B) To establish solar research centre
(C) To increase government funding and international support
(D) All of the above

**114** In which year National Action Plan on Climate Change was launched?
(A) 2000 (B) 2003 (C) 2008 (D) 2012

**115** How many missions were launched under NAPCC in 2008?
(A) Six (B) Eight
(C) Eleven (D) Fifteen

**116** Which of the following is a part of National Action Plan on Climate Change?
I. National Mission for a Green India.
II. National Water Mission.
III. National Solar Mission.
IV. National Mission for Sustainable Agriculture.
**Codes**
(A) Only I (B) II and III
(C) I and IV (D) All of these

**117** The work of forests includes
(A) These provide oxygen to breathe
(B) These reduce greenhouse gases
(C) These hold soil at its place
(D) All of the above

**118** India has protected areas about
(A) 500 (B) 615
(C) 771 (D) 815

**119** Nagoya Protocol is related to
(A) climate change
(B) ozone depletion
(C) hazardous waste
(D) biodiversity

**120** Which of the following statements are indicative of the vision of Blue revolution?
I. Promoting development of Botanical Gardens.
II. Creating an enabling environment for the full potential of fisheries in the country.
III. Improving the income status of fish farmers keeping in view the sustainability concerns.
IV. Encouraging scientific research in forestry to increase the vegetative cover.
V. Promoting integrated development of fisheries of the country.
VI. Undertaking research in new areas like marine fin fish.
Select the correct answer using the codes given below.
(A) II, IV and V (B) II, III and I
(C) II, III and V (D) I, IV and VI

## National and International Efforts/ Agreements to Conserve Environment

**121** Consider the following statements regarding environment.

I. According to the Environment Protection Act, 1986 environment includes water, air and land.

II. The flora, fauna and microorganisms as well as the man-made structure in our surroundings have a bidirectional interaction with us directly or indirectly.

Which of the above statements is/are correct?

(A) Only I (B) Only II
(C) Both I and II (D) Neither I nor II

**122** Match List I with List II.

| List I | List II |
|---|---|
| A. Rio Summit | 1. 1997 |
| B. Johannesburg Earth Summit | 2. 1972 |
| C. Kyoto Protocol | 3. 1992 |
| D. Stockholm Conference | 4. 2002 |

**Codes**

| | A | B | C | D |
|---|---|---|---|---|
| (A) | 3 | 4 | 1 | 2 |
| (B) | 1 | 2 | 3 | 4 |
| (C) | 4 | 3 | 2 | 1 |
| (D) | 2 | 1 | 4 | 3 |

**123** Kyoto protocol is related to

(A) ozone depletion (B) hazardous waste
(C) climate change (D) nuclear energy

**124** The main aim of Kyoto protocol is to

(A) require concessions from all countries involved equally in greenhouse gas emission
(B) required increases in nuclear power generation
(C) would have resulted in overall increases in greenhouse emissions
(D) reduce emissions of six greenhouse gases to levels lower than those of 1990

**125** In order to avoid catastrophic consequences of climate change, there is general agreement among the countries of the world to limit the rise in average surface temperature of Earth compared to that of pre-industrial times by

(A) 1.5 °C to 2°C
(B) 2.0 °C to 3.5°C
(C) 0.5 °C to 1.0 °C
(D) 0.25 °C to 0.5°C

**126** Consider the following statement(s) is/are incorrect with regarded to the Environment Protection Act 1986.

(A) The Act empowers both the centre and the state to take all such measures as it deem necessary.
(B) The Act provides provision for penalties.
(C) If a failure or violation occurs for more than one year the offender may be punished with imprisonment which may be extended to 7 years.
(D) For each failure or violation punishment included a prison term up to 5 years.

**127** National Disaster Management Plan, 2016 is based on which priority themes of the Sendai Framework.

(A) Understanding disaster risk
(B) Improving disaster risk
(C) Investing in disaster risk reduction and disaster preparedness
(D) All of the above

**128** In which year India became a contracting party to the Ramsar Convention?

(A) 1980 (B) 1981
(C) 1975 (D) 1971

**129** Match the following.

| List I (Ramsar Sites) | List II (State) |
|---|---|
| A. Ashtamudi Wetland | 1. Jammu and Kashmir |
| B. Hokera Wetland | 2. Himachal Pradesh |
| C. Renuka Wetland | 3. Madhya Pradesh |
| D. Bhoj Wetland | 4. Kerala |

**Codes**

| | A | B | C | D |
|---|---|---|---|---|
| (A) | 1 | 2 | 3 | 4 |
| (B) | 4 | 3 | 2 | 1 |
| (C) | 4 | 1 | 2 | 3 |
| (D) | 3 | 4 | 1 | 2 |

**130** The effects of cyclones can be mitigated through effective and efficient mitigation policies and strategies, They are

I. installation of early warning systems.
II. developing communication infrastructure.
III. developing shelter belts.
IV. developing community cyclone shelters.

Select the correct answer using the codes given below.

(A) I, II and IV
(B) I, III and IV
(C) II, III and IV
(D) All of these

**131** In which year the Convention of Biological diversity enacted?
(A) 1997 (B) 1998
(C) 1992 (D) 1999

**132** In what ways the Paris Agreement (CoP 21, 2015) was different from the Kyoto protocol?
(A) It provided a framework for all countries to take steps to curb climate change
(B) The agreement covered all crucial areas and balanced agreement including miligation adaptation, loss and damage technology
(C) Development and transfer and capacity building
(D) Both (A) and (B)

**133** How many countries joined International Solar Alliance (2015) in 2016?
(A) 130 (B) 121 (C) 125 (D) 120

**134** What were the key outcomes of Bonn, Germany (CoP 23, 2017)?
(A) It was agreed that the financial issues regarding the climate change must be adressed and rich countries must take the responsibility of it
(B) It was decided that the negotiation will keep working for one year and finalsi rule book by December, 2018
(C) It was also decided that the Adaptation fund under Kyoto protocol can become the part of the Paris Agreement to deal with the financial crunch
(D) All of the above

**135** Where was CoP 24, 2018 held?
(A) Bonn, Germany
(B) Katowice, Polland
(C) Lima, Peru
(D) Rio de Janerio, Brazil

**136** Which of the following were the focal issues of Marrakech climate change conference, 2016?
(A) Water scarcity
(B) Water cleanliness
(C) Water related sustainability
(D) All of the above

**137** What is the main objective of convention on biodiversity?
(A) The conservation of biological diversity
(B) The sustainable use of the components of biological diversity
(C) The fair and equitable sharing of the benefits Grising out of the utilisation of generic resources
(D) All of the above

**138** When was Marrakech climate change conference was held?
(A) 2018 (B) 2017
(C) 2016 (D) 2014

**139** What after measures were taken to control climate change?
(a) Carban Ofteset (b) Carbon tax
(c) Carbon Trading (d) All of the above

**140** Which of the following statement (s) is/are correct about carbon tax?
(A) It is a reduction in emission of carbon dioxide
(B) It is another form of carbon pricing
(C) It is a tax on energy sources which emits carbon dioxide
(D) It is a process of removing carbon from the atmosphere and storing it in carbon sink

**141** Where and when was the convention for the protection of the ozone layer held?
(A) Stockholm, 1972 (B) Vienna, 1985
(C) Basel, 1989 (D) Nagoya 2010

# *Previous Years' Questions*

## UGC NET-June 2019

1 One of the main outcomes of the Rio+20 conference was to develop a set of:
(A) Sustainable Development Goals
(B) Millennium Development Goals
(C) National Development Strategy
(D) National Land Restoration Strategy

2 The time frame for the implementation of Millennium Development Goals was:
(A) 2000–2005 (B) 2000–2015
(C) 2005–2010 (D) 2000–2012

3 Oligotrophic lakes are characterised by:
(A) High level of nutrients
(B) Low level of nutrients
(C) Absence of nutrients
(D) High level of organic matter

4 With increase in temperature, the dissolved oxygen content in a water body will:
(A) decreases
(B) increases
(C) remain constant
(D) may increase or decrease depending on the temperature range

5 Consider the following statements in the context of Millennium Development Goals (MDGs) adopted by the United Nations.
1. Eradicate extreme poverty and hunger.
2. Improve maternal health.
3. Responsible consumption and production.
4. Reduce child mortality.

Choose the correct answer from the options given below.
(A) 1, 2 and 3 (B) 2, 3 and 4
(C) 1, 2 and 4 (D) 1, 3 and 4

6 **Assertion** (A) Night time temperature in the central parts of a city are generally higher than those over the surrounding rural areas.

**Reason** (R) Radiation losses over the urban areas are less than that over the rural areas.
Choose the correct answer from the options given below:
(A) Both (A) and (R) are true and (R) is the correct explanation of (A)
(B) Both (A) and (R) are true, but (R) is not the correct explanation of (A)
(C) (A) is true, but (R) is false
(D) (A) is false, but (R) is true

7 Which of the following disasters belongs to the category of nuclear disasters?
1. Fukushima disaster
2. Chernobyl disaster
3. Three mile Island incident
4. The love canal disaster

Choose your answer from the options given below:
(A) (1), (2) and (3)
(B) (1), (2) and (3)
(C) (1), (3) and (4)
(D) (2), (3) and (4)

8 The Paris Agreement aims to limit the temperature rise in this century by how many degrees Celsius above the pre-industrial levels?
(A) 1° C (B) 2° C (C) 0.5°C (D) 3° C

9 **Statement I** Most of the member countries in the International Solar Alliance are located between the Tropic of Cancer and Tropic of Capricorn.

**Statement II** Japan is a member country of the International Solar Alliance.

Which of the above statement is/are correct?
(A) I only
(B) II only
(C) Both I and II
(D) Neither I nor II

10 **Assertion** (A) High concentration of ozone in the troposphere is desirable.

**Reason** (R) Ozone present in the atmosphere protects the living organisms on the surface of Earth from the harmful ultraviolet radiation of the Sun.

Choose the correct answer from the options given below.
(A) Both (A) and (R) are true and (R) is the correct explanation of (A)
(B) Both (A) and (R) true, but (R) is not the correct explanation of (A)
(C) (A) is true, but (R) is false
(D) (A) is false, but (R) is true

11 Algal blooms in oligotrophic lakes are:
(A) very frequent
(B) frequent
(C) very rare
(D) widespread

**12** Which of the following are priority areas in relation to the Sustainable Development Goals?
1. No poverty
2. Zero hunger
3. Reducing urbanisation
4. Peace, justice and strong institution

Choose the correct answer from the options given below:
(A) (1), (2)
(B) (1), (3), (4)
(C) (2), (3), (4)
(D) (1), (2), (4)

**13** **Assertion** (A) Methemoglobinemia is a condition in which blood is not able to carry and deliver enough oxygen to the body.
**Reason** (R) Consuming drinking water with high nitrate levels may cause methemoglobinemia.
Choose the correct answer from the options given below.
(A) Both (A) and (R) are true and (R) is the correct explanation of (A)
(B) Both (A) and (R) are true, but (R) is not the correct explanation of (A)
(C) (A) is true, but (R) is false
(D) (A) is false, but (R) is true

**14** In the last few years, India has been affected by which of the following tropical cyclones?
(A) Gaja, Hudhud, Bhima
(B) Hudhud, Bhima, Ockhi
(C) Gaja, Hudhud, Ockhi
(D) Gaja, Bhima, Ockhi

**15** Which pollutant is the major source of marine pollution?
(A) Agricultural run-off
(B) Oil spill
(C) Industrial wastewater
(D) Sewage

**16** Permafrost is defining characteristic of which biome?
(A) Taiga (B) Tundra
(C) Grassland (D) Desert

**17** The mangroves exist in:
(A) Fresh water system
(B) Temperate areas
(C) Semi-arid areas
(D) Saline waters

**18** Which of the following statements best explains the concept of sustainable development?
(A) Use of natural resources minimally
(B) Use of natural resources for our benefit
(C) Use of natural resources judiciously so that they are available for further generations
(D) Preserve our natural resources for our future generation

**19** Chemical oxygen demand in eutrophic water is
(A) low (B) high
(C) medium (D) extremely low

**20** Montreal protocol aims at
(A) reduction in emissions of greenhouse gases
(B) phasing out ozone depleting substances
(C) prohibiting transboundary movement of hazardous waste
(D) enhancing cooperation among UN member states for peaceful uses of nuclear energy

**21** SMTP is an acronym for:
(A) Simple Mail Transport Protocol
(B) Simple Mail Terminal Protocol
(C) Simple Mail Transfer Protocol
(D) Simple Mail Transition Protocol

**22** **Statement I** Earthquake 'A' is 5 on Richter scale and Earthquake 'B' is 8 on the same scale. Earthquake 'B' has 1000 times the wave amplitude compared to 'A'.
**Statement II** The energy released in 'B' is three times that of 'A'.
Choose the correct option:
(A) Statement I is correct and Statement II is incorrect
(B) Statements I and II are correct
(C) Statement II is correct and I is incorrect
(D) Statements I and II are incorrect

**23** Taj Mahal is mainly threatened by the deleterious effects of:
(A) Sulphur dioxide (B) Chlorine
(C) Oxygen (D) Hydrogen

**24** In large parts of Eastern India, the ground water is contaminated by:
(A) Arsenic (B) Lead (C) Mercury (D) Nickel

**25** Efficiency of electrical power generation is least amongst the following sources of energy in case of:
(A) Solar (B) Wind
(C) Geothermal (D) Nuclear

**26** During the period 2014-2018, which zone exhibits cyclic variation?
(A) East zone (B) West zone
(C) Central zone (D) South zone

**27** Choose the set of non-renewable resources.
(A) Uranium, natural gas, oil
(B) Natural gas, uranium, phosphates
(C) Petroleum, uranium, geothermal energy
(D) Shale gas, uranium, soil

**28** One of the parameters used to characterise the air quality at a location is PM2.5. Here, the suffix '2.5' refers to:
(A) average number of suspected particles in 10 $cm^3$ of air
(B) size of suspended particles in certain units
(C) concentration of oxides of sulphur and nitrogen
(D) concentration of suspended particles in 2.5 m3 of air

**29** Which of the following diseases are due to polluted water?
1. Giardiasis 2. Dengue
3. Amoebiasis 4. Typhoid

Choose the correct answer from the options given below
(A) 1, 2 and 4 (B) 2, 3 and 4
(C) 1, 2, 3 arid 4 (D) 1, 3 and 4

**30** Which of the following is non-vehicular pollutant?
(A) Chlorofluorocarbon (B) Carbon monoxide
(C) Hydrocarbon (D) Particular matter

**31** Which of the following is the largest sink of $_2$ gas?
(A) Forests (B) Oceans
(C) Ice sheets (D) Grasslands

## UGC NET- July 2018

**32** **Assertion** (A) Indoor air pollution is a serious health hazard.

**Reason** (R) The dispersal of air pollutants is rather limited in indoor environment.

Choose the correct answer from the codes given below.
(A) (A) is true and (R) is false
(B) Both (A) and (R) are false
(C) Both (A) and (R) are true and (R) is the correct explanation of (A)
(D) Both (A) and (R) are true, but R is not the correct explanation of (A)

**33** Which of the following is considered as major source of pollution in rivers of India?
(A) Agricultural run-off
(B) Thermal power plants
(C) Unregulated small scale industry
(D) Untreated sewage

**34** 'Fly-ash' produced in thermal power plants is an eco-friendly resource for use in
I. agriculture as micro-nutrient.
II. wasteland development.
III. dam and water holding structures.
IV. brick industry.

Choose the correct answer from the codes given below.
(A) I, III and IV (B) I, II, III and IV
(C) I, II and IV (D) II, III and IV

**35** Which of the following types of natural disasters has no definite beginning and end?
(A) Hurricanes (B) Droughts
(C) Earthquakes (D) Landslides

## UGC NET-December 2018

**36** Recently in Brazil, a bacterium exhibited antibiotic resistance, which was not reported previously
(A) *Pseudomonas* species
(B) *Salmonella* species
(C) *Klebsiella* species
(D) *Streptococcus* species

**37** One of the following has a positive human influence on the environment?
(A) Deforestation (B) over population
(C) Pollution (D) Conservation

**38** **Assertion** (A) The environmental impact of soil erosion can best be mitigated by removing vegetative cover only from the specific site in which construction is to take place.

**Reason** (R) The environmental impact of soil erosion can also be mitigated by disturbing the vegetation in adjacent areas as little as possible.
(A) Both (A) and (R) are true and (R) is the correct explanation of (A)
(B) Both (A) and (R) are true, but (R) is not correct explanation of (A)
(C) (A) is true, but (R) is false
(D) (A) is false, but (R) is true

**39** **Assertion** (A) Hydropower is an exhaustible energy resource.

**Reason** (R) The power of falling water would neither diminish nor get exhausted.

(A) Both (A) and (R) are true and (R) is the correct explanation of (A)

(B) Both (A) and (R) are true but (R) is not the correct explanation of (A)

(C) (A) is true, but (R) is false

(D) Both (A) and (R) is false

**40** In the scheme of life, soil is an essential resource of life, as it plays the following roles.

(i) It is a reservoir of carbon.

(ii) It is the medium for growth of food and energy for the animal world.

(iii) It provides oxygen to the biotic community

(iv) It is a natural reservoir for the huge amount of water.

Select the correct answer from the above.

(A) (i), (ii) and (iii)

(B) (i), (ii) and (iv)

(C) (ii), (iii) and (iv)

(D) (i), (iii) and (iv)

## UGC NET-June 2017

**41** Which of the following is a source of emissions leading to the eventual formation of surface ozone as a pollutant?

(A) Transport sector

(B) Refrigeration and air-conditioning

(C) Wetlands

(D) Fertilizers

**42** **Assertion** (A) Sustainable development is critical to well-being of human society.

**Reason** (R) Environmentally sound policies do not harm the environment or deplete the natural resources.

Choose the correct code.

(A) Both (A) and (R) are correct and (R) is the correct explanation of (A)

(B) Both (A) and (R) are correct but (R) is not the correct explanation of (A)

(C) (A) is true and (R) is false

(D) (A) is false and (R) is true

## UGC NET-November 2017

**43** **Assertion** (A) In urban areas, smog episodes occur frequently in winters.

**Reason** (R) In winters, a lot of biomass is burnt by people for heating purposes or to keep themselves warm.

Choose the correct answer from the codes given below.

(A) Both (A) and (R) are true, but (R) is not the correct explanation of (A)

(B) (A) is true, but (R) is false

(C) Both (A) and (R) is false

(D) Both (A) and (R) are true and (R) is the correct explanation of (A)

**44** Which of the following pollutants is the major cause of respiratory diseases?

(A) Nitrogen oxides

(B) Carbon monoxide

(C) Volatile organic compounds

(D) Suspended find particles

**45** Which of the following pollutant gases is not produced both naturally and as a result of industrial activity?

(A) Nitrous oxide

(B) Methane

(C) Carbon dioxide

(D) Chlorofluorocarbons

**46** Among the following fuels of energy, which is the most environment friendly?

(A) Biogas (B) CNG

(C) Hydrogen (D) Ethanol

**47** Occurrence of natural hazards is affected by

I. land use changes.

II. drainage and construction.

III. ozone depletion.

IV. climate change.

Choose the correct answer from the codes given below.

(A) I, II and III (B) I, II and IV

(C) II, III and IV (D) I, III and IV

## UGC NET-January 2017

**48** The dominant source of pollutant due to oxides of nitrogen ($NO_x$) in urban areas is

(A) road transport

(B) commercial sector

(C) energy use in industry

(D) power plants

**49** Which of the following is not a water-borne disease?
(A) Typhoid (B) Hepatitis
(C) Cholera (D) Dengue

**50** Which of the following natural hazards is not hydro-meteorological?
(A) Snow avalanche (B) Sea erosion
(C) Tropical cyclone (D) Tsunami

**51** In which country, the recent international agreement on phasing out Hydro Fluoro Carbons (HCFs) was signed?
(A) Rawanda (B) Morocco
(C) South Africa (D) Algeria

## UGC NET-July 2016

**52** Which of the following is the largest source of water pollution in major rivers of India?
(A) Untreated sewage
(B) Agriculture run-off
(C) Unregulated small scale industries
(D) Religious practices

**53** **Assertion** (A) Conserving our soil resources is critical to human survival.
**Reason** (R) Soil is home to many microorganisms and contains minerals.
Choose the correct code.
(A) Both (A) and (R) are correct and (R) is the correct explanation of (A)
(B) Both (A) and (R) are correct, but (R) is not the correct explanation of (A)
(C) (A) is true and (R) is false
(D) (A) is false and (R) is true

**54** Identify the air pollutant in urban areas which irritates eyes and also respiratory tract of human beings.
(A) Particulate matter
(B) Oxides of nitrogen
(C) Surface ozone
(D) Carbon monoxide

**55** Sustainable development goals have specific targets to be achieved by?
(A) 2022 (B) 2030
(C) 2040 (D) 2050

## UGC NET-June 2015

**56** India's contribution to total global carbon dioxide emissions is about
(A) ~ 3% (B) ~6%
(C) ~10% (D) ~15%

**57** In the recently launched Air Quality Index in India, which of the following pollutants is not included?
(A) Carbon monoxide
(B) Fine particulate matter
(C) Ozone
(D) Chlorofluorocarbons

**58** Which of the following combinations represent renewable natural resources?
(A) Fertile soil, fresh water and natural gas
(B) Clean air, phosphates and biological diversity
(C) Fishes, fertile soil and fresh water
(D) Oil, forests and tides

**59** Two earthquakes A and B happen to be of magnitude 5 and 6, respectively on Richter scale. The ratio of the energies released $E_B / E_A$ will be approximately
(A) ~8 (B) ~16 (C) ~32 (D) ~64

**60** The factors which are most important in determining the impact of anthropogenic activities on environment are
(A) population, affluence per person, land available per person
(B) population, affluence per person and the technology used for exploiting resources
(C) atmospheric conditions, population and forest cover
(D) population, forest cover and land available per person

## UGC NET-December 2015

**61** The most hazardous metal pollutant of automobile exhausts is
(A) mercury (B) cadmium
(C) lead (D) copper

**62** Inside rural homes, the source/sources of nitrogen oxide pollution may be
I. Unvented gas stoves
II. Wood stoves
III. Kerosene heaters
Select the correct answer using the codes given below.
(A) Only II (B) I and II
(C) II and III (D) I, II and III

**63** Which of the following pollutants can cause cancer in humans?
(A) Ozone (B) Pesticides
(C) Mercury (D) Lead

**64** Which of the following phenomena is not a natural hazard?
(A) Chemical contamination
(B) Wildfire
(C) Lightning
(D) Landslide

**65** As part of National Climate Change Policy, Indian Government is planning to raise the installed capacity of renewable energy by the year 2030 to
(A) 350 GW (B) 175 GW
(C) 200 GW (D) 250 GW

**66** **Assertion** (A) Population control measures do not necessarily help in checking environmental degradation.
**Reason** (R) The relationship between population growth and environmental degradations is rather complex.
(A) A is false, but R is true
(B) Both A and R are true and R is the correct explanation of A
(C) Both A and R are true, but R is not the correct explanation of A
(D) A is true, but R is false

# ANSWERS

## Chapter Practice

| | | | | | | | | | |
|---|---|---|---|---|---|---|---|---|---|
| 1 (B) | 2 (D) | 3 (C) | 4 (D) | 5 (C) | 6 (B) | 7 (B) | 8 (D) | 9 (C) | 10 (C) |
| 11 (B) | 12 (C) | 13 (C) | 14 (D) | 15 (C) | 16 (D) | 17 (B) | 18 (D) | 19 (A) | 20 (A) |
| 21 (B) | 22 (B) | 23 (D) | 24 (C) | 25 (D) | 26 (D) | 27 (D) | 28 (D) | 29 (D) | 30 (D) |
| 31 (A) | 32 (D) | 33 (A) | 34 (D) | 35 (C) | 36 (B) | 37 (A) | 38 (B) | 39 (D) | 40 (C) |
| 41 (D) | 42 (D) | 43 (B) | 44 (A) | 45 (D) | 46 (A) | 47 (D) | 48 (D) | 49 (B) | 50 (B) |
| 51 (C) | 52 (D) | 53 (D) | 54 (A) | 55 (B) | 56 (D) | 57 (B) | 58 (D) | 59 (C) | 60 (B) |
| 61 (B) | 62 (C) | 63 (C) | 64 (A) | 65 (A) | 66 (D) | 67 (D) | 68 (B) | 69 (B) | 70 (A) |
| 71 (A) | 72 (B) | 73 (D) | 74 (D) | 75 (B) | 76 (C) | 77 (C) | 78 (D) | 79 (D) | 80 (D) |
| 81 (A) | 82 (A) | 83 (D) | 84 (C) | 85 (C) | 86 (D) | 87 (D) | 88 (D) | 89 (D) | 90 (D) |
| 91 (B) | 92 (A) | 93 (B) | 94 (A) | 95 (B) | 96 (C) | 97 (A) | 98 (D) | 99 (A) | 100 (B) |
| 101 (A) | 102 (C) | 103 (B) | 104 (C) | 105 (B) | 106 (C) | 107 (B) | 108 (D) | 109 (A) | 110 (C) |
| 111 (B) | 112 (A) | 113 (C) | 114 (D) | 115 (B) | 116 (D) | 117 (D) | 118 (D) | 119 (A) | 120 (A) |
| 121 (C) | 122 (A) | 123 (A) | 124 (D) | 125 (B) | 126 (D) | 127 (A) | 128 (B) | 129 (C) | 130 (D) |
| 131 (C) | 132 (D) | 133 (B) | 134 (D) | 135 (B) | 136 (D) | 137 (D) | 138 (C) | 139 (D) | 140 (C) |
| 141 (B) | | | | | | | | | |

## Previous Years' Questions

| | | | | | | | | | |
|---|---|---|---|---|---|---|---|---|---|
| 1 (A) | 2 (B) | 3 (B) | 4 (A) | 5 (C) | 6 (A) | 7 (A) | 8 (B) | 9 (C) | 10 (D) |
| 11 (C) | 12 (D) | 13 (A) | 14 (C) | 15 (B) | 16 (C) | 17 (D) | 18 (D) | 19 (A) | 20 (B) |
| 21 (C) | 22 (A) | 23 (A) | 24 (A) | 25 (C) | 26 (A) | 27 (A) | 28 (B) | 29 (D) | 30 (A) |
| 31 (B) | 32 (A) | 33 (D) | 34 (D) | 35 (B) | 36 (B) | 37 (D) | 38 (B) | 39 (A) | 40 (B) |
| 41 (A) | 42 (B) | 43 (A) | 44 (D) | 45 (D) | 46 (C) | 47 (B) | 48 (A) | 49 (D) | 50 (D) |
| 51 (A) | 52 (A) | 53 (B) | 54 (C) | 55 (B) | 56 (B) | 57 (A) | 58 (C) | 59 (C) | 60 (B) |
| 61 (C) | 62 (D) | 63 (B) | 64 (A) | 65 (D) | 66 (A) | | | | |

# UNIT 10

# *Higher Education System*

CHAPTER ANALYSIS

This unit is based on the updated syllabus of NTA UGC Net covering the important topics related to Higher Education System. After going through the chapter you will be able to understand about the institutions of higher learning and education in ancient India, evolution of higher learning & research in post-independence India, oriental, conventional and non-conventional programs, policies ,governance and administration.

Every year 4 to 5 questions are asked from this unit in NTA UGC Net exam, which are based on educational committees, structure of higher education, polices, governance etc.

## EDUCATION

Education plays an important role in the development of human resources of a nation. Its importance has been realised since time immemorial and continues right upto today. It plays an important role in economic, cultural and social development. Education is a lifelong learning process. Education is both acquisition of knowledge and experiences as well as the development of skills, values, habits and attitudes which help to lead a worthwhile life in this world. It helps in the holistic development of the child personality.

IN THIS UNIT

- Institutions of Higher Learning and Education in Ancient India
- Evolution of Higher Learning and Research in Post Independence India
- Oriental, Conventional and Non-conventional Learning Programmes in India
- Professional, Technical and Skill Based Education
- Value Education and Environmental Education
- Policies, Governance and Administration

### Definitions of Education

In the words of **Pestalozzi**, "Education is natural, harmonious and progressive development of man's innate power."

According to **Swami Dayanand**, "Education is a supreme and most important moral process for the development of mankind."

In the words of **Aristotle**, "Education is the creation of sound mind in a sound body."

According to **Sri Aurobindo**, "Education means helping the growing soul to draw out that is in itself."

According to **John Dewey**, "Education is the process of continuous reconstruction of experience."

### → Four Pillars of Education

The United Nations Educational, Scientific and Cultural Organisation (UNESCO) states that education throughout life is based on four pillars that are :

- **Learning to Know** : It implies learning how to learn by developing one's concentration, memory skills and ability to think.
- **Learning to Do** : It means putting knowledge and learning into practice innovatively through skills development and practical know how . Development of competence life skills, personal qualities, aptitudes and attitudes.
- **Learning to Live Together** : It involves the development of social skills and values.
- **Learning to Be** : It involves activities that foster personal development (body, mind and spint) and contribute to creativity, personal discovery and an appreciation of the inherent value provided by these pursuits.

Education is the process of training an individual through various experiences of life draws out the best within him. "Education frequently takes place in formal and informal settings. Thus, we can say that education is the process of facilitating learning or the aquisition of basic knowledge, skills, values, beliefs and habits which teaches us to be a true human being.

# TYPES OF EDUCATION

Education frequently takes place in formal and informal settings.

## 1. Informal Education

Informal education is a general term of education that can occur outside of a structured curriculum not systematically organised, not observed any formalities, rules and regulations and discipline. It is the type of knowledge that one gains through several life experiences and encounters that one faces throughout their life by the means of conversation and exploration. The knowledge that one obtains in this type of education is given by parents and elders.It does not contain the theoretical knowledge of the books and knowledge is gained outside the classroom under the influence of society and community.

Informal education is an educative activity which is neither pre-planned nor deliberate. The child learns many habits, manners and patterns while living with others or moving in different spheres like home, society groups, etc. It is not imparted by any specialised agencies. Informal education is not given by any fixed time table.

Informal education would also include all incidental learning that takes place while at work or at play and during travels as well as spontaneous learning through films, radio and television.

## 2. Formal Education

It is a classroom based education provided by trained teachers in a systematic way within school, higher education institute or university. Formal education is fixed and limited to a period meant for teaching and learning with a fixed point of entry and exit. It takes place full time and does not permit other parallel activites. It observes strict discipline.

The student and the teacher both are aware of the fact and engage themselves in the process of education. It may however be said that any process of teaching which involves, supervision, set plan, instruction, definite aims and principles amounts to formal education.

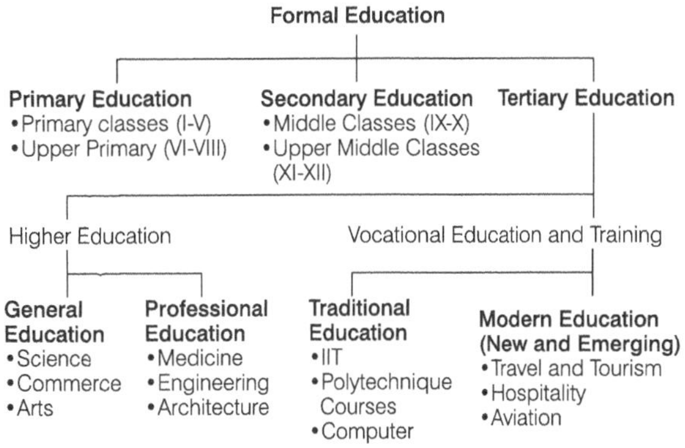

### (i) Primary Education

It is the first stage of formal education after pre-school and before secondary school. Primary education provides students with basic understanding of various subjects as well as the skills that they will use throughout their lives.

In India in regards to primary education the 86th Constitutional Amendment 2002 inserted Article 21A in the Constitution, making the Right to Education a Fundamental Right.

The right of children to free and compulsory Education Act 2009 became operative in the country on 1st April, 2010.

The act has major provisions such as

- Every child between the age of six to fourteen years shall have a right to free and compulsory education in neighbourhood school till completion of elementary education.
- No child shall be liable to pay any kind of fee or charges or expenses.
- The Central and State Governments shall have concurrent responsibility for providing funds for carrying out the provisions of this act.

### (ii) Secondary Education

Secondary education focuses on the education of the children aged between 14 to 18. It helps the students to develop a sense of their constitutional rights and duties. At the same time, it develops a logical approach as the students get acquainted with various subjects including maths, science, social studies, english, etc.

Secondary education is split into 2 parts – Secondary (grades 9-10) and Higher Secondary (grades 11-12) with a standardized nationwide examination at the end of grade 10 and grade 12 (usually informally referred to as "board exams").

### (iii) Tertiary Education

It is the tertiary level of education that comes after primary and secondary education. The form of education at this stage is optional higher education which also includes vocational education. The Ministry of Human Resources and Development has defined higher education in two ways.

1. It is a ten year school education and a minimum 3-year duration course.
2. It is obtained after twelve years of school education studies or equivalent study.

Tertiary education is of many types such general, vocational, professional or technical. Higher education is provided by universities, colleges and institutes of technology etc.

There are mainly three levels of higher of education

(i) Graduate level

(ii) Post graduate level

(iii) Research Level which includes research in Ph.D Fellowship for post Doctorate.

Some higher institutes related to higher education offers diploma such as PGDBA, PGDCA, Chartered Accountancy etc. Students who are not interested in higher education can opt for vocational courses which are employment oriented. Examination in vocational education is conducted by All India and State Boards.

# EDUCATION SYSTEM IN INDIA

The history of higher education in India can be understood as per its growth through certain periods which are mentioned below.

## Education in Ancient Period

The history of education in India can be traced to the ancient era. Education in ancient India began around 3rd century BC with elements of religious training and impart of traditional knowledge. In ancient India both formal and informal ways of education system existed. Indigenous education was imparted at home, in temples, pathshalas, tols, chatuspadis and gurukuls.

Education in India dates back to its early civilisation where teaching and learning processes revolved around the **Gurukul system**. This system was based on residential concept wherein the students were educated under the tutorship of a teacher in different areas of religion and philosophy.

The main source of teaching in the ancient education was Vedic literature which represented the most important and intrinsic part of life of the Indian people. In Vedic period, the teacher or Guru used to give knowledge to their pupil on the basis of Vedic literature which consisted of eight different forms such as, Four Vedas, Six Vedangas, Four Upavedas, Four Brahmanas, One Hundred and Eight Upanishads, Six systems of Philosophy, Bhagwad Gita and Three Smritis.

Sanskrit formed the basis of delivering Vedic education. Students were taught in the form of Shruti (listening) and Smriti (memorising).

During Vedic period, pupils used to go to **Gurukuls** (which were the formal institutions of learning) and resided there in order to gain education.

In Gurukul system of education majority of the pupils were boys or male, but there was also a provision for the girl's education.

Apart from Gurukula, Parishads (Academies), Viharas and Sammelans (Conferences) were also among many institutions of higher education.

## Objectives of Education

- Inculcation of spirit of piety and righteousness.
- Formation of good and moral character.
- Preservation and spread of ancient culture.
- Inculcation of social and civic duties.
- Stress on the perfection of the physical, mental and intellectual personality of the student.
- Communication of loyalty and righteousness.

## Examination and Titles

The examination was oral during vedic period. The guru used to verbally ask questions and then decided whether the disciple had attained the knowledge. In vedic period students were not given any certificate. His ability was his certificate. But the students who use to complete 12 years course in Gurukuls or had knowledge of any one Veda were given the title of graduates. For those who completed 24 years course or had knowledge of 2 vedas were given the title of Vasue. For those who had knowledge of 16 years course or were well versed in any three Vedas were given the title Rudra. Those who completed 48 years of course and had knowledge of four vedas were given title of Aditya.

## Four Vedas

There are four types of Vedas which are discussed below:

1. **Rigveda** It is the principal and oldest of the four vedas. It is an ancient Indian collection of vedic hymns. It is counted as one of the four sacred Hindu writings. The Rigveda has 1,028 hymns and 10,600 years. Rigveda mainly contains various hymns for praying to vedic Gods such as Agni, Indra, etc.
2. **Samveda** It is the veda of melodies and chants. It is an ancient vedic text and part of the scriptures of Hinduism. It consists of 1,549 verses.
3. **Yajurveda** It is the veda primarily of prose mantras for worship. It is a compilation of ritual offering formulae that were said by priest.
4. **Atharveda** It is the text belonging to the Atharvan and Angirasa poets. It has about 760 hymns and about 160 of the hymns common with the Rigveda. It is sometimes called Veda of magical formulae. Atharveda has been a primary source for information about vedic culture, customs, beliefs and aspirations of everyday vedic life as well associated with king and governance.

## Types of Teachers

1. **Acharya** A teacher to teach Vedas without charging fee from the students.
2. **Upadhyaya** To earn his livelihood such teachers taught only a portion of the Veda or Vedangas.
3. **Charakas** Wandering scholars who visit the nation for higher knowledge, usually regarded as possible source of knowledge

by Satapatha Brahmana. Hiuen Tsang gained the knowledge this way.

4. **Guru** used to lead a grihastha life by imparting education and by maintaining his family.
5. **Yaujanasatika** They were famous for their profound scholarship, students from distant places would visit them to seek education.
6. **Sikshaka** Instruction in arts such as dancing.

### Methods of Teaching

1. **Oral Teaching** Due to a lack of printing and writing material, especially paper, the books were handwritten. During the Vedic period, there were very fewer books, so teaching was mainly oral. The teacher taught the lessons to the students using spoken words.

   The students listened to the teacher with attention and devotion and committed the texts by heart.
2. **The Question-Answer Method** During the Vedic period, the questions-answer method and discussion were common. The Pupil asked questions and Guru explained. Through this method, the students had to learn their subjects.
3. **Agra-Shishya or Pupil Teacher System** It was a normal practice in Ashrams and Gurukulas that intelligent senior pupil was deputed by the Gurus to teach junior students. This system helped both the pupil-teacher and the students.

## Institutions of Higher Learning

Educational institutions acquired great prominence during ancient period the famous institution of higher learning are as follows

1. **Nalanda** As a Buddhist centre of learning from 427 CE to 1197 CE, Nalanda has been known as one of the first great residential universities in recorded history. Established by Shakraditya of the Gupta Dynasty in the Modern Bihar, Nalanda made unique contributions to the evolution, expansion and refinement for Indian culture.

   The subjects taught at Nalanda covered every field of learning ranging from fine arts to the art of war.

   The library of Nalanda university was the largest library of the ancient world.

   At the beginning of the 12th century the Muslim invader Bakhtiyar Khilji ruined the university.

   In 2010, The Parliament of India passed a bill, approved the plan to restore the ancient Nalanda University as a modern Nalanda International university dedicated for post graduate research.
2. **Taxila or Takshashila** As a chief centre of learning in 6th Century BC, it is often described as the first university established all across the globe. Taxila was not only the centre of higher education but was also an important centre of Brahmanical education with over 60 courses pertaining to different subjects being taught here.

   Taxila was famous for producing many well known scholars including Panini, Grammarian, Kautilya, Charaka (Father of Medicare) and even the ministers of Chandragupta Maurya.
3. **Vikramshila** It was set up-and established by the emperor Dharmpala of Pal dynasty in the 8th century in the Northern Magadha. This university was famous for religious teachings and here 108 scholars were appointed as the incharge of the various temples.

   The main subjects of the study were Vyakaran, logic, philosophy, Tantra Shastra and Karma Kanda later on Tantra Shastra gained prominence. The university was destroyed by Bakhtiyar Khilji in 1203 AD.
4. **Vallabhi** It was another education centre of Buddhist period. It was the capital seat of Maitraka kings between 475 AD and 755 AD. It can aptly be regarded as the rival of Nalanda in fame and educational importance. Hiuen Tsang, I-Tsing found Valabhi in the western side of India.

This university was known for its training in secular subjects and had students from all over the world.

5. **Jagaddala** Pal King, Raja Ram Pal of Bengal constructed a monastery and named it as Jagaddala. It remained as the centre of Buddhist education for about 100 years. It was destroyed during the invasion in 1203 CE. Jagaddala housed many scholars notable for their knowledge.
6. **Mithila** In the upanishadic age Mithila became a prominent seat of Brahmanical system of education. It was named as Videha. From 12th century to 15th century, Mithila had been an important centre of learning and culture. Besides literature and fine arts, scientific subjects and Nyaya Shastra were also taught.
7. **Odantapuri** This university had been established long before the king of Pala dynasty came into power in Magadha. It was a major centre of learning for Buddhism, Jainism and Hinduism.
8. **Nadia** situated at the confluence of Ganga and Jalangi rivers in Bengal, Nadia was an important centre for trade and business as well as learning and culture. Also called as Navadweep, education at this university was imparted at three centres namely Navadweep, Shantipur and Gopalpura.
9. **Salotgi** An important centre of learning in Karnataka. This college was richly endowed in 945 CE by Narayana the minister of Krishna III. It had 27 hostels for the students who hailed from different provinces.
9. **Ujjain** It is situated in Madhya Pradesh. This university was famous for its secular learning including mathematics and astronomy.
10. **Ennayiram** located in Tamil Nadu. This university provided free boarding and tuition to 340 students and became an important centre of learning alongwith Sringeri and Kanchi.

In the seventh century BC Banaras became one of the most important centres of education in Eastern India that provided the traditional Vedic education among the students.

## Education in Medieval Period

Arab and Central Asian people brought Muslim education to the sub-continent during medieval period. It was the time when customs, cultures and traditions of Arab and Central Asian region mingled with those of the Indian inhabitants. With the advent of Mahmud of Ghazni in A.D. 1001, Muhammad Ghauri in A.D. 1175, the educational institutions of the Hindu and the Buddhist religion were destroyed.

Arabic and Persian got prominence and Muslim education system came into existence. It was the time when Urdu was popularised by the Delhi Sultanate. Institutes of Muslim education were attached to Masjids and the education system was based on Islamic principles, law and social convention.

During this period, education received great patronage from the state. The Muslim rulers established many Maqtabas, Madrassa and Libraries etc, to impart education to all.

The Mughal Rulers established many residential colleges for postgraduate studies in different subjects and advanced studies were made in various branches of learning like Mathematics, Geometry, Astronomy, Physics, Philosophy, History, Grammar and Literature etc.

## Education in Modern Period

The major changes in the traditional style of higher education were brought by the Europeans starting from 1600 AD. The British successfully controlled much part of India by 1800 AD under East India Company and established formal system of higher education which continues till date.

There were three main agents of modern education in India :

1. The British government or East India Company.
2. Christian missionaries.
3. Indian intellectuals and reformers.

The Britishers did not only want some educated Indians who could assist them in the administration of land, but also wanted to understand the local customs and laws well, so institutions were established to impart education. Warren Hastings established the Calcutta Madrassa in 1781 for the teaching of Muslim law. In 1791, a Sanskrit College was started in Varanasi by Jonathan Duncan for the study of Hindu philosophy and law system.

Many schools were started in India with the purpose of Christianising and 'civilizing' the native Indians.

Further, many schemes and acts were passed to promote school and university education in India by the Britishers.

# EVOLUTION OF HIGHER LEARNING AND RESEARCH IN PRE-INDEPENDENCE PERIOD

The development of higher education in India can be traced back to the period of British rule in India. The British enacted and setup many committees or commissions as well as acts. Some of them are as follows

## Charter Act, 1813

The Charter Act of 1813 was the first step towards education being made an objective of the government. The Act sanctioned a sum of ₹ 1 lakh towards the education of Indians in British ruled India. The act also gave impetus to the missonaries who were given official permission to come to India.

The Act incorporated the principle of promoting knowledge of modern sciences in the country. In 1817 Calcutta college was set-up by Raja Rammohan Roy, imparting English education in western humanities and sciences.

## Elphinstone Report, 1823

According to this report, Elphinstone Institution was set-up by British in 1834 in Bombay which marked the beginning of higher education in India. The report recommended the appointment of district examination officers, school supervisors and training to teachers.

## Lord Macaulay's Minute, 1835

In 1835, under Lord Wlliam Bentinck, it was decided to introduce English as the medium of instruction. Macaulay minutes refer to his proposal of education for the Indians. It focused upon English education instead of traditional Indian learning, he told oriental culture was 'defective' and 'unholy'.

He believed in educating a few upper and middle class students. Ultimately, education would trickle down to the masses. This was called infiltration theory. He wished to create a class of Indians who were Indian in colour and blood but English in taste and affiliation.

In this way, he played an important role in building the modern education.

## Wood's Despatch, 1854

In 1854, Charles Wood prepared a despatch on the educational system for India. Considered the Magna Carta of English education in India, this document was the first comprehensive plan for spreading of education in India.

In 1857, universities at Calcutta, Bombay and Madras were setup and later, departments of education were setup in all provinces.

The Bethune school founded by J.E.D Bethune at Calcutta in 1849, was the first school to educate women. An agriculture Institute at Pusa (Bihar) and an Engineering Institute at Roorkee were also started.

## Hunter Commission, 1882-1883

In 1882, the British Government appointed a commission under the Chairmanship of WW Hunter to review the progress of education since the Despatch of 1854 in India.

The Hunter Commission recommended that responsibility for primary education must be given to Local and Municipal Boards. It also recommended grants-in-aid for promoting private participation in secondary education.

The commission emphasised for female education especially outside the presidency town and segregated primary from higher education.

Teaching-cum-examining Universities were set up such as Punjab University in 1882 and Allahabad University in 1887.

## Universities Commission, 1902

On 27th January, 1902, University Commissioner was appointed under the Presidency of Sir Thomas Raleigh by Lord Curzon. The purpose of the Commission was to inquire into the condition and prospects of universities in India and to recommend proposals for improving their Constitution and working.

As a result of the report of the recommendations of the Commission, the Indian Universities Act was passed in 1904. The main objective of the Act was to improve the condition of education in India and upgrade the system to a better level. So, a strict supervision on colleges and universities was suggested.

The Governor-General was now empowered to decide a university's limit and also affiliation between universities and colleges.

## National Council of Education, 1906

In 1906, an organisation was found by Indian nationalists in Bengal to promote science and technology as part of a Swadeshi Industrialisation Movement. This organization was called 'The National Council of Education'. Its main purpose was to provide education on national lines and under national control. Teachers were national; curriculum was based on national cultural heritage and aimed at national development in all directions i.e. economic, moral and material.

It established the Bengal National College and Bengal Technical Institute, which later merged to form Jadavpur University.

## Government Resolution on Education Policy, 1913

The Resolution of 1913 pointed out the desirability of smaller universities which would be residential and teaching and possibly based on linguistic division. The Patna, Lucknow and Rangoon Universities were set up due to local patriotism, Aligarh and Banaras Universities due to religion basis and Dacca University was set up due to both.

In its 1913 Resolution on Education Policy, the Government refused to take up the responsibility of compulsory education, but accepted the policy of removal of illiteracy and urged provincial governments to take early steps to provide free elementary education to the poorer and more backward sections.

## Saddler Commission, 1917-1919

Also called the Calcutta University Commission, this Commission was set up to study and report on problems of Calcutta University but its recommendations were applicable more or less to other universities too.

The Commission recommended that for the improvement of university education, improvement of secondary education was a necessary precondition. A separate board should be set up for administration and control of secondary and intermediate education. As a result, it became a precursor to 10+2+3 system and the setting up of Central Advisory Board of Education (CABE).

The Commission recommended that female education should be based on scientific and technological education and teachers' training including those for professional and vocational colleges should be extended.

## Education under Dyarchy, 1919

Under Montagu-Chelmsford reforms, education was shifted to provincial ministries and the government stopped taking direct interest in educational matters, while government grants, liberally sanctioned since 1902, were now stopped.

Financial difficulties prevented any substantial expansion but still education grew, especially under philanthropic efforts.

## Hartog Committee, 1929

An increase in number of schools and colleges had led to deterioration of education standards. The Hartog Committee was set up to report on development of education. The Committee emphasised on primary education and recommended to divert average students to vocational courses after VIII standard.

## Sapru Committee, 1934

The Sapru Committee was appointed by the United Province Government to enquire into the causes of unemployment.

It concluded that the mass unemployment was due to the system of education which prepared students only for examinations and degrees and not for life.

## Wood and Abbott Report, 1937

In pursuance of the recommendations of the Hartog Committee, the CABE (Central Advisory Board of Education) was revived in 1935. In its first meeting in December 1935, the CABE resolved to reorganise the existing system of education in schools.

Accordingly, both **Albert Abbott** and **Wood** were invited to advise the government on certain problems of educational reorganisation and particularly on problems of vocational education in 1936.

In 1937, the Abbott-Wood Report proposed that at university level, English should be the medium of instruction and recommended polytechnic education and establishment of vocational teacher-training colleges.

Its recommendations were the milestone in the direction of vocational studies and establishment of a Vocational Training College at Delhi.

## Wardha Scheme of Basic Education, 1937

The Congress had organised a National Conference on Education in October 1937 in Wardha. In the light of the resolutions passed there, Zakir Hussain Committee formulated a detailed national scheme for basic education or Nai Talim.

The main principle behind this scheme was 'learning through activity'. It was based on Gandhiji's ideas.

## Sergeant Plan of Education, 1944

Also known as Scheme of Post War Educational Development. The Sergeant Plan was worked out by the Central Advisory Board of Education in 1944.

It recommended

- pre-primary education for 3-6 years age group.
- free, universal and compulsory elementary education for 6-11 years age group.
- a university course of 3 years after higher secondary.
- high schools to be of two types (i) technical and vocational, and (ii) academic.
- The establishment of a University Grants Commission with its foundation in the University Grants Committee. It was established in the year 1945.

# Post-Independence Period

After attaining independence in 1947, the main task of the Government of India was to have a rapid socio-economic development and reconstruction of Indian society. The Government realised and recognised the important role of education in achieving its objective. The development of higher education after independence can be traced through the following commissions and committees.

## Radha Krishnan Commission, 1948

Also known as University Education Commission. This Commission was set up to report on university education in the country. Its recommendations proved to be of immense significance in establishing an educational system for independent India.

It recommended the following

- There should be 12 years of pre-university educational course.
- Higher education should have three main objectives namely; central education, liberal education and occupational education.

- A university degree should not be considered essential for administrative services.
- University education should be placed in 'concurrent list'.
- A University Grants Commission (UGC) should be set up to look after university education in the country.
- English as the medium of instruction for higher studies should not be removed in haste.

## Mudaliar Commission, 1952

The Commission was set up to enquire into the status of secondary education in India and hence is also called as Secondary Education Commission. It recommended to design a better curriculum pattern and life oriented syllabus. It also laid emphasis on setting up of multi-purpose schools and giving vocational training to students.

## Committee on Emotional Integration, 1961

This Committee was set up under the chairmanship of Dr Sampurnanad to study the role of educational programmes for youth in general and students in schools and colleges in order to strengthen the process of emotional integration.

The committee recommended that through the medium of education, the qualities of sacrifice and tolerance should be evolved in student behaviour so that the feeling of national unity may be fostered.

## Kothari Education Commission, 1964-66

A Commission was set up under Dr DS Kothari by Government of India to advise on the national pattern of education. Titled as 'Education and National Development' report, it was a very progressive report. Its recommendation included the following

- Free, universal and compulsory education upto the age of 14.
- A three language-formula i.e, Mother tongue, Hindi and English and also development of regional languages.
- Investment of 6% of national income on education.
- Training and quality of teachers.
- Development of education for agriculture and industry.

## Three Language Formula, 1968

The three language formula for language learning was formulated in 1968 by the ministry of Education, Government of India in consultation with states.

The three language formula provided for the study of Hindi, English and modern language (preferably one of the Southern languages) in the Hindi speaking states and Hindi, English and the Regional language in the non-Hindi speaking states.

## 42nd Amendment Act, 1976

The Indian Constitution has provisions to ensure that the state provides education to all its citizens. The Indian Constitution in its original enactment defined education as a state subject. Under Article 42 of the Constitution, an Amendment was added in 1976 and education became a concurrent list subject which enables the central government to legislate it in the manner suited to it.

## Adiseshiah Review Committee, 1978

The President of National Council of Education, Research and Training, appointed a Committee with Malcom S. Adiseshiah, the Vice-Chancellor of the University of Madras to review the curriculum of +2 standard education in the schools. The Committee made the following major recommendations:

(i) Semester system of education at +1 and +2 stage.
(ii) Priority to rural areas for establishing schools.
(iii) Encouragement to the teachers for in-service and pre-service training to improve the standard of education.
(iv) The framing of syllabi and subject combination as per the needs of the students and requirements of the states.

## 10+2+3 Education System, 1986

On the recommendation of the Education Commission 1964-66, the 10 + 2 + 3 structure was incorporated in the statement of the National Policy on Education, 1986.

In 1973, the Government of India ministry of Education and social welfare, appointed a National committee to formulate practical measures for introducing the proposed educational structure all over the country.

As a result of the report of the committee a beginning was made by the Central Board of Secondary Education, New Delhi to introduce this pattern. Since then the scheme has been accepted in principle by all the States and Union Territories.

## Acharya Ramamurti Committee, 1990

Acharya Ramamurti headed the review committee of 1990, popularly known as Ramamurti Review Committee for evaluating the progress of the National Policy on Education 1968. It recommended several changes which included the introduction of a common school system, promotion of women education and socially useful productive work.

## Gnanam Committee, 1993

The Committee was related to financial administration for the universities. It recommended flexibility and autonomy for ensuring academic excellence and asked for restricting the undesirable growth of deemed universities. It also emphasised the necessity of a National Commission on Higher Education and research to regulate the quality of education and to encourage research in university system.

## Sam Pitroda Committee, 2005

It was constituted on 13th June, 2005 and is also famous as National Knowledge Commission (NKC). It has recommended following

- Revise the curricula of existing universities.
- A central board of undergraduate education should be established, along with state boards of undergraduate education.
- An Independent Regulatory Authority for Higher Education (IRAHE) should be formed.
- The UGC should focus on disbursement of grants and maintaining public institutions of higher learning.

## Yashpal Committee, 2008

The Committee was set up to advise on renovation and rejuvenation of Higher education in 2008 under the chairmanship of Yashpal.

Key recommendations of Yashpal Committee are

- The academic functions of all the professional bodies (such as UGC, AICTE, MCI and BCI) should be subsumed under apex body for higher education called the National Commission for Higher Education and Research (NCHER), formed through constitutional amendment.
- Establish a National Education Tribunal with powers to adjudicate disputes among stakeholders within institutions.
- Vocational education sector should be brought within the purview of universities.
- Quantum of central financial support to state funded universities should be enhanced substantially on an incentive pattern.

## Sharma Committee, 2009

Looking at the declining quality and quantum of scientific research in India, an empowered committee under the Chairman of Prof MM Sharma was established.

Key recommendations of Sharma Committee are

- To promote excellence in research in higher education by supporting research programmes of the university and college teachers in various disciplines.
- Establishment of Indian Institute of Science, Education and Research (IISER) to promote scientific research.
- Atleast ₹ 500 crores be spent on research in basic sciences every year by the UGC.

## Dr Anil Kakodkar Committee, 2010

The Committee was set up by Government of India to recommend strategies to improve technical education in India. It recommended 2% budget in every institution to be earmarked for research.

## KB Pawar Committee, 2012

The KB Pawar Committee constituted by the UGC has recommended four models of Public-Private Partnership (PPP) in higher education.

They are

**Model I : Basic Infrastructure Model**

Under this model, infrastructure is provided by the private sector while the operations and management are in the hands of the government which make payments to the private investor, annually.

**Model II : Outsourcing Model**

Under this model, providing infrastructural facilities as well as operating and managing the institution are the responsibilities of the private sector. The government only pays the private investor for these services.

**Model III : Equity/ Hybrid Model**

Under this type of partnership, spending on infrastructure is borne by both, the government and the private sector. The responsibility of operating and managing the affairs of the institution is with the private sector.

**Model IV : Reserve Outsourcing Model**

Under this model, investment in infrastructure is done by the government while operations and management are looked after by the private sector.

## Subramanian Committee on New Education Policy, 2016

Under T.S.R Subramanian a committee for Evolution of the New Education Policy (NEP) was constituted by the Ministry of Human Resource Development (MHRD) in October, 2015. It submitted its report on 7th May, 2016. The committee proposed some important features for the development of education. Some of the important features are given below

- An Indian Education Service (IES) should be established as an All India Service.
- The outlay on education should be raised to atleast 6% of GDP without further loss of time.
- There should be minimum eligibility condition with 50% marks at graduate level for entry to B.Ed courses and Teacher Entrance Test (TET) should be made compulsory for recruitment of teachers.
- Compulsory certification should be made mandatory for teachers in government and private with provision for renewal in every 10 years based on independent external testing.
- It is also recommended in this committee that the Top 200 foreign universities should be allowed to open campuses in India and give the same degree which is acceptable in the home country of the said university.
- Other recommendations of the committee include ICT in Education, the Right to Education (RTE) Act, 2009, National Higher Education Promotion and Management Act (NHEPMA), Early Childhood Care (ECCE) and so on.

## New Education Policy, 2020

On 26th August, 2020, the Central Government cleared the New Education Policy (NEP) based on the report of former ISRO scientist Dr. K. Kasturirangan. The government after rejecting the recommendations of TSR Subramanium Committee on Education had constituted this committee in 2017.

The latest policy is Third Education Policy to be implemented in the country and will replace the erstwhile policy of 1986.

# EDUCATION IN POST-INDEPENDENCE INDIA

| | |
|---|---|
| 1947 | • India achieves independence. |
| 1948-49 | • **University Education Commission** constituted; given Report. |
| 1950 | • India becomes a Republic. **Free and compulsory education** enshrined as one of the **Directive Principles of State Policy** in the new Constitution. |
| 1951 | • Decennial Census yields a Literacy Rate (5+) of 18.3% (overall), 8.9% (female).<br>• First **Indian Institute of Technology** (IIT) established at Kharagpur. |
| 1952-53 | • Secondary Education Commission Constituted; gives Report. |
| 1956 | • University Grants Commission ((UGC) established by Act of Parliament.<br>• Indian Institute of Technology (Kharagpur) Act passed by Parliament.<br>• Pandit Jawaharlal Nehru delivers the First Convocation, address at the first IIT (Kharagpur). |
| 1958 | • Second IIT established at Mumbai. |
| 1959 | • Third and Fourth IITs established at Kanpur and Chennai, respectively. |
| 1961 | • NCERT established.<br>• Institutes of Technology Act passed by Parliament to provide a common legal framework for all IITs.<br>• First two Indian Institutes of Management (IIMs) set up at Ahmedabad and Kolkata. |
| 1963 | • Fifth IIT established at Delhi. |
| 1964-66 | • Education Commission constituted; gives Report. |
| 1968 | • First **National Policy on Education** (NPE) adopted, in the light of the recommendations the Educational Commission. |
| 1963 | • **Third IIM established at Bangalore**. |
| 1975 | • Integrated Child Development Services (ICDS) Scheme launched to provide for holistic development of children up to the age of six years. |
| 1976 | • Constitution amended to change **"Education"** from being a "**State**" subject to a **"Concurrent"** one. |
| 1984 | • Fourth IIM established at Lucknow. |
| 1985 | • **Indira Gandhi National Open University** (IGNOU) established by an Act of Parliament. |
| 1986 | • New National Policy on Education (NPE) adopted. |
| 1987-88 | • Many large centrally assisted schemes like "Operation Blackboard", "Education Technology", "Vocationalisation of Secondary Education", etc., launched in pursuance of NPE, 1986. |
| 1992 | • **NPE, 1986, revised**, based on a review by the Acharya Ramamurti Committee. |
| 1993 | • **National Council of Teacher Education** (NCTE) vested with statutory status by an Act of Parliament. |
| 1994 | • **District Primary Education Programme** (DPEP) launched to universalize primary education in selected districts.<br>• **National Assessment and Accreditation Council** (NAAC) established by UGC (with headquarters at Bangalore) to assess and accredit institutions of higher education. |
| 1994 | • **National Board of Accreditation** (NBA) established by AICTE to periodically evaluate technical institutions and programmes.<br>• **Sixth IIT** established at **Guwahati**. |
| 1995 | • Centrally-assisted Mid-Day Meal Scheme launched in government and semi-government primary schools all over the country, with central assistance by way of free food grains. |
| 1996 | • Fifth IIM established at Kozhikode. |
| 1998 | • Sixth IIM established at Indore. |

| | |
|---|---|
| 2001 | • Decennial Census yields Literacy Rate (7+) of 65.4% (overall), 53.7% (female).<br>• **Sarva Shiksha Abhiyan** (SSA) launched to universalize elementary education of good quality all over the country.<br>• **University of Roorkee** converted into **(the seventh)** IIT. |
| 2002 | • **Constitution amended to make Free and Compulsory Education** of all children in the age of 6-14 years as a Fundamental Right. |
| 2003 | • 17 Regional Colleges of Engineering converted into **National Institutes of Technology**, fully funded by the Central Government.<br>• **Education Cess** levied for raising additional finance needed to fulfill government's commitment to universalize quality basis education. |
| 2004 | • **Mid-Day Meal** scheme revised to provide central assistance to meet cooking cost as well.<br>• **EDUSAT**, a satellite dedicated to education, launched. |
| 2005 | • National Commission for Minority Education Institutions established by Act of Parliament. |
| 2006 | • Two **Indian Institutes of Science Education & Research** (IISERs) established at Kolkata and Pune, respectively. |
| 2007 | • Seventh Indian Institute of Management established at Shillong.<br>• One Indian Institute of Science Education & Research (IISER) established at Mohali.<br>• The National Institutes of Technology (NITs) brought under a common statutory framework by established NIT Act.<br>• Rashtriya Sanskrit Parishad constituted.<br>• The Central Education Institutions (Reservation in Admission) Act notified. |
| 2009 | • Right to Education Act. |
| 2013 | • Rashtriya Uchchatar Shiksha Abhiyan (RUSA) to transform the current status of state higher educational institutions.<br>• It focusses on promotion of autonomy and governance reform in institutions and increase gross enrolment to 30% by 2020. |
| 2014 | • Padhe Bharat Badhe Bharat with a special focus on improving language development and to create interest in mathematics among students up to class 8. |
| 2015 | • National Institutional Ranking Framework<br>• (NIRF) launched.<br>• It ranked Institutions on parameter of included Overall Universities, Engineering Colleges, Management, Pharmacy, Medical, Architecture and Law. |
| 2016 | • Institute of Eminence was launched to empower Higher Educational Institutions and help them become world class teaching and research institutions.<br>• As of 2020, 16 institutes of both public and private category have been granted eminence status. |
| 2018 | • Samagra Shiksha scheme was launched to holistically cover all aspects of school education. |
| | • Scheme focuses on improving quality of education, enhancing the learning outcomes and using technology to empower children and teachers. |
| 2019 | • Pradhan Mantri Innovative Learning Programme (DHRUV) was launched to identify and encourage talented children to enrich their skills and knowledge.<br>• RTE Amendment Act, 2019 scraps the no-detention policy and allows for the reintroduction of examinations for primary schools. |
| 2020 | • New Education Policy, launched by Union Cabinet.<br>• It addresses the five challenges of Indian education (access, equity, quality, affordability and accountability) in the comprehensive way. |

# STRUCTURE OF HIGHER EDUCATION IN INDIA

India has one of the largest higher education institutions in the world. Structure of institutions for higher learning and research in India can be divided in the following categories

**Structure of Higher Learning**

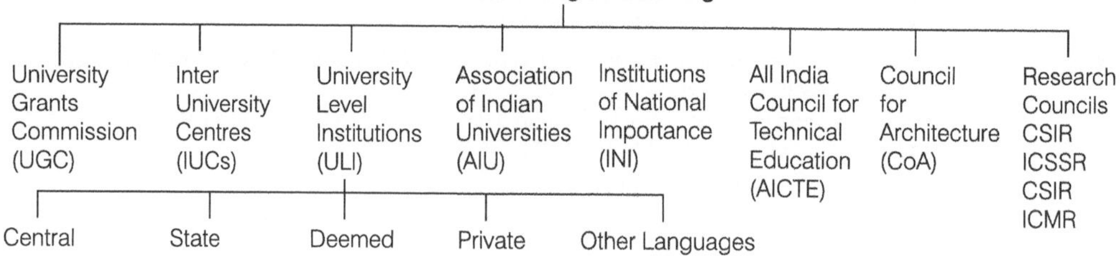


## 1. University Grants Commission (UGC)

The University Grant Commission (UGC) came into existence on 28th December, 1953 and became a statutory organisation of the Government of India through an Act of Parliament in 1956.

The functions of UGC are discussed below

- It discharges the constitutional mandate of coordination, determination, and maintenance of standards of teaching, examination and research in the field of university education and also release of grants.
- It serves as a vital link between the Union and State Governments and the institutions of higher learning.
- It monitors developments in the field of college and university education.
- It advises Central and State Governments on the measures necessary for the improvement of university education.
- It frames regulations on the minimum standards of education.

### Structure of UGC

The UGC has the right to appoint its own staff subject to rules made by the Central Government. The commission consists of chairman, vice chairman and 10 other members. The term of the chairman is upto 5 years or until he/she attains the age of 65 years, whichever is earlier. The term of Vice chairman/ President is 3 years.

The commission consists of 2 offices of the Central Government, the Secretary of Education and Secretary of Finance.

In addition, three members are working university professors. Other members are selected from the fields of agriculture technology, scientific, industry and engineering.

UGC has 6 regional offices in Bengaluru, Bhopal, Guwahati, Hyderabad, Kolkata and Pune. The head office of UGC is in New Delhi. Dr. C.D. Deshmukh first chairman of UGC Statutory Body from 1956-1961.

## 2. Inter University Centres (IUCs)

The UGC establishes autonomous Inter University Centres within the university system under Clause 12(CCC) of the UGC Act.

It provides common advanced centralised facilities/services for universities which are not able to invest in infrastructure and other inputs. It also plays a vital role in offering the best expertise in each field to teachers and resources across the country.

The Nuclear Science Centre at New Delhi (now called Inter University Accelerator Centre) was the first research centre established in 1994. As of now, six inter-university centres are functioning within the university system. They are as follows

(i) Inter University Accelerator Centre (IUAC), New Delhi.

(ii) Inter University Centre for Astronomy and Astro-physics (IUCAA), Pune.

(iii) UGC-DAE Consortium for Scientific Research (UGC-DAECSR), Indore.

(iv) Information and Library Network (INFLIBNET), Ahmedabad.

(v) Consortium for Educational Communication (CEC), New Delhi.

(vi) National Assessment and Accreditation Council (NAAC), Bangalore (Bengaluru).

## Universities

The word 'university' is derived from the Latin term 'universitas magistrorum et scholarium', which means "community of teachers and scholars". Universities are institution of higher (or tertiary) education and research, which awards academic degrees in various academic disciplines.

They are centers of learning where all types of academic and non-academic disciplines are taught, tested and evaluated, so that one is provided with standard degrees.

Universities in India are Apex institutions established by an Act of Parliament or State Legislatures functioning under the UGC. They typically provide undergraduate and postgraduate education and conduct research in various fields.

## Internal Structure of Universities

Universities in India are autonomous institutions. They have their own administrative structures and management styles.The President of India is the Visitor of all Central Universities, except the Vishwa Bharati, where the Prime Minister is the Visitor.

In case of State universities, the Governor of the respective State is the Chancellor. Both the Visitor and the Chancellor normally do not have any administrative role in the day-to-day functioning of the University.

The Vice-Chancellor is the most important functionary who is the Chief Executive and Academic Authority of a University. He/she deals with the management and administration of the universities falling under the university and submits a report to the Chancellor.

# 3. Universities Level Institutions (ULI)

Mainly, there are four categories of University in India

### (i) Central Universities

Central Universities are established by an Act of Parliament and are under the purview of the Department of Higher Education in the Ministry of Human Resource Development. Central Universities are covered by the Central Universities Act, 2009, which regulates their purpose, powers, governance, etc, and established 16 new universities.

The list of central universities published by the UGC includes 53 central universities

| University | State | Location | Estd. |
|---|---|---|---|
| Rajiv Gandhi University | Arunachal Pradesh | Itanagar | 1985 (2007) |
| Assam University | Assam | Silchar | 1994 |
| Tezpur University | Assam | Tezpur | 1994 |
| Central University of South Bihar | Bihar | Gaya | 2009 |
| Mahatma Gandhi Central University | Bihar | Motihari | 2016 |
| Nalanda University | Bihar | Rajgir, Nalanda | 2010 |
| Dr Rajendra Prasad Central Agricultural University | Bihar | Pusa | 1905 (2016) |
| Guru Ghasidas Vishwavidyalaya | Chhattisgarh | Bilaspur | 1983 (2009) |
| Indira Gandhi National Open University | Delhi | New Delhi | 1985 |
| Jamia Millia Islamia | Delhi | New Delhi | 1920 (1988) |
| Jawaharlal Nehru University, Delhi | Delhi | New Delhi | 1969 |

| University | State | Location | Estd. |
|---|---|---|---|
| South Asian University | Delhi | New Delhi | 2010 |
| University of Delhi | Delhi | New Delhi | 1922 |
| Central University of Gujarat | Gujarat | Gandhinagar | 2009 |
| Central University of Haryana | Haryana | Mahendragarh | 2009 |
| Central University of Himachal Pradesh | Himachal Pradesh | Dharamsala | 2009 |
| Central University of Jammu | Jammu and Kashmir | Jammu | 2011 |
| Central University of Kashmir | Jammu and Kashmir | Srinagar | 2009 |
| Central University of Jharkhand | Jharkhand | Ranchi | 2009 |
| Central University of Karnataka | Karnataka | Gulbarga | 2009 |
| Central University of Kerala | Kerala | Kasaragod | 2009 |
| Dr. Hari Singh Gour University | Madhya Pradesh | Sagar | 1946 (2009) |
| Indira Gandhi National Tribal University | Madhya Pradesh | Amarkantak | 2007 |
| Mahatma Gandhi Antarrashtriya Hindi Vishwavidyalaya | Maharashtra | Wardha | 1997 |
| Central Agricultural University | Manipur | Imphal | 1993 |
| Manipur University | Manipur | Imphal | 1980 (2005) |
| National Sports University | Manipur | Imphal | 2018 |
| North-Eastern Hill University | Meghalaya | Shillong | 1973 |
| Mizoram University | Mizoram | Aizawl | 2000 |
| Nagaland University | Nagaland | Lumami | 1994 |
| Central University of Orissa, Koraput | Odisha | Koraput | 2009 |
| Pondicherry University | Puducherry | Pondicherry | 1985 |
| Central University of Punjab | Punjab | Bathinda | 2009 |
| Central University of Rajasthan | Rajasthan | Ajmer | 2009 |
| Sikkim University | Sikkim | Gangtok | 2007 |
| Central University of Tamil Nadu | Tamil Nadu | Thiruvarur | 2009 |
| Indian Maritime University | Tamil Nadu | Chennai | 2008 |
| English and Foreign Languages University | Telangana | Hyderabad | 1958 (2007) |
| Maulana Azad National Urdu University | Telangana | Hyderabad | 1998 |
| University of Hyderabad | Telangana | Hyderabad | 1974 |
| Tripura University | Tripura | Agartala | 1987 |
| Aligarh Muslim University | Uttar Pradesh | Aligarh | 1920 |
| University of Allahabad | Uttar Pradesh | Allahabad | 1887 |
| Babasaheb Bhimrao Ambedkar University | Uttar Pradesh | Lucknow | 1996 |
| Banaras Hindu University | Uttar Pradesh | Varanasi | 1916 |
| Rajiv Gandhi National Aviation University | Uttar Pradesh | Raebareli | 2013 |
| Rani Lakshmi Bai Central Agricultural University | Uttar Pradesh | Jhansi | 2014 |
| Hemwati Nandan Bahuguna Garhwal University | Uttarakhand | Srinagar | 1973 (2009) |
| Vishva-Bharati University | West Bengal | Santiniketan | 1921 |

## (ii) State Universities

The State Universities are established by an Act of a State Legislature. They are run and funded by the State Government of each of the states of India.

However, following the 42nd Constitutional Amendment, 1976 it became the part of concurrent list. As a result, Section 12 (B) of the UGC Act of 1956, State Universities became fit to receive UGC grants.

As on 20th December, 2018, the UGC lists 412 state universities out of which 242 universities are fit to receive Central/UGC assistance.

State universities dominate university or higher education accounting for almost 50% of the universities found in the country and for 85% of total enrollment. Interestingly, Uttar Pradesh has the most State universities in India.

## (iii) Deemed Universities

An Institution of Higher Education, which is working at a very high standard in specific area of study can be declared as a Deemed University by the Central Government on the recommendation of UGC under Section 3 of the UGC Act, 1956. Deemed Universities enjoy full autonomy in respect of courses, syllabus, admission and fees. But they do not have the right to affiliate colleges.

Indian Institute of Science, Bangalore and Indian Agricultural Research Institute, Delhi were the first two institutes to be granted a deemed status in 1958.

Among the private institutions, Manipal Academy of Higher Education (MAHE) was the first to be granted a Deemed University Status in 1993.

UGC currently lists 124 institutions as deemed universities. The state with the most number of deemed universities is Tamil Nadu with 28 deemed universities.

### → Meta Universities

- During the 12th plan, UGC has initiated a concept of Meta University. The Meta University concept marks a paradigm shift in higher education in India. It is based on the premise that the 'whole is greater than the sum of the parts'.
- The main purpose of the Meta University is to share learning resources with different universities by using the latest technologies available in order to enable the students to benefit from the learning resources available in different institutions.
- Meta University represents the second generation universities that are free from the concepts of physical boundary and conditions while being able to operate on a virtual or digital platform.
- Taking the advantage of innovation and flexibility in the domain of technology, UGC initiated the concept of Meta University in its 12th Five Year Plan.
- The concept of Meta University was First Introduced in India by University of Delhi and Jamia Milia Islamia. Both the top universities started a 2- year joint degree program "Master of Mathematics Education" from the academic session 2015.

## (iv) Private Universities

A university established through the state or central act by a sponsoring body including a registered company, a trust, or a registered society under Section 25 of the Companies Act, 1956 is called a Private University.

Private universities are regulated under the UGC (establishment and maintenance of standards in private universities regulation) 2003. Thus, they are competent to award degrees, frame syllabus and the admission procedure, etc., with the approval of the statutory council. As of now, there are 356 private universities that are recognised by the UGC and Sikkim Manipal University, notified in 1995, is the oldest Private University in India.

## (v) Language Universities

India has six language universities out of which three are deemed to be universities and three are central universities. The deemed universities are for promotion of Sanskrit and the three central universities are one each for the promotion of English and foreign language, Hindi and Urdu.

1. Shri Lal Bahadur Shastri Rashtriya Sanskrit Vidyapeeth New Delhi.
2. Rashtriya Sanskrit Vidyapeeth, Tirupati.
3. English and Foreign Languages University, Hyderabad.
4. Mahatma Gandhi Antarrashtriya Hindi Vishwavidyalaya, Wardha.
5. Maulana Azad National Urdu University Hyderabad.
6. Rashtriya Sanskrit Sansthan, New Delhi.

## 4. Association of Indian Universities (AIU)

Association of Indian Universities (AIU) is a forum where the members of universities exchange their ideas, views and matters of common concern.

The idea of bringing together all the universities on a common platform was convened by Lord Reading, the then Viceroy of India, at Shimla in 1924.

It got its present name i.e., Association of Indian Universities (AIU) in 1973. The membership includes Traditional universities, Open universities, Professional universities, Institutes of National Importance and Deemed universities. In addition, there is a provision of granting of Associate Membership to universities of neighbouring countries.

It serves as an inter-university organisation and acts as a bureau of information as well as facilitates communication. It helps universities to maintain their autonomous character and publishes universities Handbook.

## 5. Institutions of National Importance (INI)

Institutions of National Importance (INI) is a status that may be conferred to a premier public higher educational institutions in India by an act of Parliament.

It serves as a pivotal player in developing highly skilled personnel within the specified region of the country. It receives special recognition and funding from the Government of India.

Academy of Scientific and Innovative Research, IITs, IIMs AIIMs, and so on are examples of the Institutions of National Importance.

## 6. All India Council for Technical Education (AICTE)

The All India Council for Technical Education (AICTE) is a statutory body and national level council for technical education, under department of higher education.

It was first established in November 1945 as an advisory body. But was given statutory status by an Act of Parliament in 1987.

AICTE is responsible for proper planning and coordinated development of the technical education and management education system in India.

AICTE is assisted by 10 Statutory Boards of Studies namely

1. Undergraduation studies in Engineering and Technology
2. Post Graduation and Research in Engineering and Technology
3. Management Studies
4. Vocational Education
5. Technical Education
6. Pharmaceutical Education
7. Architecture
8. Hotel Management and Catering Technology
9. Information Technology
10. Town and Country Planning

The AICTE has its headquarters in New Delhi and its regional offices are at Kanpur, Chandigarh, Gurgaon (Gurugram), Mumbai, Bhopal, Baroda, Kolkata, Guwahati, Bengaluru, Hyderabad, Chennai and Thiruvananthapuram.

AICTE is vested with statutory authority for planning, formulation and maintenance of norms and standards, quality assurance through school accreditation, funding in priority areas, monitoring and evaluation, maintaining parity of certification, awards and ensuring coordination and integrated development as well as management of technical education in the country.

## 7. Council of Architecture (CoA)

The Council of Architecture (CoA) has been constituted by the Government of India under the provisions of the Architects Act 1972. It was enacted by the Parliament and came into force on 1st September, 1972.

The Act provides for registration of architects, standards of education, recognised qualifications and standards of practice to be complied with by the practicing architects.

The COA is charged with the responsibility to regulate the education and practice of profession throughout India besides maintaining the register of architects.

### → National Institute of Education Planning and Administration (NIEPA)

NIEPA (deemed to be University) is now renamed as National University of Educational Planning and Administration (NUEPA). It was established by the Ministry of Human Resource Development. It is a premier organisation dealing with capacity building and research in planning and management of education not only in India but also in South Asia.

It is associated with the UNESCO's regional centre for Educational Planners and Administration started in 1962. It was in 1970 that the institute was taken over by Government of India and renamed as National Staff College for Educational Planners and Administration. The institute with the present name was rechristened in 1979.

The NUEPA as an autonomous organisation emphasises on planning, management and capacity building in educational policy, through research, training, consultancy and dissemination. The NUEPA structure is based on nine academic and one administrative unit.

## 8. Famous Research Councils

The Research Councils established for carrying out cutting edge research and development activities in diverse areas or fields. Today, India boasts a significant key contribution to global research and development. There are various research councils in India, some of which are mentioned below

### Indian Council of Agricultural Research, 1929

Formerly, known as Imperial Council of Agricultural Research, the Indian Council of Agricultural Research is an autonomous organisation under the Department of Agricultural Research and Education. This council is the open body for co-ordinating, guiding and managing research and education in agriculture including horticulture, fisheries and animal science in the entire country.

(i) **Indian Council of Social Science Research, 1969** (ICSSR) It was established in 1969 for promoting social science research, strengthening different disciplines, and improving the quality and quantum of research and its utilisation in national policy formulation.

(ii) **Indian Council of Historical Research, 1972** (ICHR) It is an autonomous organisation which was established under Societies Registration Act in 1972. The main objectives of the ICHR are to give a proper direction to historical research and to encourage and foster objective and scientific writing in history.

It has a broad view of history so as to include in its fold the history of science and technology, economy, art, literature, philosophy, etc and allied subjects containing strong historical bias and contents. The ICHR has established two regional centres one at Bengaluru and the other at Guwahati with a view to reach out the far flung areas of the country.

(iii) **Indian Council of Philosophical Research, 1977** (ICPR) It was set up in 1977 under Department of Higher Education in Ministry of Human Resource Development as an autonomous organisation for the promotion of research in philosophy and allied discipline. The Governing Body (GB) and the Research Project Committee (RPC) are the main authorities of the council.

(iv) **Project of History of Indian Science, Philosophy and Culture, 1990** (PHISPC) It was launched in the year 1990 under the aegis of Indian Council of Philosophical Research (ICPR). The project was initiated with the basic objective of undertaking inter disciplinary study so that inter-connection between science, philosophy and culture is developed. From 1st April, 1997, PHISPC was officially de-linked from ICPR for greater autonomy to complete the project by the stipulated period, and is now affiliated to Centre for-Studies in Civilisations (CSC). Government of India has recognised CSC as the nodal agency for the purpose of funding the ongoing project of PHISPC.

(v) **National Council of Rural Institute, 1995** (NCRI) It is a registered autonomous society fully funded by the Central Government. It was established on 19th October, 1995 with its headquarters at Hyderabad. Its main objectives are to promote rural higher education on the lines of Mahatma Gandhi's vision for education so as to take up challenges of micro planning for transformation of rural areas as envisaged in National Policy on Education (NPE), 1986.

## SCHEMES OR PROGRAMMES RELATED TO HIGHER EDUCATION

The Government of India has launched a number of schemes and programmes for the development of Higher Education in India. Some of which are given below

- **National Research Professorship, 1949** (NRP) Government of India has initiated the scheme of NRP in 1949 to honour distinguished academics and scholars in recognition of their contribution to knowledge.
- **Scheme of Integrating Persons with Disabilities in the Mainstream of Technical and Vocational Education, 1999-2000** Caters to around 50 polytechnics in the country and provides them with grants-in-aid aimed at facilitating greater integration of disabled individuals into higher education.
- **Technical Education Quality Improvement Programme, 2002** (TEQIP) This scheme was launched by MHRD in 2002 to upscale and support the quality of technical education. TEQIP Phase-I and Phase-II were implemented with the assistance of World Bank. Phase-III was launched with the help of World Bank for the upgradation of polytechnics in the country.
- **National E-library, 2006** The E-library have been envisaged as an online portal that will democratise access to knowledge by ensuring that quality content from central universities and premier educational institutions are available in a, digital format. This can be easily accessed by students, working professional and researchers across the country.
- **Rashtriya Uchchtar Shiksha Abhiyan** (RUSA) Rashtriya Uchchtar Shiksha Abhiyan is a centrally sponsored scheme launched in 2013 to raise the standards of state universities and its affiliated colleges. It aims at providing strategic funding to eligible state higher educational institutions. The central funding (in the ratio of 60 : 40 for general category states; 90 : 10 for special category states and 100% for Union Territories) is based on norms and is outcome dependent.

  RUSA places emphasis on the improvement of the quality of teaching-learning processes in order to produce employable and competitive graduates, post-graduates and Ph.Ds.

- **Scheme of Pandit Madan Mohan Malaviya National Mission on Teachers and Teaching** (PMMM NMTT), **2014** The purpose of this scheme is to raise the quantity and quality of teaching staff across schools and colleges. It also aims to create better institutional frameworks in order to cultivate change in the positive direction.
- **Swami Vivekananda Scholarship for Single Girl Child, 2014** UGC has introduced this scheme for research in social sciences with an aim to compensate direct costs of higher education especially for such girls who happen to be the only girl child in their family.
- **Unnat Bharat Abhiyan, 2014** This scheme enables processes to connect institutes of higher education with local communities. IITs, IISERs, NIT, etc. adopted villages and developed appropriate rural technologies for sustainable development through people's participation.
- **Bachelor of Vocational Studies, 2014** UGC has initiated this scheme for Bachelor degree with multiple courses at Diploma/Advanced Diploma under National Skill Qualification Framework (NSQF).
  The scheme will enhance the employability of youth and maintain their competitiveness through provisions of multi- entry, multi-exit learning opportunities and vertical mobility.
- **Study Webs of Active-learning for Young Aspiring Minds, 2014** (SWAYAM) It is a Massive Open Online Courses (MOOCs) initiative on a country level platform with a comprehensive academic structure. This platform offers the courses such as engineering, humanities and social sciences, etc., to be used by learners at large.
- **National Quality Renaissance Initiative** (NQRI), **2014** This scheme is initiated to aware and promote the quality assurance mentioning for higher education or higher institutions. It is the initiative of National Assessment and Accrediation Council (NAAC).
- **Ishan Uday, 2014** Scholarship Scheme for students of North-East: The UGC launched a special scholarship scheme for students of North-East Region.
- **Ishan Vikas, 2014** Academic Exposure of North-East students: This has been launched with a plan to bring selected college and school students from North-Eastern States. It is to bring students in close contact with IITs, NITs and IISERs during their vacation period for academic exposure.
- **Campus Connect, 2014** It aims at generating quality content as well as providing connectivity to the institutes. To assess it under the National Mission on Education Through Information and Communication Technology (NMEICT) Scheme.
- **The Uchchtar Avishkar Yojana** (UAY), **2015** It has been launched to promote industry specific need based research. This is to keep up the competitiveness of Indian industry in the global market.
- **Global Initiative of Academic Networks** (GIAN), **2015** An initiative launched to garner best international knowledge and experience into the country's higher education. This is to enable students and faculty to interact with best academic and industry experts across the world.
- **Kaushal Kendras, 2015** It is a skill development initiative scheme of the government of India for recognition and standradisation of skills. It includes the setup of Kaushal Kendras. These Kendras formulate courses at post graduate level keeping in mind the need of
  - industry in specialised areas.
  - instructional design curriculum design and contents in the areas of skill development.
  - pedagogy, assessment for skill development education and training.
  - trained faculty in the areas of skill development.
  - entrepreneurship.
- **IMPRINT Scheme, 2015** It is first of its kind MHRD supported scheme to address major science and engineering challenges and boost original scientific research in 10 technology identified domains in the country. It was launched in 2015.

- **Impactful Policy Research in Social Sciences** (IMPRESS), **2018** A web portal of the scheme launched in 2018. Under the scheme 1500 research projects will be awarded for 2 years. It is to support the social science research in the higher educational institutions. And to enable research to guide policy making.
- **Revitalising Infrastructure and System in Education** (RISE), **2018** It is a scheme announed in 2018. It aims to lend low cost funds to government higher educational institutions. Under it all centrally funded institutes including Central universities, IITs IIMs, NTSs and IISER can borrow ₹ 1,00,000 crore corpus over 4 years to build new infrastructure.
- **The Prime Minister's Research Fellowship** (PMRF), **2018** This scheme was initiated in 2018. The scheme is aimed at attracting the talent of pool of the country to doctoral (Ph.D) programmes of Indian Institute of Technology (IITs). Indian Institute of Sciences is for carrying out research in cutting edge science and technology domains with focus on national priorities.

  The following would be the fellowship for the PMRFs.

| Year | Amount (₹) |
|---|---|
| 1 Year | 70, 000 |
| 2 Year | 70,000 |
| 3 Year | 75,000 |
| 4 Year | 80,000 |
| 5 Year | 80,000 |

  Apart from this each fellowship would be eligible for a research grant of ₹ 2 lakh per year.

The major objectives are to

- improve the overall quality of existing state institutions by ensuring that all institutions conform to prescribed norms and standards. Adopt accreditation as a mandatory quality insurance framework.
- ensure academic and examination reforms in the higher educational institutions.
- enable conversion of some of the universities into research universities at par with the best in the world.
- ensure adequate availability of quality faculty in all.
- higher educational institutions and ensure capacity building at all levels of employment.
- expand the institutional base by creating additional capacity in existing institutions. Establishing new institutions in order to achieve enrolment targets.
- creating opportunities for students from rural areas to get access to better quality institutions setting up institutions in un-served and undeserved areas.

## ACCREDITATION OF HIGHER EDUCATION INSTITUTIONS

Accreditation is a process by which higher learning institutions get evaluated on their education standards by a board of members. Criteria for assessment of quality in education includes

- Overall mission of the college
- Objectives and goals
- Students requirement for admissions
- Service availability to students
- Quality of education and reputation of the faculty
- Curricular aspects
- Teaching-learning and evaluation
- Infrastructure and learning resources.
- Student support and progression.
- Organisation and management

### 1. National Assessment and Accreditation Council, 1994

National Assessment and Accreditation Council (NAAC) was established by the University Grants Commission (UGC) to assess and accredit institutions of higher learning in the country.

NAAC was originally formed in 1992 as a result of recommendation from National Policy on Education-1986 which emphasised on deteriorating quality of higher education in the country. NAAC is an autonomous body funded by the UGC, Government of India opened in 1994. Its headquarter is in Bengaluru.

### NAAC Objectives

- To assess and accredit institutions of higher learning.
- To grade institutions of higher education and their programmes.
- To stimulate the academic environment and quality of teaching and research in these institutions.
- To help institutions realise their academic objectives.
- To promote necessary changes, innovations and reforms in all aspects of institutions.
- To encourage innovations, self evaluation and accountability in higher education.

NAAC has been constantly and consciously changing its methodology as per the need of the hour. The new methodology was formed, framed and implemented from 1st April, 2007.

Under the new methodology, introduced by NAAC, the higher education institutions are assessed as accredited by a two-step approach. In the first step, the institution is required to seek 'Institutional Eligibility for Quality Assessment (IEQA). The second step is the assessment and accreditation of the institute under the grades 'A', 'B' and 'C' for accredited institutions and 'D' for those which are not accredited.

**National Board of Accreditation** (NBA) It was established by AICTE in 1994 as an autonomous body headquartered in Delhi. Its function is to periodically conduct evaluation of technical courses offered in India. It has the authority to recognise or derecognise institutions or programmes in India.

## 2. National Agriculture Education Accreditation Board, 1996

Set up by the Indian Council of Agricultural Research. The National Agricultural Education Accreditation Board undertakes the accreditation to ensure the quality of higher agricultural education in agricultural universities and its constituent colleges.

NAEAB undertakes the following accreditation programme:

- To assist people, prospective students, educational institutions, governments and other concerned agencies in identifying institutions and programmes which meet the minimum norms and standards of the Council.
- To provide guidance for the improvement of the existing agricultural education institutions/ programmes.
- To develop new institutions/programmes.

Accreditation of agricultural universities is a continuous process and since the Constitution of the Board in 1996, about 43 agricultural Universities have been accredited.

## 3. National Institutional Ranking Framework (NIRF), 2015

The National Institutional Ranking Framework (NIRF) is a methodology adopted by the Ministry of Human Resource Development (MHRD), Government of India in order to rank institutions of higher education in India. The framework was approved by the MHRD on 29th September, 2015 .

There are separate rankings for various types of institutions depending on their areas of operation like universities and colleges, engineering institutions, management institutions, pharmacy institutions and architecture institutions. The framework uses several parameters for ranking purposes such as resources, research and stakeholder perception.

These parameters have been grouped into five clusters and these clusters were assigned certain weightages. The weightage depends on the type of institutions. About 3500 institutions voluntarily participated in the first round of rankings.

The National Institutions Ranking Framework, 2019 released in April by the MHRD ranked the institutions into the categories. The institutions with top ranks are as follows

(i) **Overall Ranking** (1) IIT Madras (2) Indian Institute of Science, Bengaluru (3) IIT Delhi.

(ii) **University Ranking** (1) Indian Institute of Science (IISc), Bengaluru, (2) Jawaharlal Nehru University (Delhi), (3) Banaras Hindu University (Varanasi).

(iii) **College Ranking** (1) Delhi University (DU) Miranda House (2) Lady Shri Ram College for Women, (3) Hindu College.

(iv) **Engineering Ranking** (1) IIT Madras, (2) IIT, Delhi, (3) IIT Mumbai at third place.

(v) **Management Ranking** (1) Indian Institute of Management, Ahmedabad ranked at the top management institute, (2) IIM Bangalore (3) IIM Calcutta third position.

(vi) **Medical Ranking** (1) All India Institute of Medical Science, New Delhi (2) Post Graduate Institute of Medical Education and Research, Chandigarh (3) Christian Medical College, Tamil Nadu ranked as number three.

(vii) **Pharmacy Ranking** (1) Jamia Hamdard, Delhi, (2) Punjab University, Chandigarh, (3) National Institute of Pharmaceutical Education and Research.

(viii) **Architecture Ranking** (1) The Indian Institute of Technology (IIT), Kharagpur, (2) IIT Roorkee, (3) National Institute of Technology, Calicut.

(ix) **Law Ranking** (1) National Law School of India University, Bangalore, (2) National Law University, Delhi, (3) Nalsar University of Law, Hyderabad.

## All India Survey on Higher Education (2018-19)

Ministry of Human Resource Development has endeavored to conduct an annual web-based All India Survey on Higher Education (AISHE) since 2010-11. The survey covers all the Institutions in the country engaged in imparting the higher education.

All India Survey on Higher Education (AISHE) report for 2018-19 was released by the Ministry of Human Resource Development. Survey covers all institutions of higher education in the country registered with AISHE Code.

Its key findings were

- The Gross Enrollment Ratio (GER) increased marginally from 25.8 to 26.3 in 2018. GER for SCs has shown a growth from 21.8 to 23.0 and STs from 15.9 to 17.2.
- Increase in the number of universities from 903 in 2017 to 993 in 2018 and also the increase in number of faculty from 13.88 lakh to 14.16 lakh.
- At under graduate level, the 35.9% of the total enrollment was in arts and social science and 16.5% and 14.1% in science and commerce.
- Uttar Pradesh comes out with highest number of enrollment followed by Maharashtra and Tamil Nadu.

## Other Agencies or Bodies Related to Higher Education

There are some other agencies that govern the higher, technical as well as professional education in India. Each of these agencies is in-charge of regulating different types of education in India, like the general education, medical education, technical education, etc. Some of these are

1. **Medical Council of India** (MCI) It was founded in 1933 with its headquarters at New Delhi. The council grants recognition of medical qualifications, gives accreditation to medical schools, grants registration to medical practitioners and monitors medical practice in India.
2. **Central Hindi Directorate** It was set up in 1960 to develop Hindi as a link language throughout India under the provisions of Article 351 of the Constitution of India. It is located at New Delhi with regional offices at Chennai, Kolkata, Hyderabad and Guwahati.

3. **Commission for Scientific and Technical Terminology, 1961** It was constituted to define scientific and technical terms in all Indian languages.
4. **Bar Council of India** (BCI) It is a statutory body created by the Parliament under the Advocates Act, 1961 for regulating and representing the Indian Bar i.e., the law practices and the legal profession in India. Bar Council of India performs various activities related to law. These functions cover everything that is of legal nature, e.g. legal education, law profession, law bodies and any other matter.
5. **National Council for Teacher Education** (NCTE) It is a statutory body formed to overlook standards, procedures and processes in the Indian education system. It was established in 1973 as an advisory body for the Central and State Governments, on matters related to teacher education. It became a statutory body through the National Council for Teacher Education Act, 1993 on 17th August, 1995. Its headquarters is located in New Delhi. It has 4 regional offices.
6. **The Rehabilitation Council of India** (RCI) It was set up as a registered society in 1986. On September, 1992 the RCI Act was enacted by Parliament and it became a statutory body on 22nd June, 1993.

   The mandate given to RCI is to regulate and monitor services given to persons with disability, to standardise syllabi and to maintain a central rehabilitation register for all qualified professionals and personnel working in the field of rehabilitation and special education.
7. **National Translation Mission** (NTM), **2008** It was set up with the objective of functioning as a clearing house for all translation activities of Central Institute of Indian Languages (CIIL). Mysore is the nodal organisation for operating this mission.
8. **Higher Education Funding Agency** (HEFA) HEFA is an autonomous body which was established to finance creation of capital assets in premier educational institutions of India. HEFA was incorporated in May 2017 as a joint venture between the Ministry of Human Resource Development and Canara Bank with an agreed equity participation in the ratio of 91% and 9%, respectively.

   HEFA is registered as a non-profit company under Section 8 of the Companies Act 2013. It aims at financing the building of educational infrastructure and R & D infrastructure and thereby enabling the institutions to reach top rankings globally.
9. **National Testing Agency** (NTA) It was established in 2017 to conduct entrance examination for various higher educational institutions in India. It is registered as a society under Indian Societies Act, 1860.

   Until recently, the CBSE conducted NET exam in 84 subjects at 91 selected cities spread across the country, from December 2018, the UGC-NET is conducted by NTA.
10. **Regional Language Centres** (RLC) RLCs were established to implement the three language formula of the government. They are located at Pune, Mysore, Patiala, Bhubaneswar, Guwahati, Solan and Lucknow.

# ORIENTAL, CONVENTIONAL AND NON-CONVENTIONAL LEARNING PROGRAMMES IN INDIA

Oriental, conventional and non-conventional learning programmes are designed to provide education and skills to youth population and prepare them for employment. These learning programmes are discussed below

## Oriental Learning Programmes in India

Oriental studies is an academic field of study that embraces near Eastern and Far Eastern societies and cultures, languages, people, history and archeology. In recent terminology, such studies are called Middle Eastern studies and Asian studies. Traditional Oriental studies in Europe is focused on the discipline of Islamic studies.

With the disappearance of the Gurukula System and ancient universities, it became necessary to evolve a method by which the ancient knowledge and wisdom could be revived and preserved. In the 19th and 20th centuries, the Western scholars took upon them the word of such a revival.

Hence, a long journey of the preservation of the ancient knowledge and education system, culture, etc., started with the establishment of institutes and libraries.

## Oriental Research Institutes

There are around 16 institutes/universities whose work is consisted chiefly in collecting and collating rare manuscripts in the oriental languages (like Prakrit and Sanskrit) dealing with religion, philosophy, literature, grammar, arts and science, editing them and publishing them with or without translations and explanatory notes.

These universities are–

1. Adyar Library and Research Centre (Madras)
2. Asiatic Society
3. Bhandarkar Oriental Research Institute (Pune)
4. Ganganath Jha Kendriya Sanskrit Vidyapeeth (Allahabad)
5. Kuppuswami Sastri Research Institute (Madras)
6. Madras Sanskrit College (Chennai)
7. Mythic Society (Bangalore)
8. Oriental Institute (Baroda)
9. Oriental Manuscripts Library (Trivandum)
10. Oriental Research Institute (Mysore)
11. Oriental Research Institute (Tirupati)
12. Sanskrit Academy (Madras)
13. Sanskrit Sahitya Parishad (Kolkata)
14. Government Sanskrit College (Kolkata)
15. Saraswati Mahal Library (Tanjavur)
16. Vishveshvaranand Vishvabandhu Institute of Sanskrit and Indological Studies

# Conventional Learning Programmes in India

These learning programmes include all those courses which are imparted in colleges and universities. In these programmes, courses which are career and employment oriented taught along with intellectual skills. e.g. Graduation, M.B.A, L.L.B and so on.

## Characteristics of Conventional Learning Programmes

- These programmes include all the objectives of education like knowledge, comprehension and opportunities for employment.
- In these programmes the main emphasis is given on progressive education.
- In these programmes learning is based on holistic view, self-control, self-realisation and cultural values.
- Although through these courses chances of employment are adequate but take a long time to be accomplished.
- It is an on-campus education with fixed time which requires regular attendance, working under prescribed curriculum.
- Emphasis is more on teaching while the students learn through listening and observation.
- Student assessment happens in traditional ways.

# Non-conventional Learning Programmes in India

Non-conventional Learning Programmes in India are different from conventional learning programmes. Under this programme teaching programmes are done in the form of Online Education (E - Learning), Open and distance education, etc.

These programmes include both advanced methods and complex learning aspects through which learning becomes more effective for learners. These teaching methods can be Correspondence education, open schools and so on.

These also include online mode and optional courses. These programmes fulfill the demand of modern society and encourage employment oriented learning. Different degree, diploma and certificate courses are available under such conventional programs.

Non-conventional learning programs target unemployed youth, school dropouts, under-privileged sections including tribal and minority population.

## Characteristics of Non-Conventional Learning Programmes

- The programs are learner oriented.
- There is no fixed curriculum, but the knowledge is employment oriented.
- They are cost effective.

## Distance Education

Distance education or distance learning is the education of students who may not always be physically present in the school. The University of Delhi established a School of Correspondence Courses and Continuing Education, to cater to the increasing demand of higher education which cannot be met by conventional education. This university involved courses wherein the student corresponded with the school via post.

Further, Massive Open Online Courses (MOOCs), offering large-scale interactive participation and open access through the World Wide Web or other network technologies, are recent educational modes in distance education.

## Objectives of Distance Learning

- Effective utilisation of intellectual resources, minimising wastage of time in scouting for opportunities or desired items of knowledge appropriate to the requirement.
- Certification of attainments of any kind at any level acquired through formal or non-formal means in conventional or non-conventional fields.
- Any-time availability of desired knowledge at appropriate levels of comprehension to all for self-paced learning.
- Platform for sharing of ideas and techniques and pooling of knowledge resources.

## Characteristics of Distance Education

1. **Cost Effective** These Distance Learning Courses are quite affordable as compare to the traditional college degrees.
2. **Flexibility** By opting for Distance Learning programme, you have the opportunity to make your time table to study in accordance with your convenience. As all the course material is available offline as well online, there is no need to go to the library or market.
3. **Wide Range of Courses** With wide range of courses available, students have the freedom to select in accordance with their convenience. For instance, they can opt for a degree course, diploma or certification.
4. **Career Growth** With distance education program, one can participate in other activities including jobs or family, etc. With distance education, no break will occur and there will be a continuous growth in academics as well as career.
5. **No Commutation** With Distance Learning programme, you have the option to study from home as well as take classroom education. Most of the reputed Distance Learning providers offer classroom teaching on weekends. Thus, you can take the classes as well as faculty assistance.

## Modes of Distance Education

- Correspondence education
- Radio and Television
- Open Universities
- In -service teacher education programme

# Correspondence Education

The emergence of correspondence education or postal course was largely linked to employment opportunities. The courses fulfilled the purpose of providing vocational training of the laymen and workers. With industrialisation, there was a huge demand for skilled labourer's the number of which was not high. Hence, in order to train the laymen, institutes sprang up to teach the workers the required skill for employment.

In 1982, the term 'correspondence education' was changed to Distance Education and the Council was henceforth came to be known as the International Council for Distance Education (ICDE).

Today, distance education involves online education wherein the learning was either completely distance learning, or a combination of distance learning and traditional classroom instruction (called hybrid or blended).

**→ Distance Education Council (DEC)**

It was an organisation based in New Delhi which is responsible for the promotion and coordination of the open university and distance education. The council was constituted under the Indira Gandhi National Open University Act, 1985.

The Vice-Chancellor of IGNOU is the ex-officio chairperson of DEC. In June 2013, University Grants Commission (UGC) has taken over DEC by establishing Distance Education Bureau which govern the distance education programmes in India.

## Open Universities

The term open university usually refers to a university with an open-door academic policy, i.e. no entry requirements.

It is a non-formal system of education and caters to the needs of higher education. It is distance education which is provided on part-time basis as well with the application of latest innovations in educational technology.

The goal of open universities is to offer everyone equal opportunities to develop their abilities, to improve their level of education and to retrain for a new career. Hence, it has a capacity of thousands of students.

### Characteristics of Open Universities

1. These universities follow no-classroom teaching method. Their classes are either online or the teaching material is sent to homes. Thus, their fee is affordable for all poor, working professionals, non-working people, etc.
2. Open Universities offer access to quality education and skill development to learners in remote areas as well as those who are medically not fit to attend classes on daily basis.
3. Another important feature of Open Universities, is that there's no age limit as such. Any person from any walk of life at any age can pursue higher education.
4. Open Universities function under UGC's purview hence, the degrees and certificates awarded are UGC approved and valid in every regard.
5. Open Universities offer relaxation in the duration of a programme. e.g. a three-year programme can be completed in six years.

### Structure of Open University in India

The structure of open university officials working at higher positions is –

- Chancellor
- Two Vice-Chancellors in university-one sees academics and the other finances.
- In every district there is one study centre.
- For assisting Vice-Chancellor there are five Directors.
- Besides Directors two principals to be appointed whose level will be of Professor and Reader.
- The financial matter to be borne by State University and UGC.
- Both open and distance learning are today combined to be called the open and distance learning. In the present scenario, the ODL holds a special place in the education system as many prestiguous universities like IGNOU reaches out to the students located even in the farthest of corners.

## Indira Gandhi National Open University, IGNOU

IGNOU was established by an Act of Parliament in 1985 in New Delhi and has continuously striven to build an inclusive knowledge society through inclusive education.

It has tried to increase the Gross Enrolment Ratio (GER) by offering high-quality teaching through the Open and Distance Learning (ODL) mode.

### Objectives of IGNOU

- To provide access for all sections of society.
- To provide continual professional development and training to all sectors of the economy.

### Functions of IGNOU

- To provide access to higher education to all segments of the society.
- To offer high-quality, innovative and need-based programme at different levels for all those who require them.
- Reach out to the disadvantaged by offering programmes in all parts of the country at affordable costs.
- To promote, coordinate and regulate the standards of education offered through open and distance learning in the country.

Indira Gandhi National Open University functions provide seamless access to sustainable and learner-centric quality education, skill upgradation and training to all by using innovative technologies and methodologies and ensuring convergence of existing systems for large scale human resource development, required for promoting integrated national development and global understanding.

### IGNOU International Activities

IGNOU is offering distance education programme in collaboration with UNESCO and international institutes for capacity building in many parts of Africa.

IGNOU plays an active role in SAARC consortium for open and distance learning and global mega universities network.

### Centres of IGNOU Study Centres

The Indira Gandhi National open university has opened study centres within country and abroad including far flung areas for higher education. These are 142 centres which are providing counselling and the university has asked many organisations to open such centres.

## State Open Universities (SOUs)

Open Universities set up by the respective state grants are called State Open Universities. These are single mode institutions, meaning they provide education only in the distance mode.

Such universities cater to people who are unable to pursue regular courses due to various reasons becoming instrumental in shaping the career growth of learner who are already employed. The first open university was Dr. B.R. Ambedkar Open University, Hyderabad which was set up in August 1982.

There are 13 State Open Universities that are

1. Dr BR Ambedkar Open University, BRAOU, Hyderabad
2. Vardhman Mahaveer Open University VMOU, Kota
3. Nalanda Open University, NOU, Patna
4. Yashwantrao Chavan Maharashtra Open University, YCMOU, Nashik
5. Madhya Pradesh Bhoj Open University, MPBOU, Bhopal
6. Dr. Babasaheb Ambedkar Open University (BAOU), Ahmedabad
7. Karnataka State Open University, Mysore
8. Netaji Subhash Open University, Kolkata
9. UP Rajarshi Tandon Open University, Prayagraj, Allahabad
10. Tamil Nadu Open University, Chennai
11. Pt. Sunderlal Sharma Open University, Bilaspur
12. Uttarakhand Open University, Haldwani
13. Krishna Kanta Handiqui State Open University, Guwahati

### → Commonwealth of Learning

Commonwealth of Learning (CoL) was established through a Memorandum of Understanding between Governments of Commonwealth of Learning in 1988.

The CoL is an intergovernmental organisation created by Commonwealth Heads of Government to encourage the development and sharing of open learning, distance education knowledge, resources and technologies. CoL is helping developing nations to improve access to quality education and training, CoL has located its Commonwealth Educational Media Centre for Asia (CEMCA) in India.

### SAKSHAT

A one step education portal has been launched on October 30th, 2006, to facilitate lifelong learning for students, teachers and those in employment or in pursuit of knowledge free of cost to them. The content development task for SAKSHAT was looked after by the Content Advisory Committee (CAC).

The main vision of SAKSHAT is to cater to the learning needs of more than 50 crore people through National Mission in Education through Information and Communication Technology (ICT). The scheme is to provide connectivity to all institutions of higher learning.

# PROFESSIONAL EDUCATION

Professional education is a programme that develops individuals to acquire special competencies for professional practice and develop skills in youths.

It includes all those educational courses which provide training for livelihood. Professional education is the component of technical education programme.

The aim of this education system is to enable youths to get employment in government and non-government sectors after getting degree or diploma.

Professional education includes curriculum based on banking, media, management, tourism, teaching, aviation, etc. These curriculum enable youths to get jobs opportunity in different sectors like auditing, editing, hotel management, finance management, managers and so on. This education system enables students to become responsible for their life.

Important professional courses are

- BBA
- MBA
- MCA in Management
- Mass Communication / Journalism
- Master's in Data Analytics
- B.Ed
- M.Ed
- Hospitality
- Global Marketing Management
- Air Hostess Courses and so on

## Specialized Professional Bodies

Professional councils are responsible for recognition of courses, promotion of professional institutions and providing grants to undergraduate programs and various awards. The statutory professional councils of India are:

- All India Council of Technical Education (AICTE)
- Medical Council of India (MCI)
- Indian Council for Agricultural Research (ICAR)
- National Council for Teacher Education (NCTE)
- Dental Council of India (DCI)
- Pharmacy Council of India (PCI)
- Indian Nursing Council (INC)
- Bar Council of India (BCI)
- Central Council of Homeopathy (CCH)
- Central Council for Indian Medicine (CCIM)
- Council Of Architecture (COA)
- Distance Education Council (DEC)
- Rehabilitation Council of India (RCI)
- National Council for Rural Institutes (NCRI)
- State Councils of Higher Education (SCHE)

# TECHNICAL EDUCATION

Technical education imparts knowledge of a specific trade, craft or profession, especially in the field of science, engineering and technology. Such education plays a very important role in the human development. It creates skilled manpower, improves the quality of life and enhances industrial productivity.

Centres of technical training can be seen from the British period when first engineering college was established in the Uttar Pradesh in 1847 for the training of Civil Engineers at Roorkee. It is now located in Uttarakhand. The Indian Institute of Science was established in 1909 in order to provide research work and education in the field of engineering and science.

The first degree classes were started in University of Banaras in 1917, which provided degrees in different disciplines like mechanical engineering, electrical engineering and metallurgy, which was founded by Pt. Madan Mohan Malaviya.

Keeping the importance of technical education in mind, many institutions along with AICTE were setup. Some of them are –

### (i) Indian Institutes of Technology (IITs)

IITs are apex institutions for engineering education and research. They are governed by the Institutes of Technology Act, 1961 which has declared them as institutions of national importance and lays down their powers, duties and framework for governance.

The first IIT was set up in Kharagpur in 1951 and soon later in Bombay (1958), Madras (1959), Kanpur (1959) and Delhi (1963). The University of Roorkee was converted to IIT Roorkee in 2001.

### (ii) National Institutes of Technology (NITs)

During the Second Five-Year Plan (1956–60) in India, a number of industrial projects were contemplated. To ensure enough supply of trained personnels to meet the demand for these projects, a decision was taken to start the Regional Engineering Colleges (RECs), at the rate of one per each major state. Thus, government opened 8 RECs in 1960, two in each region.

In 2002, Ministry of Human Resource Development decided to upgrade RECs to "National Institutes of Technology" (NITs). They are governed by the National Institutes of Technology Act, 2007, which declared them as institutions of national importance and lays down their powers, duties and framework for governance. The Act lists 31 NITs that exist today.

### (iii) Indian Institutes of Information Technology (IIITs)

These are a group of institutes of higher education focused on information technology. The IIITs at Gwalior, Allahabad, Jabalpur and Kancheepuram were set up by the Ministry of Human Resource Development (MHRD) to provide UG as well as PG education.

Besides the government funded IIITs, in 2010 the Union Cabinet approved a scheme for setting up twenty more IIITs, based on the Public-Private Partnership (PPP) model, funded by the Central Government, State Government and industry partners in the ratio 50:35:15. There are 23 IIITs located at different places in Indian states.

### (iv) National Institutes of Technical Teachers' Training and Research (NITTTRs)

It is a group of autonomous institutions established by Ministry of Human Resource Development to improve the quality of engineering education system in India. Located at Bhopal, Chandigarh, Chennai and Kolkata in mid 1960s. They trained polytechnic teachers to undertake activities in the areas of education, planning and management.

It also fosters research in the inter-disciplinary area of engineering education and offers consultancy and extension services for the total development of engineering colleges, polytechnic colleges, vocational institutions, industry, service sector and the community at large.

## Indian Institutes of Management (IIMs)

IIMs are a group of 20 public, autonomous institutes of management education and research in India. They primarily offer post graduate, doctoral and executive education programmes. The establishment of IIMs was initiated by Jawaharlal Nehru. They are registered as societies under the Indian Societies Registration Act.

There are 20 IIMs located in different regions of Indian states/UTs.

Indian Institute of Management, Calcutta was the first IIM to be set up on 13th November, 1961 and soon later in Ahmedabad on 16th December, 1961.

## Skill Based Education

This type of education includes such courses which provide training and skills in different disciplines. Duration of these courses can be from 6 months to 2 years. The main objective of this education is to develop skills in students and enable them to achieve a suitable carrer option in life.

Skill based courses are Fashion Designing, Tourism, Food Processing, Garment technology, Software development, Hospitality management and IIT courses like Carpenter, Cutting, Technology technician, Electrician, Photography, Embroidery Needle Work, Health Sanitary Inspector and so on.

For the development of such education, the government has introduced various programmes including NVEQF, KAUSHAL, PMKVY, etc. These programmes target groups for skill development for all.

**→PMKVY**

In 2015, Pradhan Mantri Kaushal Vikas Yojana (PMKVY) was launched by Government of India in all states of the country. Under this programme the Ministry of Skill Development and Entrepreneurship is providing Oriental courses to students who have passed 12th level. It is also providing employment to these youths.

## Industrial Training Institutes (ITIs)

These are post-secondary schools which provide skill education and training to students.These are constituted by Directorate General of Employment and Training (DGET), Ministry of Skill Development and Entrepreneurship, Indian Government. After completion of the training, trainees/students have to pass the All India Trade Test (AITT) and they then get the National Trade Certificate (NTC).

As in April, 2016 there are around 13105 ITIs, out of these, the number of Government ITIs are 2293, while the private ITIs are 10812.

# VALUE EDUCATION

Value education is the process by which people give moral values to each other. According to CV Good, value education is the aggregate of all the process by means of which a person develops abilities and other form of behaviour of the positive values in the society in which he lives.

## Need for Imparting Value Education

- Developing societies like India face a conflict between tradition and modernisation.
- Globalisation has made societies more complex and less homogeniety.
- India is a multi-lingual, multi-cultural and multi-religious country.
- To make a society truly inclusive.
- To make children sensitive to the environment.
- To encourage greater exposition in the field of science and technology.
- To realise values that are enshrined in our Constitution such as justice, liberty, equality and fundamental duties.

### Objectives of Value Education

- To improve the integral growth of human beings.
- To create attitudes and improvement towards sustainable lifestyle.
- To increase awareness about our national history, our cultural heritage, constitutional rights, national integration, community development and environment.
- To create and develop awareness about the values and their significance and role.
- To know about various living and non-living organisms and their interaction with the environment.
- Developing tolerance towards various religions and promoting an understanding of different religious faith.

## Types of Values Introduced in the Colleges

Types of values to be introduced in the colleges by the University are

1. **Human Values** It means what is enriching and good for individuals. These are practiced by individuals alone, irrespective of his/her social relationship. It is mentored by senior faculty members.
2. **Community or Social Values** It implies what is good for the society. These values discuss the basis of the relationship of an individual with other people.
3. **Cultural Values** It means involvement and survival of the culture. The practice of such values is very essential for the growth and survival of any culture.
4. **Institutional Values** It includes political and moral values.

## Key Developments in Value Education

An awareness for the inculcation of right values in India have been grown since independence. Thus, some of the important developments in value education have been elaborated below

- **University Education Commission** (1948) The Commission considered both the philosophical and practical aspects of value-oriented education and made certain valuable proposals for reform. But they were implemented only in a small number of institutions.
- **Sri Prakash Committee** (1959) The Central Advisory Board of Education appointed a special committee on religious and moral instruction under Sri Prakash Committee.
  The Committee noted that learning of such moral and spiritual values is very essential and school should provide for reading about the lives of great religious leaders and later in higher stages of education.
- **National Education Commission** (1964-1966) It is popularly known as Kothari Commission. It recommended direct moral instruction which must be provided aside from all education.
- **National Policy on Education** (NPE), (1986 and 1992). It is constituted to promote education amongst India's people. It advocated education as a tool for social and moral values that are oriented toward unity and integration of our people.
- **National Value Education Centre** To promote value education in technological and professional Institutions. National Value Education Centre has been established in IIT Delhi.
- **Chavan's Committee's Report** (1999) It provided impetus to resume work on value orientation of education.
- **National Curriculum Framework** (2000, 2005) Both the NCFs of 2000 and 2005 reaffirm the commitment to promote values that foster peace, humanity and tolerance.

# ENVIRONMENTAL EDUCATION

Environmental education is a process which allows us to become more knowledgeable about environment issues. It motivates one to explore environmental issues, take action to improve the environment. It makes the students aware of the environmental issues and their causes and effects.

## Objectives of Environmental Education

- Creating awareness about environmental problems among people.
- Imparting basic knowledge about the environment and its allied problems.
- Developing an attitude of concern for the environment.
- Motivating people to participate in environment protection and environment improvement.
- Acquiring skills to help the concerned individuals in indentifying and solving environmental problems.
- Striving to attain harmony with Nature.

## Need for Imparting Environment at Education

- It is important to give information about sustainable development.

- There are many issues like pollution ,waste disposal, degradation of environment, global warming, depletion of ozone layer and loss of biodiversity, etc which need to be minimised by proper strategy and management policies.
- To change the careless attitude of people and make them responsible citizens.
- To prepare such a conceptual framework which may help to make people aware about their environment.

## Key Development of Environmental Education

Through 42nd amendment in 1976, the Government of India incorporated environmental concerns in the Indian Constitution. After the establishment of Ministry of Environment and Forests, the growing concerns about the environment in India provoked the Government to introduce Environmental Education at all levels of education.

In 1983-84 the Ministry of Environment and Forest launched the Environment Education, Awareness and Training scheme to enhance people's understanding regarding the human - environment relationship and to enhance skills and capabilities to protect the environment and improve it.

In 1991, the Supreme Court of India gave a ruling that Environmental Education course should be mandatory at under graduate level, which provided an opportunity to introduce sustainable development issues to higher education.

It also gave directions to the University Grants Commission (UGC) for providing grants for higher education and making policy framework for higher educational institutions to facilitate and ensure the delivery of the Environmental Education (EE) course.

There are many higher education institutions and universities which are imparting EE at higher level such as Indian Institute of Technology (IIT), Schools of Planning and Architecture, etc.

These institutions provide different courses in Environmental Education like, M.Arch in Sustainable Built Environment, M.Arch in Environmental design, Social ecology, etc.

# POLICIES

Policies can be understood as a course of action that involves making decisions and specific plans by institutions. Policies are directed towards a common goal. They are made by organisations after thorough discussions and careful study of the identified problem. In India, the education policies are taken by both the central and state governments. After making policies, the process goes through many stages-implementation, analysis and evaluation.

In India, different policies regarding education has been taken from time to time. The important policies on education are listed below:

## National Policy on Education (NPE), 1968

The NPE is based on the recommendations of the Kothari Commission (1964-66). However, in 1967 the government constituted a Committee of Members of Parliament on Education, popularly known as **Sapru Committee** to prepare the draft of a statement on the National Policy on Education (NPE).

The draft prepared by the committee was considered and approved by the CABE. It was on this basis that the Government of India announced the NPE 1968.

Following are the main features of NPE, 1968

- It emphasised the need for raising the standards of education at all levels.
- It suggested the new universities to be established only after proper planning and provisions of adequate funds.
- It emphasised on strengthening of post-graduate teaching and research as well as of centres of advanced study.

## National Policy on Education, 1986

The New National Policy on Education was announced in May 1986. It comprised of 12 parts and discussed in detail the essential characteristics of a national system of education. A review of National Education Policy, 1986 Programme of Action was done by Rama Murti Committee.

The recommendations were

- It provided for a common educational structure like 10 + 2 + 3.
- It suggested strengthening of adult education, vocational education, gradual replacement of affiliating system by autonomous colleges, setting up of open university and rural university system and fortifying technical and management education.

## National Education Policy, 1992 (NPE, 1992)

The NPE-1986 was modified by the P.V Narasimha Rao Government in 1992. It was adopted in 2005 which was recognised as "Common Minimum Programme" by the UPA government under Prime Minister Manmohan Singh.

Salient Features of NPE , 1992 are as follows

- It implemented All India Bases Common Entrance Examination for admission in all professional and technical programmes in India.
- The Indian Government laid down a Three - Exam Scheme for admission to Engineering and Architecture/Planning programmes such as : JEE, AIEEE at the National Level and SLEEE State Level Engineering Entrance Examinations.
- In this policy, State Level Institutions have option to join AIEEE.

## National Education Policy, 2016

The draft of National Education Policy (NEP) 2016 was released by the MHRD. The focus of the policy is to address gender discrimination, the creation of educational tribunals, and a common curriculum for Science, Mathematics and English.

The salient features of NEP-2016 regarding higher education are as follows

- At the national level, a teacher education university will be set up covering various aspects of teacher education and faculty development.
- Keeping in view special importance of Sanskrit, facilities for teaching Sanskrit at the school and university stages will be offered on more liberal scale.
- An independent mechanism for administering the National Higher Education Fellowship Programme will be put in place.
- A quality assurance mechanism for accreditation of all universities/institutions offering ODL/MOOCs will be put in place to ensure quality, promote innovation and reshape and modernise the ODL/MOOCs courses and programmes.
- In order to promote innovation, creativity and entrepreneurship, 100 more incubation centres will be established in HEIs over a period of next 5 years.

## New Education Policy, 2020

On 26th August, 2020, the Central Government cleared the New Education Policy (NEP) based on the report of former ISRO scientist Dr. K. Kasturirangan. The government after rejecting the recommendations of TSR Subramanium Committee on Education had constituted this committee in 2017. The latest policy is Third Education Policy to be implemented in the country and will replace the erstwhile policy of 1986.

The salient features of NEP is given below:

- The Ministry of Human Resource Development has been renamed as Ministry of Education. It will bring more clarity about the role and mandate of the Ministry.
- In context of school education, it provides for a "5 + 3 + 3 + 4" design corresponding to the age groups 3-8 years (foundational stage), 8-11 (preparatory), 11-14 (middle), and 14-18 (secondary). Apart from providing continuity to school education, it will bring pre- school under the ambit of school education.

- The other reforms in school education includes, overhauling the curriculum, "easier" Board exams, a reduction in the syllabus to retain "core essentials" and thrust on "experiential learning and critical thinking". The students till class 5 are also advised to be taught in mother tongue at school.
- In higher education, following reforms has been suggested:
  - Replacing UGC and AICTE with the Higher Education Commission of India (HECI).
  - Allowing reputed Foreign Institutions to open their campuses.
  - Re-introduction of four-year multi-disciplinary Bachelors' program, with exist option.
  - Discontinuation of M. Phil program.
  - Constitution of National Research Foundation (NRF) to enhance the pace of research in the country.
  - Flexibility to Institutions to offer different design for Master's program.
  - Phasing out of all institutions offering single streams and all universities and colleges must aim to become multi-disciplinary by 2040.
- In teacher training, following reforms has been suggested:
  - Large number of merit-based scholarships shall be instituted across the country for studying quality 4-year integrated B.Ed. courses.
  - The TETs will also be extended to cover teachers across all stages (Foundational, Preparatory, Middle and Secondary) of school education.
  - For Continuous Professional Development (CPD), teachers will be given opportunities for self-improvement and to learn the latest innovations and advances in their professions.
  - A National Professional Standards for Teachers (NPST) will be developed by 2022, after consultation with all the stakeholders.
- A new National Assessment Centre, PARAKH (Performance, Assessment, Review and Analysis of Knowledge for Holistic Development) will be set up as standard setting body.
- The government has decided to implement all these reforms in gradual manner till 2040. Further, the expenditure in education will be raised to 6% of GDP to upscale the quality and meet the rising demands from the education sector.

# GOVERNANCE AND ADMINISTRATION

Governance refers to a way or a process of governing. It relates to public management and their related issues. It is a definite political system or an order that is written in the Constitution. The Constitution of a country details the basic structure of its governance. 'Constitution' word is derived from Latin word 'Constituere' which means 'to establish'. It is a body of fundamental principles according to which a state or an organisation functions.

The Indian Constitution was written in 2 years, 11 months and 18 days. Its written draft was completed on 26 November, 1949 and was enforced on 26 January, 1950. Our Constitution has a Preamble which consists of the words Sovereign, Socialist, Secular and Democratic Republic. There are 465 articles which are divided into 25 Parts and 12 Schedules. It is the lengthiest written Constitution in the world.

## Formation of Indian Constitution

- Idea of Constituent Assembly proposed by M.N. Roy in 1934.
- First Constituent Assembly composed in November, 1946 under Cabinet Mission.
- First meeting of the Assembly held on 9 December, 1946 and was presided by Dr. Sachidanand Sinha.
- The Assembly had 389 members.
- On 11 December, 1946, Dr. Rajendra Prasad elected as permanent President of the Assembly.

- On 13 December, 1946, Jawahar Lal Nehru presented an objective resolution that later became the 'Preamble' of Indian Constitution.
- The Constitution Draft was discussed in the Constituent Assembly for 11 sessions (165 days).

## Features of Different Constitutions

Indian Constitution is a blend of different Constitutions. Features of other Constitutions are included in Constitution in it according to the needs of our country. The features borrowed from other Constitutions are as follows:

| Sources | Features |
|---|---|
| Australia | • Concurrent List<br>• Cooperative Federalism<br>• Joint sitting of 2 Houses |
| Canada | • Federal System<br>• Advisory jurisdiction of Supreme Court |
| French | • Republic<br>• Liberty, Equality and Fraternity |
| Ireland | • Directive Principles of State Policy<br>• Presidential Election |
| Russia | • Fundamental Duties<br>• Ideals of Social, Economic and Political Justice |
| South Africa | • Procedure of Constitutional Amendments<br>• Electing Rajya Sabha members |
| UK | • Election of Prime Minister and Council of Ministers<br>• Parliamentary system of government<br>• Two Houses of Parliament<br>• Legislative Procedures<br>• Single Citizenship<br>• Jurisdiction of Courts<br>• Rule of Law |
| USA | • Fundamental Rights<br>• President as Executive Head<br>• Impeachment of President<br>• Vice-President<br>• Independent Judiciary<br>• Written Constitution |
| Germany | • Suspension of Fundamental Rights during Emergency |
| Japan | • Law on which the Supreme Court functions |

## Schedules of the Constitution

There are twelve Schedules of the Constitution of India. They are as follows:

| Nos. | Features |
|---|---|
| First Schedule | • Formation of states, union territories and their jurisdiction. |
| Second Schedule | • Salaries of President, Governors, Speakers, Chairman of Rajya Sabha, Judges of Supreme Court and High Court, LAG. |
| Third Schedule | • Oaths and affirmations of Union Ministers, Member of Parliament, State Legislature, Judges of Supreme Court and High Court, Comptroller and Auditor General. |
| Fourth Schedule | • Allocation of seats for states and UTs in Rajya Sabha. |
| Fifth Schedule | • Adminsitration and control of scheduled areas and tribes. |
| Sixth Schedule | • Administration and control of tribal areas of Assam, Meghalaya, Mizoram and Tripura. |
| Seventh Schedule | • Allocation of powers and junctions between Union (central) and State.<br>• **List I** Union 100 subjects.<br>• **List II** State 61 subjects.<br>• **List III** Concurrent 52 subjects. |
| Eighth Schedule | • Languages recognized by the Constitution.<br>• At present, there are 22 recognised languages. |
| Ninth Schedule | • Acts related to land reforms, land tenure, railways, industry and property.<br>• Added in 1985 by 52nd Constitutional Amendment. |
| Tenth Schedule | • Provisions related to disqualification of members due to defection also known as Anti-Defection Law.<br>• Added in 1985 by 52nd Constitutional Amendment. |
| Eleventh Schedule | • Added by 73rd Amendment in 1992.<br>• Related to power and responsibility of Panchayats. |
| Twelfth Schedule | • Added by 74th Amendment in 1992.<br>• Related to power, responsibility and authority of Municipalities. |

## Articles

Articles related to education are listed below :

**Article 21A** is related to Right to elementary education.

**Article 29(3)** provides that no citizen will be deprived of the right to admission in any state or state aided or self-finance educational institutions on the basis of any religion, race, caste, etc.

**Article (30)** states that the state shall not in granting aid to educational institutions maintained by state or receiving aid out of state funds on grounds of religion, race, caste, language or any of them.

**Article 30(1)** says that religious or linguistic minorities will enjoy the right to establishment and administration of educational institutions of their interest.

**Article 30(2)** states that state will not discriminate in providing assistance to educational institutions run by minorities.

**Article (41)** of the Constitution provides that all citizens have equal right to education. It states that state shall within the limits of its economic capacity and development make effective provisions for right to work and education.

**Article (45)** declares free and compulsory education for children upto 14 years of age. 93rd Constitutional Amendment in 2001 added to Article (45) says that state will look after and provide education to all children until they attain the age of 6 years.

**Article (46)** provides that state will promote with special care the education and economic interests of the weaker sections of the people, especially SC/ST. The Constitution Eighty Sixth Amendment Act, 2002 inserted Article (21A) in the Constitution provide free and compulsory education of all children in the age group of six to fourteen years as a fundamental right. The right to children to free and compulsory education Act, 2009.

**Article (66)** is related to research institute of science and technology of higher education.

**Article 28(1)** No religious instruction shall be provided in any educational institution wholly maintained out of state funds.

**Article (350)(a)** says that it shall be the endeavour of every state and of every local authority within the state to provide adequate facilities for instruction in the mother tongue at the primary stage of education to children belonging to linguistic minority groups.

Education is listed in the Concurrent List of Seventh Schedule of the Indian Constitution. Thus, both the centre and state have the authority to make legislations on it. If any dispute occurs the upper hand goes to the centre.

There is another body called CABE that plays an important role in educational governance. The responsibilities that each of these bodies have are–

1. **Central Government** The Government of India has controlled the education through following functions
   - It lays down the National Policy on Education.
   - It provides grants to UGC.
   - It establishes Central Universities and Institutions of national importance.
   - It declares an educational institution as deemed university on the recommendation of the UGC.
2. **State Government** The State Government performs the following functions
   - States have also set up state councils and advisory boards to provide guidelines for proper functioning of higher education institutions in the states.
   - These state councils coordinate the roles of government, universities and apex regulatory agencies for higher education within the state.
3. **Central Advisory Board of Education** (CABE) It is the highest advisory body to advise the Central and State Governments in the field of education. It was established in 1920 and its present form is continued from 1994.

It plays a pivotal role in reviewing educational development, determining the changes required to improve the system and monitoring the implementation.

## Administrative Process of Education

The main components of educational administrative process are

1. **Decision Making** It is a continuous process at all levels to ensure smooth functioning of an organisation. This is true of the university also for the effective functioning.

   At a university level it includes varied and diversified decision making into various aspects such as what courses to be, what recruitment procedure are to be adopted for selecting academic/non-academic staff, etc.
2. **Planning** It is an important management function that helps in setting institutional goods which help to achieve the desired results which are used for assessing the performance. In educational institutions too such planning is carried out to fulfil the requirements of the institutions. Good planning ensures the success of the institute. Thus, planning contributes to the smoothness, ease and efficiency of the administrative process for the institute.
3. **Organisation** These are social units deliberately constructed and reconstructed to seek specific goals universities, colleges and training institutions may well be considered as social organisations.

   Educational organisations mean two things one is the educational institution and the other is the organisation of resources.
4. **Communication** It is one of the basic elements of administrative process and is central to all functions.
5. **Directing** It is essential that there must be an authority or an order of a policy for providing direction for the programmes.
6. **Coordination** It is an important activity of educational administration which ensures close interrelation and integration of all the functional activities of the educational institutions.
7. **Budgeting** Budgeting in higher education examines the budget process as faced by colleges and university in an increasingly complex process. Budget is prepared in the university/college with regard to the income/ expenditure of a year.

   On the basis of the budget the economic policies are formulated and executed.
8. **Evaluation** It is the final stage in the administrative process. Under the process of evaluation the university administration evaluates the educational policies, achievement in comparison to the previous year.

# Chapter Practice

## Education System During Ancient, Medieval and Modern Period and its Types

1 Why education is considered important?
(A) It plays an important role in economic, cultural and social development
(B) It helps in the development of skills attitudes, habits and values
(C) It helps in the holistic development of child personality
(D) All of the above

2 "Education is natural, harmonious and progressive development of man's innate power." Who said this?
(A) John Dewey
(B) Pestalozzi
(C) Aristotle
(D) Rabindranath Tagore

3 Which of the following is/are not the characteristic(s) of informal education?
(A) It takes place outside the classroom
(B) It is provided by agencies such as home, family or community
(C) It is provided by trained teachers in a systematic way
(D) Education can occur outside of a structured classroom

4 When the Right of Children to Free and Compulsory Education Act, 2009 became operative in the country?
(A) 1st April, 2010 (B) 1st March, 2010
(C) 1st May, 2010 (D) 1st January, 2010

5 Secondary Education comprises classes
(A) VII-VIII (B) IX-XII
(C) IX-X (D) VI-VII

6 Under which Constitutional Amendment the Right to Education has been made as a fundamental rights?
(A) 80th Amendment
(B) 86th Amendment
(C) 85th Amendment
(D) 91st Amendment

7 What was the basis of education in the ancient period of India?
(A) Philosophy (B) Religion
(C) Science (D) Both (A) and (B)

8 Which of the following language formed the basis of delivering vedic education in ancient India?
(A) Prakrit (B) Pali
(C) Sanskrit (D) Arabic

9 Consider the following statements.
I. In the Ancient period people had a belief that through religious education they would attain salvation.
II. 'Gurukul System of Education' is also known as 'Vedic System of Education.'
III. In the Vedic System of Education, pupils occupied a vital position as compared to their Guru/Teachers.
Which of the above statement(s) is/are correct?
(A) Only I (B) I and II
(C) I and III (D) All of these

10 Consider the following statements.
I. During vedic period, Gurukuls were the formal institutions of learning.
II. Gurukuls were not the residential schools.
III. During the period, there were equal number of Gurukuls for both girls and boys.
Which of the above statement(s) is/are correct?
(A) Only I (B) Only II
(C) II and III (D) All of these

11 Consider the following statements about Gurukul System of Education.
I. It was based on residential concept.
II. It provided religious and philosophical education.
III. Pupils were imparted education only through Shruti.
Which of the above statement(s) is/are correct?
(A) Only I (B) I and II
(C) II and III (D) All of these

12 Which of the following statement(s) is/are correct about Gurukul Education System?
(A) Its aim was to preserve and transmit ancient Indian Culture.
(B) It provided basically religious education.
(C) Sanskrit was the main language in the system
(D) All of the above

13 Vedic literature was consisted of
(A) One hundred and eight Upanishads
(B) Four Vedas
(C) Four Upavedas
(D) All of the above

14 Nalanda, Takshashila, Odantapuri and Jagaddala are example of Universities of the period of
(A) Ancient period (B) Medieval period
(C) Modern period (D) Pre-historic period

15 After the Vedic system of education, which system of education emerged?
(A) Education based on Buddhist studies
(B) Education based on Sutras and Epics
(C) Education based on Urdu Literature
(D) Only (A) and (C)

16 During Ancient period students were taught by which method?
(A) Only Shruti (B) Only Smriti
(C) Both (A) and (B) (D) None of these

17 Which of the following was an early education institute in India?
(A) Gurukul (B) Vedic
(C) Muslim (D) All of these

18 Which ancient university was one of the world's first residential university?
(A) Nalanda (B) Vallabhi
(C) Odantapuri (D) Takshashila

19 Name the emperor who set up and established Vikramshila University.
(A) Dharampala (B) Bhanugupta
(C) Kumargupta (D) Ashok

20 Name the University which was ruined by Bakhtiyar Khilji in 1203 AD.
(A) Nalanda (B) Vikramshila
(C) Jagaddala (D) Nadia

21 The curriculum of Nalanda, Takshashila and other ancient Universities consisted of
(A) Medicine (B) Sciences
(C) Archery (D) All of these

22 Students of which university were generally offered higher posts?
(A) Vikramshila (B) Mithila
(C) Vallabhi (D) Nadia

23 Which university of higher education was situated in Tamil Nadu?
(A) Ujjain (B) Ennayiram
(C) Odantapuri (D) Salotgi

24 Nalanda University was destroyed by
(A) Mughals (B) Huns
(C) Palas (D) Pratiharas

25 During medieval period which dynasty promoted learning, arts and literature in India ?
(A) Palas (B) Pratiharas
(C) Mughal (D) All of these

26 Mahmud of Ghazni came in India in which period?
(A) 1001 AD (B) 1009 AD
(C) 1175 AD (D) 1195 AD

27 Urdu language was popularised by which dynasty?
(A) Delhi Sultanate (B) Mughal dynasty
(C) Rashtrakutas (D) Senas

28 During Mughal period the advanced studies were comprised of
(A) Mathematics (B) Geometry
(C) Astronomy (D) All of these

29 Consider the following statements.
I. Nalanda University was brought back to its former order during the reign of Palas.
II. During this period customs, cultures and traditions of Arab and Central Asian regions mingled with those of the Indian inhabitants.
III. With the advent of Mahmud of Ghazni and Muhammad Ghauri, Arabic and Persian languages got prominance.
Which of the above statement(s) is/are correct?
(A) Only I (B) I and III
(C) II and III (D) All of these

30 During which period the British successfully controlled much part of India and established formal system of higher education?
(A) 1600 AD (B) 1700 AD
(C) 1800 AD (D) 1900 AD

31 Teaching of Muslim Law was established in
(A) 1791 (B) 1782
(C) 1778 (D) 1781

32 Consider the following statements.
I. Calcutta, Bombay and Madras learning centres were focused on generating English speaking working class for the British administrative services.

II. Modern science and engineering education flourished in India by 1909 when the Indian Institute of Science was established by Tata with focus on research in science and engineering.

III. The British model of university system continued to expand across India leading to growing number of higher learning centres by 1947.

Which of the above statement(s) is/are correct?

(A) Only I (B) II and III

(C) I and III (D) All of these

**33** The formal system of higher education was established in which period in India?

(A) Ancient (B) Medieval

(C) Modern (D) None of these

**34** Who is responsible in making English as the language of instruction across the education system in India?

(A) Lord Mountbatten

(B) Lord Bentinck

(C) Lord Macaulay

(D) Lord Dalhousie

**35** Indian Institute of Science was established in which year?

(A) 1607 (B) 1801

(C) 1899 (D) 1909

**36** **Assertion** (A) The subjects taught at Nalanda covered every field of learning.

**Reason** (R) The Government of India has decided to restore the ancient Nalanda University.

**Codes**

(A) Both (A) and (R) are true

(B) Both (A) and (R) are false

(C) (A) is true, but (R) is false

(D) (A) is false, but (R) is true

**37** Higher education is important because

(A) it provides people with opportunity to reflect on the critical, social, economic, cultural and moral issues faced by humanity

(B) it contributes to the national development through dissemination of specialised knowledge and skills

(C) it gives a person opportunity to succeed in today's global economy

(D) All of the above

## Higher Education in India

**38** Consider the following statements.

I. Higher education is the final stage of formal learning.

II. The involvement of private sector in higher education has resulted drastic changes.

III. The Right to Education Act, 2009 brought about a revolution in the education system in India.

Which of the above statement(s) is/are correct?

(A) Only I (B) I and II

(C) II and III (D) All of these

**39** Which of the following aimed to promote knowledge of modern sciences in India ?

(A) Elphinstone Report– 1823

(B) Charter Act– 1813

(C) Lord Macaulay's Minute

(D) Wood's Despatch

**40** Elphinstone Report came in which year?

(A) 1813 (B) 1823

(C) 1835 (D) 1854

**41** Which report/committee recommended the appointment of district examination officers, school supervisors and training to teachers in Indian Education System ?

(A) Charter Act

(B) Elphinstone Report

(C) Sapru Committee

(D) Hunter Commission

**42** Consider the following statements about Lord Macaulay's Minute ?

I. This famous minute favoured English as the medium of instruction.

II. However, this instruction was mainly incorporated with elementary and secondary education.

III. Lord Macaulay held the view that Indian learning was inferior to European learning.

Which of the above statements is/are correct?

(A) Only I (B) II and III

(C) I and III (D) All of these

**43** Who had the view that Indian learning was inferior to European learning?

(A) Lord Dalhousie

(B) Lord Macaulay

(C) Lord Bentinck

(D) Lord Cornwallis

44 Which of the following is considered the first comprehensive plan for spreading of education in India?
(A) Macaulay's Minute
(B) Elphinstone Report
(C) Indian University Act
(D) Wood's Despatch

45 The Bethune school, the first school to educate women, was founded by J.E.D Bethune at which place?
(A) Madras (B) Bombay
(C) Calcutta (D) Delhi

46 Whose recommendations were the milestone in the direction of vocational studies and establishment of a Vocational Training College at Delhi?
(A) Wood and Abott Report 1937
(B) Sapru Committee, 1934
(C) Hartog Committee, 1929
(D) Wardha Scheme of Basic Education, 1937

47 Which Commission/Committee emphasised for female education especially outside the presidency town in 1882-1883?
(A) Saddler Commission
(B) Hartog Commission
(C) Hunter Commission
(D) Sapru Commission

48 Which Commission/Committee recommended that responsibility for primary education must be given to Local and Municipal Boards ?
(A) Saddler Commission
(B) Hartog Committee
(C) Hunter Commission
(D) Sapru Committee

49 Where were the teaching-cum examining universities, set up under Hunter Commission, in 1882 and 1887, respectively?
(A) Calcutta, Madras (B) Punjab, Allahabad
(C) Madras, Bombay (D) Delhi, Calcutta

50 Which Commission was set up in 1904 to go into conditions and prospects of universities in India and to suggest measures for improvement in their Constitution and working ?
(A) Saddler Commission
(B) Hunter Commission
(C) Raleigh Commission
(D) None of the above

51 Under Government Resolution on Education Policy, 1913 which university was set up due to local Patriotism?
(A) Rangoon (B) Patna
(C) Lucknow (D) All of these

52 Which Committee/Commission was set up to study and report on problems of Calcutta University ?
(A) Hartog Committee
(B) Saddler Commission
(C) Sapru Committee
(D) None of the above

53 In which year under Montagu-Chelmsford reforms education was shifted to provincial ministries?
(A) 1902 (B) 1917
(C) 1918 (D) 1919

54 Which committee was appointed in 1929 to report on development of education?
(A) Sapru Committee
(B) Montague-Chelmsford Reforms
(C) Hunter Commission
(D) Hartog Committee

55 Which of the following Commission/Report proposed that at university level, English should be the medium of instruction and recommended polytechnic education and establishment of vocational teacher-training colleges?
(A) Sapru Committee
(B) Wood and Abott Report
(C) Radhakrishnan Commission
(D) Hartog Committee

56 Which Commission/Committee recommended that female education should be based on scientific and technological education?
(A) Hartog Committee
(B) Sharma Committee
(C) Gnanam Committee
(D) Saddler Commission

57 Which of the following recommended to divert average students to vocational courses after VIII standard ?
(A) Sapru Committee
(B) Hartog Committee
(C) Montagu-Chelmsford reforms
(D) None of the above

**58** The main principle of the Wardha Scheme of Basic Education was

(A) basic education or Nai Talim
(B) learning through practice
(C) learning through experience
(D) learning through activity

**59** Which of the following was/were the recommendation(s) of Sergeant Plan of Education?

I. Pre-primary education for 3-6 years age group.
II. Free, universal and compulsory elementary education for 6-11 years age group.
III. A university course of 3 years after higher secondary.

**Codes**

(A) Only I (B) I and III
(C) II and III (D) All of these

**60** Match the following.

| List I (Commission/Committee/ Policy) | List II (Year) |
|---|---|
| A. Indian University Act | 1. 1904 |
| B. Hartog Committee | 2. 1929 |
| C. Sapru Committee | 3. 1934 |
| D. Saddler Commission | 4. 1917-19 |

**Codes**

| | A | B | C | D |
|---|---|---|---|---|
| (A) | 1 | 2 | 3 | 4 |
| (B) | 2 | 3 | 1 | 4 |
| (C) | 1 | 4 | 3 | 2 |
| (D) | 4 | 1 | 2 | 3 |

**61** Who was the head of First Education Commission established by Indian Government after freedom?

(A) Dr S Radhakrishnan (B) Dr Zakir Hussain
(C) Dr DS Kothari (D) Shri Mudaliar

**62** Which of the following were the recommendations of the Radha Krishnan Commission?

I. A university degree should not be considered essential for administrative services.
II. Rural universities with Shantiniketan and Jamia Millia as their models should be established.
III. A University Grants Commission (UGC) should be set up to look after university education in the country.

Which of the above statement(s) is/are correct?

(A) Only I (B) I and III
(C) I and II (D) All of these

**63** According to Radha Krishnan Commission, the aim of Higher Education is

(A) To develop the democratic values, peace and harmony
(B) To develop great personalities who can give their contributions in politics, administration, industry and commerce
(C) Both (A) and (B)
(D) None of the above

**64** Which of the following recommended that University education should be placed in concurrent list'?

(A) Mudaliar Commission
(B) Radha Krishnan Commission
(C) Kothari Education Commission
(D) Wardha Scheme

**65** Committee on Emotional Integration (1961) was set up under the whose chairmanship?

(A) Sapru Committee
(B) Prof Yashpal
(C) Sam Pitroda
(D) Dr Sampurnanand

**66** Which commission gave the recommendation of a three language formula i.e. Mother tongue, Hindi and English and also development of regional languages?

(A) Mudaliar Commission
(B) Radha Krishnan Commission
(C) Kothari Education Commission
(D) Wardha Scheme

**67** The Kothari Commission's report was entitled on

(A) Education and National Development
(B) Learning to be adventure
(C) Diversification of Education
(D) Education and Socialisation in Democracy

**68** Which of the following is not an aim of Higher Education according to Kothari Commission?

(A) To explore new knowledge in context of truth and interpret it in terms of ancient knowledge and beliefs in contemporary needs
(B) To explore innate abilities in persons and develop them through training
(C) To promote social justice and equality
(D) To give right leadership in all the fields of life

**69** The 42nd Amendment Act made education a part of
(A) Concurrent List (B) State List
(C) Union List (D) Only (A) and (B)

**70** Which of the following recommendations were made by the Acharya Ramamurti Committee constituted in 1990?
(A) Common School System
(B) Promotion of Women Education.
(C) Socially Useful Productive Work (SUPW)
(D) All of the above

**71** Which of the following statement(s) is/are correct about Gnanam Committee, 1993?
I. It was related to financial administration for the universities.
II. It asked for restricting the undesirable growth of deemed universities.
III. It also emphasised the necessity of a National Commission on higher education and research.

**Codes**
(A) Only I (B) I and II
(C) II and III (D) All of these

**72** The title of Yashpal Committe Report (2008) is
(A) ICT is teacher education
(B) learning without burden
(C) learning through broadcasting
(D) None of the above

**73** Which Educational Committee was set up to recommend strategies to improve technical education in India?
(A) Yashpal Committee
(B) Sharma Committee
(C) Sam Pitrode Committee
(D) Dr Anil Kakodkar Committee

**74** Which of the following Models of Public-Private Partnership (PPP) was recommended by the KB Pawar Committee?
(A) Basic infrastructure model
(B) Outsourcing model
(C) Equity/Hybrid model
(D) All of the above

**75** Subramanian Committee submitted its report in which year?
(A) 1905 (B) 1995 (C) 2010 (D) 2016

**76** Ministry of Human Resource Development, MHRD, was developed in which year?
(A) 1947 (B) 1952 (C) 1975 (D) 1985

## Structure of Higher Education in India

**77** Which of the following institutions are empowered to confer or grant degrees, under the UGC Act, 1956?
I. A university established by an Act of Parliament.
II. A university established by an Act of Legislature.
III. A university/institution established by a linguistic minority.
IV. An institutions which is deemed to be university.

Select the correct answer from the codes given below.
(A) I and II (B) I, II and III
(C) I, II and IV (D) All of these

**78** Most of the Universities in India are funded by
(A) the Central Government
(B) the State Government
(C) the University Grants Commission
(D) Private bodies and individuals

**79** Which of the following statements are correct about a Central University?
I. Central University is established under an Act of Parliament.
II. The President of India Act as the visitor of the University.
III. The President has the power to nominate some members to the Executive. Committee or the Board of Management of the University.
IV. The President occasionally presides over the meeting of the Executive Committee or Court.

Select the correct answer from the codes given below.
(A) I, II and IV
(B) I, III and IV
(C) I, II and III
(D) I, II, III and IV

**80** Which of the following are Central Universities?
I. Pondicherry University
II. Viswa Bharati University
III. HNB Garhwal University
IV. Kurukshetra University

**Codes**
(A) I, II and III (B) I, III and IV
(C) II, III and IV (D) I, II and IV

81 Universities having central campus for imparting education are called
(A) Central Universities
(B) Deemed Universities
(C) Residential Universities
(D) Open Universities

82 The total number of State Universities in India are
(A) 208 (B) 300
(C) 412 (D) 401

83 The state with most State Universities is
(A) Tamil Nadu (B) Uttar Pradesh
(C) Rajasthan (D) West Bengal

84 The state with most Deemed Universities is
(A) Maharashtra (B) Gujarat
(C) Tamil Nadu (D) Karnataka

85 Which of the following institutions was the first to be granted a deemed status in 1958?
(A) Indian Institute of Science, Banglore
(B) India Agricultural Research Institute, Delhi
(C) Delhi University
(D) Both (A) and (B)

86 Deemed Universities declared by UGC under Section 3 of the UGC Act 1956, are not permitted to
(A) offer programmes in higher education and issue degrees.
(B) give affiliation to any institute of higher education
(C) open off campus and offshore campus anywhere in the country and overseas respectively without the permission of the UGC.
(D) offer distance education programmes without the approval of the Distance Education Council.

87 The difference between the University and the Deemed University is that the former
(A) is much bigger in size
(B) is established by the Act of Legislature
(C) is established by the Central Government
(D) looks after only affiliated colleges

88 Which university's concept is based on the premise that the 'whole is greater than the sum of the parts'?
(A) Central University
(B) Meta University
(C) Deemed University
(D) Innovative University

89 Which of the following University has adopted the Meta University concept?
(A) Assam University
(B) Delhi University
(C) Hyderabad University
(D) Pondicherry University

90 Which of the following institutions or organisations publishes Universities Handbook?
(A) University Grants Commission
(B) Association of Indian Universities
(C) Inter University Centres
(D) Central Advisory Board of Education

91 The headquarters of AICTE is located at
(A) Mumbai
(B) New Delhi
(C) Kolkata
(D) Bengaluru

92 The Council of Architecture came into existence in which year?
(A) 1951 (B) 1962
(C) 1972 (D) 1981

93 Which institution was established under the Societies Registration Act in 1972?
(A) PHISPC (B) ICHR
(C) NCRI (D) ICPR

94 The NCRI was hadquartered at
(A) Hyderabad (B) Mysore
(C) New Delhi (D) Bombay

95 Which of the following organisations deals with 'capacity building programme' on education planning?
(A) NCERT
(B) UGC
(C) NAAC
(D) NUEPA

96 Which of the following is/are the major objective(s) of Rashtriya Uchchatar Shiksha Abhiyan (RUSA)?
(A) To ensure academic and examination reforms in the higher educational institutions.
(B) To enable conversion of some of the universities into research universities at par with the best in the world.
(C) To create opportunities for students from rural areas to get access to better quality institutions.
(D) All of the above

**97** "This scheme was announced in 2018. It aims to lend low cost funds to government higher educational institutions." Which scheme is this?
(A) IMPRINT (B) RISE
(C) UAY (D) GIAN

**98** Which scheme/programme was launched by the Government of India in 1949 to honour distinguished academics and scholars in recognition of their contribution to knowledge?
(A) National Research Professorship
(B) Unnat Bharat Abhiyan
(C) Bachelor of Vocational Studies
(D) National Quality Renaissance Initiatives

**99** Which scholarship scheme is launched specially for North-Eastern students?
(a) Kaushal Kendra (b) Ishan Vikas
(c) Ishan Uday (d) SWAYAM

**100** For raising the educational standard of the university
(A) students opting for higher education should be selected on the basis of intellectual tests
(B) occupational and industrial development is essential with higher education
(C) state policy should be effective
(D) Both (A) and (B)

**101** National Assessment and Accreditation Council an autonomous body funded by UGC was opened in which year?
(A) 1992 (B) 1991 (C) 1994 (D) 1993

**102** Which of the following is/are the objective(s) of NAAC?
(A) To grade institutions of higher education and their programmes.
(B) To help institutions realise their academic objectives.
(C) To encourage innovations, self-evaluation and account ability in higher education.
(D) All of the above

**103** Institute of National Importance is an institution in higher education which serves as a pivotal player in developing highly skilled personnel within the specified regions of the country or state. This status can be conferred upon them by
(A) University Grants Commission
(B) An Act of Parliament
(C) All Indian Council for Technical Education
(D) All of the above

**104** Which of the following statements are correct about the National Assessment and Accreditation Council?
I. It is an autonomous institution
II. It is tasked with the responsibility of assessing and accrediting institutions of higher education.
III. It is located in Delhi.
IV. It has regional offices.
Select the correct answer from the codes given below.
(A) I and III (B) I and II
(C) I, II and IV (D) II, III and IV

**105** Who has signed an MoU for Accreditation to Teacher Education Institutions in India?
(A) NAAC and UGC
(B) NCTE and NAAC
(C) UGC and NCTE
(D) NCTE and IGNOU

**106** How many Agricultural Universities have been accredited by NAEAB?
(a) 92 (b) 46
(c) 45 (d) 43

**107** Which of the following Educational Institutions got the top rank in India in the best university category as per the National Institutional Ranking Framework (NIRF), 2018?
(A) Delhi University (B) IIT, Mumbai
(C) IISc, Bengaluru (D) IIT, Delhi

**108** Which of the following parameters are used for ranking purposes under the methodology of National Institutional Ranking Framework?
(A) Resources
(B) Research
(C) Stakeholder perception
(D) All of the above

**109** Which management institution has been ranked second as per the report of NIRF 2019?
(A) IIM, Bangalore
(B) IIM, Calcutta
(C) IIM, Ahmedabad
(D) IIM, Lucknow

**110** Which National Policy on Education (NPE) emphasized on strengthening of post-graduate teaching and research?
(A) NPE, 1968 (B) NPE, 1986
(C) NPE, 1992 (D) NPE, 2016

**111** Which government modified NPE, 1986 in 1992?
(A) PV Narsimha Rao
(B) Atal Bihari Vajpayee
(C) Charan Singh
(D) Rajiv Gandhi

**112** A review of NPE, 1986 Programme of Action was done by ..........
(A) National Commission for Teachers
(B) Yashpal Committee
(C) Rama Murti Committee
(D) Sapru Committee

**113** In NEP 2020, the current 10 + 2 system to be replaced by a new curricular structure. What is the new curricular structure?
(A) 3+4+4+5 (B) 5+3+3+4
(C) 4+3+3+5 (D) 5+4+3+3

**114** .......... will be created as an apex body for fostering a strong research culture and building research capacity across higher education as per NEP 2020.
(A) National Commission Foundation
(B) National Research Foundation
(C) Higher Commission Education
(D) None of the above

## Oriental, Conventional and Non-Conventional Learning Programmes in India

**115** Oriental studies are also called
(A) Middle Eastern studies
(B) Asian Educational studies
(C) European studies
(D) All of the above

**116** How many institutions have been set up for oriental research?
(A) 11 (B) 15 (C) 13 (D) 16

**117** The Mythic Society is located in
(A) Baroda (B) Pune
(C) Bangalore (D) Tirupati

**118** Examples of Conventional Learning Programmes is/are
(A) Graduation (B) M.B.A
(C) L.L.B (D) All of these

**119** Which of the following statement(s) is/are correct about the characteristics of Conventional Learning programmes?
I. These programmes include all the objectives of education like knowledge, comprehension and opportunities for employment.
II. In these programmes the main emphasis is given on Progressive education.
III. In these programmes learning is based on holistic view, self-control, self-realisation and cultural values.

**Codes**
(A) Only I (B) I and II
(C) Only III (D) All of these

**120** Unconventional learning programs target
(A) Married (B) Tribal
(C) Employment (D) All of these

**121** The chief objective of Distance Education is
(A) reduction of education budget.
(B) abolition of monopoly of schools.
(C) compensation of formal education.
(D) extending education among people.

**122** MOOC stands for
(A) Media Online Open Course
(B) Massachusetts Open Online Course
(C) Massive Open Online Course
(D) Myrind Open Online Course

**123** The apex body for Open and Distance Learning (ODL) system is the country is
(A) DEC (B) IGNOU
(C) MHRD (D) UGC

**124** The concept of open school imply
(A) schools where only smart children will be admitted.
(B) schools which will not be bound by a fixed curricula.
(C) schools where teaching will be done by computers.
(D) schools where teaching and learning will be open and utilise multimedia.

**125** Which one of the following councils has been disbanded in 2013?
(A) Distance Education Council (DEC)
(B) National Council for Teacher Education (NCTE)
(C) National Council of Educational Research Council (NCERT)
(D) The National Assessment and Accreditation Council (NAAC)

**126** How many Open Universities are there in India?
(A) 10 (B) 13 (C) 19 (D) 21

**127** First open university in India was
(A) Dr. B.R. Ambedkar Open University
(B) Indira Gandhi National Open University
(C) Delhi University
(D) None of the above

128 Indicate the number of Regional Offices of National Council of Teacher Education
(A) 04 (B) 05 (C) 06 (D) 08

129 Indira Gandhi Open University is located in
(A) New Delhi (B) Trivandrum
(C) Kolkata (D) Mumbai

130 Which of the following is not the function of IGNOU?
(A) To provide access to higher education to all segments of the society.
(B) To offer high-quality, innovative and need-based programme at different levels for all those who require them.
(C) Reach out to the disadvantaged by offering programmes in all parts of the country at affordable costs.
(D) All of the above

131 Exclusive educational channel of IGNOU is known as
(A) Gyan Darshan (B) Gyan Vani
(C) Door Darshan (D) Prasar Bharati

132 Which scheme was established in October, 2006, to facilitate lifelong learning for students, teachers and those-in employment or in pursuit of knowledge free of cost to them?
(A) Unnat Bharat Abhiyan
(B) SAKSHAT
(C) Technical Education Quality Improvement Programme
(D) None of the above

133 Example of professional courses is/are
(A) M.Sc in Management (B) Tourism
(C) B.Ed (D) All of these

134 Consider the following statements about professional education.
I. It is the component of technical education programme.
II. The aim of the education is to enable youths to get employment in government and non-government sectors.
III. It includes curriculum based on banking, media, management, tourism, teaching, aviation, etc.

**Codes**
(A) Only I (B) I and II
(C) II and III (D) All of these

135 Technical education covers programmes in
(A) Engineering (B) Pharmacy
(C) Town planning (D) All of these

136 The First IIT was set up in 1951 at
(A) Madras (B) Kanpur
(C) Bombay (D) Kharagpur

137 In which year the University of Roorkee was converted to IIT Roorkee?
(A) 1992 (B) 1999
(C) 2001 (D) 2006

138 There are how many IIITs is India?
(A) 19 (B) 23 (C) 26 (D) 36

139 The National Institute of Technical Teacher's Training and Research (NITTTR) is situated in
(A) Chandigarh (B) Chennai
(C) Kolkata (D) All of these

140 Which of the following was the first IIM in India?
(A) IIM, Ahmedabad
(B) IIM, Calcutta (Kolkata)
(C) IIM, Raipur
(D) IIM, Rohtak

141 The first engineering college was established at which place?
(A) Jammu and Kashmir
(B) Uttar Pradesh
(C) Tamil Nadu
(D) Kerala

142 The aim of Skill Based education is
(A) converting liberal education into vocational education
(B) preparing students for employment alongwith knowledge
(C) making liberal education job-oriented
(D) giving more importance to vocational than general education

143 In which year Pradhan Mantri Kaushal Vikas Yojana (PMKVY) was launched by the Government of India in all the states of India?
(A) 2000 (B) 2003
(C) 2010 (D) 2015

## Value Education and Environmental Education

144 Value education makes a student
(A) Good citizen
(B) Successful businessman
(C) Popular teacher
(D) Efficient manager

**145** Value education should help in
(A) increasing states income
(B) increasing teachers income
(C) controlling guardian's expenditure on child's schooling
(D) eliminating violence fanaticism

**146** Two ways of imparting value education are
(A) Incidental and accidental
(B) Systematic and non-systematic
(C) Direct and Indirect
(D) None of the above

**147** Patriotic values are included under the groups of
(A) social values (B) moral values
(C) health values (D) ultimate values

**148** Value oriented education develops
(A) character
(B) cultural values
(C) vocational efficiency
(D) All of the above

**149** What is the important value which is to be introduced in the colleges by a university?
(A) Human values (B) Social values
(C) Institutional values (D) All of these

**150** In which year the Ministry of Environment and Forest, India launched the Environment Education Awareness and Training scheme?
(A) 1961-62 (B) 1971-72
(C) 1983-84 (D) 1993-94

**151** In which year the Supreme Court of India gave a ruling that Environmental Education course should be mandatory at undergraduate level?
(A) 1961 (B) 1971 (C) 1981 (D) 1991

## Policies, Governance and Administration

**152** Which National Policy on Education is based on the recommedations of the Kothari Commission?
(A) NPE-1968 (B) NPE-1986
(C) NPE-1992 (D) MPE-2016

**153** Which National Policy on Education recommended a common educational structure i.e. 10+2+3 in Indian Education system?
(A) NPE-1968 (B) NPE-1986
(C) NPE-1992 (D) NPE-2016

**154** Which National Policy on Education recommended for implementation of All India Bases Common Entrance Examination for admission in all professional and technical programmes in India?
(A) NPE-1968 (B) NPE-1986
(C) NPE-1992 (D) NPE-2016

**155** Which of the following bodies grants funds for higher education?
(i) UGC
(ii) State Government
(iii) Municipal Corporation and Zila Parishad
(iv) Central Government
**Codes**
(A) Only (i)
(B) Only (iii) and (iv)
(C) (i), (ii) and (iv)
(D) All of the above

**156** Who is appointed by the vistor/chancellor on the recommendations of the Executive Council?
(A) The Vice-Chancellor
(B) Pro Vice Chancellor
(C) The Chancellor
(D) Deans

**157** In terms of sequential relationship, the first function requiring managerial attention is
(A) Planning (B) Coordinates
(C) Directing (D) Controlling

**158** Main functions of the administrative management are
(A) planning, organising, staffing, directing and controlling.
(B) planning, organising, directing and controlling.
(C) planning, organising, staffing and directing.
(D) planning, organising, controlling and representation.

**159** Education is listed in the Concurrent List of which Schedule in the Indian Constitution?
(A) Sixth Schedule
(B) Fifth Schedule
(C) Seventh Schedule
(D) Eight Schedule

**160** Central Advisory Board of Education (CABE) was established in ............
(A) 1994 (B) 1930
(C) 1920 (D) 1940

# *Previous Years' Questions*

## UGC NET-June 2019

**1** During which year the present system of affiliation of colleges to the Universities was introduced in India?
(A) 1857 (B) 1948
(C) 1928 (D) 1966

**2** The Constitution of India provides right to establish educational institutes of their choice by all minorities as per
(A) Article 30 (1)
(B) Article 29
(C) Article 38
(D) Article 16 (2)

**3** Which one of the following reports addressed the academic, technical and administrative problems of the examination system?
(A) Report on standards of the Educational System (1965)
(B) Report of University Education Commission (1948-49)
(C) Sargeant Report (1944)
(D) Hartog Committee Report (1929)

**4** Which one of the following universities is not among the first three that were established during 1857?
(A) Calcutta (B) Bombay
(C) Delhi (D) Madras

**5** Which one of the following coordinates, promotes and funds research activities of all social sciences disciplines?
(A) ICPR, New Delhi
(B) IIAS, Shimla
(C) ICSSR, New Delhi
(D) NUEPA, New Delhi

**6** A special focus on the problems of examination system of India formed a part of which one of the following reports?
(A) Report of the Calcutta University Commission
(B) Report of the University Education Commission (1964-66)
(C) Hartog Committee Report
(D) Report on Standards of University Education UGC (1965)

**7** In which of the following Ancient Indian universities, the culture and civilisation of Tibet was built mainly through the writings of the scholars?
(A) Nalanda (B) Vikramshila
(C) Jagaddala (D) Mithila

**8** In post-independence India, which one of the following committee/commission's report deals with all levels of education in India?
(A) Sargeant Commission
(B) Hartog Committee
(C) Kothari Commission
(D) Radha Krishnan Commission

**9** The present form of inter university board that was previously established for promoting cooperation and coordination among universities is
(A) UGC (B) AIU
(C) NUEPA (D) ICSSR

**10** The Education Commission of India that first took serious note of the problem of Brain drain was
(A) The Education Commission of India
(B) The University Education Commission
(C) The Calcutta University Commission
(D) The Sargeant Commission

**11** The report of which of the following Education Commissions carries the sub-title 'Education for National Development'?
(A) Radha Krishnan Commission
(B) Mudaliar Commission
(C) Calcutta University Education Commission
(D) Kothari Commission

**12** In which year the Modern Indian University got established?
(A) 1957 (B) 1857
(C) 1947 (D) 1964

**13** In which era given below, higher education in India got a set back?
(A) British era
(B) Buddhist era
(C) Mughal era
(D) Post-Independence era

**14** Which of the following statements represent the main functions of UGC?
1. Recognition of institutions
2. Maintenance of quality and standards
3. Appointment of Vice Chancellor
4. Giving grants to institutions
5. Making State Governments responsible for educational development

Choose the correct answer from the options given below.
(A) 1, 2 and 3 (B) 1, 3 and 4
(C) 1, 2 and 4 (D) 2, 3 and 5

**15** The main aim of the faculty recharge scheme of UGC was to
(A) Address the shortage of faculty in higher education institution
(B) Upgrade the teaching skills of the faculty
(C) Upgrade the research infrastructure for the faculty in colleges and universities
(D) Strengthen the academia - industry linkage

**16** Name the scheme which facilitates academic and research collaboration between Indian Institution and the best institution in the world.
(A) ICSSR- IMPRESS
(B) Staff Development Scheme
(C) SPARC
(D) Institutional Development Scheme

**17** Which of the following is a non-conventional learning programme in higher education?
(A) Swayam
(B) Face-to-face teaching-learning
(C) Tutorial class
(D) Seminar

**18** For the day to day administration of University, which of the following bodies is responsible?
(A) Senate
(B) Syndicate/Executive Council
(C) Student Council
(D) Academic Council

**19** Identify the scheme which aims to encourage Social Science Research in Policy relevant areas so as to provide vital inputs in policy formulation, implementation and evaluation.
(A) ICSSR Fellowship
(B) Cognitive Initiatives
(C) ICSSR- EMPRESS
(D) ICSSR Research Projects

**20** Which of the following commission/ committee in the post-independent India has paid attention all the levels of education?
(A) Radha Krishnan Commission
(B) Mudaliar Commission
(C) Kothari Commission
(D) Acharya Ramamurti Committee

**21** The purpose of Gurukul system of education is to
(A) Promote equality and excellence
(B) Minimise stress in learning
(C) Empowering for future learning
(D) Encourage self-help

**22** The scheme 'Unnat Bharat Abhiyan' aims to
(A) Increase strength of students in colleges in India
(B) Link higher educational institution in the country with at least 5 villages
(C) Increase quality in Higher Education
(D) Increase number of colleges in India

## UGC NET-December 2019

**23** In the age of four Vedas, students were admitted to the Vedas Schools after performance of which ceremony?
(A) Upanayana ceremony
(B) Ustarjana ceremony
(C) Satapatha ceremony
(D) Dhanurvidya ceremony

**24** In order to meet the new demands of market ceremony and produce competent graduates, who can compete which their counterparts in international markets the first and foremost change that needs to be introduced in the prevailing system of Indian higher education is related to
(A) Admission process
(B) Curriculum
(C) Educational technology
(D) Appointment of teachers

## UGC NET-December 2018

**25** Which of the following activity/programme in a University aims at Value Education in a holistic frame?
(A) National Cadet Corps (NCC)
(B) Yoga Education and Wellness Centres
(C) Inter-University Competitions
(D) Fine Arts and Musical Concerts

**26** For promoting Human Values through programmes of the University system in India, which of the the following activities have great potential?

(A) Association of NGOs
(B) Lectures by experts
(C) Mentoring by senior faculty members
(D) Inviting dignitaries/heads from national level organisations

**27** Which of the following statements correctly describe the functions/status of the National Institute of Educational Planning and Administration a deemed to be University?

I. Capacity building and research in planning and management of education
II. Educational Planning and Administration
III. Fully maintained by the Government of India like any Central University
IV. A Statutory Institute of Educational Planning and Administration

Select the correct answer from the codes given below.

(A) I and II
(B) I and III
(C) II and IV
(D) I and IV

**28** Which of the following bodies/units in a University has a statutory function to perform?

(A) Finance Committee
(B) Board of Studies
(C) Board of Management
(D) Research Degree Committee

**29** Which of organisation in India overseas the functioning and quality aspect of teacher education programmes?

(A) Association of Indian Universities (AIU)
(B) National Council for Teacher Education (NCTE)
(C) University Grants Commission (UGC)
(D) National Council of Educational Research and Training (NCERT)

**30** Which of the following are the goals of higher education in India?

I. Access
II. Equity
III. Quality and Excellence
IV. Relevance
V. Value based education
VI. Compulsory and free education

Select the correct answer from the codes given below.

(A) I, II, V and VI
(B) I, II, III, IV and V
(C) I, II, III, IV, V and VI
(D) I, II and V

## UGC NET-July 2018

**31** India has the largest Higher Education System in the world after

I. The United States of America
II. Australia
III. China
IV. United Kingdom (UK)

Select the correct answer from the codes given below.

(A) I, III and IV (B) I and III
(C) I, II, III and IV (D) I, II and III

## UGC NET-January 2017

**32** The purpose of value education is best served by focusing on

(A) cultural practices prevailing in the society.
(B) norms of conduct laid down by a social group.
(C) concern for human values.
(D) religious and moral practices and instructions.

## UGC NET-July 2016

**33** The best way for providing value education is through

(A) discussions on scriptural texts.
(B) lectures/discourses on values.
(C) seminars/symposia on values.
(D) mentoring/reflective sessions on values

**34** Which of the following core values among the institutions of higher education are promoted by the NAAC (National Assessment and Accreditation Council)?

I. Contributing to national development.
II. Fostering global competencies among the students.
III. Inculcating a value system among students and teachers.
IV. Promoting the optimum utilisation of the infrastructure.

**Codes**

(A) II, III and IV (B) I, II and III
(C) I, III and IV (D) All of these

## UGC NET-June 2015

**35** The total number of Central Universities in India in April 2015 was
(A) 08 (B) 14 (C) 27 (D) 43

**36** The South Asia University is situated in the city of
(A) Colombo
(B) Dhaka
(C) New Delhi
(D) Kathmandu

**37** The University Grants Commission was established with which of the following aims?
I. Promotion of research and development in higher education.
II. Identifying and sustaining institutions of potential learning.
III. Capacity building of Teachers.
IV. Providing autonomy to each and every higher educational institution of India.

Select the correct answer using the codes given below.
**Codes**
(A) I, II, III and IV (B) I, II and III
(C) II, III and IV (D) I, II and IV

**38** Which of the following are the objectives of Rashtriya Uchchatar Shiksha Abhiyan (RUSA)?
I. To improve the overall quality of state institutions.
II. To ensure adequate availability of quality faculty.
III. To create new institutions through upgradation of existing autonomous colleges.
IV. To downgrade universities with poor infrastructure into autonomous colleges.

Select the correct answer using the codes given below.
**Codes**
(A) I, II and IV (B) I, III and IV
(C) I, II and III (D) I, II, III and IV

# ANSWERS

## Chapter Practice

| | | | | | | | | | |
|---|---|---|---|---|---|---|---|---|---|
| 1 (D) | 2 (B) | 3 (C) | 4 (A) | 5 (B) | 6 (B) | 7 (D) | 8 (C) | 9 (B) | 10 (A) |
| 11 (B) | 12 (D) | 13 (D) | 14 (A) | 15 (B) | 16 (C) | 17 (A) | 18 (A) | 19 (A) | 20 (B) |
| 21 (D) | 22 (C) | 23 (B) | 24 (A) | 25 (C) | 26 (A) | 27 (A) | 28 (D) | 29 (D) | 30 (C) |
| 31 (D) | 32 (D) | 33 (C) | 34 (C) | 35 (D) | 36 (A) | 37 (D) | 38 (D) | 39 (B) | 40 (B) |
| 41 (B) | 42 (D) | 43 (B) | 44 (D) | 45 (C) | 46 (A) | 47 (C) | 48 (C) | 49 (B) | 50 (C) |
| 51 (D) | 52 (B) | 53 (D) | 54 (D) | 55 (B) | 56 (D) | 57 (B) | 58 (D) | 59 (D) | 60 (A) |
| 61 (A) | 62 (D) | 63 (C) | 64 (B) | 65 (D) | 66 (C) | 67 (A) | 68 (B) | 69 (A) | 70 (D) |
| 71 (D) | 72 (B) | 73 (D) | 74 (D) | 75 (D) | 76 (D) | 77 (C) | 78 (C) | 79 (C) | 80 (A) |
| 81 (A) | 82 (C) | 83 (B) | 84 (C) | 85 (D) | 86 (B) | 87 (D) | 88 (B) | 89 (B) | 90 (B) |
| 91 (B) | 92 (C) | 93 (B) | 94 (A) | 95 (D) | 96 (D) | 97 (B) | 98 (A) | 99 (C) | 100 (D) |
| 101 (C) | 102 (D) | 103 (B) | 104 (B) | 105 (B) | 106 (D) | 107 (B) | 108 (D) | 109 (A) | 110 (A) |
| 111 (A) | 112 (C) | 113 (B) | 114 (B) | 115 (A) | 116 (D) | 117 (C) | 118 (D) | 119 (D) | 120 (D) |
| 121 (D) | 122 (A) | 123 (D) | 124 (B) | 125 (A) | 126 (B) | 127 (A) | 128 (A) | 129 (A) | 130 (D) |
| 131 (A) | 132 (B) | 133 (D) | 134 (D) | 135 (D) | 136 (D) | 137 (C) | 138 (B) | 139 (D) | 140 (B) |
| 141 (B) | 142 (B) | 143 (D) | 144 (A) | 145 (D) | 146 (C) | 147 (A) | 148 (D) | 149 (D) | 150 (C) |
| 151 (D) | 152 (A) | 153 (B) | 154 (C) | 155 (C) | 156 (C) | 157 (A) | 158 (B) | 159 (C) | 160 (C) |

## Previous Years' Questions

| | | | | | | | | | |
|---|---|---|---|---|---|---|---|---|---|
| 1 (A) | 2 (A) | 3 (A) | 4 (C) | 5 (C) | 6 (D) | 7 (B) | 8 (C) | 9 (B) | 10 (A) |
| 11 (D) | 12 (B) | 13 (C) | 14 (C) | 15 (A) | 16 (C) | 17 (A) | 18 (B) | 19 (C) | 20 (C) |
| 21 (A) | 22 (B) | 23 (A) | 24 (B) | 25 (B) | 26 (C) | 27 (B) | 28 (C) | 29 (B) | 30 (B) |
| 31 (B) | 32 (C) | 33 (D) | 34 (B) | 35 (D) | 36 (C) | 37 (C) | 38 (C) | | |

# Practice Sets
# 1-5

# UGC

## NET/JRF/SET

# Practice Set 1

## General Paper 1 (Teaching Aptitude and Attitude)

### *Instructions*

- This paper contains fifty Multiple-Choice Questions, each question carries two marks.
- All questions are compulsory.
- Total time given for this paper is 1 hour.

**1 One of your colleagues is living in your locality but you have no affinity with him, the reason may be**

(A) his selfishness
(B) his religious faith
(C) his social rejection
(D) his miserable behaviour and rural background

**2 Maximum participation of students during teaching is possible through**

(A) Lecture method
(B) Demonstration method
(C) Inductive method
(D) Textbook method

**3 While delivering lecture if there is some disturbance in the class, then a teacher should**

(A) keep quiet for a while and then go on
(B) punish those causing disturbance
(C) not bother of what is happening in the class
(D) All of the above

**4. If a group of students enter your room and abuse you and behave violently with you, at that time how would you control your emotions?**

(A) You will feel ashamed among your teaching community.
(B) You will react in similar tone and try to assault them physically.
(C) First you will try to pacify their emotions, then ask politely about their behaviour.
(D) You will report the case to the principal with recommendation of punitive measures.

**5 Which of the following orders are the three levels of teaching?**

I. Memory Level of Teaching
II. Understanding Level of Teaching
III. Reflective Level of Teaching
IV. Pedagogical Level of Teaching

(A) I, II and III (B) II, III and IV
(C) I, III and IV (D) I, II and IV

**6 Fundamental research reflects the ability to**

(A) synthesise new ideals.
(B) expound new principles.
(C) evaluate the existing material concerning research.
(D) study the existing literature regarding various topics.

**7** Match List-I with List-II and choose the correct answer from the codes given below.

| List-I | List-II |
|---|---|
| A. Historical Method | I. Past events |
| B. Survey Method | II. Vision |
| C. Philosophical Method | III. Present events |
| D. Experimental Method | IV. Future action |

**Codes**

(A) A-I, B-III, C-II, D-IV
(B) A-I, B-II, C-III, D-IV
(C) A-I, B-III, C-II, D-IV
(D) A-II, B-III, C-I, D-IV

**8** A satisfactory statistical quantitative method should not possess one of the following qualities.

(A) Appropriateness (B) Measurability
(C) Comparability (D) Flexibility

**9** A good research question is

I. Feasible II. Clear
III. Significant IV. Ethical

**Codes**

(A) I and II (B) I, II and III
(C) II and III (D) All of these

**10** Formulation of hypothesis is not required in

I. Survey Method
II. Historical Method
III. Experimental Studies
IV. Normative Studies

**Codes**

(A) Only II (B) Both II and III
(C) I and III (D) Only IV

**Direction** (Q. Nos. 11-15) *Read the following passage and give the answers.*

Nationalism, of course, is a curious phenomenon which at a certain stage in a country's history gives life, growth and unity but, at the same time, it has a tendency to limit one, because one thinks of one's country as something different from the rest of world.

One's perceptive changes and one is continuously thinking of one's own struggles and virtues and failing to the exclusion of other thoughts. The result is that the same nationalism which is the symbol of growth for a people becomes a symbol of the cessation of that growth in mind. Nationalism, when it becomes successful sometimes goes on spreading in an aggressive way and becomes a danger internationally.

Whatever line of thought you follow, you arrive at the conclusion that some kind of balance must be found. Otherwise something that was good can turn into evil. Culture, which is essentially good become not only static but aggressive and something that breeds conflict and hatred when looked at from a wrong point of view. How are you find a balance, I don't know. Apart from the political and economic problems of the age perhaps, that is the greatest problem today because behind it there is tremendous search for something which it cannot found.

We turn to economic theories because they have an undoubted importance. It is folly to talk of culture or even of god. When human beings starve and die. Before one can talk about anything else one must provide the normal essentials of life to human beings. That is where economies comes in. Human beings today are not in mood to tolerate this suffering and starvation and inequality when they see that the burden is not equally shared. Others profit while they only bear the burden.

**11** The greatest problem in the middle of the passage refers to the question

(A) how to mitigate hardship to human beings.
(B) how to contain the dangers of aggressive nationalism.
(C) how to share the economic burden equally.
(D) how to curb international hatred

**12** Negative national feeling can make a nation

(A) selfish (B) self-centered
(C) indifferent (D) dangerous

**13** Suitable title for this passage can be

(A) Nationalism breeds unity
(B) Nationalism-a road to world unity
(C) Nationalism is not enough
(D) Nationalism and national problems

**14** 'Others' in the last sentence refers to

(A) other people (B) other nations
(C) other communities (D) other neighbours

**15** Aggressive nationalism

(A) breeds threat to international relations.
(B) leads to stunted growth
(C) endangers national unity
(D) isolates a country.

**16** The ability to communicate effectively

I. Depends on the education level.

II. It is a natural talent and cannot be learned.

III. Always depends upon the use of technology.

IV. Can be learned.

**Codes**

(A) Only IV and III (B) I, II and III

(C) All of these (D) Only IV

**17** ............. is the supreme medium to express yesterday, today, and tomorrow with its own unique language. What should be filled in the blank?

(A) Cinema (B) Radio

(C) Newspaper (D) Television

**18.** The components of Communication are

I. Message II. Channel

III. Correlation IV. Understanding

**Codes**

(A) II and III (B) IV and I

(C) I and II (D) All of these

**19.** The chronological order of non-verbal communication is

(A) Signs, symbols, codes, colours

(B) Symbols, codes, signs, colours

(C) Colours, signs, codes, symbols

(D) Codes, colours, symbols, signs

**20.** Match List-I with List-II and choose the correct answer from the codes given below.

| List-I | List-II |
|---|---|
| A. Interpretation of message by receiver. | I. Encoding |
| B. Converting an idea into form that can be transmitted. | II. Channel |
| C. Means through which message is carried. | III. Feedback |
| D. Analysing the message and reverting. | IV. Decoding |

**Codes**

(A) A-IV, B-I, C-II, D-III

(B) A-II, B-IV, C-I, D-III

(C) A-IV, B-II, C-I, D-III

(D) A-III, B-I, C-I, D-III

**21** A saving bank gives interest which compounds annually. Mr $X$ deposited ₹ 1000 and received ₹ 121 as cumulative interest at the end of second year. Rate of compound interest per annum is

(A) 10% (B) 20% (C) 10.5% (D) 20.5%

**22** If Kamal says, "Ravi's mother is the only daughter of my mother". How is kamal related to Ravi?

(A) Grand father (B) Father

(C) Brother (D) None of these

**23.** Amit walks 100 yards straight from his house which is facing north and then he walks 200 yards in the reverse direction. Further he takes a left turn and walks 100 yards. In which direction is Amit now from his original position?

(A) North-East (B) South-West

(C) North-West (D) South-East

**24** In a certain code language '1 3 4' means 'Good And Tasty' '4 7 8' means 'See Good Pictures' and '7 2 9' means 'Pictures Are Faint'. Which of the following numerical symbol stands for 'See'?

(A) 9 (B) 2

(C) 1 (D) None of these

**25** AND, COF, FPI, JQM, .....

(A) ORS (B) ORR

(C) QRS (D) PRT

**26** Elemental constitution of senses in based on the principle that

I. similar perceives similar

II. similar repels similar

III. good affects bad

IV. bad reflect bad

**Codes**

(A) I and II (B) II, III and IV

(C) Only I (D) III and IV

**27** In which pramana arthapatti is reduced by Naiyayikas?

(A) Pratyaksa (B) Anumana

(C) Upamana (D) Sabda

**28** Anumana means

(A) to make guess

(B) to draw conclusion

(C) to learn from experience

(D) to commit suicide

**29** How many pramanas are there according to Hindu philosophy?
(A) 3 (B) 3 (C) 6 (D) 8

**30** Arthapatti is a ......... term.
(A) English (B) Urdu
(C) Hindi (D) Sanskrit

**Directions** *Study the data given in the following table carefully and answer the questions* (31-35) *given below it*

**Wheat Production** (in lakh tonnes)

| States | 1986 | 1987 | 1988 | 1989 | 1990 |
|---|---|---|---|---|---|
| A | 9.0 | 10.7 | 8.9 | 11.6 | 8.4 |
| B | 14.5 | 16.3 | 16.2 | 16.4 | 16.8 |
| C | 14.9 | 15.7 | 16.8 | 16.9 | 17.8 |
| D | 7.6 | 8.4 | 7.4 | 7.9 | 8.6 |
| E | 21.0 | 22.6 | 23.2 | 22.2 | 23.9 |

**31** In 1988, which states contributed close to one-eighth of the total production of all the five states?
(A) A (B) B (C) C (D) D

**32** In which year did the production of state D falls for the first time?
(A) 1986 (B) 1987 (C) 1988 (D) 1989

**33** In which state, the production in 1989 showed the highest increase over that in 1986?
(A) A (B) B (C) C (D) D

**34** In which year does the production in state show the higher percentage of increase over that in the previous year?
(A) 1986 (B) 1987 (C) 1988 (D) 1990

**35** In which state did the production of wheat increase continuously from 1986 to 1990?
(A) A (B) B (C) C (D) D

**36** Which of the following is the appropriate definition of a computer?
(A) Computer is a machine that can process information.
(B) Computer is an electronic device that can store, retrieve and process both qualitative and quantitative data quickly and accurately.
(C) Computer is an electronic device that can store, retrieve and quickly process only quantitative data.
(D) Computer is a machine that can store, retrieve and process quickly and accurately only qualitative information.

**37** Which of the following is/are examples of operating systems?
I. Unix/BSD II. GNU/Linux
III. Windows IV. Mac OS, Mac OSX

**Codes**
(A) I, II and III (B) II, III and IV
(C) I, III and IV (D) All of these

**38** Which of the following is the appropriate format of URL of e-mail?
(A) www_mail.com (B) www@mail.com
(C) WWW@mail.com (D) www.mail.com

**39** A Hybrid computer resembles
I. Digital computer
II. Analogue computer
III. Super computer
IV. Satellite computer

**Codes**
(A) Only I (B) Only II
(C) Both I and II (D) None of these

**40** 'Banker's Algorithm' is
(A) a method to prevent the deadlock condition.
(B) a machine for capturing frequencies.
(C) a medium to spread virus.
(D) None of the above

**41** Man's urge these days has been
I. to control communicable diseases.
II. to produce bumper crops where nothing grew earlier.
III. increase of consumer facilities beyond the reach of man
(A) I alone (B) I and II
(C) I, II and III (D) I and III

**42** Earth is often struck by solar eruptions, which comprise energetic particles that are hurled away from the Sun into space. Which of the following statements reflect the effect on earth?
I. When these eruptions interact with the magnetic field, they cause beautiful auroras.
II. They breakdown radio communication and power supplies.
III. They don't affect life support system on earth.

**Codes**
(A) I only (B) I and II only
(C) II and III only (D) III only

**43** Match the following.

| | List-I | | List-II |
|---|---|---|---|
| A | Troposphere | I. | Dust particles |
| B | Stratosphere | II. | Ozone layer |
| C | Ionosphere | III. | Meteors |
| D | Exosphere | IV. | Aurora |

**Codes**

(A) A-I, B-II, C-III, D-IV
(B) A-II, B-I, C-III, D-IV
(C) A-IV, B-II, C-III, D-I
(D) None of the above

**44** Fossil fuels and mineral deposits, such as iron ore and gold ore are examples of

(A) non-renewable resources.
(B) renewable resources.
(C) Both 'A' and 'B'
(D) None of the above

**45** The structure of earth's system consists of the following. Match the following.

| | List-I (Zone) | | List-II (Chemical Character) |
|---|---|---|---|
| A. | Atmosphere | I. | Inert gases |
| B. | Biosphere | II. | Salt, freshwater, snow, and ice |
| C. | Hydrosphere | III. | Organic substances |
| D. | Lithosphere | IV. | Light silicates |

**Codes**

(A) A-II, B-III, C-I, D-IV
(B) A-I, B-III, C-II, D-IV
(C) A-II, B-I, C-III, D-IV
(D) A-IV, B-II, C-III, D-I

**46.** Who among the following gave particular attention to establishment of comprehensive institutions for the rural people starting at the early childhood level going upto the highest?

(A) Mahatma Gandhi (B) Rabindranath Tagore
(C) Vivekananda (D) Both 'A' and 'B'

**47.** IGNOU stands significantly apart from other universities because of

(A) national jurisdiction.
(B) flexible admission rules.
(C) student support services.
(D) All of these

**48.** Value education should help in

(A) increasing states income.
(B) increasing teachers income.
(C) controlling guardian's expenditure on child's schooling.
(D) eliminating violence fanaticism.

**49.** Match List I with List II and select the correct answer from the codes given below.

| | List-I (Articles) | | List-II (Institutions) |
|---|---|---|---|
| A | Article 280 | I. | Administrative Tribunals |
| B | Article 324 | II. | Election Commission |
| C | Article 323 | III. | Finance Commission |
| D | Article 315 | IV. | UPSC |

**Codes**

(A) A-I, B-II, C-III and D-IV
(B) A-III, B-II, C-I and D-IV
(C) A-II, B-III, C-IV and D-I
(D) A-II, B-IV, C-III and D-I

**50** Match List-I with List-II and select the correct answer from the codes given below.

| | List-I | | List-II |
|---|---|---|---|
| A. | National Council of Rural Institutes | I. | New Delhi |
| B. | Indian Council of Historical Research | II. | Hyderabad |
| C. | Indian Council of Philosophical Research | III. | Shimla |
| D. | Indian Institute of Advanced Study | IV. | Bangalore |

**Codes**

(A) A-II, B-IV, C-I and D-III
(B) A-II, B-IV, C-III and D-I
(C) A-II, B-III, C-IV and D-I
(D) A-II, B-I, C-IV and D-III

## ANSWERS

| | | | | | | | | | |
|---|---|---|---|---|---|---|---|---|---|
| 1 (A) | 2 (C) | 3 (A) | 4 (C) | 5 (A) | 6 (B) | 7 (A) | 8 (D) | 9 (D) | 10 (A) |
| 11 (B) | 12 (B) | 13 (C) | 14 (A) | 15 (D) | 16 (D) | 17 (A) | 18 (C) | 19 (A) | 20 (A) |
| 21 (A) | 22 (D) | 23 (D) | 24 (D) | 25 (B) | 26 (C) | 27 (B) | 28 (B) | 29 (C) | 30 (D) |
| 31 (A) | 32 (C) | 33 (A) | 34 (D) | 35 (C) | 36 (B) | 37 (D) | 38 (B) | 39 (C) | 40 (A) |
| 41 (C) | 42 (B) | 43 (A) | 44 (A) | 45 (C) | 46 (D) | 47 (D) | 48 (D) | 49 (B) | 50 (D) |

# Hints & Solutions

1 The reason may be the selfishness of the person.

2 Maximum participation of students is possible through inductive method.

3 Teacher should keep quite for a while and then go on.

4 First try to pacify their emotions and then ask politely about their behaviour.

5 Levels of teaching are Memory, Understanding and Reflective.

6 Fundamental research reflects the ability to expound new principles.

7

| | | |
|---|---|---|
| Historical Method | – | Past events |
| Survey Method | – | Present events |
| Philosophical Method | – | Vision |
| Experimental Method | – | Future action |

8 A satisfactory statistical quantitative method should not be flexible.

9 A good research question should be feasible, clear, significant and ethical.

10 Formulation of hypothesis is not required in historical method.

11 The greatest problem in the middle of the passage refers to the question as how to contain the dangers of aggressive nationalism.

12 Negative national feeling can make a nation self-centered.

13 The suitable title for this passage is 'Nationalism is not enough'.

14 'Others' in the last sentence refers to other people.

15 Aggressive nationalism always isolates a country.

16 The ability to communicate effectively can be learned.

17 Cinema is the supreme medium to express yesterday, today and tomorrow with its own unique language.

18 The components of communication are message and channel.

19 Signs, symbols, codes and colours.

20

| | |
|---|---|
| Interpretation of message by receiver. | – Decoding |
| Converting an idea into form that can be transmitted. | – Encoding |
| Means through which message is carried. | – Channel |
| Analysing the message and reverting. | – Feedback |

**21.** $$100 \times \left(1 + \frac{R}{100}\right)^2 = 121$$

$$\Rightarrow \quad \left(1 + \frac{R}{100}\right)^2 = \frac{121}{100} = \left(\frac{11}{10}\right)^2$$

$$\therefore \quad 1 + \frac{R}{100} = \frac{11}{10}$$

$$\Rightarrow \quad \frac{R}{100} = \frac{1}{10}$$

$$\Rightarrow \quad R = 10\%.$$

**22.**

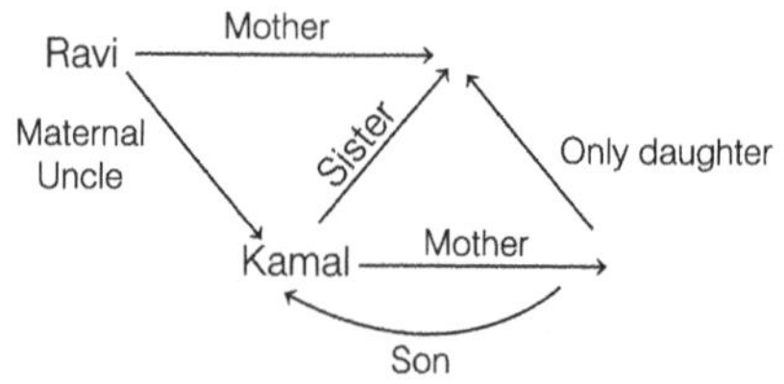


**23.** Movements of Amit are as follows

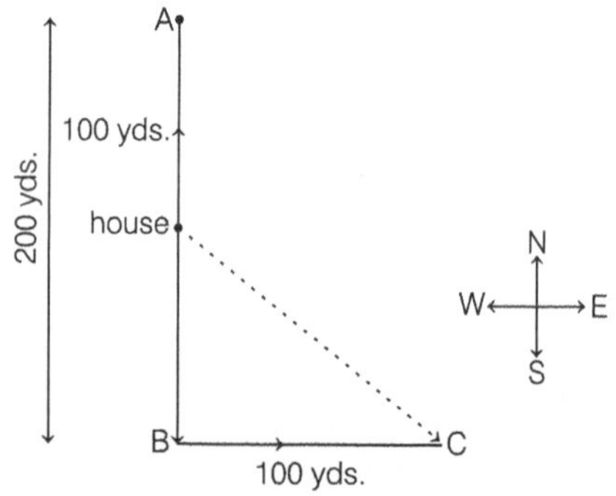


**24.** By comparing I and II we get '4' means 'Good' and by comparing II and III, we get '7' means 'Pictures'. Hence '8' means 'See'.

**25.**
$A \xrightarrow{+2} C \xrightarrow{+3} F \xrightarrow{+4} J \xrightarrow{+5}$ O

$N \xrightarrow{+1} O \xrightarrow{+1} P \xrightarrow{+1} Q \xrightarrow{+1}$ R

$D \xrightarrow{+2} F \xrightarrow{+3} I \xrightarrow{+4} M \xrightarrow{+5}$ R

**26.** Elemental constitution of senses is based on the principle that similar perceives similar.

**27.** Anumana

**28.** Anumana means to draw conclusion

**29.** According to Hindu philosophy there are 6 pramanas.

**30.** Sanskrit

**31.** Total production of all the five states in 1988 = 72.5

1/8th of 72.5 = 9 (approx).

State *A* contributes close to 1/8th of the total production of all the five states.

**32.** 1988.

**33.** Percentage increase in production of state *A* in 1989 over that in 1986 = $\frac{2.6}{9} \times 100$

$= 28.89\%$

Similar figures for the other states are 13.10, 13.42, 3.95, 5.71 respectively.

**34.** % increase of production in 1987 over that in 1986 $= \frac{1.6}{21} \times 100 = 7.62$.

Similar figures in 1988 over that in 1987 = 2.65 and in 1990 over that in 1989 is 7.66.

**35.** In state 'C' the production of wheat increased continuously from 1986 to 1990.

**36.** Computer is an electronic device that can store, retrieve and process both qualitative and quantitative data quickly and accurately.

**37.** Unix/BSD, GNU/Linux, Windows, Mac OS, Mac OSX are the examples of operating system.

**38.** www@mail.com

**39.** A hybrid computer resembles to digital and analogue computer.

**40.** 'Banker's Algorithm is a method to prevent the deadlock condition.

**41.** Man's urge is to control communicable diseases, produce bumper crops and increase consumer facilities beyond the reach of man.

**42.**
- When these eruptions interact with the magnetic field, they cause beautiful auroras.
- They breakdown radio communication and power supplies.

**43.** Troposphere – Dust particles
Stratosphere – Ozone layer
Ionosphere – Meteors
Exosphere – Aurora

**44.** Non-renewable resource.

**45.** Atmosphere – Salt, freshwater, snow, and ice
Biosphere – Inert gases
Hydrosphere – Organic substances
Lithosphere – Light silicates

**46.** Both Mahatma Gandhi and Rabindranath Tagore.

**47.** IGNOU stands significantly apart from other universities because of national jurisdiction, flexible admission rules and student support services.

**48.** Value education should help in eliminating violence fanaticism.

**49.** Article 280 – Finance Commission
Article 324 – Election Commission
Article 323 – Administrative Tribunals
Article 315 – UPSC

**50.** National Council of Rural Institutes – Hyderabad
Indian Council of Historical Research – New Delhi
Indian Council of Philosophical Research – Bangalore
Indian Institute of Advanced Study – Shimla

# UGC
## NET/JRF/SET

# Practice Set 2

## General Paper 1 (Teaching Aptitude and Attitude)

***Instructions***

- This paper contains fifty Multiple-Choice Questions, each question carries two marks.
- All questions are compulsory.
- Total time given for this paper is 1 hour.

**1.** If you get an opportunity to teach a visually challenged student alongwith normal students, what type of treatment would you like to give him in the class?
(A) Not giving extra attention because majority may suffer.
(B) Take care of him sympathetically in the classroom.
(C) You will think that blindness is his destiny and hence you cannot do anything.
(D) Arrange a seat in the front row and try to teach at a pace convenient to him.

**2.** Which of the following is not a characteristic of a good achievement test?
(A) Reliability
(B) Objectivity
(C) Ambiguity
(D) Validity

**3.** The academic performance of students can be improved if parents are encouraged to
(A) supervise the work of their wards.
(B) arrange for extra tuition.
(C) remain unconcerned about it.
(D) interact with teachers frequently.

**4.** Match List-I with List-II.

| List-I (Characteristic) | List-II (Philosophy) |
|---|---|
| A. Learning by doing | I. Naturalism |
| B. Education through environment | II. Idealism |
| C. Realisation of truth, beauty and goodness | III. Pragmatism |
| D. 'World as it is here and now' | IV. Realism |

**Codes**
(A) A-I, B-IV, C-II, D-III
(B) A-III, B-I, C-II, D-IV
(C) A-I. B-III, C-II, D-IV
(D) A- III, B-II., C-IV, D-I

**5.** Which of the following is/are the teaching maxims?
I. From psychological to logical
II. From analysis to synthesis
III. From concrete to abstract
IV. Follow nature

**Codes**
(A) I, II and III
(B) I, II and IV
(C) I, III and IV
(D) All of these

**6.** Research reports should be reviewed in the light of

I. investigator bias
II. cultural context
III. methodological factors

Which one of the following is correct?

(A) I and III (B) Only I
(C) Only III (D) I, II and III

**7.** Match List-I with List-II.

| List-I (Philosophy) | List-II (Characteristic) |
|---|---|
| A. Experimental | I. Criticism |
| B. Historical | II. Control |
| C. Case study | III. Interpretative |
| D. Ethnography | IV. Intensive |
| | V. Intuitive |

(A) A-II, B-III, C-IV, D-V
(B) A-I, B-II, C-V, D-III
(C) A-III, B-I, C-IV, D-V
(D) A- II, B-I, C-IV, D-III

**8.** In the context of survey research, the following steps are taken in a certain order.

I. Sampling
II. Inference
III. Data analysis
IV. Data collection

**Codes**

(A) II, III, I, IV (B) I, IV, III, II
(C) III, II, IV, I (D) IV, I, II, III

**9.** Which of the following variables cannot be expressed in quantitative terms.

I. Socio economic status
II. Marital status
III. Age
IV. Height

**Codes**

(A) I and II (B) II and III
(C) III and IV (D) All of these

**10.** The aims of research is/are

I. Factual II. Verifiable
III. Theoretical IV. Ambiguous

**Codes**

(A) I and II (B) II and III
(C) I, II and III (D) IV and I

**Direction** (Q. Nos. 11-15) *Read the following passage and answer the questions.*

Each day at the Shantiniketan School starts with the Saraswati Vandana. When painting competitions are held in the school, images of Hindu gods and goddesses are most common. Sanskrit is a favourite subject of many students. Nothing new about it except that the 1,200-odd students studying in the Hindu-run school are Muslims. In 1983, when Ranchodbhai Kiri started Shantiniketan in the all-Muslim Juhapura area of Ahmedabad in Gujarat, only 20 percent of the students were Muslims. But when riots involving the Muslims of Juhapura and the Hindus of nearby Jivrajpark-Vejalpur affected the locality, Hindus started migration. Today, all the students are Muslims and the school is an unparallel example of harmony. In the 2002, when a section of inflamed Muslims wanted the school closed, the parents of the students stood like a wall behind it.

Shantiniketan's principal says, "We never thought of moving the school out of the area because of the love and affection of the local Muslims. Indeed they value the high standard of education which we have set". Such is the reputation of the school that some of the local Muslim strongmen accused of involvement in communal riots are willing to protect the school during the riots.

The parents of Shantiniketan's students believe that it is the best school when it comes to the quality of the teaching. A large number of students have gone for both graduation and post graduation studies. Significantly, the only Muslim teacher in the 40-member teaching staff Husena Mansuri, teaches Sanskrit. Infact, she is so happy at the school that she recently declined the principalship of another Muslim-run school.

Some of the students' entries in a recent school painting competition mere truly move. One drew a picture of Bharat Mata with a mosque and temple, while another portrayed a boy tying rakhi to his sister. Truly, Shantiniketan is a beacon of hope that, despite the provocations from both communities, Hindus and Muslims can live side-by-side with mutual respect.

**11.** How the Shantiniketan School starts the day?

(A) National anthem (B) Prayer
(C) Saraswati Vandana (D) Puja

**12.** Write the subject which is preferred by most of the students.
(A) Hindi (B) English
(C) Sanskrit (D) Gujarati

**13.** Who protects the school during the riot times?
(A) Local Muslims (B) Hindus
(C) Politicians (D) Christians

**14.** Who is the teacher of Sanskrit?
(A) Ranchodbhai Kiri (B) Husena Mansuri
(C) Manisha Vakil (D) Husena Khatoon

**15.** What is the hope despite the communal riots?
(A) Hindus and Muslims cannot live side by side.
(B) Hindus and Muslims can live side by side.
(C) Only Hindus can live.
(D) Only Muslims can live.

**16.** The "Times of India" came into being with the amalgamation of which of these papers?
(A) The Standard and The Telegraph
(B) The Bombay Times and The Courier
(C) The Standard and The Courier
(D) Both A and B

**17.** Which of the following is 'Feedback' in newspaper's communication?
I. Articles II. Editorials
III. Letter to the Editor IV. News
**Codes**
(A) I and II (B) II and III
(C) III and IV (D) Only III

**18.** Modern communication technology is used in distance education to ensure
(A) wider and effective reach of standard material.
(B) that students are inducted to modern technology.
(C) that education is globalised and higher standards are achieved.
(D) enhancement of efficacy of teaching due to limited interpersonal links.

**19.** Video-Conferencing can be classified as one of the following types of communication.
(A) Visual one way
(B) Audio-Visual one way
(C) Audio-Visual two way.
(D) Visual two way

**20.** Which of the following are the main constituents of para language?
I. Tone
II. Pitch
III. Quality of voice
IV. Rate of speaking
**Codes**
(A) I, II and III (B) II, III and IV
(C) I, II and IV (D) All of these

**21.** The difference between the simple interest and the compound interest on ₹ 600 for 1 year at 10% per annum, reckoned half yearly is
(A) Nil (B) ₹ 6.50
(C) ₹ 4.40 (D) ₹ 1.50

**22.** Pointing to a photograph, a woman says, "This man's son's sister is my mother-in-law". How is the woman's husband related to the man in the photograph?
(A) Grandson (B) Son
(C) Son-in-law (D) None of these

**23.** The post office is in the East of the school while my house is in the South of the school. The market is in the North of the post office. If the distance of the market from the post office is equal to the distance of my house from the school, in which direction is the market with respect to my house?
(A) North (B) East
(C) North-East (D) South-West

**24.** In a certain code language
I. 'pic vic nic' means 'winter is cold'.
II. 'to nic re' means 'summer is hot'.
III. 're pic boo' means 'winter and summer'.
IV. 'vic tho pa' means 'nights are cold'.
Which word in that language represents 'summer'?
(A) nic (B) re
(C) to (D) vic

**25.** Identify the missing term
DKM, FJP, HIS, JHV, .......
(A) HGY (B) IGZ
(C) IGY (D) LGY

**26.** Perception refers primarily to
(A) Body temperature (B) Sense perception
(C) Indian philosophy (D) Sense organ

**27.** Abhava is reduced to
(A) Pratyaksa
(B) Anumana
(C) Either to pratyaksa or to anumana
(D) Neither to pratyaksa nor to anumana

**28.** Upamana gives us knowledge about
(A) two similar Vastu in the world.
(B) the relation between Vacaka and the Vacya meant by it
(C) similarity in the uses of words
(D) perceived similarity between Vastu

**29.** If the proposition "All men are not mortal" is true then which of the following inferences is correct? Choose from the code given below.
I. "All men are mortal" is true.
II. "Some men are mortal" is false.
III. "No men are mortal" is doubtful.
IV. "All men are mortal" is false.
**Codes**
(A) I, II and III (B) II, III and IV
(C) I, III and IV (D) I and III

**30.** Abhava is known by
(A) perception
(B) non-apprehension
(C) inference
(D) recognition

**Directions** *Study the following table carefully and answer the questions* (31-35) *given below it.*

**Number of Toys in Five Types Manufactured by Company over years (in 1000)**

| Years | Toys | | | | |
|---|---|---|---|---|---|
| | A | B | C | D | E |
| 1982 | 200 | 150 | 78 | 90 | 65 |
| 1983 | 150 | 180 | 100 | 105 | 70 |
| 1984 | 180 | 175 | 92 | 110 | 85 |
| 1985 | 195 | 160 | 120 | 125 | 75 |
| 1986 | 220 | 185 | 130 | 135 | 80 |

**31.** What was the percentage (approximate) increase in production of D type toys from 1983 to 1985?
(A) 10 (B) 20
(C) 19 (D) 25

**32.** In the case of which type of toys was the total production of the given five years the maximum?
(A) C (B) B (C) A (D) D

**33.** What was the percentage drop on production of A types toys from 1982 to 1984?
(A) 30 (B) 10 (C) 20 (D) 50

**34.** In the case of which type of toys was there a continuous increase in production over the years?
(A) B (B) A (C) C (D) D

**35.** The production of E type toys in 1986 was what percent of production of B type toys in 1985?
(A) 80 (B) 50 (C) 100 (D) 200

**36.** An internet e-mail message consists of
I. Message envelope
II. Message header
III. Message body
(A) I and II (B) II and III
(C) I and III (D) All of these

**37.** What should be done to successfully convert the format of an image from BMP to JPEG?
(A) Compress the file.
(B) Rename the image.
(C) Use the save as command.
(D) Change the image file extension.

**38.** Which of the following are web browsers?
I. Internet Explorer
II. Mozilla Firefox
III. Opera
IV. Safari
(A) I, II and III (B) II, III and IV
(C) I, III and IV (D) All of these

**39.** Which of the following denotes the internet hardware requirements?
I. Modem II. Hub
III. Bridge IV. Router
V. Gateway
(A) I, II and III
(B) I, III, IV and V
(C) I, IV and V
(D) I, II, III, IV and V

**40.** The data from a spreadsheet needs to be imported into a database package. Which file format would be the most appropriate when saving the spreadsheet file?

(A) CSV (B) HTML
(C) PDF (D) RTF

**41.** Which of the following statements are true in the context of particulate matter?

I. It is basically a mist move prevalent during winter weather.
II. It is more prevalent in diesel engine vehicles.
III. Long-term exposure can harm respiratory track and lung functions.

**Codes**

(A) I and II (B) I, II and III
(C) II and III (D) I and III

**42.** An ecosystem gradually merges with an adjoining one through a transitional zone is called the

(A) Ecological niche.
(B) Ecological footprint.
(C) Ecotone.
(D) Shore effect.

**43.** Favourable morphological and physiological response to a change in environment is called

(A) Preadaptation
(B) Ecotyping
(C) Formation of ecophenes
(D) Acclimatisation

**44.** Match List-I with List-II.

| List-I (Act) | List-II (Year) |
|---|---|
| A. Water (Prevention and Control of Pollution) | I. 1974 |
| B. Air (Prosecution and Control of Pollution) | II. 1981 |
| C. Wildlife Protection Act | III. 1972 |
| D. Environment Protection Act | IV. 1986 |

(A) A-I, B-II, C-III, D-IV
(B) A-I, B-III, C-II, D-IV
(C) A-IV, B-II, C-III, D-I
(D) A- IV, B-III, C-II, D-I

**45.** Tsunami occurs due to

(A) mild earthquakes and landslides in the oceans.
(B) strong earthquakes and landslides in the oceans.
(C) strong earthquakes and landslides in mountains.
(D) strong earthquakes and landslides in deserts.

**46.** The drafting committee of the Indian Constitution was headed by

(A) Dr. Rajendra Prasad.
(B) N. Gopalaswamy.
(C) Dr. B.R. Ambedkar.
(D) None of the above

**47.** Match List I with List II and select the correct answer from the codes given below.

| List-I (Institutions) | List-II (Locations) |
|---|---|
| A. National Law Institute | I. Shimla |
| B. Indian Institute of Advanced Studies | II. Bhopal |
| C. National Judicial Academy | III. Hyderabad |
| D. National Savings Institute | IV. Nagpur |

**Codes**

(A) A-III, B-II, C-IV and D-I
(B) A-I, B-II, C-III and D-IV
(C) A-IV, B-III, C-I and D-II
(D) A-III, B-I, C-II and D-IV

**48.** Match List I with List II and select the correct answer from the codes given below.

| List-I (Institutions) | List-II (Functions) |
|---|---|
| A. Parliament | I. Formulation of budget |
| B. C and AG | II. Enactment of budget |
| C. Ministry of Finance | III. Implementation of budget |
| D. Executing Departments | IV. Legality of expenditure |
| | V. Justification of income |

**Codes**

(A) A-III, B-IV, C-II and D-I
(B) A-II, B-IV, C-I and D-III
(C) A-V, B-III, C-IV and D-II
(D) A-IV, B-II, C-III and D-V

**49.** Match List-I with List-II and select the correct answer from the codes given below.

| List-I (Institutions) | List-II (Locations) |
|---|---|
| A. Dr. Hari Singh Gour University | I. Mumbai |
| B. S.N.D.T. University | II. Baroda |
| C. M.S. University | III. Jodhpur |
| D. J.N. Vyas University | IV. Sagar |

**Codes**

| | A | B | C | D | | A | B | C | D |
|---|---|---|---|---|---|---|---|---|---|
| (A) | IV | I | II | III | (B) | I | II | III | IV |
| (C) | III | I | II | IV | (D) | II | IV | I | III |

**50.** Match List-I with List-II.

| List I (Metal) | List-II (Effects) |
|---|---|
| A. Chromium | I. Thalassaemia |
| B. Arsenic | II. Itai-Itai |
| C. Cadmium | III. Dermatitis |
| D. Iron | IV. Carcinogen |

**Codes**

(A) A-IV, B-III, C-II, D-I
(B) A-IV, B-II, C-III, D-I
(C) A-I, B-III, C-II, D-IV
(D) A-I, B-II, C-III, D-IV

## ANSWERS

| | | | | | | | | | |
|---|---|---|---|---|---|---|---|---|---|
| 1 (D) | 2 (C) | 3 (D) | 4 (B) | 5 (A) | 6 (C) | 7 (C) | 8 (B) | 9 (A) | 10 (C) |
| 11 (C) | 12 (C) | 13 (A) | 14 (B) | 15 (B) | 16 (C) | 17 (D) | 18 (D) | 19 (C) | 20 (D) |
| 21 (D) | 22 (A) | 23 (C) | 24 (B) | 25 (D) | 26 (B) | 27 (C) | 28 (A) | 29 (C) | 30 (A) |
| 31 (C) | 32 (C) | 33 (B) | 34 (D) | 35 (B) | 36 (D) | 37 (C) | 38 (D) | 39 (D) | 40 (A) |
| 41 (B) | 42 (C) | 43 (C) | 44 (A) | 45 (B) | 46 (C) | 47 (D) | 48 (B) | 49 (A) | 50 (A) |

# *Hints & Solutions*

**1.** I will arrange a seat for him in front row and try to teach at a pace convenient to him.

**2.** The achievement test should not be ambiguous, it should be concrete in structure.

**3.** If the parents interact with teachers frequently, then the performance of students will be improved.

**4.**

| | | |
|---|---|---|
| Learning by doing | – | Pragmatism |
| Education through environment | – | Naturalism |
| Realisation of truth, beauty and goodness | – | Idealism |
| 'World as it is here and now' | – | Realism |

**5.** Following are the teacher maxims
- From psychological to logical.
- From analysis to synthesis.
- From concrete to abstract.

**6.** Research reports should be reviewed in the light of methodological factors.

**7.**

| | | |
|---|---|---|
| Experimental | – | Interpretative |
| Historical | – | Criticism |
| Case study | – | Intensive |
| Ethnography | – | Intuitive |

**8.** In the context of survey research, the following steps are taken in a certain order
- Sampling
- Data collection
- Data analysis
- Inference

**9.** Socio economic status and Marital status cannot be expressed in quantitative terms.

**10.** The aims of research are Factual, Verifiable and Theoretical.

**11.** Shantiniketan school starts the day by Saraswati Vandana.

**12.** The subject which was preferred by most of the students was Sanskrit.

**13.** Local Muslims protects the school during the riot times.

**14.** Husena Mansuri is the teacher of Sanskrit.

**15.** The hope despite the communal riots is that Hindus and Muslims can live side by side with peace.

**16.** The "Times of India" came into being with the amalgamation of The Standard and The Courier.

**17.** Letter to the Editor is the only feedback in newspaper communication.

**18.** Modern communication technology is used to enhance efficacy of teaching due to limited interpersonal links.

**19.** Video-conferencing is an Audio-visual two way type of communication.

**20.** Following are the main constituents of para language
- Tone
- Pitch
- Quality of voice
- Rate of speaking

**21.** $S.I = ₹\left(600 \times 1 \times \frac{10}{100}\right) = ₹\ 60.$

$$C.I = ₹\left\{\left[600 \times \left(1 + \frac{5}{100}\right)^2\right] - 600\right\}$$

$$= ₹\ \frac{123}{2} = ₹\ 61.50$$

$\therefore$ (C.I) – (S.I) = ₹ 1.50

**22.**

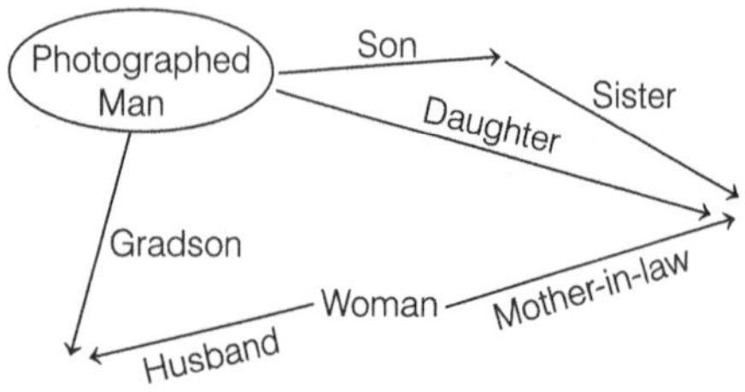


**23.** The positions of school, house, post office and market are as follows

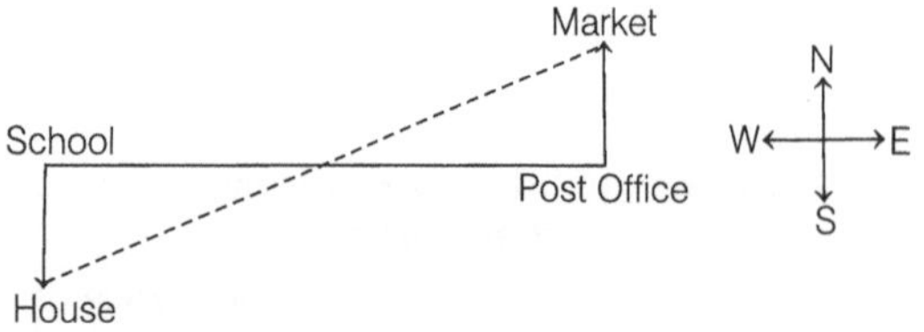


Hence, the market is in the North-East of my house.

**24.** From I and II 're' means summer.

**25.** $D \xrightarrow{+2} F \xrightarrow{+2} H \xrightarrow{+2} J \xrightarrow{+2}$ L

$K \xrightarrow{-1} J \xrightarrow{-1} I \xrightarrow{-1} H \xrightarrow{-1}$ G

$M \xrightarrow{+3} P \xrightarrow{+3} S \xrightarrow{+3} V \xrightarrow{+3}$ Y

**26.** Sense Perception

**27.** Either Pratyaksha or to Anumana.

**28.** two similar vastu in the world.

**29.**
- "All men are mortal" is true.
- "No men are mortal" is doubtful.
- "All men are mortal" is false.

**30.** Abhava is known by Perception.

**31.** Production of D type toys in 1983 = 1,05,000.

Production of D type toys in 1985 = 1,25,000

$$\text{Percentage increase} = \frac{20000}{105000} \times 100 = 19.05$$

$$= 19\% \text{ (app)}$$

**32.** Total production of A types toys from 1982-86 = 945 thousand.

Total production of B types toys from 1982-86 = 850 thousand

Total production of C types toys from 1982-86 = 520 thousands

Total production of D types toys from 1982-86 = 565 thousand

Total production of E types toys from 1982-86 = 375 thousand.

Hence, it was maximum for A types toys.

**33.** Drop in production of A types toys from 1982 to 1984 = 20000

$$\text{Percentage drop} = \frac{20000}{200000} \times 100 = 10\%.$$

**34.** From the table, it is obvious that there is a continuous increase in production of D type of toys.

**35.** If the required number is $x$, then by hypothesis 80,000 = $x$% of 160000

or $$80000 = \frac{x}{100} \times 160000$$

$$\therefore \quad x = \frac{80000 \times 100}{160000} = 50$$

**36.** An internet e-mail message consists of
- Message envelope
- Message header
- Message body

**37.** Use the save as command.

**38.** Internet Explorer, Mozilla Firefox, Opera and Safari all are Web browsers.

**39.** Following are the Internet hardware requirements
- Modem
- Hub
- Bridge
- Router
- Gateway

**40.** CSV

**41.**
- It is basically a mist move prevalent during winter weather.
- It is more prevalent in diesel engine vehicles.
- Long-term exposure can harm respiratory track and lung functions.

**42.** An ecosystem gradually merges with an adjoining one through a transitional zone is called the Ecotone.

**43.** Favourable morphological and physiological response to a change in environment is called formation of ecophenes.

**44.**

| | | |
|---|---|---|
| Water (Prevention and Control of Pollution) | – | 1974 |
| Air (Prosecution and Control of Pollution) | – | 1981 |
| Wildlife Protection Act | – | 1972 |
| Environment Protection Act | – | 1986 |

**45.** Tsunami occurs due to strong earthquakes and landslides in the oceans.

**46.** Drafting Committee of the Indian Constitution was headed by B.R. Ambedkar.

**47.**

| | | |
|---|---|---|
| National Law Institute | – | Hyderabad |
| Indian Institute of Advanced Studies | – | Shimla |
| National Judicial Academy | – | Bhopal |
| National Savings Institute | – | Nagpur |

**48.**

| | |
|---|---|
| Parliament | – Enactment of budget |
| C and AG | – Legality of expenditure |
| Ministry of Finance | – Formulation of budget |
| Executing Departments | – Implementation of budget |

**49.**

| | | |
|---|---|---|
| Dr. Hari Singh Gour University | – | Sagar |
| S.N.D.T. University | – | Mumbai |
| M.S. University | – | Baroda |
| J.N. Vyas University | – | Jodhpur |

**50.**

| | | |
|---|---|---|
| Chromium | – | Carcinogen |
| Arsenic | – | Dermatitis |
| Cadmium | – | Itai-Itai |
| Iron | – | Thalassaemia |

# UGC
## NET/JRF/SET

# Practice Set 3

## General Paper 1 (Teaching Aptitude and Attitude)

### *Instructions*

- This paper contains fifty Multiple-Choice Questions, each question carries two marks.
- All questions are compulsory.
- Total time given for this paper is 1 hour.

**1.** Which of the following skills are needed for present day teacher to adjust effectively with the classroom teaching?

I. Knowledge of technology
II. Use of technology in teaching learning
III. Knowledge of students needs
IV. Content mastery

**Codes**

(A) I and III (B) II and III
(C) II, III and IV (D) II and IV

**2.** In a classroom, a communicator's trust level is determined by

(A) the change of voice level
(B) the use of abstract concepts
(C) eye contact
(D) the use of hyperbola

**3. Assertion** (A) For an effective classroom communication at times it is desirable to use the projection technology.

**Reason** (R) Using the projection technology facilitates extensive coverage of course contents.

(A) Both 'A' and 'R' are true, and 'R' is the correct explanation.
(B) Both 'A' and 'R' are true, but 'R' is not the correct explanation.
(C) 'A' is true, but 'R' is false.
(D) 'A' is false, but 'R' is true.

**4.** In a lively classroom situation, there is likely to be

(A) occasional roars of laughter.
(B) complete silence.
(C) frequent teacher-student dialogue.
(D) loud discussion among students.

**5.** The teacher has been glorified by the phrase "Friend, philosopher and guide" because

(A) he has to play all vital roles in the context of society.
(B) he transmits the high value of humanity to students.
(C) he is the great reformer of the society.
(D) he is a great patriot.

**6.** Survey study aims at

I. knowing facts about the existing situation.
II. comparing the present status with the standard norms.
III. criticising the existing situation.

IV. identifying the means of improving the existing situation.

**Codes**

(A) I and II only (B) I, II and III
(C) I, II, III and IV (D) II and III only

**7.** A researcher divides his population into certain groups and fixes the size of the sample from each group. It is called

(A) cluster sample (B) stratified sample
(C) quota sample (D) All of these

**8.** Area (cluster) sampling technique is used when

(A) population is scattered and large size of the sample is to be drawn.
(B) population is heterogeneous.
(C) long survey is needed.
(D) Both (A) and (C)

**9.** The research antagonistic to ex-post facto research is

(A) experimental studies.
(B) library researches.
(C) normative researches.
(D) All of the above

**10.** A researcher divides the populations into PG graduates and 10 + 2 students and using the random digit table he selects some of them from each. This is technically called

(A) stratified sampling.
(B) stratified random sampling.
(C) representative sampling.
(D) None of these

**Direction** (Q. Nos. 11-15) *Read the passage and answer the following questions.*

James Madison said, "A people who mean to be their own governors must arm themselves with power that knowledge gives. "In India, the Official Secrets Act, 1923 was a convenient smoke screen to deny members of the public access to information. Public functioning has traditionally been shrouded in secrecy. But in a democracy in which people govern themselves, it is necessary to have more openness. In the maturing of our democracy, right to information is a major step forward; it enables citizens to participate fully in the decision-making process that affects their lives so profoundly. It is in this context that the address of the Prime Minister in the Lok Sabha is significant. He said, "I would only like to see that everyone, particularly our civil servants, should see the Bill in a positive spirit; not as a draconian law for paralyzing Government, but as an instrument for improving Government-Citizen interface resulting in a friendly, caring and effective Government functioning for the good of our People." He further said, "This is an innovative Bill, where there will be scope to review its functioning as we gain experience. Therefore, this is a piece of legislation, whose working will be kept under constant reviews.".

The Commission, in its Report, has dealt with the application of the Right to Information in Executive, Legislature and Judiciary. The judiciary could be a pioneer in implementing the Act in letter and spirit because much of the work that the Judiciary does is open to public scrutiny, Government of India has sanctioned an e-governance project in the Judiciary for about ₹ 700 crores which would bring about systematic classification, standardisation and categorisation of records. This would help the judiciary to fulfil its mandate under the Act. Similar capacity building would be required in all other public authorities. The transformation from non-transparency to transparency and public accountability is the responsibility of all three organs of State.

**11.** A person gets power

(A) by acquiring knowledge.
(B) from the Official Secrets Act, 1923.
(C) through openings.
(D) by denying public information.

**12.** Right to Information is a major step forward to

(A) enable citizens to participate fully in the decision making process.
(B) to make the people aware of the Act.
(C) to gain knowledge of administration.
(D) to make the people Government friendly.

**13.** The Prime Minister considered the Bill

(A) to provide power to the civil servants.
(B) as an instrument for improving Government-citizen interface resulting in a friendly, caring and effective Government.
(C) a draconian law against the officials.
(D) to check the harrassment of the people.

**14.** The Commission made the Bill effective by
(A) extending power to the executive authorities.
(B) combining the executive and legislative power.
(C) recognising Judiciary a pioneer in implementing the act in letter and spirit.
(D) educating the people before its implementation.

**15.** The Prime Minister considered the Bill innovative and hoped that
(A) it could be reviewed based on the experience gained on its functioning.
(B) the civil servants would see the Bill in a positive spirit.
(C) it would not be considered as a draconian law for paralyzing Government.
(D) All of the above

**16.** Public communication tends to occur within a more
(A) complex structure.
(B) political structure.
(C) convenient structure.
(D) formal structure.

**17.** Which of the following is the objective of mass media?
I. To provide information.
II. To convey cultural and educational programmes.
III. To entertain people.
IV. To establish social contact and linkage.

Select the correct answer from the codes given below.

(A) I and II (B) II, III, IV
(C) II and III (D) All of the above

**18.** Classroom communication is normally considered as
(A) effective (B) cognitive
(C) affective (D) selective

**19.** The oldest newspaper in India is
(A) Times of India (B) Hindu
(C) Tribune (D) Statesman

**20.** Which of the following statements regarding the term e-Governance is/are True?

**M** e-Citizenship will include the implementation of ICT for facilitation of government services relating to citizenship.

**N** e-Help refers to the facilitation of disaster and crisis management using ICT.

Select the correct answer using the codes given below.

(A) Both M and N (B) Only M
(C) Only N (D) Neither M nor N

**21.** A school boy was misdirected from his way while returning to his home. In order to reach his home he first moved 3 km in South direction and then turned to his left. 2 km from there he moved to his left and walked 3 km. After this, he again turned to his left and moved 1 km. Finally he reached his home. The home of the boy was in which direction from his school?
(A) West (B) North
(C) East (D) South

**22.** Looking at a portrait of a man, Arun said, "His mother is the wife of my father's son. I have no brother or sister." At whose portrait was Arun looking?
(A) His son (B) His cousin
(C) His uncle (D) None of these

**23.** The simple interest on a sum of money will be ₹ 600 after 10 years. If the principle is trebled after 5 years, what will be the total interest at the end of the tenth year?
(A) ₹ 600
(B) ₹ 900
(C) ₹ 1200
(D) Data inadequate

**24.** In a certain code language, QUEUE is written as Q22, CHURCH is written as 1UR1. Which of the following would be the most appropriate code for BANANA in that language?
(A) B5A5A (B) B5A5
(C) B55A (D) BA5A5A

**25.** 140 68 36 16 10 3
284 (A) (B) (C) (D) (E)

Which number will come in the place of (D)?
(A) 34 (B) 40
(C) 19 (D) 90

**26.** **Assertion** (A) There are more laws on the books today than ever before, and more crimes being committed than ever before.

**Reason** (R) Because to reduce crime we must eliminate the laws.

Choose the correct answer from below

(A) 'A' is true, 'R' is doubtful and 'R' is not the correct explanation of 'A'

(B) 'A' is false, 'R' is true and 'R' is the correct explanation of 'A'.

(C) 'A' is doubtful, 'R' is doubtful and 'R' is not the correct explanation of 'A'.

(D) 'A' is doubtful, 'R' is true and 'R' is not the correct explanation of 'A'.

**27.** Structure of logical arguments is based on

(A) Formal validity (B) Material truth

(C) Linguistic expression

(D) Aptness of examples

**28.** If two small circles represent the class of the 'men' and the class of the 'plants' and the big circle represents 'mortality', which one of the following figures represent the proposition 'All men are mortal'?

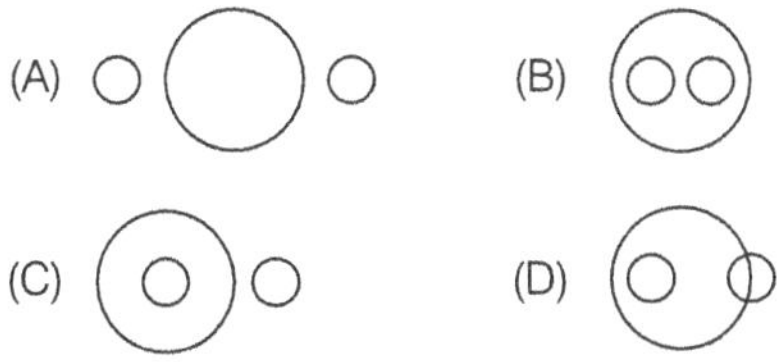


**29.** Deductive argument involves

(A) sufficient evidence.

(B) critical thinking.

(C) seeing logical relations.

(D) repeated observation.

**30.** Match the following.

| List-I | List-II |
|---|---|
| A. Perception | I. Ordinary |
| B. Inference | II. Vyapti |
| C. Comparison | III. Analogy |
| D. Verbal testimony | IV. Shalda |

**Codes**

| | A | B | C | D |
|---|---|---|---|---|
| (A) | I | II | III | IV |
| (B) | IV | III | II | I |
| (C) | I | IV | III | II |
| (D) | III | IV | II | I |

**Direction** *Study the graph carefully and answer the questions (31-35) given below.*

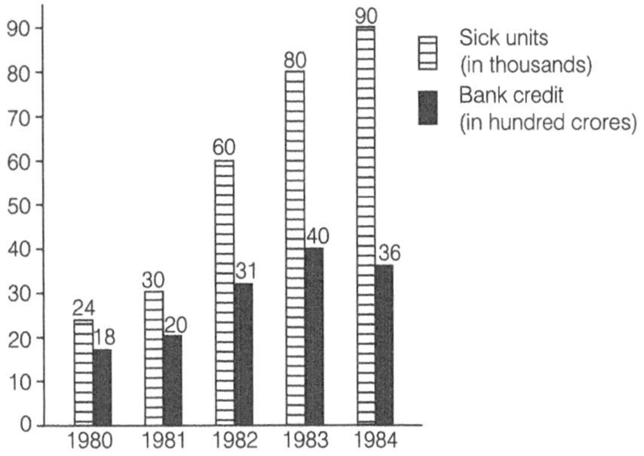


**31.** What was the percentage increase in number of sick units from 1981 to 1983?

(A) 50 (B) 150

(C) 25 (D) None of these

**32.** What was the difference in bank credit between 1981 and 1982?

(A) ₹ 5 crore (B) ₹ 50 crore

(C) ₹ 500 crore (D) ₹ 50 lac

**33.** If the bank credit is reduced to half in the year 1981, what will be the approximate bank credit per sick unit?

(A) ₹ 3 crore (B) ₹ 3 lac

(C) ₹ 30 lac (D) ₹ 4 lac

**34.** In which year was the bank credit per sick unit the maximum?

(A) 1980 (B) 1981

(C) 1982 (D) 1983

**35.** In 1983 what was the total bank credit per sick unit approximately?

(A) ₹ 32 crore (B) ₹ 71 crore

(C) ₹ 71 lac (D) ₹ 4 lac

**36.** On the keyboard of computer each character has an "ASCII" value which stands for

(A) American Stock Code for Information Interchange.

(B) American Standard Code for Information Interchange.

(C) African Standard Code for Information Interchange.

(D) Adaptable Standard Code for Information Change.

**37.** DNS in internet technology stands for
(A) Dynamic Name System.
(B) Domain Name System.
(C) Distributed Name System.
(D) None of the above

**38.** A company regularly updates a user reference guide. Some staff are confused about which of the printed document is the most current. What feature should be include in the reference guide to eliminate this confusion?
(A) Data printed
(B) Version number
(C) Authors name
(D) Copyright information

**39.** POP3 and IMAP are e-mail protocols in which
(A) one automatically gets one's mail everyday.
(B) one has to be connected to the server to read or write one's mail.
(C) one only has to be connected to the server to send and receive email.
(D) one does not need any telephone lines.

**40.** Yash tells his friends, Vaibhav (vaibhav@gmail.com), Aryan (aryan@gmail.com) and Kirti (kirti@gmail.com), date of his brother's birthday party through an E-mail as shown below.

To : vaibhav@gmail.com

CC :

BCC : aryan@gmail.com, kirti@gmail.com

Subject : Brother's Birthday Party Invitation

Hello Friend,

How are you? I hope you are alright. I want to invite you on my brother Akshay's Birthday party is on 30/01/2019.

You have to come.

Bye

Yash

Which of the following can be derived from this E-mail?
(A) Vaibhav knows that Aryan receives mail
(B) Aryan knows that Sahil receives mail
(C) Kirti knows that both Aryan and Vaibhav receive mail
(D) Vaibhav knows that Kirti receive mail

**41.** The environment which has been modified by human activities is called
(A) natural environment.
(B) anthropogenic environment.
(C) modern environment.
(D) urban environment.

**42.** The Red Data book which lists endangered species is maintained by
(A) UNO (B) WHO
(C) IUCN (D) WWF

**43.** Consider the following statements about Lithosphere.
I. It is a solid crust or the hard top layer of the earth.
II. It constitutes about 39% part of the earth.
III. It is the domain that provides us forests, lands for agriculture and human settlements.

Which of the above statements is/are correct?
(A) Only I
(B) I and II
(C) II and III
(D) All of the above

**44.** Beginning from the surface of earth, what is the sequence of different layers of atmosphere?
(A) Stratosphere, Troposphere, Ionosphere, Exosphere
(B) Troposphere, Stratosphere, Ionosphere, Exosphere
(C) Troposphere, Stratosphere, Ionosphere
(D) None of the above

**45.** Which of the following combinations represent renewable natural resources?
(A) Fertile soil, fresh water and natural gas
(B) Clean air, phosphates and biological diversity
(C) Fishes, fertile soil and fresh water
(D) Oil, forests and tides

**46.** The Fundamental Duties of a citizen include
I. Respect for the Constitution, the National Flag and the National Anthem.
II. To develop the scientific temper.
III. Respect for the Government.
IV. To protect Wildlife.

Choose the correct answer from the codes given below.

**Codes**

(A) I, II and III
(B) I, II and IV
(C) II, III and IV
(D) I, III, IV and II

**47.** Which one of the following difficulties occur in the rural area for continuing secondary education of girls?

(A) Parents do not desire to give co-education to their daughters along with boys.
(B) Poverty of parents.
(C) Help of girls in household work and work in agriculture.
(D) All of the above

**48.** The Bethune school, the first school to educate women, was founded by J.E.D Bethune at which place?

(A) Madras
(B) Bombay
(C) Calcutta
(D) Delhi

**49.** Match the List-I with the List-II and select the correct answer from the codes given below.

| | List-I (Commissions and Committees) | | List-II (Year) |
|---|---|---|---|
| A. | First Administrative Reforms Commission | I. | 2005 |
| B. | Paul H. Appleby Committee | II. | 1962 |
| C. | K. Santhanam Committee | III. | 1966 |
| D. | Second Administrative Reforms Commission | IV. | 1953 |

**Codes**

| | A | B | C | D |
|---|---|---|---|---|
| (A) | I | III | II | IV |
| (B) | III | IV | II | I |
| (C) | IV | II | III | I |
| (D) | II | I | IV | III |

**50.** Constitutionally the registration and recognition of political parties is the function performed by

(A) the State Election Commission of respective States.
(B) the Law Ministry of Government of India.
(C) the Election Commission of India.
(D) Election Department of the State Governments.

## ANSWERS

| | | | | | | | | | |
|---|---|---|---|---|---|---|---|---|---|
| 1 (C) | 2 (C) | 3 (A) | 4 (C) | 5 (B) | 6 (B) | 7 (B) | 8 (D) | 9 (A) | 10 (B) |
| 11 (A) | 12 (A) | 13 (B) | 14 (C) | 15 (D) | 16 (D) | 17 (D) | 18 (C) | 19 (A) | 20 (A) |
| 21 (C) | 22 (A) | 23 (C) | 24 (C) | 25 (C) | 26 (A) | 27 (B) | 28 (C) | 29 (C) | 30 (A) |
| 31 (D) | 32 (C) | 33 (B) | 34 (A) | 35 (D) | 36 (B) | 37 (B) | 38 (B) | 39 (B) | 40 (C) |
| 41 (B) | 42 (C) | 43 (B) | 44 (B) | 45 (B) | 46 (B) | 47 (D) | 48 (C) | 49 (B) | 50 (D) |

# UGC
## NET/JRF/SET

# Practice Set 4

## General Paper 1 (Teaching Aptitude and Attitude)

***Instructions***

- This paper contains fifty Multiple-Choice Questions, each question carries two marks.
- All questions are compulsory.
- Total time given for this paper is 1 hour.

**1.** What are required for good teaching?

I. Diagnosis II. Remedy
III. Direction IV. Feedback

Select the correct answer from the codes given below

(A) I and II (B) II, III and IV
(C) III and IV (D) All of these

**2.** Which one of the following is appropriate in respect of teacher-student relationship?

(A) Very informal and intimate
(B) Limited to classroom only
(C) Cordial and respectful
(D) Indifferent

**3.** If a group of students enter your room and abuse you and behave violently with you, at that time how would you control your emotions?

(A) First you will try to pacify their emotions, then ask politely about their behaviour.
(B) You will report the case to the principal with recommendation of punitive measures.
(C) You will feel ashamed among your teaching community.
(D) You will react in similar tone and try to assault them physically.

**4.** For a teacher, which one of the following methods would be correct for writing on the blackboard?

(A) Writing fast and as clearly as possible.
(B) Writing the matter first and then asking students to read it.
(C) Asking a question to students and then writing the answer as stated by them.
(D) Writing the important points as clearly as possible.

**5.** If a parent approaches the teacher to do some favour to his/her ward in the examination, the teacher should

(A) try to help him
(B) guide him to talk to the principal
(C) refuse politely and firmly
(D) ask him rudely to go away

**6.** Which of the following statements is/are true?
(A) In research, objectives can be worded in question form.
(B) In research, objectives can be worded in statement form.
(C) Objectives are to be stated in Chapter I of the thesis.
(D) All of the above

**7.** The study in which the investigators attempt to trace an effect is known as
(A) Survey research.
(B) 'Ex-post facto' research.
(C) Historical research.
(D) Summative research.

**8.** Generalised conclusion on the basis of a sample is technically known as
(A) Data analysis and interpretation.
(B) Parameter inference.
(C) Statistical inference.
(D) All of the above

**9.** "This research is a process of critical inquiry into past events." The statement indicates towards which type of research?
(A) Correlational research
(B) Explanatory research
(C) Historical research
(D) Ex-post facto research

**10.** The main characteristic of scientific research is
(A) empirical (B) theoretical
(C) experimental (D) All of these

**Direction** (Q. Nos. 11-15) *Read the following passage and give the answers.*

The catalytic fact of the twentieth century is uncontrollable development, consumerist society, political materialism, and spiritual devaluation. This inordinate development has led to the transcendental 'second reality' of sacred perception that biologically transcendence is a part of human life.

As the century closes, it dawns with imperative vigour that the 'first reality' of enlightened rationalism and the 'second reality' of the beyond have to be harmonised in a worthy state of man. The *de facto* values describe what we are, they portray the 'is' of our ethic, they are est values (Latin *est* means is). The ideal values tell us what we ought to be, they are *esto* values (Latin *esto* 'ought to be'). Both have to be in the ebb and flow of consciousness.

The ever new science and technology and the ever-perennial faith are two modes of one certainty, that is the wholeness of man, his courage to be, his share in being.

The materialistic foundations of science have crumbled down. Science itself has proved that matter is energy, processes are as valid as facts, and affirmed the non-materiality of the universe. The encounter of the 'two cultures', the scientific and the humane, will restore the normal vision, and will be the bedrock of a 'Science' of Understanding in the new century. It will give new meaning to the ancient perception that quantity (measure) and quality (value) coexist at the root of nature. Human endeavours cannot afford to be humanistically irresponsible.

**11.** The problem raised in the passage reflects overall on
(A) Consumerism
(B) Materialism
(C) Spiritual devaluation
(D) Inordinate development

**12.** The '*de facto*' values in the passage means
(A) What is (B) What ought to be
(C) What can be (D) Where it is

**13.** According to the passage, the 'first reality' constitutes
(A) Economic prosperity
(B) Political development
(C) Sacred perception of life
(D) Enlightened rationalism

**14.** Encounter of the 'two cultures', the scientific and the human implies
(A) Restoration of normal vision.
(B) Universe is both material and non-material.
(C) Man is superior to nature.
(D) Co-existence of quantity and quality in nature.

**15.** The contents of the passage are
(A) Descriptive (B) Prescriptive
(C) Axiomatic (D) Optional

**16.** Communication *via* new media such as computers, teleshopping, internet and mobile telephony is termed as

(A) entertainment.
(B) interactive communication.
(C) development communication.
(D) communitarian.

**17.** In downward communication, messages

(A) flow from the bottom to the top of the organisation structure.
(B) flow from the top to the bottom of the organisation structure.
(C) are meant to be exchanged between the members of the top brass.
(D) None of the above

**18.** Which of the following is not a successful communicator?

(A) One who presents material in a precise and clear way.
(B) One who is able to adopt himself according to the language of the communicatee.
(C) One who knows a lot but is somewhat reserve in his attitude.
(D) One who sometimes becomes informal before the receiver and develops rapport.

**19.** Which of the following is not true about the grapevine?

(A) It is faster at conveying information than an organisation's formal communication system.
(B) It is somewhere between 75 and 95 percent as accurate as the formal communication system.
(C) It is found in almost all organisations.
(D) Managers usually welcome its existence.

**20.** Which of the following is/are correct in respect of non-verbal communication?

I. It helps illiterate people to communicate with others easily.
II. In this communication people can repeat the verbal messages according to their need.
III. In this communication there is a great possibility in distortion of information.

Select the correct answer from the codes given below.

(A) Only I (B) I and II
(C) II and III (D) All of the above

**21.** Pointing to a photograph, a lady tells Pramod, "I am the only daughter of this lady and her son is your maternal uncle." How is the speaker related to Pramod's father?

(A) Sister-in-law
(B) Wife
(C) Either 'A' or 'B'
(D) Neither 'A' nor 'B'

**22.** The door of Danika's house is towards the east. From the backside of the house, she walks straight 100 yards then turns towards right and walks 100 yards again and after that turns towards left and stops after walking 50 yards. Now Danika is in which direction from the starting point?

(A) South-east (B) North-west
(C) North-east (D) South-west

**23.** In a certain code language

1. 'po ki top ma' means 'Usha is playing cards'.
2. 'kop ja ki ma' means 'Asha is playing tennis'.
3. 'ki top sop ho' means 'they are playing football'.
4. 'po sur kop' means 'Cards and tennis'.

Which word in that language means 'Asha'?

(A) ja (B) ma
(C) kop (D) top

**24.**

| | | | | | |
|---|---|---|---|---|---|
| 2 | 4 | 9 | 20 | 43 | 90 |
| 3 | (A) | (B) | (C) | (D) | (E) |

Which number will come in the place of (D)?

(A) 59 (B) 99
(C) 100 (D) 104

**25.** A retailer buys a sewing machine at a discount of 15% and sells it for ₹ 1955. Thus, he makes a profit of 15%. The discount is

(A) ₹ 270 (B) ₹ 290
(C) ₹ 300 (D) ₹ 280

**26.** Anuplabdhi is

(A) First pramana (B) Fourth pramana
(C) Sixth pramana (D) Not a pramana

**27.** Vyapti is an unconditional and constant relation between
(A) vyapaka and vyapya.
(B) syadhya and hetu.
(C) sabda and anumana.
(D) vyapya and vyapaka.

**28.** Vyapti is a
(A) relation and a resemblance.
(B) resemblance and recognition.
(C) relation and a rule.
(D) recognition and a rule.

**29.** "Sabda and Upamana are not independent pramana as they are reducible to anumana".
This is the view of
(A) Naiyasyikas
(B) Vaisesikas
(C) Vedanta
(D) Prabhakara Mimamsakas

**30.** The following question is based on the diagram given below. If the two small circles represent formal class-room education and distance education and the big circle stands for university system of education, which figure represents the university systems.

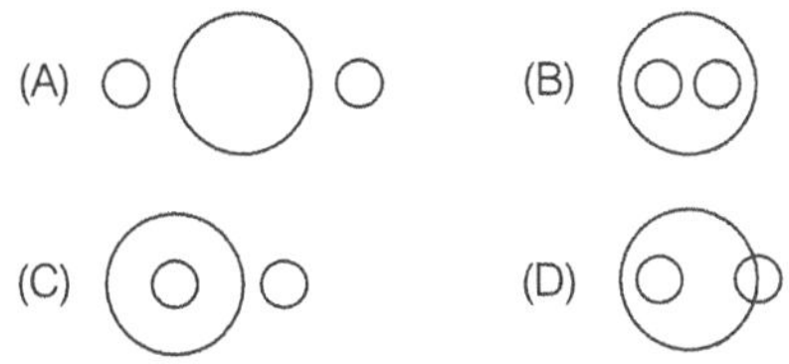


**Directions** These questions (31-34) are based on the circle graph below, which shows the expenditure incurred, in bringing out a book, by a publisher.

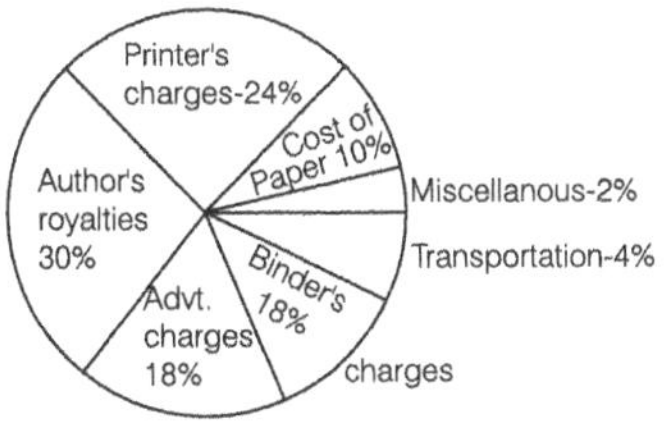


**31.** If the author's royalties amount to ₹ 30000, the binder's charges amount to ₹ .......
(A) 10500 (B) 12000
(C) 15000 (D) 18000

**32.** What should be the central angle of the sector for transportation charges?
(A) 4° (B) 8.4°
(C) 13.4° (D) 14.4°

**33.** If the advertisement charges amount to ₹ 18000, the total expenditure incurred in bringing out the books is ₹ ...............
(A) 60300 (B) 63000
(C) 90000 (D) 100000

**34.** The miscellaneous expenditure amounts to ₹ 2000 and totally 12500 copies of the book are published. What is the cost per copy at which the books must be priced, if the publishers desires a profit of 5%?
(A) ₹ 5 (B) ₹ 7.50
(C) ₹ 8 (D) ₹ 8.40

**35. Direction** Study the following graph and point out the Industrial growth rate of India

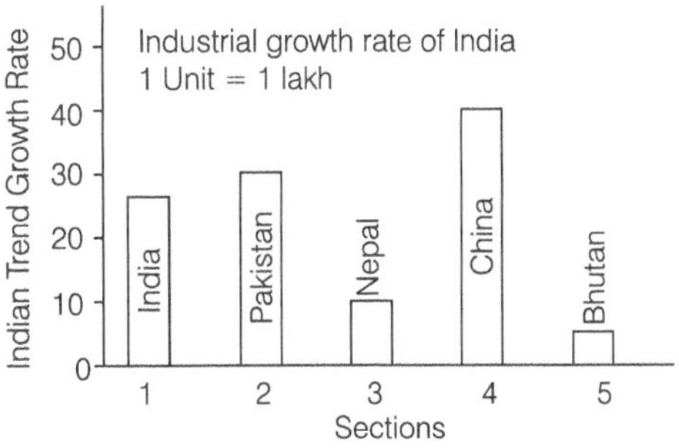


(A) 35 lakhs
(B) 40 lakhs
(C) 25 lakhs
(D) 45 lakhs

**36.** Which of the following is not related to information security on the Internet?
(A) Data Encryption
(B) Water Marking
(C) Data Hiding
(D) Information Retrieval

**37.** Which is the largest unit of storage among the following?
(A) Terabyte (B) Megabyte
(C) Kilobyte (D) Gigabyte

**38.** What do we call a network whose elements may be separated by some distance? It usually involves two or more network and dedicated high speed telephone lines.
(A) LAN (B) WAN
(C) URL (D) Server

**39.** Read the following three statements.
I. MS-word provides tool for composing, editing, formating and printing of documents.
II. Mail merge denotes the distance text boundaries and page margins.
III. Word offers Portrait-horizontally oriented.
Which of the given statement(s) is/are correct?
(A) Only I (B) Only II
(C) I and II (D) II and III

**40.** Which of the following statements is true?
(A) Smart cards do not require an operating system.
(B) Smart cards and PCs use some operating system.
(C) COS is smart card operating system.
(D) The communication between reader and card is in full duplex mode.

**41.** **Assertion** (A) Some carbonaceous aerosols may be carcinogenic.
**Reason** (R) They may contain Polycyclic Aromatic Hydrocarbons (PAHs).
(A) Both 'A' and 'R' are correct and 'R' is the correct explanation of 'A'.
(B) Both 'A' and 'R' are correct but 'R' is not the correct explanation of 'A'.
(C) 'A' is correct, but 'R' is false.
(D) 'A' is false, but 'R' is correct.

**42.** Volcanic eruptions affect
(A) atmosphere and hydrosphere.
(B) hydrosphere and biosphere.
(C) lithosphere, biosphere and atmosphere.
(D) lithosphere, hydrosphere and atmosphere.

**43.** Match List I and List II and select the correct answer from the codes given below.

| List I | List II |
|---|---|
| A. Flood | I. Lack of rainfall of sufficient duration |
| B. Drought | II. Tremors produced by the passage of vibratory waves through the rocks of the Earth |
| C. Earthquake | III. A vent through which molted substances come out |
| D. Volcano | IV. Excess rain and uneven distribution of water |

| | A | B | C | D |
|---|---|---|---|---|
| (A) | IV | I | II | III |
| (B) | II | III | IV | I |
| (C) | III | IV | II | I |
| (D) | IV | III | I | II |

**44.** What is/are the causes/cause of climate change?
I. Forest destruction
II. Volcanic activity
III. Earthquake
IV. Burning of fossil fuels.
**Codes**
(A) Only I (B) I and III
(C) I, II and IV (D) II and III

**45.** What is meant by ex-situ conservation?
(A) Conservation of a species by protecting its habitat alongwith all other species living there.
(B) Conservation of forest ecosystem.
(C) Conservation of a species outside its natural habitat.
(D) Conservation of plants.

**46.** Which of the following exercises power to promulgate ordinances during the recess of the legislative?
(A) Chief Minister (B) Governor
(C) Speaker (D) Deputy Speaker

**47.** The Election Commissioner of a state can be removed from office
(A) only by the Governor.
(B) in the same manner and on the same grounds as a judge of the Supreme Court.
(C) only by the President on the advice of the Chief Justice of the concerned State.
(D) In the same manner as the Vice-President of India.

**48.** 'Parliamentary Supremacy' is a definite feature of the political system in

(A) U.K. (B) India
(C) Canada (D) Australia

**49.** Open learning institutions differ from the formal education institutions in that

(A) the former offers more courses than the latter
(B) the former offers more flexibility in choice of course
(C) the latter implements more-flexible evaluation pattern
(D) the teaching process is given more importance than the learning by open learning institutions.

**50.** When a State Government fails to comply with the directions of the Centre in the exercise of administrative power

(A) the Governor may be directed by the President to dismiss the ministry.
(B) the President can declare a national emergency and convert the federal structure into a unitary one.
(C) a Constitutional emergency can be declared in the State and the President can assume all the powers of the State Government.
(D) the Supreme Court may be asked to intervene.

## ANSWERS

| | | | | | | | | | |
|---|---|---|---|---|---|---|---|---|---|
| 1 (D) | 2 (C) | 3 (A) | 4 (D) | 5 (C) | 6 (B) | 7 (B) | 8 (D) | 9 (C) | 10 (D) |
| 11 (C) | 12 (A) | 13 (D) | 14 (B) | 15 (A) | 16 (B) | 17 (B) | 18 (C) | 19 (D) | 20 (D) |
| 21 (B) | 22 (B) | 23 (A) | 24 (A) | 25 (C) | 26 (C) | 27 (D) | 28 (C) | 29 (B) | 30 (B) |
| 31 (D) | 32 (D) | 33 (D) | 34 (D) | 35 (C) | 36 (D) | 37 (A) | 38 (A) | 39 (A) | 40 (A) |
| 41 (A) | 42 (D) | 43 (A) | 44 (C) | 45 (C) | 46 (B) | 47 (B) | 48 (A) | 49 (C) | 50 (C) |

# UGC
## NET/JRF/SET

# Practice Set 5

## General Paper 1 (Teaching Aptitude and Attitude)

***Instructions***

- This paper contains fifty Multiple-Choice Questions, each question carries two marks.
- All questions are compulsory.
- Total time given for this paper is 1 hour.

**1.** Curriculum makers have the most difficulty when
(A) there is an inflationary cycle.
(B) the nature of the student population is changing.
(C) parents are participants.
(D) teachers unions insist on input.

**2.** Which of the following statements is correct?
(A) Syllabus is a part of curriculum.
(B) Syllabus is an annexure to curriculum.
(C) Curriculum is the same in all educational institutions affiliated to a particular university.
(D) Syllabus is not the same in all educational institutions affiliated to a particular university.

**3.** The trial and error method of instruction is best enhanced by
(A) role playing.
(B) programmed instruction.
(C) an audio-visual lesson.
(D) independent study.

**4.** Which of the following statement is not correct?
(A) Lecture Method can develop reasoning.
(B) Lecture Method can develop knowledge.
(C) Lecture Method is one way process.
(D) During Lecture Method students are passive

**5.** Which one indicates evaluation?
(A) Ram got 45 marks out of 200
(B) Mohan got 38 percent marks in English
(C) Shyam got first division in final examination
(D) All of the above

**6.** Newton gave three basic laws of motion. This research is categorised as
(A) Descriptive Research
(B) Sample Survey
(C) Fundamental Research
(D) Applied Research

**7.** A group of experts in a specific area of knowledge assembled at a place and prepared a syllabus for a new course. The process may be termed as
(A) Seminar (B) Workshop
(C) Conference (D) Symposium

**8.** In the process of conducting research 'Formulation of Hypothesis" is followed by
(A) Statement of Objectives.
(B) Analysis of Data.
(C) Selection of Research Tools.
(D) Collection of Data

**9.** Research is conducted to
I. Generate new knowledge
II. Not to develop a theory
III. Obtain research degree
IV. Reinterpret existing knowledge
Which of the above are correct?
(A) I, III and II (B) III, II and IV
(C) II, I and III (D) I, III and IV

**10.** The essential qualities of a researcher are
(A) spirit of free enquiry.
(B) reliance on observation and evidence.
(C) systematisation or theorising of knowledge.
(D) All of the above

**Direction** (Q. Nos. 11-15) *Read the passage and answer the following questions.*

There was a marked difference of quality between the personages who haunted near bridge of brick and the personages who haunted the far one of stone. Those of lowest character preferred the former adjoining the town; they did not mind the glare of the public eye.

They had been of no account during their successes and though they might feel dispirited, they had no sense of shame in their ruin. Instead of sighing at their adversaries they spat, and instead of saying the iron had entered into their souls they said they were down in their luck.

The miserable's who would pause on the remoter bridge of a politer stamp persons who did not know how to get rid of the weary time. The eyes of his species were mostly directed over the parapet upon the running water below. While one on the town ward bridge did not mind who saw him so, and kept his back to parapet to survey the passer-by, one on this never faced the road, never turned his head at coming foot-steps, but, sensitive on his own condition, watched the current whenever a stranger approached, as if some strange fish interested him, though every finned thing had been poached out of the rivers years before.

**11.** In this passage the author is trying to
(A) explain the difference between the construction of the two bridges.
(B) describe the way different sections of people like to dress.
(C) explain the variety of ways in which strangers can be treated.
(D) describe how people of different classes behaved when unhappy.

**12.** People belonging to lower strata in their moments of distress
(A) remembered the days of glory.
(B) dressed shabbily to earn sympathy.
(C) visited the brick made bridge.
(D) felt ashamed of their failures.

**13.** The attitude of lowly and genteel towards strangers was
(A) virtually the same.
(B) entirely different.
(C) completely indifferent.
(D) virulently hostile

**14.** The bridge of stone was frequented by
(A) all the sections of society.
(B) those fond of fishing
(C) the sophisticated but luckless
(D) None of the above

**15.** The two bridges were known
(A) for their similar design
(B) for being equidistant from town
(C) for being haunted places
(D) for attracting dejected people to them

**16.** Which one of the following is correct?
(A) Communication is not a mere transmission, it aims at understanding.
(B) Efficient communication minimises time and cost involved in the exchange process.
(C) Communication is a process involving a sender who sends a message, a channel through which a message is transmitted and a receiver.
(D) All of the above

**17.** Dyadic communication is the transfer of messages from a person
(A) to another person and vice versa.
(B) to a group of persons.
(C) to a mass audience.
(D) None of the above

**18.** A negative reaction to a mediated communication is described as
(A) flak (B) fragmented feedback
(C) passive response (D) non-conformity

**19.** Which of the following statements is not connected with communication?
(A) Medium is the message.
(B) The world is an electronic cocoon.
(C) Information is power.
(D) Telepathy is technology.

**20.** The term 'DAVP' stands for
(A) Directorate of Advertising and Vocal Publicity.
(B) Division of Audio-Visual Publicity.
(C) Department of Audio-Visual Publicity.
(D) Directorate of Advertising and Visual Publicity.

**21.** Given that
I. P is the brother of Q
II. R is the father of P
III. S is the brother of T
IV. T is the daughter of Q.
Then, uncle of D is
(A) P (B) Q (C) R (D) T

**22.** The ratio of Meena's age and Kamla's age is 3 : 5 and the sum of their ages is 80 years. The ratio of their ages after 10 years will be
(A) 2 : 3 (B) 1 : 2 (C) 3 : 2 (D) 3 : 5

**23.** If PICTURE is coded as tuvwxyz, then PIERCE would be coded as
(A) tuzyzv (B) tzuvzy
(C) tuzyvz (D) tzuvyz

**24.** If South-East becomes North-East and North-West becomes South-West and all the rest directions are changed in the same manner, then what will be the direction for West?
(A) North (B) North-West
(C) South (D) East

**25.** In the series 3, 11, 23, 39, 59, .... the next term will be
(A) 63 (B) 73 (C) 83 (D) 93

**26.** **Assertion** (A) Man is a rational being.
**Reason** (R) Man is a social being.
(A) Both 'A' and 'R' are true and 'R' is the correct explanation of 'A'
(B) Both 'A' and 'R' are true but 'R' is not the correct explanation of 'A'.
(C) 'A' is true but 'R' is false.
(D) 'A' is false but 'R' is true.

**27.** Among the following statements **two** are contradictory to each other. Select the direct code that represents them.
Statements
I. All poets are philosophers.
II. Some poets are philosophers.
III. Some poets are not philosophers.
IV. No philosopher is a poet.
**Codes**
(A) I and II (B) I and IV
(C) I and III (D) II and III

**28.** Consider the following **Assertion** (A) and **Reason** (R) and select the correct code given below.
(A) : No man is perfect.
(R) : Some men are not perfect.
(A) Both 'A' and 'R' are true and 'R' provides sufficient reason for 'A'.
(B) 'A' is true but 'R' is false.
(C) 'A' is false but 'R' is true.
(D) Both 'A' and 'R' are true but 'R' does not provide sufficient reason for 'A'.

**29.** The following question is based on the diagram given below. If the two small circles represent formal class-room education and distance education and the big circle stands for university system of education, which figure represents the university systems.

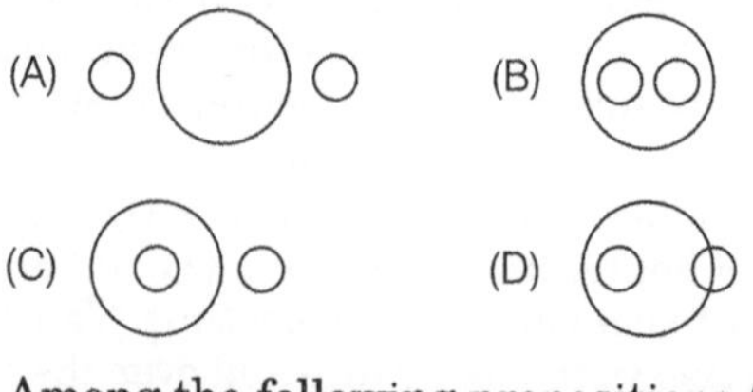


**30.** Among the following propositions two are related in such a way that they cannot both be true but can both be false. Select the code that states those two propositions.
Propositions
I. Every student is attentive
II. Some students are attentive
III. Students are never attentive
IV. Some students are not attentive
**Codes**
(A) I and II (B) I and III
(C) II and III (D) III and IV

**Directions** (31-35) The following graph shows the quarterly price index of a textile company during 1984-85. Examine it carefully and answer questions 134-138.

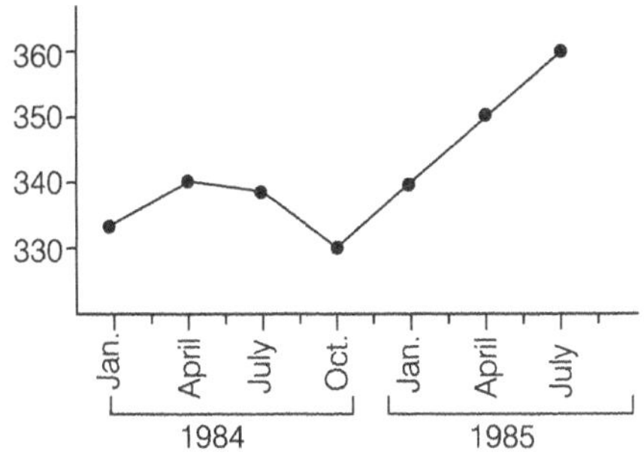


**31.** During which quarter was the rate of increase of price index the maximum?
(A) October 1984-January 1985
(B) January 1984-April 1984
(C) April 1985-July 1985
(D) January 1985-April 1985

**32.** In which of the following months, was the price index maximum?
(A) April 1984
(B) July 1984
(C) April 1985
(D) July 1985

**33.** During which of the following quarters, did the price index remains the same throughout
(A) April 1985—July 1984.
(B) April 1984-October 1984.
(C) July 1984-January 1985.
(D) None of the above

**34.** The increase in price index was approximately the same during the periods
(A) October-December, 1984 and April-June, 1985
(B) January-March, 1984 and October-December, 1984.
(C) January-March, 1985 and April-June, 1985.
(D) None of the above

**35.** Approximately, what is the percentage of increase in price index during the period January 1984-July 1985?
(A) 7% (B) 8%
(C) 10% (D) 7.5%

**36.** A computer network allows sharing of resources. The software resources exist in the form of files of data, which need to be moved between two specific computer systems for the purpose of sharing
(A) Address for communication
(B) A secure means for moving data in the form of electronic signals
(C) Both 'A' and 'B'
(D) Either 'A' or 'B'

**37.** A communication network which is used by large organisations over regional, national or global area is called
(A) LAN (B) WAN
(C) MAN (D) VAN

**38.** 1 byte is equal to
(A) 2 bits (B) 8 bits
(C) 16 bits (D) 32 bits

**39.** Which of the following are examples of input devices?
(A) Visual display unit, dot matrix printer laser printer.
(B) Keyboard, mouse, optical mark reader.
(C) Arithmetic and logic unit, control unit.
(D) RAM, ROM, PROM.

**40.** Unix, DOS, Windows are examples of
(A) application programs.
(B) operating systems.
(C) word processors.
(D) commercial computer brands.

**41.** **Assertion** (A) In the world as a whole, the environment has degraded during past several decades.
**Reason (R)** The population of the world has been growing significantly.
(A) 'A' is correct, 'R' is correct and 'R' is the correct explanation of 'A'.
(B) 'A' is correct, 'R' is correct and 'R' is not the correct explanation of 'A'.
(C) 'A' is correct, but 'R' is false.
(D) 'A' is false, but 'R' is correct.

**42.** Climate change has implications for
I. soil moisture.
II. forest fires.
III. biodiversity.
IV. groundwater

Identify the correct combinations according to the code

(A) I and III (B) I, II and III
(C) I, III and IV (D) All of these

**43.** DDT was banned in world in 1972. When was the use of DDT banned for agricultural purposes in India?

(A) 1992 (B) 1974
(C) 1962 (D) 1989

**44.** To generate environmental awareness, Paryavaran Vahini Scheme was launched in

(A) 1986 (B) 1992 (C) 1998 (D) 1994

**45.** The country which hosted first World Earth Summit (June 1992) on conservation of environment was

(A) Brazil (B) Spain (C) Peru (D) India

**46.** The recommendation of National Knowledge Commission for the establishment of 1500 Universities is to

(A) create more teaching jobs.
(B) ensure increase in student enrolment in higher education.
(C) replace or substitute the privately managed higher education institutions by public institutions.
(D) enable increased movement of students from rural areas to urban areas.

**47.** The enrolment in higher education in India is contributed both by Formal System of Education and by System of Distance Education. Distance education contributes

(A) 50% of formal system.
(B) 25% of formal system.
(C) 10% of the formal system.
(D) Distance education systems contribution is not taken into account while considering the figures of enrolment in higher education.

**48.** Match List-I with List-II and select the correct answer from the codes given below.

| List-I (Institutions) | List-II (Locations) |
|---|---|
| A. NALSAR University of Law | I. Shimla |
| B. Indian Institute of Advanced Studies | II. Bhopal |
| C. National Judicial Academy | III. Hyderabad |
| D. National Savings Institute | IV. New Delhi |

**Codes**

| | A | B | C | D |
|---|---|---|---|---|
| (A) | III | II | IV | I |
| (B) | I | II | III | IV |
| (C) | IV | III | I | II |
| (D) | III | I | II | IV |

**49.** The accreditation process by National Assessment and Accreditation Council (NAAC) differs from that of National Board of Accreditation (NBA) in terms of

(A) Disciplines covered by both being the same, there is duplication of efforts.
(B) One has institutional grading approach and the other has programme grading approach.
(C) Once get accredited by NBA or NAAC, the institution is free from renewal of grading, which is not a progressive decision.
(D) This accreditation amounts to approval of minimum standards in the quality of education in the institution concerned.

**50.** The Right to Information Act, 2005 makes the provision of

(A) dissemination of all types of information by all Public authorities to any person.
(B) establishment of central, state and district level information commissions as an appellate body.
(C) transparency and accountability in public authorities.
(D) All of the above

## ANSWERS

| | | | | | | | | | |
|---|---|---|---|---|---|---|---|---|---|
| 1 (B) | 2 (A) | 3 (D) | 4 (A) | 5 (D) | 6 (C) | 7 (B) | 8 (D) | 9 (D) | 10 (D) |
| 11 (D) | 12 (C) | 13 (B) | 14 (C) | 15 (D) | 16 (B) | 17 (A) | 18 (C) | 19 (D) | 20 (D) |
| 21 (A) | 22 (A) | 23 (C) | 24 (C) | 25 (C) | 26 (B) | 27 (B) | 28 (D) | 29 (B) | 30 (B) |
| 31 (C) | 32 (D) | 33 (D) | 34 (D) | 35 (D) | 36 (C) | 37 (B) | 38 (B) | 39 (B) | 40 (B) |
| 41 (B) | 42 (D) | 43 (D) | 44 (B) | 45 (A) | 46 (B) | 47 (B) | 48 (D) | 49 (B) | 50 (D) |